PENGUIN A

# LITERATURE
## A Pocket Anthology

SECOND CANADIAN EDITION

Edited by **R. S. GWYNN** *Lamar University*

**WANDA CAMPBELL** *Acadia University*

PEARSON
Longman

Toronto

**Library and Archives Canada Cataloguing in Publication**

Literature: a pocket anthology / edited by R. S. Gwynn, Wanda Campbell. — 2nd Canadian ed.

(Penguin academics)
Includes index.
ISBN 978-0-321-42798-4

1. Literature—Collections. I. Gwynn, R. S. II. Campbell, Wanda, 1963– III. Series.

PN6014.L576 2008      808.8      C2006-906968-9

Original edition published by Pearson Longman, a division of Pearson Education, Inc., Upper Saddle River, NJ. Copyright © 2005 by Pearson Education, Inc. This edition is authorized for sale in Canada only.

ISBN-13: 978-0-321-42798-4
ISBN-10: 0-321-42798-X

Editor-in-Chief, Vice-President of Sales: Kelly Shaw
Acquisitions Editor: Chris Helsby
Marketing Manager: Leigh-Anne Graham
Developmental Editor: Charlotte Morrison-Reed
Production Editor: Richard di Santo
Copy Editor: Sharon Kirsch
Proofreaders: Barbara Czarnecki, Nancy Carroll
Production Coordinator: Sharlene Ross
Composition: Integra
Art Director: Julia Hall
Interior and Cover Design: Susanna Brusikiewicz
Cover Image: Getty Images / Russell Kaye / Sandra-Lee Phipps

5      12 11 10

Printed and bound in Canada.

PENGUIN
ACADEMICS

PEARSON
Longman

# Contents

## Fiction 37

## Introduction to Fiction 39

## Poetry  367

## Introduction to Poetry  369

## Drama   709

## Introduction to Drama   711

# *Preface*

When the *Pocket Anthology* series first appeared a decade ago, the chief aim was to offer a clear alternative to the anthologies of fiction, poetry, and drama that were available at the time. We are very pleased to offer new Canadian editions of the *Pocket Anthology* series. This volume, *Literature: A Pocket Anthology*, incorporates the contents of the Canadian editions of *Fiction: A Pocket Anthology*, *Poetry: A Pocket Anthology*, and *Drama: A Pocket Anthology*.

    *Literature* addresses the four wishes and concerns most commonly expressed by both instructors and students. First, of course, is the **variety** of selections it contains. Admittedly, a pocket anthology has to be very selective in its contents, so we are especially proud that the 40 stories, over 200 poems, and eight plays in this book include both established canonical writers from the 16th century to the present as well as many new voices which reflect the diversity of gender, ethnic background, and national origin that is essential to any study of contemporary literature. We are also pleased that nearly one half of the selections in *Literature* are by women, and that Canadian, international, and minority writers also comprise nearly one half of its contents. Every inhabited continent is represented, and in this Canadian edition we are especially pleased to include works from every province as well as First Nation, Quebecois, Acadian, and Diaspora writers from many ethnic backgrounds. Students will find engaging works from a variety of periods and styles, works that can be studied in conjunction with works of art, and works by writers under the age of 35. More important, the contents of *Literature* have been shaped by the advice of experienced instructors who have cited the stories, poems, and plays that are most often taught and that possess proven appeal to students. The editors have also made a strong effort to include a number of works that reflect contemporary social questions and thus will easily stimulate classroom discussion and writing assignments. We strongly believe that the works in this new edition of *Literature* will provide a reading experience that is not only educational but thought-provoking and enjoyable as well.

Our second aim is **flexibility**—a book that can be used as a primary text in a variety of courses, ranging from introduction to literature to literary theory to creative writing. In addition to its generous selection of stories, poems, and plays, *Literature* contains biographical headnotes for authors, an introduction that covers the techniques and terminology of each of the three major literary genres, and a concise section on writing about literature and on research procedures. As an aid to student writing assignments, *Literature* also contains an appendix that groups works from all three genres thematically and provides suggestions for the application of a range of critical approaches. A *Question Book* for the Canadian edition, available to instructors on request, offers ideas for discussion questions and writing topics, as well as some additional background information.

The third goal is **affordability.** The Canadian edition of *Literature* reflects the original claims of the *Pocket Anthology* series, that these books represent "a new standard of value." Because of its affordability, *Literature* may be easily supplemented in individual courses with handbooks of grammar and usage, manuals of style, introductions to critical theory, textbooks on research methods, or instructional texts in creative writing.

Finally, we stress **portability.** A semester is a short time, and few courses can cover more than a fraction of the material that many bulkier collections contain. Because the focus of *Literature* is on primary texts, we are able to offer roughly the same number of poems, stories, and plays as much larger books. While *Literature* still may be a snug fit in most pockets, we trust that instructors and their students will be grateful for a book that is a more manageable size.

In its second edition, the *Pocket Anthology* series offers increased Canadian content, an updated critical framework, and enhanced audio/visual pedagogy with the addition of **MyLiteratureLab** at no extra charge. This extensive website provides a number of resources that will be of interest to users of this new edition. It contains interactive readings and lectures on a variety of well-known works, biographical information about authors, a glossary of literary and critical terms, and many other useful multimedia resources for your course.

In closing, we would like to express our gratitude to the instructors who reviewed all or part of the Canadian *Pocket Anthology* series and offered invaluable recommendations for improvements:

Julia Denholm, Langara College
Cecily Devereux, University of Alberta
Fraser Easton, University of Waterloo
Thomas Ezzy, Dawson College
Melanie Fahlman Reid, Capilano College
Gordon Fulton, University of Victoria
James Gifford, University of Lethbridge
Christopher E. Gittings, University of Alberta
Kathleen Irwin, University of Regina
Tobi Kazakewich, University of Ottawa
Christine Kerr, Champlain Regional College
Ric Knowles, University of Guelph
Jean-François Leroux, University of Ottawa
Kathy McConnell, Dalhousie University
Ninian Mellamphy, University of Western Ontario
Paul Milton, Okanagan University College
Paul Matthew St. Pierre, Simon Fraser University
Dawn Neill, University of Victoria
Catherine Nelson-McDermott, University of British Columbia
Miriam Pirbhai, Wilfred Laurier University
Nicole C. Rosevere, University of Winnipeg
Mary Silcox, McMaster University
Anna Smol, Mt. St. Vincent University
Cheryl Suzack, University of Alberta
Eleanor Ty, Wilfred Laurier University
Paul Tyndall, University of British Columbia
Lynn Wells, University of Regina
Patricia Whiting, University of Ottawa
Lorraine York, McMaster University

*R. S. Gwynn*
*Lamar University*

*Wanda Campbell*
*Acadia University*

**Wanda Campbell** has edited several other books, including *The Poetry of John Strachan* and *Hidden Rooms: Early Canadian Women Poets*. She has authored two collections of poetry, *Sky Fishing* and *Haw [Thorn]* and has published academic articles, fiction, and poetry in journals across Canada. She teaches Literature and Creative Writing at Acadia University in Wolfville, Nova Scotia.

**R. S. Gwynn** has edited several other books, including *Literature: A Pocket Anthology*, *Drama: A Pocket Anthology*, *Fiction: A Pocket Anthology*, *The Longman Anthology of Short Fiction* (with Dana Gioia), and *Contemporary American Poetry: A Pocket Anthology* (with April Lindner). He has also authored five collections of poetry, including *No Word of Farewell: Selected Poems, 1970–2000*. In 2004 he was awarded the Michael Braude Award for verse from the American Academy of Arts and Letters.

Professor Gwynn teaches at Lamar University in Beaumont, Texas.

# *Introduction to Literature*

## Explore, Experiment, Expand:
## Three Reasons to Study Literature

"In our Canadian schools we undertake to teach literature, and we certainly do teach it with a vengeance." Thus wrote Canadian poet Archibald Lampman in 1892. He went on to describe how students were asked to approach literary classics such as *Paradise Lost.*

> *They hunt up all the allusions; they make themselves acquainted with parallel passages; they discuss it historically, geographically, critically; they tear and worry and torture the lines of the great poem till they are littered out as dry and innutritive as a worm-eaten codfish.*

The study of literature may have changed since then, but the tough questions remain. What's the point of this? Why do we have to study literature? What value is this study? As a way of introducing *Literature: A Pocket Anthology*, three words have been chosen—explore, experiment, expand—to suggest some good reasons why the study of literature is invaluable to any educational experience.

### *Explore*

"We are such stuff / As dreams are made on; and our little life / Is rounded with a sleep," says Shakespeare's great magician Prospero. Our experience of the world is limited by time and place, and even the most resolute traveller can only superficially come to know the complex blends of cultures that make up our world. The act of reading literature allows us a means of imaginatively entering minds and civilizations that may seem distant to us but actually are only as remote as a turn of the page. True, we may never travel to Africa, but by reading a story by Ama Ata Aidoo we can learn something about customs that in some ways remind us of our own but in others seem foreign and strange. A poem by a Canadian poet like Alden Nowlan may bring with it the shock of recognition we reserve for those experiences that touch us most deeply. In literature we are allowed the possibility of inhabiting, for a brief time, lives and minds that are not our own. We can see the world through the eyes of people of a gender, culture, historical era, and social class that may resemble or vastly differ from our own. The perspectives and subjects we explore in literature are as varied and sometimes as troubling as life itself, but in investigating them we can broaden our understanding of life in ways that other fields of academic study cannot equal. We might eventually agree that the insight that we gain from a literary experience is equal or even superior to the experience itself. According to Joseph Gold, "We can use what we read to unravel the mystery of our own lives and feelings."

## *Experiment*

Literature does not write itself, and even the most vivid experience does not automatically translate into a memorable poem, story, or play. To the writer, every event that he or she considers as a likely subject presents a problem in literary form. Which of the genres—drama, fiction, or poetry—can best depict an experience, and which of each genre's innumerable sub-types—comedy or tragedy, short story or novel, open-form poem or sonnet—will work best? To study literature is to learn that every play, story, or poem that has ever been written involves some kind of experiment in literary technique, and much of the study of literature must be given over to questioning why artists make the choices that they do. Edgar Allan Poe once wrote an essay, "The Philosophy of Composition," about how he came to write his famous poem "The Raven," in which he explained in detail the decisions that he made about rhythm, language, setting, and even the sounds of individual words. But many readers have found that "The Raven," or for that matter any successful piece of literature, adds up to more than the sum of its parts; not even the creator has the last word on what the experiment has uncovered. As serious readers, our job is often to go beneath the surface to reveal the underlying structures and meanings. We may never write a short story, poem, or play ourselves, but in being entertained and perhaps instructed by a writer's skill with words, we gain some insight into one of the greatest human mysteries—the motives and methods of those who make art literally out of nothing. To read literature with the goal of learning how it is made is to understand literature not as life itself but as an artful imitation of it. As Richard Wilbur, observing his own daughter's attempts to write a short story, says to her, "It is always a matter, my darling, / Of life or death." And then he adds, "as I had forgotten."

## *Expand*

We expand our understanding by reading, by discussing what we have read, and by writing about it. When talking about a poem in a classroom group, students are often surprised to find that the way one reads a certain passage is not quite the same as a classmate's interpretation and that both differ from the instructor's. Literature is not a science and many of the meanings we attach to individual works remain largely matters of speculation. This is not to claim that all interpretations, no matter how far-fetched, are equally valid; it is only to observe that complex works of literature offer different channels of interpretation for readers, as any survey of available criticism of a given text will quickly demonstrate. The student's chance to speak his or her piece most often takes the form of the essay answer on an examination, in the theme or thesis paper, or in the research project. The job of making assertions, backing them up with references to the text, and locating support from outside sources remains the primary way through which students may demonstrate that their initial attempts to understand a story, poem, or play have grown and deepened. In analyzing, researching, and writing about literature, we expand our minds as we realize that none of us has the final word. As in life, the qualifications and adjustments we make as we respond to literary works teach us something about the necessity of not taking things at face value; there is always one more question to ask, one more possibility to weigh and test.

It is no coincidence that the three words that have been chosen all begin with the prefix *ex-*, which means "out of." One of the most common questions from students that we have heard over the years is "What are we supposed to get *out of* this (story, poem, play)?" If you have really savoured the full experience that good literature offers, then the first thing you should get "out of" will be your own skin—when you do that you will answer your own question. For a few moments you may lose your own identity and see through the eyes of an Elizabethan Englishman, a modern Nigerian, or a contemporary Canadian woman, and you may just find that in some significant way your own manner of looking at the world will never be quite the same again. In beginning our study of literature, we must first look at the different literary genres—fiction, poetry, and drama—and discuss their different methods and techniques. Each genre, or type, of literature has its own history and terminology, some of which may be shared with other genres. In the introductory discussions of fiction, poetry, and drama that follow, certain important terms appear in boldface type. An index of critical terms is found at the end of this book.

# Writing About Literature

## First Considerations

"Writing is no trouble: you just jot down ideas as they occur to you. The jotting is simplicity itself—it is the occurring which is difficult." Stephen Leacock's tongue-in-cheek description of the writing process draws attention to the necessity for preparation. Other writers draw attention to the necessity for polishing. "I can't write five words but that I change seven," says Dorothy Parker. It takes work to transform "jotting" into an essay that is correct, coherent, and convincing. You might have had the discouraging experience of having your first effort returned by your instructor with a bewildering array of correction symbols and a grade that was lower than any you had ever received for your writing. But then you realized that there were certain skills you would have to learn if you were ever going to become a persuasive writer. You corrected your spelling errors, matched your instructor's corrections to those in your handbook, revised mistakes in usage, punctuation, and grammar, and polished your first draft and handed it in again. This time, when it was returned, you were pleased to find fewer correction marks and a couple of encouraging bits of praise in your margins. If you weren't exactly assured that you had permanently mastered every fine point of composition, at least you now had some hope that, with practice, hard work, and careful application of the skills you were learning, your writing would improve and the improvement would be rewarded.

Everyone has been there. Even your instructor was once a student in an introductory writing class, and very few instructors are candid enough to have preserved their own early writing efforts to display to their students. But the problem is no longer your instructor's. She has survived the process to acquire an advanced degree, and her job now is to teach you the writing skills that she has acquired. You have some confidence in your own ability, but you also have begun to suspect that writing about literature is quite a bit more demanding than writing about your own life. An introduction to literature course places equal weight on your demonstrated skills as a writer and on your ability to go beyond what you have discussed in the classroom to formulate critical responses to the works that you have read. You might have written thesis papers and completed research projects that you were assigned in high school, but you still do not feel entirely confident about your ability to write about literature. You enjoy reading stories, poems, and plays, but you may find expressing your thoughts about their meaning or their literary merit intimidating. With these thoughts in mind, here are a few general strategies that may help you to write successful critical papers.

## Topic into Thesis

Writing assignments differ greatly, and your instructions may range from general (*Discuss the roles of three minor characters in any of the plays we have read*) to very specific (*Contrast, in at least 500 words, the major differences in the plot, characterization, and setting between Alice Munro's short story "Boys and Girls" and the 1983 film version of the story directed by Don McBrearty*). In some cases, especially in essay-type examinations, your instructor may give the whole class the same topic; in others, you may be allowed considerable freedom in selecting one. Length requirements may range from a single paragraph to the standard 500-word thesis (in some cases written during a single class period) to a full-scale research paper of three or four times that length. The assignment will probably require that you support your assertions with quotes from the story, poem, or play; or it may require that you add further supporting evidence from secondary critical sources. There is no way to predict the precise kinds of papers you may have to write in a literature course; however, there are a few simple guidelines to remember that may help you make the prewriting process easier.

Consider a typical assignment for an essay on poetry: *Discuss any two poems in our textbook that share a similar theme.* Although this topic allows you some latitude in selecting the poems you wish to write about, paradoxically, it is just this type of assignment that may cause you the most distress. Why is this so? Simply because there are over two hundred poems in this book, and it is usually impossible for the typical class to cover more than a fraction of that number in the time allotted during the semester to the study of poetry. Before despairing, though, consider the different ways the topic could be limited. Instead of "two poems" you might narrow the field by selecting a more specific group, for example, "two ballads," "two war poems," or "two poems by African-American poets." Suppose you settle on a group that is limited, yet still allows some selection. Choosing "two sonnets by Shakespeare" would allow you to pick from a total of four sonnets included here. In the same way, the second half of the assignment—to find two sonnets with a similar theme—can be limited in various ways. After reading the sonnets, you might observe that sonnets 18 and 30 deal with friendship. Reading the same group of sonnets a second time, you might be struck by how sonnets 18, 73, and 130 deal with physical beauty and its loss. Or, a third time, you might notice that sonnets 30 and 73 possess a depressed tone that sometimes verges on self-pity. After weighing your options and deciding which two sonnets you feel most comfortable discussing, you might formulate a thesis sentence: "In two of his sonnets, Shakespeare stresses that ideal love should be based on more than mere physical beauty." Always keep in mind that the process of choosing, limiting, and developing a topic and thesis sentence should follow the same steps that you would use in other courses. To aid you in locating stories, poems, and plays that share similarities, the appendix at the end of this book groups works thematically.

What is next? A certain amount of informal preparation is always useful: It may be helpful to brainstorm by taking notes on random ideas and refining those ideas further through discussing them with your peers and instructor. Many composition and introduction to literature courses now include group discussion and peer review of rough drafts as part of the writing process. Even if your class does not use formal group discussion as part of its prewriting activities, there is still nothing to prevent you from talking over your ideas with your classmates or scheduling a conference with your instructor. The conference, especially, is a good idea because it allows you to get a clearer sense of what is expected from you. In many cases, after a conference with your instructor, you may discover that you could have limited your topic even further or that you could have selected other more pertinent examples to support your thesis.

## Explication, Analysis, Reviewing

In general, writing assignments on literature fall into three broad categories: explication, analysis, and reviewing. Explication, which literally means "an unfolding" and is also known as "close reading," is a painstaking analysis of the details of a piece of writing. Because of its extremely limited focus—only on the specific words that the author uses—explication is a consistent favourite for writing assignments on individual poems. In such assignments, the writer attempts to discuss every possible nuance of meaning that a poet has employed. The most useful aid to explication is the dictionary; a full-scale assignment of this type may even involve using the multi-volume *Oxford English Dictionary* to demonstrate how a word in a poem might have once possessed a meaning different from its present one or to support your contention that a phrase may have several possible meanings. Explication assignments are also possible in writing about fiction and drama. You might be expected to focus closely on a single short passage from a story, for example, explicating the passages describing Mr. Kapasi in Jhumpa Lahiri's "Interpreter of Maladies," or you might be limited to one scene from a play, being asked to discuss how Othello's speeches in Act I, Scene 3, reveal both his strengths of character and the weaknesses that will prove his undoing. Many useful critical sources are available to support assignments of this type, and some of them are mentioned later in the section on research methods.

Analysis uses the same general techniques of explication, that is, the use of specific details from the text to support your statements. But where explication attempts to exhaust the widest possible range of meanings, analysis is more selective in its focus, requiring that you examine how a single element—a theme, a technique, a structural device—functions in a single work or in a related group of works. Instead of being assigned to explicate A. M. Klein's "Portrait of the Poet as Landscape" (a formidable task given its length and complexity), you might be asked to analyze only the poet's use of allusions, or to examine his imagery, or to focus exclusively on the structure of his free verse. Analysis assignments often take the form of comparison–contrast essays *(Compare and contrast the motivations and actions of the female protagonists of "Simple Recipes" and "Boys and Girls")* or essays that combine definition with example–illustration *(Define the ballad and discuss ballads written by three poets of this century, showing their links to the tradition of this type of poem)*. In the case of these examples, general reference books like William Harmon and C. Hugh Holman's *A Handbook to Literature* or the exhaustive *The New Princeton Encyclopedia of Poetry and Poetics* will help you to establish your definitions and an overall context for your examples.

The third category, reviewing, is less common in introductory literature courses. A review is a first-hand reaction to a performance or a publication and combines literary analysis with the techniques of journalism. A review of a play or film would evaluate the theatrical elements—acting, direction, sets, etc.—of the performance. Reviews are largely descriptive reporting, but they should also provide evaluation and recommendation. Many of the stories and plays in this volume have been filmed, and you could be asked to discuss how one of them has been adapted for a different medium. Even a local production of a play that you are reading in class is a possibility, and you might find yourself jotting down notes on how the quiet young woman who sits beside you in chemistry lab has transformed herself into the vibrant role of Ibsen's Nora. It is even possible that you might find yourself reviewing a public reading given by a poet or fiction writer whose works you first encountered in this book, and you might find yourself commenting on the distance between the image that the writer projects in the poems or stories and his or her actual "stage presence" as a performer. On the purely literary side, book reviews of new collections of stories and poems regularly appear in periodicals or the literary sections of major newspapers (like *The New York Times Book Review* and *The Globe and Mail*), and it is simple enough to find many excellent models should you be assigned to write a paper of this type.

One last word of warning: Note that nowhere above are primarily biographical essays about authors listed as possible writing assignments. Research assignments might ask you to discuss how the particular circumstances of a writer's life might have influenced his or her works, but for the most part biographical information should reside in the background, not the foreground, of literary analysis. An explication of a single poem that begins "Bronwen Wallace was born in 1945 in Kingston . . ." gives the erroneous impression that you are writing about the poet's life instead of about her work. Try to find a more direct (and original) way of opening your paper.

## Critical Approaches

Although many instructors of introduction to literature classes stress a formalist approach (or "close reading") to literary works, other instructors may lecture from a distinct critical perspective and ask their students to employ these techniques in their writing. You might be encouraged to apply a certain kind of critical strategy—feminist criticism or a post-colonial perspective—to the works you have studied. An instructor might stress that you should emphasize the socio-economic situation and concerns of a fiction writer and his characters. Or you may be asked to explore how female poets employ visual images that differ from those used by men. The appendix to this book, *Literature: Thematic and Critical Approaches*, provides suggestions about how works may be grouped together for analysis using various critical methods. Here you will find some brief notes on seven of the most often used areas of literary criticism and some advice on how to use the thematic listings to find stories, poems, and plays that might best profit from analysis that employs a specific critical approach. Applying complicated critical theories to individual works is a demanding assignment, and frequent instructor–student conferences may not just be helpful—they may be essential.

## Style and Content

Style is the major stumbling block that many students encounter in writing an effective piece of literary analysis. They may be aware that their vocabulary and sentence structure are less sophisticated than those found in the primary and secondary materials being discussed, and thus they sometimes try to overcompensate by adopting, usually without much success, the language of professional critics. This practice can result in garbled sentences and jargon-filled writing. It is much better to write simple, direct sentences, avoiding slang and contractions and using only words you understand.

Writing in a style with which you are comfortable allows you to make clear transitions between your own writing and the sources that you are citing for supporting evidence. In introducing a quotation from a critic, use a phrase like "As [the critic's name] notes in his essay on . . ." to guide the reader from your own style into one that is very different. Never include a statement from a critical work that you do not understand yourself, and do not hesitate to go on for a sentence or two after a supporting quotation to explain it in your own words. Remember that literary criticism has its own technical vocabulary and that many of these literary terms are discussed elsewhere in this book. Proper terminology should be used instead of homemade substitutes. Thus, to talk about the "high point of the storyline" instead of "the climax of the plot" or the "style of the rhythm and rhyme" instead of "the formal strategies of the poem" is to invite an unfavourable response.

As far as the content of your paper is concerned, try to avoid eccentric personal responses for which you can find no critical support. This rule holds for all types of literature but is especially true if you are writing about poetry. Because poetry compresses language and detail, you may have to fill in more than a few blank spaces to make sense of a poem. Good poems often *suggest* information instead of explicitly stating it; the shorter the poem, the more that may be suggested. If you do not begin by determining a poem's dramatic situation—the basic *who*, *what*, *where*, and *when* of a poem—you will not have established the basis on which your subsequent remarks must be anchored. It is possible for a student to go far astray on a poem as straightforward as Earle Birney's "El Greco: *Espolio*" because he or she failed to notice the poem's most important detail, that it is about the painting mentioned in the title.

In writing about other genres, you may have a brilliant intuition that Mrs. Mallard is not really dead at the end of Kate Chopin's "The Story of an Hour," but you may encounter difficulty in finding support for these conclusion either in the text or in the work of critics. Also, do not try, unless you are specifically asked to take a biographical approach, to make close connections between an author's work and the events of his or her life; literature and autobiography are not identical. Some perfectly decent people (Robert Browning is one example) have relished creating characters who are masterpieces of madness or evil, and some perfectly awful people have created beautiful works of literature. It may be the professional biographer's job to judge literary merit on the basis of what he or she perceives as the moral virtues or lack thereof of a writer, but unless you are specifically asked to take a biographical approach, you should probably limit your remarks to the text that you are analyzing.

## Writing About Fiction

As mentioned previously, an explication assignment on a single short story demands close attention to detail because it focuses on the subtleties of a writer's language. "Close reading" means exactly that: You should carefully weigh every word in the passage you are explicating. Typically, an explication assignment might ask you to look carefully at a key section of a short story, explaining how it contains some element upon which the whole story hinges and without which it could not succeed. Suppose, for example, that you are asked to explicate the opening paragraph of John Cheever's "Reunion" and are explicitly requested to explain what the paragraph conveys beyond obvious expository information. After poring over the paragraph several times, you might decide that it contains ample foreshadowing of the disastrous events that are about to occur. In particular you might cite such phrases as "his secretary wrote to say" or "my mother divorced him" as Cheever's way of dropping hints about the father's unstable personality. Then you might go on to mention Charlie's forebodings of his own "doom," all leading up to the aroma of pre-lunch cocktails that Charlie notices when he and his father embrace. Any explication demands that you quote extensively from the text, explaining why certain choices of words and details are important and speculating about why the writer made these choices.

A typical analysis assignment in short fiction might ask you to explain what a "rites of passage" story is and demonstrate that "Reunion" has most of the characteristics of the type. Here you might want to first define the initiation story, using your lecture notes, general literary reference books, and your familiarity with other stories from popular sources like fairy tales or motion pictures. After demonstrating that this type of story is indeed well-established and describing its chief characteristics, you might then focus on such matters in "Reunion" as Charlie's age, his naive expectations, his disillusioning experience, and his eventual "passage" out of his father's life at the end of the story. A slightly more complicated analysis assignment might involve writing a comparison and contrast paper about two texts or performing a comparative analysis of more than two. Generally, comparison seeks out common ground between two subjects whereas contrast finds differences; most papers of this type will do both, first pointing out the similarities before going on to demonstrate how each story represents a variation on the theme. Comparison–contrast essays may examine a single story, analyzing two characters' approaches to a similar situation, or even a single character's "before and after" view of another character or event. Or these essays may compare and contrast two or more works that have common threads. If you are examining a single author in depth, you might be required to locate other stories that deal with similar themes. Because Cheever writes extensively about alcoholism, family tensions, and divorce, you might choose several of his stories that reflect the same basic themes as "Reunion." Even more demanding might be a topic asking you to find stories (or even poems or plays) by other authors to compare or contrast. Among the stories in this book, there are several examples of initiation stories, and others that deal with tensions between parents and children. Assignments in comparative analysis require careful selection and planning, and it is essential to find significant examples of both similarities and differences to support your thesis.

## Writing About Poetry

Because explication of a poem involves careful close reading on a line-by-line basis, an assignment of this type will usually deal with a relatively short poem or a passage from a longer one. Some poems yield most of their meaning on a single reading; others, however, may contain complexities and nuances that deserve a careful inspection of how the poet utilizes all of the resources at his or her command. A typical explication examines both form and content and how they are related. Because assignments in analysis usually involve many of the same techniques as explication, we will look at explication more closely. Poetry explications usually require much more familiarity with the technical details of poems than do those about fiction and drama, so following is a checklist of questions that you might ask before explicating a poem. The answers apply to a poem from this book, William Shakespeare's "Sonnet 73."

## Form

1. How many lines does the poem contain? How are they arranged into stanzas? Is either the whole poem or the stanza an example of a traditional poetic form?

> Shakespeare's "Sonnet 73" contains fourteen
> lines, printed as one stanza but grammatically
> divided into three quatrains of four lines each fol-
> lowed by a concluding couplet that is characteristic
> of an English sonnet, in contrast to the octave and
> sestet division of an Italian sonnet.

2. Is there anything striking in the visual arrangement of the poem—indentation, spacing, etc.? Are capitalization and punctuation unusual?

> Capitalization and punctuation are standard
> in the poem, and Shakespeare follows the tradi-
> tional practice of capitalizing the first word of
> each line.

3. In what metre, if any, is the poem written? Does the poet use any notable examples of substitution in the metre? Are the lines primarily end-stopped or enjambed?

> The metre is fairly regular iambic pentameter
> ("That time / of year / thou mayst / in me / behold")
> with occasional substitution of trochees, particularly
> to emphasize the opening word of a line ("Bare ru- /
> ined choirs, ‖ / where late / the sweet / birds
> sang.")
> Enjambment occurs at the ends of lines one, two,
> and five. This has the effect of masking the regular
> metre and rhymes and enforcing a quiet conversational
> tone, an effect that is assisted by the caesurae in
> lines two, four, eight, and thirteen. The caesura in
> this penultimate line emphasizes the direct involve-
> ment of the listener who must now apply the lesson
> that nothing lasts forever directly to strengthening
> the relationship with the persona. The couplet at the
> end of an English sonnet is often a commentary on

the preceding quatrains that brings the poem to an
epigrammatic close.

**4. What is the rhyme scheme, if any, of the poem? What types of rhyme
are used?**

> The rhyme scheme of this poem is <u>ababcdcdefefgg</u>.
> Shakespeare uses exact masculine rhyme, though it
> could be argued that, in addition to the rhyming of
> "strong" and "long," the last words of lines thirteen
> and fourteen, "love more" and "leave ere," are slant
> or near rhymes.

**5. Are significant sound patterns evident? Is there any repetition of
whole lines, phrases, or words?**

> Alliteration is present in "<u>by</u> and <u>by</u> <u>b</u>lack
> night" in line seven and "<u>s</u>econd <u>s</u>elf, that <u>s</u>eals" in
> line eight, and there are also instances of assonance
> ("sh<u>a</u>ke ag<u>ai</u>nst"; "t<u>a</u>ke aw<u>ay</u>") and consonance ("you<u>th</u>
> do<u>th</u>"; "tha<u>t</u> which i<u>t</u>"). However, these sound pat-
> terns do not call excessive attention to themselves
> or depart from the poem's quiet reflective tone.
> "Sonnet 73" contains repetition in the three differ-
> ent metaphors used to explore the aging process, and
> the emphasis on the listener's evolving perception,
> "in me behold," "in me thou see'st" (twice) and "This
> thou perceiv'st." An instance of parallel phrasing
> occurs in line two, "or none, or few."

## Content

**1. To what genre (lyric, narrative, dramatic) does the poem belong?
Does it contain elements of more than one genre?**

> The sonnet form has traditionally been used for
> lyric poetry, and this is a lyric poem, but it also
> contains narrative elements in the aging of the per-
> sona, and dramatic elements in that the persona is
> directly addressing a listener who is encouraged to
> love deeply because time is passing.

2. Who is the persona of the poem? Is there an auditor? If so, who? What is the relationship between persona and auditor? Does the poem have a specific setting? If so, where and when is it taking place? Is there any action that has taken place before the poem opens? What actions take place during the poem?

> The persona here is the speaker who is describing his own aging process through a variety of metaphors to inspire his younger friend to love well against the inevitable end of the relationship. Considerable research and speculation have been directed toward the mystery of the unnamed auditor in Shakespeare's sonnets. Sonnets 1 to 126 appear to be directed toward a handsome young aristocrat whose identity has never been firmly established. Subsequent sonnets seem directed toward a "Dark Lady," and others toward a rival poet. The sonnets were probably written over a number of years, many before 1598, but some perhaps right up to the date of first publication in 1609, when Shakespeare was fifty-five. The setting is not explicitly stated, though the "bare ruined choirs" are a reminder of specific events in English history. In 1534, the Act of Supremacy declared that King Henry VIII was the Supreme Head of the Church of England. Roman Catholic monasteries throughout England were dissolved and their vast lands and goods were turned over to the king. Some confiscated church buildings were destroyed or vandalized, and left in ruins. Choirs are the areas of the church where the choirs once sang, and here the persona is comparing them to the empty branches of a winter tree after the birds have flown south, and to the bare, shaking arms of an old man.

3. Does the poem contain any difficulties with grammar or syntax? What individual words or phrases are striking because of their denotation or connotation?

> The syntax of "Sonnet 73" is relatively straight-forward, though it contains several inversions in

which the words do not appear in the expected order.
A paraphrase of the opening line might be "you see in
me that time of year . . ." The three quatrains and
the one couplet are each distinct grammatical units
containing a single sentence. The only exception to
the commas dividing the clauses is the semi-colon in
line six, a punctuation mark now generally used only
where one could use a period instead. The poem's
vocabulary is not unusual, though Shakespeare uses
"thou" instead of "you" and "ere" instead of "before."
Night is described as "Death's second self" because it
brings darkness and sleep which, although temporary,
resemble the permanent sleep of death. One other element to note is Shakespeare's use of syncope, or the
use of an apostrophe in place of an absent letter, so
that a word like "perceivest," which would ordinarily
be three syllables, becomes the two-syllable "perceiv'st" for the sake of preserving the metre.

**4. Does the poem use any figures of speech? If so, how do they add to the overall meaning? Is the action of the poem to be taken literally, symbolically, or both ways?**

"Sonnet 73" makes marvellously complex use of
metaphor, comparing growing old to autumn, twilight,
and the dying of a fire. The image of autumn is
developed through the loss of leaves, which symbolically indicates the loss of youthful vitality, but
might also, on the literal level, be analogous to
balding! The shivering caused by wind and cold suggests the shaking of hands and voice that sometimes
accompany aging. Even though the metaphors are
largely visual, Shakespeare also employs the tactile
and the auditory more fully to evoke the experience
he is describing. "Black night" is personified as a
thief who steals the twilight, and is further
described as "Death's second self." In Greek mythology, the personification of night is Nyx, who gives
birth to Thanatos (death) and his twin brother,
Hypnos (sleep).

In the third quatrain the persona compares himself to glowing embers in the ashes, all that remains
of the bright fire of youth amidst the greying (both
literal and symbolic) of age. Paradoxically, the wood
is turned to ash by the very flame it feeds. The time
frame becomes increasingly urgent in each successive
quatrain, from the dying of the year, to the dying
of the day, to the dying of the fire. This last event
may take only moments as the final spark flickers
out. Similarly, the setting becomes increasingly
intimate, moving from outdoors to indoors, and bringing the poem full circle as the bare boughs of the
opening stanza may well become the logs that have
now turned to ash.

5. Is the title of the poem appropriate? What are its subject, tone of
voice, and theme? Is the theme stated or implied?

Generally, titles of poems provide vitally
important clues about significance and meaning but,
as far as we know, Shakespeare did not title his
sonnets. The numbers we use have been added for the
sake of identification, and do not necessarily represent Shakespeare's intentions for the ordering of
his sonnet sequence. In the absence of a title by
the author, poems are often referred to by the first
line of the poem inside square brackets to indicate
that this is not original to the author.

Shakespeare's subject matter, the necessity of
caring intensely for those we will not always have
with us, is powerfully evoked through comparisons
between human beings and the familiar processes of
nature. Critics have noted that the theme of separation haunts many of Shakespeare's sonnets, and this
one is no exception, but the obsession with the passing of time is tempered by the ways that such knowledge inspires us to live and love more fully. An
awareness of mortality should result not in despair
but in a re-evaluation of priorities, for example,
those prompted by such questions as "What would you

do if you knew you only had a month to live?" The
poet's metaphors, though sobering, contain a ray of
hope in that winter gives way to spring, night gives
way to dawn, and fires can be rekindled. Though
friends and lovers may be parted by distance or
death, love itself endures.

Your instructor may ask you to employ specific strategies in your explication and may require a certain type of organization for the paper. It is
important not just to identify formal elements and figures of speech but
to consider how these contribute to our understanding of the poem. Any
written text represents a series of choices on the part of the author. You
should assume that the poet has made particular choices for particular
reasons, and seek to explain what those reasons might be, using evidence from the poem to support your arguments in a coherent and
careful way. In writing the body of the explication, you will probably
proceed through the poem from beginning to end, summarizing and
paraphrasing some lines and quoting others fully when you feel an
explanation is required. It should be stressed that there are many ways,
in theory, to approach a poem and that no two explications of the same
poem will agree in every detail. Some instructors may favour an explication that links the poem to events in the author's life, to the socio-
historical context in which it was written, or to some other critical
approach.

An assignment in analysis, which looks closely at the way a single
element—dramatic situation, metre, form, imagery, one or more figures of speech, theme—functions in poetry, would probably require
that you write on two or more poems; in such cases a comparison–
contrast or definition–illustration paper may be called for. An assignment of this type might examine two related poems by the same
poet, or it might inspect the way that several poets have used a poetic
device or theme.

Comparison–contrast essays look for both similarities and differences in two poems. Definition–illustration papers usually begin with a
general discussion of the topic, say, a popular theme like the *carpe diem*
motif, and then go on to illustrate how this motif may be found in several different poems. Assignments in analysis often lead to longer papers
that may require the use of secondary sources.

# Writing About Drama

A review of a play is an evaluation of an actual performance and will focus less on the text of the play itself (especially if it is a well-known one) than on the actors' performances, the overall direction of the production, and the elements of staging. Because reviews are, first, news stories, basic information about the time and place of production should be given at the beginning of the review. A short summary of the play's plot might follow, and subsequent paragraphs will evaluate the performers and the production. Remember that a review is chiefly a *recommendation*, either positive or negative, to readers. Films of many of the plays in this book are available on videotape or DVD, and you might also be asked to review one of these versions, paying attention to the ways in which directors have "opened up" the action by utilizing the complex technical resources of motion pictures. Excellent examples of drama and film reviews can be found in almost any major newspaper, in the pages of popular magazines like *Time* or *Maclean's*, or on the Internet.

Explication assignments, like the examples from fiction and poetry given earlier, will probably require that you pay close attention to a selected passage, giving a detailed account of all the fine shadings of language in a scene or perhaps a single speech. Because Shakespeare's poetry is often full of figurative language that may not be fully understood until it has been subjected to explication, close reading of one of the monologues or soliloquies in *Othello* would be a likely choice for this type of writing assignment. Or you might be asked to explicate selected passages for a common thread of imagery, for example, identifying the various kinds of birds to which the condescending Helmer metaphorically compares his wife Nora throughout *A Doll's House*.

Analysis assignments typically hinge on only one of the elements of the play, like plot or characterization, or on a concept set forth by a critic. For example, you might be asked to explain Aristotle's statements about reversal and recognition and then apply his terminology to a twentieth-century play like *Death of a Salesman*. Here you would attempt to locate relevant passages from the play to support Aristotle's contentions about the importance of these reversals in the best plots. Or you might be asked to provide a summary of his comments about the tragic hero and then apply this definition to a character like Othello. Again, comparison and contrast schemes are useful. You might be asked to contrast two or more characters in a single play (the different dreams and aspirations of the seven women in *The Rez Sisters*) or to compare characters in two different plays (Othello as he is portrayed by Shakespeare and Djanet Sears).

## The Process of Research: The Library and the Internet

Research is a time-consuming and sometimes frustrating process, but a few general principles may help you to streamline it. First, bear in mind that about ninety percent of the time you spend on assembling research materials will take place through effective use of library catalogues and other computer databases. If you rush off to consult a book on the fifth-floor shelves every time you locate a mention of something that is potentially useful to you, you may gain more expertise in climbing steps than in conducting effective research. Thus, use the reference room to assemble the "shopping list" of items you will have to find in other parts of the library. Also, remember that the online index has greatly enhanced the mechanics of research. It may be frustrating to learn that an article you spotted in a musty index and found, after a long search, in a bound volume of a journal could have been downloaded and printed out in seconds from an electronic database.

Most contemporary students have literally grown up writing with computers and are familiar with the Internet. Still, a few words about the use of the Internet for online research may be helpful. In recent years, the Internet has facilitated the chores of research, and many online databases, reference works, and periodicals may be quickly located using search engines like Google *(www.google.ca)*. The Internet also holds a wealth of information in the form of individual Web sites devoted to authors, many of which are run by universities or private organizations. Navigating the Internet can be a forbidding task, and a book like Lester Faigley's *The Longman Guide to the Web* is an invaluable traveller's companion. Students should be aware, however, that Web sites vary widely in quality. Some are legitimate sources displaying sound scholarship; others are little more than "fan pages" that may contain erroneous or misleading information. Online information, like any other kind of research material, should be carefully evaluated before using it.

Careful documentation of your sources is essential; if you use any material other than what is termed "common knowledge" you must cite it in your paper. Common knowledge includes biographical information, an author's publications, prizes and awards received, and other information that can be found in more than one reference book. Anything else—direct quotes or material you have put in your own words by paraphrasing—requires both a parenthetical citation in the body of your paper and an entry on your works cited pages.

The first step in successful research is very simple: Read the assigned text before looking for secondary sources. After you have read the story, poem, or play that you have been assigned, you may have already begun to formulate a workable thesis sentence. If you have done this before beginning your research, you will eliminate any number of missteps and repetitions. Next, perform a subject search for books that will be useful to you. If, for example, you are writing on one of John Keats's odes, a subject search may reveal one or more books devoted solely to this single type of poem. Library catalogues are set up in different configurations, but many of them allow multiple "keyword" searches; a command like FIND KEATS AND ODE will automatically find all books in the library that mention both subjects. If you are unfamiliar with your terminology and do not know, for example, how an ode differs from other kinds of poems, you should consult a reference book containing a discussion of literary terms. After you have located books and reference sources that will be of use, check the journals that publish literary criticism. The standard index for these is the *MLA International Bibliography*, which is available both in bound volumes and in online versions. A reference librarian may also direct you to other indexes such as the *Literary Criticism Index*, the *Canadian Periodical Index*, the *Humanities Index*, the *Essay & General Literature Index*, and the *Annual Bibliography of English Language & Literature (ABELL)*. It is a good idea to check indexes like these early in your research. No single university library carries all of the journals listed in the *MLA International Bibliography*, and you may discover that getting a reprint through interlibrary services can take a week or more.

Once you have located and assembled your sources, you can decide which of them will be most valuable to you. Again, if you have already formulated your thesis and perhaps completed a tentative outline as well, you can move more swiftly. One useful addition to every library is a photocopier, which removes the tedious chore of taking notes by hand. Note cards may still be useful if you want to try different arrangements of your material, but most students have happily discarded them as relics of the distant past.

It is impossible to guess what research materials will be available in any given library, but most university libraries contain many different kinds of indexes and reference books for literary research. If you are writing about a living writer, particularly recommended are three popular reference sets published by Gale Research: *Dictionary of Literary Biography (DLB)*, *Contemporary Authors (CA)*, and *Contemporary Literary Criticism (CLC)*. Both of the latter two reference works are also available in editions that cover the nineteenth and twentieth centuries. These will provide you both with useful overviews of careers and with generous samples of criticism about the authors. *DLB* and *CA* articles also contain extensive bibliographies of other relevant sources; *CLC* contains reprints of book reviews and relevant passages from critical works. Similar to these reference works are those in the *Critical Survey* series from Magill Publishers, multi-volume sets that focus on short and long fiction, poetry, drama, and film. Another reliable source of information on individual writers can be found in several series of critical books published by Twayne Publishers, which can be located in a subject search. The *Oxford Companion to Canadian Literature*, the *Encyclopaedia of Literature in Canada*, and the multi-volume reference work *Canadian Writers and Their Works* are also helpful resources. The *MLA* index will direct you to articles on authors in scholarly journals, including a number of journals that deal specifically with Canadian literature, such as *Studies in Canadian Literature/Études en littérature canadienne (SCL/ÉLC)*, *Essays on Canadian Writing*, and *Canadian Poetry: Studies, Documents, Reviews*. *Poetry Criticism* and *Short Story Criticism* are multi-volume reference works that reprint excerpts from critical essays and books. There are several popular indexes of book reviews, including the annual *Book Review Digest* and the *Canadian Book Review Annual*. Two reference sources providing examples of professional drama reviews are *The New York Times Theater Reviews*, *1920–1970* (and subsequent volumes) and the *Canadian Theatre Review*. Popular magazines containing book, drama, and film reviews (and occasionally poetry reviews as well) include *Time*, *Newsweek*, and *Maclean's*, and these reviews are indexed in the *Readers' Guide to*

*Periodical Literature* or *Canadian Periodicals*. Also, yearbooks like *Theatre World* or the *Dictionary of Literary Biography Yearbook* provide a wealth of information about the literary activities of a given year.

## Quotation and Citation

First, a warning about plagiarism. Few students knowingly plagiarize, and those who do usually are not successful at it. An instructor who has read four or five weak papers from a student is likely to be suspicious if the same student suddenly begins to sound like an officer of the Modern Language Association, writing, with no citations, about "paradigms" or "*différence*" in the "*texte.*" A definition of "common knowledge," the kind of information that does not require a citation, is given above. Otherwise, any *opinion* about a writer and his or her work must be followed by a citation indicating its source. If the opinion is directly quoted, paraphrased, or even summarized in passing, then you should still include a citation. To do less than this is to commit an act of plagiarism, for which the penalties are usually severe. Internet materials, which are so easily cut and pasted into a manuscript, provide an easy temptation but are immediately noticeable. Nothing is easier to spot in a paper than an uncited "lift" from a source; in most cases the vocabulary and sentence structure will be radically different from the rest of the paper.

You should always support the general statements you make about a story, poem, or play by quoting directly from the text or, if required, by using secondary sources for additional critical opinion. *The MLA Handbook for Writers of Research Papers* (6th ed.), which is found in the reference section of almost any library, contains standard formats for bibliographies and manuscripts; indeed, most of the writing handbooks used in university courses provide guidelines for both MLA and APA style. If you have doubts or if you have not been directed to use a certain format, ask your instructor which one he or she prefers.

The type of parenthetical citation used in MLA-style format to indicate the source of quotations is simple to learn and dispenses with such tedious and repetitive chores as footnotes and endnotes. In using parenthetical citations remember that your goal is to direct your reader from the quoted passage in the paper to the corresponding entry on your works cited pages and from there, if necessary, to the book or periodical from which the quote was taken. A good parenthetical citation gives only the *minimal* information needed to accomplish this task. Here are a few typical examples from student papers on fiction, poetry, and drama. The first discusses Cheever's "Reunion":

> Cheever moves very quickly to indicate that the
> "Reunion" may well be memorable but will not be
> happy. As soon as father and son enter the first
> restaurant and are seated, Charlie's father
> begins to act strangely: "We sat down, and my
> father hailed the waiter in a loud voice.
> 'Kellner!' he shouted. 'Garcon! Cameriere! You!' His
> boisterousness in the empty restaurant seemed out of
> place" (518).

Here you should note a couple of conventions of writing about fiction and literature in general. One is that the present tense is used in speaking of the events of the story; in general, use the present tense throughout your critical writing, except when you are giving biographical or historical information. Second, note the use of single and double quotation marks. Double quotes from the story are changed to single quotes here because they appear within the writer's own quotation marks. The parenthetical citation lists only a page number, for earlier in this paper the writer has mentioned Cheever by name and the context makes it clear that the quotation comes from the story. Only one work by Cheever appears among the works cited entries. If several works by Cheever had been listed there, the parenthetical citation would clarify which one was being referred to by adding a shortened form of the book's title: (*Stories* 518). The reader finds the following entry among the sources:

> Cheever, John. <u>The Stories of John Cheever</u>. New York:
>     Knopf, 1978.

Similarly, quotes and paraphrases from secondary critical sources should follow the same rules of common sense:

> Cheever's daughter Susan, in her candid memoir
> of her father, observes that the author's alcoholism
> followed an increasingly destructive pattern:
>> Long before I was even aware that he was
>> alcoholic, there were bottles hidden all over
>> the house, and even outside in the privet

> hedge and the garden shed. Drink was his cru-
> cible, his personal hell. As early as the
> 1950s [. . .] he spent a lot of energy trying
> not to drink before 4 p.m., and then before
> noon, and then before 10 a.m., and then
> before breakfast. (43)
>
> But she goes on to observe that Cheever's drinking
> had not yet affected his skills as a writer.

This quotation is longer than four lines, so it is indented ten spaces. Indented quotes of this type do not require quotation marks. Also note how ellipses in square brackets are used to omit extraneous information. Because the author of the quotation is identified, only the page number is included in the parenthetical citation. The reader knows where to look among the sources:

> Cheever, Susan. <u>Home Before Dark</u>. Boston: Houghton,
> 1984.

Notice that a paraphrase of the same passage requires the citation as well:

> Cheever's daughter Susan, in her candid memoir
> of her father, observes that the author's alcoholism
> followed an increasingly destructive pattern. She
> notes that as a child she found bottles hidden in the
> house, in outbuildings, and even in the hedge. She
> recalls that he spent a great deal of energy simply
> not trying to drink before a certain hour, at first
> before 4 p.m. but eventually before breakfast (43).

To simplify parenthetical citations, it is recommended that quotations from secondary sources be introduced, whenever possible, in a manner that identifies the author so that only the page number of the quotation needed inside of the parentheses.

Slightly different conventions govern quotations from poetry, like this one from *The Riverside Shakespeare:*

> In describing the season in which "yellow
> leaves, or none, or few, do hang / Upon those boughs"
> (1856), Shakespeare inverts the expected progression
> of the falling leaves.

Here you should note a couple of conventions for writing about poetry. One is that, again, the present tense is used in discussing the poem; second, note how only parts of lines are quoted here to support the sentence and how those parts fit smoothly into the author's sentence structure. In general, brackets and ellipses [ . . .] are not necessary at the beginning or end of these quotations because it is clear that they are quoted fragmentarily; they should, however, be used if something is omitted from the middle of a quote ("black night [ . . .] Death's second self"). The virgule or slash (/) is used to indicate line breaks; a double slash (//) indicates stanza breaks. Quotes of up to three lines should be treated in this manner. If a quote is longer than three lines, it should be indented ten spaces (with no quotation marks) and printed as it appears in the original poem.

> Shakespeare's use of seasonal imagery to convey mortality can be compared with lines from Canadian poet Margaret Avison's twentieth-century sonnet "Snow."
>> ... snow's legend: colour of mourning
>> Along the yellow Yangtze where the wheel
>> Spins an indifferent stasis that's death's warning.
>> Asters of tumbled quietness reveal
>> their petals. (17)

The parenthetical citation here lists only a page number because only one work by Avison appears in the list of works cited (note that the *MLA Handbook* suggests that you also include line numbers, a practice that is probably unnecessary in discussing a short poem). If several works by the poet had been listed among the works cited, the parenthetical citation would clarify which one was being referred to by adding the book's title in a complete or shortened form: *(Winter Sun* 17). The reader finds the following entry among the sources:

Avison, Margaret. <u>Winter Sun</u>. Toronto: U of Toronto
    P, 1960.

As in the example from the Cheever story, the parenthetical citation here lists only a page number because only one work by Avison appears in the list of works cited. If you are dealing with a classic poem that can be found in many editions (an ode by Keats or a Shakespeare sonnet, for example), the *MLA Handbook* recommends using line numbers instead of page numbers inside the parentheses. This practice should also be followed if you have included a copy of the poem that you are explicating with the paper.

Quoting from a play follows similar procedures. These examples discuss *Othello:*

> In a disarming display of modesty before the Venetian senators, Othello states that his military background has not prepared him to act as an eloquent spokesman in his own defence, readily admitting that "little shall I grace my cause / In speaking for myself" (1.3.90-91).

Classic poetic dramas like *Othello* may be cited by act, scene, and line numbers instead of by page numbers. The reader knows that Shakespeare is the author, so the citation here will simply direct him or her to the edition of Shakespeare listed in the works cited pages at the end of the paper. Also note that verse dramas should be quoted in the same manner as poems; quotations of more than three lines should be indented ten spaces. In this paper, a scene involving dialogue is quoted:

> In the climactic scene of *Othello*, Shakespeare's practice of fragmenting his blank verse lines into two or more parts emphasizes the violence that is about to occur:
>
> | | |
> |---|---|
> | OTHELLO. | He hath confessed. |
> | DESDEMONA. | What, my lord? |
> | OTHELLO. | That he hath used thee. |
> | DESDEMONA. | How? Unlawfully? |
> | OTHELLO. | Ay. |
> | DESDEMONA. | He will not say so. (5.2.72-74) |

If you are quoting from a prose drama, you would cite a page number from the edition of the play that you used:

> In <u>A Doll's House</u> Ibsen wants to demonstrate
> immediately that Nora and Helmer share almost child-
> like attitudes toward each other. "Is that my little
> lark twittering out there?" is Helmer's initial line
> in the play (43).

Remember that common sense is the best test to apply to any parenthetical citation. Have you given the reader enough information in the citation to locate the source from which the quote was taken?

# Sample Works Cited Entries

Here are formats for some of the most commonly accessed types of materials used in literary research. More detailed examples may be found in the *MLA Handbook for Writers of Research Papers*.

### A BOOK BY A SINGLE AUTHOR

Thien, Madeleine. <u>Simple Recipes</u>. Toronto:
    McClelland, 2001.

- Author's name, reversed for alphabetization, followed by a period.
- Full name of the book underlined or italicized and
  followed by a period.
- Publication information, including city of publication followed by a colon, publisher's name in a
  concise form followed by a comma, and year of
  publication followed by a period.

Carrier, Roch. <u>The Hockey Sweater and Other Stories</u>.
    Trans. Sheila Fischman. Toronto: Anansi, 1979.

### A BOOK WITH AUTHOR AND EDITOR

Shakespeare, William. <u>The Riverside Shakespeare</u>. Ed.
    G. Blakemore Evans. 2nd ed. Boston: Houghton
    Mifflin, 1997.
Woolf, Virginia. <u>The Complete Shorter Fiction of
    Virginia Woolf</u>. Ed. Susan Dick. San Diego:
    Harcourt, 1985.

## A Casebook or Collection of Critical Essays

Kolin, Philip C. ed. <u>Othello: New Critical Essays</u>.
   New York: Routledge, 2002.
Murphy, Brenda and Susan C. W. Abbotson.
   <u>Understanding Death of a Salesman: A Student
   Casebook to Issues, Sources, and Historical
   Documents</u>. Westport, CT: Greenwood, 1999.

## An Individual Selection from a Casebook or Edited Collection

Kruk, Laurie. "Hands and Mirrors: Gender Reflections
   in the Short Stories of Alistair MacLeod and
   Timothy Findley." <u>Dominant Impressions: Essays
   on the Canadian Short Story</u>. Eds. Gerald Lynch
   and Angela Arnold Robinson. Ottawa: U of Ottawa
   P, 1999. 137-50.
Stott, Rebecca. "'How Do I Love Thee?': Love and
   Marriage." <u>Elizabeth Barrett Browning</u>. Eds.
   Simon Avery and Rebecca Stott. London: Longman,
   2003. 134-55.

## A Poem, Play, or Story Reprinted in an Anthology or Textbook

Clarke, George Elliott. "Casualties." <u>Fiery
   Spirits & Voices: Canadian Writers of African
   Descent</u>. Ed. Ayanna Black. Toronto: Harper
   Collins, 2000. 257.
Lahiri, Jhumpa. "Interpreter of Maladies."
   <u>Literature: A Pocket Anthology</u>. 2nd Canadian ed.
   Eds. R. S. Gwynn and Wanda Campbell. Toronto:
   Pearson, 2008. 334-53.

## An Article in a Reference Book

"Margaret Avison." <u>Encyclopedia of Literature in
   Canada</u>. Toronto: U of Toronto P, 2002. 53-55.
"Aidoo, Ama Ata." <u>Encyclopedia of Post-Colonial
   Literatures in English</u>. 2nd ed. London:
   Routledge, 2005.

## An Article in a Scholarly Journal

Compton, Anne. "Writing Paintings and Thinking
Physics: Anne Simpson's Poetry." <u>Canadian
Literature</u>. 185 (2005): 30–42.
McGill, Robert. "Where Do You Think You Are? Alice
Munro's Open Houses." <u>Mosaic</u>. 35.4 (2002):
103–19.

## A Book Review in a Periodical or Newspaper

Creelman, David. "Seeking Private Nowlan." Rev. of <u>If
I Could Turn and Meet Myself: The Life of Alden
Nowlan</u>, by Patrick Toner. <u>The Fiddlehead</u>. 204
(2000): 222–24.
Babstock, Ken. "Awesome Avison." Rev. of <u>Concrete and
Wild Carrot</u>, by Margaret Avison. <u>The Globe and
Mail</u>. 21 June 2003: D13.

## Online Article or Review

Nothof, Anne. "The Artist as Moving Target in Sharon
Pollock's Moving Pictures." <u>WWR Magazine</u>. Summer
2005. 1 July 2006 <http://www.crcstudio.arts.
ualberta.ca/wwr_magazine_online/summer_05/>.
Keith, W. J. "The Poetry of Alden Nowlan: A Critical
Reassessment." <u>Canadian Poetry</u>. 53 (2003): 9–32.
1 July 2006 <http://www.canadianpoetry.ca/
cpjrn/vol53/keith.htm>.

## Interview

McKay, Don. "The Appropriate Gesture, or Regular
Dumb-Ass Guy Looks at Bird." <u>Where the Words
Come From: Canadian Poets in Conversation</u>. Ed.
Tim Bowling. Roberts Creek, BC: Nightwood,
2002. 44–61.
Sears, Djanet. Interview. <u>Canadian Adaptations
of Shakespeare</u>. Mar. 2004. 15 July 2006
<http://www.canadianshakespeares.ca/
i_dsears.cfm>.

### FILM, VIDEO, OR AUDIO RECORDING

<u>Act Without Words I</u>. Dir. Karel Reisz. DVD. Beckett
     on Film, 2002.
<u>Boys and Girls</u>. Dir. Don McBrearty. Videocassette.
     Atlantis/CBC, 1983.

### A WEB SITE

Mariotti, Meg. "The Lady of Shalott: Pre-Raphaelite
     Attitudes Toward Woman in Society." <u>The</u>
     <u>Victorian Web</u>. 1 Aug. 2006 <http://www.
     victorianweb.org/painting/prb/mariotti12.html>.
<u>Beckett on Film.</u> 15 Aug. 2006 <http::://www.
     beckettonfilm.com/>.

### AN ONLINE REFERENCE BOOK

"Sharon Pollock." <u>Canadian Theatre Encyclopedia</u>.
     1 July 2006 <http://www.canadiantheatre.com/.>
"Sonnet." *The Concise Oxford Dictionary of Literary
     Terms*. Christopher Baldick. Oxford U P, 1996.
     *Oxford Reference Online*. 19 July 2006 <http://
     www.oxfordreference.com>/views/ENTRY.html?
     subview=Main&entry=t56.e913>.

# The Annotated Bibliography

Many instructors consider the research paper a semester-long project and grade students' intermediate steps in the process—preliminary research, mastery of MLA-style formats, rough drafts, etc. One of the most popular types of intermediate assignments is to have students assemble a preliminary bibliography of different types of research materials—primary sources by the writer, reference book articles, book reviews, critical essays on the writer's work, interviews, Internet Web sites, and other materials. Although many of these sources may not actually be used in the works cited section of the final paper, students can gain an overview of an author's career, his or her chief concerns, and the critical reaction to the work by assembling such a bibliography. Brief annotation of the sources, which follows each entry, ensures that the students have inspected the material to see whether or not it will be useful in the final paper. Below are the first six entries in a sample annotated bibliography on a fictitious poet, "Marion Kirstein."

ANNOTATED BIBLIOGRAPHY

Cary, Jason. "Conspiracy Theories in Verse: Marion
      Kirstein on Form, Meter, and Rime." Saturday
      Review. 5 May 1973: 14–15.

In this early article/interview, Kirstein argues that
      prevailing fashions in verse have made it almost
      impossible for older poets to publish work in
      many magazines. Kirstein stresses that his own
      magazine, *Inner Vision*, remains open to these poets.

Collins, Michael .T. "The Poetry of Marion Kirstein."
      World Literature Today. 61.1 (1997): 55–58.

A 1500-word overview of Kirstein's career. Collins
      draws special attention to Kirstein's "unfashion-
      able" use of traditional forms like the sonnet.

Goodman, Thomas. "Marion Kirstein." American Poets
      Since World War II. Dictionary of Literary
      Biography. Vol. 5. 1980. 294–97.

This critical and biographical essay contains pho-
      tographs of Kirstein and sample manuscript
      pages. It pays particular attention to the
      influence of John Phillips, Kirstein's under-
      graduate creative writing teacher at Meridian
      College.

Hooper, Jeremy. "Marion Kirstein." Critical Survey of
      Poetry. 1982. 1167–76.

A 2500-word overview of Kirstein's career. Hooper is
      more interested in Kirstein's controversial
      political subject matter than in his poetic
      practices.

Kaye, Marilyn. Rev. of The Forsaken Cry, by Marion
      Kirstein. New York Times Book Review. 22 Mar.
      1984: 24.

A 250-word review of Kirstein's third book of poetry.
    Kaye praises Kirstein's formal technique but feels
    that his political sympathies are out of date.

Kirstein, Marion. "Be Still." <u>New Poets of England and
    America: Second Selection</u>. Eds. Donald Hall and
    Robert Pack. New York: Meridian, 1962. 149-51.

This three-hundred-line blank verse poem about the
    death of the poet's father appeared in
    Kirstein's first collection, <u>Afterglow</u>.

## Final Considerations

Finally, some basic matters of common sense are worth pondering. Consider the first impression the paper that you are about to turn in will make on your instructor, who may have to read, mark, and grade up to half a million words of student writing in a single semester. No instructor, with the clock ticking past midnight and the coffee growing cold, likes trying to read an essay in scrawled handwriting, with pieces of its torn edges, hastily ripped from a spiral notebook, drifting to the carpet. If your instructor does allow handwritten work, try to present a copy that can be read without extensive training in cryptographic analysis; in other words, make sure your writing is legible. But do not go to the opposite extreme and present a masterpiece of computer wizardry, complete with multiple sizes, shapes, and colours of fonts. In a word, plain vanilla is always the safest flavour to choose. Handwritten work should be done on one side of standard-ruled notebook paper, leaving generous margins on both the right-hand side and the bottom of the pages. In most cases, it will be required that your work be word-processed or typed. Your final copy should be double-spaced, using a letter-quality printer set at the highest resolution. Choose a standard typewriter-style font (Courier and Times Roman 12-point type are the most widely used), and do not expect a faint, smeared, draft-quality printout to receive as much attention as a readable manuscript printed on good-quality paper. Do not put your paper in any kind of folder or binder unless you are specifically asked to do so. You may have been given specific instructions about title pages and page numbering, so be sure to follow them.

It goes without saying that you should proofread your final draft carefully, paying particular attention to some of the special problems in writing mechanics (punctuation and verb tenses are two of the most common) that arise in critical papers. And, please, remember two things about the computer: First, a paper that has not been spell-checked is absolute proof of lack of diligence; second, even the most sophisticated spell checker cannot distinguish between "there" and "their" or "it's" and "its." Errors in proper nouns, such as the names of authors or publishers, also must be checked manually. Writing assignments are graded both for content and for their demonstration that the writer knows the basics of composition. A spelling error on the title page is not the best introduction to the body of your paper, and even the most original insights into a literary work will not receive due credit if the rules of standard English are consistently ignored. Be sure you allow yourself enough time to develop and polish your essay because, as the review below indicates, there are many steps to the process.

1. **Read**—Know your primary material well before you look at secondary sources.
2. **Research**—The nature of the assignment will determine the degree of research required.
3. **Review**—A focused pattern of argument should emerge as you review your rough notes.
4. **Write**—Formulate a working thesis and a tentative outline, and write a rough first draft.
5. **Reorganize**—Prove your arguments by including the right supporting material in the right place.
6. **Refine**—Pay particular attention to your introduction, thesis, transitions, and conclusion.
7. **Rewrite**—Think about style as well as substance. Formal essays demand formal language.
8. **Revise**—Check paragraphing, grammar, punctuation, verb tenses, agreement, and spelling.
9. **Reference**—All quotations should be carefully integrated and carefully documented.
10. **Reread**—Have you followed all the guidelines? Is the paper correct, coherent, and convincing?

Effective writing requires a long process involving topic selection, assembly of support, organization, rough drafts, and final adjustments. By the time you have finished printing out your final draft, you may feel that you have not only exhausted the topic, but that it has exhausted *you*. Still, the most important element that you can bring to any assignment is the simplest one: *care*. May your efforts be rewarded!

# Fiction

# Introduction to Fiction

## The Telling of the Tale

Alice Munro writes that "a story is more like a house [than a road]. Everybody knows what a house does, how it encloses space and makes connections between one enclosed space and another and presents what is outside in a new way." Stories are dwellings we love to build, to visit, and to inhabit. To respond to the simple magic of the storyteller's art is to enact one of the human race's oldest rituals, but before we can begin to examine the elements of literary fiction we must bear in mind that literature in its written form is historically a recent innovation; indeed, its two most common modern forms, the short story and the novel, have been in existence for little more than two centuries. Yet long before the invention of writing, for thousands of years ancient peoples developed complex **oral traditions** of literature; these stories, dealing with the creation of the cosmos and the origins of gods and goddesses, formed a body of **myths**, supernatural narratives widely believed to be true by the people of a given culture, and **legends,** popular stories about characters and events that may contain trace elements of historical truth. Even in modern societies, elements of this primitive folklore survive in regional or ethnic tales passed on through the generations, most often taking the written form of **folk tales** collected by literary scholars; **fairy tales,** like Charles Perrault's "Beauty and the Beast" or Hans Christian Andersen's "The Little Mermaid"; **beast fables** with animal characters; or **parables** like those found in the Gospels. Many of these, especially the fables and parables, are to some degree **didactic,** with the narrative events illustrating a **moral** that is either stated or implied. A fable is a short, non-realistic narrative that is told to illustrate a universal moral concept. A parable is similar but generally contains realistic characters and events. Thus, Aesop's fable of the tortoise and the hare, instead of telling us something about animal behaviour, illustrates the virtue of persistence against seemingly unbeatable competition. The parable of the Good Samaritan tells the story of a man who is robbed and beaten and eventually rescued by a stranger of another ethnicity in order to define the concept of "neighbour" for a questioning lawyer.

Even in modern societies, other ancient forms of oral literature still enjoy a good state of health. These include **anecdotes,** accounts of single incidents usually involving a well-known person, and **riddles** and **jokes** of all types, which often seem to spring into circulation overnight and often unwittingly mirror the basic situations and coarse humour of venerable **fabliaux**—short, realistic tales from the Middle Ages that often turn on a bawdy situation. Recently, much attention has been given to **urban legends,** so named by folklorist Jan Brunvand, which are short narratives involving grotesque incidents that are widely accepted as true. When myths and legends are assembled around the exploits of a great hero, the result is the **folk epic,** a long narrative in elevated style that is generally considered a starting point for any culture's literary history. Like most types of oral folk literature, epics were originally composed in verse for the sake of memorization, but they otherwise contain the same elements as modern literary forms like the short story and novel. For example, the individual **episodes** of Homer's *Odyssey*—such as Odysseus outwitting the Cyclops or his adventures with the sorceress Circe—can stand alone as exciting tales and also can fit into the larger structure of the epic, like chapters in a novel. Later authors, living in societies that had invented writing, consciously imitated the style of folk epics in composing **literary epics;** the *Aeneid* by Virgil (70–19 B.C.) and *The Divine Comedy* by Dante (1265–1321) are two famous examples. In the Middle Ages, **romances,** written in both verse and prose, gained great popularity among all social classes. These tales of chivalry involving a knightly hero and a series of exciting, if improbable, adventures were ridiculed by Miguel de Cervantes (1547–1616) in *Don Quixote*, a realistic account of an impoverished Spanish gentleman driven mad by reading too many romances. The eventual form that Cervantes gave Don Quixote's adventures was perhaps influenced by **picaresque novels** like the anonymous *Lazarillo of Tormes* (c. 1450), which involved a young orphan (or *pícaro*, Spanish for "rascal") in a series of loosely connected adventures. These picaresque tales are rightly considered the ancestors of modern realistic fiction. Many novels, from Mark Twain's *The Adventures of Huckleberry Finn* to J. D. Salinger's *The Catcher in the Rye* and Aritha Van Herk's *No Fixed Address*, borrow their structure from the picaresque novel, and the modern short story is indebted to its often stark level of realism.

## The Short Story

There is no agreement on the precise origins of the modern short story. One important influence in its development was the Italian **novella** of the late Middle Ages and Renaissance. The most famous collection of these realistic prose narratives is *The Decameron* by Giovanni Boccaccio (1313–1375). *The Decameron*, in which the individual stories are narrated by young men and women who have taken to the country to escape a plague, is an example of a **frame tale,** in which the stories are "framed" by a larger narrative. The famous Arabian collection *A Thousand and One Nights* is one of the earliest examples of this genre (a structure that is resurrected in films like *Pulp Fiction* and *Magnolia*). In translation, these tales were popular in other countries and widely imitated. In writing his plays, William Shakespeare frequently borrowed from Italian writers; his tragedy *Othello* takes its plot from a sensational novella by Giraldi Cinthio. We still use the term novella for short stories that are long enough (usually over 15 000 words) to be published separately in book form. Count Leo Tolstoy's *The Death of Ivan Ilyich* is a classic Russian example, and Ernest Hemingway's *The Old Man and the Sea* is one of the best-known novellas in American literature.

The first half of the nineteenth century is the great period of the growth of the short story as a distinct **literary genre,** or type, and its rise takes place in many countries at roughly the same time. Many reasons for this rapid development could be put forth, but perhaps the most important was the literary market established by newspapers and magazines aimed at middle-class audiences. The United States, with its increasingly high rate of literacy and expanding middle class, led the way in this period; Washington Irving's tales, like "Rip Van Winkle" and "The Legend of Sleepy Hollow," were among the first American writings to attain international popularity. Edgar Allan Poe, the first great theorist of the short story and one of its notable practitioners in this period, supported himself primarily (although not very prosperously) as a magazine editor and contributor, and thus had a large personal stake in promoting short fiction. Poe's influential review of Nathaniel Hawthorne's *Twice-Told Tales* in 1842 first stated the theory that a short story ought to be a unified artistic creation, as carefully shaped as a sonnet.

> *A skillful literary artist has constructed a tale. If wise, he has not fashioned his thoughts to accommodate his incidents; but having conceived, with deliberate care, a certain unique or single effect to be wrought out, he then invents such incidents—he then combines such events as may best aid him in establishing this preconceived effect. If his very initial sentence tend not to the outbringing of this effect, then he has failed in his first step. In the whole composition there should be no word written, of which the tendency, direct or indirect, is not to the one pre-established design. And by such means, with such care and skill, a picture is at length painted which leaves in the mind of him who contemplates it with a kindred art, a sense of the fullest satisfaction.*

This idea of the *single effect* is perhaps Poe's most important contribution to the development of the short story as a serious literary genre. Most of Hawthorne's and Poe's stories are perhaps more properly termed **tales,** narratives that contain elements that are exotic or supernatural and that depart from the level of ordinary experience. Poe himself established many of the conventions of the horror, science fiction, and detective tales still being written and read today. **Formula fiction,** which rigidly follows the clichés and conventions of a particular genre, is sometimes half-affectionately called **pulp fiction** (the source of the title for Quentin Tarantino's film), a reminder of the low-grade paper once used in inexpensive magazines. Still, the tale remains a lively tradition among serious artists as well. Among the contemporary stories collected in this volume, selections by Borges, Barthelme, Carrier, Walker, King, Shields, and others show their debt to the tradition of the tale.

The short story continued to develop in the nineteenth century, and its evolution was part of the larger literary movement of **realism,** which profoundly influenced the arts in the middle years of the nineteenth century. Defined as the "truthful treatment of material" by William Dean Howells, realism focused on unidealized explorations of common everyday life expressed in clear and direct prose. It has been rightly noted that realism represents the effect of democracy on literary history. Celebrating its appearance as early as 1837, Ralph Waldo Emerson noted, "The literature of the poor, the feelings of the child, the philosophy of the street, the meaning of household life, are the topics of the time." **Naturalism,** an outgrowth of realism that emerged in the second half of the nineteenth century, also proved influential because it joined realistic treatments of everyday life with understandings of human behaviour drawn from the new sciences of psychology and sociology. Both realism and naturalism remain vital currents in contemporary short fiction, as stories here by Alistair MacLeod and Jhumpa Lahiri will attest.

The twentieth century saw the short story rise to its highest level of popularity and just as rapidly decline in its influence as a literary form. In the second half of the century, many of the established magazines that regularly ran serious fiction ceased publication. Reading tastes have changed, and there is increased competition from movies, television, and the Internet. Still, the pages of so-called little magazines and literary quarterlies continue to provide outlets for publication, and new writers seem undeterred by the prospect of being paid with little more than what one disgruntled writer has called "two free copies of what I've already got." Almost every writer of short fiction prominent today first appeared in small-circulation periodicals of this type, and many have continued to publish in magazines that can offer, instead of money, prestige and a discriminating readership numbering in the hundreds. Indeed, the little magazines traditionally have been hospitable to many kinds of **experimental fiction** that editors of commercial magazines would never have considered. If the quantity of contemporary short fiction being published has shrunk from what it was in prior decades, the quality, one might argue, has remained the same or even improved. When we look at lists of recent winners of the Governor General's Award and the Man Booker, Pulitzer, and Nobel prizes, we discover many writers who have counted the short story as their first genre.

## Reading and Analyzing Short Fiction

We read for many reasons. In our daily lives most of our reading is strictly utilitarian—it is part of our jobs or education—or informational, as we scan the headlines of a daily newspaper for current events, business trends, or sports scores. We read short stories and other types of fiction for differing reasons. Sometimes our motive is simply to be entertained and to pass the time. Reading matter of this type is usually termed **escapist literature** and includes such popular categories as romance and detective novels, science fiction tales, westerns, and gothic novels. But literary fiction offers more than entertainment, making us think while engaging our imaginations. A short story that we can treat as a serious work of art will not yield all of its subtlety at first glance; in order to understand and appreciate its author's achievement fully we may have to examine its components—its plot, characterization, point of view, theme, setting, style, and symbolism—noting how each part contributes to the story's overall effect. Flannery O'Connor has warned that discussing story writing in terms of plot, character, and theme is like trying to describe the expression on a face by saying where the eyes, nose, and mouth are, and yet it is one way to explore the layered complexity of a story. The following exploration of aspects of the short story draws examples from "Reunion," a brief story by a modern American master of the genre, John Cheever (p. 162).

## *Plot*

In his discussion of tragedy in the *Poetics*, Aristotle (384–322 B.C.) gives first importance to plot as an element of a play, and most readers would agree that it holds a similar position in a work of fiction. Indeed, if we tell a friend about a short story we have enjoyed, we will probably give a **synopsis,** or brief summary, of its incidents. In the case of a very brief story like "Reunion," this synopsis is only a few sentences long:

> *In "Reunion" the narrator, a teenaged boy travelling by train, meets his estranged father during a stop for lunch in New York City. Over the course of an hour and a half, the father's alcoholism and potentially abusive personality are revealed. The story ends with the narrator boarding his train, indicating that this was the last time he saw his father, possibly by choice.*

Plot, according to Raymond Bradbury, "is no more than footprints left in the snow *after* your characters have run by on their way to incredible destinations." More simply, **plot** may be defined as a story's sequence of incidents, arranged in dramatic order. One is tempted to insert the word "chronological," but doing so would exclude many stories that depart from this strict ordering of events. Although its use is more characteristic in longer works like novels, many stories employ the **flashback** to narrate incidents in the past. Michael Winter's "Archibald the Arctic" begins with the policemen arriving at Gabriel English's door and then goes back in time to relate events that led up to that moment. Margaret Atwood's "Happy Endings" dispenses with a single plot line entirely, offering numerous possibilities for the fates of her characters. Conversely, writers sometimes use **foreshadowing** to provide hints of future actions in the story; an effective use of foreshadowing prevents a story's outcome from seeming haphazard or contrived. Of course, the manner in which stories handle time is largely illusory. During scenes with dialogue and action, time is slowed down by descriptive and explanatory phrases. At other times, stories cover gaps in chronology or leap over uneventful periods with transitional phrases and passages; the opening sentence of the second paragraph of "Reunion" ("We went out of the station and up a side street to a restaurant") compresses into a second or two an action that in reality would have taken at least several minutes. Even though "Reunion" does not take serious liberties with chronological time as we experience it, the ninety minutes of action in the story are compressed into about ten minutes of the reader's time. A plot like this, in which the action is more or less continuous within a single day, is called a **unified plot;** one that stretches over weeks or even longer periods and thus consists of isolated scenes connected by a thin tissue of transitional devices is called an **episodic plot.**

When we speak of the **dramatic structure** of a story, we refer to the exact way in which our emotional involvement in its plot is increased and relaxed. As Janet Burroway observes of the short story in *Writing Fiction*, "*Only* trouble is interesting." If we are not quickly engaged by the situation of a story and caught up in its plot, then we pronounce the cruellest of all critical verdicts on it by closing the book. The first part of this dramatic structure is the **exposition,** which provides the reader with essential information—who, what, when, where—he or she needs to know before continuing. Although writers of sophisticated fiction may try to disguise the fact, they often begin their stories with a version of the "Once upon a time" opening common to fairy tales. A variation on this type of beginning, called the **in medias res** ("in the middle of things") opening after the conventions of the old epic poems, may actually open with a "blind" bit of action before supplying its context.

The exposition of "Reunion" is fairly straightforward; in the first paragraph we learn who (Charlie and his father), what (a lunchtime meeting between trains), when (noon to 1:30 P.M.), and where (in and near Grand Central Station in Manhattan). Cheever might have begun the story with a slightly more "dramatic" sentence ("At twelve o'clock sharp I saw him coming through the crowd"), but he would have had to provide the essential contextual information in short order to avoid unnecessarily confusing the reader.

Exposition in a story usually describes a stable situation, even if it is not an entirely happy one. Charlie tells us that his parents' divorce is three years old and that he has not seen his father in that time. If he had not taken the step of writing the letter arranging the "reunion," that state of affairs might have gone on indefinitely. The appearance of "trouble" constitutes the second part of a plot, the **complication,** which is the appearance of some circumstance or event that shakes up the stable situation and begins the **rising action** of the story. Complication in a story may be either external or internal, or a combination of the two. A stroke of fortune that affects a character, such as illness or accident, is a typical example of an external complication, a problem that the character cannot ignore. An internal complication, in contrast, may not be immediately apparent, for it may result from a character's deep-seated uncertainties, dissatisfactions, and fears. The external complication in "Reunion" is the father's series of confrontations with waiters; the internal complication is Charlie's growing sense of pity and revulsion. Typically, the complication of a plot is heightened by **conflict** between two characters who have different personalities and goals. Charlie is overjoyed to see his father at the beginning of the story but, despite his knowledge that he will grow up to "be something like him," Charlie is more than eager to escape his father's company at the end, perhaps in an unconscious effort to run away from his own "future and [his]doom."

The body of a story is called the rising action and usually contains a number of scenes, involving action and dialogue, that build to **moments of crisis**—points in the story where a resolution of the complication momentarily seems at hand but quickly disappears. Aristotle used the term **peripety** for these moments of reversal, as the hopes of the characters rise and fall. Thus, in "Reunion" all that needs to be resolved, at least on the surface, is for the characters to order lunch, eat, and return in time for the departing train. The father's increasingly obnoxious behaviour, however, keeps postponing this resolution until the reunion has turned from a happy occasion into something very different. Unlike most stories, "Reunion" has a rising action as rigidly structured as a joke, with its four similar restaurant scenes that gradually escalate in absurdity as the father's senseless rage increases.

The central moment of crisis in a plot is the **climax,** or moment of greatest tension, which inaugurates the **falling action** of the story, in which the built-up tension is finally released. Some stories, particularly those involving a heavy use of suspense, have a steep "dramatic curve" and the writer uses all of his or her skills to impel the reader toward the final confrontation. Among writers included in this anthology, Edgar Allan Poe is the master of this kind of plot construction. Often one encounters the **trick ending** (also called the **O. Henry ending** after the pen name of William Sidney Porter, a popular writer of the late nineteenth century). A climax such as this depends on a quick reversal of the situation from an unexpected source; its success is always relative to the degree to which the reader is surprised when it occurs. The ending of Kate Chopin's "The Story of an Hour" hits both its protagonist and its reader with the same surprise. More typically, modern short stories instead rely on climactic devices that are somewhat subtler than unexpected plot twists. Many modern writers have followed James Joyce's lead in building not to a climactic event but to a moment of spiritual insight or revelation, what Joyce termed an **epiphany.** Epiphanies can take many forms, from an overheard chance remark that seems significant in the context of the story to a character's unpitying gaze at himself in a mirror. In the hands of a melodramatic writer insistent on sentimental happy endings, "Reunion" might have concluded with Charlie delivering a "tough love" sermon to his father, who would then fall to his knees and beg his son's forgiveness, having seen the error of his ways. Cheever's more realistic method of climax is, in this case, to avoid the confrontation altogether as Charlie escapes to his train.

The final part of a plot is the **dénouement,** or **resolution.** The French term literally refers to the untying of a knot, and we might compare the emotional release of a story's ending to a piece of cloth that has been twisted tighter and tighter and is then untwisted as the action winds down. The dénouement returns the characters to another stable situation. Just as fairy tales traditionally end with "And they lived happily ever after," many stories conclude with an indication of what the future holds for the characters. In the case of "Reunion," we return to the estrangement between Charlie and his father that existed at the beginning of the story, although this time all indications are that it will be a permanent one. A story's dénouement may be termed either closed or open. A **closed dénouement** ties up everything neatly and explains all unanswered questions the reader might have; a typical example is the "Elementary, my dear Watson" explanation of any remaining loose ends, which is provided by the sleuth Sherlock Holmes in the final paragraphs of Arthur Conan Doyle's famous tales. An **open dénouement** leaves us with a few tantalizing questions; the last phrase of "Reunion," which consciously mirrors the story's opening sentence, does not explicitly state *why* Charlie never sees his father again. Was it strictly his own choice? Did the father die soon after their meeting? Were other factors involved? We do not know, of course, and such an ending invites us to speculate.

One final word about plots: The fledgling writer attempting to invent a totally original plot is doomed to failure, and it is no exaggeration to say that there is nothing (or at least not much) new under the sun where plots of short stories are concerned. As Willa Cather maintains, "There are only two or three human stories and they go on repeating themselves as fiercely as if they had never happened before." Plots may be refurbished with new characters and settings, but they still draw on what psychologist Carl Jung called **archetypes,** universal types of characters and situations that all human beings carry in their unconscious mind. Plots deriving from these archetypes may be found in ancient mythologies, in fairy tales, and even in contemporary fiction. Among the most familiar are the triangle plot, a love story involving three people; the quest plot, which is unified around a group of characters on a journey; and the transformation plot, in which a weak or physically unattractive character changes radically in the course of the story. "Reunion" is an example of one of the most widely used of all archetypal plots, the **initiation story.** In a plot of this type, the main character, usually a child or adolescent, undergoes an experience (or **rite of passage**) that prepares him or her for adulthood. In this book, such stories as James Joyce's "Araby," Alice Munro's "Boys and Girls," Michael Winter's "Archibald the Arctic," and Madeleine Thien's

"Simple Recipes" share the same archetype, although they differ in many other respects.

## *Characterization*

Every story hinges on the actions undertaken by its main character, or **protagonist,** a term drawn from ancient Greek tragedy (literally "first debater") that is more useful in discussions of fiction than such misleading terms as hero or heroine. Additionally, stories may contain an opposing character, or **antagonist,** with whom the protagonist is drawn into conflict. In many modern stories, there is little, in any traditional sense, that is heroic about the protagonists; it may be more accurate to use a negative term, **anti-hero,** to designate one who occupies centre stage but otherwise seems incapable of fitting the traditional heroic mould. Indeed, writers of the last century have often been so reluctant to seem didactic in presenting characters that are "moral beacons" that they go to the opposite extreme in presenting protagonists whom we regard with pity or even disgust, rather than with admiration.

A character in a short story may be termed either a **flat character** or a **round character,** depending on the depth of detail the writer supplies. In "Reunion," the father is essentially a flat character, rendered with a few quick strokes of the pen and reduced to a single personality trait, his alcoholic rudeness. Minor flat characters in stories are often **stock characters,** stereotypes who may be necessary to advance the plot but otherwise are not deserving of more than the barest outlines of description. Round characters are given more than one trait, some of which may even seem contradictory, and are explored in depth as the author delves into the character's past and even into his or her unconscious mind. Characters of this type, usually a story's protagonist, begin to approach the level of complexity that we associate with real human beings.

**Development** and **motivation** are also important in any consideration of a story's characters. Characters can be either **static** or **dynamic,** depending on the degree to which they change in the course of the story. In "Reunion," the father is a static character. His personality was fixed long before the story opens, and there seems no likelihood that he will ever alter his course. But Charlie does attain some understanding in the course of the story, even if it is at the cost of his own disillusionment with what he wants his father to be. If development in a character is usually clear in a story, then motivation—the reasons the reader is given for a character's actions—may not be so obvious. In many cases, an author will simply tell us what is going on in a character's mind, but in others we are denied access to this level of understanding. Although we can speculate, playing the amateur psychiatrist, about Charlie's father's strange behaviour, we are not given any direct insight into his own view of his actions. In some stories, writers may try to plug directly into a character's thoughts by using **interior monologue,** a direct presentation of thought that is somewhat like a soliloquy in drama, or **stream-of-consciousness,** an attempt to duplicate raw sensory data in the same disordered state that the mind receives it. As useful as these last two devices can be in explaining motivation, they sometimes place excessive demands on readers' patience, for they require sifting through a jumble of thoughts and impressions whose significance is unclear.

**Description** of characters also helps us to understand the author's intent. In real life we are told from an early age not to judge people by external appearance, but in fiction the opposite is more often the case: Physical description is invariably a sign of what lurks beneath the surface. Given the brevity of most short stories, these physical details may be minimal but revealing in the author's choice of particulars. Cheever has Charlie describe his father at first as only "a big, good-looking man." Remarkably, the author then uses his protagonist's sense of smell to make the character vivid: Charlie breathes in "a rich compound of whiskey, after-shave lotion, shoe polish, woolens, and the rankness of a mature male." In that burst of imagery, we may momentarily overlook the most important item in the list, the evidence that Charlie's father has been drinking in the morning. Other elements may add to our understanding of characters in a story. Many writers take particular care in naming their characters in such a way as to draw attention to aspects of their personalities. This device (often termed **characternym**) is sometimes obvious—as with Alice Walker's character Myop—and sometimes not; in Alice Munro's "Boys and Girls," the boy who inherits the role of violence and power in the story is named Laird, the Scottish word for the proprietor of a landed estate. Similarly, actions in a story, such as speech patterns and mannerisms, may also disclose personality traits. A character's misuse of grammar or stilted vocabulary can *show* us a great deal more about his or her background and self-image than a whole page of background information or analysis. Charlie's father's gestures and loud attempts at ordering in various foreign languages grow more embarrassing until his tongue-tied request for two "Bibson Geefeaters" (a Beefeater Gibson is a potent martini made from a well-known brand of gin) comes as the punchline to a grotesque joke on himself.

## *Point of View*

When we speak of a politician's **point of view** on an issue, we mean his or her attitude toward it, pro or con. In fiction, however, the term point of view is employed in a specialized sense, referring to the question of authority in the story. Every story has a **narrator,** a voice that provides the reader with information about and insight into characters and incidents; but in some cases the identity of this voice of authority is not immediately apparent. The narrative voice may be that of a character in the story, or it may come from outside the story. Being too literal-minded about the matter of point of view is usually a mistake, and we usually have to accept certain **narrative conventions** without questioning them too seriously if we are to enjoy reading stories. Thus, when we finish reading a detective story narrated by the sleuth him- or herself, we do not worry ourselves speculating about when such a busy character found time to jot down the events of the story. Similarly, we accept as a convention the fact that a narrator may suddenly jump from simply recording a conversation to telling us what one of its participants is thinking. Very early in our lives we learn how stories are told, just as we have been conditioned to make a mental transition while watching a movie, when our perspective shifts in the blink of an eye from one character's frightened stare, to the flashing barrel of a gun, to a hand clutching a chest, to another character's sneer of triumph.

Almost all narrative points of view can be classified as either first person or third person. In **first-person narration,** the narrator is a **participant** in the action. He or she may be either a major character (which is the case with Charlie in "Reunion") or a minor character, who may be close to the event in time or distant from it. Although it is never directly stated, it seems likely that the adult Charlie is narrating an account of something that happened years before; thus, his repeated phrase about the last time he saw his father has a finality about it that goes far beyond a simple statement like "The last time I saw my father was a week ago in Grand Central Station." In general, first-person stories may seem more immediate than third-person stories, but they are limited by the simple fact that the narrator must be present at all times and must also have some knowledge of what is going on. If, for example, an attempt had been made to tell "Reunion" from the point of view of one of the restaurant waiters, the narrator might have had to resort to eavesdropping on Charlie and his father in order to report their circumstances. The ability of the narrator to tell the story accurately is also important. An **unreliable narrator**, either through naïveté, ignorance, or impaired mental processes, relates events in such a distorted manner that the reader, who has come to recognize the narrator's unreliability, literally has to turn the character's reporting on its head to make sense. Imagine how we would read "Reunion" if it had been told from the boozy, self-deluding point of view of Charlie's father.

**Third-person narration,** by definition, employs a **non-participant** narrator, a voice of authority that never reveals its source and is capable of moving from place to place to describe action and report dialogue. In third-person stories, the question of reliability is rarely an issue, but the matter of **omniscience,** the degree to which the "all-knowing" narrator can reveal the thoughts of characters, is. **Total omniscience** means that the narrator knows everything about the characters' lives—their pasts, presents, and futures—and may reveal the thoughts of anyone in the story. An **editorial point of view** goes even farther, allowing the godlike author to comment directly on the action (also called **authorial intrusion**). Most contemporary authors avoid total omniscience in short fiction, perhaps sensing that a story's strength is dissipated if more than one perspective is used. Instead, they employ **limited omniscience,** also called **selective omniscience** or the **method of central intelligence,** thereby limiting themselves to the thoughts and perceptions of a single character. This point of view is perhaps the most flexible of all because it allows the writer to compromise between the immediacy of first-person narration and the mobility of third-person narration. A further departure from omniscience is the **dramatic point of view** (also called the **objective point of view**). Here the narrator simply reports dialogue and action with minimal interpretation and does not delve into characters' minds. As the name implies, the dramatic point of view approximates the experience of reading a play; readers are provided only with set descriptions, stage directions, and dialogue, and thus must supply motivations that are based solely on this external evidence.

Technically, other points of view are possible, although they are rarely used. Stories have been told in the second person using "you" but they are rare. A plural point of view also may be employed, but such points of view are difficult to sustain and may quickly prove distracting to readers. Also, there is an unwritten rule that point of view should be consistent throughout a story, although occasionally a writer may utilize multiple perspectives to illustrate how the "truth" of any incident is always relative to the way in which it is witnessed.

## Theme

We have already discussed the manner in which fables and other types of didactic literature make their purpose clear by explicitly stating a moral or interpretation at the end of the story. Literary fiction, however, is usually much more subtle in revealing its **theme,** the overall meaning the reader derives from the story. Most of the early reading we did as children probably fell into two distinct categories—sheer entertainment or overt didacticism—with very little middle ground. Thus, many readers, coming to serious fiction for the first time, want either to avoid the tedious search for a "message" or to complain, "If the author was trying to say that, then why didn't she just come right out and *say* it!" To complicate matters further, the theoretical manner in which we analyze stories and the preconceptions we bring to bear on them may result in multiple interpretations of meaning. No single statement of theme is likely to be the "correct" one, although it is fair to say that some seem more likely than others. In fact, according to Flannery O'Connor, "When anybody asks what a story is about, the only proper thing is to tell him to read the story. The meaning of fiction is not abstract meaning but experienced meaning, and the purpose of making statements about the meaning is only to help you to experience that meaning more fully."

What, then, is the theme of "Reunion"? A reader insistent on a moral might denounce Charlie's father, commenting on alcohol's destructive effects. Another reader, slightly more charitable, might recognize alcoholism as a disease and feel some amount of sympathy for the father. Yet another, perhaps entirely too self-righteous, might fault Charlie for running away from his father, interpreting the older man's actions as a subconscious cry for help. If we investigate Cheever's own troubled biography and note his own serious problems with both parenthood and alcoholism, we may read the story as a psychological confession, with Cheever himself simultaneously playing the roles of father and son. With so many possibilities before us, it is perhaps best to summarize a story's theme broadly:

> *"Reunion," like most initiation stories, is about growth through loss of innocence. Children have to learn, often through painful experience, that they are not responsible for their parents' well-being, and sometimes they must distance themselves from their parents in order to survive.*

Such a statement does not encompass every possible nuance of the story's theme, but it does at least provide us with a starting point for arguing about the finer points of Cheever's meaning.

Still, many modern authors are not always reticent about revealing their themes. Alistair MacLeod says that he begins all his work with ideas, and that his story "The Boat" is about choice. Alice Walker's commitment to rendering African-American experience and Margaret Atwood's feminism are rarely hidden in these authors' stories and poems. Many modern stories are in fact **allegorical tales,** in which the literal events point to a parallel sequence of symbolic ideas. In many stories the literal setting of the story is a **microcosm,** a "small world" that reflects the tensions of the larger world outside. Thus, despite their outward sophistication, many of the stories included here reveal their debt to the ancient ethical functions of fables and parables.

## Setting

Novelists can lavish pages of prose on details of setting, just as they can describe characters down to such minutiae as the contents of their pockets. But short-story writers, hemmed in by limitations of space, rarely have such luxury and must ordinarily limit themselves to very selective descriptions of time and place. When a writer goes into great detail in his or her descriptions (for example, as Guy de Maupassant does in the opening sentences of "The Piece of String") it is likely that **atmosphere,** the emotional aura surrounding a certain setting, is more important to him or her than the actual physical locale.

**Setting** is simply the time and place of a story, and in most cases the details of description are given to the reader directly by the narrator.

A story may employ multiple locations in its different scenes, and its time frame may encompass a few hours or many years. "Reunion" is a story with relatively few details of setting. Because Cheever wrote his stories almost exclusively for *The New Yorker*, it is not necessary for him to describe the interior of Grand Central Station to an audience doubtless familiar with it; excessive details here would probably be irrelevant. Similarly, he spends no more than a sentence or two describing each of the restaurants: One has "a lot of horse tack on the walls," one is "Italian," and the other two are not described at all. The time setting is also relatively unimportant here. We know that the action is taking place during the lunch hour on a weekday, probably in the summer, but as far as a more specific time is concerned, we know little or nothing. "Reunion" could be taking place today or fifty years ago or, for that matter, twenty years from now.

Some stories, however, depend on their **locale** or time setting much more heavily and thus demand fuller exposition of setting. **Historical fiction** usually pays great attention to the altered landscapes and customs of bygone eras. A writer who carelessly lets an alarm clock go off in a story set in the early 1800s has committed an anachronism that may be only slightly more obvious than another writer's use of contemporary slang in the same setting. **Local colour fiction** depends heavily on the unique characteristics of a particular area, usually a rural one that is off the beaten path. Such places have become increasingly rare in contemporary writing, but locales such as Guy Vanderhaeghe's prairie or Ama Ata Aidoo's rural Ghana still possess intrinsic interest. Some writers first established their reputations as practitioners of **regionalism,** setting most of their work in a particular area or part of the country. Alistair MacLeod shows, in virtually every one of his stories, his deep connections to Cape Breton. Gabriel García Márquez continually draws us into the strange world of Colombian villages cut off from the contemporary world—places where past and present, history and folklore, natural and supernatural, seamlessly join in what has been labelled **magic realism.**

Stories contain both specific and general settings. The specific setting is the precise time(s) and place(s) where the action takes place. The general setting of a story, what is called its **enveloping action,** is its sense of the "times" and how its characters interact with events and social currents in the larger world. We have already mentioned how the specific setting of a story often is a microcosm that reflects the doings of society at large. It is impossible to read stories by Alice Walker and not be made aware of the social changes that have transformed the rural American South in the last thirty years. Stories sometimes depend on readers' ability to bring their knowledge of history and culture to bear on the events taking place. In reading Timothy Findley's "Stones," younger readers may be unaware of the widespread impact of the two world wars that older readers can painfully recall.

## Style and Symbol

**Style** in fiction refers equally to the characteristics of language in a particular story and to the same characteristics in a writer's complete works. The more individual a writer's style is, the easier it is to write a **parody,** or satirical imitation, of it, as the well-publicized annual "Faux Faulkner" and "International Imitation Hemingway" contests attest. A detailed analysis of the style in an individual story might include attention to such matters as diction, sentence structure, punctuation (or the lack thereof), and use of figurative language. In English we usually make a distinction between the differing qualities of words—standard versus slang usage, Latinate versus Germanic vocabulary, abstract versus concrete diction, and so on. While such matters are most meaningful in the context of an individual story or an author's work in general, we can clearly see the difference between one character who says, "I have profited to a great degree from the educational benefits of the realm of experience," and another who says, "I graduated from the school of hard knocks." However, in analyzing style we must be sensitive to the literary fashions of periods other than our own; it is senseless to fault Poe for "flowery diction" when we compare his use of language with that of his contemporaries. The prevailing fashion in fiction today is for the unadorned starkness of writers like Raymond Carver, a type of literature that has been disparagingly called "K-Mart realism" by one critic. Still, one should not be surprised if, as we move forward in a new century, fashions shift and writers compete to outdo Faulkner at his most ornate.

The style of "Reunion" is for the most part straightforward, with few flourishes of vocabulary (if we except the foreign phrases) or sentence structure. About the only significant departure from this plain style is in the opening paragraph, where Charlie momentarily rises to a slightly elevated rhetorical plateau: "as soon as I saw him I felt that he was my father, my flesh and blood, my future and my doom." The **tone** of the story, or what we can indirectly determine about the author's own feelings about its events from his choice of words, is also carefully controlled. Cheever avoids the twin pitfalls of sentimentality on the one hand and cynicism on the other by deftly walking an emotional tightrope. After the opening paragraph, at no point does Charlie tell us how he feels; instead he lets his father's actions speak for themselves. There are points in "Reunion" where we may laugh, but it is an uncomfortable laugh at which we probably feel a little guilty. The possible tones available for use in any given story may run through the whole range of human emotions, from outright comedy or satirical contempt to pathos of the most wrenching sort. It is possible for an unwary reader to fail to appreciate the keen edge of Guy de Maupassant's irony or the profound skepticism of Jorge Luis Borges, but this failure should not be laid at the feet of the writers. Appreciation of a writer's tone of voice can often be slow to develop, coming only after the experience of reading a wide range of stories and comparing how irony may or may not be present in them.

Like tone of voice, symbolism in stories is often a troublesome affair for beginning readers, as is indicated by the oft-heard phrase "hidden meanings." Are authors doing their best to conceal, rather than reveal, the significance of actions and things in their works? Usually they are not, but a superficial reading of a story may barely scratch the surface of its full complexity. **Symbolism,** by which we mean the use of one thing (usually a concrete object) to suggest another (usually an abstract idea), may occur in any of the elements discussed above: A plot or character or setting may have some symbolic value. There is little heavy symbolism in "Reunion," but if we think about the title, with its suggestions of emotional warmth, and the opening setting, a busy train station, we can see that Cheever has chosen his title carefully, and it has both ironic and symbolic overtones.

If the details of a plot seem consistently symbolic, with each detail clearly pointing the way to some obvious larger meaning, then we are reading **allegory.** Hawthorne's "The Birthmark" invites an allegorical reading because of the many abstract ideas suggested by Georgiana's birthmark, said to resemble "a crimson stain" and a tiny "human hand."

Or, using another approach to symbolism, in a given story, an author may employ a **traditional symbol,** a thing that most members of a culture instantly recognize as possessing a shared symbolic meaning. We may recognize a white gown or a red rose symbolizing, on the one hand, innocence and, on the other, romantic love without having to think very deeply about either. Familiarity with an individual author's works may also help us to recognize a **private symbol,** a symbol that the author has made his or her own by repeated usage. Other writers may use certain colours, situations, and actions repeatedly; it is hard to read much of Poe's fiction without becoming aware of the personal horror that small, confined spaces represent for the author. Finally, we may identify an **incidental symbol** in a story. This may be a thing or action that ordinarily would not have deeper meaning but acquires one in a particular story. How can we learn to spot these symbols? Paying close attention to the way an author repeats certain details or otherwise points to their significance perhaps in the title or in the conclusion is the key. Understanding what a symbol *means* is often less important than merely realizing that it *exists*. The exact meaning of an incidental symbol is usually open to interpretation and multiple interpretations of its implications do not necessarily contradict one another.

The variety of short stories in this collection is testimony to the versatility of the form. The short story has been called "a fierce pleasure" by Raymond Carver, "a musical composition" by Katherine Mansfield, and "an art of snapshots" by Alice Munro. That there are as many definitions of the form as there are practitioners can perhaps be explained by the fact that the short story is a dynamic hybrid. According to V. S. Pritchett, "It owes much to the quickness, the objectivity and cutting of the cinema; it owes much to the poet on the one hand and the newspaper reporter on the other; something also to the dramatic compression of the theatre, and everything to the restlessness, the alert nerve, the scientific eye and the short breath of contemporary life."

*Nathaniel Hawthorne (1804–1864) was born in Salem, Massachusetts, tracing his heritage back to the earliest settlers. One of his Puritan ancestors, John Hathorne, was a magistrate who assisted the prosecution during the infamous Salem witch trials that appear in Hawthorne's novel* The Scarlet Letter *(1850). His collection of short stories* Twice-Told Tales *(1837) was the subject of an enthusiastic review by Edgar Allan Poe. A dedicated craftsman, Hawthorne was a moralist who did not shrink from depicting the dark side of human nature, and his often painful examinations of American history and conscience have set the tone for many subsequent generations of writers. "The Birthmark," written in 1843 and published in* Mosses from an Old Manse *(1846), explores the perils of attempting to improve upon nature.*

# Nathaniel Hawthorne
# The Birthmark

In the latter part of the last century there lived a man of science, an eminent proficient in every branch of natural philosophy, who not long before our story opens had made experience of a spiritual affinity more attractive than any chemical one. He had left his laboratory to the care of an assistant, cleared his fine countenance from the furnace smoke, washed the stain of acids from his fingers, and persuaded a beautiful woman to become his wife. In those days when the comparatively recent discovery of electricity and other kindred mysteries of Nature seemed to open paths into the region of miracle, it was not unusual for the love of science to rival the love of woman in its depth and absorbing energy. The higher intellect, the imagination, the spirit, and even the heart might all find their congenial aliment in pursuits which, as some of their ardent votaries believed, would ascend from one step of powerful intelligence to another, until the philosopher should lay his hand on the secret of creative force and perhaps make new worlds for himself. We know not whether Aylmer possessed this degree of faith in man's ultimate control over Nature. He had devoted himself, however, too unreservedly to scientific studies ever to be weaned from them by any second passion. His love for his young wife might prove the stronger of the two; but it could only be by intertwining itself with his love of science, and uniting the strength of the latter to his own.

Such a union accordingly took place, and was attended with truly remarkable consequences and a deeply impressive moral. One day, very soon after their marriage, Aylmer sat gazing at his wife with a trouble in his countenance that grew stronger until he spoke.

"Georgiana," said he, "has it never occurred to you that the mark upon your cheek might be removed?"

"No, indeed," said she, smiling; but perceiving the seriousness of his manner, she blushed deeply. "To tell you the truth it has been so often called a charm that I was simple enough to imagine it might be so."

"Ah, upon another face perhaps it might," replied her husband; "but never on yours. No, dearest Georgiana, you came so nearly perfect from the hand of Nature that this slightest possible defect, which we hesitate whether to term a defect or a beauty, shocks me, as being the visible mark of earthly imperfection."

"Shocks you, my husband!" cried Georgiana, deeply hurt; at first reddening with momentary anger, but then bursting into tears. "Then why did you take me from my mother's side? You cannot love what shocks you!"

To explain this conversation it must be mentioned that in the centre of Georgiana's left cheek there was a singular mark, deeply interwoven, as it were, with the texture and substance of her face. In the usual state of her complexion—a healthy though delicate bloom—the mark wore a tint of deeper crimson, which imperfectly defined its shape amid the surrounding rosiness. When she blushed it gradually became more indistinct, and finally vanished amid the triumphant rush of blood that bathed the whole cheek with its brilliant glow. But if any shifting motion caused her to turn pale there was the mark again, a crimson stain upon the snow, in what Aylmer sometimes deemed an almost fearful distinctness. Its shape bore not a little similarity to the human hand, though of the smallest pygmy size. Georgiana's lovers were wont to say that some fairy at her birth hour had laid her tiny hand upon the infant's cheek, and left this impress there in token of the magic endowments that were to give her such sway over all hearts. Many a desperate swain would have risked life for the privilege of pressing his lips to the mysterious hand. It must not be concealed, however, that the impression wrought by this fairy sign manual varied exceedingly, according to the difference of temperament in the beholders. Some fastidious persons—but they were exclusively of her own sex—affirmed that the bloody hand, as they chose to call it, quite destroyed the effect of Georgiana's beauty, and rendered her countenance even hideous. But it would be as reasonable to say that one of those small blue stains which sometimes occur in the purest statuary marble would convert the Eve of Powers[1] to a monster. Masculine observers, if the birthmark did not heighten their admiration, contented themselves with wishing it away, that the world might possess one living specimen of ideal loveliness without the semblance of a flaw. After his marriage,—for he thought little or nothing of the matter before,—Aylmer discovered that this was the case with himself.

Had she been less beautiful,—if Envy's self could have found aught else to sneer at,—he might have felt his affection heightened by the prettiness of this mimic hand, now vaguely portrayed, now lost, now stealing forth again and glimmering to and fro with every pulse of emotion that throbbed within her heart; but seeing her otherwise so perfect, he found this one defect grow more and more intolerable with every moment of their united lives. It was the fatal flaw of humanity which Nature, in one shape or another, stamps ineffaceably on all her productions, either to imply that they are temporary and finite, or that their perfection must be wrought by toil and pain. The crimson hand expressed the ineludible gripe in which mortality clutches the highest and purest of earthly mould, degrading them into kindred with the lowest, and even with the very brutes, like whom their visible frames return to dust. In this manner, selecting it as the symbol of his wife's liability to sin, sorrow, decay, and death, Aylmer's sombre imagination was not long in rendering the birthmark a frightful object, causing him more trouble and horror than ever Georgiana's beauty, whether of soul or sense, had given him delight.

At all the seasons which should have been their happiest, he invariably and without intending it, nay, in spite of a purpose to the contrary, reverted to this one disastrous topic. Trifling as it at first appeared, it so connected itself with innumerable trains of thought and modes of feeling that it became the central point of all. With the morning twilight Aylmer opened his eyes upon his wife's face and recognized the symbol of imperfection; and when they sat together at the evening hearth his eyes wandered stealthily to her cheek, and beheld, flickering with the blaze of the wood fire, the spectral hand that wrote mortality where he would fain have worshipped. Georgiana soon learned to shudder at his gaze. It needed but a glance with the peculiar expression that his face often

[1]*Eve of Powers:* Hiram Powers (1805–1873), American sculptor, was famous for his white marble sculpture of Eve entitled *Eve Before the Fall.*

wore to change the roses of her cheek into a deathlike paleness, amid which the crimson hand was brought strongly out, like a bass-relief of ruby on the whitest marble.

Late one night when the lights were growing dim, so as hardly to betray the stain on the poor wife's cheek, she herself, for the first time, voluntarily took up the subject.

"Do you remember, my dear Aylmer," said she, with a feeble attempt at a smile, "have you any recollection of a dream last night about this odious hand?"

"None! none whatever!" replied Aylmer, starting; but then he added, in a dry, cold tone, affected for the sake of concealing the real depth of his emotion, "I might well dream of it; for before I fell asleep it had taken a pretty firm hold of my fancy."

"And you did dream of it?" continued Georgiana, hastily; for she dreaded lest a gush of tears should interrupt what she had to say. "A terrible dream! I wonder that you can forget it. Is it possible to forget this one expression?—'It is in her heart now; we must have it out!' Reflect, my husband; for by all means I would have you recall that dream."

The mind is in a sad state when Sleep, the all-involving, cannot confine her spectres within the dim region of her sway, but suffers them to break forth, affrighting this actual life with secrets that perchance belong to a deeper one. Aylmer now remembered his dream. He had fancied himself with his servant Aminadab, attempting an operation for the removal of the birthmark; but the deeper went the knife, the deeper sank the hand, until at length its tiny grasp appeared to have caught hold of Georgiana's heart; whence, her husband was inexorably resolved to cut or wrench it away.

When the dream had shaped itself perfectly in his memory, Aylmer sat in his wife's presence with a guilty feeling. Truth often finds its way to the mind close muffled in robes of sleep, and then speaks with uncompromising directness of matters in regard to which we practise an unconscious self-deception during our waking moments. Until now he had not been aware of the tyrannizing influence acquired by one idea over his mind, and of the lengths which he might find in his heart to go for the sake of giving himself peace.

"Aylmer," resumed Georgiana, solemnly, "I know not what may be the cost to both of us to rid me of this fatal birthmark. Perhaps its removal may cause cureless deformity; or it may be the stain goes as deep as life itself. Again: do we know that there is a possibility, on any terms, of unclasping the firm gripe of this little hand which was laid upon me before I came into the world?"

"Dearest Georgiana, I have spent much thought upon the subject," hastily interrupted Aylmer. "I am convinced of the perfect practicability of its removal."

"If there be the remotest possibility of it," continued Georgiana, "let the attempt be made at whatever risk. Danger is nothing to me; for life, while this hateful mark makes me the object of your horror and dis-gust,—life is a burden which I would fling down with joy. Either remove this dreadful hand, or take my wretched life! You have deep science. All the world bears witness of it. You have achieved great wonders. Cannot you remove this little, little mark, which I cover with the tips of two small fingers? Is this beyond your power, for the sake of your own peace, and to save your poor wife from madness?"

"Noblest, dearest, tenderest wife," cried Aylmer, rapturously, "doubt not my power. I have already given this matter the deepest thought— thought which might almost have enlightened me to create a being less perfect than yourself. Georgiana, you have led me deeper than ever into the heart of science. I feel myself fully competent to render this dear cheek as faultless as its fellow; and then, most beloved, what will be my triumph when I shall have corrected what Nature left imperfect in her fairest work! Even Pygmalion,[2] when his sculptured woman assumed life, felt not greater ecstasy than mine will be."

"It is resolved, then," said Georgiana, faintly smiling. "And, Aylmer, spare me not, though you should find the birthmark take refuge in my heart at last."

Her husband tenderly kissed her cheek—her right cheek—not that which bore the impress of the crimson hand.

The next day Aylmer apprised his wife of a plan that he had formed whereby he might have opportunity for the intense thought and constant watchfulness which the proposed operation would require; while Georgiana, likewise, would enjoy the perfect repose essential to its success. They were to seclude themselves in the extensive apartments

---

[2]*Pygmalion:* In Greek mythology, Pygmalion was a skilled sculptor who fell in love with his own creation of a perfect maiden carved in ivory, and prayed to Aphrodite for a wife like her. Aphrodite caused his sculpture to come alive, and creator and creation were married.

occupied by Aylmer as a laboratory, and where, during his toilsome youth, he had made discoveries in the elemental powers of Nature that had roused the admiration of all the learned societies in Europe. Seated calmly in this laboratory, the pale philosopher had investigated the secrets of the highest cloud region and of the profoundest mines; he had satisfied himself of the causes that kindled and kept alive the fires of the volcano; and had explained the mystery of fountains, and how it is that they gush forth, some so bright and pure, and others with such rich medicinal virtues, from the dark bosom of the earth. Here, too, at an earlier period, he had studied the wonders of the human frame, and attempted to fathom the very process by which Nature assimilates all her precious influences from earth and air, and from the spiritual world, to create and foster man, her masterpiece. The latter pursuit, however, Aylmer had long laid aside in unwilling recognition of the truth—against which all seekers sooner or later stumble—that our great creative Mother, while she amuses us with apparently working in the broadest sunshine, is yet severely careful to keep her own secrets, and, in spite of her pretended openness, shows us nothing but results. She permits us, indeed, to mar, but seldom to mend, and, like a jealous patentee, on no account to make. Now, however, Aylmer resumed these half-forgotten investigations; not, of course, with such hopes or wishes as first suggested them; but because they involved much physiological truth and lay in the path of his proposed scheme for the treatment of Georgiana.

As he led her over the threshold of the laboratory, Georgiana was cold and tremulous. Aylmer looked cheerfully into her face, with intent to reassure her, but was so startled with the intense glow of the birthmark upon the whiteness of her cheek that he could not restrain a strong convulsive shudder. His wife fainted.

"Aminadab! Aminadab!" shouted Aylmer, stamping violently on the floor.

Forthwith there issued from an inner apartment a man of low stature, but bulky frame, with shaggy hair hanging about his visage, which was grimed with the vapors of the furnace. This personage had been Aylmer's underworker during his whole scientific career, and was admirably fitted for that office by his great mechanical readiness, and the skill with which, while incapable of comprehending a single principle, he executed all the details of his master's experiments. With his vast strength, his shaggy hair, his smoky aspect, and the indescribable earthiness that incrusted him, he seemed to represent man's physical nature; while Aylmer's slender figure, and pale, intellectual face, were no less apt a type of the spiritual element.

"Throw open the door of the boudoir, Aminadab," said Aylmer, "and burn a pastil."

"Yes, master," answered Aminadab, looking intently at the lifeless form of Georgiana; and then he muttered to himself, "If she were my wife, I'd never part with that birthmark."

When Georgiana recovered consciousness she found herself breathing an atmosphere of penetrating fragrance, the gentle potency of which had recalled her from her deathlike faintness. The scene around her looked like enchantment. Aylmer had converted those smoky, dingy, sombre rooms, where he had spent his brightest years in recondite pursuits, into a series of beautiful apartments not unfit to be the secluded abode of a lovely woman. The walls were hung with gorgeous curtains, which imparted the combination of grandeur and grace that no other species of adornment can achieve; and as they fell from the ceiling to the floor, their rich and ponderous folds, concealing all angles and straight lines, appeared to shut in the scene from infinite space. For aught Georgiana knew, it might be a pavilion among the clouds. And Aylmer, excluding the sunshine, which would have interfered with his chemical processes, had supplied its place with perfumed lamps, emitting flames of various hue, but all uniting in a soft, impurpled radiance. He now knelt by his wife's side, watching her earnestly, but without alarm; for he was confident in his science, and felt that he could draw a magic circle round her within which no evil might intrude.

"Where am I? Ah, I remember," said Georgiana, faintly; and she placed her hand over her cheek to hide the terrible mark from her husband's eyes.

"Fear not, dearest!" exclaimed he. "Do not shrink from me! Believe me, Georgiana, I even rejoice in this single imperfection, since it will be such a rapture to remove it."

"Oh, spare me!" sadly replied his wife. "Pray do not look at it again. I never can forget that convulsive shudder."

In order to soothe Georgiana, and, as it were, to release her mind from the burden of actual things, Aylmer now put in practice some of the light and playful secrets which science had taught him among its profounder lore. Airy figures, absolutely bodiless ideas, and forms of unsubstantial beauty came and danced before her, imprinting their momentary footsteps on beams of light. Though she had some indistinct idea of the method of these optical phenomena, still the illusion was almost perfect enough to warrant the belief that her husband possessed sway over the spiritual world. Then again, when she felt a wish to look forth from her seclusion, immediately, as if her thoughts were answered, the procession of external existence flitted across a screen. The scenery and the figures of actual life were perfectly represented, but with that bewitching, yet indescribable difference which always makes a picture, an image, or a shadow so much more attractive than the original. When wearied of this, Aylmer bade her cast her eyes upon a vessel containing a quantity of earth. She did so, with little interest at first; but was soon startled to perceive the germ of a plant shooting upward from the soil. Then came the slender stalk; the leaves gradually unfolded themselves; and amid them was a perfect and lovely flower.

"It is magical!" cried Georgiana. "I dare not touch it."

"Nay, pluck it," answered Aylmer,—"pluck it, and inhale its brief perfume while you may. The flower will wither in a few moments and leave nothing save its brown seed vessels; but thence may be perpetuated a race as ephemeral as itself."

But Georgiana had no sooner touched the flower than the whole plant suffered a blight, its leaves turning coal-black as if by the agency of fire.

"There was too powerful a stimulus," said Aylmer, thoughtfully.

To make up for this abortive experiment, he proposed to take her portrait by a scientific process of his own invention. It was to be effected by rays of light striking upon a polished plate of metal. Georgiana assented; but, on looking at the result, was affrighted to find the features of the portrait blurred and indefinable; while the minute figure of a hand appeared where the cheek should have been. Aylmer snatched the metallic plate and threw it into a jar of corrosive acid.

Soon, however, he forgot these mortifying failures. In the intervals of study and chemical experiment he came to her flushed and exhausted, but seemed invigorated by her presence, and spoke in glowing language of the resources of his art. He gave a history of the long dynasty of the alchemists, who spent so many ages in quest of the universal solvent by which the golden principle might be elicited from all things vile and base. Aylmer appeared to believe that, by the plainest scientific logic, it was altogether within the limits of possibility to discover this long-sought medium; "but," he added, "a philosopher who should go deep enough to acquire the power would attain too lofty a wisdom to stoop to the exercise of it." Not less singular were his opinions in regard to the elixir vitae. He more than intimated that it was at his option to concoct a liquid that should prolong life for years, perhaps interminably; but that it would produce a discord in Nature which all the world, and chiefly the quaffer of the immortal nostrum, would find cause to curse.

"Aylmer, are you in earnest?" asked Georgiana, looking at him with amazement and fear. "It is terrible to possess such power, or even to dream of possessing it."

"Oh, do not tremble, my love," said her husband. "I would not wrong either you or myself by working such inharmonious effects upon our lives; but I would have you consider how trifling, in comparison, is the skill requisite to remove this little hand."

At the mention of the birthmark, Georgiana, as usual, shrank as if a redhot iron had touched her cheek.

Again Aylmer applied himself to his labors. She could hear his voice in the distant furnace room giving directions to Aminadab, whose harsh, uncouth, misshapen tones were audible in response, more like the grunt or growl of a brute than human speech. After hours of absence, Aylmer reappeared and proposed that she should now examine his cabinet of chemical products and natural treasures of the earth. Among the former he showed her a small vial, in which, he remarked, was contained a gentle yet most powerful fragrance, capable of impregnating all the breezes that blow across a kingdom. They were of inestimable value, the contents of that little vial; and, as he said so, he threw some of the perfume into the air and filled the room with piercing and invigorating delight.

"And what is this?" asked Georgiana, pointing to a small crystal globe containing a gold-colored liquid. "It is so beautiful to the eye that I could imagine it the elixir of life."

"In one sense it is," replied Aylmer; "or, rather, the elixir of immortality. It is the most precious poison that ever was concocted in this world. By its aid I could apportion the lifetime of any mortal at whom you might point your finger. The strength of the dose would determine whether he were to linger out years, or drop dead in the midst of a breath. No king on his guarded throne could keep his life if I, in my private station, should deem that the welfare of millions justified me in depriving him of it."

"Why do you keep such a terrific drug?" inquired Georgiana in horror.

"Do not mistrust me, dearest," said her husband, smiling; "its virtuous potency is yet greater than its harmful one. But see! here is a powerful cosmetic. With a few drops of this in a vase of water, freckles may be washed away as easily as the hands are cleansed. A stronger infusion would take the blood out of the cheek, and leave the rosiest beauty a pale ghost."

"Is it with this lotion that you intend to bathe my cheek?" asked Georgiana, anxiously.

"Oh, no," hastily replied her husband; "this is merely superficial. Your case demands a remedy that shall go deeper."

In his interviews with Georgiana, Aylmer generally made minute inquiries as to her sensations and whether the confinement of the rooms and the temperature of the atmosphere agreed with her. These questions had such a particular drift that Georgiana began to conjecture that she was already subjected to certain physical influences, either breathed in with the fragrant air or taken with her food. She fancied likewise, but it might be altogether fancy, that there was a stirring up of her system—a strange, indefinite sensation creeping through her veins, and tingling, half painfully, half pleasurably, at her heart. Still, whenever she dared to look into the mirror, there she beheld herself pale as a white rose and with the crimson birthmark stamped upon her cheek. Not even Aylmer now hated it so much as she.

To dispel the tedium of the hours which her husband found it necessary to devote to the processes of combination and analysis, Georgiana turned over the volumes of his scientific library. In many dark old tomes she met with chapters full of romance and poetry. They were the works of philosophers of the middle ages, such as Albertus Magnus, Cornelius Agrippa, Paracelsus, and the famous friar who created the prophetic Brazen Head.[3] All these antique naturalists stood in advance of their centuries, yet were imbued with some of their credulity, and therefore were believed, and perhaps imagined themselves to have acquired from the investigation of Nature a power above Nature, and from physics a sway

---

[3] *Albertus Magnus* (c.1200–1280) and *Cornelius Agrippa* (1486–1535) of Germany, and *Paracelsus* (1490–1541) of Switzerland were all philosophers of the Middle Ages interested in the natural sciences, alchemy, and the supernatural. The *famous friar* is Roger Bacon (c.1214–1294), an English philosopher and scientist who was said to have created a head of brass that could speak with great wisdom.

over the spiritual world. Hardly less curious and imaginative were the early volumes of the Transactions of the Royal Society, in which the members, knowing little of the limits of natural possibility, were continually recording wonders or proposing methods whereby wonders might be wrought.

But to Georgiana the most engrossing volume was a large folio from her husband's own hand, in which he had recorded every experiment of his scientific career, its original aim, the methods adopted for its development, and its final success or failure, with the circumstances to which either event was attributable. The book, in truth, was both the history and emblem of his ardent, ambitious, imaginative, yet practical and laborious life. He handled physical details as if there were nothing beyond them; yet spiritualized them all, and redeemed himself from materialism by his strong and eager aspiration towards the infinite. In his grasp the veriest clod of earth assumed a soul. Georgiana, as she read, reverenced Aylmer and loved him more profoundly than ever, but with a less entire dependence on his judgment than heretofore. Much as he had accomplished, she could not but observe that his most splendid successes were almost invariably failures, if compared with the ideal at which he aimed. His brightest diamonds were the merest pebbles, and felt to be so by himself, in comparison with the inestimable gems which lay hidden beyond his reach. The volume, rich with achievements that had won renown for its author, was yet as melancholy a record as ever mortal hand had penned. It was the sad confession and continual exemplification of the shortcomings of the composite man, the spirit burdened with clay and working in matter, and of the despair that assails the higher nature at finding itself so miserably thwarted by the earthly part. Perhaps every man of genius in whatever sphere might recognize the image of his own experience in Aylmer's journal.

So deeply did these reflections affect Georgiana that she laid her face upon the open volume and burst into tears. In this situation she was found by her husband.

"It is dangerous to read in a sorcerer's books," said he with a smile, though his countenance was uneasy and displeased. "Georgiana, there are pages in that volume which I can scarcely glance over and keep my senses. Take heed lest it prove as detrimental to you."

"It has made me worship you more than ever," said she.

"Ah, wait for this one success," rejoined he, "then worship me if you will. I shall deem myself hardly unworthy of it. But come, I have sought you for the luxury of your voice. Sing to me, dearest."

So she poured out the liquid music of her voice to quench the thirst of his spirit. He then took his leave with a boyish exuberance of gayety, assuring her that her seclusion would endure but a little longer, and that the result was already certain. Scarcely had he departed when Georgiana felt irresistibly impelled to follow him. She had forgotten to inform Aylmer of a symptom which for two or three hours past had begun to excite her attention. It was a sensation in the fatal birthmark, not painful, but which induced a restlessness throughout her system. Hastening after her husband, she intruded for the first time into the laboratory.

The first thing that struck her eye was the furnace, that hot and feverish worker, with the intense glow of its fire, which by the quantities of soot clustered above it seemed to have been burning for ages. There was a distilling apparatus in full operation. Around the room were retorts, tubes, cylinders, crucibles, and other apparatus of chemical research. An electrical machine stood ready for immediate use. The atmosphere felt oppressively close, and was tainted with gaseous odors which had been tormented forth by the processes of science. The severe and homely simplicity of the apartment, with its naked walls and brick pavement, looked strange, accustomed as Georgiana had become to the fantastic elegance of her boudoir. But what chiefly, indeed almost solely, drew her attention, was the aspect of Aylmer himself.

He was pale as death, anxious and absorbed, and hung over the furnace as if it depended upon his utmost watchfulness whether the liquid which it was distilling should be the draught of immortal happiness or misery. How different from the sanguine and joyous mien that he had assumed for Georgiana's encouragement!

"Carefully now, Aminadab; carefully, thou human machine; carefully, thou man of clay!" muttered Aylmer, more to himself than his assistant. "Now, if there be a thought too much or too little, it is all over."

"Ho! ho!" mumbled Aminadab. "Look, master! look!"

Aylmer raised his eyes hastily, and at first reddened, then grew paler than ever, on beholding Georgiana. He rushed towards her and seized her arm with a gripe that left the print of his fingers upon it.

"Why do you come hither? Have you no trust in your husband?" cried he, impetuously. "Would you throw the blight of that fatal birthmark over my labors? It is not well done. Go, prying woman, go!"

"Nay, Aylmer," said Georgiana with the firmness of which she possessed no stinted endowment, "it is not you that have a right to complain. You mistrust your wife; you have concealed the anxiety with which you watch the development of this experiment. Think not so unworthily of me, my husband. Tell me all the risk we run, and fear not that I shall shrink; for my share in it is far less than your own."

"No, no, Georgiana!" said Aylmer, impatiently; "it must not be."

"I submit," replied she calmly. "And, Aylmer, I shall quaff whatever draught you bring me; but it will be on the same principle that would induce me to take a dose of poison if offered by your hand."

"My noble wife," said Aylmer, deeply moved, "I knew not the height and depth of your nature until now. Nothing shall be concealed. Know, then, that this crimson hand, superficial as it seems, has clutched its grasp into your being with a strength of which I had no previous conception. I have already administered agents powerful enough to do aught except to change your entire physical system. Only one thing remains to be tried. If that fail us we are ruined."

"Why did you hesitate to tell me this?" asked she.

"Because, Georgiana," said Aylmer, in a low voice, "there is danger."

"Danger? There is but one danger—that this horrible stigma shall be left upon my cheek!" cried Georgiana. "Remove it, remove it, whatever be the cost, or we shall both go mad!"

"Heaven knows your words are too true," said Aylmer, sadly. "And now, dearest, return to your boudoir. In a little while all will be tested."

He conducted her back and took leave of her with a solemn tenderness which spoke far more than his words how much was now at stake. After his departure Georgiana became rapt in musings. She considered the character of Aylmer, and did it completer justice than at any previous moment. Her heart exulted, while it trembled, at his honorable love—so pure and lofty that it would accept nothing less than perfection nor miserably make itself contented with an earthlier nature than he had dreamed of. She felt how much more precious was such a sentiment than that meaner kind which would have borne with the imperfection for her sake, and have been guilty of treason to holy love by degrading its perfect idea to the level of the actual; and with her whole spirit she prayed that, for a single moment, she might satisfy his highest and deepest conception. Longer than one moment she well knew it could not be; for his spirit was ever on the march, ever ascending, and each instant required something that was beyond the scope of the instant before.

The sound of her husband's footsteps aroused her. He bore a crystal goblet containing a liquor colorless as water, but bright enough to be the draught of immortality. Aylmer was pale; but it seemed rather the consequence of a highly-wrought state of mind and tension of spirit than of fear or doubt.

"The concoction of the draught has been perfect," said he, in answer to Georgiana's look. "Unless all my science have deceived me, it cannot fail."

"Save on your account, my dearest Aylmer," observed his wife, "I might wish to put off this birthmark of mortality by relinquishing mortality itself in preference to any other mode. Life is but a sad possession to those who have attained precisely the degree of moral advancement at which I stand. Were I weaker and blinder it might be happiness. Were I stronger, it might be endured hopefully. But, being what I find myself, methinks I am of all mortals the most fit to die."

"You are fit for heaven without tasting death!" replied her husband. "But why do we speak of dying? The draught cannot fail. Behold its effect upon this plant."

On the window seat there stood a geranium diseased with yellow blotches, which had overspread all its leaves. Aylmer poured a small quantity of the liquid upon the soil in which it grew. In a little time, when the roots of the plant had taken up the moisture, the unsightly blotches began to be extinguished in a living verdure.

"There needed no proof," said Georgiana, quietly. "Give me the goblet. I joyfully stake all upon your word."

"Drink, then, thou lofty creature!" exclaimed Aylmer, with fervid admiration. "There is no taint of imperfection on thy spirit. Thy sensible frame, too, shall soon be all perfect."

She quaffed the liquid and returned the goblet to his hand.

"It is grateful," said she with a placid smile. "Methinks it is like water from a heavenly fountain; for it contains I know not what of unobtrusive fragrance and deliciousness. It allays a feverish thirst that had parched me for many days. Now, dearest, let me sleep. My earthly senses are closing over my spirit like the leaves around the heart of a rose at sunset."

She spoke the last words with a gentle reluctance, as if it required almost more energy than she could command to pronounce the faint and lingering syllables. Scarcely had they loitered through her lips ere she was lost in slumber. Aylmer sat by her side, watching her aspect with the emotions proper to a man the whole value of whose existence was involved in the process now to be tested. Mingled with this mood, however, was the philosophic investigation characteristic of the man of science. Not the minutest symptom escaped him. A heightened flush of the cheek, a slight irregularity of breath, a quiver of the eyelid, a hardly perceptible tremor through the frame,—such were the details which, as the moments passed, he wrote down in his folio volume. Intense thought had set its stamp upon every previous page of that volume, but the thoughts of years were all concentrated upon the last.

While thus employed, he failed not to gaze often at the fatal hand, and not without a shudder. Yet once, by a strange and unaccountable impulse, he pressed it with his lips. His spirit recoiled, however, in the very act; and Georgiana, out of the midst of her deep sleep, moved uneasily and murmured as if in remonstrance. Again Aylmer resumed his watch. Nor was it without avail. The crimson hand, which at first had been strongly visible upon the marble paleness of Georgiana's cheek, now grew more faintly outlined. She remained not less pale than ever; but the birthmark, with every breath that came and went, lost somewhat of its former distinctness. Its presence had been awful; its departure was more awful still. Watch the stain of the rainbow fading out the sky, and you will know how that mysterious symbol passed away.

"By Heaven! it is well-nigh gone!" said Aylmer to himself, in almost irrepressible ecstasy. "I can scarcely trace it now. Success! success! And now it is like the faintest rose color. The lightest flush of blood across her cheek would overcome it. But she is so pale!"

He drew aside the window curtain and suffered the light of natural day to fall into the room and rest upon her cheek. At the same time he heard a gross, hoarse chuckle, which he had long known as his servant Aminadab's expression of delight.

"Ah, clod! ah, earthly mass!" cried Aylmer, laughing in a sort of frenzy, "you have served me well! Matter and spirit—earth and heaven—have both done their part in this! Laugh, thing of the senses! You have earned the right to laugh."

These exclamations broke Georgiana's sleep. She slowly unclosed her eyes and gazed into the mirror which her husband had arranged for that purpose. A faint smile flitted over her lips when she recognized how barely perceptible was now that crimson hand which had once blazed forth with such disastrous brilliancy as to scare away all their happiness. But then her eyes sought Aylmer's face with a trouble and anxiety that he could by no means account for.

"My poor Aylmer!" murmured she.

"Poor? Nay, richest, happiest, most favored!" exclaimed he. "My peerless bride, it is successful! You are perfect!"

"My poor Aylmer," she repeated, with a more than human tenderness, "you have aimed loftily; you have done nobly. Do not repent that with so high and pure a feeling, you have rejected the best the earth could offer. Aylmer, dearest Aylmer, I am dying!"

Alas! it was too true! The fatal hand had grappled with the mystery of life, and was the bond by which an angelic spirit kept itself in union with a mortal frame. As the last crimson tint of the birthmark—that sole token of human imperfection—faded from her cheek, the parting breath of the now perfect woman passed into the atmosphere, and her soul, lingering a moment near her husband, took its heavenward flight. Then a hoarse, chuckling laugh was heard again! Thus ever does the gross fatality of earth exult in its invariable triumph over the immortal essence which, in this dim sphere of half development, demands the completeness of a higher state. Yet, had Aylmer reached a profounder wisdom, he need not thus have flung away the happiness which would have woven his mortal life of the selfsame texture with the celestial. The momentary circumstance was too strong for him; he failed to look beyond the shadowy scope of time, and, living once for all in eternity, to find the perfect future in the present.

*—1846*

*Edgar Allan Poe (1809–1849) has become so much the captive of his own legend that his name summons up visions of a mad genius who has little in common with the meticulous craftsman of criticism, fiction, and poetry whose influence on world literature has been immense. Born in Boston, Poe was the child of actors and orphaned at age two. Nevertheless, he lived a privileged childhood as the ward of John Allan, a wealthy Richmond merchant who gave Poe his middle name. After a profligate year at the University of Virginia, successful military service (under an assumed name), and an abortive stay at West Point, Poe broke with his foster father, married his young cousin, and set about a literary career, succeeding as editor of several prominent magazines. However, his irregular habits and a drinking problem, which grew more pronounced following the death of his wife in 1847, led to his mysterious death in Baltimore at the age of thirty-nine. Poe's poetry and short fiction have influenced writers as diverse as Charles Baudelaire and Stephen King. Similarly, Poe's literary criticism has been extremely influential; his tightly structured "The Cask of Amontillado" is a good example of his theory of the "single effect" produced by a well-crafted short story.*

# Edgar Allan Poe
# The Cask of Amontillado[1]

The thousand injuries of Fortunato I had borne as I best could; but when he ventured upon insult, I vowed revenge. You, who so well know the nature of my soul, will not suppose, however, that I gave utterance to a threat. *At length* I would be avenged; this was a point definitely settled—but the very definitiveness with which it was resolved precluded the idea of risk. I must not only punish, but punish with impunity. A wrong is unredressed when retribution overtakes its redresser. It is equally unredressed when the avenger fails to make himself felt as such to him who has done the wrong.

It must be understood that neither by word nor deed had I given Fortunato cause to doubt my good will. I continued, as was my wont, to smile in his face, and he did not perceive that my smile *now* was at the thought of his immolation.

He had a weak point—this Fortunato—although in other regards he was a man to be respected and even feared. He prided himself on

---

[1]*Cask:* barrel. *Amontillado:* dry sherry from Montilla, Spain.

his connoisseurship in wine. Few Italians have the true virtuoso spirit. For the most part their enthusiasm is adopted to suit the time and opportunity—to practise imposture upon the British and Austrian *millionaires*. In painting and gemmary Fortunato, like his countrymen, was a quack—but in the matter of old wines he was sincere. In this respect I did not differ from him materially; I was skilful in the Italian vintages myself, and bought largely whenever I could.

It was about dusk, one evening during the supreme madness of the carnival season, that I encountered my friend. He accosted me with excessive warmth, for he had been drinking much. The man wore motley. He had on a tight-fitting parti-striped dress, and his head was surmounted by the conical cap and bells. I was so pleased to see him that I thought I should never have done wringing his hand.

I said to him—'My dear Fortunato, you are luckily met. How remarkably well you are looking to-day! I But I have received a pipe[2] of what passes for Amontillado, and I have my doubts.'

'How?' said he. 'Amontillado? A pipe? Impossible! And in the middle of the carnival!'

'I have my doubts', I replied; 'and I was silly enough to pay the full Amontillado price without consulting you in the matter. You were not to be found, and I was fearful of losing a bargain.'

'Amontillado!'

'I have my doubts.'

'Amontillado!'

'And I must satisfy them.'

'Amontillado!'

'As you are engaged, I am on my way to Luchesi. If any one has a critical turn, it is he. He will tell me—'

'Luchesi cannot tell Amontillado from Sherry.'

'And yet some fools will have it that his taste is a match for your own.'

'Come, let us go.'

'Whither?'

'To your vaults.'

'My friend, no; I will not impose upon your good nature. I perceive you have an engagement. Luchesi—'

'I have no engagement;—come.'

[2]*pipe:* large cask holding 477 litres.

'My friend, no. It is not the engagement, but the severe cold with which I perceive you are afflicted. The vaults are insufferably damp. They are encrusted with nitre.'

'Let us go, nevertheless. The cold is merely nothing. Amontillado! You have been imposed upon. And as for Luchesi, he cannot distinguish Sherry from Amontillado.'

Thus speaking, Fortunato possessed himself of my arm. Putting on a mask of black silk, and drawing a *roquelaire*[3] closely about my person, I suffered him to hurry me to my palazzo.

There were no attendants at home; they had absconded to make merry in honor of the time. I had told them that I should not return until the morning, and had given them explicit orders not to stir from the house. These orders were sufficient, I well knew, to insure their immediate disappearance, one and all, as soon as my back was turned.

I took from their sconces two flambeaux, and giving one to Fortunato, bowed him through several suites of rooms to the archway that led into the vaults. I passed down a long and winding staircase, requesting him to be cautious as he followed. We came at length to the foot of the descent, and stood together on the damp ground of the catacombs of the Montresors.

The gait of my friend was unsteady, and the bells upon his cap jingled as he strode.

'The pipe,' said he.

'It is farther on,' said I; 'but observe the white web-work which gleams from these cavern walls.'

He turned towards me, and looked into my eyes with two filmy orbs that distilled the rheum of intoxication.

'Nitre?' he asked, at length.

'Nitre,' I replied. 'How long have you had that cough?'

'Ugh! ugh! ugh!—ugh! ugh! ugh!—ugh! ugh! ugh!—ugh! ugh! ugh!—ugh! ugh! ugh!'

My poor friend found it impossible to reply for many minutes.

'It is nothing', he said, at last.

'Come', I said, with decision, 'we will go back; your health is precious. You are rich, respected, admired, beloved; you are happy, as once I was.

[3]*roquelaire:* knee-length man's cloak.

You are a man to be missed. For me it is no matter. We will go back; you will be ill, and I cannot be responsible. Besides, there is Luchesi—,'

'Enough,' he said; 'the cough is a mere nothing; it will not kill me. I shall not die of a cough.'

'True—true,' I replied; 'and, indeed, I had no intention of alarming you unnecessarily—but you should use all proper caution. A draught of this Médoc will defend us from the damps.'

Here I knocked off the neck of a bottle which I drew from a long row of its fellows that lay upon the mould.

'Drink,' I said, presenting him the wine.

He raised it to his lips with a leer. He paused and nodded to me familiarly, while his bells jingled.

'I drink,' he said, 'to the buried that repose around us.'

'And I to your long life.'

He again took my arm, and we proceeded.

'These vaults,' he said, 'are extensive.'

'The Montresors,' I replied, 'were a great and numerous family.'

'I forget your arms.'

'A huge human foot d'or, in a field azure; the foot crushes a serpent rampant whose fangs are imbedded in the heel.'

'And the motto?'

'*Nemo me impune lacessit.*'[4]

'Good!' he said.

The wine sparkled in his eyes and bells jingled. My own fancy grew warm with the Médoc. We had passed through walls of piled bones, with casks and puncheons intermingling, into the inmost recesses of the catacombs. I paused again, and this time I made bold to seize Fortunato by an arm above the elbow.

'The nitre!' I said; 'see, it increases. It hangs like moss upon the vaults. We are below the river's bed. The drops of moisture trickle among the bones. Come, we will go back ere it is too late. Your cough—'

'It is nothing,' he said; 'let us go on. But first, another draught of the Médoc.'

I broke and reached him a flaçon of De Grâve. He emptied it at a breath. His eyes flashed with a fierce light. He laughed and threw the bottle upwards with a gesticulation I did not understand.

---

[4]*Nemo me impune lacessit:* No one provokes me with impunity.

I looked at him in surprise. He repeated the movement—a grotesque one.

'You do not comprehend?' he said.

'Not I,' I replied.

'Then you are not of the brotherhood.'

'How?'

'You are not of the masons.'[5]

'Yes, yes,' I said, 'yes, yes.'

'You? Impossible! A mason?'

'A mason,' I replied.

'A sign,' he said.

'It is this,' I answered, producing a trowel from beneath the folds of my *roquelaire*.

'You jest,' he exclaimed, recoiling a few paces. 'But let us proceed to the Amontillado.'

'Be it so,' I said, replacing the tool beneath the cloak, and again offering him my arm. He leaned upon it heavily. We continued our route in search of the Amontillado. We passed through a range of low arches, descended, passed on, and descending again, arrived at a deep crypt, in which the foulness of the air caused our flambeaux rather to glow than flame.

At the most remote end of the crypt there appeared another less spacious. Its walls had been lined with human remains, piled to the vault overhead, in the fashion of the great catacombs of Paris. Three sides of this interior crypt were still ornamented in this manner. From the fourth the bones had been thrown down, and lay promiscuously upon the earth, forming at one point a mound of some size. Within the wall thus exposed by the displacing of the bones, we perceived a still interior recess, in depth about four feet, in width three, in height six or seven. It seemed to have been constructed for no especial use within itself, but formed merely the interval between two of the colossal supports of the roof of the catacombs, and was backed by one of their circumscribing walls of solid granite.

It was in vain that Fortunato, uplifting his dull torch, endeavored to pry into the depth of the recess. Its termination the feeble light did not enable us to see.

[5]*mason:* member of the secret society of Freemasons.

'Proceed,' I said; 'herein is the Amontillado. As for Luchesi—'

'He is an ignoramus,' interrupted my friend, as he stepped unsteadily forward, while I followed immediately at his heels. In an instant he had reached the extremity of the niche, and finding his progress arrested by the rock, stood stupidly bewildered. A moment more and I had fettered him to the granite. In its surface were two iron staples, distant from each other about two feet, horizontally. From one of these depended a short chain, from the other a padlock. Throwing the links about his waist, it was but the work of a few seconds to secure it. He was too much astounded to resist. Withdrawing the key I stepped back from the recess.

'Pass your hand,' I said, 'over the wall; you cannot help feeling the nitre. Indeed it is *very* damp. Once more let me *implore* you to return. No? Then I must positively leave you. But I must first render you all the little attentions in my power.'

'The Amontillado!' ejaculated my friend, not yet recovered from his astonishment.

'True,' I replied; 'the Amontillado.'

As I said these words I busied myself among the pile of bones of which I have before spoken. Throwing them aside, I soon uncovered a quantity of building stone and mortar. With these materials and with the aid of my trowel, I began vigorously to wall up the entrance of the niche.

I had scarcely laid the first tier of the masonry when I discovered that the intoxication of Fortunato had in a great measure worn off. The earliest indication I had of this was a low moaning cry from the depth of the recess. It was *not* the cry of a drunken man. There was then a long and obstinate silence. I laid the second tier, and the third, and the fourth; and then I heard the furious vibrations of the chain. The noise lasted for several minutes, during which, that I might hearken to it with the more satisfaction, I ceased my labors and sat down upon the bones. When at last the clanking subsided, I resumed the trowel, and finished without interruption the fifth, the sixth, and the seventh tier. The wall was now nearly upon a level with my breast. I again paused, and holding the flambeaux over the mason-work, threw a few feeble rays upon the figure within.

A succession of loud and shrill screams, bursting suddenly from the throat of the chained form, seemed to thrust me violently back. For a brief moment I hesitated—I trembled. Unsheathing my rapier, I began to grope with it about the recess: but the thought of an instant reassured me. I placed my hand upon the solid fabric of the catacombs, and felt satisfied. I reapproached the wall. I replied to the yells of him who clamored. I re-echoed—I aided—I surpassed them in volume and in strength. I did this, and the clamorer grew still.

It was now midnight, and my task was drawing to a close. I had completed the eighth, the ninth, and the tenth tier. I had finished a portion of the last and the eleventh; there remained but a single stone to be fitted and plastered in. I struggled with its weight; I placed it partially in its destined position. But now there came from out the niche a low laugh that erected the hairs upon my head. It was succeeded by a sad voice, which I had difficulty in recognising as that of the noble Fortunato. The voice said—

'Ha! ha! ha!—he! he!—a very good joke indeed—an excellent jest. We will have many a rich laugh about it at the palazzo—he! he! he!—over our wine—he! he! he!'

'The Amontillado!' I said.

'He! he! he!—he! he! he!—yes, the Amontillado. But is it not getting late? Will not they be awaiting us at the palazzo, the Lady Fortunato and the rest? Let us be gone.'

'Yes,' I said, 'let us be gone.'

'*For the love of God, Montresor!*'

'Yes,' I said, 'for the love of God!'

But to these words I hearkened in vain for a reply. I grew impatient. I called aloud—

'Fortunato!'

No answer. I called again—

'Fortunato!'

No answer still. I thrust a torch through the remaining aperture and let it fall within. There came forth in return only a jingling of the bells. My heart grew sick—on account of the dampness of the catacombs. I hastened to make an end of my labor. I forced the last stone into its position; I plastered it up. Against the new masonry I re-erected the old rampart of bones. For the half of a century no mortal has disturbed them. *In pace requiescat!*[6]

*—1846*

---

[6]*In pace requiescat!* Rest in peace!

**Guy de Maupassant (1850–1893)** *did not consider a literary career until he was almost thirty years of age. After military service he worked as a French government clerk until 1882. The great influence on his development as a writer was the novelist Gustave Flaubert, who introduced Maupassant to other Parisian literary figures. Maupassant died young, a victim of a self-destructive lifestyle that led to syphilis, attempted suicide, and madness, but during his most productive decade (1880–1890) he produced over three hundred stories, six novels, poetry, travel writing, and a play. Maupassant's focus on the unglamorous realities of both rural and urban life marks him as one of the masters of literary naturalism, and his careful plot construction and attention to detail set high standards for later writers of short fiction.*

# *Guy de Maupassant*
# The Piece of String

Along all the roads around Goderville the peasants and their wives were coming toward the town because it was market day. The men were proceeding with slow steps, the whole body bent forward at each movement of their long twisted legs, deformed by their hard work, by the weight on the plow which, at the same time, raised the left shoulder and swerved the figure, by the reaping of the wheat which made the knees spread to make a firm "purchase," by all the slow and painful labors of the country. Their blouses, blue, "stiff-starched," shining as if varnished, ornamented with a little design in white at the neck and wrists, puffed about their bony bodies, seemed like balloons ready to carry them off. From each of them a head, two arms, and two feet protruded.

Some led a cow or a calf by a cord, and their wives, walking behind the animal, whipped its haunches with a leafy branch to hasten its progress. On their arms they carried large baskets from which, in some cases, chickens and, in others, ducks thrust out their heads. And they walked with a quicker, livelier step than their husbands. Their spare straight figures were wrapped in scanty little shawls, pinned over their flat bosoms, and their heads were enveloped in white cloths glued to the hair and surmounted by caps.

Then a wagon passed at the jerky trot of a nag, shaking strangely, two men seated side by side and a woman in the bottom of the vehicle, the latter holding on to the sides to lessen the hard jolts.

In the public square of Goderville there was a crowd, a throng of human beings and animals mixed together. The horns of the cattle, the tall hats with the long nap of the rich peasant, and the headgear of the peasant women rose above the surface of the assembly. And the clamorous, shrill, screaming voices made a continuous and savage din which sometimes was dominated by the robust lungs of some countryman's laugh, or the long lowing of a cow tied to the wall of a house.

All that smacked of the stable, the dairy and the dirt heap, hay and sweat, giving forth that unpleasant odor, human and animal, peculiar to the people of the field.

Maître Hauchecome, of Breaute, had just arrived at Goderville, and he was directing his steps toward the public square, when he perceived upon the ground a little piece of string. Maître Hauchecome, economical like a true Norman, thought that everything useful ought to be picked up, and he bent painfully, for he suffered from rheumatism. He took the bit of thin cord from the ground and began to roll it carefully when he noticed Maître Malandain, the harness-maker, on the threshold of his door, looking at him. They had heretofore had business together on the subject of a halter, and they were on bad terms, being both good haters. Maître Hauchecome was seized with a sort of shame to be seen thus by his enemy, picking a bit of string out of the dirt. He concealed his "find" quickly under his blouse, then in his trousers' pocket; then he pretended to be still looking on the ground for something which he did not find, and he went toward the market, his head forward, bent double by his pains.

He was soon lost in the noisy and slowly moving crowd, which was busy with interminable bargainings. The peasants milked, went and came, perplexed, always in fear of being cheated, not daring to decide, watching the vendor's eye, ever trying to find the trick in the man and the flaw in the beast.

The women, having placed their great baskets at their feet, had taken out the poultry which lay upon the ground, tied together by the feet, with terrified eyes and scarlet crests.

They heard offers, stated their prices with a dry air and impassive face, or perhaps, suddenly deciding on some proposed reduction, shouted to the customer who was slowly going away: "All right, Maître Authirne, I'll give it to you for that."

Then little by little the square was deserted, and when the Angelus rang at noon, those who had stayed too long, scattered to their shops.

At Jourdain's the great room was full of people eating, as the big court was full of vehicles of all kinds, carts, gigs, wagons, dump carts, yellow with dirt, mended and patched, raising their shafts to the sky like two arms, or perhaps with their shafts in the ground and their backs in the air.

Just opposite the diners seated at the table, the immense fireplace, filled with bright flames, cast a lively heat on the backs of the row on the right. Three spits were turning on which were chickens, pigeons, and legs of mutton; and an appetizing odor of roast beef and gravy dripping over the nicely browned skin rose from the hearth, increased the jovialness, and made everybody's mouth water.

All the aristocracy of the plow ate there, at Maître Jourdain's, tavern keeper and horse dealer, a rascal who had money.

The dishes were passed and emptied, as were the jugs of yellow cider. Everyone told his affairs, his purchases, and sales. They discussed the crops. The weather was favorable for the green things but not for the wheat.

Suddenly the drum beat in the court, before the house. Everybody rose except a few indifferent persons, and ran to the door, or to the windows, their mouths still full and napkins in their hands.

After the public crier had ceased his drum-beating, he called out in a jerky voice, speaking his phrases irregularly:

"It is hereby made known to the inhabitants of Goderville, and in general to all persons present at the market, that there was lost this morning, on the road to Benzeville, between nine and ten o'clock, a black leather pocketbook containing five hundred francs and some business papers. The finder is requested to return same with all haste to the mayor's office or to Maître Fortune Houlbreque of Manneville. There will be twenty francs reward."

Then the man went away. The heavy roll of the drum and the crier's voice were again heard at a distance.

Then they began to talk of this event discussing the chances that Maître Houlbreque had of finding or not finding his pocketbook.

And the meal concluded. They were finishing their coffee when a chief of the gendarmes appeared upon the threshold.

He inquired: "Is Maître Hauchecome, of Breaute, here?"

Maître Hauchecome, seated at the other end of the table, replied: "Here I am."

And the officer resumed: "Maître Hauchecome, will you have the goodness to accompany me to the mayor's office? The mayor would like to talk to you."

The peasant, surprised and disturbed, swallowed at a draught his tiny glass of brandy, rose, and, even more bent than in the morning, for the first steps after each rest were specially difficult, set out, repeating: "Here I am, here I am."

The mayor was awaiting him, seated on an armchair. He was the notary of the vicinity, a stout, serious man, with pompous phrases.

"Maître Hauchecome," said he, "you were seen this morning to pick up, on the road to Benzeville, the pocketbook lost by Maître Houlbreque, of Manneville."

The countryman, astounded, looked at the mayor, already terrified by this suspicion resting on him without his knowing why.

"Me? Me? Me pick up the pocketbook?"

"Yes, you, yourself."

"Word of honor, I never heard of it."

"But you were seen."

"I was seen, me? Who says he saw me?"

"Monsieur Malandain, the harness-maker."

The old man remembered, understood, and flushed with anger.

"Ah, he saw me, the clodhopper, he saw me pick up this string, here, M'sieu' the Mayor." And rummaging in his pocket he drew out the little piece of string.

But the mayor, incredulous, shook his head.

"You will not make me believe, Maître Hauchecome, that Monsieur Malandain, who is a man worthy of credence, mistook this cord for a pocketbook."

The peasant, furious, lifted his hand, spat at one side to attest his honor, repeating: "It is nevertheless the truth of the good God, the sacred truth, M'sieu' the Mayor. I repeat it on my soul and my salvation."

The mayor resumed: "After picking up the object, you stood like a stilt, looking a long while in the mud to see if any piece of money had fallen out."

The good, old man choked with indignation and fear.

"How anyone can tell—how anyone can tell—such lies to take away an honest man's reputation! How can anyone—"

There was no use in his protesting; nobody believed him. He was confronted with Monsieur Malandain, who repeated and maintained his affirmation. They abused each other for an hour. At his own request, Maître Hauchecome was searched; nothing was found on him.

Finally the mayor, very much perplexed, discharged him with the warning that he would consult the public prosecutor and ask for further orders.

The news had spread. As he left the mayor's office, the old man was surrounded and questioned with a serious or bantering curiosity, in which there was no indignation. He began to tell the story of the string. No one believed him. They laughed at him.

He went along, stopping his friends, beginning endlessly his statement and his protestations, showing his pockets turned inside out, to prove that he had nothing.

They said: "Old rascal, get out!"

And he grew angry, becoming exasperated, hot, and distressed at not being believed, not knowing what to do and always repeating himself.

Night came. He must depart. He started on his way with three neighbors to whom he pointed out the place where he had picked up the bit of string; and all along the road he spoke of his adventure.

In the evening he took a turn in the village of Breaute, in order to tell it to everybody. He only met with incredulity.

It made him ill at night.

The next day about one o'clock in the afternoon, Marius Paumelle, a hired man in the employ of Maître Breton, husbandman at Ymanville, returned the pocketbook and its contents to Maître Houlbreque of Manneville.

This man claimed to have found the object in the road; but not knowing how to read, he had carried it to the house and given it to his employer.

The news spread through the neighborhood. Maître Hauchecome was informed of it. He immediately went the circuit and began to recount his story completed by the happy climax. He was in triumph.

"What grieved me so much was not the thing itself, as the lying. There is nothing so shameful as to be placed under a cloud on account of a lie."

He talked of his adventure all day long; he told it on the highway to people who were passing by, in the wine-shop to people who were drinking there, and to persons coming out of church the following Sunday. He stopped strangers to tell them about it. He was calm now, and yet something disturbed him without his knowing exactly what it was. People had the air of joking while they listened. They did not seem convinced. He seemed to feel that remarks were being made behind his back.

On Tuesday of the next week he went to the market at Goderville, urged solely by the necessity he felt of discussing the case.

Malandain, standing at his door, began to laugh on seeing him pass. Why?

He approached a farmer from Crequetot, who did not let him finish, and giving him a thump in the stomach said to his face: "You big rascal."

Then he turned his back on him.

Maître Hauchecome was confused. Why was he called a big rascal?

When he was seated at the table, in Jourdain's tavern he commenced to explain "the affair."

A horse dealer from Monvilliers called to him: "Come, come, old sharper, that's an old trick; I know all about your piece of string!"

Hauchecome stammered: "But since the pocketbook was found."

But the other man replied: "Shut up, papa, there is one that finds, and there is one that reports. At any rate you are mixed up with it."

The peasant stood choking. He understood. They accused him of having had the pocketbook returned by a confederate, by an accomplice.

He tried to protest. All the table began to laugh.

He could not finish his dinner and went away, in the midst of jeers.

He went home ashamed and indignant, choking with anger and confusion, the more dejected that he was capable with his Norman cunning of doing what they had accused him of, and even boasting of it as of a good turn. His innocence to him, in a confused way, was impossible to prove, as his sharpness was known. And he was stricken to the heart by the injustice of the suspicion.

Then he began to recount the adventures again, prolonging his history every day, adding each time new reasons, more energetic protestations, more solemn oaths which he imagined and prepared in his hours of solitude, his whole mind given up to the story of the string. He was believed so much the less as his defense was more complicated and his arguing more subtle.

"Those are lying excuses," they said behind his back.

He felt it, consumed his heart over it, and wore himself out with useless efforts. He wasted away before their very eyes.

The wags now made him tell about the string to amuse them, as they make a soldier who has been on a campaign tell about his battles. His mind, touched to the depth, began to weaken.

Toward the end of December he took to his bed.

He died in the first days of January, and in the delirium of his death struggles he kept claiming his innocence, reiterating:

"A piece of string, a piece of string—look—here it is, M'sieu' the Mayor."

*—1883*

---

*Kate Chopin (1851–1904) was virtually forgotten for most of the twentieth century, except as a chronicler of life among the Louisiana Creoles and Cajuns, but she has since been rediscovered, initially by feminist critics and subsequently by general readers. Born in St. Louis, Chopin spent the 1870s in rural Louisiana as the wife of a cotton broker from New Orleans. After her husband's death in 1883, she returned to St. Louis with her six children and began her literary career. Much of her later work is remarkable for its frank depiction of women's sexuality, and Chopin became the subject of controversy after the appearance of her most important novel,* The Awakening *(1899). The negative reception of that work caused Chopin to suffer social ostracism and effectively ended her active career as a writer.*

## Kate Chopin
# The Story of an Hour

Knowing that Mrs. Mallard was afflicted with a heart trouble, great care was taken to break to her as gently as possible the news of her husband's death.

It was her sister Josephine who told her, in broken sentences, veiled hints that revealed in half concealing. Her husband's friend Richards was there, too, near her. It was he who had been in the newspaper office when intelligence of the railroad disaster was received, with Brently Mallard's name leading the list of "killed." He had only taken the time to assure himself of its truth by a second telegram, and had hastened to forestall any less careful, less tender friend in bearing the sad message.

She did not hear the story as many women have heard the same, with a paralyzed inability to accept its significance. She wept at once, with sudden, wild abandonment, in her sister's arms. When the storm of grief had spent itself she went away to her room alone. She would have no one follow her.

There stood, facing the open window, a comfortable, roomy arm-chair. Into this she sank, pressed down by a physical exhaustion that haunted her body and seemed to reach into her soul.

She could see in the open square before her house the tops of trees that were all aquiver with the new spring life. The delicious breath of rain was in the air. In the street below a peddler was crying his wares. The notes of a distant song which some one was singing reached her faintly, and countless sparrows were twittering in the eaves.

There were patches of blue sky showing here and there through the clouds that had met and piled above the other in the west facing her window.

She sat with her head thrown back upon the cushion of the chair quite motionless, except when a sob came up into her throat and shook her, as a child who has cried itself to sleep continues to sob in its dreams.

She was young, with a fair, calm face, whose lines bespoke repression and even a certain strength. But now there was a dull stare in her eyes, whose gaze was fixed away off yonder on one of those patches of blue sky. It was not a glance of reflection, but rather indicated a suspension of intelligent thought.

There was something coming to her and she was waiting for it, fearfully. What was it? She did not know; it was too subtle and elusive to name. But she felt it, creeping out of the sky, reaching toward her through the sounds, the scents, the color that filled the air.

Now her bosom rose and fell tumultuously. She was beginning to recognize this thing that was approaching to possess her, and she was striving to beat it back with her will—as powerless as her two white slender hands would have been.

When she abandoned herself a little whispered word escaped her slightly parted lips. She said it over and over under her breath: "Free, free, free!" The vacant stare and the look of terror that had followed it went from her eyes. They stayed keen and bright. Her pulses beat fast, and the coursing blood warmed and relaxed every inch of her body.

She did not stop to ask if it were not a monstrous joy that held her. A clear and exalted perception enabled her to dismiss the suggestion as trivial.

She knew that she would weep again when she saw the kind, tender hands folded in death; the face that had never looked save with love upon her, fixed and gray and dead. But she saw beyond that bitter moment a long procession of years to come that would belong to her absolutely. And she opened and spread her arms out to them in welcome.

There would be no one to live for her during those coming years; she would live for herself. There would be no powerful will bending her in that blind persistence with which men and women believe they have a right to impose a private will upon a fellow creature. A kind intention or a cruel intention made the act seem no less a crime as she looked upon it in that brief moment of illumination.

And yet she had loved him—sometimes. Often she had not. What did it matter! What could love, the unsolved mystery, count for in face of this possession of self-assertion which she suddenly recognized as the strongest impulse of her being.

"Free! Body and soul free!" she kept whispering.

Josephine was kneeling before the closed door with her lips to the keyhole, imploring for admission. "Louise, open the door! I beg; open the door—you will make yourself ill. What are you doing, Louise? For heaven's sake open the door."

"Go away. I am not making myself ill." No; she was drinking in a very elixir of life through that open window.

Her fancy was running riot along those days ahead of her. Spring days and summer days, and all sorts of days that would be her own. She breathed a quick prayer that life might be long. It was only yesterday she had thought with a shudder that life might be long.

She arose at length and opened the door to her sister's importunities. There was a feverish triumph in her eyes, and she carried herself unwittingly like a goddess of Victory. She clasped her sister's waist, and together they descended the stairs. Richards stood waiting for them at the bottom.

Some one was opening the front door with a latchkey. It was Brently Mallard who entered, a little travel-stained, composedly carrying his gripsack and umbrella. He had been far from the scene of the accident, and did not even know there had been one. He stood amazed at Josephine's piercing cry; at Richards' quick motion to screen him from the view of his wife.

But Richards was too late.

When the doctors came they said she had died of heart disease—of joy that kills.

*—1894*

---

*Oscar Wilde (1854–1900) was an Irish-born writer best known for his play* The Importance of Being Earnest *(1895); but he also wrote poems and fiction including the novel* The Picture of Dorian Gray *(1891), and beloved fairy tales such as "The Selfish Giant" and "The Happy Prince." In 1895 he was tried for homosexuality and sentenced to imprisonment with hard labour for two years. After his release, crushed financially and physically, Wilde lived out his last years in Paris under an assumed name. In her story "Mr. Wilde's Second Chance," Joanna Russ speculates on the choices open to Wilde in the era in which he lived.*

## Oscar Wilde

# The Sphinx without a Secret: An Etching

One afternoon I was sitting outside the Café de la Paix, watching the splendour and shabbiness of Parisian life, and wondering over my vermouth at the strange panorama of pride and poverty that was passing before me, when I heard some one call my name. I turned round, and saw Lord Murchison. We had not met since we had been at college together, nearly ten years before, so I was delighted to come across him again, and we shook hands warmly. At Oxford we had been great friends. I had liked him immensely, he was so handsome, so high-spirited, and so honourable. We used to say of him that he would be the best of fellows, if he did not always speak the truth, but I think we really admired him all the more for his frankness. I found him a good deal changed. He looked anxious and puzzled, and seemed to be in doubt about something. I felt it could not be modern scepticism, for Murchison was the stoutest of Tories, and believed in the Pentateuch[1] as firmly as he believed in the House of Peers; so I concluded that it was a woman, and asked him if he was married yet.

'I don't understand women well enough,' he answered.

'My dear Gerald,' I said, 'women are meant to be loved, not to be understood.'

'I cannot love where I cannot trust,' he replied.

'I believe you have a mystery in your life, Gerald,' I exclaimed; 'tell me about it.'

'Let us go for a drive,' he answered, 'it is too crowded here. No, not a yellow carriage, any other colour—there, that dark-green one will do;' and in a few moments we were trotting down the boulevard in the direction of the Madeleine.

'Where shall we go to?' I said.

'Oh, anywhere you like!' he answered—'to the restaurant in the Bois; we will dine there, and you shall tell me all about yourself.'

'I want to hear about you first,' I said. 'Tell me your mystery.'

He took from his pocket a little silver-clasped morocco case, and handed it to me. I opened it. Inside there was the photograph of a woman. She was tall and slight, and strangely picturesque with her large vague eyes and loosened hair. She looked like a *clairvoyante*, and was wrapped in rich furs.

'What do you think of that face?' he said; 'is it truthful?'

I examined it carefully. It seemed to me the face of some one who had a secret, but whether that secret was good or evil I could not say. Its beauty was a beauty moulded out of many mysteries—the beauty, in fact, which is psychological, not plastic—and the faint smile that just played across the lips was far too subtle to be really sweet.

'Well,' he cried impatiently, 'what do you say?'

'She is the Gioconda[2] in sables,' I answered. 'Let me know all about her.'

'Not now,' he said; 'after dinner;' and began to talk of other things.

When the waiter brought us our coffee and cigarettes I reminded Gerald of his promise. He rose from his seat, walked two or three times

---

[1]*Pentateuch:* first five books of the Old Testament.
[2]*Gioconda:* Leonardo da Vinci's *Mona Lisa* (1507).

up and down the room, and, sinking into an armchair, told me the following story:—

'One evening,' he said, 'I was walking down Bond Street about five o'clock. There was a terrific crush of carriages, and the traffic was almost stopped. Close to the pavement was standing a little yellow brougham, which, for some reason or other, attracted my attention. As I passed by there looked out from it the face I showed you this afternoon. It fascinated me immediately. All that night I kept thinking of it, and all the next day. I wandered up and down that wretched Row, peering into every carriage, and waiting for the yellow brougham; but I could not find *ma belle inconnue*, and at last I began to think she was merely a dream. About a week afterwards I was dining with Madame de Rastail. Dinner was for eight o'clock; but at half-past eight we were still waiting in the drawing-room. Finally the servant threw open the door, and announced Lady Alroy. It was the woman I had been looking for. She came in very slowly, looking like a moonbeam in grey lace, and, to my intense delight, I was asked to take her in to dinner. After we had sat down I remarked quite innocently, "I think I caught sight of you in Bond Street some time ago, Lady Alroy." She grew very pale, and said to me in a low voice, "Pray do not talk so loud; you may be overheard." I felt miserable at having made such a bad beginning, and plunged recklessly into the subject of the French plays. She spoke very little, always in the same low musical voice, and seemed as if she was afraid of some one listening. I fell passionately, stupidly in love, and the indefinable atmosphere of mystery that surrounded her excited my most ardent curiosity. When she was going away, which she did very soon after dinner, I asked her if I might call and see her. She hesitated for a moment, glanced round to see if any one was near us, and then said, "Yes; to-morrow at a quarter to five." I begged Madame de Rastail to tell me about her; but all that I could learn was that she was a widow with a beautiful house in Park Lane, and as some scientific bore began a dissertation on widows, as exemplifying the survival of the matrimonially fittest, I left and went home.

'The next day I arrived at Park Lane punctual to the moment, but was told by the butler that Lady Alroy had just gone out. I went down to the club quite unhappy and very much puzzled, and after long consideration wrote her a letter, asking if I might be allowed to try my chance some other afternoon. I had no answer for several days, but at last I got a little note saying she would be at home on Sunday at four, and with this extraordinary postscript: "Please do not write to me here again; I will explain when I see you." On Sunday she received me, and was perfectly charming; but when I was going away she begged of me if I ever had occasion to write to her again, to address my letter to "Mrs. Knox, care of Whittaker's Library, Green Street." "There are reasons," she said, "why I cannot receive letters in my own house."

'All through the season I saw a great deal of her, and the atmosphere of mystery never left her. Sometimes I thought that she was in the power of some man, but she looked so unapproachable that I could not believe it. It was really very difficult for me to come to any conclusion, for she was like one of those strange crystals that one sees in museums, which are at one moment clear, and at another clouded. At last I determined to ask her to be my wife: I was sick and tired of the incessant secrecy that she imposed on all my visits, and on the few letters I sent her. I wrote to her at the library to ask her if she could see me the following Monday at six. She answered yes, and I was in the seventh heaven of delight. I was infatuated with her: in spite of the mystery, I thought then—in consequence of it, I see now. No; it was the woman herself I loved. The mystery troubled me, maddened me. Why did chance put me in its track?'

'You discovered it, then?' I cried.

'I fear so,' he answered. 'You can judge for yourself.'

'When Monday came round I went to lunch with my uncle, and about four o'clock found myself in the Marylebone Road. My uncle, you know, lives in Regent's Park. I wanted to get to Piccadilly, and took a short cut through a lot of shabby little streets. Suddenly I saw in front of me Lady Alroy, deeply veiled and walking very fast. On coming to the last house in the street, she went up the steps, took out a latch-key, and let herself in. "Here is the mystery," I said to myself; and I hurried on and examined the house. It seemed a sort of place for letting lodgings. On the doorstep lay her handkerchief, which she had dropped. I picked it up and put it in my pocket. Then I began to consider what I should do. I came to the conclusion that I had no right to spy on her, and I drove down to the club. At six I called to see her. She was lying on a sofa, in a tea-gown of silver tissue looped up by some strange moon-stones that she always wore. She was looking quite lovely. "I am so glad to see you," she said; "I have not been out all day." I stared at her in amazement, and pulling the handkerchief out of my pocket, handed it to her. "You dropped this in Cumnor Street this afternoon, Lady Alroy,"

I said very calmly. She looked at me in terror, but made no attempt to take the handkerchief. "What were you doing there?" I asked. "What right have you to question me?" she answered. "The right of a man who loves you," I replied; "I came here to ask you to be my wife." She hid her face in her hands, and burst into floods of tears. "You must tell me," I continued. She stood up, and, looking me straight in the face, said, "Lord Murchison, there is nothing to tell you."—"You went to meet some one," I cried; "this is your mystery." She grew dreadfully white, and said, "I went to meet no one."—"Can't you tell the truth?" I exclaimed. "I have told it," she replied. I was mad, frantic; I don't know what I said, but I said terrible things to her. Finally I rushed out of the house. She wrote me a letter the next day; I sent it back unopened, and started for Norway with Alan Colville. After a month I came back, and the first thing I saw in the *Morning Post* was the death of Lady Alroy. She had caught a chill at the Opera, and had died in five days of congestion of the lungs. I shut myself up and saw no one. I had loved her so much, I had loved her so madly. Good God! how I had loved that woman!'

'You went to the street, to the house in it?' I said.

'Yes,' he answered.

'One day I went to Cumnor Street. I could not help it; I was tortured with doubt. I knocked at the door, and a respectable-looking woman opened it to me. I asked her if she had any rooms to let. "Well, sir," she replied, "the drawing-rooms are supposed to be let; but I have not seen the lady for three months, and as rent is owing on them, you can have them."—"Is this the lady?" I said, showing the photograph. "That's her, sure enough," she exclaimed; "and when is she coming back, sir?"—"The lady is dead," I replied. "Oh, sir, I hope not!" said the woman; "she was my best lodger. She paid me three guineas a week merely to sit in my drawing-rooms now and then."—"She met some one here?" I said; but the woman assured me that it was not so, that she always came alone, and saw no one. "What on earth did she do here?" I cried. "She simply sat in the drawing-room, sir, reading books, and sometimes had tea," the woman answered. I did not know what to say, so I gave her a sovereign and went away. Now, what do you think it all meant? You don't believe the woman was telling the truth?'

'I do.'

'Then why did Lady Alroy go there?'

'My dear Gerald,' I answered, 'Lady Alroy was simply a woman with a mania for mystery. She took these rooms for the pleasure of going there with her veil down, and imagining she was a heroine. She had a passion for secrecy, but she herself was merely a Sphinx without a secret.'

'Do you really think so?'

'I am sure of it,' I replied.

He took out the morocco case, opened it, and looked at the photograph. 'I wonder?' he said at last.

*—1891*

---

*Anton Chekhov (1860–1904) was the grandchild of Russian serfs but showed great understanding of and sympathy for the upper-class characters, like those in his masterpiece* The Cherry Orchard *(1904), who could see their world ending in the decades before the Russian Revolution. After early education in his native town of Taganrog, Chekhov entered the University of Moscow, where he took a medical degree in 1884. Except for occasional service during epidemics, Chekhov practised only rarely, preferring to earn his living as a regular contributor of stories to humour magazines. His first play,* Ivanov, *was produced in 1887, beginning for Chekhov a career as a dramatist that flourished in the last decade of his life, when he allied himself with the Moscow Art Theatre and its influential director, Konstantin Stanislavsky. Chekhov's early stories were primarily comic, but those of his mature period, like his plays, are remarkable for their emotional depth. Chekhov's objectivity and realism, qualities that he perhaps gained from his medical studies, continue to make him one of the most modern of nineteenth-century authors; there are rarely easy morals in Chekhov's works. The "unheroic heroes and heroines" whom he depicts with sympathy and gentle irony foreshadow many of the key literary themes of the twentieth century.*

## *Anton Chekhov*

# An Upheaval

Mashenka Pavletsky, a young girl who had only just finished her studies at a boarding school, returning from a walk to the house of the Kushkins, with whom she was living as a governess, found the household in a terrible turmoil. Mihailo, the porter who opened the door to her, was excited and red as a crab.

Translated by Constance Garnett.

Loud voices were heard from upstairs.

"Madame Kushkin is in a fit, most likely, or else she has quarrelled with her husband," thought Mashenka.

In the hall and in the corridor she met maidservants. One of them was crying. Then Mashenka saw, running out of her room, the master of the house himself, Nikolay Sergeitch, a little man with a flabby face and a bald head, though he was not old. He was red in the face and twitching all over. He passed the governess without noticing her, and throwing up his arms, exclaimed:

"Oh, how horrible it is! How tactless! How stupid! How barbarous! Abominable!"

Mashenka went into her room, and then, for the first time in her life, it was her lot to experience in all its acuteness the feeling that is so familiar to persons in dependent positions, who eat the bread of the rich and powerful, and cannot speak their minds. There was a search going on in her room. The lady of the house, Fedosya Vassilyevna, a stout, broad-shouldered, uncouth woman with thick black eyebrows, a faintly perceptible moustache, and red hands, who was exactly like a plain, illiterate cook in face and manners, was standing, without her cap on, at the table, putting back into Mashenka's work-bag balls of wool, scraps of materials, and bits of papers. . . . Evidently the governess's arrival took her by surprise, since, on looking round and seeing the girl's pale and astonished face, she was a little taken aback, and muttered:

"*Pardon.* I . . . I upset it accidentally. . . . My sleeve caught in it . . ."

And saying something more, Madame Kushkin rustled her long skirts and went out. Mashenka looked round her room with wondering eyes, and, unable to understand it, not knowing what to think, shrugged her shoulders, and turned cold with dismay. What had Fedosya Vassilyevna been looking for in her work-bag? If she really had, as she said, caught her sleeve in it and upset everything, why had Nikolay Sergeitch dashed out of her room so excited and red in the face? Why was one drawer of the table pulled out a little way? The money-box, in which the governess put away ten kopeck pieces and old stamps, was open. They had opened it, but did not know how to shut it, though they had scratched the lock all over. The whatnot with her books on it, the things on the table, the bed—all bore fresh traces of a search. Her linen-basket, too. The linen had been carefully folded, but it was not in the same order as Mashenka had left it when she went out. So the search had been thorough, most thorough. But what was it for? Why? What had happened? Mashenka remembered the excited porter, the general turmoil which was still going on, the weeping servant-girl; had it not all some connection with the search that had just been made in her room? Was she not mixed up in something dreadful? Mashenka turned pale, and feeling cold all over, sank on to her linen-basket.

A maidservant came into the room.

"Liza, you don't know why they have been rummaging in my room?" the governess asked her.

"Mistress has lost a brooch worth two thousand," said Liza.

"Yes, but why have they been rummaging in my room?"

"They've been searching every one, miss. They've searched all my things, too. They stripped us all naked and searched us. . . . God knows, miss, I never went near her toilet-table, let alone touching the brooch. I shall say the same at the police-station."

"But . . . why have they been rummaging here?" the governess still wondered.

"A brooch has been stolen, I tell you. The mistress has been rummaging in everything with her own hands. She even searched Mihailo, the porter, herself. It's a perfect disgrace! Nikolay Sergeitch simply looks on and cackles like a hen. But you've no need to tremble like that, miss. They found nothing here. You've nothing to be afraid of if you didn't take the brooch."

"But Liza, it's vile . . . it's insulting," said Mashenka, breathless with indignation. "It's so mean, so low! What right had she to suspect me and to rummage in my things?"

"You are living with strangers, miss," sighed Liza. "Though you are a young lady, still you are . . . as it were . . . a servant. . . . It's not like living with your papa and mamma."

Mashenka threw herself on the bed and sobbed bitterly. Never in her life had she been subjected to such an outrage, never had she been so deeply insulted. . . . She, well-educated, refined, the daughter of a teacher, was suspected of theft; she had been searched like a street-walker! She could not imagine a greater insult. And to this feeling of resentment was added an oppressive dread of what would come next. All sorts of absurd ideas came into her mind. If they could suspect her of theft, then they might arrest her, strip her naked, and search her, then lead her through the street with an escort of soldiers, cast her into a cold, dark cell with mice and wood lice, exactly like the dungeon in which Princess Tarakanov was imprisoned. Who would stand up for her? Her parents lived far away in the Provinces; they had not the money to come to her. In the capital she was as solitary as in a desert, without friends or kindred. They could do what they liked with her.

"I will go to all the courts and all the lawyers," Mashenka thought, trembling. "I will explain to them, I will take an oath. . . . They will believe that I could not be a thief!"

Mashenka remembered that under the sheets in her basket she had some sweetmeats, which, following the habits of her schooldays, she had put in her pocket at dinner and carried off to her room. She felt hot all over, and was ashamed at the thought that her little secret was known to the lady of the house; all this terror, shame, resentment, brought on an attack of palpitation of the heart, which set up a throbbing in her temples, in her heart, and deep down in her stomach.

"Dinner is ready," the servant summoned Mashenka.

"Shall I go, or not?"

Mashenka brushed her hair, wiped her face with a wet towel and went into the dining-room. There they had already begun dinner. At one end of the table sat Fedosya Vassilyevna with a stupid, solemn, serious face; at the other end Nikolay Sergeitch. At the sides there were the visitors and the children. The dishes were handed by two footmen in swallowtails and white gloves. Everyone knew that there was an upset in the house, that Madame Kushkin was in trouble, and everyone was silent. Nothing was heard but the sound of munching and the rattle of spoons on the plates.

The lady of the house, herself, was the first to speak.

"What is the third course?" she asked the footman in a weary, injured voice.

"*Esturgeon à la russe*,"[1] answered the footman.

"I ordered that, Fenya," Nikolay Sergeitch hastened to observe. "I wanted some fish. If you don't like it, *ma chère*, don't let them serve it. I just ordered it. . . ."

Fedosya Vassilyevna did not like dishes that she had not ordered herself, and now her eyes filled with tears.

"Come, don't let us agitate ourselves," Mamikov, her household doctor, observed in a honeyed voice, just touching her arm, with a smile as

---

[1]*Esturgeon à la russe:* sturgeon, cooked in the Russian manner.

honeyed. "We are nervous enough as it is. Let us forget the brooch! Health is worth more than two thousand roubles!"

"It's not the two thousand I regret," answered the lady, and a big tear rolled down her cheek. "It's the fact itself that revolts me! I cannot put up with thieves in my house. I don't regret it—I regret nothing; but to steal from me is such ingratitude! That's how they repay me for my kindness. . . ."

They all looked into their plates, but Mashenka fancied after the lady's words that every one was looking at her. A lump rose in her throat; she began crying and put her handkerchief to her lips.

"*Pardon,*" she muttered. "I can't help it. My head aches. I'll go away."

And she got up from the table, scraping her chair awkwardly, and went out quickly, still more overcome with confusion.

"It's beyond everything!" said Nikolay Sergeitch, frowning. "What need was there to search her room? How out of place it was!"

"I don't say she took the brooch," said Fedosya Vassilyevna, "but can you answer for her? To tell the truth, I haven't much confidence in these learned paupers."

"It really was unsuitable, Fenya. . . . Excuse me, Fenya, but you've no kind of legal right to make a search."

"I know nothing about your laws. All I know is that I've lost my brooch. And I will find the brooch!" She brought her fork down on the plate with a clatter, and her eyes flashed angrily. "And you eat your dinner, and don't interfere in what doesn't concern you!"

Nikolay Sergeitch dropped his eyes mildly and sighed. Meanwhile Mashenka, reaching her room, flung herself on her bed. She felt now neither alarm nor shame, but she felt an intense longing to go and slap the cheeks of this hard, arrogant, dull-witted, prosperous woman.

Lying on her bed she breathed into her pillow and dreamed of how nice it would be to go and buy the most expensive brooch and fling it into the face of this bullying woman. If only it were God's will that Fedosya Vassilyevna should come to ruin and wander about begging, and should taste all the horrors of poverty and dependence, and that Mashenka, whom she had insulted, might give her alms! Oh, if only she could come in for a big fortune, could buy a carriage, and could drive noisily past the windows so as to be envied by that woman!

But all these were only dreams, in reality there was only one thing left to do—to get away as quickly as possible, not to stay another hour in this place. It was true it was terrible to lose her place, to go back to her parents, who had nothing; but what could she do? Mashenka could not bear the sight of the lady of the house nor of her little room; she felt stifled and wretched here. She was so disgusted with Fedosya Vassilyevna, who was so obsessed by her illnesses and her supposed aristocratic rank, that everything in the world seemed to have become coarse and unattractive because this woman was living in it. Mashenka jumped up from the bed and began packing.

"May I come in?" asked Nikolay Sergeitch at the door; he had come up noiselessly to the door, and spoke in a soft, subdued voice. "May I?"

"Come in."

He came in and stood still near the door. His eyes looked dim and his red little nose was shiny. After dinner he used to drink beer, and the fact was perceptible in his walk, in his feeble, flabby hands.

"What's this?" he asked, pointing to the basket.

"I am packing. Forgive me, Nikolay Sergeitch, but I cannot remain in your house. I feel deeply insulted by this search!"

"I understand. . . . Only you are wrong to go. . . . Why should you? They've searched your things, but you . . . what does it matter to you? You will be none the worse for it."

Mashenka was silent and went on packing. Nikolay Sergeitch pinched his moustache, as though wondering what he should say next, and went on in an ingratiating voice:

"I understand, of course, but you must make allowances. You know my wife is nervous, headstrong; you mustn't judge her too harshly."

Mashenka did not speak.

"If you are so offended," Nikolay Sergeitch went on, "well, if you like, I'm ready to apologize. I ask your pardon."

Mashenka made no answer, but only bent lower over her box. This exhausted, irresolute man was of absolutely no significance in the household. He stood in the pitiful position of a dependent and hanger-on, even with the servants, and his apology meant nothing either.

"H'm . . . You say nothing! That's not enough for you. In that case, I will apologize for my wife. In my wife's name. . . . She behaved tact-lessly, I admit it as a gentleman . . ."

Nikolay Sergeitch walked about the room, heaved a sigh, and went on:

"Then you want me to have it rankling here, under my heart. . . . You want my conscience to torment me. . . ."

"I know it's not your fault, Nikolay Sergeitch," said Mashenka, looking him full in the face with her big tear-stained eyes. "Why should you worry yourself?"

"Of course, no. . . . But still, don't you . . . go away. I entreat you."

Mashenka shook her head. Nikolay Sergeitch stopped at the window and drummed on a pane with his fingertips.

"Such misunderstandings are simply torture to me," he said. "Why, do you want me to go down on my knees to you, or what? Your pride is wounded, and here you've been crying and packing up to go; but I have pride, too, and you do not spare it! Or do you want me to tell you what I would not tell at Confession? Do you? Listen; you want me to tell you what I won't tell the priest on my deathbed?"

Mashenka made no answer.

"I took my wife's brooch," Nikolay Sergeitch said quickly. "Is that enough now? Are you satisfied? Yes, I . . . took it. . . . But, of course, I count on your discretion. . . . For God's sake, not a word, not half a hint to any one!"

Mashenka, amazed and frightened, went on packing; she snatched her things, crumpled them up, and thrust them anyhow into the box and the basket. Now, after this candid avowal on the part of Nikolay Sergeitch, she could not remain another minute, and could not understand how she could have gone on living in the house before.

"And it's nothing to wonder at," Nikolay Sergeitch went on after a pause. "It's an everyday story! I need money, and she . . . won't give it to me. It was my father's money that bought this house and everything, you know! It's all mine, and the brooch belonged to my mother, and . . . it's all mine! And she took it, took possession of everything. . . . I can't go to law with her, you'll admit. . . . I beg you most earnestly, overlook it . . . stay on. *Tout comprendre, tout pardonner.*[2] Will you stay?"

"No!" said Mashenka resolutely, beginning to tremble. "Let me alone, I entreat you!"

"Well, God bless you!" sighed Nikolay Sergeitch, sitting down on the stool near the box. "I must own I like people who still can feel resentment, contempt, and so on. I could sit here forever and look at your indignant face. . . . So you won't stay, then? I understand. . . . it's bound to be so. . . . Yes, of course. . . . It's all right for you, but for me—wo-o-o-o! . . . I can't

---

[2]*Tout comprendre, tout pardonner:* All is understood, all is forgiven.

stir a step out of this cellar. I'd go off to one of our estates, but in every one of them there are some of my wife's rascals ... stewards, experts, damn them all! They mortgage and remortgage. . . . You mustn't catch fish, must keep off the grass, mustn't break the trees."

"Nikolay Sergeitch!" his wife's voice called from the drawing-room. "Agnia, call your master!"

"Then you won't stay?" asked Nikolay Sergeitch, getting up quickly and going toward the door. "You might as well stay, really. In the evenings I could come and have a talk with you. Eh? Stay! If you go, there won't be a human face left in the house. It's awful!"

Nikolay Sergeitch's pale, exhausted face besought her, but Mashenka shook her head, and with a wave of his hand he went out.

Half an hour later she was on her way.

*—1917*

---

*Stephen Leacock (1869–1944) was born in Swanmore, England, but immigrated to Ontario with his family in 1876. Though he published in the field of political science, he was best known for his humour writing, most notably* Sunshine Sketches of a Little Town *(1912), a collection of affectionate satires of small-town Canadian life based on Orillia, a town on the shore of Lake Simcoe, where Leacock spent his summer holidays.* Idle Adventures of the Arcadian Rich *(1914), a darker collection based on life in Montreal, where Leacock taught at McGill University, soon followed. The explicitly Canadian content of these accomplished works might have meant that they were not as popular internationally as Leacock's other comic collections, including* Literary Lapses *(1910),* Nonsense Novels *(1911), and* The Dry Pickwick *(1932).*

## Stephen Leacock
# Ho for Happiness: A Plea for Lighter and Brighter Literature

"Why is it," said some one in conversation the other day, "that all the really good short stories seem to contain so much sadness and suffering and to turn so much on crime and wickedness? Why can't they be happy all the time?"

No one present was able to answer the question. But I thought it over afterwards, and I think I see why it is so. A happy story, after all, would make pretty dull reading. It may be all right in real life to have everything come along just right, with happiness and good luck all the time, but in fiction it would never do.

Stop, let me illustrate the idea. Let us make up a story which is happy all the time and contrast it as it goes along with the way things happen in the really good stories.

Harold Herald never forgot the bright October morning when the mysterious letter, which was to alter his whole life, arrived at his downtown office.

His stenographer brought it in to him and laid it on his desk.

"A letter for you," she said. Then she kissed him and went out again.

Harold sat for some time with the letter in front of him. Should he open it? After all, why not?

He opened the letter. Then the idea occurred to him to read it. "I might as well," he thought.

"Dear Mr. Herald" (so ran the letter), "if you will have the kindness to call at this office, we shall be happy to tell you something to your great advantage."

The letter was signed John Scribman. The paper on which it was written bore the heading "Scribman, Scribman & Company, Barristers, Solicitors, etc., No. 13 Yonge St."

A few moments later saw Harold on his way to the lawyers' office. Never had the streets looked brighter and more cheerful than in this perfect October sunshine. In fact, they never had been.

Nor did Harold's heart misgive him and a sudden suspicion enter his mind as Mr. Scribman, the senior partner, rose from his chair to greet him. Not at all. Mr. Scribman was a pleasant, middle-aged man whose countenance behind his gold spectacles beamed with goodwill and good nature.

"Ah, Mr. Harold Herald," he said, "or perhaps, you will let me call you simply Harold. I didn't like to give you too much news in one short letter. The fact is that our firm has been entrusted to deliver to you a legacy, or rather a gift. . . . Stop, stop!" continued the lawyer, as Harold was about to interrupt with questions, " . . . our client's one request was that his name would not be divulged. He thought it would be so much nicer for you just to have the money and not know who gave it to you."

Harold murmured his assent.

Mr. Scribman pushed a bell.

"Mr. Harold Herald's money, if you please," he said.

A beautiful stenographer wearing an American Beauty rose at her waist entered the room carrying a silken bag.

"There is half a million dollars here in five-hundred-dollar bills," said the lawyer. "At least, we didn't count them; but that is what our client said. Did you take any?" he asked the stenographer.

"I took out a few last night to go to the theatre with," admitted the girl with a pretty blush.

"Monkey!" said Mr. Scribman. "But that's all right. Don't bother with a receipt, Harold. Come along with me: my daughter is waiting for us down below in the car to take us to lunch."

Harold thought he had never seen a more beautiful girl than Alicia Scribman. In fact he hadn't. The luxurious motor, the faultless chauffeur, the presence of the girl beside him and the bag of currency under the seat, the sunlit streets filled with happy people with the bright feeling of just going back to work, full of lunch—the sight of all this made Harold feel as if life were indeed a pleasant thing.

"After all," he mused, "how little is needed for our happiness! Half a million dollars, a motor-car, a beautiful girl, youth, health—surely one can be content with that . . ."

It was after lunch at the beautiful country home of the Scribmans that Harold found himself alone for a few minutes with Miss Scribman.

He rose, walked over to her and took her hand, kneeling on one knee and pulling up his pants so as not to make a crease in them.

"Alicia!" he said. "Ever since I first saw you, I have loved you. I want to ask you if you will marry me?"

"Oh, Harold," said Alicia, leaning forward and putting both her arms about his neck with one ear against the upper right-hand end of his cheekbone. "Oh, Harold!"

"I can, as you know," continued Harold, "easily support you."

"Oh, that's all right," said Alicia. "As a matter of fact, I have much more than that of my own, to be paid over to me when I marry."

"Then you will marry me?" said Harold rapturously.

"Yes, indeed," said Alicia, "and it happens so fortunately just now, as papa himself is engaged to marry again and so I shall be glad to have a new home of my own. Papa is marrying a charming girl, but she is so much younger than he is that perhaps she would not want a grown-up stepdaughter."

Harold made his way back to the city in a tumult of happiness. Only for a moment was his delirium of joy brought to a temporary standstill.

As he returned to his own apartment, he suddenly remembered that he was engaged to be married to his cousin Winnie. . . . The thing had been entirely washed out of his mind by the flood-tide of his joy.

He seized the telephone.

"Winnie," he said, "I am so terribly sorry. I want to ask you to release me from our engagement. I want to marry someone else."

"That's all right, Hal!" came back Winnie's voice cheerfully. "As a matter of fact, I want to do the same thing myself. I got engaged last week to the most charming man in the world, a little older, in fact quite a bit older than I am, but ever so nice. He is a wealthy lawyer and his name is Walter Scribman. . . ."

The double wedding took place two weeks later, the church being smothered with chrysanthemums and the clergyman buried under Canadian currency. Harold and Alicia built a beautiful country home at the other side—the farthest-away side—of the city from the Scribmans'. A year or so after their marriage, they had a beautiful boy, and then another, then a couple of girls (twins), and then they lost count.

There. Pretty dull reading it makes. And yet, I don't know. There's something about it, too. In the real stories Mr. Scribman would have been a crook, and Harold would have either murdered Winnie or been accused of it, and the stenographer with the rose would have stolen the money instead of just taking it, and it wouldn't have happened in bright, clear October weather but in dirty old November—oh, no, let us have romance and happiness, after all. It may not be true, but it's better.

*—1932*

*Emily Carr (1871–1945) was born in Victoria, British Columbia, to English parents. Associated with the Group of Seven, she is known as Canada's most famous female painter for her efforts to make a visual record of Haida and Tlingit culture in coastal British Columbia. When Carr suffered a heart attack in 1937, she turned more and more to writing. Her first collection of short stories, entitled* Klee Wyck *(1942) or "Laughing One" — after the Native name she was given — was based on her earlier visits to First Nation villages, including one called Kitwancool in the Queen Charlotte Islands. This book won a Governor General's Award and was followed by six more largely autobiographical books of lean and vivid prose, four of which were published posthumously.*

## Emily Carr
# Kitwancool

When the Indians told me about the Kitwancool totem poles, I said:

"How can I get to Kitwancool?"

"Dunno," the Indians replied.

White men told me about the Kitwancool poles too, but when I told them I wanted to go there, they advised me—"Keep out." But the thought of those old Kitwancool poles pulled at me. I was at Kitwangak, twenty or so miles from Kitwancool.

Then a halfbreed at Kitwangak said to me, "The young son of the Kitwancool Chief is going in tomorrow with a load of lumber. I asked if he would take you; he will."

"How can I get out again?"

"The boy is coming back to Kitwangak after two days."

The Chief's son Aleck was shy, but he spoke good English. He said I was to be at the Hudson's Bay store at eight the next morning.

I bought enough food and mosquito oil to last me two days; then I sat in front of the Hudson's Bay store from eight to eleven o'clock, waiting. I saw Aleck drive past to load his lumber. The wagon had four wheels and a long pole. He tied the lumber to the pole and a sack of oats to the lumber; I was to sit on the oats. Rigged up in front somehow was a place for the driver—no real seat, just a couple of coal-oil boxes bound to some boards. Three men sat on the two boxes. The road was terrible. When we bumped, the man on the down side of the boxes fell off.

A sturdy old man trudged behind the wagon. Sometimes he rode a bit on the end of the long pole, which tossed him up and down like a see-saw. The old man carried a gun and walked most of the way.

The noon sun burnt fiercely on our heads. The oat-sack gave no support to my back, and my feet dangled. I had to clutch the corner of the oat-sack with one hand to keep from falling off—with the other I held my small griffon dog. Every minute I thought we would be pitched off the pole. You could seldom see the old man because of clouds of yellow dust rolling behind the wagon. The scrub growth at the road-side smelt red hot.

The scraggy ponies dragged their feet heavily; sweat cut rivers through the dust that was caked on their sides.

One of the three men on the front seat of the wagon seemed to be a hero. The other men questioned him all the way, though generally Indians do not talk as they travel. When one of the men fell off the seat he ran round the wagon to the high side and jumped up again and all the while he did not stop asking the hero questions. There were so many holes in the road and the men fell off so often that they were always changing places, like birds on a roost in cold weather.

Suddenly we gave such an enormous bump that we all fell off together, and the horses stopped. When the wheels were not rattling any more we could hear water running. Then the old man came out of the clouds of dust behind us and said there was a stream close by.

We threw ourselves on-to our stomachs, put our lips to the water and drank like horses. The Indians took the bits out of their horses' mouths and gave them food. Then the men crawled under the wagon to eat their lunch in its shade; I sat by the shadiest wheel. It was splendid to put my legs straight out and have the earth support them and the wheel support my back. The old man went to sleep.

After he woke and after the horses had pulled the wagon out of the big hole, we rumbled on again.

When the sun began to go down we were in woods, and the clouds of mosquitoes were as thick as the clouds of dust, but more painful. We let them eat us because, after bumping for seven hours, we were too tired to fight.

At last we came to a great dip where the road wound around the edge of a ravine shaped like an oblong bowl. There were trees growing in this earth bowl. It seemed to be bottomless. We were level with the tree-tops as we looked down. The road was narrow—its edges broken.

I was afraid and said, "I want to walk."

Aleck waved his hand across the ravine. "Kitwancool," he said and I saw some grey roofs on the far side of the hollow. After we had circled the ravine and climbed the road on the other side we would be there, unless we were lying dead in that deep bowl.

I said again, "I want to walk."

"Village dogs will kill you and the little dog," said Aleck. But I did walk around the bend and up the hill, until the village was near. Then I rode into Kitwancool on the oat-sack.

The dogs rushed out in a pack. The village people came out too. They made a fuss over the hero-man, clustering about him and jabbering. They paid no more attention to me than to the oat-sack. All of them went into the nearest house taking Aleck, the hero, the old man and the other man with them, and shut the door.

I wanted to cry, sticking alone up there on top of the oats and lumber, the sagging horses in front and the yapping dogs all round, nobody to ask about anything and very tired. Aleck had told me I could sleep on the verandah of his father's house, because I only had a cot and a tent-fly with me, and bears came into the village often at night. But how did I know which was his father's house? The dogs would tear me if I got down and there was no one to ask, anyway.

Suddenly something at the other end of the village attracted the dogs. The pack tore off and the dust hid me from them.

Aleck came out of the house and said, "We are going to have dinner in this house now." Then he went in again and shut the door.

The wagon was standing in the new part of the village. Below us, on the right, I could see a row of old houses. They were dim, for the light was going, but above them, black and clear against the sky stood the old totem poles of Kitwancool. I jumped down from the wagon and came to them. That part of the village was quite dead. Between the river and the poles was a flat of green grass. Above, stood the houses, grey and broken. They were in a long, wavering row, with wide, windowless fronts. The totem poles stood before them there on the top of a little bank above the green flat. There were a few poles down on the flat too, and some graves that had fences round them and roofs over the tops.

When it was almost dark I went back to the wagon.

The house of Aleck's father was the last one at the other end of the new village. It was one great room like a hall and was built of new logs. It had seven windows and two doors; all the windows were propped open with blue castor-oil bottles.

I was surprised to find that the old man who had trudged behind our wagon was Chief Douse—Aleck's father.

Mrs. Douse was more important than Mr. Douse; she was a chieftain-ess in her own right, and had great dignity. Neither of them spoke to me that night. Aleck showed me where to put my bed on the verandah and I hung the fly over it. I ate a dry scrap of food and turned into my blankets. I had no netting, and the mosquitoes tormented me.

My heart said into the thick dark, "Why did I come?"

And the dark answered, "You know."

In the morning the hero-man came to me and said, "My mother-in-law wishes to speak with you. She does not know English words so she will talk through my tongue."

I stood before the tall, cold woman. She folded her arms across her body and her eyes searched my face. They were as expressive as if she were saying the words herself instead of using the hero's tongue.

"My mother-in-law wishes to know why you have come to our village."

"I want to make some pictures of the totem poles."

"What do you want our totem poles for?"

"Because they are beautiful. They are getting old now, and your people make very few new ones. The young people do not value the poles as the old ones did. By and by there will be no more poles. I want to make pictures of them, so that your young people as well as the white people will see how fine your totem poles used to be."

Mrs. Douse listened when the young man told her this. Her eyes raked my face to see if I was talking "straight". Then she waved her hand towards the village.

"Go along," she said through the interpreter, "and I shall see." She was neither friendly nor angry. Perhaps I was going to be turned out of this place that had been so difficult to get into.

The air was hot and heavy. I turned towards the old village with the pup Ginger Pop at my heels. Suddenly there was a roar of yelpings, and I saw my little dog putting half a dozen big ones to rout down the village street. Their tails were flat, their tongues lolled and they yelped. The Douses all rushed out of their house to see what the noise was about, and we laughed together so hard that the strain, which before had been between us, broke.

The sun enriched the old poles grandly. They were carved elaborately and with great sincerity. Several times the figure of a woman that held a child was represented. The babies had faces like wise little old men. The mothers expressed all womanhood—the big wooden hands holding the child were so full of tenderness they had to be distorted enormously in order to contain it all. Womanhood was strong in Kitwancool. Perhaps, after all, Mrs. Douse might let me stay.

I sat in front of a totem mother and began to draw—so full of her strange, wild beauty that I did not notice the storm that was coming, till the totem poles went black, flashed vividly white and then went black again. Bang upon bang, came the claps of thunder. The hills on one side tossed it to the hills on the other; sheets of rain washed over me. I was beside a grave down on the green flat; some of the pickets of its fence were gone, so I crawled through on to the grave with Ginger Pop in my arms to shelter under its roof. Stinging nettles grew on top of the grave with mosquitoes hiding under their leaves. While I was beating down the nettles with my easel, it struck the head of a big wooden bear squatted on the grave. He startled me. He was painted red. As I sat down upon him my foot hit something that made a hollow rattling noise. It was a shaman's rattle. This then must be a shaman's, a medicine-man's grave, and this the rattle he had used to scare away evil spirits. Shamen worked black magic. His body lay here just a few feet below me in the earth. At the thought I made a dash for the broken community house on the bank above. All the Indian horses had got there first and taken for their shelter the only corner of the house that had any roof over it.

I put my stool near the wall and sat upon it. The water ran down the wall in rivers. The dog shivered under my coat—both of us were wet to the skin. My sketch sack was so full of water that when I emptied it on to the ground it made the pool we sat in bigger.

After two hours the rain stopped suddenly. The horses held their bones stiff and quivered their skins. It made the rain fly out of their coats and splash me. One by one they trooped out through a hole in the wall. When their hooves struck the baseboard there was a sodden thud. Ginger Pop shook himself too, but I could only drip. Water poured from the eyes of the totems and from the tips of their carved noses. New little rivers trickled across the green flat. The big river was whipped to froth. A blur like boiling mist hung over it.

When I got back to the new village I found my bed and things in a corner of the Douses' great room. The hero told me, "My mother-in-law says you may live in her house. Here is a rocking-chair for you."

Mrs. Douse acknowledged my gratitude stolidly. I gave Mr. Douse a dollar and asked if I might have a big fire to dry my things and make tea. There were two stoves—the one at their end of the room was alight. Soon, mine too was roaring and it was cosy. When the Indians accepted me as one of themselves, I was very grateful.

The people who lived in that big room of the Douses were two married daughters, their husbands and children, the son Aleck and an orphan girl called Lizzie. The old couple came and went continually, but they ate and slept in a shanty at the back of the new house. This little place had been made round them. The floor was of earth and the walls were of cedar. The fire on the ground sent its smoke through a smoke-hole in the roof. Dried salmon hung on racks. The old people's mattress was on the floor. The place was full of themselves—they had breathed themselves into it as a bird, with its head under its wing, breathes itself into its own cosiness. The Douses were glad for their children to have the big fine house and be modern but this was the right sort of place for themselves.

Life in the big house was most interesting. A baby swung in its cradle from the rafters; everyone tossed the cradle as he passed and the baby cooed and gurgled. There was a crippled child of six—pinched and white under her brown skin; she sat in a chair all day. And there was Orphan Lizzie who would slip out into the wet bushes and come back with a wild strawberry or a flower in her grubby little hand, and, kneeling by the sick child's chair, would open her fingers suddenly on the surprise.

There was no rush, no scolding, no roughness in this household. When anyone was sleepy he slept; when they were hungry they ate; if they were sorry they cried, and if they were glad they sang. They enjoyed Ginger Pop's fiery temper, the tilt of his nose and particularly the way he kept the house free of Indian dogs. It was Ginger who bridged the gap between their language and mine with laughter. Ginger's snore was the only sound in that great room at night. Indians sleep quietly.

Orphan Lizzie was shy as a rabbit but completely unselfconscious. It was she who set the food on the big table and cleared away the dishes. There did not seem to be any particular meal-times. Lizzie always took a long lick at the top of the jam-tin as she passed it.

The first morning I woke at the Douses', I went very early to wash myself in the creek below the house. I was kneeling on the stones brushing my teeth. It was very cold. Suddenly I looked up—Lizzie was close by me watching. When I looked up, she darted away like a fawn, leaving her water pails behind. Later, Mrs. Douse came to my corner of the house, carrying a tin basin; behind her was Lizzie with a tiny glass cream pitcher full of water, and behind Lizzie was the hero.

"My mother-in-law says the river is too cold for you to wash in. Here is water and a basin for you."

Everyone watched my washing next morning. The washing of my ears interested them most.

One day after work I found the Douse family all sitting round on the floor. In the centre of the group was Lizzie. She was beating something in a pail, beating it with her hands; her arms were blobbed with pink froth to the elbows. Everyone stuck his hand into Lizzie's pail and hooked out some of the froth in the crook of his fingers, then took long delicious licks. They invited me to lick too. It was "soperlallie", or soap berry. It grows in the woods; when you beat the berry it froths up and has a queer bitter taste. The Indians love it.

For two days from dawn till dark I worked down in the old part of the village. On the third day Aleck was to take me back to Kitwangak. But that night it started to rain. It rained for three days and three nights without stopping; the road was impossible. I had only provisioned for two days, had been here five and had given all the best bits from my box to the sick child. All the food I had left for the last three days was hard tack and raisins. I drank hot water, and rocked my hunger to the tune of the rain beating on the window. Ginger Pop munched hard tack unconcerned—amusing everybody.

The Indians would have shared the loaf and jam-tin with me, but I did not tell them that I had no food. The thought of Lizzie's tongue licking the jam-tin stopped me.

When it rained, the Indians drowsed like flies, heavy as the day itself.

On the sixth day of my stay in Kitwancool the sun shone again, but we had to wait a bit for the puddles to drain.

I straightened out my obligations and said goodbye to Mr. and Mrs. Douse. The light wagon that was taking me out seemed luxurious after the thing I had come in on. I climbed up beside Aleck. He gathered his reins and "giddapped".

Mrs. Douse, followed by her husband, came out of the house and waved a halt. She spoke to Aleck.

"My mother wants to see your pictures."

"But I showed her every one before they were packed."

At the time I had thought her stolidly indifferent.

"My mother wishes to see the pictures again."

I clambered over the back of the wagon, unpacked the wet canvases and opened the sketchbooks. She went through them all. The two best poles in the village belonged to Mrs. Douse. She argued and discussed with her husband. I told Aleck to ask if his mother would like to have me give her pictures of her poles. If so, I would send them through the Hudson's Bay store at Kitwangak. Mrs. Douse's neck loosened. Her head nodded violently and I saw her smile for the first time.

Repacking, I climbed over the back of the seat to Aleck.

"Giddap!"

The reins flapped: we were off. The dust was laid; everything was keen and fresh; indeed the appetites of the mosquitoes were very keen.

When I got back to Kitwangak the Mounted Police came to see me.

"You have been in to Kitwancool?"

"Yes."

"How did the Indians treat you?"

"Splendidly."

"Learned their lesson, eh?" said the man. "We have had no end of trouble with those people—chased missionaries out and drove surveyors off with axes—simply won't have whites in their village. I would never have advised anyone going in—particularly a woman. No, I would certainly have said, 'Keep out'."

"Then I am glad I did not ask for your advice," I said. "Perhaps it is because I am a woman that they were so good to me."

"One of the men who went in on the wagon with you was straight from jail, a fierce, troublesome customer."

Now I knew who the hero was.

*—1941*

---

*Lucy Maud Montgomery (1874–1942) was born and raised in Prince Edward Island, the setting for most of her books, including* Anne of Green Gables *(1908), the international best-seller about the red-haired heroine with the vivid imagination.* The Story Girl *(1911) was the last of her books to be written on the Island, and includes the experiences of her own great-grandmother. After her marriage in 1911, Montgomery moved to Ontario, where she lived for the remainder of her life, continuing to write prolifically, producing twenty-two books of fiction and hundreds of short stories and poems, as well as extensive journals.*

## Lucy Maud Montgomery
# How Betty Sherman Won a Husband

The rest of us did not share the Story Girl's enthusiasm regarding our call on Mr. Campbell. We secretly dreaded it. If, as was said, he detested children, who knew what sort of a reception we might meet?

Mr. Campbell was a rich, retired farmer, who took life easily. He had visited New York and Boston, Toronto and Montreal; he had even been as far as the Pacific coast. Therefore he was regarded in Carlisle as a much travelled man; and he was known to be "well read" and intelligent. But it was also known that Mr. Campbell was not always in a good humour. If he liked you there was nothing he would not do for you; if he disliked you—well, you were not left in ignorance of it. In short, we had the impression that Mr. Campbell resembled the famous little girl with the curl in the middle of her forehead. "When he was good, he was very, very good, and when he was bad he was horrid." What if this were one of his horrid days?

"He can't *do* anything to us, you know," said the Story Girl. "He may be rude, but that won't hurt any one but himself."

"Hard words break no bones," observed Felix philosophically.

"But they hurt your feelings. *I* am afraid of Mr. Campbell," said Cecily candidly.

"Perhaps we'd better give up and go home," suggested Dan.

"You can go home if you like," said the Story Girl scornfully. "But *I* am going to see Mr. Campbell. I know I can manage him. But if I have to go alone, and he gives me anything, I'll keep it all for my own collection, mind you."

That settled it. We were not going to let the Story Girl get ahead of us in the matter of collecting.

Mr. Campbell's housekeeper ushered us into his parlour and left us. Presently Mr. Campbell himself was standing in the doorway, looking us over. We took heart of grace. It seemed to be one of his good days, for there was a quizzical smile on his broad, clean-shaven, strongly-featured face. Mr. Campbell was a tall man, with a massive head, well thatched with thick, black hair, gray-streaked. He had big, black eyes, with many wrinkles around them, and a thin, firm, long-lipped mouth. We thought him handsome, for an old man.

His gaze wandered over us with uncomplimentary indifference until it fell on the Story Girl, leaning back in an armchair. She looked like a slender red lily in the unstudied grace of her attitude. A spark flashed into Mr. Campbell's black eyes.

"Is this a Sunday School deputation?" he inquired rather ironically.

"No. We have come to ask a favour of you," said the Story Girl.

The magic of her voice worked its will on Mr. Campbell, as on all others. He came in, sat down, hooked his thumb into his vest pocket, and smiled at her.

"What is it?" he asked.

"We are collecting for our school library, and we have called to ask you for a contribution," she replied.

"Why should *I* contribute to your school library?" demanded Mr. Campbell.

This was a poser for us. Why should he, indeed? But the Story Girl was quite equal to it. Leaning forward, and throwing an indescribable witchery into tone and eyes and smile, she said,

"Because a lady asks you."

Mr. Campbell chuckled.

"The best of all reasons," he said. "But see here, my dear young lady, I'm an old miser and curmudgeon, as you may have heard. I *hate* to part with my money, even for a good reason. And I *never* part with any of it, unless I am to receive some benefit from the expenditure. Now, what earthly good could I get from your three by six school library? None whatever. But I shall make you a fair offer. I have heard from my housekeeper's urchin of a son that you are a 'master hand' to tell stories. Tell me one, here and now. I shall pay you in proportion to the entertainment you afford me. Come now, and do your prettiest."

There was a fine mockery in his tone that put the Story Girl on her mettle instantly. She sprang to her feet, an amazing change coming over her. Her eyes flashed and burned; crimson spots glowed in her cheeks.

"I shall tell you the story of the Sherman girls, and how Betty Sherman won a husband," she said.

We gasped. Was the Story Girl crazy? Or had she forgotten that Betty Sherman was Mr. Campbell's own great-grandmother, and that her method of winning a husband was not exactly in accordance with maidenly traditions.

But Mr. Campbell chuckled again.

"An excellent test," he said. "If you can amuse *me* with that story you must be a wonder. I've heard it so often that it has no more interest for me than the alphabet."

"One cold winter day, eighty years ago," began the Story Girl without further parley, "Donald Fraser was sitting by the window of his new house, playing his fiddle for company, and looking out over the white, frozen bay before his door. It was bitter, bitter cold, and a storm was brewing. But, storm, or no storm, Donald meant to go over the bay that evening to see Nancy Sherman. He was thinking of her as he played 'Annie Laurie,' for Nancy was more beautiful than the lady of the song. 'Her face, it is the fairest that e'er the sun shone on,' hummed Donald— and oh, he thought so, too! He did not know whether Nancy cared for him or not. He had many rivals. But he knew that if she would not come to be the mistress of his new house no one else ever should. So he sat there that afternoon and dreamed of her, as he played sweet old songs and rollicking jigs on his fiddle.

"While he was playing a sleigh drove up to the door, and Neil Campbell came in. Donald was not overly glad to see him, for he suspected where he was going. Neil Campbell, who was Highland Scotch and lived down at Berwick, was courting Nancy Sherman, too; and, what was far worse, Nancy's father favoured him, because he was a richer man than Donald Fraser. But Donald was not going to show all he thought—Scotch people never do—and he pretended to be very glad to see Neil, and made him heartily welcome.

"Neil sat down by the roaring fire, looking quite well satisfied with himself. It was ten miles from Berwick to the bay shore, and a call at a half way house was just the thing. Then Donald brought out the whisky. They always did that eighty years ago, you know. If you were a woman, you could give your visitors a dish of tea; but if you were a man and did not offer them a 'taste' of whisky, you were thought either very mean or very ignorant.

" 'You look cold,' said Donald, in his great, hearty voice. 'Sit nearer the fire, man, and put a bit of warmth in your veins. It's bitter cold the day. And now tell me the Berwick news. Has Jean McLean made up with her man yet? And is it true that Sandy McQuarrie is to marry Kate Ferguson? 'Twill be a match now! Sure, with her red hair, Sandy will not be like to lose his bride past finding.'

"Neil had plenty of news to tell. And the more whisky he drank the more he told. He didn't notice that Donald was not taking much. Neil talked on and on, and of course he soon began to tell things it would have been much wiser not to tell. Finally he told Donald that he was going over the bay to ask Nancy Sherman that very night to marry him. And if she would have him, then Donald and all the folks should see a wedding that *was* a wedding.

"Oh, wasn't Donald taken aback! This was more than he had expected. Neil hadn't been courting Nancy very long, and Donald never dreamed he would propose to her *quite* so soon.

"At first Donald didn't know what to do. He felt sure deep down in his heart, that Nancy liked *him*. She was very shy and modest, but you know a girl can let a man see she likes him without going out of her way. But Donald knew that if Neil proposed first he would have the best chance. Neil was rich and the Shermans were poor, and old Elias Sherman would have the most to say in the matter. If he told Nancy she must take Neil Campbell she would never dream of disobeying him. Old Elias Sherman was a man who had to be obeyed. But if Nancy had only promised some one else first her father would not make her break her word.

"Wasn't it a hard plight for poor Donald? But he was a Scotchman, you know, and it's pretty hard to stick a Scotchman long. Presently a twinkle came into his eyes, for he remembered that all was fair in love and war. So he said to Neil, oh, so persuasively,

" 'Have some more, man, have some more. 'Twill keep the heart in you in the teeth of that wind. Help yourself. There's plenty more where that came from.'

"Neil didn't want *much* persuasion. He took some more, and said slyly,

" 'Is it going over the bay the night that yourself will be doing?'

"Donald shook his head.

" 'I had thought of it,' he owned, 'but it looks a wee like a storm, and my sleigh is at the blacksmith's to be shod. If I went it must be on Black Dan's back, and he likes a canter over the ice in a snow-storm as little as I. His own fireside is the best place for a man to-night, Campbell. Have another taste, man, have another taste.'

"Neil went on 'tasting,' and that sly Donald sat there with a sober face, but laughing eyes, and coaxed him on. At last Neil's head fell forward on his breast, and he was sound asleep. Donald got up, put on his overcoat and cap, and went to the door.

" 'May your sleep be long and sweet, man,' he said, laughing softly, 'and as for the waking, 'twill be betwixt you and me.'

"With that he untied Neil's horse, climbed into Neil's sleigh, and tucked Neil's buffalo robe about him.

" 'Now, Bess, old girl, do your bonniest,' he said. 'There's more than you know hangs on your speed. If the Campbell wakes too soon Black Dan could show you a pair of clean heels for all your good start. On, my girl.'

"Brown Bess went over the ice like a deer, and Donald kept thinking of what he should say to Nancy—and more still of what she would say to him. *Suppose* he was mistaken. *Suppose* she said 'no!'

" 'Neil will have the laugh on me then. Sure he's sleeping well. And the snow is coming soon. There'll be a bonny swirl on the bay ere long.

I hope no harm will come to the lad if he starts to cross. When he wakes up he'll be in such a fine Highland temper that he'll never stop to think of danger. Well, Bess, old girl, here we are. Now, Donald Fraser, pluck up heart and play the man. Never flinch because a slip of a lass looks scornful at you out of the bonniest dark-blue eyes on earth.'

"But in spite of his bold words Donald's heart was thumping as he drove into the Sherman yard. Nancy was there, milking a cow by the stable door, but she stood up when she saw Donald coming. Oh, she was very beautiful! Her hair was like a skein of golden silk, and her eyes were as blue as the gulf water when the sun breaks out after a storm. Donald felt more nervous than ever. But he knew he must make the most of his chance. He might not see Nancy alone again before Neil came. He caught her hand and stammered out,

" 'Nan, lass, I love you. You may think 'tis a hasty wooing, but that's a story I can tell you later maybe. I know well I'm not worthy of you, but if true love could make a man worthy there'd be none before me. Will you have me, Nan?'

"Nancy didn't *say* she would have him. She just *looked* it, and Donald kissed her right there in the snow.

"The next morning the storm was over. Donald knew that Neil must be soon on his track. He did not want to make the Sherman house the scene of a quarrel, so he resolved to get away before the Campbell came. He persuaded Nancy to go with him to visit some friends in another settlement. As he brought Neil's sleigh up to the door he saw a black speck far out on the bay and laughed.

" 'Black Dan goes well, but he'll not be quick enough,' he said.

"Half an hour later Neil Campbell rushed into the Sherman kitchen and oh, how angry he was! There was nobody there but Betty Sherman, and Betty was not afraid of him. She was never afraid of anybody. She was very handsome, with hair as brown as October nuts and black eyes and crimson cheeks; and she had always been in love with Neil Campbell herself.

" 'Good morning, Mr. Campbell,' she said, with a toss of her head. 'It's early abroad you are. And on Black Dan, no less! Was I mistaken in thinking that Donald Fraser said once that his favourite horse should never be backed by any man but him? But doubtless a fair exchange is no robbery, and Brown Bess is a good mare in her way.'

" 'Where is Donald Fraser?' said Neil, shaking his fist. 'It's him I'm seeking, and it's him I will be finding. Where is he, Betty Sherman?'

" 'Donald Fraser is far enough away by this time,' mocked Betty. 'He is a prudent fellow, and has some quickness of wit under that sandy thatch of his. He came here last night at sunset, with a horse and sleigh not his own, or lately gotten, and he asked Nan in the stable yard to marry him. Did a man ask *me* to marry him at the cow's side, with a milking pail in my hand, it's a cold answer he'd get for his pains. But Nan thought differently, and they sat late together last night, and 'twas a bonny story Nan wakened me to hear when she came to bed—the story of a braw lover who let his secret out when the whisky was above the wit, and then fell asleep while his rival was away to woo and win his lass. Did you ever hear a like story, Mr. Campbell?'

" 'Oh, yes,' said Neil fiercely. 'It is laughing at me over the country side and telling that story that Donald Fraser will be doing, is it? But when I meet him it is not laughing he will be doing. Oh, no. There will be another story to tell!'

" 'Now, don't meddle with the man,' cried Betty. 'What a state to be in because one good-looking lass likes sandy hair and gray eyes better than Highland black and blue! You have not the spirit of a wren, Neil Campbell. Were I you, I would show Donald Fraser that I could woo and win a lass as speedily as any Lowlander of them all; that I would! There's many a girl would gladly say "yes" for your asking. And here stands one! Why not marry *me*, Neil Campbell? Folks say I'm as bonny as Nan—and I could love you as well as Nan loves her Donald—ay, and ten times better!'

"What do you suppose the Campbell did? Why, just the thing he ought to have done. He took Betty at her word on the spot; and there was a double wedding soon after. And it is said that Neil and Betty were the happiest couple in the world—happier even than Donald and Nancy. So all was well because it ended well!"

The Story Girl curtsied until her silken skirts swept the floor. Then she flung herself in her chair and looked at Mr. Campbell, flushed, triumphant, daring.

The story was old to us. It had once been published in a Charlottetown paper, and we had read in Aunt Olivia's scrap-book, where the Story Girl had learned it. But we had listened entranced.

I have written down the bare words of the story, as she told it; but I can never reproduce the charm and colour and spirit she infused into it. It *lived* for us. Donald and Neil, Nancy and Betty, were there in that room with us. We saw the flashes of expression on their faces, we heard their voices, angry or tender, mocking or merry, in Lowland and Highland accent. We realized all the mingled coquetry and feeling and defiance and archness in Betty Sherman's daring speech. We had even forgotten all about Mr. Campbell.

That gentleman, in silence, took out his wallet, extracted a note therefrom, and handed it gravely to the Story Girl.

"There are five dollars for you," he said, "and your story was well worth it. You *are* a wonder. Some day you will make the world realize it. I've been about a bit, and heard some good things, but I've never enjoyed anything more than that threadbare old story I heard in my cradle. And now, will you do me a favour?"

"Of course," said the delighted Story Girl.

"Recite the multiplication table for me," said Mr. Campbell.

We stared. Well might Mr. Campbell be called eccentric. What on earth did he want the multiplication table recited for? Even the Story Girl was surprised. But she began promptly, with twice one and went through it to twelve times twelve. She repeated it simply, but her voice changed from one tone to another as each in succession grew tired. We had never dreamed that there was so much in the multiplication table. As she announced it, the fact that three times three was nine was exquisitely ridiculous, five times six almost brought the tears to our eyes, eight times seven was the most tragic and frightful thing ever heard of, and twelve times twelve rang like a trumpet call to victory.

Mr. Campbell nodded his satisfaction.

"I thought you could do it," he said. "The other day I found this statement in a book. 'Her voice would have made the multiplication table charming!' I thought of it when I heard yours. I didn't believe it before, but I do now."

Then he let us go.

"You see," said the Story Girl as we went home, "you need never be afraid of people."

"But we are not all Story Girls," said Cecily.

That night we heard Felicity talking to Cecily in their room.

"Mr. Campbell never noticed one of us except the Story Girl," she said, "but if *I* had put on *my* best dress as she did maybe she wouldn't have taken all the attention."

"Could you ever do what Betty Sherman did, do you suppose?" asked Cecily absently.

"No; but I believe the Story Girl could," answered Felicity rather snappishly.

*—1911*

---

*James Joyce (1882–1941) is best known for his masterpiece,* Ulysses, *the complex modernist novel of a single day in the life of Dublin that shortly after its appearance in 1922 became both a classic and the subject of a landmark censorship case, which its publishers eventually won. Joyce's lifelong quarrel with the provincial concerns of Irish religious, cultural, and literary life (all touched on in his long story "The Dead") led him to permanent Continental self-exile in Zurich and Paris. Most readers would associate Joyce with his pioneering of experimental techniques such as the fragmentary observations found in his early* Epiphanies *(posthumously published in 1956), his use of interior monologue and stream-of-consciousness, and the complicated linguistic games of* Finnegan's Wake *(1939), forgetting that his earlier works lie squarely in the realm of traditional fiction.* Dubliners *(1914), his collection of short stories of life in his native city, remains an imposing achievement, as does his autobiographical novel,* A Portrait of the Artist as a Young Man *(1916).*

# *James Joyce*
## Araby

North Richmond Street, being blind, was a quiet street except at the hour when the Christian Brothers' School set the boys free. An uninhabited house of two storeys stood at the blind end, detached from its neighbours in a square ground. The other houses of the street, conscious of decent lives within them, gazed at one another with brown imperturbable faces.

The former tenant of our house, a priest, had died in the back drawing-room. Air, musty from having been long enclosed, hung in all the rooms, and the waste room behind the kitchen was littered with old useless papers. Among these I found a few paper-covered books, the pages of which were curled and damp: *The Abbot*, by Walter Scott, *The Devout Communicant* and *The Memoirs of Vidocq*. I liked the last best because its leaves were yellow. The wild garden behind the house contained a central apple-tree and a few straggling bushes under one of which I found the late tenant's rusty bicycle-pump. He had been a very charitable priest; in his will he had left all his money to institutions and the furniture of his house to his sister.

When the short days of winter came dusk fell before we had well eaten our dinners. When we met in the street the houses had grown sombre. The space of sky above us was the colour of ever-changing violet and towards it the lamps of the street lifted their feeble lanterns. The cold air stung us and we played till our bodies glowed. Our shouts echoed in the silent street. The career of our play brought us through the dark muddy lanes behind the houses where we ran the gantlet of the rough tribes from the cottages, to the back doors of the dark dripping gardens where odours arose from the ashpits, to the dark odorous stables where a coachman smoothed and combed the horse or shook music from the buckled harness. When we returned to the street light from the kitchen windows had filled the areas. If my uncle was seen turning the corner we hid in the shadow until we had seen him safely housed. Or if Mangan's sister came out on the doorstep to call her brother in to his tea we watched her from our shadow peer up and down the street. We waited to see whether she would remain or go in and, if she remained, we left our shadow and walked up to Mangan's steps resignedly. She was waiting for us, her figure defined by the light from the half-opened door. Her brother always teased her before he obeyed and I stood by the railings looking at her. Her dress swung as she moved her body and the soft rope of her hair tossed from side to side.

Every morning I lay on the floor in the front parlour watching her door. The blind was pulled down to within an inch of the sash so that I could not be seen. When she came out on the doorstep my heart leaped. I ran to the hall, seized my books and followed her. I kept her brown figure always in my eye and, when we came near the point at which our ways diverged, I quickened my pace and passed her. This happened morning after morning. I had never spoken to her, except for a few casual words, and yet her name was like a summons to all my foolish blood.

Her image accompanied me even in places the most hostile to romance. On Saturday evenings when my aunt went marketing I had to go to carry some of the parcels. We walked through the flaring streets, jostled by drunken men and bargaining women, amid the curses of labourers, the shrill litanies of shop-boys who stood on guard by the barrels of pigs' cheeks, the nasal chanting of street-singers, who sang a *come-all-you* about O'Donovan Rossa, or a ballad about the troubles in our native land. These noises converged in a single sensation of life for me: I imagined that I bore my chalice safely through a throng of foes. Her name sprang to my lips at moments in strange prayers and praises which I myself did not understand. My eyes were often full of tears (I could not tell why) and at times a flood from my heart seemed to pour itself out into my bosom. I thought little of the future. I did not know whether I would ever speak to her or not or, if I spoke to her, how I could tell her of my confused adoration. But my body was like a harp and her words and gestures were like fingers running upon the wires.

One evening I went into the back drawing-room in which the priest had died. It was a dark rainy evening and there was no sound in the house. Through one of the broken panes I heard the rain impinge upon the earth, the fine incessant needles of water playing in the sodden beds. Some distant lamp or lighted window gleamed below me. I was thankful that I could see so little. All my senses seemed to desire to veil themselves and, feeling that I was about to slip from them, I pressed the palms of my hands together until they trembled, murmuring: *O love! O love!* many times.

At last she spoke to me. When she addressed the first words to me I was so confused that I did not know what to answer. She asked me was I going to *Araby*. I forget whether I answered yes or no. It would be a splendid bazaar, she said; she would love to go.

—And why can't you? I asked.

While she spoke she turned a silver bracelet round and round her wrist. She could not go, she said, because there would be a retreat that week in her convent. Her brother and two other boys were fighting for their caps and I was alone at the railings. She held one of the spikes, bowing her head towards me. The light from the lamp opposite our door caught the white curve of her neck, lit up her hair that rested there and, falling, lit up the hand upon the railing. It fell over one side of her dress and caught the white border of a petticoat, just visible as she stood at ease.

—It's well for you, she said.

—If I go, I said, I will bring you something.

What innumerable follies laid waste my waking and sleeping thoughts after that evening! I wished to annihilate the tedious intervening days. I chafed against the work of school. At night in my bedroom and by day in the classroom her image came between me and the page I strove to read. The syllables of the word *Araby* were called to me through the silence in which my soul luxuriated and cast an Eastern enchantment over me. I asked for leave to go to the bazaar Saturday night. My aunt was surprised and hoped it was not some Freemason affair. I answered few questions in class. I watched my master's face pass from amiability to sternness; he hoped I was not beginning to idle. I could not call my wandering thoughts together. I had hardly any patience with the serious work of life which, now that it stood between me and my desire, seemed to me child's play, ugly monotonous child's play.

On Saturday morning I reminded my uncle that I wished to go to the bazaar in the evening. He was fussing at the hallstand, looking for the hat-brush, and answered me curtly:

—Yes, boy, I know.

As he was in the hall I could not go into the front parlour and lie at the window. I left the house in bad humour and walked slowly towards the school. The air was pitilessly raw and already my heart misgave me.

When I came home to dinner my uncle had not yet been home. Still it was early. I sat staring at the clock for some time and, when its ticking began to irritate me, I left the room. I mounted the staircase and gained the upper part of the house. The high cold empty gloomy rooms liberated me and I went from room to room singing. From the front window I saw my companions playing below in the street. Their cries reached me weakened and indistinct and, leaning my forehead against the cool glass, I looked over at the dark house where she lived. I may have stood there for an hour, seeing nothing but the brown-clad figure cast by my imagination, touched discreetly by the lamplight at the curved neck, at the hand upon the railings and at the border below the dress.

When I came downstairs again I found Mrs Mercer sitting at the fire. She was an old garrulous woman, a pawnbroker's widow, who collected used stamps for some pious purpose. I had to endure the gossip of the tea-table. The meal was prolonged beyond an hour and still my uncle did not come. Mrs Mercer stood up to go: she was sorry she couldn't wait any longer, but it was after eight o'clock and she did not like to be out late, as the night air was bad for her. When she had gone I began to walk up and down the room, clenching my fists. My aunt said:

—I'm afraid you may put off your bazaar for this night of Our Lord.

At nine o'clock I heard my uncle's latchkey in the hall-door. I heard him talking to himself and heard the hallstand rocking when it had received the weight of his overcoat. I could interpret these signs. When he was midway through his dinner I asked him to give me the money to go to the bazaar. He had forgotten.

—The people are in bed and after their first sleep now, he said.

I did not smile. My aunt said to him energetically:

—Can't you give him the money and let him go? You've kept him late enough as it is.

My uncle said he was very sorry he had forgotten. He said he believed in the old saying: *All work and no play makes Jack a dull boy*. He asked me where I was going and, when I had told him a second time he asked me did I know *The Arab's Farewell to his Steed*. When I left the kitchen he was about to recite the opening lines of the piece to my aunt.

I held a florin tightly in my hand as I strode down Buckingham Street towards the station. The sight of the streets thronged with buyers and glaring with gas recalled to me the purpose of my journey. I took my seat in a third-class carriage of a deserted train. After an intolerable delay the train moved out of the station slowly. It crept onward among ruinous houses and over the twinkling river. At Westland Row Station a crowd of people pressed to the carriage doors; but the porters moved them back, saying that it was a special train for the bazaar. I remained alone in the bare carriage. In a few minutes the train drew up beside an improvised wooden platform. I passed out on to the road and saw by the lighted dial of a clock that it was ten minutes to ten. In front of me was a large building which displayed the magical name.

I could not find any sixpenny entrance and, fearing that the bazaar would be closed, I passed in quickly through a turnstile, handing a shilling to a weary-looking man. I found myself in a big hall girdled at half its height by a gallery. Nearly all the stalls were closed and the greater part of the hall was in darkness. I recognised a silence like that which pervades a church after a service. I walked into the centre of the bazaar timidly. A few people were gathered about the stalls which were still open. Before a curtain, over which the words *Café Chantant* were written in coloured lamps, two men were counting money on a salver. I listened to the fall of the coins.

Remembering with difficulty why I had come I went over to one of the stalls and examined porcelain vases and flowered tea-sets. At the door of the stall a young lady was talking and laughing with two young gentlemen. I remarked their English accents and listened vaguely to their conversation.

—O, I never said such a thing!

—O, but you did!

—O, but I didn't!

—Didn't she say that?

—Yes. I heard her.

—O, there's a . . . fib!

Observing me the young lady came over and asked me did I wish to buy anything. The tone of her voice was not encouraging; she seemed to have spoken to me out of a sense of duty. I looked humbly at the great jars that stood like eastern guards at either side of the dark entrance to the stall and murmured:

—No, thank you.

The young lady changed the position of one of the vases and went back to the two young men. They began to talk of the same subject. Once or twice the young lady glanced at me over her shoulder.

I lingered before her stall, though I knew my stay was useless, to make my interest in her wares seem the more real. Then I turned away slowly and walked down the middle of the bazaar. I allowed the two pennies to fall against the sixpence in my pocket. I heard a voice call from one end of the gallery that the light was out. The upper part of the hall was now completely dark.

Gazing up into the darkness I saw myself as a creature driven and derided by vanity; and my eyes burned with anguish and anger.

*—1914*

*Virginia Woolf (1882–1941) was born Virginia Stephen into a literary household in London, England. Despite not receiving the education granted to her brothers, she became an important writer, critic, and essayist who, along with her husband, Leonard Woolf, founded a press that published early works of Katherine Mansfield and T. S. Eliot and translations of Sigmund Freud. She was an innovator in the form of prose fiction known as stream-of-consciousness in novels such as* Mrs. Dalloway *(1925),* To the Lighthouse *(1927), and* The Waves *(1931), and in her short fiction gathered in* Monday and Tuesday *(1921) and* A Haunted House *(1944). Her feminist concerns appear in non-fiction books such as* A Room of One's Own *(1929) and* Three Guineas *(1938). Struggling with the fragile mental health that had plagued her for much of her life, she drowned herself in 1941.*

# Virginia Woolf
# A Haunted House

Whatever hour you woke there was a door shutting. From room to room they went, hand in hand, lifting here, opening there, making sure— a ghostly couple.

"Here we left it," she said. And he added, "Oh, but here too!" "It's upstairs," she murmured. "And in the garden," he whispered. "Quietly," they said, "or we shall wake them."

But it wasn't that you woke us. Oh, no. "They're looking for it; they're drawing the curtain," one might say, and so read on a page or two. "Now they've found it," one would be certain, stopping the pencil on the margin. And then, tired of reading, one might rise and see for oneself, the house all empty, the doors standing open, only the wood pigeons bubbling with content and the hum of the threshing machine sounding from the farm. "What did I come in here for? What did I want to find?" My hands were empty. "Perhaps it's upstairs then?" The apples were in the loft. And so down again, the garden still as ever, only the book had slipped into the grass.

But they had found it in the drawing-room. Not that one could ever see them. The window panes reflected apples, reflected roses; all the leaves were green in the glass. If they moved in the drawing-room, the apple only turned its yellow side. Yet, the moment after, if the door was opened, spread about the floor, hung upon the walls, pendant from the ceiling—what? My hands were empty. The shadow of a thrush crossed the carpet; from the deepest wells of silence the wood pigeon drew its bubble of sound. "Safe, safe, safe," the pulse of the house beat softly. "The treasure buried; the room . . ." the pulse stopped short. Oh, was that the buried treasure?

A moment later the light had faded. Out in the garden then? But the trees spun darkness for a wandering beam of sun. So fine, so rare, coolly sunk beneath the surface the beam I sought always burnt behind the glass. Death was the glass; death was between us; coming to the woman first, hundreds of years ago, leaving the house, sealing all the windows; the rooms were darkened. He left it, left her, went North, went East, saw the stars turned in the Southern sky; sought the house, found it dropped beneath the Downs. "Safe, safe, safe," the pulse of the house beat gladly. "The Treasure yours."

The wind roars up the avenue. Trees stoop and bend this way and that. Moonbeams splash and spill wildly in the rain. But the beam of the lamp falls straight from the window. The candle burns stiff and still. Wandering through the house, opening the windows, whispering not to wake us, the ghostly couple seek their joy.

"Here we slept," she says. And he adds, "Kisses without number." "Waking in the morning—" "Silver between the trees—" "Upstairs—" "In the garden—" "When summer came—" "In winter snowtime—" The doors go shutting far in the distance, gently knocking like the pulse of a heart.

Nearer they come; cease at the doorway. The wind falls, the rain slides silver down the glass. Our eyes darken; we hear no steps beside us; we see no lady spread her ghostly cloak. His hands shield the lantern. "Look," he breathes. "Sound asleep. Love upon their lips."

Stooping, holding their silver lamp above us, long they look and deeply. Long they pause. The wind drives straightly; the flame stoops slightly. Wild beams of moonlight cross both floor and wall, and, meeting, stain the faces bent; the faces pondering; the faces that search the sleepers and seek their hidden joy.

"Safe, safe, safe," the heart of the house beats proudly. "Long years—" he sighs. "Again you found me." "Here," she murmurs, "sleeping; in the garden reading; laughing, rolling apples in the loft. Here we left our treasure—" Stooping, their light lifts the lids upon my eyes. "Safe! safe! safe!" the pulse of the house beats wildly. Waking, I cry "Oh, is this *your* buried treasure? The light in the heart."

*—1921*

*D. H. Lawrence (1885–1930) was born in Nottinghamshire, England, the son of a coal miner and a teacher. His first novel,* The White Peacock *(1911), was followed by* Sons and Lovers *(1913),* The Rainbow *(1915), and* Women in Love *(1920). His interest in Freudian psychology and human sexuality made him controversial during his career and perhaps still overshadows his skills as a chronicler of English life in villages forever altered by the Industrial Revolution.* Lady Chatterley's Lover *(1928), with its frank language and depictions of sex, remains a landmark in the battle against literary censorship, and an unexpurgated edition did not appear in England until thirty years after the author's death. Lawrence also published numerous collections of poetry and short stories. "The Horse Dealer's Daughter" reflects both his interest in the dynamics of desire and his symbolic technique.*

## D. H. Lawrence
# The Horse Dealer's Daughter

"Well, Mabel, and what are you going to do with yourself?" asked Joe, with foolish flippancy. He felt quite safe himself. Without listening for an answer, he turned aside, worked a grain of tobacco to the tip of his tongue, and spat it out. He did not care about anything, since he felt safe himself.

The three brothers and the sister sat round the desolate breakfast-table, attempting some sort of desultory consultation. The morning's post had given the final tap to the family fortunes, and all was over. The dreary dining-room itself, with its heavy mahogany furniture, looked as if it were waiting to be done away with.

But the consultation amounted to nothing. There was a strange air of ineffectuality about the three men, as they sprawled at table, smoking and reflecting vaguely on their own condition. The girl was alone, a rather short, sullen-looking young woman of twenty-seven. She did not share the same life as her brothers. She would have been good-looking, save for the impressive fixity of her face, 'bull-dog', as her brothers called it.

There was a confused tramping of horses' feet outside. The three men all sprawled round in their chairs to watch. Beyond the dark holly bushes that separated the strip of lawn from the high-road, they could see a cavalcade of shire horses swinging out of their own yard, being taken for exercise. This was the last time. These were the last horses that would go through their hands. The young men watched with critical, callous look. They were all frightened at the collapse of their lives, and the sense of disaster in which they were involved left them no inner freedom.

Yet they were three fine, well-set fellows enough. Joe, the eldest, was a man of thirty-three, broad and handsome in a hot, flushed way. His face was red, he twisted his black moustache over a thick finger, his eyes were shallow and restless. He had a sensual way of uncovering his teeth when he laughed, and his bearing was stupid. Now he watched the horses with a glazed look of helplessness in his eyes, a certain stupor of downfall.

The great draught-horses swung past. They were tied head to tail, four of them, and they heaved along to where a lane branched off from the high-road, planting their great hoofs floutingly in the fine black mud, swinging their great rounded haunches sumptuously, and trotting a few sudden steps as they were led into the lane, round the corner. Every movement showed a massive, slumbrous strength, and a stupidity which held them in subjection. The groom at the head looked back, jerking the leading rope. And the cavalcade moved out of sight up the lane, the tail of the last horse, bobbed up tight and stiff, held out taut from the swinging great haunches as they rocked behind the hedges in a motion-like sleep.

Joe watched with glazed hopeless eyes. The horses were almost like his own body to him. He felt he was done for now. Luckily he was engaged to a woman as old as himself, and therefore her father, who was steward of a neighbouring estate, would provide him with a job. He would marry and go into harness. His life was over, he would be a subject animal now.

He turned uneasily aside, the retreating steps of the horses echoing in his ears. Then, with foolish restlessness, he reached for the scraps of bacon-rind from the plates, and making a faint whistling sound, flung them to the terrier that lay against the fender. He watched the dog swallow them, and waited till the creature looked into his eyes. Then a faint grin came on his face, and in a high, foolish voice he said:

"You won't get much more bacon, shall you, you little b——?"

The dog faintly and dismally wagged its tail, then lowered its haunches, circled round, and lay down again.

There was another helpless silence at the table. Joe sprawled uneasily in his seat, not willing to go till the family conclave was dissolved. Fred Henry, the second brother, was erect, clean-limbed, alert. He had watched the passing of the horses with more *sang-froid*.[1] If he was an animal, like Joe, he was an animal which controls, not one which is controlled. He was master of any horse, and he carried himself with a well-tempered air of mastery. But he was not master of the situations of life. He pushed his coarse brown moustache upwards, off his lip, and glanced irritably at his sister, who sat impassive and inscrutable.

"You'll go and stop with Lucy for a bit, shan't you?" he asked. The girl did not answer.

"I don't see what else you can do," persisted Fred Henry.

"Go as a skivvy," Joe interpolated laconically.

The girl did not move a muscle.

"If I was her, I should go in for training for a nurse," said Malcolm, the youngest of them all. He was the baby of the family, a young man of twenty-two, with a fresh, jaunty *museau*.[2]

But Mabel did not take any notice of him. They had talked at her and round her for so many years, that she hardly heard them at all.

The marble clock on the mantelpiece softly chimed the half-hour, the dog rose uneasily from the hearth-rug and looked at the party at the breakfast-table. But still they sat on in ineffectual conclave.

"Oh, all right," said Joe suddenly, apropos of nothing. "I'll get a move on."

He pushed back his chair, straddled his knees with a downward jerk, to get them free, in horsey fashion, and went to the fire. Still he did not go out of the room; he was curious to know what the others would do or say. He began to charge his pipe, looking down at the dog and saying in a high, affected voice:

"Going wi' me? Going wi' me are ter? Tha't goin' further than tha counts on just now, dost hear?"

The dog faintly wagged its tail, the man stuck out his jaw and covered his pipe with his hands, and puffed intently, losing himself in the tobacco, looking down all the while at the dog with an absent brown eye. The dog looked up at him in mournful distrust. Joe stood with his knees stuck out, in real horsey fashion.

[1]*sang-froid:* literally "cold blood," with cool indifference.
[2]*museau:* face.

"Have you had a letter from Lucy?" Fred Henry asked of his sister.

"Last week," came the neutral reply.

"And what does she say?"

There was no answer.

"Does she *ask* you to go and stop there?" persisted Fred Henry.

"She says I can if I like."

"Well, then, you'd better. Tell her you'll come on Monday."

This was received in silence.

"That's what you'll do then, is it?" said Fred Henry, in some exasperation.

But she made no answer. There was a silence of futility and irritation in the room. Malcolm grinned fatuously.

"You'll have to make up your mind between now and next Wednesday," said Joe loudly, "or else find yourself lodgings on the kerbstone."

The face of the young woman darkened, but she sat on immutable.

"Here's Jack Ferguson!" exclaimed Malcolm, who was looking aimlessly out of the window.

"Where?" exclaimed Joe loudly.

"Just gone past."

"Coming in?"

Malcolm craned his neck to see the gate.

"Yes," he said.

There was a silence. Mabel sat on like one condemned, at the head of the table. Then a whistle was heard from the kitchen. The dog got up and barked sharply. Joe opened the door and shouted:

"Come on."

After a moment a young man entered. He was muffled up in overcoat and a purple woollen scarf, and his tweed cap, which he did not remove, was pulled down on his head. He was of medium height, his face was rather long and pale, his eyes looked tired.

"Hello, Jack! Well, Jack!" exclaimed Malcolm and Joe. Fred Henry merely said: "Jack."

"What's doing?" asked the newcomer, evidently addressing Fred Henry.

"Same. We've got to be out by Wednesday. Got a cold?"

"I have—got it bad, too."

"Why don't you stop in?"

"*Me* stop in? When I can't stand on my legs, perhaps I shall have a chance." The young man spoke huskily. He had a slight Scotch accent.

"It's a knock-out, isn't it," said Joe, boisterously, "if a doctor goes round croaking with a cold. Looks bad for the patients, doesn't it?"

The young doctor looked at him slowly.

"Anything the matter with *you*, then?" he asked sarcastically.

"Not as I know of. Damn your eyes, I hope not. Why?"

"I thought you were very concerned about the patients, wondered if you might be one yourself."

"Damn it, no, I've never been patient to no flaming doctor, and hope I never shall be," returned Joe.

At this point Mabel rose from the table, and they all seemed to become aware of her existence. She began putting the dishes together. The young doctor looked at her, but did not address her. He had not greeted her. She went out of the room with the tray, her face impassive and unchanged.

"When are you off then, all of you?" asked the doctor.

"I'm catching the eleven-forty," replied Malcolm. "Are you goin' down wi' th' trap, Joe?"

"Yes, I've told you I'm going down wi' th' trap, haven't I?"

"We'd better be getting her in then. So long, Jack, if I don't see you before I go," said Malcolm, shaking hands.

He went out, followed by Joe, who seemed to have his tail between his legs.

"Well, this is the devil's own," exclaimed the doctor, when he was left alone with Fred Henry. "Going before Wednesday, are you?"

"That's the orders," replied the other.

"Where, to Northampton?"

"That's it."

"The devil!" exclaimed Fergusson, with quiet chagrin.

And there was silence between the two.

"All settled up, are you?" asked Fergusson.

"About."

There was another pause.

"Well, I shall miss yer, Freddy, boy," said the young doctor.

"And I shall miss thee, Jack," returned the other.

"Miss you like hell," mused the doctor.

Fred Henry turned aside. There was nothing to say. Mabel came in again, to finish clearing the table.

"What are *you* going to do, then, Miss Pervin?" asked Fergusson. "Going to your sister's, are you?"

Mabel looked at him with her steady, dangerous eyes, that always made him uncomfortable, unsettling his superficial ease.

"No," she said.

"Well, what in the name of fortune *are* you going to do? Say what you mean to do," cried Fred Henry, with futile intensity.

But she only averted her head, and continued her work. She folded the white table-cloth, and put on the chenille cloth.

"The sulkiest bitch that ever trod!" muttered her brother.

But she finished her task with perfectly impassive face, the young doctor watching her interestedly all the while. Then she went out.

Fred Henry stared after her, clenching his lips, his blue eyes fixing in sharp antagonism, as he made a grimace of sour exasperation.

"You could bray her into bits, and that's all you'd get out of her," he said, in a small, narrowed tone.

The doctor smiled faintly.

"What's she *going* to do, then?" he asked.

"Strike me if *I* know!" returned the other.

There was a pause. Then the doctor stirred.

"I'll be seeing you to-night, shall I?" he said to his friend.

"Ay—where's it to be? Are we going over to Jessdale?"

"I don't know. I've got such a cold on me. I'll come round to the 'Moon and Stars', anyway."

"Let Lizzie and May miss their night for once, eh?"

"That's it—if I feel as I do now."

"All's one——"

The two young men went through the passage and down to the back door together. The house was large, but it was servantless now, and desolate. At the back was a small bricked house-yard and beyond that a big square, gravelled fine and red, and having stables on two sides. Sloping, dank, winter-dark fields stretched away on the open sides.

But the stables were empty. Joseph Pervin, the father of the family, had been a man of no education, who had become a fairly large horse dealer. The stables had been full of horses, there was a great turmoil and come-and-go of horses and of dealers and grooms. Then the kitchen was full of servants. But of late things had declined. The old man had married a second time, to retrieve his fortunes. Now he was dead and everything was gone to the dogs, there was nothing but debt and threatening.

For months, Mabel had been servantless in the big house, keeping the home together in penury for her ineffectual brothers. She had kept house for ten years. But previously it was with unstinted means. Then, however brutal and coarse everything was, the sense of money had kept her proud, confident. The men might be foul-mouthed, the women in the kitchen might have bad reputations, her brothers might have illegitimate children. But so long as there was money, the girl felt herself established, and brutally proud, reserved.

No company came to the house, save dealers and coarse men. Mabel had no associates of her own sex, after her sister went away. But she did not mind. She went regularly to church, she attended to her father. And she lived in the memory of her mother, who had died when she was fourteen, and whom she had loved. She had loved her father, too, in a different way, depending upon him, and feeling secure in him, until at the age of fifty-four he married again. And then she had set hard against him. Now he had died and left them all hopelessly in debt.

She had suffered badly during the period of poverty. Nothing, however, could shake the curious, sullen, animal pride that dominated each member of the family. Now, for Mabel, the end had come. Still she would not cast about her. She would follow her own way just the same. She would always hold the keys of her own situation. Mindless and persistent, she endured from day to day. Why should she think? Why should she answer anybody? It was enough that this was the end, and there was no way out. She need not pass any more darkly along the main street of the small town, avoiding every eye. She need not demean herself any more, going into the shops and buying the cheapest food. This was at an end. She thought of nobody, not even of herself. Mindless and persistent, she seemed in a sort of ecstasy to be coming nearer to her fulfilment, her own glorification, approaching her dead mother, who was glorified.

In the afternoon she took a little bag, with shears and sponge and a small scrubbing-brush, and went out. It was a grey, wintry day, with saddened, dark green fields and an atmosphere blackened by the smoke of foundries not far off. She went quickly, darkly along the causeway, heeding nobody, through the town to the churchyard.

There she always felt secure, as if no one could see her, although as a matter of fact she was exposed to the stare of everyone who passed along under the churchyard wall. Nevertheless, once under the shadow of the great looming church, among the graves, she felt immune from the world, reserved within the thick churchyard wall as in another country.

Carefully she clipped the grass from the grave, and arranged the pinky white, small chrysanthemums in the tin cross. When this was done, she took an empty jar from a neighbouring grave, brought water, and carefully, most scrupulously sponged the marble headstone and the coping-stone.

It gave her sincere satisfaction to do this. She felt in immediate contact with the world of her mother. She took minute pains, went through the park in a state bordering on pure happiness, as if in performing this task she came into a subtle, intimate connection with her mother. For the life she followed here in the world was far less real than the world of death she inherited from her mother.

The doctor's house was just by the church. Fergusson, being a mere hired assistant, was slave to the country-side. As he hurried now to attend to the out-patients in the surgery, glancing across the graveyard with his quick eye, he saw the girl at her task at the grave. She seemed so intent and remote, it was like looking into another world. Some mystical element was touched in him. He slowed down as he walked, watching her as if spellbound.

She lifted her eyes, feeling him looking. Their eyes met. And each looked again at once, each feeling, in some way, found out by the other. He lifted his cap and passed on down the road. There remained distinct in his consciousness, like a vision, the memory of her face, lifted from the tombstone in the churchyard; and looking at him with slow, large, portentous eyes. It *was* portentous, her face. It seemed to mesmerise him. There was a heavy power in her eyes which laid hold of his whole being, as if he had drunk some powerful drug. He had been feeling weak and done before. Now the life came back into him, he felt delivered from his own fretted, daily self.

He finished his duties at the surgery as quickly as might be, hastily filling up the bottles of the waiting people with cheap drugs. Then, in perpetual haste, he set off again to visit several cases in another part of his round, before tea-time. At all times he preferred to walk if he could, but particularly when he was not well. He fancied the motion restored him.

The afternoon was falling. It was grey, deadened, and wintry, with a slow, moist, heavy coldness sinking in and deadening all the faculties. But why should he think or notice? He hastily climbed the hill and turned across the dark green fields, following the black cinder-track. In the distance, across a shallow dip in the country, the small town was clustered like smouldering ash, a tower, a spire, a heap of low, raw, extinct houses. And on the nearest fringe of the town, sloping into the dip, was Oldmeadow, the Pervins' house. He could see the stables and the outbuildings distinctly, as they lay towards him on the slope. Well, he would not go there many more times! Another resource would be lost to him, another place gone: the only company he cared for in the alien, ugly little town he was losing. Nothing but work, drudgery, constant hastening from dwelling to dwelling among the colliers and the iron-workers. It wore him out, but at the same time he had a craving for it. It was a stimulant to him to be in the homes of the working people, moving, as it were, through the innermost body of their life. His nerves were excited and gratified. He could come so near, into the very lives of the rough, inarticulate, powerfully emotional men and women. He grumbled, he said he hated the hellish hole. But as a matter of fact it excited him, the contact with the rough, strongly-feeling people was a stimulant applied direct to his nerves.

Below Oldmeadow, in the green, shallow, soddened hollow of fields, lay a square, deep pond. Roving across the landscape, the doctor's quick eye detected a figure in black passing through the gate of the field, down towards the pond. He looked again. It would be Mabel Pervin. His mind suddenly became alive and attentive.

Why was she going down there? He pulled up on the path on the slope above, and stood staring. He could just make sure of the small black figure moving in the hollow of the failing day. He seemed to see her in the midst of such obscurity, that he was like a clairvoyant, seeing rather with the mind's eye than with ordinary sight. Yet he could see her positively enough, whilst he kept his eye attentive. He felt, if he looked away from her, in the thick, ugly falling dusk, he would lose her altogether.

He followed her minutely as she moved, direct and intent, like something transmitted rather than stirring in voluntary activity, straight down the field towards the pond. There she stood on the bank for a moment. She never raised her head. Then she waded slowly into the water.

He stood motionless as the small black figure walked slowly and deliberately towards the centre of the pond, very slowly, gradually moving deeper into the motionless water, and still moving forward as the water got up to her breast. Then he could see her no more in the dusk of the dead afternoon.

"There!" he exclaimed. "Would you believe it?"

And he hastened straight down, running over the wet, soddened fields, pushing through the hedges, down into the depression of callous wintry obscurity. It took him several minutes to come to the pond. He stood on the bank, breathing heavily. He could see nothing. His eyes seemed to penetrate the dead water. Yes, perhaps that was the dark shadow of her black clothing beneath the surface of the water.

He slowly ventured into the pond. The bottom was deep, soft clay, he sank in, and the water clasped dead cold round his legs. As he stirred he could smell the cold, rotten clay that fouled up into the water. It was objectionable in his lungs. Still, repelled and yet not heeding, he moved deeper into the pond. The cold water rose over his thighs, over his loins, upon his abdomen. The lower part of his body was all sunk in the hideous cold element. And the bottom was so deeply soft and uncertain, he was afraid of pitching with his mouth underneath. He could not swim, and was afraid.

He crouched a little, spreading his hands under the water and moving them round, trying to feel for her. The dead cold pond swayed upon his chest. He moved again, a little deeper, and again, with his hands underneath, he felt all around under the water. And he touched her clothing. But it evaded his fingers. He made a desperate effort to grasp it.

And so doing he lost his balance and went under, horribly, suffocating in the foul earthy water, struggling madly for a few moments. At last, after what seemed an eternity, he got his footing, rose again into the air and looked around. He gasped, and knew he was in the world. Then he looked at the water. She had risen near him. He grasped her clothing, and drawing her nearer, turned to take his way to land again.

He went very slowly, carefully, absorbed in the slow progress. He rose higher, climbing out of the pond. The water was now only about his legs; he was thankful, full of relief to be out of the clutches of the pond. He lifted her and staggered on to the bank, out of the horror of wet, grey clay.

He laid her down on the bank. She was quite unconscious and running with water. He made the water come from her mouth, he worked to restore her. He did not have to work very long before he could feel the breathing begin again in her; she was breathing naturally. He worked a little longer. He could feel her live beneath his hands; she was coming back. He wiped her face, wrapped her in his overcoat, looked round into the dim, dark grey world, then lifted her and staggered down the bank and across the fields.

It seemed an unthinkably long way, and his burden so heavy he felt he would never get to the house. But at last he was in the stable-yard, and then in the house-yard. He opened the door and went into the house. In the kitchen he laid her down on the hearth-rug and called. The house was empty. But the fire was burning in the grate.

Then again he kneeled to attend to her. She was breathing regularly, her eyes were wide open and as if conscious, but there seemed something missing in her look. She was conscious in herself, but unconscious of her surroundings.

He ran upstairs, took blankets from a bed, and put them before the fire to warm. Then he removed her saturated, earthy-smelling clothing, rubbed her dry with a towel, and wrapped her naked in the blankets. Then he went into the dining-room, to look for spirits. There was a little whisky. He drank a gulp himself, and put some into her mouth.

The effect was instantaneous. She looked full into his face, as if she had been seeing him for some time, and yet had only just become conscious of him.

"Dr. Fergusson?" she said.

"What?" he answered.

He was divesting himself of his coat, intending to find some dry clothing upstairs. He could not bear the smell of the dead, clayey water, and he was mortally afraid for his own health.

"What did I do?" she asked.

"Walked into the pond," he replied. He had begun to shudder like one sick, and could hardly attend to her. Her eyes remained full on him, he seemed to be going dark in his mind, looking back at her helplessly.

The shuddering became quieter in him, his life came back to him, dark and unknowing, but strong again.

"Was I out of my mind?" she asked, while her eyes were fixed on him all the time.

"Maybe, for the moment," he replied. He felt quiet, because his strength had come back. The strange fretful strain had left him.

"Am I out of my mind now?" she asked.

"Are you?" he reflected a moment. "No," he answered truthfully, "I don't see that you are." He turned his face aside. He was afraid now, because he felt dazed, and felt dimly that her power was stronger than his, in this issue. And she continued to look at him fixedly all the time. "Can you tell me where I shall find some dry things to put on?" he asked.

"Did you dive into the pond for me?" she asked.

"No," he answered. "I walked in. But I went in overhead as well."

There was silence for a moment. He hesitated. He very much wanted to go upstairs to get into dry clothing. But there was another desire in him. And she seemed to hold him. His will seemed to have gone to sleep, and left him, standing there slack before her. But he felt warm inside himself. He did not shudder at all, though his clothes were sodden on him.

"Why did you?" she asked.

"Because I didn't want you to do such a foolish thing," he said.

"It wasn't foolish," she said, still gazing at him as she lay on the floor, with a sofa cushion under her head. "It was the right thing to do. *I* knew best, then."

"I'll go and shift these wet things," he said. But still he had not the power to move out of her presence, until she sent him. It was as if she had the life of his body in her hands, and he could not extricate himself. Or perhaps he did not want to.

Suddenly she sat up. Then she became aware of her own immediate condition. She felt the blankets about her, she knew her own limbs. For a moment it seemed as if her reason were going. She looked round, with wild eye, as if seeking something. He stood still with fear. She saw her clothing lying scattered.

"Who undressed me?" she asked, her eyes resting full and inevitable on his face.

"I did," he replied, "to bring you round."

For some moments she sat and gazed at him awfully, her lips parted. "Do you love me, then?" she asked.

He only stood and stared at her, fascinated. His soul seemed to melt.

She shuffled forward on her knees, and put her arms round him, round his legs, as he stood there, pressing her breasts against his knees and thighs, clutching him with strange, convulsive certainty, pressing his thighs against her, drawing him to her face, her throat, as she looked up at him with flaring, humble eyes of transfiguration, triumphant in first possession.

"You love me," she murmured, in strange transport, yearning and triumphant and confident. "You love me. I know you love me, I know."

And she was passionately kissing his knees, through the wet clothing, passionately and indiscriminately kissing his knees, his legs, as if unaware of everything.

He looked down at the tangled wet hair, the wild, bare, animal shoulders. He was amazed, bewildered, and afraid. He had never thought of loving her. He had never wanted to love her. When he rescued her and restored her, he was a doctor, and she was a patient. He had had no single personal thought of her. Nay, this introduction of the personal element was very distasteful to him, a violation of his professional honour. It was horrible to have her there embracing his knees. It was horrible. He revolted from it, violently. And yet—and yet—he had not the power to break away.

She looked at him again, with the same supplication of powerful love, and that same transcendent, frightening light of triumph. In view of the delicate flame which seemed to come from her face like a light, he was powerless. And yet he had never intended to love her. He had never intended. And something stubborn in him could not give way.

"You love me," she repeated, in a murmur of deep, rhapsodic assurance. "You love me."

Her hands were drawing him, drawing him down to her. He was afraid, even a little horrified. For he had, really, no intention of loving her. Yet her hands were drawing him towards her. He put out his hand quickly to steady himself, and grasped her bare shoulder. A flame seemed to burn the hand that grasped her soft shoulder. He had no intention of loving her: his whole will was against his yielding. It was horrible. And yet wonderful was the touch of her shoulders, beautiful the shining of her face. Was she perhaps mad? He had a horror of yielding to her. Yet something in him ached also.

He had been staring away at the door, away from her. But his hand remained on her shoulder. She had gone suddenly very still. He looked down at her. Her eyes were now wide with fear, with doubt, the light was dying from her face, a shadow of terrible greyness was returning. He could not bear the touch of her eyes' question upon him, and the look of death behind the question.

With an inward groan he gave way, and let his heart yield towards her. A sudden gentle smile came on his face. And her eyes, which never left his face, slowly, slowly filled with tears. He watched the strange water rise in her eyes, like some slow fountain coming up. And his heart seemed to burn and melt away in his breast.

He could not bear to look at her any more. He dropped on his knees and caught her head with his arms and pressed her face against his throat. She was very still. His heart, which seemed to have broken, was burning with a kind of agony in his breast. And he felt her slow, hot tears wetting his throat. But he could not move.

He felt the hot tears wet his neck and the hollows of his neck, and he remained motionless, suspended through one of man's eternities. Only now it had become indispensable to him to have her face pressed close to him; he could never let her go again. He could never let her head go away from the close clutch of his arm. He wanted to remain like that for ever, with his heart hurting him in a pain that was also life to him. Without knowing, he was looking down on her damp, soft brown hair.

Then, as it were suddenly, he smelt the horrid stagnant smell of that water. And at the same moment she drew away from him and looked at him. Her eyes were wistful and unfathomable. He was afraid of them, and he fell to kissing her, not knowing what he was doing. He wanted her eyes not to have that terrible, wistful, unfathomable look.

When she turned her face to him again, a faint delicate flush was glowing, and there was again dawning that terrible shining of joy in her eyes, which really terrified him, and yet which he now wanted to see, because he feared the look of doubt still more.

"You love me?" she said, rather faltering.

"Yes." The word cost him a painful effort. Not because it wasn't true. But because it was too newly true, the *saying* seemed to tear open again his newly-torn heart. And he hardly wanted it to be true, even now.

She lifted her face to him, and he bent forward and kissed her on the mouth, gently, with the one kiss that is an eternal pledge. And as he kissed her his heart strained again in his breast. He never intended to love her. But now it was over. He had crossed over the gulf to her, and all that he had left behind had shrivelled and become void.

After the kiss, her eyes again slowly filled with tears. She sat still, away from him, with her face drooped aside, and her hands folded in her lap. The tears fell very slowly. There was complete silence. He too sat there motionless and silent on the hearth-rug. The strange pain of his heart that was broken seemed to consume him. That he should love her? That this was love! That he should be ripped open in this way! Him, a doctor! How they would all jeer if they knew! It was agony to him to think they might know.

In the curious naked pain of the thought he looked again to her. She was sitting there drooped into a muse. He saw a tear fall, and his heart flared hot. He saw for the first time that one of her shoulders was quite uncovered, one arm bare, he could see one of her small breasts; dimly, because it had become almost dark in the room.

"Why are you crying?" he asked, in an altered voice.

She looked up at him, and behind her tears the consciousness of her situation for the first time brought a dark look of shame to her eyes.

"I'm not crying, really," she said, watching him, half frightened.

He reached his hand, and softly closed it on her bare arm.

"I love you! I love you!" he said in a soft, low vibrating voice, unlike himself.

She shrank, and dropped her head. The soft, penetrating grip of his hand on her arm distressed her. She looked up at him.

"I want to go," she said. "I want to go and get you some dry things."

"Why?" he said. "I'm all right."

"But I want to go," she said. "And I want you to change your things."

He released her arm, and she wrapped herself in the blanket, looking at him rather frightened. And still she did not rise.

"Kiss me," she said wistfully.

He kissed her, but briefly, half in anger.

Then, after a second, she rose nervously, all mixed up in the blanket. He watched her in her confusion as she tried to extricate herself and wrap herself up so that she could walk. He watched her relentlessly, as she knew. And as she went, the blanket trailing, and as he saw a glimpse of her feet and her white leg, he tried to remember her as she was when he had wrapped her in the blanket. But then he didn't want to remember, because she had been nothing to him then, and his nature revolted from remembering her as she was when she was nothing to him.

A tumbling, muffled noise from within the dark house startled him. Then he heard her voice: "There are clothes." He rose and went to the foot of the stairs, and gathered up the garments she had thrown down. Then he came back to the fire, to rub himself down and dress. He grinned at his own appearance when he had finished.

The fire was sinking, so he put on coal. The house was now quite dark, save for the light of a street-lamp that shone in faintly from beyond the holly trees. He lit the gas with matches he found on the mantelpiece. Then he emptied the pockets of his own clothes, and threw all his wet things in a heap into the scullery. After which he gathered up her sodden clothes, gently, and put them in a separate heap on the copper-top in the scullery.

It was six o'clock on the clock. His own watch had stopped. He ought to go back to the surgery. He waited, and still she did not come down. So he went to the foot of the stairs and called:

"I shall have to go."

Almost immediately he heard her coming down. She had on her best dress of black voile, and her hair was tidy, but still damp. She looked at him—and in spite of herself, smiled.

"I don't like you in those clothes," she said.

"Do I look a sight?" he answered.

They were shy of one another.

"I'll make you some tea," she said.

"No, I must go."

"Must you?" And she looked at him again with the wide, strained, doubtful eyes. And again, from the pain of his breast, he knew how he loved her. He went and bent to kiss her, gently, passionately, with his heart's painful kiss.

"And my hair smells so horrible," she murmured in distraction. "And I'm so awful, I'm so awful! Oh no, I'm too awful." And she broke into bitter, heart-broken sobbing. "You can't want to love me, I'm horrible."

"Don't be silly, don't be silly," he said, trying to comfort her, kissing her, holding her in his arms. "I want you, I want to marry you, we're going to be married, quickly, quickly—to-morrow if I can."

But she only sobbed terribly, and cried:

"I feel awful. I feel awful. I feel I'm horrible to you."

"No, I want you, I want you," was all he answered, blindly, with that terrible intonation which frightened her almost more than her horror lest he should *not* want her.

—*1922*

---

*Katherine Mansfield (1888–1923) was born in Wellington, New Zealand, and chose the short story as her primary vehicle for exploring the psychological lives of her characters, particularly women and children. Her collections include* Bliss *(1920) and* The Garden Party *(1922), in which this story appears. Influenced by Chekhov, she was interested in the significance of small details, and the aptness of expression. Of "Miss Brill" she wrote, "I chose not only the length of every sentence, but even the sound of every sentence—I chose the rise and fall of every paragraph to fit her—and to fit her on that day at that very moment." Mansfield lived an unconventional life as a New Woman travelling throughout England, France, and Italy, making friends with D. H. Lawrence and Virginia Woolf. She died of tuberculosis at age thirty-five.*

## *Katherine Mansfield*
# Miss Brill

Although it was so brilliantly fine—the blue sky powdered with gold and great spots of light like white wine splashed over the Jardins Publiques—Miss Brill was glad that she had decided on her fur. The air was motionless, but when you opened your mouth there was just a faint chill, like a chill from a glass of iced water before you sip, and now and again a leaf came drifting—from nowhere, from the sky. Miss Brill put up her hand and touched her fur. Dear little thing! It was nice to feel it again. She had taken it out of its box that afternoon, shaken out the moth-powder, given it a good brush, and rubbed the life back into the dim little eyes. "What has been happening to me?" said the sad little eyes. Oh, how sweet it was to see them snap at her again from the red eiderdown! . . . But the nose, which was of some black composition, wasn't at all firm. It must have had a knock, somehow. Never mind—a little dab of black sealing-wax when the time came—when it was absolutely necessary. . . . Little rogue! Yes, she really felt like that about it. Little rogue biting its tail just by her left ear. She could have taken it off and laid it on her lap and stroked it. She felt a tingling in her hands and arms, but that came from walking, she supposed. And when she breathed, something light and sad—no, not sad, exactly—something gentle seemed to move in her bosom.

There were a number of people out this afternoon, far more than last Sunday. And the band sounded louder and gayer. That was because the Season had begun. For although the band played all the year round on Sundays, out of season it was never the same. It was like some one playing with only the family to listen; it didn't care how it played if there weren't any strangers present. Wasn't the conductor wearing a new coat, too? She was sure it was new. He scraped with his foot and flapped his arms like a rooster about to crow, and the bandsmen sitting in the green rotunda blew out their cheeks and glared at the music. Now there came a little "flutey" bit—very pretty!—a little chain of bright drops. She was sure it would be repeated. It was; she lifted her head and smiled.

Only two people shared her "special" seat: a fine old man in a velvet coat, his hands clasped over a huge carved walking-stick, and a big old woman, sitting upright, with a roll of knitting on her embroidered apron. They did not speak. This was disappointing, for Miss Brill always looked forward to the conversation. She had become really quite expert, she thought, at listening as though she didn't listen, at sitting in other people's lives just for a minute while they talked round her.

She glanced, sideways, at the old couple. Perhaps they would go soon. Last Sunday, too, hadn't been as interesting as usual. An Englishman and his wife, he wearing a dreadful Panama hat and she button boots. And she'd gone on the whole time about how she ought to wear spectacles; she knew she needed them; but that it was no good getting any; they'd be sure to break and they'd never keep on. And he'd been so patient. He'd suggested everything—gold rims, the kind that curved round your ears, little pads inside the bridge. No, nothing would please her. "They'll always be sliding down my nose!" Miss Brill had wanted to shake her.

The old people sat on the bench, still as statues. Never mind, there was always the crowd to watch. To and fro, in front of the flower-beds and the band rotunda, the couples and groups paraded, stopped to talk, to greet, to buy a handful of flowers from the old beggar who had his tray fixed to the railings. Little children ran among them, swooping and laughing; little boys with big white silk bows under their chins, little girls, little French dolls, dressed up in velvet and lace. And sometimes a tiny staggerer came suddenly rocking into the open from under the trees, stopped, stared, as suddenly sat down "flop," until its small high-stepping mother, like a young hen, rushed scolding to its rescue. Other people sat on the benches and green chairs, but they were nearly always the same, Sunday after Sunday, and—Miss Brill had often noticed—there was something funny about nearly all of them. They were odd, silent, nearly all old, and from the way they stared they looked as though they'd just come from dark little rooms or even—even cupboards!

Behind the rotunda the slender trees with yellow leaves down drooping, and through them just a line of sea, and beyond the blue sky with gold-veined clouds.

Tum-tum-tum tiddle-um! tiddle-um! tum tiddley-um tum ta! blew the band.

Two young girls in red came by and two young soldiers in blue met them, and they laughed and paired and went off arm-in-arm. Two peasant women with funny straw hats passed, gravely, leading beautiful smoke-coloured donkeys. A cold, pale nun hurried by. A beautiful woman came along and dropped her bunch of violets, and a little boy ran after to hand them to her, and she took them and threw them away as if they'd been poisoned. Dear me! Miss Brill didn't know whether to admire that or not! And now an ermine toque and a gentleman in grey met just in front of her. He was tall, stiff, dignified, and she was wearing the ermine toque she'd bought when her hair was yellow. Now everything, her hair, her face, even her eyes, was the same colour as the shabby ermine, and her hand, in its cleaned glove, lifted to dab her lips, was a tiny yellowish paw. Oh, she was so pleased to see him—delighted! She rather thought they were going to meet that afternoon. She described where she'd been—everywhere, here, there, along by the sea. The day was so charming—didn't he agree? And wouldn't he, perhaps? . . . But he shook his head, lighted a cigarette, slowly breathed a great deep puff into her face, and, even while she was still talking and laughing, flicked the match away and walked on. The ermine toque was alone; she smiled more brightly than ever. But even the band seemed to know what she was feeling and played more softly, played tenderly, and the drum beat, "The Brute! The Brute!" over and over. What would she do? What was going to happen now? But as Miss Brill wondered, the ermine toque turned, raised her hand as though she'd seen some one else, much nicer, just over there, and pattered away. And the band changed again and played more quickly, more gaily than ever, and the old couple on Miss Brill's seat got up and marched away, and such a funny old man with long whiskers hobbled along in time to the music and was nearly knocked over by four girls walking abreast.

Oh, how fascinating it was! How she enjoyed it! How she loved sitting here, watching it all! It was like a play. It was exactly like a play. Who could believe the sky at the back wasn't painted? But it wasn't till a little brown dog trotted on solemn and then slowly trotted off, like a little "theatre" dog, a little dog that had been drugged, that Miss Brill discovered what it was that made it so exciting. They were all on the stage. They weren't only the audience, not only looking on; they were acting. Even she had a part and came every Sunday. No doubt somebody would have noticed if she hadn't been there; she was part of the performance after all. How strange she'd never thought of it like that before! And yet it explained why she made such a point of starting from home at just the same time each week—so as not to be late for the performance—and it also explained why she had quite a queer, shy feeling at telling her English pupils how she spent her Sunday afternoons. No wonder! Miss Brill nearly laughed out loud. She was on the stage. She thought of the old invalid gentleman to whom she read the newspaper four afternoons a week while he slept in the garden. She had got quite used to the frail head on the cotton pillow, the hollowed eyes, the open mouth and the high pinched nose. If he'd been dead she mightn't have noticed for weeks; she wouldn't have minded. But suddenly he knew he was having the paper read to him by an actress! "An actress!" The old head lifted; two points of light quivered in the old eyes. "An actress—are ye?" And Miss Brill smoothed the newspaper as though it were the manuscript of her part and said gently: "Yes, I have been an actress for a long time."

The band had been having a rest. Now they started again. And what they played was warm, sunny, yet there was just a faint chill—a something, what was it?—not sadness—no, not sadness—a something that made you want to sing. The tune lifted, lifted, the light shone; and it seemed to Miss Brill that in another moment all of them, all the whole company, would begin singing. The young ones, the laughing ones who were moving together, they would begin, and the men's voices, very resolute and brave, would join them. And then she too, she too, and the others on the benches—they would come in with a kind of accompaniment—something low, that scarcely rose or fell, something so beautiful—moving. . . . And Miss Brill's eyes filled with tears and she looked smiling at all the other members of the company. Yes, we understand, we understand, she thought—though what they understood she didn't know.

Just at that moment a boy and a girl came and sat down where the old couple had been. They were beautifully dressed; they were in love. The hero and heroine, of course, just arrived from his father's yacht. And still soundlessly singing, still with that trembling smile, Miss Brill prepared to listen.

"No, not now," said the girl. "Not here, I can't."

"But why? Because of that stupid old thing at the end there?" asked the boy. "Why does she come here at all—who wants her? Why doesn't she keep her silly old mug at home?"

"It's her fu-fur which is so funny," giggled the girl. "It's exactly like a fried whiting."

"Ah, be off with you!" said the boy in an angry whisper. Then: "Tell me, ma petite chérie—"

"No, not here," said the girl. "Not *yet*."

On her way home she usually bought a slice of honey-cake at the baker's. It was her Sunday treat. Sometimes there was an almond in her slice, sometimes not. It made a great difference. If there was an almond it was like carrying home a tiny present—a surprise—something that might very well not have been there. She hurried on the almond Sundays and struck the match for the kettle in quite a dashing way.

But to-day she passed the baker's by, climbed the stairs, went into the little dark room—her room like a cupboard—and sat down on the red eiderdown. She sat there for a long time. The box that the fur came out of was on the bed. She unclasped the necklet quickly; quickly, without looking, laid it inside. But when she put the lid on she thought she heard something crying.

*—1922*

**Ernest Hemingway (1899–1961)** *completely embodied the public image of the successful writer for so long that nearly half a century after his suicide it is difficult to separate the celebrity from the serious artist, the sportsman from the stylist whose influence on the short story and novel continues to be felt. The terse, stripped-down quality of his prose renders modern alienation with stark, concrete details. Born the son of a doctor in a middle-class suburb of Chicago, wounded as a volunteer ambulance driver in Italy during World War I, he worked as a reporter in Kansas and Toronto, moving to Paris in the early 1920s, where he was at the centre of a group of American expatriate writers referred to as the "Lost Generation." Sojourns in Europe, Africa, America, and Cuba inspired his long fiction—from his first successful novel,* The Sun Also Rises *(1926), to his Pulitzer Prize–winning* The Old Man and the Sea *(1952)—as well as several collections of short fiction and nonfiction. He won the Nobel Prize in 1954.*

## Ernest Hemingway
# Hills like White Elephants

The hills across the valley of the Ebro were long and white. On this side there was no shade and no trees and the station was between two lines of rails in the sun. Close against the side of the station there was the warm shadow of the building and a curtain, made of strings of bamboo beads, hung across the open door into the bar, to keep out flies. The American and the girl with him sat at a table in the shade, outside the building. It was very hot and the express from Barcelona would come in forty minutes. It stopped at this junction for two minutes and went on to Madrid.

"What should we drink?" the girl asked. She had taken off her hat and put it on the table.

"It's pretty hot," the man said.

"Let's drink beer."

"*Dos cervezas,*" the man said into the curtain.

"Big ones?" a woman asked from the doorway.

"Yes. Two big ones."

The woman brought two glasses of beer and two felt pads. She put the felt pads and the beer glasses on the table and looked at the man and the girl. The girl was looking off at the line of hills. They were white in the sun and the country was brown and dry.

"They look like white elephants," she said.

"I've never seen one," the man drank his beer.

"No, you wouldn't have."

"I might have," the man said. "Just because you say I wouldn't have doesn't prove anything."

The girl looked at the bead curtain. "They've painted something on it," she said. "What does it say?"

"Anis del Toro. It's a drink."

"Could we try it?"

The man called "Listen" through the curtain. The woman came out from the bar.

"Four reales."

"We want two Anis del Toro."

"With water?"

"Do you want it with water?"

"I don't know," the girl said. "Is it good with water?"

"It's all right."

"You want them with water?" asked the woman.

"Yes, with water."

"It tastes like licorice," the girl said and put the glass down.

"That's the way with everything."

"Yes," said the girl. "Everything tastes of licorice. Especially all the things you've waited so long for, like absinthe."

"Oh, cut it out."

"You started it," the girl said. "I was being amused. I was having a fine time."

"Well, let's try and have a fine time."

"All right. I was trying. I said the mountains looked like white elephants. Wasn't that bright?"

"That was bright."

"I wanted to try this new drink: That's all we do, isn't it—look at things and try new drinks?"

"I guess so."

The girl looked across at the hills.

"They're lovely hills," she said. "They don't really look like white elephants. I just meant the coloring of their skin through the trees."

"Should we have another drink?"

"All right."

The warm wind blew the bead curtain against the table.

"The beer's nice and cool," the man said.

"It's lovely," the girl said.

"It's really an awfully simple operation, Jig," the man said. "It's not really an operation at all."

The girl looked at the ground the table legs rested on.

"I know you wouldn't mind it, Jig. It's really not anything. It's just to let the air in."

The girl did not say anything.

"I'll go with you and I'll stay with you all the time. They just let the air in and then it's all perfectly natural."

"Then what will we do afterward?"

"We'll be fine afterward. Just like we were before."

"What makes you think so?"

"That's the only thing that bothers us. It's the only thing that's made us unhappy."

The girl looked at the bead curtain, put her hand out and took hold of two of the strings of beads.

"And you think then we'll be all right and be happy."

"I know we will. You don't have to be afraid. I've known lots of people that have done it."

"So have I," said the girl. "And afterward they were all so happy."

"Well," the man said, "if you don't want to you don't have to. I wouldn't have you do it if you didn't want to. But I know it's perfectly simple."

"And you really want to?"

"I think it's the best thing to do. But I don't want you to do it if you don't really want to."

"And if I do it you'll be happy and things will be like they were and you'll love me?"

"I love you now. You know I love you."

"I know. But if I do it, then it will be nice again if I say things are like white elephants, and you'll like it?"

"I'll love it. I love it now but I just can't think about it. You know how I get when I worry."

"If I do it you won't ever worry?"

"I won't worry about that because it's perfectly simple."

"Then I'll do it. Because I don't care about me."

"What do you mean?"

"I don't care about me."

"Well, I care about you."

"Oh, yes. But I don't care about me. And I'll do it and then everything will be fine."

"I don't want you to do it if you feel that way."

The girl stood up and walked to the end of the station. Across, on the other side, were fields of grain and trees along the banks of the Ebro. Far away, beyond the river, were mountains. The shadow of a cloud moved across the field of grain and she saw the river through the trees.

"And we could have all this," she said. "And we could have everything and every day we make it more impossible."

"What did you say?"

"I said we could have everything."

"We can have everything."

"No, we can't."

"We can have the whole world."

"No, we can't."

"We can go everywhere."

"No, we can't. It isn't ours any more."

"It's ours."

"No, it isn't. And once they take it away, you never get it back."

"But they haven't taken it away."

"We'll wait and see."

"Come on back in the shade," he said. "You mustn't feel that way."

"I don't feel any way," the girl said. "I just know things."

"I don't want you to do anything that you don't want to do——"

"Nor that isn't good for me," she said. "I know. Could we have another beer?"

"All right. But you've got to realize——"

"I realize," the girl said. "Can't we maybe stop talking?"

They sat down at the table and the girl looked across at the hills on the dry side of the valley and the man looked at her and at the table.

"You've got to realize," he said, "that I don't want you to do it if you don't want to. I'm perfectly willing to go through with it if it means anything to you."

"Doesn't it mean anything to you? We could get along."

"Of course it does. But I don't want anybody but you. I don't want any one else. And I know it's perfectly simple."

"Yes, you know it's perfectly simple."

"It's all right for you to say that, but I do know it."

"Would you do something for me now?"

"I'd do anything for you."

"Would you please please please please please please please stop talking?"

He did not say anything but looked at the bags against the wall of the station. There were labels on them from all the hotels where they had spent nights.

"But I don't want you to," he said, "I don't care anything about it."

"I'll scream," the girl said.

The woman came out through the curtains with two glasses of beer and put them down on the damp felt pads. "The train comes in five minutes," she said.

"What did she say?" asked the girl.

"That the train is coming in five minutes."

The girl smiled brightly at the woman, to thank her.

"I'd better take the bags over to the other side of the station," the man said. She smiled at him.

"All right. Then come back and we'll finish the beer."

He picked up the two heavy bags and carried them around the station to the other tracks. He looked up the tracks but could not see the train. Coming back, he walked through the barroom, where people waiting for the train were drinking. He drank an Anis at the bar and looked at the people. They were all waiting reasonably for the train. He went out through the bead curtain. She was sitting at the table and smiled at him.

"Do you feel better?" he asked.

"I feel fine," she said. "There's nothing wrong with me. I feel fine."

*—1927*

*Jorge Luis Borges (1899–1986) is perhaps the most original writer in Spanish of the twentieth century, and many of his experiments anticipate the "metafiction" and "cyberpunk" techniques of today's avant-garde. Born in Buenos Aires, Borges was caught with his parents in Switzerland during World War I, a circumstance that happily led to a multilingual education. Borges was equally fluent in English (he was an expert in Anglo-Saxon literature) and his native Spanish, and he also learned French, German, and Latin. In his early career he was associated with a group of avant-garde experimental poets who attempted, in the pages of literary magazines like Sur, to connect the provincial Argentine reading public with the main currents of modernism. Borges himself translated the works of complex American poets like e. e. cummings and Wallace Stevens into Spanish. Borges turned to fiction in his forties, and his paradoxical allegories of time and being, although widely discussed, were never aimed at large popular audiences. A vocal opponent of the Nazis (who had many supporters in Argentina) and of the Perón dictatorship, Borges was dismissed from several positions because of his politics. After the fall of Perón in 1955, Borges served a distinguished term as director of Argentina's national library, despite progressive deterioration of his sight, which left him almost totally blind. In his later years he travelled and lectured in the United States and oversaw the translation of his works into English.*

# Jorge Luis Borges
# The Book of Sand

. . . thy rope of sands . . . [1]

—George Herbert (1593–1623)

The line consists of an infinite number of points; the plane, of an infinite number of lines; the volume, of an infinite number of planes; the hypervolume, of an infinite number of volumes . . . No—this, *more geometrico*, is decidedly not the best way to begin my tale. To say that the story is true is by now a convention of every fantastic tale; mine, nevertheless, *is* true.

I live alone, in a fifth-floor apartment on Calle Belgrano. One evening a few months ago, I heard a knock at my door. I opened it, and a stranger stepped in. He was a tall man, with blurred, vague features, or perhaps my nearsightedness made me see him that way. Everything about him spoke of honest poverty: he was dressed in gray, and carried a gray valise. I immediately sensed that he was a foreigner. At first

[1] *thy rope of sands:* line from Herbert's poem "The Collar" (1633).

I thought he was old; then I noticed that I had been misled by his sparse hair, which was blond, almost white, like the Scandinavians'. In the course of our conversation, which I doubt lasted more than an hour, I learned that he hailed from the Orkneys.

I pointed the man to a chair. He took some time to begin talking. He gave off an air of melancholy, as I myself do now.

"I sell Bibles," he said at last.

"In this house," I replied, not without a somewhat stiff, pedantic note, "there are several English Bibles, including the first one, Wyclif's. I also have Cipriano de Valera's, Luther's (which is, in literary terms, the worst of the lot), and a Latin copy of the Vulgate. As you see, it isn't exactly Bibles I might be needing."

After a brief silence he replied.

"It's not only Bibles I sell. I can show you a sacred book that might interest a man such as yourself. I came by it in northern India, in Bikaner."

He opened his valise and brought out the book. He laid it on the table. It was a clothbound octavo volume that had clearly passed through many hands. I examined it; the unusual heft of it surprised me. On the spine was printed *Holy Writ*, and then *Bombay*.

"Nineteenth century, I'd say," I observed.

"I don't know," was the reply. "Never did know."

I opened it at random. The characters were unfamiliar to me. The pages, which seemed worn and badly set, were printed in double columns, like a Bible. The text was cramped, and composed into versicles. At the upper corner of each page were Arabic numerals. I was struck by an odd fact: the even-numbered page would carry the number 40,514, let us say, while the odd-numbered page that followed it would be 999. I turned the page; the next page bore an eight-digit number. It also bore a small illustration, like those one sees in dictionaries: an anchor drawn in pen and ink, as though by the unskilled hand of a child.

It was at that point that the stranger spoke again.

"Look at it well. You will never see it again."

There was a threat in the words, but not in the voice.

I took note of the page, and then closed the book. Immediately I opened it again. In vain I searched for the figure of the anchor, page after page. To hide my discomfiture, I tried another tack.

"This is a version of Scripture in some Hindu language, isn't that right?"

"No," he replied.

Then he lowered his voice, as though entrusting me with a secret.

"I came across this book in a village on the plain, and I traded a few rupees and a Bible for it. The man who owned it didn't know how to read. I suspect he saw the Book of Books as an amulet. He was of the lowest caste; people could not so much as step on his shadow without being defiled. He told me his book was called the Book of Sand because neither sand nor this book has a beginning or an end."

He suggested I try to find the first page.

I took the cover in my left hand and opened the book, my thumb and forefinger almost touching. It was impossible: several pages always lay between the cover and my hand. It was as though they grew from the very book.

"Now try to find the end."

I failed there as well.

"This can't be," I stammered, my voice hardly recognizable as my own.

"It can't be, yet it *is*," the Bible peddler said, his voice little more than a whisper. "The number of pages in this book is literally infinite. No page is the first page; no page is the last. I don't know why they're numbered in this arbitrary way, but perhaps it's to give one to understand that the terms of an infinite series can be numbered any way whatever."

Then, as though thinking out loud, he went on.

"If space is infinite, we are anywhere, at any point in space. If time is infinite, we are at any point in time."

His musings irritated me, "You," I said, "are a religious man, are you not?"

"Yes, I'm Presbyterian. My conscience is clear. I am certain I didn't cheat that native when I gave him the Lord's Word in exchange for his diabolic book."

I assured him he had nothing to reproach himself for, and asked whether he was just passing through the country. He replied that he planned to return to his own country within a few days. It was then that I learned he was a Scot, and that his home was in the Orkneys. I told him I had great personal fondness for Scotland because of my love for Stevenson and Hume.

"And Robbie Burns," he corrected.

As we talked I continued to explore the infinite book.

"Had you intended to offer this curious specimen to the British Museum, then?" I asked with feigned indifference.

"No," he replied, "I am offering it to you," and he mentioned a great sum of money.

I told him, with perfect honesty, that such an amount of money was not within my ability to pay. But my mind was working; in a few moments I had devised my plan.

"I propose a trade," I said. "You purchased the volume with a few rupees and the Holy Scripture; I will offer you the full sum of my pension, which I have just received, and Wyclif's black-letter Bible. It was left to me by my parents."

"A black-letter Wyclif!" he murmured.

I went to my bedroom and brought back the money and the book. With a bibliophile's zeal he turned the pages and studied the binding.

"Done," he said.

I was astonished that he did not haggle. Only later was I to realize he had entered my house already determined to sell the book. He did not count the money, but merely put the bills into his pocket.

We chatted about India, the Orkneys, and the Norwegian jarls that had once ruled those islands. Night was falling when the man left. I have never seen him since, nor do I know his name.

I thought of putting the Book of Sand in the space left by the Wyclif, but I chose at last to hide it behind some imperfect volumes of the *Thousand and One Nights.*

I went to bed but could not sleep. At three or four in the morning I turned on the light. I took out the impossible book and turned its pages. On one, I saw an engraving of a mask. There was a number in the corner of the page—I don't remember now what it was—raised to the ninth power.

I showed no one my treasure. To the joy of possession was added the fear that it would be stolen from me, and to that, the suspicion that it might not be truly infinite. Those two points of anxiety aggravated my already habitual misanthropy. I had but few friends left, and those, I stopped seeing. A prisoner of the Book, I hardly left my house. I examined the worn binding and the covers with a magnifying glass, and rejected the possibility of some artifice. I found that the small illustrations were spaced at two-thousand-page intervals. I began noting them down in an alphabetized notebook, which was very soon filled. They never repeated themselves. At night, during the rare intervals spared me by insomnia, I dreamed of the book.

Summer was drawing to a close, and I realized that the book was monstrous. It was cold consolation to think that I, who looked upon it with my eyes and fondled it with my ten flesh-and-bone fingers, was no less monstrous than the book. I felt it was a nightmare thing, an obscene thing, and that it defiled and corrupted reality.

I considered fire, but I feared that the burning of an infinite book might be similarly infinite, and suffocate the planet in smoke.

I remembered reading once that the best place to hide a leaf is in the forest. Before my retirement I had worked in the National Library, which contained nine hundred thousand books; I knew that to the right of the lobby a curving staircase descended into the shadows of the basement, where the maps and periodicals are kept. I took advantage of the librarians' distraction to hide the Book of Sand on one of the library's damp shelves; I tried not to notice how high up, or how far from the door.

I now feel a little better, but I refuse even to walk down the street the library's on.[2]

*—1971*

---

[2]In Spanish, the story ends with "Calle Mexico," the street location of Argentina's National Library, where Borges was director, but the allusion has been explained for foreign readers.

*John Cheever (1912–1982) was associated with* The New Yorker *for most of his creative life. It was the magazine that first published most of his short stories. Cheever's examinations of the tensions of life in white-collar suburbia take many forms —from naturalism to outright fantasy —but virtually all of his fiction is suffused with a melancholy that is often fuelled by marital tensions, failed social aspirations, and what one story aptly calls "the sorrows of gin." Born in Quincy, Massachusetts, Cheever was expelled from Thayer Academy at seventeen, an event that formed the subject of his first published story, and he worked almost exclusively as a writer of fiction for the rest of his life, with occasional periods spent teaching at universities and writing for television. His most original writing is arguably in his short stories, but novels like the National Book Award-winning* The Wapshot Chronicle *(1957),* The Wapshot Scandal *(1964),* Bullet Park *(1969), and* Falconer *(1977) brought him to the attention of large audiences.* The Stories of John Cheever *won the Pulitzer Prize in 1979. In recent years his daughter, Susan Cheever, has published a memoir,* Home Before Dark, *and an edition of her father's journals, both of which chronicle Cheever's long struggles with alcoholism and questions of sexual identity.*

## John Cheever
# Reunion

The last time I saw my father was in Grand Central Station. I was going from my grandmother's in the Adirondacks to a cottage on the Cape that my mother had rented, and I wrote my father that I would be in New York between trains for an hour and a half, and asked if we could have lunch together. His secretary wrote to say that he would meet me at the information booth at noon, and at twelve o'clock sharp I saw him coming through the crowd. He was a stranger to me—my mother divorced him three years ago and I hadn't been with him since—but as soon as I saw him I felt that he was my father, my flesh and blood, my future and my doom. I knew that when I was grown I would be something like him; I would have to plan my campaigns within his limitations. He was a big, good-looking man, and I was terribly happy to see him again. He struck me on the back and shook my hand. "Hi, Charlie," he said. "Hi, boy. I'd like to take you up to my club, but it's in the Sixties, and if you have to catch an early train I guess we'd better get something to eat around here." He put his arm around me, and I smelled my father the way my mother sniffs a rose. It was a rich compound of whiskey, after-shave lotion, shoe polish, woolens, and the rankness of a mature male. I hoped that someone would see us together. I wished that we could be photographed. I wanted some record of our having been together.

We went out of the station and up a side street to a restaurant. It was still early, and the place was empty. The bartender was quarreling with a delivery boy, and there was one very old waiter in a red coat down by the kitchen door. We sat down, and my father hailed the waiter in a loud voice. "*Kellner!*" he shouted. "*Garçon! Cameriere! You!*" His boisterousness in the empty restaurant seemed out of place. "Could we have a little service here!" he shouted. "Chop-chop." Then he clapped his hands. This caught the waiter's attention, and he shuffled over to our table.

"Were you clapping your hands at me?" he asked.

"Calm down, calm down, *sommelier,*" my father said. "If it isn't too much to ask of you—if it wouldn't be too much above and beyond the call of duty, we would like a couple of Beefeater Gibsons."

"I don't like to be clapped at," the waiter said.

"I should have brought my whistle," my father said. "I have a whistle that is audible only to the ears of old waiters. Now, take out your little pad and your little pencil and see if you can get this straight: two Beefeater Gibsons. Repeat after me: two Beefeater Gibsons."

"I think you'd better go somewhere else," the waiter said quietly.

"That," said my father, "is one of the most brilliant suggestions I have ever heard. Come on, Charlie, let's get the hell out of here!"

I followed my father out of that restaurant into another. He was not so boisterous this time. Our drinks came, and he cross-questioned me about the baseball season. He then struck the edge of his empty glass with his knife and began shouting again. "*Garçon! Kellner! Cameriere! You!* Could we trouble you to bring us two more of the same."

"How old is the boy?" the waiter asked.

"That," my father said, "is none of your God-damned business."

"I'm sorry, sir," the waiter said, "but I won't serve the boy another drink."

"Well, I have some news for you," my father said. "I have some very interesting news for you. This doesn't happen to be the only restaurant in New York. They've opened another on the corner. Come on, Charlie."

He paid the bill, and I followed him out of that restaurant into another. Here the waiters wore pink jackets like hunting coats, and there was a lot of horse tack on the walls. We sat down, and my father began to shout again. "Master of the hounds! Tallyhoo and all that sort of thing. We'd like a little something in the way of a stirrup cup. Namely, two Bibson Geefeaters."

"Two Bibson Geefeaters?" the waiter asked, smiling.

"You know damned well what I want," my father said angrily. "I want two Beefeater Gibsons, and make it snappy. Things have changed in jolly old England. So my friend the duke tells me. Let's see what England can produce in the way of a cocktail."

"This isn't England," the waiter said.

"Don't argue with me," my father said. "Just do as you're told."

"I just thought you might like to know where you are," the waiter said.

"If there is one thing I cannot tolerate," my father said, "it is an impudent domestic. Come on, Charlie."

The fourth place we went to was Italian. *"Buon giorno,"* my father said. *"Per favore, possiamo avere due cocktail americani, forti, forti. Molto gin, poco vermut."*[1]

"I don't understand Italian," the waiter said.

"Oh, come off it," my father said. "You understand Italian, and you know damned well you do. *Vogliamo due cocktail americani. Subito."*

The waiter left us and spoke with the captain, who came over to our table and said, "I'm sorry, sir, but this table is reserved."

"All right," my father said. "Get us another table."

"All the tables are reserved," the captain said.

"I get it," my father said. "You don't desire our patronage. Is that it? Well, the hell with you. *Vada all' inferno.* Let's go, Charlie."

"I have to get my train," I said.

"I'm sorry, sonny," my father said. "I'm terribly sorry." He put his arm around me and pressed me against him. "I'll walk you back to the station. If there had only been time to go up to my club."

"That's all right, Daddy," I said.

"I'll get you a paper," he said. "I'll get you a paper to read on the train."

Then he went up to a newsstand and said, "Kind sir, will you be good enough to favor me with one of your God-damned, no-good,

[1] The father is ordering drinks in Italian.

ten-cent afternoon papers?" The clerk turned away from him and stared at a magazine cover. "Is it asking too much, kind sir," my father said, "is it asking too much for you to sell me one of your disgusting specimens of yellow journalism?"

"I have to go, Daddy," I said. "It's late."

"Now, just wait a second, sonny," he said. "I want to get a rise out of this chap."

"Goodbye, Daddy," I said, and I went down the stairs and got my train, and that was the last time I saw my father.

—*1962*

*Maya Angelou (b. 1928) was born Marguerite Ann Johnson in St. Louis, Missouri, but went in 1931 to live with her grandmother in Stamps, Arkansas, a childhood she describes in the best-seller* I Know Why the Caged Bird Sings *(1970). Five more volumes of autobiography followed, culminating with* A Song Flung Up to Heaven *(2002). While working as a nightclub singer, Angelou adopted her professional name, which combined a childhood nickname with the name of her first husband. She has published more than thirty books, including several collections of poetry and plays, books for children, and personal essays. She is also an actor, director, educator, and civil rights activist.*

# Maya Angelou
# *from* I Know Why the Caged Bird Sings

The Angel of the candy counter had found me out at last, and was exacting excruciating penance for all the stolen Milky Ways, Mounds, Mr. Goodbars and Hersheys with Almonds. I had two cavities that were rotten to the gums. The pain was beyond the bailiwick of crushed aspirins or oil of cloves. Only one thing could help me, so I prayed earnestly that I'd be allowed to sit under the house and have the building collapse on my left jaw. Since there was no Negro dentist in Stamps, nor doctor either, for that matter, Momma had dealt with previous toothaches by pulling them out (a string tied to the tooth with the other end looped over her fist), pain killers and prayer. In this particular instance the medicine had proved ineffective; there wasn't enough enamel left to hook a string on, and the prayers were being ignored because the Balancing Angel was blocking their passage.

I lived a few days and nights in blinding pain, not so much toying with as seriously considering the idea of jumping in the well, and Momma decided I had to be taken to a dentist. The nearest Negro dentist was in Texarkana, twenty-five miles away, and I was certain that I'd be dead long before we reached half the distance. Momma said we'd go to Dr. Lincoln, right in Stamps, and he'd take care of me. She said he owed her a favor.

I knew that there were a number of whitefolks in town that owed her favors. Bailey and I had seen the books which showed how she had lent money to Blacks and whites alike during the Depression, and most still owed her. But I couldn't aptly remember seeing Dr. Lincoln's name, nor had I ever heard of a Negro's going to him as a patient. However, Momma said we were going, and put water on the stove for our baths. I had never been to a doctor, so she told me that after the bath (which would make my mouth feel better) I had to put on freshly starched and ironed underclothes from inside out. The ache failed to respond to the bath, and I knew then that the pain was more serious than that which anyone had ever suffered.

Before we left the Store, she ordered me to brush my teeth and then wash my mouth with Listerine. The idea of even opening my clamped jaws increased the pain, but upon her explanation that when you go to a doctor you have to clean yourself all over, but most especially the part that's to be examined, I screwed up my courage and unlocked my teeth. The cool air in my mouth and the jarring of my molars dislodged what little remained of my reason. I had frozen to the pain, my family nearly had to tie me down to take the toothbrush away. It was no small effort to get me started on the road to the dentist. Momma spoke to all the passersby, but didn't stop to chat. She explained over her shoulder that we were going to the doctor and she'd "pass the time of day" on our way home.

Until we reached the pond the pain was my world, an aura that haloed me for three feet around. Crossing the bridge into whitefolks' country, pieces of sanity pushed themselves forward. I had to stop moaning and start walking straight. The white towel, which was drawn under my chin and tied over my head, had to be arranged. If one was dying, it had to be done in style if the dying took place in whitefolks' part of town.

On the other side of the bridge the ache seemed to lessen as if a whitebreeze blew off the whitefolks and cushioned everything in their neighborhood—including my jaw. The gravel road was smoother, the stones smaller and the tree branches hung down around the path and nearly covered us. If the pain didn't diminish then, the familiar yet strange sights hypnotized me into believing that it had.

But my head continued to throb with the measured insistence of a bass drum, and how could a toothache pass the calaboose,[1] hear the songs of the prisoners, their blues and laughter, and not be changed? How could one or two or even a mouthful of angry tooth roots meet a wagonload of powhite-trash children, endure their idiotic snobbery and not feel less important?

Behind the building which housed the dentist's office ran a small path used by servants and those tradespeople who catered to the butcher and Stamps' one restaurant. Momma and I followed that lane to the backstairs of Dentist Lincoln's office. The sun was bright and gave the day a hard reality as we climbed up the steps to the second floor.

Momma knocked on the back door and a young white girl opened it to show surprise at seeing us there. Momma said she wanted to see Dentist Lincoln and to tell him Annie was there. The girl closed the door firmly. Now the humiliation of hearing Momma describe herself as if she had no last name to the young white girl was equal to the physical pain. It seemed terribly unfair to have a toothache and a headache and have to bear at the same time the heavy burden of Blackness.

It was always possible that the teeth would quiet down and maybe drop out of their own accord. Momma said we would wait. We leaned in the harsh sunlight on the shaky railings of the dentist's back porch for over an hour.

He opened the door and looked at Momma. "Well, Annie, what can I do for you?"

He didn't see the towel around my jaw or notice my swollen face.

Momma said, "Dentist Lincoln. It's my grandbaby here. She got two rotten teeth that's giving her a fit."

She waited for him to acknowledge the truth of her statement. He made no comment, orally or facially.

---

[1] *calaboose:* prison.

"She had this toothache purt' near four days now, and today I said, 'Young lady, you going to the Dentist.' "

"Annie?"

"Yes, sir, Dentist Lincoln."

He was choosing words the way people hunt for shells. "Annie, you know I don't treat nigra, colored people."

"I know, Dentist Lincoln. But this here is just my little grandbaby, and she ain't gone be no trouble to you . . ."

"Annie, everybody has a policy. In this world you have to have a policy. Now, my policy is I don't treat colored people."

The sun had baked the oil out of Momma's skin and melted the Vaseline in her hair. She shone greasily as she leaned out of the dentist's shadow.

"Seem like to me, Dentist Lincoln, you might look after her, she ain't nothing but a little mite. And seems like maybe you owe me a favor or two."

He reddened slightly. "Favor or no favor. The money has all been repaid to you and that's the end of it. Sorry, Annie." He had his hand on the doorknob. "Sorry." His voice was a bit kinder on the second "Sorry," as if he really was.

Momma said, "I wouldn't press on you like this for myself but I can't take No. Not for my grandbaby. When you come to borrow my money you didn't have to beg. You asked me, and I lent it. Now, it wasn't my policy. I ain't no moneylender, but you stood to lose this building and I tried to help you out."

"It's been paid, and raising your voice won't make me change my mind. My policy . . ." He let go of the door and stepped nearer Momma. The three of us were crowded on the small landing. "Annie, my policy is I'd rather stick my hand in a dog's mouth than in a nigger's."

He had never once looked at me. He turned his back and went through the door into the cool beyond. Momma backed up inside herself for a few minutes. I forgot everything except her face which was almost a new one to me. She leaned over and took the doorknob, and in her everyday soft voice she said, "Sister, go on downstairs. Wait for me. I'll be there directly."

Under the most common of circumstances I knew it did no good to argue with Momma. So I walked down the steep stairs, afraid to look back and afraid not to do so. I turned as the door slammed, and she was gone.

*Momma walked in that room as if she owned it. She shoved that silly nurse aside with one hand and strode into the dentist's office. He was sitting in his chair, sharpening his mean instruments and putting extra sting into his medicines. Her eyes were blazing like live coals and her arms had doubled themselves in length. He looked up at her just before she caught him by the collar of his white jacket.*

*"Stand up when you see a lady, you contemptuous scoundrel." Her tongue had thinned and the words rolled off well enunciated. Enunciated and sharp like little claps of thunder.*

*The dentist had no choice but to stand at R.O.T.C.[2] attention. His head dropped after a minute and his voice was humble. "Yes, ma'am, Mrs. Henderson."*

*"You knave, do you think you acted like a gentleman, speaking to me like that in front of my granddaughter?" She didn't shake him, although she had the power. She simply held him upright.*

*"No, ma'am, Mrs. Henderson."*

*"No, ma'am, Mrs. Henderson, what?" Then she did give him the tiniest of shakes, but because of her strength the action set his head and arms to shaking loose on the ends of his body. He stuttered much worse than Uncle Willie. "No, ma'am. Mrs. Henderson, I'm sorry."*

*With just an edge of her disgust showing, Momma slung him back in his dentist's chair. "Sorry is as sorry does, and you're about the sorriest dentist I ever laid my eyes on." (She could afford to slip into the vernacular because she had such eloquent command of English.)*

*"I didn't ask you to apologize in front of Marguerite, because I don't want her to know my power, but I order you, now and herewith. Leave Stamps by sundown."*

*"Mrs. Henderson, I can't get my equipment ..." He was shaking terribly now.*

*"Now, that brings me to my second order. You will never again practice dentistry. Never! When you get settled in your next place, you will be a vegetarian caring for dogs with the mange, cats with the cholera and cows with the epizootic.[3] Is that clear?"*

*The saliva ran down his chin and his eyes filled with tears. "Yes, ma'am. Thank you for not killing me. Thank you, Mrs. Henderson."*

---

[2]*R.O.T.C.:* Reserve Officers' Training Corps.
[3]*epizootic:* cattle plague.

*Momma pulled herself back from being ten feet tall with eight-foot arms and said, "You're welcome for nothing, you varlet, I wouldn't waste a killing on the likes of you."*

*On her way out she waved her handkerchief at the nurse and turned her into a crocus sack of chicken feed.*

Momma looked tired when she came down the stairs, but who wouldn't be tired if they had gone through what she had. She came close to me and adjusted the towel under my jaw (I had forgotten the toothache; I only knew that she made her hands gentle in order not to awaken the pain). She took my hand. Her voice never changed. "Come on, Sister."

I reckoned we were going home where she would concoct a brew to eliminate the pain and maybe give me new teeth too. New teeth that would grow overnight out of my gums. She led me toward the drugstore, which was in the opposite direction from the Store. "I'm taking you to Dentist Baker in Texarkana."

I was glad after all that that I had bathed and put on Mum and Cashmere Bouquet talcum powder. It was a wonderful surprise. My toothache had quieted to solemn pain, Momma had obliterated the evil white man, and we were going on a trip to Texarkana, just the two of us.

On the Greyhound she took an inside seat in the back, and I sat beside her. I was so proud of being her granddaughter and sure that some of her magic must have come down to me. She asked if I was scared. I only shook my head and leaned over on her cool brown upper arm. There was no chance that a dentist, especially a Negro dentist, would dare hurt me then. Not with Momma there. The trip was uneventful, except that she put her arm around me, which was very unusual for Momma to do.

The dentist showed me the medicine and the needle before he deadened my gums, but if he hadn't I wouldn't have worried. Momma stood right behind him. Her arms were folded and she checked on everything he did. The teeth were extracted and she bought me an ice cream cone from the side window of a drug counter. The trip back to Stamps was quiet, except that I had to spit into a very small empty snuff can which she had gotten for me and it was difficult with the bus humping and jerking on our country roads.

At home, I was given a warm salt solution, and when I washed out my mouth I showed Bailey the empty holes, where the clotted blood sat like filling in a pie crust. He said I was quite brave, and that was my cue to reveal our confrontation with the peckerwood[4] dentist and Momma's incredible powers.

I had to admit that I didn't hear the conversation, but what else could she have said than what I said she said? What else done? He agreed with my analysis in a lukewarm way, and I happily (after all, I'd been sick) flounced into the Store. Momma was preparing our evening meal and Uncle Willie leaned on the door sill. She gave her version.

"Dentist Lincoln got right uppity. Said he'd rather put his hand in a dog's mouth. And when I reminded him of the favor, he brushed it off like a piece of lint. Well, I sent Sister downstairs and went inside. I hadn't never been in his office before, but I found the door to where he takes out teeth, and him and the nurse was in there thick as thieves. I just stood there till he caught sight of me." Crash bang the pots on the stove. "He jumped just like he was sitting on a pin. He said, 'Annie, I done tole you, I ain't gonna mess around in no niggah's mouth.' I said, 'Somebody's got to do it then,' and he said, 'Take her to Texarkana to the colored dentist' and that's when I said, 'If you paid me my money I could afford to take her.' He said, 'It's all been paid.' I tole him everything but the interest had been paid. He said, ''Twasn't no interest.' I said, ''Tis now. I'll take ten dollars as payment in full.' You know, Willie, it wasn't no right thing to do, 'cause I lent that money without thinking about it.

"He tole that little snippity nurse of his'n to give me ten dollars and make me sign a 'paid in full' receipt. She gave it to me and I signed the papers. Even though by rights he was paid up before, I figger, he gonna be that kind of nasty, he gonna have to pay for it."

Momma and her son laughed and laughed over the white man's evilness and her retributive sin.

I preferred, much preferred, my version.

*—1969*

---

[4] *peckerwood:* slang for white person.

*Gabriel García Márquez (b. 1928) is the author of a brilliant serio-comic historical novel,* One Hundred Years of Solitude *(1967). It is one of the landmarks of contemporary fiction, and rapidly became an international best-seller. "Magic realism" is the term that is often used to describe the author's unique blend of folklore, historical fact, naturalism, and fantasy, much of it occurring in the fictional village of Macondo. A native of Colombia, García Márquez, the eldest of twelve children, was born in Aracéataca, a small town that is the model for the isolated, decaying settlements found in his fiction. Trained as a journalist, García Márquez has lived in France, Spain, and Mexico, where he has written collections of short fiction and non-fiction as well as novels. He was awarded the Nobel Prize in 1982, and his novels* Love in the Time of Cholera *(1988) and* Memories of My Melancholy Whores *(2005) have reached a wide audience.*

## Gabriel García Márquez
# A Very Old Man with Enormous Wings

On the third day of rain they had killed so many crabs inside the house that Pelayo had to cross his drenched courtyard and throw them into the sea, because the newborn child had a temperature all night and they thought it was due to the stench. The world had been sad since Tuesday. Sea and sky were a single ash-gray thing and the sands of the beach, which on March nights glimmered like powdered light, had become a stew of mud and rotten shellfish. The light was so weak at noon that when Pelayo was coming back to the house after throwing away the crabs, it was hard for him to see what it was that was moving and groaning in the rear of the courtyard. He had to go very close to see that it was an old man, a very old man, lying face down in the mud, who, in spite of his tremendous efforts, couldn't get up, impeded by his enormous wings.

Frightened by that nightmare, Pelayo ran to get Elisenda, his wife, who was putting compresses on the sick child, and he took her to the rear of the courtyard. They both looked at the fallen body with mute stupor. He was dressed like a ragpicker. There were only a few faded hairs left on his bald skull and very few teeth in his mouth, and his pitiful condition of a drenched great-grandfather had taken away any sense

Translated by Gregory Rabassa.

of grandeur he might have had. His huge buzzard wings, dirty and half-plucked, were forever entangled in the mud. They looked at him so long and so closely that Pelayo and Elisenda very soon overcame their surprise and in the end found him familiar. Then they dared speak to him, and he answered in an incomprehensible dialect with a strong sailor's voice. That was how they skipped over the inconvenience of the wings and quite intelligently concluded that he was a lonely castaway from some foreign ship wrecked by the storm. And yet, they called in a neighbor woman who knew everything about life and death to see him, and all she needed was one look to show them their mistake.

"He's an angel," she told them. "He must have been coming for the child, but the poor fellow is so old that the rain knocked him down."

On the following day everyone knew that a flesh-and-blood angel was held captive in Pelayo's house. Against the judgment of the wise neighbor woman, for whom angels in those times were the fugitive survivors of a celestial conspiracy, they did not have the heart to club him to death. Pelayo watched over him all afternoon from the kitchen, armed with his bailiff's club, and before going to bed he dragged him out of the mud and locked him up with the hens in the wire chicken coop. In the middle of the night, when the rain stopped, Pelayo and Elisenda were still killing crabs. A short time afterward the child woke up without a fever and with a desire to eat. Then they felt magnanimous and decided to put the angel on a raft with fresh water and provisions for three days and leave him to his fate on the high seas. But when they went out into the courtyard with the first light of dawn, they found the whole neighborhood in front of the chicken coop having fun with the angel, without the slightest reverence, tossing him things to eat through the openings in the wire as if he weren't a supernatural creature but a circus animal.

Father Gonzaga arrived before seven o'clock, alarmed at the strange news. By that time onlookers less frivolous than those at dawn had already arrived and they were making all kinds of conjectures concerning the captive's future. The simplest among them thought that he should be named mayor of the world. Others of sterner mind felt that he should be promoted to the rank of five-star general in order to win all wars. Some visionaries hoped that he could be put to stud in order to implant on earth a race of winged wise men who could take charge of the universe. But Father Gonzaga, before becoming a priest, had been a robust woodcutter. Standing by the wire, he reviewed his catechism in an instant and asked them to open the door so that he could take a close look at that pitiful man who looked more like a huge decrepit hen among the fascinated chickens. He was lying in a corner drying his open wings in the sunlight among the fruit peels and breakfast leftovers that the early risers had thrown him. Alien to the impertinences of the world, he only lifted his antiquarian eyes and murmured something in his dialect when Father Gonzaga went into the chicken coop and said good morning to him in Latin. The parish priest had his first suspicion of an impostor when he saw that he did not understand the language of God or know how to greet His ministers. Then he noticed that seen close up he was much too human: he had an unbearable smell of the outdoors, the back side of his wings was strewn with parasites and his main feathers had been mistreated by terrestrial winds, and nothing about him measured up to the proud dignity of angels. Then he came out of the chicken coop and in a brief sermon warned the curious against the risks of being ingenuous. He reminded them that the devil had the bad habit of making use of carnival tricks in order to confuse the unwary. He argued that if wings were not the essential element in determining the difference between a hawk and an airplane, they were even less so in the recognition of angels. Nevertheless, he promised to write a letter to his bishop so that the latter would write to his primate so that the latter would write to the Supreme Pontiff in order to get the final verdict from the highest courts.

His prudence fell on sterile hearts. The news of the captive angel spread with such rapidity that after a few hours the courtyard had the bustle of a marketplace and they had to call in troops with fixed bayonets to disperse the mob that was about to knock the house down. Elisenda, her spine all twisted from sweeping up so much marketplace trash, then got the idea of fencing in the yard and charging five cents admission to see the angel.

The curious came from far away. A traveling carnival arrived with a flying acrobat who buzzed over the crowd several times, but no one paid any attention to him because his wings were not those of an angel but, rather, those of a sidereal[1] bat. The most unfortunate invalids on earth came in search of health: a poor woman who since childhood had been counting her heartbeats and had run out of numbers, a Portuguese man

[1]*sidereal:* coming from the stars.

who couldn't sleep because the noise of the stars disturbed him, a sleep-walker who got up at night to undo the things he had done while awake; and many others with less serious ailments. In the midst of that shipwreck disorder that made the earth tremble, Pelayo and Elisenda were happy with fatigue, for in less than a week they had crammed their rooms with money and the line of pilgrims waiting their turn to enter still reached beyond the horizon.

The angel was the only one who took no part in his own act. He spent his time trying to get comfortable in his borrowed nest, befuddled by the hellish heat of the oil lamps and sacramental candles that had been placed along the wire. At first they tried to make him eat some mothballs, which according to the wisdom of the wise neighbor woman, were the food prescribed for angels. But he turned them down, just as he turned down the papal lunches that the penitents brought him, and they never found out whether it was because he was an angel or because he was an old man that in the end he ate nothing but eggplant mush. His only supernatural virtue seemed to be patience. Especially during the first days, when the hens pecked at him, searching for the stellar parasites that proliferated in his wings, and the cripples pulled out feathers to touch their defective parts with, and even the most merciful threw stones at him, trying to get him to rise so they could see him standing. The only time they succeeded in arousing him was when they burned his side with an iron for branding steers, for he had been motionless for so many hours that they thought he was dead. He awoke with a start, ranting in his hermetic language and with tears in his eyes, and he flapped his wings a couple of times, which brought on a whirlwind of chicken dung and lunar dust and a gale of panic that did not seem to be of this world. Although many thought that his reaction had been one not of rage but of pain, from then on they were careful not to annoy him, because the majority understood that his passivity was not that of a hero taking his ease but that of a cataclysm in repose.

Father Gonzaga held back the crowd's frivolity with formulas of maidservant inspiration while awaiting the arrival of a final judgment on the nature of the captive. But the mail from Rome showed no sense of urgency. They spent their time finding out if the prisoner had a navel, if his dialect had any connection with Aramaic, how many times he could fit on the head of a pin, or whether he wasn't just a Norwegian with wings. Those meager letters might have come and gone until the end of time if a providential event had not put an end to the priest's tribulations.

It so happened that during those days, among so many other carnival attractions, there arrived in town the traveling show of the woman who had been changed into a spider for having disobeyed her parents. The admission to see her was not only less than the admission to see the angel, but people were permitted to ask her all manner of questions about her absurd state and to examine her up and down so that no one would ever doubt the truth of her honor. She was a frightful tarantula the size of a ram and with the head of a sad maiden. What was most heart-rending, however, was not her outlandish shape but the sincere affliction with which she recounted the details of her misfortune. While still practically a child she had sneaked out of her parents' house to go to a dance, and while she was coming back through the woods after having danced all night without permission, a fearful thunderclap rent the sky in two and through the crack came the lightning bolt of brimstone that changed her into a spider. Her only nourishment came from the meatballs that charitable souls chose to toss into her mouth. A spectacle like that, full of so much human truth and with such a fearful lesson, was found to defeat without even trying that of a haughty angel who scarcely deigned to look at mortals. Besides, the few miracles attributed to the angel showed a certain mental disorder, like the blind man who didn't recover his sight but grew three new teeth, or the paralytic who didn't get to walk, but almost won the lottery, and the leper whose sores sprouted sunflowers. Those consolation miracles, which were more like mocking fun, had already ruined the angel's reputation when the woman who had been changed into a spider finally crushed him completely. That was how Father Gonzaga was cured forever of his insomnia and Pelayo's courtyard went back to being as empty as during the time it had rained for three days and crabs walked through the bedrooms.

The owners of the house had no reason to lament. With the money they saved they built a two-story mansion with balconies and gardens and high netting so that crabs wouldn't get in during the winter, and with iron bars on the windows so that angels wouldn't get in. Pelayo also set up a rabbit warren close to town and gave up his job as bailiff for good, and Elisenda bought some satin pumps with high heels and many dresses of iridescent silk, the kind worn on Sunday by the most desirable women in those times. The chicken coop was the only thing that didn't receive any attention. If they washed it down with creolin and burned tears of myrrh inside it every so often, it was not in homage to the angel but to drive away the dungheap stench that still hung everywhere like a ghost and was turning the new house into an old one. At first, when the child learned to walk, they were careful that he not get too close to the chicken coop. But then they began to lose their fears and got used to the smell, and before the child got his second teeth he'd gone inside the chicken coop to play, where the wires were falling apart. The angel was no less standoffish with him than with other mortals, but he tolerated the most ingenious infamies with the patience of a dog who had no illusions. They both came down with chicken pox at the same time. The doctor who took care of the child couldn't resist the temptation to listen to the angel's heart, and he found so much whistling in the heart and so many sounds in his kidneys that it seemed impossible for him to be alive. What surprised him most, however, was the logic of his wings. They seemed so natural on that completely human organism that he couldn't understand why other men didn't have them too.

When the child began school it had been some time since the sun and rain had caused the collapse of the chicken coop. The angel went dragging himself about here and there like a stray dying man. They would drive him out of the bedroom with a broom and a moment later find him in the kitchen. He seemed to be in so many places at the same time that they grew to think that he'd been duplicated, that he was reproducing himself all through the house, and the exasperated and unhinged Elisenda shouted that it was awful living in that hell full of angels. He could scarcely eat and his antiquarian eyes had also become so foggy that he went about bumping into posts. All he had left were the bare cannulae[2] of his last feathers. Pelayo threw a blanket over him and extended him the charity of letting him sleep in the shed, and only then did they notice that he had a temperature at night, and was delirious with the tongue twisters of an old Norwegian. That was one of the few times they became alarmed, for they thought he was going to die and not even the wise neighbor woman had been able to tell them what to do with dead angels.

---

[2]*cannulae:* the tubular pieces by which feathers are attached to a body.

And yet he not only survived his worst winter, but seemed improved with the first sunny days. He remained motionless for several days in the farthest corner of the courtyard, where no one would see him, and at the beginning of December some large, stiff feathers began to grow on his wings, the feathers of a scarecrow, which looked more like another misfortune of decrepitude. But he must have known the reason for those changes, for he was quite careful that no one should notice them, that no one should hear the sea chanteys that he sometimes sang under the stars. One morning Elisenda was cutting some bunches of onions for lunch when a wind that seemed to come from the high seas blew into the kitchen. Then she went to the window and caught the angel in his first attempts at flight. They were so clumsy that his fingernails opened a furrow in the vegetable patch and he was on the point of knocking the shed down with the ungainly flapping that slipped on the light and couldn't get a grip on the air. But he did manage to gain altitude. Elisenda let out a sigh of relief, for herself and for him, when she saw him pass over the last houses, holding himself up in some way with the risky flapping of a senile vulture. She kept watching him even when she was through cutting the onions and she kept on watching until it was no longer possible for her to see him, because then he was no longer an annoyance in her life but an imaginary dot on the horizon of the sea.

—*1968*

*Ursula K. Le Guin (b. 1929), the daughter of an anthropologist and a folklorist, is often called a science fiction writer because of classics like* The Left Hand of Darkness *(1969) and the* Earthsea *books; but her work might best be termed speculative fiction, in which she ponders important questions about the meaning of culture, gender, language, and survival. She uses a variety of techniques such as fantasy, realism, and magic realism in her novels and collections of short fiction, which include* The Compass Rose *(1982) and* Changing Planes *(2003). Le Guin has also published many works for children and collections of poetry, including* Incredible Good Fortune: New Poems *(2006).*

# Ursula K. Le Guin
## Sur[1]

A Summary Report of the *Yelcho* Expedition
to the Antarctic, 1909–1910

Although I have no intention of publishing this report, I think it would be nice if a grandchild of mine, or somebody's grandchild, happened to find it some day; so I shall keep it in the leather trunk in the attic, along with Rosita's christening dress and Juanito's silver rattle and my wedding shoes and finneskos.[2]

The first requisite for mounting an expedition—money—is normally the hardest to come by. I grieve that even in a report destined for a trunk in the attic of a house in a very quiet suburb of Lima I dare not write the name of the generous benefactor, the great soul without whose unstinting liberality the *Yelcho*[3] Expedition would never have been more than the idlest excursion into daydream. That our equipment was the best and most modern—that our provisions were plentiful and fine—that a ship of the Chilean Government, with her brave officers and gallant crew, was twice sent halfway round the world for our convenience: all this is due to that benefactor whose name, alas! I must not say, but whose happiest debtor I shall be till death.

When I was little more than a child my imagination was caught by a newspaper account of the voyage of the *Belgica*, which, sailing south from Tierra del Fuego, became beset by ice in the Bellingshausen Sea

---

[1]*Sur:* Spanish for "south."
[2]*finneskos:* reindeer-skin boots.
[3]*Yelcho:* Chilean steamer that later rescued the stranded crew of Ernest Shackleton in 1916.

and drifted a whole year with the floe, the men aboard her suffering a great deal from want of food and from the terror of the unending winter darkness. I read and reread that account, and later followed with excitement the reports of the rescue of Dr. Nordenskjold from the South Shetland Isles by the dashing Captain Irizar of the *Uruguay*; and the adventures of the *Scotia* in the Weddell Sea. But all these exploits were

### The Map in the Attic[4]

[4]The female explorers rename places after women such as pioneer British nurse **Florence Nightingale** (1820–1910), or South American figures such as **Concolorcorvo**, pseudonym of Alonso Carrio de la Vandera (1715–1778), who wrote *El Lazarillo: A Guide for Inexperienced Travellers;* **Garcilaso** (1539–1616), writer and son of a Spanish conquistador and Inca princess; Spanish poet **Ercilla** (1533–1595); and South American revolutionaries **Francisco de Miranda** (1750–1816) and **Simon Bolivar** (1783–1830). The treeless plains of South America are called **pampas.**

to me but forerunners of the British National Antarctic Expedition of 1902–1904, in the *Discovery*; and the wonderful account of that expedition by Captain Scott.[5] This book, which I ordered from London and reread a thousand times, filled me with longing to see with my own eyes that strange continent, last Thule of the South, which lies on our maps and globes like a white cloud, a void, fringed here and there with scraps of coastline, dubious capes, supposititious islands, headlands that may or may not be there: Antarctica. And the desire was as pure as the polar snows: to go, to see—no more, no less. I deeply respect the scientific accomplishments of Captain Scott's expedition, and have read with passionate interest the findings of physicists, meteorologists, biologists, etc.; but having had no training in any science, nor any opportunity for such training, my ignorance obliged me to forego any thought of adding to the body of scientific knowledge concerning Antarctica; and the same is true for all the members of my expedition. It seems a pity; but there was nothing we could do about it. Our goal was limited to observation and exploration. We hoped to go a little farther, perhaps, and see a little more; if not, simply to go and to see. A simple ambition, I think, and essentially a modest one.

Yet it would have remained less than an ambition, no more than a longing, but for the support and encouragement of my dear cousin and friend Juana —— ——. (I use no surnames, lest this report fall into strangers' hands at last, and embarrassment or unpleasant notoriety thus be brought upon unsuspecting husbands, sons, etc.) I had lent Juana my copy of *The Voyage of the Discovery*, and it was she who, as we strolled beneath our parasols across the Plaza de Armas after Mass one Sunday in 1908, said, "Well, if Captain Scott can do it, why can't we?"

It was Juana who proposed that we write Carlota —— in Valparaiso. Through Carlota we met our benefactor, and so obtained our money, our ship, and even the plausible pretext of going on retreat in a Bolivian convent, which some of us were forced to employ (while the rest of us said we were going to Paris for the winter season). And it was my Juana who in the darkest moments remained resolute, unshaken in her determination to achieve our goal.

[5]*Captain Scott:* British explorer Robert Falcon Scott (1866–1912) made two expeditions to Antarctica, the second ending in death.

And there were dark moments, especially in the early months of 1909—times when I did not see how the Expedition would ever become more than a quarter ton of pemmican gone to waste and a lifelong regret. It was so very hard to gather our expeditionary force together! So few of those we asked even knew what we were talking about—so many thought we were mad, or wicked, or both! And of those few who shared our folly, still fewer were able, when it came to the point, to leave their daily duties and commit themselves to a voyage of at least six months, attended with not inconsiderable uncertainty and danger. An ailing parent; an anxious husband beset by business cares; a child at home with only ignorant or incompetent servants to look after it: these are not responsibilities lightly to be set aside. And those who wished to evade such claims were not the companions we wanted in hard work, risk, and privation.

But since success crowned our efforts, why dwell on the setbacks and delays, or the wretched contrivances and downright lies that we all had to employ? I look back with regret only to those friends who wished to come with us but could not, by any contrivance, get free—those we had to leave behind to a life without danger, without uncertainty, without hope.

On the seventeenth of August, 1909, in Punta Arenas, Chile, all the members of the Expedition met for the first time: Juana and I, the two Peruvians; from Argentina, Zoe, Berta, and Teresa; and our Chileans, Carlota and her friends Eva, Pepita, and Dolores. At the last moment I had received word that Maria's husband, in Quito, was ill, and she must stay to nurse him, so we were nine, not ten. Indeed, we had resigned ourselves to being but eight, when, just as night fell, the indomitable Zoe arrived in a tiny pirogue manned by Indians, her yacht having sprung a leak just as it entered the Strait of Magellan.

That night before we sailed we began to get to know one another; and we agreed, as we enjoyed our abominable supper in the abominable seaport inn of Punta Arenas, that if a situation arose of such urgent danger that one voice must be obeyed without present question, the unenviable honor of speaking with that voice should fall first upon myself: if I were incapacitated, upon Carlota: if she, then upon Berta. We three were then toasted as "Supreme Inca," "La Araucana," and "The Third Mate," among a lot of laughter and cheering. As it came out, to my very great pleasure and relief, my qualities as a "leader" were never tested; the nine of us worked things out amongst us from beginning to end without any orders being given by anybody, and only two or three times with recourse to a vote by voice or show of hands. To be sure, we argued a good deal. But then, we had time to argue. And one way or another the arguments always ended up in a decision, upon which action could be taken. Usually at least one person grumbled about the decision, sometimes bitterly. But what is life without grumbling, and the occasional opportunity to say, "I told you so"? How could one bear housework, or looking after babies, let alone the rigors of sledge-hauling in Antarctica, without grumbling? Officers—as we came to understand aboard the *Yelcho*—are forbidden to grumble; but we nine were, and are, by birth and upbringing, unequivocally and irrevocably, all crew.

Though our shortest course to the southern continent, and that originally urged upon us by the captain of our good ship, was to the South Shetlands and the Bellingshausen Sea, or else by the South Orkneys into the Weddell Sea, we planned to sail west to the Ross Sea, which Captain Scott had explored and described, and from which the brave Ernest Shackleton had returned only the previous autumn. More was known about this region than any other portion of the coast of Antarctica, and though that more was not much, yet it served as some insurance of the safety of the ship, which we felt we had no right to imperil. Captain Pardo had fully agreed with us after studying the charts and our planned itinerary; and so it was westward that we took our course out of the Strait next morning.

Our journey half round the globe was attended by fortune. The little *Yelcho* steamed cheerily along through gale and gleam, climbing up and down those seas of the Southern Ocean that run unbroken round the world. Juana, who had fought bulls and the far more dangerous cows on her family's *estancia,*[6] called the ship *"la vaca valiente,"* because she always returned to the charge. Once we got over being seasick we all enjoyed the sea voyage, though oppressed at times by the kindly but officious protectiveness of the captain and his officers, who felt that we were only "safe" when huddled up in the three tiny cabins which they had chivalrously vacated for our use.

---

[6]*estancia:* Spanish for ranch.
[7]*"la vaca valiente":* the courageous cow.

We saw our first iceberg much farther south than we had looked for it, and saluted it with Veuve Clicquot at dinner. The next day we entered the ice pack, the belt of floes and bergs, broken loose from the land ice and winter-frozen seas of Antarctica, which drifts northward in the spring. Fortune still smiled on us: our little steamer, incapable, with her unreinforced metal hull, of forcing a way into the ice, picked her way from lane to lane without hesitation, and on the third day we were through the pack, in which ships have sometimes struggled for weeks and been obliged to turn back at last. Ahead of us now lay the dark grey waters of the Ross Sea, and beyond that, on the horizon, the remote glimmer, the cloud-reflected whiteness of the Great Ice Barrier.

Entering the Ross Sea a little east of Longitude West 160°, we came in sight of the Barrier at the place where Captain Scott's party, finding a bight in the vast wall of ice, had gone ashore and sent up their hydrogen-gas balloon for reconnaissance and photography. The towering face of the Barrier, its sheer cliffs and azure and violet water-worn caves, all were as described, but the location had changed: instead of a narrow bight there was a considerable bay, full of the beautiful and terrific orca whales playing and spouting in the sunshine of that brilliant southern spring.

Evidently masses of ice many acres in extent had broken away from the Barrier (which—at least for most of its vast extent—does not rest on land but floats on water) since the *Discovery*'s passage in 1902. This put our plan to set up camp on the Barrier itself in a new light; and while we were discussing alternatives, we asked Captain Pardo to take the ship west along the Barrier face towards Ross Island and McMurdo Sound. As the sea was clear of ice and quite calm, he was happy to do so, and, when we sighted the smoke plume of Mount Erebus, to share in our celebration—another half case of Veuve Clicquot.

The *Yelcho* anchored in Arrival Bay, and we went ashore in the ship's boat. I cannot describe my emotions when I set foot on the earth, on that earth, the barren, cold gravel at the foot of the long volcanic slope. I felt elation, impatience, gratitude, awe, familiarity. I felt that I was home at last. Eight Adélie penguins immediately came to greet us with many exclamations of interest not unmixed with disapproval. "Where on earth have you been? What took you so long? The Hut is around this way. Please come this way. Mind the rocks!" They insisted on our going to visit Hut Point, where the large structure built by Captain Scott's party stood, looking just as in the photographs and drawings that illustrate his book. The area about it, however, was disgusting—a kind of graveyard of seal skins, seal bones, penguin bones, and rubbish, presided over by the mad, screaming skua gulls. Our escorts waddled past the slaughterhouse in all tranquillity, and one showed me personally to the door, though it would not go in.

The interior of the hut was less offensive, but very dreary. Boxes of supplies had been stacked up into a kind of room within the room; it did not look as I had imagined it when the *Discovery* party put on their melodramas and minstrel shows in the long winter night. (Much later, we learned that Sir Ernest had rearranged it a good deal when he was there just a year before us.) It was dirty, and had about it a mean disorder. A pound tin of tea was standing open. Empty meat tins lay about; biscuits were spilled on the floor; a lot of dog turds were underfoot— frozen, of course, but not a great deal improved by that. No doubt the last occupants had had to leave in a hurry, perhaps even in a blizzard. All the same, they could have closed the tea tin. But housekeeping, the art of the infinite, is no game for amateurs.

Teresa proposed that we use the hut as our camp. Zoe counterproposed that we set fire to it. We finally shut the door and left it as we had found it. The penguins appeared to approve, and cheered us all the way to the boat.

McMurdo Sound was free of ice, and Captain Pardo now proposed to take us off Ross Island and across to Victoria Land, where we might camp at the foot of the Western Mountains, on dry and solid earth. But those mountains, with their storm-darkened peaks and hanging cirques and glaciers, looked as awful as Captain Scott had found them on his western journey, and none of us felt much inclined to seek shelter among them.

Aboard the ship that night we decided to go back and set up our base as we had originally planned, on the Barrier itself. For all available reports indicated that the clear way south was across the level Barrier surface until one could ascend one of the confluent glaciers to the high plateau which appears to form the whole interior of the continent. Captain Pardo argued strongly against this plan, asking what would become of us if the Barrier "calved"—if our particular acre of ice broke away and started to drift northward. "Well," said Zoe, "then you won't have to come so far to meet us." But he was so persuasive on this theme that he persuaded himself into leaving one of the *Yelcho*'s boats with us when we camped, as a means of escape. We found it useful for fishing, later on.

My first steps on Antarctic soil, my only visit to Ross Island, had not been pleasure unalloyed. I thought of the words of the English poet:

> *Though every prospect pleases,*
> *And only Man is vile.*[8]

But then, the backside of heroism is often rather sad; women and servants know that. They know also that the heroism may be no less real for that. But achievement is smaller than men think. What is large is the sky, the earth, the sea, the soul. I looked back as the ship sailed east again that evening. We were well into September now, with ten hours or more of daylight. The spring sunset lingered on the twelve-thousand-foot peak of Erebus and shone rosy gold on her long plume of steam. The steam from our own small funnel faded blue on the twilit water as we crept along under the towering pale wall of ice.

On our return to "Orca Bay"—Sir Ernest, we learned years later, had named it the Bay of Whales—we found a sheltered nook where the Barrier edge was low enough to provide fairly easy access from the ship. The *Yelcho* put out her ice anchor, and the next long, hard days were spent in unloading our supplies and setting up our camp on the ice, a half kilometer in from the edge: a task in which the *Yelcho*'s crew lent us invaluable aid and interminable advice. We took all the aid gratefully, and most of the advice with salt.

The weather so far had been extraordinarily mild for spring in this latitude; the temperature had not yet gone below $-20°$ Fahrenheit, and there was only one blizzard while we were setting up camp. But Captain Scott had spoken feelingly of the bitter south winds on the Barrier, and we had planned accordingly. Exposed as our camp was to every wind, we built no rigid structures above ground. We set up tents to shelter in while we dug out a series of cubicles in the ice itself, lined them with hay insulation and pine boarding, and roofed them with canvas over bamboo poles, covered with snow for weight and insulation. The big central room was instantly named Buenos Aires by our Argentineans, to whom the center, wherever one is, is always Buenos Aires. The heating

[8]*And only Man is vile:* lines from the hymn "From Greenland's Icy Mountains" (1819) by Reginald Heber.

and cooking stove was in Buenos Aires. The storage tunnels and the privy (called Punta Arenas) got some back heat from the stove. The sleeping cubicles opened off Buenos Aires, and were very small, mere tubes into which one crawled feet first; they were lined deeply with hay and soon warmed by one's body warmth. The sailors called them "coffins" and "wormholes," and looked with horror on our burrows in the ice. But our little warren or prairie-dog village served us well, permitting us as much warmth and privacy as one could reasonably expect under the circumstances. If the *Yelcho* was unable to get through the ice in February, and we had to spend the winter in Antarctica, we certainly could do so, though on very limited rations. For this coming summer, our base—Sudamérica del Sur, South South America, but we generally called it the Base—was intended merely as a place to sleep, to store our provisions, and to give shelter from blizzards.

To Berta and Eva, however, it was more than that. They were its chief architect-designers, its most ingenious builder-excavators, and its most diligent and contented occupants, forever inventing an improvement in ventilation, or learning how to make skylights, or revealing to us a new addition to our suite of rooms dug in the living ice. It was thanks to them that our stores were stowed so handily, that our stove drew and heated so efficiently, and that Buenos Aires, where nine people cooked, ate, worked, conversed, argued, grumbled, painted, played the guitar and banjo, and kept the Expedition's library of books and maps, was a marvel of comfort and convenience. We lived there in real amity; and if you simply had to be alone for a while, you crawled into your sleeping hole head first.

Berta went a little farther. When she had done all she could to make South South America livable, she dug out one more cell just under the ice surface, leaving a nearly transparent sheet of ice like a greenhouse roof; and there, alone, she worked at sculptures. They were beautiful forms, some like a blending of the reclining human figure with the subtle curves and volumes of the Weddell seal, others like the fantastic shapes of ice cornices and ice caves. Perhaps they are there still, under the snow, in the bubble in the Great Barrier. There where she made them they might last as long as stone. But she could not bring them north. That is the penalty for carving in water.

Captain Pardo was reluctant to leave us, but his orders did not permit him to hang about the Ross Sea indefinitely, and so at last, with many earnest injunctions to us to stay put—make no journeys—take no risks—beware of frostbite—don't use edge tools—look out for cracks in the ice—and a heartfelt promise to return to Orca Bay on the twentieth of February, or as near that date as wind and ice would permit, the good man bade us farewell, and his crew shouted us a great goodbye cheer as they weighed anchor. That evening, in the long orange twilight of October, we saw the topmast of the *Yelcho* go down the north horizon, over the edge of the world, leaving us to ice, and silence, and the Pole.

That night we began to plan the Southern Journey.

The ensuing month passed in short practice trips and depot-laying. The life we had led at home, though in its own way strenuous, had not fitted any of us for the kind of strain met with in sledge-hauling at ten or twenty degrees below freezing. We all needed as much working-out as possible before we dared undertake a long haul.

My longest exploratory trip, made with Dolores and Carlota, was southwest towards Mount Markham, and it was a nightmare—blizzards and pressure ice all the way out, crevasses and no view of the mountains when we got there, and white weather and sastrugi[9] all the way back. The trip was useful, however, in that we could begin to estimate our capacities; and also in that we had started out with a very heavy load of provisions, which we depoted at 100 and 130 miles SSW of Base. Thereafter other parties pushed on farther, till we had a line of snow cairns and depots right down to Latitude 83° 43', where Juana and Zoe, on an exploring trip, had found a kind of stone gateway opening on a great glacier leading south. We established these depots to avoid, if possible, the hunger that had bedevilled Captain Scott's Southern Party, and the consequent misery and weakness. And we also established to our own satisfaction—intense satisfaction—that we were sledgehaulers at least as good as Captain Scott's husky dogs. Of course we could not have expected to pull as much or as fast as his men. That we did so was because we were favored by much better weather than Captain Scott's party ever met on the Barrier; and also the quantity and quality of our food made a very considerable difference. I am sure that the fifteen percent of dried fruits in our pemmican helped prevent scurvy; and the potatoes, frozen and dried according to an ancient Andean Indian method, were very nourishing yet very light and compact—perfect

---

[9]*sastrugi:* wind-formed ridges of snow.

sledging rations. In any case, it was with considerable confidence in our capacities that we made ready at last for the Southern Journey.

The Southern Party consisted of two sledge teams: Juana, Dolores, and myself; Carlota, Pepita, and Zoe. The support team of Berta, Eva, and Teresa set out before us with a heavy load of supplies, going right up onto the glacier to prospect routes and leave depots of supplies for our return journey. We followed five days behind them, and met them returning between Depot Ercilla and Depot Miranda (see map). That "night"—of course there was no real darkness—we were all nine together in the heart of the level plain of ice. It was the fifteenth of November, Dolores's birthday. We celebrated by putting eight ounces of pisco in the hot chocolate, and became very merry. We sang. It is strange now to remember how thin our voices sounded in that great silence. It was overcast, white weather, without shadows and without visible horizon or any feature to break the level; there was nothing to see at all. We had come to that white place on the map, that void, and there we flew and sang like sparrows.

After sleep and a good breakfast the Base Party continued north, and the Southern Party sledged on. The sky cleared presently. High up, thin clouds passed over very rapidly from southwest to northeast, but down on the Barrier it was calm and just cold enough, five or ten degrees below freezing, to give a firm surface for hauling.

On the level ice we never pulled less than eleven miles, seventeen kilometers, a day, and generally fifteen or sixteen miles, twenty-five kilometers. (Our instruments, being British made, were calibrated in feet, miles, degrees Fahrenheit, etc., but we often converted miles to kilometers because the larger numbers sounded more encouraging.) At the time we left South America, we knew only that Mr. Shackleton had mounted another expedition to the Antarctic in 1908, had tried to attain the Pole but failed, and had returned to England in June of the current year, 1909. No coherent report of his explorations had yet reached South America when we left; we did not know what route he had gone, or how far he had got. But we were not altogether taken by surprise when, far across the featureless white plain, tiny beneath the mountain peaks and the strange silent flight of the rainbow-fringed cloud wisps, we saw a fluttering dot of black. We turned west from our course to visit it: a snow heap nearly buried by the winter's storms—a flag on a bamboo pole, a mere shred of threadbare cloth—an empty oilcan—and a few footprints standing some inches above the ice. In some conditions of weather the snow compressed under one's weight remains when the surrounding soft snow melts or is scoured away by the wind; and so these reversed footprints had been left standing all these months, like rows of cobbler's lasts—a queer sight.

We met no other such traces on our way. In general I believe our course was somewhat east of Mr. Shackleton's. Juana, our surveyor, had trained herself well and was faithful and methodical in her sightings and readings, but our equipment was minimal—a theodolite on tripod legs, a sextant with artificial horizon, two compasses, and chronometers. We had only the wheel meter on the sledge to give distance actually travelled.

In any case, it was the day after passing Mr. Shackleton's waymark that I first saw clearly the great glacier among the mountains to the southwest, which was to give us a pathway from the sea level of the Barrier up to the altiplano, ten thousand feet above. The approach was magnificent: a gateway formed by immense vertical domes and pillars of rock. Zoe and Juana had called the vast ice river that flowed through that gateway the Florence Nightingale Glacier, wishing to honor the British, who had been the inspiration and guide of our expedition; that very brave and very peculiar lady seemed to represent so much that is best, and strangest, in the island race. On maps, of course, this glacier bears the name Mr. Shackleton gave it, the Beardmore.

The ascent of the Nightingale was not easy. The way was open at first, and well marked by our support party, but after some days we came among terrible crevasses, a maze of hidden cracks, from a foot to thirty feet wide and from thirty to a thousand feet deep. Step by step we went, and step by step, and the way always upward now. We were fifteen days on the glacier. At first the weather was hot, up to 20° F., and the hot nights without darkness were wretchedly uncomfortable in our small tents. And all of us suffered more or less from snowblindness just at the time when we wanted clear eyesight to pick our way among the ridges and crevasses of the tortured ice, and to see the wonders about and before us. For at every day's advance more great, nameless peaks came into view in the west and southwest, summit beyond summit, range beyond range, stark rock and snow in the unending noon.

We gave names to these peaks, not very seriously, since we did not expect our discoveries to come to the attention of geographers. Zoe had a gift for naming, and it is thanks to her that certain sketch maps in various suburban South American attics bear such curious features as "Bolívar's Big Nose," "I Am General Rosas," "The Cloudmaker," "Whose Toe?" and "Throne of Our Lady of the Southern Cross." And when at last we got up onto the altiplano, the great interior plateau, it was Zoe who called it the pampa, and maintained that we walked there among vast herds of invisible cattle, transparent cattle pastured on the spindrift snow, their gauchos, the restless, merciless winds. We were by then all a little crazy with exhaustion and the great altitude—twelve thousand feet—and the cold and the wind blowing and the luminous circles and crosses surrounding the suns, for often there were three or four suns in the sky, up there.

That is not a place where people have any business to be. We should have turned back; but since we had worked so hard to get there, it seemed that we should go on, at least for a while.

A blizzard came with very low temperatures, so we had to stay in the tents, in our sleeping bags, for thirty hours, a rest we all needed; though it was warmth we needed most, and there was no warmth on that terrible plain anywhere at all but in our veins. We huddled close together all that time. The ice we lay on is two miles thick.

It cleared suddenly and became, for the plateau, good weather: twelve below zero and the wind not very strong. We three crawled out of our tent and met the others crawling out of theirs. Carlota told us then that her group wished to turn back. Pepita had been feeling very ill; even after the rest during the blizzard, her temperature would not rise above 94°. Carlota was having trouble breathing. Zoe was perfectly fit, but much preferred staying with her friends and lending them a hand in difficulties to pushing on towards the Pole. So we put the four ounces of pisco which we had been keeping for Christmas into the breakfast cocoa, and dug out our tents, and loaded our sledges, and parted there in the white daylight on the bitter plain.

Our sledge was fairly light by now. We pulled on to the south. Juana calculated our position daily. On the twenty-second of December, 1909, we reached the South Pole. The weather was, as always, very cruel. Nothing of any kind marked the dreary whiteness. We discussed leaving some kind of mark or monument, a snow cairn, a tent pole and flag; but there seemed no particular reason to do so. Anything we could do, anything we were, was insignificant, in that awful place. We put up the tent for shelter for an hour and made a cup of tea, and then struck

"90° Camp."[10] Dolores, standing patient as ever in her sledging harness, looked at the snow; it was so hard frozen that it showed no trace of our footprints coming, and she said, "Which way?"

"North," said Juana.

It was a joke, because at that particular place there is no other direction. But we did not laugh. Our lips were cracked with frostbite and hurt too much to let us laugh. So we started back, and the wind at our backs pushed us along, and dulled the knife edges of the waves of frozen snow.

All that week the blizzard wind pursued us like a pack of mad dogs. I cannot describe it. I wished we had not gone to the Pole. I think I wish it even now. But I was glad even then that we had left no sign there, for some man longing to be first might come some day, and find it, and know then what a fool he had been, and break his heart.

We talked, when we could talk, of catching up to Carlota's party, since they might be going slower than we. In fact they had used their tent as a sail to catch the following wind and had got far ahead of us. But in many places they had built snow cairns or left some sign for us; once Zoe had written on the lee side of a ten-foot sastrugi, just as children write on the sand of the beach at Miraflores, "This Way Out!" The wind blowing over the frozen ridge had left the words perfectly distinct.

In the very hour that we began to descend the glacier, the weather turned warmer, and the mad dogs were left to howl forever tethered to the Pole. The distance that had taken us fifteen days going up we covered in only eight days going down. But the good weather that had aided us descending the Nightingale became a curse down on the Barrier ice, where we had looked forward to a kind of royal progress from depot to depot, eating our fill and taking our time for the last three hundred-odd miles. In a tight place on the glacier I lost my goggles—I was swinging from my harness at the time in a crevasse—and then Juana had broken hers when we had to do some rock climbing coming down to the Gateway. After two days in bright sunlight with only one pair of snow goggles to pass amongst us, we were all suffering badly from snowblindness. It became acutely painful to keep lookout for landmarks or depot flags, to take sightings, even to study the compass, which had to be laid down on the snow to steady the needle. At Concolorcorvo Depot, where there was a particularly good

[10] *"90° camp"*: location of the South Pole at 90 degrees latitude, 0 degrees longitude.

supply of food and fuel, we gave up, crawled into our sleeping bags with bandaged eyes, and slowly boiled alive like lobsters in the tent exposed to the relentless sun. The voices of Berta and Zoe were the sweetest sound I ever heard. A little concerned about us, they had skied south to meet us. They led us home to Base.

We recovered quite swiftly, but the altiplano left its mark. When she was very little, Rosita asked if a dog "had bitted Mama's toes." I told her Yes, a great, white, mad dog named Blizzard! My Rosita and my Juanito heard many stories when they were little, about that fearful dog and how it howled, and the transparent cattle of the invisible gauchos, and a river of ice eight thousand feet high called Nightingale, and how Cousin Juana drank a cup of tea standing on the bottom of the world under seven suns, and other fairy tales.

We were in for one severe shock when we reached Base at last. Teresa was pregnant. I must admit that my first response to the poor girl's big belly and sheepish look was anger—rage—fury. That one of us should have concealed anything, and such a thing, from the others! But Teresa had done nothing of the sort. Only those who had concealed from her what she most needed to know were to blame. Brought up by servants, with four years' schooling in a convent, and married at sixteen, the poor girl was still so ignorant at twenty years of age that she had thought it was "the cold weather" that made her miss her periods. Even this was not entirely stupid, for all of us on the Southern Journey had seen our periods change or stop altogether as we experienced increasing cold, hunger, and fatigue. Teresa's appetite had begun to draw general attention; and then she had begun, as she said pathetically, "to get fat." The others were worried at the thought of all the sledge-hauling she had done, but she flourished, and the only problem was her positively insatiable appetite. As well as could be determined from her shy references to her last night on the hacienda with her husband, the baby was due at just about the same time as the *Yelcho*, the twentieth of February. But we had not been back from the Southern Journey two weeks when, on February 14, she went into labor.

Several of us had borne children and had helped with deliveries, and anyhow most of what needs to be done is fairly self-evident; but a first labor can be long and trying, and we were all anxious, while Teresa was frightened out of her wits. She kept calling for her José till she was as hoarse as a skua. Zoe lost all patience at last and said, "By God, Teresa, if you say 'José!' once more I hope you have a penguin!" But what she had, after twenty long hours, was a pretty little red-faced girl.

Many were the suggestions for that child's name from her eight proud midwife-aunts: Polita, Penguina, McMurdo, Victoria. . . . But Teresa announced, after she had had a good sleep and a large serving of pemmican, "I shall name her Rosa—Rosa del Sur," Rose of the South. That night we drank the last two bottles of Veuve Clicquot (having finished the pisco at 88° 30' South) in toasts to our little Rose.

On the nineteenth of February, a day early, my Juana came down into Buenos Aires in a hurry. "The ship," she said, "the ship has come," and she burst into tears—she who had never wept in all our weeks of pain and weariness on the long haul.

Of the return voyage there is nothing to tell. We came back safe.

In 1912 all the world learned that the brave Norwegian Amundsen[11] had reached the South Pole; and then, much later, came the accounts of how Captain Scott and his men had come there after him, but did not come home again.

Just this year, Juana and I wrote to the captain of the *Yelcho*, for the newspapers have been full of the story of his gallant dash to rescue Sir Ernest Shackleton's men from Elephant Island, and we wished to congratulate him, and once more to thank him. Never one word has he breathed of our secret. He is a man of honor, Luis Pardo.

I add this last note in 1929. Over the years we have lost touch with one another. It is very difficult for women to meet, when they live so far apart as we do. Since Juana died, I have seen none of my old sledge-mates, though sometimes we write. Our little Rosa del Sur died of the scarlet fever when she was five years old. Teresa had many other children. Carlota took the veil in Santiago ten years ago. We are old women now, with old husbands, and grown children, and grandchildren who might some day like to read about the Expedition. Even if they are rather ashamed of having such a crazy grandmother, they may enjoy sharing in the secret. But they must not let Mr. Amundsen know! He would be terribly embarrassed and disappointed. There is no need for him or anyone else outside the family to know. We left no footprints, even.

*—1982*

[11]*Amundsen:* Roald Amundsen (1872–1928) of Norway was the first man to reach the South Pole, on December 14, 1911.

*Timothy Findley (1930–2002) was born in Toronto, and moved from an acting to a writing career that included ten novels, three short-story collections, and several plays. Violence and the human struggle to survive it have been among his most enduring subjects, from his third novel,* The Wars *(1977), which earned him his first Governor General's Award, to this story from the collection* Stones *(1988). Whether in work that is self-reflexive and surreal or work that is more closely tied to history, Findley maintains that fiction is all about "achieving the clarity obscured by facts."*

# Timothy Findley
## Stones

We lived on the outskirts of Rosedale, over on the wrong side of Yonge Street. This was the impression we had, at any rate. Crossing the streetcar tracks put you in another world.

One September, my sister, Rita, asked a girl from Rosedale over to our house after school. Her name was Allison Pritchard and she lived on Cluny Drive. When my mother telephoned to see if Allison Pritchard could stay for supper, Mrs Pritchard said she didn't think it would be appropriate. That was the way they talked in Rosedale: very polite; oblique and cruel.

Over on our side—the west side—of Yonge Street, there were merchants—and this, apparently, made the difference to those whose houses were in Rosedale. People of class were not meant to live in the midst of commerce.

Our house was on Gibson Avenue, a cul-de-sac with a park across the road. My bedroom window faced a hockey rink in winter and a football field in summer. Cy, my brother, was a star in either venue. I was not. My forte, then, was the tricycle.

Up at the corner, there was an antique store on one side and a variety shop on the other. In the variety shop, you could spend your allowance on penny candy, Eskimo pies and an orange drink I favoured then called *Stubby*. *Stubby* came in short, fat bottles and aside from everything else—the thick orange flavour and the ginger in the bubbles —there was something wonderfully satisfying in the fact that it took both hands to hold it up to your lips and tip it down your throat.

Turning up Yonge Street, beyond the antique store, you came to The Women's Bakery, Adam's Grocery, Oskar Schickel, the butcher and

Max's Flowers. We were Max's Flowers. My mother and my father wore green aprons when they stood behind the counter or went back into the cold room where they made up wreaths for funerals, bouquets for weddings and corsages for dances at the King Edward Hotel. Colonel Matheson, retired, would come in every morning on his way downtown and pick out a boutonnière from the jar of carnations my mother kept on the counter near the register. Once, when I was four, I caused my parents untold embarrassment by pointing out that Colonel Matheson had a large red growth on the end of his nose. The "growth" was nothing of the sort, of course, but merely the result of Colonel Matheson's predilection for gin.

Of the pre-war years, my overall memory is one of perfect winters, heavy with snow and the smell of coal- and wood-smoke mingling with the smell of bread and cookies rising from The Women's Bakery. The coal-smoke came from our furnaces and the wood-smoke—mostly birch and maple—came to us from the chimneys of Rosedale, where it seemed that every house must have a fireplace in every room.

Summers all smelled of grass being cut in the park and burning tar from the road crews endlessly patching the potholes in Yonge Street. The heat of these summers was heroic and the cause of many legends. Mister Schickel, the butcher, I recall once cooked an egg on the sidewalk outside his store. My father, who was fond of Mister Schickel, made him a bet of roses it could not be done. I think Mister Schickel's part of the bet was pork chops trimmed of excess fat. When the egg began to sizzle, my father slapped his thigh and whistled and he sent my sister, Rita, in to get the flowers. Mister Schickel, however, was a graceful man and when he placed his winnings in the window of his butcher shop, he also placed a card that read: *Thanks to Max's Flowers one dozen roses.*

The Great Depression held us all in thrall, but its effects on those of us who were used to relative poverty—living on the west side of Yonge Street—were not so debilitating as they were on the far side in Rosedale. The people living there regarded money as something you had—as opposed to something you went out and got—and they were slower to adjust to what, for them, was the unique experience of deprivation.

I remember, too, that there always seemed to be a tramp at the door: itinerants asking if—for the price of a meal, or the meal itself—they could carry out the ashes, sweep the walks or pile the baskets and pails in which my father brought his flowers from the market and the greenhouse.

Our lives continued in this way until about the time I was five—in August of 1939. Everyone's life, I suppose, has its demarcation lines—its latitudes and longitudes passing through time. Some of these lines define events that everyone shares—others are confined to personal—even to secret lives. But the end of summer 1939 is a line drawn through the memory of everyone who was then alive. We were all about to be pitched together into a melting pot of violence from which a few of us would emerge intact and the rest of us would perish.

My father joined the army even before the war had started. He went downtown one day and didn't come back till after suppertime. I noticed that he hadn't taken the truck but had ridden off on the streetcar. I asked my mother why he had worn his suit on a weekday and she replied *because today is special.* But that was all she said.

At the table, eating soufflé and salad, my brother, Cy—who was nine years old that summer—talked about the World's Fair in New York City and pictures he'd seen of the future in magazines. The Great World's Fair was a subject that had caught all our imaginations with its demonstrations of new appliances, aeroplanes and motor cars. Everything was "streamlined" in 1939; everything designed with swept-back lines as if we were all preparing to shoot off into space. Earlier that summer, the King and Queen of England had come to Canada, riding on a streamlined train whose blue-painted engine was sleek and slim as something in a silver glove. In fact, the King and Queen had arrived in Toronto just up Yonge Street from where we lived. We got permission from the Darrow family, who lived over Max's Flowers, to stand on the roof and watch the parade with its Mounties in scarlet and its Black Watch Band and the King and Queen, all blue and white and smiling, sitting in an open Buick called a *McLaughlin—built,* according to Cy, *right here in Canada!* For one brief moment while all these symbols of who we were went marching past, the two communities—one on either side of Yonge Street—were united in a surge of cheering and applause. But after the King and Queen were gone, the ribbon of Yonge Street divided us again. It rained.

Now, Cy and Rita were arguing over the remnants in the soufflé dish. Cy held the classic belief that what was in the dish was his by virtue of his being the eldest child. He also held the classic belief that girls were meant to be second in everything. Rita, who was always hungry but never seemed to gain an ounce, held none of these beliefs and was capable of fighting Cy for hours on end when our parents weren't present. With Mother at the table, however, the argument was silenced by her announcement that the soufflé dish and all the delicious bits of cheese and egg that clung to its sides would be set aside for our father.

Then—or shortly thereafter—our father did indeed arrive, but he said he wasn't hungry and he wanted to be left alone with Mother.

In half an hour the children were called from the kitchen where we had been doing the dishes and scooping up the remains of the meal. I— the child my mother called *The Rabbit*—had been emptying the salad bowl, stuffing my mouth with lettuce, tomatoes and onion shards and nearly choking in the process. We all went into the sitting-room with food on our lips and tea towels in our hands: Father's three little Maxes —Cy and Rita and Ben. He looked at us then, as he always did, with a measure of pride he could never hide and a false composure that kept his lips from smiling, but not his eyes. I look back now on that moment with some alarm when I realize my father was only twenty-seven years old—an age I have long survived and doubled.

"Children, I have joined the army," he said—in his formal way, as if we were his customers. "I am going to be a soldier."

Our mother had been weeping before we entered the room, but she had dried her eyes because she never allowed us to witness her tears. Now, she was smiling and silent. After a moment, she left the room and went out through the kitchen into the garden where, in the twilight, she found her favourite place and sat in a deck-chair amidst the flowers.

Cy, for his part, crowed with delight and yelled with excitement. He wanted to know if the war would last until he was a man and could join our father at the front.

Father, I remember, told him the war had not yet begun and the reason for his enlistment was precisely so that Cy and I could not be soldiers. "There will be no need for that," he said.

Cy was immensely disappointed. He begged our father to make the war go on till 1948, when he would be eighteen.

Our father only laughed at that.

"The war," he said, "will be over in 1940."

I went out then and found our mother in the garden.

"What will happen to us while he's away?" I asked.

"Nothing," she said. And then she said: "come here."

I went and leaned against her thigh and she put her arm around my shoulder and I could smell the roses somewhere behind us. It was getting dark.

"Look up there," she said. "The stars are coming out. Why don't you count them?"

This was her way of distracting me whenever my questions got out of hand. Either she told me to count the stars or go outside and dig for China. *There's a shovel in the shed*, she would tell me. *You get started and I will join you.* Just as if we would be in China and back by suppertime.

But that night in August, 1939, I wasn't prepared to bite. I didn't want to dig for China and I didn't want to count the stars. I'd dug for China so many times and had so many holes in the yard that I knew I would never arrive; it was much too far and, somehow, she was making a fool of me. As for the stars: "I counted them last night," I told her. "And the night before."

"Oh?" she said—and I felt her body tense, though she went on trying to inject a sense of ease when she spoke. "So tell me," she said. "How many are there?"

"Twelve," I said.

"Ah," she said. And sighed. "Just twelve. I thought there might be more than twelve."

"I mean twelve zillion," I said with great authority.

"Oh," she said. "I see. And you counted them all?"

"Unh-hunh."

For a moment she was quiet. And then she said: "what about that one there?"

One week later, the war began. But my father had already gone.

On the 14th of February, 1943, my father was returned. He came back home from the war. He did this on a Sunday and I recall the hush that fell upon our house, as indeed it seemed to have fallen over all the city. Only the sparrows out in the trees made sound.

We had gone downtown to the Exhibition Grounds to meet him. The journey on the streetcar took us over an hour, but Mother had splurged and hired a car and driver to take us all home. The car, I remember, embarrassed me. I was afraid some friend would see me being driven— sitting up behind a chauffeur.

A notice had come that told us the families of all returning soldiers would be permitted to witness their arrival. I suspect the building they used for this was the one now used to house the Royal Winter Fair and other equestrian events. I don't remember what it was called and I'm not inclined to inquire. It was enough that I was there that once—and once remains enough.

We sat in the bleachers, Cy and Rita and Mother and me, and there was a railing holding us back. There must have been over a thousand people waiting to catch a glimpse of someone they loved—all of them parents, children or wives of the men returning. I was eight years old that February—almost nine and feeling I would never get there. Time was like a field of clay and all the other children I knew appeared to have cleared it in a single bound while I was stuck in the mud and barely able to lift my feet. I hated being eight and dreaded being nine. I wanted to be ten—the only dignified age a child could be, it seemed to me. Cy, at ten, had found a kind of silence I admired to the point of worship. Rita, who in fact was ten that year and soon to be eleven, had also found a world of silence in which she kept her self secreted—often behind closed doors. Silence was a sign of valour.

The occasion was barely one for public rejoicing. The men who were coming home were mostly casualties whose wounds, we had been warned, could be distressing and whose spirit, we had equally been warned, had been damaged in long months of painful recuperation. Plainly, it was our job to lift their spirits and to deny the severity of their wounds. Above all else, they must not be allowed to feel they could not rejoin society at large. A man with no face must not be stared at.

Our father's wounds were greater by far than we had been told. There was not a mark on his body, but—far inside—he had been destroyed. His mind had been severely damaged and his spirit had been broken. No one had told me what this might have made of him. No one had said *he may never be kind again.* No one had said *he will never sleep again without the aid of alcohol.* No one had said *he will try to kill your mother.* No one had said *you will not be sure it's him when you see him.* Yet all these things were true.

I had never seen a military parade without a band. The effect was eerie and upsetting. Two or three officers came forward into the centre of the oval. Somebody started shouting commands and a sergeant-major, who could not yet be seen, was heard outside the building counting off the steps.

I wanted drums. I wanted bugles. Surely this ghostly, implacable sound of marching feet in the deadening sand was just a prelude to everyone standing up and cheering and the music blaring forth. But, no. We all stood up, it is true, the minute the first of the columns rounded the wooden corner of the bleachers and came into sight. But no one uttered a sound. One or two people threw their hands up over their mouths—as if to stifle cries—but most of us simply stood there—staring in disbelief.

Nurses came with some of the men, supporting them. Everyone was pale in the awful light—and the colours of their wounds and bruises were garish and quite unreal. There was a predominance of yellow flesh and dark maroon scars and of purple welts and blackened scabs. Some men wore bandages—some wore casts and slings. Others used canes and crutches to support themselves. A few had been the victims of fire, and these wore tight, blue skull-caps and collarless shirts and their faces and other areas of uncovered skin were bright with shining ointments and dressings.

It took a very great while for all these men and women—perhaps as many as two hundred of them—to arrive inside the building and make their way into the oval. They were being lined up in order of columns—several long lines, and each line punctuated here and there with attendant nurses. The voices of the sergeant-major and of the adjutant who was taking the parade were swallowed up in the dead acoustics, and—far above us—pigeons and sparrows moved among the girders and beams that supported the roof. I still had not seen Father.

At last, because my panic was spreading out of control, I tugged my mother's elbow and whispered that I couldn't see him. Had there been a mistake and he wasn't coming at all?

"No," she told me—looking down at me sideways and turning my head with her ungloved fingers. "There he is, there," she said. "But don't say anything yet. He may not know we're here."

My father's figure could only be told because of his remarkable height. He was six feet four and had always been, to me, a giant. But now his height seemed barely greater than the height of half a dozen other men who were gathered out in the sand. His head was bowed, though once or twice he lifted his chin when he heard the commands.

His shoulders, no longer squared, were rounded forward and dipping towards his centre. His neck was so thin I thought that someone or something must have cut over half of it away. I studied him solemnly and then looked up at my mother.

She had closed her eyes against him because she could not bear to look.

Later on that night, when everyone had gone to bed but none of us had gone to sleep, I said to Cy: "what is it?"

"What?"

"That's happened to Dad. . . ."

Cy didn't answer for a moment and then he said: "Dieppe."

I didn't understand. I thought it was a new disease.

We were told the next day not to mention at school that our father had come back home. Nothing was said about why it must be kept a secret. That was a bitter disappointment. Other children whose fathers had returned from overseas were always the centre of attention. Teachers, beaming smiles and patting heads, would congratulate them just as if they had won a prize. Classmates pestered them with questions: *what does he look like? Have you seen his wounds? How many Germans did he kill?* But we had none of this. All we got was: *what did you do on the weekend?*

*Nothing.*

All day Monday, Father remained upstairs. Our parents' bedroom was on the second floor directly over the sitting-room. Also, directly underneath the bedroom occupied by Cy and me. We had heard our mother's voice long into the night, apparently soothing him, telling him over and over again that everything was going to be all right.

We could not make out her words, but the tone of her voice was familiar. Over time, she had sat with each of us, deploying her comforts in all the same cadences and phrases, assuring us that pains and aches and sicknesses would pass.

Because we could not afford to lose the sale of even one flower, neither the single rose bought once a week by Edna Holmes to cheer her ailing sister, nor the daily boutonnière of Colonel Matheson—our mother had persuaded Mrs Adams, the grocer's wife, to tend the store while she "nipped home" once every hour to see to Father's needs.

It was only later that we children realized what those needs entailed. He was drinking more or less constantly in every waking hour, and our mother's purpose was first to tempt him with food—which he refused— and then to make certain that his matches and cigarettes did not set fire to the house.

On the Wednesday, Father emerged from his shell around two o'clock in the afternoon. We were all at school, of course, and I have only the account of what follows from my mother. When she returned at two, Mother found that Father had come down into the hallway, fully dressed in civilian clothes. He had already donned his greatcoat when she arrived. She told me that, at first, he had seemed to be remarkably sober. He told her he wanted to go outside and walk in the street. He wanted to go and see the store, he said.

"But you can't wear your greatcoat, David," she told him.

"Why?"

"Because you're in civilian dress. You know that's not allowed. A man was arrested just last week."

"I wasn't here last week," said my father.

"Nevertheless," my mother told him, "this man was arrested because it is not allowed."

"But I'm a soldier!" my father yelled.

My mother had to play this scene with all the care and cunning she could muster. The man who had been arrested had been a deserter. All that winter, desertions had been increasing and there had been demon- strations of overt disloyalty. People had shouted *down with the King!* and had booed the Union Jack. There were street gangs of youths who called themselves *Zombies* and they hung around the Masonic Temple on Yonge Street and the Palais Royale at Sunnyside. Some of these young men were in uniform, members of the Home Guard: reserves who had been promised, on joining up, they would not be sent overseas. They may have disapproved of the war, but they did not disapprove of fighting. They waited outside the dancehalls, excessively defensive of their manhood, challenging the servicemen who were dancing inside to *come out fighting and show us your guts!* Men had been killed in such encounters and the encounters had been increasing. The government was absolutely determined to stamp these incidents out before they spread across the country. These were the darkest hours of the war and morale, both in and out of the Forces, was at its lowest ebb. If my father had appeared on the street with his military greatcoat worn over his civilian clothes, it would have been assumed he was a *Zombie* or a deserter and he would have been arrested instantly. Our neighbours would have turned him in, no matter who he was. Our patriotism had come to that.

"I don't have a civilian overcoat," my father said. "And don't suggest that I put on my uniform, because I won't. My uniform stinks of sweat and I hate it."

"Well, you aren't going out like that," my mother said. "That's all there is to it. Why not come to the kitchen and I'll fix you a sandwich. . . ."

"I don't want a goddamned sandwich," my father yelled at her. "I want to see the store!"

At this point, he tore off his greatcoat and flung it onto the stairs. And then, before my mother could prevent him, he was out the door and running down the steps.

My mother—dressed in her green shop apron and nothing but a scarf to warm her—raced out after him.

What would the neighbours think? What would the neighbours say? How could she possibly explain?

By the time she had reached the sidewalk, my father had almost reached the corner. But, when she got to Yonge Street, her fears were somewhat allayed. My father had not gone into Max's Flowers but was standing one door shy of it, staring into the butcher's window.

"What's going on here?" he said, as my mother came abreast of him.

Mother did not know what he meant.

"Where is Mister Schickel, Lily?" he asked her.

She had forgotten that, as well.

"Mister Schickel has left," she told him—trying to be calm—trying to steer my father wide of the butcher's window and in towards their own front stoop.

"Left?" my father shouted. "He's only just managed to pay off his mortgage! And who the hell is this imposter, Reilly?"

"Reilly?"

"Arthur Reilly the bloody butcher!" My father pointed at and read the sign that had replaced *Oskar Schickel, Butcher* in the window.

"Mister Reilly has been there most of the winter, David. Didn't I write and tell you that?" She knew very well she hadn't.

My father blinked at the meagre cuts of rationed meat displayed beyond the glass and said: "what happened to Oskar, Lily? Tell me."

And so, she had to tell him, like it or not.

Mister Schickel's name was disagreeable—stuck up there on Yonge Street across from Rosedale—and someone from Park Road had thrown a stone through the window.

There. It was said.

"But Oskar wasn't a German," my father whispered. "He was a Canadian."

"But his name was German, David."

My father put his fingers against the glass and did not appear to respond to what my mother had said.

At last my mother pulled at his arm. "Why not come back home," she said. "You can come and see the shop tomorrow."

My father, while my mother watched him, concentrated very hard and moved his finger over the dusty glass of Oskar Schickel's store.

"What are you doing, David?"

"Nothing," said my father. "Setting things right, that's all."

Then he stepped back and said to her: "now—we'll go home."

What he had written was:

*Oskar Schickel: Proprietor in absentia.*

Mother said that Mrs Reilly rushed outside as soon as they had reached the corner and she washed the window clean.

This was the only remaining decent thing my father did until the day he died.

The rest was all a nightmare.

I had never seen Dieppe. I had seen its face in photographs. I had read all the books and heard all the stories. The battle, of which my father had been a victim, had taken place in August of 1942—roughly six months before he was returned to us. Long since then, in my adult years, I have seen that battle, or seen its parts, through the medium of documentary film. It was only after Cy and Rita had vetted these films that I was able to watch. Till then, I had been afraid I would catch my father's image unawares—fearful that somehow our eyes would meet in that worst of moments. I couldn't bear the thought of seeing him destroyed. So, I had seen all this—the photographs, the books, the films—but I had never seen the town of Dieppe itself until that day in May of 1987 when I took my father's ashes there to scatter them.

Before I can begin this ending, I have to make it clear that the last thing I want to provoke is the sentimental image of a wind-blown stretch of rocky beach with a rainbow of ashes arching over the stones and blowing out to sea. If you want that image, let me tell you that had been the way it was when Cy, my brother, and Rita, my sister, and I went walking, wading into the ocean south of Lunenburg, Nova Scotia— where our mother had been born—to cast her ashes into the air above the Atlantic. Then there was almost music and we rejoiced because our mother had finally gained her freedom from a life that had become intolerable. But in Dieppe, when I shook my father's ashes out of their envelope, there was no rejoicing. None.

I felt, in fact, as if I had brought the body of an infidel into a holy place and laid it down amongst the true believers. Still, this was what my father had wanted—and how could I refuse him? Neither Cy nor Rita would do it for him. *Gone*, they had said. *Good riddance.*

And so it fell to me.

I was always the least informed. I was always the most inquisitive. During my childhood, nobody told me—aside from the single word *Dieppe*—what it was that had happened to my father. And yet, perhaps because I knew the least and because I was the youngest and seemed the most naïve and willing, it was more than often me he focused on.

His tirades would begin in silence—the silence we had been warned of when he first returned. He would sit at the head of the table, eating a piece of fish and drinking from a glass of beer. The beer was always dark in colour. Gold.

Our dining-room had a window facing west. Consequently, winter sunsets in particular got in his eyes.

*Curtain*, he would say at his plate—and jab his fork at me.

If I didn't understand because his mouth was full, my mother would reach my sleeve and pull it with her fingers. *The curtain, Ben*, she would say. *Your father's eyes.*

*Yes, ma'am.* Down I'd get and pull the curtain.

Then, no sooner would I be reseated than my father—still addressing his plate—would mumble *lights*. And I would rise and turn on the lights. Then, when I was back at last in my chair, he would look at me and say, without apparent rancour, *why don't you tell me to shove the goddamn curtain up my ass?*

You will understand my silence in response to this if you understand that—before he went away—the worst my father had ever said in our presence had been *damn* and *hell*. The ultimate worst had been *Christ!* when he'd nearly sliced his finger off with a knife. Then, however, he hadn't known that anyone was listening. And so, when he started to talk this way—and perhaps especially at table—it paralyzed me.

Cy or Mother would sometimes attempt to intervene, but he always cut them off with something worse than he'd said to me. Then he would turn his attention back in my direction and continue. He urged me to refuse his order, then to upbraid him, finally to openly defy him—call him the worst of the words he could put in my mouth and hit him. Of course, I never did any of these things, but the urging, the cajoling and ultimately the begging never ceased.

One night, he came into the bedroom where I slept in the bunk-bed over Cy and he shouted at me *why don't you fight back?* Then he dragged my covers off and threw me onto the floor against the bureau. All this was done in the dark, and after my mother had driven me down in the truck to the Emergency Ward of Wellesley Hospital, the doctors told her that my collar-bone was broken. I heard my mother saying *yes, he fell out of bed.*

Everyone—even I—conspired to protect him. The trouble was, my father had no wish to protect himself. At least, it seemed that way until a fellow veteran of Dieppe turned up one day in the shop and my father turned on him with a pair of garden shears and tried to drive him back onto Yonge Street. Far from being afraid of my father, the other man took off his jacket and threw it in my father's face and all the while he stood there, the man was yelling at my father: *Coward! Coward! Yellow Bastard!*

Then, he turned around and walked away. The victor.

Thinking for sure the police would come, my mother drew the blind and closed the shop for the rest of the day.

But that was not the end of it. She gathered us together out on the porch and Cy was told to open a can of pork and beans and to make what our mother called a *passel of toast.* He and Rita and I were to eat this meal in the kitchen, after which Cy, who'd been handed a dollar bill my mother had lifted from the till, was to take us down to the Uptown

Theatre where an Abbott and Costello film was playing. All these ordinary things we did. Nonetheless, we knew that our father had gone mad.

It was summer then and when the movie was over, I remember Cy and Rita and I stood on the street and the sidewalks gave off heat and the air around us smelled of peanuts and popcorn and Cy said: "I don't think it's safe to go home just yet." For almost an hour, we wandered on Yonge Street, debating what we should do and, at last, we decided we would test the waters by going and looking at the house and listening to see if there was any yelling.

Gibson Avenue only has about twenty houses, most of them semi-detached—and all of them facing south and the park. The porches and the stoops that night were filled with our neighbours drinking beer from coffee cups and fanning themselves with paper plates and folded bits of the *Daily Star.* They were drinking out of cups—you could smell the beer—because the law back then forbade the public consumption, under any circumstance, of alcohol. Whatever you can hide does not exist.

Passing, we watched our neighbours watching us—the Matlocks and the Wheelers and the Conrads and the Bolts—and we knew they were thinking *there go the Max kids and David Max, their father, tried to kill a man today in his store with gardening shears. . . .*

"Hello, Cy."

"Hello."

"Ben. Rita."

"Hi."

"Good-night . . ."

We went and stood together on the sidewalk out in front of our house.

Inside, everything seemed to be calm and normal. The lights were turned on in their usual distribution—most of them downstairs. The radio was playing. Someone was singing *Praise the Lord and Pass the Ammunition.*

Cy went up the steps and turned the handle. He was brave—but I'd always known that. Rita and I were told to wait on the porch.

Two minutes passed—or five—or ten—and finally Cy returned. He was very white and his voice was dry, but he wasn't shaking and all he said was: "you'd best come in. I'm calling the police."

Our father had tried to kill our mother with a hammer. She was lying on the sofa and her hands were broken because she had used them trying to fend off the blows.

Father had disappeared. The next day, he turned himself in because, as he told the doctors, he had come to his senses. He was kept for a year and a half—almost until the war was over—at the Asylum for the Insane on Queen Street. None of us children was allowed to visit him there—but our mother went to see him six months after he had been committed. She told me they sat in a long, grey room with bars on all the windows. My father wore a dressing gown and hadn't shaved. Mother said he couldn't look her in the eyes. She told him that she forgave him for what he had done. But my father never forgave himself. My mother said she never saw his eyes again.

Two weeks after our father had tried to kill our mother, a brick was thrown through the window of Max's Flowers. On the brick, a single word was printed in yellow chalk.

*Murderer.*

Mother said: "there's no way around this, now. I'm going to have to explain."

That was how we discovered what had gone wrong with our father at Dieppe.

Our mother had known this all along, and I still have strong suspicions Cy had found it out and maybe Rita before our mother went through the formal procedure of sitting us down and telling us all together. Maybe they had thought I was just too young to understand. Maybe Cy and maybe Rita hadn't known. Maybe they had only guessed. At any rate, I had a very strong sense that I was the only one who received our mother's news in a state of shock.

Father had risen, since his enlistment in 1939, all the way up from an NCO to the rank of captain. Everyone had adored him in the army. He was what they called a natural leader. His men were particularly fond of him and they would, as the saying goes, have followed him anywhere. Then came Dieppe. All but a handful of those who went into battle there were Canadians. This was our Waterloo. Our Gettysburg.

There isn't a single history book you can read—there isn't a single man who was there who won't tell you—there isn't a single scrap of evidence in any archive to suggest that the battle of Dieppe was anything but a total and appalling disaster. Most have called it a slaughter.

Dieppe is a port and market town on the coast of Normandy in northern France. In 1942, the British High Command had chosen it to be the object of a practice raid in preparation for the invasion of Europe. The Allies on every front were faltering, then. A gesture was needed, and even the smallest of victories would do.

And so, on the 19th of August, 1942, the raid on Dieppe had taken place—and the consequent carnage had cost the lives of over a thousand Canadians. Over two thousand were wounded or taken prisoner. Five thousand set out; just over one thousand came back.

My father never left his landing craft.

He was to have led his men ashore in the second wave of troops to follow the tanks—but, seeing the tanks immobilized, unable to move because the beaches were made of stone and the stones had jammed the tank tracks—and seeing the evident massacre of the first wave of troops whose attempt at storming the shore had been repulsed by machine-gun fire from the cliffs above the town—my father froze in his place and could not move. His men—it is all too apparent—did not know what to do. They had received no order to advance and yet, if they stayed, they were sitting ducks.

In the end, though a handful escaped by rushing forward into the water, the rest were blown to pieces when their landing craft was shelled. In the meantime, my father had recovered enough of his wits to crawl back over the end of the landing craft, strip off his uniform and swim out to sea where he was taken on board a British destroyer sitting offshore.

The destroyer, H.M.S. *Berkley*, was ultimately hit and everyone on board, including my father—no one knowing who he was—was transferred to another ship before the *Berkley* was scuttled where she sat. My father made it all the way back to England, where his burns and wounds were dressed and where he debated taking advantage of the chaos to disappear, hoping that, in the long run, he would be counted among the dead.

His problem was, his conscience had survived. He stayed and, as a consequence, he was confronted by survivors who knew his story. He was dishonourably discharged and sent home to us. Children don't understand such things. The only cowards they recognize are figures cut from comic books or seen on movie screens.

Fathers cannot be cowards.

It is impossible.

His torment and his grief were to lead my father all the way to the grave. He left our mother, in the long run, though she would not have wished him to do so and he lived out his days in little bars and back-street beer parlours, seeking whatever solace he could find with whores and derelicts whose stories might have matched his own. The phone would ring and we would dread it. Either it was him or news of him—either his drunken harangue or the name of his most recent jail.

He died in the Wellesley Hospital, the place where I was born—and when he was dying he asked to see his children. Cy and Rita "could not be reached," but I was found—where he'd always found me—sitting within yelling distance. Perhaps this sounds familiar to other children—of whatever age—whose parents, whether one of them or both of them, have made the mistake of losing faith too soon in their children's need to love.

I would have loved a stone.

If only he had known.

He sensed it, maybe, in the end. He told me he was sorry for every-thing—and meant it. He told me the names of all his men and he said he had walked with them all through hell, long since their deaths, to do them honour. He hoped they would understand him, now.

I said they might.

He asked if his ashes could be put with theirs.

*Why not*, I thought. *A stone among stones.*

The beaches at Dieppe can throw you off balance. The angle at which they slope into the water is both steep and dangerous. At high tide you can slide into the waves and lose your footing before you've remembered how to swim. The stones are treacherous. But they are also beautiful.

My father's ashes were contraband. You can't just walk about with someone's remains, in whatever form, in your suitcase. Stepping off the *Sealink* ferry, I carried my father in an envelope addressed to myself in Canada. This was only in case I was challenged. There was hardly more than a handful of him there. I had thrown the rest of him into the English Channel as the coast of Normandy was coming into view. It had been somewhat more than disconcerting to see the interest his ashes caused amongst the gulls and other sea birds. I had hoped to dispose of him in a private way, unnoticed. But a woman with two small children came and stood beside me at the railing and I heard her explain that *this nice gentleman is taking care of our feathered friends.* I hoped that, if my father was watching, he could laugh. I had to look away.

The ferry arrived in the early afternoon and—once I had booked myself into La Présidence Hotel—I went for a walk along the promenade above the sea-wall. It being May, the offshore breeze was warm and filled with the faintest scent of apple trees in bloom.

I didn't want to relive the battle. I hadn't come to conjure ghosts. But the ghosts and the battle are palpable around you there, no matter what your wishes are. The sound of the tide rolling back across the stones is all the cue you need to be reminded of that summer day in 1942. I stood that evening, resting my arms along the wall and thinking *at last, my father has come ashore.*

In the morning, before the town awoke, I got up in the dark and was on the beach when the sun rose inland beyond the cliffs. I wore a thick woollen sweater, walking shorts and a pair of running shoes. The envelope was in my pocket.

The concierge must have thought I was just another crazy North American off on my morning run. He grunted as I passed and I pretended not to know that he was there. Out on the beach, I clambered over retaining walls and petrified driftwood until I felt I was safely beyond the range of prying eyes.

The stones at Dieppe are mostly flint—and their colours range from white through yellow to red. The red stones look as if they have been washed in blood and the sight of them takes your breath away. I hunkered down above them, holding all that remained of my father in my fist. He felt like a powdered stone—pummelled and broken.

I let him down between my fingers, feeling him turn to paste—watching him divide and disappear.

He is dead and he is gone.

Weekends, our parents used to take us walking under the trees on Crescent Road. This was on the Rosedale side of Yonge Street. My brother Cy and I were always dressed in dark blue suits whose rough wool shorts would chafe against our thighs. Our knee socks—also blue—were turned down over thick elastic garters. Everything itched and smelled of Sunday. Cy had cleats on his shoes because he walked in such a way as to wear his heels *to the bone,* as my mother said—and causing much expense. The cleats made a wondrous clicking noise and you could always hear him coming. I wanted cleats, but I was refused because, no matter how I tried, I couldn't walk like that.

The houses sat up neat as pins beyond their lawns—blank-eyed windows, steaming chimneys—havens of wealth and all the mysteries of wealth.

Father often walked behind us. I don't know why. Mother walked in front with Rita. Rita always wore a dress that was either red or blue beneath her princess coat and in the wintertime she wore a sort of woollen cloche that was tied with a knitted string beneath her chin. Her Mary Jane shoes were just like Shirley Temple's shoes—which, for a while, was pleasing to Rita; then it was not. Rita always had an over-powering sense of image.

After the advent of our father's return, she said from the corner of her mouth one Sunday as we walked on Crescent Road that she and Cy and I had been named as if we were manufactured products: *Cy Max Office Equipment; Rita Max Household Appliances* and *Ben Max Watches*. This, she concluded, was why our father had always walked behind us. Proudly, he was measuring our performance. Now, he had ceased to walk behind us and our mother led us forward dressed in black.

*Tick. Tick. Tick.* That's me. The Ben Max Watch.

I have told our story. But I think it best—and I like it best—to end with all of us moving there beneath the trees in the years before the war. Mister and Mrs David Max out walking with their children any Sunday afternoon in any kind of weather but the rain.

Colonel Matheson, striding down his walk, is caught and forced to grunt acknowledgment that we are there. He cannot ignore us, after all. We have seen him every weekday morning, choosing his boutonnière and buying it from us.

*—1988*

*Chinua Achebe (b. 1930) was born in Ogidi, Nigeria, and, after graduation from University College in Ibadan and study at London University, was employed by the Nigerian Broadcasting Service, where he served for years as a producer. After the appearance of his first novel,* Things Fall Apart, *in 1958 (the title is taken from William Butler Yeats's apocalyptic poem "The Second Coming") he became one of the most widely acclaimed writers to emerge from the former British colonies of Africa. The author of several novels as well as a collection of short stories, Achebe draws heavily on the oral traditions of his native country, but he has been successful in adapting European fictional techniques to deal with subjects like the degradations imposed by colonialism and the relative failure of most post-colonial governments to materially improve on the past for the betterment of the lives of their citizens.*

## Chinua Achebe
# Dead Men's Path

Michael Obi's hopes were fulfilled much earlier than he had expected. He was appointed headmaster of Ndume Central School in January 1949. It had always been an unprogressive school, so the Mission authorities decided to send a young and energetic man to run it. Obi accepted this responsibility with enthusiasm. He had many wonderful ideas and this was an opportunity to put them into practice. He had had sound secondary school education which designated him a "pivotal teacher" in the official records and set him apart from the other headmasters in the mission field. He was outspoken in his condemnation of the narrow views of these older and often less-educated ones.

"We shall make a good job of it, shan't we?" he asked his young wife when they first heard the joyful news of his promotion.

"We shall do our best," she replied. "We shall have such beautiful gardens and everything will be just *modern* and delightful. . . ." In their two years of married life she had become completely infected by his passion for "modern methods" and his denigration of "these old and superannuated people in the teaching field who would be better employed as traders in the Onitsha market." She began to see herself already as the admired wife of the young headmaster, the queen of the school.

The wives of the other teachers would envy her position. She would set the fashion in everything. . . . Then, suddenly, it occurred to her that there might not be other wives. Wavering between hope and fear, she asked her husband, looking anxiously at him.

"All our colleagues are young and unmarried," he said with enthusiasm which for once she did not share. "Which is a good thing," he continued.

"Why?"

"Why? They will give all their time and energy to the school."

Nancy was downcast. For a few minutes she became skeptical about the new school; but it was only for a few minutes. Her little personal misfortune could not blind her to her husband's happy prospects. She looked at him as he sat folded up in a chair. He was stoop-shouldered and looked frail. But he sometimes surprised people with sudden bursts of physical energy. In his present posture, however, all his bodily strength seemed to have retired behind his deep-set eyes, giving them an extraordinary power of penetration. He was only twenty-six, but looked thirty or more. On the whole, he was not unhandsome.

"A penny for your thoughts, Mike," said Nancy after a while, imitating the woman's magazine she read.

"I was thinking what a grand opportunity we've got at last to show these people how a school should be run."

Ndume School was backward in every sense of the word. Mr. Obi put his whole life into the work, and his wife hers too. He had two aims. A high standard of teaching was insisted upon, and the school compound was to be turned into a place of beauty. Nancy's dream-gardens came to life with the coming of the rains, and blossomed. Beautiful hibiscus and allamanda hedges in brilliant red and yellow marked out the carefully tended school compound from the rank neighborhood bushes.

One evening as Obi was admiring his work he was scandalized to see an old woman from the village hobble right across the compound, through a marigold flower-bed and the hedges. On going up there he found faint signs of an almost disused path from the village across the school compound to the bush on the other side.

"It amazes me," said Obi to one of his teachers who had been three years in the school, "that you people allowed the villagers to make use of this footpath. It is simply incredible." He shook his head.

"The path," said the teacher apologetically, "appears to be very important to them. Although it is hardly used, it connects the village shrine with their place of burial."

"And what has that got to do with the school?" asked the headmaster.

"Well, I don't know," replied the other with a shrug of the shoulders. "But I remember there was a big row some time ago when we attempted to close it."

"That was some time ago. But it will not be used now," said Obi as he walked away. "What will the Government Education Officer think of this when he comes to inspect the school next week? The villagers might, for all I know, decide to use the schoolroom for a pagan ritual during the inspection."

Heavy sticks were planted closely across the path at the two places where it entered and left the school premises. These were further strengthened with barbed wire.

Three days later the village priest of *Ani* called on the headmaster. He was an old man and walked with a slight stoop. He carried a stout walking-stick which he usually tapped on the floor, by way of emphasis, each time he made a new point in his argument.

"I have heard," he said after the usual exchange of cordialities, "that our ancestral footpath has recently been closed. . . ."

"Yes," replied Mr. Obi. "We cannot allow people to make a highway of our school compound."

"Look here, my son," said the priest bringing down his walking-stick, "this path was here before you were born and before your father was born. The whole life of this village depends on it. Our dead relatives depart by it and our ancestors visit us by it. But most important, it is the path of children coming in to be born. . . ."

Mr. Obi listened with a satisfied smile on his face.

"The whole purpose of our school," he said finally, "is to eradicate just such beliefs as that. Dead men do not require footpaths. The whole idea is just fantastic. Our duty is to teach your children to laugh at such ideas."

"What you say may be true," replied the priest, "but we follow the practices of our fathers. If you reopen the path we shall have nothing to quarrel about. What I always say is: let the hawk perch and let the eagle perch." He rose to go.

"I am sorry," said the young headmaster. "But the school compound cannot be a thoroughfare. It is against our regulations. I would suggest your constructing another path, skirting our premises. We can even get our boys to help in building it. I don't suppose the ancestors will find the little detour too burdensome."

"I have no more words to say," said the old priest, already outside.

Two days later a young woman in the village died in childbed. A diviner was immediately consulted and he prescribed heavy sacrifices to propitiate ancestors insulted by the fence.

Obi woke up next morning among the ruins of his work. The beautiful hedges were torn up not just near the path but right round the school, the flowers trampled to death and one of the school buildings pulled down. . . . That day, the white Supervisor came to inspect the school and wrote a nasty report on the state of the premises but more seriously about the "tribal-war situation developing between the school and the village, arising in part from the misguided zeal of the new headmaster."

*—1953*

*Alice Munro (b. 1931) was born on a farm in Wingham, Ontario, and educated at the University of Western Ontario, where she received her degree in 1952. Her first book,* Dance of the Happy Shades, *appeared in 1968, and she has continued regularly to publish collections of short stories. Asked about her devotion to short fiction, Munro told* Contemporary Authors: *"I never intended to be a short story writer — I started writing them because I didn't have time to write anything else — I had three children. And then I got used to writing short stories, so I see my materials that way, and now I don't think I'll ever write a novel." Parent–child and marital relations and the discovery of personal freedom are constant themes in Munro's work. Munro has won both the Governor General's Award and the Canadian Booksellers' Award, befitting her status as one of Canada's most distinguished writers.* Selected Stories *appeared in 1996, and* The Love of a Good Woman *was published in 1998. Her collection* Runaway *won the 2004 Giller Prize and she was named one of the world's most influential people in 2005 by* Time *magazine.*

### Alice Munro
# Boys and Girls

My father was a fox farmer. That is, he raised silver foxes, in pens; and in the fall and early winter, when their fur was prime, he killed them and skinned them and sold their pelts to the Hudson's Bay Company or the Montreal Fur Traders. These companies supplied us with heroic calendars to hang, one on each side of the kitchen door. Against a background of cold blue sky and black pine forests and treacherous northern rivers, plumed adventurers planted the flags of England or of France; magnificent savages bent their backs to the portage.

For several weeks before Christmas, my father worked after supper in the cellar of our house. The cellar was whitewashed, and lit by a hundred-watt bulb over the worktable. My brother Laird and I sat on the top step and watched. My father removed the pelt inside-out from the body of the fox, which looked surprisingly small, mean and rat-like, deprived of its arrogant weight of fur. The naked, slippery bodies were collected in a sack and buried at the dump. One time the hired man, Henry Bailey, had taken a swipe at me with this sack, saying, "Christmas present!" My mother thought that was not funny. In fact she disliked the whole pelting operation—that was what the killing, skinning, and preparation of the furs was called—and wished it did not have to take place in the house. There was the smell. After the pelt had been stretched inside-out on a long board my father scraped away delicately, removing the little clotted webs of blood vessels, the bubbles of fat; the smell of blood and animal fat, with the strong primitive odour of the fox itself, penetrated all parts of the house. I found it reassuringly seasonal, like the smell of oranges and pine needles.

Henry Bailey suffered from bronchial troubles. He would cough and cough until his narrow face turned scarlet, and his light blue, derisive eyes filled up with tears; then he took the lid off the stove, and, standing well back, shot out a great clot of phlegm—hsss—straight into the heart of the flames. We admired him for this performance and for his ability to make his stomach growl at will, and for his laughter, which was full of high whistlings and gurglings and involved the whole faulty machinery of his chest. It was sometimes hard to tell what he was laughing at, and always possible that it might be us.

After we had been sent to bed we could still smell fox and still hear Henry's laugh, but these things, reminders of the warm, safe, brightly lit downstairs world, seemed lost and diminished, floating on the stale cold air upstairs. We were afraid at night in the winter. We were not afraid of *outside* though this was the time of year when snowdrifts curled around our house like sleeping whales and the wind harassed us all night, coming up from the buried fields, the frozen swamp, with its old bugbear chorus of threats and misery. We were afraid of *inside*, the room where we slept. At this time the upstairs of our house was not finished. A brick chimney went up one wall. In the middle of the floor was a square hole, with a wooden railing around it; that was where the stairs came up. On the other side of the stairwell were the things that nobody had any use for any more—a soldiery roll of linoleum, standing on end, a wicker baby carriage, a fern basket, china jugs and basins with cracks in them, a picture of the Battle of Balaclava, very sad to look at. I had told Laird, as soon as he was old enough to understand such things, that bats and skeletons lived over there; whenever a man escaped from the county jail, twenty miles away, I imagined that he had somehow let himself in the window and was hiding behind the linoleum. But we had rules to keep us safe. When the light was on, we were safe as long as we did not step off the square of worn carpet which defined our bedroom-space; when the light was off no place was safe but the beds themselves. I had to turn out the light kneeling on the end of my bed, and stretching as far as I could to reach the cord.

In the dark we lay on our beds, our narrow life rafts, and fixed our eyes on the faint light coming up the stairwell, and sang songs. Laird sang "Jingle Bells," which he would sing any time, whether it was Christmas or not, and I sang "Danny Boy." I loved the sound of my own voice, frail and supplicating, rising in the dark. We could make out the tall frosted shapes of the windows now, gloomy and white. When I came to the part, *When I am dead, as dead I well may be*—a fit of shivering caused not by the cold sheets but by pleasurable emotion almost silenced me. *You'll kneel and say, an Ave there above me*—What was an Ave? Every day I forgot to find out.

Laird went straight from singing to sleep. I could hear his long, satisfied, bubbly breaths. Now for the time that remained to me, the most perfectly private and perhaps the best time of the whole day, I arranged myself tightly under the covers and went on with one of the stories I was telling myself from night to night. These stories were about myself, when I had grown a little older; they took place in a world that was recognizably mine, yet one that presented opportunities for courage, boldness and self-sacrifice, as mine never did. I rescued people from a bombed building (it discouraged me that the real war had gone on so far away from Jubilee). I shot two rabid wolves who were menacing the schoolyard (the teachers cowered terrified at my back). I rode a fine horse spiritedly down the main street of Jubilee, acknowledging the townspeople's gratitude for some yet-to-be-worked-out piece of heroism (nobody ever rode a horse there, except King Billy in the Orangemen's Day parade). There was always riding and shooting in these stories, though I had only been on a horse twice—bareback because we did not own a saddle—and the second time I had slid right around and dropped under the horse's feet; it had stepped placidly over me. I really was learning to shoot, but I could not hit anything yet, not even tin cans on fence posts.

Alive, the foxes inhabited a world my father made for them. It was surrounded by a high guard fence, like a medieval town, with a gate that was padlocked at night. Along the streets of this town were ranged large, sturdy pens. Each of them had a real door that a man could go through, a wooden ramp along the wire, for the foxes to run up and down on, and a kennel—something like a clothes chest with airholes—where they slept and stayed in winter and had their young. There were feeding and watering dishes attached to the wire in such a way that they could be emptied and cleaned from the outside. The dishes were made of old tin cans, and the ramps and kennels of odds and ends of old lumber. Everything was tidy and ingenious; my father was tirelessly inventive and his favourite book in the world was *Robinson Crusoe*. He had fitted a tin drum on a wheelbarrow, for bringing water down to the pens. This was my job in summer, when the foxes had to have water twice a day. Between nine and ten o'clock in the morning, and again after supper, I filled the drum at the pump and trundled it down through the barnyard to the pens, where I parked it, and filled my watering can and went along the streets. Laird came too, with his little cream and green gardening can, filled too full and knocking against his legs and slopping water on his canvas shoes. I had the real watering can, my father's, though I could only carry it three-quarters full.

The foxes all had names, which were printed on a tin plate and hung beside their doors. They were not named when they were born, but when they survived the first year's pelting and were added to the breeding stock. Those my father had named were called names like Prince, Bob, Wally and Betty. Those I had named were called Star or Turk, or Maureen or Diana. Laird named one Maud after a hired girl we had when he was little, one Harold after a boy at school, and one Mexico, he did not say why.

Naming them did not make pets out of them, or anything like it. Nobody but my father ever went into the pens, and he had twice had blood-poisoning from bites. When I was bringing them their water they prowled up and down on the paths they had made inside their pens, barking seldom—they saved that for nighttime, when they might get up a chorus of community frenzy—but always watching me, their eyes burning, clear gold, in their pointed, malevolent faces. They were beautiful for their delicate legs and heavy, aristocratic tails and the bright fur sprinkled on dark down their backs—which gave them their name—but especially for their faces, drawn exquisitely sharp in pure hostility, and their golden eyes.

Besides carrying water I helped my father when he cut the long grass, and the lamb's quarter and flowering money-musk, that grew between the pens. He cut with the scythe and I raked into piles. Then he took a pitchfork and threw fresh-cut grass all over the top of the pens, to keep the foxes cooler and shade their coats, which were browned by too much sun. My father did not talk to me unless it was about the job we were doing. In this he was quite different from my mother, who, if she was feeling cheerful, would tell me all sorts of things—the name of a dog she had had when she was a little girl, the names of boys she had gone out with later on when she was grown up, and what certain dresses of hers had looked like—she could not imagine now what had become of them. Whatever thoughts and stories my father had were private, and I was shy of him and would never ask him questions. Nevertheless I worked willingly under his eyes, and with a feeling of pride. One time a feed salesman came down into the pens to talk to him and my father said, "Like to have you meet my new hired man." I turned away and raked furiously, red in the face with pleasure.

"Could of fooled me," said the salesman. "I thought it was only a girl."

After the grass was cut, it seemed suddenly much later in the year. I walked on stubble in the earlier evening, aware of the reddening skies, the entering silences, of fall. When I wheeled the tank out of the gate and put the padlock on, it was almost dark. One night at this time I saw my mother and father standing talking on the little rise of ground we called the gangway, in front of the barn. My father had just come from the meathouse; he had his stiff bloody apron on, and a pail of cut-up meat in his hand.

It was an odd thing to see my mother down at the barn. She did not often come out of the house unless it was to do something—hang out the wash or dig potatoes in the garden. She looked out of place, with her bare lumpy legs, not touched by the sun, her apron still on and damp across the stomach from the supper dishes. Her hair was tied up in a kerchief, wisps of it falling out. She would tie her hair up like this in the morning, saying she did not have time to do it properly, and it would stay tied up all day. It was true, too; she really did not have time. These days our back porch was piled with baskets of peaches and grapes and pears, bought in town, and onions and tomatoes and cucumbers grown at home, all waiting to be made into jelly and jam and preserves, pickles and chili sauce. In the kitchen there was a fire in the stove all day, jars clinked in boiling water, sometimes a cheesecloth bag was strung on a pole between two chairs, straining blue-black grape pulp for jelly. I was given jobs to do and I would sit at the table peeling peaches that had been soaked in the hot water, or cutting up onions, my eyes smarting and streaming. As soon as I was done I ran out of the house, trying to get out of earshot before my mother thought of what she wanted me to do next. I hated the hot dark kitchen in summer, the green blinds and the flypapers, the same old oilcloth table and wavy mirror and bumpy linoleum. My mother was too tired and preoccupied to talk to me, she had no heart to tell about the Normal School Graduation Dance; sweat trickled over her face and she was always counting under her breath, pointing at jars, dumping cups of sugar. It seemed to me that work in the house was endless, dreary and peculiarly depressing; work done out of doors, and in my father's service, was ritualistically important.

I wheeled the tank up to the barn, where it was kept, and I heard my mother saying, "Wait till Laird gets a little bigger, then you'll have a real help."

What my father said I did not hear. I was pleased by the way he stood listening, politely as he would to a salesman or a stranger, but with an air of wanting to get on with his real work. I felt my mother had no business down here and I wanted him to feel the same way. What did she mean about Laird? He was no help to anybody. Where was he now? Swinging himself sick on the swing, going around in circles, or trying to catch caterpillars. He never once stayed with me till I was finished.

"And then I can use her more in the house," I heard my mother say. She had a dead-quiet, regretful way of talking about me that always made me uneasy. "I just get my back turned and she runs off. It's not like I had a girl in the family at all."

I went and sat on a feed bag in the corner of the barn, not wanting to appear when this conversation was going on. My mother, I felt, was not to be trusted. She was kinder than my father and more easily fooled, but you could not depend on her, and the real reasons for the things she said and did were not to be known. She loved me, and she sat up late at night making a dress of the difficult style I wanted, for me to wear when school started, but she was also my enemy. She was always plotting. She was plotting now to get me to stay in the house more, although she knew I hated it (*because* she knew I hated it) and keep me from working for my father. It seemed to me she would do this simply out of perversity, and to try her power. It did not occur to me that she could be lonely, or jealous. No grown-up could be; they were too fortunate. I sat and kicked my heels monotonously against a feedbag, raising dust, and did not come out till she was gone.

At any rate, I did not expect my father to pay any attention to what she said. Who could imagine Laird doing my work—Laird remembering the padlock and cleaning out the watering-dishes with a leaf on the end of a stick, or even wheeling the tank without it tumbling over? It showed how little my mother knew about the way things really were.

I have forgotten to say what the foxes were fed. My father's bloody apron reminded me. They were fed horsemeat. At this time most farmers still kept horses, and when a horse got too old to work, or broke a leg or got down and would not get up, as they sometimes did, the owner would call my father, and he and Henry went out to the farm in the truck. Usually they shot and butchered the horse there, paying the farmer from five to twelve dollars. If they had already too much meat on hand, they would bring the horse back alive, and keep it for a few days or weeks in our stable, until the meat was needed. After the war the farmers were buying tractors and gradually getting rid of horses altogether, so it sometimes happened that we got a good healthy horse, that there was just no use for any more. If this happened in the winter we might keep the horse in our stable till spring, for we had plenty of hay and if there was a lot of snow—and the plow did not always get our road cleared—it was convenient to be able to go to town with a horse and cutter.

The winter I was eleven years old we had two horses in the stable. We did not know what names they had had before, so we called them Mack and Flora. Mack was an old black workhorse, sooty and indifferent. Flora was a sorrel mare, a driver. We took them both out in the cutter. Mack was slow and easy to handle. Flora was given to fits of violent alarm, veering at cars and even at other horses, but we loved her speed and high-stepping, her general air of gallantry and abandon. On Saturdays we went down to the stable and as soon as we opened the door on its cosy, animal-smelling darkness Flora threw up her head, rolled her eyes, whinnied despairingly and pulled herself through a crisis of nerves on the spot. It was not safe to go into her stall; she would kick.

This winter also I began to hear a great deal more on the theme my mother had sounded when she had been talking in front of the barn. I no longer felt safe. It seemed that in the minds of the people around me there was a steady undercurrent of thought, not to be deflected, on this one subject. The word *girl* had formerly seemed to me innocent and unburdened, like the word *child*; now it appeared that it was no such thing. A girl was not, as I had supposed, simply what I was; it was what I had to become. It was a definition, always touched with emphasis, with reproach and disappointment. Also it was a joke on me. Once Laird and I were fighting, and for the first time ever I had to use all my strength against him; even so, he caught and pinned my arm for a moment, really hurting me. Henry saw this, and laughed, saying, "Oh, that there Laird's gonna show you, one of these days!" Laird was getting a lot bigger. But I was getting bigger too.

My grandmother came to stay with us for a few weeks and I heard other things. "Girls don't slam doors like that." "Girls keep their knees together when they sit down." And worse still, when I asked some questions, "That's none of girls' business." I continued to slam the doors and sit as awkwardly as possible, thinking that by such measures I kept myself free.

When spring came, the horses were let out in the barnyard. Mack stood against the barn wall trying to scratch his neck and haunches, but Flora trotted up and down and reared at the fences, clattering her hooves against the rails. Snow drifts dwindled quickly, revealing the hard grey and brown earth, the familiar rise and fall of the ground, plain and bare after the fantastic landscape of winter. There was a great feeling of opening-out, of release. We just wore rubbers now, over our shoes; our feet felt ridiculously light. One Saturday we went out to the stable and found all the doors open, letting in the unaccustomed sunlight and fresh air. Henry was there, just idling around looking at his collection of calendars which were tacked up behind the stalls in a part of the stable my mother had probably never seen.

"Come to say goodbye to your old friend Mack?" Henry said. "Here, you give him a taste of oats." He poured some oats into Laird's cupped hands and Laird went to feed Mack. Mack's teeth were in bad shape. He ate very slowly, patiently shifting the oats around in his mouth, trying to find a stump of a molar to grind it on. "Poor old Mack," said Henry mournfully. "When a horse's teeth's gone, he's gone. That's about the way."

"Are you going to shoot him today?" I said. Mack and Flora had been in the stable so long I had almost forgotten they were going to be shot.

Henry didn't answer me. Instead he started to sing in a high, trembly, mocking-sorrowful voice, *Oh, there's no more work, for poor Uncle Ned, he's gone where the good darkies go.* Mack's thick, blackish tongue worked diligently at Laird's hand. I went out before the song was ended and sat down on the gangway.

I had never seen them shoot a horse, but I knew where it was done. Last summer Laird and I had come upon a horse's entrails before they were buried. We had thought it was a big black snake, coiled up in the sun. That was around in the field that ran up beside the barn. I thought that if we went inside the barn, and found a wide crack or a knothole to look through, we would be able to see them do it. It was not something I wanted to see; just the same, if a thing really happened, it was better to see it, and know.

My father came down from the house, carrying the gun.

"What are you doing here?" he said.

"Nothing."

"Go on up and play around the house."

He sent Laird out of the stable. I said to Laird, "Do you want to see them shoot Mack?" and without waiting for an answer led him around to the front door of the barn, opened it carefully, and went in. "Be quiet or they'll hear us," I said. We could hear Henry and my father talking in the stable, then the heavy, shuffling steps of Mack being backed out of his stall.

In the loft it was cold and dark. Thin, crisscrossed beams of sunlight fell through the cracks. The hay was low. It was a rolling country, hills and hollows, slipping under our feet. About four feet up was a beam going around the walls. We piled hay up in one corner and I boosted Laird up and hoisted myself. The beam was not very wide; we crept along it with our hands flat on the barn walls. There were plenty of knotholes, and I found one that gave me the view I wanted—a corner of the barnyard, the gate, part of the field. Laird did not have a knothole and began to complain.

I showed him a widened crack between two boards. "Be quiet and wait. If they hear you you'll get us in trouble."

My father came in sight carrying the gun. Henry was leading Mack by the halter. He dropped it and took out his cigarette papers and tobacco; he rolled cigarettes for my father and himself. While this was going on Mack nosed around in the old, dead grass along the fence.

Then my father opened the gate and they took Mack through. Henry led Mack away from the path to a patch of ground and they talked together, not loud enough for us to hear. Mack again began searching for a mouthful of fresh grass, which was not to be found. My father walked away in a straight line, and stopped short at a distance which seemed to suit him. Henry was walking away from Mack too, but sideways, still negligently holding on to the halter. My father raised the gun and Mack looked up as if he had noticed something and my father shot him.

Mack did not collapse at once but swayed, lurched sideways and fell, first on his side; then he rolled over on his back and, amazingly, kicked his legs for a few seconds in the air. At this Henry laughed, as if Mack had done a trick for him. Laird, who had drawn a long, groaning breath of surprise when the shot was fired, said out loud, "He's not dead." And it seemed to me it might be true. But his legs stopped, he rolled on his side again, his muscles quivered and sank. The two men walked over and looked at him in a businesslike way; they bent down and examined his forehead where the bullet had gone in, and now I saw his blood on the brown grass.

"Now they just skin him and cut him up," I said. "Let's go." My legs were a little shaky and I jumped gratefully down into the hay. "Now you've seen how they shoot a horse," I said in a congratulatory way, as if I had seen it many times before. "Let's see if any barn cat's had kittens in the hay." Laird jumped. He seemed young and obedient again. Suddenly I remembered how, when he was little, I had brought him into the barn and told him to climb the ladder to the top beam. That was in the spring, too, when the hay was low. I had done it out of a need for excitement, a desire for something to happen so that I could tell about it. He was wearing a little bulky brown and white checked coat, made down from one of mine. He went all the way up, just as I told him, and sat down on the top beam with the hay far below him on one side, and the barn floor and some old machinery on the other. Then I ran screaming to my father, "Laird's up on the top beam!" My father came, my mother came, my father went up the ladder talking very quietly and brought Laird down under his arm, at which my mother leaned against the ladder and began to cry. They said to me, "Why weren't you watching him?" but nobody ever knew the truth. Laird did not know enough to tell. But whenever I saw the brown and white checked coat hanging in the closet, or at the bottom of the rag bag, which was where it ended up, I felt a weight in my stomach, the sadness of unexorcized guilt.

I looked at Laird who did not even remember this, and I did not like the look on this thin, winter-pale face. His expression was not frightened or upset, but remote, concentrating. "Listen," I said, in an unusually bright and friendly voice, "you aren't going to tell, are you?"

"No," he said absently.

"Promise."

"Promise," he said. I grabbed the hand behind his back to make sure he was not crossing his fingers. Even so, he might have a nightmare; it might come out that way. I decided I had better work hard to get all thoughts of what he had seen out of his mind—which, it seemed to me, could not hold very many things at a time. I got some money I had saved and that afternoon we went into Jubilee and saw a show, with Judy Canova, at which we both laughed a great deal. After that I thought it would be all right.

Two weeks later I knew they were going to shoot Flora. I knew from the night before, when I heard my mother ask if the hay was holding out all right, and my father said, "Well, after tomorrow there'll just be the cow, and we should be able to put her out to grass in another week." So I knew it was Flora's turn in the morning.

This time I didn't think of watching it. That was something to see just one time. I had not thought about it very often since, but sometimes when I was busy, working at school, or standing in front of the mirror combing my hair and wondering if I would be pretty when I grew up, the whole scene would flash into my mind: I would see the easy, practised way my father raised the gun, and hear Henry laughing when Mack kicked his legs in the air. I did not have any great feeling of horror and opposition, such as a city child might have had; I was too used to seeing the death of animals as a necessity by which we lived. Yet I felt a little ashamed, and there was a new wariness, a sense of holding-off, in my attitude to my father and his work.

It was a fine day, and we were going around the yard picking up tree branches that had been torn off in winter storms. This was something we had been told to do, and also we wanted to use them to make a teepee. We heard Flora whinny, and then my father's voice and Henry's shouting, and we ran down to the barnyard to see what was going on.

The stable door was open. Henry had just brought Flora out, and she had broken away from him. She was running free in the barnyard, from one end to the other. We climbed up on the fence. It was exciting to see her running, whinnying, going up on her hind legs, prancing and threatening like a horse in a Western movie, an unbroken ranch horse, though she was just an old driver, an old sorrel mare. My father and Henry ran after her and tried to grab the dangling halter. They tried to work her into a corner, and they had almost succeeded when she made a run between them, wild-eyed, and disappeared around the corner of the barn. We heard the rails clatter down as she got over the fence, and Henry yelled, "She's into the field now!"

That meant she was in the long L-shaped field that ran up by the house. If she got around the center, heading towards the lane, the gate was open; the truck had been driven into the field this morning. My father shouted to me, because I was on the other side of the fence, nearest the lane, "Go shut the gate!"

I could run very fast. I ran across the garden, past the tree where our swing was hung, and jumped across a ditch into the lane. There was the open gate. She had not got out, I could not see her up on the road; she must have run to the other end of the field. The gate was heavy. I lifted it out of the gravel and carried it across the roadway. I had it half-way across when she came in sight, galloping straight towards me. There was just time to get the chain on. Laird came scrambling through the ditch to help me.

Instead of shutting the gate, I opened it as wide as I could. I did not make any decision to do this, it was just what I did. Flora never slowed down; she galloped straight past me, and Laird jumped up and down, yelling, "Shut it, shut it!" even after it was too late. My father and Henry appeared in the field a moment too late to see what I had done. They only saw Flora heading for the township road. They would think I had not got there in time.

They did not waste any time asking about it. They went back to the barn and got the gun and the knives they used, and put these in the truck; then they turned the truck around and came bouncing up the field toward us. Laird called to them, "Let me go too, let me go too!" and Henry stopped the truck and they took him in. I shut the gate after they were all gone.

I supposed Laird would tell. I wondered what would happen to me. I had never disobeyed my father before, and I could not understand why I had done it. Flora would not really get away. They would catch up with her in the truck. Or if they did not catch her this morning somebody would see her and telephone us this afternoon or tomorrow. There was no wild country here for her to run to, only farms. What was more, my father had paid for her, we needed the meat to feed the foxes, we needed the foxes to make our living. All I had done was make more work for my father who worked hard enough already. And when my father found out about it he was not going to trust me any more; he would know that I was not entirely on his side. I was on Flora's side, and that made me no use to anybody, not even to her. Just the same, I did not regret it; when she came running at me and I held the gate open, that was the only thing I could do.

I went back to the house, and my mother said, "What's all the commotion?" I told her that Flora had kicked down the fence and got away. "Your poor father," she said, "now he'll have to go chasing over the countryside. Well, there isn't any use planning dinner before one." She put up the ironing board. I wanted to tell her, but thought better of it and went upstairs and sat on my bed.

Lately I had been trying to make my part of the room fancy, spreading the bed with old lace curtains, and fixing myself a dressing-table with some leftovers of cretonne for a skirt. I planned to put up some kind of barricade between my bed and Laird's, to keep my section separate from his. In the sunlight, the lace curtains were just dusty rags. We did not sing at night any more. One night when I was singing Laird said, "You sound silly," and I went right on but the next night I did not start. There was not so much need to anyway, we were no longer afraid. We knew it was just old furniture over there, old jumble and confusion. We did not keep to the rules. I still stayed awake after Laird was asleep and told myself stories, but even in these stories something different was happening, mysterious alterations took place. A story might start off in the old way, with a spectacular danger, a fire or wild animals, and for a while I might rescue people; then things would change around, and instead, somebody would be rescuing me. It might be a boy from our class at school, or even Mr. Campbell, our teacher, who tickled girls under the arms. And at this point the story concerned itself at great length with what I looked like—how long my hair was, and what kind of dress I had on; by the time I had these details worked out the real excitement of the story was lost.

It was later than one o'clock when the truck came back. The tarpaulin was over the back, which meant there was meat in it. My mother had to heat dinner up all over again. Henry and my father had changed from their bloody overalls into ordinary working overalls in the barn, and they washed their arms and necks and faces at the sink, and splashed water on their hair and combed it. Laird lifted his arm to show off a streak of blood. "We shot old Flora," he said, "and cut her up in fifty pieces."

"Well I don't want to hear about it," my mother said. "And don't come to my table like that."

My father made him go and wash the blood off.

We sat down and my father said grace and Henry pasted his chewing gum on the end of his fork, the way he always did; when he took it off he would have us admire the pattern. We began to pass the bowls of steaming, overcooked vegetables. Laird looked across the table at me and said proudly, distinctly, "Anyway it was her fault Flora got away."

"What?" my father said.

"She could of shut the gate and she didn't. She just open' it up and Flora run out."

"Is that right?" my father said.

Everybody at the table was looking at me. I nodded, swallowing food with great difficulty. To my shame, tears flooded my eyes.

My father made a curt sound of disgust. "What did you do that for?"

I did not answer. I put down my fork and waited to be sent from the table, still not looking up.

But this did not happen. For some time nobody said anything, then Laird said matter-of-factly, "She's crying."

"Never mind," my father said. He spoke with resignation, even good humour, the words which absolved and dismissed me for good. "She's only a girl," he said.

I didn't protest that, even in my heart. Maybe it was true.

*—1968*

*Donald Barthelme (1931–1989) was born in Philadelphia but lived in New York City and Texas. An innovator on the frontier between modernism and postmodernism, he produced four novels, including* Snow White *(1967) and* Paradise *(1986), and over one hundred short stories gathered in collections such as* City Life *(1970),* Sixty Stories *(1981), and* Overnight to Many Distant Cities *(1983). His fiction makes use of collage techniques incorporating high and low culture, realism and fable, and the bizarre and familiar fragments that make up the disjointed debris of contemporary life, often without regard to the conventions of plot, character, and setting.*

# *Donald Barthelme*
# The Glass Mountain

1. I was trying to climb the glass mountain.

2. The glass mountain stands at the corner of Thirteenth Street and Eighth Avenue.

3. I had attained the lower slope.

4. People were looking up at me.

5. I was new in the neighborhood.

6. Nevertheless I had acquaintances.

7. I had strapped climbing irons to my feet and each hand grasped a sturdy plumber's friend.

8. I was 200 feet up.

9. The wind was bitter.

10. My acquaintances had gathered at the bottom of the mountain to offer encouragement.

11. "Shithead."

12. "Asshole."

13. Everyone in the city knows about the glass mountain.

14. People who live here tell stories about it.

15. It is pointed out to visitors.

16. Touching the side of the mountain, one feels coolness.

17. Peering into the mountain, one sees sparkling blue-white depths.

18. The mountain towers over that part of Eighth Avenue like some splendid, immense office building.

19. The top of the mountain vanishes into the clouds, or on cloudless days, into the sun.

20. I unstuck the righthand plumber's friend leaving the lefthand one in place.

21. Then I stretched out and reattached the righthand one a little higher up, after which I inched my legs into new positions.

22. The gain was minimal, not an arm's length.

23. My acquaintances continued to comment.

24. "Dumb motherfucker."

25. I was new in the neighborhood.

26. In the streets were many people with disturbed eyes.

27. Look for yourself.

28. In the streets were hundreds of young people shooting up in door-ways, behind parked cars.

29. Older people walked dogs.

30. The sidewalks were full of dogshit in brilliant colors: ocher, umber, Mars yellow, sienna, viridian, ivory black, rose madder.

31. And someone had been apprehended cutting down trees, a row of elms broken-backed among the VWs and Valiants.

32. Done with a power saw, beyond a doubt.

33. I was new in the neighborhood yet I had accumulated acquaintances.

34. My acquaintances passed a brown bottle from hand to hand.

35. "Better than a kick in the crotch."

36. "Better than a poke in the eye with a sharp stick."

37. "Better than a slap in the belly with a wet fish."

38. "Better than a thump on the back with a stone."

39. "Won't he make a splash when he falls, now?"

40. "I hope to be here to see it. Dip my handkerchief in the blood."

41. "Fart-faced fool."

42. I unstuck the lefthand plumber's friend leaving the righthand one in place.

43. And reached out.

44. To climb the glass mountain, one first requires a good reason.

45. No one has ever climbed the mountain on behalf of science, or in search of celebrity, or because the mountain was a challenge.

46. Those are not good reasons.

47. But good reasons exist.

48. At the top of the mountain there is a castle of pure gold, and in a room in the castle tower sits . . .

49. My acquaintances were shouting at me.

50. "Ten bucks you bust your ass in the next four minutes!"

51. . . . a beautiful enchanted symbol.

52. I unstuck the righthand plumber's friend leaving the lefthand one in place.

53. And reached out.

54. It was cold there at 206 feet and when I looked down I was not encouraged.

55. A heap of corpses both of horses and riders ringed the bottom of the mountain, many dying men groaning there.

56. "A weakening of the libidinous interest in reality has recently come to a close." (Anton Ehrenzweig)[1]

---

[1]*Anton Ehrenzweig*: the author of the *Hidden Order of Art: A Study in the Psychology of Artistic Imagination*.

57. A few questions thronged into my mind.

58. Does one climb a glass mountain, at considerable personal discomfort, simply to disenchant a symbol?

59. Do today's stronger egos still *need* symbols?

60. I decided that the answer to these questions was "yes."

61. Otherwise what was I doing there, 206 feet above the power-sawed elms, whose white meat I could see from my height?

62. The best way to fail to climb the mountain is to be a knight in full armor—one whose horse's hoofs strike fiery sparks from the sides of the mountain.

63. The following-named knights had failed to climb the mountain and were groaning in the heap: Sir Giles Guilford, Sir Henry Lovell, Sir Albert Denny, Sir Nicholas Vaux, Sir Patrick Grifford, Sir Gisbourne Gower, Sir Thomas Grey, Sir Peter Coleville, Sir John Blunt, Sir Richard Vernon, Sir Walter Willoughby, Sir Stephen Spear, Sir Roger Faulconbridge, Sir Clarence Vaughan, Sir Hubert Ratcliffe, Sir James Tyrrel, Sir Walter Herbert, Sir Robert Brakenbury, Sir Lionel Beaufort, and many others.[2]

64. My acquaintances moved among the fallen knights.

65. My acquaintances moved among the fallen knights, collecting rings, wallets, pocket watches, ladies' favors.

66. "Calm reigns in the country, thanks to the confident wisdom of everyone." (M. Pompidou)[3]

67. The golden castle is guarded by a lean-headed eagle with blazing rubies for eyes.

68. I unstuck the lefthand plumber's friend, wondering if—

69. My acquaintances were prising out the gold teeth of not-yet-dead knights.

---

[2]Names of knights taken from the history plays of William Shakespeare including *The Tragedy of King Richard the Third* and *The Famous History of the Life of King Henry the Eighth.*
[3]*Monsieur Georges Pompidou* (1911–1974): president of France from 1969 to 1974. During the French student–worker revolt of May 1968, he was instrumental in negotiating an end to the strikes and restoring law and order.

70. In the streets were people concealing their calm behind a façade of vague dread.

71. "The conventional symbol (such as the nightingale, often associated with melancholy), even though it is recognized only through agreement, is not a sign (like the traffic light) because, again, it presumably arouses deep feelings and is regarded as possessing properties beyond what the eye alone sees." *(A Dictionary of Literary Terms)*

72. A number of nightingales with traffic lights tied to their legs flew past me.

73. A knight in pale pink armor appeared above me.

74. He sank, his armor making tiny shrieking sounds against the glass.

75. He gave me a sideways glance as he passed me.

76. He uttered the word *"Muerte"* [4] as he passed me.

77. I unstuck the righthand plumber's friend.

78. My acquaintances were debating the question, which of them would get my apartment?

79. I reviewed the conventional means of attaining the castle.

80. The conventional means of attaining the castle are as follows: "The eagle dug its sharp claws into the tender flesh of the youth, but he bore the pain without a sound, and seized the bird's two feet with his hands. The creature in terror lifted him high up into the air and began to circle the castle. The youth held on bravely. He saw the glittering palace, which by the pale rays of the moon looked like a dim lamp; and he saw the windows and balconies of the castle tower. Drawing a small knife from his belt, he cut off both the eagle's feet. The bird rose up in the air with a yelp, and the youth dropped lightly onto a broad balcony. At the same moment a door opened, and he saw a courtyard filled with flowers and trees, and there, the beautiful enchanted princess." *(The Yellow Fairy Book)*[5]

---

[4]*Muerte:* Spanish for "Death."
[5]*Yellow Fairy Book:* Scottish scholar Andrew Lang (1844–1912) edited numerous volumes of fairy stories named after colours.

81. I was afraid.

82. I had forgotten the Bandaids.

83. When the eagle dug its sharp claws into my tender flesh—

84. Should I go back for the Bandaids?

85. But if I went back for the Bandaids I would have to endure the contempt of my acquaintances.

86. I resolved to proceed without the Bandaids.

87. "In some centuries, his [man's] imagination has made life an intense practice of all the lovelier energies." (John Masefield)[6]

88. The eagle dug its sharp claws into my tender flesh.

89. But I bore the pain without a sound, and seized the bird's two feet with my hands.

90. The plumber's friends remained in place, standing at right angles to the side of the mountain.

91. The creature in terror lifted me high in the air and began to circle the castle.

92. I held on bravely.

93. I saw the glittering palace, which by the pale rays of the moon looked like a dim lamp; and I saw the windows and balconies of the castle tower.

94. Drawing a small knife from my belt, I cut off both the eagle's feet.

95. The bird rose up in the air with a yelp, and I dropped lightly onto a broad balcony.

96. At the same moment a door opened, and I saw a courtyard filled with flowers and trees, and there, the beautiful enchanted symbol.

97. I approached the symbol, with its layers of meaning, but when I touched it, it changed into only a beautiful princess.

[6]*John Masefield* (1878–1967): an English poet who wandered the world doing odd jobs including a stint as a bartender's assistant in New York. He was Poet Laureate of England from 1930 until his death.

98. I threw the beautiful princess headfirst down the mountain to my acquaintances.

99. Who could be relied upon to deal with her.

100. Nor are eagles plausible, not at all, not for a moment.

*—1970*

---

*Carol Shields (1935–2003) was born in Oak Park, Illinois, but moved to Canada in her twenties, living primarily in Manitoba and British Columbia. She is best known for her novels, including* The Stone Diaries *(1993), which won both the Governor General's Award and the Pulitzer Prize, and* Unless *(2000). However, she also published a number of short-story collections, including* Various Miracles *(1985) and* Dressing Up for the Carnival *(2001), which explore the extraordinary beneath the ordinary, especially in the unrecorded lives of women.*

# *Carol Shields*
## Words

When the world first started heating up, an international conference was held in Rome to discuss ways of dealing with the situation.

Ian's small northern country—small in terms of population, that is, not in size—sent him to the meetings as a junior observer, and it was there he met Isobel, who was representing her country as a full-fledged delegate. She wore a terrible green dress the first time he saw her, and rather clumsy shoes, but he could see that her neck was slender, her waist narrow and her legs long and brown. For so young a woman, she was astonishingly articulate; in fact, it was her voice more than anything else that he fell in love with—its hills and valleys and its pliant, easy-sided wit. It was a voice that could be distinguished in any gathering, being both sweet and husky and having an edging of contralto merriment that seemed to Ian as rare and fine as a border of gold leaf.

They played truant, missing half the study sessions, the two of them lingering instead over tall, cool drinks in the cafe they found on the Via Traflori. There, under a cheerful striped canopy, Isobel leaned across a little table and placed long, ribbony Spanish phrases into Ian's mouth, encouraging and praising him when he got them right. And he, in his somewhat stiff northern voice, gave back the English equivalents: table, chair, glass, cold, hot, money, street, people, mouth. In the evenings, walking in the gardens in front of the institute where the conference was being held, they turned to each other and promised with their eyes, and in two languages as well, to love each other for ever.

The second International Conference was held ten years later. The situation had become grave. One could use the word *crisis* and not be embarrassed. Ian—by then married to Isobel, who was at home with the children—attended every session, and he listened attentively to the position papers of various physicists, engineers, geographers and linguists from all parts of the world. It was a solemn but distinguished assembly; many eminent men and women took their places at the lectern, including the spidery old Scottish demographer who years earlier had made the first correlation between substrata temperatures and highly verbalized societies. In every case, these speakers presented their concerns with admirable brevity, each word weighted and frugally chosen, and not one of them exceeded the two-minute time limitation. For by now no one really doubted that it was the extravagance and proliferation of language that had caused the temperature of the earth's crust to rise, and in places—California, Japan, London—to crack open and form long ragged lakes of fire. The evidence was everywhere and it was incontrovertible; thermal maps and measurements, sonar readings, caloric separations, a network of subterranean monitoring systems—all these had reinforced the integrity of the original Scottish theories.

But the delegates, sitting in the plenary session of the second International Conference, still were reluctant to take regulatory action. It was partly a case of heads-in-the-sand; it was—human nature being what it is—partly a matter of political advantage or commercial gain. There lingered, too, a somewhat surprising nostalgia for traditional liberties and for the old verbal order of the world. Discussion at the conference had gone around and around all week, pointless and wasteful, and it looked very much as though the final meeting would end in yet another welter of indecision and deferral. It was at that point that Ian, seated in the front row, rose and requested permission to speak.

He was granted a one-minute slot on the agenda. In fact, he spoke for several minutes, but his eloquence, his sincerity (and no doubt his strong, boyish appearance, his shaggy hair and his blue eyes) seemed to merit an exception. Certainly not one person sitting in that gathering had any wish to stop him.

It was unfortunate, tragic some thought, that a freak failure in the electronic system—only a plug accidentally pulled from its socket—prevented his exact words from being recorded, but those who were present remembered afterward how passionately he pleaded his love for the planet. (In truth—though who could know this?—he was thinking chiefly of his love for Isobel and his two children.)

We are living in a fool's dream, he told his fellow delegates, and the time has come for us to wake up. Voluntary restraints were no longer adequate to preserve the little earth, which was the only home we know. Halfway measures like the old three-hour *temps tranquilles* were next to useless since they were never, or almost never, enforced. The evening curfew-lingua was ridiculously lenient. Abuses of every sort abounded, particularly the use of highly percussive words or words that were redolent with emotional potency, even though it had been established that these two classes of words were particularly damaging to bedrock and shales. Multilingualism continued to flourish. Wasteful antiphonic structures were actually on the increase in the more heavily populated regions, as was the use of elaborate ceremonial metaphor. It was as though, by refusing to make linguistic sacrifices, the human race had willed its own destruction.

When he finished speaking, the applause was prolonged and powerful. It perhaps held an element of shame, too; this young man had found the courage to say at last what should have been said long before. One after another the delegates rose to their feet, and soon their clapping fell into a steady rhythmic beat which had the effect of holding Ian hostage on the platform. The chairman whispered into his ear, begging him for a few additional words.

He assented. He could not say no. And, in a fever that was remarkably similar to the fever he had suffered as a child during a severe case of measles, or like the fever of love he had succumbed to ten years earlier in Rome, he announced to the audience, holding up a hand for attention, that he would be the first to take a vow of complete silence for the sake of the planet that had fathered him.

Almost at once he regretted his words, but hubris kept him from recanting for the first twenty-four hours and, after that, a kind of stubbornness took over. Isobel met him at the airport with the words, "You went too far." Later, after a miserable, silent attempt at lovemaking, she said, "I'll never forgive you." His children, clamoring to hear about his moment of heroism, poked at him, at his face and chest and arms, as though he were inert. He tried to tell them with his eyes that he was still their father, that he still loved them.

"Leave him alone," Isobel said sharply. "He might as well be a stranger now. He's no different than anyone else."

She became loud and shrewish. When his silent followers arrived at their door—and in time there were thousands of them, each with the same blank face and gold armband—she admitted them with bad grace. She grew garrulous. She rambled on and on, bitter and blaming, sometimes incoherent, sometimes obscene, sometimes reverting to a coarse, primitive schoolyard Spanish, sometimes shouting to herself or cursing into the mirror or chanting oaths—anything to furnish the emptiness of the house with words. She became disoriented. The solid plaster of the walls fell away from her, melting into a drift of vapor. There seemed to be no shadows, no sense of dimension, no delicate separation between one object and another. Privately she pleaded with her husband for an act of apostasy. Later she taunted him. "Show me you're still human," she would say. "Give me just one word." The word *betrayal* came frequently out of her wide mobile mouth, and so did the scornful epithet *martyr*.

But time passes and people forget. She forgot, finally, what it was that had betrayed her. Next she forgot her husband's name. Sometimes she forgot that she had a husband at all, for how could anything be said to exist, she asked herself loudly, hoarsely—even a husband, even one's self—if it didn't also exist in the shape of a word.

He worried that she might be arrested, but for some reason, his position probably, she was always let off with a warning. In their own house she ignored him, passing him on the stairs without a look, or crossing in front of him as though he were a stuffed chair. Often she disappeared for hours, venturing out alone into the heat of the night, and he began to suspect she had taken a lover.

The thought preyed on him, though in fact he had long since forgotten the word for *wife* and also the word for *fidelity*. One night, when she left the house, he attempted to follow her, but clearly she was suspicious because she walked very quickly, looking back over her shoulder, making a series of unnecessary turns and choosing narrow old streets whose curbs were blackened by fire. Within minutes he lost sight of her; soon after that he was driven back by the heat.

The next night he tried again, and this time he saw her disappear into an ancient, dilapidated building, the sort of enclosure, he remembered, where children had once gone to learn to read and write. Unexpectedly he felt a flash of pity; what a sad place for a tryst. He waited briefly, then entered the building and went up a flight of smoldering stairs which seemed on the point of collapse. There he found a dim corridor, thick with smoke, and a single room at one end.

Through the door he heard a waterfall of voices. There must have been a dozen people inside, all of them talking. The talk seemed to be about poetry. Someone—a woman—was giving a lecture. There were interruptions, a discussion, some laughter. He heard his wife's voice, her old gilt-edged contralto, asking a question, and the sound of it made him draw in his breath so sharply that something hard, like a cinder or a particle of gravel, formed in his throat.

It stayed stubbornly lodged there all night. He found it painful to breathe, and even Isobel noticed how he thrashed about in bed, gasping wildly for air. In the morning she called a doctor, who could find nothing wrong, but she remained uneasy, and that evening she stayed home and made him cups of iced honey-and-lemon tea to ease his throat. He took her hand at one point and held it to his lips as though it might be possible to find the air he needed inside the crevices of her skin. By now the scraping in his throat had become terrible, a raw agonizing rasp like a dull knife sawing through limestone. She looked at his face from which the healthy, blood-filled elasticity had gone out and felt herself brushed by a current of air or what might have been the memory of a name.

He began to choke violently, and she heard something grotesque come out of his mouth, a sound that was only half-human, but which rode on a curious rhythmic wave that for some reason stirred her deeply. She imagined it to be the word *Isobel*. "Isobel?" she asked, trying to remember its meaning. He said it a second time, and this time the syllables were more clearly formed.

The light of terror came into his eyes, or perhaps the beginning of a new fever; she managed to calm him by stroking his arm. Then she called the children inside the house, locked the doors and windows against the unbearable heat, and they began, hands linked, at the beginning where they had begun before—with table, chair, bed, cool, else, other, sleep, face, mouth, breath, tongue.

Slowly, patiently.

*—1985*

*Alistair MacLeod (b. 1936) was born in Saskatchewan but in 1946 moved back to the family farm in Cape Breton, a place that became the setting for much of his fiction, including two short-story collections,* The Lost Salt Gift of Blood *(1976) and* As Birds Bring Forth the Sun *(1986), as well as the novel* No Great Mischief *(1999), which won the prestigious IMPAC Dublin award. Noted for his exceptional craftsmanship and a generous and humane approach to his characters, he has expressed an interest in literature that rises from and goes back to the people.*

## Alistair MacLeod
# The Boat

There are times even now, when I awake at four o'clock in the morning with the terrible fear that I have overslept; when I imagine that my father is waiting for me in the room below the darkened stairs or that the shorebound men are tossing pebbles against my window while blowing their hands and stomping their feet impatiently on the frozen steadfast earth. There are times when I am half out of bed and fumbling for socks and mumbling for words before I realize that I am foolishly alone, that no one waits at the base of the stairs and no boat rides restlessly in the waters by the pier.

At such times only the grey corpses on the overflowing ashtray beside my bed bear witness to the extinction of the latest spark and silently await the crushing out of the most recent of their fellows. And then because I am afraid to be alone with death, I dress rapidly, make a great to-do about clearing my throat, turn on both faucets in the sink and proceed to make loud splashing ineffectual noises. Later I go out and walk the mile to the all-night restaurant.

In the winter it is a very cold walk and there are often tears in my eyes when I arrive. The waitress usually gives a sympathetic little shiver and says, "Boy, it must be really cold out there; you got tears in your eyes."

"Yes," I say, "it sure is; it really is."

And then the three or four of us who are always in such places at such times make uninteresting little protective chit-chat until the dawn reluctantly arrives. Then I swallow the coffee which is always bitter and leave with a great busy rush because by that time I have to worry about being late and whether I have a clean shirt and whether my car will start and about all the other countless things one must worry about when he teaches at a great Midwestern university. And I know then that that day will go by as have all the days of the past ten years, for the call and the voices and the shapes and the boat were not really there in the early morning's darkness and I have all kinds of comforting reality to prove it. They are only shadows and echoes, the animals a child's hands make on the wall by lamplight, and the voices from the rain barrel; the cuttings from an old movie made in the black and white of long ago.

I first became conscious of the boat in the same way and at almost the same time that I became aware of the people it supported. My earliest recollection of my father is a view from the floor of gigantic rubber boots and then of being suddenly elevated and having my face pressed against the stubble of his cheek, and of how it tasted of salt and of how he smelled of salt from his red-soled rubber boots to the shaggy whiteness of his hair.

When I was very small, he took me for my first ride in the boat. I rode the half-mile from our house to the wharf on his shoulders and I remember the sound of his rubber boots galumphing along the gravel beach, the tune of the indecent little song he used to sing, and the odour of the salt.

The floor of the boat was permeated with the same odour and in its constancy I was not aware of change. In the harbour we made our little circle and returned. He tied the boat by its painter, fastened the stern to its permanent anchor and lifted me high over his head to the solidity of the wharf. Then he climbed up the little iron ladder that led to the wharf's cap, placed me once more upon his shoulders and galumphed off again.

When we returned to the house everyone made a great fuss over my precocious excursion and asked, "How did you like the boat?" "Were you afraid in the boat?" "Did you cry in the boat?" They repeated "the boat" at the end of all their questions and I knew it must be very important to everyone.

My earliest recollection of my mother is of being alone with her in the mornings while my father was away in the boat. She seemed to be always repairing clothes that were "torn in the boat," preparing food "to be eaten in the boat" or looking for "the boat" through our kitchen window which faced upon the sea. When my father returned about noon, she would ask, "Well, how did things go in the boat today?" It was the first question I remember asking: "Well, how did things go in the boat today?" "Well, how did things go in the boat today?"

The boat in our lives was registered at Port Hawkesbury. She was what Nova Scotians called a Cape Island boat and was designed for the small inshore fishermen who sought the lobsters of the spring and the mackerel of summer and later the cod and haddock and hake. She was thirty-two feet long and nine wide, and was powered by an engine from a Chevrolet truck. She had a marine clutch and a high speed reverse gear and was painted light green with the name *Jenny Lynn* stencilled in black letters on her bow and painted on an oblong plate across her stern. Jenny Lynn had been my mother's maiden name and the boat was called after her as another link in the chain of tradition. Most of the boats that berthed at the wharf bore the names of some female member of their owner's household.

I say this now as if I knew it all then. All at once, all about boat dimensions and engines, and as if on the day of my first childish voyage I noticed the difference between a stencilled name and a painted name. But of course it was not that way at all, for I learned it all very slowly and there was not time enough.

I learned first about our house which was one of about fifty which marched around the horseshoe of our harbour and the wharf which was its heart. Some of them were so close to the water that during a storm the sea spray splashed against their windows while others were built farther along the beach as was the case with ours. The houses and their people, like those of the neighbouring towns and villages, were the result of Ireland's discontent and Scotland's Highland Clearances[1] and America's War of Independence. Impulsive emotional Catholic Celts who could not

---

[1]*Highland Clearances:* The sometimes violent removal of tenants so Scottish landowners could introduce sheep in the early 1800s is referred to as the "Highland Clearances."

bear to live with England and shrewd determined Protestant Puritans who, in the years after 1776, could not bear to live without.

The most important room in our house was one of those oblong old-fashioned kitchens heated by a wood- and coal-burning stove. Behind the stove was a box of kindlings and beside it a coal scuttle. A heavy wooden table with leaves that expanded or reduced its dimensions stood in the middle of the floor. There were five wooden homemade chairs which had been chipped and hacked by a variety of knives. Against the east wall, opposite the stove, there was a couch which sagged in the middle and had a cushion for a pillow, and above it a shelf which contained matches, tobacco, pencils, odd fish-hooks, bits of twine, and a tin can filled with bills and receipts. The south wall was dominated by a window which faced the sea and on the north there was a five-foot board which bore a variety of clothes hooks and the burdens of each. Beneath the board there was a jumble of odd footwear, mostly of rubber. There was also, on this wall, a barometer, a map of the marine area and a shelf which held a tiny radio. The kitchen was shared by all of us and was a buffer zone between the immaculate order of ten other rooms and the disruptive chaos of the single room that was my father's.

My mother ran her house as her brothers ran their boats. Everything was clean and spotless and in order. She was tall and dark and powerfully energetic. In later years she reminded me of the women of Thomas Hardy, particularly Eustacia Vye, in a physical way. She fed and clothed a family of seven children, making all of the meals and most of the clothes. She grew miraculous gardens and magnificent flowers and raised broods of hens and ducks. She would walk miles on berry-picking expeditions and hoist her skirts to dig for clams when the tide was low. She was fourteen years younger than my father, whom she had married when she was twenty-six and had been a local beauty for a period of ten years. My mother was of the sea as were all of her people, and her horizons were the very literal ones she scanned with her dark and fearless eyes.

Between the kitchen clothes rack and barometer, a door opened into my father's bedroom. It was a room of disorder and disarray. It was as if the wind which so often clamoured about the house succeeded in entering this single room and after whipping it into turmoil stole quietly away to renew its knowing laughter from without.

My father's bed was against the south wall. It always looked rumpled and unmade because he lay on top of it more than he slept within any folds it might have had. Beside it, there was a little brown table. An archaic goose-necked reading light, a battered table radio, a mound of wooden matches, one or two packages of tobacco, a deck of cigarette papers and an overflowing ashtray cluttered its surface. The brown larvae of tobacco shreds and the grey flecks of ash covered both the table and the floor beneath it. The once-varnished surface of the table was disfigured by numerous black scars and gashes inflicted by the neglected burning cigarettes of many years. They had tumbled from the ashtray unnoticed and branded their statements permanently and quietly into the wood until the odour of their burning caused the snuffing out of their lives. At the bed's foot there was a single window which looked upon the sea.

Against the adjacent wall there was a battered bureau and beside it there was a closet which held his single ill-fitting serge suit, the two or three white shirts that strangled him and the square black shoes that pinched. When he took off his more friendly clothes, the heavy woollen sweaters, mitts and socks which my mother knitted for him and the woollen and doeskin shirts, he dumped them unceremoniously on a single chair. If a visitor entered the room while he was lying on the bed, he would be told to throw the clothes on the floor and take their place upon the chair.

Magazines and books covered the bureau and competed with the clothes for domination of the chair. They further overburdened the heroic little table and lay on top of the radio. They filled a baffling and unknowable cave beneath the bed, and in the corner by the bureau they spilled from the walls and grew up from the floor.

The magazines were the most conventional: *Time, Newsweek, Life, Maclean's Family Herald, Reader's Digest.* They were the result of various cut-rate subscriptions or of the gift subscriptions associated with Christmas, "the two whole years for only $3.50."

The books were more varied. There were a few hard-cover magnificents and bygone Book-of-the-Month wonders and some were Christmas or birthday gifts. The majority of them, however, were used paperbacks which came from those second-hand bookstores which advertise in the backs of magazines: "Miscellaneous Used Paperbacks 10¢ Each." At first he sent for them himself, although my mother resented the expense, but in later years they came more and more often from my sisters who had moved to the cities. Especially at first they were very weird and varied. Mickey Spillane and Ernest Haycox vied with Dostoyevsky and Faulkner, and the Penguin Poets edition of Gerard Manley Hopkins arrived in the same box as a little book on sex technique called *Getting the Most Out of Love.* The former had been assiduously annotated by a very fine hand using a very blue-inked fountain pen while the latter had been studied by someone with very large thumbs, the prints of which were still visible in the margins. At the slightest provocation it would open almost automatically to particularly graphic and well-smudged pages.

When he was not in the boat, my father spent most of his time lying on the bed in his socks, the top two buttons of his trousers undone, his discarded shirt on the ever-ready chair and the sleeves of the woollen Stanfield underwear, which he wore both summer and winter, drawn half way up to his elbows. The pillows propped up the whiteness of his head and the goose-necked lamp illuminated the pages in his hands. The cigarettes smoked and smouldered on the ashtray and on the table and the radio played constantly, sometimes low and sometimes loud. At midnight and at one, two, three and four, one could sometimes hear the radio, his occasional cough, the rustling thud of a completed book being tossed to the corner heap, or the movement necessitated by his sitting on the edge of the bed to roll the thousandth cigarette. He seemed never to sleep, only to doze, and the light shone constantly from his window to the sea.

My mother despised the room and all it stood for and she had stopped sleeping in it after I was born. She despised disorder in rooms and in houses and in hours and in lives, and she had not read a book since high school. There she had read *Ivanhoe* and considered it a colossal waste of time. Still the room remained, like a solid rock of opposition in the sparkling waters of a clear deep harbour, opening off the kitchen where we really lived our lives, with its door always open and its contents visible to all.

The daughters of the room and of the house were very beautiful. They were tall and willowy like my mother and had her fine facial features set off by the reddish copper-coloured hair that had apparently once been my father's before it turned to white. All of them were very clever in school and helped my mother a great deal about the house. When they were young they sang and were very happy and very nice to me because I was the youngest and the family's only boy.

My father never approved of their playing about the wharf like the other children, and they went there only when my mother sent them on an errand. At such times they almost always overstayed, playing screaming games of tag or hide-and-seek in and about the fishing shanties, the piled traps and tubs of trawl, shouting down to the perch that swam languidly about the wharf's algae-covered piles, or jumping in and out of the boats that tugged gently at their lines. My mother was never uneasy about them at such times, and when her husband criticized her she would say, "Nothing will happen to them there," or "They could be doing worse things in worse places."

By about the ninth or tenth grade my sisters one by one discovered my father's bedroom and then the change would begin. Each would go into the room one morning when he was out. She would go with the ideal hope of imposing order or with the more practical objective of emptying the ashtray, and later she would be found spellbound by the volume in her hand. My mother's reaction was always abrupt, bordering on the angry. "Take your nose out of that trash and come and do your work," she would say, and once I saw her slap my youngest sister so hard that the print of her hand was scarletly emblazoned upon her daughter's cheek while the broken-spined paperback fluttered uselessly to the floor.

Thereafter my mother would launch a campaign against what she had discovered but could not understand. At times although she was not overly religious she would bring in God to bolster her arguments, saying, "In the next world God will see to those who waste their lives reading useless books when they should be about their work." Or without theological aid, "I would like to know how books help anyone to live a life." If my father were in, she would repeat the remarks louder than necessary, and her voice would carry into his room where he lay upon his bed. His usual reaction was to turn up the volume of the radio, although that action in itself betrayed the success of the initial thrust.

Shortly after my sisters began to read the books, they grew restless and lost interest in darning socks and baking bread, and all of them eventually went to work as summer waitresses in the Sea Food Restaurant. The restaurant was run by a big American concern from Boston and catered to the tourists that flooded the area during July and August. My mother despised the whole operation. She said the restaurant was not run by "our people," and "our people" did not eat there, and that it was run by outsiders for outsiders.

"Who are these people anyway?" she would ask, tossing back her dark hair, "and what do they, though they go about with their cameras for a hundred years, know about the way it is here, and what do they care about me and mine, and why should I care about them?"

She was angry that my sisters should even conceive of working in such a place and more angry when my father made no move to prevent it, and she was worried about herself and about her family and about her life. Sometimes she would say softly to her sisters, "I don't know what's the matter with my girls. It seems none of them are interested in any of the right things." And sometimes there would be bitter savage arguments. One afternoon I was coming in with three mackerel I'd been given at the wharf when I heard her say, "Well I hope you'll be satisfied when they come home knocked up and you'll have had your way."

It was the most savage thing I'd ever heard my mother say. Not just the words but the way she said them, and I stood there in the porch afraid to breathe for what seemed like the years from ten to fifteen, feeling the damp moist mackerel with their silver glassy eyes growing clammy against my leg.

Through the angle in the screen door I saw my father who had been walking into his room wheel around on one of his rubber-booted heels and look at her with his blue eyes flashing like clearest ice beneath the snow that was his hair. His usually ruddy face was drawn and grey, reflecting the exhaustion of a man of sixty-five who had been working in those rubber boots for eleven hours on an August day, and for a fleeting moment I wondered what I would do if he killed my mother while I stood there in the porch with those three foolish mackerel in my hand. Then he turned and went into his room and the radio blared forth the next day's weather forecast and I retreated under the noise and returned again, stamping my feet and slamming the door too loudly to signal my approach. My mother was busy at the stove when I came in, and did not raise her head when I threw the mackerel in a pan. As I looked into my father's room, I said, "Well how did things go in the boat today?" and he replied, "Oh not too badly, all things considered." He was lying on his back and lighting the first cigarette and the radio was talking about the Virginia coast.

All of my sisters made good money on tips. They bought my father an electric razor which he tried to use for a while and they took out even more magazine subscriptions. They bought my mother a great many clothes of the type she was very fond of, the wide-brimmed hats and the brocaded dresses, but she locked them all in trunks and refused to wear any of them.

On one August day my sisters prevailed upon my father to take some of their restaurant customers for an afternoon ride in the boat. The tourists with their expensive clothes and cameras and sun glasses awkwardly backed down the iron ladder at the wharf's side to where my father waited below, holding the rocking *Jenny Lynn* in snug against the wharf with one hand on the iron ladder and steadying his descending passengers with the other. They tried to look both prim and wind-blown like the girls in the Pepsi-Cola ads and did the best they could, sitting on the thwarts where the newspapers were spread to cover the splattered blood and fish entrails, crowding to one side so that they were in danger of capsizing the boat, taking the inevitable pictures or merely trailing their fingers through the water of their dreams.

All of them liked my father very much and, after he'd brought them back from their circles in the harbour, they invited him to their rented cabins which were located high on a hill overlooking the village to which they were so alien. He proceeded to get very drunk up there with the beautiful view and the strange company and the abundant liquor, and late in the afternoon he began to sing.

I was just approaching the wharf to deliver my mother's summons when he began, and the familiar yet unfamiliar voice that rolled down from the cabins made me feel as I had never felt before in my young life or perhaps as I had always felt without really knowing it, and I was ashamed yet proud, young yet old and saved yet forever lost, and there was nothing I could do to control my legs which trembled nor my eyes which wept for what they could not tell.

The tourists were equipped with tape recorders and my father sang for more than three hours. His voice boomed down the hill and bounced off the surface of the harbour, which was an unearthly blue on that hot August day, and was then reflected to the wharf and the fishing shanties where it was absorbed amidst the men who were baiting their lines for the next day's haul.

He sang all the old sea chanties which had come across from the old world and by which men like him had pulled ropes for generations, and he sang the East Coast sea songs which celebrated the sealing vessels of Northumberland Strait and the long liners of the Grand Banks, and of Anticosti, Sable Island, Grand Manan, Boston Harbor, Nantucket and Block Island. Gradually he shifted to the seemingly unending Gaelic drinking songs with their twenty or more verses and inevitable refrains, and the men in the shanties smiled at the coarseness of some of the verses and at the thought that the singer's immediate audience did not know what they were applauding nor recording to take back to staid old Boston. Later as the sun was setting he switched to the laments and the wild and haunting Gaelic war songs of those spattered Highland ancestors he had never seen, and when his voice ceased, the savage melancholy of three hundred years seemed to hang over the peaceful harbour and the quiet boats and the men leaning in the doorways of their shanties with their cigarettes glowing in the dusk and the women looking to the sea from their open windows with their children in their arms.

When he came home he threw the money he had earned on the kitchen table as he did with all his earnings but my mother refused to touch it and the next day he went with the rest of the men to bait his trawl in the shanties. The tourists came to the door that evening and my mother met them there and told them that her husband was not in although he was lying on the bed only a few feet away with the radio playing and the cigarette upon his lips. She stood in the doorway until they reluctantly went away.

In the winter they sent him a picture which had been taken on the day of the singing. On the back it said, "To Our Ernest Hemingway" and the "Our" was underlined. There was also an accompanying letter telling how much they had enjoyed themselves, how popular the tape was proving and explaining who Ernest Hemingway was. In a way it almost did look like one of those unshaven, taken-in-Cuba pictures of Hemingway. He looked both massive and incongruous in the setting. His bulky fisherman's clothes were too big for the green and white lawn chair in which he sat, and his rubber boots seemed to take up all of the well-clipped grass square. The beach umbrella jarred with his sunburned face and because he had already been singing for some time, his lips which chapped in the winds of spring and burned in the water glare of summer had already cracked in several places, producing tiny flecks of blood at their corners and on the whiteness of his teeth. The bracelets of brass chain which he wore to protect his wrists from chafing seemed abnormally large and his broad leather belt had been slackened and his heavy shirt and underwear were open at the throat revealing an uncultivated wilderness of white chest hair bordering on the semi-controlled stubble of his neck and chin. His blue eyes had looked directly into the camera and his hair was whiter than the two tiny clouds which hung over his left shoulder. The sea was behind him and its immense blue flatness stretched out to touch the arching blueness of the sky. It seemed very far away from him or else he was so much in the foreground that he seemed too big for it.

Each year another of my sisters would read the books and work in the restaurant. Sometimes they would stay out quite late on the hot summer nights and when they came up the stairs my mother would ask them many long and involved questions which they resented and tried to avoid. Before ascending the stairs they would go into my father's room and those of us who waited above could hear them throwing his clothes off the chair before sitting on it or the squeak of the bed as they sat on its edge. Sometimes they would talk to him a long time, the murmur of their voices blending with the music of the radio into a mysterious vapour-like sound which floated softly up the stairs.

I say this again as if it all happened at once and as if all of my sisters were of identical ages and like so many lemmings going into another sea and, again, it was of course not that way at all. Yet go they did, to Boston, to Montreal, to New York with the young men they met during the summers and later married in those far-away cities. The young men were very articulate and handsome and wore fine clothes and drove expensive cars and my sisters, as I said, were very tall and beautiful with their copper-coloured hair and were tired of darning socks and baking bread.

One by one they went. My mother had each of her daughters for fifteen years, then lost them for two and finally forever. None married a fisherman. My mother never accepted any of the young men, for in her eyes they seemed always a combination of the lazy, the effeminate, the dishonest and the unknown. They never seemed to do any physical work and she could not comprehend their luxurious vacations and she did not know whence they came nor who they were. And in the end she did not really care, for they were not of her people and they were not of her sea.

I say this now with a sense of wonder at my own stupidity in thinking I was somehow free and would go on doing well in school and playing and helping in the boat and passing into my early teens while streaks of grey began to appear in my mother's dark hair and my father's rubber boots dragged sometimes on the pebbles of the beach as he trudged home from the wharf. And there were but three of us in the house that had at one time been so loud.

Then during the winter that I was fifteen he seemed to grow old and ill at once. Most of January he lay upon the bed, smoking and reading and listening to the radio while the wind howled about the house and the needle-like snow blistered off the ice-covered harbour and the doors flew out of people's hands if they did not cling to them like death.

In February when the men began overhauling their lobster traps he still did not move, and my mother and I began to knit lobster trap headings in the evenings. The twine was as always very sharp and harsh, and blisters formed upon our thumbs and little paths of blood snaked quietly down between our fingers while the seals that had drifted down from distant Labrador wept and moaned like human children on the ice-floes of the Gulf.

In the daytime my mother's brother who had been my father's partner as long as I could remember also came to work upon the gear. He was a year older than my mother and was tall and dark and the father of twelve children.

By March we were very far behind and although I began to work very hard in the evenings I knew it was not hard enough and that there were but eight weeks left before the opening of the season on May first. And I knew that my mother worried and my uncle was uneasy and that all of our very lives depended on the boat being ready with her gear and two men, by the date of May the first. And I knew then that *David Copperfield* and *The Tempest* and all of those friends I had dearly come to love must really go forever. So I bade them all good-bye.

The night after my first full day at home and after my mother had gone upstairs he called me into his room where I sat upon the chair beside his bed. "You will go back tomorrow," he said simply.

I refused then, saying I had made my decision and was satisfied.

"That is no way to make a decision," he said, "and if you are satisfied I am not. It is best that you go back." I was almost angry then and told him as all children do that I wished he would leave me alone and stop telling me what to do.

He looked at me a long time then, lying there on the same bed on which he had fathered me those sixteen years before, fathered me his only son, out of who knew what emotions when he was already fifty-six and his hair had turned to snow. Then he swung his legs over the edge of the squeaking bed and sat facing me and looked into my own dark eyes with his of crystal blue and placed his hand upon my knee. "I am not telling you to do anything," he said softly, "only asking you."

The next morning I returned to school. As I left, my mother followed me to the porch and said, "I never thought a son of mine would choose useless books over the parents that gave him life."

In the weeks that followed he got up rather miraculously and the gear was ready and the *Jenny Lynn* was freshly painted by the last two weeks of April when the ice began to break up and the lonely screaming gulls returned to haunt the silver herring as they flashed within the sea.

On the first day of May the boats raced out as they had always done, laden down almost to the gunwales with their heavy cargoes of traps. They were almost like living things as they plunged through the waters of the spring and manoeuvred between the still floating icebergs of crystal-white and emerald green on their way to the traditional grounds that they sought out every May. And those of us who sat that day in the high school on the hill, discussing the water imagery of Tennyson, watched them as they passed back and forth beneath us until by afternoon the piles of traps which had been stacked upon the wharf were no longer visible but were spread about the bottoms of the sea. And the *Jenny Lynn* went too, all day, with my uncle tall and dark, like a latter-day Tashtego[2] standing at the tiller with his legs wide apart and guiding her deftly between the floating pans of ice and my father in the stern standing in the same way with his hands upon the ropes that lashed the cargo to the deck. And at night my mother asked, "Well, how did things go in the boat today?"

And the spring wore on and the summer came and school ended in the third week of June and the lobster season on July first and I wished that the two things I loved so dearly did not exclude each other in a manner that was so blunt and too clear.

At the conclusion of the lobster season my uncle said he had been offered a berth on a deep sea dragger and had decided to accept.

[2]*Tashtego:* a Native American harpooner in Herman Melville's novel *Moby-Dick* (1851) about the pursuit of a great white whale.

We all knew that he was leaving the *Jenny Lynn* forever and that before the next lobster season he would buy a boat of his own. He was expecting another child and would be supporting fifteen people by the next spring and could not chance my father against the family that he loved.

I joined my father then for the trawling season, and he made no protest and my mother was quite happy. Through the summer we baited the tubs of trawl in the afternoon and set them at sunset and revisited them in the darkness of the early morning. The men would come tramping by our house at four A.M. and we would join them and walk with them to the wharf and be on our way before the sun rose out of the ocean where it seemed to spend the night. If I was not up they would toss pebbles to my window and I would be very embarrassed and tumble downstairs to where my father lay fully clothed atop his bed, reading his book and listening to his radio and smoking his cigarette. When I appeared he would swing off his bed and put on his boots and be instantly ready and then we would take the lunches my mother had prepared the night before and walk off toward the sea. He would make no attempt to wake me himself.

It was in many ways a good summer. There were few storms and we were out almost every day and we lost a minimum of gear and seemed to land a maximum of fish and I tanned dark and brown after the manner of my uncles.

My father did not tan—he never tanned—because of his reddish complexion, and the salt water irritated his skin as it had for sixty years. He burned and reburned over and over again and his lips still cracked so that they bled when he smiled, and his arms, especially the left, still broke out into the oozing salt-water boils as they had ever since as a child I had first watched him soaking and bathing them in a variety of ineffectual solutions. The chafe-preventing bracelets of brass linked chain that all the men wore about their wrists in early spring were his the full season and he shaved but painfully and only once a week.

And I saw then, that summer, many things that I had seen all my life as if for the first time and I thought that perhaps my father had never been intended for a fisherman either physically or mentally. At least not in the manner of my uncles; he had never really loved it. And I remembered that, one evening in his room when we were talking about *David Copperfield*, he had said that he had always wanted to go to the university and I had dismissed it then in the way one dismisses his father's saying he would like to be a tight-rope walker, and we had gone on to talk about the Peggottys and how they loved the sea.

And I thought then to myself that there were many things wrong with all of us and all our lives and I wondered why my father, who was himself an only son, had not married before he was forty and then I wondered why he had. I even thought that perhaps he had had to marry my mother and checked the dates on the flyleaf of the Bible where I learned that my oldest sister had been born a prosaic eleven months after the marriage, and I felt myself then very dirty and debased for my lack of faith and for what I had thought and done.

And then there came into my heart a very great love for my father and I thought it was very much braver to spend a life doing what you really do not want rather than selfishly following forever your own dreams and inclinations. And I knew then that I could never leave him alone to suffer the iron-tipped harpoons which my mother would forever hurl into his soul because he was a failure as a husband and a father who had retained none of his own. And I felt that I had been very small in a little secret place within me and that even the completion of high school was for me a silly shallow selfish dream.

So I told him one night very resolutely and very powerfully that I would remain with him as long as he lived and we would fish the sea together. And he made no protest but only smiled through the cigarette smoke that wreathed his bed and replied, "I hope you will remember what you've said."

The room was now so filled with books as to be almost Dickensian, but he would not allow my mother to move or change them and he continued to read them, sometimes two or three a night. They came with great regularity now, and there were more hard covers, sent by my sisters who had gone so long ago and now seemed so distant and so prosperous, and sent also pictures of small red-haired grandchildren with baseball bats and dolls which he placed upon his bureau and which my mother gazed at wistfully when she thought no one would see. Red-haired grandchildren with baseball bats and dolls who would never know the sea in hatred or in love.

And so we fished through the heat of August and into the cooler days of September when the water was so clear we could almost see the bottom and the white mists rose like delicate ghosts in the early morning dawn. And one day my mother said to me, "You have given added years to his life."

And we fished on into October when it began to roughen and we could no longer risk night sets but took our gear out each morning and returned at the first sign of the squalls; and on into November when we lost three tubs of trawl and the clear blue water turned to a sullen grey and the trochoidal[3] waves rolled rough and high and washed across our bows and decks as we ran within their troughs. We wore heavy sweaters now and the awkward rubber slickers and the heavy woollen mitts which soaked and froze into masses of ice that hung from our wrists like the limbs of gigantic monsters until we thawed them against the exhaust pipe's heat. And almost every day we would leave for home before noon, driven by the blasts of the northwest wind, coating our eyebrows with ice and freezing our eyelids closed as we leaned into a visibility that was hardly there, charting our course from the compass and the sea, running with the waves and between them but never confronting their towering might.

And I stood at the tiller now, on these homeward lunges, stood in the place and in the manner of my uncle, turning to look at my father and to shout over the roar of the engine and the slop of the sea to where he stood in the stern, drenched and dripping with the snow and the salt and the spray and his bushy eyebrows caked in ice. But on November twenty-first, when it seemed we might be making the final run of the season, I turned and he was not there and I knew even in that instant that he would never be again.

On November twenty-first the waves of the grey Atlantic are very very high and the waters are very cold and there are no signposts on the surface of the sea. You cannot tell where you have been five minutes before and in the squalls of snow you cannot see. And it takes longer than you would believe to check a boat that has been running before a gale and turn her ever so carefully in a wide and stupid circle, with timbers creaking and straining, back into the face of storm. And you know that it is useless and that your voice does not carry the length of the boat and that even if you knew the original spot, the relentless waves would carry such a burden perhaps a mile or so by the time you could return. And you know also, the final irony, that

---

[3]In geometry, a trochoid is a curve connected to a rolling circle.

your father like your uncles and all the men that form your past, cannot swim a stroke.

The lobster beds off the Cape Breton coast are still very rich and now, from May to July, their offerings are packed in crates of ice, and thundered by the gigantic transport trucks, day and night, through New Glasgow, Amherst, Saint John and Bangor and Portland and into Boston where they are tossed still living into boiling pots of water, their final home.

And though the prices are higher and the competition tighter, the grounds to which the *Jenny Lynn* once went remain untouched and unfished as they have for the last ten years. For if there are no signposts on the sea in storm there are certain ones in calm and the lobster bottoms were distributed in calm before any of us can remember and the grounds my father fished were those his father fished before him and there were others before and before and before. Twice the big boats have come from forty and fifty miles, lured by the promise of the grounds, and strewn the bottom with their traps and twice they have returned to find their buoys cut adrift and their gear lost and destroyed. Twice the Fisheries Officer and the Mounted Police have come and asked many long and involved questions and twice they have received no answers from the men leaning in the doors of their shanties and the women standing at their windows with their children in their arms. Twice they have gone away saying: "There are no legal boundaries in the Marine area"; "No one can own the sea"; "Those grounds don't wait for anyone."

But the men and the women, with my mother dark among them, do not care for what they say, for to them the grounds are sacred and they think they wait for me.

It is not an easy thing to know that your mother lives alone on an inadequate insurance policy and that she is too proud to accept any other aid. And that she looks through her lonely window onto the ice of winter and the hot flat calm of summer and the rolling waves of fall. And that she lies awake in the early morning's darkness when the rubber boots of the men scrunch upon the gravel as they pass beside her house on their way down to the wharf. And she knows that the footsteps never stop, because no man goes from her house, and she alone of all the Lynns has neither son nor son-in-law that walks toward the boat that will take him to the sea. And it is not an easy thing to know that your mother looks upon the sea with love and on you with bitterness because the one has been so constant and the other so untrue.

But neither is it easy to know that your father was found on November twenty-eighth, ten miles to the north and wedged between two boulders at the base of the rock-strewn cliffs where he had been hurled and slammed so many many times. His hands were shredded ribbons as were his feet which had lost their boots to the suction of the sea, and his shoulders came apart in our hands when we tried to move him from the rocks. And the fish had eaten his testicles and the gulls had pecked out his eyes and the white-green stubble of his whiskers had continued to grow in death, like the grass on graves, upon the purple, bloated mass that was his face. There was not much left of my father, physically, as he lay there with the brass chains on his wrists and the seaweed in his hair.

—*1976*

*Roch Carrier (b. 1937) is best known for his short story "The Hockey Sweater," an excerpt of which appears on the Canadian five-dollar bill. Born in the village of Sainte-Justine, Quebec, he continued his education in New Brunswick, Montreal, and Paris. In 1968, he published the novel* La Guerre, Yes Sir! *and later went on to publish more than a dozen other novels and collections of short short stories, or* contes—*as they are called in the French- Canadian tradition. He has also worked as a teacher, a dramatist, and the National Librarian of Canada.*

## *Roch Carrier*
# Perhaps the Trees Do Travel

There were those who had travelled like migratory birds and those who lived rooted to the earth, like trees. Some had gone very far. I remember hearing the story of a man who had gone to the place where the sky meets the earth: he'd had to bend down so he wouldn't bump his head against the sky. The man had suddenly felt lonely and he'd written to his wife. The stamp cost a thousand dollars. Some people had gone to New York; another visited a brother in Montana; my grandfather had sailed on the Atlantic Ocean; a family had migrated to Saskatchewan; and men went to cut timber in the forests of Maine or Abitibi. When these people came home in their new clothes, even the trees on the main street were a little envious of the travellers.

And there were those who had never gone away. Like old Herménégilde. He was so old he'd seen the first house being built in our village. He was old, but his mustache was still completely black. It was a huge mustache that hid his nose, his mouth and his chin. I can still see old Herménégilde's mustache like a big black cloud over our village. Our parents used to say of him that he was healthy as a horse; all the storms of life had been unable to bend his upright, solid pride. At the end of his life he possessed nothing but a small frame house. All his children were gone. Old Herménégilde had spent his whole life without ever going outside the village limits. And he was very proud of having lived that way, rooted to the soil of our village. To indicate the full extent of his pride he would say:

'I've lived my whole life and never needed strangers!'

Old Herménégilde had never gone running off to the distant forests, he had never gone to the neighbouring villages to buy or sell animals. He'd found his wife in the village. Old Herménégilde used to say:

'The good Lord gave us everything we need to get by right here in our village! How come people have to go running off somewheres else where it ain't no better?'

He recalled a proverb written by a very old French poet and repeated it in his own way:

'The fellow next door's grass always looks a heck of a lot greener than your own.'

Old Herménégilde had never been inside an automobile.

'I'm in no rush to die,' he said. 'I want to do it on foot, like a man.'

One morning a black car longer than the one driven by Monsieur Cassidy, the undertaker, stopped with a jolt in front of old Herménégilde's house. A son he hadn't seen for a good many years got out of the car, all dressed in black, as Monsieur Cassidy usually was.

'You coming to my burial, my boy?' asked old Herménégilde.

'No,' said the son. 'I came to take you on a trip.'

Moving from one trade, one job to another, the son had become the private chauffeur to a businessman from Montreal; before he could ask himself what was happening, old Herménégilde, who had never been in a car before, was pushed onto the leather seat of a Cadillac that pawed the ground like a horse.

'Father,' said the son, 'you can't die before you see the world a little.'

'I've seen everything a man needs to see,' said old Herménégilde.

The son's long black car carried him off at a speed he'd never experienced. To avoid seeing that he was going beyond the village limits, old Herménégilde closed his eyes. And with his eyes closed the old man didn't see that he was driving through the neighbouring village, where a number of old men had gone to get their wives; he didn't see Mont Orignal, the highest mountain in the region; he didn't see the ten villages the black car drove through at a speed no runaway horse had ever reached. Tobie, his son, was talking, but he didn't want to listen.

'I'm your son and I know you've spent your whole life as if you were in jail. But you gotta see the world before you die and I'm the one that'll take you out of that jail. Nowadays there's no such thing as distance. My boss, he gets up in Montreal, he opens his eyes in Toronto, he eats his breakfast in New York and then comes back to Montreal to go to sleep. That's what I call living! You gotta keep up with the times. We know the world turns. And you gotta turn with it. I never stop travelling. I know the world. I know life. But you, you've never lived in modern times. It's something you gotta see.'

'A man can go as far as he wants,' said old Herménégilde, 'but he always stays in the same pair of boots.'

'I'm not what you'd call a good son,' said Tobie, 'but I'm the one that's gonna show you the world. That'll be one good thing I've done in my life.'

So then old Herménégilde understood that he was no longer allowed to keep his eyes closed. They had entered Quebec City. In a single glance the old man took in houses taller than the church, more people in the street than for a religious procession and cars swarming everywhere, like ants. His son drove him in front of an immense château, a real château whose name he'd heard when people talked about the rich—the Château Frontenac; then he showed him something much older than he was, older even than his late father—the houses built by the first Frenchmen.

The black car stopped in front of a large garden. Tobie helped his father get out.

'Now people won't be able to say you died without ever setting foot on the Plains of Abraham. This is where we lost our country . . .'

And then it was time to go home. In the car, the son noticed the old Herménégilde was keeping his eyes closed.

'Father, don't shut your eyes, look at the people.'

'I seen too much,' said the old man, 'you showed me too many things today.'

As soon as the son had left old Herménégilde at his house, he hurried off again in the long black car, summoned by other journeys in the vast modern world.

For long months, behind his big black mustache and his closed eyes, old Herménégilde waited for the long black car to return.

—*1979*

---

*Joanna Russ (b. 1937) was born in New York. She has combined feminism and speculative fiction in novels such as* The Female Man *(1975) and* The Two of Them *(1978). Her short-story collections include* Extra (Ordinary) People *(1984) and* The Hidden Side of the Moon *(1987). She has also published non-fiction works, including* How to Suppress Women's Writing *(1983) and* The Country You Have Never Seen *(2005). In 1895, the Irish writer Oscar Wilde was imprisoned for homosexuality, and Russ speculates on what choice he might have made had he been given a second chance.*

## *Joanna Russ*
# Mr. Wilde's Second Chance

*This is a tale told to me by a friend after the Cointreau and the music as we sat in the dusk waiting for the night to come.*

When Oscar Wilde (he said) died, his soul was found too sad for heaven and too happy for hell. A tattered spirit with the look of a debased street imp led him through miles of limbo into a large, foggy room, very like (for what he could see of it) a certain club in London. His small, grimy scud of a guide went up to a stand something like that used by ladies for embroidery or old men for chess, and there it stopped, spinning like a top.

"Yours!" it squeaked.

"Mine?"

But it was gone. On the stand was a board like the kind used for children's games, and nearby a dark lady in wine-colored silk moved pieces over a board of her own. The celebrated writer bent to watch her—she chanced to look up—it was Ada R—, the victim of the most celebrated scandal of the last decade. She had died of pneumonia or a broken heart in Paris; no one knew which. She gave him, out of her black eyes, a look so tragic, so shrinking, so haunted, that the poet (the most courteous of men, even when dead) bowed and turned away. The board before him was a maze of colored squares and meandering lines, and on top was written "O. O'F. Wilde" in coronet script, for this was his life's pattern and each man or woman in the room labored over a board on which was figured the events of his life. Each was trying to rearrange his life into a beautiful and ordered picture, and when he had done that he would be free to live again. As you can imagine, it was both exciting and horribly anxious, this reliving, this being down on the board and at the same time a dead—if not damned—soul in a room the size of all Aetna,[1] but queerly like a London club when it has just got dark and they have lit the lamps. The lady next to Wilde was pale as glass. She was almost finished. She raised one arm—her dark sleeve swept across the board—and in an instant her design was in ruins. Mr. Wilde picked up several of the pieces that had fallen and handed them to the lady.

"If you please," she said. "You are still holding my birthday and my visits to my children."

The poet returned them.

"You are generous," said she. "But then everyone here is generous. They provide everything. They provide all of one's life."

The poet bowed.

"Of course, it is not easy," said the lady. "I try very hard. But I cannot seem to finish anything. I am not sure if it is the necessary organizing ability that I lack or perhaps the aesthetic sense; something ugly always seems to intrude. . . ." She raised her colored counters in both hands, with the grace that had once made her a favorite of society.

"I have tried several times before," she said.

It was at this point that the poet turned and attempted to walk away from his second chance, but wherever he went the board preceded him.

---

[1] *Aetna:* the Latin spelling of Etna (from the Greek for "I burn"), the highest active volcano in Europe, situated on the east coast of Sicily.

It interposed itself between him and old gentlemen in velvet vests; it hovered in front of ladies; it even blossomed briefly at the elbow of a child. Then the poet seemed to regain his composure; he began to work at the game; he sorted and matched and disposed, although with what public in view it was not possible to tell. The board—which had been heavily overlaid in black and purple (like a drawing by one of Mr. Wilde's contemporaries)—began to take on the most delicate stipple of color. It breathed wind and shadow like the closes of a park in June. It spread itself like a fan.

O. O'F. Wilde, the successful man of letters, was strolling with his wife in Hyde Park in the year nineteen-twenty-five. He was sixty-nine years old. He had written twenty books where Oscar Wilde had written one, fifteen plays where the degenerate and debauché had written five, innumerable essays, seven historical romances, three volumes of collected verse, had given many public addresses (though not in the last few years), and had received a citation (this was long in the past) from Queen Victoria herself. The tulips of Hyde Park shone upon the Wildes with a mild and equable light. O. O'F. Wilde, who had written twenty books, and—needless to say—left his two sons an unimpeachable reputation, started, clutched at his heart, and died.

"That is beautiful, sir, beautiful," said a voice in the poet's ear. A gentleman—who was not a *gentleman*—stood at his elbow. "Seldom," said the voice, "have we had one of our visitors, as you might say, complete a work in such a short time, and such a beautiful work, too. And such industry, sir!" The gentleman was beside himself. "Such enthusiasm! Such agreeable docility! You know, of course, that few of our guests display such an excellent attitude. Most of our guests—"

"Do you think so?" said Mr. Wilde curiously.

"Lovely, sir! Such agreeable color. Such delicacy."

"I see," said Mr. Wilde.

"I'm so glad you do, sir. Most of our guests don't. Most of our guests, if you'll permit me the liberty of saying so, are not genteel. Not genteel at all. But you, sir—"

Oscar Wilde, poet, dead at forty-four, took his second chance from the table before him and broke the board across his knee. He was a tall, strong man for all his weight, nearly six feet tall.

*"And then?" I said.*

*"And then," said my friend, "I do not know what happened."*

"Perhaps," said I, "they gave him his second chance, after all. Perhaps they had to."

"Perhaps," said my friend, "they did nothing of the kind. . . . "I wish I knew," he added. "I only wish I knew!"

And there we left it.

—*1981*

---

*Raymond Carver (1938–1988) built a reputation as a master of the contemporary short story that was still growing at the end of his life, which came prematurely after a long struggle with cancer. A native of Clatskanie, Oregon, Carver worked at a number of unskilled jobs in his early years. Married and the father of two before he was twenty, he knew the working class more intimately than have most American writers. Carver's publishing career is bracketed by collections of poetry, and the compression of language he learned as a poet may in part account for the lean quality of his prose, which has been called, perhaps unfairly and inaccurately, "minimalist." Loving the "brevity and intensity" of the short story, he published five collections, including* What We Talk About When We Talk About Love *(1981) and* Elephant *(1988). He felt the title story of the collection* Cathedral *(1983) marked a turning point in his writing in a different, more detailed and hopeful direction, perhaps reflecting his personal victory over alcoholism, his successful relationship with the poet Tess Gallagher, and increasing critical acclaim.*

# *Raymond Carver*
## Cathedral

This blind man, an old friend of my wife's, he was on his way to spend the night. His wife had died. So he was visiting the dead wife's relatives in Connecticut. He called my wife from his in-laws'. Arrangements were made. He would come by train, a five-hour trip, and my wife would meet him at the station. She hadn't seen him since she worked for him one summer in Seattle ten years ago. But she and the blind man had kept in touch. They made tapes and mailed them back and forth. I wasn't enthusiastic about his visit. He was no one I knew. And his being blind bothered me. My idea of blindness came from the movies. In the movies, the blind moved slowly and never laughed. Sometimes they were led by seeing-eye dogs. A blind man in my house was not something I looked forward to.

That summer in Seattle she had needed a job. She didn't have any money. The man she was going to marry at the end of the summer was in officers' training school. He didn't have any money, either. But she was in love with the guy, and he was in love with her, etc. She'd seen something in the paper: HELP WANTED—*Reading to Blind Man*, and a telephone number. She phoned and went over, was hired on the spot. She'd worked with this blind man all summer. She read stuff to him, case studies, reports, that sort of thing. She helped him organize his little office in the county social-service department. They'd become good friends, my wife and the blind man. How do I know these things? She told me. And she told me something else. On her last day in the office, the blind man asked if he could touch her face. She agreed to this. She told me he touched his fingers to every part of her face, her nose—even her neck! She never forgot it. She even tried to write a poem about it. She was always trying to write a poem. She wrote a poem or two every year, usually after something really important had happened to her.

When we first started going out together, she showed me the poem. In the poem, she recalled his fingers and the way they had moved around over her face. In the poem, she talked about what she had felt at the time, about what went through her mind when the blind man touched her nose and lips. I can remember I didn't think much of the poem. Of course, I didn't tell her that. Maybe I just don't understand poetry. I admit it's not the first thing I reach for when I pick up something to read.

Anyway, this man who'd first enjoyed her favors, the officer-to-be, he'd been her childhood sweetheart. So okay. I'm saying that at the end of the summer she let the blind man run his hands over her face, said goodbye to him, married her childhood etc., who was now a commissioned officer, and she moved away from Seattle. But they'd kept in touch, she and the blind man. She made the first contact after a year or so. She called him up one night from an Air Force base in Alabama. She wanted to talk. They talked. He asked her to send him a tape and tell him about her life. She did this. She sent the tape. On the tape, she told the blind man about her husband and about their life together in the military. She told the blind man she loved her husband but she didn't like it where they lived and she didn't like it that he was a part of the military-industrial thing. She told the blind man she'd written a poem and he was in it. She told him that she was writing a poem about what it was like to be an Air Force officer's wife. The poem wasn't finished yet. She was still writing it. The blind man made a tape. He sent her the tape. She made a tape. This went on for years. My wife's officer was posted to one base and then another. She sent tapes from Moody AFB, McGuire, McConnell, and finally Travis, near Sacramento, where one night she got to feeling lonely and cut off from people she kept losing in that moving-around life. She got to feeling she couldn't go it another step. She went in and swallowed all the pills and capsules in the medicine chest and washed them down with a bottle of gin. Then she got into a hot bath and passed out.

But instead of dying, she got sick. She threw up. Her officer—why should he have a name? he was the childhood sweetheart, and what more does he want?—came home from somewhere, found her, and called the ambulance. In time, she put it all on a tape and sent the tape to the blind man. Over the years, she put all kinds of stuff on tapes and sent the tapes off lickety-split. Next to writing a poem every year, I think it was her chief means of recreation. On one tape, she told the blind man she'd decided to live away from her officer for a time. On another tape, she told him about her divorce. She and I began going out, and of course she told her blind man about it. She told him everything, or so it seemed to me. Once she asked me if I'd like to hear the latest tape from the blind man. This was a year ago. I was on the tape, she said. So I said okay, I'd listen to it. I got us drinks and we settled down in the living room. We made ready to listen. First she inserted the tape into the player and adjusted a couple of dials. Then she pushed a lever. The tape squeaked and someone began to talk in this loud voice. She lowered the volume. After a few minutes of harmless chitchat, I heard my own name in the mouth of this stranger, this blind man I didn't even know! And then this: "From all you've said about him, I can only conclude—" But we were interrupted, a knock at the door, something, and we didn't ever get back to the tape. Maybe it was just as well. I'd heard all I wanted to.

Now this same blind man was coming to sleep in my house.

"Maybe I could take him bowling," I said to my wife. She was at the draining board doing scalloped potatoes. She put down the knife she was using and turned around.

"If you love me," she said, "you can do this for me. If you don't love me, okay. But if you had a friend, any friend, and the friend came to visit, I'd make him feel comfortable." She wiped her hands with the dish towel.

"I don't have any blind friends," I said.

"You don't have *any* friends," she said. "Period. Besides," she said, "goddamn it, his wife's just died! Don't you understand that? The man's lost his wife!"

I didn't answer. She'd told me a little about the blind man's wife. Her name was Beulah. Beulah! That's a name for a colored woman.

"Was his wife a Negro?" I asked.

"Are you crazy?" my wife said. "Have you just flipped or something?" She picked up a potato. I saw it hit the floor, then roll under the stove. "What's wrong with you?" she said. "Are you drunk?"

"I'm just asking," I said.

Right then my wife filled me in with more detail than I cared to know. I made a drink and sat at the kitchen table to listen. Pieces of the story began to fall into place.

Beulah had gone to work for the blind man the summer after my wife had stopped working for him. Pretty soon Beulah and the blind man had themselves a church wedding. It was a little wedding—who'd want to go to such a wedding in the first place?—just the two of them, plus the minister and the minister s wife. But it was a church wedding just the same. It was what Beulah had wanted, he'd said. But even then Beulah must have been carrying the cancer in her glands. After they had been inseparable for eight years—my wife's word, *inseparable*—Beulah's health went into a rapid decline. She died in a Seattle hospital room, the blind man sitting beside the bed and holding on to her hand. They'd married, lived and worked together, slept together—had sex, sure—and then the blind man had to bury her. All this without his having ever seen what the goddamned woman looked like. It was beyond my understanding. Hearing this, I felt sorry for the blind man for a little bit. And then I found myself thinking what a pitiful life this woman must have led. Imagine a woman who could never see herself as she was seen in the eyes of her loved one. A woman who could go on day after day and never receive the smallest compliment from her beloved. A woman whose husband could never read the expression on her face, be it misery or something better. Someone who could wear makeup or not—what difference to him? She could, if she wanted, wear green eye-shadow around one eye, a straight pin in her nostril, yellow slacks and purple shoes, no matter. And then to slip off into death, the blind man's hand on her hand, his blind eyes streaming tears—I'm imagining now—her last thought maybe this: that he never even knew what she looked like, and she on an express to the grave. Robert was left with a small insurance policy and half of a twenty-peso Mexican coin. The other half of the coin went into the box with her. Pathetic.

So when the time rolled around, my wife went to the depot to pick him up. With nothing to do but wait—sure, I blamed him for that—I was having a drink and watching the TV when I heard the car pull into the drive. I got up from the sofa with my drink and went to the window to have a look.

I saw my wife laughing as she parked the car. I saw her get out of the car and shut the door. She was still wearing a smile. Just amazing. She went around to the other side of the car to where the blind man was already starting to get out. This blind man, feature this, he was wearing a full beard! A beard on a blind man! Too much, I say. The blind man reached into the back seat and dragged out a suitcase. My wife took his arm, shut the car door, and, talking all the way, moved him down the drive and then up the steps to the front porch. I turned off the TV. I finished my drink, rinsed the glass, dried my hands. Then I went to the door.

My wife said, "I want you to meet Robert. Robert, this is my husband. I've told you all about him." She was beaming. She had this blind man by his coat sleeve.

The blind man let go of his suitcase and up came his hand.

I took it. He squeezed hard, held my hand, and then he let it go.

"I feel like we've already met," he boomed.

"Likewise," I said. I didn't know what else to say. Then I said, "Welcome. I've heard a lot about you." We began to move then, a little group, from the porch into the living room, my wife guiding him by the arm. The blind man was carrying his suitcase in his other hand. My wife said things like, "To your left here, Robert. That's right. Now watch it, there's a chair. That's it. Sit down right here. This is the sofa. We just bought this sofa two weeks ago."

I started to say something about the old sofa. I'd liked that old sofa. But I didn't say anything. Then I wanted to say something else, small-talk, about the scenic ride along the Hudson. How going *to* New York, you should sit on the right-hand side of the train, and coming *from* New York, the left-hand side.

"Did you have a good train ride?" I said. "Which side of the train did you sit on, by the way?"

"What a question, which side!" my wife said. "What's it matter which side?" she said.

"I just asked," I said.

"Right side," the blind man said. "I hadn't been on a train in nearly forty years. Not since I was a kid. With my folks. That's been a long time. I'd nearly forgotten the sensation. I have winter in my beard now," he said. "So I've been told, anyway. Do I look distinguished, my dear?" the blind man said to my wife.

"You look distinguished, Robert," she said. "Robert," she said. "Robert, it's just so good to see you."

My wife finally took her eyes off the blind man and looked at me. I had the feeling she didn't like what she saw. I shrugged.

I've never met, or personally known, anyone who was blind. This blind man was late forties, a heavy-set, balding man with stooped shoulders, as if he carried a great weight there. He wore brown slacks, brown shoes, a light-brown shirt, a tie, a sports coat. Spiffy. He also had this full beard. But he didn't use a cane and he didn't wear dark glasses. I'd always thought dark glasses were a must for the blind. Fact was, I wished he had a pair. At first glance, his eyes looked like anyone else's eyes. But if you looked close, there was something different about them. Too much white in the iris, for one thing, and the pupils seemed to move around in the sockets without his knowing it or being able to stop it. Creepy. As I stared at his face, I saw the left pupil turn in toward his nose while the other made an effort to keep in one place. But it was only an effort, for that eye was on the roam without his knowing it or wanting it to be.

I said, "Let me get you a drink. What's your pleasure? We have a little of everything. It's one of our pastimes."

"Bub, I'm a Scotch man myself," he said fast enough in this big voice.

"Right," I said. Bub! "Sure you are. I knew it."

He let his fingers touch his suitcase, which was sitting alongside the sofa. He was taking his bearings. I didn't blame him for that.

"I'll move that up to your room," my wife said.

"No, that's fine," the blind man said loudly. "It can go up when I go up."

"A little water with the Scotch?" I said.

"Very little," he said.

"I knew it," I said.

He said, "Just a tad. The Irish actor, Barry Fitzgerald? I'm like that fellow. When I drink water, Fitzgerald said, I drink water. When I drink whiskey, I drink whiskey." My wife laughed. The blind man brought his hand up under his beard. He lifted his beard slowly and let it drop.

I did the drinks, three big glasses of Scotch with a splash of water in each. Then we made ourselves comfortable and talked about Robert's travels. First the long flight from the West Coast to Connecticut, we covered that. Then from Connecticut up here by train. We had another drink concerning that leg of the trip.

I remembered having read somewhere that the blind didn't smoke because, as speculation had it, they couldn't see the smoke they exhaled. I thought I knew that much and that much only about blind people. But this blind man smoked his cigarette down to the nubbin and then lit another one. This blind man filled his ashtray and my wife emptied it.

When we sat down at the table for dinner, we had another drink. My wife heaped Robert's plate with cube steak, scalloped potatoes, green beans. I buttered him up two slices of bread. I said, "Here's bread and butter for you." I swallowed some of my drink. "Now let us pray," I said, and the blind man lowered his head. My wife looked at me, her mouth agape. "Pray the phone won't ring and the food doesn't get cold," I said.

We dug in. We ate everything there was to eat on the table. We ate like there was no tomorrow. We didn't talk. We ate. We scarfed. We grazed that table. We were into serious eating. The blind man had right away located his foods, he knew just where everything was on his plate. I watched with admiration as he used his knife and fork on the meat. He'd cut two pieces of meat, fork the meat into his mouth, and then go all out for the scalloped potatoes, the beans next, and then he'd tear off a hunk of buttered bread and eat that. He'd follow this up with a big drink of milk. It didn't seem to bother him to use his fingers once in a while, either.

We finished everything, including half a strawberry pie. For a few moments, we sat as if stunned. Sweat beaded on our faces. Finally, we got up from the table and left the dirty plates. We didn't look back. We took ourselves into the living room and sank into our places again.

Robert and my wife sat on the sofa. I took the big chair. We had us two or three more drinks while they talked about the major things that had come to pass for them in the past ten years. For the most part, I just listened. Now and then I joined in. I didn't want him to think I'd left the room, and I didn't want her to think I was feeling left out. They talked of things that had happened to them—to them!—these past ten years. I waited in vain to hear my name on my wife's sweet lips: "And then my dear husband came into my life"—something like that. But I heard nothing of the sort. More talk of Robert. Robert had done a little of everything, it seemed, a regular blind jack-of-all-trades. But most recently he and his wife had had an Amway distributorship, from which, I gathered, they'd earned their living, such as it was. The blind man was also a ham radio operator. He talked in his loud voice about conversations he'd had with fellow operators in Guam, in the Philippines, in Alaska, and even in Tahiti. He said he'd have a lot of friends there if he ever wanted to go visit those places. From time to time, he'd turn his blind face toward me, put his hand under his beard, ask me something. How long had I been in my present position? (Three years.) Did I like my work? (I didn't.) Was I going to stay with it? (What were the options?) Finally, when I thought he was beginning to run down, I got up and turned on the TV.

My wife looked at me with irritation. She was heading toward a boil. Then she looked at the blind man and said, "Robert, do you have a TV?"

The blind man said, "My dear, I have two TVs. I have a color set and a black-and-white thing, an old relic. It's funny, but if I turn the TV on, and I'm always turning it on, I turn on the color set. It's funny, don't you think?"

I didn't know what to say to that. I had absolutely nothing to say to that. No opinion. So I watched the news program and tried to listen to what the announcer was saying.

"This is a color TV," the blind man said. "Don't ask me how, but I can tell."

"We traded up a while ago," I said.

The blind man had another taste of his drink. He lifted his beard, sniffed it, and let it fall. He leaned forward on the sofa. He positioned his ashtray on the coffee table, then put the lighter to his cigarette. He leaned back on the sofa and crossed his legs at the ankles.

My wife covered her mouth, and then she yawned. She stretched. She said, "I think I'll go upstairs and put on my robe. I think I'll change into something else. Robert, you make yourself comfortable," she said.

"I'm comfortable," the blind man said.

"I want you to feel comfortable in this house," she said.

"I am comfortable," the blind man said.

After she'd left the room, he and I listened to the weather report and then to the sports roundup. By that time, she'd been gone so long I didn't know if she was going to come back. I thought she might have gone to bed. I wished she'd come back downstairs. I didn't want to be left alone with a blind man. I asked him if he wanted another drink, and he said sure. Then I asked if he wanted to smoke some dope with me. I said I'd just rolled a number. I hadn't, but I planned to do so in about two shakes.

"I'll try some with you," he said.

"Damn right," I said. "That's the stuff."

I got our drinks and sat down on the sofa with him. Then I rolled us two fat numbers. I lit one and passed it. I brought it to his fingers. He took it and inhaled.

"Hold it as long as you can," I said. I could tell he didn't know the first thing.

My wife came back downstairs wearing her pink robe and her pink slippers.

"What do I smell?" she said.

"We thought we'd have us some cannabis," I said.

My wife gave me a savage look. Then she looked at the blind man and said, "Robert, I didn't know you smoked."

He said, "I do now, my dear. There's a first time for everything. But I don't feel anything yet."

"This stuff is pretty mellow," I said. "This stuff is mild. It's dope you can reason with," I said. "It doesn't mess you up."

"Not much it doesn't, bub," he said, and laughed.

My wife sat on the sofa between the blind man and me. I passed her the number. She took it and toked and then passed it back to me. "Which way is this going?" she said. Then she said, "I shouldn't be smoking this. I can hardly keep my eyes open as it is. That dinner did me in. I shouldn't have eaten so much."

"It was the strawberry pie," the blind man said. "That's what did it," he said, and he laughed his big laugh. Then he shook his head.

"There's more strawberry pie," I said.

"Do you want some more, Robert?" my wife said.

"Maybe in a little while," he said.

We gave our attention to the TV. My wife yawned again. She said, "Your bed is made up when you feel like going to bed, Robert. I know you must have had a long day. When you're ready to go to bed, say so." She pulled his arm. "Robert?"

He came to and said, "I've had a real nice time. This beats tapes, doesn't it?"

I said, "Coming at you," and I put the number between his fingers. He inhaled, held the smoke, and then let it go. It was like he'd been doing it since he was nine years old.

"Thanks, bub," he said. "But I think this is all for me. I think I'm beginning to feel it," he said. He held the burning roach out for my wife.

"Same here," she said. "Ditto. Me, too." She took the roach and passed it to me. "I may just sit here for a while between you two guys with my eyes closed. But don't let me bother you, okay? Either one of you. If it bothers you, say so. Otherwise, I may just sit here with my eyes closed until you're ready to go to bed," she said. "Your bed's made up, Robert, when you're ready. It's right next to our room at the top of the stairs. We'll show you up when you're ready. You wake me up now, you guys, if I fall asleep." She said that and then she closed her eyes and went to sleep.

The news program ended. I got up and changed the channel. I sat back down on the sofa. I wished my wife hadn't pooped out. Her head lay across the back of the sofa, her mouth open. She'd turned so that her robe had slipped away from her legs, exposing a juicy thigh. I reached to draw her robe back over her, and it was then that I glanced at the blind man. What the hell! I flipped the robe open again.

"You say when you want some strawberry pie," I said.

"I will," he said.

I said, "Are you tired? Do you want me to take you up to your bed? Are you ready to hit the hay?"

"Not yet," he said. "No, I'll stay up with you, bub. If that's all right. I'll stay up until you're ready to turn in. We haven't had a chance to talk. Know what I mean? I feel like me and her monopolized the evening." He lifted his beard and he let it fall. He picked up his cigarettes and his lighter.

"That's all right," I said. Then I said. "I'm glad for the company."

And I guess I was. Every night I smoked dope and stayed up as long as I could before I fell asleep. My wife and I hardly ever went to bed at the same time. When I did go to sleep, I had these dreams. Sometimes I'd wake up from one of them, my heart going crazy.

Something about the church and the Middle Ages was on the TV. Not your run-of-the-mill TV fare. I wanted to watch something else. I turned to the other channels. But there was nothing on them, either. So I turned back to the first channel and apologized.

"Bub, it's all right," the blind man said. "It's fine with me. Whatever you want to watch is okay. I'm always learning something. Learning never ends. It won't hurt me to learn something tonight. I got ears," he said.

We didn't say anything for a time. He was leaning forward with his head turned at me, his right ear aimed in the direction of the set. Very disconcerting. Now and then his eyelids drooped and then they snapped open again. Now and then he put his fingers into his beard and tugged, like he was thinking about something he was hearing on the television.

On the screen, a group of men wearing cowls was being set upon and tormented by men dressed in skeleton costumes and men dressed as devils. The men dressed as devils wore devil masks, horns, and long tails. This pageant was part of a procession. The Englishman who was narrating the thing said it took place in Spain once a year. I tried to explain to the blind man what was happening.

"Skeletons," he said. "I know about skeletons," he said, and he nodded.

The TV showed this one cathedral. Then there was a long, slow look at another one. Finally, the picture switched to the famous one in Paris, with its flying buttresses and its spires reaching up to the clouds. The camera pulled away to show the whole of the cathedral rising above the skyline.

There were times when the Englishman who was telling the thing would shut up, would simply let the camera move around over the cathedrals. Or else the camera would tour the countryside, men in fields walking behind oxen. I waited as long as I could. Then I felt I had to say something. I said, "They're showing the outside of this cathedral now.

Gargoyles. Little statues carved to look like monsters. Now I guess they're in Italy. Yeah, they're in Italy. There's paintings on the walls of this one church."

"Are those fresco paintings, bub?" he asked, and he sipped from his drink.

I reached for my glass. But it was empty. I tried to remember what I could remember. "You're asking me are those frescoes?" I said, "That's a good question. I don't know."

The camera moved to a cathedral outside Lisbon. The differences in the Portuguese cathedral compared with the French and Italian were not that great. But they were there. Mostly the interior stuff. Then something occurred to me, and I said, "Something has occurred to me. Do you have any idea what a cathedral is? What they look like, that is? Do you follow me? If somebody says cathedral to you, do you have any notion what they're talking about? Do you know the difference between that and a Baptist church, say?"

He let the smoke dribble from his mouth. "I know they took hundreds of workers fifty or a hundred years to build," he said. "I just heard the man say that, of course. I know generations of the same families worked on a cathedral. I heard him say that, too. The men who began their life's work on them, they never lived to see the completion of their work. In that wise, bub, they're no different from the rest of us, right?" He laughed. Then his eyelids drooped again. His head nodded. He seemed to be snoozing. Maybe he was imagining himself in Portugal. The TV was showing another cathedral now. This one was in Germany. The Englishman's voice droned on. "Cathedrals," the blind man said. He sat up and rolled his head back and forth. "If you want the truth, bub, that's about all I know. What I just said. What I heard him say. But maybe you could describe one to me? I wish you'd do it. I'd like that. If you want to know, I really don't have a good idea."

I stared hard at the shot of the cathedral on the TV. How could I even begin to describe it? But say my life depended on it. Say my life was being threatened by an insane guy who said I had to do it or else.

I stared some more at the cathedral before the picture flipped off into the countryside. There was no use. I turned to the blind man and said, "To begin with, they're very tall." I was looking around the room for clues. "They reach way up. Up and up. Toward the sky. They're so big, some of them, they have to have these supports. To help hold them

up, so to speak. These supports are called buttresses. They remind me
of viaducts, for some reason. But maybe you don't know viaducts,
either? Sometimes the cathedrals have devils and such carved into the
front. Sometimes lords and ladies. Don't ask me why this is," I said.

He was nodding. The whole upper part of his body seemed to be
moving back and forth.

"I'm not doing so good, am I?" I said.

He stopped nodding and leaned forward on the edge of the sofa. As
he listened to me, he was running his fingers through his beard. I wasn't
getting through to him, I could see that. But he waited for me to go on
just the same. He nodded, like he was trying to encourage me. I tried to
think what else to say. "They're really big," I said. "They're massive.
They're built of stone. Marble, too, sometimes. In those olden days,
when they built cathedrals, men wanted to be close to God. In those
olden days, God was an important part of everyone's life. You could tell
this from their cathedral-building. I'm sorry," I said, "but it looks like
that's the best I can do for you. I'm just no good at it."

"That's all right, bub," the blind man said. "Hey, listen. I hope you
don't mind my asking you. Can I ask you something? Let me ask you a
simple question, yes or no. I'm just curious and there's no offense.
You're my host. But let me ask if you are in any way religious? You
don't mind my asking?"

I shook my head. He couldn't see that, though. A wink is the same as
a nod to a blind man. "I guess I don't believe in it. In anything.
Sometimes it's hard. You know what I'm saying?"

"Sure, I do," he said.

"Right," I said.

The Englishman was still holding forth. My wife sighed in her sleep.
She drew a long breath and went on with her sleeping.

"You'll have to forgive me," I said. "But I can't tell you what a
cathedral looks like. It just isn't in me to do it. I can't do any more than
I've done."

The blind man sat very still, his head down, as he listened to me.

I said, "The truth is, cathedrals don't mean anything special to me.
Nothing. Cathedrals. They're something to look at on late-night TV.
That's all they are."

It was then that the blind man cleared his throat. He brought something up. He took a handkerchief from his back pocket. Then he said,

"I get it, bub. It's okay. It happens. Don't worry about it," he said. "Hey, listen to me. Will you do me a favor? I got an idea. Why don't you find us some heavy paper? And a pen. We'll do something. We'll draw one together. Get us a pen and some heavy paper. Go on, bub, get the stuff," he said.

So I went upstairs. My legs felt like they didn't have any strength in them. They felt like they did after I'd done some running. In my wife's room, I looked around. I found some ballpoints in a little basket on her table. And then I tried to think where to look for the kind of paper he was talking about.

Downstairs, in the kitchen, I found a shopping bag with onion skins in the bottom of the bag. I emptied the bag and shook it. I brought it into the living room and sat down with it near his legs. I moved some things, smoothed the wrinkles from the bag, spread it out on the coffee table.

The blind man got down from the sofa and sat next to me on the carpet.

He ran his fingers over the paper. He went up and down the sides of the paper. The edges, even the edges. He fingered the corners.

"All right," he said. "All right, let's do her."

He found my hand, the hand with the pen. He closed his hand over my hand. "Go ahead, bub, draw," he said. "Draw. You'll see. I'll follow along with you. It'll be okay. Just begin now like I'm telling you. You'll see. Draw," the blind man said.

So I began. First I drew a box that looked like a house. It could have been the house I lived in. Then I put a roof on it. At either end of the roof, I drew spires. Crazy.

"Swell," he said. "Terrific. You're doing fine," he said. "Never thought anything like this could happen in your lifetime, did you, bub? Well, it's a strange life, we all know that. Go on now. Keep it up."

I put in windows with arches. I drew flying buttresses. I hung great doors. I couldn't stop. The TV station went off the air. I put down the pen and closed and opened my fingers. The blind man felt around over the paper. He moved the tips of his fingers over the paper, all over what I had drawn, and he nodded.

"Doing fine," the blind man said.

I took up the pen again, and he found my hand. I kept at it. I'm no artist. But I kept drawing just the same.

My wife opened up her eyes and gazed at us. She sat up on the sofa, her robe hanging open. She said, "What are you doing? Tell me, I want to know."

I didn't answer her.

The blind man said, "We're drawing a cathedral. Me and him are working on it. Press hard," he said to me. "That's right. That's good," he said. "Sure. You got it, bub. I can tell. You didn't think you could. But you can, can't you? You're cooking with gas now. You know what I'm saying? We're going to really have us something here in a minute. How's the old arm?" he said. "Put some people in there now. What's a cathedral without people?"

My wife said, "What's going on? Robert, what are you doing? What's going on?"

"It's all right," he said to her. "Close your eyes now," the blind man said to me.

I did it. I closed them just like he said.

"Are they closed?" he said. "Don't fudge."

"They're closed," I said.

"Keep them that way," he said. He said, "Don't stop now. Draw."

So we kept on with it. His fingers rode my fingers as my hand went over the paper. It was like nothing else in my life up to now.

Then he said, "I think that's it. I think you got it," he said. "Take a look. What do you think?"

But I had my eyes closed. I thought I'd keep them that way for a little longer. I thought it was something I ought to do.

"Well?" he said. "Are you looking?"

My eyes were still closed. I was in my house. I knew that. But I didn't feel like I was inside anything.

"It's really something," I said.

—*1981*

*Margaret Atwood (b. 1939) is a leading figure among Canadian writers, with a huge international following. Equally skilled as a poet and fiction writer, she has used her considerable reputation to support a variety of causes, including PEN International. Born in Ottawa, Ontario, she graduated from the University of Toronto in 1962, and later did graduate work at Radcliffe and Harvard. She has authored over a dozen poetry collections, a dozen novels, including the dystopias* The Handmaid's Tale *(1985) and* Oryx and Crake *(2003), and half a dozen collections of short fiction, including* The Tent *(2006). She has also written literary criticism, including* Survival: A Thematic Guide to Canadian Literature *(1972), and several books for children. Her long list of awards includes the Giller Prize, the Man Booker Prize, and the Governor General's Award. She continues to be an inventive and prolific writer of works that reflect her feminist concerns, her interest in classical and popular mythology, and her increasing concern for the future of humanity.*

# *Margaret Atwood*
# Happy Endings

> John and Mary meet.
> *What happens next?*
> *If you want a happy ending, try A.*

## A

John and Mary fall in love and get married. They both have worthwhile and remunerative jobs which they find stimulating and challenging. They buy a charming house. Real estate values go up. Eventually, when they can afford live-in help, they have two children, to whom they are devoted. The children turn out well. John and Mary have a stimulating and challenging sex life and worthwhile friends. They go on fun vacations together. They retire. They both have hobbies which they find stimulating and challenging. Eventually they die. This is the end of the story.

## B

Mary falls in love with John but John doesn't fall in love with Mary. He merely uses her body for selfish pleasure and ego gratification of a tepid kind. He comes to her apartment twice a week and she cooks him dinner, you'll notice that he doesn't even consider her worth the price of a dinner out, and after he's eaten the dinner he fucks her and after that he falls asleep, while she does the dishes so he won't think she's untidy, having all those dirty dishes lying around, and puts on fresh lipstick so she'll look good when he wakes up, but when he wakes up he doesn't even notice, he puts on his socks and his shorts and his pants and his shirt and his tie and his shoes, the reverse order from the one in which he took them off. He doesn't take off Mary's clothes, she takes them off herself, she acts as if she's dying for it every time, not because she likes sex exactly, she doesn't, but she wants John to think she does because if they do it often enough surely he'll get used to her, he'll come to depend on her and they will get married, but John goes out the door with hardly so much as a good-night and three days later he turns up at six o'clock and they do the whole thing over again.

Mary gets run-down. Crying is bad for your face, everyone knows that and so does Mary but she can't stop. People at work notice. Her friends tell her John is a rat, a pig, a dog, he isn't good enough for her, but she can't believe it. Inside John, she thinks, is another John, who is much nicer. This other John will emerge like a butterfly from a cocoon, a Jack from a box, a pit from a prune, if the first John is only squeezed enough.

One evening John complains about the food. He has never complained about the food before. Mary is hurt.

Her friends tell her they've seen him in a restaurant with another woman, whose name is Madge. It's not even Madge that finally gets to Mary: it's the restaurant. John has never taken Mary to a restaurant. Mary collects all the sleeping pills and aspirins she can find, and takes them and a half a bottle of sherry. You can see what kind of a woman she is by the fact that it's not even whiskey. She leaves a note for John. She hopes he'll discover her and get her to the hospital in time and repent and then they can get married, but this fails to happen and she dies.

John marries Madge and everything continues as in A.

C

John, who is an older man, falls in love with Mary, and Mary, who is only twenty-two, feels sorry for him because he's worried about his hair falling out. She sleeps with him even though she's not in love with him. She met him at work. She's in love with someone called James, who is twenty-two also and not yet ready to settle down.

John on the contrary settled down long ago: this is what is bothering him. John has a steady, respectable job and is getting ahead in his field, but Mary isn't impressed by him, she's impressed by James, who has a motorcycle and a fabulous record collection. But James is often away on his motorcycle, being free. Freedom isn't the same for girls, so in the meantime Mary spends Thursday evenings with John. Thursdays are the only days John can get away.

John is married to a woman called Madge and they have two children, a charming house which they bought just before the real estate values went up, and hobbies which they find stimulating and challenging, when they have the time. John tells Mary how important she is to him, but of course he can't leave his wife because a commitment is a commitment. He goes on about this more than is necessary and Mary finds it boring, but older men can keep it up longer so on the whole she has a fairly good time.

One day James breezes in on his motorcycle with some top-grade California hybrid and James and Mary get higher than you'd believe possible and they climb into bed. Everything becomes very underwater, but along comes John, who has a key to Mary's apartment. He finds them stoned and entwined. He's hardly in any position to be jealous, considering Madge, but nevertheless he's overcome with despair. Finally he's middle-aged, in two years he'll be bald as an egg and he can't stand it. He purchases a handgun, saying he needs it for target practice—this is the thin part of the plot, but it can be dealt with later—and shoots the two of them and himself.

Madge, after a suitable period of mourning, marries an understanding man called Fred and everything continues as in A, but under different names.

D

Fred and Madge have no problems. They get along exceptionally well and are good at working out any little difficulties that may arise. But their charming house is by the seashore and one day a giant tidal wave approaches. Real estate values go down. The rest of the story is about what caused the tidal wave and how they escape from it. They do, though thousands drown, but Fred and Madge are virtuous and lucky. Finally on high ground they clasp each other, wet and dripping and grateful, and continue as in A.

E

Yes, but Fred has a bad heart. The rest of the story is about how kind and understanding they both are until Fred dies. Then Madge devotes herself to charity work until the end of A. If you like, it can be "Madge," "cancer," "guilty and confused," and "bird watching."

F

If you think this is all too bourgeois, make John a revolutionary and Mary a counterespionage agent and see how far that gets you. Remember, this is Canada. You'll still end up with A, though in between you may get a lustful brawling saga of passionate involvement, a chronicle of our times, sort of.

You'll have to face it, the endings are the same however you slice it. Don't be deluded by any other endings, they're all fake, either deliberately fake, with malicious intent to deceive, or just motivated by excessive optimism if not by downright sentimentality.

The only authentic ending is the one provided here:

*John and Mary die. John and Mary die. John and Mary die.*

So much for endings. Beginnings are always more fun. True connoisseurs, however, are known to favor the stretch in between, since it's the hardest to do anything with.

That's about all that can be said for plots, which anyway are just one thing after another, a what and a what and a what.

Now try How and Why.

*—1983*

*Ama Ata Aidoo (b. 1942) was born the daughter of a chief in central Ghana and went on to study at the University of Ghana, where she produced her first play. She has since become an important African writer, producing plays, poems, short stories, and novels that explore questions of political and cultural autonomy as well as women's liberation. Though Ghana received independence in 1957, the period that followed was one of disillusionment. In "The Message," a story from No Sweetness Here (1970), Aidoo explores the challenging intersection between Western and African cultures with wit and insight.*

## Ama Ata Aidoo
# The Message

"Look here my sister, it should not be said but they say they opened her up."

"They opened her up?"

"Yes, opened her up."

"And the baby removed?"

"Yes, the baby removed."

"Yes, the baby removed."-

"I say . . ."

"They do not say, my sister."

"Have you heard it?"

"What?"

"This and this and that . . ."

"A-a-ah! that is it . . ."

"*Meewuo!*"

"They don't say *meewuo* . . ."

"And how is she?"

"Am I not here with you? Do I know the highway which leads to Cape Coast?"

"Hmmm . . ."

"And anyway how can she live? What is it like even giving birth with a stomach which is whole . . . eh? . . . I am asking you. And if you are always standing on the brink of death who go to war with a stomach that is whole, then how would she do whose stomach is open to the winds?"

"Oh, *poo*, pity . . ."

"I say . . ."

My little bundle, come. You and I are going to Cape Coast today.

I am taking one of her own cloths with me, just in case. These people on the coast do not know how to do a thing and I am not going to have anybody mishandling my child's body. I hope they give it to me. Horrible things I have heard done to people's bodies. Cutting them up and using them for instructions. Whereas even murderers still have decent burials.

I see Mensima coming. . . . And there is Nkama too . . . and Adwoa Meenu. . . . Now they are coming to . . . "*poo* pity" me. Witches, witches, witches . . . they have picked mine up while theirs prosper around them, children, grandchildren and great-grandchildren—theirs shoot up like mushrooms.

"Esi, we have heard of your misfortune . . ."

"That our little lady's womb has been opened up . . ."

"And her baby removed . . ."

Thank you very much.

"Has she lived through it?"

I do not know.

"Esi, bring her here, back home whatever happens."

*Yoo,* thank you. If the government's people allow it, I shall bring her home.

"And have you got ready your things?"

Yes. . . . No.

I cannot even think well.

It feels so noisy in my head. . . . Oh my little child. . . . I am wasting time. . . . And so I am going . . .

Yes, to Cape Coast.

No, I do not know anyone there now but do you think no one would show me the way to this big hospital . . . if I asked around?

Hmmm . . . it's me has ended up like this. I was thinking that everything was alright now. . . . *Yoo.* And thank you too. Shut the door for me when you are leaving. You may stay too long outside if you wait for me, so go home and be about your business. I will let you know when I bring her in.

"Maami Amfoa, where are you going?"

My daughter, I am going to Cape Coast.

"And what is our old mother going to do with such swift steps? Is it serious?"

My daughter, it is very serious.

"Mother, may God go with you."

*Yoo*, my daughter.

"Eno, and what calls at this hour of the day?"

They want me in Cape Coast.

"Does my friend want to go and see how much the city has changed since we went there to meet the new Wesleyan Chairman, twenty years ago?"

My sister, do you think I have knees to go parading on the streets of Cape Coast?

"Is it heavy?"

Yes, very heavy indeed. They have opened up my grandchild at the hospital, *hi, hi, hi.* . . .

"Eno *due, due, due* . . . I did not know. May God go with you. . . ."

Thank you. *Yaa.*

"O, the world!"

"It's her grandchild. The only daughter of her only son. Do you remember Kojo Amisa who went to sodja and fell in the great war, overseas?"

"Yes, it's his daughter. . . ."

. . . O, *poo*, pity.

"Kobina, run to the street, tell Draba Anan to wait for Nana Amfoa."

". . . Draba Anan, Draba, my mother says I must come and tell you to wait for Nana Amfoa."

"And where is she?"

"There she comes."

"Just look at how she hops like a bird . . . does she think we are going to be here all day? And anyway we are full already . . ."

O, you drivers!

"What have drivers done?"

"And do you think it shows respect when you speak in this way? It is only that things have not gone right; but she could, at least have been your mother. . . ."

"But what have I said? I have not insulted her. I just think that only Youth must be permitted to see Cape Coast, the town of the Dear and Expensive. . . ."

"And do you think she is going on a peaceful journey? The only daughter of her only son has been opened up and her baby removed from her womb."

O . . . God.

O

O

O

*Poo*, pity.

"Me . . . *poo*—pity, I am right about our modern wives I always say they are useless as compared with our mothers."

"You drivers!"

"Now what have your modern wives done?"

"Am I not right what I always say about them?"

"You go and watch them in the big towns. All so thin and dry as sticks—you can literally blow them away with your breath. No decent flesh anywhere. Wooden chairs groan when they meet with their hard exteriors."

"O you drivers. . . ."

"But of course all drivers . . ."

"What have I done? Don't all my male passengers agree with me? These modern girls. . . . Now here is one who cannot even have a baby in a decent way. But must have the baby removed from her stomach. *Tchiaa!*"

"What . . ."

"Here is the old woman."

"Whose grandchild . . . ?"

"Yes."

"Nana, I hear you are coming to Cape Coast with us."

Yes my master.

"We nearly left you behind but we heard it was you and that it is a heavy journey you are making."

Yes my master . . . thank you my master.

"Push up please . . . push up. Won't you push up? Why do you all sit looking at me with such eyes as if I was a block of wood?"

"It is not that there is nowhere to push up to. Five fat women should go on that seat, but look at you!"

"And our own grandmother here is none too plump herself. . . . Nana, if they won't push, come to the front seat with me."

". . . *Hei*, scholar, go to the back. . . ."

". . . And do not scowl on me. I know your sort too well. Something tells me you do not have any job at all. As for that suit you are wearing and looking so grand in, you hired or borrowed it. . . ."

"Oh you drivers!"

Oh you drivers . . .

The scholar who read this telegram thing, said it was made about three days ago. My lady's husband sent it. . . . Three days. . . . God—that is too long ago. Have they buried her . . . where? Or did they cut her up. . . . I should not think about it . . . or something will happen to me. Eleven or twelve . . . Efua Panyin, Okuma, Kwame Gyasi and who else? But they should not have left me here. Sometimes . . . ah, I hate this nausea. But it is this smell of petrol. Now I have remembered I never could travel in a lorry. I always was so sick. But now I hope at least that will not happen. These young people will think it is because I am old and they will laugh. At least if I knew the child of my child was alive, it would have been good. And the little things she sent me. . . . Sometimes some people like Mensima and Nkansa make me feel as if I had been a barren woman instead of only one with whom infant-mortality pledged friendship . . .

I will give her that set of earrings, bracelet and chain which Odwumfo Ata made for me. It is the most beautiful and the most expensive thing I have. . . . It does not hurt me to think that I am going to die very soon and have them and their children gloating over my things. After all what did they swallow my children for? It does not hurt me at all. If I had been someone else, I would have given them all away before I died. But it does not matter. They can share their own curse. Now, that is the end of me and my roots. . . . Eternal death has worked like a warrior rat, with diabolical sense of duty, to gnaw my bottom. Everything is finished now. The vacant lot is swept and the scraps of old sugar-cane pulp, dry sticks and bunches of hair burnt . . . how it reeks, the smoke!

"O, Nana do not weep . . ."

"Is the old woman weeping?"

"If the only child of your only child died, won't you weep?"

"Why do you ask me? Did I know her grandchild is dead?"

"Where have you been, not in this lorry? Where were your ears when we were discussing it?"

"I do not go putting my mouth in other people's affairs . . ."

"So what?"

"So go and die."

"*Hei, hei,* it is prohibited to quarrel in my lorry."

"Draba, here is me, sitting quiet and this lady of muscles and bones being cheeky to me."

"Look, I can beat you."

"Beat me . . . beat me . . . let's see."

"*Hei,* you are not civilised, eh?"

"Keep quiet and let us think, both of you, or I will put you down."

"Nana, do not weep. There is God above."

Thank you my master.

"But we are in Cape Coast already."

*Meewuo!* My God, hold me tight or something will happen to me.

My master, I will come down here.

"O Nana, I thought you said you were going to the hospital. . . . We are not there yet."

I am saying maybe I will get down here and ask my way around.

"Nana, you do not know these people, eh? They are very impudent here. They have no use for old age. So they do not respect it. Sit down, I will take you there."

Are you going there, my master?

"No, but I will take you there."

Ah, my master, your old mother thanks you. Do not shed a tear when you hear of my death . . . my master, your old mother thanks you.

I hear there is somewhere where they keep corpses until their owners claim them . . . if she has been buried, then I must find her husband . . . Esi Amfoa, what did I come to do under this sky? I have buried all my children and now I am going to bury my only grandchild!

"Nana we are there."

Is this the hospital?

"Yes, Nana. What is your child's name?"

Esi Amfoa. Her father named her after me.

"Do you know her European name?"

No, my master.

"What shall we do?"

". . . *Ei* lady, Lady Nurse, we are looking for somebody."

"You are looking for somebody and can you read? If you cannot, you must ask someone what the rules in the hospital are. You can only come and visit people at three o'clock."

Lady, please. She was my only grandchild . . .

"Who? And anyway, it is none of our business."

"Nana, you must be patient . . . and not cry . . ."

"Old woman, why are you crying, it is not allowed here. No one must make any noise . . ."

My lady, I am sorry but she was all I had.

"Who? Oh, are you the old woman who is looking for somebody?"

Yes.

"Who is he?"

She was my granddaughter—the only child of my only son.

"I mean, what was her name?"

Esi Amfoa.

"Esi Amfoa . . . Esi Amfoa. I am sorry, we do not have anyone whom they call like that here."

Is that it?

"Nana, I told you they may know only her European name here."

My master, what shall we do then?

"What is she ill with?"

She came here to have a child . . .

". . . And they say, they opened her stomach and removed the baby."

"Oh . . . oh, I see."

My Lord, hold me tight so that nothing will happen to me now.

"I see. It is the Caesarean case."

"Nurse, you know her?"

And when I take her back, Anona Ebusuafo will say that I did not wait for them to come with me . . .

"Yes. Are you her brother?"

"No. I am only the driver who brought the old woman."

"Did she bring all her clan?"

"No. She came alone."

"Strange thing for a villager to do."

I hope they have not cut her up already.

"Did she bring a whole bag full of cassava and plantain and kenkey?"

"No. She has only her little bundle."

"Follow me. But you must not make any noise. This is not the hour for coming here . . ."

My master, does she know her?

"Yes."

I hear it is very cold where they put them . . .

It was feeding time for new babies. When old Esi Amfoa saw young Esi Amfoa, the latter was all neat and nice. White sheets and all. She did not see the beautiful stitches under the sheets. "This woman is a tough bundle," Dr. Gyamfi had declared after the identical twins had been removed, the last stitches had been threaded off and Mary Koomson, alias Esi Amfoa, had come to.

The old woman somersaulted into the room and lay groaning, not screaming, by the bed. For was not her last pot broken? So they lay them in state even in hospitals and not always cut them up for instruction?

The Nursing Sister was furious. Young Esi Amfoa spoke. And this time old Esi Amfoa wept loud and hard—wept all her tears.

Scrappy nurse-under-training, Jessy Treeson, second-generation-Cape-Coaster-her-grandmother-still-remembered-at-Egyaa No. 7 said, "As for these villagers," and giggled.

Draba Anan looked hard at Jessy Treeson, looked hard at her, all of her: her starched uniform, apron and cap . . . and then dismissed them all. . . . "Such a cassava stick . . . but maybe I will break my toe if I kicked at her buttocks," he thought.

And by the bed the old woman was trying hard to rise and look at the only pot which had refused to get broken.

*—1970*

**Thomas King (b. 1943)** *was born in California of Cherokee and Greek descent. Since 1980 he has spent much of his time in Canada, most recently as professor of Native literature at the University of Guelph. In "A Coyote Columbus Story," origi-nally published for children in 1992, and then in a collection intended for adults,* One Good Story, That One *(1993), he plays with both oral traditions and the Trickster figure of Native mythology. His fiction includes* Medicine River *(1990),* Green Grass, Running Water *(1993),* Truth and Bright Water *(1999), and* A Short History of Indians in Canada: Stories *(2005).*

## *Thomas King*
# A Coyote Columbus Story

You know, Coyote came by my place the other day. She was going to a party. She had her party hat and she had her party whistle and she had her party rattle.

I'm going to a party, she says.

Yes, I says, I can see that.

It is a party for Christopher Columbus, says Coyote. That is the one who found America. That is the one who found Indians.

Boy, that Coyote is one silly Coyote. You got to watch out for her. Some of Coyote's stories have got Coyote tails and some of Coyote's stories are covered with scraggy Coyote fur but all of Coyote's stories are bent.

Christopher Columbus didn't find America, I says. Christopher Columbus didn't find Indians, either. You got a tail on that story.

Oh no, says Coyote. I read it in a book.

Must have been a Coyote book, I says.

No, no, no, no, says Coyote. It was a history book. Big red one. All about how Christopher Columbus sailed the ocean blue looking for America and the Indians.

Sit down, I says. Have some tea. We're going to have to do this story right. We're going to have to do this story now.

It was all Old Coyote's fault, I tell Coyote, and here is how the story goes. Here is what really happened.

So.

Old Coyote loved to play ball, you know. She played ball all day and all night. She would throw the ball and she would hit the ball and she would run and catch the ball. But playing ball by herself was boring, so she sang a song and she danced a dance and she thought about playing ball and pretty soon along came some Indians. Old Coyote and the Indians became very good friends. You are sure a good friend, says those Indians. Yes, that's true, says Old Coyote.

But, you know, whenever Old Coyote and the Indians played ball, Old Coyote always won. She always won because she made up the rules. That sneaky one made up the rules and she always won because she could do that.

That's not fair, says the Indians. Friends don't do that.

That's the rules, says Old Coyote. Let's play some more. Maybe you will win the next time. But they don't.

You keep changing the rules, says those Indians.

No, no, no, no, says Old Coyote. You are mistaken. And then she changes the rules again.

So, after a while, those Indians find better things to do.

Some of them go fishing.

Some of them go shopping.

Some of them go to a movie.

Some of them go on a vacation.

Those Indians got better things to do than play ball with Old Coyote and those changing rules.

So, Old Coyote doesn't have anyone to play with.

So, she has to play by herself.

So, she gets bored.

When Old Coyote gets bored, anything can happen. Stick around. Big trouble is coming, I can tell you that.

Well. That silly one sings a song and she dances a dance and she thinks about playing ball. But she's thinking about changing those rules, too, and she doesn't watch what she is making up out of her head. So pretty soon, she makes three ships.

Hmmmm, says Old Coyote, where did those ships come from?

And pretty soon, she makes some people on those ships.

Hmmmm, says Old Coyote, where did those people come from?

And pretty soon, she makes some people on the beach with flags and funny-looking clothes and stuff.

Hooray, says Old Coyote. You are just in time for the ball game.

Hello, says one of the men in silly clothes and red hair all over his head. I am Christopher Columbus. I am sailing the ocean blue looking for China. Have you seen it?

Forget China, says Old Coyote. Let's play ball.

It must be around here somewhere, says Christopher Columbus. I have a map.

Forget the map, says Old Coyote. I'll bat first and I'll tell you the rules as we go along.

But that Christopher Columbus and his friends don't want to play ball. We got work to do, he says. We got to find China. We got to find things we can sell.

Yes, says those Columbus people, where is the gold?

Yes, they says, where is that silk cloth?

Yes, they says, where are those portable color televisions?

Yes, they says, where are those home computers?

Boy, says Old Coyote, and that one scratches her head. I must have sung that song wrong. Maybe I didn't do the right dance. Maybe I thought too hard. These people I made have no manners. They act as if they have no relations.

And she is right. Christopher Columbus and his friends start jumping up and down in their funny clothes and they shout so loud that Coyote's ears almost fall off.

Boy, what a bunch of noise, says Coyote. What bad manners. You guys got to stop jumping and shouting or my ears will fall off.

We got to find China, says Christopher Columbus. We got to become rich. We got to become famous. Do you think you can help us?

But all Old Coyote can think about is playing ball.

I'll let you bat first, says Old Coyote.

No time for games, says Christopher Columbus.

I'll let you make the rules, cries Old Coyote.

But those Columbus people don't listen. They are too busy running around, peeking under rocks, looking in caves, sailing all over the place. Looking for China. Looking for stuff they can sell.

I got a monkey, says one.

I got a parrot, says another.

I got a fish, says a third.

I got a coconut, says a fourth.

That stuff isn't worth poop, says Christopher Columbus. We can't sell those things in Spain. Look harder.

But all they find are monkeys and parrots and fish and coconuts. And when they tell Christopher Columbus, that one he squeezes his ears and he chews his nose and grinds his teeth. He grinds his teeth so hard, he gets a headache, and, then, he gets cranky.

And then he gets an idea.

Say, says Christopher Columbus. Maybe we could sell Indians.

Yes, says his friends, that's a good idea. We could sell Indians, and they throw away their monkeys and parrots and fish and coconuts.

Wait a minute, says the Indians, that is not a good idea. That is a bad idea. That is a bad idea full of bad manners.

When Old Coyote hears this bad idea, she starts to laugh. Who would buy Indians, she says, and she laughs some more. She laughs so hard, she has to hold her nose on her face with both her hands.

But while that Old Coyote is laughing, Christopher Columbus grabs a big bunch of Indian men and Indian women and Indian children and locks them up in his ships.

When Old Coyote stops laughing and looks around, she sees that some of the Indians are missing. Hey, she says, where are those Indians? Where are my friends?

I'm going to sell them in Spain, says Christopher Columbus. Somebody has to pay for this trip. Sailing over the ocean blue isn't cheap, you know.

But Old Coyote still thinks that Christopher Columbus is playing a trick. She thinks it is a joke. That is a good joke, she says, trying to make me think that you are going to sell my friends. And she starts to laugh again.

Grab some more Indians, says Christopher Columbus.

When Old Coyote sees Christopher Columbus grab some more Indians, she laughs even harder. What a good joke, she says. And she laughs some more. She does this four times and when she is done laughing, all the Indians are gone. And Christopher Columbus is gone and Christopher Columbus's friends are gone, too.

Wait a minute, says old Coyote. What happened to my friends? Where are my Indians? You got to bring them back. Who's going to play ball with me?

But Christopher Columbus didn't bring the Indians back and Old Coyote was real sorry she thought him up. She tried to take him back. But, you know, once you think things like that, you can't take them back. So you have to be careful what you think.

So. That's the end of the story.

Boy, says Coyote. That is one sad story.

Yes, I says. It's sad alright. And things don't get any better, I can tell you that.

What a very sad story, says Coyote. Poor Old Coyote didn't have anyone to play ball with. That one must have been lonely. And Coyote begins to cry.

Stop crying, I says. Old Coyote is fine. Some blue jays come along after that and they play ball with her

Oh, good, says Coyote. But what happened to the Indians? There was nothing in that red history book about Christopher Columbus and the Indians.

Christopher Columbus sold the Indians, I says, and that one became rich and famous.

Oh, good, says Coyote. I love a happy ending. And that one blows her party whistle and that one shakes her party rattle and that one puts her party hat back on her head. I better get going, she says, I'm going to be late for the party.

Okay, I says. Just remember how that story goes. Don't go messing it up again. Have you got it straight, now?

You bet, says Coyote. But if Christopher Columbus didn't find America and he didn't find Indians, who found these things?

Those things were never lost, I says. Those things were always here. Those things are still here today.

By golly, I think you are right, says Coyote.

Don't be thinking, I says. This world has enough problems already without a bunch of Coyote thoughts with tails and scraggy fur running around bumping into each other.

Boy, that's the truth. I can tell you that.

*—1993*

**Alice Walker (b. 1944)** *wrote the Pulitzer Prize–winning epistolary novel* The Color Purple *(1982). The book and its 1985 film version have made her the most famous living African-American writer, perhaps the most widely read of any American woman of colour. A native of Eatonton, Georgia, Walker was the eighth child of an impoverished farm couple. She attended Spelman College in Atlanta and Sarah Lawrence College on scholarships, graduating in 1965. Walker began her literary career as a poet, eventually publishing six volumes of verse. Walker's short-story collections and novels, including* The Temple of My Familiar *(1989) and* Possessing the Secret of Joy *(1992), which takes as its subject the controversial practice of female circumcision among African tribes, have continued to reach large audiences and have solidified her reputation as one of the major figures in contemporary literature. Walker has coined the term "womanist" to stand for the Black feminist concerns of much of her fiction. Her latest works include the novel* Now Is the Time to Open Your Heart *(2004) and* Collected Poems *(2005). Like so much of Walker's writing, the story "The Flowers" from* In Love and Trouble *(1973) challenges a myopic world view.*

## Alice Walker

# The Flowers

It seemed to Myop as she skipped lightly from hen house to pigpen to smokehouse that the days had never been as beautiful as these. The air held a keenness that made her nose twitch. The harvesting of the corn and cotton, peanuts and squash, made each day a golden surprise that caused excited little tremors to run up her jaws.

Myop carried a short, knobby stick. She struck out at random at chickens she liked, and worked out the beat of a song on the fence around the pigpen. She felt light and good in the warm sun. She was ten, and nothing existed for her but her song, the stick clutched in her dark brown hand, and the tat-de-ta-ta-ta of accompaniment.

Turning her back on the rusty boards of her family's sharecropper cabin, Myop walked along the fence till it ran into the stream made by the spring. Around the spring, where the family got drinking water, silver ferns and wildflowers grew. Along the shallow banks pigs rooted. Myop watched the tiny white bubbles disrupt the thin black scale of soil and the water that silently rose and slid away down the stream.

She had explored the woods behind the house many times. Often, in late autumn, her mother took her to gather nuts among the fallen leaves.

*Today she made her own path, bouncing this way and that way, vaguely keeping an eye out for snakes. She found, in addition to various common but pretty ferns and leaves, an armful of strange blue flowers with velvety ridges and a sweetsuds bush full of the brown, fragrant buds.*

*By twelve o'clock, her arms laden with sprigs of her findings, she was a mile or more from home. She had often been as far before, but the strangeness of the land made it not as pleasant as her usual haunts. It seemed gloomy in the little cove in which she found herself. The air was damp, the silence close and deep.*

*Myop began to circle back to the house, back to the peacefulness of the morning. It was then she stepped smack into his eyes. Her heel became lodged in the broken ridge between brow and nose, and she reached down quickly, unafraid, to free herself. It was only when she saw his naked grin that she gave a little yelp of surprise.*

*He had been a tall man. From feet to neck covered a long space. His head lay beside him. When she pushed back the leaves and layers of earth and debris Myop saw that he'd had large white teeth, all of them cracked or broken, long fingers, and very big bones. All his clothes had rotted away except some threads of blue denim from his overalls. The buckles of the overalls had turned green.*

*Myop gazed around the spot with interest. Very near where she'd stepped into the head was a wild pink rose. As she picked it to add to her bundle she noticed a raised mound, a ring, around the rose's root. It was the rotted remains of a noose, a bit of shredding plowline, now blending benignly into the soil. Around an overhanging limb of a great spreading oak clung another piece. Frayed, rotted, bleached, and frazzled—barely there—but spinning restlessly in the breeze. Myop laid down her flowers.*

*And the summer was over.*

*—1973*

*Lise Bissonnette (b. 1945) was born in Northern Quebec and was for many years the publisher of Montreal's influential newspaper* Le Devoir. *Considered an exceptional journalist and editor, she has also written three novels,* Following the Summer *(1993),* Affairs of Art *(1996), and* An Appropriate Place *(2003), and a collection of stories,* Cruelties *(1998). She is known for her advocacy of feminist and separatist concerns, and now serves as CEO of La Grande Bibliothèque du Québec.*

# *Lise Bissonnette*
# Dresses

It ought to be worn with patent-leather pumps, a string of pearls, and most important, with your hair in a coil, the kind that ripples halfway down the back as it comes undone.

I had high-heeled shoes in a matte, smoky grey-black, harlequin glasses, a rhinestone necklace, and hair as straight as we imagined the nuns' would be under their coifs.

It crossed my mind to throw myself into the water; I tried in vain to feel the urge. On the wire hanger with its scrawny shoulders, the little black dress murmured a call to sin. We'd see.

It had been sewn miles away from the boarding school, during the Christmas holidays. I'd been allowed to choose a Vogue pattern, something my mother consented to only for grand occasions, but on this one we were silent. There comes an age when we pass from taffeta to soft crepe; I wanted it to be dark, she merely warned me not to iron it on the right side, that would make the seams shiny. The hem stopped just below the knee, the sleeves at the elbow, the only fullness was at the bosom, where it was draped over as yet non-existent points. At the last fitting my brother had whistled. The legs, he said, weren't bad.

But now, standing at my bedroom closet, Michèle was gazing at it with the pout of a connoisseur. She'd been dealing with boys for a long time now and if I was able to stand up to her, it was through literature. Jean-Jacques Rousseau was on the Index; I could quote him word for word. Borrowed from the Ottawa library, from which they no longer dared ban us, his *Confessions* under my pillow was considered to be the

Translated by Sheila Fischman.

first licentious book to reach our dormitory. I also claimed to know the loves of Claudel and I invented some for Charles Péguy.[1] I impressed the readers of *Seventeen*, including Michèle, who got along fairly well in Latin too.

My black dress was declared to be too sober. It's true, I didn't dare tell anyone where I'd got the image. That of the wife of Yousuf Karsh,[2] a hieratic beauty I'd brushed up against late that fall. The city was so boring in those days that even Churchill's photographer attended the Jeunesses Musicales concerts. I did mental dictation as I listened to the pianists, an odd little habit that took the soul out of Chopin and left me free to observe this high society among whom she stood alone. So white in her black silk that you could hardly see the pearls around her neck. At intermission, I saw her lean her head towards a man whose chin disappeared into his cravat, a layer of softness for a voice entangled in its accent: "Vould you come mit me to see ze artist after ze concert?" She had the remarkable power of not responding, or of responding so briefly that it seemed she hadn't. I wanted to be long, lithe, and unattainable.

Michèle decided otherwise. Of course I'd wanted this black dress so someone would touch me, while she wanted to correct the faint melancholy of this basic garment, which actually looked rather feminine. In English, and passing ourselves off as a pair of hotheads from Hull, after lengthy explorations we bought first the red shoes and then the matching bag. There was no money left for a perm, but we did that at home quite successfully. Glasses were unthinkable, a myopic gaze being in any case more flattering, and she was going to lend me the earrings and necklace of fake gold I turned out to be allergic to.

On the evening in question, she found a man with dark hair and a friend to take us to the Club Chaudière. I wasn't ugly; a cross between a poodle and a bluish Siamese cat, I felt vague and strong. "You're more sensual than I am," Michèle decreed, promising herself that she'd borrow the dress the following Saturday. We claimed we were going to the movies, a double bill that the chaplain pretended to check on.

[1] *Charles Péguy* (1873–1914): French poet and philosopher known for his contribution to French intellectual life, through his writings, his socialist and religious beliefs, and his *Fortnightly Notebooks*, the small but significant journal he founded.
[2] *Yousuf Karsh* (1908–2002): American-Canadian photographer known for his portraits of famous people including Churchill and Hemingway.

The boy was as inane as Péguy would have been at a *bal musette*.[3] He had thick lips and a kiss curl, and he was a compulsive hand-holder (his was damp). Nothing could have been longer than the drive home, complete with the ritual of the backseat Michèle had warned me to go along with.

I came across as a future nun while I dreamed of wantonness in soft crepe. I thought of jumping in the water, I searched in vain for the desire to do so.

Spring came to me on Ste. Catherine Street. A slenderness under woollen clothes, a warm glimmer on a motorbike, an evil thread of violin music through the window of a Tourist Room, dust in an ambulance's wake. I didn't intend to feel provincial for very long.

It was still dark as shopkeepers pushed their displays into the middle of the sidewalk, series of dresses all the same except for the colours in the pattern, hung crowded together on racks, with a piece of cardboard at one end where "$5.00 each/chaque" was written in felt pen. Surrounded by the smells of plastic and of sour winter, squashed into a cupboard where half a mirror jutted out over some packages, I tried on one that moved like daylight itself. Green spangles were woven into the grey weft, the neckline was round, the sleeves short, and the waist was barely caught in the plastic belt, a thin twist in the same green.

Straight and without a fold, it fell like jersey, and it was. Mid-season, I thought, listening to myself in silence. It's fluid, jersey, you grow taller when you pour yourself into it, and its two consonants rub against your skin. You feel like Michelle Tisseyre[4] entertaining in her garden on the first evenings that aren't so cool. "Shall I bring you a sweater?" "No, perhaps another few drops of port." And the man's arm brushes against your shoulder as he pours. There'll always be time to go inside.

I felt as if I were twenty years old; I was dismantling the pleasure of it in advance.

The little man with the moustache was keeping an eye on both the sidewalk and the boutique; he saw none of my beauty, which was

---

[3]*bal musette:* French dance hall with music provided by an accordion band.
[4]*Michelle Tisseyre* (1918– ): Montreal-born star of French radio and television, who worked on the *Encyclopédie de la femme canadienne* (1965) and "La Collection des deux solitudes," intended to bring the work of Canadian English writers to francophone readers.

camouflaged by a winter coat once more when I paid. The jersey would be for other eyes, that very evening.

The bag was light, so light, as far as the corner of the street. For there are limits to frivolity and I had five dollars less for the unexpected— a bookstore that was also displaying its wares in the sun. I spent a long time leafing through the pamphlets published by Éditions du Jour, they were blaring rages unknown in my Ottawa-area boarding school. The door was open and I worked up the courage to go inside as far as the first section of shelves, which disappeared into the half-light of noon. The bookseller was affable and I was terrified by his voice, that of an examiner in search of brilliant students. "You're studying philosophy at your age? Nonsense, I imagine." I hadn't said a word and he was confirming the limits of Thomism,[5] an insight that struck me as original.

It cost me a dollar and twenty cents for the brand-new paperback edition of *The Situation of the Worker*, Simone Weil's journal of her days as a factory worker, a double volume with a red-and-black cover, blood and night. Henri Tranquille had just sold me my first book worthy of the name, and entrance into the world of women who had rebelled, which would lead me later to the world of both George Sand and Rosa Luxemburg.

But I certainly wasn't there yet, though I was in fine form, with my book and my dress in my bookbag. At 101 St. Joseph Boulevard West, I was the last of the regional representatives to take my place at the table where we were to discuss secularism and the Parent report on Quebec's education system. Though at school you couldn't shut me up on the subject, which I used to harass a professor of pedagogy, I would be silent in the presence of the boys, some of whom were about to meet with the minister, Paul Gérin-Lajoie. I would write the press release, however, which only *Le Devoir* would run, abridged: "Through its president, the Presse étudiante nationale (PEN) declares that democratization of the education system must be the primary objective of any reform."

I was thanked as they left the premises for their dinners in Outremont.[6] The only people still there were middle class, the Gestetner operators and stamp-lickers, ready for the night on the town they'd been promised for months. I relinquished Simone Weil and my woollies,

[5]*Thomism:* the doctrines of Thomas Aquinas (c.1225–1274) that synthesize theology and philosophy.
[6]*Outremont:* an attractive and affluent community named for its location beyond (*outre*) Mont Royal, the mountain that gives Montreal its name.

the dress clung tenderly—jersey is uncrushable. Jersey for jazz, jersey for the knee offered under the table. To a skinny boy whose blue eyes were looking elsewhere.

Peel Street, second floor, the trumpet blasting into the piano, the beer as bitter as it was illegal at my age. And I plunged forever into the atrocious solitude of a woman who wanted to be one and wasn't. For what the skinny blue-eyed boy saw all around were Juliettes in black sweaters, black skirts, and black stockings, their hair as straight as the very notion of despair, sooty lashes, souls in hell. My green spangles caught in my throat, and my short sleeves undressed me roughly. The sun was totally out of fashion. I spent hours and a night suffering from the springtime that I'd misread so badly.

On the bus home the next day, Simone Weil taught me about detachment from material goods. In vain. I'd felt as if I were twenty years old, and I had dismantled the pleasure of it in advance.

"You aren't going to wear that for making free love!" Rose-Aimée's cry came not from the heart but from the throat. A fluttering of nerves, hers were fierce and accustomed to scandal. As usual, she was speaking as much to the ceiling as to me, with that way she had of pushing both instruction and morality with her chin, of holding high the tablets of the law. Of all of us, she was the only one who had a boyfriend, a deathly pale member of the Catholic student movement with whom she actively practised purity and preached about it so, she made us loathe it.

Facing the closets we were emptying in preparation for packing our bags in June, she finally encountered evil elsewhere than in sermons. Displayed before her was a long nightgown in which a young woman could die a martyr or live condemned to hell: it was a question of what I might have had in mind when I chose it: deep pink percale, with the bodice cut from a piece of lace crocheted by a grandmother I'd never known. Cream and satin was the ribbon that snaked its way through the lace to cinch the empire waist, and the wide pleats fell like those of Josephine de Beauharnais[7] or St. Cecile, patron of music, depending. Rose-Aimée obviously suspected me of designing this wonder and having it made for purposes other than elegant sleep, especially since I'd never

[7]*Josephine de Beauharnais* (1763–1814): After the death of her first husband she became wife to Napoleon Bonaparte and empress of France.

worn it. But she was mistaken. I'd wanted it for no particular reason, for an image, to bring beauty into the tedium of the dormitories.

Still, I was about to wear it for the first time, finally. I'd recently met a young man whose natural shyness went well with my desire to be done with regional activities. His name was Roger, I forgave him for it, and in his slow way of moving one could sense the necessary aptitude for practising existentialism. He was long and pensive, with blue-green eyes and a pianist's hands. During meetings he drew. At the movie he stroked my fingers, on the street his fingers brushed my neck, and he said all kinds of intelligent things about the futility of the world. He'd introduced me to his mother, a mistake. Her enthusiasm had put a little too much colour into the shades of grey where we were silent about our feelings.

He had the use of an apartment that belonged to a friend of his in Montreal, where I was going the next day for a final meeting before the summer holidays. He would be alone, he'd take care of the wine, cheese, and candles, we would eat and sleep there, just the two of us. Not another word had been said. But never was a lace-topped pink night-gown so appropriate as for this occasion. The whole dormitory was in on the secret, and with the exception of Rose-Aimée they all agreed. "Don't forget perfume," Michèle had fussed. She lent it to me with a new reverence. She didn't know any boys who had the use of an apart-ment; I was the first one to cross that particular threshold.

As for free love, you'd have had to be warped to threaten me with it. There were still so many kisses to discover before I got there, so many acts to perform, so many murmurs to commence. I felt nothing but impatience for a window open onto the noise of Dorchester Boulevard, for a pink gown that moves all down its length, for the bitterness of the wine, for the silence we'd flow into before nightfall, and its hours that would be what they would be. We would open them one by one.

And so there I was at seventeen and a half, draped in pink, drinking Spanish Iago, and chatting about Auguste Comte.[8] I'd become acquainted with him at the same time as with Roger, who considered him to be the spiritual father of Jean-Paul Sartre, and I nearly fell genuinely in love with this long, lean boy buried under his words, who bestowed them on me without vanity. We talked about everything except ourselves, even as

---

[8]*Auguste Comte* (1798–1857): French thinker known as the founder of sociology and positivism, a philosophical system that confines itself to knowledge gained through the scientific method of observation and experimentation.

we moved closer together in the low armchair that we never dared to abandon for the big bed in the next room. I was excited enough to palpitate a little, I would have untied a ribbon, perhaps I did so just before he finally told me into my hair that his heart was strange and a stranger. He traced the lace with his finger: "I love a boy, this is his place, I can't leave him . . ." His cheek was hollow in the lamplight, his body tense. Was he expecting to see me slip away from him, outside this place, outside of us? But I was filled with contentment. The night passed serenely now, I was fascinated by this man's confession, I was penetrating much deeper than I'd expected into the forbidden, I could put off the decisions of my body, which wasn't serious because it was seventeen years old.

At dawn we went to the mountain to watch the sunrise. The mosquitoes were preparing for a humid day and real summer. We stretched out in the short grass, I imagined us upright and impossible like Tristan and Isolde, who slept with a sword between them.

Roger disturbed the arrangement when he put his hand on my stomach; he was as free now as he was chaste, he could touch a girl.

That was what brought a bellow from the policeman on horseback who was passing by, he drove us from the earthly paradise with words as religious as those of Rose-Aimée. To him I owe the long kiss that my false lover placed defiantly on my neck, love was as free as the air that was gilding both man and beast, we laughed, we were hungry. Life was going to be irresistible.

*—1999*

*Jamaica Kincaid (b. 1949) was born Elaine Potter Richardson in Antigua, a Caribbean island that did not achieve independence from Britain until 1981. She left Antigua at seventeen to be an au pair in New York, taking on a new name that was both a removal and reminder of her ties to the West Indies. "Girl" was first published in* The New Yorker *and then in the collection* At the Bottom of the River *(1983). Her style, often closer to poetry than prose, has been compared to that of Gertrude Stein. Describing writing as a "kind of self-rescuing," she has published several autobiographical novels, including* Annie John *(1985),* Lucy *(1990),* Autobiography of My Mother *(1996), and* Mr. Potter *(2002), as well as works of non-fiction, including* My Brother *(1997) and* Among Flowers: A Walk in the Himalaya *(2005).*

## Jamaica Kincaid

## Girl

Wash the white clothes on Monday and put them on the stone heap; wash the color clothes on Tuesday and put them on the clothesline to dry; don't walk barehead in the hot sun; cook pumpkin fritters in very hot sweet oil; soak your little cloths right after you take them off; when buying cotton to make yourself a nice blouse, be sure that it doesn't have gum on it, because that way it won't hold up well after a wash; soak salt fish overnight before you cook it; is it true that you sing benna[1] in Sunday school?; always eat your food in such a way that it won't turn someone else's stomach; on Sundays try to walk like a lady and not like the slut you are so bent on becoming; don't sing benna in Sunday school; you mustn't speak to wharf-rat boys, not even to give directions; don't eat fruits on the street—flies will follow you; *but I don't sing benna on Sundays at all and never in Sunday school;* this is how to sew on a button; this is how to make a buttonhole for the button you have just sewed on; this is how to hem a dress when you see the hem coming down and so to prevent yourself from looking like the slut I know you are so bent on becoming; this is how you iron your father's khaki shirt so that it doesn't have a crease; this is how you iron your father's khaki pants so that they don't have a crease; this is how you grow okra—far from the house, because okra tree harbors red ants; when you are growing dasheen, make sure it gets plenty of water or else it makes your

---

[1] *benna:* popular music, calypso.

throat itch when you are eating it; this is how you sweep a corner; this is how you sweep a whole house; this is how you sweep a yard; this is how you smile to someone you don't like too much; this is how you smile to someone you don't like at all; this is how you smile to someone you like completely; this is how you set a table for tea; this is how you set a table for dinner; this is how you set a table for dinner with an important guest; this is how you set a table for lunch; this is how you set a table for breakfast; this is how to behave in the presence of men who don't know you very well, and this way they won't recognize immediately the slut I have warned you against becoming; be sure to wash every day, even if it is with your own spit; don't squat down to play marbles—you are not a boy, you know; don't pick people's flowers—you might catch something; don't throw stones at blackbirds, because it might not be a blackbird at all; this is how to make a bread pudding; this is how to make doukona;[2] this is how to make pepper pot; this is how to make a good medicine for a cold; this is how to make a good medicine to throw away a child before it even becomes a child; this is how to catch a fish; this is how to throw back a fish you don't like, and that way something bad won't fall on you; this is how to bully a man; this is how a man bullies you; this is how to love a man, and if this doesn't work there are other ways, and if they don't work don't feel too bad about giving up; this is how to spit up in the air if you feel like it, and this is how to move quick so that it doesn't fall on you; this is how to make ends meet; always squeeze bread to make sure it's fresh; *but what if the baker won't let me feel the bread?*; you mean to say that after all you are really going to be the kind of woman who the baker won't let near the bread?

—*1983*

---

[2]*doukona:* a spicy pudding, often made from plantains and wrapped in a plantain or banana leaf.

*Guy Vanderhaeghe (b. 1951) was born in Esterhazy, Saskatchewan, and continues to explore the truth and mythology of Western life in such award-winning novels as* The Englishman's Boy *(1996) and* The Last Crossing *(2001). His debut collection of stories,* Man Descending *(1982), won the Governor General's Award, and he has continued to work in the form, publishing* The Trouble with Heroes *(1983) and* Things as They Are? *(1992). He counts Alice Munro and John Updike among his influences and combines a love of history, popular culture, and complex characterization in his fiction. Describing himself as a "Big Sky Guy," he credits Saskatoon with making him feel both valued and grounded.*

## Guy Vanderhaeghe
# The Home Place

It was early morning, so early that Gil MacLean loaded the colt into the truck box under a sky still scattered with faint stars. The old man circled the truck once, checking the tailgate, the tires, and the knot in the halter shank, tottering around on legs stiff as stilts, shoulders hunched to keep the chill off him. He was sixty-nine and mostly cold these days.

A hundred yards behind him one window burned yellow in the dark house. That was his son Ronald, asleep under the bare light bulb and the airplanes. Whenever Ronald fled Darlene, the woman Gil MacLean referred to as the "back-pages wife," he slunk back to his father's house in the dead of night to sleep in a room lit up like a Christmas tree. To her father-in-law, Darlene was the back-pages wife because Ronald had found her advertising herself in the classified section of a farm newspaper, right alongside sale notices for second-hand grain augers and doubtful chain-saws.

Dawn found the old man in a temper, a mood. It was the mare he had wanted when he rattled oats in the pail and whistled, but it was the gelding which had been lured. The mare, wiser and warier, had hung back. So this morning he had a green, rough-broke colt to ride. There was nothing for it, though. He needed a horse because his mind was made up to repair Ronald's fences. They were a disgrace.

Generally that was the way to catch what you wanted, shake a little bait. It was what Darlene had done with Ronald, but she hadn't fooled Gil MacLean for a second. He knew how it was.

Four years ago his son and Darlene married after exchanging honeyed letters for six months. Ronald never breathed a word to him about any wedding. When Ronald's mother was alive she used to say Ronald was too much under his father's thumb. But the one time he slipped out from beneath it, look at the result.

One morning Ronald had driven off in the pick-up. Twelve hours later he phoned from Regina to announce that he and his bride were bound for Plentywood, Montana, to honeymoon. Ronald was thirty-eight then, had never been married, had never been engaged, had never even had a date that his father could recollect. It was a shock and a mystery. The way Gil figured it, Ronald must have proposed by mail before he ever met face to face with Darlene. Ronald didn't have it in him to offer himself in the flesh to someone with whom he was actually acquainted. He would be too shy, too embarrassed for that.

The old man folded himself into the cab of the truck, joint by joint. "The best work, the worst sleep," he muttered to Ronald's lighted window as he drove under it. In the east there were mares' tails on the horizon, fine as the vapour trails of jets, reddened by the rising sun.

It was Gil MacLean's speculation that his son married only to get his hands on land. Not land of Darlene's, she was a waif and a pauper and had none, but his land, Gil MacLean's land. He never entertained the idea that Ronald might have married out of loneliness, or lust, or any feeling of the remotest kin to either. Just land. That was why he was sometimes troubled, wondering what share of responsibility was his to bear for Ronald's current unhappiness. Maybe he ought to have transferred the title sooner, but he had never trusted the boy's judgment. Events appeared to have confirmed his suspicions. Ronald had his own farm now, a wedding present. A married man needed land, so his father gave him the farm that the MacLeans had always called the "home place." It gave Gil satisfaction to see it pass from father to son and he thought it might bring Ronald luck.

The home place consisted of the original quarter Gil's father had homesteaded, the pre-emption, and another 320 acres picked up cheap from a Finnish immigrant who went to pieces when his wife ran off on him. Over the years the MacLean family acquired other holdings but the home place was special. Situated in a valley, it was a mix of rich bottom land and steep, wooded hills. In the spring, down by the river, blizzards of gulls floated in the wake of tractor and disker, pursuing easy pickings, while hawks rode the air high above the lean hills and, shrieking, fell to plunder these lazy storms of white birds. To Gil it had all been beautiful. It was all he had ever wanted, to possess that place and those sights. A day spent away from the farm made him restless, cranky. Returning to it, even after the briefest absence, he acted oddly, dodging through the wires of a fence in his city clothes to wade about in his crop, hands running back and forth lightly over the bearded heads the way another man might absent-mindedly stroke a cat. Or he might suddenly strike off for the hills with all the energy and purpose of someone hurrying off to keep an appointment, tie flying over his shoulder.

His wife used to say: "Gil's gone off to satisfy himself that nobody so much as shifted a cup of dirt on this place when he was away."

What Gil never confided to his wife was that he felt more present in the land than he did in his own flesh, his own body. Apart from it he had no real existence. When he looked in a mirror he stood at a great distance from what he regarded, but with the land it was different. All that he had emptied of himself into it, he recognized.

The road to the home place ran due east without deviating a hair, rising and falling regularly as a sleeper's breath as it made its way over a succession of bare hills. The emerging sun drew his eyes into a squint when he topped a rise; the blue shadows in the hollows forced them wide again. In the back of the truck the slither and clatter of iron shoes was unremitting. The colt was either highly strung or lacked balance. If it lost its footing and fell it would be a task to get on its feet again; the box was narrow and there was little room for manoeuvring. He'd have to go back and get Ronald out of bed to help him.

Turning Ronald out of bed was not an easy job. Despite his son's difficulties falling asleep, once he was gone he wasn't likely to stir. Often he didn't wake before noon. Gil, on the other hand, roused to the slightest sound. That first night the gritty scraping of the shoes on the stairs had been enough to jerk him out of a dreamless sleep. He'd never been one to lock doors, he had only himself to thank that a night intruder was climbing up to him. It was like the television and its stories of grinning madmen invading houses and arming themselves with drapery cords and butcher knives to strangle and stab. The old man bunched up his pillow and held it out before him, ready to parry the first knife thrust. The footsteps, however, went on past his door. Only when the toilet flushed did he realize it had to be Ronald.

He simply shook in bed for several minutes, too angry and too relieved to ask himself what his son might be up to. Finally he grew calm and curiosity prodded him out into the hallway to investigate. The light was on in Ronald's old bedroom and the door stood ajar.

Ronald was lying flat on his back on the bed, staring up at his model airplanes. As a teenager, even as a young man, he had exhibited little interest in anything other than building models of airplanes from kits, squeezing tubes of glue, pasting on decals, and painting engine cowlings with brushes whose tips he sucked into needle points. The models had never been removed. Forty or more of them hung suspended from the ceiling on fine wires; his room was almost exactly as he had left it when he chose Darlene. Flying Fortresses, Mustangs, Zeros, Spitfires, Messerschmitts, a whole catalogue of war planes dangled there. The light in the bedroom was also as harsh, pitiless, and glaring as it had ever been. When Ronald was fourteen he had unscrewed the bulb in the ceiling fixture and replaced it with a more powerful one. He also dispensed with the shade because he wanted the models hanging beneath the light bulb to cast their shadows on his bedspread and linoleum in the way fighter planes and bombers passing between sun and earth print their images on country lanes and city squares. These shadows were repeated everywhere about the room, and in their midst lay Ronald, gazing up into the strong light, gazing up at undercarriages and silhouettes.

"What's all this, Ronald?" his father said. "This is a hell of a time to pay a visit. It's past two."

Ronald said: "I can't stand it. I can't sleep there no longer." He kept his eyes fixed on the planes as he spoke.

Gil knew there was talk going around town about his son and his daughter-in-law, all of it unfortunate. Darlene had come stamped with the word trouble; he'd seen it from day one. The old man sighed and took a seat on the straight-back chair beside the dresser. Ronald was not exactly the forthcoming type, he was prepared to wait him out.

After a considerable stretch of silence his son said: "I should never have left." Gil knew what he meant. Ronald wasn't saying he ought not to have left Darlene; he was saying he should not have abandoned this room and the comfort and solace of those planes that could not fly.

It was strange that, given all the worrying he had done about Ronald and Darlene, Gil had never seen the real danger. Now he did. The realization of what might lie ahead was like an attack of some kind. Before he could proceed it was necessary to relieve the pressure prodding his breastbone and robbing him of breath. He arched his back and squeezed his eyes tight until it eased and he could speak. And speak he did, urgently, for a solid hour without interruption and with a drying mouth. He said it was the government and the courts. They'd gone and changed the marriage property laws so that the women ended up with half of everything these days. Did Ronald know what that meant? Darlene could lay claim to a half share of the home place. "No divorce, Ronald," he repeated. "No divorce. Don't let that bitch break up the home place. Don't you give her that satisfaction." Only when he had wrung this promise out of Ronald did he cease arguing. For a moment he was overcome by his son's loyalty. He patted the back of his hand and murmured: "Thank you. Thank you."

In a month, however, Ronald came creeping back up the stairs. In baffled rage and fear of the future, Gil shouted through his bedroom door: "Don't expect any sympathy from me if you won't try to adjust!"

Ronald explained that he had a problem going to sleep in the same room, the same house as Darlene. That's the reason he came home every once in a while, to relax and catch up on his sleep. Not that it was easy for him to get to sleep in his old room either, but there he could manage it. What he did was stare up at the glowing bulb and planes until the moment arrived when he could feel the sun hot on his back and suddenly he was winged and soaring, flying into sleep, released, sometimes for twelve hours at a time.

Ronald had been paying his visits to his father's to sleep for a year. About the time they started he commenced on improvements to the home place. This meant pushing bush and clearing land up top, above the valley, in the hills. Gil had pointed out this was nothing but sheer craziness. Marginal land like that was suitable only for pasture, cropping it would never repay the cost of breaking and if the hillsides were stripped of cover they would erode. But Ronald, who was usually willing to be advised, wouldn't listen to his father. A cunning, stubborn look stole over his face when he said: "We'll see. I hired another dozer. Pretty soon the brush piles will be dry and ready to burn."

All spring Ronald fired his huge, gasoline-laced bonfires of scrub oak and poplar. The gusty roar of flames was like constant static in his ears, heat crumpled the air around him and stained it a watery yellow, greasy black clouds mounted indolently into the purity of blue skies. The scars of the dozer blades fresh on the earth made the old man indignant. In places the soil had been cut so deep that streaks of rubbly gravel were exposed.

"You won't grow wheat in that," Gil MacLean shouted. "So what'll it be? Carrots?"

Smiling oddly, Ronald said: "I'm not growing nothing. I'll open a pit and peddle gravel to the Department of Highways by the yard."

"That's not farming," his father returned, disgusted. "That's mining."

It was all Ronald had any interest in at present, pushing bush, clawing up roots, burning. His face appeared hot, scorched. His eyes were forever weepy and red, their lids puffy and swollen, lashes singed away. The ends of his hair had crinkled, crisped, and gone white in the furnace-heat. Everything else Ronald neglected. He hadn't yet done his summer fallow and his cattle were continually straying. This morning Gil was determined to mend Ronald's fences because he was ashamed of what the neighbours would think with his son's cows belly-deep in their crops.

The old man crested the last rise and the valley spread itself out at his feet. There were days when he would pull his truck over to the shoulder of the road and look with deep satisfaction at the slow river and the sombre quilt of green and black fields, look until he had his fill. From such a height the home place looked fatter and richer than with your nose shoved in it. Up close dirt was dirt. There was no time for stopping and admiring this morning though. He was in a hurry.

Gil entered his son's property by a little-used side gate because he didn't want Darlene spying his truck and reporting his doings to Ronald. He parked, unloaded the horse, and slung a duffel bag of tools and a coil of barbed wire on the saddle. Within minutes he was riding down an old trail they had hauled hay on in summer and wood in winter in his father's time. Neither of those things would be possible now, encroaching wild rose and chokecherry bushes had narrowed it so a loaded wagon couldn't pass. The occasional sapling had taken root between the old ruts. Sunlight and sparrows strayed amid the poplar leaves overhead. Ronald's dozers hadn't reached this far yet, hadn't peeled all this back. Maybe his money would run out before they could, that was Gil's fervent hope.

It was eight o'clock before Gil located the first break in the fence. The wires were rotten with rust and would have to be replaced. He set to work. The old man ought not to have been taken by surprise. He knew the very nature of a young horse was unpredictability. It happened when he was playing out sixty yards of wire, lazy-man style, one end of the coil dallied round the horn, the horse walking it out. It could have been the sound the wire made hissing and writhing after them through the grass and weeds. It could have been that a barb nicked the gelding's hocks. Suddenly the colt froze in its tracks, laid back its ears, and trembled all over like a leaf.

Gil had been a horseman all his life, nearly all of his seventy years. He knew what was coming and he fought with all his strength to keep the gelding from pulling its head down between its forelegs. If the colt managed to get its head down it would be able to buck. It managed. An old man's strength was not sufficient. The horse squealed, wriggled, snapped out its hind legs. Gil's lower plate popped out of his mouth. The sky tilted. He fell.

It was bad luck to get snarled in the wire. The colt dragged him several hundred yards, the old man skipping and bounding and tumbling along behind like a downed water-skier without the presence of mind to relinquish his grip on the tow rope.

When it had winded itself the horse came to a halt, stood rolling its eyes and snorting. The old man began to paw himself feebly, searching his pockets for a pair of fencing pliers with which to cut himself out of the jumble of wire. Using the pliers, he had to move cautiously and deliberately so as not to excite the skittish colt. Nevertheless, when the final strand of wire parted with a twang the colt kicked him twice in a convulsion of fear before trotting off a stone's throw away. There it circled about anxiously, stepping on the ends of the dragging reins and bruising its mouth.

The old man lay still, taking stock. There seemed to be a lot of blood, the wire had cut him in many places. He sat up and the blood gushed out of his nose and mouth and spilled down his jacket front. He peered about him, dazed. The colt had dragged him to a desolate place. Ronald's dozers had been at work. Here there was nothing but bare, black earth engraved by caterpillar treads, piles of stones, and the remains of bonfires, charred tree trunks furred in white powdery ash.

While he sat up the blood continued to pour from his mouth and nose. It was better to lie back down. He was feeling weak but he told himself that was because he had taken nothing that morning but a cup of instant coffee. "I'll rest and my strength will come back," he told himself.

Gil closed his eyes and became aware of the powerful scents of sage, milkweed, grass. How was this possible in a place scoured clean? Then he realized they were coming from his clothes, had been ground into them by the dragging.

During the next three hours he tried a number of times to sit himself up, but the blood always ran so freely from his mouth he resigned the attempt. "Not yet," he muttered to himself. "In a while." He had little sense of passing time. There was only thirst and the stiff, scratchy ache of the wounds on his face, hands, legs.

When the sun shone directly down into his face he realized it was noon. The bright light in his eyes and the time of day made him think of Ronald. He would be waking now, looking up at his airplanes.

He had asked Ronald: "What is it with you? Why do you stare up at those planes?" And Ronald had said: "I like to pretend I'm up there, high enough to look down on something or somebody for once in my life."

Gil had laughed as if it were a joke, but it was an uneasy laugh.

Suddenly the old man was seized by a strange panic.

Making a great effort, he sat himself up. It was as if he hoped the force of gravity would pull everything he just now thought and saw down out of his head, drain it away. What he saw was Ronald's lashless eyes, singed hair, red burning face. What he thought was that such a face belonged to a man who wished to look down from a great height on fire, on ruin, on devastation, on dismay.

When the old man collapsed back into the wire he saw that face hovering above, looking down on him.

"You've got no right to look down on me," he said to the burning sky. "I came to fix your fences. I gave you the home place and showed you how to keep it."

His vehement voice filled the clearing and argued away the afternoon. It became harsher and louder when the sun passed out of Gil's vision and he could not raise himself to follow its course. The horse grew so accustomed to this steady shouting and calling out that only when it suddenly stopped did the gelding prick its ears, swing its head, and stare.

*—1992*

*Diane Schoemperlen (b. 1954) is from Thunder Bay, Ontario. She is noted for challenging the conventions of realistic fiction with unconventional structures, points of view, premises, and plots, but beneath the playful use of imagery and language are deeper explorations of the human condition. In her novels, including* In the Language of Love *(1994) and* Our Lady of the Lost and Found *(2001), and in several collections of short fiction, including the Governor General's Award–winning* Forms of Devotion *(1998), she widens our notion of what constitutes a story, finding epiphany in unexpected places.*

# Diane Schoemperlen
# Forms of Devotion

Strangely enough we are all seeking a form of devotion which fits our sense of wonder.

—J. Marks, *Transition*

## I. FAITH

The faithful are everywhere. They climb into their cars each morning and drive undaunted into the day. They sail off to work, perfectly confident that they will indeed get there: on time, intact. It does not occur to them that they could just as well be broadsided by a Coca-Cola delivery truck running the red light at the corner of Johnson and Main. They do not imagine the bottles exploding, the windshield shattering, their chests collapsing, the blood spurting out of their ears. They just drive. The same route every day, stop and go, back and forth, and yes, they get there: safe and sound. In the same unremarkable manner, they get home again too. Then they start supper without ever once marvelling at the fact that they have survived. It does not occur to them that the can of tuna they are using in the casserole might be tainted and they could all be dead of botulism by midnight.

They are armed with faith. They trust, if not in God exactly, then in the steadfast notion of everyday life. They do not expect to live forever of course, but they would not be entirely surprised if they did. On a daily basis, death strikes them mostly as a calamity which befalls other people, people who are probably evil, careless, or unlucky: just in the wrong place at the wrong time.

On weekend mornings, the faithful take their children to the park and assume they will not be abducted or fondled behind the climber by a pervert in a trench coat. In the afternoons, they work in their gardens, quite confident that those tiny seeds will eventually produce more tomatoes, zucchini, and green beans than they will know what to do with. They dig in the dirt and believe in the future. They put up preserves, save for retirement, and look forward to being grandparents. After they retire, they plan to buy a motorhome and travel.

When they go to bed at night, they assume that their white houses will stay standing, their green gardens will keep growing, their pink babies will keep breathing, and the yellow sun will rise in the morning just as it always does. Many of the faithful are women, giving birth being, after all, the ultimate act of pure faith. When their sons and daughters (whose as yet embryonic faith may temporarily fail them) wake sobbing from nightmares and wail, "Mommy, I dreamed you were dead. You won't die, will you?" these faithful mothers say, in all honesty, "Don't worry, I won't." The faithful sleep soundly.

If ever they find themselves feeling unhappy or afraid (as sometimes they do because, although faithful, they are also still human), they assume this too shall pass. They expect to be safe. They expect to be saved in the long run. They are devoted to the discharge of their daily lives. It does not occur to them that the meaning of life may be open to question.

## II. MEMORY

Remember to put out the garbage, pick up the dry cleaning, defrost the pork chops (the ground beef, the chicken thighs, the fillet of sole). Remember to feed the dog (the cat, the hamster, the goldfish, the canary). Remember the first smile, the first step, the first crush, the first kiss. Remember the bright morning, the long hot afternoon, the quiet evening, the soft bed, gentle rain in the night. Also remember the pain, the disappointments, the humiliations, the broken hearts, and an eclectic assortment of other sorrows. Take these tragedies in stride and with dignity. Do not tear your hair out. Forgive and forget and get on with it. The faithful look back fondly.

They are only passingly familiar with shame, guilt, torment, chaos, existentialism, and metaphysics. The consciences of the faithful are clear. They are not the ones spending millions of dollars on self-help books and exercise videos. They know they've done the best they could. If and when the faithful make mistakes, they know how to forgive themselves without requiring years of expensive therapy in the process.

In the summer, remember the winter: snow sparkling in clear sunlight, children in puffy snowsuits building snowmen and sucking icicles. Remember hockey rinks, rosy cheeks, Christmas carols, wool socks, and hot chocolate with marshmallows. In the winter, remember the summer: tidy green grass beneath big blue sky, long-limbed children playing hide-and-go-seek and running through sprinklers. Remember barbecues, sailboats, flowers, strawberries, and pink lemonade. The faithful can always find something to look forward to. The faithful never confuse the future with the past.

## III. KNOWLEDGE

The knowledge of the faithful is vast. They know how to change a tire on a deserted highway in the middle of the night without getting dirty or killed. They know how to bake a birthday cake in the shape of a bunny rabbit with gumdrop eyes and a pink peppermint nose. They know how to unplug a clogged drain with baking soda and vinegar.

They know how to paint the hallway, refinish the hardwood floors, wallpaper the bedroom, insulate the attic, reshingle the roof, and install a new toilet. They know how to build a campfire and pitch a tent single-handedly. They know how to tune up the car, repair the furnace, and seal the storm windows to prevent those nasty and expensive winter drafts.

They know how to prepare dinner for eight in an hour and a half for less than twenty dollars. They know how to sew, knit, crochet, and cut hair. They know how to keep themselves, their houses, their cars, and their children clean, very clean. They do not resent having to perform the domestic duties of family life. They may even enjoy doing the laundry, washing the walls, cleaning the oven, and grocery shopping.

They know how to make love to the same person for twenty years without either of them getting bored. They know how to administer CPR and the Heimlich manoeuvre. They know how and when to have fun.

The faithful know exactly what to say at funerals, weddings, and cocktail parties. They know when to laugh and when to cry and they never get these two expressions of emotion mixed up. The faithful know they are normal and they're damn proud of it. What they don't know won't hurt them.

## IV. INNOCENCE

The faithful are so innocent. Despite all evidence to the contrary, they believe that deep down everybody is just like them, or could be. They believe in benevolence, their own and other people's. They think that, given half a chance, even hardened criminals and manic-depressives can change. They are willing to give everyone a second chance. For the faithful, shaking off doubt is as easy as shaking a rug.

The faithful believe in law and order. They still look up to policemen, lawyers, teachers, doctors, and priests. They believe every word these people say. They even believe what the radio weatherman says in the forecast right after the morning news. It does not occur to them that these authority figures could be wrong, corrupt, or just plain stupid. Mind you, even the faithful are beginning to have serious reservations about politicians.

The faithful take many miraculous things for granted. Things like skin, electricity, trees, water, fidelity, the dogged revolution of the earth around the sun. They believe in beauty as a birthright and surround themselves with it whenever they can. They believe in interior decorating and makeup. They never underestimate the degree of happiness to be engendered by renovating the kitchen, placing fresh-cut flowers on the table, purchasing a set of fine silver, a mink coat, a minivan, or miscellaneous precious jewels. The faithful still believe you get what you pay for.

The faithful take things at face value. They do not search for hidden meanings or agendas. They are not skeptical, cynical, or suspicious. They are not often ironic. The faithful are the angels among us.

## V. STRENGTH

The faithless say the faithful are fools. Obviously it must be getting more and more difficult to keep the faith these days. Read the paper. Watch the news. Wonder what the world is coming to. All things considered, it has become harder to believe than to despair.

The faithless say the faithful are missing the point. But secretly the faithless must admit that if indeed, as they allege, there is no point (no purpose, no reason, no hope), then the faithful aren't missing a thing.

The faithless say the faithful are living minor lives, trivial, mundane, frivolous, blind. But secretly the faithless must envy the faithful, wondering if they themselves are simply too faint-hearted for faith.

While the faithless gaze into the abyss, fretting, moaning, and brooding, the faithful are busy getting on with their lives: labouring, rejoicing, carving Hallowe'en pumpkins, roasting Christmas and Thanksgiving turkeys, blowing out birthday candles year after year, and kissing each other wetly at midnight on New Year's Eve.

No matter what, the faithful know how to persevere. They are masters of the rituals that protect them. To the faithful, despair is a foreign language which they have neither the time nor the inclination to learn. The faithful frequently sing in the shower.

The faithful understand the value of fortitude. They carry always with them the courage of their convictions. They do not go to extremes but they could perform miracles if they had to. The faithful will not be crushed by the weight of the world. The faithful are sturdy and brave.

## VI. IMAGINATION

The faithful have their imaginations well in hand. They do not lie awake at night imagining earthquakes, tornadoes, flash floods, or nuclear war. They do not deal in cataclysms. They do not entertain the possibility of being axed to death in their beds by a psychokiller on the loose from the psychiatric hospital on the eastern edge of town. They do not lie there wide-eyed for hours picturing malignant cells galloping through their uteruses, their intestines, their prostate glands, or their brains. To the faithful, a headache is a headache, not a brain tumour. They do not imagine themselves rotting away from the inside out. They do not have detailed sexual fantasies about the mailman, the aerobics instructor, or their children's Grade Two teacher. The nights of the faithful are peaceful. Even their nightmares have happy endings. The faithful wake up smiling. Their subconsciouses are clear.

Imagine perfect health, financial security, your mortgage paid off, a new car every second year. Imagine mowing the lawn on Sunday afternoon and enjoying it. Imagine raking leaves in the fall without having to contemplate the futility of daily life. Imagine your grandchildren sitting at your knee while you tell them the story of your life.

The faithful are seldom haunted by a pesky sense of impending doom. They imagine that their lives are unfolding as they were meant to. They imagine that they are free. They imagine finding their feet planted squarely on the road to heaven. The faithful are prepared to live happily ever after.

Imagine laughing in the face of the future.

Imagine belonging to the fine fierce tribe of the faithful.

## VII. PRAYER

Pray for sunshine, pray for rain. Pray for peace. Pray for an end to the suffering of the unfortunate. Pray silently in a language simple enough for a child to understand. It is not necessary to get down on your knees with your eyes closed, your hands clasped. It is not necessary to hold your breath. Pray while you are cooking dinner, doing the dishes, washing the floor, holding your sleeping child in your arms. Pray with your heart, not just your mouth.

The faithful know how to pray to whatever gods they may worship. The faithful are praying all the time, every step of the way. Their prayers are not the sort that begin with the word *Please*. They do not bargain with their gods for personal favours. They do not make promises they can't keep, to their gods or anyone else. They do not beg for money, power, easy answers, or a yellow Porsche. They do not beseech, petition, implore, solicit, entreat, adjure, or snivel. They do not throw themselves upon the unreliable mercy of the pantheon. They are not dramatic zealots. The faithful are dignified, stalwart, and patient. All things come to them who will but wait. They are committed to simply enduring in a perpetual state of grace. Their faith itself is a never-ending benediction. The faithful may or may not go to church on Sunday. Their faith is their business.

The prayers of the faithful are mostly wordless forms of devotion. Actions speak louder than language. The faithful are reverent, humble, blessed. They are always busy having a religious experience. The faithful are seldom alarmed or afraid. The faithful barely have time to notice that all their prayers have been answered.

## VIII. ABUNDANCE

The faithful have more than enough of everything. They are never stingy. They believe in abundance and they know how to share the wealth. They give regularly to local and international charities and to most panhandlers. They give their old clothes and toys to the poor. The faithful are always generous. Of course they can afford to be. Of course there's more where that came from.

Every evening at dinner the faithful cry, "More, more, let's have some more!" The table is completely covered with heavy oval platters of meat and giant bowls of mashed potatoes and garden salad. They always have dessert. They prefer their children soft and plump. The faithful never bite off more than they can chew.

The days of the faithful are as full as their stomachs. They have energy to burn. They never whine about having too much to do. They like to be busy. They do not need time to think. Their bounty abounds. Their homes and their hearts are always full. Full of exuberance or solemnity, whichever current circumstances may require. The cups of the faithful frequently runneth over.

The arms of the faithful are always open. They have time for everyone. The faithful know how to share both the triumphs and the sorrows of others. They've always got the coffee on, blueberry muffins in the oven, a box of Kleenex handy just in case. The faithful know how to listen and they only offer advice when they're asked.

The faithful know how to count their blessings, even if it takes all day. They have all the time in the world. They know when to thank their lucky stars. The faithful are privileged but they are not smug.

## IX. WISDOM

The faithful are uncommonly wise. They are indefatigably glad to be alive. To the faithful everything matters. It does not occur to them that their whole lives may well end up having been nothing but a waste of time. The faithful are always paying attention. They know how to revel in the remarkable treasures of the everyday: a pink rose blooming below the window, a ham and cheese omelette steaming on the plate, a white cat washing her face in the sun, a new baby with eyes the colour of sand, a double rainbow in the western sky after a long hard rain. The faithful love rainbows and pots of gold. They know how to take pleasure wherever they can find it. The faithful are always exclaiming, "Look, look, look at that!" To the faithful nothing is mundane.

The faithful are everywhere. See if you can spot them: in the bank lineup on Friday afternoon, at McDonald's having hamburgers and chocolate milkshakes with their children, in the park walking the dog at seven o'clock on a January morning, at the hardware store shopping for a socket wrench and a rake. The faithful may be right in your own backyard.

The faithful are thankful for small pleasures and small mercies.

The faithful are earnest.

The faithful are easily amused.

The faithful do or do not know how lucky they are.

The faithful frequently cry at parades.

The faithful are not afraid of the dark because they have seen the light. Nothing is lost on the faithful. As far as they are concerned, wonders will never cease. The faithful are convinced that the best is yet to come.

## X. HOPE

The hope of the faithful is a tonic. Their eyes are bright, their skin is clear, their hair is shiny, and their blood flows vigorously through all of their veins. Even in times of adversity, the faithful know how to take heart. At the tiniest tingle of possibility, the faithful are not afraid to get their hopes up. They believe in divine providence. It all depends on how you define *divine*. The faithful are not fools. Although the faithless would dispute this, the faithful live in the real world just as much as anyone. They know all about hoping against hope. But they are not troubled by paradox. They are immune to those fits of despair which can cripple and dumbfound.

Concerning matters both big and small, the faithful have always got hope. Their whole lives are forms of perpetual devotion to the promise which hope extends. The faithful breathe hope like air, drink it like water, eat it like popcorn. Once they start, they can't stop.

Hope for world peace. Hope for a drop in the crime rate, shelter for the homeless, food for the hungry, rehabilitation for the deranged. Hope your son does well on his spelling test. Hope your team wins the World Series. Hope your mother does not have cancer. Hope the pork chops are not undercooked. Hope your best friend's husband is not having an affair with his secretary. Hope you win the lottery. Hope the rain stops tomorrow. Hope this story has a happy ending.

The hope of the faithful is infinite, ever expanding to fill the space available. Faith begets hope. Hope begets faith. Faith and hope beget power.

The faithful lean steadily into the wind.

*—1994*

**Michael Winter (b. 1965)** *was born in England but moved to Newfoundland at the age of ten, a dual heritage reflected in the name of his narrator Gabriel English. Winter grew up in Corner Brook, though he now divides his time between St. John's and Toronto. Part of the new wave of Newfoundland fiction, Winter's works include* Creaking in Their Skins *(1994),* One Last Good Look *(1999), and* The Big Why *(2004). "Archibald the Arctic" is the title of a book written by Archibald Fleming (1883–1953), an Anglican missionary to the Inuit.*

## *Michael Winter*
# Archibald the Arctic

Early on New Year's Day my mother woke me to say, calmly, that two police officers were at the door. She said this in the same way she'd say there's a fried egg sandwich in the oven. I was seventeen, home for Christmas, staying in Junior's room, in his bed in fact. I had been out with Geoff Doyle and Skizicks the night before, we ended up on Crow Hill throwing our empties down on the tracks, enjoying the wet distant crumple they made, waiting for the fireworks to sputter into the cold dark air. I remember Skizicks, who is a year older and knew we were virgins, saying he'd screwed Heidi Miller against the wall in behind Tim Horton's. Over the course of two long minutes we counted the reports of eleven shotguns, sounding small, disorganized and lonely.

I walked to the porch in my cold jeans, barefoot. I was hungry and my head hurt. I worked my mouth. The police officers were still outside. I opened the screen door. The white metal handle was frosty. Snow was drifting lightly onto their new fur hats, their epaulets, sliding off the waxed cruiser which hummed quietly in behind my father's car. There were no lights flashing. The driveway needed to be shovelled. Doyle would be up in his window, if he was up. The officers were facing each other, conversing. Their footprints were the first to our door in the new year. They looked fit and very awake.

Are you Gabriel English?

Yes.

We have a warrant for your arrest, son.

I knew there was something you could say here. I searched for the proper wording.

Can I ask what the charge is?

We'll discuss that at the station.

Am I under arrest?

This is what my father had taught us. When the law wants you, ask if you're under arrest. I was glad I could remember it.

We'd prefer to formally charge you down at the station, son, after we've cleared a few things up.

My father, who had been in the bathroom shaving, came to the door. He was still in his undervest, mopping his neck and chin with a white towel. He wasn't wearing his glasses, which gave him a relaxed look. He said, Would it be all right, fellas, if the boy had some breakfast? I'll bring him down right after.

The way he dried himself with the towel showed off his massive, pale biceps, his thick wrists. The thickness was well-earned. There was a beat and then the older officer said that would be fine. He decided to look at my father for a moment and then they turned and made new footprints back to the cruiser.

My father turned to me and said, Well what a way to start the new year. He said this in a way that reassured me. He knew already that I hadn't done anything, that I wasn't capable of doing a bad thing. He was confident about this, all he knew about me was good things. I was the good son. His impression reinforced a faith in my own innocence. It made me realize what must have happened and suddenly I got upset.

It's Junior, isn't it, he said.

I suspect it's Junior, Dad.

And why do you suspect him.

He knew that I must be in league with Junior, had information that we'd kept from him. Over breakfast I told him what I knew. He listened as if, while the particulars of the event were new to him, they fit into the larger maze which was the interlaced lives of his sons. He said, They're going to begin with a presumption. That you've been driving. And you haven't. Be flat out with that and the rest hold to your chin. He said, People in charge like to figure things out. They don't appreciate confessions.

We drove to the police station, which was a bunker below the Sir Richard Squires building. The building housed the first elevator in Newfoundland.

I liked the Up and Down arrows by the elevator buttons. That was my earliest appreciation of technology's ability to appear prescient.

I thought it was a considerate touch by the makers. The elevator was the avenue to Corner Brook's public library, which my father had introduced to me before I could read. I would pick up books Junior had chosen, like *Archibald the Arctic* and stare at the riddle of print. Junior loved the northern explorers—of men eating their dogs, and each other.

The lobby was glass on three sides, with nine storeys of brick pressing down on it. My father took me to the sixth floor once, to a government office where he had some tax business. I could see the Bowater mill, the neck of the bay twisting around the town of Curling, the swans (the whitest things in town) drifting below in the reservoir which cooled the mill's furnaces, the secondary schools on the landscaped hill to the east. I was uneasy in the building, I was convinced the glass footing would topple. I worried for the commissionaire stationed at his desk by the fountain.

The fountain stood in the centre of the lobby behind an iron railing. It drizzled water over its scalloped and flared glass edges.

A boy was carefully tossing a penny in. The fountain was a silent, enormous presence, a wordless example of grander things one could value and live for. I loved the fountain even when no one and nothing told me it was worthy of love.

My father leaned against the rail. He said if he had guts, he'd sell everything and help the poor in Calcutta. That was his base belief about what was right. His weakness drove him to self-interest, to preserving family and constantly bettering our material position. He could appreciate decorative flourishes, but never allowed himself to get carried away.

My mother would say I have these thoughts because we emigrated from England. My mother has given a lot of time to such considerations. She cultivates hindsight, and researches the repercussions of certain acts. Perhaps if I had grown up where I was born, had not felt strange in my own skin, I wouldn't be so sensitive in the world. In the house I spoke with an English accent, outside I pronounced words the way Doyle and Skizicks said them. I said brakfest, chimley, sove you a seat. I was aware of the boundary between blood bond and friends, between house and world. Junior was different. He managed to be pure Newfoundlander.

My father and I walked down to the police station and I began my brief story of never having driven a Japanese car in Alberta and the officer nodded as if he knew the truth of the matter only too well, that my arrest was a technicality, that a million brothers a month pretend to be younger brothers and he was going to add this latest infraction to the pile. I was free to go.

The station, below the library, was a place I had been to only once before, when Doyle and Skizicks and I were accused of breaking a window. We were kicking stones down Valley Road and a neighbour's window crashed in. We ran. We ran home. Junior said, When you're in trouble, where do you run?

Home.

No Gabe, always run away from home.

I found the station small and casual. It didn't look hard to break out of. There were three cells in the back that I could only hear.

I never spoke to Junior about this arrest. He had left to go back to Alberta on Boxing Day. He was plugging dynamite holes in Fort MacMurray.

My father has cried twice—once when a German shepherd we had ran from his knee and was crushed by a snow plough, the other when Junior left to work in the tar sands. It doesn't hurt me to think of him crying for Junior and not for my departure, or even crying for a dog we rescued from the pound, a thin, shivering creature who knew who to thank for fattening him up. He became too fierce in protecting us. Crying is an irrational act and should never be resented. I know Junior's life is a riskier thing. I know that my parents trust my good senses (I am named executor of their wills). There will be greater love attached to wilder men.

Before Christmas I went out with Junior to a cabin belonging to one of the Brads. Junior knew three men named Brad, and my mother had begun to disbelieve him. That the Brads had other names. She would answer the phone and say, No, he's off somewhere with one of the Brads. As if that was a joke and she wasn't to be fooled. But I believe they were all called Brad. I think perhaps naming someone Brad is not a good idea.

Brad picked us up in his black and gold Trans Am and tried his best to charm our mother who appreciated the gesture but still kept her opinion. I sat in the back and we detoured down Mountbatten Road. We stopped at a house with blue aluminum siding. Brad honked his horn and a screen door opened with two women waving and smiling and pointing a finger to indicate one moment. Brad popped the trunk from inside and waited.

Me: Who are they.

Junior: Our wool blankets.

The girls climbed in the back and I remembered Linda from a party Junior had at the house. She had come into my bedroom, sat on the floor with a beer, and told me how she loved Junior to bits.

They nudged me with their hips to get their seat belts on. I was in the middle. Then Linda smiled: You're gonna be our chaperon, Gabe. Danielle leaned forward and pulled on Brad's hair and kissed him on the ear and I could see the perfect contour of her breast.

Brad Pynn had a cabin up in Pynn's Brook. Junior liked to go snow-mobiling and drinking up there over the holidays. He'd flown into town, gotten his presents giftwrapped by Linda at the hardware store he used to work at, and invited her to Brad's.

Brad and Junior had an old plan to rob the small bank above Co-op grocery on Main Street. I don't mind revealing this because, to my know-ledge, they never pulled the heist and now, I believe, the bank is closed. It was a small bank, used by members of the Co-op. It was less formal than other banks. There were just desks, rather than counters with glass. You could walk right into the safe if you were quick. Junior was convinced you could pull off that job. The only problem was, everyone knew him. And if you did it with someone like a Brad Pynn, you could never be sure if he'd blow too much money one night, or brag, or betray you.

This bank scheme was something that always came up after a few beers, or during a vial of oil and a sewing needle, which Junior had out in the front seat, spreading the green oil over a cigarette paper on his knee. The joint was passed and I had to take it from Danielle, smoke, and hand it to Linda. Danielle kept pressing my knee saying, Look at that, if she saw a cute house, or a crow on the melted road that refused to lift. She'd press my knee then slide her hand a little up my thigh, as though she'd forgotten it was my thigh. Linda put her arm along the back window to make more shoulder room. They were quite relaxed.

Junior had a sawed-off shotgun between his legs which I watched him load with a red number four shell. He asked Brad to roll down his window. Cold air pummelled into the car. Junior clicked the chamber closed. He lifted the barrel up to Brad's windowsill, pushed off the safety, stared back at us and said, Watch this.

He saw Danielle's hand on my thigh and Linda's arm around my neck and paused.

There were three black objects ahead standing in the snow on Brad's side of the highway. Brad kept the speedometer at the limit. Junior didn't aim, just pointed at the grade and estimated the distance. He fired and the crows flew up alertly. Brad swerved.

Jesus, June.

He slipped off the road, hit bare ice, fishtailed, adjusted for the swing, pumped the brakes a little, and straightened up. The blast echoed inside the car. Junior was laughing until he saw that Linda and Danielle were horrified. We all saw, through a thin veil of trees, a line of cabins.

Oh, honey. Sorry about that.

Linda clenched her jaw and stared out her window. Her arms crossed and flexed.

Brad owned a Gold Wing which he parked and chained into the cabin over winter, and this bike he straddled and drank beer from and turned on the stereo embedded in the ruby fibreglass windjammer and would have started it up if Junior hadn't, at Brad's request, drained the cylinders and cleaned his valves and left the engine to hibernate in drenched oil.

Brad and June took the purple Arctic Cat for a bomb down the lake to ice fish and to hunt with the sawed-off. They carried a small auger and they had slugs in case of a moose. The girls and I played Scrabble and drank rum mixed with Tang crystals. I missed touching their arms and hips. They were about twenty, both attending the Career Academy and slowly becoming disappointed. But that winter they were still bright, talkative Newfoundland women who wore friendship rings and small twinkling earrings and could imagine ways to have fun and succeed. They'd spent summers working in the fish plant in Curling and winters wearing white skates on ponds like Little Rapids. I could tell they enjoyed me and while each on her own might have been bored with my company, together they shared a glee in flirting, in egging me on. In their eyes I was a man in the making, and I accepted this. Women like a confidence no matter what the confidence is.

Linda said, You're going to be something, aren't you. You're like your brother, but you're smarter and gentle.

Ah Linda he's shy, boy.

And Danielle put her arm around my neck and felt my ear. Her collarbone lifted a white bra strap. Shy? Why you got nothing to be shy about.

She slipped her hand down to my waist.

Have you ever done the dirty? she said.

I didn't have to answer and they laughed and loved the fact that now they were getting into this.

You know something me and Linda have wanted to do?

Linda felt my crotch. She put a hand in my jeans pocket.

Wow. Danielle. Guess what he's not wearing.

Go way.

Danielle slipped her hand in my other pocket. This pocket had the lining torn and her warm, probing hand clasped directly and gently.

Oh Linda we've got a fine young man on our hands.

A growing boy.

Linda unbuttoned my jeans. I shifted in my chair and prayed that the skidoo would be loud. I tried to recall the sound it made as it buzzed up the lake. But as it was, even if Brad and Junior came in the door, nothing could be seen above the table. Nothing except an astonished boy and two eager, laughing women leaning in to him.

Last fall Junior hit a moose. This was six days after the mandatory seat belt law had been established, and it was this law which had saved his life. Dad and I found him unconscious, pinned behind the wheel of his orange-and-chrome VW Bug. Eight hundred pounds of moose had rolled over the bonnet, crumpled the windshield, bent the doorframes and lay bleeding in his lap. The ambulance service had to wait for the jaws of life to free him. He'd loved the Bug, it had lived its previous life in salt-free Florida. Investigators measured skid marks, the animal was towed off with two canvas cables, its injuries charted, witnesses signed statements and it was declared that Junior had been driving with abandon under severe winter conditions.

He bought a Rabbit then, and two weeks later he rammed into the back of an eighteen-wheeler; the Rabbit was dragged four hundred metres before the semi braked. The trucker was furious, he hadn't even seen Junior he was that far up his ass. Up your wind tunnel, Junior said, looking for an opportunity to pass. The trucker wanted to smack him. He would have if my father hadn't stretched his big hands in an obvious way.

Junior began giving up on a Datsun, an old, whipped car. He was motoring around town, scouting for other drivers' infractions. Someone running a red light. If he saw anything, he drove into it. He was making money, he said, from other people's insurance.

When the Datsun had built up a nest egg he asked if I wanted to go for a ride. This was after supper, in early December. He'd decided, he said, to retire the vehicle. The insurance company had declared it a liability and he had to write it off before the calendar year.

We drove to the empty, carefully ploughed parking lot behind the school my father taught at. The street lamps were just flickering on. It was terminally ill, Junior said, and we had to put it out of its misery.

He revved up the motor, spun on the slightly icy pavement, and swaggered the car towards a ploughed mound of snow at the edge of the lot.

Hold on, Gabe.

The headlights lurched, grew in concentration against the bank as we accelerated and approached. The car exploded into compact snow, driving in a few feet, snow smacking against the windshield, the hill absorbed our blow. The motor muffled, hummed, still ran happily. If it had a tail it would be wagging.

Junior shifted into reverse, hit the wipers, spun wide, and galloped for the opposite end of the lot, dipsy doodling around a street-light pole on the way, swinging on the ice and slamming sideways into the far bank of snow.

I had to get out and push this time. The exhaust was clogged with snow. I watched as Junior aimed for a sturdier bank pressed against the school. The car whined horribly. There was no give in the snow. The seat belt cut against his chest as he came up hard on a hidden concrete post. A crease formed in the hood of the car, the grill burst open and jets of water spouted up, dousing the windshield and melting then freezing the snow on the hood. The motor kept running as if nothing had happened. I ran to him.

Can't kill a fucking Datsun, man.

Junior got out to reconsider his approach. I reminded him that if he went through with this demolition we'd have to walk home. He popped the hood (it opened at the windshield) and cranked up the heat to transfer valuable degrees over from the engine. Then he said, Come look at this.

We stood on the front bumper and stared into the dark classroom. On the board were the yellow chalk drawings our father made of various projects: tables, lamps, chairs. There were angles and choice of wood screw and the correct use of a plane and a clamp. The work tables were cleared, the tools all hanging in their racks, the cement floor swept with sawdust and water. Everything in order.

We drove home with the broken radiator, my eyes fixed to the temperature gauge, which hovered past the orange bar.

It was then Junior asked me for a favour. We were parked, the lights shut off, the engine ticking to the cold. He said his insurance was sky-high. What we'd do, he said, is insure his next car in my name and he'd be a second driver. It would save him a hell of a lot of cash.

At the time I wasn't driving anything and when you're not using something, it's hard to feel the importance of giving it away. There was a mature air about Junior needing my help in the adult world. But a warning hunch spread through my body. I knew there would be repercussions, though I could not articulate them. It all seemed reasonable, he just needed to borrow my driver's license for an hour.

It wasn't just the insurance, the police told me. The car was registered in my name too. I had an overdrawn bank account. There was a bad prairie loan. A lien on a leased Ford pickup. In Alberta, his entire life had become my life. He was living under the name Gabriel English. It was as if he never expected me to live a life, so he'd better do it for me.

*—1999*

*Jhumpa Lahiri (b. 1967) was born in London, England, to Bengali parents but has lived most of her life in the United States. The sense of exile created by being connected to but not fully belonging to three different continents is a theme of much of her work, including her debut short-story collection,* The Interpreter of Maladies *(2000), which won the Pulitzer Prize, and her novel* The Namesake *(2003), which was made into a film in 2006.*

## Jhumpa Lahiri
# Interpreter of Maladies

At the tea stall Mr. and Mrs. Das bickered about who should take Tina to the toilet. Eventually Mrs. Das relented when Mr. Das pointed out that he had given the girl her bath the night before. In the rearview mirror Mr. Kapasi watched as Mrs. Das emerged slowly from his bulky white Ambassador, dragging her shaved, largely bare legs across the back seat. She did not hold the little girl's hand as they walked to the rest room.

They were on their way to see the Sun Temple at Konarak.[1] It was a dry, bright Saturday, the mid-July heat tempered by a steady ocean breeze, ideal weather for sightseeing. Ordinarily Mr. Kapasi would not have stopped so soon along the way, but less than five minutes after he'd picked up the family that morning in front of Hotel Sandy Villa, the little girl had complained. The first thing Mr. Kapasi had noticed when he saw Mr. and Mrs. Das, standing with their children under the portico of the hotel, was that they were very young, perhaps not even thirty. In addition to Tina they had two boys, Ronny and Bobby, who appeared very close in age and had teeth covered in a network of flashing silver wires. The family looked Indian but dressed as foreigners did, the children in stiff, brightly colored clothing and caps with translucent visors. Mr. Kapasi was accustomed to foreign tourists; he was assigned to them regularly because he could speak English. Yesterday he had driven an elderly couple from Scotland, both with spotted faces and fluffy white hair so thin it exposed their sunburnt scalps. In comparison, the tanned, youthful faces of Mr. and Mrs. Das were all the more striking. When he'd introduced himself, Mr. Kapasi

---

[1]*Konarak:* village in Orissa state, eastern India.

had pressed his palms together in greeting, but Mr. Das squeezed hands like an American so that Mr. Kapasi felt it in his elbow. Mrs. Das, for her part, had flexed one side of her mouth, smiling dutifully at Mr. Kapasi, without displaying any interest in him.

As they waited at the tea stall, Ronny, who looked like the older of the two boys, clambered suddenly out of the back seat, intrigued by a goat tied to a stake in the ground.

"Don't touch it," Mr. Das said. He glanced up from his paperback tour book, which said "INDIA" in yellow letters and looked as if it had been published abroad. His voice, somehow tentative and a little shrill, sounded as though it had not yet settled into maturity.

"I want to give it a piece of gum," the boy called back as he trotted ahead.

Mr. Das stepped out of the car and stretched his legs by squatting briefly to the ground. A clean-shaven man, he looked exactly like a magnified version of Ronny. He had a sapphire blue visor, and was dressed in shorts, sneakers, and a T-shirt. The camera slung around his neck, with an impressive telephoto lens and numerous buttons and markings, was the only complicated thing he wore. He frowned, watching as Ronny rushed toward the goat, but appeared to have no intention of intervening. "Bobby, make sure that your brother doesn't do anything stupid."

"I don't feel like it," Bobby said, not moving. He was sitting in the front seat beside Mr. Kapasi, studying a picture of the elephant god taped to the glove compartment.

"No need to worry," Mr. Kapasi said. "They are quite tame." Mr. Kapasi was forty-six years old, with receding hair that had gone completely silver, but his butterscotch complexion and his unlined brow, which he treated in spare moments to dabs of lotus-oil balm, made it easy to imagine what he must have looked like at an earlier age. He wore gray trousers and a matching jacket-style shirt, tapered at the waist, with short sleeves and a large pointed collar, made of a thin but durable synthetic material. He had specified both the cut and the fabric to his tailor—it was his preferred uniform for giving tours because it did not get crushed during his long hours behind the wheel. Through the windshield he watched as Ronny circled around the goat, touched it quickly on its side, then trotted back to the car.

"You left India as a child?" Mr. Kapasi asked when Mr. Das had settled once again into the passenger seat.

"Oh, Mina and I were both born in America," Mr. Das announced with an air of sudden confidence. "Born and raised. Our parents live here now, in Assansol. They retired. We visit them every couple years." He turned to watch as the little girl ran toward the car, the wide purple bows of her sundress flopping on her narrow brown shoulders. She was holding to her chest a doll with yellow hair that looked as if it had been chopped, as a punitive measure, with a pair of dull scissors. "This is Tina's first trip to India, isn't it, Tina?"

"I don't have to go to the bathroom anymore," Tina announced.

"Where's Mina?" Mr. Das asked.

Mr. Kapasi found it strange that Mr. Das should refer to his wife by her first name when speaking to the little girl. Tina pointed to where Mrs. Das was purchasing something from one of the shirtless men who worked at the tea stall. Mr. Kapasi heard one of the shirtless men sing a phrase from a popular Hindi love song as Mrs. Das walked back to the car, but she did not appear to understand the words of the song, for she did not express irritation, or embarrassment, or react in any other way to the man's declarations.

He observed her. She wore a red-and-white-checkered skirt that stopped above her knees, slip-on shoes with a square wooden heel, and a close-fitting blouse styled like a man's undershirt. The blouse was decorated at chest-level with a calico appliqué in the shape of a strawberry. She was a short woman with small hands like paws, her frosty pink fingernails painted to match her lips, and was slightly plump in her figure. Her hair, shorn only a little longer than her husband's, was parted far to one side. She was wearing large dark brown sunglasses with a pinkish tint to them, and carried a big straw bag, almost as big as her torso, shaped like a bowl, with a water bottle poking out of it. She walked slowly, carrying some puffed rice tossed with peanuts and chili peppers in a large packet made from newspapers. Mr. Kapasi turned to Mr. Das.

"Where in America do you live?"

"New Brunswick, New Jersey."

"Next to New York?"

"Exactly. I teach middle school there."

"What subject?"

"Science. In fact, every year I take my students on a trip to the Museum of Natural History in New York City. In a way we have a lot in common, you could say, you and I. How long have you been a tour guide, Mr. Kapasi?"

"Five years."

Mrs. Das reached the car. "How long's the trip?" she asked, shutting the door.

"About two and a half hours," Mr. Kapasi replied.

At this Mrs. Das gave an impatient sigh, as if she had been traveling her whole life without pause. She fanned herself with a folded Bombay film magazine written in English.

"I thought that the Sun Temple is only eighteen miles north of Puri," Mr. Das said, tapping on the tour book.

"The roads to Konarak are poor. Actually it is a distance of fifty-two miles," Mr. Kapasi explained.

Mr. Das nodded, readjusting the camera strap where it had begun to chafe the back of his neck.

Before starting the ignition, Mr. Kapasi reached back to make sure the cranklike locks on the inside of each of the back doors were secured. As soon as the car began to move the little girl began to play with the lock on her side, clicking it with some effort forward and backward, but Mrs. Das said nothing to stop her. She sat a bit slouched at one end of the back seat, not offering her puffed rice to anyone. Ronny and Tina sat on either side of her, both snapping bright green gum.

"Look," Bobby said as the car began to gather speed. He pointed with his finger to the tall trees that lined the road. "Look."

"Monkeys!" Ronny shrieked. "Wow!"

They were seated in groups along the branches, with shining black faces, silver bodies, horizontal eyebrows, and crested heads. Their long gray tails dangled like a series of ropes among the leaves. A few scratched themselves with black leathery hands, or swung their feet, staring as the car passed.

"We call them the hanuman," Mr. Kapasi said. "They are quite common in the area."

As soon as he spoke, one of the monkeys leaped into the middle of the road, causing Mr. Kapasi to brake suddenly. Another bounced onto the hood of the car, then sprang away. Mr. Kapasi beeped his horn. The children began to get excited, sucking in their breath and covering their faces partly with their hands. They had never seen monkeys outside of a zoo, Mr. Das explained. He asked Mr. Kapasi to stop the car so that he could take a picture.

While Mr. Das adjusted his telephoto lens, Mrs. Das reached into her straw bag and pulled out a bottle of colorless nail polish, which she proceeded to stroke on the tip of her index finger.

The little girl stuck out a hand. "Mine too. Mommy, do mine too."

"Leave me alone," Mrs. Das said, blowing on her nail and turning her body slightly. "You're making me mess up."

The little girl occupied herself by buttoning and unbuttoning a pinafore on the doll's plastic body.

"All set," Mr. Das said, replacing the lens cap.

The car rattled considerably as it raced along the dusty road, causing them all to pop up from their seats every now and then, but Mrs. Das continued to polish her nails. Mr. Kapasi eased up on the accelerator, hoping to produce a smoother ride. When he reached for the gearshift the boy in front accommodated him by swinging his hairless knees out of the way. Mr. Kapasi noted that this boy was slightly paler than the other children. "Daddy, why is the driver sitting on the wrong side in this car, too?" the boy asked.

"They all do that here, dummy," Ronny said.

"Don't call your brother a dummy," Mr. Das said. He turned to Mr. Kapasi. "In America, you know . . . it confuses them."

"Oh yes, I am well aware," Mr. Kapasi said. As delicately as he could, he shifted gears again, accelerating as they approached a hill in the road. "I see it on *Dallas*, the steering wheels are on the left-hand side."

"What's *Dallas*?" Tina asked, banging her now naked doll on the seat behind Mr. Kapasi.

"It went off the air," Mr. Das explained. "It's a television show."

They were all like siblings, Mr. Kapasi thought as they passed a row of date trees. Mr. and Mrs. Das behaved like an older brother and sister, not parents. It seemed that they were in charge of the children only for the day; it was hard to believe they were regularly responsible for anything other than themselves. Mr. Das tapped on his lens cap, and his tour book, dragging his thumbnail occasionally across the pages so that they made a scraping sound. Mrs. Das continued to polish her nails. She had still not removed her sunglasses. Every now and then Tina renewed her plea that she wanted her nails done, too, and so at one point

Mrs. Das flicked a drop of polish on the little girl's finger before depositing the bottle back inside her straw bag.

"Isn't this an air-conditioned car?" she asked, still blowing on her hand. The window on Tina's side was broken and could not be rolled down.

"Quit complaining," Mr. Das said. "It isn't so hot."

"I told you to get a car with air-conditioning," Mrs. Das continued. "Why do you do this, Raj, just to save a few stupid rupees. What are you saving us, fifty cents?"

Their accents sounded just like the ones Mr. Kapasi heard on American television programs, though not like the ones on *Dallas*.

"Doesn't it get tiresome, Mr. Kapasi, showing people the same thing every day?" Mr. Das asked, rolling down his own window all the way. "Hey, do you mind stopping the car. I just want to get a shot of this guy."

Mr. Kapasi pulled over to the side of the road as Mr. Das took a picture of a barefoot man, his head wrapped in a dirty turban, seated on top of a cart of grain sacks pulled by a pair of bullocks. Both the man and the bullocks were emaciated. In the back seat Mrs. Das gazed out another window, at the sky, where nearly transparent clouds passed quickly in front of one another.

"I look forward to it, actually," Mr. Kapasi said as they continued on their way. "The Sun Temple is one of my favorite places. In that way it is a reward for me. I give tours on Fridays and Saturdays only. I have another job during the week."

"Oh? Where?" Mr. Das asked.

"I work in a doctor's office."

"You're a doctor?"

"I am not a doctor. I work with one. As an interpreter."

"What does a doctor need an interpreter for?"

"He has a number of Gujarati patients. My father was Gujarati, but many people do not speak Gujarati in this area, including the doctor. And so the doctor asked me to work in his office, interpreting what the patients say."

"Interesting. I've never heard of anything like that," Mr. Das said.

Mr. Kapasi shrugged. "It is a job like any other."

"But so romantic," Mrs. Das said dreamily, breaking her extended silence. She lifted her pinkish brown sunglasses and arranged them on top of her head like a tiara. For the first time, her eyes met Mr. Kapasi's in the rearview mirror: pale, a bit small, their gaze fixed but drowsy.

Mr. Das craned to look at her. "What's so romantic about it?"

"I don't know. Something." She shrugged, knitting her brows together for an instant. "Would you like a piece of gum, Mr. Kapasi?" she asked brightly. She reached into her straw bag and handed him a small square wrapped in green-and-white-striped paper. As soon as Mr. Kapasi put the gum in his mouth a thick sweet liquid burst onto his tongue.

"Tell us more about your job, Mr. Kapasi," Mrs. Das said.

"What would you like to know, madame?"

"I don't know," she shrugged, munching on some puffed rice and licking the mustard oil from the corners of her mouth. "Tell us a typical situation." She settled back in her seat, her head tilted in a patch of sun, and closed her eyes. "I want to picture what happens."

"Very well. The other day a man came in with a pain in his throat."

"Did he smoke cigarettes?"

"No. It was very curious. He complained that he felt as if there were long pieces of straw stuck in his throat. When I told the doctor he was able to prescribe the proper medication."

"That's so neat."

"Yes," Mr. Kapasi agreed after some hesitation.

"So these patients are totally dependent on you," Mrs. Das said. She spoke slowly, as if she were thinking aloud. "In a way, more dependent on you than the doctor."

"How do you mean? How could it be?"

"Well, for example, you could tell the doctor that the pain felt like a burning, not straw. The patient would never know what you had told the doctor, and the doctor wouldn't know that you had told the wrong thing. It's a big responsibility."

"Yes, a big responsibility you have there, Mr. Kapasi," Mr. Das agreed.

Mr. Kapasi had never thought of his job in such complimentary terms. To him it was a thankless occupation. He found nothing noble in interpreting people's maladies, assiduously translating the symptoms of so many swollen bones, countless cramps of bellies and bowels, spots on people's palms that changed color, shape, or size. The doctor, nearly half his age, had an affinity for bell-bottom trousers and made humorless jokes about the Congress party. Together they worked in a stale little infirmary where Mr. Kapasi's smartly tailored clothes clung to him in the heat, in spite of the blackened blades of a ceiling fan churning over their heads.

The job was a sign of his failings. In his youth he'd been a devoted scholar of foreign languages, the owner of an impressive collection of dictionaries. He had dreamed of being an interpreter for diplomats and dignitaries, resolving conflicts between people and nations, settling disputes of which he alone could understand both sides. He was a self-educated man. In a series of notebooks, in the evenings before his parents settled his marriage, he had listed the common etymologies of words, and at one point in his life he was confident that he could converse, if given the opportunity, in English, French, Russian, Portuguese, and Italian, not to mention Hindi, Bengali, Orissi, and Gujarati. Now only a handful of European phrases remained in his memory, scattered words for things like saucers and chairs. English was the only non-Indian language he spoke fluently anymore. Mr. Kapasi knew it was not a remarkable talent. Sometimes he feared that his children knew better English than he did, just from watching television. Still, it came in handy for the tours.

He had taken the job as an interpreter after his first son, at the age of seven, contracted typhoid—that was how he had first made the acquaintance of the doctor. At the time Mr. Kapasi had been teaching English in a grammar school, and he bartered his skills as an interpreter to pay the increasingly exorbitant medical bills. In the end the boy had died one evening in his mother's arms, his limbs burning with fever, but then there was the funeral to pay for, and the other children who were born soon enough, and the newer, bigger house, and the good schools and tutors, and the fine shoes and the television, and the countless other ways he tried to console his wife and to keep her from crying in her sleep, and so when the doctor offered to pay him twice as much as he earned at the grammar school, he accepted. Mr. Kapasi knew that his wife had little regard for his career as an interpreter. He knew it reminded her of the son she'd lost, and that she resented the other lives he helped, in his own small way, to save. If ever she referred to his position, she used the phrase "doctor's assistant," as if the process of interpretation were equal to taking someone's temperature, or changing a bedpan. She never asked him about the patients who came to the doctor's office, or said that his job was a big responsibility.

For this reason it flattered Mr. Kapasi that Mrs. Das was so intrigued by his job. Unlike his wife, she had reminded him of its intellectual challenges. She had also used the word "romantic." She did not behave in a romantic way toward her husband, and yet she had used the word to describe him. He wondered if Mr. and Mrs. Das were a bad match, just as he and his wife were. Perhaps they, too, had little in common apart from three children and a decade of their lives. The signs he recognized from his own marriage were there—the bickering, the indifference, the protracted silences. Her sudden interest in him, an interest she did not express in either her husband or her children, was mildly intoxicating. When Mr. Kapasi thought once again about how she had said "romantic," the feeling of intoxication grew.

He began to check his reflection in the rearview mirror as he drove, feeling grateful that he had chosen the gray suit that morning and not the brown one, which tended to sag a little in the knees. From time to time he glanced through the mirror at Mrs. Das. In addition to glancing at her face he glanced at the strawberry between her breasts, and the golden brown hollow in her throat. He decided to tell Mrs. Das about another patient, and another: the young woman who had complained of a sensation of raindrops in her spine, the gentleman whose birthmark had begun to sprout hairs. Mrs. Das listened attentively, stroking her hair with a small plastic brush that resembled an oval bed of nails, asking more questions, for yet another example. The children were quiet, intent on spotting more monkeys in the trees, and Mr. Das was absorbed by his tour book, so it seemed like a private conversation between Mr. Kapasi and Mrs. Das. In this manner the next half hour passed, and when they stopped for lunch at a roadside restaurant that sold fritters and omelette sandwiches, usually something Mr. Kapasi looked forward to on his tours so that he could sit in peace and enjoy some hot tea, he was disappointed. As the Das family settled together under a magenta umbrella fringed with white and orange tassels, and placed their orders with one of the waiters who marched about in tricornered caps, Mr. Kapasi reluctantly headed toward a neighboring table.

"Mr. Kapasi, wait. There's room here," Mrs. Das called out. She gathered Tina onto her lap, insisting that he accompany them. And so, together, they had bottled mango juice and sandwiches and plates of onions and potatoes deep-fried in graham-flour batter. After finishing two omelette sandwiches Mr. Das took more pictures of the group as they ate.

"How much longer?" he asked Mr. Kapasi as he paused to load a new roll of film in the camera.

"About half an hour more."

By now the children had gotten up from the table to look at more monkeys perched in a nearby tree, so there was a considerable space between Mrs. Das and Mr. Kapasi. Mr. Das placed the camera to his face and squeezed one eye shut, his tongue exposed at one corner of his mouth. "This looks funny. Mina, you need to lean in closer to Mr. Kapasi."

She did. He could smell a scent on her skin, like a mixture of whiskey and rosewater. He worried suddenly that she could smell his perspiration, which he knew had collected beneath the synthetic material of his shirt. He polished off his mango juice in one gulp and smoothed his silver hair with his hands. A bit of the juice dripped onto his chin. He wondered if Mrs. Das had noticed.

She had not. "What's your address, Mr. Kapasi?" she inquired, fishing for something inside her straw bag.

"You would like my address?"

"So we can send you copies," she said. "Of the pictures." She handed him a scrap of paper which she had hastily ripped from a page of her film magazine. The blank portion was limited, for the narrow strip was crowded by lines of text and a tiny picture of a hero and heroine embracing under a eucalyptus tree.

The paper curled as Mr. Kapasi wrote his address in clear, careful letters. She would write to him, asking about his days interpreting at the doctor's office, and he would respond eloquently, choosing only the most entertaining anecdotes, ones that would make her laugh out loud as she read them in her house in New Jersey. In time she would reveal the disappointment of her marriage, and he his. In this way their friendship would grow, and flourish. He would possess a picture of the two of them, eating fried onions under a magenta umbrella, which he would keep, he decided, safely tucked between the pages of his Russian grammar. As his mind raced, Mr. Kapasi experienced a mild and pleasant shock. It was similar to a feeling he used to experience long ago when, after months of translating with the aid of a dictionary, he would finally read a passage from a French novel, or an Italian sonnet, and understand the words, one after another, unencumbered by his own efforts. In those moments Mr. Kapasi used to believe that all was right with the world, that all struggles were rewarded, that all of life's mistakes made sense in the end. The promise that he would hear from Mrs. Das now filled him with the same belief.

When he finished writing his address Mr. Kapasi handed her the paper, but as soon as he did so he worried that he had either misspelled his name, or accidentally reversed the numbers of his postal code. He dreaded the possibility of a lost letter, the photograph never reaching him, hovering somewhere in Orissa, close but ultimately unattainable. He thought of asking for the slip of paper again, just to make sure he had written his address accurately, but Mrs. Das had already dropped it into the jumble of her bag.

They reached Konarak at two-thirty. The temple, made of sandstone, was a massive pyramid-like structure in the shape of a chariot. It was dedicated to the great master of life, the sun, which struck three sides of the edifice as it made its journey each day across the sky. Twenty-four giant wheels were carved on the north and south sides of the plinth. The whole thing was drawn by a team of seven horses, speeding as if through the heavens. As they approached, Mr. Kapasi explained that the temple had been built between A.D. 1243 and 1255, with the efforts of twelve hundred artisans, by the great ruler of the Ganga dynasty, King Narasimhadeva the First, to commemorate his victory against the Muslim army.

"It says the temple occupies about a hundred and seventy acres of land," Mr. Das said, reading from his book.

"It's like a desert," Ronny said, his eyes wandering across the sand that stretched on all sides beyond the temple.

"The Chandrabhaga River once flowed one mile north of here. It is dry now," Mr. Kapasi said, turning off the engine.

They got out and walked toward the temple, posing first for pictures by the pair of lions that flanked the steps. Mr. Kapasi led them next to one of the wheels of the chariot, higher than any human being, nine feet in diameter.

"'The wheels are supposed to symbolize the wheel of life,'" Mr. Das read. "'They depict the cycle of creation, preservation, and achievement of realization.' Cool." He turned the page of his book. "'Each wheel is divided into eight thick and thin spokes, dividing the day into eight equal parts. The rims are carved with designs of birds and animals, whereas the medallions in the spokes are carved with women in luxurious poses, largely erotic in nature.'"

What he referred to were the countless friezes of entwined naked bodies, making love in various positions, women clinging to the necks of men, their knees wrapped eternally around their lovers' thighs. In addition to these were assorted scenes from daily life, of hunting and trading, of deer being killed with bows and arrows and marching warriors holding swords in their hands.

It was no longer possible to enter the temple, for it had filled with rubble years ago, but they admired the exterior, as did all the tourists Mr. Kapasi brought there, slowly strolling along each of its sides. Mr. Das trailed behind, taking pictures. The children ran ahead, pointing to figures of naked people, intrigued in particular by the Nagamithunas, the half-human, half serpentine couples who were said, Mr. Kapasi told them, to live in the deepest waters of the sea. Mr. Kapasi was pleased that they liked the temple, pleased especially that it appealed to Mrs. Das. She stopped every three or four paces, staring silently at the carved lovers, and the processions of elephants, and the topless female musicians beating on two-sided drums.

Though Mr. Kapasi had been to the temple countless times, it occurred to him, as he, too, gazed at the topless women, that he had never seen his own wife fully naked. Even when they had made love she kept the panels of her blouse hooked together, the string of her petticoat knotted around her waist. He had never admired the backs of his wife's legs the way he now admired those of Mrs. Das, walking as if for his benefit alone. He had, of course, seen plenty of bare limbs before, belonging to the American and European ladies who took his tours. But Mrs. Das was different. Unlike the other women, who had an interest only in the temple, and kept their noses buried in a guidebook, or their eyes behind the lens of a camera, Mrs. Das had taken an interest in him.

Mr. Kapasi was anxious to be alone with her, to continue their private conversation, yet he felt nervous to walk at her side. She was lost behind her sunglasses, ignoring her husband's requests that she pose for another picture, walking past her children as if they were strangers. Worried that he might disturb her, Mr. Kapasi walked ahead, to admire, as he always did, the three life-sized bronze avatars of Surya, the sun god, each emerging from its own niche on the temple facade to greet the sun at dawn, noon, and evening. They wore elaborate headdresses, their languid, elongated eyes closed, their bare chests draped with carved chains and amulets. Hibiscus petals, offerings from previous visitors, were strewn at their gray-green feet. The last statue, on the northern wall of the temple, was Mr. Kapasi's favorite. This Surya had a tired expression, weary after a hard day of work, sitting astride a horse with folded legs. Even his horse's eyes were drowsy. Around his body were smaller sculptures of women in pairs, their hips thrust to one side.

"Who's that?" Mrs. Das asked. He was startled to see that she was standing beside him.

"He is the Astachala-Surya," Mr. Kapasi said. "The setting sun."

"So in a couple of hours the sun will set right here?" She slipped a foot out of one of her square-heeled shoes, rubbed her toes on the back of her other leg.

"That is correct."

She raised her sunglasses for a moment, then put them back on again. "Neat."

Mr. Kapasi was not certain exactly what the word suggested, but he had a feeling it was a favorable response. He hoped that Mrs. Das had understood Surya's beauty, his power. Perhaps they would discuss it further in their letters. He would explain things to her, things about India, and she would explain things to him about America. In its own way this correspondence would fulfill his dream, of serving as an interpreter between nations. He looked at her straw bag, delighted that his address lay nestled among its contents. When he pictured her so many thousands of miles away he plummeted, so much so that he had an overwhelming urge to wrap his arms around her, to freeze with her, even for an instant, in an embrace witnessed by his favorite Surya. But Mrs. Das had already started walking.

"When do you return to America?" he asked, trying to sound placid.

"In ten days."

He calculated: A week to settle in, a week to develop the pictures, a few days to compose her letter, two weeks to get to India by air. According to his schedule, allowing room for delays, he would hear from Mrs. Das in approximately six weeks' time.

The family was silent as Mr. Kapasi drove them back, a little past four-thirty, to Hotel Sandy Villa. The children had bought miniature granite versions of the chariot's wheels at a souvenir stand, and they turned them round in their hands. Mr. Das continued to read his book. Mrs. Das untangled Tina's hair with her brush and divided it into two little ponytails.

Mr. Kapasi was beginning to dread the thought of dropping them off. He was not prepared to begin his six-week wait to hear from Mrs. Das. As he stole glances at her in the rearview mirror, wrapping elastic bands around Tina's hair, he wondered how he might make the tour last a little longer. Ordinarily he sped back to Puri using a shortcut, eager to return home, scrub his feet and hands with sandalwood soap, and enjoy the evening newspaper and a cup of tea that his wife would serve him in silence. The thought of that silence, something to which he'd long been resigned, now oppressed him. It was then that he suggested visiting the hills at Udayagiri and Khandagiri, where a number of monastic dwellings were hewn out of the ground, facing one another across a defile. It was some miles away, but well worth seeing, Mr. Kapasi told them.

"Oh yeah, there's something mentioned about it in this book," Mr. Das said. "Built by a Jain king, or something."

"Shall we go then?" Mr. Kapasi asked. He paused at a turn in the road. "It's to the left."

Mr. Das turned to look at Mrs. Das. Both of them shrugged.

"Left, left," the children chanted.

Mr. Kapasi turned the wheel, almost delirious with relief. He did not know what he would do or say to Mrs. Das once they arrived at the hills. Perhaps he would tell her what a pleasing smile she had. Perhaps he would compliment her strawberry shirt, which he found irresistibly becoming. Perhaps, when Mr. Das was busy taking a picture, he would take her hand.

He did not have to worry. When they got to the hills, divided by a steep path thick with trees, Mrs. Das refused to get out of the car. All along the path, dozens of monkeys were seated on stones, as well as on the branches of the trees. Their hind legs were stretched out in front and raised to shoulder level, their arms resting on their knees.

"My legs are tired," she said, sinking low in her seat. "I'll stay here."

"Why did you have to wear those stupid shoes?" Mr. Das said. "You won't be in the pictures."

"Pretend I'm there."

"But we could use one of these pictures for our Christmas card this year. We didn't get one of all five of us at the Sun Temple. Mr. Kapasi could take it."

"I'm not coming. Anyway, those monkeys give me the creeps."

"But they're harmless," Mr. Das said. He turned to Mr. Kapasi. "Aren't they?"

"They are more hungry than dangerous," Mr. Kapasi said. "Do not provoke them with food, and they will not bother you."

Mr. Das headed up the defile with the children, the boys at his side, the little girl on his shoulders. Mr. Kapasi watched as they crossed paths with a Japanese man and woman, the only other tourists there, who paused for a final photograph, then stepped into a nearby car and drove away. As the car disappeared out of view some of the monkeys called out, emitting soft whooping sounds, and then walked on their flat black hands and feet up the path. At one point a group of them formed a little ring around Mr. Das and the children. Tina screamed in delight. Ronny ran in circles around his father. Bobby bent down and picked up a fat stick on the ground. When he extended it, one of the monkeys approached him and snatched it, then briefly beat the ground.

"I'll join them," Mr. Kapasi said, unlocking the door on his side. "There is much to explain about the caves."

"No. Stay a minute," Mrs. Das said. She got out of the back seat and slipped in beside Mr. Kapasi. "Raj has his dumb book anyway." Together, through the windshield, Mrs. Das and Mr. Kapasi watched as Bobby and the monkey passed the stick back and forth between them.

"A brave little boy," Mr. Kapasi commented.

"It's not so surprising," Mrs. Das said.

"No?"

"He's not his."

"I beg your pardon?"

"Raj's. He's not Raj's son."

Mr. Kapasi felt a prickle on his skin. He reached into his shirt pocket for the small tin of lotus-oil balm he carried with him at all times, and applied it to three spots on his forehead. He knew that Mrs. Das was watching him, but he did not turn to face her. Instead he watched as the figures of Mr. Das and the children grew smaller, climbing up the steep path, pausing every now and then for a picture, surrounded by a growing number of monkeys.

"Are you surprised?" The way she put it made him choose his words with care.

"It's not the type of thing one assumes," Mr. Kapasi replied slowly. He put the tin of lotus-oil balm back in his pocket.

"No, of course not. And no one knows, of course. No one at all. I've kept it a secret for eight whole years." She looked at Mr. Kapasi, tilting her chin as if to gain a fresh perspective. "But now I've told you."

Mr. Kapasi nodded. He felt suddenly parched, and his forehead was warm and slightly numb from the balm. He considered asking Mrs. Das for a sip of water, then decided against it.

"We met when we were very young," she said. She reached into her straw bag in search of something, then pulled out a packet of puffed rice. "Want some?"

"No, thank you."

She put a fistful in her mouth, sank into the seat a little, and looked away from Mr. Kapasi, out the window on her side of the car. "We married when we were still in college. We were in high school when he proposed. We went to the same college, of course. Back then we couldn't stand the thought of being separated, not for a day, not for a minute. Our parents were best friends who lived in the same town. My entire life I saw him every weekend, either at our house or theirs. We were sent upstairs to play together while our parents joked about our marriage. Imagine! They never caught us at anything, though in a way I think it was all more or less a setup. The things we did those Friday and Saturday nights, while our parents sat downstairs drinking tea . . . I could tell you stories, Mr. Kapasi."

As a result of spending all her time in college with Raj, she continued, she did not make many close friends. There was no one to confide in about him at the end of a difficult day, or to share a passing thought or a worry. Her parents now lived on the other side of the world, but she had never been very close to them, anyway. After marrying so young she was overwhelmed by it all, having a child so quickly, and nursing, and warming up bottles of milk and testing their temperature against her wrist while Raj was at work, dressed in sweaters and corduroy pants, teaching his students about rocks and dinosaurs. Raj never looked cross or harried, or plump as she had become after the first baby.

Always tired, she declined invitations from her one or two college girlfriends, to have lunch or shop in Manhattan. Eventually the friends stopped calling her, so that she was left at home all day with the baby, surrounded by toys that made her trip when she walked or wince when she sat, always cross and tired. Only occasionally did they go out after Ronny was born, and even more rarely did they entertain. Raj didn't mind; he looked forward to coming home from teaching and watching television and bouncing Ronny on his knee. She had been outraged when Raj told her that a Punjabi friend, someone whom she had once met but did not remember, would be staying with them for a week for some job interviews in the New Brunswick area.

Bobby was conceived in the afternoon, on a sofa littered with rubber teething toys, after the friend learned that a London pharmaceutical company had hired him, while Ronny cried to be freed from his playpen. She made no protest when the friend touched the small of her back as she was about to make a pot of coffee, then pulled her against his crisp navy suit. He made love to her swiftly, in silence, with an expertise she had never known, without the meaningful expressions and smiles Raj always insisted on afterward. The next day Raj drove the friend to JFK. He was married now, to a Punjabi girl, and they lived in London still, and every year they exchanged Christmas cards with Raj and Mina, each couple tucking photos of their families into the envelopes. He did not know that he was Bobby's father. He never would.

"I beg your pardon, Mrs. Das, but why have you told me this information?" Mr. Kapasi asked when she had finally finished speaking, and had turned to face him once again.

"For God's sake, stop calling me Mrs. Das. I'm twenty-eight. You probably have children my age."

"Not quite." It disturbed Mr. Kapasi to learn that she thought of him as a parent. The feeling he had had toward her, that had made him check his reflection in the rearview mirror as they drove, evaporated a little.

"I told you because of your talents." She put the packet of puffed rice back into her bag without folding over the top.

"I don't understand," Mr. Kapasi said.

"Don't you see? For eight years I haven't been able to express this to anybody, not to friends, certainly not to Raj. He doesn't even suspect it. He thinks I'm still in love with him. Well, don't you have anything to say?"

"About what?"

"About what I've just told you. About my secret, and about how terrible it makes me feel. I feel terrible looking at my children, and at

Raj, always terrible. I have terrible urges, Mr. Kapasi, to throw things away. One day I had the urge to throw everything I own out the window, the television, the children, everything. Don't you think it's unhealthy?"

He was silent.

"Mr. Kapasi, don't you have anything to say? I thought that was your job."

"My job is to give tours, Mrs. Das."

"Not that. Your other job. As an interpreter."

"But we do not face a language barrier. What need is there for an interpreter?"

"That's not what I mean. I would never have told you otherwise. Don't you realize what it means for me to tell you?"

"What does it mean?"

"It means that I'm tired of feeling so terrible all the time. Eight years, Mr. Kapasi, I've been in pain eight years. I was hoping you could help me feel better, say the right thing. Suggest some kind of remedy."

He looked at her, in her red plaid skirt and strawberry T-shirt, a woman not yet thirty, who loved neither her husband nor her children, who had already fallen out of love with life. Her confession depressed him, depressed him all the more when he thought of Mr. Das at the top of the path, Tina clinging to his shoulders, taking pictures of ancient monastic cells cut into the hills to show his students in America, unsuspecting and unaware that one of his sons was not his own. Mr. Kapasi felt insulted that Mrs. Das should ask him to interpret her common, trivial little secret. She did not resemble the patients in the doctor's office, those who came glassy-eyed and desperate, unable to sleep or breathe or urinate with ease, unable, above all, to give words to their pains. Still, Mr. Kapasi believed it was his duty to assist Mrs. Das. Perhaps he ought to tell her to confess the truth to Mr. Das. He would explain that honesty was the best policy. Honesty, surely, would help her feel better, as she'd put it. Perhaps he would offer to preside over the discussion, as a mediator. He decided to begin with the most obvious question, to get to the heart of the matter, and so he asked, "Is it really pain you feel, Mrs. Das, or is it guilt?"

She turned to him and glared, mustard oil thick on her frosty pink lips. She opened her mouth to say something, but as she glared at Mr. Kapasi some certain knowledge seemed to pass before her eyes, and she stopped. It crushed him; he knew at that moment that he was not even important enough to be properly insulted. She opened the car door and began walking up the path, wobbling a little on her square wooden heels, reaching into her straw bag to eat handfuls of puffed rice. It fell through her fingers, leaving a zigzagging trail, causing a monkey to leap down from a tree and devour the little white grains. In search of more, the monkey began to follow Mrs. Das. Others joined him, so that she was soon being followed by about half a dozen of them, their velvety tails dragging behind.

Mr. Kapasi stepped out of the car. He wanted to holler, to alert her in some way, but he worried that if she knew they were behind her, she would grow nervous. Perhaps she would lose her balance. Perhaps they would pull at her bag or her hair. He began to jog up the path, taking a fallen branch in his hand to scare away the monkeys. Mrs. Das continued walking, oblivious, trailing grains of puffed rice. Near the top of the incline, before a group of cells fronted by a row of squat stone pillars, Mr. Das was kneeling on the ground, focusing the lens of his camera. The children stood under the arcade, now hiding, now emerging from view.

"Wait for me," Mrs. Das called out. "I'm coming."

Tina jumped up and down. "Here comes Mommy!"

"Great," Mr. Das said without looking up. "Just in time. We'll get Mr. Kapasi to take a picture of the five of us."

Mr. Kapasi quickened his pace, waving his branch so that the monkeys scampered away, distracted, in another direction.

"Where's Bobby?" Mrs. Das asked when she stopped.

Mr. Das looked up from the camera. "I don't know. Ronny, where's Bobby?"

Ronny shrugged. "I thought he was right here."

"Where is he?" Mrs. Das repeated sharply. "What's wrong with all of you?"

They began calling his name, wandering up and down the path a bit. Because they were calling, they did not initially hear the boy's screams. When they found him, a little farther down the path under a tree, he was surrounded by a group of monkeys, over a dozen of them, pulling at his T-shirt with their long black fingers. The puffed rice Mrs. Das had spilled was scattered at his feet, raked over by the monkeys' hands. The boy was silent, his body frozen, swift tears running down his startled face. His bare legs were dusty and red with welts from where one of the monkeys struck him repeatedly with the stick he had given to it earlier.

"Daddy, the monkey's hurting Bobby," Tina said.

Mr. Das wiped his palms on the front of his shorts. In his nervousness he accidentally pressed the shutter on his camera; the whirring noise of the advancing film excited the monkeys, and the one with the stick began to beat Bobby more intently. "What are we supposed to do? What if they start attacking?"

"Mr. Kapasi," Mrs. Das shrieked, noticing him standing to one side. "Do something, for God's sake, do something!"

Mr. Kapasi took his branch and shooed them away, hissing at the ones that remained, stomping his feet to scare them. The animals retreated slowly, with a measured gait, obedient but unintimidated. Mr. Kapasi gathered Bobby in his arms and brought him back to where his parents and siblings were standing. As he carried him he was tempted to whisper a secret into the boy's ear. But Bobby was stunned, and shivering with fright, his legs bleeding slightly where the stick had broken the skin. When Mr. Kapasi delivered him to his parents, Mr. Das brushed some dirt off the boy's T-shirt and put the visor on him the right way. Mrs. Das reached into her straw bag to find a bandage which she taped over the cut on his knee. Ronny offered his brother a fresh piece of gum. "He's fine. Just a little scared, right, Bobby?" Mr. Das said, patting the top of his head.

"God, let's get out of here," Mrs. Das said. She folded her arms across the strawberry on her chest. "This place gives me the creeps."

"Yeah. Back to the hotel, definitely," Mr. Das agreed.

"Poor Bobby," Mrs. Das said. "Come here a second. Let Mommy fix your hair." Again she reached into her straw bag, this time for her hairbrush, and began to run it around the edges of the translucent visor. When she whipped out the hairbrush, the slip of paper with Mr. Kapasi's address on it fluttered away in the wind. No one but Mr. Kapasi noticed. He watched as it rose, carried higher and higher by the breeze, into the trees where the monkeys now sat, solemnly observing the scene below. Mr. Kapasi observed it too, knowing that this was the picture of the Das family he would preserve forever in his mind.

*—2000*

*Richard Van Camp (b. 1971) is a member of the Dogrib First Nation from Fort Smith, Northwest Territories. He has written a novel,* The Lesser Blessed *(1996), a collection of short stories,* Angel Wing Splash Pattern *(2002), and books for children in collaboration with Cree artist George Littlechild. Of his work, which has been widely anthologized and adapted for radio, he says, "I braid the oral tradition I grew up with and combine it with what I see today."*

# *Richard Van Camp*

# the uranium leaking from port radium and rayrock mines is killing us

and the girl with sharp knees sits in her underwear. She is shivering. The bus is cold. The man at the gun store has seagull eyes. Freckles grow on the wrong side of his face. This town has the biggest Canadian flag anywhere. It is always tangled and never waves. For grass this playground has human hair. It never grows on Sundays. The kids that play here are cold and wet. They are playing in their underwear. They are singing with cold tongues. They have only seven fingers to hide with.

Those are rotting clouds. This is the other side of rain. The band plays but there is no sound. I snap my finger but there is no sound.

There is someone running on the highway. There is no one in the field. Nobody knows the cats here. No one knows their names.

They are letting the librarian's right eye fuse shut. There is a pencil stabbed thru her bun. She can read "I didn't pop my balloon the grass did" in my library book. She looks into me. One eye is pink. The other is blue.

My father said take the bus. There is yellow tape around my house. A finger is caught in the engine but they only rev it harder. There are cold hands against my back. I want to kiss Pocahontas before she dies at age 21. Someone is stealing the dogs of this town while doctors hold babies high in black bags. My mother's voice is a dull marble rolling down her mouth, stolen to her lap, not even bouncing, not even once. She has sprayed metal into her hair. I am sitting on a red seat. My hands open with rawhide.

This is the ear I bled from. There is a child walking in the field. He is walking with a black gun.

In my girlfriend's fist is a promise. She does not raise herself to meet me. Her socks are always dirty. She is selling me a broken bed so she can lie on plywood. Her feet are always cold. The coffee we drink is cold. The bus driver does not wave goodbye. Why are there only children on this bus? Why are we wet and cold? Why are we only in our underwear?

I want to run but I have no legs. The tongue that slides from my mouth is blue.

Friday is the loneliest day of the week she says. The blanket she knitted this winter is torn upon us. She laughs at me with blue eyes. She says if you walk in the rain no one can tell you're crying. The soup we drink after is cold. The popcorn we eat after is cold. Someone is crying in the basement. Someone is crying next door.

The dream we have is something running on four legs, running on pavement towards us. It is running from the highway. It is a dead caribou running on dead legs. I meet its eyes but there are only antlers. In between the antlers is an eye. It too is cold and watching. Its eye is the color of blue.

The plants here have no flowers. The trees themselves are black. The fish are rolling sideways. Rain has started to fall.

The child with the black gun sees my house. He is walking backwards towards me. He swings his head. His eyes are blue. *Can you please sing with me?*

The bus driver does not wave goodbye.

The band is playing but all I hear is galloping.

I snap my finger.

My eyes are blue.

All I can hear is galloping . . .

*—1996*

**Author's Note:**
For those of you who don't know, the Northwest Territories was home to the world's first uranium mine: Port Radium (1932–1960), located in Sahtu Dene territory. The uranium that was used by the US Government to develop the World War II Atom Bomb technology and ferocity behind the detonation over Hiroshima and Nagasaki came from a number of places: American and African mines and Port Radium. The US Government ordered 918 tonnes of uranium from Port Radium. Later, Uranium 2308 was harvested from Rayrock mines (1955–1957) in Dogrib territory in the NWT and was sold to Atomic Research of

Canada. Despite the Canadian government's knowledge in 1931 and 1932 of the serious health hazards associated with exposure to the dust from high-grade radioactive ores, Dene men, referred to as "coolies," were used to transport the radioactive ore along the 2,100-kilometre route called the "Highway of the Atom" without warnings. Many of the Dene later developed cancer. Additionally, 1.7 million tons of radioactive tailings were dumped into the Sahtu (Great Bear Lake)—the ninth largest lake in the world and home to the world's largest trout fishing.

---

*Madeleine Thien (b. 1974) is the Vancouver-born daughter of Chinese-Malaysian immigrants, who cites Alice Munro, Michael Ondaatje, and Michael Ignatieff as important literary influences. Her first collection of stories, the award-winning* Simple Recipes *(2001), explores the complexity of relationships, often from a child's perspective. Her debut novel,* Certainty *(2006), takes readers to wartorn Asia in search of answers. Thien, whose fiction illustrates her belief that humans "can understand each other," has also written for children and now makes her home in Quebec City.*

## *Madeleine Thien*
# Simple Recipes

There is a simple recipe for making rice. My father taught it to me when I was a child. Back then, I used to sit up on the kitchen counter watching him, how he sifted the grains in his hands, sure and quick, removing pieces of dirt or sand, tiny imperfections. He swirled his hands through the water and it turned cloudy. When he scrubbed the grains clean, the sound was as big as a field of insects. Over and over, my father rinsed the rice, drained the water, then filled the pot again.

The instructions are simple. Once the washing is done, you measure the water this way—by resting the tip of your index finger on the surface of the rice. The water should reach the bend of your first knuckle. My father did not need instructions or measuring cups. He closed his eyes and felt for the waterline.

Sometimes I still dream my father, his bare feet flat against the floor, standing in the middle of the kitchen. He wears old buttoned shirts and faded sweatpants drawn at the waist. Surrounded by the gloss of the kitchen counters, the sharp angles of the stove, the fridge, the shiny sink, he looks out of place. This memory of him is so strong, sometimes it stuns me, the detail with which I can see it.

Every night before dinner, my father would perform this ritual— rinsing and draining, then setting the pot in the cooker. When I was older, he passed this task on to me but I never did it with the same care. I went through the motions, splashing the water around, jabbing my finger down to measure the water level. Some nights the rice was a mushy gruel. I worried that I could not do so simple a task right. "Sorry," I would say to the table, my voice soft and embarrassed. In answer, my father would keep eating, pushing the rice into his mouth as if he never expected anything different, as if he noticed no difference between what he did so well and I so poorly. He would eat every last mouthful, his chopsticks walking quickly across the plate. Then he would rise, whistling, and clear the table, every motion so clean and sure, I would be convinced by him that all was well in the world.

My father is standing in the middle of the kitchen. In his right hand he holds a plastic bag filled with water. Caught inside the bag is a live fish.

The fish is barely breathing, though its mouth opens and closes. I reach up and touch it through the plastic bag, trailing my fingers along the gills, the soft, muscled body, pushing my finger overtop the eyeball. The fish looks straight at me, flopping sluggishly from side to side.

My father fills the kitchen sink. In one swift motion he overturns the bag and the fish comes sailing out with the water. It curls and jumps. We watch it closely, me on my tiptoes, chin propped up on the counter. The fish is the length of my arm from wrist to elbow. It floats in place, brushing up against the sides of the sink.

I keep watch over the fish while my father begins the preparations for dinner. The fish folds its body, trying to turn or swim, the water nudging overtop. Though I ripple tiny circles around it with my fingers, the fish stays still, bobbing side-to-side in the cold water.

For many hours at a time, it was just the two of us. While my mother worked and my older brother played outside, my father and I sat on the couch, flipping channels. He loved cooking shows. We watched *Wok with Yan*, my father passing judgement on Yan's methods. I was enthralled when Yan transformed orange peels into swans. My father sniffed. "I can do that," he said. "You don't have to be a genius to do that." He placed a sprig of green onion in water and showed me how it bloomed like a flower. "I know many tricks like this," he said. "Much more than Yan."

Still, my father made careful notes when Yan demonstrated Peking Duck. He chuckled heartily at Yan's punning. "Take a wok on the wild side!" Yan said, pointing his spatula at the camera.

"Ha ha!" my father laughed, his shoulders shaking. "*Wok* on the wild side!"

In the mornings, my father took me to school. At three o'clock, when we came home again, I would rattle off everything I learned that day. "The brachiosaurus," I informed him, "eats only soft vegetables."

My father nodded. "That is like me. Let me see your forehead." We stopped and faced each other in the road. "You have a high forehead," he said, leaning down to take a closer look. "All smart people do."

I walked proudly, stretching my legs to match his steps. I was over-joyed when my feet kept time with his, right, then left, then right, and we walked like a single unit. My father was the man of tricks, who sat for an hour mining a watermelon with a circular spoon, who carved the rind into a castle.

My father was born in Malaysia and he and my mother immigrated to Canada several years before I was born, first settling in Montreal, then finally in Vancouver. While I was born into the persistence of the Vancouver rain, my father was born in the wash of a monsoon country. When I was young, my parents tried to teach me their language but it never came easily to me. My father ran his thumb gently over my mouth, his face kind, as if trying to see what it was that made me different.

My brother was born in Malaysia but when he immigrated with my parents to Canada the language left him. Or he forgot it, or he refused it, which is also common, and this made my father angry. "How can a child forget a language?" he would ask my mother. "It is because the child is lazy. Because the child chooses not to remember." When he was twelve years old, my brother stayed away in the afternoons. He drummed the soccer ball up and down the back alley, returning home only at dinner time. During the day, my mother worked as a sales clerk at the Woodward's store downtown, in the building with the red revolv-ing W on top.

In our house, the ceilings were yellowed with grease. Even the air was heavy with it. I remember that I loved the weight of it, the air that was dense with the smell of countless meals cooked in a tiny kitchen, all those good smells jostling for space.

The fish in the sink is dying slowly. It has a glossy sheen to it, as if its skin is made of shining minerals. I want to prod it with both hands, its body tense against the pressure of my fingers. If I hold it tightly, I imagine I will be able to feel its fluttering heart. Instead, I lock eyes with the fish. *You're feeling verrrry sleepy,* I tell it. *You're getting verrrry tired.*

Beside me, my father chops green onions quickly. He uses a cleaver that he says is older than I am by many years. The blade of the knife rolls forward and backward, loops of green onion gathering in a pyramid beside my father's wrist. When he is done, he rolls his sleeve back from his right hand, reaches in through the water and pulls the plug.

The fish in the sink floats and we watch it in silence. The water level falls beneath its gills, beneath its belly. It drains and leaves the sink dry. The fish is lying on its side, mouth open and its body heaving. It leaps sideways and hits the sink. Then up again. It curls and snaps, lunging for its own tail. The fish sails into the air, dropping hard. It twitches violently.

My father reaches in with his bare hands. He lifts the fish out by the tail and lays it gently on the counter.

While holding it steady with one hand, he hits the head with the flat of the cleaver. The fish falls still and he begins to clean it.

In my apartment, I keep the walls scrubbed clean. I open the windows and turn the fan on whenever I prepare a meal. My father bought me a rice cooker when I first moved into my own apartment, but I use it so rarely it stays in the back of the cupboard, the cord wrapped neatly around its belly. I have no longing for the meals themselves, but I miss the way we sat down together, our bodies leaning hungrily forward while my father, the magician, unveiled plate after plate. We laughed and ate, white steam fogging my mother's glasses until she had to take them off and lay them on the table. Eyes closed, she would eat, crunchy vegetables gripped in her chopsticks, the most vivid green.

My brother comes into the kitchen and his body is covered with dirt. He leaves a thin trail of it behind as he walks. The soccer ball, muddy from outside, is encircled in one arm. Brushing past my father, his face is tense.

Beside me, my mother sprinkles garlic onto the fish. She lets me slide one hand underneath the fish's head, cradling it, then bending it backwards so that she can fill the fish's insides with ginger. Very carefully, I turn the fish over. It is firm and slippery, and beaded with tiny, sharp scales.

At the stove, my father picks up an old teapot. It is full of oil and he pours the oil into the wok. It falls in a thin ribbon. After a moment, when the oil begins crackling, he lifts the fish up and drops it down into the wok. He adds water and the smoke billows up. The sound of the fish frying is like tires on gravel, a sound so loud it drowns out all other noises. Then my father steps out from the smoke. "Spoon out the rice," he says as he lifts me down from the counter.

My brother comes back into the room, his hands muddy and his knees the colour of dusty brick. His soccer shorts flutter against the backs of his legs. Sitting down, he makes an angry face. My father ignores him.

Inside the cooker, the rice is flat like a pie. I push the spoon in, turning the rice over, and the steam shoots up in a hot mist and condenses on my skin. While my father moves his arms delicately over the stove, I begin dishing the rice out: first for my father, then my mother, then my brother, then myself. Behind me the fish is cooking quickly. In a crockery pot, my father steams cauliflower, stirring it round and round.

My brother kicks at a table leg.

"What's the matter?" my father asks.

He is quiet for a moment, then he says, "Why do we have to eat fish?"

"You don't like it?"

My brother crosses his arms against his chest. I see the dirt lining his arms, dark and hardened. I imagine chipping it off his body with a small spoon.

"I don't like the eyeball there. It looks sick."

My mother tuts. Her nametag is still clipped to her blouse. It says *Woodward's*, and then, *Sales Clerk*. "Enough," she says, hanging her purse on the back of the chair. "Go wash your hands and get ready for supper."

My brother glares, just for a moment. Then he begins picking at the dirt on his arms. I bring plates of rice to the table. The dirt flies off his skin, speckling the tablecloth. "Stop it," I say crossly.

"*Stop it*," he says, mimicking me.

"Hey!" My father hits his spoon against the counter. It *pings*, high-pitched. He points at my brother. "No fighting in this house."

My brother looks at the floor, mumbles something, and then shuffles away from the table. As he moves farther away, he begins to stamp his feet.

Shaking her head, my mother takes her jacket off. It slides from her shoulders. She says something to my father in the language I can't understand. He merely shrugs his shoulders. And then he replies, and I think his words are so familiar, as if they are words I should know, as if maybe I did know them once but then I forgot them. The language that they speak is full of soft vowels, words running together so that I can't make out the gaps where they pause for breath.

My mother told me once about guilt. Her own guilt she held in the palm of her hands, like an offering. But your guilt is different, she said. You do not need to hold on to it. Imagine this, she said, her hands running along my forehead, then up into my hair. Imagine, she said. Picture it, and what do you see?

A bruise on the skin, wide and black.

A bruise, she said. Concentrate on it. Right now, it's a bruise. But if you concentrate, you can shrink it, compress it to the size of a pinpoint. And then, if you want to, if you see it, you can blow it off your body like a speck of dirt.

She moved her hands along my forehead.

I tried to picture what she said. I pictured blowing it away like so much nothing, just these little pieces that didn't mean anything, this complicity that I could magically walk away from. She made me believe in the strength of my own thoughts, as if I could make appear what had never existed. Or turn it around. Flip it over so many times you just lose sight of it, you lose the tail end and the whole thing disappears into smoke.

My father pushes at the fish with the edge of his spoon. Underneath, the meat is white and the juice runs down along the side. He lifts a piece and lowers it carefully onto my plate.

Once more, his spoon breaks skin. Gingerly, my father lifts another piece and moves it towards my brother.

"I don't want it," my brother says.

My father's hand wavers. "Try it," he says, smiling. "Take a wok on the wild side."

"No."

My father sighs and places the piece on my mother's plate. We eat in silence, scraping our spoons across the dishes. My parents use chopsticks, lifting their bowls and motioning the food into their mouths. The smell of food fills the room.

Savouring each mouthful, my father eats slowly, head tuned to the flavours in his mouth. My mother takes her glasses off, the lenses fogged, and lays them on the table. She eats with her head bowed down, as if in prayer.

Lifting a stem of cauliflower to his lips, my brother sighs deeply. He chews, and then his face changes. I have a sudden picture of him drowning, his hair waving like grass. He coughs, spitting the mouthful back onto his plate. Another cough. He reaches for his throat, choking.

My father slams his chopsticks down on the table. In a single movement, he reaches across, grabbing my brother by the shoulder. "I have tried," he is saying. "I don't know what kind of son you are. To be so ungrateful." His other hand sweeps by me and bruises into my brother's face.

My mother flinches. My brother's face is red and his mouth is open. His eyes are wet.

Still coughing, he grabs a fork, tines aimed at my father, and then in an unthinking moment, he heaves it at him. It strikes my father in the chest and drops.

"I hate you! You're just an asshole, you're just a fucking asshole chink!" My brother holds his plate in his hands. He smashes it down and his food scatters across the table. He is coughing and spitting. "I wish you weren't my father! I wish you were dead."

My father's hand falls again. This time pounding downwards. I close my eyes. All I can hear is someone screaming. There is a loud voice. I stand awkwardly, my hands covering my eyes.

"Go to your room," my father says, his voice shaking.

And I think he is talking to me so I remove my hands.

But he is looking at my brother. And my brother is looking at him, his small chest heaving.

A few minutes later, my mother begins clearing the table, face weary as she scrapes the dishes one by one over the garbage.

I move away from my chair, past my mother, onto the carpet and up the stairs.

Outside my brother's bedroom, I crouch against the wall. When I step forward and look, I see my father holding the bamboo pole between his hands. The pole is smooth. The long grains, fine as hair, are pulled together, at intervals, jointed. My brother is lying on the floor, as if thrown down and dragged there. My father raises the pole into the air.

I want to cry out. I want to move into the room between them, but I can't.

It is like a tree falling, beginning to move, a slow arc through the air. The bamboo drops silently. It rips the skin on my brother's back. I cannot hear any sound. A line of blood edges quickly across his body.

The pole rises and again comes down. I am afraid of bones breaking. My father lifts his arms once more.

On the floor, my brother cries into the carpet, pawing at the ground. His knees folded into his chest, the crown of his head burrowing down. His back is hunched over and I can see his spine, little bumps on his skin.

The bamboo smashes into bone and the scene in my mind bursts into a million white pieces.

My mother picks me up off the floor, pulling me across the hall, into my bedroom, into bed. Everything is wet, the sheets, my hands, her body, my face, and she soothes me with words I cannot understand because all I can hear is screaming. She rubs her cool hands against my forehead. "Stop," she says. "Please stop," but I feel loose, deranged, as if everything in the known world is ending right here.

In the morning, I wake up to the sound of oil in the pan and the smell of French toast. I can hear my mother bustling around, putting dishes in the cupboards.

No one says anything when my brother doesn't come down for breakfast. My father piles French toast and syrup onto a plate and my mother pours a glass of milk. She takes everything upstairs to my brother's bedroom.

As always, I follow my father around the kitchen. I track his footprints, follow behind him and hide in the shadow of his body. Every so often, he reaches down and ruffles my hair with his hands. We cast a spell, I think. The way we move in circles, how he cooks without thinking because this is the task that comes to him effortlessly. He smiles down at me, but when he does this, it somehow breaks the spell. My father stands in place, hands dropping to his sides as if he has forgotten what he was doing mid-motion. On the walls, the paint is peeling and the floor, unswept in days, leaves little pieces of dirt stuck to our feet.

My persistence, I think, my unadulterated love, confuse him. With each passing day, he knows I will find it harder to ignore what I can't comprehend, that I will be unable to separate one part of him from another. The unconditional quality of my love for him will not last forever, just as my brother's did not. My father stands in the middle of the kitchen, unsure. Eventually, my mother comes downstairs again and puts her arms around him and holds him, whispering something to him, words that to me are meaningless and incomprehensible. But she offers them to him, sound after sound, in a language that was stolen from some other place, until he drops his head and remembers where he is.

Later on, I lean against the door frame upstairs and listen to the sound of a metal fork scraping against a dish. My mother is already there, her voice rising and falling. She is moving the fork across the plate, offering my brother pieces of French toast.

I move towards the bed, the carpet scratchy, until I can touch the wooden bed-frame with my hands.

My mother is seated there, and I go to her, reaching my fingers out to the buttons on her cuff and twisting them over to catch the light.

"Are you eating?" I ask my brother.

He starts to cry. I look at him, his face half hidden in the blankets.

"Try and eat," my mother says softly.

He only cries harder but there isn't any sound. The pattern of sunlight on his blanket moves with his body. His hair is pasted down with sweat and his head moves forward and backward like an old man's.

At some point I know my father is standing at the entrance of the room but I cannot turn to look at him. I want to stay where I am, facing the wall. I'm afraid that if I turn around and go to him, I will be complicit, accepting a portion of guilt, no matter how small that piece. I do not know how to prevent this from happening again, though now I know, in the end, it will break us apart. This violence will turn all my love to shame and grief. So I stand there, not looking at him or my brother.

Even my father, the magician, who can make something beautiful out of nothing, he just stands and watches.

A face changes over time, it becomes clearer. In my father's face, I have seen everything pass. Anger that has stripped it of anything recognizable, so that it is only a face of bones and skin. And then, at other times, so much pain that it is unbearable, his face so full of grief it might dissolve. How to reconcile all that I know of him and still love him? For a long time, I thought it was not possible. When I was a child, I did not love my father because he was complicated, because he was human, because he needed me to. A child does not know yet how to love a person that way.

How simple it should be. Warm water running over, the feel of the grains between my hands, the sound of it like stones running along the pavement. My father would rinse the rice over and over, sifting it between his fingertips, searching for the impurities, pulling them out. A speck, barely visible, resting on the tip of his finger.

If there were some recourse, I would take it. A cupful of grains in my open hand, a smoothing out, finding the impurities, then removing them piece by piece. And then, to be satisfied with what remains.

Somewhere in my memory, a fish in the sink is dying slowly. My father and I watch as the water runs down.

*—2001*

# Poetry

# *Introduction to Poetry*

## An Anecdote: Where Poetry Starts

Poetry readings are popular because they lift a curtain to give a behind-the-scenes glimpse of the poetic process. The poet probably will not look as we expect a poet to look. Surprisingly, he or she may not even begin with a poem. This time, a man in a chambray shirt adjusts his glasses and, in a relaxed voice, tells an anecdote about his younger daughter and an overdue science project. When he moves from the background story into reading the poem itself, there is little change in his volume level, and his tone remains conversational. The students find that the poem, which they had discussed in class only a couple of days before, takes on new meaning when its origins are explained by the poet himself. They find themselves listening attentively to his words, even laughing out loud several times. The hour goes by quickly, and at its end their applause, like that of the rest of the audience, is long and sincere.

At the next class meeting, the instructor asks for reactions to the reading. Although some of the class members are slightly critical, faulting the speaker for his informal manner and his failure to maintain eye contact with the room, most of the remarks are positive. The comments that surface most often have to do with how much more meaningful the poems in the textbook become when the poet explains how he came to write them. They now know that one poem is actually spoken in the voice of the poet's dead father and that another is addressed to a friend who was paralyzed in an automobile accident. Although these things could perhaps be inferred from the poems alone, the students are unanimous in their opinion that knowing the details beforehand adds a great deal to the first impression a poem makes. As one student puts it, "It's just that a poem makes a lot more sense when you know who's talking and when and where it's supposed to be taking place."

"It always helps to know where poetry starts," adds one of her classmates.

## Speaker, Listener, and Context

The situation described above is hardly unique. Instructors have long been encouraging their students to attend events like the one described, and the poetry reading has become, for many, the closest encounter students will have with this complex and often perplexing art form. But what students often find at such readings, sometimes to their amazement, is that poetry need not be intimidating or obscure. Poems that are *performed* provide a gentle reminder that the roots of poetry, like those of all literature, have their origins in the **oral tradition.** In ancient societies, stories and poems were passed down from generation to generation and recited for all members of the tribe, from the wizened elders to the youngest children. For most of its long history, poetry has been a popular art form aimed at *audiences* (remember that the word audience means "hearers"). It is only recently, in the last three or four decades, that its most visible signs of life are to be found on campuses. Still, it is perhaps worth noting that we are exposed daily to a great deal of poetry in oral form, primarily through the medium of recorded song lyrics. The unique qualities of poetry throughout the ages—its ability to tell stories or summarize complicated emotions in a few well-chosen words—are demonstrated whenever we memorize the lines of a popular song and sing them to ourselves.

Of course, poetry written primarily for the page may be more demanding than song lyrics. Writers of popular songs aim at a wide commercial audience, and this simple fact of economics, added to the fact that the lyrics are not intended primarily for publication but for being recorded as a song with all the resources of studio technology, can make song lyrics appear simple and repetitive in print. There are, of course, exceptions like Leonard Cohen, whose work has received acclaim from both literary critics and the music industry. A poem will exist primarily as a printed text, although its effect may be enhanced greatly through a skillful oral performance in which the poet can also explain the background of the poem, its setting and speaker, and the circumstances under which it was written. In general, these details, so crucial to understanding a poem yet so often only implied when the poem appears in print, are called the **dramatic situation** of a poem. Situation can be summed up in a question: *Who is speaking to whom under what circumstances?* If the poet fails to provide us with clues or if we are careless in picking up the information that is provided, then we may begin reading with no sense of reference and, thus, may go far astray. Even such words as "on," "upon," or "to" in titles can be crucial to our understanding of dramatic situation, telling us something about an event or object that provided the stimulus for the poem or about the identity of the "you" addressed in the poem.

An illustration may be helpful. Suppose we look at what is arguably the most widely known poem ever written by a Canadian: John McCrae's "In Flanders Fields." It is a poem that many Canadians can recite because of its use on Remembrance Day. As Margaret Atwood said of this poem, "as a Canadian born in 1939, I had 'In Flanders Fields' hammered into my head at an early age, and will doubtless never be able to shake the notion that what one properly does with torches is to hold them high: otherwise you get haunted." Despite the controversy of the closing call to arms, it is still a powerful evocation of the sacrifices of the Great War, an event that many believe marked Canada's coming of age.

## In Flanders Fields

In Flanders fields the poppies blow
Between the crosses, row on row
That mark our place; and in the sky
The larks, still bravely singing, fly
Scarce heard amid the guns below.

We are the Dead. Short days ago
We lived, felt dawn, saw sunset glow,
Loved and were loved, and now we lie
In Flanders fields.

Take up our quarrel with the foe:
To you from failing hands we throw

The torch; be yours to hold it high.
If ye break faith with us who die
We shall not sleep, though poppies grow
In Flanders fields.

The poem is an example of **occasional verse,** a poem that is written about or for an important event (or occasion), sometimes private but usually of some public significance. Although poems of this type are not often printed on the front pages of newspapers as they once were, they are still being written. The author of "In Flanders Fields," John McCrae (1872–1918), was a medical doctor who wrote poetry as an avocation. Yet like many men and women who are not professional writers, McCrae was so deeply moved by an event that he witnessed that occasional poetry was the only medium through which he could express his feelings.

Now let's go back to our question about dramatic situation, taking it one part at a time: *Who is speaking?* A technical word that is often used to designate the speaker of a poem is **persona** (plural: **personae**), a word that meant "mask" in ancient Greek. In this case, it is not the poet, who is still alive at the time of the writing of the poem, but rather his fallen comrades in arms, "the Dead," who are speaking. According to some accounts, the poem was inspired by the death of McCrae's friend Lieutenant Alexis Helmer, who was killed by an enemy shell on May 2, 1915. The voice-from-the-grave device, used by Hardy and others for ironic purposes, was here used to evoke emotion. The unusual perspective gained extra poignancy when on January 28, 1918, McCrae himself died of pneumonia and meningitis at the front, worn down from having treated the wounded from some of the war's most horrific battles, Ypres, Somme, and Vimy Ridge. He was buried at Wimereux, France, and within the year the war that claimed the life of eight and a half million soldiers was over.

It is important to look at poems carefully to see if they give any evidence that the speaker is someone other than the poet. Poems like "The Death of the Ball Turret Gunner" by Randall Jarrell or "The River-Merchant's Wife: A Letter" by Ezra Pound have titles that identify personae who are, respectively, a soldier who has died and a young bride. In neither case is the persona to be identified with the poet. Other poems may be somewhat more problematical. Edgar Allan Poe's "The Raven," like many of Poe's short stories, is spoken by a persona who is not to be

identified with the author, even though he shares many of the same mor-
bid preoccupations of Poe's other characters. Even in the work of Sylvia
Plath, a poet usually associated with an extremely candid form of autobiographical poetry known as **confessional poetry,** it is a mistake to
assume that there is no invention in the creation of characters. Sometimes
poems have more than one persona, which is the case with Dudley
Randall's "Ballad of Birmingham," a poem that opens with a dialogue
between mother and daughter. In other poems, for instance in many ballads, the voice may simply be a third-person **narrator** such as we might
find in a short story or novel. Thus, although it is perhaps true that many
poems (including the majority of those included here) are in fact spoken
by the poet out of his or her most private feelings, it is not a good idea to
leap too quickly to the assumption that the persona of a poem is identical
to the poet and shares his or her views. Conclusions about the degree to
which a poem is autobiographical can be verified only by research and
familiarity with a poet's other works.

To return to our question: Who is speaking *to whom?* Another
useful term is **auditor,** the person or persons spoken to in a poem. Some
poems identify no auditor; others clearly do specify an auditor or auditors, in most cases identified by name or by the second-person pronoun
"you" (or "thee/thou" in older poetry). Again, the title may give clues:
Poe's "To Helen" is addressed to the famous beauty of Homeric legend;
as we discover in the final stanza of the villanelle by Dylan Thomas, "Do
Not Go Gentle into That Good Night" is a plea from son to father. (The
figure of speech **apostrophe**—discussed later in this introduction—is
used when a non-human, inanimate, or abstract thing is directly
addressed.) Relatively few poems are addressed directly to the reader, so
when we read the opening of William Shakespeare's Sonnet 18 ("Shall I
compare thee to a summer's day?") we should keep in mind that he is
addressing not us but another individual, in this case a young male
friend who is referred to in many of the sonnets.

Now the final part of the question: Who is speaking to whom *under
what circumstances?* First, we might ask if there is a relationship, either
implied or stated, between persona and auditor. Obviously many love
poems take the form of verbal transactions between two parties and,
because relationships have their ups and downs, these shifts of mood are
reflected in the poetry. A "courtship ritual" poem such as Andrew
Marvell's "To His Coy Mistress" is a witty argument in favour of the

couple's engaging in sexual relations. An example from poetry about marital love is Matthew Arnold's "Dover Beach," which ends with the plea "Ah, love, let us be true / To one another" as the only hope for stability the persona can find in a world filled with uncertainty and fear. Other questions relating to circumstances of the dramatic situation might concern the poem's physical setting (if any), time (of day, year, historical era), even such matters as weather. Pauline Johnson's "The Idlers" provides a good example of a poem in which the setting, a canoe drifting through the languorous heat of a Canadian July, symbolically reinforces the erotic tension between the idlers. The shift in setting from the springtime idyll to the "cold hillside" in John Keats's "La Belle Dame sans Merci" cannot be overlooked in discussing the persona's disillusionment. Of course, many poems are explicitly occasional, like Dionne Brand's "Blues Spiritual for Mammy Prater," and may even contain an **epigraph** (a brief explanatory statement or quotation) or a **dedication,** which explains the setting. Sometimes footnotes or even outside research may be necessary. Joy Kogawa's poem "When I Was a Little Girl" will make little sense to readers if they do not know that Kogawa and her family, along with many other Japanese Canadians, were separated from their homes and possessions after the 1941 attack on Pearl Harbor.

To return, then, one final time to "In Flanders Fields," let us apply our question to the poem. We have already determined that the "we" in the poem refers to the soldiers who are dead. Who is the "you" mentioned in the final stanza? It seems that "you" would refer in part to the soldiers who were still alive to carry on, including McCrae himself. Though well aware of the grim realities of battle, McCrae wrote, "I am going because I think every bachelor, especially if he has experience of war, ought to go. I am really rather afraid, but more afraid to stay at home with my conscience." But the poem was also addressed to potential soldiers and supporters on the home front. In fact, Victory Loan Bonds, which used lines from the final stanza of McCrae's poem in their advertisements, raised $400 million for the war effort. Why would McCrae, who wrote, "It was HELL all the time. We really expected to die in our tracks," encourage others to join the fray? There is clearly a shift from the elegiac tone of the first stanzas to a call to arms that contrasts strongly with Wilfred Owen's assertion that dying for one's country is never sweet. Few people have argued that "In Flanders Fields" is a great poem. Still, it is an effective piece of verse that reveals one aspect of a formative event in Canadian history. As Paul Fussell writes in *The Great War and Modern Memory*, "it is an interesting poem because it manages to accumulate the maximum number of well-known motifs and images" before disintegrating into a "vicious and stupid" propaganda argument against peace. There may be ways to redeem the poem by suggesting that the foe in McCrae's poem is not the kaiser's army, but rather war itself. Language, often layered and ambiguous, becomes particularly so in times of propaganda. As George Elliott Clarke has argued in "Casualties," his poem about the 1991 Gulf conflict, "the first casualty of war is language."

## Lyric, Narrative, Dramatic

The starting point for all literary criticism in Western civilization is Aristotle's *Poetics*, a work dating from the fourth century B.C. Although Aristotle's remarks on drama, and tragedy in particular, are more complete than his analysis of other types of literature, he does mention three main types of poetry: lyric, epic, and dithyrambic. In doing so, Aristotle outlines for the first time a theory of literature based on **genres,** or separate categories delineated by distinct style, form, and content. This three-fold division remains useful today, although in two cases different terminology is employed. The first genre, **lyric poetry,** originally comprised brief poems that were meant to be sung or chanted to the accompaniment of a lyre. Today we still use the word "lyrics" in a specialized sense when referring to the words of a song, but lyric poetry has become such a large category that it includes virtually all poems that are primarily *about* a subject and contain little narrative content. The subject of a lyric poem may be the poet's emotions, an abstract idea, a satirical insight, or a description of a person or place. The persona in a lyric is usually closely identified with the poet himself or herself. Because we tend to identify the essence of poetry with personal, subjective expression of feelings or ideas, lyric poetry remains the largest genre, with a number of subtypes. Among them are the **epigram,** a short, satirical lyric usually aimed at a specific person; the **elegy,** a lyric on the occasion of a death; and the **ode,** a long lyric in elevated language on a serious theme.

Aristotle's second genre, the **epic,** has been expanded to include all types of **narrative poetry,** that is, poetry whose main function is to tell a story. Like prose fiction, narrative poems have plots, characters, setting, and point of view and may be discussed in the same terms as, say, a short story. The epic is a long narrative poem about the exploits of a hero. **Folk epics** like the *Iliad* or *Beowulf* were originally intended for public recitation and existed in oral form for a long time before they were transcribed. Little or nothing is known about the authors of folk epics; even Homer, the purported author of the *Iliad* and the *Odyssey*, is primarily a legendary character. **Literary epics,** like Dante's *Inferno* or Milton's *Paradise Lost,* differ in that they are the products of known authors who *wrote* their poems for publication. **Ballads** generally are shorter narratives with song-like qualities that often include rhyme and repeated refrains. **Folk ballads,** like folk epics, come from the oral tradition and are usually published anonymously; "Sir Patrick Spens" is a typical example. **Art** or **literary ballads** are conscious imitations of the ballad style by later poets and are generally somewhat more sophisticated than folk ballads in their techniques. Examples of this popular genre include Keats's "La Belle Dame sans Merci," and ballads continue to be written and sung to this day. There are also other types of narrative poetry that have been popular through the centuries. **Metrical romances,** verse tales of the exploits of knights, were a popular genre during the Middle Ages and the Renaissance; Edmund Spenser's *The Faerie Queene* is one of the most ambitious examples of the type. At the opposite extreme are **mock-heroic narratives** like Lord Byron's *Don Juan,* which spoof the conventions of epic poetry for comic or satirical effect. **Realistic narratives** of medium length (under one thousand lines) have been popular since the early nineteenth century and are sometimes discussed as "poetic novels" or "short stories in verse."

There is no exact contemporary analogue for Aristotle's third category, **dithyrambic** poetry. This type of poem, composed to be chanted at religious rituals by a chorus, was the forerunner of tragedy. Today this third type is usually called **dramatic poetry,** because it has perhaps as much in common with the separate genre of drama as with lyric and narrative poetry. In general, the persona in a dramatic poem is an invented character not to be identified with the poet. The poem is presented as a speech or dialogue that might be acted out like a soliloquy or scene from a play. The **dramatic monologue** is a speech for a single character, usually delivered to a silent auditor. Browning's "My Last Duchess" is a famous example. A dramatic monologue sometimes implies, in the words of its persona, a distinct setting and interplay between persona and auditor. Tom Wayman's poem "Did I Miss Anything?" in which an instructor provides various answers to this question frequently asked by students after missing a class, is a witty twist on this convention. Dramatic poetry can also take the form of **dialogue poetry,** in which two personae speak alternately as in Dudley Randall's "Ballad of Birmingham." A popular type of dialogue poem that originated in the Middle Ages was the *débat,* or mock-debate, in which two characters, usually personified abstractions like the Soul and the Body, argued their respective merits.

Although it is easy enough to find examples of "pure" lyrics, narratives, and dramatic monologues, sometimes the distinctions among the three major types may become blurred, even in the same poem. "In Flanders Fields," for example, contains elements of all three genres. The opening stanza, with its vivid re-creation of the battlefields and cemeteries of Flanders, is closest to lyric poetry. The second stanza, describing the fate of the soldiers, is primarily narrative, and the final stanza, with its call for participation on the part of the listeners, is dramatic. Still, the three-fold division is useful in discussing a single author's various ways of dealing with subjects or in comparing examples of one type by separate authors.

## The Language of Poetry

One of the most persistent myths about poetry is that its language is artificial, "flowery," and essentially different from the language that people speak every day. Although these beliefs may be true of some poetry, one can easily find numerous examples that demonstrate poetic diction of an entirely different sort. It is impossible to characterize poetic language narrowly, for poetry, which is after all the art of language, covers the widest possible range of linguistic possibilities. For example, here are several passages from different poets, all describing birds:

> Hail to thee, blithe Spirit!
> 　Bird thou never wert—
> That from Heaven, or near it,
> 　Pourest thy full heart
> In profuse strains of unpremeditated art.

> Higher still and higher
> 　From the earth thou springest

Like a cloud of fire;
   The blue deep thou wingest,
And singing still dost soar, and soaring ever singest.

Percy Bysshe Shelley, "To a Skylark"

I caught this morning morning's minion, king-
dom of daylight's dauphin, dapple-dawn-drawn Falcon, in his riding
Of the rolling level underneath him steady air, and striding
High there, how he rung upon the rein of a wimpling wing
In his ecstasy!

Gerard Manley Hopkins, "The Windhover"

On the stiff twig up there
Hunches a wet black rook
Arranging and rearranging its feathers in the rain.

Sylvia Plath, "Black Rook in Rainy Weather"

Lower down, Merlins slice the air with wings that say crisp crisp,
precise as sushi chefs, while Sharp-shins alternately glide and flap,
hunting as they go, each line break poised, ready to pivot like a
point guard. . . .

Don McKay, "Icarus"

Of these quotes, only Shelley's from the early nineteenth century
possesses the stereotypical characteristics of what we mean when we
use the term "poetic" in a negative sense. Poetry, like any other art
form, follows fashions that change over the years; by Shelley's day, the
use of "thee" and "thou" and their related verb forms ("wert" and
"wingest") had come full circle from their original use as a familiar
form of the second person, employed to address intimates and servants, to an artificially heightened grammatical form reserved for
prayers and poetry. Hopkins's language, from a poem of the 1870s, is
artificial in an entirely different way; here the poet's **idiom,** the personal use of words that marks his poetry, is highly idiosyncratic;
indeed, it would be hard to mistake a poem by Hopkins, with its
muscular monosyllables and rich texture of sound patterns, with one
by any other poet. When we move to the contemporary period, we can

find little difference between the language of many poems and conversational speech, as Plath's lines indicate. McKay's comparison of falcons and hawks to sushi chefs and basketball players strikes us as especially contemporary.

Still, in reading a poem, particularly one from the past, we should be aware of certain problems that may impede our understanding. **Diction** refers to the individual words in a poem and may be classified in several ways. A poem's **level of diction** can range from slang at one extreme to formal usage at the other. Now, when most poems use a level of diction that stays in the middle of the scale, these distinctions are useful only when a poet is being self-consciously formal (perhaps for ironic effect) or going to the opposite extreme to imitate the language of the streets. In past eras the term **poetic diction** was used to indicate a level of speech somehow refined above ordinary usage and, thus, somehow superior to it. Today the same term would most likely be used as a way of criticizing a poet's language. We should keep in mind that the slang of one era may become the standard usage of another, as is the case with "OK," which has become a universal expression. A good dictionary is useful in many ways, particularly in dealing with **archaisms** (words that are no longer in common use) and other words that may not be familiar to the reader. Take, for example, the opening lines of Edgar Allan Poe's "To Helen":

> Helen, thy beauty is to me
> Like those Nicean barks of yore,
> That gently, o'er a perfumed sea,
> The weary, way-worn wanderer bore
> To his own native shore.

Several words here may give trouble to the average contemporary reader. First, "o'er," like "ne'er" or similar words like "falt'ring" and "glimm'ring," is simply a contraction; this dropping of a letter, called **syncope,** is done for the sake of maintaining the poem's metre. "Barks of yore" will probably send most of us to the dictionary, for our sense of "bark" as either the outer surface of a tree or the noise that a dog makes does not fit here; likewise, "yore" is unfamiliar, possibly archaic. Looking up the literal sense of a word in a dictionary discloses its **denotation,** or literal meaning. Thus, we find that "barks" are small sailing ships and that "yore" refers to the distant past. Of course, Poe could have said "ships of the past" or a similar phrase, but his word choice was perhaps dictated by **connotation,** the implied meaning or feel that some words have acquired; it may be that even in Poe's day "barks of yore" had a remote quality that somehow evoked ancient Greece in a way that, say, "ancient ships" would not. But what are we to make of "Nicean," a proper adjective that sounds geographical but does not appear in either the dictionary or gazetteer? In this case we have encountered an example of a **coinage,** or **neologism,** a word made up by the poet. Speculation on the source of "Nicean" has ranged from Nice, in the south of France, to Phoenician, but it is likely that Poe simply coined the word for its exotic sound. Similarly, we might note that the phrase "weary, way-worn wanderer" contains words that seem to have been chosen primarily for their alliterated sounds.

When we put a poem into our own words, we **paraphrase** it, a practice that is often useful when passages are hard to understand. Other than diction, **syntax,** the order of words in a sentence, may also give readers problems. Syntax in poetry, particularly in poems that use rhyme, is likely to be different from that of both speech and prose; if a poet decides to rhyme in a certain pattern, then word order may be modified to fit the formal design, and this can present difficulties to readers in understanding the grammar of a passage. The passage from Poe's poem presents few difficulties of this order but does contain one example of **inversion,** words that fall out of their expected order (a related syntactical problem lies in **ellipsis,** words that are consciously omitted by the poet). If we do not allow for this, we are likely to be confused by "the weary, way-worn wanderer bore / To his own native shore." The wanderer bore *what?* A quick mental sentence diagram shows that "wanderer" is the direct object of "bore," not its subject. A good paraphrase should simplify both diction and syntax: "Helen, to me your beauty is like those Nicean (?) ships of the ancient past that carried the weary, travel-worn wanderer gently over a perfumed sea to his own native land." In paraphrasing, only the potentially troublesome words and phrases should be substituted, leaving the original language as intact as possible. Paraphrasing is a useful first step toward unfolding a poem's literal sense, but it obviously takes few of a poet's specific nuances of language into account; words like "thin," "slender," and "skinny" may denote the same thing, but each has its own connotation, and poets are particularly attuned to such nuances. "Poetry," Robert Frost famously remarked, "is what is lost in translation."

Several other matters relevant to poetic language are worth mentioning. **Etymology,** the study of the sources of words, is a particularly rewarding topic in English because our language has such an unusually rich history—just compare an unabridged French dictionary with its English counterpart. Old English (or Anglo-Saxon), the ancient language of the British Isles, was part of the Germanic family of languages. When the Norman French successfully invaded Britain in 1066 they brought with them their own language, part of the Romance language family (all originally derived from Latin). By the time of Chaucer's death in 1400 these two linguistic traditions had merged into a single language, Middle English, that can be read today, despite its differences in spelling, pronunciation, and vocabulary. We can still, however, distinguish the words that show their Germanic heritage from those of Latinate origin, and despite the fact that English is rich in synonyms, the Germanic and Latinate words often have different connotations. "Smart" (from the Old English *smeart*) is not quite the same as "intelligent" (from the Latin *intellegent*). A "map-maker" is subtly different from a "cartographer"—ask yourself which would have ink on his fingers. Although a poet's preference for words of a certain origin is not always immediately clear, we can readily distinguish the wide gulf that separates a statement like "I live in a house with my folks" from "I abide in a residence with my parents."

A final tension exists in poems between their use of **concrete diction** and **abstract diction.** Concrete words denote that which can be perceived by the senses, and the vividness of a poem's language resides primarily in the way it uses **imagery,** sensory details denoting specific physical experiences. Because sight is the most important of the five senses, **visual imagery** ("a dim light"; "a dirty rag"; "a golden daffodil") predominates in poems, but we should also be alert for striking examples of the other types of imagery: **auditory** ("a pounding surf"), **tactile** ("a scratchy beard"), **olfactory** ("the scent of apple blossoms"), and **gustatory** ("the bitter tang of gin"). The use of specific imagery has always been crucial for poetry. In the early twentieth century, a group of poets led by Americans Ezra Pound and H. D. (Hilda Doolittle) pioneered a poetic movement called **imagism,** in which concrete details predominate in short descriptive poems (see Ezra Pound's "In a Station of the Metro"). "Go in fear of abstractions," commanded Pound, and his friend William Carlos Williams modified the remark to become a poetic credo: "No ideas but in things."

Still, for some poets abstract words remain important because they carry the burden of a poem's overall meaning or theme. More often than not, one can expect to encounter the largest number of abstract words near the conclusion of poems. Probably the most famous abstract statement in English poetry, John Keats's "'Beauty is truth, truth beauty,' —that is all / Ye know on earth, and all ye need to know" appears in the last two lines of "Ode on a Grecian Urn," a fifty-line poem that is filled with lush, sensory details of description. Two other devices sometimes govern a poet's choice of words. **Onomatopoeia** refers to individual words like "buzz" or "thud" whose meanings are closely related to their sounds. Auditory imagery in a poem can often be enhanced by the use of onomatopoeic words. In some cases, however, a whole line can be called onomatopoeic, even if it contains no single word that illustrates the device. Archibald Lampman uses these lines to describe the "City of the End of Things": "The beat, the thunder and the hiss / Cease not, and change not, night nor day." Here the repetition of similar sounds helps to imitate the grim, noisy routine of a city dominated by machines. A second device is the **pun,** the use of one word to imply the additional meaning of a similar-sounding word (the formal term is **paranomasia**). Thus, when Anne Bradstreet compares her first book to an illegitimate child, she addresses the book in this manner: "If for thy father asked, say thou hadst none; / And for thy mother, she alas is poor, / Which caused her thus to send thee out of door." The closeness of the interjection "alas" to the article and noun "a lass" is hardly coincidental. Poets in Bradstreet's day considered the pun a staple of their repertoire, even in serious poetry, but contemporary poets are more likely to use it primarily for comic effect.

## Figurative Language

We use figurative language in everyday speech without thinking of the poetic functions of the same devices. We can always relate experience in a purely literal fashion: "His table manners were deplorable. Mother scolded him severely, and Dad said some angry words to him. He left the table embarrassed and with his feelings hurt." But a more vivid way of saying the same thing might employ language used not in the literal but in the figurative sense. Thus, another version might run, "He made an absolute pig of himself. Mother jumped on his back about it, and Dad scorched his ears. You should have seen him slink off like a scolded puppy." At least four comparisons are made here in an attempt to describe one character's table manners, his mother's scolding, his father's words, and the manner in which the character retreated from the table. In every case, the thing being described, what is called the **tenor** of the figure of speech, is linked with a concrete image, or **vehicle.** By making comparisons we apply what we know to what is new to us, inevitably enhancing our understanding of both.

Traditionally, figurative language was divided into two categories: rhetorical figures in which the order or pattern of words changes and tropes (turns) in which the meaning of the words changes, often involving some kind of comparison, either explicit or implied. Thus, two of the figures in the above example specifically compare aspects of the character's behaviour to animal behaviour. The other two imply parental words that were delivered with strong physical force or extreme anger. Both rhetorical figures and tropes are now generally referred to as figures of speech. Some of the most common are:

**Metaphor:** a direct comparison between two unlike things. Metaphors may take several forms.

> His words were sharp knives.
> The sharp knife of his words cut through the silence.
> He spoke sharp, cutting words.
> His words knifed through the still air.
> "I will speak daggers to her . . ." *(William Shakespeare)*

**Simile:** a comparison using "like," "as," or "than" as a connective device.

> Because she was old and useless,
> Like a paddle broken and warped . . . *(D. C. Scott)*

**Conceit:** an extended or far-fetched metaphor, in most cases comparing things that apparently have almost nothing in common. A **Petrarchan conceit,** named after the first great master of the sonnet, is a clichéd comparison usually relating to a woman's beauty (Shakespeare's Sonnet 130 parodies this type of trope). The **metaphysical conceit** refers to the extended comparisons favoured by such so-called metaphysical poets as John Donne and George Herbert. The conceit in Donne's "Holy Sonnet 14" compares the heart to a town under enemy control.

I, like an usurped town, to another due *(John Donne)*

**Hyperbole:** an overstatement, a comparison using conscious exaggeration.

And I will luve thee still, my dear,
Till a' the seas gang dry. *(Robert Burns)*

**Allusion:** a metaphor making a direct comparison to a historical or literary event or character, a myth, a biblical reference, and so forth.

Order streamed from Noah in blue triangles . . . *(Anne Carson)*

**Metonymy:** use of a related object to stand for the thing actually being talked about.

And O ye high-flown quills that soar the skies,
And ever with your prey still catch your praise. *(Anne Bradstreet)*

Here, Bradstreet speaks of critics who may be hostile to her work. She identifies them as "quills," referring to their quill pens.

**Synecdoche:** use of a part for the whole, or vice versa.

Friends, Romans, countrymen: lend me your ears.
*(William Shakespeare)*

**Personification:** giving human characteristics to non-human things or to abstractions.

Thou still unravished bride of quietness . . . *(John Keats)*

**Apostrophe:** a variety of personification in which a non-human thing, abstraction, or person not physically present is directly addressed as if it could respond.

> Acadie, my too beautiful desecrated love . . .
> *(Herménégilde Chiasson)*

**Paradox:** an apparent contradiction or illogical statement.

> This is the beauty
> of strength broken by strength
> and still strong. *(A. J. M. Smith)*

**Oxymoron:** a short paradox, usually consisting of an adjective and noun with conflicting meanings.

> Yet from those flames / No light, but rather darkness visible . . .
> *(John Milton)*

**Synesthesia:** a conscious mixing of two different types of sensory experience.

> With Blue—uncertain stumbling Buzz— *(Emily Dickinson)*

# Symbolism

Related to the figurative devices are the various types of symbolism that may occur in poems. Symbolism is important in fiction, but its use in poetry is perhaps even more complex. In many cases, a poem may seem so simple on the surface that we feel impelled to read deeper meanings into it. Robert Frost's "Stopping by Woods on a Snowy Evening" is a classic case in point. There is nothing wrong with searching for larger significance in a poem, but the reader should perhaps be wary of leaping to conclusions about symbolic meanings before fully exhausting the literal sense of a poem. Whatever the case, both symbolism and allegory share the demand that the reader supply abstract or general meanings to the specific concrete details of the poem.

The simplest form that this substitution takes occurs in **allegory,** which appears in poetry as well as prose. An allegory is usually a narrative that exists on at least two levels simultaneously, a concrete, literal level and a second level of abstract meaning; throughout an allegory a consistent sequence of parallels exists between the literal and the abstract. Christina Rossetti's "Goblin Market," for example, has been interpreted on feminist, economic, creative, and religious levels.

Many poems contain symbolic elements that are somewhat more elusive in meaning than the simple one-for-one equivalences presented by allegory. A **symbol,** then, is any concrete thing or action in a poem that implies a meaning beyond its literal sense. Many of these things or actions are called **traditional symbols,** that is, symbols that hold roughly the same meanings for members of a given society. Certain flowers, colours, natural objects, and religious emblems possess meanings that we can generally agree on, though these can change from culture to culture. In the West the colour associated with mourning is black, whereas in the Chinese tradition, white is associated with death—a difference that Margaret Avison explores in her poem "Snow." Other types of symbols can be identified in poems that are otherwise not allegorical. A **private symbol** is one that has acquired certain meanings from a single poet's repeated use of it. William Butler Yeats's use of "gyres" is explained in some of his prose writings as a symbol for the turning of historical cycles, and his use of the word in his poems obviously goes beyond the literal level. Some visionary poets like Yeats and William Blake devised complicated private symbolic systems, a sort of alternative mythology, and understanding the full import of these symbols becomes primarily the task of critics who have specialized in these poets. Other poets may employ **incidental symbols,** things that are not usually considered symbolic but may be in a particular poem, or symbolic acts, situations or responses that seem of greater than literal import. As noted earlier, one of the most famous poems using these two devices is Robert Frost's "Stopping by Woods on a Snowy Evening." In this poem some readers see the "lovely, dark and deep" woods as both inviting and threatening, and want to view the persona's rejection of their allure ("But I have promises to keep / And miles to go before I sleep") as some sort of life-affirming act. Frost himself was not particularly helpful in guiding his readers, often scoffing at those who had read too much metaphysical portent into such a simple lyric, although in other poems he presents objects such as a rock wall between neighbouring farms or an abandoned woodpile in a manner that leads the reader to feel that these objects obviously possess some larger significance. Many modern poems remain so enigmatic that readers have consistently returned to them seeking new interpretations. Poems like these were to a degree influenced by the symbolists, a group of French poets of the late nineteenth century, who deliberately wrote poems filled with vague nuances subject to multiple interpretations. Such American attempts at symbolist experiments as Wallace Stevens's "Thirteen Ways of Looking at a Blackbird" continue to perplex and fascinate readers, particularly those who are versed in recent schools of interpretation that focus on the indeterminacy of a poetic text.

## Tone of Voice

Even the simplest statement is subject to multiple interpretations if it is delivered in several different tones of voice. Consider the shift in emphasis between saying "*I* gave you the money," "I *gave* you the money," and "I gave *you* the money." Even a seemingly innocent compliment like "You look lovely this morning" takes on a different meaning if it is delivered by a woman to her obviously hung-over husband. Still, these variations in **tone,** the speaker's implied attitude toward the words he or she says, depend primarily on vocal inflection. Because a poet only rarely gets the opportunity to elucidate his or her tones in a public performance, it is possible that readers may have difficulties in grasping the tone of a poem printed on the page, though the lineation (division into lines) gives some clues about where to place the emphasis, as in William Carlos Williams's poem "To a Poor Old Woman." Still, many poems establish their tone quite clearly from the outset. The opening of George Elliott Clarke's "Casualties" ("Snow annihilates all beauty / this merciless January") establishes a harsh tone of criticism toward the disguises we find for the cruelties we perpetrate. Keats's initial apostrophe in "Ode on a Grecian Urn" ("Thou still unravished bride of quietness, / Thou foster-child of silence and slow time . . .") strikes the reader as both passionate and reverent in the poet's response to an undamaged artifact of the ancient past. Thus, in many cases we can relate the tone of voice in poems to the emotions we employ in our own speech, and we would have to violate quite a few rules of common sense to argue that Clarke is being flippant or that Keats is speaking sarcastically.

**Irony** is the element of tone by which a poet may imply an attitude that is in fact contrary to what his or her words appear to say. Of course, the simplest form of irony is **sarcasm,** the wounding tone of voice we use to imply exactly the opposite of what we say: "That's really a *great* excuse!" or "What a *wonderful* performance!" For obvious reasons, sarcasm is appropriate primarily to spoken language. It has become almost universal to follow a bit of gentle sarcasm in an e-mail message with a symbolic :) to indicate that the remark is not to be taken "straight." **Verbal irony** is the conscious manipulation of tone by which the poet's actual attitude is the opposite of what he says. Verbal irony is also a conspicuous feature of **verse satire,** poetry that exists primarily to mock or ridicule, although often with serious intent. One famous example, in the form of a short satirical piece, or **epigram,** is Sarah N. Cleghorn's "The Golf Links," a poem written before the advent of child labour laws:

> The golf links lie so near the mill
> That almost every day
> The laboring children can look out
> And see the men at play.

Here the weight of the verbal irony falls on two words, "labouring" and "play," and the way each is incongruously applied to the wrong group of people.

"The Golf Links," taken as a whole, also represents a second form of irony, **situational irony,** in which the setting of the poem (labouring children watching playing adults) contains a built-in incongruity. **Dramatic irony,** the third type of irony, occurs when the persona of a poem is less aware of the full import of his or her words than is the reader.

## Repetition: Sounds and Schemes

Because poetry uses language at its most intense level, we are aware of the weight of individual words and phrases to a degree that is usually lacking when we read prose. Poets have long known that the meanings that they attempt to convey often depend as much on the sound of the words as their meanings. We have already mentioned one sound device, onomatopoeia. Consider how much richer the experience of "the murmuring of innumerable bees" is than a synonymous phrase, "the low sound of a lot of bees." It has often been said that all art aspires to the condition of music in the way that it affects an audience on some unconscious, visceral level. By carefully exploiting the repetition of sound devices, a poet may attempt to produce some of the same effects that the musical composer does.

Of course, much of this sonic level of poetry is subjective; what strikes one listener as pleasant may overwhelm the ear of another. Still, it is useful to distinguish between a poet's use of **euphony,** a series of pleasant sounds, and **cacophony,** sounds that are deliberately unpleasant. Note the following passages from Alexander Pope's "An Essay on Criticism," a didactic poem that attempts to illustrate many of the devices poets use:

> Soft is the strain when Zephyr gently blows,
> And the smooth stream in smoother numbers flows . . .

The repetition of the initial consonant sounds is called **alliteration,** and here Pope concentrates on the *s* sound. The vowel sounds are generally long: str*ai*n, bl*ow*s, sm*oo*th, and fl*ow*s. Here the description of the gentle west wind is assisted by the generally pleasing sense of euphony. But Pope, to illustrate the opposite quality, follows this couplet with a second:

> But when loud surges lash the sounding shore,
> The hoarse, rough verse should like the torrent roar.

Now the wind is anything but gentle, and the repetition of the *r* sounds in su*r*ges, sho*r*e, hoa*r*se, *r*ough, ve*r*se, to*r*rent, and *r*oa*r* forces the reader to speak from the back of the throat, making sounds that are anything but euphonious.

Repetition of sounds has no inherent meaning value (although some linguists may argue that certain sounds do stimulate particular emotions), but this repetition does call attention to itself and can be particularly effective when a poet wishes to emphasize a certain passage. We have already mentioned alliteration. Other sound patterns are **assonance,** the repetition of similar vowel sounds (st*ee*p, *e*ven, rec*ei*ve, v*ea*l), and **consonance,** the repetition of similar consonant sounds (du*ck*, tor*que*, stri*ke*, tri*ck*le). It should go without saying that spelling has little to do with any sound pattern; an initial *f* will alliterate with an initial *ph*.

**Rhyme** is the most important sound device, and our pleasure in deftly executed rhymes goes beyond mere sound to include the pleasure we take when an unexpected word is magically made to fit with another. There are several types of rhyme. **Masculine rhyme** occurs between single stressed syllables: *fleece*, re*lease*, sur*cease*, *niece*, and so on. **Feminine rhyme,** also called **double rhyme,** matches two syllables, the first stressed and the second usually unstressed: *stinging*, *upbringing*, *flinging*. **Triple rhyme** goes further: *slithering*, *withering*. **Slant rhyme** (also called **near rhyme** and **off rhyme**) contains hints of sound repetition (sometimes related to assonance and consonance): *chill*, *dull*, and *sale* are possibilities, although poets often grant themselves considerable leeway in counting as rhyming words pairs that often have only the slightest similarity. When rhymes fall in a pattern in a poem and are **end rhymes,** occurring at the ends of lines, it is then convenient to assign letters to the sounds and speak of a **rhyme scheme.** Thus, a stanza of four lines ending with *heaven*, *hell*, *bell*, *eleven* would be said to have a rhyme scheme of *abba*. Rhymes may also occasionally be found in the interior of lines, which is called **internal rhyme.** Note how both end and internal rhymes work in the complex stanza which Poe uses in "The Raven."

More complicated patterns of repetition involve more than mere sounds but whole phrases and grammatical units. Ancient rhetoricians, teaching the art of public speaking, identified several of these, and they are also found in poetry. **Parallel structure** is simply the repetition of grammatically similar phrases or clauses: Tennyson's "To strive, to seek, to find, and not to yield." **Anaphora** and **epistrophe** are repeated words or phrases at, respectively, the beginning and end of lines. This passage from Lorna Crozier's "Packing for the Future: Instructions" illustrates anaphora:

> There may be water.
> There may be stones.
> There may be high places . . .

**Antithesis** is the matching of parallel units that contain contrasting meanings, such as "Man proposes, God disposes." Although such rhetorical schemes are perhaps more native to the orator, the poet can still make occasional effective use of them.

# Metre and Rhythm

The subject of poetic metre and rhythm can be a difficult one, to say the least, and it is doubtless true that such phrases as *trochaic octameter* or *spondaic substitution* have an intimidating quality. Still, discussions of metre need not be limited to experts, and even beginning readers should be able to apply a few of the metrical principles that are commonly found in poetry written in English.

First, let us distinguish between two terms that are often used synonymously: **poetry** and **verse.** Poetry refers to a whole genre of literature and thus stands with fiction and drama as one of the three major types of writing, whereas verse refers to a mode of writing in lines of a certain length; thus, many poets still retain the old practice of capitalizing the first word of each line to indicate its integrity as a unit of composition. Virtually any piece of writing can be versified (and sometimes rhymed as well). Especially useful are bits of **mnemonic verse,** in which information like the number of days in the months (thirty days has September . . .) or simple spelling rules ("I before E / Except after C . . .") is cast in a form that is easy to remember. Although it is not strictly accurate to do so, many writers use verse to denote metrical writing that somehow does not quite measure up to the level of true poetry; phrases like **light verse** or **occasional verse** (lines written for a specific occasion, like a birthday or anniversary) are often used in this manner.

If a writer is unconcerned about the length of individual lines and is governed only by the width of the paper being used, then he or she is writing not verse but **prose.** All verse is metrical writing; prose is not. However, there is a body of writing called **prose poetry,** writing that uses language in a poetic manner but avoids any type of metre; Carolyn Forché's "The Colonel" is one example. Perhaps the simplest way to think of **metre** in verse is to think of its synonym, **measure** (think of the use of metre in words like "kilometre"). Thus, metre refers to the method by which a poet determines line length.

When we talk about metre in poetry we ordinarily mean that the poet is employing some kind of consistent **prosody,** or system of measurement. There are many possible prosodies, depending on what the poet decides to count as the unit of measurement in the line, but only three of these systems are common in English poetry. Perhaps the simplest is

**syllabic verse.** In verse of this type, the length of the line is determined by counting the total number of syllables the line contains (Sylvia Plath's "Metaphors," for one example, uses lines of nine syllables, a witty metaphor for the poem's subject, pregnancy). Much French poetry of the past was written in twelve-syllable lines, or **Alexandrines,** and in English **octosyllabic** denotes a line of eight syllables. Because English is a language of strong stresses, most of our poets have favoured other prosodic systems, but syllabic poetry has been attempted by many poets, among them Marianne Moore and Dylan Thomas. Moore, in particular, often wrote in **quantitative syllabics,** that is, stanzas containing the same number of lines with identical numbers of syllables in the corresponding lines of different stanzas. Moore's "The Fish" uses stanzas made of lines of one, three, nine, six, and nine syllables, respectively.

More natural to the English language is **accentual** verse, a prosodic system in which only accented or strongly stressed syllables are counted in a line, which can also contain a varying number of unaccented syllables. Much folk poetry, perhaps intended to be recited to the beat of a percussion instrument, retains this stress-based pattern, and the oldest verse in the British tradition, Anglo-Saxon poetry like *Beowulf,* is composed in four-stress lines that were recited to musical accompaniment. Many of the verses we recall from nursery rhymes, children's chanting games ("Red rover, red rover, / Send [any name from one to four syllables can be substituted here] right over"), and sports cheers ("Two, four, six, eight. Who do we appreciate?") retain the strong sense of rhythmical pulse that characterizes much accentual verse, a fact we recognize when we clap our hands and move rhythmically to the sound of the words. Indeed, the lyrics to much current rap music are actually composed to a four-stress accentual line, and the stresses, or "beats," can be heard plainly when we listen or dance. Gerard Manley Hopkins, attempting to recapture some of the flavour of Anglo-Saxon verse, pioneered a type of accentual prosody that he called **sprung rhythm,** in which he counted only the strong stresses in his lines. Accentual metres still supply possibilities for contemporary poets; indeed, what often appears to be free verse is revealed, on closer inspection, to be a poem written in accentual metre. Richard Wilbur's "The Writer," for example, is written in a stanza containing lines of three, five, and three strong stresses, respectively, but the stresses do not overwhelm the reader insistently.

**Accentual-syllabic verse** is the most important prosodic system in English, dominating our poetry for the five centuries from Chaucer's time down to the early years of the twentieth century. Even though free verse has become the prevailing style in which poetry is now written, accentual-syllabic verse still has many able practitioners. An accentual-syllabic prosody is somewhat more complicated than the two systems we have mentioned, because it requires that the poet count both the strongly stressed syllables and the total number of syllables in the line. Because stressed and unstressed syllables alternate fairly regularly in this system, four **metrical feet,** representing the most common patterns, designate the subdivisions of rhythm that make up the line (think of a yardstick divided into three feet). These feet are the **iamb** (or **iambic foot**), one unstressed and one stressed syllable; the **trochee** (or **trochaic foot**), one stressed and one unstressed syllable; the **anapest** (or **anapestic foot**), two unstressed syllables and one stressed syllable; and the **dactyl** (or **dactylic foot**), one stressed and two unstressed syllables. The first two of these, iambic and trochaic, are called **double metres;** the second two, **triple metres.** Iambic and anapestic metres are sometimes called **rising metres** because they "rise" toward the stressed syllable; trochaic and dactylic metres are called **falling metres** for the opposite reason. Simple repetition of words or phrases can give us the sense of how these lines sound in a purely schematic sense. The **breve** (∪) and **ictus** (◠) are used to denote unstressed and stressed syllables, respectively.

*Iambic:*

   ∪ ◠   ∪ ◠   ∪ ◠
   release / release / release

   ∪ ◠   ∪ ◠   ∪ ◠
   to fall / into / despair

   ∪ ◠   ∪ ◠   ∪ ◠ ∪
   Marie / discov / ers candy

*Trochaic:*

   ◠ ∪   ◠ ∪   ◠ ∪   ◠ ∪
   melting / melting / melting / melting

   ◠ ∪   ◠ ∪   ◠ ∪   ◠ ∪
   Peter / disa / greed en / tirely

   ◠ ∪   ◠ ∪   ◠ ∪   ◠
   clever / writing / filled the / page

*Anapestic:*

　　∪　∪　／　　∪　∪　／
to the top / to the top

　∪　∪　／　　∪　∪　／
a retriev / er appeared

　∪　∪　／　　∪　∪　　／　∪
and a ter / ri ble thunder

*Dactylic:*

／　∪　∪　　／　∪　∪　　／　∪　∪　　／　∪　∪　　／　∪　∪
shivering / shivering / shivering / shivering / shivering

／　∪　∪　　／　∪　∪　　／　∪　∪　　／　∪　∪　　／　∪∪
terribly / ill with the / symptoms of / viral pneu / monia

／　∪　∪　　／　∪　∪　　／　∪　∪　　／　∪∪　　／
note how the / minister / whispered at / Emily's / grave

Because each of these lines contains a certain number of feet, a second specialized term is used to denote how many times a pattern is repeated in a line:

| | |
|---|---|
| one foot | monometer |
| two feet | dimeter |
| three feet | trimeter |
| four feet | tetrameter |
| five feet | pentameter |
| six feet | hexameter |
| seven feet | heptameter |
| eight feet | octameter |

Thus, in the examples above, the first set of lines is iambic trimeter; the second, trochaic tetrameter; the third, anapestic dimeter; and the fourth, dactylic pentameter. The third lines in the iambic and anapestic examples are **hypermetrical;** that is, they contain an extra unstressed syllable, or **feminine ending.** Conversely, the third lines in the trochaic and dactylic examples are missing one and two unstressed final syllables, respectively, a common practice called **catalexis.** Although over thirty combinations of foot type and number per line theoretically are possible, relatively few are ordinarily encountered in poetry. The iambic foot is most common in English, followed by the anapest and the trochee; the dactylic foot is relatively rare. Line lengths tend to be from three to five feet, with anything shorter or longer used only sparingly. Still, there are famous exceptions like Poe's "The Raven," which is composed in trochaic octameter.

Metre denotes regularity, the "blueprint" for a line from which the poet works. Because iambic pentameter is the most common metre used in English poetry, our subsequent discussion will focus on poems written in it. Most poets quickly learn that a metronomic regularity, five iambic feet marching in lockstep line after line, is not a virtue and quickly becomes predictable. Thus, there are several ways by which poets can add variety to their lines so that the actual **rhythm** of the line, what is actually heard, plays a subtle counterpoint against the regularity of the metre. One way is to vary the placement of the **caesura** (‖), or pause, within a line (usually indicated by a mark of punctuation). Another is by mixing **end-stopped lines,** which clearly pause at their conclusion, with **enjambed** lines (or *enjambment*), which run on into the next line with no pause.

Another technique of varying regularity is **metrical substitution,** where feet of a different type are substituted for what the metre calls for. In iambic metre, trochaic feet are often encountered at the beginnings of lines, or after a caesura. Two other feet, the **pyrrhic** ( ∪ ∪ ), consisting of two unstressed syllables, and the **spondee** ( ′ ′ ), consisting of two stressed syllables, are also commonly substituted. The poem "Metrical Feet," which Samuel Taylor Coleridge wrote for his sons, illustrates some of these variations.

How far can a poet depart from the pattern without losing contact with the original metre? That question is impossible to answer in general terms. The following scansion will probably strike us at first as a far departure from regular iambic pentameter:

′ ‖ ′ / ∪ ‖ ′ ′ / ∪ ∪ ‖ ‖ / ′ ∪ / ∪ ′

Yet it is actually the opening line of one of Shakespeare's most often quoted passages, Mark Antony's funeral oration from *Julius Caesar:*

Friends, ‖ Ro / mans, ‖ coun / trymen, ‖ / lend me / your ears

Poets who have learned to use the full resources of metre do not consider it a restraint; instead, they are able to stretch the pattern to its limits without breaking it. A good analogy might be made between poetry and dance. Beginning dancers watch their feet and count the steps while making them; after considerable practice, the movements become second nature, and a skillful pair of partners can add dips and passes without losing the basic step of the music.

## Free Verse and Open Form

Nothing has been so exhaustively debated in poetry as the exact nature of **free verse.** The simplest definition may be the best: Free verse is verse with no consistent metrical pattern. As Ezra Pound put it, "some poems may have form as a tree has form, some as water poured into a vase." Fixed forms serve as the vase that holds the subject matter in a predetermined shape, whereas free verse grows organically, branching out according to the demands of the material. In free verse, line length is a subjective decision made by the poet, and length may be determined by grammatical phrases, the poet's own sense of individual "breath-units," or even by the visual arrangement of lines on the page. Clearly, it is easier to speak of what free verse is not than to explain what it is. Even its practitioners do not seem very happy with the term free verse, which is derived from the French *vers libre* movement established by French poets of the late nineteenth century such as Rimbaud and Laforgue, who were rebelling against the strictness of established French verse patterns. The extensive use of free verse is a fairly recent phenomenon in the history of poetry. Even though there are many examples of free verse from the past (including the Psalms, Ecclesiastes, and the Song of Solomon from the King James Bible), the modern history of free verse begins in 1855 with the publication of Walt Whitman's *Leaves of Grass*, and subsequent poets who have used free verse have written lines that vary widely in syllable count. As this anthology reveals, contemporary poetry has been enriched by a variety of influences from around the world. International and indigenous voices have contributed their own rhythms both in English and in translation. Good free verse, as T. S. Eliot remarked, still contains some kind of "ghost of meter," and its rhythms can be terse and clipped or lushly sensuous. The poet who claims that free verse is somehow easier to write than metrical verse would find many arguments to the contrary. As Eliot said, "No verse is free for the poet who wants to do a good job."

All poems have form, the arrangement of the poem on the page that differentiates it from prose. Sometimes this arrangement indicates that the poet is following a preconceived plan—a metrical pattern, a rhyme scheme, a purely visual design like that of **concrete** or **spatial poetry,** or a scheme like that of **acrostic verse,** in which the first letters of the lines spell a message. An analysis of poetic form notes how the lines are arranged, how long they are, and how they are grouped into blocks, or **stanzas.** Further analysis might reveal the existence of types of repetition, rhyme, or the use of a **refrain,** or a repeated line or groups of lines. A large number of the poems composed in the twentieth and twenty-first centuries have been written in **open form,** which simply means that there is no strict pattern of regularity in the elements mentioned above; that is, there is no consistent metre and no rhyme scheme. Still, even a famous poem in open form like William Carlos Williams's "The Red Wheelbarrow" can be described in formal terms:

> so much depends
> upon
>
> a red wheel
> barrow
>
> glazed with rain
> water
>
> beside the white
> chickens.

Here we observe that the eight-line poem is divided into **uniform stanzas** of two lines each (or couplets). Line length varies between four and two syllables per line. The odd-numbered lines each contain three words; the even, one. Although there is no apparent use of rhyme or repetition here, many poems in open form contain some rhyme and metrical regularity. A type of free verse called **dispersed,** or "open," verse isolates words across the page in fragmented lines, but even among the discontinuous and seemingly scattered lines, one can often discern a pattern of multiple margins or other strategies of emphasis.

Unlike open form, **closed form** denotes the existence of some kind of regular pattern of metre, stanza, rhyme, or repetition. **Stanza forms** are consistent patterns in the individual units of the poem (stanza means "room" in Italian); **fixed forms** are patterns that encompass a complete poem, for example, a sonnet or a villanelle. **Traditional forms** are patterns that have been used for long periods of time and thus may be associated with certain subjects, themes, or types of poems; the sonnet is one example, for it has been used primarily (but by no means exclusively) for lyric poetry. Sometimes poems that are in traditional fixed forms in the original language, like Émile Nelligan's sonnet "Les Angéliques" ("Evening Bells"), are translated into free verse. **Nonce forms** are patterns that originate in an individual poem and have not been widely used by other poets. Of course, it goes without saying that every traditional form was at first a nonce form; the Italian poet (now lost to memory) who first wrote a lyric consisting of fourteen rhymed eleven-syllable lines could not have foreseen that in subsequent centuries poets the world over would produce literally millions of sonnets that are all variations on the original model. Some of the most common stanza and fixed forms are briefly discussed herein.

# Stanza Forms

**Blank verse** is not, strictly speaking, a stanza form because it consists of individual lines of iambic pentameter that do not rhyme. However, long poems in blank verse may be arranged into verse **paragraphs,** or stanzas with a varying number of lines. Blank verse originally appeared in English with the Earl of Surrey's translation of the *Aeneid* in the fifteenth century; it has been used extensively for narrative and dramatic purposes since then, particularly in epics like Milton's *Paradise Lost* and in Shakespeare's plays. Also written in stanzas of varying lengths is the **irregular ode,** a poem that employs lines of varying lengths (although usually of a regular rhythm that is iambic or matches one of the other feet) and an irregular rhyme scheme.

Paired rhyming lines (*aabbcc . . .*) are called **couplets,** although they are only rarely printed as separate stanzas. **Short couplets** have a metre of iambic tetrameter (and are sometimes called **octosyllabic couplets**). If their rhymes are predominantly feminine and seem chosen for comic effect, they may be called **Hudibrastic couplets** after Samuel Butler's satirical poem *Hudibras* of the late 1600s. **Heroic couplets** have a metre of iambic pentameter and take their name from John Dryden's translation of the *Aeneid* (1697) and Alexander Pope's hugely successful translation of Homer's *Iliad* and *Odyssey* (1720–1726); all three of these are "heroic" or epic poems. Heroic couplets have also been used effectively in satirical poems like Alexander Pope's "mock epic" *The Dunciad* and even in dramatic monologues like Robert Browning's "My Last Duchess," where the rhymes are so effectively buried by enjambment that the poem approximates speech. Two other couplet forms, both rare, are **poulter's measure,** rhyming pairs of alternating lines of iambic hexameter and iambic heptameter, and **fourteeners,** pairs of iambic heptameter (fourteen-syllable) lines which, because a natural caesura usually falls after the fourth foot, closely resemble common metre (see below). A three-line stanza is called a **tercet.** If it rhymes in an *aaa bbb . . .* pattern, it is a **triplet;** sometimes triplets appear in poems written in heroic couplets, especially at the end of sections or where special emphasis is desired. Iambic pentameter tercets rhyming *aba bcb cdc . . .* form **terza rima,** a pattern invented by Dante for *The Divine Comedy.*

A four-line stanza is known as a **quatrain.** Alternating lines of tetrameter and trimeter in any foot, rhyming *abcb* or *abab*, make up a **ballad stanza;** if the feet are strictly iambic, then the quatrain is called **common metre,** the form of many popular hymns like "Amazing Grace." **Long metre,** also widely used in hymns, consists of iambic tetrameter lines rhyming *abcb* or *abab;* **short metre** has a similar rhyme scheme but contains first, second, and fourth lines of iambic trimeter and a third line of iambic tetrameter. The ***In Memoriam* stanza,** named after Tennyson's long poetic sequence, is iambic tetrameter rhyming *abba.* The ***Rubaiyat* stanza,** an import from Persia, consists of lines of either iambic tetrameter or pentameter, rhyming *aaba bbcb . . .;* Edward FitzGerald's translation *The Rubaiyat of Omar Khayyam* employs this form. Four lines of iambic pentameter rhyming *abab* are known as an **English quatrain,** also known as the **elegiac stanza** (after Thomas Gray's "Elegy Written in a Country Churchyard"). Lines of the same metre rhyming *abba* make up an **Italian quatrain.** One other unusual quatrain stanza is an import from ancient Greece, the **Sapphic stanza,** named after the poet Sappho. The Sapphic stanza consists of three **hendecasyllabic** (eleven-syllable) lines of this pattern:

$$\prime \ \cup \ / \ \prime \ \cup \ / \ \prime \ \cup \ \cup \ / \ \prime \ \cup \ / \ \prime \ \cup$$

and a fourth line called an **Adonic,** which is five syllables long and consists of one dactylic foot and one trochaic foot. The Sapphic stanza is usually unrhymed. The quatrain stanza is also used in another import, the **pantoum,** a poem in which the second and fourth lines of the first stanza become the first and third of the second, and the second and fourth of the second become the first and third of the fourth, and so on. Pantoums may be written in any metre and may or may not employ rhyme.

A five-line stanza is known as a **quintet** and is relatively rare in English poetry. The **sestet,** or six-line stanza, can be found with a number of different metres and rhyme schemes. A seven-line stanza is called a **septet;** one septet stanza form is **rime royal,** seven lines of iambic pentameter rhyming *ababbcc.* An eight-line stanza is called an **octave;** one widely used stanza of this length is **ottava rima,** iambic pentameter lines rhyming *abababcc.* Another octave form is the **Monk's Tale stanza,** named after one of Chaucer's tales. It is iambic pentameter and rhymes *ababbcbc.* The addition of a ninth line, rhyming *c* and having a metre of iambic hexameter, makes a **Spenserian stanza,** named after Edmund Spenser, the poet who invented it for *The Faerie Queene,* a long metrical romance.

## Fixed Forms

**Fixed forms** are combinations of metre, rhyme scheme, and repetition that constitute complete poems. One familiar three-line fixed form is the **haiku,** a Japanese import consisting of lines of five, seven, and five syllables, respectively. Related to the haiku is the **tanka,** which adds two additional seven-syllable lines.

Two five-line fixed forms are the **limerick** and the **cinquain.** The limerick consists of anapestic trimeter in lines one, two, and five, and anapestic dimeter in lines three and four. The rhymes, *aabba*, are usually double rhymes used for comic effect.

A cinquain, the invention of American poet Adelaide Crapsey (1878–1914), consists of five unrhymed lines of two, four, six, eight, and two syllables, respectively. The most important of the fixed forms is the **sonnet,** which consists of fourteen lines of rhymed iambic pentameter. The original form of the sonnet is called the **Italian sonnet,** or the **Petrarchan sonnet,** after the fourteenth-century poet who popularized it. An Italian sonnet is usually cast in two stanzas, an octave rhyming *abbaabba* and a sestet with a variable rhyme scheme; *cdcdcd, cdecde,* and *cddcee* are some of the possible patterns. A **volta,** or "turn," usually a conjunction or conjunctive adverb like "but" or "then," may appear at the beginning of the sestet, signifying a slight change of direction in thought. Many Italian sonnets have a strong logical connection between octave and sestet problem/solution, cause/effect, question/answer and the volta helps to clarify the transition. The **English sonnet,** also known as the **Shakespearean sonnet** after its prime exemplar, was developed in the sixteenth century after the sonnet was imported to England and employs a different rhyme scheme that takes into consideration the relative scarcity of rhymes in English (compared with Italian). The English sonnet has a rhyme scheme of *ababcdcdefefgg* and is usually printed as a single stanza. The pattern of three English quatrains plus a heroic couplet often forces a slightly different organizational scheme on the poet, although many of Shakespeare's sonnets still employ a strong volta at the beginning of the ninth line. Other English sonnets may withhold the turn until the beginning of the closing couplet. A third sonnet type, relatively rare, is the **Spenserian sonnet,** named after Edmund Spenser, author of *Amoretti,* one of the earliest sonnet sequences in English. The Spenserian sonnet rhymes *ababbcbccdcdee.* Many other sonnets have been written over the years that have other rhyme schemes, often hybrids of the Italian and English types. These are usually termed **nonce sonnets;** Shelley's "Ozymandias," with its unusual rhyme scheme of *ababacdcedefef,* is one notable example. A fourteen-line stanza rhyming *aba bcb cdc ded ee* has been called a **terza rima sonnet.**

Several other fixed forms, all French imports, have appeared frequently in English poetry. The **rondeau** has fifteen lines of iambic tetrameter or pentameter arranged in three stanzas: *aabba aabR aabbaR;* the *R* here stands for the unrhymed refrain, which repeats the first few words of the poem's first line. A maddeningly complex variation is the thirty-one line **rondeau redoublé,** through which Wendy Cope wittily manoeuvres in her poem of the same name. The **villanelle** is a nineteen-line poem, usually written in iambic pentameter, employing two refrain lines, $A_1$ and $A_2$, in a pattern of five tercets and a final quatrain: $A_1bA_2\ abA_1\ abA_2\ abA_1\ abA_2\ abA_1A_2$. "Do Not Go Gentle into That Good Night" by Dylan Thomas is a famous example. A related form, also nineteen lines long, is the **terzanelle,** which uses several more repeating lines (capitalized here): $A_1BA_2\ bCB\ cDC\ dED\ eFE\ f\ A_1FA_2$. The **ballade** is twenty-eight lines of iambic tetrameter employing a refrain that appears at the end of its three octaves and final quatrain, or **envoy:** *ababbcbC ababbcbC ababbcbC bcbC*. Obviously the rhyming demands of the villanelle, the terzanelle, and the ballade pose serious challenges to English-language poets. A final fixed form is the thirty-nine-line **sestina,** which may be either metred or in free verse and uses a complicated sequence repeating, in different order, the six words that end the lines of the initial stanza. The sequence for the first six sestets is *123456 615243 364125 532614 451362 246531*. A final tercet uses three words in the interior of the lines and three at the ends in the pattern *(2)5(4)3(6)1*. Many sestinas hinge on the poet's choice of six end words that have multiple meanings and can serve as more than one part of speech. There are many other less familiar types of stanza forms and fixed forms. Lewis Turco's *The Book of Forms* and Miller Williams's *Patterns of Poetry* are two reference sources that are useful in identifying them.

## Literary History and Poetic Conventions

What a poet attempts to do in any given poem is always governed by the tension that exists between originality and convention, or between the poet's desire, in Ezra Pound's famous phrase, to "make it new," and the various stylistic devices that other poets and readers are familiar with through their understanding of the poetic tradition which has become increasingly international and diverse. Examples of diversity from this anthology include Canadian poet P. K. Page's building a poem around lines from a poem by Chilean poet Pablo Neruda, along with Québécois and Acadian poets in translation, First Nations voices from Canada, the United States, and Australia, and international poets who combine a number of traditions within their work. If we look at some of the most obscure passages of Pound's *Cantos* (a single page may contain passages in several foreign languages), we may think that the poet has departed about as far from conventional modes of expression as possible, leaving his audience far behind him. Yet it is important to keep two facts in mind. First, this style was not arrived at overnight; Pound's early poetry is relatively traditional and should present little difficulty to most readers. He arrived at the style of the *Cantos* after a twenty-year apprenticeship to the styles of writers as different as Li-Po, Robert Browning, and William Butler Yeats. Second, by the time Pound was writing his mature poetry the modernist movement was in full flower, forcing the public not only to read poems but also to look at paintings and sculpture and to listen to music in ways that would have been unimaginable only a decade or two earlier. When we talk about the stylistic conventions of any given literary period, we should keep in mind that poets are rarely willing to go much beyond what they have educated their audiences to understand. This mutual sense of agreement is the essence of poetic convention.

One should be wary of making sweeping generalizations about "schools" of poetry or the shared conventions of literary periods. In any era, there is always a significant amount of diversity among nations and even among individual poets. Further, an anthology of this limited scope, which by its very nature must exclude most long poems, is likely to contribute to a misleading view of literary history and the development of poetry. When we read Shakespeare's or Milton's sonnets, we should not forget that the major reputations of these authors rest on poetry of a very different sort. The neoclassical era in English poetry, stretching from the late seventeenth century until almost the end of the eighteenth, is poorly represented in this anthology because the satires of John Dryden and Alexander Pope do not readily lend themselves to being excerpted. Edgar Allan Poe once claimed that a long poem is "simply a contradiction in terms," but the continued high reputations of *The Faerie Queene, Paradise Lost,* and *Don Juan* demonstrate that Poe's was far from the last word on the subject. bp Nichol, represented in this anthology by two very brief concrete poems, also wrote *The Martyrology,* a poem that extends over nine volumes.

The earliest poems in this volume, all anonymous, represent poetry's links to the oral folk tradition, from the songs and orature of the First Nations of North America to popular English ballads. The poets of the Tudor (1485–1558) and Elizabethan (1558–1603) eras excelled at lyric poetry; Sir Thomas Wyatt and Henry Howard, Earl of Surrey, had imported the sonnet form from Italy, and the form was perfected during this period. Much of the love poetry of the age is characterized by conventional imagery, so-called Petrarchan conceits, which Shakespeare satirizes brilliantly in his Sonnet 130 ("My mistress' eyes are nothing like the sun").

The poetry of the first half of the seventeenth century has several major schools: a smooth lyricism influenced by dramatist Ben Jonson; a serious body of devotional poetry by John Donne, George Herbert, and John Milton; and the metaphysical style, which uses complex extended metaphors or metaphysical conceits—Donne and Herbert are its chief exemplars, followed by early American poets such as Anne Bradstreet. Shortly after the English Restoration in 1660, a profound period of conservatism began in the arts, and the neoclassical era, lasting through most of the eighteenth century, drew heavily on Greek and Roman models. Poetry written during this period—the age of Jonathan Swift and Alexander Pope—was dominated by one form, the heroic couplet; the genres of epic and satire; and an emphasis on human reason as the poet's chief guide. Never has the private voice been so subordinated to the public as in this period when, as Pope put it, a poet's highest aspiration should be to utter "What oft was thought, but ne'er so well expressed."

The first inklings of the romantic era coincide with the American and French revolutions, and poets of the latter half of the eighteenth century like William Blake exhibit some of its characteristics. But it was not until the publication of *Lyrical Ballads,* a 1798 book containing the best early work of William Wordsworth and Samuel Taylor Coleridge, that the romantic era can be said to have truly flowered. Wordsworth's famous formulation of a poem as "the spontaneous overflow of powerful feeling recollected in tranquillity" remains one of romanticism's key definitions, with its emphasis on emotion and immediacy and reflection; Wordsworth's own poetry, with its focus on the natural world, was tremendously influential. Most of the English and North American poets of the first half of the nineteenth century had ties to romanticism in its various guises, and even a poet as late as Walt Whitman (b. 1819) inherited many of its liberal, democratic attitudes. Poets of the Victorian era (1837–1901), such as Alfred, Lord Tennyson and Elizabeth Barrett Browning, continued to explore many of the same themes and genres as their romantic forebears, but certainly much of the optimism of the early years of the century had dissipated by the time poets like Matthew Arnold, Thomas Hardy, and William Butler Yeats, with their omnipresent irony and pessimism, arrived on the scene in the century's last decades.

The twentieth century and the beginning of the twenty-first have been ruled by the upheavals that modernism caused in every art form. If anything characterized the first half of the twentieth century, it was its tireless experimentation with the forms of poetry. There is a continuum in poetry from early beginnings through to the present day, but Ezra Pound, H. D., and T. S. Eliot, to mention only three chief modernists, published poetry that would have totally mystified readers of their grandparents' day, just as Picasso and Matisse produced paintings that represented radical breaks with the visual forms of the past. Although many of the experiments of movements like imagism and surrealism seem not much more than historical curiosities today, they parallel the unusual directions that most of the other arts took during the same period.

For the sake of convenience more than anything else, it has been useful to refer to the era following the end of World War II as the postmodern era. Certainly many of the hard-won modernist gains—open form and increased candour in language and subject matter—have been taken for granted by poets writing in the contemporary period. The confessional poem, a frankly autobiographical narrative that reveals what poets in earlier ages might have striven desperately to conceal, surfaced in the late 1950s in the works of Robert Lowell, Sylvia Plath, and Anne Sexton, and remains one of the chief contemporary genres. Postmodernism incorporates an eclectic mix of styles while denying the supremacy of any one mode of expression. Often abandoning or playing with conventional formal structures and questioning the stability of meaning, postmodern works draw attention to their own status as constructs. As the selections here will attest, there is considerable variety to be found in the contemporary scene both in North America and around the world, and it will perhaps be many years before critics have the necessary historical distance to assess the unique characteristics of the present period.

*This traditional song is taken from a collection by John Robert Colombo,* Poems of the Inuit *(1981), based on the work of Knud Rasmussen. According to Daniel David Moses and Terry Goldie, editors of* An Anthology of Canadian Native Literature in English *(1998), in which this song appears, it should be considered as a "sample of a recording process which comments on both cultures involved."*

## *Inuit Traditional Song*
# Magic Words/Aua

To Lighten Heavy Loads

I speak with the mouth of Qeqertuanaq, and say.
I will walk with leg muscles strong as the sinews on the shin of
    a little caribou calf.
I will walk with leg muscles strong as the sinews on the shin of
    a little hare.                                                                 5
I will take care not to walk toward the dark.
I will walk toward the day.

—*Date Unknown*

*This selection from editor John Robert Colombo's* Songs of the Indians *(1985) bears the heritage of both the Native oral tradition and the folklorists who have translated and recorded it.*

## *Southern First Nations*
## *Traditional Orature*
# Fragment of a Song

There was a woman, long, long ago:
she came out of a hole.
In it dead people were buried.
She made her house in a tree;
She was dressed in leaves,                                                         5

All long ago.
When she walked among the dry leaves
Her feet were so covered
The feet were invisible.
She walked through the woods,                                    10
Singing all the time,
'I want company; I'm lonesome!'
A wild man heard her:
From afar over the lakes and mountains
He came to her.                                                 15
She saw him; she was afraid;
She tried to flee away,
For he was covered with the rainbow;
Colour and light were his garments.
She ran, and he pursued rapidly;                                20
He chased her to the foot of a mountain.
He spoke in a strange language;
She could not understand him at first.
He would make her tell where she dwelt.
They married; they had two children.                            25
One of them was a boy.
He was blind from his birth,
But he frightened his mother by his sight.
He could tell her what was coming,
What was coming from afar.                                      30
What was near he could not see.
He could see the bear and the moose
Far away beyond the mountains;
He could see through everything.

—*Date Unknown*

*Some of the popular ballads and lyrics of England and Scotland, composed for the most part between 1300 and 1500, were first collected in their current forms by Thomas Percy, whose* Reliques of Ancient English Poetry *(1765) helped to revive interest in folk poetry. Francis James Child (1825–1896), an American, gathered over a thousand variant versions of the three hundred–odd core of poems. The Romantic poets of the early nineteenth century showed their debt to the folk tradition by writing imitative "art ballads" (see Keats's "La Belle Dame sans Merci"), which incorporate many of their stylistic devices.*

## *Anonymous*
# Western Wind

Western wind, when will thou blow,
    The small rain down can rain?
Christ, if my love were in my arms
    And I in my bed again!

                                          *—1450?*

# Sir Patrick Spens

The king sits in Dumferling town,
    Drinking the blude-reid° wine:
"O whar will I get guid sailor,
    To sail this ship of mine?"

Up and spak an eldern knicht,°                     5
    Sat at the king's richt° knee:
"Sir Patrick Spens is the best sailor
    That sails upon the sea."

The king has written a braid° letter,
    And signed it wi' his hand,               10
And sent it to Sir Patrick Spens,
    Was walking on the sand.

---

**2 blude-reid** blood-red   **5 eldern knicht** elderly knight   **6 richt** right   **9 braid** long

The first line that Sir Patrick read,
 A loud lauch° lauched he;
The next line that Sir Patrick read,      15
 The tear blinded his ee.°

"O wha is this has done this deed,
 This ill deed done to me,
To send me out this time o' the year,
 To sail upon the sea?        20

"Mak haste, mak haste, my mirry men all,
 Our guid ship sails the morn."
"O say na sae,° my master dear,
 For I fear a deadly storm.

"Late, late yestre'en° I saw the new moon,   25
 Wi' the auld moon in hir arm,
And I fear, I fear, my dear master,
 That we will come to harm."

O our Scots nobles wer richt laith°
 To weet° their cork-heeled shoon,°    30
But lang or a'° the play were played,
 Their hats they swam aboon.°

O lang, lang may their ladies sit,
 Wi' their fans into their hand,
Or ere they see Sir Patrick Spens     35
 Come sailing to the land.

O lang, lang may the ladies stand, .
 Wi' their gold kems° in their hair,
Waiting for their ain dear lords,
 For they'll see them na mair.      40

Half o'er, half o'er to Aberdour
 It's fifty fadom deep,
And there lies guid Sir Patrick Spens
 Wi' the Scots lords at his feet.

               *—1500?*

---

**14 lauch** laugh **16 ee** eye **23 na sae** not so **25 yestre'en** last evening **29 laith** loath **30 weet**
wet **shoon** shoes **31 lang or a'** long before **32 Their hats they swam aboon** their hats swam
above them **38 kems** combs

*Sir Thomas Wyatt (1503?–1542) served Henry VIII as a diplomat in Italy. Wyatt read the love poetry of Petrarch (1304–1374) and is generally credited with having imported both the fashions of these lyrics — hyperbolic "conceits" or metaphorical descriptions of the woman's beauty and the lover's suffering — and their form, the sonnet, to England. "They Flee from Me," an example of one of his original lyrics, displays Wyatt's unique grasp of the rhythms of speech.*

## Sir Thomas Wyatt
# They Flee from Me

They flee from me, that sometime did me seek,
With naked foot stalking in my chamber.
I have seen them gentle, tame and meek,
That now are wild, and do not remember
That sometime they put themself in danger                          5
To take bread at my hand; and now they range,
Busily seeking with a continual change.

Thanked be Fortune it hath been otherwise,
Twenty times better; but once in special,
In thin array, after a pleasant guise,°                            10
When her loose gown from her shoulders did fall,
And she me caught in her arms long and small,
And therewith all sweetly did me kiss
And softly said, "Dear heart, how like you this?"

It was no dream, I lay broad waking.                               15
But all is turned, thorough° my gentleness,
Into a strange fashion of forsaking;
And I have leave to go, of her goodness,
And she also to use newfangleness.
But since that I so kindely° am served,                            20
I fain° would know what she hath deserved.

—1557

---

**10 guise** appearance   **16 thorough** through   **20 kindely** in this manner   **21 fain** gladly

*Queen Elizabeth I (1533–1603) was an amateur poet who drew praise from the members of her court, many of whom were also versifiers. A few of her lyrics survive, as do translations she made from the Roman writers Seneca and Horace. Her reign (1558–1603) established England as a world power and also nurtured the talents of Edmund Spenser, William Shakespeare, Christopher Marlowe, and Ben Jonson.*

## Queen Elizabeth I
# When I Was Fair and Young

When I was fair and young, and favor gracèd me,
Of many was I sought, their mistress for to be;
But I did scorn them all, and answered them therefore,
    "Go, go, go seek some otherwhere!
                Importune me no more!"     5

How many weeping eyes I made to pine with woe,
How many sighing hearts, I have no skill to show;
Yet I the prouder grew, and answered them therefore,
    "Go, go, go seek some otherwhere!
                Importune me no more!"     10

Then spake fair Venus' son,° that proud victorious boy,
And said, "Fine dame, since that you be so coy,
I will so pluck your plumes that you shall say no more,
    'Go, go, go seek some otherwhere!
                Importune me no more!'"     15

When he had spake these words, such change grew in my breast
That neither night nor day since that, I could take any rest.
Then lo! I did repent that I had said before,
    "Go, go, go seek some otherwhere!
                Importune me no more!"     20

—1585

---

11 **Venus' son** Eros or Cupid, god of love

*Edmund Spenser (1552–1599) was born in London, and spent most of his adult life in Ireland, where he held a variety of minor government posts.* The Faerie Queene, *a long allegorical romance about Elizabethan England, was uncompleted at his death. The eighty-odd sonnets that make up the sequence called* Amoretti *are generally thought to detail his courtship of his second wife, Elizabeth Boyle, whom he married in 1594.*

## *Edmund Spenser*
# Amoretti: Sonnet 75

One day I wrote her name upon the strand,
But came the waves and washèd it away:
Agayne I wrote it with a second hand,°
But came the tyde, and made my paynes his pray.
"Vayne man," sayd she, "that doest in vaine assay,°       *5*
A mortall thing so to immortalize,
For I my selve shall lyke° to this decay
And eek° my name bee wypèd out lykewize."
"Not so," quod° I, "let baser things devize
To dy in dust, but you shall live by fame:       *10*
My verse your vertues rare shall eternize,
And in the hevens wryte your glorious name.
Where whenas death shall all the world subdew
Our love shall live, and later life renew."

          —*1595*

**3 second hand** second time   **5 assay** attempt   **7 lyke** be similar to   **8 eek** also   **9 quod** said

*William Shakespeare (1564–1616) first printed his sonnets in 1609, during the last years of his active career as a playwright, but they had circulated privately a dozen years before. Given the lack of concrete details about Shakespeare's life outside the theatre, critics have found the sonnets fertile ground for biographical speculation, and the sequence of 154 poems does contain distinct characters—a handsome youth to whom most of the first 126 sonnets are addressed, a "Dark Lady" who figures strongly in the remaining poems, and the poet himself, whose name is the source of many puns in the poems. There is probably no definitive "key" to the sonnets, but there is also little doubt that their place is secure among the monuments of English lyric verse.*

# William Shakespeare
## Sonnet 18

Shall I compare thee to a summer's day?
Thou art more lovely and more temperate:
Rough winds do shake the darling buds of May,
And summer's lease hath all too short a date:
Sometimes too hot the eye of heaven shines,                    5
And often is his gold complexion dimmed;
And every fair from fair° sometimes declines,
By chance or nature's changing course untrimmed:°
But thy eternal summer shall not fade,
Nor lose possession of that fair thou ow'st;°                  10
Nor shall death brag thou wander'st in his shade,
When in eternal lines to time thou grow'st:
So long as men can breathe, or eyes can see,
So long lives this, and this gives life to thee.

—*1609*

**7 fair from fair** every fair thing from its fairness   **8 untrimmed** stripped   **10 ow'st** ownest

# Sonnet 30

When to the sessions° of sweet silent thought
I summon up remembrance of things past,
I sigh the lack of many a thing I sought,
And with old woes new wail my dear time's waste:
Then can I drown an eye, unused to flow,                    5
For precious friends hid in death's dateless° night,
And weep afresh love's long since canceled woe,
And moan the expense of many a vanished sight:
Then can I grieve at grievances foregone,
And heavily from woe to woe tell o'er                      10
The sad account of fore-bemoanèd moan,
Which I new pay as if not paid before.
But if the while I think on thee, dear friend,
All losses are restored and sorrows end.

                                                        —1609

# Sonnet 73

That time of year thou mayst in me behold
When yellow leaves, or none, or few, do hang
Upon those boughs which shake against the cold,
Bare ruined choirs, where late the sweet birds sang.
In me thou see'st the twilight of such day                 5
As after sunset fadeth in the west;
Which by and by black night doth take away,
Death's second self, that seals up all in rest.
In me thou see'st the glowing of such fire,
That on the ashes of his youth doth lie,                   10
As the deathbed whereon it must expire,
Consumed with that which it was nourished by.
This thou perceiv'st, which makes thy love more strong,
To love that well which thou must leave ere long.

                                                        —1609

**1 sessions** as in sessions of a court of law   **6 dateless** endless

# Sonnet 130

My mistress' eyes are nothing like the sun;
Coral is far more red than her lips' red;
If snow be white, why then her breasts are dun;
If hairs be wires, black wires grow on her head.
I have seen roses damasked,° red and white,                    5
But no such roses see I in her cheeks;
And in some perfumes is there more delight
Than in the breath that from my mistress reeks.
I love to hear her speak, yet well I know
That music hath a far more pleasing sound;                    10
I grant I never saw a goddess go;
My mistress, when she walks, treads on the ground.
And yet, by heaven, I think my love as rare
As any she belied° with false compare.°

—*1609*

---

*John Donne (1572–1631) was trained in the law for a career in government service, but Donne became the greatest preacher of his day, ending his life as dean of St. Paul's Cathedral in London. Only two of Donne's poems and a handful of his sermons were printed during his life, but both circulated widely in manuscript and his literary reputation among his contemporaries was considerable. His poetry falls into two distinct periods: the witty love poetry of his youth and the sober religious meditations of his maturity. In both, however, Donne shows remarkable originality in rhythm, diction, and the use of metaphor and conceit, which marks him as the chief poet of what has become commonly known as the metaphysical style.*

## *John Donne*
# Song

Go and catch a falling star,
  Get with child a mandrake root,°

---

**5 damasked** multi-coloured    **14 belied** lied about    **compare** comparisons
**2 mandrake** root forked like the lower half of the human body and said to shriek when pulled from the ground

Tell me where all past years are,
   Or who cleft the Devil's foot,
Teach me to hear mermaids singing,                      5
Or to keep off envy's stinging,
      And find
      What wind
Serves to advance an honest mind.

If thou beest born to strange sights,               10
   Things invisible to see,
Ride ten thousand days and nights,
   Till age snow white hairs on thee,
Thou, when thou return'st, wilt tell me,
All strange wonders that befell thee,              15
      And swear,
      No where
Lives a woman true, and fair.

If thou find'st one, let me know,
   Such a pilgrimage were sweet;              20
Yet do not, I would not go,
   Though at next door we might meet;
Though she were true, when you met her,
And last till you write your letter,
      Yet she                       25
      Will be
False, ere I come, to two, or three.

                                   —*1633*

# Holy Sonnet 14

Batter my heart, three-personed God; for You
As yet but knock, breathe, shine, and seek to mend;
That I may rise, and stand, o'erthrow me, and bend
Your force to break, blow, burn, and make me new.
I, like an usurped town, to another due,                                     5
Labor to admit You, but O, to no end;
Reason, Your viceroy in me, me should defend,
But is captived, and proves weak or untrue.
Yet dearly I love You, and would be lovèd fain,°
But am betrothed unto Your enemy.                                            10
Divorce me, untie or break that knot again;
Take me to You, imprison me, for I,
Except You enthrall me, never shall be free,
Nor ever chaste, except You ravish me.

—*1633*

---

*Robert Hayman (1575–1629) was born in Devonshire, England, and came to
Harbour Grace, Newfoundland, in 1621 as governor. Here he wrote* Quodlibets
*(1628), one of the earliest books of poetry about North America to be written in English.
A quodlibet is a musical medley or a scholastic debate based on questions; both meanings
apply to Hayman's efforts to celebrate Newfoundland and encourage settlement.*

## *Robert Hayman*
# The Four Elements
# in Newfoundland

TO THE WORSHIPFUL CAPTAIN JOHN MASON, WHO DID
WISELY AND WORTHILY GOVERN THERE DIVERS YEARS.

The Air in Newfoundland is wholesome, good;
The Fire as sweet as any made of wood;

**9 fain** gladly

The Waters, very rich, both salt and fresh;
The Earth more rich, you know it no less.
Where all are good, Fire, Water, Earth, and Air,                    5
What man made of these four would not live there?

—1628

*Mary Wroth (1587?–1651) was the niece of Sir Philip Sidney and the cousin of Sir Walter Raleigh, both distinguished poets and courtiers. A friend of poet Ben Jonson, who dedicated* The Alchemist *to her, she was prominent in the court of King James I. Her prose romance,* Urania *(1621), stirred controversy because of its similarities to actual people and events. Wroth may have fallen into disfavour at court after the publication of* Urania, *and few facts are known about her later life.*

## Mary Wroth

# [In this strange labyrinth how shall I turn?]

In this strange labyrinth how shall I turn?
    Ways° are on all sides, while the way I miss:
    If to the right hand, there in love I burn,
    Let me go forward, therein danger is.
If to the left, suspicion hinders bliss:                            5
    Let me turn back, shame cries I ought return:
    Nor faint, though crosses° with my fortunes kiss.
    Stand still is harder, although sure to mourn.
Thus let me take the right, or left hand way,
    Go forward, or stand still, or back retire:                     10
    I must these doubts endure without allay°
    Or help, but travail find for my best hire
Yet that which most my troubled sense doth move,
Is to leave all and take the thread of Love°

—1621

2 **ways** paths    7 **crosses** troubles    11 **allay** alleviation    14 **Love** an allusion to the myth of Theseus, who, with the help of Ariadne, unrolled a thread behind him as he entered the labyrinth of Crete

*George Herbert (1593–1633) was the great master of the English devotional lyric. Herbert was born into a distinguished family, which included his mother, the formidable literary patroness Lady Magdalen Herbert, and his brother, the poet and statesman Edward, Lord Herbert of Cherbury. Like John Donne, with whom he shares the metaphysical label, Herbert early aimed at a political career but turned to the clergy, spending several happy years as rector of Bemerton before his death at age forty. The Temple, which contains most of his poems, was published posthumously in 1633.*

## George Herbert
# Easter Wings

Lord, who createdst man in wealth and store,°
Though foolishly he lost the same,
Decaying more and more
Till he became
Most poor:　　　　　　　　　5
With Thee
O let me rise
As larks, harmoniously,
And sing this day Thy victories:
Then shall the fall further the flight in me.　　10

My tender age in sorrow did begin;
And still with sicknesses and shame
Thou didst so punish sin,
That I became
Most thin.　　　　　　　　　15
With Thee
Let me combine,
And feel this day thy victory;
For, if I imp my wing on thine,°
Affliction shall advance the flight in me.　　20

—*1633*

---

**1 store** abundance　**19 imp my wing on thine** to graft feathers from a strong wing onto a weak one, a term from falconry

*John Milton (1608–1674) is best known as the London-born author of* Paradise
Lost *(1667), the great epic poem that sought to "justify the ways of God to men"
(Book 1.122) in twelve "books" of blank verse. Though he also wrote prose, lyric
poetry, sonnets, and powerful elegies such as "Lycidas," Milton is principally
remembered for his verse epics, which, because of the blindness of his later years, he
composed in his head and dictated to assistants.*

## John Milton
# Paradise Lost, Book X: 720–770

"O miserable of happy! Is this the end                              720
Of this new glorious world, and me so late
The glory of that glory? who now, become
Accursed of blessèd, hide me from the face
Of God, whom to behold was then my height
Of happiness! Yet well, if here would end                          725
The misery; I deserved it, and would bear
My own deservings; but this will not serve.
All that I eat or drink, or shall beget,
Is propagated curse.° O voice, once heard
Delightfully, 'Increase and multiply,'                             730
Now death to hear! for what can I increase
Or multiply but curses on my head?
Who, of all ages to succeed, but, feeling
The evil on him brought by me, will curse
My head: 'Ill fare our ancestor impure!                            735
For this we may thank Adam!' but his thanks
Shall be the execration;° so besides
Mine own that bide upon me, all from me
Shall with a fierce reflux on me redound,
On me, as on their natural center, light                           740
Heavy, though in their place. O fleeting joys

**729 propagated curse** multiplied curse   **737 execration** curses

Of Paradise, dear bought with lasting woes!
Did I request thee, Maker, from my clay
To mold me man? Did I solicit thee
From darkness to promote me, or here place          745
In this delicious garden? As my will
Concurred not to my being, it were but right
And equal to reduce me to my dust,
Desirous to resign and render back
All I received, unable to perform          750
Thy terms too hard, by which I was to hold
The good I sought not. To the loss of that,
Sufficient penalty, why hast thou added
The sense of endless woes? Inexplicable
Thy justice seems; yet to say truth, too late          755
I thus contèst; then should have been refused
Those terms whatever, when they were proposed.
Thou didst accept them; wilt thou enjoy the good,
Then cavil the conditions? And though God
Made thee without thy leave, what if thy son          760
Prove disobedient, and reproved, retort,
'Wherefore didst thou beget me? I sought it not.'
Wouldst thou admit for his contempt of thee
That proud excuse? Yet him not thy election,
But natural necessity begot.          765
God made thee of choice his own, and of his own
To serve him; thy reward was of his grace;
Thy punishment then justly is at his will.
Be it so, for I submit; his doom is fair,
That dust I am and shall to dust return.          770

—*1667*

*Anne Bradstreet (1612–1672) was an American Puritan who was one of the first settlers of the Massachusetts Bay Colony, along with her husband, Simon, later governor of the colony.* The Tenth Muse Lately Sprung Up in America, *published abroad by a relative without her knowledge, was the first American book of poetry published in England, and the circumstances of its appearance lie behind the witty tone of "The Author to Her Book."*

## Anne Bradstreet
# The Author to Her Book

Thou ill-formed offspring of my feeble brain,
Who after birth didst by my side remain,
Till snatched from thence by friends, less wise than true,
Who thee abroad, exposed to public view,
Made thee in rags, halting to th' press° to trudge,     5
Where errors were not lessened (all may judge).
At thy return my blushing was not small,
My rambling brat (in print) should mother call,
I cast thee by as one unfit for light,
Thy visage was so irksome in my sight;     10
Yet being mine own, at length affection would
Thy blemishes amend, if so I could:
I washed thy face, but more defects I saw,
And rubbing off a spot still made a flaw.
I stretched thy joints to make thee even feet,°     15
Yet still thou run'st more hobbling than is meet;
In better dress to trim thee was my mind,
But nought save homespun cloth i' th' house I find.
In this array 'mongst vulgars° may'st thou roam.
In critic's hands beware thou dost not come,     20
And take thy way where yet thou art not known;
If for thy father asked, say thou hadst none;
And for thy mother, she alas is poor,
Which caused her thus to send thee out of door.

—*1678*

---

**5 press** printing press; also a clothes closet or chest   **15 even feet** a pun on metrical feet
**19 vulgars** common people, i.e., average readers

*Richard Lovelace (1618–1658) was a Cavalier lyricist who was a staunch supporter of Charles I, serving as a soldier in Scotland and France. He composed many of his poems in prison following the English Civil War.*

### Richard Lovelace

# To Lucasta, Going to the Wars

Tell me not, sweet, I am unkind
That from the nunnery
Of thy chaste breast and quiet mind,
To war and arms I fly.

True, a new mistress now I chase,          5
The first foe in the field;
And with a stronger faith embrace
A sword, a horse, a shield.

Yet this inconstancy is such
As you too shall adore;          10
I could not love thee, dear, so much,
Loved I not honor more.

—*1649*

*Andrew Marvell (1621–1678) was widely known for the playful sexual wit of this most famous example of the* carpe diem *poem in English. Marvell was a learned Latin scholar who moved in high circles of government under both the Puritans and Charles II, serving as a member of parliament for two decades. Oddly, Marvell was almost completely forgotten as a lyric poet for almost two hundred years after his death, although today he is considered the last of the great exemplars of the metaphysical style.*

# *Andrew Marvell*

# To His Coy Mistress

Had we but world enough, and time,
This coyness,° lady, were no crime.
We would sit down, and think which way
To walk, and pass our long love's day.
Thou by the Indian Ganges' side                                    5
Shouldst rubies find; I by the tide
Of Humber° would complain. I would
Love you ten years before the flood,
And you should, if you please, refuse
Till the conversion of the Jews.°                                   10
My vegetable° love should grow
Vaster than empires, and more slow;
An hundred years should go to praise
Thine eyes, and on thy forehead gaze;
Two hundred to adore each breast,                                  15
But thirty thousand to the rest;
An age at least to every part,
And the last age should show your heart.
For, lady, you deserve this state,°
Nor would I love at lower rate.                                    20
    But at my back I always hear
Time's wingèd chariot hurrying near;
And yonder all before us lie
Deserts of vast eternity.

2 **coyness** here, artificial sexual reluctance    7 **Humber** an English river near Marvell's home
10 **conversion of the Jews** at the end of time    11 **vegetable** flourishing    19 **state** estate

Thy beauty shall no more be found;                                    *25*
Nor, in thy marble vault, shall sound
My echoing song; then worms shall try°
That long-preserved virginity,
And your quaint° honor turn to dust,
And into ashes all my lust:                                           *30*
The grave's a fine and private place,
But none, I think, do there embrace.
    Now therefore, while the youthful hue
Sits on thy skin like morning glow,
And while thy willing soul transpires                                 *35*
At every pore with instant fires,
Now let us sport us while we may,
And now, like amorous birds of prey,
Rather at once our time devour
Than languish in his slow-chapped° power.                             *40*
Let us roll all our strength and all
Our sweetness up into one ball,
And tear our pleasures with rough strife
Thorough the iron gates of life:
Thus, though we cannot make our sun                                   *45*
Stand still, yet we will make him run.

—*1681*

27 **try** test   29 **quaint** too subtle   40 **chapped** jawed

*Margaret Cavendish (1623?–1673) Best known for* Poems and Fancies: Written by the Right Honourable, the Lady Newcastle *(1653), this English noblewoman also wrote plays, fiction, biography, and essays on science, while battling objections to her writing career. In poems like "Nature's Cook," she offers a witty combination of domestic imagery and vivid personification.*

## Margaret Cavendish
# Nature's Cook

*Death* is the *Cook of Nature:* and we find
*Meat* dressed several ways to please her *Mind.*
Some *Meats she* roasts with *Fevers, burning hot,*
And some *she* boils with *Dropsies* in a *Pot.*
Some for *Jelly* consuming by degrees,                                    5
And some with *Ulcers,* Gravy out to squeeze.
Some *Flesh* as *Sage she* stuffs with *Gouts* and *Pains,*
Others for tender *Meat* hang up in *Chains.*
Some in the *Sea she pickles* up to keep,
Others, as *Brawn* is soused, those in *Winesteep.*                       10
Some with the *Pox,* chops *Flesh,* and *Bones* so small,
Of which *She* makes a *French Fricasse* withall.
Some on *Gridirons* of *Calentures*° is broiled
And some is trodden on, and so quite spoiled.
But those are *baked,* when smothered they do die,                        15
By *Hectic Fevers* some *Meat* She doth *fry.*
In *Sweat* sometimes *she stews* with *savoury smell,*
A *Hodge-Podge* of *Diseases* tasteth well.
*Brains* dressed with *Apoplexy* to *Nature's* wish,
Or swims with *Sauce* of *Megrimes*° in a *Dish.*                         20
And *Tongues* she dries with *Smoke* with *Stomachs* ill,
Which as the second *Course* she sends up still.
Then *Death* cuts *Throats,* for *Blood-puddings* to make,
And puts them in the *Guts,* which *Colics* rack.

---

**13 Calentures** tropical fevers similar to sunstroke   **20 Megrimes** migraine headaches

Some hunted are by *Death*, for *Deer* that's red,         25
Or *Stall-fed Oxen*, knocked on the *Head*.
Some for *Bacon* by *Death* are *Singed*, or *scaled*,
Then powdered up with *Phlegm*, and *Rheum* that's salt.

*—1653*

---

**John Dryden (1631–1700)** *excelled at long forms—verse dramas like* All for Love, *his version of Shakespeare's* Antony and Cleopatra, *his translation of Virgil's* Aeneid, *political allegories like* Absalom and Achitophel, *and* MacFlecknoe, *the first great English literary satire. Dryden's balance and formal conservatism introduced the neoclassical style to English poetry, a manner that prevailed for a century after his death. He became poet laureate of England in 1668.*

## *John Dryden*

# Epigram on Milton

Three poets, in three distant ages born,
Greece,° Italy,° and England did adorn.
The first in loftiness of thought surpassed,
The next in majesty, in both the last:
The force of Nature could no farther go;         5
To make a third, she joined the former two.

*—1688*

---

2 **Greece** i.e., Homer   **Italy** i.e., Virgil

*Aphra Behn (1640–1689) Considered England's first professional woman writer,
Behn is most remembered for eighteen plays, including* The Rover *(1677), and for
her novel* Oroonoko *(1688), set in Surinam, which she visited as a young woman.
She may have been the daughter of Mary Wroth's illegitimate daughter, but many
details of her life remain mysterious. Her surprising career did include international
travel and a stint as a spy. In her poetry, she often treated "scandalous" topics such
as impotence and adultery with great wit, but here in this song from her play*
Abdelazer, *or* The Moor's Revenge *(1676), she looks at the darker side of love.*

## *Aphra Behn*
# Love Armed

Love in fantastic triumph sat
Whilst bleeding hearts around him flowed,
For whom fresh pains he did create
And strange tyrannic power he showed.

From thy bright eyes he took the fires                                      5
Which round about in sport he hurled,
But 'twas from mine he took desires
Enough t'undo the amorous world.

From me he took his sighs and tears,
From thee his pride and cruelty;                                            10
From me his languishments and fears.
And every killing dart° from thee.

Thus thou and I the God have armed
And set him up a deity;
But my poor heart alone is harmed,                                          15
Whilst thine the victor is, and free.

—*1676*

---

**12 killing dart** The Roman god of love, Cupid (from the Latin cupido meaning "desire"), was
portrayed with a bow he used to shoot arrows into the hearts of his victims.

***Anne Finch (1661–1720)*** *From a prominent English family, the well-educated Finch served Mary of Modena, the second wife of James II. After his deposition, she retired to the countryside in Kent and continued to write poetry, some of which appeared in* Miscellany Poems on Several Occasions *(1713). She was admired by Swift and Wordsworth for her nature lyrics and her wit. She also wrote poems about the role of women, like this one in which Adam is "posed" (puzzled and perplexed) by his new partner.*

## *Anne Finch*
# Adam Posed

Could our first father, at his toilsome plough,
Thorns in his path, and labor on his brow,
Clothed only in a rude, unpolished skin,
Could he a vain fantastic nymph have seen,
In all her airs, in all her antic graces,                                              5
Her various fashions, and more various faces;
How had it posed that skill, which late assigned
Just appellations° to each several kind,
A right idea of the sight to frame;
T'have guessed from what new element she came;                      10
T'have hit the wavering form, or given this thing a name!

—*1709*

---

**8 just appellations** In Genesis 2:19–20, Adam chooses names for all the animals.

*Jonathan Swift (1667–1745), the author of* Gulliver's Travels, *stands unchallenged as the greatest English prose satirist, but his poetry too is remarkable in the unsparing realism of its best passages. Like many poets of the neoclassical era, Swift adds tension to his poetry by ironically emphasizing parallels between the heroic past and the familiar characters and scenes of contemporary London. A native of Dublin, Swift returned to Ireland in his maturity as dean of St. Patrick's Cathedral.*

## Jonathan Swift
# A Description of a City Shower

Careful observers may foretell the hour
(By sure prognostics)° when to dread a shower:
While rain depends,° the pensive cat gives o'er
Her frolics, and pursues her tail no more.
Returning home at night, you'll find the sink°                    5
Strike your offended sense with double stink.
If you be wise, then go not far to dine;
You'll spend in coach hire more than save in wine.
A coming shower your shooting corns presage,
Old achès throb, your hollow tooth will rage.                     10
Sauntering in coffeehouse is Dulman° seen;
He damns the climate and complains of spleen.°
      Meanwhile the South, rising with dabbled wings,
A sable cloud athwart the welkin° flings,
That swilled more liquor than it could contain,                  15
And, like a drunkard, gives it up again.
Brisk Susan whips her linen from the rope,
While the first drizzling shower is borne aslope:
Such is that sprinkling which some careless quean°
Flirts on you from her mop, but not so clean:                    20
You fly, invoke the gods; then turning, stop
To rail; she singing, still whirls on her mop.

2 **prognostics** forecasts  3 **depends** is imminent  5 **sink** sewer  11 **Dulman** i.e., dull man
12 **spleen** mental depression  14 **welkin** sky  19 **quean** ill-mannered woman

Not yet the dust had shunned the unequal strife,
But, aided by the wind, fought still for life,
And wafted with its foe by violent gust,                                    25
'Twas doubtful which was rain and which was dust.
Ah! where must needy poet seek for aid,
When dust and rain at once his coat invade?
Sole coat, where dust cemented by the rain
Erects the nap, and leaves a mingled stain.                               30
    Now in contiguous drops the flood comes down,
Threatening with deluge this devoted° town.
To shops in crowds the daggled° females fly,
Pretend to cheapen° goods, but nothing buy.
The Templar° spruce, while every spout's abroach,°                        35
Stays till 'tis fair, yet seems to call a coach.
The tucked-up sempstress walks with hasty strides,
While streams run down her oiled umbrella's sides.
Here various kinds, by various fortunes led,
Commence acquaintance underneath a shed.                                  40
Triumphant Tories and desponding Whigs°
Forget their feuds, and join to save their wigs.
Boxed in a chair° the beau impatient sits,
While spouts run clattering o'er the roof by fits,
And ever and anon with frightful din                                      45
The leather sounds; he trembles from within.
So when Troy chairmen bore the wooden steed,
Pregnant with Greeks impatient to be freed
(Those bully Greeks, who, as the moderns do,
Instead of paying chairmen, run them through),                            50
Laocoön° struck the outside with his spear,
And each imprisoned hero quaked for fear.
    Now from all parts the swelling kennels° flow,
And bear their trophies with them as they go:
Filth of all hues and odors seem to tell                                  55
What street they sailed from, by their sight and smell.

---

**32 devoted** doomed    **33 daggled** spattered    **34 cheapen** inspect prices of    **35 Templar** law
student    **abroach** pouring    **41 Tories . . . Whigs** rival political factions    **43 chair** sedan chair
**51 Laocoön** For his attempt to warn the Trojans, he was crushed by sea serpents sent by Poseidon.
**53 kennels** storm drains

They, as each torrent drives with rapid force,
From Smithfield° or St. Pulchre's shape their course,
And in huge confluence joined at Snow Hill ridge,
Fall from the conduit prone to Holborn Bridge.                    *60*
Sweepings from butchers' stalls, dung, guts, and blood,
Drowned puppies, stinking sprats,° all drenched in mud,
Dead cats, and turnip tops, come tumbling down the flood.

—*1710*

---

*Henry Kelsey (1667–1771) Born in England, Kelsey joined the Hudson's Bay Company as a young man and spent much of his life in Canada. This is the poetic record of the voyage he took in 1690 from Churchill, Manitoba, on Hudson Bay deep into the interior. He and his Native guides travelled by canoe and on foot across the prairie, making him the first European to see what is now Saskatchewan. He makes particular note of elements of economic interest to the fur trade.*

## Henry Kelsey
# Now Reader Read . . .

FROM HENRY KELSEY HIS BOOK BEING THE GIFT OF JAMES HUBBUD IN THE YEAR OF OUR LORD 1693

Now Reader Read for I am well assur'd
Thou dost not know the hardships I endur'd
In this same desert where Ever that I have been
Nor wilt thou me believe without that thou had seen
The Emynent Dangers that did often me attend                     *5*
But still I lived in hopes that once it would amend
And makes me free from hunger & from Cold
Likewise many other things which I cannot here unfold
For many times I have often been oppresst
With fears & Cares that I could not take my rest                  *10*
Because I was alone & no friend could find
And once that in my travels I was left behind

---

58 **Smithfield** site of London cattle exchange   62 **sprats** small fish

Which struck fear & terror into me
But still I was resolved this same Country for to see
Although through many dangers I did pass                          15
Hoped still to undergo them at the Last
Now Considering that it was my dismal fate
for to repent I thought it now too late
Trusting still unto my masters Consideration
Hoping they will Except of this my small Relation                 20
Which here I have pend & still will Justifie
Concerning of those Indians & their Country
If this wont do farewell to all as I may say
And for my living i'll seek some other way
In sixteen hundred & ninety'th year                               25
I set forth as plainly may appear
Through Gods assistance for to understand
The natives language & to see their land
And for my masters interest I did soon
Sett from the house the twealth of June                           30
Then up the River I with heavy heart
Did take my way & from all English part
To live amongst the Natives of this place
If god permits me for one two years space
The Inland Country of Good report hath been                       35
By Indians but by English yet not seen
Therefore I on my Journey did not stay
But making all the hast I could upon our way
Gott on the borders of the stone Indian Country
I took possession on the tenth Instant July                       40
And for my masters I speaking for them all
This neck of land I deerings point did call
Distance from hence by Judgement at the lest
From the house six hundred miles southwest
Through Rivers which run strong with falls                        45
thirty three Carriages five lakes in all
The ground begins for to be dry with wood
Poplo & birch with ash thats very good
For the Natives of that place which knows
No use of Better than their wooden Bows                           50

According to the use & custom of this place
In September I brought those Natives to a peace
But I had no sooner from those Natives turnd my back
Some of the home Indians° came upon their track
And for old grudges & their minds to fill                                      55
Came up with them Six tents of which they kill'd
This ill news kept secrett was from me
Nor none of those home Indians did I see
Untill that they their murder all had done
And the Chief acter was he thats called the Sun                         60
So far I have spoken concerning of the spoil
And now will give account of that same Country soile
Which hither part is very thick of wood
Affords small nutts with little cherryes very good
Thus it continues till you leave the woods behind            65
And then you have beast of severall kind
The one is a black a Buffillo great
Another is an outgrown Bear which is good meat
His skin to gett I have used all the ways I can
He is mans food & he makes food of man                           70
His hide they would not me it preserve
But said it was a god & they should Starve
This plain affords nothing but Beast & grass
And over it in three days time we past
getting unto the woods on the other side                             75
It being about forty six miles wide
This wood is poplo ridges with small ponds of water
there is beavour in abundance but no Otter
with plains & ridges in the Country throughout
Their Enemies many whom they cannot rout                    80
But now of late they hunt their Enemies
And with our English guns do make them flie
At deerings point after the frost
I set up their a Certain Cross
In token of my being there                                               85

---

**54 home Indians** Kelsey's term for the Natives already trading at the Hudson's Bay Company post at York Factory

Cut out on it the date of year
And Likewise for to veryfie the same
added to it my master sir Edward deerings name
So having no more to trouble you withall I am
Sir your most obedient & faithful Servant at Command 90

—*1693*

---

*Alexander Pope (1688–1744) was a tiny man who was afflicted in childhood by a crippling disease. Pope was the dominant poet of eighteenth–century England, excelling as a master of mock-epic satire in "The Rape of the Lock" and "The Dunciad." Both his much-quoted "An Essay on Criticism" (1711) and "An Essay on Man" (1733–1734) are written in heroic couplets indicative of a neo-classical aesthetic.*

# *Alexander Pope*
## *from* An Essay on Man

    1. Know then thyself, presume not God to scan,
The proper study of mankind is Man.
Placed on this isthmus of a middle state,
A being darkly wise, and rudely great:
With too much knowledge for the skeptic side, 5
With too much weakness for the Stoic's pride,
He hangs between; in doubt to act, or rest;
In doubt to deem himself a god, or beast;
In doubt his mind or body to prefer,
Born but to die, and reasoning but to err; 10
Alike in ignorance, his reason such,
Whether he thinks too little, or too much:
Chaos of thought and passion, all confused;
Still by himself abused, or disabused;
Created half to rise, and half to fall; 15

Great lord of all things, yet a prey to all;
Sole judge of truth, in endless error hurled:
The glory, jest, and riddle of the world!

—*1733*

---

*Christopher Smart (1722–1771) was educated, like Thomas Gray, at
Cambridge, but fell victim to religious mania and insanity yet continued to write
throughout his life.* Jubilate Agno *("Rejoice in the Lamb") is a long meditation
on the immanence of God, even in such insignificant forms as Smart's cat Jeoffry.
The poem is one of the earliest examples of free verse in English.*

## *Christopher Smart*
# *from* Jubilate Agno

For I will consider my Cat Jeoffry.
For he is the servant of the Living God, duly and daily serving him.
For at the first glance of the glory of God in the East he worships in
    his way.
For is this done by wreathing his body seven times round with
    elegant quickness.
For then he leaps up to catch the musk,° which is the blessing of
    God upon his prayer.        *5*
For he rolls upon prank to work it in.
For having done duty and received blessing he begins to
    consider himself.
For this he performs in ten degrees.
For first he looks upon his forepaws to see if they are clean.
For secondly he kicks up behind to clear away there.      *10*
For thirdly he works it upon stretch with the forepaws
    extended.
For fourthly he sharpens his paws by wood.
For fifthly he washes himself.
For sixthly he rolls upon wash.

---

**5 musk** scented object or toy

For seventhly he fleas himself, that he may not be
    interrupted upon the beat.° 15
For eighthly he rubs himself against a post.
For ninthly he looks up for his instructions.
For tenthly he goes in quest of food.
For having considered God and himself he will consider his
    neighbor.
For if he meets another cat he will kiss her in kindness. 20
For when he takes his prey he plays with it to give it a chance.
For one mouse in seven escapes by his dallying.
For when his day's work is done his business more properly
    begins.
For he keeps the Lord's watch in the night against the
    adversary.°
For he counteracts the powers of darkness by his electrical
    skin and glaring eyes. 25
For he counteracts the Devil, who is death, by brisking about
    the life.
For in his morning orisons he loves the sun and the sun loves him.
For he is of the tribe of Tiger.
For the Cherub Cat is a term° of the Angel Tiger.
For he has the subtlety and hissing of a serpent, which in
    goodness he suppresses. 30
For he will not do destruction if he is well-fed, neither will he
    spit without provocation.
For he purrs in thankfulness when God tells him he's a good Cat.
For he is an instrument for the children to learn benevolence
    upon.
For every house is incomplete without him, and a blessing is
    lacking in the spirit.

—ca. 1760

15 **beat** accustomed path   24 **adversary** i.e., Satan   29 **term** immature version

*Mary Leapor (1722–1746) A working-class upbringing in Marston St. Lawrence in England, and her work as a kitchen maid, put Leapor in a good position to comment on the role of women in her time. Her* Poems upon Several Occasions *(1748) was published after she died of measles at the age of 24.*

# *Mary Leapor*
# An Essay on Woman

Woman, a pleasing but a short-lived flower,
Too soft for business and too weak for power:
A wife in bondage, or neglected maid;
Despised, if ugly; if she's fair, betrayed.
'Tis wealth alone inspires every grace,                              5
And calls the raptures to her plenteous face.
What numbers for those charming features pine,
If blooming acres round her temples twine!
Her lip the strawberry, and her eyes more bright
Than sparkling Venus° in a frosty night;                              10
Pale lilies fade and, when the fair appears,
Snow turns a negro and dissolves in tears,
And, where the charmer treads her magic toe,
On English ground Arabian odours grow;
Till mighty Hymen° lifts his sceptred rod,                           15
And sinks her glories with a fatal nod,
Dissolves her triumphs, sweeps her charms away,
And turns the goddess to her native clay.
   But, Artemisia,° let your servant sing
What small advantage wealth and beauties bring.                      20
Who would be wise, that knew Pamphilia's fate?
Or who be fair, and joined to Sylvia's mate?
Sylvia, whose cheeks are fresh as early day,
As evening mild, and sweet as spicy May:
And yet that face her partial husband tires,                         25
And those bright eyes, that all the world admires.

---

**10 Venus** the Roman goddess of love   **15 Hymen** the Greek god of marriage   **19 Artemisia**, etc. women's names. Pamphilia, meaning "all-loving," may refer to Mary Wroth's sonnet sequence *Pamphilia to Amphilanthus.*

Pamphilia's wit who does not strive to shun,
Like death's infection or a dog-day's sun?
The damsels view her with malignant eyes,
The men are vexed to find a nymph so wise:                    30
And wisdom only serves to make her know
The keen sensation of superior woe.
The secret whisper and the listening ear,
The scornful eyebrow and the hated sneer,
The giddy censures of her babbling kind,                      35
With thousand ills that grate a gentle mind,
By her are tasted in the first degree,
Though overlooked by Simplicus and me.
Does thirst of gold a virgin's heart inspire,
Instilled by nature or a careful sire?                        40
Then let her quit extravagance and play,
The brisk companion and expensive tea,
To feast with Cordia in her filthy sty
On stewed potatoes or on mouldy pie;
Whose eager eyes stare ghastly at the poor,                   45
And fright the beggars from her hated door;
In greasy clouts she wraps her smoky chin,
And holds that pride's a never-pardoned sin.
    If this be wealth, no matter where it falls;
But save, ye Muses, save your Mira's° walls:                  50
Still give me pleasing indolence and ease,
A fire to warm me and a friend to please.
    Since, whether sunk in avarice or pride,
A wanton virgin or a starving bride,
Or wondering crowds attend her charming tongue,               55
Or, deemed an idiot, ever speaks the wrong;
Though nature armed us for the growing ill
With fraudful cunning and a headstrong will;
Yet, with ten thousand follies to her charge,
Unhappy woman's but a slave at large.                         60

*—1748*

---

50 **Mira** Leapor's pen name

*Phillis Wheatley (1753–1784) Purchased from a slave ship as a child by the man whose last name she adopted, Wheatley showed herself to be an avid student while working as Mrs. Wheatley's personal servant. Sometimes criticized for her admiration of Western culture and the Christian religion, she is praised by Alice Walker for "keeping the notion of song alive" against tremendous odds. Her* Poems on Various Subjects, Religious and Moral *was published in England in 1773 and in America in 1786.*

## Phillis Wheatley
# On Being Brought from Africa to America

'Twas mercy brought me from my pagan land,
Taught my benighted° soul to understand
That there's a God, that there's a Savior too:
Once I redemption neither sought nor knew.
Some view that sable race with scornful eye:                    5
"Their color is a diabolic dye."
Remember, Christians, Negroes black as Cain°
May be refined and join the angelic strain.

—*1773*

**2 benighted** involved in intellectual or moral darkness   **7 Cain** Adam and Eve's son Cain, the first murderer, was marked and sent to wander the earth (Genesis 4:13–16). Some interpreted this story as the origin of the Blacks.

**William Blake (1757–1827)** *was a poet, painter, engraver, and visionary. Blake does not fit easily into any single category, although his political sympathies link him to the later romantic poets. His first book,* Poetical Sketches, *attracted little attention, but his mature works, starting with* Songs of Innocence *and* Songs of Experience, *combine poetry with his own remarkable illustrations and are unique in English literature. Thought mad by many in his own day, Blake anticipated many future directions of both literature and modern psychology.*

## William Blake
# The Tyger

Tyger! Tyger! burning bright
In the forests of the night,
What immortal hand or eye
Could frame thy fearful symmetry?

In what distant deeps or skies          5
Burnt the fire of thine eyes?
On what wings dare he aspire?
What the hand, dare seize the fire?

And what shoulder, & what art,
Could twist the sinews of thy heart?          10
And when thy heart began to beat,
What dread hand? & what dread feet?

What the hammer? what the chain?
In what furnace was thy brain?
What the anvil? what dread grasp          15
Dare its deadly terrors clasp?

When the stars threw down their spears,
And water'd heaven with their tears,
Did he smile his work to see?
Did he who made the Lamb make thee?          20

Tyger! Tyger! burning bright
In the forests of the night,
What immortal hand or eye,
Dare frame thy fearful symmetry?

*—1794*

# The Sick Rose

O Rose, thou art sick.
The invisible worm
That flies in the night
In the howling storm

Has found out thy bed                                                    5
Of crimson joy,
And his dark secret love
Does thy life destroy.

*—1794*

---

*Robert Burns (1759–1796) was a Scot known in his day as the "Ploughman Poet" and was one of the first English poets to put dialect to serious literary purpose. Chiefly known for his realistic depictions of peasant life, he was also an important lyric poet who prefigured many of the later concerns of the romantic era.*

## Robert Burns
# A Red, Red Rose

O my luve's like a red, red rose,
   That's newly sprung in June;
O my luve's like the melodie
   That's sweetly played in tune.

As fair art thou, my bonnie lass,      *5*
   So deep in luve am I;
And I will luve thee still, my dear,
   Till a' the seas gang° dry.

Till a' the seas gang dry, my dear,
   And the rocks melt wi' the sun;      *10*
O I will luve thee still, my dear,
   While the sands o' life shall run.

And fare thee weel, my only luve,
   And fare thee weel awhile!
And I will come again, my luve      *15*
   Though it were ten thousand mile.

*—1791*

---

*William Wordsworth (1770–1850) is generally considered the first of the English romantics. Lyrical Ballads, the 1798 volume that introduced both his poetry and Samuel Taylor Coleridge's to a wide readership, remains one of the most influential collections of poetry ever published. Wordsworth's preface to the revised edition of 1800 contains the famous romantic formulation of poetry as the "spontaneous overflow of powerful feelings," a theory exemplified in short lyrics like "I Wandered Lonely as a Cloud" and in longer meditative pieces like "Tintern Abbey." Wordsworth served as poet laureate from 1843 to his death.*

## *William Wordsworth*
# I Wandered Lonely as a Cloud

I wandered lonely as a cloud
That floats on high o'er vales and hills,
When all at once I saw a crowd,
A host, of golden daffodils;

**8 gang** go

Beside the lake, beneath the trees,⁣      5
Fluttering and dancing in the breeze.

Continuous as the stars that shine
And twinkle on the milky way,
They stretched in never-ending line
Along the margin of a bay:      10
Ten thousand saw I at a glance,
Tossing their heads in sprightly dance.

The waves beside them danced, but they
Outdid the sparkling waves in glee;
A poet could not but be gay,      15
In such a jocund company;
I gazed—and gazed—but little thought
What wealth the show to me had brought:

For oft, when on my couch I lie
In vacant or in pensive mood,      20
They flash upon that inward eye
Which is the bliss of solitude;
And then my heart with pleasure fills,
And dances with the daffodils.

—*1807*

# The World Is Too Much with Us

The world is too much with us; late and soon,
Getting and spending, we lay waste our powers;
Little we see in Nature that is ours;
We have given our hearts away, a sordid boon!°
This Sea that bares her bosom to the moon;      5

**4 sordid boon** corrupted gift

The winds that will be howling at all hours,
And are up-gathered now like sleeping flowers;
For this, for every thing, we are out of tune;
It moves us not.—Great God! I'd rather be
A Pagan suckled in a creed outworn;                                   10
So might I, standing on this pleasant lea,
Have glimpses that would make me less forlorn;
Have sight of Proteus° rising from the sea;
Or hear old Triton° blow his wreathèd horn.

—*1807*

*Samuel Taylor Coleridge (1772–1834), inspired but erratic, did his best work,
like Wordsworth, during the great first decade of their friendship, the period that produced* Lyrical Ballads. *Coleridge's later life is a tragic tale of financial and marital
problems, unfinished projects, and a ruinous addiction to opium. A brilliant critic,
Coleridge lectured on Shakespeare and other writers and wrote the* Biographia
Literaria, *perhaps the greatest literary autobiography ever written.*

# Samuel Taylor Coleridge
## Kubla Khan°

### OR A VISION IN A DREAM,° A FRAGMENT

In Xanadu did Kubla Khan
A stately pleasure-dome decree:
Where Alph, the sacred river, ran
Through caverns measureless to man

---

13 **Proteus** old man of the sea capable of changing shape   14 **Triton** sea god who blows on a
conch shell
**Kubla Khan** ruler of China (1216–1294)   **vision in a dream** Coleridge's own account tells how he
took opium for an illness and slept for three hours, during which time he envisioned a complete poem
of some three hundred lines. When he awoke, he began to write down the details of his dream. "At
this moment he was unfortunately called out by a person on business from Porlock, and detained by
him above an hour, and on his return to the room found, to his no small surprise and mortification,
that though he still retained some vague and dim recollection of the general purport of the vision, yet,
with the exception of some eight or ten scattered lines and images, all the rest had passed away like
the images on the surface of a stream into which a stone has been cast . . ." [Coleridge's note].

Down to a sunless sea.      *5*
So twice five miles of fertile ground
With walls and towers were girdled round:
And there were gardens bright with sinuous rills,
Where blossomed many an incense-bearing tree;
And here were forests ancient as the hills,      *10*
Enfolding sunny spots of greenery.

But oh! that deep romantic chasm which slanted
Down the green hill athwart a cedarn cover!
A savage place! as holy and enchanted
As e'er beneath a waning moon was haunted      *15*
By woman wailing for her demon lover!
And from this chasm, with ceaseless turmoil seething,
As if this earth in fast thick pants were breathing,
A mighty fountain momently was forced:
Amid whose swift half-intermitted burst      *20*
Huge fragments vaulted like rebounding hail,
Or chaffy grain beneath the thresher's flail:
And 'mid these dancing rocks at once and ever
It flung up momently the sacred river.
Five miles meandering with a mazy motion      *25*
Through wood and dale the sacred river ran,
Then reached the caverns measureless to man,
And sank in tumult to a lifeless ocean:
And 'mid this tumult Kubla heard from far
Ancestral voices prophesying war!      *30*

    The shadow of the dome of pleasure
      Floated midway on the waves;
      Where was heard the mingled measure
      From the fountain and the caves.
It was a miracle of rare device,      *35*
A sunny pleasure-dome with caves of ice!

    A damsel with a dulcimer
      In a vision once I saw:
      It was an Abyssinian maid,
      And on her dulcimer she played,      *40*

Singing of Mount Abora.
Could I revive within me
Her symphony and song,
To such a deep delight 'twould win me,
That with music loud and long,                                45
I would build that dome in air,
That sunny dome! those caves of ice!
And all who heard should see them there,
And all should cry, Beware! Beware!
His flashing eyes, his floating hair!                         50
Weave a circle round him thrice,
And close your eyes with holy dread,
For he on honey-dew hath fed,
And drunk the milk of Paradise.

                                                        —1797–98

# Metrical Feet

### LESSON FOR A BOY

Trōchĕe trips frŏm lŏng tŏ shōrt;
From long to long in solemn sort
Slōw Spōndēe stālks; strōng fŏ͞ot! yet ill able
Ēvĕr tŏ cōme ŭp wĭth Dāctўl trĭsўllăblĕ.
Ĭ āmbĭcs mārch frŏm shŏrt tŏ lōng—                             5
Wĭth ă lēap ănd ă bo͞und thĕ swĭft Ănăpĕsts thrōng;
One syllable long, with one short at each side,
Ămphĭbrăchўs hāstes wĭth ă stātelў stride—
Fīrst ănd lāst bēĭng lōng, mĭddlĕ shŏrt, Ămphĭmācer
Strīkes hĭs thūndērĭng ho͞ofs līke ă pro͞ud hĭgh-brĕd Rācer.   10
If Derwent° be innocent, steady, and wise,
And delight in the things of earth, water, and skies;
Tender warmth at his heart, with these meters to show it,

---

**11 Derwent** Coleridge's younger son

With sound sense in his brains, may make Derwent a poet—
May crown him with fame, and must win him the love          15
Of his father on earth and his Father above.
            My dear, dear child!
Could you stand upon Skiddaw,° you would not from its whole ridge
See a man who so loves you as your fond S. T. Coleridge.

                                   *—1806*

*George Gordon, Lord Byron (1788–1824) attained flamboyant celebrity status, leading an unconventional lifestyle that contributed to his notoriety. Byron was the most widely read of all the English romantic poets, but his verse romances and mock-epic poems like* Don Juan *have not proved as popular in this century. An English aristocrat who was committed to revolutionary ideals, Byron died while lending military assistance to the cause of Greek freedom.*

## *George Gordon, Lord Byron*

# When a Man Hath No Freedom to Fight for at Home

When a man hath no freedom to fight for at home,
    Let him combat for that of his neighbors;
Let him think of the glories of Greece and of Rome,
    And get knock'd on the head for his labors.

To do good to mankind is the chivalrous plan,          5
    And is always as nobly requited;
Then battle for freedom wherever you can,
    And, if not shot or hang'd, you'll get knighted.

                                   *—1824*

---

**18 Skiddaw** mountain in England's lake country

*Percy Bysshe Shelley (1792–1822)*, like his friend Byron, has not found as much favour in recent eras as the other English romantics, although his political liberalism anticipates many currents of our own day. Perhaps his unbridled emotionalism is sometimes too intense for modern readers. His wife, Mary Wollstonecraft Shelley, will be remembered as the author of the classic horror novel Frankenstein.

## Percy Bysshe Shelley
# When the Lamp Is Shattered

When the lamp is shattered
The light in the dust lies dead—
   When the cloud is scattered
The rainbow's glory is shed—
   When the lute is broken          5
Sweet tones are remembered not—
   When the lips have spoken
Loved accents are soon forgot.

   As music and splendour
Survive not the lamp and the lute,     10
   The heart's echoes render
No song when the spirit is mute—
   No song—but sad dirges
Like the wind through a ruined cell,
   Or the mournful surges          15
That ring the dead seaman's knell.

   When hearts have once mingled
Love first leaves the well-built nest—
   The weak one is singled
To endure what it once possest.       20
   O Love! who bewailest
The frailty of all things here,
   Why choose you the frailest
For your cradle, your home and your bier?

Its passions will rock thee                                    *25*
As the storms rock the ravens on high—
    Bright Reason will mock thee
Like the Sun from a wintry sky—
    From thy nest every rafter
Will rot, and thine eagle home                                 *30*
    Leave thee naked to laughter,
When leaves fall and cold winds come.

                                                    *—1824*

# Ozymandias°

I met a traveler from an antique land
Who said: Two vast and trunkless legs of stone
Stand in the desert. . . . Near them, on the sand,
Half sunk, a shattered visage lies, whose frown,
And wrinkled lip, and sneer of cold command,              *5*
Tell that its sculptor well those passions read
Which yet survive, stamped on these lifeless things,
The hand that mocked them, and the heart that fed:
And on the pedestal these words appear:
"My name is Ozymandias, king of kings:                    *10*
Look on my works, ye Mighty, and despair!"
Nothing beside remains. Round the decay
Of that colossal wreck, boundless and bare
The lone and level sands stretch far away.

                                                    *—1818*

**Ozymandias** Ramses II of Egypt (c. 1250 B.C.)

*John Keats (1795–1821) is now perhaps the most admired of all the major roman-
tics. Certainly his tragic death from tuberculosis in his twenties gives poignancy to
thoughts of the doomed young poet writing feverishly in a futile race against time; "Here
lies one whose name was writ in water" are the words he chose for his own epitaph. Many
of Keats's poems are concerned with glimpses of the eternal, whether a translation of an
ancient epic poem or a pristine artifact of a vanished civilization.*

## John Keats
# La Belle Dame sans Merci°

O what can ail thee, Knight at arms,
    Alone and palely loitering?
The sedge has withered from the Lake
    And no birds sing!

O what can ail thee, Knight at arms,                            5
    So haggard, and so woebegone?
The squirrel's granary is full
    And the harvest's done.

I see a lily on thy brow
    With anguish moist and fever dew,                      10
And on thy cheeks a fading rose
    Fast withereth too.

"I met a Lady in the Meads,
    Full beautiful, a faery's child,
Her hair was long, her foot was light,                   15
    And her eyes were wild.

"I made a Garland for her head,
    And bracelets too, and fragrant Zone;°
She looked at me as she did love
    And made sweet moan.                                 20

**La Belle Dame sans Merci** "the beautiful lady without pity"  **18 Zone** belt

"I set her on my pacing steed
    And nothing else saw all day long,
For sidelong would she bend and sing
    A faery's song.

"She found me roots of relish sweet,          *25*
    And honey wild, and manna dew,
And sure in language strange she said
    'I love thee true.'

"She took me to her elfin grot°
    And there she wept and sighed full sore,    *30*
And there I shut her wild wild eyes
    With kisses four.

"And there she lullèd me asleep,
    And there I dreamed, Ah Woe betide!
The latest dream I ever dreamt          *35*
    On the cold hill side.

"I saw pale Kings, and Princes too,
    Pale warriors, death-pale were they all;
They cried, 'La belle Dame sans merci
    Hath thee in thrall!'          *40*

"I saw their starved lips in the gloam
    With horrid warning gapèd wide,
And I awoke, and found me here
    On the cold hill's side.

"And this is why I sojourn here          *45*
    Alone and palely loitering;
Though the sedge is withered from the Lake,
    And no birds sing."

                    *—1819*

29 **grot** cave

# Ode on a Grecian Urn

### 1

Thou still unravished bride of quietness,
 Thou foster-child of silence and slow time,
Sylvan historian, who canst thus express
 A flowery tale more sweetly than our rhyme:
What leaf-fringed legend haunts about thy shape      5
  Of deities or mortals, or of both,
   In Tempe or the dales of Arcady?°
  What men or gods are these? What maidens loath?°
What mad pursuit? What struggle to escape?
   What pipes and timbrels?° What wild ecstasy?     10

### 2

Heard melodies are sweet, but those unheard
 Are sweeter; therefore, ye soft pipes, play on;
Not to the sensual ear, but, more endeared,
 Pipe to the spirit ditties of no tone:
Fair youth, beneath the trees, thou canst not leave     15
  Thy song, nor ever can those trees be bare;
   Bold Lover, never, never canst thou kiss,
Though winning near the goal—yet, do not grieve;
   She cannot fade, though thou hast not thy bliss,
  Forever wilt thou love, and she be fair!       20

### 3

Ah, happy, happy boughs! that cannot shed
 Your leaves, nor ever bid the Spring adieu;
And, happy melodist, unwearièd,
 Forever piping songs forever new;
More happy love! more happy, happy love!       25
  Forever warm and still to be enjoyed,
   Forever panting, and forever young;

---

**7 Tempe or the dales of Arcady** idealized Greek settings   **8 loath** reluctant   **10 timbrels** tambourines

All breathing human passion far above,
    That leaves a heart high-sorrowful and cloyed,
        A burning forehead, and a parching tongue.    *30*

    4

Who are these coming to the sacrifice?
    To what green altar, O mysterious priest,
Lead'st thou that heifer lowing at the skies,
    And all her silken flanks with garlands dressed?
What little town by river or sea shore,    *35*
    Or mountain-built with peaceful citadel,
        Is emptied of this folk, this pious morn?
And, little town, thy streets forevermore
    Will silent be; and not a soul to tell
        Why thou art desolate, can e'er return.    *40*

    5

O Attic° shape! Fair attitude! with brede°
    Of marble men and maidens overwrought,
With forest branches and the trodden weed;
    Thou, silent form, dost tease us out of thought
As doth eternity: Cold Pastoral!    *45*
    When old age shall this generation waste,
        Thou shalt remain, in midst of other woe
    Than ours, a friend to man, to whom thou say'st,
"Beauty is truth, truth beauty,"—that is all
        Ye know on earth, and all ye need to know.    *50*

    *—1819*

**41 Attic** Greek    **brede** ornamental pattern

*Susanna Moodie (1803–1885) was born in Suffolk, England, and is best known for* Roughing It in the Bush *(1852), her prose account of her arrival and settlement in Upper Canada in 1832, which later inspired Margaret Atwood's* Journals of Susanna Moodie *(1970). This poem first appeared in the* Literary Garland *in 1847, then in* Roughing It in the Bush *as an epigraph to Moodie's chapter on Brian, who practised a method of hunting that requires absolute stillness.*

### Susanna Moodie
# Brian, the Still-Hunter

O'er memory's glass I see his shadow flit,
Though he was gathered to the silent dust
Long years ago. A strange and wayward man,
That shunn'd companionship, and lived apart;
The leafy covert of the dark brown woods,                    5
The gleamy lakes, hid in their gloomy depths,
Whose still, deep waters never knew the stroke
Of cleaving oar, or echoed to the sound
Of social life, contained for him the sum
Of human happiness. With dog and gun                         10
Day after day he track'd the nimble deer
Through all the tangled mazes of the forest.

—*1847*

*Elizabeth Barrett Browning (1806–1861) was already a famous poet when she met her husband-to-be, Robert Browning, who had been corresponding with her on literary matters. She originally published her famous sonnet sequence, written in the first years of her marriage, in the guise of a translation of Portuguese poems, perhaps to mask their personal revelations.*

## Elizabeth Barrett Browning

# Sonnets from the Portuguese, 1

I thought once how Theocritus had sung
Of the sweet years, the dear and wish'd-for years,
Who each one in a gracious hand appears
To bear a gift for mortals, old or young:
And, as I mus'd it in his antique tongue,        5
I saw, in gradual vision through my tears,
The sweet, sad years, the melancholy years,
Those of my own life, who by turns had flung
A shadow across me. Straightway I was 'ware,
So weeping, how a mystic Shape did move        10
Behind me, and drew me backward by the hair;
And a voice said in mastery, while I strove,—
"Guess now who holds thee!"—"Death," I said. But, there,
The silver answer rang—"Not Death, but Love."

—*1812*

# Sonnets from the Portuguese, 43

How do I love thee? Let me count the ways.
I love thee to the depth and breadth and height
My soul can reach, when feeling out of sight
For the ends of Being and ideal Grace.
I love thee to the level of everyday's        5

Most quiet need, by sun and candle-light.
I love thee freely, as men strive for Right;
I love thee purely, as they turn from Praise.
I love thee with the passion put to use
In my old griefs, and with my childhood's faith.                              *10*
I love thee with a love I seemed to lose
With my lost saints—I love thee with the breath,
Smiles, tears, of all my life!—and, if God choose,
I shall but love thee better after death.

*—1845–46*

---

*Edgar Allan Poe (1809–1849) has survived his own myth as a deranged, drug-crazed genius, despite the wealth of evidence to the contrary that can be gleaned from his brilliant, though erratic, career as a poet, short-story writer, critic, and editor. Poe's brand of romanticism seems at odds with that of other American poets of his day, and is perhaps more in keeping with the spirit of Coleridge than that of Wordsworth. "The Raven" has been parodied perhaps more than any other American poem, yet it still retains a powerful hold on its audience.*

## Edgar Allan Poe
# The Raven

Once upon a midnight dreary, while I pondered, weak and weary,
Over many a quaint and curious volume of forgotten lore—
While I nodded, nearly napping, suddenly there came a tapping,
As of some one gently rapping, rapping at my chamber door.
"'Tis some visitor," I muttered, "tapping at my chamber door—              *5*
                    Only this and nothing more."

Ah, distinctly I remember it was in the bleak December;
And each separate dying ember wrought its ghost upon the floor.
Eagerly I wished the morrow;—vainly I had sought to borrow
From my books surcease of sorrow—sorrow for the lost Lenore—              *10*
For the rare and radiant maiden whom the angels name Lenore—
                    Nameless *here* for evermore.

And the silken, sad, uncertain rustling of each purple curtain
Thrilled me—filled me with fantastic terrors never felt before;
So that now, to still the beating of my heart, I stood repeating      *15*
"'Tis some visitor entreating entrance at my chamber door;—
Some late visitor entreating entrance at my chamber door;—
                This it is and nothing more."

Presently my soul grew stronger; hesitating then no longer,
"Sir," said I, "or Madam, truly your forgiveness I implore;      *20*
But the fact is I was napping, and so gently you came rapping,
And so faintly you came tapping, tapping at my chamber door,
That I scarce was sure I heard you"—here I opened wide the door;—
                Darkness there and nothing more.

Deep into that darkness peering, long I stood there wondering,
    fearing,      *25*
Doubting, dreaming dreams no mortal ever dared to dream before;
But the silence was unbroken, and the stillness gave no token,
And the only word there spoken was the whispered word, "Lenore?"
This I whispered, and an echo murmured back the word, "Lenore!"
                Merely this and nothing more.      *30*

Back into the chamber turning, all my soul within me burning,
Soon again I heard a tapping somewhat louder than before.
"Surely," said I, "surely that is something at my window lattice;
Let me see, then, what thereat is, and this mystery explore—
Let my heart be still a moment and this mystery explore;—      *35*
                'Tis the wind and nothing more!"

Open here I flung the shutter, when, with many a flirt and flutter,
In there stepped a stately Raven of the saintly days of yore;
Not the least obeisance made he; not a minute stopped or stayed he;
But, with mien of lord or lady, perched above my chamber door—      *40*
Perched upon a bust of Pallas° just above my chamber door—
                Perched, and sat, and nothing more.

**41 Pallas** Athena, goddess of wisdom

Then this ebony bird beguiling my sad fancy into smiling,
By the grave and stern decorum of the countenance it wore,
"Though thy crest be shorn and shaven, thou," I said, "art sure no
    craven,                                                 45
Ghastly grim and ancient Raven wandering from the Nightly shore—
Tell me what thy lordly name is on the Night's Plutonian° shore!"
                       Quoth the Raven, "Nevermore."

Much I marvelled this ungainly fowl to hear discourse so plainly,
Though its answer little meaning—little relevancy bore;                50
For we cannot help agreeing that no living human being
Ever yet was blessed with seeing bird above his chamber door—
Bird or beast upon the sculptured bust above his chamber door,
                  With such name as "Nevermore."

But the Raven, sitting lonely on the placid bust, spoke only       55
That one word, as if his soul in that one word he did outpour.
Nothing farther then he uttered—not a feather then he fluttered—
Till I scarcely more than muttered, "Other friends have flown
    before—
On the morrow *he* will leave me, as my Hopes have flown before."
                Then the bird said, "Nevermore."     60

Startled at the stillness broken by reply so aptly spoken,
"Doubtless," said I, "what it utters is its only stock and store
Caught from some unhappy master whom unmerciful Disaster
Followed fast and followed faster till his songs one burden bore—
Till the dirges of his Hope that melancholy burden bore       65
              Of 'Never—nevermore.' "

But the Raven still beguiling all my sad fancy into smiling,
Straight I wheeled a cushioned seat in front of bird and bust and
    door;
Then, upon the velvet sinking, I betook myself to linking
Fancy unto fancy, thinking what this ominous bird of yore—     70
What this grim, ungainly, ghastly, gaunt, and ominous bird of yore
              Meant in croaking "Nevermore."

**47 Plutonian** after Pluto, Roman god of the underworld

This I sat engaged in guessing, but no syllable expressing
To the fowl whose fiery eyes now burned into my bosom's core;
This and more I sat divining, with my head at ease reclining    75
On the cushion's velvet lining that the lamp-light gloated o'er,
But whose velvet-violet lining with the lamp-light gloating o'er,
　　　　　*She* shall press, ah, nevermore!

Then, methought, the air grew denser, perfumed from an unseen
　　censer
Swung by seraphim whose foot-falls tinkled on the tufted floor.    80
"Wretch," I cried, "thy God hath lent thee—by these angels he
　　hath sent thee.
Respite—respite and nepenthe° from thy memories of Lenore;
Quaff, oh quaff this kind nepenthe and forget this lost Lenore!"
　　　　　Quoth the Raven, "Nevermore."

"Prophet!" said I, "thing of evil!—prophet still, if bird or devil!—    85
Whether Tempter sent, or whether tempest tossed thee here ashore,
Desolate yet all undaunted, on this desert land enchanted—
On this home by Horror haunted—tell me truly, I implore—
Is there—*is* there balm in Gilead?—tell me—tell me, I implore!"
　　　　　Quoth the Raven, "Nevermore."    90

"Prophet!" said I, "thing of evil!—prophet still, if bird or devil!
By that Heaven that bends above us—by that God we both adore—
Tell this soul with sorrow laden if, within the distant Aidenn,°
It shall clasp a sainted maiden whom the angels name Lenore—
Clasp a rare and radiant maiden whom the angels name Lenore."    95
　　　　　Quoth the Raven, "Nevermore."

"Be that word our sign of parting, bird or fiend!" I shrieked,
　　upstarting—
"Get thee back into the tempest and the Night's Plutonian shore!
Leave no black plume as a token of that lie thy soul hath spoken!
Leave my loneliness unbroken!—quit the bust above my door!    100
Take thy beak from out my heart, and take thy form from off my
　　door!"
　　　　　Quoth the Raven, "Nevermore."

**82 nepenthe** drug causing forgetfulness　**93 Aidenn** Eden

And the Raven, never flitting, still is sitting, *still* is sitting
On the pallid bust of Pallas just above my chamber door;
And his eyes have all the seeming of a demon's that is dreaming,          105
And the lamp-light o'er him streaming throws his shadow on
    the floor;
And my soul from out that shadow that lies floating on the floor
                           Shall be lifted—nevermore!

                                         *—1845*

# To Helen

Helen, thy beauty is to me
    Like those Nicean° barks of yore,
That gently, o'er a perfumed sea
    The weary, way-worn wanderer bore
    To his own native shore.          5

On desperate seas long wont to roam,
    Thy hyacinth° hair, thy classic face
Thy Naiad° airs have brought me home
    To the glory that was Greece
And the grandeur that was Rome.          10

Lo! in yon brilliant window-niche
    How statue-like I see thee stand!
    The agate lamp within thy hand,
Ah! Psyche,° from the regions which
    Are Holy Land!          15

                                           *—1831*

---

**2 Nicean** possibly of Nice (in the South of France); or Phoenician     **7 hyacinth** reddish, like the flower of Greek myth     **8 Naiad** water nymph     **14 Psyche** the soul

*Alfred Lord Tennyson (1809–1892) became the most famous English poet of his era with the 1850 publication of* In Memoriam, *a sequence of poems on the death of his friend Arthur Hallam. As poet laureate, he was an official apologist for Victorian England, but he often returned to the past for inspiration — to classical Greece for poems such as "Ulysses" and to Arthurian England for "The Lady of Shalott," a poem that has inspired many painters, including the Pre-Raphaelites.*

## *Alfred Lord Tennyson*
# The Lady of Shalott

### I

On either side the river lie
Long fields of barley and of rye,
That clothe the wold° and meet the sky;
And thro' the field the road runs by
  To many-tower'd Camelot;°         5
And up and down the people go,
Gazing where the lilies blow
Round an island there below,
  The island of Shalott.

Willows whiten, aspens quiver,           10
Little breezes dusk and shiver
Thro' the wave that runs forever
By the island in the river
  Flowing down to Camelot.
Four gray walls, and four gray towers,       15
Overlook a space of flowers,
And the silent isle imbowers
  The Lady of Shalott.

By the margin, willow-veil'd
Slide the heavy barges trail'd          20
By slow horses; and unhail'd

---

**3 wold** rolling uplands   **5 Camelot** King Arthur's legendary castle

The shallop° flitteth silken-sail'd
    Skimming down to Camelot:
But who hath seen her wave her hand?
Or at the casement seen her stand?            *25*
Or is she known in all the land,
    The Lady of Shalott?

Only reapers, reaping early
In among the bearded barley,
Hear a song that echoes cheerly           *30*
From the river winding clearly,
    Down to tower'd Camelot:
And by the moon the reaper weary,
Piling sheaves in uplands airy,
Listening, whispers "'Tis the fairy       *35*
    Lady of Shalott."

    II

There she weaves by night and day
A magic web with colors gay.
She has heard a whisper say,
A curse is on her if she stay           *40*
    To look down to Camelot.
She knows not what the curse may be,
And so she weaveth steadily,
And little other care hath she,
    The Lady of Shalott.           *45*

And moving thro' a mirror clear
That hangs before her all the year,
Shadows of the world appear.
There she sees the highway near
    Winding down to Camelot:         *50*
There the river eddy whirls,
And there the surly village churls,
And the red cloaks of market girls,
    Pass onward from Shalott.

---

**22 shallop** open boat propelled by oars or sail

Sometimes a troop of damsels glad,          *55*
An abbot on an ambling pad,°
Sometimes a curly shepherd lad,
Or long-hair'd page in crimson clad,
     Goes by to tower'd Camelot;
And sometimes through the mirror blue     *60*
The knights come riding two and two:
She hath no loyal knight and true,
     The Lady of Shalott.

But in her web she still delights
To weave the mirror's magic sights,     *65*
For often thro' the silent nights
A funeral, with plumes and lights
     And music, went to Camelot;
Or when the moon was overhead,
Came two young lovers lately wed:     *70*
"I am half-sick of shadows," said
     The Lady of Shalott.

### III

A bow-shot from her bower-eaves,
He rode between the barley-sheaves,
The sun came dazzling thro' the leaves,     *75*
And flamed upon the brazen greaves°
     Of bold Sir Lancelot.
A red-cross knight for ever kneel'd
To a lady in his shield,
That sparkled on the yellow field,     *80*
     Beside remote Shalott.

The gemmy bridle glitter'd free,
Like to some branch of stars we see
Hung in the golden Galaxy.
The bridle bells rang merrily     *85*
     As he rode down to Camelot:

---

**56 ambling pad** horse moving leisurely    **76 greaves** armour for the shins

And from his blazon'd baldric° slung
A mighty silver bugle hung,
And as he rode his armour rung,
    Beside remote Shalott.             *90*

All in the blue unclouded weather
Thick-jewel'd shone the saddle-leather,
The helmet and the helmet-feather
Burn'd like one burning flame together,
    As he rode down to Camelot.          *95*
As often thro' the purple night,
Below the starry clusters bright,
Some bearded meteor, trailing light,
    Moves over still Shalott.

His broad clear brow in sunlight glow'd;     *100*
On burnish'd hooves his war-horse trode;
From underneath his helmet flow'd
His coal-black curls as on he rode,
    As he rode down to Camelot.
From the bank and from the river         *105*
He flash'd into the crystal mirror,
"Tirra lirra," by the river
    Sang Sir Lancelot.

She left the web, she left the loom,
She made three paces thro' the room,       *110*
She saw the water-lily bloom,
She saw the helmet and the plume,
    She look'd down to Camelot.
Out flew the web and floated wide;
The mirror crack'd from side to side;       *115*
"The curse is come upon me," cried
    The Lady of Shalott.

---

**87 baldric** ornamented sash worn diagonally across the chest

IV

In the stormy east wind straining,
The pale yellow woods were waning,
The broad stream in his banks complaining,          *120*
Heavily the low sky raining
    Over tower'd Camelot;
Down she came and found a boat
Beneath a willow left afloat,
And round about the prow she wrote          *125*
    *The Lady of Shalott.*

And down the river's dim expanse
Like some bold seër in a trance,
Seeing all his own mischance—
With a glassy countenance          *130*
    Did she look to Camelot.
And at the closing of the day
She loosed the chain, and down she lay;
The broad stream bore her far away,
    The Lady of Shalott.          *135*

Lying, robed in snowy white
That loosely flew to left and right—
The leaves upon her falling light—
Thro' the noises of the night
    She floated down to Camelot;          *140*
And as the boat-head wound along
The willowy hills and fields among,
They heard her singing her last song,
    The Lady of Shalott.

Heard a carol, mournful, holy,          *145*
Chanted loudly, chanted lowly,
Till her blood was frozen slowly,
And her eyes were darken'd wholly,
    Turn'd to tower'd Camelot.

For ere she reach'd upon the tide                    *150*
The first house by the waterside,
Singing in her song she died,
    The Lady of Shalott.

Under tower and balcony,
By garden wall and gallery,                          *155*
A gleaming shape she floated by,
Dead-pale between the houses high,
    Silent into Camelot.
Out upon the wharfs they came,
Knight and burgher,° lord and dame,                  *160*
And round the prow they read her name,
    *The Lady of Shalott.*

Who is this? and what is here?
And in the lighted palace near
Died the sound of royal cheer;                       *165*
And they cross'd themselves for fear,
    All the knights at Camelot:
But Lancelot mused a little space;
He said, "She has a lovely face;
God in his mercy lend her grace,                     *170*
    The Lady of Shalott."

                                       —*1832*

**160 burgher** citizen

*Robert Browning (1812–1889) wrote many successful dramatic monologues that are his lasting legacy, for he brings the genre to a level of achievement rarely equalled. Less regarded during his lifetime than his contemporary Tennyson, he has consistently risen in the esteem of modern readers. Often overlooked in his gallery of often grotesque characters are his considerable metrical skills and ability to simulate speech while working in demanding poetic forms.*

# Robert Browning
## My Last Duchess

FERRARA°

That's my last duchess painted on the wall,
Looking as if she were alive. I call
That piece a wonder, now: Frà Pandolf's° hands
Worked busily a day, and there she stands.
Will't please you sit and look at her? I said          5
"Frà Pandolf" by design, for never read
Strangers like you that pictured countenance,
The depth and passion of its earnest glance,
But to myself they turned (since none puts by
The curtain I have drawn for you, but I)          10
And seemed as they would ask me, if they durst,
How such a glance came there; so, not the first
Are you to turn and ask thus. Sir, 'twas not
Her husband's presence only, called that spot
Of joy into the Duchess' cheek: perhaps          15
Frà Pandolf chanced to say "Her mantle laps
Over my lady's wrist too much," or "Paint
Must never hope to reproduce the faint
Half-flush that dies along her throat": such stuff
Was courtesy, she thought, and cause enough          20
For calling up that spot of joy. She had
A heart—how shall I say?—too soon made glad,
Too easily impressed; she liked whate'er

**Ferrara** The speaker is probably Alfonso II d'Este, Duke of Ferrara (1533–158?). **3 Frà Pandolf** an imaginary painter

She looked on, and her looks went everywhere.
Sir, 'twas all one! My favor at her breast,                        *25*
The dropping of the daylight in the West,
The bough of cherries some officious fool
Broke in the orchard for her, the white mule
She rode with round the terrace—all and each
Would draw from her alike the approving speech,              *30*
Or blush, at least. She thanked men—good! but thanked
Somehow—I know not how—as if she ranked
My gift of a nine-hundred-years-old name
With anybody's gift. Who'd stoop to blame
This sort of trifling? Even had you skill                          *35*
In speech—which I have not—to make your will
Quite clear to such an one, and say, "Just this
Or that in you disgusts me; here you miss,
Or there exceed the mark"—and if she let
Herself be lessoned so, nor plainly set                            *40*
Her wits to yours, forsooth, and made excuse,
—E'en then would be some stooping; and I choose
Never to stoop. Oh sir, she smiled, no doubt,
Whene'er I passed her; but who passed without
Much the same smile? This grew; I gave commands;          *45*
Then all smiles stopped together. There she stands
As if alive. Will't please you rise? We'll meet
The company below, then. I repeat,
The Count your master's° known munificence
Is ample warrant that no just pretense                             *50*
Of mine for dowry will be disallowed;
Though his fair daughter's self, as I avowed
At starting, is my object. Nay, we'll go
Together down, sir. Notice Neptune, though,
Taming a sea horse, thought a rarity,                              *55*
Which Claus of Innsbruck cast in bronze for me!

*—1842*

---

**49 Count your master's** The auditor is apparently an envoy sent to arrange a marriage between the
Duke of Ferrara and a count's daughter.

**Emily Brontë (1818–1848)** *Although best known for her fiercely passionate novel,* Wuthering Heights *(1847), set on the Yorkshire moors of England where she was raised, Brontë also wrote poetry that, according to her sister Charlotte, possessed "a peculiar music—wild, melancholy and elevating." The poetry of Charlotte, Emily, and Anne Brontë first appeared in* Poems by Currer, Ellis, and Acton Bell *(1846), but the book's poor reception inspired the three sisters to try writing novels.*

## *Emily Brontë*
# [Ah! why, because the dazzling sun]

Ah! why, because the dazzling sun
Restored my earth to joy
Have you° departed, every one,
And left a desert sky?

All through the night, your glorious eyes          5
Were gazing down in mine,
And with a full heart's thankful sighs
I blessed that watch divine!

I was at peace, and drank your beams
As they were life to me                              10
And revelled in my changeful dreams
Like petrel° on the sea.

Thought followed thought—star followed star
Through boundless regions on,
While one sweet influence, near and far,             15
Thrilled through and proved us one.

Why did the morning rise to break
So great, so pure a spell,
And scorch with fire the tranquil cheek
Where your cool radiance fell?                        20

---

**3 you** The poet is addressing the stars.   **12 petrel** small seabirds

Blood-red he rose, and arrow-straight
His fierce beams struck my brow:
The soul of Nature sprang elate,
But mine sank sad and low!

My lids closed down—yet through their veil                     25
I saw him blazing still;
And bathe in gold the misty dale,
And flash upon the hill.

I turned me to the pillow then
To call back Night, and see                                    30
Your worlds of solemn light, again
Throb with my heart and me!

It would not do—the pillow glowed
And glowed both roof and floor,
And birds sang loudly in the wood,                             35
And fresh winds shook the door.

The curtains waved, the wakened flies
Were murmuring round my room,
Imprisoned there, till I should rise
And give them leave to roam.                                   40

O Stars and Dreams and Gentle Night;
O Night and Stars return!
And hide me from the hostile light
That does not warm, but burn—

That drains the blood of suffering men;                        45
Drinks tears, instead of dew:
Let me sleep through his blinding reign,
And only wake with you!

—1845

*Alexander McLachlan (1818–1896) Known as the "Burns of Canada," McLachlan immigrated from Scotland to Ontario in 1840. He struggled as a farmer, eventually returning to tailoring, the profession for which he had trained. He also wrote five books of poetry between 1846 and 1874. Though he often celebrated the beauty of his adopted country, in this poem, he reveals the plight of the poor and the hypocrisy of those who fail to help.*

## *Alexander McLachlan*
# We Live in a Rickety House

We live in a rickety house,
    In a dirty dismal street,
Where the naked hide from day,
    And thieves and drunkards meet.

And pious folks with their tracts,°                   5
    When our dens they enter in,
They point to our shirtless backs,
    As the fruits of beer and gin.

And they quote us texts, to prove
    That our hearts are hard as stone;              10
And they feed us with the fact,
    That the fault is all our own.

And the parson comes and prays—
    He's very concerned 'bout our souls;
But he never asks, in the coldest days,          15
    How we may be off for coals.

It will be long ere the poor
    Will learn their grog° to shun;
While it's raiment, food and fire,
    And religion all in one.                   20

**5 tracts** short pamphlets on religious topics   **18 grog** alcohol

I wonder some pious folks
    Can look us straight in the face,
For our ignorance and crime
    Are the Church's shame and disgrace.

We live in a rickety house,                        25
    In a dirty dismal street,
Where the naked hide from day,
    And thieves and drunkards meet.

                                         —*1861*

---

*Walt Whitman (1819–1892) pioneered the use of free verse, which established him as one of the forebears of modern poetry, but his subject matter, often dealing with sexual topics, and his unsparing realism were equally controversial in his day. An admirer of Emerson, he adapted many of the ideas of transcendentalism in* Song of Myself, *his first major sequence, and also incorporated many of Emerson's calls for poets to use American subjects and patterns of speech.* Leaves of Grass, *which he revised from 1855 until his death, expanded to include virtually all of his poems, including the graphic poems he wrote while serving as a volunteer in Civil War army hospitals.*

# Walt Whitman
## *from* Song of Myself

### 1

I celebrate myself, and sing myself,
And what I assume you shall assume,
For every atom belonging to me as good belongs to you.

I loaf and invite my soul,
I lean and loaf at my ease observing a spear of summer grass.     5

My tongue, every atom of my blood, formed from this soil,
    this air,
Born here of parents born here from parents the same, and their
    parents the same,

I, now thirty-seven years old in perfect health begin,
Hoping to cease not till death.

Creeds and schools in abeyance,                                                    10
Retiring back a while sufficed at what they are, but never forgotten,
I harbor for good or bad, I permit to speak at every hazard,
Nature without check with original energy.

52

The spotted hawk swoops by and accuses me, he complains of my gab and
    my loitering.                                                1331

I too am not a bit tamed, I too am untranslatable,
I sound my barbaric yawp° over the roofs of the world.

The last scud of day holds back for me,
It flings my likeness after the rest and true as any on the shadowed
    wilds,                                                          1335
It coaxes me to the vapor and the dusk.

I depart as air, I shake my white locks at the runaway sun,
I effuse my flesh in eddies, and drift it in lacy jags.

I bequeath myself to the dirt to grow from the grass I love,
If you want me again look for me under your boot-soles.             1340

You will hardly know who I am or what I mean,
But I shall be good health to you nevertheless,
And filter and fiber your blood.

Failing to fetch me at first keep encouraged,
Missing me one place search another,                                        1345
I stop somewhere waiting for you.

—*1881*

1333 **yawp** harsh hoarse cry

*Matthew Arnold (1822–1888) was the son of the headmaster of Rugby School and himself served as an inspector of schools during much of his adult life. An influential essayist as well as a poet, Arnold was unsparing in his criticism of middle-class "Philistinism." At least part of "Dover Beach" is thought to date from his honeymoon in 1851.*

## Matthew Arnold
# Dover Beach

The sea is calm tonight.
The tide is full, the moon lies fair
Upon the straits; on the French coast the light
Gleams and is gone; the cliffs of England stand,
Glimmering and vast, out in the tranquil bay.                    5
Come to the window, sweet is the night-air!
Only, from the long line of spray
Where the sea meets the moon-blanched land,
Listen! you hear the grating roar
Of pebbles which the waves draw back, and fling,                 10
At their return, up the high strand,
Begin, and cease, and then again begin,
With tremulous cadence slow, and bring
The eternal note of sadness in.

Sophocles° long ago                                              15
Heard it on the Aegean, and it brought
Into his mind the turbid ebb and flow
Of human misery; we
Find also in the sound a thought,
Hearing it by this distant northern sea.                         20

The Sea of Faith
Was once, too, at the full, and round earth's shore
Lay like the folds of a bright girdle° furled.
But now I only hear

---

**15 Sophocles** Athenian tragic poet (496–406 B.C.)   **23 girdle** sash

Its melancholy, long, withdrawing roar, 25
Retreating, to the breath
Of the night-wind, down the vast edges drear
And naked shingles° of the world.

Ah, love, let us be true
To one another! for the world, which seems 30
To lie before us like a land of dreams,
So various, so beautiful, so new,
Hath really neither joy, nor love, nor light,
Nor certitude, nor peace, nor help for pain;
And we are here as on a darkling plain 35
Swept with confused alarms of struggle and flight,
Where ignorant armies clash by night.

—*1867*

---

*Emily Dickinson (1830–1886) has been reinvented with each generation, and readers' views of her have ranged between two extremes —one perceiving her as the abnormally shy "Belle of Amherst" making poetry out of her own neuroses and another seeing her as a protofeminist carving out a world of her own in self-willed isolation. What remains is her brilliant poetry —unique, original, and marked with the stamp of individual talent. Dickinson published only seven poems during her life- time, but left behind hundreds of poems in manuscript at her death. Published by her relatives, they were immediately popular, but it was not until the edition of Thomas Johnson in 1955 that they were read with Dickinson's eccentric punctuation and capitalization intact.*

## *Emily Dickinson*
# [I died for Beauty—but was scarce

I died for Beauty—but was scarce
Adjusted in the Tomb
When One who died for Truth, was lain
In an adjoining Room—

**28 shingles** beach pebbles

He questioned softly "Why I failed?"                                    5
"For Beauty," I replied—
"And I—for Truth—Themself are One—
We Brethren, are," He said—

And so, as Kinsmen, met a Night—
We talked between the Rooms—                                          10
Until the Moss had reached our lips—
And covered up—our names—

                                                                    —*1890*

# [I had been hungry, all the Years—]

I had been hungry, all the Years—
My Noon had Come—to dine—
I trembling drew the Table near—
And touched the Curious Wine—

'Twas this on Tables I had seen—                                       5
When turning, hungry, Home
I looked in Windows, for the Wealth
I could not hope—for Mine—

I did not know the ample Bread—
'Twas so unlike the Crumb                                             10
The Birds and I, had often shared
In Nature's—Dining Room—

The Plenty hurt me—'twas so new—
Myself felt ill—and odd—
As Berry—of a Mountain Bush—                                         15
Transplanted—to the Road—

Nor was I hungry—so I found
That Hunger—was a way
Of Persons outside Windows—
The Entering—takes away—                                        *20*

                                                            *—1891*

---

*Christina Rossetti (1830–1894) was the younger sister of the Pre-Raphaelite painter Dante Gabriel Rossetti, who illustrated one of her most famous poems, "Goblin Market" (1862). Explored from many critical perspectives (feminist, religious, psychological, economic, creative, etc.), this poem reveals new dimensions of a poet once defined by her invalidism and devotional poetry. Christina Rossetti published six collections of poetry, as well as short stories, works for children, and religious essays.*

## Christina Rossetti
# Goblin Market

Morning and evening
Maids heard the goblins cry:
"Come buy our orchard fruits,
Come buy, come buy:
Apples and quinces,                                              *5*
Lemons and oranges,
Plump unpecked cherries—
Melons and raspberries,
Bloom-down-cheeked peaches,
Swart-headed° mulberries,                                        *10*
Wild free-born cranberries,
Crab-apples, dewberries,
Pine-apples, blackberries,
Apricots, strawberries—
All ripe together                                               *15*

---

**10 swart-headed** dark

In summer weather—
Morns that pass by,
Fair eves that fly;
Come buy, come buy;
Our grapes fresh from the vine,                                    20
Pomegranates full and fine,
Dates and sharp bullaces,°
Rare pears and greengages,
Damsons and bilberries,
Taste them and try:                                                25
Currants and gooseberries,
Bright-fire-like barberries,
Figs to fill your mouth,
Citrons from the South,
Sweet to tongue and sound to eye,                                  30
Come buy, come buy."

Evening by evening
Among the brookside rushes,
Laura bowed her head to hear,
Lizzie veiled her blushes:                                         35
Crouching close together
In the cooling weather,
With clasping arms and cautioning lips,
With tingling cheeks and finger-tips.
"Lie close," Laura said,                                           40
Pricking up her golden head:
We must not look at goblin men,
We must not buy their fruits:
Who knows upon what soil they fed
Their hungry thirsty roots?"                                       45
"Come buy," call the goblins
Hobbling down the glen.
"O! cried Lizzie, Laura, Laura,
You should not peep at goblin men."
Lizzie covered up her eyes                                         50

**22 bullaces** type of plum as are greengages and damsons

Covered close lest they should look;
Laura reared her glossy head,
And whispered like the restless brook:
"Look, Lizzie, look, Lizzie,
Down the glen tramp little men.                                    55
One hauls a basket,
One bears a plate,
One lugs a golden dish
Of many pounds' weight.
How fair the vine must grow                                        60
Whose grapes are so luscious;
How warm the wind must blow
Through those fruit bushes."
"No," said Lizzie, "no, no, no;
Their offers should not charm us,                                  65
Their evil gifts would harm us."
She thrust a dimpled finger
In each ear, shut eyes and ran:
Curious Laura chose to linger
Wondering at each merchant man.                                    70
One had a cat's face,
One whisked a tail,
One tramped at a rat's pace,
One crawled like a snail,
One like a wombat prowled obtuse and furry,                        75
One like a ratel° tumbled hurry-scurry.
Lizzie heard a voice like voice of doves
Cooing all together:
They sounded kind and full of loves
In the pleasant weather.                                           80

Laura stretched her gleaming neck
Like a rush-imbedded swan,
Like a lily from the beck,°
Like a moonlit poplar branch,
Like a vessel at the launch                                        85
When its last restraint is gone.

**76 ratel** honey badger    **83 beck** stream

Backwards up the mossy glen
Turned and trooped the goblin men,
With their shrill repeated cry,
"Come buy, come buy."                                    90
When they reached where Laura was
They stood stock still upon the moss,
Leering at each other,
Brother with queer brother;
Signalling each other,                                   95
Brother with sly brother.
One set his basket down,
One reared his plate;
One began to weave a crown
Of tendrils, leaves, and rough nuts brown               100
(Men sell not such in any town);
One heaved the golden weight
Of dish and fruit to offer her:
"Come buy, come buy," was still their cry.
Laura stared but did not stir,                          105
Longed but had no money:
The whisk-tailed merchant bade her taste
In tones as smooth as honey,
The cat-faced purr'd,
The rat-paced spoke a word                              110
Of welcome, and the snail-paced even was heard;
One parrot-voiced and jolly
Cried "Pretty Goblin" still for "Pretty Polly";
One whistled like a bird.

But sweet-tooth Laura spoke in haste:                   115
"Good folk, I have no coin;
To take were to purloin:
I have no copper in my purse,
I have no silver either,
And all my gold is on the furze°                        120
That shakes in windy weather

**120 furze** bush bearing yellow flowers

Above the rusty heather."
"You have much gold upon your head,"
They answered altogether:
"Buy from us with a golden curl."                                    125
She clipped a precious golden lock,
She dropped a tear more rare than pearl,
Then sucked their fruit globes fair or red:
Sweeter than honey from the rock,
Stronger than man-rejoicing wine,                                    130
Clearer than water flowed that juice;
She never tasted such before,
How should it cloy with length of use?
She sucked and sucked and sucked the more
Fruits which that unknown orchard bore,                              135
She sucked until her lips were sore;
Then flung the emptied rinds away,
But gathered up one kernel stone,
And knew not was it night or day
As she turned home alone.                                            140

Lizzie met her at the gate
Full of wise upbraidings:
"Dear, you should not stay so late,
Twilight is not good for maidens;
Should not loiter in the glen                                        145
In the haunts of goblin men.
Do you not remember Jeanie,
How she met them in the moonlight,
Took their gifts both choice and many,
Ate their fruits and wore their flowers                             150
Plucked from bowers
Where summer ripens at all hours?
But ever in the moonlight
She pined and pined away;
Sought them by night and day,                                        155
Found them no more, but dwindled and grew gray;
Then fell with the first snow,
While to this day no grass will grow

Where she lies low:
I planted daisies there a year ago                    *160*
That never blow.
You should not loiter so."
"Nay hush," said Laura.
"Nay hush, my sister:
I ate and ate my fill,                                *165*
Yet my mouth waters still;
To-morrow night I will
Buy more," and kissed her.
"Have done with sorrow;
I'll bring you plums to-morrow                        *170*
Fresh on their mother twigs,
Cherries worth getting;
You cannot think what figs
My teeth have met in,
What melons, icy-cold                •                *175*
Piled on a dish of gold
Too huge for me to hold,
What peaches with a velvet nap,
Pellucid grapes without one seed:
Odorous indeed must be the mead                       *180*
Whereon they grow, and pure the wave they drink,
With lilies at the brink,
And sugar-sweet their sap."

Golden head by golden head,
Like two pigeons in one nest                          *185*
Folded in each other's wings,
They lay down, in their curtained bed:
Like two blossoms on one stem,
Like two flakes of new-fallen snow,
Like two wands of ivory                               *190*
Tipped with gold for awful° kings.
Moon and stars beamed in at them,        ·
Wind sang to them lullaby,
Lumbering owls forbore to fly,

**191 awful** inspiring awe

Not a bat flapped to and fro                                          *195*
Round their rest:
Cheek to cheek and breast to breast
Locked together in one nest.

Early in the morning
When the first cock crowed his warning,                               *200*
Neat like bees, as sweet and busy,
Laura rose with Lizzie:
Fetched in honey, milked the cows,
Aired and set to rights the house,
Kneaded cakes of whitest wheat,                                       *205*
Cakes for dainty mouths to eat,
Next churned butter, whipped up cream,
Fed their poultry, sat and sewed;
Talked as modest maidens should
Lizzie with an open heart,                                            *210*
Laura in an absent dream,
One content, one sick in part;
One warbling for the mere bright day's delight,
One longing for the night.

At length slow evening came—                                          *215*
They went with pitchers to the reedy brook;
Lizzie most placid in her look,
Laura most like a leaping flame.
They drew the gurgling water from its deep
Lizzie plucked purple and rich golden flags,                          *220*
Then turning homeward said: "The sunset flushes
Those furthest loftiest crags;
Come, Laura, not another maiden lags,
No wilful squirrel wags,
The beasts and birds are fast asleep."                                *225*
But Laura loitered still among the rushes
And said the bank was steep.

And said the hour was early still,
The dew not fallen, the wind not chill:
Listening ever, but not catching                                      *230*

The customary cry,
"Come buy, come buy,"
With its iterated jingle
Of sugar-baited words:
Not for all her watching                                          235
Once discerning even one goblin
Racing, whisking, tumbling, hobbling;
Let alone the herds
That used to tramp along the glen,
In groups or single,                                             240
Of brisk fruit-merchant men.

Till Lizzie urged, "O Laura, come,
I hear the fruit-call, but I dare not look:
You should not loiter longer at this brook:
Come with me home.                                               245
The stars rise, the moon bends her arc,
Each glow-worm winks her spark,
Let us get home before the night grows dark;
For clouds may gather even
Though this is summer weather,                                   250
Put out the lights and drench us through;
Then if we lost our way what should we do?"

Laura turned cold as stone
To find her sister heard that cry alone,
That goblin cry,                                                 255
"Come buy our fruits, come buy."
Must she then buy no more such dainty fruit?
Must she no more such succous pasture find,
Gone deaf and blind?
Her tree of life drooped from the root:                          260
She said not one word in her heart's sore ache;
But peering thro' the dimness, naught discerning,
Trudged home, her pitcher dripping all the way;
So crept to bed, and lay
Silent 'til Lizzie slept;                                        265

Then sat up in a passionate yearning,
And gnashed her teeth for balked desire, and wept
As if her heart would break.

Day after day, night after night,
Laura kept watch in vain,                                                      270
In sullen silence of exceeding pain.
She never caught again the goblin cry:
"Come buy, come buy,"
She never spied the goblin men
Hawking their fruits along the glen:                                           275
But when the noon waxed bright
Her hair grew thin and gray;
She dwindled, as the fair full moon doth turn
To swift decay, and burn
Her fire away.                                                                 280

One day remembering her kernel-stone
She set it by a wall that faced the south;
Dewed it with tears, hoped for a root,
Watched for a waxing shoot,
But there came none;                                                           285
It never saw the sun,
It never felt the trickling moisture run:
While with sunk eyes and faded mouth
She dreamed of melons, as a traveller sees
False waves in desert drouth                                                   290
With shade of leaf-crowned trees,
And burns the thirstier in the sandful breeze.

She no more swept the house,
Tended the fowls or cows,
Fetched honey, kneaded cakes of wheat,                                         295
Brought water from the brook:
But sat down listless in the chimney-nook
And would not eat.

Tender Lizzie could not bear
To watch her sister's cankerous° care,                    *300*
Yet not to share.
She night and morning
Caught the goblins' cry:
"Come buy our orchard fruits,
Come buy, come buy."                                       *305*
Beside the brook, along the glen
She heard the tramp of goblin men,
The voice and stir
Poor Laura could not hear;
Longed to buy fruit to comfort her,                        *310*
But feared to pay too dear,

She thought of Jeanie in her grave,
Who should have been a bride;
But who for joys brides hope to have
Fell sick and died                                         *315*
In her gay prime,
In earliest winter-time,
With the first glazing rime,
With the first snow-fall of crisp winter-time.

Till Laura, dwindling,                                     *320*
Seemed knocking at Death's door:
Then Lizzie weighed no more
Better and worse,
But put a silver penny in her purse,
Kissed Laura, crossed the heath with clumps of furze       *325*
At twilight, halted by the brook,
And for the first time in her life
Began to listen and look.

Laughed every goblin
When they spied her peeping:                               *330*
Came towards her hobbling,
Flying, running, leaping,
Puffing and blowing,

**300 cankerous** eating away

Chuckling, clapping, crowing,
Clucking and gobbling, 335
Mopping and mowing,
Full of airs and graces,
Pulling wry faces,
Demure grimaces,
Cat-like and rat-like, 340
Ratel and wombat-like,
Snail-paced in a hurry,
Parrot-voiced and whistler,
Helter-skelter, hurry-skurry,
Chattering like magpies, 345
Fluttering like pigeons,
Gliding like fishes,—
Hugged her and kissed her;
Squeezed and caressed her;
Stretched up their dishes, 350
Panniers and plates:
"Look at our apples
Russet and dun,
Bob at our cherries
Bite at our peaches, 355
Citrons and dates,
Grapes for the asking,
Pears red with basking
Out in the sun,
Plums on their twigs; 360
Pluck them and suck them,
Pomegranates, figs."

"Good folk," said Lizzie,
Mindful of Jeanie,
"Give me much and many";— 365
Held out her apron,
Tossed them her penny.
"Nay, take a seat with us,
Honor and eat with us,"

They answered grinning;                                          *370*
"Our feast is but beginning.
Night yet is early,
Warm and dew-pearly,
Wakeful and starry:
Such fruits as these                                             *375*
No man can carry;
Half their bloom would fly,
Half their dew would dry,
Half their flavor would pass by.
Sit down and feast with us,                                      *380*
Be welcome guest with us,
Cheer you and rest with us."
"Thank you," said Lizzie; "but one waits
At home alone for me:
So, without further parleying,                                   *385*
If you will not sell me any
Of your fruits though much and many,
Give me back my silver penny
I tossed you for a fee."
They began to scratch their pates,                               *390*
No longer wagging, purring,
But visibly demurring,
Grunting and snarling.
One called her proud,
Cross-grained, uncivil;                                          *395*
Their tones waxed loud,
Their looks were evil.
Lashing their tails
They trod and hustled her,
Elbowed and jostled her,                                         *400*
Clawed with their nails,
Barking, mewing, hissing, mocking,
Tore her gown and soiled her stocking,
Twitched her hair out by the roots,
Stamped upon her tender feet,                                    *405*
Held her hands and squeezed their fruits
Against her mouth to make her eat.

White and golden Lizzie stood,
Like a lily in a flood,
Like a rock of blue-veined stone                      *410*
Lashed by tides obstreperously,—
Like a beacon left alone
In a hoary roaring sea,
Sending up a golden fire,—
Like a fruit-crowned orange-tree                    *415*
White with blossoms honey-sweet
Sore beset by wasp and bee,—
Like a royal virgin town
Topped with gilded dome and spire
Close beleaguered by a fleet                       *420*
Mad to tear her standard down.

One may lead a horse to water,
Twenty cannot make him drink.
Though the goblins cuffed and caught her,
Coaxed and fought her,                            *425*
Bullied and besought her,
Scratched her, pinched her black as ink,
Kicked and knocked her,
Mauled and mocked her,
Lizzie uttered not a word;                       *430*
Would not open lip from lip
Lest they should cram a mouthful in;
But laughed in heart to feel the drip
Of juice that syruped all her face,
And lodged in dimples of her chin,              *435*
And streaked her neck which quaked like curd.
At last the evil people,
Worn out by her resistance,
Flung back her penny, kicked their fruit
Along whichever road they took,              *440*
Not leaving root or stone or shoot.
Some writhed into the ground,
Some dived into the brook
With ring and ripple.

Some scudded on the gale without a sound,                                    445
Some vanished in the distance.

In a smart, ache, tingle,
Lizzie went her way;
Knew not was it night or day;
Sprang up the bank, tore through the furze,                                  450
Threaded copse and dingle,
And heard her penny jingle
Bouncing in her purse,—
Its bounce was music to her ear.
She ran and ran                                                              455
As if she feared some goblin man
Dogged her with gibe or curse
Or something worse:
But not one goblin skurried after,
Nor was she pricked by fear;                                                 460
The kind heart made her windy-paced
That urged her home quite out of breath with haste
And inward laughter.

She cried "Laura," up the garden,
"Did you miss me?                                                            465
Come and kiss me.
Never mind my bruises,
Hug me, kiss me, suck my juices
Squeezed from goblin fruits for you,
Goblin pulp and goblin dew.                                                  470
Eat me, drink me, love me;
Laura, make much of me:
For your sake I have braved the glen
And had to do with goblin merchant men."

Laura started from her chair,                                                475
Flung her arms up in the air,
Clutched her hair:
"Lizzie, Lizzie, have you tasted
For my sake the fruit forbidden?
Must your light like mine be hidden,                                         480

Your young life like mine be wasted,
Undone in mine undoing,
And ruined in my ruin;
Thirsty, cankered, goblin-ridden?"
She clung about her sister,                                    *485*
Kissed and kissed and kissed her:
Tears once again
Refreshed her shrunken eyes,
Dropping like rain
After long sultry drouth;                                      *490*
Shaking with anguish, fear, and pain,
She kissed and kissed her with a hungry mouth.

Her lips began to scorch,
That juice was wormwood to her tongue,
She loathed the feast:                                         *495*
Writhing as one possessed she leaped and sung,
Rent all her robe, and wrung
Her hands in lamentable haste,
And beat her breast.
Her locks streamed like the torch                              *500*
Borne by a racer at full speed,
Or like the mane of horses in their flight,
Or like an eagle when she stems° the light
Straight toward the sun,
Or like a caged thing freed,                                   *505*
Or like a flying flag when armies run.

Swift fire spread through her veins, knocked at her heart,
Met the fire smouldering there
And overbore its lesser flame,
She gorged on bitterness without a name:                       *510*
Ah! fool, to choose such part
Of soul-consuming care!
Sense failed in the mortal strife:
Like the watch-tower of a town
Which an earthquake shatters down,                             *515*

**503 stems** makes headway against

Like a lightning-stricken mast,
Like a wind-uprooted tree
Spun about,
Like a foam-topped water-spout
Cast down headlong in the sea,                               520
She fell at last;
Pleasure past and anguish past,
Is it death or is it life ?

Life out of death.
That night long Lizzie watched by her,                      525
Counted her pulse's flagging stir,
Felt for her breath,
Held water to her lips, and cooled her face
With tears and fanning leaves:
But when the first birds chirped about their eaves,         530
And early reapers plodded to the place
Of golden sheaves,
And dew-wet grass
Bowed in the morning winds so brisk to pass,
And new buds with new day                                   535
Opened of cup-like lilies on the stream,
Laura awoke as from a dream,
Laughed in the innocent old way,
Hugged Lizzie but not twice or thrice;
Her gleaming locks showed not one thread of gray,           540
Her breath was sweet as May,
And light danced in her eyes.

Days, weeks, months, years
Afterwards, when both were wives
With children of their own;                                 545
Their mother-hearts beset with fears,
Their lives bound up in tender lives;
Laura would call the little ones
And tell them of her early prime,
Those pleasant days long gone                               550
Of not-returning time:
Would talk about the haunted glen,

The wicked, quaint fruit-merchant men,
Their fruits like honey to the throat,
But poison in the blood;                                                         555
(Men sell not such in any town);
Would tell them how her sister stood
In deadly peril to do her good,
And win the fiery antidote:
Then joining hands to little hands                                              560
Would bid them cling together,
"For there is no friend like a sister,
In calm or stormy weather,
To cheer one on the tedious way,
To fetch one if one goes astray,                                                 565
To lift one if one totters down,
To strengthen whilst one stands."

                                                                    —*1830*

---

*Thomas Hardy (1840–1928), after the disappointing response to his novel* Jude
the Obscure *in 1895, returned to his first love, writing poetry for the last thirty years
of his long life. The language and life of Hardy's native Wessex inform both his novels
and poems. His subject matter is very much of the nineteenth century, but his ironic,
disillusioned point of view marks him as one of the chief predecessors of modernism.*

## *Thomas Hardy*
# The Convergence
# of the Twain

LINES ON THE LOSS OF THE TITANIC

1

      In a solitude of the sea
      Deep from human vanity,
And the Pride of Life that planned her, stilly couches she.

2

Steel chambers, late the pyres
Of her salamadrine fires,°                                    5
Cold currents thrid,° and turn to rhythmic tidal lyres.

3

Over the mirrors meant
To glass the opulent
The sea-worm crawls—grotesque, slimed, dumb, indifferent.

4

Jewels in joy designed                                        10
To ravish the sensuous mind
Lie lightless, all their sparkles bleared and black and blind.

5

Dim moon-eyed fishes near
Gaze at the gilded gear
And query: "What does this vaingloriousness down here?"        15

6

Well: while was fashioning
This creature of cleaving wing,
The Immanent Will° that stirs and urges everything

7

Prepared a sinister mate
For her—so gaily great—                                       20
A Shape of Ice, for the time far and dissociate.

8

And as the smart ship grew
In stature, grace, and hue,
In shadowy silent distance grew the Iceberg too.

---

**5 salamandrine fires** The salamander, according to legend, could live in fire.   **6 thrid** thread
**18 Immanent Will** term used by Hardy for fate

**9**

     Alien they seemed to be:         25
     No mortal eye could see
The intimate welding of their later history,

**10**

     Or sign that they were bent
     By paths coincident
On being anon twin halves of one august event,       30

**11**

     Till the Spinner of the Years
     Said "Now!" And each one hears,
And consummation comes, and jars two hemispheres.

*—1912*

---

*Gerard Manley Hopkins (1844–1889) was an English Jesuit priest who developed elaborate theories of poetic metre (what he called "sprung rhythm") and language to express his own spiritual ardour. Most of his work was posthumously printed through the efforts of his Oxford friend and later correspondent Robert Bridges, who was poet laureate.*

## Gerard Manley Hopkins
# God's Grandeur

The world is charged with the grandeur of God.
   It will flame out, like shining from shook foil;°
   It gathers to a greatness, like the ooze of oil
Crushed.° Why do men then now not reck his rod?
Generations have trod, have trod, have trod;     5
   And all is seared with trade; bleared, smeared with toil;
   And wears man's smudge and shares man's smell: the soil
Is bare now, nor can foot feel, being shod.

---

**2 foil** gold leaf    **4 Crushed** Hopkins is referring to olive oil.

And for all this, nature is never spent;
   There lives the dearest freshness deep down things;       *10*
And though the last lights off the black West went
    Oh, morning, at the brown brink eastward, springs—
Because the Holy Ghost over the bent
    World broods with warm breast and with ah! bright wings.

                         *—1877*

# Pied Beauty

Glory be to God for dappled things—
    For skies of couple-color as a brinded° cow;
       For rose-moles all in stipple upon trout that swim;
Fresh-firecoal chestnut-falls;° finches' wings;
    Landscape plotted and pieced—fold, fallow, and plough;      *5*
      And all trades, their gear and tackle and trim.
All things counter, original, spare, strange;
    Whatever is fickle, freckled (who knows how?)
      With swift, slow; sweet, sour; adazzle, dim;
He fathers-forth whose beauty is past change:          *10*
       Praise him.

                         *—1877*

---

**2 brinded** streaked   **4 Fresh-firecoal chestnut-falls** According to the poet, chestnuts have a red colour.

*Isabella Valancy Crawford (1850–1887) Born in Dublin, Ireland, Crawford came with her family to Canada in 1858, and lived in various Ontario locations, finally settling in Toronto, where she published her only book of verse,* Old Spookses' Pass, Malcolm's Katie, and Other Poems *(1884). Long dismissed, she is now considered an important and versatile early Canadian poet. Though Crawford published "The Dark Stag" separately, the lyric is part of a long unfinished poem known as "Hugh and Ion."*

# Isabella Valancy Crawford
# The Dark Stag

A startl'd stag the blue grey night
Leaps down beyond dark pines
Behind, a length of yellow light,
    The Hunter's arrow shines
His moccasins are stain'd with red           5
    He bends upon his knee
From cov'ring peaks his shafts are sped
The blue mists plume his mighty head!
    Well may the dark stag flee!

The pale moon like a snow-white doe        10
    Bounds by his dappl'd flank;
They beat the stars down as they go
    As wood-bells growing rank.
The winds lift dew-laps from the ground
    Leap from dry shaking reeds         15
Their hoarse bays shake the cedars round—
With keen cries on the trail they bound—
    Swift, swift the dark stag speeds!

Roar the rent lakes, as through the waves
    Their silver warriors plunge        20
As vaults from core of crystal caves
    The vast, fierce Maskelonge.°
Red torches of the sumach glow
    Fall's council fires are lit

**22 Maskelonge** a large pike prized by fishermen

The bittern, squaw-like scolds the air                            25
The wild duck splashes loudly, where
   The waving rice-spears knit.

Shaft after shaft the red sun speeds—
   Rent the stag's dappl'd side,
His breast to fangs of hoarse winds bleeds              30
   He staggers on the tide.
He feels the hungry waves of space
   Rush at him high and blue
The white spray smites his dusky face
Swifter the sun's swift arrows race                            35
   And pierce his strong heart through.

Away! his white doe far behind
   Lies wounded on the plain
Yells at his flank the nimblest wind—
   His large tears fall like rain                         40
Like lily-pads shall clouds grow white
   About his darkling way
From her bald nest upon the height
The red-ey'd eagle sees his flight
He falters—turns—the antler'd night                        45
   The black stag stands at bay!

His feet are in the waves of space
   His antlers broad and dun,
He low'rs, and turns his velvet face
   To front the hunter sun,
He stamps the lilied clouds and high,                        50
   His branches fill the west—
The lean stork sails across the sky—
The shy loon shrieks to see him die
   The winds leap at his breast.

His antlers fall—once more he spurns
   The hoarse hounds of the day                    55
His blood upon the crisp blue burns
   Reddens the mounting spray.

His branches smite the wave—with cries       *60*
    The shrill winds pausing, flag
He sinks in space—red glow the skies;
The brown earth crimsons as he dies,
    The stout and lusty stag!

                                      *—1883*

---

*Charles G. D. Roberts (1860–1943) Born in New Brunswick, Roberts was raised by the Tantramar Marshes, which are the subject of this poem on the theme of change, written in the tradition of Wordsworth. One of the most prolific of the "Confederation Poets," who included Archibald Lampman and Duncan Campbell Scott, Roberts was also known for his sonnets and animal stories.*

# *Charles G. D. Roberts*
# Tantramar° Revisited

Summers and summers have come, and gone with the flight of the
    swallow;
Sunshine and thunder have been, storm, and winter, and frost;
Many and many a sorrow has all but died from remembrance,
Many a dream of joy fall'n in the shadow of pain.
Hands of chance and change have marred, or moulded, or
    broken,                                                  *5*
Busy with spirit or flesh, all I most have adored;
Even the bosom of Earth is strewn with heavier shadows,—
Only in these green hills, aslant to the sea, no change!
Here where the road that has climbed from the inland valleys and
    woodlands,
Dips from the hill-tops down, straight to the base of the hills,—   *10*
Here, from my vantage-ground, I can see the scattering houses,
Stained with time, set warm in orchards, meadows, and wheat,
Dotting the broad bright slopes outspread to southward and
    eastward,
Wind-swept all day long, blown by the south-east wind.

**Tantramar** a fertile area of marshes and rivers flowing into Chignecto Bay and the Bay of Fundy where New Brunswick and Nova Scotia join, near the childhood home of Charles G. D. Roberts

Skirting the sunbright uplands stretches a riband° of meadow,     *15*
Shorn of the labouring grass, bulwarked well from the sea,
Fenced on its seaward border with long clay dikes from
    the turbid
Surge and flow of the tides vexing the Westmoreland shores.
Yonder, toward the left, lie broad the Westmoreland
    marshes,—
Miles on miles they extend, level, and grassy, and dim,     *20*
Clear from the long red sweep of flats to the sky in the
    distance,
Save for the outlying heights, green-rampired° Cumberland
    Point;
Miles on miles outrolled, and the river-channels divide them,—
Miles on miles of green, barred by the hurtling gusts.

Miles on miles beyond the tawny bay is Minudie.°     *25*
There are the low blue hills; villages gleam at their feet.
Nearer a white sail shines across the water, and nearer
Still are the slim, grey masts of fishing boats dry on the flats.
Ah, how well I remember those wide red flats, above
    tide-mark
Pale with scurf° of the salt, seamed and baked in the sun!     *30*
Well I remember the piles of blocks and ropes, and the net-reels
Wound with the beaded nets, dripping and dark from the sea!
Now at this season the nets are unwound; they hang from
    the rafters
Over the fresh-stowed hay in upland barns, and the wind
Blows all day through the chinks, with the streaks of sunlight,
    and sways them     *35*
Softly at will; or they lie heaped in the gloom of a loft.

Now at this season the reels are empty and idle; I see them
Over the lines of the dikes, over the gossiping grass.
Now at this season they swing in the long strong wind,
    thro' the lonesome
Golden afternoon, shunned by the foraging gulls.     *40*

---

**15 riband** ribbon   **22 green-rampired** The green slopes are like ramparts or fortifications.
**25 Minudie** village that lies across the Bay of Fundy in Nova Scotia   **30 scurf** flaky deposits

Near about sunset the crane will journey homeward above
    them;
Round them, under the moon, all the calm night long,
Winnowing soft grey wings of marsh-owls wander and wander,
Now to the broad, lit marsh, now to the dusk of the dike.
Soon, thro' their dew-wet frames, in the live keen freshness of
    morning,         *45*
Out of the teeth of the dawn blows back the awakening wind.
Then, as the blue day mounts, and the low-shot shafts of the
    sunlight
Glance from the tide to the shore, gossamers jewelled with dew
Sparkle and wave, where late sea-spoiling fathoms of drift-net
Myriad-meshed, uploomed sombrely over the land.         *50*

Well I remember it all. The salt, raw scent of the margin;
While, with men at the windlass, groaned each reel, and the net,
Surging in ponderous lengths, uprose and coiled in its station;
Then each man to his home,—well I remember it all!

Yet, as I sit and watch, this present peace of the landscape,—    *55*
Stranded boats, these reels empty and idle, the hush,
One grey hawk slow-wheeling above yon cluster of haystacks,—
More than the old-time stir this stillness welcomes me home.
Ah, the old-time stir, how once it stung me with rapture,—
Old-time sweetness, the winds freighted with honey and salt!    *60*
Yet will I stay my steps and not go down to the marshland,—
Muse and recall far off, rather remember than see,—
Lest on too close sight I miss the darling illusion,
Spy at their task even here the hands of chance and change.

                        *—1886*

*Pauline Johnson (1861–1913) Born on the Six Nations Reserve near Brantford, Ontario, Johnson was the daughter of an Englishwoman and a Mohawk chief, a mixed heritage that defined her poetry and her performance career, which included extensive touring across Canada and internationally. Her collections include* The White Wampum *(1895),* Canadian Born *(1903), and* Flint and Feather *(1912).*

# Pauline Johnson
## The Idlers

The sun's red pulses beat,
Full prodigal of heat,
Full lavish of its lustre unrepressed;
But we have drifted far
From where his kisses are,                                    5
And in this landward-lying shade we let our paddles rest.

The river, deep and still,
The maple-mantled hill,
The little yellow beach whereon we lie,
The puffs of heated breeze,                                  10
All sweetly whisper—These
Are days that only come in a Canadian July.

So, silently we two
Lounge in our still canoe,
Nor fate, nor fortune matters to us now:                    15
So long as we alone
May call this dream our own,
The breeze may die, the sail may droop, we care not
      when or how.

Against the thwart, near by,
Inactively you lie,                                          20
And all too near my arm your temple bends.
Your indolently crude,
Abandoned attitude,
Is one of ease and art, in which a perfect languor blends.

Your costume, loose and light,                                                25
Leaves unconcealed your might
Of muscle, half-suspected, half defined;
And falling well aside,
Your vesture opens wide,
Above your splendid sunburnt throat that pulses unconfined.      30

With easy unreserve,
Across the gunwale's curve,
Your arm superb is lying, brown and bare;
Your hand just touches mine
With import firm and fine,                                                    35
(I kiss the very wind that blows about your tumbled hair).

Ah! Dear, I am unwise
In echoing your eyes
Whene'er they leave their far-off gaze, and turn
To melt and blur my sight;                                                    40
For every other light
Is servile to your cloud-grey eyes, wherein cloud shadows burn.

But once the silence breaks,
But once your ardour wakes
To words that humanize this lotus-land;°                              45
So perfect and complete
Those burning words and sweet,
So perfect is the single kiss your lips lay on my hand.

The paddles lie disused,
The fitful breeze abused,                                                     50
Has dropped to slumber, with no after-blow;
And hearts will pay the cost,
For you and I have lost
More than the homeward blowing wind that died an hour ago.

*—1890*

---

**45 lotus-land** In Homer's *Odyssey* (9.82–87) veterans of the Trojan War become forgetful of the homeward way after eating the fruit of the lotus, an episode also explored in Alfred Tennyson's poem "The Lotos-Eaters."

*Archibald Lampman (1861–1899) Born in Morpeth, Canada West, Lampman worked in the Post Office in Ottawa, and wrote several fine collections of poetry, including* Among the Millet *(1888),* Lyrics of Earth *(1895), and* Alcyone *(1899), in which this grim vision of an urban dystopia appears.*

# Archibald Lampman
# The City of the End of Things°

Beside the pounding cataracts
Of midnight streams unknown to us
'Tis builded in the leafless tracts
And valleys huge of Tartarus.°
Lurid and lofty and vast it seems;                        5
It hath no rounded name that rings,
But I have heard it called in dreams
The City of the End of Things.

Its roofs and iron towers have grown
None knoweth how high within the night,             10
But in its murky streets far down
A flaming terrible and bright
Shakes all the stalking shadows there,
Across the walls, across the floors,
And shifts upon the upper air                             15
From out a thousand furnace doors;
And all the while an awful sound
Keeps roaring on continually,
And crashes in the ceaseless round
Of a gigantic harmony.                                      20
Through its grim depths re-echoing
And all its weary height of walls,

---

**The City of the End of Things** Originally the poem was titled "The Issue of Things That Are."
**4 Tartarus** in Greek mythology, the lowest part of Hades, or hell

With measured roar and iron ring,
The inhuman music lifts and falls.
Where no thing rests and no man is,                          *25*
And only fire and night hold sway;
The beat, the thunder and the hiss
Cease not, and change not, night nor day.

And moving at unheard commands,
The abysses and vast fires between,                          *30*
Flit figures that with clanking hands
Obey a hideous routine;
They are not flesh, they are not bone,
They see not with the human eye,
And from their iron lips is blown                            *35*
A dreadful and monotonous cry;
And whoso of our mortal race
Should find that city unaware,
Lean Death would smite him face to face,
And blanch him with its venomed air:                         *40*
Or caught by the terrific spell,
Each thread of memory snapt and cut,
His soul would shrivel and its shell
Go rattling like an empty nut.

It was not always so, but once,                              *45*
In days that no man thinks upon,
Fair voices echoed from its stones,
The light above it leaped and shone:
Once there were multitudes of men,
That built that city in their pride,                         *50*
Until its might was made, and then
They withered age by age and died.
But now of that prodigious race,
Three only in an iron tower,
Set like carved idols face to face,                          *55*
Remain the masters of its power;
And at the city gate a fourth,
Gigantic and with dreadful eyes,

Sits looking toward the lightless north,
Beyond the reach of memories;                                                60
Fast rooted to the lurid floor,
A bulk that never moves a jot,
In his pale body dwells no more,
Or mind or soul,—an idiot!
But sometime in the end those three                                          65
Shall perish and their hands be still,
And with the master's touch shall flee
Their incommunicable skill.
A stillness absolute as death
Along the slacking wheels shall lie,                                         70
And, flagging at a single breath,
The fires shall moulder out and die.
The roar shall vanish at its height,
And over that tremendous town
The silence of eternal night                                                75
Shall gather close and settle down.
All its grim grandeur, tower and hall,
Shall be abandoned utterly,
And into rust and dust shall fall
From century to century;                                                    80
Nor ever living thing shall grow,
Nor trunk of tree, nor blade of grass;
No drop shall fall, no wind shall blow,
Nor sound of any foot shall pass:
Alone of its accursèd state,                                                85
One thing the hand of Time shall spare,
For the grim Idiot at the gate
Is deathless and eternal there.

—*1895*

***Duncan Campbell Scott (1862–1947)*** *Born in Ottawa, Scott began to write after meeting Archibald Lampman, producing seven volumes of poetry, including* The Magic House *(1893) and* The Green Cloister *(1935), as well as collections of short stories. Many of his poems reflect his experiences in his controversial work as an official with the Department of Indian Affairs.*

## Duncan Campbell Scott

# The Forsaken

### I

Once in the winter
Out on a lake
In the heart of the north-land,
Far from the Fort
And far from the hunters,                                    5
A Chippewa woman
With her sick baby,
Crouched in the last hours
Of a great storm.
Frozen and hungry,                                           10
She fished through the ice
With a line of the twisted
Bark of the cedar,
And a rabbit-bone hook
Polished and barbed;                                         15
Fished with the bare hook
All through the day,
Fished and caught nothing;
While the young chieftain
Tugged at her breasts,                                       20
Or slept in the lacings
Of the warm *tikanagan.*°
All the lake-surface
Streamed with the hissing
Of millions of iceflakes,                                    25
Hurled by the wind;

**22 tikanagan** Cree word for a cradle board used to carry an infant

Behind her the round
Of a lonely island
Roared like a fire
With the voice of the storm                                    30
In the deeps of the cedars.
Valiant, unshaken,
She took of her own flesh,
Baited the fish-hook,
Drew in a grey-trout,                                          35
Drew in his fellows,
Heaped them beside her,
Dead in the snow.
Valiant, unshaken,
She faced the long distance,                                   40
Wolf-haunted and lonely,
Sure of her goal
And the life of her dear one;
Tramped for two days,
On the third in the morning,                                   45
Saw the strong bulk
Of the Fort by the river,
Saw the wood-smoke
Hang soft in the spruces,
Heard the keen yelp                                            50
Of the ravenous huskies
Fighting for whitefish:
Then she had rest.

### II

Years and years after,
When she was old and withered,                                 55
When her son was an old man
And his children filled with vigour,
They came in their northern tour on the verge of winter,
To an island in a lonely lake.
There one night they camped, and on the morrow               60
Gathered their kettles and birch-bark°

**61 birch-bark** waterproof birch-bark bowls or buckets

Their rabbit-skin robes and their mink-traps,
Launched their canoes and slunk away through the islands,
Left her alone forever,
Without a word of farewell,                                    65
Because she was old and useless,
Like a paddle broken and warped,
Or a pole that was splintered.
Then, without a sigh,
Valiant, unshaken,                                            70
She smoothed her dark locks under her kerchief,
Composed her shawl in state,
Then folded her hands ridged with sinews and corded
        with veins,
Folded them across her breasts spent with the nourishing
        of children,
Gazed at the sky past the tops of the cedars,                75
Saw two spangled nights arise out of the twilight,
Saw two days go by filled with the tranquil sunshine,
Saw, without pain, or dread, or even a moment of longing:
Then on the third great night there came thronging and
        thronging
Millions of snowflakes out of a windless cloud;             80
They covered her close with a beautiful crystal shroud,
Covered her deep and silent.
But in the frost of the dawn,
Up from the life below,
Rose a column of breath                                       85
Through a tiny cleft in the snow,
Fragile, delicately drawn,
Wavering with its own weakness,
In the wilderness a sign of the spirit,
Persisting still in the sight of the sun                      90
Till day was done.
Then all light was gathered up by the hand of God and hid in His
        breast,
Then there was born a silence deeper than silence,
Then she had rest.

                                                        —*1905*

***William Butler Yeats (1865–1939)*** *is considered the greatest Irish poet and provides an important link between the late romantic era and early modernism. His early poetry, focusing on Irish legend and landscape, is regional in the best sense of the term, but his later work, with its prophetic tone and symbolist texture, moves on a larger stage. Yeats lived in London for many years and was at the centre of British literary life. He was awarded the Nobel Prize in 1923.*

## *William Butler Yeats*
# Sailing to Byzantium°

### 1

That is no country for old men. The young
In one another's arms, birds in the trees
—Those dying generations—at their song,
The salmon-falls, the mackerel-crowded seas,
Fish, flesh, or fowl, commend all summer long                  5
Whatever is begotten, born, and dies.
Caught in that sensual music all neglect
Monuments of unaging intellect.

### 2

An aged man is but a paltry thing,
A tattered coat upon a stick, unless                              10
Soul clap its hands and sing, and louder sing
For every tatter in its mortal dress,
Nor is there singing school but studying
Monuments of its own magnificence;
And therefore I have sailed the seas and come                   15
To the holy city of Byzantium.

### 3

O sages standing in God's holy fire
As in the gold mosaic of a wall,
Come from the holy fire, perne in a gyre,°
And be the singing-masters of my soul.                          20

**Byzantium** Constantinople or Istanbul, capital of the Eastern Roman Empire    **19 perne in a gyre**
descend in a spiral; the gyre for Yeats was a private symbol of historical cycles

Consume my heart away; sick with desire
And fastened to a dying animal
It knows not what it is; and gather me
Into the artifice of eternity.

4

Once out of nature I shall never take                                    *25*
My bodily form from any natural thing,
But such a form as Grecian goldsmiths make
Of hammered gold and gold enameling
To keep a drowsy Emperor awake;
Or set upon a golden bough to sing                                        *30*
To lords and ladies of Byzantium
Of what is past, or passing, or to come.

                                                                *—1927*

# The Second Coming

Turning and turning in the widening gyre°
The falcon cannot hear the falconer;
Things fall apart; the center cannot hold;
Mere anarchy is loosed upon the world,
The blood-dimmed tide is loosed, and everywhere         *5*
The ceremony of innocence is drowned;
The best lack all conviction, while the worst
Are full of passionate intensity.

Surely some revelation is at hand;
Surely the Second Coming is at hand.                          *10*
The Second Coming! Hardly are those words out
When a vast image out of *Spiritus Mundi°*
Troubles my sight: somewhere in the sands of the desert
A shape with lion body and the head of a man,
A gaze blank and pitiless as the sun,                         *15*
Is moving its slow thighs, while all about it

---

**1 gyre** see note to "Sailing to Byzantium"   **12 Spiritus Mundi** World-Spirit

Reel shadows of the indignant desert birds.
The darkness drops again; but now I know
That twenty centuries of stony sleep
Were vexed to nightmare by a rocking cradle,                    *20*
And what rough beast, its hour come round at last,
Slouches towards Bethlehem to be born?

—*1921*

---

*Sophia Almon Hensley (1866–1946) Born in Bridgetown, Nova Scotia, Hensley was encouraged by Charles G. D. Roberts to develop as a poet. She published five collections of poetry, including* The Way of a Woman *(1928), in which this World War I poem, first published in 1918, appeared, as well as a novel and non-fiction studies of social issues affecting women.*

# *Sophia Almon Hensley*
## Courage°

Leave me alone here, proudly, with my dead,
    Ye mothers of brave sons adventurous;
He who once prayed: "If it be possible°
    Let this cup pass," will arbitrate for us.
Your boy with iron nerves and careless smile                   *5*
    Marched gaily by, and dreamed of glory's goal;
Mine had blanched cheek, straight mouth, and close-
        gripped hands,
    And prayed that somehow he might save his soul.
I do not grudge your ribbon or your cross,°
    The price of these my soldier, too, has paid;               *10*
I hug a prouder knowledge to my heart,
    The mother of the boy who was afraid!

He was a tender child with nerves so keen
    They doubled pain and magnified the sad,

---

**Courage** This poem was first published under the title "Somewhere in France."   **3 If it be possible** the prayer of Jesus in the Garden of Gethsemane on the night before he was crucified (Matthew 26:39)   **9 ribbon or your cross** military medals for courage, such as the Victoria Cross

He hated cruelty and things obscene,                              *15*
    And in all high and holy things was glad.
And so he gave what others could not give,
    The one supremest sacrifice he made,

A thing your brave boy could not understand;
    He gave his all because he was afraid.                    *20*
Like a machine he fed the shining shell
    Into a hungry maw from sun to sun;
And when at last the hour struck, and he fell,
    He smiled, and murmured: "Thank God, it is done."
Ye glory well, ye mothers of brave sons                           *25*
    Eager and sinewy, in the part they played;
And England will remember, and repay,
    And history will see their names arrayed.
But God looked down upon my soldier-boy
    Who set his teeth, and did his bit, and prayed,           *30*
And understands why I am proud to be
    The mother of the boy who was afraid!

                                                              *—1918*

---

*Edwin Arlington Robinson (1869–1935) wrote many poems set in "Tilbury," a re-creation of his hometown of Gardiner, Maine. These poems continue to present readers with a memorable cast of eccentric characters who somehow manifest universal human desires. Robinson languished in poverty and obscurity for many years before his reputation began to flourish as a result of the interest taken in his work by President Theodore Roosevelt, who obtained a government job for Robinson and wrote a favourable review of one of his books.*

## *Edwin Arlington Robinson*
# Richard Cory

Whenever Richard Cory went down town,
We people on the pavement looked at him:
He was a gentleman from sole to crown,
Clean favored, and imperially slim.

And he was always quietly arrayed,                                    5
And he was always human when he talked;
But still he fluttered pulses when he said,
"Good-morning," and he glittered when he walked.

And he was rich—yes, richer than a king—
And admirably schooled in every grace:                               10
In fine, we thought that he was everything
To make us wish that we were in his place.

So on we worked, and waited for the light,
And went without the meat, and cursed the bread;
And Richard Cory, one calm summer night,                             15
Went home and put a bullet through his head.

—*1896*

---

*Paul Laurence Dunbar (1872–1906), a native of Dayton, Ohio, was one of the first Black poets to make a mark in American literature. Many of his dialect poems reflect a sentimentalized view of life in the South, which he did not know directly. However, he was also capable of powerful expressions of racial protest. The last line of his poem "Sympathy" appears as the title of Maya Angelou's autobiography.*

## *Paul Laurence Dunbar*
# Sympathy

I know what the caged bird feels, alas!
    When the sun is bright on the upland slopes;
When the wind stirs soft through the springing grass,
And the river flows like a stream of glass;
    When the first bird sings and the first bud opens,    5
And the faint perfume from its chalice steals—
I know what the caged bird feels!

I know why the caged bird beats his wing
    Till its blood is red on the cruel bars;
For he must fly back to his perch and cling            10

When he fain would be on the bough a-swing;
    And a pain still throbs in the old, old scars
And they pulse again with a keener sting—
I know why he beats his wing!

I know why the caged bird sings, ah me,                    15
    When his wing is bruised and his bosom sore,—
When he beats his bars and he would be free;
It is not a carol of joy or glee,
    But a prayer that he sends from his heart's deep core,
But a plea, that upward to Heaven he flings—              20
I know why the caged bird sings!

                                                    *—1893*

---

*Robert Frost (1874–1963), during the second half of his long life, was a public figure who attained a popularity unmatched by any American poet of the last century. His reading at the inauguration of John F. Kennedy in 1961 capped an impressive career that included four Pulitzer Prizes. Unattracted by the more exotic aspects of modernism, Frost nevertheless remains a poet who speaks eloquently to contemporary uncertainties about humanity's place in a universe that does not seem to care much for its existence. While Frost is rarely directly an autobiographical poet, his work always bears the stamp of his powerful personality and identification with the New England landscape.*

## *Robert Frost*
# Neither Out Far nor In Deep

The people along the sand
All turn and look one way.
They turn their back on the land.
They look at the sea all day.

As long as it takes to pass                               5
A ship keeps raising its hull;

The wetter ground like glass
Reflects a standing gull.

The land may vary more;
But wherever the truth may be—                                    10
The water comes ashore,
And the people look at the sea.

They cannot look out far.
They cannot look in deep.
But when was that ever a bar                                      15
To any watch they keep?

—1936

# Stopping by Woods on a Snowy Evening

Whose woods these are I think I know.
His house is in the village though;
He will not see me stopping here
To watch his woods fill up with snow.

My little horse must think it queer                               5
To stop without a farmhouse near
Between the woods and frozen lake
The darkest evening of the year.

He gives his harness bells a shake
To ask if there is some mistake.                                  10
The only other sound's the sweep
Of easy wind and downy flake.

The woods are lovely, dark and deep,
But I have promises to keep,
And miles to go before I sleep,                                   15
And miles to go before I sleep.

—1923

*Katherine Hale (1878–1956) Born Amelia Beers Warnock in Galt, Ontario, Hale published widely under her pen name. She wrote six collections of poetry, including* Morning in the West *(1923) and* The Island and Other Poems *(1934), a book about Isabella Valancy Crawford, and several prose works on Canadian history.*

# *Katherine Hale*
## This Oblivion

One dear to him is moving towards the river;
Her broad-brimmed hat and dress of faded blue,
Her sketch book under a protecting arm.
Slowly she disappears, hid by the grasses,
Fading in light of the dim, blue-grey day.                                5
Ah, so he faded as his tie with earth
Was loosed, and he slipped down
Hidden, as she is now. But the dim green
That floats and weaves above his secret place
Will not return him, not for any grace                                   10
Of wildest supplication. Yet she comes,
Risen from the grasses, back along the road,
Her little disappearance traced in form,
Her morning told in colour and in line.
Self-tranced she walks into the world again                              15
Renewed by this oblivion.
But, oh, for him, bound in a blinding sleep,
What recompense?
I see no recompense that such negation brings
Or—is there song that endless silence sings                             20
Faintly, below these grasses strong and deep?

                                                                *—1950*

*Émile Nelligan (1879–1941) Influenced by the symbolist poets of France, the Montreal-born Nelligan made a significant contribution to poetry in Quebec, though most of his poems were written in a three-year period before 1899, when a mental breakdown led to institutionalization for the remainder of his life. The first collection of his poetry,* Émile Nelligan et son oeuvre, *was published in 1903.*

# *Émile Nelligan*
# Evening Bells

Some evenings I roamed the moors, beyond the bounds
Of my home village, lost in the great rosy hills'
Calm pride, and down the wind the Angels shook the bells
Of churches in long waves of melancholy sound.

And in a shepherd-poet's dreamy, romantic mood               5
In the perfume of roses I used to breathe their prayer,
While in the dying gold my flocks of mania
Aimlessly wandered through forests of sandalwood.

Thus in this life where I follow my lonely path
I have kept in my mind a corner of old earth,               10
That evening countryside whose glow I see again;

While you, my heart, within your private reach of moor,
Recall the long-ago angelus, voiceless, faint:
That winging of bronze birds flown from the chapel towers.

—*1903*

Translated by P. F. Widdows.

*Wallace Stevens (1879–1955) was a lawyer specializing in surety bonds and rose to be a vice-president of the Hartford Accident and Indemnity Company. His poetry was collected for the first time in* Harmonium *when he was forty-five, and while he published widely during his lifetime, his poetry was only slowly recognized as the work of a major modernist whose originality has not been surpassed. Stevens's idea of poetry as a force taking the place of religion has had a profound influence on poets and critics of this century.*

*Wallace Stevens*

# Thirteen Ways of Looking at a Blackbird

### I

Among twenty snowy mountains,
The only moving thing
Was the eye of the blackbird.

### II

I was of three minds,
Like a tree                                                                         5
In which there are three blackbirds.

### III

The blackbird whirled in the autumn winds.
It was a small part of the pantomime.

### IV

A man and a woman
Are one.                                                                            10
A man and a woman and a blackbird
Are one.

### V

I do not know which to prefer,
The beauty of inflections
Or the beauty of innuendoes,                                                        15
The blackbird whistling
Or just after.

### VI
Icicles filled the long window
With barbaric glass.
The shadow of the blackbird                                     20
Crossed it, to and fro.
The mood
Traced in the shadow
An indecipherable cause.

### VII
O thin men of Haddam,°                                          25
Why do you imagine golden birds?
Do you not see how the blackbird
Walks around the feet
Of the women about you?

### VIII
I know noble accents                                           30
And lucid, inescapable rhythms;
But I know, too,
That the blackbird is involved
In what I know.

### IX
When the blackbird flew out of sight,                          35
It marked the edge
Of one of many circles.

### X
At the sight of blackbirds
Flying in a green light,
Even the bawds of euphony                                      40
Would cry out sharply.

### XI
He rode over Connecticut
In a glass coach.
Once, a fear pierced him,
In that he mistook                                             45

**25 Haddam** town in Connecticut

The shadow of his equipage
For blackbirds.

### XII

The river is moving.
The blackbird must be flying.

### XIII

It was evening all afternoon.                                                    50
It was snowing
And it was going to snow.
The blackbird sat
In the cedar-limbs.

*—1923*

# The Motive for Metaphor

You like it under the trees in autumn,
Because everything is half dead.
The wind moves like a cripple among the leaves
And repeats words without meaning.

In the same way, you were happy in spring,                                       5
With the half colors of quarter-things,
The slightly brighter sky, the melting clouds,
The single bird, the obscure moon—

The obscure moon lighting an obscure world
Of things that would never be quite expressed,                                   10
Where you yourself were never quite yourself
And did not want nor have to be,

Desiring the exhilarations of changes:
The motive for metaphor, shrinking from
The weight of primary noon,                                                      15
The A B C of being,

The ruddy temper, the hammer
Of red and blue, the hard sound—
Steel against intimation—the sharp flash,
The vital, arrogant, fatal, dominant X.                          20

—1947

---

**E. J. Pratt (1882–1964)** *Born in Western Bay, Newfoundland, Pratt went on to teach at Victoria College, University of Toronto. The publication of his second volume,* Newfoundland Verse *(1923), marked a new direction in Canadian poetry. Pratt also published several long poems that deal with pivotal events in Canadian history, including* Brébeuf and His Brethren *(1940) and* Towards the Last Spike *(1952).*

# E. J. Pratt
# From Stone to Steel

From stone to bronze, from bronze to steel
Along the road-dust of the sun,
Two revolutions of the wheel
From Java to Geneva° run.

The snarl Neanderthal is worn                                    5
Close to the smiling Aryan lips,
The civil polish of the horn
Gleams from our praying finger tips.

The evolution of desire
Has but matured a toxic wine,                                    10
Drunk long before its heady fire
Reddened Euphrates or the Rhine.

Between the temple and the cave
The boundary lies tissue-thin:
The yearlings still the altars crave                             15
As satisfaction for a sin.

---

**4 Java to Geneva** Java was then the site of the discovery of the oldest human fossils. Geneva is the Swiss city associated with peace and humane conduct during war.

The road goes up, the road goes down—
Let Java or Geneva be—
But whether to the cross or crown,
The path lies through Gethsemane.°                                        20

—1932

---

*William Carlos Williams (1883–1963), like his friend Wallace Stevens, followed an unconventional career for a poet, working until his death as a pediatrician in Rutherford, New Jersey. Williams is modern poetry's greatest proponent of the American idiom. His plain-spoken poems have been more widely imitated than those of any other American poet of the twentieth century, perhaps because he represents a homegrown modernist alternative to the intellectualized Europeanism of T. S. Eliot and Ezra Pound (a friend of his from college days). In his later years, Williams assisted many younger poets, among them Allen Ginsberg, for whose controversial book* Howl *he wrote an introduction.*

# William Carlos Williams
## The Red Wheelbarrow

so much depends
upon

a red wheel
barrow

glazed with rain                                                          5
water

beside the white
chickens.

—1923

---

**20 Gethsemane** the garden where Christ prayed before his crucifixion, asking to be released from the suffering to come

# To a Poor Old Woman

munching a plum on
the street a paper bag
of them in her hand

They taste good to her
They taste good                                                    5
to her. They taste
good to her

You can see it by
the way she gives herself
to the one half                                                   10
sucked out in her hand

Comforted
a solace of ripe plums
seeming to fill the air
They taste good to her                                            15

—1935

---

*Ezra Pound (1885–1972) was the greatest international proponent of modern poetry. Born in Idaho and reared in Philadelphia, he emigrated to England in 1909, where he befriended Yeats, promoted the early work of Frost, and discovered Eliot. Pound's early promotion of the imagist movement assisted a number of important poetic principles and reputations, including those of H. D. (Hilda Doolittle) and, later, William Carlos Williams. Pound's support of Mussolini during World War II, expressed in controversial radio broadcasts, caused him to be held for over a decade after the war as a mental patient in the United States, after which he returned to Italy for the final years of his long and controversial life.*

## *Ezra Pound*
# In a Station of the Metro

The apparition of these faces in the crowd;
Petals on a wet, black bough.

—1916

# The River-Merchant's Wife: A Letter°

While my hair was still cut straight across my forehead
I played about the front gate, pulling flowers.
You came by on bamboo stilts, playing horse,
You walked about my seat, playing with blue plums.
And we went on living in the village of Chokan:                5
Two small people, without dislike or suspicion.
At fourteen I married My Lord you.
I never laughed, being bashful
Lowering my head, I looked at the wall.
Called to, a thousand times, I never looked back.           10

At fifteen I stopped scowling,
I desired my dust to be mingled with yours
Forever and forever and forever.
Why should I climb the lookout?

At sixteen you departed,                                    15
You went into far Ku-to-yen, by the river of swirling eddies,
And you have been gone five months.
The monkeys make sorrowful noise overhead.

You dragged your feet when you went out.
By the gate now, the moss is grown, the different mosses,   20
Too deep to clear them away!
The leaves fall early this autumn, in wind.
The paired butterflies are already yellow with August
Over the grass in the West garden;
They hurt me. I grow older.                                 25
If you are coming down through the narrows of the river Kiang,
Please let me know beforehand,
And I will come out to meet you
    As far as Cho-Fu-Sa.

—*1915*

**The River-Merchant's Wife: A Letter** imitation of a poem by Li-Po (A.D. 701–762)

*H. D. (Hilda Doolittle) (1886–1961) was born in Bethlehem, Pennsylvania. Hilda Doolittle was a college friend of both William Carlos Williams and Ezra Pound and moved to Europe permanently in 1911. With her husband, Richard Aldington, H. D. was an important member of the imagist group promoted by Pound.*

## *H. D. (Hilda Doolittle)*
# Helen°

All Greece hates
the still eyes in the white face,
the lustre as of olives
where she stands,
and the white hands.                                        5

All Greece reviles
the wan face when she smiles,
hating it deeper still
when it grows wan and white,
remembering past enchantments                               10
and past ills.

Greece sees unmoved,
God's daughter, born of love,
the beauty of cool feet
and slenderest knees,                                       15
could love indeed the maid,
only if she were laid,
white ash amid funereal cypresses.

—*1924*

**Helen** The beautiful daughter of Leda and Zeus, who was given to Paris, the Prince of Troy, by Aphrodite. Her husband, the Greek leader Menelaus, waged the Trojan War to bring her back.

*Marianne Moore (1887–1972) called her own work poetry—unconventional and marked with the stamp of a rare personality—because, as she put it, there was no other category for it. For four years she was editor of the* Dial, *one of the chief modernist periodicals. Moore's wide range of reference, which can leap from the commonplace to the wondrous within a single poem, reflects her unique set of personal interests—which range from exotic natural species to baseball.*

## *Marianne Moore*
# The Fish

wade
through black jade.
    Of the crow-blue mussel-shells, one keeps
    adjusting the ash-heaps;
        opening and shutting itself like              5

an
injured fan.
    The barnacles which encrust the side
    of the wave, cannot hide
        there for the submerged shafts of the       10

sun,
split like spun
    glass, move themselves with spotlight swiftness
    into the crevices—
        in and out, illuminating             15

the
turquoise sea
    of bodies. The water drives a wedge
    of iron through the iron edge
        of the cliff; whereupon the stars,       20

pink
rice-grains, ink-
    bespattered jelly-fish, crabs like green
    lilies, and submarine
        toadstools, slide each on the other.     25

All
external
    marks of abuse are present on this
    defiant edifice—
        all the physical features of                         30
ac-
cident—lack
    of cornice, dynamite grooves, burns, and
    hatchet strokes, these things stand
        out on it; the chasm-side is                         35
dead.
Repeated
    evidence has proved that it can live
    on what can not revive
        its youth. The sea grows old in it.

*—1921*

---

*T. S. Eliot (1888–1965) was the author of* The Waste Land, *one of the most famous and difficult modernist poems, and became an international figure. Born in St. Louis and educated at Harvard, he moved to London in 1914, where he remained for the rest of his life, becoming a British subject in 1927. This chief prophet of modern despair turned to the Church of England in later life and wrote successful dramas on religious themes. As a critic and influential editor, Eliot dominated poetic taste in England and America for over twenty-five years. He was awarded the Nobel Prize in 1948.*

## T. S. Eliot
# Journey of the Magi°

'A cold coming we had of it,
Just the worst time of the year
For a journey, and such a long journey:
The ways deep and the weather sharp,
The very dead of winter.'°                         5

**Magi** Wise Men mentioned in Matthew 2:1–2   **1–5 'A cold . . . winter'** The quotation marks indicated Eliot's source, a sermon by Lancelot Andrewes (1555–1626).

And the camels galled, sore-footed, refractory,
Lying down in the melting snow.
There were times we regretted
The summer palaces on slopes, the terraces,
And the silken girls bringing sherbet.                                    *10*
Then the camel men cursing and grumbling
And running away, and wanting their liquor and women,
And the night-fires going out, and the lack of shelters,
And the cities hostile and the towns unfriendly
And the villages dirty and charging high prices:                          *15*
A hard time we had of it.
At the end we preferred to travel all night,
Sleeping in snatches,
With the voices singing in our ears, saying
That this was all folly.                                                  *20*

Then at dawn we came down to a temperate valley,
Wet, below the snow line, smelling of vegetation;
With a running stream and a water-mill beating the darkness,
And three trees on the low sky.
And an old white horse galloped away in the meadow.                       *25*
Then we came to a tavern with vine-leaves over the lintel,
Six hands at an open door dicing for pieces of silver,
And feet kicking the empty wine-skins.
But there was no information, and so we continued
And arrived at evening, not a moment too soon                             *30*
Finding the place; it was (you may say) satisfactory.

All this was a long time ago, I remember,
And I would do it again, but set down
This° set down
This: were we led all that way for                                        *35*
Birth or Death? There was a Birth, certainly,
We had evidence and no doubt. I had seen birth and death,
But had thought they were different; this Birth was
Hard and bitter agony for us, like Death, our death.

---

**33–34 set down . . . This** The Magus is dictating his memoirs to a scribe.

We returned to our places, these Kingdoms,             *40*
But no longer at ease here, in the old dispensation,°
With an alien people clutching their gods.
I should be glad of another death.

                                          *—1927*

# The Love Song of J. Alfred Prufrock

> *S'io credesse che mia risposta fosse*
> *A persona che mai tornasse al mondo,*
> *Questa fiamma staria senza più scosse.*
> *Ma perciocche giammai di questo fondo*
> *Non tornò vivo alcun, s'i'odo il vero,*
> *Senza tema d'infamia ti rispondo.°*

Let us go then, you° and I,
When the evening is spread out against the sky
Like a patient etherised upon a table;
Let us go, through certain half-deserted streets,
The muttering retreats                                 *5*
Of restless nights in one-night cheap hotels
And sawdust restaurants with oyster-shells:
Streets that follow like a tedious argument
Of insidious intent
To lead you to an overwhelming question . . .           *10*
Oh, do not ask, "What is it?"
Let us go and make our visit.

In the room the women come and go
Talking of Michelangelo.°

---

41 **old dispensation** world before the birth of Christ
**S'io credesse . . . rispondo** From Dante's *Inferno* (Canto 27). The speaker is Guido da Montefeltro: "If I thought I spoke to someone who would return to the world, this flame would tremble no longer. But, if what I hear is true, since no one has ever returned alive from this place I can answer you without fear of infamy."  **1 you** Eliot said that the auditor of the poem was a male friend of Prufrock.
14 **Michelangelo** Italian painter and sculptor (1475–1564)

The yellow fog that rubs its back upon the window-panes,     *15*
The yellow smoke that rubs its muzzle on the window-panes,
Licked its tongue into the corners of the evening,
Lingered upon the pools that stand in drains,
Let fall upon its back the soot that falls from chimneys,
Slipped by the terrace, made a sudden leap,     *20*
And seeing that it was a soft October night,
Curled once about the house, and fell asleep.

And indeed there will be time
For the yellow smoke that slides along the street,
Rubbing its back upon the window-panes;     *25*
There will be time, there will be time
To prepare a face to meet the faces that you meet;
There will be time to murder and create,
And time for all the works and days of hands
That lift and drop a question on your plate:     *30*
Time for you and time for me,
And time yet for a hundred indecisions,
And for a hundred visions and revisions,
Before the taking of a toast and tea.

In the room the women come and go     *35*
Talking of Michelangelo.

And indeed there will be time
To wonder, "Do I dare?" and, "Do I dare?"—
Time to turn back and descend the stair,
With a bald spot in the middle of my hair—     *40*
(They will say: "How his hair is growing thin!")
My morning coat, my collar mounting firmly to the chin,
My necktie rich and modest, but asserted by a simple pin—
(They will say: "But how his arms and legs are thin!")
Do I dare     *45*
Disturb the universe?
In a minute there is time
For decisions and revisions which a minute will reverse.

For I have known them all already, known them all:
Have known the evenings, mornings, afternoons,       *50*
I have measured out my life with coffee spoons;
I know the voices dying with a dying fall
Beneath the music from a farther room.
      So how should I presume?

And I have known the eyes already, known them all—       *55*
The eyes that fix you in a formulated phrase,
And when I am formulated, sprawling on a pin,
When I am pinned and wriggling on the wall,
Then how should I begin
To spit out all the butt-ends of my days and ways?       *60*
      And how should I presume?

And I have known the arms already, known them all—
Arms that are braceleted and white and bare
(But in the lamplight, downed with light brown hair!)
Is it perfume from a dress       *65*
That makes me so digress?
Arms that lie along a table, or wrap about a shawl.
    And should I then presume?
    And how should I begin?

   . . . . .

Shall I say, I have gone at dusk through narrow streets,       *70*
And watched the smoke that rises from the pipes
Of lonely men in shirtsleeves, leaning out of windows? . . .

I should have been a pair of ragged claws
Scuttling across the floors of silent seas.

   . . . . .

And the afternoon, the evening, sleeps so peacefully!       *75*
Smoothed by long fingers,
Asleep . . . tired . . . or it malingers,
Stretched on the floor, here beside you and me.
Should I, after tea and cakes and ices,
Have the strength to force the moment to its crisis?       *80*
But though I have wept and fasted, wept and prayed,

Though I have seen my head (grown slightly bald) brought in
    upon a platter,
I am no prophet°—and here's no great matter;
I have seen the moment of my greatness flicker,
And I have seen the eternal Footman hold my coat, and
    snicker,                                     *85*
        And in short, I was afraid.

And would it have been worth it, after all,
After the cups, the marmalade, the tea,
Among the porcelain, among some talk of you and me,
Would it have been worth while,                        *90*
To have bitten off the matter with a smile,
To have squeezed the universe into a ball
To roll it towards some overwhelming question,
To say: "I am Lazarus,° come from the dead,
Come back to tell you all, I shall tell you all"—        *95*
If one, settling a pillow by her head,
        Should say: "That is not what I meant at all;
        That is not it, at all."

And would it have been worth it, after all,
Would it have been worth while,                       *100*
After the sunsets and the dooryards and the sprinkled streets,
After the novels, after the teacups, after the skirts that trail
    along the floor—
And this, and so much more?—
It is impossible to say just what I mean!
But as if a magic lantern° threw the nerves in patterns on
    a screen:                                        *105*
Would it have been worth while
If one, settling a pillow or throwing off a shawl,
And turning toward the window, should say:
        "That is not it at all,
        That is not what I meant, at all."           *110*

    . . . . .

**82–83 my head . . . no prophet** allusion to John the Baptist    **94 Lazarus** raised from the dead in
John 11:1–44    **105 magic lantern** old-fashioned slide projector

No! I am not Prince Hamlet, nor was meant to be;
Am an attendant lord, one that will do
To swell a progress, start a scene or two,
Advise the prince; no doubt, an easy tool,
Deferential, glad to be of use,                                              115
Politic, cautious, and meticulous;
Full of high sentence, but a bit obtuse;
At times, indeed, almost ridiculous—
Almost, at times, the Fool.°

I grow old . . . I grow old . . .                                            120
I shall wear the bottoms of my trousers rolled.

Shall I part my hair behind? Do I dare to eat a peach?
I shall wear white flannel trousers, and walk upon the beach.
I have heard the mermaids singing, each to each.

I do not think that they will sing to me.                                    125

I have seen them riding seaward on the waves
Combing the white hair of the waves blown back
When the wind blows the water white and black.
We have lingered in the chambers of the sea
By sea-girls wreathed with seaweed red and brown                             130
Till human voices wake us, and we drown.

—*1917*

---

**111–119 not Prince Hamlet . . . the Fool** The allusion is probably to Polonius, a character in
*Hamlet.*

*Edna St. Vincent Millay (1892–1950) was extremely popular in the 1920s, when her sonnets seemed the ultimate expression of the liberated sexuality of what was then called the New Woman. Neglected for many years, her poems have recently generated renewed interest, and it seems likely that she will eventually regain her status as one of the most important female poets of the twentieth century.*

## Edna St. Vincent Millay

# What Lips My Lips Have Kissed, and Where, and Why

What lips my lips have kissed, and where, and why,
I have forgotten, and what arms have lain
Under my head till morning; but the rain
Is full of ghosts tonight, that tap and sigh
Upon the glass and listen for reply,                          5
And in my heart there stirs a quiet pain
For unremembered lads that not again
Will turn to me at midnight with a cry.
Thus in the winter stands the lonely tree,
Nor knows what birds have vanished one by one,              10
Yet knows its boughs more silent than before:
I cannot say what loves have come and gone,
I only know that summer sang in me
A little while, that in me sings no more.

*—1923*

*Wilfred Owen (1893–1918) was killed in the trenches only a few days before the armistice that ended World War I. Owen showed more promise than any other English poet of his generation. A decorated officer whose nerves broke down after exposure to battle, he met Siegfried Sassoon at Craiglockhart military hospital. His work was posthumously collected by his friend. A novel by Pat Barker,* Regeneration *(also made into a film), deals with their poetic and personal relationship.*

## *Wilfred Owen*
# Dulce et Decorum Est°

Bent double, like old beggars under sacks,
Knock-kneed, coughing like hags, we cursed through sludge,
Till on the haunting flares we turned our backs
And towards our distant rest began to trudge.
Men marched asleep. Many had lost their boots          5
But limped on, blood-shod. All went lame; all blind;
Drunk with fatigue; deaf even to the hoots
Of tired, outstripped Five-Nines° that dropped behind.

Gas! Gas! Quick, boys!—An ecstasy of fumbling
Fitting the clumsy helmets just in time;          10
But someone still was yelling out and stumbling
And flound'ring like a man in fire or lime . . .
Dim, through the misty panes and thick green light,°
As under a green sea, I saw him drowning.

In all my dreams, before my helpless sight,          15
He plunges at me, guttering, choking, drowning.

If in some smothering dreams you too could pace
Behind the wagon that we flung him in,
And watch the white eyes writhing in his face,
His hanging face, like a devil's sick of sin;          20
If you could hear, at every jolt, the blood
Come gargling from the froth-corrupted lungs,

---

**Dulce et Decorum Est (pro patria mori)** from the Roman poet Horace: "It is sweet and proper to die for one's country"   **8 Five-Nines** German artillery shells (59 mm)   **13 misty panes and thick green light** i.e., through the gas mask

Obscene as cancer, bitter as the cud
Of vile, incurable sores on innocent tongues,—
My friend,° you would not tell with such high zest          25
To children ardent for some desperate glory,
The old Lie: Dulce et decorum est
Pro patria mori.

—*1920*

# Disabled

He sat in a wheeled chair, waiting for dark,
And shivered in his ghastly suit of grey,
Legless, sewn short at elbow. Through the park
Voices of boys rang saddening like a hymn,
Voices of play and pleasure after day,                       5
Till gathering sleep had mothered them from him.

About this time Town used to swing so gay
When glow-lamps budded in the light blue trees,
And girls glanced lovelier as the air grew dim,—
In the old times, before he threw away his knees.           10
Now he will never feel again how slim
Girls' waists are, or how warm their subtle hands;
All of them touch him like some queer disease.

There was an artist silly for his face,
For it was younger than his youth, last year.               15
Now, he is old; his back will never brace;
He's lost his color very far from here,
Poured it down shell-holes till the veins ran dry,
And half his lifetime lapsed in the hot race,
And leap of purple spurted from his thigh.                  20

---

**25 my friend** The poem was originally addressed to Jessie Pope, a writer of patriotic verse.

One time he liked a blood-smear down his leg,
After the matches,° carried shoulder-high
It was after football, when he'd drunk a peg,°
He thought he'd better join.—He wonders why.
Someone had said he'd look a god in kilts,                    25
That's why; and may be, too, to please his Meg;
Aye, that was it, to please the giddy jilts°
He asked to join. He didn't have to beg;
Smiling they wrote his lie; aged nineteen years.

Germans he scarcely thought of; all their guilt,            30
And Austria's, did not move him. And no fears
Of Fear came yet. He thought of jeweled hilts
For daggers in plaid socks; of smart salutes;
And care of arms; and leave; and pay arrears;
*Esprit de corps;* and hints for young recruits.            35
And soon, he was drafted out with drums and cheers.

Some cheered him home, but not as crowds cheer Goal.
Only a solemn man who brought him fruits
*Thanked* him; and then inquired about his soul.
Now, he will spend a few sick years in Institutes,          40
And do what things the rules consider wise,
And take whatever pity they may dole.
Tonight he noticed how the women's eyes
Passed from him to the strong men that were whole.
How cold and late it is! Why don't they come                45
And put him into bed? Why don't they come?

*—1917*

---

**22 matches** soccer, called "football" in England    **23 peg** drink, usually brandy and soda
**27 jilts** contemptuous term for girls or young women

*Bertolt Brecht (1898–1956) is the German poet and playwright best known for his epic drama using "alienation effects" that reminded audiences they were viewing theatre and not reality. Born in Bavaria, he studied medicine and served in an army hospital in 1918. His greatest plays were written while in exile from Nazi Germany, first in Scandinavia (1933–1941) and then in the United States (1941–1947). Arguing that "all great poems have the quality of documents," he wrote over 1500 poems about the public and private upheavals of the tumultuous first half of the twentieth century.*

## *Bertolt Brecht*
# The God of War

I saw the old god of war stand in a bog between chasm and
    rockface.
He smelled of free beer and carbolic and showed his testicles to
adolescents, for he had been rejuvenated by several professors.
In a hoarse wolfish voice he declared his love for everything
young. Nearby stood a pregnant woman, trembling.          5
    And without shame he talked on and presented himself as
a great one for order. And he described how everywhere he
put barns in order, by emptying them.
And as one throws crumbs to sparrows, he fed poor people
with crusts of bread which he had taken away from poor       10
people.
    His voice was now loud, now soft, but always hoarse.
    In a loud voice he spoke of great times to come, and in a soft voice
he taught the women how to cook crows and sea-gulls. Meanwhile
his back was unquiet, and he kept looking round, as though     15
afraid of being stabbed.

    And every five minutes he assured his public that he would
take up very little of their time.

—*1939*

Translated by Michael Hamburger.

*Dorothy Parker (1893–1967), as a humorist, journalist, and poet, was for many years associated with* The New Yorker *as both author and critic. Along with Robert Benchley, James Thurber, and E. B. White, she epitomizes the hard-edged humour that made that magazine unique among American periodicals.*

## *Dorothy Parker*
# One Perfect Rose

A single flow'r he sent me, since we met.
All tenderly his messenger he chose;
Deep-hearted, pure, with scented dew still wet—
One perfect rose.

I knew the language of the floweret;      5
"My fragile leaves," it said, "his heart enclose."
Love long has taken for his amulet
One perfect rose.

Why is it no one sent me yet
One perfect limousine, do you suppose?      10
Ah no, it's always just my luck to get
One perfect rose.

—*1926*

*e. e. cummings (1894–1962) was the son of a Harvard professor and Unitarian clergyman. Edward Estlin Cummings served as a volunteer ambulance driver in France during World War I. Cummings's experimentation with the typographical aspects of poetry reveals his serious interest in cubist painting, which he studied in Paris in the 1920s. A brilliant satirist, he also excelled as a writer of lyrical poems whose unusual appearance and idiosyncratic grammar, spelling, and punctuation often overshadow their traditional themes.*

## e. e. cummings

# [pity this busy monster,manunkind]

pity this busy monster,manunkind,

not. Progress is a comfortable disease:
your victim (death and life safely beyond)

plays with the bigness of his littleness
—electrons° deify one razorblade                                         5
into a mountainrange; lenses extend

unwish through curving wherewhen till unwish
returns on its unself.
                      A world of made
is not a world of born—pity poor flesh

and trees,poor stars and stones,but never this                          10
fine specimen of hypermagical

ultraomnipotence. We doctors know

a hopeless case if—listen: there's a hell
of a good universe next door; let's go

—*1944*

5 **electrons** in an electron microscope

# [l(a]

l(a

le
af
fa

ll

s)
one
l

iness

—1958

*F. R. Scott (1899–1985) was born in Quebec City, settling eventually in Montreal, where he was a professor at McGill's faculty of law. Influential in politics, poetry, and translation, he helped to shape Canadian culture while exposing it to satire.* The Collected Poems of F. R. Scott *(1981) was awarded the Governor General's Award.*

## *F. R. Scott*
# Laurentian Shield

Hidden in wonder and snow, or sudden with summer,
This land stares at the sun in a huge silence
Endlessly repeating something we cannot hear.
Inarticulate, arctic,
Not written on by history, empty as paper,                    5
It leans away from the world with songs in its lakes
Older than love, and lost in the miles.

This waiting is wanting.
It will choose its language

When it has chosen its technic,                                    *10*
A tongue to shape the vowels of its productivity.

*A language of flesh and of roses.°*

Now there are pre-words,
Cabin syllables,
Nouns of settlement                                                *15*
Slowly forming, with steel syntax,
The long sentence of its exploitation.

The first cry was the hunter, hungry for fur,
And the digger for gold, nomad, no-man, a particle;
Then the bold commands of monopoly, big with machines,             *20*
Carving their kingdoms out of the public wealth;
And now the drone of the plane, scouting the ice,
Fills all the emptiness with neighbourhood
And links our future over the vanished pole.

But a deeper note is sounding, heard in the mines,                 *25*
The scattered camps and the mills, a language of life,
And what will be written in the full culture of occupation
Will come, presently, tomorrow,
From millions whose hands can turn this rock into children.

—*1954*

12 *A language of flesh and of roses* a line from British poet Stephen Spender

*A. J. M. Smith (1902–1980) was born in Montreal and became a founder of the Canadian modernist movement through his work as a poet, editor, and critic. This poem, originally subtitled "Group of Seven," first appeared in the* McGill Fortnightly Review, *which Smith began with F. R. Scott. His poetry collections include* News of the Phoenix *(1943) and* The Classic Shade *(1978).*

## A. J. M. Smith
# The Lonely Land

Cedar and jagged fir
uplift sharp barbs
against the gray
and cloud-piled sky;
and in the bay                                              5
blown spume and windrift
and thin, bitter spray
snap
at the whirling sky;
and the pine trees                                          10
lean one way.

A wild duck calls
to her mate,
and the ragged
and passionate tones                                        15
stagger and fall,
and recover,
and stagger and fall,
on these stones—
are lost                                                    20
in the lapping of water
on smooth, flat stones.

This is a beauty
of dissonance,
this resonance                                              25
of stony strand,
this smoky cry

curled over a black pine
like a broken
and wind-battered branch                                                  30
when the wind
bends the tops of the pines
and curdles the sky
from the north.

This is the beauty                                                        35
of strength
broken by strength
and still strong.

—*1926*

***Earle Birney (1904–1995)*** *was born in Alberta and travelled extensively
throughout his life. A Chaucerian scholar and a poetic innovator, he published over
fifteen collections of poetry, including the award-winning* David and Other
Poems *(1945),* Collected Poems *(1975), and* Last Makings *(1991), as well
as two novels and various non-fiction works on writing and writers.*

## *Earle Birney*
# El Greco: *Espolio*°

The carpenter is intent on the pressure of his hand

on the awl      and the trick of pinpointing his strength
through the awl to the wood      which is tough
He has no effort to spare for despoilings
or to worry if he'll be cut in on the dice                                5
His skill is vital to the scene      and the safety of the state
Anyone can perform the indignities      It's his hard arms
and craft that hold the eyes of the convict's women
There is the problem of getting the holes exact

**El Greco:** *Espolio* The Spanish painter known as El Greco (1541–1614) was famous for painting
intensely expressive religious scenes like *Espolio* (from the Latin for "despoiling"), which shows Christ
just before his clothes are torn away and he is crucified. Birney focuses on the figure of the
carpenter in the right foreground, who is preparing the cross.

(in the middle of this elbowing crowd)                                         *10*
and deep enough to hold the spikes .
after they've sunk through those bared feet
and inadequate wrists he knows are waiting behind him
He doesn't sense perhaps that one of the hands
Is held in a curious gesture over him—                                         *15*
giving      or asking      forgiveness?—
but he'd scarcely take time to be puzzled by poses
Criminals come in all sorts
as anyone knows who makes crosses
are as mad or sane as those who decide on their killings      *20*
Our one at least has been quiet so far
though they say he talked himself into this trouble
a carpenter's son who got notions of preaching
Well here's a carpenter's son who'll have carpenter sons
God willing      and build what's wanted                                        *25*
temples or tables      mangers or crosses
and shape them decently
working alone in that firm and profound abstraction
which blots out the bawling of rag-snatchers
To construct with hands      knee-weight      braced thigh      *30*
keeps the back turned from death

But it's too late now for the other carpenter's boy
to return to this peace before the nails are hammered

*Point Grey 1960*
*—1962*

***Pablo Neruda (1904–1973)** Born in Parral, Chile, as Neftali Ricardo Reyes y Basoalto, Neruda helped to shape Latin American literature and politics, winning the Nobel Prize in 1971. From 1948 until 1952, when Chile lifted its ban on communism, Neruda lived in exile in the USSR, Europe, and Mexico. Considered the people's poet, he published several accessible collections, including* Residence on Earth *(tr. 1946),* The Elementary Odes *(tr. 1961), and a volume of love poems.*

## *Pablo Neruda*
# In Praise of Ironing

Poetry is pure white:
it emerges from the water covered with drops,
all wrinkled, in a heap.
It has to be spread out, the skin of this planet,
has to be ironed, the sea in its whiteness;                     5
and the hands keep on moving,
smoothing the holy surfaces.
So are things accomplished.
Each day, hands re-create the world,
fire is married to steel,                                       10
and the canvas, the linens and the cottons return
from the skirmishing of the laundries;
and out of light is born a dove.
Out of the froth once more comes chastity.

—*1962*

Translated by Alastair Reid.

*W. H. Auden (1907–1973) was already established as an important younger British poet before he moved to America in 1939 (he later became a U.S. citizen). As an important transatlantic link between two literary cultures, Auden was one of the most important literary figures and cultural spokespersons in the English-speaking world for almost forty years, giving a name to the post-war era when he dubbed it "The Age of Anxiety" in a poem. In his last years he returned briefly to Oxford, where he occupied the poetry chair.*

## *W. H. Auden*
# Musée des Beaux Arts°

About suffering they were never wrong,
The Old Masters: how well they understood
Its human position; how it takes place
While someone else is eating or opening a window or just
    walking dully along;
How, when the aged are reverently, passionately waiting       5
For the miraculous birth, there always must be
Children who did not specially want it to happen, skating
On a pond at the edge of the wood:
They never forgot
That even the dreadful martyrdom must run its course       10
Anyhow in a corner, some untidy spot
Where the dogs go on with their doggy life and the torturer's
    horse
Scratches its innocent behind on a tree.

In Brueghel's *Icarus*,° for instance: how everything turns away
Quite leisurely from the disaster; the ploughman may       15
Have heard the splash, the forsaken cry,
But for him it was not an important failure; the sun shone
As it had to on the white legs disappearing into the green
Water; and the expensive delicate ship that must have seen
Something amazing, a boy falling out of the sky,       20
Had somewhere to get to and sailed calmly on.

*—1938*

**Musée des Beaux Arts** Museum of Fine Arts    **14 Brueghel's *Icarus*** In this painting (c. 1550) the famous event from Greek myth is almost inconspicuous among the other details Auden mentions.

*Theodore Roethke (1908–1963) was born in Michigan. Roethke was an influential teacher of poetry at the University of Washington for many years. His father was the owner of a greenhouse, and Roethke's childhood closeness to nature was an important influence on his mature poetry. His periodic nervous breakdowns, the result of bipolar manic-depression, presaged his early death.*

## Theodore Roethke
# Root Cellar

Nothing would sleep in that cellar, dank as a ditch,
Bulbs broke out of boxes hunting for chinks in the dark,
Shoots dangled and drooped,
Lolling obscenely from mildewed crates,
Hung down long yellow evil necks, like tropical snakes.      5
And what a congress of stinks!—
Roots ripe as old bait,
Pulpy stems, rank, silo-rich,
Leaf-mold, manure, lime, piled against slippery planks.
Nothing would give up life:      10
Even the dirt kept breathing a small breath.

—*1948*

*Louis Zukofsky (1904–1978) was born in New York to Jewish immigrants. Though once influential through his association with the Objectivist movement of the 1930s and his impact on the Black Mountain Poets, Zukofsky's own work is now experiencing a critical revival. His major achievement is the long poem "A," which he worked on throughout his life, but he also published numerous volumes of short poems and critical essays.*

## Louis Zukofsky
# Mantis

Mantis! praying mantis! since your wings' leaves
And your terrified eyes, pins, bright, black and poor
Beg—"Look, take it up" (thoughts' torsion)! "save it!"
I who can't bear to look, cannot touch,—You—

You can—but no one sees you steadying lost                         5
In the cars' drafts on the lit subway stone.

Praying mantis, what wind-up brought you, stone
On which you sometimes prop, prey among leaves
(Is it love's food your raised stomach prays?), lost
Here, stone holds only seats on which the poor          10
Ride, who rising from the news may trample you—
The shops' crowds a jam with no flies in it.

Even the newsboy who now sees knows it
No use, papers make money, makes stone, stone,
Banks, "it is harmless," he says moving on—You?          15
Where will he put *you*? There are no safe leaves
To put you back in here, here's news! too poor
Like all the separate poor to save the lost.

Don't light on my chest, mantis! do—you're lost,
Let the poor laugh at my fright, then see it:          20
My shame and theirs, you whom old Europe's poor
Call spectre, strawberry, by turns; a stone—
You point—they say—you lead lost children—leaves
Close in the paths men leave, saved, safe with you.

Killed by thorns (once men), who now will save you          25
Mantis? what male love bring a fly, be lost
Within your mouth, prophetess, harmless to leaves
And hands, faked flower,—the myth is: dead, bones, it
Was assembled, apes wing in wind: On stone,
Mantis, you will die, touch, beg, of the poor.          30

Android, loving beggar, dive to the poor
As your love would even without head to you,
Graze like machined wheels, green, from off this stone
And preying on each terrified chest, lost
Say, I am old as the globe, the moon, it          35
Is my old shoe, yours, be free as the leaves.

Fly, mantis, on the poor, arise like leaves
The armies of the poor, strength: stone on stone
And build the new world in your eyes, Save it!

                                                        —*1934*

*A. M. Klein (1909–1972) Born in the Ukraine, Klein came as an infant to Montreal with his family and went on to become a lawyer and poet. His collections* Hath Not a Jew . . . *(1940) and the satiric* Hitleriad *(1944), and his novel* The Second Scroll *(1951), draw on his Jewish heritage, whereas the award-winning* The Rocking Chair *(1948) also explores French Quebec. After a breakdown in 1954, he withdrew from writing and public activity for the remainder of his life.*

## A. M. Klein

# Portrait of the Poet as Landscape

### I

Not an editorial-writer, bereaved with bartlett,°
mourns him, the shelved Lycidas.°
No actress squeezes a glycerine tear for him.
The radio broadcast lets his passing pass.
And with the police, no record. Nobody, it appears,          5
either under his real name or his alias,
missed him enough to report.

It is possible that he is dead, and not discovered.
It is possible that he can be found some place
in a narrow closet, like the corpse in a detective story,          10
standing, his eyes staring, and ready to fall on his face.
It is also possible that he is alive
and amnesiac, or mad, or in retired disgrace,
or beyond recognition lost in love.

We are sure only that from our real society          15
he has disappeared; he simply does not count,
except in the pullulation° of vital statistics—
somebody's vote, perhaps, an anonymous taunt

---

**1 bartlett** *Bartlett's Familiar Quotations*   **2 Lycidas** In his poem "Lycidas" (1637), John Milton mourns the drowning death of his Cambridge schoolmate Edward King (1612–1637).
**17 pullulation** breeding, rapid increase

of the Gallup poll, a dot in a government table—
but not felt, and certainly far from eminent—                    20
in a shouting mob, somebody's sigh.

O, he who unrolled our culture from his scroll—
the prince's quote, the rostrum-rounding roar—
who under one name made articulate
heaven, and under another the seven-circled air,°      25
is, if he is at all, a number, an x,
a Mr Smith in a hotel register,—
incognito, lost, lacunal.°

    II

The truth is he's not dead, but only ignored—
like the mirroring lenses forgotten on a brow          30
that shine with the guilt of their unnoticed world.
The truth is he lives among neighbours, who, though
    they will allow
him a passable fellow, think him eccentric, not solid,
a type that one can forgive, and for that matter, forgo.

Himself he has his moods, just like a poet.            35
Sometimes, depressed to nadir, he will think all lost,
will see himself as throwback, relict,° freak,
his mother's miscarriage, his great-grandfather's ghost,
and he will curse his quintuplet senses, and their tutors
in whom he put, as he should not have put, his trust.  40

Then he will remember his travels over that body—
the torso verb, the beautiful face of the noun,
and all those shaped and warm auxiliaries!
A first love it was, the recognition of his own.
Dear limbs adverbial, complexion of adjective,         45
dimple and dip of conjugation!

And then remember how this made a change in him
affecting for always the glow and growth of his being;

---

**25 seven-circled air** Before Copernicus, Ptolemy's system of the universe showed circles around the
earth for the moon, the five known planets, and the sun. Perhaps also an allusion to the Muslim belief
that Allah created seven heavens.  **28 lacunal** resembling an empty space  **37 relict** leftover organism surviving in a changed environment

how suddenly was aware of the air, like shaken tinfoil,°
of the patents of nature, the shock of belated seeing,                    *50*
the lonelinesses peering from the eyes of crowds;
the integers of thought; the cube-roots of feeling.

Thus, zoomed to zenith, sometimes he hopes again,
and sees himself as a character, with a rehearsed role:
the Count of Monte Cristo,° come for his revenges;          *55*
the unsuspected heir, with papers; the risen soul;
or the chloroformed prince awaking from his flowers;
or—deflated again—the convict on parole.

   III

He is alone; yet not completely alone.
Pins on a map of a colour similar to his,                    *60*
each city has one, sometimes more than one;
here, caretakers of art, in colleges;
in offices, there, with arm-bands, and green-shaded;
and there, pounding their catalogued beats in libraries,—

everywhere menial, a shadow's shadow.                       *65*
And always for their egos—their outmoded art.
Thus, having lost the bevel in the ear,
they know neither up nor down, mistake the part
for the whole, curl themselves in a comma,
talk technics, make a colon their eyes. They distort—       *70*

such is the pain of their frustration—truth
to something convolute and cerebral.
How they do fear the slap of the flat of the platitude!
Now Pavlov's victims,° their mouths water at bell,
the platter empty.                                          *75*
          See they set twenty-one jewels
into their watches; the time they do not tell!

---

**49 tinfoil** See Gerard Manley Hopkins's poem "God's Grandeur" (p. 497).    **55 Count of Monte
Cristo** *The Count of Monte Cristo* (1844) is a novel by Alexandre Dumas, in which a wrongfully
imprisoned man escapes to take revenge on those who made him suffer.    **74 Pavlov's victims**
Russian physiologist Ivan Pavlov (1849–1936) was famous for his experiments on the conditioned
reflex, including making a dog salivate at the sound of a bell.

Some, patagonian° in their own esteem,
and longing for the multiplying word,
join party and wear pins, now have a message,                    *80*
an ear, and the convention-hall's regard.
Upon the knees of ventriloquists, they own,
of their dandled brightness, only the paint and board.

And some go mystical, and some go mad.
One stares at a mirror all day long, as if                       *85*
to recognize himself; another courts
angels,—for here he does not fear rebuff;
and a third, alone, and sick with sex, and rapt,
doodles him symbols convex and concave.

O schizoid solitudes! O purities                                 *90*
curdling upon themselves! Who live for themselves,
or for each other, but for nobody else;
desire affection, private and public loves;
are friendly, and then quarrel and surmise
the secret perversions of each other's lives.                    *95*

    IV

He suspects that something has happened, a law
been passed, a nightmare ordered. Set apart,
he finds himself, with special haircut and dress,
as on a reservation. Introvert.
He does not understand this; sad conjecture                      *100*
muscles and palls thrombotic on his heart.

He thinks an imposter, having studied his personal
    biography,
his gestures, his moods, now has come forward to pose
in the shivering vacuums his absence leaves.
Wigged with his laurel, that other, and faked with his face,     *105*
he pats the heads of his children, pecks his wife,
and is at home, and slippered, in his house.

---

**78 patagonian** Natives of the Patagonia area in Argentina were described by early explorers as the
world's tallest people.

So he guesses at the impertinent silhouette
that talks to his phone-piece and slits open his mail.
Is it the local tycoon who for a hobby                                    *110*
plays poet, he so epical in steel?
The orator, making a pause? Or is that man
he who blows his flash of brass in the jittering hall?

Or is he cuckolded by the troubadour
rich and successful out of celluloid?                                    *115*
Or by the don who unrhymes atoms? Or
the chemist death built up? Pride, lost impostor'd pride,
it is another, another, whoever he is,
who rides where he should ride.

     V

*Fame*, the adrenalin: to be talked about;                               *120*
to be a verb; to be introduced as *The*:
to smile with endorsement from slick paper; make
caprices anecdotal; to nod to the world; to see
one's name like a song upon the marquees played;
to be forgotten with embarrassment; to be—                               *125*
to be.

It has its attractions, but is not the thing;
nor is it the ape mimesis° who speaks from the tree
ancestral; nor the merkin° joy . . .
Rather it is stark infelicity                                            *130*
which stirs him from his sleep, undressed, asleep
to walk upon roofs and window-sills and defy
the gape of gravity.

     VI

Therefore he seeds illusions. Look, he is
the nth Adam taking a green inventory                                     *135*
in world but scarcely uttered, naming, praising,
the flowering fiats° in the meadow, the

---

**128 mimesis** imitation    **129 merkin** pubic wig for women; also slang for "American"
**137 fiats** commands from the Latin, "let it be done"

syllabled fur, stars aspirate, the pollen
whose sweet collision sounds eternally.                        140
For to praise

the world—he, solitary man—is breath
to him. Until it has been praised, that part
has not been. Item by exciting item—
air to his lungs, and pressured blood to his heart.—          145
they are pulsated, and breathed, until they map,
not the world's, but his own body's chart!

And now in imagination he has climbed
another planet, the better to look
with single camera view upon this earth—                      150
its total scope, and each afflated° tick,
its talk, its trick, its tracklessness—and this,
this, he would like to write down in a book!

To find a new function for the *déclassé* craft
archaic like the fletcher's;° to make a new thing;            155
to say the word that will become sixth sense;
perhaps by necessity and indirection bring
new forms to life, anonymously, new creeds—
O, somehow pay back the daily larcenies of the lung!

These are not mean ambitions. It is already something         160
merely to entertain them. Meanwhile, he
makes of his status as zero a rich garland,
a halo of his anonymity,
and lives alone, and in his secret shines
like phosphorus. At the bottom of the sea.                    165

                                                       —*1948*

---

**151 afflated** breathed upon, inspired    **155 fletcher's** arrow maker's

*Dorothy Livesay (1909–1996) Born in Winnipeg, Livesay lived and worked in Montreal, Vancouver, and Zambia. The publication of* **Green Pitcher** *(1928) and the many collections that followed marked her as an important contributor to modern Canadian poetry. Her style ranged from imagism to what she called the "documentary" poem that creates dialogue between historical material and the poet's own thoughts.*

## Dorothy Livesay

# The Three Emilys°

These women crying in my head
Walk alone, uncomforted:
The Emilys, these three
Cry to be set free—
And others whom I will not name                                    5
Each different, each the same.

Yet they had liberty!
Their kingdom was the sky:
They batted clouds with easy hand,
Found a mountain for their stand;                                 10
From wandering lonely they could catch
The inner magic of a heath—
A lake their palette, any tree
Their brush could be.

And still they cry to me                                          15
As in reproach—
I, born to hear their inner storm
Of separate man in woman's form,
I yet possess another kingdom, barred
To them, these three, this Emily.                                 20
I move as mother in a frame,
My arteries

**The Three Emilys** British poet and novelist Emily Brontë (1818–1878), American poet Emily Dickinson (1830–1886), and Canadian painter Emily Carr (1871–1945). Unlike Livesay, none of the three married or had children.

Flow the immemorial way
Towards the child, the man;
And only for a brief span                                          25
Am I an Emily on mountain snows
And one of these.

And so the whole that I possess
Is still much less—
They move triumphant through my head:                              30
I am the one
Uncomforted.

—*1953*

---

*Charles Olson (1910–1970) was born in Worcester, Massachusetts, and educated at Harvard. In his influential essay "Projective Verse" (1950), he argued that "a poem is energy transferred from where the poet got it . . . to the reader" and that the ear and the breath are essential to poetry. He and other avant-garde poets associated with North Carolina's Black Mountain College were known as the "Black Mountain Poets."*

## *Charles Olson*
# The Ring of

it was the west wind caught her up, as
she° rose
from the genital
wave, and bore her from the delicate
foam, home                                                          5
to her isle

and those lovers
of the difficult, the hours
of the golden day welcomed her, clad her, were
as though they had made her, were wild                              10

---

**2 she** Aphrodite, goddess of love in Greek mythology and Botticelli's *Birth of Venus* (1485)

to bring this new thing born
of the ring of the sea pink
& naked, this girl, brought her
to the face of the gods, violets
in her hair                                                                      *15*

Beauty, and she
said no to zeus & them all, all were not or
was it she chose the ugliest
to bed with, or was it straight
and to expiate the nature of beauty, was it?                    *20*

knowing hours, anyway,
she did not stay long, or the lame
was only one part, & the handsome
mars had her     And the child
had that name, the arrow of                                              *25*
as the flight of, the move of
his mother who adorneth

with myrtle the dolphin and words
they rise, they do who
are born of like                                                                    *30*
elements

                                                                            —*1953*

*Elizabeth Bishop (1911–1979) was from Worcester, Massachusetts, but time spent with maternal grandparents in a Nova Scotia coastal village inspired some memorable poems. Always highly regarded as a "poet's poet," she won the Pulitzer Prize in 1956, but her reputation has continued to increase since the publication of* The Complete Poems 1927–1979 *(1983). She travelled widely and lived in Brazil for many years before returning to the United States to teach at Harvard during the last years of her life.*

## Elizabeth Bishop

# At the Fishhouses

Although it is a cold evening,
down by one of the fishhouses
an old man sits netting,
his net, in the gloaming almost invisible
a dark purple-brown,                                                    5
and his shuttle worn and polished.
The air smells so strong of codfish
it makes one's nose run and one's eyes water.
The five fishhouses have steeply peaked roofs
and narrow, cleated gangplanks slant up                                 10
to storerooms in the gables
for the wheelbarrows to be pushed up and down on.
All is silver: the heavy surface of the sea,
swelling slowly as if considering spilling over,
is opaque, but the silver of the benches,                               15
the lobster pots, and masts, scattered
among the wild jagged rocks,
is of an apparent translucence
like the small old buildings with an emerald moss
growing on their shoreward walls.                                       20
The big fish tubs are completely lined
with layers of beautiful herring scales
and the wheelbarrows are similarly plastered
with creamy iridescent coats of mail,
with small iridescent flies crawling on them.                           25

Up on the little slope behind the houses,
set in the sparse bright sprinkle of grass,
is an ancient wooden capstan,°
cracked, with two long bleached handles
and some melancholy stains, like dried blood,                    *30*
where the ironwork has rusted.
The old man accepts a Lucky Strike.°
He was a friend of my grandfather.
We talk of the decline in the population
and of codfish and herring                                        *35*
while he waits for a herring boat to come in.
There are sequins on his vest and on his thumb.
He has scraped the scales, the principal beauty,
from unnumbered fish with that black old knife,
the blade of which is almost worn away.                          *40*

Down at the water's edge, at the place
where they haul up the boats, up the long ramp
descending into the water, thin silver
tree trunks are laid horizontally
across the gray stones, down and down                            *45*
at intervals of four or five feet.

Cold dark deep and absolutely clear,
element bearable to no mortal,
to fish and to seals . . . One seal particularly
I have seen here evening after evening.                          *50*
He was curious about me. He was interested in music;
like me a believer in total immersion,
so I used to sing him Baptist hymns.
I also sang "A Mighty Fortress Is Our God."
He stood up in the water and regarded me                         *55*
steadily, moving his head a little.
Then he would disappear, then suddenly emerge
almost in the same spot, with a sort of shrug
as if it were against his better judgment.
Cold dark deep and absolutely clear,                             *60*

**28 capstan** mechanism for winding cable    **32 Lucky Strike** brand of American cigarettes

the clear gray icy water . . . Back, behind us,
the dignified tall firs begin.
Bluish, associating with their shadows,
a million Christmas trees stand
waiting for Christmas. The water seems suspended                    65
above the rounded gray and blue-gray stones.
I have seen it over and over, the same sea, the same,
slightly, indifferently swinging above the stones,
icily free above the stones,
above the stones and then the world.                                70
If you should dip your hand in,
your wrist would ache immediately,
your bones would begin to ache and your hand would burn
as if the water were a transmutation of fire
that feeds on stones and burns with a dark gray flame.              75
If you tasted it, it would first taste bitter,
then briny, then surely burn your tongue.
It is like what we imagine knowledge to be:
dark, salt, clear, moving, utterly free,
drawn from the cold hard mouth                                      80
of the world, derived from the rocky breasts
forever, flowing and drawn, and since
our knowledge is historical, flowing, and flown.

—*1955*

# One Art

The art of losing isn't hard to master;
so many things seem filled with the intent
to be lost that their loss is no disaster.

Lose something every day. Accept the fluster
of lost door keys, the hour badly spent.                            5
The art of losing isn't hard to master.

Then practice losing farther, losing faster:
places, and names, and where it was you meant
to travel. None of these will bring disaster.

I lost my mother's watch. And look! my last, or                   *10*
next-to-last, of three loved houses went.
The art of losing isn't hard to master.

I lost two cities, lovely ones. And, vaster,
some realms I owned, two rivers, a continent.
I miss them, but it wasn't a disaster.                            *15*

—Even losing you (the joking voice, a gesture
I love) I shan't have lied. It's evident
the art of losing's not too hard to master
though it may look like *(Write* it!) like disaster.

                                                          *—1976*

---

*Allen Curnow (1911–2001) was born in Timaru, New Zealand, and is considered
one of that country's leading poets. In poems like "Landfall in Unknown Seas" he
explores the history of his island homeland. His numerous books of poetry span a
long career from* Valley of Decision *(1933) to* Bells of Saint Babel's *(2001).*

## Allen Curnow
# Landfall in Unknown Seas

THE 300TH ANNIVERSARY OF THE DISCOVERY OF NEW ZEALAND
BY ABEL TASMAN, 13 DECEMBER 1642

I

Simply by sailing in a new direction
You could enlarge the world.
                                You picked your captain,
Keen on discoveries, tough enough to make them,
Whatever vessels could be spared from other                       *5*
More urgent service for a year's adventure;
Took stock of the more probable conjectures
About the Unknown to be traversed, all
Guesses at golden coasts and tales of monsters
To be digested into plain instructions                            *10*
For likely and unlikely situations.

All this resolved and done, you launched the whole
On a fine morning, the best time of year,
Skies widening and the oceanic furies
Subdued by summer illumination; time                                15
To go and to be gazed at going
On a fine morning, in the Name of God
Into the nameless waters of the world.

O you had estimated all the chances
Of business in those waters, the world's waters                     20
Yet unexploited.
                    But more than the sea-empire's
Cannon, the dogs of bronze and iron barking
From Timor to the Straits, backed up the challenge.
Between you and the South an older enmity                            25
Lodged in the searching mind, that would not tolerate
So huge a hegemony of ignorance.
There, where your Indies had already sprinkled
Their tribes like ocean rains, you aimed your voyage;
Like them invoked your God, gave seas to history                    30
And islands to new hazardous tomorrows.

    II

Suddenly exhilaration
Went off like a gun, the whole
Horizon, the long chase done,
Hove to. There was the seascape                                     35
Crammed with coast, surprising
As new lands will, the sailor
Moving on the face of the waters,
Watching the earth take shape
Round the unearthly summits, brighter                               40
Than its emerging colour.

Yet this, no far fool's errand,
Was less than the heart desired,
In its old Indian dream
The glittering gulfs ascending                                      45

Past palaces and mountains
Making one architecture.
Here the uplifted structure,
Peak and pillar of cloud—
O splendour of desolation—reared                    *50*
Tall from the pit of the swell,
With a shadow, a finger of wind, forbade
Hopes of a lucky landing.

Always to islanders danger
Is what comes over the sea;                          *55*
Over the yellow sands and the clear
Shallows, the dull filament
Flickers, the blood of strangers:
Death discovered the Sailor
O in a flash, in a flat calm,                        *60*
A clash of boats in the bay
And the day marred with murder.
The dead required no further
Warning to keep their distance;
The rest, noting the failure,                        *65*
Pushed on with a reconnaissance
To the north; and sailed away.

### III

Well, home is the Sailor, and that is a chapter
In a schoolbook, a relevant yesterday
We thought we knew all about, being much apter       *70*
    To profit, sure of our ground,
No murderers mooring in our Golden Bay.

But now there are no more islands to be found
And the eye scans risky horizons of its own
In unsettled weather, and murmurs of the drowned     *75*
    Haunt their familiar beaches—
Who navigates us towards what unknown

But not improbable provinces? Who reaches
A future down for us from the high shelf

Of spiritual daring? Not those speeches            *80*
    Pinning on the Past like a decoration
For merit that congratulates itself,

O not the self-important celebration
Or most painstaking history, can release
The current of a discoverer's elation            *85*
    And silence the voices saying,
'Here is the world's end where wonders cease.'

Only by a more faithful memory, laying
On him the half-light of a diffident glory,
The Sailor lives, and stands beside us, paying            *90*
    Out into our time's wave
The stain of blood that writes an island story.

—*1943*

---

*Irving Layton (1912–2006) was born in Romania to a Jewish family but came to Montreal as an infant, eventually changing his name from Lazarovitch to Layton. He is one of Canada's best-known poets as much for his feisty personality as for his exuberant poetry. In more than forty collections, including the award-winning* A Red Carpet for the Sun *(1959) and* Collected Poems *(1971), he has explored his hope that love and imagination are two ways to dominate reality.*

## *Irving Layton*
# The Fertile Muck

There are brightest apples on those trees
    but until I, fabulist, have spoken
they do not know their significance
or what other legends are hung like garlands
    on their black boughs twisting            *5*
like a rumour. The wind's noise is empty.

Nor are the winged insects better off
    though they wear my crafty eyes
wherever they alight. Stay here, my love;

you will see how delicately they deposit
    me on the leaves of elms
or fold me in the orient dust of summer.

And if in August joiners and bricklayers
    are thick as flies around us
building expensive bungalows for those
who do not need them, unless they release
    me roaring from their moth-proofed cupboards
their buyers will have no joy, no ease.

I could extend their rooms for them without cost
    and give them crazy sundials
to tell the time with, but I have noticed
how my irregular footprint horrifies them
    evenings and Sunday afternoons:
they spray for hours to erase its shadow.

How to dominate reality? Love is one way;
    imagination another. Sit here
beside me, sweet; take my hard hand in yours.
We'll mark the butterflies disappearing over the hedge
    with tiny wristwatches on their wings:
our fingers touching the earth, like two Buddhas.

—1956

*(line numbers: 10, 15, 20, 25, 30)*

---

*Muriel Rukeyser (1913–1980) was born and lived in New York, and sought in her poetry to offer a female-centred vision to counteract the violence of Western culture. Her poetic career ranged from* Theory of Flight *(1935) to* Collected Poems *(1978).*

## *Muriel Rukeyser*
# Myth

Long afterward, Oedipus, old and blinded, walked the
roads.    He smelled a familiar smell.    It was
the Sphinx.    Oedipus said, "I want to ask one question.

Why didn't I recognize my mother?"     "You gave the
wrong answer," said the Sphinx.     "But that was what     5
made everything possible," said Oedipus.     "No," she said.
"When I asked, What walks on four legs in the morning,
two at noon, and three in the evening, you answered,
Man.     You didn't say anything about woman."
"When you say Man," said Oedipus, "you include women     10
too. Everyone knows that."     She said, "That's what
you think."

*—1973*

---

*Dudley Randall (1914–2000) was the founder of Broadside Press, a Black-owned
publishing firm that eventually attracted important writers like Gwendolyn Brooks
and Don L. Lee. For most of his life a resident of Detroit, Randall spent many years
working in that city's library system before taking a similar position at the
University of Detroit.*

# Dudley Randall
# Ballad of Birmingham

ON THE BOMBING OF A CHURCH IN BIRMINGHAM, ALABAMA, 1963°

"Mother dear, may I go downtown
Instead of out to play,
And march the streets of Birmingham
In a Freedom March today?"

"No, baby, no, you may not go,     5
For the dogs are fierce and wild,
And clubs and hoses, guns and jail
Aren't good for a little child."

"But, mother, I won't be alone.
Other children will go with me,     10

**Birmingham, Alabama, 1963** during the height of the civil rights movement

And march the streets of Birmingham
To make our country free."

"No, baby, no, you may not go,
For I fear those guns will fire.
But you may go to church instead                                   15
And sing in the children's choir."

She has combed and brushed her night-dark hair,
And bathed rose petal sweet,
And drawn white gloves on her small brown hands,
And white shoes on her feet.                                       20

The mother smiled to know her child
Was in the sacred place,
But that smile was the last smile
To come upon her face.

For when she heard the explosion,                                  25
Her eyes grew wet and wild.
She raced through the streets of Birmingham
Calling for her child.

She clawed through bits of glass and brick,
Then lifted out a shoe.                                            30
"O, here's the shoe my baby wore,
But, baby, where are you?"

*—1969*

*William Stafford (1914–1993) was one of the most prolific poets of the post-war era. Stafford published in virtually every magazine in the United States. Raised in Kansas as a member of the pacifist Church of the Brethren, Stafford served in a camp for conscientious objectors during World War II. His first book did not appear until he was in his forties, but he published over thirty collections before his death at age seventy-nine.*

## *William Stafford*
# Traveling Through the Dark

Traveling through the dark I found a deer
dead on the edge of the Wilson River road.
It is usually best to roll them into the canyon:
that road is narrow; to swerve might make more dead.

By glow of the tail-light I stumbled back of the car          5
and stood by the heap, a doe, a recent killing;
she had stiffened already, almost cold.
I dragged her off; she was large in the belly.

My fingers touching her side brought me the reason—
her side was warm; her fawn lay there waiting,          10
alive, still, never to be born.
Beside that mountain road I hesitated.

The car aimed ahead its lowered parking lights;
under the hood purred the steady engine.
I stood in the glare of the warm exhaust turning red;          15
around our group I could hear the wilderness listen.

I thought hard for us all—my only swerving—
then pushed her over the edge into the river.

—1960

*Dylan Thomas (1914–1953) was a legendary performer of his and others' poetry. His popularity in the United States led to several collegiate reading tours, punctuated with outrageous behaviour and self-destructive drinking that led to his early death in New York City, the victim of what the autopsy report labelled "insult to the brain." The Wales of his childhood remained a constant source of inspiration for his poetry and for radio dramas like* Under Milk Wood, *which was turned into a film by fellow Welshman Richard Burton and his wife at the time, Elizabeth Taylor.*

## Dylan Thomas
# Do Not Go Gentle into That Good Night

Do not go gentle into that good night,
Old age should burn and rave at close of day;
Rage, rage against the dying of the light.

Though wise men at their end know dark is right,
Because their words had forked no lightning they                    5
Do not go gentle into that good night.

Good men, the last wave by, crying how bright
Their frail deeds might have danced in a green bay,
Rage, rage against the dying of the light.

Wild men who caught and sang the sun in flight,                     10
And learn, too late, they grieved it on its way,
Do not go gentle into that good night.

Grave men, near death, who see with blinding sight
Blind eyes could blaze like meteors and be gay,
Rage, rage against the dying of the light.                          15

And you, my father, there on the sad height,
Curse, bless, me now with your fierce tears, I pray,
Do not go gentle into that good night.
Rage, rage against the dying of the light.

—1952

# Fern Hill

Now as I was young and easy under the apple boughs
About the lilting house and happy as the grass was green,
    The night above the dingle starry,
        Time let me hail and climb
      Golden in the heydays of his eyes,              5
And honored among wagons I was prince of the apple towns
And once below a time I lordly had the trees and leaves
        Trail with daisies and barley
    Down the rivers of the windfall light.

And as I was green and carefree, famous among the barns    10
About the happy yard and singing as the farm was home,
    In the sun that is young once only,
        Time let me play and be
      Golden in the mercy of his means,
And green and golden I was huntsman and herdsman, the calves 15
Sang to my horn, the foxes on the hills barked clear and cold,
        And the sabbath rang slowly
    In the pebbles of the holy streams.

All the sun long it was running, it was lovely, the hay
Fields high as the house, the tunes from the chimneys, it was air  20
    And playing, lovely and watery
        And fire green as grass.
    And nightly under the simple stars
As I rode to sleep the owls were bearing the farm away,
All the moon long I heard, blessed among stables, the night-jars  25
    Flying with the ricks, and the horses
      Flashing into the dark.

And then to awake, and the farm, like a wanderer white
With the dew, come back, the cock on his shoulder: it was all
    Shining, it was Adam and maiden,            30
        The sky gathered again
    And the sun grew round that very day.
So it must have been after the birth of the simple light
In the first, spinning place, the spellbound horses walking warm

Out of the whinnying green stable                                     35
    On to the fields of praise.

And honored among foxes and pheasants by the gay house
Under the new made clouds and happy as the heart was long,
    In the sun born over and over,
        I ran my heedless ways,                                       40
    My wishes raced through the house high hay
And nothing I cared, at my sky blue trades, that time allows
In all his tuneful turning so few and such morning songs
    Before the children green and golden
        Follow him out of grace,                                      45

Nothing I cared, in the lamb white days, that time would take me
Up to the swallow thronged loft by the shadow of my hand,
    In the moon that is always rising,
        Nor that riding to sleep
    I should hear him fly with the high fields                        50
And wake to the farm forever fled from the childless land.
Oh as I was young and easy in the mercy of his means,
        Time held me green and dying
    Though I sang in my chains like the sea.

                                                                *—1946*

*Randall Jarrell (1914–1965) excelled as both a poet and a (sometimes brutally honest) reviewer of poetry. Ironically, the author of what is perhaps the best-known poem to have emerged from World War II did not see combat during the war: He served as a control tower officer in stateside bases. A native of Nashville, Kentucky, Jarrell studied at Vanderbilt University and followed his mentor, John Crowe Ransom, to Kenyon College in 1937, where he befriended another student, Robert Lowell.*

## *Randall Jarrell*
# The Death of the Ball Turret° Gunner

From my mother's sleep I fell into the State,
And I hunched in its belly till my wet fur froze.
Six miles from earth, loosed from its dream of life,
I woke to black flak and the nightmare fighters.
When I died they washed me out of the turret with a hose.          5

—*1945*

*John Ciardi (1916–1986) was born in Boston, the son of Italian immigrants. He was an aerial gunner with the U.S. Army Air Corps (1942–1945), returning to teach at Harvard and other universities until 1961. He has written over forty collections of poetry for adults and children, a critically acclaimed translation of Dante's* Divine Comedy, *and several prose works that have helped to make poetry more widely accessible.*

## *John Ciardi*
# To Lucasta,° About That War

A long winter from home the gulls blew
    on their brinks, the tankers slid
    over the hump where the wolf packs hid

---

**Ball Turret** A Plexiglas sphere set into the belly of a heavy bomber; Jarrell noted the similarity between the gunner and a fetus in the womb.
**Lucasta** See Richard Lovelace's poem of 1649.

like voodoo talking, the surf threw
bundles with eyes ashore. I did                                          5
what booze brought me, and it wasn't you.

I was almost bored. I watched and told time
as enforced, a swag-man
under the clock. The bloat-bags ran
wet from nowhere, selling three-for-a-dime                               10
and nobody buying. Armies can
type faster than men die, I'm

told, and can prove. Didn't I find
time there, and more, to count
all, triplicate, and still walk guard-mount                              15
on the gull- and drum-wind
over the hump? I did, and won't
deny several (or more) pig-blind

alleys with doors, faces, dickers,
which during, the ships slid                                             20
over the humps where the packs hid.
And talking voodoo and snickers
over the edge of their welts, I did
what I could with (they called them) knickers;

and it was goddam good,                                                  25
and not bad either. It
was war (they called it) and it lit
a sort of skyline somehow in the blood,
and I typed the dead out a bit
faster than they came, or anyone should,                                 30

and the gulls blew high on their brinks,
and the ships slid, and the surf threw,
and the army initialled, and you
were variously, and straight and with kinks,
raped, fondled, and apologized to—                                       35
which is called (as noted) war. And it stinks.

*—1959*

*Anne Hébert (1916–2000) was born in a small village not far from Quebec City and is one of Quebec's best known writers, though she lived for many years in Paris. She is probably best known for her novels, including* Kamouraska *(1970) and* Un Habit de lumière *(1998), but has also written plays and poems, including this one translated by F. R. Scott.*

## *Anne Hébert*
# Snow

Snow puts us in a dream on vast plains without track or colour

Beware, my heart, snow puts us in the saddle on steeds of foam

Proclaim the coronation of childhood, snow consecrates us on high seas, dreams fulfilled, all sails set

Snow puts us in a trance, a widespread whiteness, flaring plumes pierced by the red eye of this bird

My heart; a point of fire under palms of frost flows the marvelling blood.                                                                                5

—*1960*

Translated by F.R. Scott.

*P. K. Page (b. 1916) was born in England and raised on the Canadian prairies. She lived abroad in Australia and Brazil, settling finally in British Columbia. A visual artist and a poet, she has published over a dozen books, including the two-volume collected poems* The Hidden Room *(1997) and* Hand Luggage *(2006). "Planet Earth" is based on lines from Pablo Neruda's poem "In Praise of Ironing."*

## *P. K. Page*
# Planet Earth

*It has to be spread out, the skin of this planet,*
*has to be ironed, the sea in its whiteness;*
*and the hands keep on moving,*
*smoothing the holy surfaces.*

In Praise of Ironing, *Pablo Neruda*

It has to be loved the way a laundress loves her linens,
the way she moves her hands caressing the fine muslins
knowing their warp and woof,
like a lover coaxing, or a mother praising.
It has to be loved as if it were embroidered                   5
with flowers and birds and two joined hearts upon it.
It has to be stretched and stroked.
It has to be celebrated.
O this great beloved world and all the creatures in it.
*It has to be spread out, the skin of this planet.*            10

The trees must be washed, and the grasses and mosses.
They have to be polished as if made of green brass.
The rivers and little streams with their hidden cresses
and pale-coloured pebbles
and their fool's gold                                          15
must be washed and starched or shined into brightness,.
the sheets of lake water
smoothed with the hand
and the foam of the oceans pressed into neatness.
*It has to be ironed, the sea in its whiteness.*               20

and pleated and goffered, the flower-blue sea
the protean, wine-dark, grey, green, sea
with its metres of satin and bolts of brocade.
And sky—such an O! overhead—night and day
must be burnished and rubbed                                   25
by hands that are loving
so the blue blazons forth
and the stars keep on shining
within and above
*and the hands keep on moving.*                                30

It has to be made bright, the skin of this planet
till it shines in the sun like gold leaf.
Archangels then will attend to its metals
and polish the rods of its rain.
Seraphim will stop singing hosannas                            35

to shower it with blessings and blisses and praises
and, newly in love,
we must draw it and paint it
our pencils and brushes and loving caresses
*smoothing the holy surfaces.*                                    40

—*1994*

*Robert Lowell (1917–1977) was born into a prominent Boston family and became known for his autobiographical poetry and his political activism. His poetry collections include the Pulitzer Prize–winning* Lord Weary's Castle *(1947) and* The Dolphin *(1973), as well as the influential* Life Studies *(1959). He was repeatedly hospitalized for severe manic depression.*

# Robert Lowell
## Water

It was a Maine lobster town—
each morning boatloads of hands
pushed off for granite
quarries on the islands,

and left dozens of bleak                                    5
white frame houses stuck
like oyster shells
on a hill of rock,

and below us, the sea lapped
the raw little match-stick                                    10
mazes of a weir,
where the fish for bait were trapped.

Remember? We sat on a slab of rock.
From this dance in time,
it seems the color                                    15
of iris, rotting and turning purpler,

but it was only
the usual gray rock
turning the usual green
when drenched by the sea.                                                    20

The sea drenched the rock
at our feet all day,
and kept tearing away
flake after flake.

One night you dreamed                                                        25
you were a mermaid clinging to a wharf-pile,
and trying to pull
off the barnacles with your hands.

We wished our two souls
might return like gulls                                                      30
to the rock. In the end,
the water was too cold for us.

*—1964*

---

**Gwendolyn Brooks (1917–2000)** *was the first African American to win a
Pulitzer Prize for poetry. Brooks reflected many changes in Black culture during her
long career, and she wrote about the stages of her own life candidly in* From the
Mecca, *her literary autobiography. Brooks was the last poetry consultant of the
Library of Congress before that position became poet laureate of the United States. At
the end of her life Brooks was one of the most honoured and beloved of American poets.*

## Gwendolyn Brooks
# First Fight. Then Fiddle.

First fight. Then fiddle. Ply the slipping string
With feathery sorcery; muzzle the note
With hurting love; the music that they wrote
Bewitch, bewilder. Qualify to sing
Threadwise. Devise no salt, no hempen thing                                   5

For the dear instrument to bear. Devote
The bow to silks and honey. Be remote
A while from malice and from murdering.
But first to arms, to armor. Carry hate
In front of you and harmony behind. 10
Be deaf to music and to beauty blind.
Win war. Rise bloody, maybe not too late
For having first to civilize a space
Wherein to play your violin with grace.

—*1949*

---

**Margaret Avison (b. 1918)** *was born in Galt, Ontario, and grew up on the prairies. Her conversion to Christianity in 1963 is reflected in collections like* The Dumfounding *(1966) and* Sunblue *(1978). Her other collections include the award-winning* Winter Sun *(1960),* No Time *(1989),* Concrete and Wild Carrot *(2002),* Always Now *(in three volumes), and* Momentary Dark *(2006).*

## *Margaret Avison*
# Snow

Nobody stuffs the world in at your eyes.
The optic heart must venture: a jail-break
And re-creation. Sedges and wild rice
Chase rivery pewter. The astonished cinders quake
With rhizomes.° All ways through the electric air 5
Trundle candy-bright disks; they are desolate
Toys if the soul's gates seal, and cannot bear,
Must shudder under, creation's unseen freight.
But soft, there is snow's legend: colour of mourning
Along the yellow Yangtze° where the wheel 10

---

**5 rhizomes** plant stems that run along the ground and send out both roots and leaves    **10 Yangtze** longest river in China

Spins an indifferent stasis that's death's warning.
Asters of tumbled quietness reveal
Their petals. Suffering this starry blur
The rest may ring your change,° sad listener.

—1960

---

Al Pur∂y (1918–2000) Identified as the People's Poet and the Voice of the Land,
Purdy was born in Wooler, Ontario, but travelled widely across Canada, celebrating
its places and people in memorable poems such as "Lament for the Dorsets" and
"The Country North of Belleville." His collections include The Cariboo Horses
(1965), Collected Poems (1986), and Beyond Remembering (2000).

## Al Pur∂y
# A Handful of Earth

TO RENÉ LÉVESQUE°

Proposal:
let us join Quebec
if Quebec won't join us
I don't mind in the least
being governed from Quebec City                                    5
by Canadiens instead of Canadians
in fact the fleur-de-lis
            and maple leaf
are only symbols
and our true language                                              10
speaks from inside
the land itself

---

**14 ring your change** To ring the changes is to go through all the changes in ringing a peal of bells; to
go through all the possible variations of a process.
**René Lévesque** (1922–1987) became leader of the separatist Parti Québécois in 1967 and served as
premier of Quebec from 1976 to 1985.

Listen:
you can hear soft wind blowing
among tall fir trees on Vancouver Island                                    15
it is the same wind we knew
whispering along Côte des Neiges
on the island of Montreal
when we were lovers and had no money
Once flying in a little Cessna 180                                          20
above that great spine of mountains
where a continent attempts the sky
I wondered who owns this land
and knew that no one does
for we are tenants only                                                     25

Go back a little:
to hip-roofed houses on the Isle d'Orléans
and scattered along the road to Chicoutimi
the remaining few log houses in Ontario
sod huts of sunlit prairie places                                          30
dissolved in rain long since
the stones we laid atop of one another
a few of which still stand
those origins
in which children were born                                                35
in which we loved and hated
in which we built a place to stand on
and now must tear it down?
—and here I ask all the oldest questions
of myself                                                                   40
the reasons for being alive
the way to spend this gift and thank the giver
but there is no way

I think of the small dapper man
chain-smoking at PQ headquarters                                           45
Lévesque
on Avenue Christophe Colomb in Montreal
where we drank coffee together six years past

I say to him now: my place is here
whether Côte des Neiges Avenue Christophe Colomb          *50*
Yonge Street Toronto Halifax or Vancouver
this place is where I stand
where all my mistakes were made
when I grew awkwardly and knew what I was
and that is Canadian or Canadien          *55*
it doesn't matter which to me

Sod huts break the prairie skyline
then melt in rain
the hip-roofed houses of New France as well
but French no longer          *60*
nor are we any longer English
—limestone houses
lean-tos and sheds our fathers built
in which our mothers died
before the forests tumbled down          *65*
ghost habitations
only this handful of earth
for a time at least
I have no other place to go

                              *—1977, rev. 1978*

***Lawrence Ferlinghetti (b. 1919)*** *Born in Yonkers, New York, Ferlinghetti received a doctorate from the Sorbonne and settled in San Francisco, where he established the City Lights Bookstore. He has published* A Far Rockaway of the Heart *(1997) and* Loud Prayer *(1998), but it is* A Coney Island of the Mind *(1958), from which this poem is taken, that remains one of the quintessential documents of the Beat Generation.*

## *Lawrence Ferlinghetti*
# In Goya's° greatest scenes we seem to see

In Goya's greatest scenes we seem to see
                              the people of the world
          exactly at the moment when
                    they first attained the title of
                              'suffering humanity'          5
          They writhe upon the page
                              in a veritable rage
                                   of adversity
               Heaped up
                    groaning with babies and bayonets          10
                              under cement skies
               in an abstract landscape of blasted trees
                    bent statues bats wings and beaks
                         slippery gibbets
                    cadavers and carnivorous cocks          15
               and all the final hollering monsters
                    of the
                         'imagination of disaster'
               they are so bloody real
                    it is as if they really still existed          20

And they do

               Only the landscape is changed

**Goya** Goya y Lucientes (1746–1828), Spanish painter known for his tortured paintings and etchings of violence and madness, including a series entitled "The Disasters of War"

They still are ranged along the roads
   plagued by legionaires
            false windmills and demented roosters    *25*
They are the same people
           only further from home
  on freeways fifty lanes wide
         on a concrete continent
              spaced with bland billboards    *30*
      illustrating imbecile illusions of happiness
The scene shows fewer tumbrils°
       but more maimed citizens
              in painted cars
  and they have strange license plates    *35*
and engines
    that devour America
                               *—1958*

---

*Oodgeroo of the Tribe Noonuccal (1920–1993) was born Kath Walker on Stradbroke Island off the Queensland coast of Australia. Taking her Aboriginal name, she became a prominent activist for Aboriginal rights and a poet whose collections include* We Are Going *(1964) and* Stradbroke Dreaming *(1972).*

# Oodgeroo of the Tribe Noonuccal (Kath Walker)

# We Are Going

FOR GRANNIE COOLWELL

They came in to the little town
A semi-naked band subdued and silent,
All that remained of their tribe.
They came here to the place of their old bora ground°
Where now the many white men hurry about like ants.    *5*

---

**32 tumbrils** dung carts or instruments of punishment
**4 bora ground** site of Aboriginal initiation ceremony in which a boy is admitted to manhood

Notice of estate agent reads: "Rubbish May Be Tipped Here."
Now it half covers the traces of the old bora ring.
They sit and are confused, they cannot say their thoughts:
"We are as strangers here now, but the white tribe are the
    strangers.
We belong here, we are of the old ways.                     *10*
We are the corroboree° and the bora ground,
We are the old sacred ceremonies, the laws of the elders.
We are the wonder tales of Dream Time,° the tribal legends
    told.
We are the past, the hunts and the laughing games, the
    wandering camp fires.
We are the lightning-bolt over Gaphembah Hill°             *15*
Quick and terrible,
And the Thunderer after him, that loud fellow.
We are the quiet daybreak paling the dark lagoon.
We are the shadow-ghosts creeping back as the camp fires
    burn low.
We are nature and the past, all the old ways               *20*
Gone now and scattered.
The scrubs are gone, the hunting and the laughter.
The eagle is gone, the emu° and the kangaroo are gone
    from this place.
The bora ring is gone.
The corroboree is gone.                               *25*
And we are going."

*—1964*

---

**11 corroboree** public performance of songs and dances celebrating Aboriginal mythology and spirituality    **13 Dream Time** the time beyond living memory, when the world came into being    **15 Gaphembah Hill** hill near Moongalba on Stradbroke Island, home of the author, off southeastern Queensland in Australia    **23 emu** large flightless bird of Australia

*Richard Wilbur (b. 1921) will be remembered by posterity as perhaps the most skillful metricist and exponent of wit that American poetry has produced. His highly polished poetry — against the grain of much contemporary writing — is a monument to his craftsmanship and intelligence. Perhaps the most honoured of all living American poets, Wilbur served as poet laureate of the United States in 1987. His translations of the verse dramas of Molière and Racine are regularly performed throughout the world.*

## Richard Wilbur
# The Writer

In her room at the prow of the house
Where light breaks, and the windows are tossed with linden,
My daughter is writing a story.

I pause in the stairwell, hearing
From her shut door a commotion of typewriter-keys 5
Like a chain hauled over a gunwale.

Young as she is, the stuff
Of her life is a great cargo, and some of it heavy:
I wish her a lucky passage.

But now it is she who pauses, 10
As if to reject my thought and its easy figure.
A stillness greatens, in which

The whole house seems to be thinking,
And then she is at it again with a bunched clamor
Of strokes, and again is silent. 15

I remember the dazed starling
Which was trapped in that very room, two years ago;
How we stole in, lifted a sash

And retreated, not to affright it;
And how for a helpless hour, through the crack of the door, 20
We watched the sleek, wild, dark

And iridescent creature
Batter against the brilliance, drop like a glove
To the hard floor, or the desk-top.

And wait then, humped and bloody,                               25
For the wits to try it again; and how our spirits
Rose when, suddenly sure,

It lifted off from a chair-back,
Beating a smooth course for the right window
And clearing the sill of the world.                             30

It is always a matter, my darling,
Of life or death, as I had forgotten. I wish
What I wished you before, but harder.

—*1976*

---

*Philip Larkin (1922–1985) was perhaps the last British poet to establish a sig-
nificant body of readers in the United States. The general pessimism of his work is
mitigated by a wry sense of irony and brilliant formal control. For many years he
was a librarian at the University of Hull, and he was also a dedicated fan and critic
of jazz.*

## Philip Larkin
# Water

If I were called in
To construct a religion
I should make use of water.

Going to church
Would entail a fording                                          5
To dry, different clothes;

My liturgy would employ
Images of sousing,
A furious devout drench,

And I should raise in the east 10
A glass of water
Where any-angled light
Would congregate endlessly.

—*1954*

*Denise Levertov (1923–1999) was an outspoken opponent of U.S. involvement in
the Vietnam War, an activity that has tended to overshadow her accomplishments as
a lyric poet. Born of Jewish and Welsh parents in England, she emigrated to the
United States during World War II.*

## Denise Levertov
# In Mind

There's in my mind a woman
of innocence, unadorned but

fair-featured, and smelling of
apples or grass. She wears

a utopian smock or shift, her hair 5
is light brown and smooth, and she

is kind and very clean without
ostentation—
                but she has
no imagination. 10

                And there's a
turbulent moon-ridden girl

or old woman, or both,
dressed in opals and rags, feathers

and torn taffeta, 15
who knows strange songs—

but she is not kind.

—*1964*

*Maxine Kumin (b. 1925) was born in Philadelphia and educated at Radcliffe. Kumin was an early literary ally and friend of Anne Sexton, with whom she co-authored several children's books. The winner of the 1973 Pulitzer Prize, Kumin has preferred a rural life raising horses for some years. Her increased interest in the natural world has paralleled the environmental awareness of many of her readers.*

## *Maxine Kumin*
# Noted in the *New York Times*

*Lake Buena Vista, Florida, June 16, 1987*

Death claimed the last pure dusky seaside sparrow
today, whose coastal range was narrow,
as narrow as its two-part buzzy song.
From hummocks lost to Cape Canaveral
this mouselike skulker in the matted grass,         5
a six-inch bird, plain brown, once thousands strong,
sang *toodle-raeee azhee*, ending on a trill
before the air gave way to rocket blasts.

It laid its dull white eggs (brown specked) in small
neat cups of grass on plots of pickleweed,         10
bulrushes, or salt hay. It dined
on caterpillars, beetles, ticks, the seeds
of sedges. Unremarkable
the life it led with others of its kind.

Tomorrow we can put it on a stamp,         15
a first-day cover with Key Largo rat,
Schaus swallowtail, Florida swamp
crocodile, and fading cotton mouse.
How simply symbols replace habitat!
The tower frames of Aerospace         20
quiver in the flush of another shot
where, once indigenous, the dusky sparrow
soared trilling twenty feet above its burrow.

—*1989*

*Allen Ginsberg (1926–1997) became the chief poetic spokesman of the Beat
Generation. He was a force —as poet and celebrity —who continued to outrage and
delight four decades after the appearance of* Howl, *the monumental poem describing
how Ginsberg saw: "the best minds of my generation destroyed by madness."
Ginsberg's poems are cultural documents that provide a key to understanding the radical changes in American life, particularly among youth, that began in the mid-1950s.*

## Allen Ginsberg
# A Supermarket in California

What thoughts I have of you tonight, Walt Whitman, for I walked
down the sidestreets under the trees with a headache self-conscious
looking at the full moon.

In my hungry fatigue, and shopping for images, I went into
the neon fruit supermarket, dreaming of your enumerations!

What peaches and what penumbras?° Whole families shopping at
night! Aisles full of husbands! Wives in the avocados, babies
in the tomatoes!—and you, García Lorca,° what were you doing down
by the watermelons?

I saw you, Walt Whitman, childless, lonely old grubber,
poking among the meats in the refrigerator and eyeing the
grocery boys.

I heard you asking questions of each: Who killed the pork
chops? What price bananas? Are you my Angel?                    5

I wandered in and out of the brilliant stacks of cans
following you, and followed in my imagination by the store
detective.

We strode down the open corridors together in our solitary
fancy tasting artichokes, possessing every frozen delicacy, and
never passing the cashier.

**3 penumbras** shadows   **3 García Lorca** Federico García Lorca, Spanish poet (1899–1936)

Where are we going, Walt Whitman? The doors close in an
hour. Which way does your beard point tonight?
    (I touch your book and dream of our odyssey in the super-
market and feel absurd.)
    Will we walk all night through solitary streets? The trees add
shade to shade, lights out in the houses, we'll both be lonely.       *10*
    Will we stroll dreaming of the lost America of love past blue
automobiles in driveways, home to our silent cottage?
    Ah, dear father, graybeard, lonely old courage-teacher, what
America did you have when Charon° quit poling his ferry and
you got out on a smoking bank and stood watching the boat
disappear on the black waters of Lethe?°

*—1956*

---

**Robert Kroetsch (b. 1927)** *was born in Heisler, Alberta, and has explored life on
the prairies and Canada's north through a variety of playful postmodern novels,
including* The Studhorse Man *(1969) and* The Man from the Creeks *(1998),
and long poems collected in* Completed Field Notes *(1989).*

*Robert Kroetsch*
# Stone Hammer Poem

### 1

This stone
become a hammer
of stone, this maul
is the colour
of bone (no,                         *5*
bone is the colour
of this stone maul).

---

12 **Charon** ferryman of Hades   **Lethe** river in Hades, means forgetfulness

The rawhide loops
are gone, the
hand is gone, the                                                    *10*
buffalo's skull
is gone;

the stone is
shaped like the skull
of a child.                                                          *15*

    2

This paperweight on my desk

where I begin
this poem    was

found in a wheatfield
lost (this hammer,                                                   *20*
this poem).

Cut to a function,
this stone was
(the hand is    gone—

    3

Grey, two-headed,                                                    *25*
the pemmican maul°

fell from the travois° or
a boy playing    lost it in
the prairie wool or
a squaw    left it in                          *30*
the brain of a buffalo or

It is a million
years older than
the hand that
chipped stone or                                                     *35*
raised slough
water (or blood) or

**26 pemmican maul** stone hammer used by Natives to make pemmican, a preparation of lean meat dried, pounded, and pressed into cakes   **27 travois** type of Native sledge

4

This stone maul
was found.

In the field                                          *40*
my grandfather
thought
was his

my father
thought was his                                       *45*

5

It is a stone
old as the last
Ice Age, the
retreating/the
recreating ice,                                        *50*
the retreating
buffalo, the
retreating Indians

(the saskatoons bloom
white (infrequently                                    *55*
the chokecherries the
highbush cranberries the
pincherries bloom
white along the barbed
wire fence (the                                        *60*
pemmican      winter

6

This stone maul
stopped a plow
long enough for one
*Gott im Himmel.*°                                     *65*

The Blackfoot (the
Cree?) not

---

**65 *Gott im Himmel*** German for "God in Heaven"

finding the maul
cursed.

? did he curse 70
? did he try to
go back
? what happened
I have to/I want
to know (not know) 75
? WHAT HAPPENED

    7

The poem
is the stone
chipped and hammered
until it is shaped 80
like the stone
hammer, the maul.

    8

Now the field is
mine because
I gave it
(for a price) 85

to a young man
(with a growing son)
who did not

notice that the land 90
did not belong

to the Indian who
gave it to the Queen
(for a price) who
gave it to the CPR° 95
(for a price) which

**95 CPR** The Canadian Pacific Railway laid rail from east to west and promoted commerce by selling land along the tracks to farmers.

gave it to my grandfather
(for a price) who
gave it to my father
(50 bucks an acre
*Gott im Himmel* I cut                                                100
down all the trees I
picked up all the stones) who

gave it to his son
(who sold it)                                                        105

    9

This won't
surprise you.

My grandfather
lost the stone maul.

    10

My father (retired)                                                  110
grew raspberries.
He dug in his potato patch.
He drank one glass of wine
each morning.
He was lonesome                                                      115
for death.

He was lonesome for the
hot wind on his face, the smell
of horses, the distant
hum of a threshing machine,                                          120
the oilcan he carried, the weight
of a crescent wrench in his hind pocket.

He was lonesome for his absent
sons and his daughters,
for his wife, for his own                                            125
brothers and sisters and

his own mother and father.

He found the stone maul
on a rockpile in the
north-west corner of what          *130*
he thought of
as his wheatfield.

He kept it (the
stone maul) on the railing
of the back porch in          *135*
a raspberry basket.

### 11

I keep it
on my desk
(the stone).

Sometimes I use it          *140*
in the (hot) wind
(to hold down paper)

smelling a little of cut
grass or maybe even of
ripening wheat or of          *145*
buffalo blood hot
in the dying sun.

Sometimes I write
my poems for that

stone hammer.          *150*

—*1975*

*Phyllis Webb (b. 1927) was born in Victoria. After living in Montreal and Toronto, she eventually moved back to British Columbia. Her poetry—gathered in collections such as* Naked Poems *(1965),* Water and Light: Ghazals and Anti-Ghazals *(1984), and the award- winning* Selected Poems: The Vision Tree *(1982)—has been referred to as metaphysical, existential, feminist, and minimalist.*

## *Phyllis Webb*
# Leaning

I am half-way up the stairs
of the Leaning Tower of Pisa.

Don't go down. You are in this
with me too.

I am leaning out of the Leaning                                    5
Tower heading into the middle distance

where a fur-blue star contracts, becomes
the ice-pond Brueghel's° figures are skating on.

North Magnetic pulls me like a flower
out of the perpendicular                                          10

angles me into outer space
an inch at a time, the slouch

of the ground, do you hear that?
the hiccup of the sludge about the stone.

(Rodin° in Paris, his amanuensis, a torso . . .)                  15
 I must change my life or crunch

over in vertigo, hands
bloodying the inside tower walls

lichen and dirt under the fingernails
Parsifal° vocalizing in the crazy night                          20

---

**8 Brueghel** Pieter Brueghel the Elder (1525–1569), Flemish painter known for his landscapes and scenes of peasant life    **15 Rodin** Auguste Rodin (1840–1917), French sculptor famous for *The Thinker*    **20 Parsifal** The composer Richard Wagner (1813–1883) used the story of the Arthurian knight Perceval as the basis for his last opera, *Parsifal* (1882).

my sick head on the table where I write
slumped one degree from the horizontal

the whole culture leaning . . .

the phalloi of Mies,° Columbus returning
stars all shot out—                                                                25

And now this. Smelly tourists
shuffling around my ears

climbing into the curvature.
They have paid good lira to get in here.

So have I. So did Einstein and Bohr.°                                    30
Why should we ever come down, ever?

And you, are you still here

tilting in this stranded ark
blind and seeing in the dark.

                                                                                    *—1984*

---

*Martin Carter (1927–1997) Considered Guyana's greatest poet, Carter was involved in politics, the struggle for independence from the British, and the social well-being of his people, all themes that emerge in his revolutionary poetry gathered in* Poems of Succession *(1977) and other collections.*

## Martin Carter
# University of Hunger

is the university of hunger the wide waste.
is the pilgrimage of man the long march.
The print of hunger wanders in the land.
The green tree bends above the long forgotten.
The plains of life rise up and fall in spasms.                          5
The huts of men are fused in misery.

24 **Mies** Ludwig Mies van der Rohe (1886–1969), German-born architect who was known for his skyscrapers    30 **Einstein and Bohr** Albert Einstein (1879–1955) and Neils Bohr (1885–1962) were quantum physicists who took part in the making of the atomic bomb.

They come treading in the hoofmarks of the mule
passing the ancient bridge
the grave of pride
the sudden flight                                                              10
the terror and the time.

They come from the distant village of the flood
passing from middle air to middle earth
in the common hours of nakedness.
Twin bars of hunger mark their metal brows                                     15
twin seasons mock them
parching drought and flood.

is the dark ones
the half sunken in the land.
is they who had no voice in the emptiness                                      20
in the unbelievable
in the shadowless.

They come treading on the mud floor of the year
mingling with dark heavy waters
and the sea sound of the eyeless flitting bat.                                 25
O long is the march of men and long is the life
and wide is the span.
O cold is the cruel wind blowing.
O cold is the hoe in the ground.

They come like sea birds                                                       30
flapping in the wake of a boat
is the torture of sunset in purple bandages
is the powder of fire spread like dust in the twilight
is the water melodies of white foam on wrinkled sand.

The long streets of night move up and down                                     35
baring the thighs of a woman
and the cavern of generation.
The beating drum returns and dies away.
The bearded men fall down and go to sleep.
The cocks of dawn stand up and crow like bugles.                               40

is they who rose early in the morning
watching the moon die in the dawn.
is they who heard the shell blow and the iron clang.
is they who had no voice in the emptiness
in the unbelievable                                                    45
in the shadowless.
O long is the march of men and long is the life
and wide is the span.

—*1977*

---

**John Ashbery (b. 1927)** *was born in upstate New York and educated at Harvard University. His first full-length book,* Some Trees, *was chosen by W. H. Auden as winner of the Yale Younger Poets Award in 1956. The author of over twenty books of poetry, Ashbery is now seen as the chief inheritor of the symbolist tradition brought to American locales by Wallace Stevens.*

## *John Ashbery*
# Paradoxes and Oxymorons

The poem is concerned with language on a very plain level.
Look at it talking to you. You look out a window
Or pretend to fidget. You have it but you don't have it.
You miss it, it misses you. You miss each other.

The poem is sad because it wants to be yours, and cannot.          5
What's a plain level? It is that and other things,
Bringing a system of them into play. Play?
Well, actually, yes, but I consider play to be

A deeper outside thing, a dreamed role-pattern,
As in the division of grace these long August days               10
Without proof. Open-ended. And before you know
It gets lost in the steam and chatter of typewriters.

It has been played once more. I think you exist only
To tease me into doing it, on your level, and then you aren't there
Or have adopted a different attitude. And the poem                    15
Has set me softly down beside you. The poem is you.

—*1981*

---

*Anne Sexton (1928–1974) lived a tortured life of mental illness and family troubles, becoming the model of the confessional poet. A housewife with two small daughters, she began writing poetry as the result of a program on public television, later taking a workshop from Robert Lowell, in which Sylvia Plath was a fellow student. For fifteen years until her suicide, she was a vibrant, exciting presence in American poetry. A controversial biography of Sexton by Diane Wood Middlebrook appeared in 1991.*

## *Anne Sexton*
# Cinderella

You always read about it:
the plumber with twelve children
who wins the Irish Sweepstakes.
From toilets to riches.
That story.                                                          5

Or the nursemaid,
some luscious sweet from Denmark
who captures the oldest son's heart.
From diapers to Dior.
That story.                                                          10

Or a milkman who serves the wealthy,
eggs, cream, butter, yogurt, milk,
the white truck like an ambulance
who goes into real estate
and makes a pile.                                                    15
From homogenized to martinis at lunch.

Or the charwoman
who is on the bus when it cracks up
and collects enough from the insurance.
From mops to Bonwit Teller.                                          *20*
That story.

Once
the wife of a rich man was on her deathbed
and she said to her daughter Cinderella:
Be devout. Be good. Then I will smile                               *25*
down from heaven in the seam of a cloud.
The man took another wife who had
two daughters, pretty enough
but with hearts like blackjacks.
Cinderella was their maid.                                          *30*
She slept on the sooty hearth each night
and walked around looking like Al Jolson.
Her father brought presents home from town,
jewels and gowns for the other women
but the twig of a tree for Cinderella.                              *35*
She planted that twig on her mother's grave
and it grew to a tree where a white dove sat.
Whenever she wished for anything the dove
would drop it like an egg upon the ground.
The bird is important, my dears, so heed him.                       *40*

Next came the ball, as you all know.
It was a marriage market.
The prince was looking for a wife.
All but Cinderella were preparing
and gussying up for the big event.                                  *45*
Cinderella begged to go too.
Her stepmother threw a dish of lentils
into the cinders and said: Pick them
up in an hour and you shall go.
The white dove brought all his friends;                             *50*
all the warm wings of the fatherland came,
and picked up the lentils in a jiffy.
No, Cinderella, said the stepmother,

you have no clothes and cannot dance.
That's the way with stepmothers.                                          55

Cinderella went to the tree at the grave
and cried forth like a gospel singer:
Mama! Mama! My turtledove,
send me to the prince's ball!
The bird dropped down a golden dress                                      60
and delicate little gold slippers.
Rather a large package for a simple bird.
So she went. Which is no surprise.
Her stepmother and sisters didn't
recognize her without her cinder face                                     65
and the prince took her hand on the spot
and danced with no other the whole day.

As nightfall came she thought she'd
better get home. The prince walked her home
and she disappeared into the pigeon house                                 70
and although the prince took an axe and broke
it open she was gone. Back to her cinders.
These events repeated themselves for three days.
However on the third day the prince
covered the palace steps with cobbler's wax                               75
And Cinderella's gold shoe stuck upon it.
Now he would find whom the shoe fit
and find his strange dancing girl for keeps.
He went to their house and the two sisters
were delighted because they had lovely feet.                              80
The eldest went into a room to try the slipper on
but her big toe got in the way so she simply
sliced it off and put on the slipper.
The prince rode away with her until the white dove
told him to look at the blood pouring forth.                              85
That is the way with amputations.
They don't just heal up like a wish.
The other sister cut off her heel
but the blood told as blood will.
The prince was getting tired.                                             90

He began to feel like a shoe salesman.
But he gave it one last try.
This time Cinderella fit into the shoe
like a love letter into its envelope.

At the wedding ceremony                                                   *95*
the two sisters came to curry favor
and the white dove pecked their eyes out.
Two hollow spots were left
like soup spoons.

Cinderella and the prince                                                  *100*
lived, they say, happily ever after,
like two dolls in a museum case
never bothered by diapers or dust,
never arguing over the timing of an egg,
never telling the same story twice,                                         *105*
never getting a middle-aged spread,
their darling smiles pasted on for eternity
Regular Bobbsey Twins.
That story.

*—1970*

# The Starry Night

> *That does not keep me from having a terrible*
> *need of—shall I say the word—religion. Then I*
> *go out at night to paint the stars.*
>
> —Vincent Van Gogh in a letter to his brother

The town does not exist
except where one black-haired tree slips
up like a drowned woman into the hot sky.
The town is silent. The night boils with eleven stars
Oh starry starry night! This is how                                         *5*
I want to die.

It moves. They are all alive.
Even the moon bulges in its orange irons

to push children, like a god, from its eye.
The old unseen serpent swallows up the stars.        10
Oh starry starry night! This is how
I want to die:

into that rushing beast of the night,
sucked up by that great dragon, to split
from my life with no flag,                            15
no belly,
no cry.

—1962

---

*A. K. Ramanujan (1929–1993) was born and educated in Mysore in South India. He was a poet in both Kannada and English, a scholar, professor, translator, and editor. His poetry collections in English include* The Striders *(1966),* Relations *(1971),* Second Sight *(1986), and the posthumous* Collected Poems *(1995). He also co-edited* The Oxford Anthology of Modern Indian Poetry *(1994).*

## A. K. Ramanujan
# A River

In Madurai,
              city of temples and poets
who sang of cities and temples:

every summer
a river dries to a trickle                            5
in the sand,
baring the sand-ribs,
straw and women's hair
clogging the watergates
at the rusty bars                                     10
under the bridges with patches
of repair all over them,
the wet stones glistening like sleepy
crocodiles, the dry ones
shaven water-buffaloes lounging in the sun.           15

The poets sang only of the floods.

He was there for a day
when they had the floods.
People everywhere talked
of the inches rising,                                      *20*
of the precise number of cobbled steps
run over by the water, rising
on the bathing places,
and the way it carried off three village houses,
one pregnant woman                                         *25*
and a couple of cows
named Gopi and Brinda, as usual.

The new poets still quoted
the old poets, but no one spoke
in verse                                                   *30*
of the pregnant woman
drowned, with perhaps twins in her,
kicking at blank walls
even before birth.

He said:                                                   *35*
the river has water enough
to be poetic
about only once a year
and then
it carries away                                            *40*
in the first half-hour
three village houses,
a couple of cows
named Gopi and Brinda
and one pregnant woman                                     *45*
expecting identical twins
with no moles on their bodies,
with different-coloured diapers

to tell them apart.

*—1966*

*Adrienne Rich (b. 1929) was born in Baltimore, Maryland, of Jewish heritage. Her first book of poetry,* A Change of World *(1951), was introduced by W. H. Auden. After dedicating time to marriage and motherhood, she returned to writing powerful poetry and prose that was increasingly political and concerned with feminist and lesbian themes. In all, she has written over twenty books of poetry, including the landmark work* Diving into the Wreck *(1973),* An Atlas of the Difficult World *(1991),* Midnight Salvage *(1999), and* The School Among the Ruins *(2004). Her work has earned her many awards, including the Lannan Foundation Lifetime Achievement Award. She lives in California.*

## *Adrienne Rich*
# Power

Living     in the earth-deposits     of our history
Today a backhoe divulged     out of a crumbling flank of earth
one bottle     amber     perfect     a hundred-year-old
cure for fever     or melancholy     a tonic
for living on this earth     in the winters of this climate          5

Today I was reading about Marie Curie:
she must have known she suffered     from radiation sickness
her body bombarded for years     by the element
she had purified
It seems she denied to the end                                        10
the source of the cataracts on her eyes
the cracked and suppurating skin     of her finger-ends
till she could no longer hold     a test-tube or a pencil

She died     a famous woman     denying
her wounds                                                            15
denying
her wounds     came     from the same source as her power

*—1978*

*D. G. Jones (b. 1929) was born in Ontario but has spent much of his life in Quebec. He has earned Governor General's Awards both for his translations and for his own poetry, of which he has published over ten collections. In his complex suite of thirteen acrostic poems, Jones celebrates the love between early Canadian poet Archibald Lampman and Katherine Waddell.*

# *D. G. Jones*

# Kate, These Flowers . . .

(THE LAMPMAN POEMS)

### I

You picked the dead bloom
expertly, leaving one star
lifting, long-stemmed, above cascading
leaves
  my day's star          *5*

Oh, Archie, you're a fool, she said

What colours are the vireo?°
Deep garden lights, the reflected lights of
apple leaves
   my dear         *10*
your shadowed flesh

like grave eyes in the afternoon
it is, under all pain, silent
laughter
   bird, flower        *15*
you, Kate, briefly on a day in June

### II

Kisses are knowledge, Kate
aphasia confounds us with a new
tongue
   too Pentecostal; too      *20*

---

**7 vireo** small songbirds

Eleusinian,° perhaps, for us
moderate Anglicans

You blush and the immoderate blood
riots like a rose
                 we are both                    25
exposed
      I who hate Sundays

dream how I will boldly
rush out and overnight paint
Ottawa crimson                                       30
           I come
secretly to the fold, would find
election° in your mouth

                                                 —*1977*

---

*Ted Hughes (1930–1998) was a native of Yorkshire, England. He never ventured far from the natural world of his childhood for his subject matter. Hughes was married to Sylvia Plath until her death in 1963;* Birthday Letters, *a book of poems about their troubled relationship, appeared in 1998. At the time of his death, Hughes was the British poet laureate.*

## *Ted Hughes*
# The Thought-Fox

I imagine this midnight moment's forest:
Something else is alive
Beside the clock's loneliness
And this blank page where my fingers move.

Through the window I see no star;                        5
Something more near
Though deeper within darkness
Is entering the loneliness:

**21 Eleusinian** celebrations near Athens in honour of the fertility goddess Demeter
**33 election** to be chosen

Cold, delicately as the dark snow,
A fox's nose touches twig, leaf;                              *10*
Two eyes serve a movement, that now
And again now, and now, and now

Sets neat prints into the snow
Between trees, and warily a lame
Shadow lags by stump and in hollow                           *15*
Of a body that is bold to come

Across clearings, an eye,
A widening deepening greenness,
Brilliantly, concentratedly,
Coming about its own business                                *20*

Till, with a sudden sharp hot stink of fox
It enters the dark hole of the head.
The window is starless still; the clock ticks,
The page is printed.

—*1957*

---

*Kamau Brathwaite (b. 1930) In many of his poems, including "Colombe,"*
*Brathwaite explores the influence of colonization and slavery on his native Barbados.*
*His collections include* The Arrivants *(1973),* Middle Passages *(1992), and*
Born to Slow Horses *(2005), which won the Griffin Poetry Prize for 2006.*

# *Kamau Brathwaite*
# Colombe

**C**olumbus from his after-
deck watched stars, absorbed in water,
melt in liquid amber drifting

through my summer air                                        *5*
Now with morning shadows lifting
beaches stretched before him cold & clear

Birds circled flapping flag & mizzen
mast.   birds harshly hawking.   without fear
Discovery he sailed for.   was so near                    *10*

### ℭ

olumbus from his after-
deck watched heights he hoped for
rocks he dreamed.   rise solid from my simple water

Parrots screamed. Soon he would touch              *15*
our land.   his charted mind's desire
The blue sky blessed the morning with its fire

But did his vision
fashion as he watched the shore
the slaughter that his soldiers                          *20*

furthered here?   Pike
point & musket butt
hot splintered courage.   bones

cracked with bullet shot
tipped black boot in my belly.   the                      *25*
whips uncurled desire?

### ℭ

olumbus from his after-
deck saw bearded fig trees.   yellow pouis
blazed like pollen & thin                                 *30*

waterfalls suspended in the green
as his eyes climbed towards the highest ridges
where our farms were hidden

Now he was sure
he heard soft voices mocking in the leaves                *35*
What did this journey mean.   this

new world mean.   dis
covery? or a return to terrors
he had sailed from.   known before?

I watched him pause                                    *40*

Then he was splashing silence
Crabs snapped their claws
and scattered as he walked towards our shore

—*1992*

---

**Derek Walcott (b. 1930)** *is a native of the tiny Caribbean island of St. Lucia in the West Indies. Walcott combines a love of the tradition of English poetry with the exotic surfaces of tropical life. In many ways, his life and career have constituted a study in divided loyalties, which are displayed in his ambivalent poems about life in the United States, where he has lived and taught for many years. Walcott was awarded the Nobel Prize in 1992.*

## *Derek Walcott*

# Central America

Helicopters are cutlassing the wild bananas.
Between a nicotine thumb and forefinger
brittle faces crumble like tobacco leaves.
Children waddle in vests, their legs bowed,
little shrimps curled under their navels.                    *5*
The old men's teeth are stumps in a charred forest.
Their skins grate like the iguana's.
Their gaze like slate stones.
Women squat by the river's consolations
where children wade up to their knees,                       *10*
and a stick stirs up a twinkling of butterflies.
Up there, in the blue acres
of forest, flies circle their fathers.
In spring, in the upper provinces
of the Empire, yellow tanagers                               *15*
float up through the bare branches.
There is no distinction in these distances.

—*1987*

*Miller Williams (b. 1930) won the Poet's Prize in 1990 for* Living on the Surface, *a volume of selected poems. A skillful translator of both Giuseppe Belli, a Roman poet of the early nineteenth century, and Nicanor Parra, a contemporary Chilean, Williams has written many poems about his travels throughout the world yet has retained the relaxed idiom of his native Arkansas.*

# *Miller Williams*
## The Book

I held it in my hands while he told the story.

He had found it in a fallen bunker,
a book for notes with all the pages blank.
He took it to keep for a sketchbook and diary.

He learned years later, when he showed the book                5
to an old bookbinder, who paled, and stepped back
a long step and told him what he held,
what he had laid the days of his life in.
It's bound, the binder said, in human skin.

I stood turning it over in my hands,                           10
turning it in my head. Human skin.

What child did this skin fit? What man, what woman?
Dragged still full of its flesh from what dream?

Who took it off the meat? Some other one
who stayed alive by knowing how to do this?                    15

I stared at the changing book and a horror grew,
I stared and a horror grew, which was, which is,
how beautiful it was until I knew.

—*1989*

*Linda Pastan (b. 1932) served as poet laureate of Maryland, where she has lived and taught for many years. Her first book,* A Perfect Circle of Sun, *appeared in 1971, and ten more collections have been published since. Her straightforward language belies the discipline of her craft, in which each poem "goes through something like 100 revisions."*

# Linda Pastan
## Ethics

In ethics class so many years ago
our teacher asked this question every fall:
if there were a fire in a museum
which would you save, a Rembrandt painting
or an old woman who hadn't many                                        5
years left anyhow? Restless on hard chairs
caring little for pictures or old age
we'd opt one year for life, the next for art
and always half-heartedly. Sometimes
the woman borrowed my grandmother's face                               10
leaving her usual kitchen to wander
some drafty, half imagined museum.
One year, feeling clever, I replied
why not let the woman decide herself?
Linda, the teacher would report, eschews                               15
the burdens of responsibility.
This fall in a real museum I stand
before a real Rembrandt, old woman,
or nearly so, myself. The colors
within this frame are darker than autumn,                              20
darker even than winter—the browns of earth,
though earth's most radiant elements burn
through the canvas. I know now that woman
and painting and season are almost one
and all beyond saving by children.                                     25

—1981

*Sylvia Plath (1932–1963), whose troubled personal life is often difficult to separate from her poetry, is almost always read as an autobiographical and confessional poet. Brilliant and precocious, she served a long apprenticeship to the tradition of modern poetry before attaining her mature style in the final two years of her life. Only one collection,* The Colossus, *appeared in her lifetime, and her fame has mainly rested on her posthumous books of poetry and the success of her lone novel,* The Bell Jar. *She committed suicide in 1963. Plath has been the subject of many biographical studies, reflecting the intense interest that readers, especially women, have in her life and work.*

## Sylvia Plath
# Black Rook in Rainy Weather

On the stiff twig up there
Hunches a wet black rook
Arranging and rearranging its feathers in the rain.
I do not expect a miracle
Or an accident                                                    5

To set the sight on fire
In my eye, nor seek
Any more in the desultory weather some design,
But let spotted leaves fall as they fall,
Without ceremony, or portent                                     10

Although, I admit, I desire,
Occasionally, some backtalk
From the mute sky, I can't honestly complain:
A certain minor light may still
Leap incandescent                                                15

Out of kitchen table or chair
As if a celestial burning took
Possession of the most obtuse objects now and then—
Thus hallowing an interval
Otherwise inconsequent                                           20

By bestowing largesse, honor,
One might say love. At any rate, I now walk

Wary (for it could happen
Even in this dull, ruinous landscape); skeptical,
Yet politic; ignorant                                                     25

Of whatever angel may choose to flare
Suddenly at my elbow. I only know that a rook
Ordering its black feathers can so shine
As to seize my senses, haul
My eyelids up, and grant                                                  30

A brief respite from fear
Of total neutrality. With luck,
Trekking stubborn through this season
Of fatigue, I shall
Patch together a content                                                  35

Of sorts. Miracles occur,
If you care to call those spasmodic
Tricks of radiance miracles. The wait's begun again,
The long wait for the angel,
For that rare, random descent.°                                          40

                                                                *—1960*

# Metaphors

I'm a riddle in nine syllables,
An elephant, a ponderous house,
A melon strolling on two tendrils.
O red fruit, ivory, fine timbers!
This loaf's big with its yeasty rising.                                   5
Money's new-minted in this fat purse.
I'm a means, a stage, a cow in calf.
I've eaten a bag of green apples,
Boarded the train there's no getting off.

                                                                *—1960*

---

**40 descent** In the Bible, the crippled and blind gathered around the pool of Bethesda, where an angel would sometimes descend and stir the waters. The first in would be healed (John 5:4).

*Alden Nowlan (1933–1983) grew up in Nova Scotia in impoverished circum-stances. He quit school in Grade 5 but continued to educate himself through reading, and went on to become a journalist and to publish novels and short stories that evoke a Maritime world at once harsh and human, as well as over ten collections of poetry, including* Bread, Wine and Salt *(1965),* I Might Not Tell Everybody This *(1982), and* An Exchange of Gifts *(1985).*

## Alden Nowlan
# The Bull Moose

Down from the purple mist of trees on the mountain,
lurching through forests of white spruce and cedar,
stumbling through tamarack swamps,
came the bull moose
to be stopped at last by a pole-fenced pasture.                              5

Too tired to turn or, perhaps, aware
there was no place left to go, he stood with the cattle.
They, scenting the musk of death, seeing his great head
like the ritual mask of a blood god, moved to the other end
of the field and waited.                                                     10

The neighbours heard of it, and by afternoon
cars lined the road.    The children teased him
with alder switches and he gazed at them
like an old tolerant collie.    The women asked
if he could have escaped from a Fair.                                        15

The oldest man in the parish remembered seeing
a gelded moose yoked with an ox for plowing.
The young men snickered and tried to pour beer
down his throat, while their girl friends
took their pictures.                                                         20

And the bull moose let them stroke his tick-ravaged flanks,
let them pry open his jaws with bottles, let a giggling girl
plant a little purple cap
of thistles on his head.

When the wardens came, everyone agreed it was a shame     *25*
to shoot anything so shaggy and cuddlesome.
He looked like the kind of pet
women put to bed with their sons.

So they held their fire.   But just as the sun dropped in the river
the bull moose gathered his strength                         *30*
like a scaffolded king, straightened and lifted his horns
so that even the wardens backed away as they raised their rifles.
When he roared, people ran to their cars.   All the young men
leaned on their automobile horns as he toppled.

                                                        *—1970*

# The Broadcaster's Poem

I used to broadcast at night
alone in a radio station
but I was never good at it,
partly because my voice wasn't right
but mostly because my peculiar                               *5*
metaphysical stupidity
made it impossible
for me to keep believing
there was somebody listening
when it seemed I was talking                                 *10*
only to myself in a room no bigger
than an ordinary bathroom.
I could believe it for a while
and then I'd get somewhat
the same feeling as when you                                 *15*
start to suspect you're the victim
of a practical joke.
                    So one part of me
was afraid another part
might blurt out something                                    *20*
about myself so terrible

that even I had never until
that moment suspected it.
       This was like the fear
of bridges and other                            25
high places: Will I take off my glasses
and throw them
into the water, although I'm
half-blind without them?
Will I sneak up behind                       30
myself and push?
            Another thing:
as a reporter
I covered an accident in which a train
ran into a car, killing                     35
three young men, one of whom
was beheaded. The bodies looked
boneless, as such bodies do.
More like mounds of rags.
And inside the wreckage                 40
where nobody could get at it
the car radio
was still playing.
          I thought about places
the disc jockey's voice goes             45
and the things that happen there
and of how impossible it would be for him
to continue if he really knew.

                                   —*1974*

*Jacques Godbout (b. 1933) was born in Montreal and has worked as a screenwriter, professor of French and philosophy, playwright, novelist, essayist, and poet. He has directed over thirty films, including four dramatic features, and published nine novels, including* Salut Galarneau! *(1967) and* Une Histoire Américaine *(1986), as well as half a dozen collections of poetry, including* Souvenirs Shop *(1984).*

# *Jacques Godbout*
# Trees

Trees we have given you a thousand names

In a tree-hollow I have hidden a silver coin
They will find it when they are sixteen

Under torn-away bark in the tree's wood
I too have carved the words love liberty friendship          5
A fantasy without respect for its dignity
I wanted very much to write peace
But there was no more space
So I looked around
The forest had gone to bed and under the sleeping trunks          10
Ready for the pulping stone the papermaking
The C-I-L factories and One Hundred Industries
I slipped You your name

I hid in a hollow tree
Watchful as a big cat for the sound of footsteps          15
When they are twenty they will find me
With my head between my legs
And my bones bleached because I waited for you,
What will they make from my bones?
Perhaps some games          20
Or drawings done on sand

When the forests rise up as in
a Shakespearean tragedy at the cinema

Translated by John Glassco.

And when they have also walked
When trees have shattered the concrete                                  25
Of launching pads
When sequoias have strangled the steel structures
(mosses and lianas parasites    control instruments)
What will they make with my money?

A goddess perhaps                                                        30
Or a charm against boredom

They will see an army of blacks with bronze trumpets
Sit down on a rocket's tip
To make it fall
Carried away by sound and by their own flesh                            35
They will find in tree-hollows
Their homesickness for lianas and drums

Trees we have given you a thousand names
And streets too
That we love                                                            40

In tree-hollows and shaded streets
In rock-gardens and courtyard moss
We have hidden a silver coin
Our dear friendship our love even
However it may be that others invent prisons                            45
And the iron of angelic hate

Almond trees tender bougainvilleas
We used to make love in your shade

Perhaps you will grant us
The secret of your light                                                50

                                                                  —*1960*

*Leonard Cohen (b. 1934) was born in Montreal of Jewish heritage, and has had a long, successful career as a poet, singer, and songwriter whose songs have been widely recorded. He has published two novels,* The Favourite Game *(1963) and* Beautiful Losers *(1966), and several collections of poetry, including* Flowers for Hitler *(1964),* Book of Mercy *(1984), and* Book of Longing *(2006). He has lived as a Zen monk, been honoured with numerous literary and music awards, and recorded more than fourteen albums.*

# *Leonard Cohen*

# The Future

Give me back my broken night
my mirrored room, my secret life
It's lonely here,
there's no one left to torture
Give me absolute control                                    5
over every living soul
And lie beside me, baby,
that's an order!

Give me crack and anal sex
Take the only tree that's left                              10
and stuff it up the hole
in your culture
Give me back the Berlin Wall
give me Stalin and St Paul
I've seen the future, brother:                              15
it is murder.

*Things are going to slide in all directions*
*Won't be nothing*
*Nothing you can measure any more*
*The blizzard of the world*                                 20
*has crossed the threshold*
*and it has overturned*
*the order of the soul*
*When they said REPENT*
*I wonder what they meant*                                  25

You don't know me from the wind
you never will, you never did
I'm the little jew
who wrote the bible
I've seen the nations rise and fall                    30
I've heard their stories, heard them all
but love's the only engine of survival

Your servant here, he has been told
to say it clear, to say it cold:
It's over, it ain't going                              35
any further
And now the wheels of heaven stop
you feel the devil's riding crop
Get ready for the future:
it is murder.                                          40

*Things are going to slide in all directions*

There'll be the breaking
of the ancient western code
Your private life will suddenly explode
There'll be phantoms                                   45
there'll be fires on the road
and the white man dancing

You'll see your woman
hanging upside down
her features covered by her fallen gown               50
and all the lousy little poets
coming round
trying to sound like Charlie Manson

Give me back the Berlin Wall
give me Stalin and St Paul                              55
Give me Christ
or give me Hiroshima
Destroy another fetus now
We don't like children anyhow
I've seen the future, baby:                            60
it is murder.

Things are going to slide in all directions
Won't be nothing
Nothing you can measure any more
The blizzard of the world                                    65
has crossed the threshold
and it has overturned
the order of the soul
When they said REPENT
I wonder what they meant                                      70

—*1993 (recorded 1992)*

*Pat Lowther (1935–1975) grew up in Vancouver and spent her life on the West Coast. Her poetry collections include* A Difficult Flowering *(1968) and* Milk Stone *(1974). In 1975 her body was discovered in a creek near Squamish, British Columbia, and her husband was convicted of her murder.* A Stone Diary *(1976) and* Final Instructions *(1980) were published posthumously.*

## Pat Lowther
# Octopus

The octopus is beautifully
functional as an umbrella;
at rest a bag of rucked skin
sags like an empty scrotum
his jelled eyes sad and bored                                5

but taking flight: look
how lovely purposeful
in every part:
the jet vent smooth
as modern plumbing                                           10
the webbed pinwheel of tentacles
moving in perfect accord
like a machine dreamed
by Leonardo

—*1977*

*George Bowering (b. 1935) was born in Penticton, British Columbia, and was a member of the Tish movement inspired by the Black Mountain Poets. He has published over thirty books of poetry, as well as numerous books of criticism and award-winning fiction. He was named Canada's first poet laureate in 2000. Baseball, one of his most enduring metaphors, appears in this poem from Blonds on Bikes (1997).*

## George Bowering
# Play & Work & Art

When you play the infield,
especially on diamonds like the one at Woodlands Park,
you bend over at the inning's beginning
& pick up stones
to throw thru the wire fence.                                              5

One day near second base at Woodlands Park
I bent over & picked up a pointy pebble
I raised to my eye, rubbed the dust off,
& it was an arrowhead.

Right there, East Side Vancouver.                                          10

Months later, sitting here with a sore baseball back
I thought about baseball as play
& arrow-making as work.

Then I thought again.

Making an arrowhead to kill a fish or deer                                 15
to feed a family or a people
is still interesting, is still making.
It is not a nuisance. You can see it

coming, like a ground ball, which
if you're over fifty, is no sure thing,                                    20
which is enough like work, like work & pain
in a life you are getting thru.

—*1997*

*Joy Kogawa (b. 1935) was born in Vancouver, of Japanese heritage. This poem, like the novel* Obasan *(1981), for which she is best known, deals with her experience of the evacuation and internment of Japanese Canadians after Pearl Harbor. Her books of poetry include* A Choice of Dreams *(1974) and* A Song of Lilith *(2000).*

## Joy Kogawa
# When I Was a Little Girl

When I was a little girl
We used to walk together
Tim, my brother who wore glasses,
And I, holding hands
Tightly as we crossed the bridge            5
And he'd murmur, "You pray now"
—being a clergyman's son—
Until the big white boys
Had kicked on past.
Later we'd climb the bluffs                  10
Overhanging the ghost town
And pick the small white lilies
And fling them like bombers
Over Slocan.

—*1974*

*Fred Chappell (b. 1936) wrote the prize-winning epic-length poem* Midquest *(1981), a complex autobiographical sequence heavily indebted to Dante for its formal structure. A versatile writer of both poetry and prose, Chappell brilliantly displays his classical learning in unusual contexts.*

## *Fred Chappell*
# Narcissus and Echo°

Shall the water not remember  *Ember*
my hand's slow gesture, tracing above  *of*
its mirror my half-imaginary  *airy*
portrait? My only belonging  *longing*
is my beauty, which I take  *ache*                                   5
away and then return as love  *of*
teasing playfully the one being  *unbeing.*

whose gratitude I treasure  *Is your*
moves me. I live apart  *heart*
from myself, yet cannot  *not*                                      10
live apart. In the water's tone,  *stone?*
that brilliant silence, a flower  *Hour,*
whispers my name with such slight  *light,*
moment, it seems filament of air,  *fare*
the world become cloudswell.  *well.*                               15

—*1985*

**Narcissus and Echo** In the myth, the vain Narcissus drowned attempting to embrace his own reflection in the water. Echo, a nymph who loved him, pined away until only her voice remained.

*Marge Piercy (b. 1936) was a political radical during her student days at the University of Michigan. Piercy has continued to be outspoken on political, cultural, and sexual issues. Her phrase "to be of use" has become a key measure by which feminist writers and critics have gauged the meaning of their own life experiences.*

## Marge Piercy
# Barbie Doll

This girlchild was born as usual
and presented dolls that did pee-pee
and miniature GE stoves and irons
and wee lipsticks the color of cherry candy.
Then in the magic of puberty, a classmate said:                    5
You have a great big nose and fat legs.

She was healthy, tested intelligent
possessed strong arms and back,
abundant sexual drive and manual dexterity.
She went to and fro apologizing.                                   10
Everyone saw a fat nose on thick legs.

She was advised to play coy,
exhorted to come on hearty,
exercise, diet, smile and wheedle.
Her good nature wore out                                           15
like a fan belt.
So she cut off her nose and her legs
and offered them up.

In the casket displayed on satin she lay
with the undertaker's cosmetics painted on,                        20
a turned-up putty nose,
dressed in a pink and white nightie.
Doesn't she look pretty? everyone said.
Consummation at last.
To every woman a happy ending.                                     25

—1982

> ***Robert Phillips (b. 1938)*** *laboured for over thirty years as a New York advertising executive, a remarkable fact when one considers his many books of poetry, fiction, and criticism and the numerous books he has edited. He currently lives in Houston, where he teaches in the creative writing program at the University of Houston.*

## *Robert Phillips*

# Compartments

Which shall be final?
       Pine box in a concrete vault,
urn on a mantel?

Last breath a rattle,
       stuffed in a black body bag,                5
he's zipped head to toe.

At the nursing home,
       side drawn to prevent a fall—
in a crib again.

His dead wife's false teeth                    10
       underfoot in their bedroom.
Feel the piercing chill.

Pink flamingo lawn,
       a Florida trailer park:
one space he'll avoid.                    15

The box they gave him
       on retirement held a watch
that measures decades.

The new bifocals
       rest in their satin-lined case,            20
his body coffined.

Move to the suburbs.
       Crowded train at seven-oh-two,
empty head at night.

New playpen, new crib,
        can't compete with the newness
of the newborn child.                                                    *25*

Oak four-poster bed
        inherited from family—
Jack Frost defrosted.                                                    *30*

Once he was pink-slipped.
        Dad helped out: "A son's a son,
Son, from womb to tomb."

Fourteen-foot ceilings,
        parquet floors, marble fireplace,                                *35*
proud first apartment.

The Jack Frost Motel,
        its very name a portent
for their honeymoon.

Backseat of a car,                                                       *40*
        cursing the inventor of
nylon pantyhose.

First-job cubicle.
        Just how many years before
a window office?                                                         *45*

College quad at noon,
        chapel bells, frat men, coeds,
no pocket money.

his grandfather's barn.
        After it burned to the ground,                                   *50*
the moon filled its space.

His favorite tree—
        the leaves return to branches?
No, butterflies light.

Closet where he hid                                                      *55*
        to play with himself. None knew?
Mothball orgasms.

Chimney that he scaled
     naked to sweep for his Dad:
Blake's soot-black urchin.                             60

The town's swimming pool
     instructor, throwing him in
again and again . . .

Kindergarten play
     ground: swings, slides, rings, jungle gym.     65
Scraped knees, molester.

Red, blue and green birds
     mobilize over his crib,
its sides a tall fence.

Two months premature,                          70
     he incubates by light bulbs,
like a baby chick.

He is impatient,
     curled in foetal position,
floating in darkness.                              75

*—2000*

**Margaret Atwood (b. 1939)** *is a leading figure among Canadian writers, with a huge international following. She is equally skilled as a poet and fiction writer, and has used her considerable reputation to support a variety of causes, including PEN International. Born in Ottawa, she graduated from the University of Toronto in 1962 and later did graduate work at Radcliffe and Harvard. She has authored over a dozen poetry collections, including* Eating Fire: Selected Poems, 1965–1995 *(1998); a dozen novels, including* The Handmaid's Tale *(1985) and* The Penelopiad *(2005); as well as half a dozen collections of short fiction, including* The Tent *(2006). She has also written literary criticism, including* Survival: A Thematic Guide to Canadian Literature *(1972), and several books for children. Her long list of awards includes the Giller Prize, the Booker Prize, and the Governor General's Award. She continues to be an inventive and prolific writer of works that reflect her feminist concerns, her interest in classical and popular mythology, and her increasing concern for the future of the planet.*

# Margaret Atwood
# [you fit into me]

you fit into me
like a hook into an eye

a fish hook
an open eye

—1971

# Death of a Young Son
# by Drowning

He, who navigated with success
the dangerous river of his own birth
once more set forth

on a voyage of discovery
into the land I floated on                                                5
but could not touch to claim.

His feet slid on the bank,
the currents took him;
he swirled with ice and trees in the swollen water

and plunged into distant regions,                               10
his head a bathysphere;
through his eyes' thin glass bubbles

he looked out, reckless adventurer
on a landscape stranger than Uranus
we have all been to and some remember.                          15

There was an accident; the air locked,
he was hung in the river like a heart.
They retrieved the swamped body,

cairn of my plans and future charts,
with poles and hooks                                            20
from among the nudging logs.

It was spring, the sun kept shining, the new grass
lept to solidity;
my hands glistened with details.

After the long trip I was tired of waves.                       25
My foot hit rock. The dreamed sails
collapsed, ragged.

      I planted him in this country
      like a flag.

*—1970*

# Notes Towards a Poem That Can Never Be Written

FOR CAROLYN FORCHÉ

i

This is the place
you would rather not know about,
this is the place that will inhabit you,
this is the place you cannot imagine,
this is the place that will finally defeat you                                    5

where the word *why* shrivels and empties
itself. This is famine.

ii

There is no poem you can write
about it, the sandpits
where so many were buried                                                         10
& unearthed, the unendurable
pain still traced on their skins.

This did not happen last year
or forty years ago but last week.
This has been happening,                                                          15
this happens.

We make wreaths of adjectives for them,
we count them like beads,
we turn them into statistics & litanies
and into poems like this one.                                                     20

Nothing works.
They remain what they are.

iii

The woman lies on the wet cement floor
under the unending light,
needle marks on her arms put there                                    *25*
to kill the brain
and wonders why she is dying.

She is dying because she said.
She is dying for the sake of the word.
It is her body, silent                                                *30*
and fingerless, writing this poem.

iv

It resembles an operation
but it is not one

nor despite the spread legs, grunts
& blood, is it a birth.                                               *35*

Partly it's a job,
partly it's a display of skill
like a concerto.

It can be done badly
or well, they tell themselves.                                        *40*

Partly it's an art.

v

The facts of this world seen clearly
are seen through tears;
why tell me then
there is something wrong with my eyes?                                *45*

To see clearly and without flinching,
without turning away,
this is agony, the eyes taped open
two inches from the sun.

What is it you see then?                                               *50*
Is it a bad dream, a hallucination?
Is it a vision?
What is it you hear?

The razor across the eyeball
is a detail from an old film.      *55*
It is also a truth.
Witness is what you must bear.

   vi

In this country you can say what you like
because no one will listen to you anyway,
it's safe enough, in this country you can try to write      *60*
the poem that can never be written,
the poem that invents
nothing and excuses nothing,
because you invent and excuse yourself each day.

Elsewhere, this poem is not invention.      *65*
Elsewhere, this poem takes courage.
Elsewhere, this poem must be written
because the poets are already dead.

Elsewhere, this poem must be written
as if you are already dead,      *70*
as if nothing more can be done
or said to save you.

Elsewhere you must write this poem
because there is nothing more to do.

                                          *—1981*

*Patrick Lane (b. 1939) was born in Nelson, British Columbia, and has travelled widely describing an ungentle but inspiring world. He has published over twenty collections of poetry, including* Beware the Months of Fire *(1974),* Poems New and Selected *(1978), which won a Governor General's Award, and* Go Leaving Strange *(2004).*

## Patrick Lane

# Because I Never Learned

FOR JOHN

Because I never learned how
to be gentle and the country
I lived in was hard with dead
animals and men I didn't question
my father when he told me                              5
to step on the kitten's head
after the bus had run over
its hind quarters.

Now, twenty years later,
I remember only:                                       10
the silence of the dying
when the fragile skull collapsed
under my hard bare heel,
the curved tongue in the dust
that would never cry again                             15
and the small of my father's back
as he walked tall away.

—*1974*

*Seamus Heaney (b. 1939) was born in the troubled country of Northern Ireland. Heaney has largely avoided the type of political differences that have divided his homeland. Instead, he has chosen to focus on the landscape of the rural Ireland he knew while growing up as a farmer's son. Since 1982, Heaney has taught part of the year at Harvard University. He was awarded the Nobel Prize for Literature in 1995.*

# Seamus Heaney
# Digging

Between my finger and my thumb
The squat pen rests; snug as a gun.

Under my window, a clean rasping sound
When the spade sinks into gravelly ground:
My father, digging. I look down                                    5

Till his straining rump among the flowerbeds
Bends low, comes up twenty years away
Stooping in rhythm through potato drills°
Where he was digging.

The coarse boot nestled on the lug, the shaft                     10
Against the inside knee was levered firmly.
He rooted out tall tops, buried the bright edge deep
To scatter new potatoes that we picked
Loving their cool hardness in our hands.

By God, the old man could handle a spade.                         15
Just like his old man.

My grandfather cut more turf in a day
Than any other man on Toner's bog.
Once I carried him milk in a bottle
Corked sloppily with paper. He straightened up                    20
To drink it, then fell to right away

---

**8 drills** furrows

Nicking and slicing neatly, heaving sods
Over his shoulder, going down and down
For the good turf. Digging.

The cold smell of potato mould, the squelch and slap          25
Of soggy peat, the curt cuts of an edge
Through living roots awaken in my head.
But I've no spade to follow men like them.

Between my finger and my thumb
The squat pen rests.                                          30
I'll dig with it.

—*1980*

*Florence Cassen Mayers (b. 1940) is a widely published poet and children's author. Her "ABC" books include children's guides to baseball and to the National Basketball Association.*

## *Florence Cassen Mayers*
# All-American Sestina

One nation, indivisible
two-car garage
three strikes you're out
four-minute mile
five-cent cigar                                               5
six-string guitar

six-pack Bud
one-day sale
five-year warranty
two-way street                                                10
fourscore and seven years ago
three cheers

three-star restaurant
sixty-
four-dollar question                                        *15*
one-night stand
two-pound lobster
five-star general

five-course meal
three sheets to the wind                                    *20*
two bits
six-shooter
one-armed bandit
four-poster

four-wheel drive                                            *25*
five-and-dime
hole in one
three-alarm fire

sweet sixteen
two-wheeler                                                 *30*

two-tone Chevy
four rms, hi flr, w/vu
six-footer
high five
three-ring circus                                           *35*
one-room schoolhouse

two thumbs up, five-karat diamond
Fourth of July, three-piece suit
six feet under, one-horse town

                                                  *—1996*

***Robert Hass (b. 1941)*** *was born and raised in San Francisco and now teaches at the University of California at Berkeley. His first book,* Field Guide, *was chosen for the Yale Series of Younger Poets in 1973. He has collaborated with Nobel Prize–winner Czeslaw Milosz on English translations of the latter's poetry.*

## *Robert Hass*

# Picking Blackberries with a Friend Who Has Been Reading Jacques Lacan°

August dust is here. Drought
stuns the road,
but juice gathers in the berries.

We pick them in the hot
slow-motion of midmorning.                                          5
Charlie is exclaiming:

for him it is twenty years ago
and raspberries and Vermont.
We have stopped talking

about *L'Histoire de la vérité,*°                                    10
about subject and object
and the mediation of desire.

Our ears are stoppered
in the bee-hum. And Charlie,
laughing wonderfully,                                               15

beard stained purple
by the word *juice,*
goes to get a bigger pot.

—*1979*

**Jacques Lacan** French psychoanalyst and literary theorist   **10 *L'Histoire de la vérité*** *The History of Truth,* by Lacan

*Gwendolyn MacEwan (1941–1987) was born in Toronto and published more than ten books of poetry, including* The Shadow-Maker *(1969) and* Afterworlds *(1987), both of which won Governor General's Awards. Many of her poems reveal a fascination with the magic and mythologies beneath the mundane surfaces of history and place.*

# Gwendolyn MacEwan
## Water

When you think of it, water is everything. Or rather,
Water ventures into everything and becomes everything.
     It has
All tastes and moods imaginable; water is history
And the end of the world is water also.                                   5
                    I have tasted water
From London to Miransah. In France it tasted
Of Crusaders' breastplates, swords, and tunnels of rings
On ladies' fingers.
              In the springs of Lebanon water had          10
No color, and was therefore all colors,
                       outside of Damascus
It disguised itself as snow and let itself be chopped
And spooned onto the stunned red grapes of summer.

For years I have defended water, even though I am told          15
           there are other drinks.
Water will never lie to you, even when it insinuates itself
Into someone else's territory. Water has style.

Water has no conscience and no shame; water
           thrives on water, is self-quenching.          20
It often tastes of brine and ammonia, and always
Knows its way back home.

When you want to travel very far, do as the Bedouin do—
Drink to overflowing when you can,

                                    and then                          25
Go sparingly between wells.

                                                          —1982


# Poem Improvised Around a First Line*

the smoke in my bedroom which is always burning
worsens you, motorcycle Icarus;
you are black and leathery and lean and
you cannot distinguish between sex and nicotine

anytime, it's all one thing for you—                          5
cigarette, phallus, sacrificial fire—
all part of that grimy flight
on wings axlegreased from Toronto to Buffalo
for the secret beer over the border—

now I long to see you fullblown and black                     10
over Niagara, your bike burning and in full flame
and twisting and pivoting over Niagara
and falling finally into Niagara,
and tourists coming to see your black leather wings
hiss and swirl in the steaming current—                       15

now I long to give up cigarettes
and change the sheets on my carboniferous bed;
O baby, what Hell to be Greek in this country—
without wings, but burning anyway

                                                          —1966


*The first line around which it was improvised has disappeared. [G. MacEwan]

*Don McKay (b. 1942) was born in Owen Sound, Ontario, but has lived on both coasts of Canada, most recently in British Columbia. He has published eleven books of highly crafted poetry, including the Governor General's Award–winning* Night Field *(1991) and* Another Gravity *(2000). In* Strike/Slip *(2006) he once again explores the intersection between the human and the natural world.*

## Don McKay

# Icarus°

isn't sorry. We do not find him
doing penance, writing out the golden mean for all
eternity, or touring its high schools to tell student bodies
not to do what he done
done. Over and over he rehearses flight                                    5
and fall, tuning his moves, entering
with fresh rush into the mingling of the air
with spirit. This is his practice
and his prayer: to be translated into air, as air
with each breath enters lungs,                                             10
then blood. He feels resistance gather in his stiff
strange wings, angles his arms to shuck the sweet lift
from the drag, runs the full length
of a nameless corridor, his feet striking the paving stones
less and less heavily, then                                                15
they're bicycling above the ground,
a few shallow beats and he's up,
he's out of the story and into the song.

At the melting point of wax, which now he knows
the way Doug Harvey° knows the blue line,                                   20
he will back-beat to create a pause, hover for maybe fifty
hummingbird heartbeats and then
lose it, tumbling into freefall, shedding feathers

---

**Icarus** In Greek mythology, Icarus is the son of Daedalus, who fashioned wings for them both to escape from Crete. Icarus flew too close to the sun, melting the wax that held his wings together, and fell into the sea. (See W. H. Auden's poem "Musée des Beaux Arts.") **20 Doug Harvey** Doug Harvey (1924–1989) played hockey for the Montreal Canadiens and was the seven-time winner of the Norris Trophy for the best defenceman.

like a lover shedding clothes. He may glide
in the long arc of a Tundra Swan or pull up sharp                    25
to Kingfisher into the sea which bears his name.° Then,
giving it the full Ophelia, drown.

On the shore
the farmer ploughs his field, the dull ship
sails away, the poets moralize about our                             30
insignificance. But Icarus is thinking tremolo and
backflip, is thinking
next time with a half-twist
and a tuck and isn't
sorry.                                                               35

                                   *

Repertoire, technique. The beautiful contraptions bred from
ingenuity and practice, and the names by which he claims
them, into which—lift-off, loop-the-loop—they seem to
bloom. Icarus could write a book. Instead he will stand for
hours in that musing half-abstracted space, watching. During     40
fall migrations he will often climb to the edge of a north-south
running ridge where the soaring hawks find thermals like
naturally occurring laughter, drawing his eyebeam up an
unseen winding stair until they nearly vanish in the depth of
sky. Lower down, Merlins° slice the air with wings that say       45
crisp crisp, precise as sushi chefs, while Sharp-shins
alternately glide and flap, hunting as they go, each line break
poised, ready to pivot like a point guard or Robert Creeley.°
Icarus notices how the Red-tails and Broadwings separate
their primaries° to spill a little air, giving up just enough lift to   50
break their drag up into smaller trailing vortices. What does
this remind him of? He thinks of the kind of gentle teasing
that can dissipate a dark mood so it slips off as a bunch of
skirmishes and quirks. Maybe that. Some little gift to

---

26 **the sea which bears his name** In ancient times, the part of the Aegean Sea into which Icarus
reportedly fell was called the Icarian Sea. **45 Merlins** Merlins are small falcons. Sharp-shins, Red-
tails, and Broadwings are hawks. **48 Robert Creeley** Point guards are some of basketball's quickest
and most skilled players. Robert Creeley (b. 1926) is an American poet known as a master technician.
**50 primaries** main flight feathers

acknowledge the many claims of drag and keep its big    *55*
imperative at bay. Icarus knows all about that one.

In the spring he heads for a slough and makes himself a blind
out of wolf willow and aspen, then climbs inside to let the
marsh-mind claim his thinking. The soft splashdowns of
Scaup and Bufflehead,° the dives which are simple shrugs and    *60*
vanishings; the Loon's wing, thin and sharp for flying in the
underwater world, and the broad wing of the Mallard,
powerful enough to break the water's grip with one sweep, a
guffaw which lifts it straight up into the air. Icarus has
already made the mistake of trying this at home, standing on    *65*
a balustrade in the labyrinth and fanning like a manic
punkah,° the effort throwing him backward off his perch and
into a mock urn which the Minotaur° had, more than once,
used as a pisspot. Another gift of failure. Now his watching is
humbler, less appropriative, a thoughtless thinking amid fly    *70*
drone and dragonfly dart. Icarus will stay in the blind until
his legs cramp up so badly that he has to move. He is really
too large to be a foetus for more than an hour. He unbends
creakily, stretches, and walks home, feeling gravity's pull
upon him as a kind of wealth.    *75*

\*

Sometimes Icarus dreams back into his early days with
Daedalus in the labyrinth. Then he reflects upon the
Minotaur, how seldom they saw him—did they ever?—while
they shifted constantly from no-place to no-place, setting up
false campsites and leaving decoy models of themselves.    *80*
Sometimes they would come upon these replicas in strange
postures, holding their heads in their laps or pointing to their
private parts. Once they discovered two sticks stuck like horns
in a decoy's head, which Daedalus took to be the worst of
omens. Icarus was not so sure.    *85*

---

**60 Scaup and Bufflehead** water birds  **67 punkah** large cloth fan suspended from the rafters
**68 Minotaur** half-man, half-bull who was confined in the labyrinth built by the father of Icarus
and who devoured the Athenian children who fed him

For today's replay he imagines himself sitting in a corridor
reflecting on life as a Minotaur (*The* Minotaur) while waiting
for his alter ego to come bumbling by. They were, he realizes,
both children of technology—one its *enfant terrible*, the other
the rash adolescent who, they will always say, should never      90
have been given a pilot's licence in the first place. What will
happen when they finally meet? Icarus imagines dodging like
a Barn Swallow, throwing out enough quick banter to deflect
his rival's famous rage and pique his interest. How many
Minotaurs does it take to screw in a light bulb? What did the    95
queen say to the machine? Should he wear two sticks on his
head, or save that for later? He leaps ahead to scenes out of
the Hardy Boys and Tom Sawyer. They will chaff and boast
and punch each other on the arm. They will ridicule the weird
obsessions of their parents. As they ramble, cul-de-sacs turn    100
into secret hideouts and the institutional corridors take on the
names of birds and athletes. They discover some imperfections in the rock face, nicks and juts which Daedalus
neglected to chisel off, and which they will use to climb,
boosting and balancing each other until they fall off. Together  105
they will scheme and imagine. Somehow they will find a way
to put their brute heads° in the clouds.

—*2000*

---

**107 brute heads** In the *Divine Comedy*, Dante writes "Consider your origins. You were not made that
you might live as brutes, but so as to follow virtue and knowledge." (Inferno 26. 118)

*Sharon Olds (b. 1942) was born in San Francisco but makes her home in New York City. In eight collections of poetry, including* Strike Sparks: Selected Poems *(2004), she displays tremendous candour in dealing with the intimacies of family relations covering three generations, a subject matter that has made her one of the chief contemporary heirs to the confessional tradition.*

## Sharon Olds

# I Go Back to May 1937

I see them standing at the formal gates of their colleges,
I see my father strolling out
under the ochre sandstone arch, the
red tiles glinting like bent
plates of blood behind his head, I                                          5
see my mother with a few light books at her hip
standing at the pillar made of tiny bricks with the
wrought-iron gate still open behind her, its
sword-tips black in the May air,
they are about to graduate, they are about to get married,     10
they are kids, they are dumb, all they know is they are
innocent, they would never hurt anybody.
I want to go up to them and say Stop,
don't do it—she's the wrong woman,
he's the wrong man, you are going to do things                   15
you cannot imagine you would ever do,
you are going to do bad things to children,
you are going to suffer in ways you never heard of,
you are going to want to die. I want to go
up to them there in the late May sunlight and say it,            20
her hungry pretty blank face turning to me,
her pitiful beautiful untouched body,
his arrogant handsome blind face turning to me,
his pitiful beautiful untouched body,
but I don't do it. I want to live. I                                         25

take them up like the male and female
paper dolls and bang them together
at the hips like chips of flint as if to
strike sparks from them, I say
Do what you are going to do, and I will tell about it.                    *30*

—*1987*

---

*Daphne Marlatt (b. 1942) was born in Australia and grew up in Malaysia, but went to Vancouver in 1951 and has remained there. She has published several collections of poems of place, including* Steveston *(1974), and poems of passion, including* Touch to My Tongue *(1984) and* This Tremor Love Is *(2001), as well as the novel* Ana Historic *(1988).*

## Daphne Marlatt

# (is love enough?)

> *Salt through the earth conduct the sea*
> —*Olga Broumas°*

such green glistening, a sparrow preening a far-stretched
wing, light full of pleasure-chirping, feathered bodies at
home in earth's soft voltage & newness written over your face
waking from dream, each blade, each leaf encased still in the
wet from last night's rain                                                  *5*

is love enough when the breast milk a mother jets in the
urgent mouth of her baby is laced with PCBs°?

hungry you said, for love, for light, armfuls of daffodils we
refuse to gather standing luminous, pale ears listening, ochre
trumpets at the heart darkness pools, & the radio, as we sit          *10*
on a paint-blistered deck in brilliant sun reports that snow,
whiter than chalk on the highest shelf of the Rockies is
sedimented with toxins

---

**Olga Broumas** Olga Broumas (b. 1949), Greek poet who deals with Sapphic themes in collections such as *Beginning with O* **7 PCBs** PCBs (polychlorinated biphenyl) are chemical compounds widely used in industry prior to 1970. Because they resist decomposition, they remain in water and soil for many years, entering and endangering the food chain.

the dead, the dying—we imprint our presence everywhere on
every wall & rock                                                    15

what is love in the face of such loss?

since dawn, *standing by my bed*, she wrote, *in gold sandals . . .*
*that very/moment* half-awake in a whisper of light her
upturned face given to presence, a woman involved, a circle of
women she taught how to love, how to pay a fine attention         20
raising simply & correctly the fleeting phases of what is, arrives

we get these glimpses, you said, grizzlies begging at human
doorways, two cubs & a mother so thin her ribs showed
prominent under ratty fur, shot now that our salmon rivers
run empty, rivers that were never ours to begin with—            25

& the sea, the sea goes out a long way in its unpublished
killing ground

this webwork—what we don't know about the body, what we
don't know may well be killing us—well : spring : stream :
river, these powerful points you set your fingers on, drawing      30
current through blockages, moving inward, not out, to see

chi° equally in
*the salt sea and fields thick with bloom*
inner channels & rivers

a sea full of apparent islands, no jetting-off point, no            35
airborne leap possible

without the body all these bodies
interlaced

                                                                *—2001*

---

32 **chi** the life force discussed in Chinese philosophy

*Michael Ondaatje (b. 1943) was born in Sri Lanka, eventually coming to Canada in 1962. Best known for his novels, including* The English Patient *(1992), which was turned into an Oscar-winning feature film, he is also the author of several poetry collections, including* The Cinnamon Peeler *(1992), and cross-genre works like* The Collected Works of Billy the Kid *(1970) and the autobiographical* Running in the Family *(1982).*

# Michael Ondaatje
# Sweet like a Crow

FOR HETTI COREA, 8 YEARS OLD

> The Sinhalese° are beyond a doubt one of the
> least musical people in the world. It would be
> quite impossible to have less sense of pitch, line,
> or rhythm
>
> —Paul Bowles

Your voice sounds like a scorpion being pushed
through a glass tube
like someone has just trod on a peacock
like wind howling in a coconut
like a rusty bible, like someone pulling barbed wire                    5
across a stone courtyard, like a pig drowning,
a vattacka being fried
a bone shaking hands
a frog singing at Carnegie Hall.
Like a crow swimming in milk,                                          10
like a nose being hit by a mango
like the crowd at the Royal-Thomian match,
a womb full of twins, a pariah dog
with a magpie in its mouth
like the midnight jet from Casablanca                                  15

---

**Sinhalese** natives of Sri Lanka

like Air Pakistan curry,
a typewriter on fire, like a spirit in the gas
which cooks your dinner,
like a hundred pappadans° being crunched, like someone
uselessly trying to light *3 Roses* matches in a dark room,                    *20*
the clicking sound of a reef when you put your head into the sea,
a dolphin reciting epic poetry to a sleepy audience,
the sound of a fan when someone throws brinjals° at it,
like pineapples being sliced in the Pettah market
like betel juice° hitting a butterfly in mid-air                    *25*
like a whole village running naked onto the street
and tearing their sarongs, like an angry family
pushing a jeep out of the mud, like dirt on the needle,
like 8 sharks being carried on the back of a bicycle
like 3 old ladies locked in the lavatory                    *30*
like the sound I heard when having an afternoon sleep
and someone walked through my room in ankle bracelets.

*—1982*

---

**Craig Raine (b. 1944)** *early in his career displayed a comic surrealism that was responsible for so many imitations that critic James Fenton dubbed him the founder of the "Martian School" of contemporary poetry. He was born in Bishop Auckland, England.*

## Craig Raine
# A Martian Sends a Postcard Home

Caxtons° are mechanical birds with many wings
and some are treasured for their markings—

they cause the eyes to melt
or the body to shriek without pain.

---

**19 pappadan**s crunchy wafer-thin appetizer     **23 brinjals** eggplant     **25 betel juice** leaf chewed
and spit like chewing tobacco
**1 Caxtons** i.e., books; after William Caxton (1422–1491), first English printer

I have never seen one fly, but                                             5
sometimes they perch on the hand.

Mist is when the sky is tired of flight
and rests its soft machine on ground:

then the world is dim and bookish
like engravings under tissue paper.                                       10

Rain is when the earth is television.
It has the property of making colours darker.

Model T is a room with the lock inside—
a key is turned to free the world

for movement, so quick there is a film                                    15
to watch for anything missed.

But time is tied to the wrist
or kept in a box, ticking with impatience.

In homes, a haunted apparatus sleeps,
that snores when you pick it up.                                          20

If the ghost cries, they carry it
to their lips and soothe it to sleep

with sounds. And yet, they wake it up
deliberately, by tickling with a finger.

Only the young are allowed to suffer                                      25
openly. Adults go to a punishment room

with water but nothing to eat.
They lock the door and suffer the noises

alone. No one is exempt
and everyone's pain has a different smell.                                30

At night, when all the colours die,
they hide in pairs

and read about themselves—
in colour, with their eyelids shut.

—*1978*

*Enid Shomer (b. 1944) grew up in Washington, D.C., but has lived most of her life in Florida. Her first collection,* Stalking the Florida Panther *(1987), explored both the Jewish traditions of her childhood and her attachment to her adopted state. She went on to publish fiction and several more collections of poetry, including* Stars at Noon: Poems from the Life of Jacqueline Cochran *(2001).*

*Enid Shomer*

# Women Bathing at Bergen-Belsen°

APRIL 24, 1945

Twelve hours after the Allies arrive
there is hot water, soap. Two women bathe
in a makeshift, open-air shower while nearby
fifteen thousand are flung naked into mass graves
by captured SS guards. Clearly legs and arms          5
are the natural handles of a corpse. The bathers,
taken late in the war, still have flesh
on their bones, still have breasts. Though nudity was
a death sentence here, they have undressed,
oblivious to the soldiers and the cameras.          10
The corpses push through the limed earth like upended
headstones. The bathers scrub their feet, bending
in beautiful curves, mapping the contours
of the body, that kingdom to which they've returned.

—*1987*

**Bergen-Belsen** German concentration camp in World War II

*bp Nichol (1944–1988) was born in Vancouver and is best known for his concrete or visual poetry, like these examples from early and late in his career. Experimentation is also evident in the* The Martyrology, *a poem that extends over nine volumes, and in the sound poetry Nichol performed with the group the Four Horsemen, of which he was a founding member.*

## *bp Nichol*
## Blues

[Author's Note:] here I'm paraphrasing an old blues—"love, oh love, oh careless love"—to slant the reading of "evol" towards "evil" and support the visually derived blues moan

—*1967*

# landscape: I

alongthehorizongrewanunbrokenlineoftrees

*—1986*

*Wendy Cope (b. 1945) lives in Winchester, England, and writes witty yet technically sophisticated poetry that reaches a wide audience. "I dislike the term 'light verse' because it is used as a way of dismissing poets who allow humour into their work. I believe that a humorous poem can also be 'serious'; deeply felt and saying something that matters."*

## Wendy Cope
# Rondeau Redoublé

There are so many kinds of awful men—
One can't avoid them all. She often said
She'd never make the same mistake again:
She always made a new mistake instead.

The chinless type who made her feel ill-bred;                      5
The practised charmer, less than charming when
He talked about the wife and kids and fled—
There are so many kinds of awful men.

The half-crazed hippy, deeply into Zen,
Whose cryptic homilies she came to dread;                          10
The fervent youth who worshipped Tony Benn—
'One can't avoid them all,' she often said.

The ageing banker, rich and overfed,
who held forth on the dollar and the yen—
Though there were many more mistakes ahead,                        15
She'd never make the same mistake again.

The budding poet, scribbling in his den
Odes not to her but to his pussy, Fred;
The drunk who fell asleep at nine or ten—
She always made a new mistake instead.                             20

And so the gambler was at least unwed
And didn't preach or sneer or wield a pen
Or hoard his wealth or take the Scotch to bed.
She'd lived and learned and lived and learned but then
There are so many kinds.                                           25

—1986

*Tom Wayman (b. 1945) was born in Hawkesbury, Ontario, but as a child moved to British Columbia, which remains his home. Wayman has published more than a dozen collections of poems, including* Did I Miss Anything? *(1993) and* My Father's Cup *(2002). He is particularly interested in poems about the workplace.*

# Tom Wayman
# Did I Miss Anything?

QUESTION FREQUENTLY ASKED BY
STUDENTS AFTER MISSING A CLASS

Nothing. When we realized you weren't here
we sat with our hands folded on our desks
in silence, for the full two hours

    Everything. I gave an exam worth
    40 per cent of the grade for this term            5
    and assigned some reading due today
    on which I'm about to hand out a quiz
    worth 50 per cent.

Nothing. None of the content of this course
has value or meaning                  10
Take as many days off as you like:
any activities we undertake as a class
I assure you will not matter either to you or me
and are without purpose

    Everything. A few minutes after we began last time    15
    a shaft of light descended and an angel
    or other heavenly being appeared
    and revealed to us what each woman or man must do
    to attain divine wisdom in this life and
    the hereafter                  20
    This is the last time the class will meet
    before we disperse to bring this good news to all people on earth

Nothing. When you are not present
how could something significant occur?

    Everything. Contained in this classroom                  *25*
    is a microcosm of human existence
    assembled for you to query and examine and ponder
    This is not the only place such an opportunity has been
        gathered

but it was one place                               *30*

And you weren't here

                                     —*1991*

---

*Bronwen Wallace (1945–1989) was born in Kingston, Ontario. She published four collections of conversational yet carefully crafted poems about the extraordinary grace in ordinary lives, including* Common Magic *(1985),* The Stubborn Particulars of Grace *(1987), and* Keep That Candle Burning Bright *(1991), which was published after her early death from cancer.*

## Bronwen Wallace
# Common Magic

Your best friend falls in love
and her brain turns to water.
You can watch her lips move,
making the customary sounds,
but you can see they're merely                    *5*
words, flimsy as bubbles rising
from some golden sea where she
swims sleek and exotic as a mermaid.

It's always like that.
You stop for lunch in a crowded               *10*
restaurant and the waitress floats
toward you. You can tell she doesn't care
whether you have the baked or french-fried
and you wonder if your voice comes
in bubbles too.                                *15*

It's not just women either. Or love
for that matter. The old man
across from you on the bus holds
a young child on his knee; he is singing
to her and his voice is a small boy                                    20
turning somersaults in the green
country of his blood.
It's only when the driver calls his stop
that he emerges into this puzzle
of brick and tiny hedges. Only then                                    25
you notice his shaking hands, his need
of the child to guide him home.

All over the city
you move in your own seasons
through the seasons of others: old women, faces                        30
clawed by weather you can't feel
clack dry tongues at passersby
while adolescents seethe
in their glassy atmospheres of anger.

In parks, the children                                                 35
are alien life-forms, rooted
in the galaxies they've grown through
to get here. Their games weave
the interface and their laughter
tickles that part of your brain where smells                           40
are hidden and the nuzzling textures of things.

It's a wonder that anything gets done
at all: a mechanic flails
at the muffler of your car
through whatever storm he's trapped inside                             45
and the mailman stares at numbers
from the haze of a distant summer.

Yet somehow letters arrive and buses
remember their routes. Banks balance.
Mangoes ripen on the supermarket shelves.                              50
Everyone manages. You gulp the thin air

of this planet as if it were the only
one you knew. Even the earth you're
standing on seems solid enough.
It's always the chance word, unthinking                    55
gesture that unlocks the face before you.
Reveals the intricate countries
deep within the eyes. The hidden
lives, like sudden miracles,
that breathe there.                                        60

                                                        —*1983*

---

*Herménégilde Chiasson* **(b. 1946)** *was born in Saint-Simon, New Brunswick, of Acadian heritage. Chiasson is a visual artist, filmmaker, playwright, and poet. His poetry collections include* Mourir à Scoudouc *(1974),* Vous *(1991),* Climats *(1996), and* Conversations *(1999), winner of the Governor General's Award. He was appointed Lieutenant-Governor of New Brunswick in 2003.*

## *Herménégilde Chiasson*
# Red

Acadie, my too beautiful desecrated love, you whom I will never take into white sheets, the sheets that you have torn to make white flags like the fields of snow that you have sold like your old fence posts, your old barns, your old legends, your old dreams, white as an old wedding dress in an old cedar chest. Acadie, my too beautiful desecrated love, who speaks on credit to say things that one must pay in cash, who borrows privileges while believing she is gaining rights. Acadie, my too beautiful desecrated love, on *stand-by* on every continent, on *stand-by* in every galaxy, divided by church steeples that are stretched too thin, filled with saints up to a heaven that is too far away. Rip off your blue dress, put red stars on your breasts, sink yourself into the sea, the red sea that is going to open as it did for the flight from Egypt, the sea belongs to us, it is true, the whole sea belongs to us because we cannot sell it, because there is no one who could buy it.

                                                        —*1974*

Translated by Fred Cogswell and Jo-Anne Elder.

**Robert Bringhurst** *(b. 1946) Born in California of Canadian parents, Bringhurst grew up in the Rockies. He has published widely in fields as diverse as Native mythology, typography, and translation, but he has also published over a dozen books of poetry, including* The Beauty of the Weapons *(1982),* The Calling *(1995), and the polyphonic masque* Ursa Major *(2003).*

# Robert Bringhurst
# Essay on Adam

There are five possibilities. One: Adam fell.
Two: he was pushed. Three: he jumped. Four:
he only looked over the edge, and one look silenced him.
Five: nothing worth mentioning happened to Adam.

The first, that he fell, is too simple. The fourth,                          5
fear, we have tried and found useless. The fifth,
nothing happened, is dull. The choice is between:
he jumped or was pushed. And the difference between these

is only an issue of whether the demons
work from the inside out or from the outside                               10
in: the one
theological question.

—1975

**M. NourbeSe Philip** *(b. 1947) was born in Tobago but moved to Canada, where she worked for several years as a lawyer before deciding to devote more time to writing. She is the author of several collections of poetry, including* Thorns *(1980),* Salmon Courage *(1983), and* She Tries Her Tongue; Her Silence Softly Breaks *(1988). Her poetry and short fiction have been widely anthologized.*

# M. NourbeSe Philip

# Discourse on the Logic of Language

WHEN IT WAS BORN, THE MOTHER HELD HER NEWBORN CHILD CLOSE: SHE BEGAN THEN TO LICK IT ALL OVER. THE CHILD WHIMPERED A LITTLE, BUT AS THE MOTHER'S TONGUE MOVED FASTER AND STRONGER OVER ITS BODY, IT GREW SILENT—THE MOTHER TURNING IT THIS WAY AND THAT UNDER HER TONGUE, UNTIL SHE HAD TONGUED IT CLEAN OF THE CREAMY WHITE SUBSTANCE COVERING ITS BODY.

English
is my mother tongue.
A mother tongue is not
not a foreign lan lan lang
language                                           5
l/anguish
anguish
—a foreign anguish.

English is
my father tongue.                                  10
A father tongue is
a foreign language,
therefore English is
a foreign language
not a mother tongue.                               15

What is my mother
tongue
my mammy tongue
my mummy tongue
my momsy tongue                                    20
my modder tongue
my ma tongue?

I have no mother
tongue
no mother to tongue                                25
no tongue to mother
to mother
tongue
me

I must therefore be tongue                         30
dumb
dumb-tongued
dub-tongued
damn dumb
tongue                                             35

*EDICT I*

*Every owner of slaves
shall, wherever possible,
ensure that his slaves
belong to as many ethno-
linguistic groups as
possible. If they can-
not speak to each other,
they cannot then foment
rebellion and revolution.*

Those parts of the brain chiefly responsible for speech are named after two learned nineteenth century doctors, the eponymous Doctors Wernicke and Broca respectively.

Dr. Broca believed the size of the brain determined intelligence; he devoted much of his time to 'proving' that white males of the Caucasian race had larger brains than, and were therefore superior to, women, Blacks and other peoples of colour. 40

Understanding and recognition of the spoken word takes place in Wernicke's area—the left temporal lobe, situated next to the auditory cortex; from there relevant information passes to Broca's area—situated in the left frontal cortex—which then forms the response and passes it on to the motor cortex. The motor cortex controls the muscles of speech. 45

THE MOTHER THEN PUT HER FINGERS INTO HER CHILD'S MOUTH—GENTLY FORCING IT OPEN; SHE TOUCHES HER TONGUE TO THE CHILD'S TONGUE, AND HOLDING THE TINY MOUTH OPEN, SHE BLOWS INTO IT—HARD. SHE WAS BLOWING WORDS—HER WORDS, HER MOTHER'S WORDS, THOSE OF HER MOTHER'S MOTHER, AND ALL THEIR MOTHERS BEFORE—INTO HER DAUGHTER'S MOUTH.

but I have
a dumb tongue                                                50
tongue dumb
father tongue
and english is
my mother tongue
is                                                           55
my father tongue
is a foreign lan lan lang
language
l/anguish
  anguish                                                    60
a foreign anguish
is english—
another tongue
my mother
      mammy             65
      mummy
      moder
      mater
      macer
      moder             70
tongue
mothertongue

tongue mother
tongue me
mothertongue me       75
mother me
touch me
with the tongue of your
lan lan lang
language
l/anguish                                                    80
  anguish
english
is a foreign anguish

**EDICT II**

*Every slave caught speaking his native language shall be severely punished. Where necessary, removal of the tongue is recommended. The offending organ, when removed, should be hung on high in a central place, so that all may see and tremble.*

A tapering, blunt-tipped, muscular, soft and fleshy organ    85
describes
(a) the penis.
(b) the tongue.
(c) neither of the above.
(d) both of the above.

In man the tongue is    90
(a) the principal organ of taste.
(b) the principal organ of articulate speech.
(c) the principal organ of oppression and exploitation.
(d) all of the above.

The tongue    95
(a) is an interwoven bundle of striated muscle running in
    three planes.
(b) is fixed to the jawbone.
(c) has an outer covering of a mucous membrane covered
    with papillae.
(d) contains ten thousand taste buds, none of which is sensitive to
    the taste of foreign words.

Air is forced out of the lungs up the throat to the larynx where    100
it causes the vocal cords to vibrate and create sound. The
metamorphosis from sound to intelligible word requires
(a) the lip, tongue and jaw all working together.
(b) a mother tongue.
(c) the overseer's whip.
(d) all of the above or none.

*—1989*

**R. S. Gwynn (b. 1948)** *is one of the editors of this volume and (with Dana Gioia) of* The Longman Anthology of Short Fiction. *He teaches at Lamar University.* No Word of Farewell: Selected Poems 1970–2000 *appeared in 2001.*

# R. S. Gwynn
## Approaching a Significant Birthday, He Peruses *The Norton Anthology of Poetry*

All human things are subject to decay.
Beauty is momentary in the mind.
The curfew tolls the knell of parting day.
If Winter comes, can Spring be far behind?

Forlorn! the very word is like a bell                    5
And somewhat of a sad perplexity.
Here, take my picture, though I bid farewell;
In a dark time the eye begins to see

The woods decay, the woods decay and fall—
Bare ruined choirs where late the sweet birds sing.      10
What but design of darkness to appall?
An aged man is but a paltry thing.

If I should die, think only this of me:
Crass casualty obstructs the sun and rain
When I have fears that I may cease to be,                 15
To cease upon the midnight with no pain

And hear the spectral singing of the moon
And strictly meditate the thankless muse.
The world is too much with us, late and soon.
It gathers to a greatness, like the ooze.                 20

Do not go gentle into the good night.
Fame is no plant that grows on mortal soil.

Again he raised the jug up to the light:
Old age hath yet his honor and his toil.

Downward to darkness on extended wings,                                    25
Break, break, break, on thy cold gray stones, O Sea,
and tell sad stories of the death of kings.
I do not think that they will sing to me.

                                                                    —1990

---

*Timothy Steele (b. 1948) has written a successful scholarly study of the rise of free verse, Missing Measures, and is perhaps the most skillful craftsman of the contemporary New Formalist poets. Born in Vermont, he has lived for a number of years in Los Angeles, where he teaches at California State University, Los Angeles.*

## Timothy Steele
# Sapphics° Against Anger

Angered, may I be near a glass of water;
May my first impulse be to think of Silence,
Its deities (who are they? do, in fact, they
          Exist? etc.).

May I recall what Aristotle says of                                        5
The subject: to give vent to rage is not to
Release it but to be increasingly prone
          To its incursions.

May I imagine being in the Inferno,
Hearing it asked: "Virgilio mio,° who's                                    10
That sulking with Achilles there?" and hearing
          Virgil say: "Dante,

---

**Sapphics** stanza form named after Sappho (c. 650 B.C.)    **10 Virgilio mio** Dante is addressing Virgil, his guide through hell.

That fellow, at the slightest provocation,
Slammed phone receivers down, and waved his arms like
A madman. What Attila did to Europe,                         *15*
　　　What Genghis Khan did

To Asia, that poor dope did to his marriage."
May I, that is, put learning to good purpose,
Mindful that melancholy is a sin, though
　　　Stylish at present.                                     *20*

Better than rage is the post-dinner quiet,
The sink's warm turbulence, the streaming platters,
The suds rehearsing down the drain in spirals
　　　In the last rinsing.

For what is, after all, the good life save that             *25*
Conducted thoughtfully, and what is passion
If not the holiest of powers, sustaining
　　　Only if mastered.

　　　　　　　　　　　　　　　　　　　*—1986*

---

**Lorna Crozier (b. 1948)** *was born in Swift Current, Saskatchewan. Her many award-winning collections include* Inventing the Hawk *(1992),* Apocrypha of Light *(2002), and* Selected Poems *(2007).* No Longer Two People *(1981) was co-authored with her partner, Patrick Lane.*

## *Lorna  Crozier*
# Packing for the Future: Instructions

Take the thickest socks.
Wherever you're going
you'll have to walk.

There may be water.
There may be stones.                                         *5*

There may be high places
you cannot go without
the hope socks bring you,
the way they hold you
to the earth.                                        10

At least one pair must be new,
must be blue as a wish
hand-knit by your mother
in her sleep.

\*

Take a leather satchel,                              15
a velvet bag and an old tin box—
a salamander painted on the lid.

This is to carry that small thing
you cannot leave. Perhaps the key
you've kept though it doesn't fit                    20
any lock you know,
the photograph that keeps you sane,
a ball of string to lead you out
though you can't walk back
into that light.                                     25

In your bag leave room for sadness,
leave room for another language.

There may be doors nailed shut.
There may be painted windows.
There may be signs that warn you                     30
to be gone. Take the dream
you've been having since
you were a child, the one
with open fields and the wind
sounding.                                            35

\*

Mistrust no one who offers you
water from a well, a songbird's feather,
something that's been mended twice.
Always travel lighter
than the heart.                                           *40*

—*1999*

---

**Jeannette C. Armstrong (b. 1948)** *Born on the Penticton Indian Reserve in British Columbia, of Okanagan heritage, Armstrong has published works including the novels* Slash *(1988) and* Whispering in Shadows *(2000), and the poetry collection* Breath Tracks *(1991).*

# Jeannette C. Armstrong
## History Lesson

Out of the belly of Christopher's ship
a mob bursts
Running in all directions
Pulling furs off animals
Shooting buffalo                                           5
Shooting each other
left and right

Father mean well
waves his makeshift wand
forgives saucer-eyed Indians                              10

Red coated knights
gallop across the prairie
to get their men
and to build a new world

Pioneers and traders                                      15
bring gifts
Smallpox, Seagrams
and Rice Krispies

Civilization has reached
the promised land.                                                    *20*

Between the snap crackle pop
of smoke stacks
and multi-coloured rivers
swelling with flower powered zee
are farmers sowing skulls and bones                                   *25*
and miners
pulling from gaping holes
green paper faces
of smiling English lady

The colossi                                                           *30*
in which they trust
while burying
breathing forests and fields
beneath concrete and steel
stand shaking fists                                                   *35*
waiting to mutilate
whole civilizations
ten generations at a blow.

Somewhere among the remains
of skinless animals                                                   *40*
is the termination
to a long journey
and unholy search
for the power
glimpsed in a garden                                                  *45*
forever closed
forever lost.

*—1991*

*Lenore Keeshig-Tobias (b. 1949)* *A member of the Chippewas of the Nawash First Nation in Ontario, Keeshig-Tobias draws on her Anishnabe heritage in her roles as storyteller and culture worker. Her published work includes the bilingual children's books* Bird Talk *(1991) and* Emma and the Trees *(1995), and contributions to* Indigena: Contemporary Native Perspectives *(1992).*

## *Lenore Keeshig-Tobias*
# How to Catch a White Man (Oops) I Mean Trickster

FROM *TRICKSTER BEYOND 1992: OUR RELATIONSHIP*

First, find yourself a forest. Any stand of ancient trees will do;
in fact, the older the better. Stand in the middle of it and tell
your stories. Soon the white man! (I mean Trickster) will
come by, carrying a big pack on his back. In that pack he
carries the voices of his women and the voices of other people     5
he has walked over with his long legs. 'I'm going to tell those
stories for you,' he'll say. 'You're far too primitive to tell them
yourself. I am going to let the world know what you think.
I am going to tell the world how you think when you think.
And I'm going to build a golf course here, too. These trees     10
are so old, and besides you're not using them trees.'

Tell him you heard some people talking about better stories
and a better place for a golf course, perhaps even a
h-y-d-r-o e-l-e-c-t-r-i-c dam, or two. Say, you could even
push for a super fantasyland golf course. Anyhow, tell him he     15
could make the stories into TV movies, docudramas, feature films.
He could write novels using the stories. He could receive all kinds
of literary awards for his great imagination, with these stories.
He could even achieve world acclaim for telling others how it is
with the 'Native Indian'. (God, how I hate that word 'Indian'.)     20

Okay, then tell him to wait there while you'll go find out more about
those stories and that other place. He'll say, 'Okay, but come right
back.' Only don't go back.

Find another forest and dig a big big hole in the middle of it, beside a pine tree. Then climb up and sit in the branches of that tree and call out saying, 'Hey, white man! (I mean Trickster. You could call him a trickster, you know. He's like that, clever. But he's not smart.) These stories are not for you, and you can't build your golf course here either.'

It won't be long and he'll come by with that great big pack and this time with his guns and tanks, too—ready to take those stories—ready to build his golf course.

Then you tell him from that tree you can see, hear everything all over the world, and know exactly what's going on, too. He'll say, 'That's new to me.' Ask him if he would like to see these things, too. Of course, he'll say, 'Yes.' Tell him to leave his heavy pack at the bottom of the tree. He won't. He'll climb up into that tree with his weapons, too. Ask him if he's comfortable. He'll say, 'I'm comfortable anywhere.' Be careful now because he'll want to sit right on top of you.

Now, tell him to close his eyes. He has to close his eyes if he is to know and see all the things you do. He has to listen to the trees and grass. Tell him it takes a while for the vision to come clear, and he should sit quietly and wait and listen. As soon as his eyes are closed, run away and watch. Get other people to watch, too. And the children. Don't forget about the children.

Of course, that man won't see anything. Never did. And he certainly won't hear anything. Never has. And after a bit he'll become uncomfortable, restless, impatient and he'll cock his gun and open his eyes. When he sees you are gone he'll get mad as heck and fall out of the tree, shooting himself in the foot, dropping his great pack and tumbling into the hole, his foot in his mouth.

That's when you run over and grab his great pack, open it up and set free the voices of the people he has walked over and the voices of his women.

Now that white man (I mean Trickster) will scramble. And he'll fight, digging himself deeper into the hole, but he won't ever get

out this time. His women will see to that. Then tell the children.
Teach them. Teach them the history of this land, the real history, 60
before 1492 and since. Those stories will guide them into the
next 500 years. Tell them not to do as the Trickster (I mean
white man) has done. And tell them to listen to the trees and
grass. The trees and the grass hold on to heaven for us.

—*1992*

---

*Stan Rogers (1949–1983) was born in Hamilton, Ontario, with family roots
in the Maritimes, a connection that appears in many of his finest lyrics about life
on and by the sea. One of Canada's best known folk singers, he toured the country
from coast to coast, penning memorable songs about the vast Canadian landscape
and the dreams of those who live there. When returning home from an American
folk festival, he died in an airline fire at the age of thirty-three.*

## *Stan Rogers*
# The *Mary Ellen Carter*

She went down last October in a pouring driving rain.
The skipper, he'd been drinking and the Mate, he felt no pain.
Too close to Three Mile Rock, and she was dealt her mortal blow,
And the *Mary Ellen Carter* settled low.
There were five of us aboard her when she finally was awash.     5
We'd worked like hell to save her, all heedless of the cost.
And the groan she gave as she went down, it caused us to proclaim
That the *Mary Ellen Carter* would rise again.

Well, the owners wrote her off; not a nickel would they spend.
She gave twenty years of service, boys, then met her sorry end.     10
But insurance paid the loss to them, they let her rest below.
Then they laughed at us and said we had to go.
But we talked of her all winter, some days around the clock,
For she's worth a quarter million, afloat and at the dock.
And with every jar that hit the bar, we swore we would remain     15
And make the *Mary Ellen Carter* rise again.

Rise again, rise again, that her name not be lost
To the knowledge of men.
Those who loved her best and were with her till the end
Will make the *Mary Ellen Carter* rise again.                    20

All spring, now, we've been with her on a barge lent by a friend.
Three dives a day in hard hat suit and twice I've had the bends.
Thank God it's only sixty feet and the currents here are slow
Or I'd never have the strength to go below.
But we've patched her rents, stopped her vents, dogged hatch
    and porthole down.                                           25
Put cables to her, 'fore and aft and girded her around.
Tomorrow, noon, we hit the air and then take up the strain.
And watch the *Mary Ellen Carter* rise again.

For we couldn't leave her there, you see, to crumble into scale.
She'd saved our lives so many times, living through the gale      30
And the laughing, drunken rats who left her to a sorry grave
They won't be laughing in another day . . .
And you, to whom adversity has dealt the final blow
With smiling bastards lying to you everywhere you go
Turn to, and put out all your strength of arm and heart
    and brain                                                    35
And like the *Mary Ellen Carter*, rise again.

Rise again, rise again—though your heart it be broken
And life about to end
No matter what you've lost, be it a home, a love, a friend.
Like the *Mary Ellen Carter*, rise again.                        40

—*1979*

*Rodney Jones (b. 1950) was born in Alabama and received important national attention when* Transparent Gestures *won the Poets' Prize in 1990. Like many younger southern poets, he often deals with the difficult legacy of racism and the adjustments that a new era have forced on both whites and Blacks.*

## *R o d n e y   J o n e s*

# Winter Retreat: Homage to Martin Luther King, Jr.

There is a hotel in Baltimore where we came together,
we black and white educated and educators,
for a week of conferences, for important counsel
sanctioned by the DOE° and the Carter administration,
to make certain difficult inquiries, to collate notes                    5
on the instruction of the disabled, the deprived,
the poor, who do not score well on entrance tests,
who, failing school, must go with mop and pail
skittering across the slick floors of cafeterias,
or climb dewy girders to balance high above cities,               10
or, jobless, line up in the bone cold. We felt
substantive burdens lighter if we stated it right.
Very delicately, we spoke in turn. We walked
together beside the still waters of behaviorism.
Armed with graphs and charts, with new strategies            15
to devise objectives and determine accountability,
we empathetic black and white shone in seminar rooms.
We enunciated every word clearly and without accent.
We moved very carefully in the valley of the shadow
of the darkest agreement error. We did not digress.            20
We ascended the trunk of that loftiest cypress
of Latin grammar the priests could never
successfully graft onto the rough green chestnut
of the English language. We extended ourselves

**4 DOE** Department of Education

with that sinuous motion of the tongue that is half                25
pain and almost eloquence. We black and white
politely reprioritized the parameters of our agenda
to impact equitably on the Seminole and the Eskimo.
We praised diversity and involvement, the sacrifices
of fathers and mothers. We praised the next white        30
Gwendolyn Brooks° and the next black Robert Burns.°
We deep made friends. In that hotel we glistened
over the *pommes au gratin*° and the *poitrine de veau.*°
The morsels of lamb flamed near where we talked.
The waiters bowed and disappeared among the ferns.          35
And there is a bar there, there is a large pool.
Beyond the tables of the drinkers and raconteurs,
beyond the hot tub brimming with Lebanese tourists
and the women in expensive bathing suits doing laps,
if you dive down four feet, swim out far enough,          40
and emerge on the other side, it is sixteen degrees.
It is sudden and very beautiful and colder
than thought, though the air frightens you at first,
not because it is cold, but because it is visible,
almost palpable, in the fog that rises from difference.     45
While I stood there in the cheek-numbing snow,
all Baltimore was turning blue. And what I remember
of that week of talks is nothing the record shows,
but the revelation outside, which was the city
many came to out of the fields, then the thought        50
that we had wanted to make the world kinder,
but, in speaking proudly, we had failed a vision.

—*1989*

---

**31 Gwendolyn Brooks** Black American poet (1917–2000)   **Robert Burns** Scottish poet (1759–1796)
**33 *pommes au gratin*** potatoes baked with cheese   ***poitrine de veau*** brisket of veal

*Carolyn Forché (b. 1950) won the Yale Younger Poets Award for her first collection,* Gathering the Tribes *(1975).* The Country Between Us *(1982), Forché's second collection, contains poems based on the poet's experiences in the wartorn country of El Salvador in the early 1980s.*

# *Carolyn Forché*
# The Colonel

What you have heard is true. I was in his house.° His wife
carried a tray of coffee and sugar. His daughter filed her nails,
his son went out for the night. There were daily papers, pet
dogs, a pistol on the cushion beside him. The moon swung
bare on its black cord over the house. On the television was a          5
cop show. It was in English. Broken bottles were embedded
in the walls around the house to scoop the kneecaps from
a man's legs or cut his hands to lace. On the windows there
were gratings like those in liquor stores. We had dinner, rack
of lamb, good wine, a gold bell was on the table for calling          10
the maid. The maid brought green mangoes, salt, a type of
bread. I was asked how I enjoyed the country. There was a
brief commercial in Spanish. His wife took everything away.
There was some talk then of how difficult it had become to
govern. The parrot said hello on the terrace. The colonel told          15
it to shut up, and pushed himself from the table. My friend
said to me with his eyes: say nothing. The colonel returned
with a sack used to bring groceries home. He spilled many
human ears on the table. They were like dried peach halves.
There is no other way to say this. He took one of them in his          20
hands, shook it in our faces, dropped it into a water glass. It
came alive there. I am tired of fooling around he said. As for the
rights of anyone, tell your people they can go fuck themselves.
He swept the ears to the floor with his arm and held the last of
his wine in the air. Something for your poetry, no? he said.          25
Some of the ears on the floor caught this scrap of his voice.
Some of the ears on the floor were pressed to the ground.

*—1978*

**1 his house** in El Salvador

*Anne Carson (b. 1950) was born in Toronto and has a reputation as both a classical scholar and a prize-winning poet. Her collections include the riddle-like* Short Talks *(1992),* Glass, Irony and God *(1995), and* Men in the Off Hours *(2000). Her evocative and erudite work, including* Autobiography of Red: A Novel in Verse *(1998) and* Decreation *(2005), often blurs the boundaries between genres.*

## Anne Carson
# God's List of Liquids

It was a November night of wind.
Leaves tore past the window.
God had the book of life open at PLEASURE

and was holding the pages down with one hand
because of the wind from the door.                              5
*For I made their flesh as a sieve*

wrote God at the top of the page
and then listed in order:
Alcohol
Blood                                                         10
Gratitude
Memory
Semen
Song
Tears                                                         15
Time.

—*1995*

# Short Talk on the Total Collection

From childhood he dreamed of being able to keep with him all the objects in the world lined up on his shelves and bookcases. He denied lack, oblivion or even the likelihood of a missing piece. Order streamed

from Noah in blue triangles and as the pure fury of his classifications
rose around him, engulfing his life they came to be called waves by
others, who drowned, a world of them.

*—1992*

**Harry Thurston (b. 1950)** *was born in Yarmouth, Nova Scotia, and was trained as a biologist. His intense interest in the natural world is reflected in his non-fiction works, including* Tidal Life: A Natural History of the Bay of Fundy *(1990), and in his poetry collections, including* If Men Lived on Earth *(1999) and* A Ship Portrait *(2005).*

# *Harry Thurston*
## Miracle

I tell my toddling daughter
not to pick the blossom,
explaining that the flower
will turn into a strawberry
in a few short weeks,                                              5
then she can pick and eat the sweet fruit.
No sooner are the words out
than I regret forestalling her pleasure—
for what is one blossom less,
and weeks to a child too long to wait.                            10
And then, too, she looks at me
as if I have told her a lie,
fashioned a twisted fairy tale.
But speaking it, for the first time in years,
I am awed by the miracle                                          15
of what really happens.

*—2000*

*Paul Muldoon (b. 1951) was born in County Armagh, Northern Ireland, and after years of working for the BBC in Belfast he moved to the United States in 1987. His many poetry collections include* Why Brownlee Left *(1980),* Poems 1968–1998 *(2001),* Moy Sand and Gravel *(2002), which won the Pulitzer Prize, and* Horse Latitudes *(2006).*

# Paul Muldoon
# Anseo

When the Master was calling the roll
At the primary school in Collegelands,
You were meant to call back *Anseo*
And raise your hand
As your name occurred.                                          5
*Anseo*, meaning here, here and now,
All present and correct,
Was the first word of Irish I spoke.
The last name on the ledger
Belonged to Joseph Mary Plunkett Ward          10
And was followed, as often as not,
By silence, knowing looks,
A nod and a wink, the Master's droll
'And where's our little Ward-of-court?'°

I remember the first time he came back          15
The Master had sent him out
Along the hedges
To weigh up for himself and cut
A stick with which he would be beaten.
After a while, nothing was spoken;          20
He would arrive as a matter of course
With an ash-plant, a salley-rod.
Or, finally, the hazel-wand
He had whittled down to a whip-lash,
Its twist of red and yellow lacquers          25

14 **Ward-of-court** minor with court-appointed guardian

Sanded and polished,
And altogether so delicately wrought
That he had engraved his initials on it.

I last met Joseph Mary Plunkett Ward
In a pub just over the Irish border.                                     30
He was living in the open,
In a secret camp
On the other side of the mountain.
He was fighting for Ireland,
Making things happen.                                                    35
And he told me, Joe Ward,
Of how he had risen through the ranks
To Quartermaster, Commandant:
How every morning at parade
His volunteers would call back *Anseo*                                   40
And raise their hands
As their names occurred.

*—1980*

---

*Christopher Dewdney (b. 1951) resides in Toronto and is the author of twelve
collections of poems that often deal with scientific subject matter in an avant-garde
way. His publications include the collections of poems* Radiant Inventories *(1988)
and* Signal Fires *(2000), as well as works of popular non-fiction, such as*
Acquainted with the Night *(2004).*

# Christopher Dewdney
# Ten Typically Geological Suicides

1. Standing naked over the vent of a thermal geyser that erupts
   periodically.

2. Throwing yourself into molten lava.

3. Placing your head at the bottom of a children's slide with a pull-string attached to a stick propping up a large granite boulder perched at the top.

4. Licking the radium from the faces of old watches.

5. Standing under a projecting horizontal ledge of limestone and waiting for the slab to fall. Constructing a small shelter to facilitate waiting in comfort.

6. Eating a lethal dose of beach sand.

7. Taping burning lumps of coal to your body.

8. Injecting liquid gold into your veins.

9. Slitting your wrists with quartz crystals.

10. Wearing a uranium belt.

*—1988*

---

**Daniel David Moses (b. 1952)** *Moses takes pride in his Delaware heritage and the Iroquoian influences of his childhood on Six Nations land near Brantford, Ontario. His work includes the poetry collections* The White Line *(1990) and* Sixteen Jesuses *(2000), and several plays. He also co-edited* An Anthology of Canadian Native Literature in English *(1998).*

# Daniel David Moses
## Inukshuk

You were built from the stones,
they say, positioned
alone against the sky
here so they might take
you for something human                                          5

checking the migrations.
That's how you manage this,

standing upright despite
the blue wind that snow is,
this close to Polaris. 10

Still, the wind worries
you some. It's your niches
which ought to be empty.
Nothing but lichen grows
there usually. Now 15

they're home to dreams. Most come
from the south, a few from
further north—but what flows
out of their mouths comes from
no direction you know. 20

They keep singing about
the Great Blue Whale the world
is; how it swims through space
having nightmares about
hunters who only hunt 25

their brothers—each after
the other's snow-white face.
*How beautiful frozen*
*flesh is! Like ivory,*
*like carved bone, like the light* 30

*of Polaris in hand.*
So it goes on and on,
the hunting refrain. Dead
silence would be better,
the Pole star overhead. 35

The wind agrees, at least
wants to stop up each niche.
How long can you stand it
—that song, the cold, the stones
that no longer hold you 40

up now that they hold you
down? Soon the migrations
recommence. How steady
are you? Dreams, so they say,
also sing on the wing.                                          45

—*1990*

---

**Rita Dove (b. 1952)** *Born in Akron, Ohio, Dove was the youngest poet and the first African American to be named poet laureate. Her collections of poetry include* Thomas and Beulah *(1986), which won the Pulitzer Prize, and* Grace Notes *(1989).* Mother Love *(1995) includes a series of loosely structured sonnets using the myth of Demeter and Persephone to explore mother-daughter relationships.*

## Rita Dove

# Persephone, Falling°

One narcissus among the ordinary beautiful
flowers, one unlike all the others! She pulled,
stooped to pull harder—
when, sprung out of the earth
on his glittering terrible                                     5
carriage, he claimed his due.
It is finished. No one heard her
No one! She had strayed from the herd.

(Remember: go straight to school.
This is important, stop fooling around!                        10
Don't answer to strangers. Stick
with your playmates. Keep your eyes down.)
This is how easily the pit
opens. This is how one foot sinks into the ground.

—*1995*

---

**Persephone, Falling** In Greek mythology, Persephone is the daughter of Demeter, goddess of the harvest, and Zeus. When the beautiful Persephone was collecting flowers on the plain of Enna, the earth suddenly opened, and Hades, the god of the underworld, rose up and took her for himself.

*Janice Kulyk Keefer (b. 1953) Born in Canada of Ukrainian heritage, Keefer is the author of more than ten books in several genres, including poetry, fiction, literary criticism, and biography. This tribute to her mother is taken from* White of the Lesser Angels *(1986).*

## Janice Kulyk Keefer
# My Mother, a Closet Full of Dresses

In Poland, needing a dress
for the potato masher to become a doll,
she cut out a patch from somebody's
Sunday skirt—black silk, good enough
to be buried in; waterfalling folds—                                    5
no one would notice. Before the whole church,
Baba bent to kiss the icons; her skirts
fanned, the missing patch a window
to her starched white drawers.
My mother whipped until she could not sit;                              10
the baba never setting foot
in church again.

In Canada, her sewing teacher
called it shameful—a girl of such gifts
entering a factory! Sent her                                           15
to design school instead, dressed
in her castoffs. My mother, slashing
stitches from priggish Liberty prints—
everyone else flaunting
palm leaves, cabbage roses.                                            20

*The Story of a Dress* at the Exhibition.
She sat in a small display-cage, designing,
cutting out, sewing a dress.
The man who grilled her on each
click of the scissors, till she bit                                    25
blistered lips, blood

drooling down her chin.
Watched for a week,
then hired her like that—
though it was still Depression,                                    *30*
designers a dime a dozen.

The wedding dress she sketched
and sewed herself: "the bride in peau de soie
with a delicate rose tint and beading
in the shape of scattered leaves."                                 *35*
Satin peignoirs from the honeymoon—
tea-coloured stains; folds creased
as with a knife.

A closet full of dresses for weddings,
anniversaries,                                                     *40*
funerals—

And occasions for which she didn't dress:
children with high fevers, and husband
off playing golf or bridge as husbands did;
the miscarriage when she bled                                      *45*
faster than the ambulance; migraines
in dark rooms at noon;
and all the nights
when she rummaged, naked,
through steel hangers in an empty closet.                          *50*

                                                    *—1986*

*Dionne Brand (b. 1953) Born in Trinidad, Brand pursued post-secondary education in Canada and now lives north of Toronto. In poetry collections such as* No Language Is Neutral *(1990), the Governor General's Award–winning* Land to Light On *(1997), and* thirsty *(2002), as well as works of fiction and non-fiction, she explores the immigrant, minority, and lesbian experiences.*

## Dionne Brand
# Blues Spiritual for Mammy Prater

ON LOOKING AT "THE PHOTOGRAPH OF MAMMY PRATER AN EX-SLAVE, 115 YEARS OLD WHEN HER PHOTOGRAPH WAS TAKEN"

she waited for her century to turn
she waited until she was one hundred and fifteen
years old to take a photograph
to take a photograph and to put those eyes in it
she waited until the technique of photography was                    5
suitably developed
to make sure the picture would be clear
to make sure no crude daguerreotype° would lose
her image
would lose her lines and most of all her eyes                       10
and her hands
she knew the patience of one hundred and fifteen years
she knew that if she had the patience,
to avoid killing a white man
that I would see this photograph                                    15
she waited until it suited her
to take this photograph and to put those eyes in it.

In the hundred and fifteen years which it took her to
wait for this photograph she perfected this pose
she sculpted it over a shoulder of pain,                            20

---

**8 daguerreotype** an early photograph named for the inventor of the process, Louis-Jacques-Mandé Daguerre (1789–1851), a French painter and physicist

a thing like despair which she never called
this name for she would not have lasted
the fields, the ones she ploughed
on the days that she was a mule, left
their etching on the gait of her legs                                25
deliberately and unintentionally
she waited, not always silently, not always patiently,
for this self portrait
by the time she sat in her black dress, white collar,
white handkerchief, her feet had turned to marble,          30
her heart burnished red,
and her eyes.
she waited one hundred and fifteen years
until the science of photography passed tin and
talbotype° for a surface sensitive enough                        35
to hold her eyes
she took care not to lose the signs
to write in those eyes what her fingers could not script
a pact of blood across a century, a decade and more
she knew then that it would be me who would find          40
her will, her meticulous account, her eyes,
her days when waiting for this photograph
was all that kept her sane
she planned it down to the day,                                        45
the light,
the superfluous photographer
her breasts,
her hands
this moment of                                                               50
my turning the leaves of a book,
noticing, her eyes.

*—1990*

---

**35 talbotype** A photographic method using light-sensitive paper and a chemical that brought developing time down from one hour to one minute. Patented by William Henry Talbot (1800–1877) of Great Britain in 1841.

*Kim Addonizio (b. 1954) was born in Washington, D.C., as Kim Addie but returned to the name her Italian grandparents abandoned when immigrating to the United States. Her poetry collections include* The Philosopher's Club *(1994) and* What Is This Thing Called Love *(2004). She has also published fiction, a guide to writing poetry, and* Dorothy Parker's Elbow: Tattoos on Writers, Writers on Tattoos *(2002).*

## *Kim Addonizio*
# First Poem for You

I like to touch your tattoos in complete
darkness, when I can't see them. I'm sure of
where they are, know by heart the neat
lines of lightning pulsing just above
your nipple, can find, as if by instinct, the blue     *5*
swirls of water on your shoulder where a serpent
twists, facing a dragon. When I pull you
to me, taking you until we're spent
and quiet on the sheets, I love to kiss
the pictures in your skin. They'll last until     *10*
you're seared to ashes; whatever persists
or turns to pain between us, they will still
be there. Such permanence is terrifying.
So I touch them in the dark; but touch them, trying.

*—1994*

***Carol Ann Duffy (b. 1955),*** *a native of Glasgow, Scotland, makes her home in Manchester, England. A popular and prolific poet, she has published over thirty collections since 1974, when her first book appeared. Many of her works have received awards, including* Rapture *(2005), and she also writes for children and the stage.*

# Carol Ann Duffy
## Prayer

Some days, although we cannot pray, a prayer
utters itself. So, a woman will lift
her head from the sieve of her hands and stare
at the minims° sung by a tree, a sudden gift.

Some nights, although we are faithless, the truth                    5
enters our hearts, that small familiar pain;
then a man will stand stock-still, hearing his youth
in the distant Latin chanting of a train.

Pray for us now. Grade I piano scales
console the lodger looking out across                                 10
a Midlands town. Then dusk, and someone calls
a child's name as though they named their loss.

Darkness outside. Inside, the radio's prayer—
Rockall. Maim. Dogger. Finisterre.°

—*1993*

---

**4 minims** half notes    **14 Rockall . . .** The BBC shipping forecast includes these four marine zones.

*Armand Ruffo (b. 1955) was born in Chapleau in Northern Ontario, a member of the Fox Lake First Nation. His Ojibwa heritage is reflected in his poetry collections* Opening the Sky *(1994) and* At Geronimo's Grave *(2001), and in the creative biographies* Grey Owl: The Mystery of Archie Belaney *(1997) and* Norval Morriseau *(2006), about the renowned Ojibwa painter.*

## *Armand Ruffo*
# Poem for Duncan Campbell Scott

(Canadian poet who 'had a long and distinguished career
in the Department of Indian Affairs, retiring in 1932.'
*The Penguin Book of Canadian Verse*)

Who is this black coat and tie?
Christian severity etched in the lines
he draws from his mouth. Clearly a noble man
who believes in work and mission. See
how he rises from the red velvet chair,                              5
rises out of the boat with the two Union Jacks
fluttering like birds of prey
and makes his way towards our tents.
This man looks as if he could walk on water
and for our benefit probably would,                                  10
if he could.

He says he comes from Ottawa way, Odawa country,
comes to talk treaty and annuity and destiny,
to make the inevitable less painful,
bearing gifts that must be had.                                      15
Notice how he speaks aloud and forthright:
    This or Nothing.
    Beware! Without title to the land
    under the Crown you have no legal right
    to be here.                                              20
Speaks as though what has been long decided wasn't.
As though he wasn't merely carrying out his duty
to God and King. But sincerely felt.

Some whisper this man lives in a house of many rooms,
has a cook and a maid and even a gardener                                    25
to cut his grass and water his flowers.
Some don't care, they don't like the look of him.
They say he asks many questions but
doesn't want to listen. Asks
much about yesterday, little about today                                      30
and acts as if he knows tomorrow.
Others don't like the way he's always busy writing
stuff in the notebook he carries. Him,
he calls it poetry
and says it will make us who are doomed                                       35
live forever.

—*1994*

---

*Anne Simpson (b. 1956) lives and teaches in Nova Scotia. Her critically
acclaimed debut poetry collection,* Light Falls Through You *(2000), was followed
by a novel,* Canterbury Beach *(2001), and* Loop *(2003), which won the prestigious Griffin Poetry Prize.*

## *Anne Simpson*
# The Body Tattoo of World History

*Whose?*

This is a boy's body. Visited, like Sainte-Thérèse, by visions.

*On his wrist*

are many heads of obscure Chinese scholars, buried to their necks
in sand. You might think of the heads as attached to bodies, or          5
sliced from them by a dozen swordsmen.

There are tiny dots to represent the hundred heads. Or perhaps the
dots signify the sand, in which the heads have disappeared.

*On his left thigh*

Alexander's famous phalanx, a box formation (moving hedge        10
of bodies) that saved the Greeks.

Who was it they were fighting?

*On his right toe*

is a tiny face, but not one any of us know. (It could be a
miniature portrait of the nameless woman who lived on the        15
Steppes and rode a horse as well as any man, hunted with
falcons, and had six children before she was twenty-four.
When her youngest child died, she put two pieces of felt over
its eyes, as she had done with five others.)

*On his neck*                                                    20

a miniature human body, bird-headed creature from the caves of
Lascaux.°

Was there ever such a thing?

*On his right earlobe*

Jumbo the elephant, killed on the railway tracks in St. Thomas,  25
Ontario, in 1885, squeezed between two trains. Its tusks became
scimitars piercing its brain, but it did not die right away.

---

22 **Lascaux** caves in central France lined with prehistoric paintings

Something remains.

*On his left eyelid*

a symbol for Planck time° that can't be deciphered easily. More
beautiful than the Big Bang° itself,                              30

this tattoo, and more original.


*The body*

is that of a boy killed in a convenience store in a small town.

The murderer was a few years older, wearing a death's head
mask, carrying a hunting knife.                              35

A tattoo of wounds.


*How perfect the flesh, just*

before a body is cremated.


*History is whatever*

*lingers.*                              40

—*2003*

---

**29 Planck time** shortest unit of time named for quantum physicist Max Planck (1858–1947)
**30 Big Bang** theory of the evolution of the universe

*George Elliott Clarke (b. 1960) was born in Windsor Plains, Nova Scotia, of Africadian heritage, a heritage he explores in several collections of poetry—among them, the Governor General's Award–winning* Execution Poems *(2001),* Blue *(2001), and* Black *(2006)—as well as in his novel* George & Rue *(2005). He is also a playwright, literary critic, anthologist, and professor of literature at the University of Toronto.*

# George Elliott Clarke
# Casualties

## JANUARY 16, 1991

Snow annihilates all beauty
this merciless January.
A white blitzkrieg, Klan—cruel,
arsons and obliterates.

Piercing lies numb us to pain.                    5
Nerves and words fail so we
can't feel agony or passion,
so we can't flinch or cry,

when we spy blurred children's
charred bodies protruding                         10
from the smoking rubble
of statistics or see a man

stumbling in a blizzard
of bullets. Everything is
normal, absurdly normal.                          15
We see, as if through a snow-

storm, darkly. Reporters
rat-a-tat-tat tactics,
stratagems. Missiles bristle
behind newspaper lines.                           20

Our minds chill; we weather
the storm, huddle in dreams.
Exposed, though, a woman,
lashed by lightning, repents

of her flesh, becomes a living         25
X-ray, "collateral damage."
The first casualty of war
is language.

        —*1992*

---

*Wanda Campbell (b. 1963) was born in South India and came to Canada at the age of ten. She has published* Sky Fishing *(1997) and* Haw [Thorn] *(2003), and edited an anthology of early Canadian women poets entitled* Hidden Rooms *(2000).*

# *Wanda Campbell*
## Woolf

> *"Virginia Woolf is the Jackie Robinson of women's writing."*
>
>         —*A Student*

the one man
in a class full of women
surprised to be
for once a minority

wearing short sleeves         5
even in winter
but bearing gifts
in his hard brown arms

knowing they both insisted
we are as good as you         10
knowing they both wanted fans
to look past the colour

of their difference
to the music of their swing
such jazz and grace                                          15
and skill at stealing

they entered the room
but found it bare
the great experiment
took its toll                                                20

she, fifty-nine, loading her pockets
with stones the size of baseballs
and walking into the stream
of the unconscious

he, fifty-three, leaning                                     25
on a cane instead of a bat
almost blind, hair white
saying I never had it made

but Jesse Jackson
calling him at his funeral                                   30
a rock in the water
ripples and waves

*—2001*

*Christian Bök (b. 1966) is a sound poet and conceptual artist from Toronto who is especially interested in language, having even invented artificial languages for television shows. His poetry collections include* Crystallography *(1994) and* Eunoia *(2001), which was named for the shortest word in the English language to contain all five vowels.*

## Christian Bök
# Vowels

loveless vessels

we vow
solo love

we see
love solve loss                                                                    5

else we see
love sow woe

selves we woo
we lose

losses we levee                                                                    10
we owe

we sell
loose vows

so we love
less well                                                                          15

so low
so level

wolves evolve

—2001

*Stephanie Bolster (b. 1969) teaches at Concordia University in Montreal. She won the Governor General's Award for her debut poetry collection,* White Stone: The Alice Poems *(1998), about the real girl behind* Alice in Wonderland. Two Bowls of Milk *(1999) and* Pavilion *(2002) were also critically acclaimed.*

### Stephanie Bolster

# Le Far-West (1955)°

*A few acres of snow.*° In a Montréal
December I come upon your few feet

of west, a tawny field grazed on
by some animals. They might be

antelope and this some view of                                5
Africa—or cows and Idaho? What

cowboy hat do you imagine
my umbrella is? You have not gone

far enough, your English Bay a mouth
drawn shut, its trees cowering                               10

under an enormous Québec
sky I cannot write, my words

small glimpses between
this branch of fir and that. How west

must have threatened to open                                 15
you. My pages nearly white

these days, I'm shutting up.
That 'I' I write no longer me

but you, alone in the midst of what
I call nothing and you home.                                 20

—1999

Le Far-West (1955) painting by Québécois artist Jean Paul Lemieux (1904–1990)   **1** *A few acres of snow* In 1759, Voltaire used this phrase to question the value of fighting over Canadian territory.

*Ryan Knighton (b. 1973) is a native of British Columbia, where he still lives and teaches. His debut poetry collection,* Swing in the Hollow *(2001), was followed by* Cars *(2002), an "auto-biography" co-written with George Bowering, and* Cockeyed *(2006), a memoir that traces Knighton's slow descent into blindness.*

# Ryan Knighton
## Braille

It is January goosebumps, it is noon-hour sand
in your sandals & sometimes, when you're four,
it's bare feet clutching barnacles
in Pender Harbour.° That same year
it's your father's whiskers on your cheek                              5
& a July heat rash on your palms. It is gravel
at 16 under balding tires & it is an eternity
of ha ha ha ha after midnight.

Once it's an itchiness from the neighbour's lawn
& maybe, having fallen that summer, it is pavement          10
under your chin—it is definitely the stitches
that followed & it is my recently shaved head.
It is never rubbing a fish the wrong way
& it is in the delicacy of spider's feet
you were afraid to touch. It is a late supper of brown rice   15
& asparagus tips on your tongue & it's any set
of particular bedtime fingertips.
Vancouver's light autumn drizzle is what it is
& it's finally pressing stars to dial God.

                                                                              *—1999*

4 **Pender Harbour** harbour north of Vancouver

**Matt Robinson (b. 1974)** *A native of Halifax, Robinson has published widely in journals and has three books of poetry:* A Ruckus of Awkward Stacking (2001), How We Play at It: A List *(2002), and* no cage contains a stare that well *(2005), a collection of hockey poems.*

## Matt Robinson

# when skates break

that ice in its liquid form is a solvent,
should not confuse matters. this is all about stains;
this game concerns itself with scars—in fact,

    the surgical violence of that first step
is merely a prelude, an introduction. a perverse                    5
baptism. i remember our knees—carpet raw

    and bloody with tape-ball hockey
and too much sleep-over sugar; rec rooms alive
and stale gear crowded with the thrill of an oilers

    game on television out east. and especially          10
now, years later, after this afternoon's failure, when
the chill anticipation of this october night has shuddered

    and cracked, given way like we imagine
our childhood ponds never did—there is still
a sense of tired awe. and the broken, old goalie skates,      15

    a grade nine remnant now retired, are propped
in the corner—their blade acne, their cracked plastic,
become something more than nostalgia; become

    a grudging admission of the ambiguity of
physics and chemistry in the face of history. become          20
a memorial to the resiliency of water in all its states.

—*2001*

*Tania Langlais (b. 1979) was born in Montreal. She won the Émile-Nelligan Award for her critically acclaimed debut poetry collection,* Douze bêtes aux chemises de l'homme *(2000). After winning first prize for poetry in the CBC Literary Awards in 2002, she went on to publish a second collection,* La Clarté s'installe comme un chat *(2004).*

## *Tania Langlais*

# [she recites one hundred times]

she recites one hundred times
the lexicon of oceans
always signing her name
above the islands
to perfectly measure                                      5
the wasted expanse
neither daughter nor delta
she said
"when you sleep in the bed
it is the andalusian° thirst of wells                      10
that you multiply
and fold up behind me"

—2006

Translated by Wanda Campbell

10 **andalusian** region in southern Spain

# Drama

# Introduction
# to Drama

## The Play's the Thing

The theatre, located in the heart of a fading downtown business district, is a relic of the silent movie era that has been restored to something approaching its former glory. Although only a few members of tonight's audience can actually remember it in its heyday, the expertise of the organist seated at the antique Wurlitzer instills a sense of false nostalgia in the crowd, now settling by twos and threes into red, plush-covered seats and looking around in search of familiar faces. Just as the setting is somewhat out of the ordinary, so is this group. Unlike movie audiences, they are for the most part older and less casually dressed. Few small children are present, and even the teenagers seem to be on their best behaviour. Oddly, no one is eating popcorn or noisily drinking pop. A mood of seriousness and anticipation hovers over the theatre, and those who have lived in the town long enough can spot the spouse or companion of one of the principal actors nervously folding a program or checking a watch.

As the organ magically descends into the recesses of the orchestra pit, the lights dim, a hush falls over the crowd, and the curtain creakily rises. There is a general murmur of approval at the ingenuity and many hours of hard work that have transformed empty space into a remarkable semblance of a turn-of-the-century upper-class drawing room. Dressed as a domestic servant, a young woman, known by face to the audience from her frequent appearances in local television commercials, enters and begins to dust a table. She hums softly to herself. A tall young man, in reality a junior partner in a local law firm, wanders in, carrying a tennis racket. The maid turns, sees him, and catches her breath, startled. "Why Mr. Fenton!" she exclaims. . . .

And the world begins.

The full experience of drama—whether at an amateur production like the little theatre performance described here or at a huge Broadway playhouse—is much more complex than that of any other form of literature. The word **drama** itself comes from a Greek word meaning "a thing that is done," and the roots of both **theatre** and **audience** call to mind the acts of seeing and hearing, respectively. Like those of other communal public activities—such as religious services, sporting events, and meetings of political or fraternal organizations—drama's own set of customs, rituals, and rules has evolved over many centuries. The exact shape of these characteristics—**dramatic conventions**—may differ from country to country or from period to period, but they all have one aim in common, namely to define and govern an art form whose essence is to be found in public performances of written texts. No other form of literature shares this primary goal. Before we can discuss drama purely as literature, we should first ponder some aspects of its unique status as "a thing that is done."

It is worth noting that dramatists are also called playwrights. Note the spelling; a "wright" is a maker, as old family names like Cartwright or Boatwright attest. If a play is in fact *made* rather than written, then a playwright is similar to an architect who has designed a unique building. The concept may be his or hers, but the construction project requires the contributions of many other hands before the sparkling steel and glass tower alters the city's skyline. In the case of a new play, money must be raised by a producer, a director must be chosen, a cast and a crew found, a set designed and built, and many hours of rehearsal completed before the curtain can be raised for the first time. Along the way, modifications to the original play may become necessary, and it is possible that the author will listen to advice from the actors, director, or stage manager and incorporate these opinions into any revisions. Professional theatre is, after all, a branch of show business, and no play will survive much beyond its premiere if it does not attract paying crowds. The dramatists we read and study so reverently today managed to reach large popular audiences in their time. Even ancient Greek playwrights like Sophocles and Euripides must have stood by surreptitiously "counting the house" as the open-air seats slowly filled, and Shakespeare prospered as part-owner of the Globe theatre to the extent that he was able to retire to his hometown at the ripe old age of forty-seven.

When compared with this rich communal experience, the solitary act of reading a play seems a poor substitute, contrary to the play's very nature (only a small category known as **closet drama** comprises plays intended to be read instead of acted). Yet dramatists like Shakespeare and Ibsen are counted among the giants of world literature, and their works are annually read by far more people than actually see these plays performed. In reading a play, we are forced to pay close attention to such matters as **set description,** particularly with a playwright like Ibsen who lavishes great attention on the design of his set; references to **properties,** or "props," that will figure in the action of the play; physical description of characters and costumes; **stage directions** indicating the movements and gestures made by actors in scenes; and any other **stage business,** that is, action without dialogue. Many modern dramatists are very scrupulous in detailing these matters; writers of earlier periods, however, provided little or no instruction. In reading Shakespeare, we are forced to concentrate on the characters' words to envision how actions and other characters were originally conceived. Reading aloud, alone or in a group, or following along in the text while listening to a recorded performance is particularly recommended for verse plays like *Othello.* Also, versions of many of the plays contained in this book are currently available on videotape or DVD. Although viewing a film is an experience of a different kind from seeing a live performance, film versions obviously provide a convenient insight into the ways in which great actors have interpreted their roles. Seeing the joy in the face of Laurence Fishburne when, as Othello, he lands triumphantly in Cyprus and rejoins his bride makes his tragic fall even more poignant.

## Origins of Drama

No consensus exists about the exact date of the birth of drama but, according to most authorities, it originated in Greece over 2500 years ago as an outgrowth of the worship of the god Dionysus, who was associated with fertility, agriculture (especially the cultivation of vineyards), and seasonal renewal. In these Dionysian festivals, a group of fifty citizens of Athens, known as a **chorus,** outfitted and trained by a leader, or **choragos,** would perform hymns of praise to the god, known as

**dithyrambic poetry.** The celebration concluded with the ritual sacrifice of a goat, or *tragos*. The two main genres of drama originally took their names from these rituals. The word comedy comes from *kômos*, the Greek term for a festivity. These primitive revels were invariably accompanied by a union of the sexes (*gamos* in Greek, a word that survives in English words like "monogamy"), perhaps in the symbolic form of a dance celebrating fertility and continuance of the race. This is an ancient custom still symbolically observed in the "fade-out kiss" that concludes most comedies. The word tragedy literally means "song of the goat," taking its name from the *tragos* that was killed on the altar (***thymele***), cooked, and shared by the celebrants with their god.

Around 600 B.C. certain refinements took place. In the middle of the sixth century B.C. an official springtime festival, known as the Greater or City Dionysia, was established in Athens, and prizes for the best dithyrambic poems were first awarded. At about the same time a special ***orchestra,*** or "dancing place," was constructed, a circular area surrounding the altar, and permanent seats, or a ***theatron*** ("seeing place"), arranged in a semicircle around the orchestra were added. At the back of the orchestra the facade of a temple (the ***skene***) and a raised "porch" in front of it (the ***proskenion,*** in later theatres the **proscenium**) served as a backdrop, usually representing the palace of the ruler; walls extending to either side of the skene, the ***parodoi,*** served to conceal backstage activity from the audience. Behind the *skene* a crane-like device called a ***mechane*** could be used to lower a god from the heavens or represent a spectacular effect like the flying chariot drawn by dragons at the conclusion of Euripides's *Medea.*

Around 535 B.C. a writer named Thespis won the annual competition with a startling innovation. Thespis separated one member of the chorus (called a *hypocrites*, or "actor") and had him engage in **dialogue,** spoken lines representing conversation, with the remaining members. If we define drama primarily as a story related through live action and recited dialogue, then Thespis may rightly be called the father of drama, and his name endures in "thespian," a synonym for actor.

The century after Thespis, from 500 to 400 B.C., saw many refinements in the way tragedies were performed and is considered the golden age of Greek drama. In that century, the careers of the three great tragic playwrights—Aeschylus (525–456 B.C.), Sophocles (c. 496–406 B.C.), and Euripides (c. 485–408 B.C.)—and the greatest comic playwright,

Aristophanes (448–380 B.C.), overlapped. It is no coincidence that in this remarkable period Athens, under the leadership of the general Pericles (d. 429 B.C.), reached the height of its wealth, influence, and cultural development and was home to the philosophers Socrates (470–399 B.C.) and Plato (427–327 B.C.). Aristotle (384–322 B.C.), the third of the great Athenian philosophers, was also a literary critic who wrote the first extended analysis of drama.

## Aristotle on Tragedy

In his *Poetics*, the earliest work of literary criticism in Western civilization, Aristotle attempts to define and classify the different literary **genres** that use rhythm, language, and harmony. He identifies four genres—epic poetry, dithyrambic poetry, comedy, and tragedy—that have in common their attempts at imitation, or *mimesis*, of various types of human activity.

Aristotle comments most fully on tragedy, and his definition of the genre demands close examination:

> A tragedy, then, is the imitation of an action that is serious and also, as having magnitude, complete in itself; in language with pleasurable accessories, each kind brought in separately in the parts of the work; in a dramatic, not in a narrative form; with incidents arousing pity and fear, wherewith to accomplish its catharsis of such emotions.

First we should note that the imitation here is of *action*. Later in the passage, when Aristotle differentiates between narrative and dramatic forms of literature, it is clear that he is referring to tragedy as a type of literature written primarily for public performance. Furthermore, tragedy must be serious and must have magnitude. By this, Aristotle implies that issues of life and death must be involved and that these issues must be of public import. In many Greek tragedies the fate of the *polis*, or city, of which the chorus is the voice, is bound up with the actions taken by the main character in the play. Despite their rudimentary form of democracy, the people of Athens would have been perplexed by a tragedy with an ordinary citizen at its centre; the magnitude of tragedy demands that only the affairs of persons of high rank are of sufficient importance for tragedy. Aristotle further requires that this imitated action possess a sense of completeness. At no point does he say that a tragedy has to end with a death or even in a state of unhappiness; he does require, however, that the audience sense that after the last words are spoken no further story cries out to be told.

The next part of the passage may confuse the modern reader. By "language with pleasurable accessories" Aristotle means the poetic devices of rhythm and, in the choral parts of the tragedy, music and dance as well. Reading the choral passages in a Greek tragedy, we are likely to forget that these passages were intended to be chanted or sung ("chorus" and "choir" share the same root word in Greek) and danced ("choreography" comes from this root as well).

The rest of Aristotle's definition dwells on the emotional effects of tragedy on the audience. Pity and fear are to be evoked—pity because we must care for the characters and to some extent empathize with them, fear because we come to realize that the fate they endure involves actions that civilized men and women most abhor. Finally, Aristotle's word **catharsis** has proven controversial over the centuries. The word literally means "a purging," but readers have debated whether Aristotle is referring to a release of harmful emotions or a transformation of them. In either case, the implication is that viewing a tragedy has a beneficial effect on an audience, perhaps because the viewers' deepest fears are brought to light in a make-believe setting. How many of us, at the end of some particularly wrenching film, have turned to a companion and said, "Thank god, it was only a movie"? The sacrificial animal from whom tragedy took its name was, after all, only a stand-in whose blood was offered to the gods as a substitute for a human subject. The protagonist of a tragedy remains, in many ways, a "scapegoat" on whose head we project our own unconscious terrors. Aristotle identifies six elements of a tragedy, and these elements are still useful in analyzing not only tragedies but other types of plays as well. In order of importance they are **plot, characterization, theme, diction, melody,** and **spectacle.** Despite the fact that *Poetics* is over two thousand years old, Aristotle's elements still provide a useful way of understanding how plays work.

# Plot

Aristotle considers plot the chief element of a play, and it is easy to see this when we consider that in discussing a film with a friend we usually give a brief summary, or **synopsis,** of the plot, stopping just short of "giving it away" by telling how the story concludes. Aristotle defines plot as "the combination of incidents, or things done in the story," going on to give the famous formulation that a plot "is that which has beginning, middle, and end." Aristotle notes that the best plots are selective in their use of material and have an internal coherence and logic. Aristotle seems to favour plays with a unified plot, that is, one that takes place in a single day; in a short play with a **unified plot** like Gwen Pharis Ringwood's *Still Stands the House*, the action is continuous and imitates the amount of time that the events would have taken in real life. By **episodic plot** we mean one that spreads its action out over a longer period of time. A play that has a unified plot, a single setting, and no subplots is said to observe the **three unities,** which critics in some past eras have virtually insisted on as ironclad rules. Although most plots are chronological, playwrights in the last half-century have experimented, sometimes radically, with such straightforward progression through time. Arthur Miller's *Death of a Salesman* effectively blends **flashbacks** to past events with his main action, as does Sharon Pollock's *Moving Pictures*, which uses three different actors to represent the same character over time.

Two other important elements of plots that Aristotle considers most successful are **reversal** (*peripeteia* in Greek, also known as **peripety**) and **recognition** (*anagnorisis* in Greek, also known as **discovery**). By reversal he means a change "from one state of things within the play to its opposite." Most plays have more than a single reversal; each episode or act builds on the main character's hopes that his or her problems will be solved, only to dash those expectations as the play proceeds. Recognition, the second term, is perhaps more properly an element of characterization because it involves a character's "change from ignorance to knowledge." If the events of the plot have not served to illuminate the character about his or her failings, then the audience is likely to feel that the story lacks depth. The kind of self-knowledge that tragedies provide is invariably accompanied by suffering and is won at great emotional cost, whereas in comedies reversals may bring relief to the characters, and recognition may bring about the happy conclusion of the play.

As with fiction, a typical plot may be broken down into several components. First comes the **exposition,** which provides the audience with essential information—who, what, when, where—that it needs to know before the play can continue. A novelist or short-story writer can present information directly with some sort of variation on the "Once upon a time" opening. But dramatists have particular problems with exposition because facts must be presented in the form of dialogue and action. Greek dramatists used the first two parts of a tragedy, a prologue and the first appearance of the chorus, to refresh the audience's familiarity with the myths being retold and to set up the initial situation of the play. Other types of drama use a single character to provide expository material. Medieval morality plays often use a "heavenly messenger" to deliver the opening speech, and some of Shakespeare's plays employ a single character named "Chorus" who speaks an introductory prologue and sets the scene for later portions of the plays as well (the film *Shakespeare in Love* captures this memorably). Occasionally, we encounter the least elegant solution to the problem of dramatic exposition, employing minor characters whose sole function is to provide background information in the play's opening scene. Countless drawing-room comedies have raised the curtain on a pair of servants in the midst of a gossipy conversation that catches the audience up on the doings of the family members who make up the rest of the cast.

The second part of a plot is called the **complication,** the interjection of some circumstance or event that shakes up the stable situation that has existed before the play's opening and begins the **rising action** of the play, during which the audience's tension and expectations become tightly intertwined and involved with the characters and the events they experience. Complication in a play may be both external and internal. A plague, a threatened invasion, or a conclusion of a war is a typical example of an external complication, an outside event that affects the characters' lives. However, many plays rely primarily on an internal complication, a single character's weakness in his or her personality. Often the complication is heightened by **conflict** between two characters whom events have forced into collision with each other. In Arthur Miller's *Death of a Salesman,* for example, the external complication stems from Willy's troubles with his boss, the internal complication is his growing depression and suicidal tendencies, and the chief conflict is with his son Biff. No matter how it is presented, the complication of the plot usually introduces a problem that the characters cannot avoid. The rising action, which constitutes the body of the play, usually contains a number of moments of **crisis,** when solutions crop up momentarily but quickly disappear. These critical moments in the scenes may take the form of the kinds of reversals discussed above, and the audience's emotional involvement in the plot generally hinges on the characters' rising and falling hopes.

The central moment of crisis in the play is the **climax,** or the moment of greatest tension, which initiates the **falling action** of the plot. Perhaps "moments" of greatest tension would be a more exact phrase, for skillful playwrights know how to wring as much tension as possible from the audience. In the best plots everything in earlier parts of the play has pointed to this scene—a duel, a suicide, a murder—and the play's highest pitch of emotion.

The final part of a plot is the **resolution,** or **dénouement.** This French word literally refers to the untying of a knot, the release of the tension that has built up during the play. The dénouement returns the play and its characters to a stable situation, though not the same one that existed at the beginning of the play, and gives some indication of what the future holds for them. A dénouement may be either closed or open. A **closed dénouement** ties up everything neatly and explains all unanswered questions the audience might have; an **open dénouement** leaves a few tantalizing loose ends.

Several other plot terms should also be noted. Aristotle mentions, not altogether favourably, plots with "double issues." The most common word for this is **subplot,** a less important story involving minor characters that may mirror the main plot of the play. Some plays, like Shakespeare's *A Midsummer Night's Dream*, may even have more than one subplot. Occasionally, a playwright finds it necessary to drop hints about coming events in the plot, perhaps to keep the audience from complaining that certain incidents have happened "out of the blue." This is called **foreshadowing.** If a climactic incident that helps to resolve the plot has not been adequately prepared for, the playwright may be accused of having resorted to a *deus ex machina* ending, which takes its name from the *mechane* that once literally lowered a god or goddess into the midst of the dramatic proceedings. An ending of this sort, like that of an old western movie in which the cavalry arrives just as the wagon train is about to be annihilated, is rarely satisfactory.

Finally, the difference between **suspense** and **dramatic irony** should be addressed. Both of these devices generate tension in the audience, although through opposite means—suspense when the audience does not know what is about to happen, dramatic irony, paradoxically, when it does. Much of our pleasure in reading a new play lies in speculating about what will happen next, but in Greek tragedy the original audience would be fully familiar with the basic outlines of the mythic story before the action even began. Dramatic irony thus occurs at moments when the audience is more knowledgeable about events than the onstage characters are. In *Othello* we are continually reminded that Iago is lying to Othello. In some plays, our foreknowledge of certain events is so strong that we may want to cry out a warning to the characters.

## Characterization

The Greek word *agon* means "debate" and refers to the central issue or conflict of a play. From *agon* we derive two words commonly used to denote the chief characters in a play: **protagonist,** literally the "first speaker," and **antagonist,** one who speaks against him. Often the word "hero" is used as a synonym for protagonist, and it is difficult not to think of Oedipus or Othello as tragic heroes. In many modern plays it may be more appropriate to speak of the protagonist as an **anti-hero** because he or she may possess few, if any, of the traditional attributes of a hero, a point that Arthur Miller discusses in his essay "Tragedy and the Common Man." Similarly, the word "villain" may bring to mind a sinister, sneering character in a top hat and opera cloak from an old-fashioned **melodrama** (a play whose complications are solved happily at the last minute by the "triumph of good over evil") and usually has little application to the complex characters one encounters in a serious play.

Aristotle, in his discussion of characterization, stresses the complexity that marks the personages in the greatest plays. Nothing grows tiresome more quickly than a perfectly virtuous man or woman at the centre of a play, and nothing is more offensive to the audience than seeing absolute innocence despoiled. Although Aristotle stresses that a successful protagonist must be better than ordinary men and women, he also insists that the protagonist be somewhat less than perfect:

> There remains, then, the intermediate kind of personage, a man not pre-eminently virtuous and just, whose misfortune, however, is brought upon him not by vice and depravity but by some error of judgment. . . .

Aristotle's word for this error is ***hamartia,*** which is commonly translated as "tragic flaw" but might more properly be termed a "great error." Whether he means some innate flaw, like a psychological defect, or simply a great mistake is open to question, but writers of tragedies have traditionally created deeply flawed protagonists. In ordinary circumstances, the protagonist's strength of character may allow him to prosper, but under the pressure of events he may crack as one small chink in his armour widens and leaves him vulnerable. A typical flaw in tragedies is ***hubris,*** arrogance or excessive pride, which leads the protagonist into errors that might have been avoided if he had listened to the advice of others. Although he does not use the term himself, Aristotle touches here on the concept of **poetic justice,** the audience's sense that virtue and vice have been fairly dealt with in the play and that the protagonist's punishment is to some degree deserved.

We should bear in mind that the greatest burden of characterization in drama falls on the actor or actress who undertakes a role. No matter how well-written a part is, in the hands of an incompetent or inappropriate performer the character will not be credible. Vocal inflection, gesture, and even the strategic use of silence are the stock in trade of actors, for it is up to them to convince us that we are involved in the sufferings and joys of real human beings. No two actors will play the same part in the same manner. The role of Othello has been played in film versions by actors as various as Orson Welles, Laurence Olivier, Anthony Hopkins, and Laurence Fishburne. Comparing these performances provides a wonderful short course in the validity of radically different approaches to the same role. In reading, there are several points to keep in mind about main characters. Physical description, while it may be minimal at best, is worth paying close attention to. To cite one example from the plays contained in this edition, Shakespeare identifies Othello simply as a "Moor," a native of North Africa. Racialization is an important cause of conflict in the play, but through the years the part has been played with equal success by both Black and white actors. The central issue in *Othello* is that the tragic hero is a cultural misfit in the Venetian society from which he takes a wife; he is a widely respected military leader but an outsider all the same. Shakespeare provides us with few other details of Othello's appearance, but we can probably assume that he is a large and powerful warrior, capable of commanding men by his mere presence. Sometimes an author will give a character a name that is an indicator of his or her personality and appearance. Willy Loman, the failed protagonist of Arthur Miller's *Death of a Salesman*, bears a surname ("low man") which contains a pun on his character, a device called a **characternym.**

**Character motivation** is another point of characterization to ponder. Why do characters act in a certain manner? What do they hope to gain from their actions? In some cases, these motives are clear enough and may be discussed openly by the characters. In other plays, motivation is more elusive, as the playwright deliberately mystifies the audience by presenting characters who perhaps are not fully aware of the reasons for their compulsions. Modern dramatists, influenced by advances in psychology, have often refused to reduce characters' actions to simple equations of cause and effect.

Two conventions that the playwright may employ in revealing motivation are **soliloquy** and **aside.** A soliloquy is a speech made by a single character on stage alone. Hamlet's soliloquies, among them some of the most famous passages in all drama, show us the process of his mind as he toys with various plans of revenge but delays putting them into action. The aside is a brief remark (traditionally delivered to the side of a raised hand) that an actor makes directly to the audience and that the other characters on stage cannot hear. Occasionally an aside reveals a reason for a character's behaviour in a scene. Neither of these devices is as widely used in today's theatre as in earlier periods, but they remain part of the dramatist's collection of techniques.

Minor characters are also of great importance in a successful play, and several different traditional types exist. A **foil,** a minor character with whom a major character sharply contrasts, is used primarily as a sounding board for ideas, as in the way Iago banters with the foolish Roderigo in *Othello.* A **confidant,** like Nora Helmer's friend Dr. Rank in Ibsen's *A Doll's House,* is a trusted friend or servant to whom a major character speaks frankly and openly; confidants fulfill in some respects one role that the chorus plays in Greek tragedy. **Stock characters** are stereotypes that are useful for advancing the plot and fleshing out the scenes, particularly in comedies. Hundreds of plays have employed a pair of innocent young lovers, sharp-tongued servants, and/or meddling mothers-in-law as part of their casts. **Allegorical characters** in morality plays like *Everyman* are clearly labelled by their names and, for the most part, are personifications of human attributes (Beauty, Good Deeds) or of theological concepts (Confession). **Comic relief** in a tragedy may be provided by minor characters like Shakespeare's fools or clowns.

# Theme

Aristotle has relatively little to say about the theme of a play, simply noting that "thought of the personages is shown in everything to be effected by their language." Because he focuses to such a large degree on the emotional side of tragedy—its stimulation of pity and fear—he seems to give less importance to the role of drama as a serious forum for the discussion of ideas, referring his readers to another of his works, *The Art of Rhetoric,* where these matters have greater prominence. Nevertheless, **theme,** the central idea or ideas that a play discusses, is important in Greek tragedy and in the subsequent history of the theatre. The trilogies of early playwrights were thematically unified around an *aition,* a Greek word for the origin of a custom; today one might find the origin of the holiday custom of gift-giving in a Nativity play.

Some dramas are explicitly **didactic** in their intent, existing with the specific aim of instructing the audience in ethical, religious, or political areas. A **morality play,** a popular type of drama in the late Middle Ages, is essentially a sermon on sin and redemption rendered in dramatic terms. More subtle in its didacticism is the **problem play** of the late nineteenth century, popularized by Ibsen, which uses the theatre as a forum for the serious debate of social issues like industrial pollution or women's rights. The **drama of ideas** of playwrights like George Bernard Shaw does not merely present social problems; it goes further, actually advancing programs of reform. In the United States during the Great Depression, Broadway theatres featured a great deal of **social drama,** in which radical social and political programs were openly propagandized. In the ensuing decades the theatre has remained a popular forum for debating issues of class, gender, and racialization, as the success of Tomson Highway's *The Rez Sisters* and many other plays will attest. Keep in mind, however, that plays are not primarily religious or political forums. If we are not entertained and moved by a play's language, action, and plot, then it is unlikely that we will respond to its message. The author who must resort to long sermons from a *raisonneur* (like Cléante, the protagonist's brother-in-law in Molière's famous comedy *Tartuffe*) who serves primarily as the voice of reason, that is, the mouthpiece for the playwright's opinions, is not likely to hold the audience's sympathy or attention for long. The best plays are complex enough that they cannot be reduced to simple "thesis statements" that sum up their meaning in a few words.

## Diction

Aristotle was also the author of the first important manual of public speaking, *The Art of Rhetoric*, so it should come as no surprise that he devotes considerable attention in the *Poetics* to the precise words, either alone or in combinations, that playwrights use. Instead of "diction," we would probably speak today of a playwright's "style" or discuss his or her handling of various levels of idiom in the dialogue. Although much of what Aristotle has to say about parts of speech and the sounds of words in Greek is of little interest to us, his emphasis on clarity and originality in the choice of words remains relevant. For Aristotle, the language of tragedy should be "poetic" in the best sense, somehow elevated above the level of ordinary speech but not so ornate that it loses the power to communicate feelings and ideas to an audience. Realism in speech is largely a matter of illusion, and close inspection of the actual lines of modern dramatists like Miller reveal a discrepancy between the carefully chosen words that characters speak in plays, often making up lengthy **monologues,** and the halting, often inarticulate ("Like, ya know what I mean?") manner in which we may express ourselves in everyday life. The language of the theatre has always been an artificial one. The idiom of plays, whether by William Shakespeare or by Sharon Pollock, *imitates* the language of life; it does not duplicate it.

Shakespeare's use of the full resources of the English language has been the standard against which all subsequent writers in the language have had to measure themselves. However, Shakespeare's language presents some special difficulties for the modern reader. His vocabulary is essentially the same as ours, but many words have changed in meaning or become obsolete over the last four hundred years. Shakespeare is also a master of different **levels of diction.** In the space of a few lines he can range from self-consciously flowery heights ("If after every tempest come such calms, / May the winds blow till they have wakened death, / And let the laboring bark climb hills of seas / Olympus-high, and duck again as low / As hell's from heaven!" exults Othello on being reunited with his bride in Cyprus) to the slangy level of the streets—he is a master of the off-colour joke and the sarcastic put-down. Responding to Roderigo's threat to drown himself, Iago says, "Come, be a man. Drown thyself? Drown cats and blind puppies." We should remember that Shakespeare's poetic drama lavishly uses figurative language; his lines abound with similes, metaphors, personifications, and hyperboles, all characteristic devices of the language of poetry. Shakespeare's theatre had little in the way of scenery and no "special effects," so a passage from *Hamlet* like "But, look, the morn, in russet mantle clad / Walks o'er the dew of yon high eastward hill" is not merely pretty or picturesque; it has the dramatic function of helping the audience visualize the welcome end of a long, fearful night.

It is true that playwrights since the middle of the nineteenth century have striven for more fidelity to reality, more verisimilitude, in the language their characters use, but even realistic dramatists often rise to rhetorical peaks that have little relationship to the way people actually speak. Ibsen began his career as a poet and, surprisingly, the first draft of Arthur Miller's "realistic" tragedy *Death of a Salesman* was largely written in verse. Samuel Beckett's play *Act Without Words I* has no words at all, and Tomson Highway makes extensive use of Cree, so playwrights continue to experiment with the tools of their trade.

## Melody

Greek tragedy was accompanied by music. None of this music survives, and we cannot be certain how it was integrated into the drama. Certainly the choral parts of the play were sung and danced, and it is likely that even the dialogue involved highly rhythmical chanting, especially in passages employing **stichomythia,** rapid alternation of single lines between two actors, a device often encountered during moments of high dramatic tension. In the original language, the different poetic rhythms used in Greek tragedy are still evident, although these are for the most part lost in English translation. At any rate, it is apparent that the skillful manipulation of a variety of **poetic metres,** combinations of line lengths and rhythms, for different types of scenes was an important part of the tragic poet's repertoire.

Both tragedies and comedies have been written in verse throughout the ages, often employing rhyme as well as rhythm. Shakespeare's *Othello* is composed, like all of his plays, largely in **blank verse,** that is, unrhymed lines of iambic pentameter (lines of ten syllables, alternating unstressed and stressed syllables). He also uses rhymed pairs of lines called **couplets,** particularly for emphasis at the close of scenes; songs (there are three in *Othello*); and even prose passages, especially when dealing with comic, or "low," characters. A study of Shakespeare's versification is beyond the scope of this discussion, but suffice it to say that a trained actor must be aware of the rhythmical patterns that Shakespeare utilized if he or she is to deliver the lines with anything approaching accuracy.

Of course, not only verse drama has rhythm. Both Sharon Pollock and Tomson Highway incorporate songs into their plays, and in *The Rez Sisters* the character of Nanabush the Trickster dances in white and dark feathers. Likewise, a double bass and cello provide an important jazz and blues backdrop to the dialogue in *Harlem Duet*. The ancient musical heritage of tragedy thus lingers on in the modern theatre and has proven resistant even to the prosaic rhythms of contemporary life.

# Spectacle

Spectacle (sometimes called *mise en scène,* French for "putting on stage") is the last of Aristotle's elements of tragedy and, in his view, the least important. By spectacle we mean the purely visual dimension of a play; in ancient Greece, this meant costumes, a few props, and effects carried out by the use of the *mechane.* Costumes in Greek tragedy were simple but impressive. The tragic mask, or *persona,* and a high-heeled boot (*cothurnus*), were apparently designed to give characters a larger-than-life appearance. Historians also speculate that the mask might have additionally served as a crude megaphone to amplify the actors' voices, a necessary feature when we consider that the open-air theatre in Athens could seat over ten thousand spectators. Other elements of set decoration were kept to a minimum, although playwrights occasionally employed a few well-chosen spectacular effects like the triumphant entrance of the victorious king in

Aeschylus's *Agamemnon*, which involves a horse-drawn chariot and brilliant red carpet on which Agamemnon walks to his death. Elizabethan drama likewise relied little on spectacular stage effects. Shakespeare's plays call for few props, and little attempt was made at historical accuracy in costumes, a noble patron's cast-off clothing dressing Caesar one week, Othello the next.

Advances in technology since Shakespeare's day have obviously facilitated more elaborate effects in what we now call **staging** than patrons of earlier centuries could have envisioned. In the nineteenth century, first gas and then electric lighting not only made effects like sunrises possible but also, through the use of different combinations of colour, added atmosphere to certain scenes. By Ibsen's day, realistic **box sets** were designed to resemble, in the smallest details, interiors of houses and apartments with an invisible "fourth wall" nearest the audience. Modern theatre has experimented in all directions with set design, from the bare stage to barely suggested walls and furnishings, from revolving stages to scenes that "break the plane" by involving the audience in the drama. Samuel Beckett is famous for the spareness of his sets, from the lone tree of *Waiting for Godot* to the "Desert. Dazzling light" of *Act Without Words I: A Mime for One Player.* Tomson Highway's *The Rez Sisters* employs music, mime, dancing, "lighting magic," and the transformation of the entire theatre into a bingo palace with Nanabush as the Bingo Master. It is fitting that Wasaychigan, the name of the fictional reserve where the play is set, means "window" in Ojibway, as Highway uses a variety of theatrical techniques to provide us a window into the dreams and realities of life on the Rez. Sharon Pollock's play begins and ends with the bodies of the actors serving as a "screen" for moving pictures, and playwright Djanet Sears makes extensive use of audio clips of individuals important to African-American history, including Martin Luther King and Malcolm X.

In today's Broadway productions, the most impressive uses of spectacle may represent anything from the catacombs beneath the Paris Opera House in *Phantom of the Opera* to ten-metre-high street barricades manned by soldiers firing muskets in *Les Misérables.* Modern technology can create virtually any sort of stage illusion; the only limitations in today's professional theatre are imagination and budget.

Before we leave our preliminary discussion, one further element should be mentioned—**setting.** For the most part specific locales in the greatest plays are less important than the universal currents that are touched. If we are interested in the particular features of middle-class marriage in Oslo in the late nineteenth century, we would perhaps do better going to sociology texts than to Ibsen's *A Doll's House.* Still, every play implies a larger sense of setting, a sense of history that is called the **enveloping action.** Life on the prairies may not be as desperate as it was during the Depression years, the context for Gwen Pharis Ringwood's *Still Stands the House,* and yet farmers continue to face similar struggles. The Rez (or Reservation) and Harlem are sufficiently important to the shaping of action and character that they appear in the titles of the plays by Highway and Sears, respectively. Even though a play from another place or time may still speak eloquently today, it also provides a capsule whose contents tell us how people lived and what they most valued when the play was written and first performed.

# Brief History and Description of Dramatic Conventions

## Greek Tragedy

By the time of Sophocles, tragedy had evolved into an art form with a complex set of conventions. Each playwright would submit a **tetralogy,** or set of four plays, to the yearly competition. The first three plays, or **trilogy,** would be tragedies, and the fourth, called a **satyr-play,** was comic, with a chorus of goat-men engaging in bawdy revels that, oddly, mocked the serious content of the preceding tragedies. Each tragedy was composed according to a prescribed formula, as ritualized as the order of worship in a contemporary church service. The tragedy begins with a **prologue** (*prologos*), "that which is said first." The prologue is an introductory scene that tells the audience important information about the play's setting, characters, and events immediately preceding the opening of the drama. The second part of the tragedy is called the ***parodos,*** the first appearance of the chorus in the play. As the members of the chorus enter the orchestra, they dance and sing more generally of the situation in which the city finds itself. Choral parts in some translations are divided into sections called **strophes** and **antistrophes,** indicating choral movements to left and right, respectively. The body of the play is made up of two types of alternating scenes. The first, an episode (*episodos*), is a passage of dialogue between two or more actors or between actors and the chorus. Each of these "acts" of the tragedy is separated from the rest by a choral **ode** (*stasimon;* pl. *stasima*) during which the chorus is alone on the orchestra, commenting, as the voice of public opinion, about the course of action being taken by the main characters. Typically there are four pairs of episodes and odes in the play. The final scene of the play is called the *exodos.* During this part, the climax occurs out of sight of the audience, and a vivid description of this usually violent scene is sometimes given by a messenger or other witness. After the messenger's speech, the protagonist reappears and the resolution of his fate is determined. In some plays, a wheeled platform called an *eccyclema* was used to move this fatal tableau into the view of the spectators. A tragedy concludes with the exit of the main characters, sometimes leaving the chorus to deliver a brief speech, or **epilogue,** a final summing-up of the play's meaning.

Although we may at first find such complicated rituals bizarre, we should keep in mind that dramatic conventions are primarily customary and artificial and have little to do with "reality" as we usually experience it. The role of the chorus (set by the time of Sophocles at fifteen members) may seem puzzling to modern readers, but in many ways the conventions of Greek tragedy are no stranger than those of contemporary musicals in which the characters burst into song and dance. What is most remarkable about the history of drama is not how much these conventions have changed but how remarkably similar they have remained for over twenty-five centuries.

## *Medieval Drama*

Drama flourished during Greek and Roman times, but after the fall of the Roman Empire (A.D. 476) it went into four centuries of eclipse, kept alive throughout Europe only by wandering troupes of actors performing various types of **folk drama.** The "Punch and Judy" puppet show, still popular in parts of Europe, is a late survivor of this tradition, as are the ancient slapstick routines of circus clowns. Even though drama was officially discouraged by the Church for a long period, when it did re-emerge it was as an outgrowth of the Roman Catholic mass, in the form of **liturgical drama.** Around the ninth century, short passages of sung dialogue between the priest and choir, called **tropes,** were added on special holidays to commemorate the event. These tropes grew more elaborate over the years until full-fledged religious pageants were being performed in front of the altar. In 1210, Pope Innocent III, wishing to restore the dignity of the services, banned such performances from the interior of the church. Moving them outside, first to the church porch and later entirely off church property, provided greater opportunity for inventiveness in action and staging.

In the fourteenth and fifteenth centuries, much of the work of putting on plays passed to the guilds, organizations of skilled craftsmen, and their productions became part of city-wide festivals in many Continental and British cities. Several types of plays evolved. **Mystery plays** were derived from Holy Scripture. **Passion plays** (some of which survive unchanged today) focused on the crucifixion of Christ. **Miracle plays** dramatized the lives of the saints. The last and most complex, **morality plays,** were dramatized sermons with allegorical characters (Everyman, Death, Good Deeds) representing various generalized aspects of human life.

## Elizabethan Drama

Although the older morality plays were still performed throughout the sixteenth century, during the time of Queen Elizabeth I (b. 1533, reigned 1558–1603) a new type of drama, typical in many ways of other innovative types of literature developed in the Renaissance, began to be produced professionally by companies of actors not affiliated with any religious institutions. This **secular drama,** beginning in short pieces called **interludes,** which may have been designed for entertainment during banquets or other public celebrations, eventually evolved into full-length tragedies and comedies designed for performance in large outdoor theatres like Shakespeare's famous Globe.

A full history of this fertile period would take many pages, but a few of its dramatic conventions are worth noting. We have already mentioned blank verse, the poetic line perfected by Shakespeare's contemporary Christopher Marlowe (1564–1593). Shakespeare wrote tragedies, comedies, and historical dramas with equal success, all characterized by passages that remain the greatest examples of poetic expression in English.

The raised platform stage in an Elizabethan theatre used little or no scenery, but relied on the author's descriptive talents to set the scene and indicate lighting and weather. The stage itself had two supporting columns, which might be used to represent trees or hiding places; a raised area at the rear, which could represent a balcony or upper story of a house; a small curtained alcove at its base; and a trap door, which could serve as a grave or hiding place. In contrast to the relatively bare stage, costumes were elaborate and acting was highly stylized, with the blank verse lines delivered at high volume and with broad gestures. Female roles were played by young boys, and the same actor might play several different minor roles in the same play.

A few more brief words about Shakespeare's plays may be in order. First, drama in Shakespeare's time was intended for performance, with publication being of only secondary importance. The texts of many of Shakespeare's plays were published in cheap editions called **quartos,** which are full of misprints and often contain widely different versions of the same play. Any play by Shakespeare contains words and passages that different editors have trouble agreeing on. Second, originality, in the sense we prize it, meant little to a playwright in a time before copyright laws; virtually every one of Shakespeare's plays is derived from an earlier source—Greek myth, history, another play or, in the case of *Othello*, an Italian short story of questionable literary merit. The true test of Shakespeare's genius rests in his ability to transform these raw materials into art. Finally, we should keep in mind that Shakespeare's plays were designed to appeal to a wide audience—educated aristocrats and slovenly "groundlings" filled the theatre—and this fact may account for the great diversity of tones and levels of language in the plays. Purists of later eras might have been dismayed by some of Shakespeare's wheezy clowns and bad puns, but for us the mixture of "high" and "low" elements gives his plays their remarkable texture.

## The Comic Genres

Shakespeare's ability to move easily between "high" and "low," between tragic and comic, should be a reminder that comedy has developed along lines parallel to tragedy and never wholly separate from it. Most of Aristotle's remarks on comedy are lost, but he does make the observation that comedy differs from tragedy in that comedy depicts men and women as worse than they are, whereas tragedy generally stresses their best qualities. During the great age of Greek tragedy, comedies were regularly performed at Athenian festivals. The greatest of the early comic playwrights was Aristophanes (c. 450–380 B.C.). The plays of Aristophanes are classified as **Old Comedy** and shared many of the same structural elements as tragedy, with scenes alternating with choral parts. Old Comedy was always satirical and usually obscene; in *Lysistrata*, written during the devastating Athenian wars with Sparta, the men of both sides are brought to their knees by the women of the two cities, who engage in a sex strike until the men relent. **New Comedy,** which evolved in the century after Aristophanes, tended to observe more traditional moral values and stressed romance. The New Comedy of Greece greatly influenced the writings of Roman playwrights like Plautus (254–184 B.C.) and Terence (190–59 B.C.). Plautus's *Miles Gloriosus* still finds favour in its modern musical adaptation, *A Funny Thing Happened on the Way to the Forum.*

Like other forms of drama, comedy virtually vanished during the early Middle Ages. Its spirit was kept alive primarily by roving companies of actors who staged improvisational dramas in the squares of towns throughout Europe. The popularity of these plays is evidenced by certain elements in the religious dramas of the same period; the *Second Shepherd's Play* (c. 1450) involves a sheep-rustler with three shepherds in an uproarious parody of the Nativity that still evokes laughter today. Even a serious play such as *Everyman* contains satirical elements in the complicated excuses that Goods and other characters contrive for not accompanying the protagonist on his journey with Death.

On the Continent, a highly stylized form of improvisational drama appeared in sixteenth-century Italy, apparently an evolution from earlier types of folk drama. ***Commedia dell'arte*** involved a cast of masked stock characters (the miserly old man, the young wife, the ardent seducer) in situations involving mistaken identity and cuckoldry. Because it was an improvisational form, *commedia dell'arte* does not survive in written texts, but its popularity influenced the direction that comedy would take in the next century. The great French comic playwright Molière (1622–1673) incorporated many of its elements into his own plays, which combine elements of **farce**, a type of comedy that hinges on broadly drawn characters and embarrassing situations usually involving sexual misconduct, with serious social satire. Comedy such as Molière's, which exposes the hypocrisy and pretensions of people in social situations, is called **comedy of manners;** as Molière put it, the main purpose of his plays was "the correction of mankind's vices."

Other types of comedy have also been popular in different eras. Shakespeare's comedies begin with the farcical complications of *The Comedy of Errors*, progress through romantic **pastoral** comedies, such as *As You Like It*, which present an idealized view of rural life, and end with the philosophical comedies of his final period, of which *The Tempest* is the greatest example. His contemporary Ben Jonson (1572–1637) favoured a type known as **comedy of humours,** a type of comedy of manners in which the conduct of the characters is determined by their underlying dominant trait (the four humours were thought to be bodily fluids whose proportions determined personality). English plays of the late seventeenth and early eighteenth centuries tended to combine the hard-edged satire of comedy of manners with varying amounts of sentimental romance. A play of this type, usually hinging on matters of inheritance and marriage, is known as a **drawing-room comedy,** and its popularity, while peaking in the midnineteenth century, endures today.

Modern comedy in English can be said to begin with Oscar Wilde (1854–1900) and George Bernard Shaw (1856–1950). Wilde's brilliant wit and skillful incorporation of paradoxical **epigrams,** witty sayings that have made him one of the most quoted authors of the nineteenth century, have rarely been equalled. Shaw, who began his career as a drama critic, admired both Wilde and Ibsen, and succeeded in combining the best elements of the comedy of manners and the problem play in his works. *Major Barbara* (1905), a typical **comedy of ideas,** frames serious discussion of war, religion, and poverty with a search for an heir to a millionaire's fortune and a suitable husband for one of his daughters. One striking development of comedy in recent times lies in its deliberate harshness. So-called **black humour,** an extreme type of satire in which barriers of taste are assaulted and pain seems the constant companion of laughter, has characterized much of the work of playwrights like Samuel Beckett (1906–1989), Eugene Ionesco (1909–1994), and Edward Albee (b. 1928).

## *Realistic Drama, the Modern Stage, and Beyond*

Realism is a term that is loosely employed as a synonym for "true to life," but in literary history it denotes a style of writing that developed in the mid-nineteenth century, first in the novels of such masters as Charles Dickens, Gustave Flaubert, and Count Lev Nikolaevich Tolstoy, and later in the dramas of Ibsen and Chekhov. Many of the aspects of dramatic realism have to do with staging and acting. The box set, with its invisible "fourth wall" facing the audience, could, with the added subtleties of artificial lighting, successfully mimic the interior of a typical middle-class home. Realistic prose drama dropped devices like the soliloquy in favour of more natural means of acting, such as those championed by Konstantin Stanislavsky (1863–1938). This Russian director worked closely with Anton Chekhov (1860–1904) to perfect a method whereby actors learned to identify with their characters' psychological problems from "inside out." This "method" acting often tries, as is the case in Chekhov's plays and, later, those of Arthur Miller, to develop a play's **subtext,** the crucial issue in the play that no one can bear to address directly. Stanislavsky's theories have influenced several generations of actors and have become standard throughout the world of the theatre. Ibsen's plays, which in fact ushered in the modern era of the theatre, are often called **problem plays** because they deal with serious, even controversial or taboo, issues in society. Shaw said that Ibsen's great originality as a playwright lay in his ability to shock the members of the audience into thinking about their own lives. As the barriers of censorship have fallen over the years, the capacity of the theatre to shock has perhaps been diminished, but writers still find it a forum admirably suited for debating the controversial issues that divide society.

World drama in the twentieth century went far beyond realism to experiment with the dreamlike atmosphere of **expressionism** (which, like the invisible walls in Miller's *Death of a Salesman*, employs distorted sets to mirror the troubled, perhaps even unbalanced, psyches of the play's characters) or **theatre of the absurd,** which depicts a world without meaning in which everything seems ridiculous. Today, playwrights are likely to combine elements from a variety of traditions to keep an audience challenged and engaged.

## Film Versions: A Note

Nothing can equal the experience of an actual stage production, but the many fine film versions of the plays in this anthology offer instructors and students the opportunity, in some cases, to explore two or three different cinematic approaches to the same material. The differences between print and film versions of plays offer students many challenging topics for discussion, analysis, and writing. Of course, the two media differ radically; in some cases noted below, the film versions, especially those from past decades, badly compromise the original plays. To cite one notorious instance regarding a play not in this anthology, Elia Kazan's celebrated film of Tennessee Williams's *A Streetcar Named Desire*, so wonderful in its sets, direction, and the performances of Marlon Brando and Vivien Leigh, tampers with the play's ending (on orders from the Hollywood Production Code office) to give the impression that Stella will take her child and leave Stanley. Williams himself wrote the screenplay, and he was aware of, if not exactly happy with, the moral standards of the times.

The late O. B. Hardison, director of the Folger Shakespeare Library, once observed two important differences between plays and films. The first is that attending a play is a social function; the audience members and the performers are aware of one another's presence, and laughter in the wrong place can signal the beginning of a disaster. But film is largely a private experience; it was with good reason that one film critic titled a collection of her reviews *A Year in the Dark*. The other chief difference, Hardison notes, is that drama is a realistic medium, whereas film is surrealistic. Watching a play, we see real persons who have a physical reality, and we see them from a uniform perspective. But film has conditioned us to its own complex vocabulary of close-ups, jump cuts, and panoramas, and we view the action from a variety of perspectives. These differences, as fundamental as they seem, are rarely noted by students (unless they have taken a film course) until the differences are pointed out. Still, film versions provide us with a wonderful time capsule in which many treasures of drama's past have been preserved. A reasoned list of some of these, most of them available on video or DVD, follows.

## *The Tragedy of Othello, the Moor of Venice*

*Othello* has proved one of Shakespeare's most popular plays on film. Orson Welles's 1952 version, thought lost for many years, was lovingly restored by his daughter Rebecca Welles and features a remastered soundtrack that remedies most of the original complaints about the poor quality of sound in the film. A fascinating film-noir study in Shakespeare, it features a bravura performance by Welles and an affecting one by Suzanne Cloutier as Desdemona. Less successful is Laurence Olivier's 1966 version, essentially a filmed version of his acclaimed Royal Shakespeare Company production. Olivier's controversial performance, which mimics West Indian speech patterns, and that of Maggie Smith as Desdemona are worth seeing, but Olivier's stage makeup, unconvincing in film close-ups, and minimal production values mar the effort. The 1980 version, starring Anthony Hopkins as Othello and Bob Hoskins as Iago, features interesting performances from the principals, despite Hopkins's distracting hairpiece. This uncut version was part of the PBS Shakespeare series and is widely available in libraries. The 1995 film, directed by Oliver Parker, has excellent performances by Laurence Fishburne and Kenneth Branagh and a sumptuous, erotic style. Contemporary students will probably find it the most satisfying of the four. The high school basketball drama "O," directed by Tim Blake Nelson and released in 2001, is based on *Othello*.

## *A Doll's House*

For some inexplicable reason *A Doll's House* was made into two films in the same year, 1973. Patrick Garland's version stars Claire Bloom as Nora and Anthony Hopkins as Torvald. Sir Ralph Richardson essays the role of Dr. Rank, and the reliable Denholm Elliott plays Krogstad. Joseph Losey's version features Jane Fonda as an energetic (and very young) Nora, David Warner as Torvald, and Trevor Howard as Dr. Rank. Most critics felt that the Losey version, which includes actual scenes that Ibsen only hints at, tried too obviously to make the play relevant to contemporary audiences. In 1992 a television production of the play was made in the United Kingdom, starring Juliet Stevenson as Nora. The 1993 Iranian film *Sara*, directed by Dariush Mehrjui and starring Niki Karimi, is an award-winning adaptation of Ibsen's play.

### *Death of a Salesman*

Miller was not pleased with the 1951 film, in which Fredric March over-acted badly as Willy Loman. Still, Mildred Dunnock, Kevin McCarthy, and Cameron Mitchell provided excellent support. Volker Schlöndorff's 1985 version has been widely acclaimed, though some viewers have found Dustin Hoffman ill-suited to the role that Miller wrote with the large-boned Lee J. Cobb in mind. John Malkovich and Kate Reid are very good, and Schlöndorff's impressionistic set designs and seamless handling of flashbacks are very impressive. A videotape of the final performance of the award-winning 1999 Broadway revival, starring Brian Dennehy and Elizabeth Franz, aired on Showtime in 2000. Dennehy brought a magnitude to the role of Willy Loman that many critics found impressive.

### *Act Without Words I: A Mime for One Player*

This short piece was made into an animated film by Pyramid Film Productions in 1970 and was performed on film by Barry Smith's Theatre of Puppets in 1982. More recently, *Act Without Words I* was filmed as part of the ambitious Beckett on Film project, in which noted directors and actors have filmed all nineteen plays. More about this project, including interviews with the participants, can be found at **www.beckettonfilm.com.** *Act Without Words I* was directed by Karl Reisz, director of such films as *The French Lieutenant's Woman* (1980) and *Sweet Dreams* (1990), and stars Sean Foley, a trained clown, who co-founded the comedy act Right Size. Of the twenty-minute film that features action and music, Reisz said, "As always with Beckett, in the agony there is pity, understanding and humanity. By using repetition, Beckett was trying to make sense of his own experience of the world."

## *The Canadian Plays*

Excerpts from *The Rez Sisters* that formed part of a cabaret performance were included in the documentary *Thank You for the Love You Gave: The Life & Times of Tomson Highway,* which first aired on CBC television in 1997. Some of Nell Shipman's films, including *Back to God's Country* (1919), are now available on DVD.

*William Shakespeare (1564–1616), the supreme writer of English, was born, baptized, and buried in the market town of Stratford-on-Avon, eighty miles from London. Son of a glove maker and merchant who was high bailiff (or mayor) of the town, he probably attended grammar school and learned to read Latin authors in the original. At eighteen he married Anne Hathaway, twenty-six, by whom he had three children, including twins. By 1592 he had become well-known and envied as an actor and playwright in London. From 1594 until he retired, he belonged to the same theatrical company, the Lord Chamberlain's Men (later renamed the King's Men in honour of their patron, James I), for whom he wrote thirty-six plays—some of them, such as* Hamlet *and* King Lear, *profound reworkings of old plays. As an actor, Shakespeare is believed to have played supporting roles, such as Hamlet's father's ghost. The company prospered, moved into the Globe Theatre in 1599, and in 1608 bought the fashionable Blackfriars as well; Shakespeare owned an interest in both theatres. When plagues shut down the theatres from 1592 to 1594, Shakespeare turned to story poems; his great* sonnets *(published only in 1609) probably also date from the 1590s. Plays were regarded as entertainments of little literary merit and Shakespeare did not bother to supervise their publication. After* The Tempest *(1611), the last play entirely from his hand, he retired to Stratford, where since 1597 he had owned the second-largest house in town. Most critics agree that when he wrote* Othello *(c. 1604), Shakespeare was at the height of his powers.*

*William Shakespeare*
# The Tragedy of Othello, the Moor of Venice

## CHARACTERS

*Othello,* the Moor
*Brabantio,* [a senator,] father to Desdemona
*Cassio,* an honorable lieutenant [to Othello]
*Iago,* [Othello's ancient,] a villain

**NOTE ON THE TEXT:** This text of *Othello* is based on that of the First Folio, or large collection, of Shakespeare's plays (1623). But there are many differences between the Folio text and that of the play's first printing in the Quarto, or small volume, of 1621 (eighteen or nineteen years after the play's first performance). Some readings from the Quarto are included. For the reader's convenience, some material has been added by the editor, David Bevington (some indications of scene, some stage directions). Such additions are enclosed in brackets. Mr. Bevington's text and notes were prepared for his book, *The Complete Works of Shakespeare,* 4th ed. (New York: HarperCollins, 1992).

Edited by David Bevington

*Roderigo*, a gulled gentleman
*Duke of Venice*
*Senators* [of Venice]
*Montano*, governor of Cyprus
*Gentlemen of Cyprus*
*Lodovico and Gratiano*, [kinsmen to Brabantio,] two noble Venetians
*Sailors*
*Clown*
*Desdemona*, [daughter to Brabantio and] wife to Othello
*Emilia*, wife to Iago
*Bianca*, a courtesan [and mistress to Cassio]
[*A Messenger*
*A Herald*
*A Musician*
*Servants, Attendants, Officers, Senators, Musicians, Gentlemen*]

[Scene: *Venice; a seaport in Cyprus*]

# ACT I

## SCENE I [VENICE. A STREET.]

*Enter Roderigo and Iago.*

**RODERIGO:**    Tush, never tell me!° I take it much unkindly
      That thou, Iago, who hast had my purse
      As if the strings were thine, shouldst know of this.°
**IAGO:**    'Sblood,° but you'll not hear me.
      If ever I did dream of such a matter,                                             5
      Abhor me.
**RODERIGO:**    Thou toldst me thou didst hold him in thy hate.
**IAGO:**    Despise me
      If I do not. Three great ones of the city,
      In personal suit to make me his lieutenant,                                   10
      Off-capped to him;° and by the faith of man,

---

**1 never tell me** (An expression of incredulity, like "tell me another one.")    **3 this** i.e., Desdemona's elopement    **4 'Sblood** by His (Christ's) blood    **11 him** i.e., Othello

I know my price, I am worth no worse a place.
But he, as loving his own pride and purposes,
Evades them with a bombast circumstance°
Horribly stuffed with epithets of war,°                                    15
And, in conclusion,
Nonsuits° my mediators. For, "Certes,"° says he,
"I have already chose my officer."
And what was he?
Forsooth, a great arithmetician,°                                         20
One Michael Cassio, a Florentine,
A fellow almost damned in a fair wife,°
That never set a squadron in the field
Nor the division of a battle° knows
More than a spinster°—unless the bookish theoric,°                        25
Wherein the togaed° consuls° can propose°
As masterly as he. Mere prattle without practice
Is all his soldiership. But he, sir, had th' election;
And I, of whom his° eyes had seen the proof
At Rhodes, at Cyprus, and on other grounds                                30
Christened° and heathen, must be beleed and calmed°
By debitor and creditor.° This countercaster,°
He, in good time,° must his lieutenant be,
And I—God bless the mark!°—his Moorship's ancient.°
**RODERIGO:** By heaven, I rather would have been his hangman.°           35
**IAGO:** Why, there's no remedy. 'Tis the curse of service;
Preferment° goes by letter and affection,°

**14 bombast circumstance** wordy evasion (Bombast is cotton padding.)    **15 epithets of war** military expressions    **17 Nonsuits** rejects the petition of    **Certes** certainly    **20 arithmetician** i.e., a man whose military knowledge is merely theoretical, based on books of tactics    **22 A . . . wife** (Cassio does not seem to be married, but his counterpart in Shakespeare's source does have a woman in his house. See also Act IV, Scene i, line 127.)    **24 division of a battle** disposition of a military unit    **25 a spinster** i.e., a housewife, one whose regular occupation is spinning    **theoric** theory    **26 togaed** wearing the toga    **consuls** counsellors, senators    **propose** discuss    **29 his** i.e., Othello's    **31 Christened** Christian    **beleed and calmed** left to leeward without wind, becalmed (A sailing metaphor.)    **32 debitor and creditor** (A name for a system of bookkeeping, here used as a contemptuous nickname for Cassio.)    **countercaster** i.e., bookkeeper, one who tallies with *counters*, or "metal disks" (Said contemptuously.)    **33 in good time** opportunely, i.e., forsooth    **34 God bless the mark** (Perhaps originally a formula to ward off evil; here an expression of impatience.)    **ancient** standard-bearer, ensign    **35 his hangman** the executioner of him    **37 Preferment** promotion    **letter and affection** personal influence and favouritism

And not by old gradation,° where each second
Stood heir to th' first. Now, sir, be judge yourself
Whether I in any just term° am affined°                                40
To love the Moor.

**RODERIGO:**   I would not follow him then.

**IAGO:**   O sir, content you.°
I follow him to serve my turn upon him.
We cannot all be masters, nor all masters                               45
Cannot be truly° followed. You shall mark
Many a duteous and knee-crooking knave
That, doting on his own obsequious bondage,
Wears out his time, much like his master's ass,
For naught but provender, and when he's old, cashiered.°                50
Whip me° such honest knaves. Others there are
Who, trimmed in forms and visages of duty,°
Keep yet their hearts attending on themselves,
And, throwing but shows of service on their lords,
Do well thrive by them, and when they have lined their coats,°          55
Do themselves homage.° These fellows have some soul,
And such a one do I profess myself. For, sir,
It is as sure as you are Roderigo,
Were I the Moor I would not be Iago.°
In following him, I follow but myself—                                  60
Heaven is my judge, not I for love and duty,
But seeming so for my peculiar° end.
For when my outward action doth demonstrate
The native° act and figure° of my heart
In compliment extern,° 'tis not long after                             65
But I will wear my heart upon my sleeve
For daws° to peck at. I am not what I am.°

---

**38 old gradation** step-by-step seniority, the traditional way    **40 term** respect    **affined** bound
**43 content you** don't you worry about that    **46 truly** faithfully    **50 cashiered** dismissed from service    **51 Whip me** whip, as far as I'm concerned    **52 trimmed . . . duty** dressed up in the mere
form and show of dutifulness    **55 lined their coats** i.e., stuffed their purses    **56 Do themselves
homage** i.e., attend to self-interest solely    **59 Were . . . Iago** i.e., if I were able to assume command, I certainly would not choose to remain a subordinate, or, I would keep a suspicious eye on a
flattering subordinate    **62 peculiar** particular, personal    **64 native** innate    **figure** shape, intent
**65 compliment extern** outward show (Conforming in this case to the inner workings and intention
of the heart.)    **67 daws** small crowlike birds, proverbially stupid and avaricious    **I am not what I
am** i.e., I am not one who wears his heart on his sleeve

**RODERIGO:** What a full° fortune does the thick-lips° owe°
    If he can carry 't thus!°
**IAGO:**                      Call up her father.
    Rouse him, make after him, poison his delight,                       70
    Proclaim him in the streets; incense her kinsmen,
    And, though he in a fertile climate dwell,
    Plague him with flies.° Though that his joy be joy,°
    Yet throw such changes of vexation° on 't
    As it may° lose some color.°                               75
**RODERIGO:** Here is her father's house. I'll call aloud.
**IAGO:** Do, with like timorous° accent and dire yell
    As when, by night and negligence,° the fire
    Is spied in populous cities.
**RODERIGO:** What ho, Brabantio! Signor Brabantio, ho!             80
**IAGO:** Awake! What ho, Brabantio! Thieves, thieves, thieves!
    Look to your house, your daughter, and your bags!
    Thieves, thieves!

    *Brabantio [enters] above [at a window].*°

**BRABANTIO:** What is the reason of this terrible summons?
    What is the matter° there?                                   85
**RODERIGO:** Signor, is all your family within?
**IAGO:** Are your doors locked?
**BRABANTIO:**                     Why, wherefore ask you this?
**IAGO:** Zounds,° sir, you're robbed. For shame, put on your gown!
    Your heart is burst; you have lost half your soul.
    Even now, now, very now, an old black ram                 90
    Is tupping° your white ewe. Arise, arise!
    Awake the snorting° citizens with the bell,
    Or else the devil° will make a grandsire of you.
    Arise, I say!

---

**68 full** swelling   **thick-lips** (Elizabethans often applied the term "Moor" to Negroes.)   **owe** own
**69 carry 't thus** carry this off   **72–73 though . . . flies** though he seems prosperous and happy
now, vex him with misery   **73 Though . . . be joy** although he seems fortunate and happy
(Repeats the idea of line 72.)   **74 changes of vexation** vexing changes   **75 As it may** that may
cause it to   **some color** some of its fresh gloss   **77 timorous** frightening   **78 and negligence**
i.e., by negligence   **83 [s.d.] at a window** (This stage direction, from the Quarto, probably calls for
an appearance on the gallery above and rearstage.)   **85 the matter** your business   **88 Zounds**
by His (Christ's) wounds   **91 tupping** covering, copulating with (Said of sheep.)   **92 snorting**
snoring   **93 the devil** (The devil was conventionally pictured as Black.)

**BRABANTIO:**   What, have you lost your wits?

**RODERIGO:**   Most reverend signor, do you know my voice?   *95*

**BRABANTIO:**   Not I. What are you?

**RODERIGO:**   My name is Roderigo.

**BRABANTIO:**   The worser welcome.

I have charged thee not to haunt about my doors.

In honest plainness thou hast heard me say   *100*

My daughter is not for thee; and now, in madness,

Being full of supper and distempering° drafts,

Upon malicious bravery° dost thou come

To start° my quiet.

**RODERIGO:**   Sir, sir, sir—

**BRABANTIO:**                    But thou must needs be sure   *105*

My spirits and my place° have in° their power

To make this bitter to thee.

**RODERIGO:**                    Patience, good sir.

**BRABANTIO:**   What tell'st thou me of robbing? This is Venice;

My house is not a grange.°

**RODERIGO:**                    Most grave Brabantio,

In simple° and pure soul I come to you.   *110*

**IAGO:**   Zounds, sir, you are one of those that will not serve God
if the devil bid you. Because we come to do you service and
you think we are ruffians, you'll have your daughter covered
with a Barbary° horse; you'll have your nephews° neigh
to you; you'll have coursers° for cousins° and jennets° for   *115*
germans.°

**BRABANTIO:**   What profane wretch art thou?

**IAGO:**   I am one, sir, that comes to tell you your daughter and
the Moor are now making the beast with two backs.

**BRABANTIO:**   Thou art a villain.

**IAGO:**                    You are—a senator.°   *120*

**BRABANTIO:**   This thou shalt answer.° I know thee, Roderigo.

---

**102 distempering** intoxicating    **103 Upon malicious bravery** with hostile intent to defy me
**104 start** startle, disrupt    **106 My spirits and my place** my temperament and my authority of
office    **have in** have it in    **109 grange** isolated country house    **110 simple** sincere
**114 Barbary** from northern Africa (and hence associated with Othello)    **nephews** i.e., grandsons
**115 coursers** powerful horses    **cousins** kinsmen    **jennets** small Spanish horses    **116 germans**
near relatives    **120 a senator** (Said with mock politeness, as though the word itself were an insult.)
**121 answer** be held accountable for

**RODERIGO:**  Sir, I will answer anything. But I beseech you,
    If't be your pleasure and most wise° consent—
    As partly I find it is—that your fair daughter,
    At this odd-even° and dull watch o' the night,        *125*
    Transported with° no worse nor better guard
    But with a knave° of common hire, a gondolier,
    To the gross clasps of a lascivious Moor—
    If this be known to you and your allowance°
    We then have done you bold and saucy° wrongs.        *130*
    But if you know not this, my manners tell me
    We have your wrong rebuke. Do not believe
    That, from° the sense of all civility,°
    I thus would play and trifle with your reverence.°
    Your daughter, if you have not given her leave,        *135*
    I say again, hath made a gross revolt,
    Tying her duty, beauty, wit,° and fortunes
    In an extravagant° and wheeling° stranger°
    Of here and everywhere. Straight° satisfy yourself.
    If she be in her chamber or your house,        *140*
    Let loose on me the justice of the state
    For thus deluding you.
**BRABANTIO:**    Strike on the tinder,° ho!
    Give me a taper! Call up all my people!
    This accident° is not unlike my dream.        *145*
    Belief of it oppresses me already.
    Light, I say, light!                  *Exit [above].*
**IAGO:**    Farewell, for I must leave you.
    It seems not meet° nor wholesome to my place°
    To be producted°—as, if I stay, I shall—        *150*
    Against the Moor. For I do know the state,
    However this may gall° him with some check,°

---

**123 wise** well-informed    **125 odd-even** between one day and the next, i.e., about midnight
**126 with** by    **127 But with a knave** than by a low fellow, a servant    **129 allowance** permission
**130 saucy** insolent    **133 from** contrary to    **civility** good manners, decency    **134 your reverence**
the respect due to you    **136 wit** intelligence    **138 extravagant** expatriate, wandering far from
home    **wheeling** roving about, vagabond    **stranger** foreigner    **139 Straight** straightway
**143 tinder** charred linen ignited by a spark from flint and steel, used to light torches or tapers (lines
144, 170)    **145 accident** occurrence, event    **149 meet** fitting    **place** position (as ensign)
**150 producted** produced (as a witness)    **152 gall** rub; oppress    **check** rebuke

Cannot with safety cast° him, for he's embarked°
With such loud reason° to the Cyprus wars,
Which even now stands in act,° that, for their souls,°          155
Another of his fathom° they have none
To lead their business; in which regard,°
Though I do hate him as I do hell pains,
Yet for necessity of present life°
I must show out a flag and sign of love,          160
Which is indeed but sign. That you shall surely find him,
Lead to the Sagittary° the raisèd search,°
And there will I be with him. So farewell.          *Exit.*

*Enter [below] Brabantio [in his nightgown°] with servants
and torches.*

**BRABANTIO:** It is too true an evil. Gone she is;
And what's to come of my despisèd time°          165
Is naught but bitterness. Now, Roderigo,
Where didst thou see her?—O unhappy girl!—
With the Moor, sayst thou?—Who would be a father!—
How didst thou know 'twas she?—O, she deceives me
Past thought!—What said she to you?—Get more tapers.          170
Raise all my kindred.—Are they married, think you?
**RODERIGO:** Truly, I think they are.
**BRABANTIO:** O heaven! How got she out? O treason of the
blood!
Fathers, from hence trust not your daughters' minds
By what you see them act. Is there not charms°          175
By which the property° of youth and maidhood
May be abused?° Have you not read, Roderigo,
Of some such thing?
**RODERIGO:**                    Yes, sir, I have indeed.

---

153 **cast** dismiss    **embarked** engaged    154 **loud reason** unanimous shout of confirmation (in the
Senate)    155 **stands in act** are going on    **for their souls** to save themselves    156 **fathom** i.e.,
ability, depth of experience    157 **in which regard** out of regard for which    159 **life** livelihood
162 **Sagittary** (An inn or house where Othello and Desdemona are staying, named for its sign of
Sagittarius, or Centaur.)    **raisèd search** search party roused out of sleep    163 **[s.d.] nightgown**
dressing gown (This costuming is specified in the Quarto text.)    165 **time** i.e., remainder of life
175 **charms** spells    176 **property** special quality, nature    177 **abused** deceived

**BRABANTIO:** Call up my brother.—O, would you had had her!—
Some one way, some another.—Do you know                              *180*
Where we may apprehend her and the Moor?
**RODERIGO:** I think I can discover° him, if you please
To get good guard and go along with me.
**BRABANTIO:** Pray you, lead on. At every house I'll call;
I may command° at most.—Get weapons, ho!                            *185*
And raise some special officers of night.—
On, good Roderigo. I will deserve° your pains.

*Exeunt.*

SCENE II [VENICE. ANOTHER STREET, BEFORE
OTHELLO'S LODGINGS.]

*Enter Othello, Iago, attendants with torches.*

**IAGO:** Though in the trade of war I have slain men,
Yet do I hold it very stuff° o' the conscience
To do no contrived° murder. I lack iniquity
Sometimes to do me service. Nine or ten times
I had thought t' have yerked° him° here under the ribs.          *5*
**OTHELLO:** 'Tis better as it is.
**IAGO:**                         Nay, but he prated,
And spoke such scurvy and provoking terms
Against your honor
That, with the little godliness I have,
I did full hard forbear him.° But, I pray you, sir,             *10*
Are you fast married? Be assured of this,
That the magnifico° is much beloved,
And hath in his effect° a voice potential°
As double as the Duke's. He will divorce you,
Or put upon you what restraint or grievance                     *15*
The law, with all his might to enforce it on,
Will give him cable.°

---

**182 discover** reveal, uncover   **185 command** demand assistance   **187 deserve** show gratitude for
**2 very stuff** essence, basic material (continuing the metaphor of *trade* from line 1)   **3 contrived**
premeditated   **5 yerked** stabbed   **him** i.e., Roderigo   **10 I . . . him** I restrained myself with
great difficulty from assaulting him   **12 magnifico** Venetian grandee, i.e., Brabantio   **13 in his**
**effect** at his command   **potential** powerful   **17 cable** i.e., scope

**OTHELLO:** Let him do his spite.
My services which I have done the seigniory°
Shall out-tongue his complaints. 'Tis yet to know°—
Which, when I know that boasting is an honor,                                    *20*
I shall promulgate—I fetch my life and being
From men of royal siege,° and my demerits°
May speak unbonneted° to as proud a fortune
As this that I have reached. For know, Iago,
But that I love the gentle Desdemona,                                            *25*
I would not my unhousèd° free condition
Put into circumscription and confine°
For the sea's worth.° But look, what lights come yond?

*Enter Cassio [and certain officers°] with torches.*

**IAGO:** Those are the raisèd father and his friends.
You were best go in.
**OTHELLO:** Not I. I must be found.                                             *30*
My parts, my title, and my perfect soul°
Shall manifest me rightly. Is it they?
**IAGO:** By Janus,° I think no.
**OTHELLO:** The servants of the Duke? And my lieutenant?
The goodness of the night upon you, friends!                                     *35*
What is the news?
**CASSIO:** The Duke does greet you, General,
And he requires your haste-post-haste appearance
Even on the instant.
**OTHELLO:** What is the matter,° think you?
**CASSIO:** Something from Cyprus, as I may divine.°
It is a business of some heat.° The galleys                                      *40*
Have sent a dozen sequent° messengers
This very night at one another's heels,

---

**18 seigniory** Venetian government    **19 yet to know** not yet widely known    **22 siege** i.e., rank
(Literally, a seat used by a person of distinction.)    **demerits** deserts    **23 unbonneted** without
removing the hat, i.e., on equal terms (? Or "with hat off," "in all due modesty.")    **26 unhousèd**
unconfined, undomesticated    **27 circumscription and confine** restriction and confinement
**28 the sea's worth** all the riches at the bottom of the sea    **[s.d.] officers** (The Quarto text calls for
"Cassio with lights, officers with torches.")    **31 My . . . soul** my natural gifts, my position or reputation, and my unflawed conscience    **33 Janus** Roman two-faced god of beginnings    **38 matter**
business    **39 divine** guess    **40 heat** urgency    **41 sequent** successive

And many of the consuls,° raised and met,
Are at the Duke's already. You have been hotly called for;
When, being not at your lodging to be found,                                45
The Senate hath sent about° three several° quests
To search you out.
**OTHELLO:**                    'Tis well I am found by you.
I will but spend a word here in the house
And go with you.                                        [*Exit.*]
**CASSIO:**            Ancient, what makes° he here?
**IAGO:**    Faith, he tonight hath boarded° a land carrack.°           50
If it prove lawful prize,° he's made forever.
**CASSIO:**    I do not understand.
**IAGO:**                    He's married.
**CASSIO:**                            To who?

[*Enter Othello.*]

**IAGO:**    Marry,° to—Come, Captain, will you go?
**OTHELLO:**    Have with you.°
**CASSIO:**    Here comes another troop to seek for you.               55

*Enter Brabantio, Roderigo, with officers and torches.*°

**IAGO:**    It is Brabantio. General, be advised.°
He comes to bad intent.
**OTHELLO:**                    Holla! Stand there!
**RODERIGO:**    Signor, it is the Moor.
**BRABANTIO:**                    Down with him, thief!

[*They draw on both sides.*]

**IAGO:**    You, Roderigo! Come, sir, I am for you.
**OTHELLO:**    Keep up° your bright swords, for the dew will rust
them.                                                   60
Good signor, you shall more command with years
Than with your weapons.

---

43 **consuls** senators    46 **about** all over the city    **several** separate    49 **makes** does
50 **boarded** gone aboard and seized as an act of piracy (with sexual suggestion)    **carrack** large
merchant ship    51 **prize** booty    53 **Marry** (An oath, originally "by the Virgin Mary"; here used
with wordplay on *married.*)    54 **Have with you** i.e., let's go    55 **[s.d.] officers and torches** (The
Quarto text calls for "others with lights and weapons.")    56 **be advised** be on your guard
60 **Keep up** keep in the sheath

**BRABANTIO:**   O thou foul thief, where hast thou stowed my
daughter?
Damned as thou art, thou hast enchanted her!
For I'll refer me° to all things of sense,°                                65
If she in chains of magic were not bound
Whether a maid so tender, fair, and happy,
So opposite to marriage that she shunned
The wealthy curlèd darlings of our nation,
Would ever have, t' incur a general mock,                                70
Run from her guardage° to the sooty bosom
Of such a thing as thou—to fear, not to delight.
Judge me the world if 'tis not gross in sense°
That thou hast practiced on her with foul charms,
Abused her delicate youth with drugs or minerals°      75
That weakens motion.° I'll have 't disputed on;°
'Tis probable and palpable to thinking.
I therefore apprehend and do attach° thee
For an abuser of the world, a practicer
Of arts inhibited° and out of warrant.°—                           80
Lay hold upon him! If he do resist,
Subdue him at his peril.

**OTHELLO:**                           Hold your hands,
Both you of my inclining° and the rest.
Were it my cue to fight, I should have known it
Without a prompter.—Whither will you that I go              85
To answer this your charge?

**BRABANTIO:**   To prison, till fit time
Of law and course of direct session°
Call thee to answer.

**OTHELLO:**                  What if I do obey?
How may the Duke be therewith satisfied,                           90
Whose messengers are here about my side
Upon some present business of the state

---

**65 refer me** submit my case    **things of sense** commonsense understandings, or, creatures possessing common sense    **71 her guardage** my guardianship of her    **73 gross in sense** obvious
**75 minerals** i.e., poisons    **76 weakens motion** impair the vital faculties    **disputed on** argued in
court by professional counsel, debated by experts    **78 attach** arrest    **80 arts inhibited** prohibited
arts, black magic    **out of warrant** illegal    **83 inclining** following, party    **88 course of direct
session** regular or specially convened legal proceedings

To bring me to him?

**OFFICER:**          'Tis true, most worthy signor.

The Duke's in council, and your noble self,

I am sure, is sent for.

**BRABANTIO:**        How? The Duke in council?      95

In this time of the night? Bring him away.°

Mine's not an idle° cause. The Duke himself,

Or any of my brothers of the state,

Cannot but feel this wrong as 'twere their own;

For if such actions may have passage free,°      100

Bondslaves and pagans shall our statesmen be.

*Exeunt.*

## SCENE III [VENICE. A COUNCIL CHAMBER.]

*Enter Duke [and] Senators [and sit at a table, with lights],
and Officers.° [The Duke and Senators are reading dispatches.]*

**DUKE:**   There is no composition° in these news

That gives them credit.

**FIRST SENATOR:**   Indeed, they are disproportioned.°

My letters say a hundred and seven galleys.

**DUKE:**   And mine, a hundred forty.

**SECOND SENATOR:**           And mine, two hundred.      5

But though they jump° not on a just° account—

As in these cases, where the aim° reports

'Tis oft with difference—yet do they all confirm

A Turkish fleet, and bearing up to Cyprus.

**DUKE:**   Nay, it is possible enough to judgment.      10

I do not so secure me in the error

But the main article I do approve°

In fearful sense.

**SAILOR** (*within*):   What ho, what ho, what ho!

---

**96 away** right along    **97 idle** trifling    **100 have passage free** are allowed to go unchecked
**[s.d.] Enter . . . Officers** (The Quarto text calls for the Duke and senators to "sit at a table with
lights and attendants.")
**1 composition** consistency    **3 disproportioned** inconsistent    **6 jump** agree.   **just** exact    **7 the
aim** conjecture    **11–12 I do not . . . approve** I do not take such (false) comfort in the discrepan-
cies that I fail to perceive the main point, i.e., that the Turkish fleet is threatening

*Enter Sailor.*

**OFFICER:** A messenger from the galleys.

**DUKE:** Now, what's the business?                                          *15*

**SAILOR:** The Turkish preparation° makes for Rhodes.
So was I bid report here to the state
By Signor Angelo.

**DUKE:** How say you by° this change?

**FIRST SENATOR:**                                  This cannot be
By no assay° of reason. 'Tis a pageant°                                      *20*
To keep us in false gaze.° When we consider
Th' importancy of Cyprus to the Turk,
And let ourselves again but understand
That, as it more concerns the Turk than Rhodes,
So may he with more facile question bear it,°                                *25*
For that° it stands not in such warlike brace,°
But altogether lacks th' abilities°
That Rhodes is dressed in°—if we make thought of this,
We must not think the Turk is so unskillful°
To leave that latest° which concerns him first,                             *30*
Neglecting an attempt of ease and gain
To wake° and wage° a danger profitless.

**DUKE:** Nay, in all confidence, he's not for Rhodes.

**OFFICER:** Here is more news.

*Enter a Messenger.*

**MESSENGER:** The Ottomites, reverend and gracious,                        *35*
Steering with due course toward the isle of Rhodes,
Have there injointed them° with an after° fleet.

**FIRST SENATOR:** Ay, so I thought. How many, as you guess?

**MESSENGER:** Of thirty sail; and now they do restem
Their backward course,° bearing with frank appearance°                      *40*
Their purposes toward Cyprus. Signor Montano,

---

**16 preparation** fleet prepared for battle    **19 by** about    **20 assay** test    **pageant** mere show
**21 in false gaze** looking the wrong way    **25 So may . . . it** so also he (the Turk) can more easily
capture it (Cyprus)    **26 For that** since    **brace** state of defence    **27 abilities** means of self-
defence    **28 dressed in** equipped with    **29 unskillful** deficient in judgment    **30 latest** last
**32 wake** stir up    **wage** risk    **37 injointed them** joined themselves    **after** second, following
**39–40 restem . . . course** retrace their original course    **40 frank appearance** undisguised intent

Your trusty and most valiant servitor,°
With his free duty° recommends° you thus,
And prays you to believe him.

DUKE: 'Tis certain then for Cyprus.      45
Marcus Luccicos, is not he in town?

FIRST SENATOR: He's now in Florence.

DUKE: Write from us to him, post-post-haste. Dispatch.

FIRST SENATOR: Here comes Brabantio and the valiant Moor.

*Enter Brabantio, Othello, Cassio, Iago, Roderigo, and
officers.*

DUKE: Valiant Othello, we must straight° employ you      50
Against the general enemy° Ottoman.
[*To Brabantio.*] I did not see you; welcome, gentle° signor.
We lacked your counsel and your help tonight.

BRABANTIO: So did I yours. Good Your Grace, pardon me;
Neither my place° nor aught I heard of business      55
Hath raised me from my bed, nor doth the general care
Take hold on me, for my particular° grief
Is of so floodgate° and o'erbearing nature
That it engluts° and swallows other sorrows
And it is still itself.°

DUKE:      Why, what's the matter?      60

BRABANTIO: My daughter! O, my daughter!

DUKE AND SENATORS:      Dead?

BRABANTIO:      Ay, to me.
She is abused,° stol'n from me, and corrupted
By spells and medicines bought of mountebanks;
For nature so preposterously to err,
Being not deficient,° blind, or lame of sense,°      65
Sans° witchcraft could not.

DUKE: Whoe'er he be that in this foul proceeding
Hath thus beguiled your daughter of herself,

---

**42 servitor** officer under your command   **43 free duty** freely given and loyal service   **recom-**
**mends** commends himself and reports to   **50 straight** straightway   **51 general enemy** universal
enemy to all Christendom   **52 gentle** noble   **55 place** official position   **57 particular** personal
**58 floodgate** i.e., overwhelming (as when floodgates are opened)   **59 engluts** engulfs   **60 is still**
**itself** remains undiminished   **62 abused** deceived   **65 deficient** defective   **lame of sense** deficient in sensory perception   **66 Sans** without

And you of her, the bloody book of law
You shall yourself read in the bitter letter                                          70
After your own sense°—yea, though our proper° son
Stood in your action.°

**BRABANTIO:**                Humbly I thank Your Grace.
Here is the man, this Moor, whom now it seems
Your special mandate for the state affairs
Hath hither brought.

**ALL:**                    We are very sorry for 't.                               75

**DUKE** [*to Othello*]: What, in your own part, can you say to
this?

**BRABANTIO:** Nothing, but this is so.

**OTHELLO:** Most potent, grave, and reverend signors,
My very noble and approved° good masters:
That I have ta'en away this old man's daughter,                              80
It is most true; true, I have married her.
The very head and front° of my offending
Hath this extent, no more. Rude° am I in my speech,
And little blessed with the soft phrase of peace;
For since these arms of mine had seven years' pith,°                         85
Till now some nine moons wasted,° they have used
Their dearest° action in the tented field;
And little of this great world can I speak
More than pertains to feats of broils and battle,
And therefore little shall I grace my cause                                  90
In speaking for myself. Yet, by your gracious patience,
I will a round° unvarnished tale deliver
Of my whole course of love—what drugs, what charms,
What conjuration, and what mighty magic,
For such proceeding I am charged withal,°                                    95
I won his daughter.

**BRABANTIO:**            A maiden never bold;
Of spirit so still and quiet that her motion

---

**71 After . . . sense** according to your own interpretation    **our proper** my own    **72 Stood . . .
action** were under your accusation    **79 approved** proved, esteemed    **82 head and front** height
and breadth, entire extent    **83 Rude** unpolished    **85 since . . . pith** i.e., since I was seven    **pith**
strength, vigour    **86 Till . . . wasted** until some nine months ago (since when Othello has evidently
not been on active duty, but in Venice)    **87 dearest** most valuable    **92 round** plain    **95 withal**
with

Blushed at herself;° and she, in spite of nature,
Of years,° of country, credit,° everything,
To fall in love with what she feared to look on!          *100*
It is a judgment maimed and most imperfect
That will confess° perfection so could err
Against all rules of nature, and must be driven
To find out practices° of cunning hell
Why this should be. I therefore vouch° again          *105*
That with some mixtures powerful o'er the blood,°
Or with some dram conjured to this effect,°
He wrought upon her.

**DUKE:**                    To vouch this is no proof,
Without more wider° and more overt test°
Than these thin habits° and poor likelihoods°          *110*
Of modern seeming° do prefer° against him.

**FIRST SENATOR:**  But Othello, speak.
Did you by indirect and forcèd courses°
Subdue and poison this young maid's affections?
Or came it by request and such fair question°          *115*
As soul to soul affordeth?

**OTHELLO:**                    I do beseech you,
Send for the lady to the Sagittary
And let her speak of me before her father.
If you do find me foul in her report,
The trust, the office I do hold of you          *120*
Not only take away, but let your sentence
Even fall upon my life.

**DUKE:**                    Fetch Desdemona hither.

**OTHELLO:**  Ancient, conduct them. You best know the place.

[*Exeunt Iago and attendants.*]

And, till she come, as truly as to heaven

---

97–98 **her . . . herself** i.e., she blushed easily at herself. (*Motion* can suggest the impulse of the soul or of the emotions, or physical movement.)    99 **years** i.e., difference in age.    **credit** virtuous reputation    102 **confess** concede (that)    104 **practices** plots    105 **vouch** assert    106 **blood** passions    107 **dram . . . effect** dose made by magical spells to have this effect    109 **more wider** fuller    **test** testimony    110 **habits** garments, i.e., appearances    **poor likelihoods** weak inferences    111 **modern seeming** commonplace assumption    **prefer** bring forth    113 **forcèd courses** means used against her will    115 **question** conversation

I do confess the vices of my blood,° 125
So justly° to your grave ears I'll present
How I did thrive in this fair lady's love,
And she in mine.

**DUKE:** Say it, Othello.

**OTHELLO:** Her father loved me, oft invited me, 130
Still° questioned me the story of my life
From year to year—the battles, sieges, fortunes
That I have passed.
I ran it through, even from my boyish days
To th' very moment that he bade me tell it, 135
Wherein I spoke of most disastrous chances,
Of moving accidents° by flood and field,
Of hairbreadth scapes i' th' imminent deadly breach,°
Of being taken by the insolent foe
And sold to slavery, of my redemption thence, 140
And portance° in my travels' history,
Wherein of antres° vast and deserts idle,°
Rough quarries,° rocks, and hills whose heads touch
heaven,
It was my hint° to speak—such was my process—
And of the Cannibals that each other eat, 145
The Anthropophagi,° and men whose heads
Do grow beneath their shoulders. These things to hear
Would Desdemona seriously incline;
But still the house affairs would draw her thence,
Which ever as she could with haste dispatch 150
She'd come again, and with a greedy ear
Devour up my discourse. Which I, observing,
Took once a pliant° hour, and found good means
To draw from her a prayer of earnest heart
That I would all my pilgrimage dilate,° 155
Whereof by parcels° she had something heard,

---

**125 blood** passions, human nature    **126 justly** truthfully, accurately    **131 Still** continually
**137 moving accidents** stirring happenings    **138 imminent . . . breach** death-threatening gaps
made in a fortification    **141 portance** conduct    **142 antres** caverns    **idle** barren, desolate
**143 Rough quarries** rugged rock formations    **144 hint** occasion, opportunity
**146 Anthropophagi** man-eaters (A term from Pliny's *Natural History*.)    **153 pliant** well-suiting
**155 dilate** relate in detail    **156 by parcels** piecemeal

But not intentively.° I did consent,
And often did beguile her of her tears,
When I did speak of some distressful stroke
That my youth suffered. My story being done,                    160
She gave me for my pains a world of sighs.
She swore, in faith, 'twas strange, 'twas passing° strange,
'Twas pitiful, 'twas wondrous pitiful.
She wished she had not heard it, yet she wished
That heaven had made her° such a man. She thanked me,          165
And bade me, if I had a friend that loved her,
I should but teach him how to tell my story,
And that would woo her. Upon this hint° I spake.
She loved me for the dangers I had passed,
And I loved her that she did pity them.                         170
This only is the witchcraft I have used.
Here comes the lady. Let her witness it.

*Enter Desdemona, Iago, [and] attendants.*

**DUKE:**   I think this tale would win my daughter too.
  Good Brabantio,
  Take up this mangled matter at the best.°                     175
  Men do their broken weapons rather use
  Than their bare hands.

**BRABANTIO:**                  I pray you, hear her speak.
  If she confess that she was half the wooer,
  Destruction on my head if my bad blame
  Light on the man!—Come hither, gentle mistress.              180
  Do you perceive in all this noble company
  Where most you owe obedience?

**DESDEMONA:**                      My noble Father,
  I do perceive here a divided duty.
  To you I am bound for life and education;°
  My life and education both do learn° me                      185
  How to respect you. You are the lord of duty;°

---

**157 intentively** with full attention, continuously    **162 passing** exceedingly    **165 made her** created her to be    **168 hint** opportunity (Othello does not mean that she was dropping hints.)
**175 Take . . . best** make the best of a bad bargain    **184 education** upbringing    **185 learn** teach
**186 of duty** to whom duty is due

I am hitherto your daughter. But here's my husband,
And so much duty as my mother showed
To you, preferring you before her father,
So much I challenge° that I may profess                                    *190*
Due to the Moor my lord.

**BRABANTIO:**   God be with you! I have done.
Please it Your Grace, on to the state affairs.
I had rather to adopt a child than get° it.
Come hither, Moor.                                                          *195*

*[He joins the hands of Othello and Desdemona.]*

I here do give thee that with all my heart°
Which, but thou hast already, with all my heart°
I would keep from thee.—For your sake,° jewel,
I am glad at soul I have no other child,
For thy escape° would teach me tyranny,                                    *200*
To hang clogs° on them.—I have done, my lord.

**DUKE:**   Let me speak like yourself,° and lay a sentence°
Which, as a grece° or step, may help these lovers
Into your favor.
When remedies° are past, the griefs are ended                             *205*
By seeing the worst, which late on hopes depended.°
To mourn a mischief° that is past and gone
Is the next° way to draw new mischief on.
What° cannot be preserved when fortune takes,
Patience her injury a mockery makes.°                                      *210*
The robbed that smiles steals something from the thief;
He robs himself that spends a bootless grief.°

**BRABANTIO:**   So let the Turk of Cyprus us beguile,
We lose it not, so long as we can smile.
He bears the sentence well that nothing bears                             *215*

---

190 **challenge** claim    194 **get** beget    196 **with all my heart** wherein my whole affection has been
engaged    197 **with all my heart** willingly, gladly    198 **For your sake** on your account
200 **escape** elopement    201 **clogs** (Literally, blocks of wood fastened to the legs of criminals or con-
victs to inhibit escape.)    202 **like yourself** i.e., as you would, in your proper temper    **lay a sentence** apply a maxim    203 **grece** step    205 **remedies** hopes of remedy    206 **which . . .
depended** which griefs were sustained until recently by hopeful anticipation    207 **mischief** misfortune, injury    208 **next** nearest    209 **What** whatever    210 **Patience . . . makes** patience laughs
at the injury inflicted by fortune (and thus eases the pain)    212 **spends a bootless grief** indulges in
unavailing grief

But the free comfort which from thence he hears,
But he bears both the sentence and the sorrow
That, to pay grief, must of poor patience borrow.°
These sentences, to sugar or to gall,
Being strong on both sides, are equivocal.°                                                    *220*
But words are words. I never yet did hear
That the bruised heart was piercèd through the ear.°
I humbly beseech you, proceed to th' affairs of state.

**DUKE:** The Turk with a most mighty preparation makes for
Cyprus. Othello, the fortitude° of the place is best known                   *225*
to you; and though we have there a substitute° of most
allowed° sufficiency, yet opinion, a sovereign mistress of
effects, throws a more safer voice on you.° You must therefore be content to slubber° the gloss of your new fortunes
with this more stubborn° and boisterous expedition.                          *230*

**OTHELLO:** The tyrant custom, most grave senators,
Hath made the flinty and steel couch of war
My thrice-driven° bed of down. I do agnize°
A natural and prompt alacrity
I find in hardness,° and do undertake                                                    *235*
These present wars against the Ottomites.
Most humbly therefore bending to your state,°
I crave fit disposition for my wife,
Due reference of place and exhibition,°
With such accommodation° and besort°                                            *240*
As levels° with her breeding.°

**DUKE:** Why, at her father's.

**BRABANTIO:**                                    I will not have it so.

**OTHELLO:** Nor I.

---

**215–218 He bears . . . borrow** a person well bears out your maxim who can enjoy its platitudinous
comfort, free of all genuine sorrow, but anyone whose grief bankrupts his poor patience is left with
your saying and his sorrow, too (*Bears the sentence* also plays on the meaning, "receives judicial
sentence.")    **219–220 These . . . equivocal** these fine maxims are equivocal, either sweet or
bitter in their application    **222 piercèd . . . ear** i.e., surgically lanced and cured by mere words
of advice    **225 fortitude** strength    **226 substitute** deputy    **227 allowed** acknowledged
**227–228 opinion . . . on you** general opinion, an important determiner of affairs, chooses you as
the best man    **229 slubber** soil, sully    **230 stubborn** harsh, rough    **233 thrice-driven**
thrice sifted, winnowed    **agnize** know in myself, acknowledge    **235 hardness** hardship
**237 bending . . . state** bowing or kneeling to your authority    **239 reference . . . exhibition**
provision of appropriate place to live and allowance of money    **240 accommodation** suitable
provision    **besort** attendance    **241 levels** equals, suits    **breeding** social position, upbringing

**DESDEMONA:**      Nor I. I would not there reside,
    To put my father in impatient thoughts
    By being in his eye. Most gracious Duke,                                245
    To my unfolding° lend your prosperous° ear,
    And let me find a charter° in your voice,
    T' assist my simpleness.
**DUKE:**   What would you, Desdemona?
**DESDEMONA:**   That I did love the Moor to live with him,                250
    My downright violence and storm of fortunes°
    May trumpet to the world. My heart's subdued
    Even to the very quality of my lord.°
    I saw Othello's visage in his mind,
    And to his honors and his valiant parts°                               255
    Did I my soul and fortunes consecrate.
    So that, dear lords, if I be left behind
    A moth° of peace, and he go to the war,
    The rites° for why I love him are bereft me,
    And I a heavy interim shall support                                    260
    By his dear° absence. Let me go with him.
**OTHELLO:**   Let her have your voice.°
    Vouch with me, heaven, I therefor beg it not
    To please the palate of my appetite,
    Nor to comply with heat°—the young affects°                           265
    In me defunct—and proper° satisfaction,
    But to be free° and bounteous to her mind.
    And heaven defend° your good souls that you think°
    I will your serious and great business scant
    When she is with me. No, when light-winged toys                       270
    Of feathered Cupid seel° with wanton dullness
    My speculative and officed instruments,°

---

**246 unfolding** explanation, proposal   **prosperous** propitious   **247 charter** privilege, authorization
**251 My . . . fortunes** my plain and total breach of social custom, taking my future by storm and dis-
rupting my whole life   **252–253 My heart's . . . lord** my heart is brought wholly into accord with
Othello's virtues; I love him for his virtues   **255 parts** qualities   **258 moth** i.e., one who consumes
merely   **259 rites** rites of love (with a suggestion, too, of "rights," sharing)   **261 dear** (1) heartfelt
(2) costly   **262 voice** consent   **265 heat** sexual passion   **young affects** passions of youth, desires
**266 proper** personal   **267 free** generous   **268 defend** forbid   **think** should think   **271 seel** i.e.,
make blind (as in falconry, by sewing up the eyes of the hawk during training)   **272 speculative . . .
instruments** eyes and other faculties used in the performance of duty

That° my disports° corrupt and taint° my business,
Let huswives make a skillet of my helm,
And all indign° and base adversities                                    275
Make head° against my estimation!°

**DUKE:**   Be it as you shall privately determine,
Either for her stay or going. Th' affair cries haste,
And speed must answer it.

**A SENATOR:**                        You must away tonight.

**DESDEMONA:**   Tonight, my lord?

**DUKE:**                        This night.

**OTHELLO:**                        With all my heart.     280

**DUKE:**   At nine i' the morning here we'll meet again.
Othello, leave some officer behind,
And he shall our commission bring to you,
With such things else of quality and respect°
As doth import° you.

**OTHELLO:**                 So please Your Grace, my ancient;     285
A man he is of honesty and trust.
To his conveyance I assign my wife,
With what else needful Your Good Grace shall think
To be sent after me.

**DUKE:**                 Let it be so.
Good night to everyone. [*To Brabantio.*] And, noble signor,     290
If virtue no delighted° beauty lack,
Your son-in-law is far more fair than black.

**FIRST SENATOR:**   Adieu, brave Moor. Use Desdemona well.

**BRABANTIO:**   Look to her, Moor, if thou hast eyes to see.
She has deceived her father, and may thee.                              295

   *Exeunt* [*Duke, Brabantio, Cassio, Senators, and officers*].

**OTHELLO:**   My life upon her faith! Honest Iago,
My Desdemona must I leave to thee.
I prithee, let thy wife attend on her,
And bring them after in the best advantage.°

---

**273 That** so that    **disports** sexual pastimes    **taint** impair    **275 indign** unworthy, shameful
**276 Make head** raise an army    **estimation** reputation    **284 of quality and respect** of importance and relevance    **285 import** concern    **291 delighted** capable of delighting    **299 in . . .
advantage** at the most favourable opportunity

Come, Desdemona. I have but an hour                                        *300*
Of love, of worldly matters and direction,°
To spend with thee. We must obey the time.°

*Exit* [*with Desdemona*].

**RODERIGO:** Iago—

**IAGO:** What sayst thou, noble heart?

**RODERIGO:** What will I do, think'st thou?                             *305*

**IAGO:** Why, go to bed and sleep.

**RODERIGO:** I will incontinently° drown myself.

**IAGO:** If thou dost, I shall never love thee after. Why, thou silly
gentleman?

**RODERIGO:** It is silliness to live when to live is torment; and       *310*
then have we a prescription° to die when death is our
physician.

**IAGO:** O villainous!° I have looked upon the world for four
times seven years, and, since I could distinguish betwixt a
benefit and an injury, I never found man that knew how to         *315*
love himself. Ere I would say I would drown myself for the
love of a guinea hen,° I would change my humanity with a
baboon.

**RODERIGO:** What should I do? I confess it is my shame to be
so fond,° but it is not in my virtue° to amend it.                 *320*

**IAGO:** Virtue? A fig!° 'Tis in ourselves that we are thus or thus.
Our bodies are our gardens, to the which our wills are gar-
deners; so that if we will plant nettles or sow lettuce, set hys-
sop° and weed up thyme, supply it with one gender° of herbs
or distract it with° many, either to have it sterile with idle-      *325*
ness° or manured with industry—why, the power and corrigible authority° of this lies in our wills. If the beam° of our
lives had not one scale of reason to poise° another of sensuality,

---

**301 direction** instructions    **302 the time** the urgency of the present crisis    **307 incontinently**
immediately, without self-restraint    **311 prescription** (1) right based on long-established custom
(2) doctor's prescription    **313 villainous** i.e., what perfect nonsense    **317 guinea hen** (A slang
term for a prostitute.)    **320 fond** infatuated    **virtue** strength, nature    **321 fig** (To give a fig
is to thrust the thumb between the first and second fingers in a vulgar and insulting gesture.)
**324 hyssop** an herb of the mint family    **gender** kind    **325 distract it with** divide it among
**326 idleness** want of cultivation    **327 corrigible authority** power to correct    **beam**
balance    **328 poise** counterbalance

the blood° and baseness of our natures would conduct
us to most preposterous conclusions. But we have reason to          330
cool our raging motions,° our carnal stings, our unbitted°
lusts, whereof I take this that you call love to be a sect or
scion.°

**RODERIGO:** It cannot be.

**IAGO:** It is merely a lust of the blood and a permission of the          335
will. Come, be a man. Drown thyself? Drown cats and blind
puppies. I have professed me thy friend, and I confess me
knit to thy deserving with cables of perdurable° toughness. I
could never better stead° thee than now. Put money in thy
purse. Follow thou the wars; defeat thy favor° with an          340
usurped° beard. I say, put money in thy purse. It cannot be
long that Desdemona should continue her love to the Moor—
put money in thy purse—nor he his to her. It was a violent
commencement in her, and thou shalt see an answerable
sequestration°—put but money in thy purse. These Moors          345
are changeable in their wills°—fill thy purse with money.
The food that to him now is as luscious as locusts° shall be to
him shortly as bitter as coloquintida.° She must change for
youth; when she is sated with his body, she will find the error
of her choice. She must have change, she must. Therefore          350
put money in thy purse. If thou wilt needs damn thyself, do
it a more delicate way than drowning. Make° all the money
thou canst. If sanctimony° and a frail vow betwixt an erring°
barbarian and a supersubtle Venetian be not too hard for my
wits and all the tribe of hell, thou shalt enjoy her. Therefore          355
make money. A pox of drowning thyself! It is clean out of the
way.° Seek thou rather to be hanged in compassing° thy joy
than to be drowned and go without her.

---

**329 blood** natural passions    **331 motions** appetites.    **unbitted** unbridled, uncontrolled
**332–333 sect or scion** cutting or offshoot    **338 perdurable** very durable    **339 stead** assist
**340 defeat thy favor** disguise your face    **341 usurped** (The suggestion is that Roderigo is not man
enough to have a beard of his own.)    **344–345 an answerable sequestration** a corresponding
separation or estrangement    **346 wills** carnal appetites    **347 locusts** fruit of the carob tree (see
Matthew 3:4), or perhaps honeysuckle    **348 coloquintida** colocynth or bitter apple, a purgative
**352 Make** raise, collect    **353 sanctimony** sacred ceremony    **353 erring** wandering, vagabond,
unsteady    **356–357 clean . . . way** entirely unsuitable as a course of action    **357 compassing**
encompassing, embracing

**RODERIGO:**  Wilt thou be fast° to my hopes if I depend on the
issue?°

360

**IAGO:**  Thou art sure of me. Go, make money. I have told thee
often, and I retell thee again and again, I hate the Moor. My
cause is hearted;° thine hath no less reason. Let us be con-
junctive° in our revenge against him. If thou canst cuckold
him, thou dost thyself a pleasure, me a sport. There are
many events in the womb of time which will be delivered.
Traverse,° go, provide thy money. We will have more of this
tomorrow. Adieu.

365

**RODERIGO:**  Where shall we meet i' the morning?

**IAGO:**  At my lodging.

370

**RODERIGO:**  I'll be with thee betimes.° [*He starts to leave.*]

**IAGO:**  Go to, farewell.—Do you hear, Roderigo?

**RODERIGO:**  What say you?

**IAGO:**  No more of drowning, do you hear?

**RODERIGO:**  I am changed.

375

**IAGO:**  Go to, farewell. Put money enough in your purse.

**RODERIGO:**  I'll sell all my land.                                    *Exit.*

**IAGO:**  Thus do I ever make my fool my purse;
For I mine own gained knowledge should profane
If I would time expend with such a snipe°
But for my sport and profit. I hate the Moor;
And it is thought abroad° that twixt my sheets
He's done my office.° I know not if 't be true;
But I, for mere suspicion in that kind,
Will do as if for surety.° He holds me well;°
The better shall my purpose work on him.
Cassio's a proper° man. Let me see now:
To get his place and to plume up° my will
In double knavery—How, how?—Let's see:
After some time, to abuse° Othello's ear
That he° is too familiar with his wife.

380

385

390

---

**359 fast** true    **360 issue** (successful) outcome    **363 hearted** fixed in the heart, heartfelt
**364 conjunctive** united    **367 Traverse** (A military marching term.)    **371 betimes** early
**380 snipe** woodcock, i.e., fool    **382 it is thought abroad** it is rumoured    **383 my office** i.e., my
sexual function as husband    **385 do . . . surety** act as if on certain knowledge    **holds me well**
regards me favourably    **387 proper** handsome    **388 plume up** put a feather in the cap of, i.e.,
glorify, gratify    **390 abuse** deceive    **391 he** i.e., Cassio

He hath a person and a smooth dispose°
To be suspected, framed to make women false.
The Moor is of a free° and open° nature,
That thinks men honest that but seem to be so,                                    *395*
And will as tenderly° be led by the nose
As asses are.
I have 't. It is engendered. Hell and night
Must bring this monstrous birth to the world's light.

                                                                              [*Exit.*]

# ACT II

## Scene I [A Seaport in Cyprus. An Open Place Near the Quay.]

*Enter Montano and two Gentlemen.*

**MONTANO:**   What from the cape can you discern at sea?
**FIRST GENTLEMAN:**   Nothing at all. It is a high-wrought
    flood.°
    I cannot, twixt the heaven and the main,°
    Descry a sail.
**MONTANO:**   Methinks the wind hath spoke aloud at land;                         *5*
    A fuller blast ne'er shook our battlements.
    If it hath ruffianed° so upon the sea,
    What ribs of oak, when mountains° melt on them,
    Can hold the mortise?° What shall we hear of this?
**SECOND GENTLEMAN:**   A segregation° of the Turkish fleet.                       *10*
    For do but stand upon the foaming shore,
    The chidden° billow seems to pelt the clouds;
    The wind-shaked surge, with high and monstrous mane,°
    Seems to cast water on the burning Bear°

---

392 **dispose** disposition   394 **free** frank, generous   **open** unsuspicious   396 **tenderly** readily
2 **high-wrought flood** very agitated sea   3 **main** ocean (also at line 41)   7 **ruffianed** raged
8 **mountains** i.e., of water   9 **hold the mortise** hold their joints together (A *mortise* is the socket
hollowed out in fitting timbers.)   10 **segregation** dispersal   12 **chidden** i.e., rebuked, repelled (by
the shore), and thus shot into the air   13 **monstrous mane** (The surf is like the mane of a wild
beast.)   14 **the burning Bear** i.e., the constellation Ursa Minor or the Little Bear, which includes
the polestar (and hence regarded as the guards of *th' ever-fixèd pole* in the next line; sometimes the
term *guards* is applied to the two "pointers" of the Big Bear or Dipper, which may be intended here.)

And quench the guards of th' ever-fixèd pole.                   15
I never did like molestation° view
On the enchafèd° flood.

MONTANO:   If that° the Turkish fleet
Be not ensheltered and embayed,° they are drowned;
It is impossible to bear it out.°                               20

*Enter a [Third] Gentleman.*

THIRD GENTLEMAN:   News, lads! Our wars are done.
The desperate tempest hath so banged the Turks
That their designment° halts.° A noble ship of Venice
Hath seen a grievous wreck° and sufferance°
On most part of their fleet.                                    25

MONTANO:   How? Is this true?

THIRD GENTLEMAN:   The ship is here put in,
A Veronesa;° Michael Cassio,
Lieutenant to the warlike Moor Othello,
Is come on shore; the Moor himself at sea,                      30
And is in full commission here for Cyprus.

MONTANO:   I am glad on 't. 'Tis a worthy governor.

THIRD GENTLEMAN:   But this same Cassio, though he speak
of comfort
Touching the Turkish loss, yet he looks sadly°
And prays the Moor be safe, for they were parted               35
With foul and violent tempest.

MONTANO:                       Pray heaven he be,
For I have served him, and the man commands
Like a full° soldier. Let's to the seaside, ho!
As well to see the vessel that's come in
As to throw out our eyes for brave Othello,                    40
Even till we make the main and th' aerial blue°
An indistinct regard.°

THIRD GENTLEMAN:   Come, let's do so,

---

**16 like molestation** comparable disturbance    **17 enchafèd** angry    **18 If that** if    **19 embayed**
sheltered by a bay    **20 bear it out** survive, weather the storm    **23 designment** design, enterprise.
**halts** is lame    **24 wreck** shipwreck    **sufferance** damage, disaster    **28 Veronesa** i.e., fitted out in
Verona for Venetian service, or possibly *Verennessa* (the Folio spelling), i.e., *verrinessa*, a cutter (from
*verrinare,* "to cut through")    **34 sadly** gravely    **38 full** perfect    **41 the main . . . blue** the sea
and the sky    **42 An indistinct regard** indistinguishable in our view

For every minute is expectancy°
Of more arrivance.°

*Enter Cassio.*

CASSIO: Thanks, you the valiant of this warlike isle,      45
That so approve° the Moor! O, let the heavens
Give him defense against the elements,
For I have lost him on a dangerous sea.
MONTANO: Is he well shipped?
CASSIO: His bark is stoutly timbered, and his pilot      50
Of very expert and approved allowance;°
Therefore my hopes, not surfeited to death,°
Stand in bold cure.°
        [*A cry*] *within*: "A sail, a sail, a sail!"
CASSIO: What noise?
A GENTLEMAN: The town is empty. On the brow o' the sea°      55
Stand ranks of people, and they cry "A sail!"
CASSIO: My hopes do shape him for° the governor.

                            [*A shot within.*]

SECOND GENTLEMAN: They do discharge their shot of
  courtesy;°
Our friends at least.
CASSIO:               I pray you, sir, go forth,
And give us truth who 'tis that is arrived.      60
SECOND GENTLEMAN: I shall.                *Exit.*
MONTANO: But, good Lieutenant, is your general wived?
CASSIO: Most fortunately. He hath achieved a maid
That paragons° description and wild fame,°
One that excels the quirks° of blazoning° pens,      65
And in th' essential vesture of creation

---

43 **is expectancy** gives expectation    44 **arrivance** arrival    46 **approve** admire, honour
51 **approved allowance** tested reputation    52 **surfeited to death** i.e., overextended, worn thin
through repeated application or delayed fulfillment    53 **in bold cure** in strong hopes of fulfillment
55 **brow o' the sea** cliff-edge    57 **My . . . for** I hope it is    58 **discharge . . . courtesy** fire a
salute in token of respect and courtesy    64 **paragons** surpasses.   **wild fame** extravagant report
65 **quirks** witty conceits   **blazoning** setting forth as though in heraldic language

Does tire the enginer.°

*Enter [Second] Gentleman.*°

                  How now? Who has put in?°

**SECOND GENTLEMAN:**  'Tis one Iago, ancient to the General.

**CASSIO:**  He's had most favorable and happy speed.

    Tempests themselves, high seas, and howling winds,             70

    The guttered° rocks and congregated sands—

    Traitors ensteeped° to clog the guiltless keel—

    As° having sense of beauty, do omit°

    Their mortal° natures, letting go safely by

    The divine Desdemona.

**MONTANO:**                  What is she?              75

**CASSIO:**  She that I spake of, our great captain's captain,

    Left in the conduct of the bold Iago,

    Whose footing° here anticipates our thoughts

    A sennight's° speed. Great Jove, Othello guard,

    And swell his sail with thine own powerful breath,         80

    That he may bless this bay with his tall° ship,

    Make love's quick pants in Desdemona's arms,

    Give renewed fire to our extinct spirits,

    And bring all Cyprus comfort!

*Enter Desdemona, Iago, Roderigo, and Emilia.*

                  O, behold,

The riches of the ship is come on shore!              85

You men of Cyprus, let her have your knees.

*[The gentlemen make curtsy to Desdemona.]*

Hail to thee, lady! And the grace of heaven

Before, behind thee, and on every hand

Enwheel thee round!

---

**66–67 in . . . enginer** in her real, God-given, beauty, (she) defeats any attempt to praise her. **enginer** engineer, i.e., poet, one who devises    **[s.d.]** *Second Gentleman* (So identified in the Quarto text here and in lines 58, 61, 68, and 96; the Folio calls him a gentleman.)    **67 put in** i.e., to harbour    **71 guttered** jagged, trenched    **72 ensteeped** lying under water    **73 As** as if    **omit** forbear to exercise    **74 mortal** deadly    **78 footing** landing    **79 sennight's** week's    **81 tall** splendid, gallant

**DESEMONA:**           I thank you, valiant Cassio.

What tidings can you tell me of my lord?                                    90

**CASSIO:** He is not yet arrived, nor know I aught

But that he's well and will be shortly here.

**DESEMONA:**   O, but I fear—How lost you company?

**CASSIO:**   The great contention of the sea and skies

Parted our fellowship.

                    [*Within*] "A sail, a sail!" [*A shot.*]

                    But hark. A sail!                                       95

**SECOND GENTLEMAN:**   They give their greeting to the citadel.

This likewise is a friend.

**CASSIO:**                    See for the news.

                    [*Exit Second Gentleman.*]

Good Ancient, you are welcome. [*Kissing Emilia.*] Welcome,
mistress.

Let it not gall your patience, good Iago,

That I extend° my manners; 'tis my breeding°                               100

That gives me this bold show of courtesy.

**IAGO:**   Sir, would she give you so much of her lips

As of her tongue she oft bestows on me,

You would have enough.

**DESEMONA:**   Alas, she has no speech!°                                    105

**IAGO:**   In faith, too much.

I find it still,° when I have list° to sleep.

Marry, before your ladyship, I grant,

She puts her tongue a little in her heart

And chides with thinking.°

**EMILIA:**                    You have little cause to say so.                110

**IAGO:**   Come on, come on. You are pictures out of doors,°

Bells° in your parlors, wildcats in your kitchens,°

Saints° in your injuries, devils being offended,

Players° in your huswifery,° and huswives° in your beds.

---

**100 extend** give scope to   **breeding** training in the niceties of etiquette   **105 she has no speech** i.e.,
she's not a chatterbox, as you allege   **107 still** always   **list** desire   **110 with thinking** i.e., in her
thoughts only   **111 pictures out of doors** i.e., silent and well-behaved in public   **112 Bells** i.e., jan-
gling, noisy, and brazen   **in your kitchens** i.e., in domestic affairs (Ladies would not do the cooking.)
**113 Saints** martyrs   **114 Players** idlers, triflers, or deceivers   **huswifery** housekeeping   **huswives**
hussies (i.e., women who are "busy" in bed, or unduly thrifty in dispensing sexual favours)

**DESDEMONA:**   O, fie upon thee, slanderer!                          115

**IAGO:**   Nay, it is true, or else I am a Turk.°

You rise to play, and go to bed to work.

**EMILIA:**   You shall not write my praise.

**IAGO:**                                            No, let me not.

**DESDEMONA:**   What wouldst write of me, if thou shouldst
praise me?

**IAGO:**   O gentle lady, do not put me to 't,                          120

For I am nothing if not critical.°

**DESDEMONA:**   Come on, essay.°—There's one gone to the
harbor?

**IAGO:**   Ay, madam.

**DESDEMONA:**   I am not merry, but I do beguile

The thing I am° by seeming otherwise.                          125

Come, how wouldst thou praise me?

**IAGO:**   I am about it, but indeed my invention

Comes from my pate as birdlime° does from frieze°—

It plucks out brains and all. But my Muse labors,°

And thus she is delivered:                          130

If she be fair and wise, fairness and wit,

The one's for use, the other useth it.°

**DESDEMONA:**   Well praised! How if she be black° and witty?

**IAGO:**   If she be black, and thereto have a wit,

She'll find a white° that shall her blackness fit.°                          135

**DESDEMONA:**   Worse and worse.

**EMILIA:**                                            How if fair and foolish?

**IAGO:**   She never yet was foolish that was fair,

For even her folly° helped her to an heir.°

**DESDEMONA:**   These are old fond° paradoxes to make fools
laugh i' th' alehouse. What miserable praise hast thou for                          140
her that's foul and foolish?

---

**116 a Turk** an infidel, not to be believed   **121 critical** censorious   **122 essay** try   **125 The thing
I am** i.e., my anxious self   **128 birdlime** sticky substance used to catch small birds   **frieze** coarse
woolen cloth   **129 labors** (1) exerts herself (2) prepares to deliver a child (with a following pun on
*delivered* in line 130)   **132 The one's . . . it** i.e., her cleverness will make use of her beauty
**133 black** dark-complexioned, brunette   **135 a white** a fair person (with word-play on "wight," a
person)   **fit** (with sexual suggestion of mating)   **138 folly** (with added meaning of "lechery, wantonness.")   **to an heir** i.e., to bear a child   **139 fond** foolish

**IAGO:** There's none so foul° and foolish thereunto,°
But does foul° pranks which fair and wise ones do.

**DESDEMONA:** O heavy ignorance! Thou praisest the worst
best. But what praise couldst thou bestow on a deserving          *145*
woman indeed, one that, in the authority of her merit, did
justly put on the vouch° of very malice itself?

**IAGO:** She that was ever fair, and never proud,
Had tongue at will, and yet was never loud,
Never lacked gold and yet went never gay,°          *150*
Fled from her wish, and yet said, "Now I may,"°
She that being angered, her revenge being nigh,
Bade her wrong stay° and her displeasure fly,
She that in wisdom never was so frail
To change the cod's head for the salmon's tail,°          *155*
She that could think and ne'er disclose her mind,
See suitors following and not look behind,
She was a wight, if ever such wight were—

**DESDEMONA:** To do what?

**IAGO:** To suckle fools° and chronicle small beer.°          *160*

**DESDEMONA:** O most lame and impotent conclusion! Do not
learn of him, Emilia, though he be thy husband. How say
you, Cassio? Is he not a most profane° and liberal° coun-
selor?

**CASSIO:** He speaks home,° madam. You may relish° him more          *165*
in° the soldier than in the scholar.

[*Cassio and Desdemona stand together, conversing intimately.*]

**IAGO** [*aside*]: He takes her by the palm. Ay, well said,° whisper.
With as little a web as this will I ensnare as great a fly as
Cassio. Ay, smile upon her, do; I will gyve° thee in thine own

---

**142 foul** ugly **thereunto** in addition **143 foul** sluttish **147 put . . . vouch** compel the
approval **150 gay** extravagantly clothed **151 Fled . . . may** avoided temptation where the choice
was hers **153 Bade . . . stay** i.e., resolved to put up with her injury patiently **155 To . . . tail**
i.e., to exchange a lacklustre husband for a sexy lover (?) (**Cod's head** is slang for "penis," and tail,
for "pudendum.") **160 suckle fools** breastfeed babies **chronicle small beer** i.e., keep petty
household accounts, keep track of trivial matters **163 profane** irreverent, ribald. **liberal** licentious, free-spoken **165 home** right to the target (A term from fencing.) **relish** appreciate
**166 in** in the character of **167 well said** well done **169 gyve** fetter, shackle

courtship.° You say true;° 'tis so, indeed. If such tricks as      *170*
these strip you out of your lieutenantry, it had been better
you had not kissed your three fingers so oft, which now
again you are most apt to play the sir° in. Very good; well
kissed! An excellent courtesy! 'Tis so, indeed. Yet again your
fingers to your lips? Would they were clyster pipes° for your      *175*
sake! [*Trumpet within.*] The Moor! I know his trumpet.
**CASSIO:**  'Tis truly so.
**DESDEMONA:**  Let's meet him and receive him.
**CASSIO:**  Lo, where he comes!

*Enter Othello and attendants.*

**OTHELLO:**  O my fair warrior!
**DESDEMONA:**                   My dear Othello!      *180*
**OTHELLO:**  It gives me wonder great as my content
    To see you here before me. O my soul's joy,
    If after every tempest come such calms,
    May the winds blow till they have wakened death,
    And let the laboring bark climb hills of seas      *185*
    Olympus-high, and duck again as low
    As hell's from heaven! If it were now to die,
    'Twere now to be most happy, for I fear
    My soul hath her content so absolute
    That not another comfort like to this      *190*
    Succeeds in unknown fate.°
**DESDEMONA:**                   The heavens forbid
    But that our loves and comforts should increase
    Even as our days do grow!
**OTHELLO:**  Amen to that, sweet powers!
    I cannot speak enough of this content.      *195*
    It stops me here; it is too much of joy.
    And this, and this, the greatest discords be

    [*They kiss.*]°

---

**170 courtship** courtesy, show of courtly manners     **You say true** i.e., that's right, go ahead
**173 the sir** i.e., the fine gentleman     **175 clyster pipes** tubes used for enemas and douches
**191 Succeeds . . . fate** i.e., can follow in the unknown future     **197 [s.d.] They kiss** (The direction
is from the Quarto.)

That e'er our hearts shall make!
IAGO [*aside*]:   O, you are well tuned now!
But I'll set down° the pegs that make this music,                    *200*
As honest as I am.°
OTHELLO:   Come, let us to the castle.
News, friends! Our wars are done, the Turks are drowned.
How does my old acquaintance of this isle?—
Honey, you shall be well desired° in Cyprus;                          *205*
I have found great love amongst them. O my sweet,
I prattle out of fashion,° and I dote
In mine own comforts.—I prithee, good Iago,
Go to the bay and disembark my coffers.°
Bring thou the master° to the citadel;                               *210*
He is a good one, and his worthiness
Does challenge° much respect.—Come, Desdemona.—
Once more, well met at Cyprus!

> *Exeunt Othello and Desdemona [and all*
> *but Iago and Roderigo].*

IAGO [*to an attendant*]:   Do thou meet me presently at the harbor. [*To Roderigo.*] Come hither. If thou be'st valiant—as,        *215*
they say, base men° being in love have then a nobility in
their natures more than is native to them—list° me. The
Lieutenant tonight watches on the court of guard.° First, I
must tell thee this: Desdemona is directly in love with him.
RODERIGO:   With him? Why, 'tis not possible.                        *220*
IAGO:   Lay thy finger thus,° and let thy soul be instructed.
Mark me with what violence she first loved the Moor, but°
for bragging and telling her fantastical lies. To love him still
for prating? Let not thy discreet heart think it. Her eye must
be fed; and what delight shall she have to look on the devil?       *225*
When the blood is made dull with the act of sport,° there

---

**200 set down** loosen (and hence untune the instrument)    **201 As . . . I am** for all my supposed
honesty    **205 desired** welcomed    **207 out of fashion** irrelevantly, incoherently (?)    **209 coffers**
chests, baggage    **210 master** ship's captain    **212 challenge** lay claim to, deserve    **216 base men**
even lowly born men    **217 list** listen to    **218 court of guard** guardhouse (Cassio is in charge of
the watch.)    **221 thus** i.e., on your lips    **222 but** only    **226 the act of sport** sex

should be, again to inflame it and to give satiety a fresh
appetite, loveliness in favor,° sympathy° in years, manners,
and beauties—all which the Moor is defective in. Now, for
want of these required conveniences,° her delicate tender-           230
ness will find itself abused,° begin to heave the gorge,° dis-
relish and abhor the Moor. Very nature° will instruct her in it
and compel her to some second choice. Now, sir, this
granted—as it is a most pregnant° and unforced position—
who stands so eminent in the degree of° this fortune as          235
Cassio does? A knave very voluble,° no further conscion-
able° than in putting on the mere form of civil and humane°
seeming for the better compassing of his salt° and most hidden loose affection.° Why, none, why, none. A slipper° and
subtle knave, a finder out of occasions, that has an eye can      240
stamp° and counterfeit advantages,° though true advantage
never present itself; a devilish knave. Besides, the knave is
handsome, young, and hath all those requisites in him that
folly° and green° minds look after. A pestilent complete
knave, and the woman hath found him° already.                    245

**RODERIGO:** I cannot believe that in her. She's full of most
blessed condition.°

**IAGO:** Blessed fig's end!° The wine she drinks is made of
grapes. If she had been blessed, she would never have loved
the Moor. Blessed pudding!° Didst thou not see her paddle         250
with the palm of his hand? Didst not mark that?

**RODERIGO:** Yes, that I did; but that was but courtesy.

**IAGO:** Lechery, by this hand. An index° and obscure° prologue
to the history of lust and foul thoughts. They met so near
with their lips that their breaths embraced together.            255
Villainous thoughts, Roderigo! When these mutualities° so

---

**228 favor** appearance   **sympathy** correspondence, similarity   **230 required conveniences** things
conducive to sexual compatibility   **231 abused** cheated, revolted   **heave the gorge** experience
nausea   **232 Very nature** her very instincts   **234 pregnant** evident, cogent   **235 in . . . of** as
next in line for   **236 voluble** facile, glib   **237 conscionable** conscientious, conscience-bound
**humane** polite, courteous   **238 salt** licentious   **239 affection** passion   **slipper** slippery
**241 an eye can stamp** an eye that can coin, create   **advantages** favourable opportunities
**244 folly** wantonness   **green** immature   **245 found him** sized him up, perceived his intent
**247 condition** disposition   **248 fig's end** (See Act I, Scene iii, line 321 for the vulgar gesture of the
fig.)   **250 pudding** sausage   **253 index** table of contents   **obscure** (i.e., the *lust and foul
thoughts* in line 254 are secret, hidden from view)   **256 mutualities** exchanges, intimacies

marshal the way, hard at hand° comes the master and main exercise, th' incorporate° conclusion. Pish! But, sir, be you ruled by me. I have brought you from Venice. Watch you° tonight; for the command, I'll lay 't upon you.° Cassio knows you not. I'll not be far from you. Do you find some occasion to anger Cassio, either by speaking too loud, or tainting° his discipline, or from what other course you please, which the time shall more favorably minister.°     *260*

RODERIGO: Well.     *265*

IAGO: Sir, he's rash and very sudden in choler,° and haply° may strike at you. Provoke him that he may, for even out of that will I cause these of Cyprus to mutiny,° whose qualification° shall come into no true taste° again but by the displanting of Cassio. So shall you have a shorter journey to your desires by the means I shall then have to prefer° them, and the impediment most profitably removed, without the which there were no expectation of our prosperity.     *270*

RODERIGO:          I will do this, if you can bring it to any opportunity.     *275*

IAGO:      I warrant° thee. Meet me by and by° at the citadel. I must fetch his necessaries ashore. Farewell.

RODERIGO: Adieu.                    *Exit.*

IAGO: That Cassio loves her, I do well believe 't;
That she loves him, 'tis apt° and of great credit.°     *280*
The Moor, howbeit that I endure him not,
Is of a constant, loving, noble nature,
And I dare think he'll prove to Desdemona
A most dear husband. Now, I do love her too,
Not out of absolute lust—though peradventure     *285*
I stand accountant° for as great a sin—
But partly led to diet° my revenge
For that I do suspect the lusty Moor
Hath leaped into my seat, the thought whereof

---

**257 hard at hand** closely following    **258 incorporate** carnal    **259 Watch you** stand watch **260 for the command . . . you** I'll arrange for you to be appointed, given orders    **262 tainting** disparaging    **264 minister** provide    **266 choler** wrath    **haply** perhaps    **268 mutiny** riot **269 qualification** appeasement    **true taste** i.e., acceptable state    **271 prefer** advance **276 warrant** assure    **by and by** immediately    **280 apt** probable    **credit** credibility **286 accountant** accountable    **287 diet** feed

Doth, like a poisonous mineral, gnaw my innards;                    *290*
And nothing can or shall content my soul
Till I am evened with him, wife for wife,
Or failing so, yet that I put the Moor
At least into a jealousy so strong
That judgment cannot cure. Which thing to do,               *295*
If this poor trash of Venice, whom I trace°
For° his quick hunting, stand the putting on,°
I'll have our Michael Cassio on the hip,°
Abuse° him to the Moor in the rank garb—°
For I fear Cassio with my nightcap° too—                    *300*
Make the Moor thank me, love me, and reward me
For making him egregiously an ass
And practicing upon° his peace and quiet
Even to madness. 'Tis here, but yet confused.
Knavery's plain face is never seen till used.                    *305*

                                                       *Exit.*


## SCENE II [CYPRUS. A STREET.]

*Enter Othello's Herald with a proclamation.*

HERALD:   It is Othello's pleasure, our noble and valiant general, that, upon certain tidings now arrived, importing the
mere perdition° of the Turkish fleet, every man put himself
into triumph:° some to dance, some to make bonfires, each
man to what sport and revels his addiction° leads him. For,          *5*
besides these beneficial news, it is the celebration of his nup-
tial. So much was his pleasure should be proclaimed. All
offices° are open, and there is full liberty of feasting from this

---

**296 trace** i.e., train, or follow (?), or perhaps *trash*, a hunting term, meaning to put weights on a
hunting dog in order to slow him down    **297 For** to make more eager    **stand . . . on** respond
properly when I incite him to quarrel    **298 on the hip** at my mercy, where I can throw him (A
wrestling term.)    **299 Abuse** slander    **rank garb** coarse manner, gross fashion    **300 with my
nightcap** i.e., as a rival in my bed, as one who gives me cuckold's horns    **303 practicing upon**
plotting against
**3 mere perdition** complete destruction    **4 triumph** public celebration    **5 addiction** inclination
**8 offices** rooms where food and drink are kept

present hour of five till the bell have told eleven. Heaven
bless the isle of Cyprus and our noble general Othello!      *10*

*Exit.*

SCENE III [CYPRUS. THE CITADEL.]

*Enter Othello, Desdemona, Cassio, and attendants.*

OTHELLO:   Good Michael, look you to the guard tonight.
Let's teach ourselves that honorable stop°
Not to outsport° discretion.
CASSIO:   Iago hath direction what to do,
But notwithstanding, with my personal eye                    *5*
Will I look to 't.
OTHELLO:              Iago is most honest.
Michael, good night. Tomorrow with your earliest°
Let me have speech with you. [*To Desdemona.*]
    Come, my dear love,
The purchase made, the fruits are to ensue;
That profit's yet to come 'tween me and you.°—              *10*
Good night.

*Exit [Othello, with Desdemona and attendants].*

*Enter Iago.*

CASSIO:   Welcome, Iago. We must to the watch.
IAGO:   Not this hour,° Lieutenant; 'tis not yet ten o' the clock.
Our general cast° us thus early for the love of his
Desdemona; who° let us not therefore blame. He hath not yet   *15*
made wanton the night with her, and she is sport for Jove.
CASSIO:   She's a most exquisite lady.
IAGO:   And, I'll warrant her, full of game.
CASSIO:   Indeed, she's a most fresh and delicate creature.
IAGO:   What an eye she has! Methinks it sounds a parley° to       *20*
provocation.

---

**2 stop** restraint   **3 outsport** celebrate beyond the bounds of   **7 with your earliest** at your earliest
convenience   **9–10 The purchase . . . you** i.e., though married, we haven't yet consummated our
love   **13 Not this hour** not for an hour yet   **14 cast** dismissed   **15 who** i.e., Othello   **20 sounds
a parley** calls for a conference, issues an invitation

**CASSIO:** An inviting eye, and yet methinks right modest.

**IAGO:** And when she speaks, is it not an alarum° to love?

**CASSIO:** She is indeed perfection.

**IAGO:** Well, happiness to their sheets! Come, Lieutenant, I have      25
a stoup° of wine, and here without° are a brace° of Cyprus
gallants that would fain have a measure° to the health of
black Othello.

**CASSIO:** Not tonight, good Iago. I have very poor and unhappy
brains for drinking. I could well wish courtesy would invent      30
some other custom of entertainment.

**IAGO:** O, they are our friends. But one cup! I'll drink for you.°

**CASSIO:** I have drunk but one cup tonight, and that was
craftily qualified° too, and behold what innovation° it makes
here.° I am unfortunate in the infirmity and dare not task      35
my weakness with any more.

**IAGO:** What, man? 'Tis a night of revels. The gallants desire it.

**CASSIO:** Where are they?

**IAGO:** Here at the door. I pray you, call them in.

**CASSIO:** I'll do 't, but it dislikes me.°                 *Exit.*     40

**IAGO:** If I can fasten but one cup upon him,
With that which he hath drunk tonight already,
He'll be as full of quarrel and offense°
As my young mistress' dog. Now, my sick fool Roderigo,
Whom love hath turned almost the wrong side out,      45
To Desdemona hath tonight caroused°
Potations pottle-deep;° and he's to watch.°
Three lads of Cyprus—noble swelling° spirits,
That hold their honors in a wary distance,°
The very elements° of this warlike isle—      50
Have I tonight flustered with flowing cups,
And they watch° too. Now, 'mongst this flock of drunkards

---

23 **alarum** signal calling men to arms (continuing the military metaphor of *parley*, line 20.)
26 **stoup** measure of liquor, two quarts    **without** outside    **brace** pair    27 **fain have a measure**
gladly drink a toast    32 **for you** in your place (Iago will do the steady drinking to keep the gallants
company while Cassio has only one cup.)    34 **qualified** diluted    **innovation** disturbance, insur-
rection    35 **here** i.e., in my head    40 **it dislikes me** i.e., I'm reluctant    43 **offense** readiness to
take offence    46 **caroused** drunk off    47 **pottle-deep** to the bottom of the tankard    **watch** stand
watch    48 **swelling** proud    49 **hold . . . distance** i.e., are extremely sensitive of their honour
50 **very elements** typical sort    52 **watch** are members of the guard

Am I to put our Cassio in some action
That may offend the isle.—But here they come.

*Enter Cassio, Montano, and gentlemen; [servants following with wine].*

If consequence do but approve my dream,°                                              55
My boat sails freely both with wind and stream.°
**CASSIO:** 'Fore God, they have given me a rouse° already.
**MONTANO:** Good faith, a little one; not past a pint, as I am a
soldier.
**IAGO:** Some wine, ho! [*He sings.*]

"And let me the cannikin° clink, clink,                                              60
    And let me the cannikin clink.
    A soldier's a man,
    O, man's life's but a span;°
Why, then, let a soldier drink."

Some wine, boys!                                                                      65
**CASSIO:** 'Fore God, an excellent song.
**IAGO:** I learned it in England, where indeed they are most
potent in potting.° Your Dane, your German, and your swag-
bellied Hollander—drink, ho!—are nothing to your English.
**CASSIO:** Is your Englishman so exquisite in his drinking?                           70
**IAGO:** Why, he drinks you,° with facility, your Dane° dead
drunk; he sweats not° to overthrow your Almain;° he gives
your Hollander a vomit ere the next pottle can be filled.
**CASSIO:** To the health of our general!
**MONTANO:** I am for it, Lieutenant, and I'll do you justice.°                        75
**IAGO:** O sweet England! [*He sings.*]

"King Stephen was and—a worthy peer,
    His breeches cost him but a crown;
He held them sixpence all too dear,
    With that he called the tailor lown.°                                            80

---

**55 If . . . dream** if subsequent events will only substantiate my scheme   **56 stream** current
**57 rouse** full draft of liquor   **60 cannikin** small drinking vessel   **63 span** brief span of time.
(Compare Psalm 39:6 as rendered in the 1928 *Book of Common Prayer*: "Thou hast made my days as
it were a span long.")   **68 potting** drinking   **71 drinks you** drinks   **your Dane** your typical
Dane   **72 sweats not** i.e., need not exert himself   **Almain** German   **75 I'll . . . justice** i.e., I'll
drink as much as you   **80 lown** lout, rascal

He was a wight of high renown,
    And thou art but of low degree.
'Tis pride° that pulls the country down;
    Then take thy auld° cloak about thee."

Some wine, ho!                                                                    85

**CASSIO:** 'Fore God, this is a more exquisite song than the
other.

**IAGO:** Will you hear 't again?

**CASSIO:** No, for I hold him to be unworthy of his place that
does those things. Well, God's above all; and there be souls
must be saved, and there be souls must not be saved.                              90

**IAGO:** It's true, good Lieutenant.

**CASSIO:** For mine own part—no offense to the General, nor
any man of quality°—I hope to be saved.

**IAGO:** And so do I too, Lieutenant.

**CASSIO:** Ay, but, by your leave, not before me; the lieutenant is            95
to be saved before the ancient. Let's have no more of this;
let's to our affairs.—God forgive us our sins!—Gentlemen,
let's look to our business. Do not think, gentlemen, I am
drunk. This is my ancient; this is my right hand, and this is
my left. I am not drunk now. I can stand well enough, and          100
speak well enough.

**GENTLEMEN:** Excellent well.

**CASSIO:** Why, very well then; you must not think then that
I am drunk.                                                          *Exit.*

**MONTANO:** To th' platform, masters. Come, let's set the
watch.°                                                                           105

                                        [*Exeunt Gentlemen.*]

**IAGO:** You see this fellow that is gone before.
He's a soldier fit to stand by Caesar
And give direction; and do but see his vice.
'Tis to his virtue a just equinox,°
The one as long as th' other. 'Tis pity of him.                                  110

---

**83 pride** i.e., extravagance in dress    **84 auld** old    **93 quality** rank    **105 set the watch** mount
the guard    **109 just equinox** exact counterpart (*Equinox* is a day on which daylight and nighttime
hours are equal.)

I fear the trust Othello puts him in,
On some odd time of his infirmity,
Will shake this island.
MONTANO:                    But is he often thus?
IAGO:   'Tis evermore the prologue to his sleep.
He'll watch the horologe a double set,°                          115
If drink rock not his cradle.
MONTANO:                    It were well
The General were put in mind of it.
Perhaps he sees it not, or his good nature
Prizes the virtue that appears in Cassio
And looks not on his evils. Is not this true?              120

*Enter Roderigo.*

IAGO [*aside to him*]:   How now, Roderigo?
I pray you, after the Lieutenant; go.          [*Exit Roderigo.*]
MONTANO:   And 'tis great pity that the noble Moor
Should hazard such a place as his own second
With° one of an engraffed° infirmity.                             125
It were an honest action to say so
To the Moor.
IAGO:                    Not I, for this fair island.
I do love Cassio well and would do much
To cure him of this evil.          . [*Cry within:* "Help! Help!"]
But, hark! What noise?

*Enter Cassio, pursuing° Roderigo.*

CASSIO:   Zounds, you rogue! You rascal!                    130
MONTANO:   What's the matter, Lieutenant?
CASSIO:   A knave teach me my duty? I'll beat the knave into a
twiggen° bottle.
RODERIGO:   Beat me?
CASSIO:   Dost thou prate, rogue? [*He strikes Roderigo.*]     135

---

115 watch . . . set stay awake twice around the clock or *horologe*     124–125 hazard . . . With risk
giving such an important position as his second in command to     125 engraffed engrafted, inveterate
129 [s.d.] pursuing (The Quarto text reads, "driving in.")     133 twiggen wicker-covered. (Cassio
vows to assail Roderigo until his skin resembles wickerwork or until he has driven Roderigo through
the holes in a wickerwork.)

**MONTANO:** Nay, good Lieutenant. [*Restraining him.*] I pray
    you, sir, hold your hand.
**CASSIO:** Let me go, sir, or I'll knock you o'er the mazard.°
**MONTANO:** Come, come, you're drunk.
**CASSIO:**                   Drunk?            [*They fight.*]
**IAGO** [*aside to Roderigo*]:   Away, I say. Go out and cry a
    mutiny.°                                      140

                       [*Exit Roderigo.*]

    Nay, good Lieutenant—God's will, gentlemen—
    Help, ho!—Lieutenant—sir—Montano—sir—
    Help, masters!°—Here's a goodly watch indeed!

    [*A bell rings.*]°

    Who's that which rings the bell?—Diablo,° ho!
    The town will rise.° God's will, Lieutenant, hold!         145
    You'll be ashamed forever.

    *Enter Othello and attendants* [*with weapons*].

**OTHELLO:** What is the matter here?
**MONTANO:**                       Zounds, I bleed still.
    I am hurt to th' death. He dies! [*He thrusts at Cassio.*]
**OTHELLO:**                  Hold, for your lives!
**IAGO:** Hold, ho! Lieutenant—sir—Montano—gentlemen—
    Have you forgot all sense of place and duty?           150
    Hold! The General speaks to you. Hold, for shame!
**OTHELLO:** Why, how now, ho! From whence ariseth this?
    Are we turned Turks, and to ourselves do that
    Which heaven hath forbid the Ottomites?°
    For Christian shame, put by this barbarous brawl!      155
    He that stirs next to carve for° his own rage
    Holds his soul light;° he dies upon his motion.°
    Silence that dreadful bell. It frights the isle

---

**138 mazard** i.e., head (Literally, a drinking vessel.)   **140 mutiny** riot   **143 masters** sirs   **[s.d.]
A bell rings** (This direction is from the Quarto, as are *Exit Roderigo* at line 122, *They fight* at line
139, and *with weapons* at line 146.)   **144 Diablo** the devil   **145 rise** grow riotous   **153–154 to
ourselves . . . Ottomites** inflict on ourselves the harm that heaven has prevented the Turks from
doing (by destroying their fleet)   **156 carve for** i.e., indulge, satisfy with his sword   **157 Holds . . .
light** i.e., places little value on his life   **upon his motion** if he moves

From her propriety.° What is the matter, masters?
Honest Iago, that looks dead with grieving,                     *160*
Speak. Who began this? On thy love, I charge thee.
**IAGO:**  I do not know. Friends all but now, even now,
In quarter° and in terms° like bride and groom
Devesting them° for bed; and then, but now—
As if some planet had unwitted men—                             *165*
Swords out, and tilting one at others' breasts
In opposition bloody. I cannot speak°
Any beginning to this peevish odds;°
And would in action glorious I had lost
Those legs that brought me to a part of it!                     *170*
**OTHELLO:**  How comes it, Michael, you are thus forgot?°
**CASSIO:**  I pray you, pardon me. I cannot speak.
**OTHELLO:**  Worthy Montano, you were wont be° civil;
The gravity and stillness° of your youth
The world hath noted, and your name is great                    *175*
In mouths of wisest censure.° What's the matter
That you unlace° your reputation thus
And spend your rich opinion° for the name
Of a night-brawler? Give me answer to it.
**MONTANO:**  Worthy Othello, I am hurt to danger.               *180*
Your officer, Iago, can inform you—
While I spare speech, which something° now offends° me—
Of all that I do know; nor know I aught
By me that's said or done amiss this night,
Unless self-charity be sometimes a vice,                        *185*
And to defend ourselves it be a sin
When violence assails us.
**OTHELLO:**                    Now, by heaven,
My blood° begins my safer guides° to rule,
And passion, having my best judgment collied,°

---

**159 propriety** proper state or condition   **163 In quarter** in friendly conduct, within bounds   **in terms** on good terms   **164 Devesting them** undressing themselves   **167 speak** explain   **168 peevish odds** childish quarrel   **171 are thus forgot** have forgotten yourself thus   **173 wont be** accustomed to be   **174 stillness** sobriety   **176 censure** judgment   **177 unlace** undo, lay open (as one might loose the strings of a purse containing reputation)   **178 opinion** reputation   **182 something** somewhat   **offends** pains   **188 blood** passion (of anger)   **guides** i.e., reason   **189 collied** darkened

Essays° to lead the way. Zounds, if I stir,                                   190
Or do but lift this arm, the best of you
Shall sink in my rebuke. Give me to know
How this foul rout° began, who set it on;
And he that is approved in° this offense,
Though he had twinned with me, both at a birth,                               195
Shall lose me. What? In a town of° war
Yet wild, the people's hearts brim full of fear,
To manage° private and domestic quarrel?
In night, and on the court and guard of safety?°
'Tis monstrous. Iago, who began 't?                                           200
MONTANO [*to Iago*]:   If partially affined,° or leagued in office,°
Thou dost deliver more or less than truth,
Thou art no soldier.
IAGO:                    Touch me not so near.
I had rather have this tongue cut from my mouth
Than it should do offense to Michael Cassio;                                  205
Yet, I persuade myself, to speak the truth
Shall nothing wrong him. Thus it is, General.
Montano and myself being in speech,
There comes a fellow crying out for help,
And Cassio following him with determined sword                                210
To execute° upon him. Sir, this gentleman

[*indicating Montano*]

Steps in to Cassio and entreats his pause.°
Myself the crying fellow did pursue,
Lest by his clamor—as it so fell out—
The town might fall in fright. He, swift of foot,                             215
Outran my purpose, and I returned, the rather°
For that I heard the clink and fall of swords
And Cassio high in oath, which till tonight
I ne'er might say before. When I came back—

---

**190 Essays** undertakes    **193 rout** riot    **194 approved in** found guilty of    **196 town of** town garrisoned for    **198 manage** undertake    **199 on . . . safety** at the main guardhouse or headquarters and on watch    **201 partially affined** made partial by some personal relationship    **leagued in office** in league as fellow officers    **211 execute** give effect to (his anger)    **212 his pause** him to stop    **216 rather** sooner

For this was brief—I found them close together                    *220*
At blow and thrust, even as again they were
When you yourself did part them.
More of this matter cannot I report.
But men are men; the best sometimes forget.°
Though Cassio did some little wrong to him,                         *225*
As men in rage strike those that wish them best,°
Yet surely Cassio, I believe, received
From him that fled some strange indignity,
Which patience could not pass.°
OTHELLO:                             I know, Iago,
Thy honesty and love doth mince this matter,                       *230*
Making it light to Cassio. Cassio, I love thee,
But nevermore be officer of mine.

*Enter Desdemona, attended.*

Look if my gentle love be not raised up.
I'll make thee an example.
DESDEMONA: What is the matter, dear?
OTHELLO:                             All's well now,                *235*
sweeting;
Come away to bed. [*To Montano.*] Sir, for your hurts,
Myself will be your surgeon.°—Lead him off.

[*Montano is led off.*]

Iago, look with care about the town
And silence those whom this vile brawl distracted.
Come, Desdemona. 'Tis the soldiers' life                           *240*
To have their balmy slumbers waked with strife.

                    *Exit* [*with all but Iago and Cassio*].

IAGO:   What, are you hurt, Lieutenant?
CASSIO:   Ay, past all surgery.
IAGO:   Marry, God forbid!

---

**224 forget** forget themselves    **226 those . . . best** i.e., even those who are well disposed    **229 pass**
pass over, overlook    **237 be your surgeon** i.e., make sure you receive medical attention

**CASSIO:**  Reputation, reputation, reputation! O, I have lost my     245
reputation! I have lost the immortal part of myself, and
what remains is bestial. My reputation, Iago, my reputation!

**IAGO:**  As I am an honest man, I thought you had received some
bodily wound; there is more sense in that than in reputation.
Reputation is an idle and most false imposition,° oft got     250
without merit and lost without deserving. You have lost no
reputation at all, unless you repute yourself such a loser.
What, man, there are more ways to recover° the General
again. You are but now cast in his mood°—a punishment
more in policy° than in malice, even so as one would beat his     255
offenseless dog to affright an imperious lion.° Sue° to him
again and he's yours.

**CASSIO:**  I will rather sue to be despised than to deceive so good
a commander with so slight,° so drunken, and so indiscreet
an officer. Drunk? And speak parrot?° And squabble? Swag-     260
ger? Swear? And discourse fustian with one's own shadow?
O thou invisible spirit of wine, if thou hast no name to be
known by, let us call thee devil!

**IAGO:**  What was he that you followed with your sword? What
had he done to you?     265

**CASSIO:**  I know not.

**IAGO:**  Is 't possible?

**CASSIO:**  I remember a mass of things, but nothing distinctly; a
quarrel, but nothing wherefore.° O God, that men should
put an enemy in their mouths to steal away their brains!     270
That we should, with joy, pleasance, revel, and applause°
transform ourselves into beasts!

**IAGO:**  Why, but you are now well enough. How came you thus
recovered?

**CASSIO:**  It hath pleased the devil drunkenness to give place to     275
the devil wrath. One unperfectness shows me another, to
make me frankly despise myself.

---

**250 false imposition** thing artificially imposed and of no real value     **253 recover** regain favour with
**254 cast in his mood** dismissed in a moment of anger     **255 in policy** done for expediency's sake
and as a public gesture     **255–256 would . . . lion** i.e., would make an example of a minor offender
in order to deter more important and dangerous offenders     **256 Sue** petition     **259 slight** worthless
**260 speak parrot** talk nonsense, rant     **269 wherefore** why     **271 applause** desire for applause

**IAGO:** Come, you are too severe a moraler.° As the time, the place, and the condition of this country stands, I could heartily wish this had not befallen; but since it is as it is, mend it for your own good.      *280*

**CASSIO:** I will ask him for my place again; he shall tell me I am a drunkard. Had I as many mouths as Hydra,° such an answer would stop them all. To be now a sensible man, by and by a fool, and presently a beast! O, strange! Every inordinate cup is unblessed, and the ingredient is a devil.      *285*

**IAGO:** Come, come, good wine is a good familiar creature, if it be well used. Exclaim no more against it. And, good Lieutenant, I think you think I love you.

**CASSIO:** I have well approved° it, sir. I drunk!      *290*

**IAGO:** You or any man living may be drunk at a time,° man. I'll tell you what you shall do. Our general's wife is now the general—I may say so in this respect, for that° he hath devoted and given up himself to the contemplation, mark, and denotement° of her parts° and graces. Confess yourself freely to her;      *295* importune her help to put you in your place again. She is of so free,° so kind, so apt, so blessed a disposition, she holds it a vice in her goodness not to do more than she is requested. This broken joint between you and her husband entreat her to splinter;° and, my fortunes against any lay° worth naming,      *300* this crack of your love shall grow stronger than it was before.

**CASSIO:** You advise me well.

**IAGO:** I protest,° in the sincerity of love and honest kindness.

**CASSIO:** I think it freely;° and betimes in the morning I will beseech the virtuous Desdemona to undertake for me. I am      *305* desperate of my fortunes if they check° me here.

**IAGO:** You are in the right. Good night, Lieutenant. I must to the watch.

**CASSIO:** Good night, honest Iago.      *Exit Cassio.*

**IAGO:** And what's he then that says I play the villain,      *310*

---

**278 moraler** moralizer    **282 Hydra** the Lernaean Hydra, a monster with many heads and the ability to grow two heads when one was cut off, slain by Hercules as the second of his twelve labours
**290 approved** proved    **291 at a time** at one time or another    **293 in . . . that** in view of this fact, that    **294–295 mark, and denotement** (Both words mean "observation.")    **295 parts** qualities
**297 free** generous    **300 splinter** bind with splints    **lay** stake, wager    **303 protest** insist, declare
**304 freely** unreservedly    **306 check** repulse

When this advice is free° I give, and honest,
Probal° to thinking, and indeed the course
To win the Moor again? For 'tis most easy
Th' inclining° Desdemona to subdue°
In any honest suit; she's framed as fruitful°                    *315*
As the free elements.° And then for her
To win the Moor—were 't to renounce his baptism,
All seals and symbols of redeemèd sin—
His soul is so enfettered to her love
That she may make, unmake, do what she list,               *320*
Even as her appetite° shall play the god
With his weak function.° How am I then a villain,
To counsel Cassio to this parallel° course
Directly to his good? Divinity of hell!°
When devils will the blackest sins put on,°                  *325*
They do suggest° at first with heavenly shows,
As I do now. For whiles this honest fool
Plies Desdemona to repair his fortune,
And she for him pleads strongly to the Moor,
I'll pour this pestilence into his ear,                        *330*
That she repeals him° for her body's lust;
And by how much she strives to do him good,
She shall undo her credit with the Moor.
So will I turn her virtue into pitch,°
And out of her own goodness make the net                    *335*
That shall enmesh them all.

*Enter Roderigo.*

How now, Roderigo?

**RODERIGO:**   I do follow here in the chase, not like a hound that
hunts, but one that fills up the cry.° My money is almost

---

**311 free** (1) free from guile (2) freely given    **312 Probal** probable, reasonable    **314 inclining**
favourably disposed    **subdue** persuade    **315 framed as fruitful** created as generous    **316 free
elements** i.e., earth, air, fire, and water, unrestrained and spontaneous    **321 her appetite** her
desire, or, perhaps, his desire for her    **322 function** exercise of faculties (weakened by his fondness
for her)    **323 parallel** corresponding to these facts and to his best interests    **324 Divinity of hell**
inverted theology of hell (which seduces the soul to its damnation)    **325 put on** further, instigate
**326 suggest** tempt    **331 repeals him** attempts to get him restored    **334 pitch** i.e., (1) foul blackness (2) a snaring substance    **338 fills up the cry** merely takes part as one of the pack

spent; I have been tonight exceedingly well cudgeled; and I
think the issue will be I shall have so much° experience for        340
my pains, and so, with no money at all and a little more wit,
return again to Venice.

IAGO:  How poor are they that have not patience!
       What wound did ever heal but by degrees?
       Thou know'st we work by wit, and not by witchcraft,          345
       And wit depends on dilatory time.
       Does 't not go well? Cassio hath beaten thee,
       And thou, by that small hurt, hast cashiered° Cassio.
       Though other things grow fair against the sun,
       Yet fruits that blossom first will first be ripe.°            350
       Content thyself awhile. By the Mass, 'tis morning!
       Pleasure and action make the hours seem short.
       Retire thee; go where thou art billeted.
       Away, I say! Thou shalt know more hereafter.
       Nay, get thee gone.                     *Exit Roderigo.*
                         Two things are to be done.                  355
       My wife must move° for Cassio to her mistress;
       I'll set her on;
       Myself the while to draw the Moor apart
       And bring him jump° when he may Cassio find
       Soliciting his wife. Ay, that's the way.                      360
       Dull not device° by coldness° and delay.         *Exit.*

# ACT III

## SCENE I [BEFORE THE CHAMBER OF OTHELLO AND DESDEMONA.]

*Enter Cassio [and] Musicians.*

CASSIO:  Masters, play here—I will content your pains°—
         Something that's brief, and bid "Good morrow, General."
         [*They play.*]

---

**340 so much** just so much and no more   **348 cashiered** dismissed from service   **349–350 Though
. . . ripe** i.e., plans that are well-prepared and set expeditiously in motion will soonest ripen into success   **356 move** plead   **359 jump** precisely   **361 device** plot   **coldness** lack of zeal
**1 content your pains** reward your efforts

[*Enter*] *Clown.*

CLOWN:  Why, masters, have your instruments been in Naples,
   that they speak i' the nose° thus?
A MUSICIAN:  How, sir, how?                                                5
CLOWN:  Are these, I pray you, wind instruments?
A MUSICIAN:  Ay, marry, are they, sir.
CLOWN:  O, thereby hangs a tail.
A MUSICIAN:  Whereby hangs a tale, sir?
CLOWN:  Marry, sir, by many a wind instrument° that I know.          10
   But, masters, here's money for you. [*He gives money.*] And
   the General so likes your music that he desires you, for love's
   sake,° to make no more noise with it.
A MUSICIAN:  Well, sir, we will not.
CLOWN:  If you have any music that may not° be heard, to 't          15
   again; but, as they say, to hear music the General does not
   greatly care.
A MUSICIAN:  We have none such, sir.
CLOWN:  Then put up your pipes in your bag, for I'll away.°
   Go, vanish into air, away!                    *Exeunt Musicians.*    20
CASSIO:  Dost thou hear, mine honest friend?
CLOWN:  No, I hear not your honest friend; I hear you.
CASSIO:  Prithee, keep up° thy quillets.° There's a poor piece of
   gold for thee. [*He gives money.*] If the gentle-woman that
   attends the General's wife be stirring, tell her there's one       25
   Cassio entreats her a little favor of speech.° Wilt thou do
   this?
CLOWN:  She is stirring, sir. If she will stir° hither, I shall seem°
   to notify unto her.
CASSIO:  Do, good my friend.                    *Exit Clown.*

*Enter Iago.*

---

3-4 **speak i' the nose** (1) sound nasal (2) sound like one whose nose has been attacked by syphilis
(Naples was popularly supposed to have a high incidence of venereal disease.)    **10 wind instrument**
(With a joke on flatulence. The *tail*, line 8, that hangs nearby the *wind instrument* suggests the penis.)
**12 for love's sake** (1) out of friendship and affection (2) for the sake of lovemaking in Othello's marriage    **15 may not** cannot    **19 I'll away** (Possibly a misprint, or a snatch of song?)    **23 keep up**
do not bring out, do not use    **quillets** quibbles, puns    **26 a little . . . speech** the favor of a brief
talk    **28 stir** bestir herself (with a play on *stirring*, "rousing herself from rest")    **seem** deem it
good, think fit

In happy time,° Iago.                                    30

**IAGO:** You have not been abed, then?

**CASSIO:** Why, no. The day had broke
Before we parted. I have made bold, Iago,
To send in to your wife. My suit to her
Is that she will to virtuous Desdemona          35
Procure me some access.

**IAGO:** I'll send her to you presently;
And I'll devise a means to draw the Moor
Out of the way, that your converse and business
May be more free.                                        40

**CASSIO.** I humbly thank you for 't.          *Exit* [*Iago*].
                                    I never knew
A Florentine° more kind and honest.

*Enter Emilia.*

**EMILIA:** Good morrow, good Lieutenant. I am sorry
For your displeasure;° but all will sure be well.
The General and his wife are talking of it,      45
And she speaks for you stoutly.° The Moor replies
That he you hurt is of great fame° in Cyprus
And great affinity,° and that in wholesome wisdom
He might not but refuse you; but he protests° he loves you
And needs no other suitor but his likings        50
To take the safest occasion by the front°
To bring you in again.

**CASSIO:**                     Yet I beseech you,
If you think fit, or that it may be done,
Give me advantage of some brief discourse
With Desdemon alone.

**EMILIA:**                     Pray you, come in.    55
I will bestow you where you shall have time
To speak your bosom° freely.

**CASSIO:** I am much bound to you.          [*Exeunt.*]

---

**30 In happy time** i.e., well-met    **42 Florentine** i.e., even a fellow Florentine. (Iago is a Venetian; Cassio is a Florentine.)    **44 displeasure** fall from favour    **46 stoutly** spiritedly    **47 fame** reputation, importance    **48 affinity** kindred, family connection    **49 protests** insists    **51 occasion . . . front** opportunity by the forelock    **57 bosom** inmost thoughts

## Scene II [The Citadel.]

*Enter Othello, Iago, and Gentlemen.*

**OTHELLO** [*giving letters*]:   These letters give, Iago, to the pilot,
  And by him do my duties° to the Senate.
  That done, I will be walking on the works;°
  Repair° there to me.
**IAGO:**                                  Well, my good lord, I'll do 't.
**OTHELLO:**   This fortification, gentlemen, shall we see 't?                    5
**GENTLEMEN:**   We'll wait upon° your lordship.                    *Exeunt.*

## Scene III [The Garden of the Citadel.]

*Enter Desdemona, Cassio, and Emilia.*

**DESDEMONA:**   Be thou assured, good Cassio, I will do
  All my abilities in thy behalf.
**EMILIA:**   Good madam, do. I warrant it grieves my husband
  As if the cause were his.
**DESDEMONA:**   O, that's an honest fellow. Do not doubt, Cassio,                    5
  But I will have my lord and you again
  As friendly as you were.
**CASSIO:**                                  Bounteous madam,
  Whatever shall become of Michael Cassio,
  He's never anything but your true servant.
**DESDEMONA:**   I know 't. I thank you. You do love my lord;                    10
  You have known him long, and be you well assured
  He shall in strangeness° stand no farther off
  Than in a politic° distance.
**CASSIO:**                                  Ay, but, lady,
  That policy may either last so long,
  Or feed upon such nice and waterish diet,°                    15
  Or breed itself so out of circumstance,°
  That, I being absent and my place supplied,°

**2 do my duties** convey my respects   **3 works** breastworks, fortifications   **4 Repair** return, come
**6 wait upon** attend
**12 strangeness** aloofness   **13 politic** required by wise policy   **15 Or . . . diet** or sustain itself at
length upon such trivial and meagre technicalities   **16 breed . . . circumstance** continually renew
itself so out of chance events, or yield so few chances for my being pardoned   **17 supplied** filled by
another person

My general will forget my love and service.

**DESDEMONA:** Do not doubt° that. Before Emilia here
I give thee warrant° of thy place. Assure thee,                    20
If I do vow a friendship I'll perform it
To the last article. My lord shall never rest.
I'll watch him tame° and talk him out of patience;°
His bed shall seem a school, his board° a shrift;°
I'll intermingle everything he does                                25
With Cassio's suit. Therefore be merry, Cassio,
For thy solicitor° shall rather die
Than give thy cause away.°

*Enter Othello and Iago [at a distance].*

**EMILIA:** Madam, here comes my lord.

**CASSIO:** Madam, I'll take my leave.                             30

**DESDEMONA:** Why, stay, and hear me speak.

**CASSIO:** Madam, not now. I am very ill at ease,
Unfit for mine own purposes.

**DESDEMONA:** Well, do your discretion.°              *Exit Cassio.*

**IAGO:** Ha? I like not that.                                    35

**OTHELLO:** What dost thou say?

**IAGO:** Nothing, my lord; or if—I know not what.

**OTHELLO:** Was not that Cassio parted from my wife?

**IAGO:** Cassio, my lord? No, sure, I cannot think it,
That he would steal away so guiltylike,                            40
Seeing you coming.

**OTHELLO:** I do believe 'twas he.

**DESDEMONA:** How now, my lord?
I have been talking with a suitor here,
A man that languishes in your displeasure.                         45

**OTHELLO:** Who is 't you mean?

**DESDEMONA:** Why, your lieutenant, Cassio. Good my lord,
If I have any grace or power to move you,
His present reconciliation take;°

---

**19 doubt** fear   **20 warrant** guarantee   **23 watch him tame** tame him by keeping him from sleeping (A term from falconry.)   **out of patience** past his endurance   **24 board** dining table   **shrift** confessional   **27 solicitor** advocate   **28 away** up   **34 do your discretion** act according to your own discretion   **49 His . . . take** let him be reconciled to you right away

For if he be not one that truly loves you,                              50
That errs in ignorance and not in cunning,°
I have no judgment in an honest face.
I prithee, call him back.

**OTHELLO:** Went he hence now?

**DESDEMONA:** Yes, faith, so humbled                                    55
That he hath left part of his grief with me
To suffer with him. Good love, call him back.

**OTHELLO:** Not now, sweet Desdemon. Some other time.

**DESDEMONA:** But shall 't be shortly?

**OTHELLO:** The sooner, sweet, for you.                                 60

**DESDEMONA:** Shall 't be tonight at supper?

**OTHELLO:** No, not tonight.

**DESDEMONA:** Tomorrow dinner,° then?

**OTHELLO:** I shall not dine at home.
I meet the captains at the citadel.                                     65

**DESDEMONA:** Why, then, tomorrow night, or Tuesday morn,
On Tuesday noon, or night, on Wednesday morn.
I prithee, name the time, but let it not
Exceed three days. In faith, he's penitent;
And yet his trespass, in our common reason°—                            70
Save that, they say, the wars must make example
Out of her best°—is not almost° a fault
T' incur a private check.° When shall he come?
Tell me, Othello. I wonder in my soul
What you would ask me that I should deny,                               75
Or stand so mammering on.° What? Michael Cassio,
That came a-wooing with you, and so many a time,
When I have spoke of you dispraisingly,
Hath ta'en your part—to have so much to do
To bring him in!° By 'r Lady, I could do much—                          80

**OTHELLO:** Prithee, no more. Let him come when he will;
I will deny thee nothing.

---

**51 in cunning** wittingly     **63 dinner** (The noontime meal.)     **70 common reason** everyday judgments     **71–72 Save . . . best** were it not that, as the saying goes, military discipline requires making an example of the very best men (*Her* refers to wars as a singular concept.)     **72 not almost** scarcely     **73 private check** even a private reprimand     **76 mammering on** wavering about     **80 bring him in** restore him to favour

**DESDEMONA:** Why, this is not a boon.
    'Tis as I should entreat you wear your gloves,
    Or feed on nourishing dishes, or keep you warm, 85
    Or sue to you to do a peculiar° profit
    To your own person. Nay, when I have a suit
    Wherein I mean to touch° your love indeed,
    It shall be full of poise° and difficult weight,
    And fearful to be granted. 90

**OTHELLO:** I will deny thee nothing.
    Whereon,° I do beseech thee, grant me this,
    To leave me but a little to myself.

**DESDEMONA:** Shall I deny you? No. Farewell, my lord.

**OTHELLO:** Farewell, my Desdemona. I'll come to thee straight.° 95

**DESDEMONA:** Emilia, come.—Be as your fancies° teach you;
    Whate'er you be, I am obedient.         *Exit [with Emilia].*

**OTHELLO:** Excellent wretch!° Perdition catch my soul
    But I do love thee! And when I love thee not,
    Chaos is come again.° 100

**IAGO:** My noble lord—

**OTHELLO:** What dost thou say, Iago?

**IAGO:** Did Michael Cassio, when you wooed my lady,
    Know of your love?

**OTHELLO:** He did, from first to last. Why dost thou ask? 105

**IAGO:** But for a satisfaction of my thought;
    No further harm.

**OTHELLO:**             Why of thy thought, Iago?

**IAGO:** I did not think he had been acquainted with her.

**OTHELLO:** O, yes, and went between us very oft.

**IAGO:** Indeed? 110

**OTHELLO:** Indeed? Ay, indeed. Discern'st thou aught in that?
    Is he not honest?

**IAGO:** Honest, my lord?

**OTHELLO:** Honest. Ay, honest.

---

**86 peculiar** particular, personal   **88 touch** test   **89 poise** weight, heaviness; or equipoise, delicate balance involving hard choice   **92 Whereon** in return for which   **95 straight** straightway   **96 fancies** inclinations   **98 wretch** (A term of affectionate endearment.)   **99–100 And . . . again** i.e., my love for you will last forever, until the end of time when chaos will return (But with an unconscious, ironic suggestion that, if anything should induce Othello to cease loving Desdemona, the result would be chaos.)

796  •  *William Shakespeare*

**IAGO:**  My lord, for aught I know.                                           *115*

**OTHELLO:**  What dost thou think?

**IAGO:**  Think, my lord?

**OTHELLO:**  "Think, my lord?" By heaven, thou echo'st me,
  As if there were some monster in thy thought
  Too hideous to be shown. Thou dost mean something.        *120*
  I heard thee say even now, thou lik'st not that,
  When Cassio left my wife. What didst not like?
  And when I told thee he was of my counsel°
  In my whole course of wooing, thou criedst "Indeed?"
  And didst contract and purse° thy brow together          *125*
  As if thou then hadst shut up in thy brain
  Some horrible conceit.° If thou dost love me,
  Show me thy thought.

**IAGO:**  My lord, you know I love you.

**OTHELLO:**  I think thou dost;                                               *130*
  And, for° I know thou'rt full of love and honesty,
  And weigh'st thy words before thou giv'st them breath,
  Therefore these stops° of thine fright me the more;
  For such things in a false disloyal knave
  Are tricks of custom,° but in a man that's just          *135*
  They're close dilations,° working from the heart
  That passion cannot rule.°

**IAGO:**                                       For° Michael Cassio,
  I dare be sworn I think that he is honest.

**OTHELLO:**  I think so too.

**IAGO:**                          Men should be what they seem;
  Or those that be not, would they might seem none!°        *140*

**OTHELLO:**  Certain, men should be what they seem.

**IAGO:**  Why, then, I think Cassio's an honest man.

**OTHELLO:**  Nay, yet there's more in this.
  I prithee, speak to me as to thy thinkings,
  As thou dost ruminate, and give thy worst of thoughts     *145*
  The worst of words.

---

**123 of my counsel** in my confidence    **125 purse** knit    **127 conceit** fancy    **131 for** because
**133 stops** pauses    **135 of custom** customary    **136 close dilations** secret or involuntary expressions or delays    **137 That passion cannot rule** i.e., that are too passionately strong to be restrained (referring to the workings), or . . . that cannot rule its own passions (referring to the heart)
**137 For** as for    **140 none** i.e., not to be men, or not seem to be honest

**IAGO:**                           Good my lord, pardon me.

Though I am bound to every act of duty,

I am not bound to that° all slaves are free to.°

Utter my thoughts? Why, say they are vile and false,

As where's the palace whereinto foul things                    *150*

Sometimes intrude not? Who has that breast so pure

But some uncleanly apprehensions

Keep leets and law days,° and in sessions sit

With° meditations lawful?°

**OTHELLO:**   Thou dost conspire against thy friend,° Iago,      *155*

If thou but think'st him wronged and mak'st his ear

A stranger to thy thoughts.

**IAGO:**                           I do beseech you,

Though I perchance am vicious° in my guess—

As I confess it is my nature's plague

To spy into abuses, and oft my jealousy°                        *160*

Shapes faults that are not—that your wisdom then,°

From one° that so imperfectly conceits,°

Would take no notice, nor build yourself a trouble

Out of his scattering° and unsure observance.

It were not for your quiet nor your good,                       *165*

Nor for my manhood, honesty, and wisdom,

To let you know my thoughts.

**OTHELLO:**                           What dost thou mean?

**IAGO:**   Good name in man and woman, dear my lord,

Is the immediate° jewel of their souls.

Who steals my purse steals trash; 'tis something, nothing;       *170*

'Twas mine, 'tis his, and has been slave to thousands;

But he that filches from me my good name

Robs me of that which not enriches him

And makes me poor indeed.

**OTHELLO:**   By heaven, I'll know thy thoughts.                  *175*

---

**148 that** that which    **free to** free with respect to    **153 Keep leets and law days** i.e., hold court, set up their authority in one's heart (*Leets* are a kind of manor court; *law days* are the days courts sit in session, or those sessions.)    **154 With** along with    **lawful** innocent    **155 thy friend** i.e., Othello    **158 vicious** wrong    **160 jealousy** suspicious nature    **161 then** on that account    **162 one** i.e., myself, Iago    **conceits** judges, conjectures    **164 scattering** random    **169 immediate** essential, most precious

**IAGO:**   You cannot, if° my heart were in your hand,
   Nor shall not, whilst 'tis in my custody.
**OTHELLO:**   Ha?
**IAGO:**           O, beware, my lord, of jealousy.
   It is the green-eyed monster which doth mock
   The meat it feeds on.° That cuckold lives in bliss         *180*
   Who, certain of his fate, loves not his wronger;°
   But O, what damnèd minutes tells° he o'er
   Who dotes, yet doubts, suspects, yet fondly loves!
**OTHELLO:**   O misery!
**IAGO:**   Poor and content is rich, and rich enough,°         *185*
   But riches fineless° is as poor as winter
   To him that ever fears he shall be poor.
   Good God, the souls of all my tribe defend
   From jealousy!
**OTHELLO:**   Why, why is this?         *190*
   Think'st thou I'd make a life of jealousy,
   To follow still the changes of the moon
   With fresh suspicions?° No! To be once in doubt
   Is once° to be resolved.° Exchange me for a goat
   When I shall turn the business of my soul         *195*
   To such exsufflicate and blown° surmises
   Matching thy inference.° 'Tis not to make me jealous
   To say my wife is fair, feeds well, loves company,
   Is free of speech, sings, plays, and dances well;
   Where virtue is, these are more virtuous.         *200*
   Nor from mine own weak merits will I draw
   The smallest fear or doubt of her revolt,°
   For she had eyes, and chose me. No, Iago,
   I'll see before I doubt; when I doubt, prove;
   And on the proof, there is no more but this—         *205*

**176 if** even if    **179–180 doth mock . . . on** mocks and torments the heart of its victim, the man who suffers jealousy    **181 his wronger** i.e., his faithless wife (The unsuspecting cuckold is spared the misery of loving his wife only to discover she is cheating on him.)    **182 tells** counts    **185 Poor . . . enough** to be content with what little one has is the greatest wealth of all (Proverbial.)    **186 fineless** boundless    **192–193 To follow . . . suspicions** to be constantly imagining new causes for suspicion, changing incessantly like the moon    **194 once** once and for all    **resolved** free of doubt, having settled the matter    **196 exsufflicate and blown** inflated and blown up, rumoured about, or, spat out and flyblown, hence, loathsome, disgusting    **197 inference** description or allegation    **202 doubt . . . revolt** fear of her unfaithfulness

Away at once with love or jealousy.

IAGO:   I am glad of this, for now I shall have reason
To show the love and duty that I bear you
With franker spirit. Therefore, as I am bound,
Receive it from me. I speak not yet of proof.                    *210*
Look to your wife; observe her well with Cassio.
Wear your eyes thus, not° jealous nor secure.°
I would not have your free and noble nature,
Out of self-bounty,° be abused.° Look to 't.
I know our country disposition well;                              *215*
In Venice they do let God see the pranks
They dare not show their husbands; their best conscience
Is not to leave 't undone, but keep 't unknown.

OTHELLO:   Dost thou say so?

IAGO:   She did deceive her father, marrying you;                 *220*
And when she seemed to shake and fear your looks,
She loved them most.

OTHELLO:                    And so she did.

IAGO:                                Why, go to,° then!
She that, so young, could give out such a seeming,°
To seel° her father's eyes up close as oak,°
He thought 'twas witchcraft! But I am much to blame.             *225*
I humbly do beseech you of your pardon
For too much loving you.

OTHELLO:   I am bound° to thee forever.

IAGO:   I see this hath a little dashed your spirits.

OTHELLO:   Not a jot, not a jot.

IAGO:                    I' faith, I fear it has.                  *230*
I hope you will consider what is spoke
Comes from my love. But I do see you're moved.
I am to pray you not to strain my speech
To grosser issues° nor to larger reach°
Than to suspicion.                                                *235*

OTHELLO:   I will not.

---

**212 not** neither   **secure** free from uncertainty   **214 self-bounty** inherent or natural goodness and generosity   **abused** deceived   **222 go to** (An expression of impatience.)   **223 seeming** false appearance   **224 seel** blind (A term from falconry.)   **oak** (A close-grained wood.)   **228 bound** indebted (but perhaps with ironic sense of "tied.")   **234 issues** significances   **reach** meaning, scope

**IAGO:**  Should you do so, my lord,
    My speech should fall into such vile success°
    Which my thoughts aimed not. Cassio's my worthy friend.
    My lord, I see you're moved.
**OTHELLO:**                    No, not much moved.                    *240*
    I do not think but Desdemona's honest.°
**IAGO:**  Long live she so! And long live you to think so!
**OTHELLO:**  And yet, how nature erring from itself—
**IAGO:**  Ay, there's the point! As—to be bold with you—
    Not to affect° many proposèd matches                    *245*
    Of her own clime, complexion, and degree,°
    Whereto we see in all things nature tends—
    Foh! One may smell in such a will° most rank,
    Foul disproportion,° thoughts unnatural.
    But pardon me. I do not in position°                    *250*
    Distinctly speak of her, though I may fear
    Her will, recoiling° to her better° judgment,
    May fall to match you with her country forms°
    And happily° repent.
**OTHELLO:**                    Farewell, farewell!
    If more thou dost perceive, let me know more.                    *255*
    Set on thy wife to observe. Leave me, Iago.
**IAGO** [*going*]:  My lord, I take my leave.
**OTHELLO:**  Why did I marry? This honest creature doubtless
    Sees and knows more, much more, than he unfolds.
**IAGO** [*returning*]:  My Lord, I would I might entreat your honor                    *260*
    To scan° this thing no farther. Leave it to time.
    Although 'tis fit that Cassio have his place—
    For, sure, he fills it up with great ability—
    Yet, if you please to hold him off awhile,
    You shall by that perceive him and his means.°                    *265*
    Note if your lady strain his entertainment°
    With any strong or vehement importunity;

---

**238 success** effect, result    **241 honest** chaste    **245 affect** prefer, desire    **246 clime . . . degree** country, colour, and social position    **248 will** sensuality, appetite    **249 disproportion** abnormality    **250 position** argument, proposition    **252 recoiling** reverting    **better** i.e., more natural and reconsidered    **253 fall . . . forms** undertake to compare you with Venetian norms of handsomeness    **254 happily repent** perhaps repent her marriage    **261 scan** scrutinize    **265 his means** the method he uses (to regain his post)    **266 strain his entertainment** urge his reinstatement

Much will be seen in that. In the meantime,
Let me be thought too busy° in my fears—
As worthy cause I have to fear I am—                                   *270*
And hold her free,° I do beseech your honor.
**OTHELLO:**   Fear not my government.°
**IAGO:**   I once more take my leave.                          *Exit.*
**OTHELLO:**   This fellow's of exceeding honesty,
And knows all qualities,° with a learnèd spirit,                      *275*
Of human dealings. If I do prove her haggard,°
Though that her jesses° were my dear heartstrings,
I'd whistle her off and let her down the wind°
To prey at fortune.° Haply, for° I am black
And have not those soft parts of conversation°                        *280*
That chamberers° have, or for I am declined
Into the vale of years—yet that's not much—
She's gone. I am abused,° and my relief
Must be to loathe her. O curse of marriage,
That we can call these delicate creatures ours                        *285*
And not their appetites! I had rather be a toad
And live upon the vapor of a dungeon
Than keep a corner in the thing I love
For others' uses. Yet, 'tis the plague of great ones;
Prerogatived° are they less than the base.°                          *290*
'Tis destiny unshunnable, like death.
Even then this forkèd° plague is fated to us
When we do quicken.° Look where she comes.

*Enter Desdemona and Emilia.*

If she be false, O, then heaven mocks itself!
I'll not believe 't.

---

**269 busy** interfering   **271 hold her free** regard her as innocent   **272 government** self-control,
conduct   **275 qualities** natures, types   **276 haggard** wild (like a wild female hawk)   **277 jesses**
straps fastened around the legs of a trained hawk   **278 I'd . . . wind** i.e., I'd let her go forever (To
release a hawk downwind was to invite it not to return.)   **279 prey at fortune** fend for herself in the
wild   **Haply, for** perhaps because   **280 soft . . . conversation** pleasing graces of social behaviour
**281 chamberers** gallants   **283 abused** deceived   **290 Prerogatived** privileged (to have honest
wives.)   **the base** ordinary citizens (Socially prominent men are especially prone to the unavoidable
destiny of being cuckolded and to the public shame that goes with it.)   **292 forkèd** (An allusion to
the horns of the cuckold.)   **293 quicken** receive life (Quicken may also mean to swarm with maggots as the body festers, as in Act IV, Scene ii, line 69, in which case lines 292–293 suggest that *even
then*, in death, we are cuckolded by *forkèd* worms.)

**DESDEMONA:**     How now, my dear Othello?                    *295*
   Your dinner, and the generous° islanders
   By you invited, do attend° your presence.
**OTHELLO:**   I am to blame.
**DESDEMONA:**               Why do you speak so faintly?
   Are you not well?
**OTHELLO:**   I have a pain upon my forehead here.           *300*
**DESDEMONA:**   Faith, that's with watching.° 'Twill away again.

[*She offers her handkerchief.*]

   Let me but bind it hard, within this hour
   It will be well.
**OTHELLO:**         Your napkin° is too little.
   Let it alone.° Come, I'll go in with you.

[*He puts the handkerchief from him, and it drops.*]

**DESDEMONA:**   I am very sorry that you are not well.        *305*

                          *Exit* [*with Othello*].

**EMILIA** [*picking up the handkerchief*]:   I am glad I have found
   this napkin.
   This was her first remembrance from the Moor.
   My wayward° husband hath a hundred times
   Wooed me to steal it, but she so loves the token—
   For he conjured her she should ever keep it—          *310*
   That she reserves it evermore about her
   To kiss and talk to. I'll have the work ta'en out,°
   And give 't Iago. What he will do with it
   Heaven knows, not I;
   I nothing but to please his fantasy.°                  *315*

   *Enter Iago.*

**IAGO:**   How now? What do you here alone?
**EMILIA:**   Do not you chide. I have a thing for you.

---

**296 generous** noble    **297 attend** await    **301 watching** too little sleep    **303 napkin** handkerchief
**304 Let it alone** i.e., never mind    **308 wayward** capricious    **312 work ta'en out** design of the
embroidery copied    **315 fantasy** whim

IAGO:   You have a thing for me? It is a common thing°—

EMILIA:   Ha?

IAGO:   To have a foolish wife.                                              *320*

EMILIA:   O, is that all? What will you give me now
For that same handkerchief?

IAGO:   What handkerchief?

EMILIA:   What handkerchief?
Why, that the Moor first gave to Desdemona;                                 *325*
That which so often you did bid me steal.

IAGO:   Hast stolen it from her?

EMILIA:   No, faith. She let it drop by negligence,
And to th' advantage° I, being here, took 't up.
Look, here 'tis.

IAGO:                          A good wench! Give it me.                     *330*

EMILIA:   What will you do with 't, that you have been so
earnest
To have me filch it?

IAGO [*snatching it*]:   Why, what is that to you?

EMILIA:   If it be not for some purpose of import,
Give 't me again. Poor lady, she'll run mad
When she shall lack° it.

IAGO:                          Be not acknown on 't.°                       *335*
I have use for it. Go, leave me.                *Exit Emilia.*
I will in Cassio's lodging lose° this napkin
And let him find it. Trifles light as air
Are to the jealous confirmations strong
As proofs of Holy Writ. This may do something.                             *340*
The Moor already changes with my poison.
Dangerous conceits° are in their natures poisons,
Which at the first are scarce found to distaste,°
But with a little act° upon the blood
Burn like the mines of sulfur.

*Enter Othello.*

---

**318 common thing** (With bawdy suggestion; *common* suggests coarseness and availability to all comers, and *thing* is a slang term for the pudendum.)   **329 to th' advantage** taking the opportunity
**335 lack** miss   **Be . . . on't** do not confess knowledge of it   **337 lose** (The Folio spelling, *loose*, is a normal spelling for "lose," but it may also contain the idea of "let go," "release.")   **342 conceits** fancies, ideas   **343 distaste** be distasteful   **344 act** action, working

I did say so.                                345
Look where he comes! Not poppy nor mandragora°
Nor all the drowsy syrups of the world
Shall ever medicine thee to that sweet sleep
Which thou owedst° yesterday.

**OTHELLO:**                    Ha, ha, false to me?

**IAGO:**  Why, how now, General? No more of that.          350

**OTHELLO:**  Avaunt! Begone! Thou hast set me on the rack.
I swear 'tis better to be much abused
Than but to know 't a little.

**IAGO:**                    How now, my lord?

**OTHELLO:**  What sense had I of her stolen hours of lust?
I saw 't not, thought it not, it harmed not me.          355
I slept the next night well, fed well, was free° and merry;
I found not Cassio's kisses on her lips.
He that is robbed, not wanting° what is stolen,
Let him not know 't and he's not robbed at all.

**IAGO:**  I am sorry to hear this.                     360

**OTHELLO:**  I had been happy if the general camp,
Pioners° and all, had tasted her sweet body,
So° I had nothing known. O, now, forever
Farewell the tranquil mind! Farewell content!
Farewell the plumèd troops and the big° wars          365
That makes ambition virtue! O, farewell!
Farewell the neighing steed and the shrill trump,
The spirit-stirring drum, th' ear-piercing fife,
The royal banner, and all quality,°
Pride,° pomp, and circumstance° of glorious war!          370
And O, you mortal engines,° whose rude throats
Th' immortal Jove's dread clamors° counterfeit,
Farewell! Othello's occupation's gone.

**IAGO:**  Is 't possible, my lord?

**OTHELLO:**  Villain, be sure thou prove my love a whore!          375

---

346 **mandragora** an opiate made of the mandrake root    349 **thou owedst** you did own    356 **free** carefree    358 **wanting** missing    362 **Pioners** diggers of mines, the lowest grade of soldiers    363 **So** provided    365 **big** stately    369 **quality** character, essential nature    370 **Pride** rich display    **circumstance** pageantry    371 **mortal engines** i.e., cannon. (*Mortal* means "deadly.")    372 **Jove's dread clamors** i.e., thunder

Be sure of it. Give me the ocular proof,
Or, by the worth of mine eternal soul,
Thou hadst been better have been born a dog
Than answer my waked wrath!

**IAGO:** Is 't come to this?

**OTHELLO:** Make me to see 't, or at the least so prove it     380
That the probation° bear no hinge nor loop
To hang a doubt on, or woe upon thy life!

**IAGO:** My noble lord—

**OTHELLO:** If thou dost slander her and torture me,
Never pray more; abandon all remorse;°     385
On horror's head horrors accumulate;°
Do deeds to make heaven weep, all earth amazed;°
For nothing canst thou to damnation add
Greater than that.

**IAGO:** O grace! O heaven forgive me!
Are you a man? Have you a soul or sense?     390
God b' wi' you; take mine office. O wretched fool,°
That lov'st to make thine honesty a vice!°
O monstrous world! Take note, take note, O world,
To be direct and honest is not safe.
I thank you for this profit,° and from hence°     395
I'll love no friend, sith° love breeds such offense.°

**OTHELLO:** Nay, stay. Thou shouldst be° honest.

**IAGO:** I should be wise, for honesty's a fool
And loses that° it works for.

**OTHELLO:** By the world,
I think my wife be honest and think she is not;     400
I think that thou art just and think thou art not.
I'll have some proof. My name, that was as fresh
As Dian's° visage, is now begrimed and black
As mine own face. If there be cords, or knives,
Poison, or fire, or suffocating streams,     405

---

**381 probation** proof   **385 remorse** pity, penitent hope for salvation   **386 horrors accumulate**
add still more horrors   **387 amazed** confounded with horror   **391 O wretched fool** (Iago addresses
himself as a fool for having carried honesty too far.)   **392 vice** failing, something overdone
**395 profit** profitable instruction   **hence** henceforth   **396 sith** since   **offense** i.e., harm to the one
who offers help and friendship   **397 Thou shouldst be** it appears that you are (But Iago replies in
the sense of "ought to be.")   **399 that** what   **403 Dian** Diana, goddess of the moon and of chastity

I'll not endure it. Would I were satisfied!

IAGO:  I see, sir, you are eaten up with passion.

I do repent me that I put it to you.

You would be satisfied?

OTHELLO:                    Would? Nay, and I will.

IAGO:  And may; but how? How satisfied, my lord?                    410

Would you, the supervisor,° grossly gape on?

Behold her topped?

OTHELLO:                    Death and damnation! O!

IAGO:  It were a tedious difficulty, I think,

To bring them to that prospect. Damn them then,°

If ever mortal eyes do see them bolster°                    415

More° than their own.° What then? How then?

What shall I say? Where's satisfaction?

It is impossible you should see this,

Were they as prime° as goats, as hot as monkeys,

As salt° as wolves in pride,° and fools as gross                    420

As ignorance made drunk. But yet I say,

If imputation and strong circumstances°

Which lead directly to the door of truth

Will give you satisfaction, you might have 't.

OTHELLO:  Give me a living reason she's disloyal.                    425

IAGO:  I do not like the office.

But sith° I am entered in this cause so far,

Pricked° to 't by foolish honesty and love,

I will go on. I lay with Cassio lately,

And being troubled with a raging tooth                    430

I could not sleep. There are a kind of men

So loose of soul that in their sleeps will mutter

Their affairs. One of this kind is Cassio.

In sleep I heard him say, "Sweet Desdemona,

Let us be wary, let us hide our loves!"                    435

And then, sir, would he grip and wring my hand,

Cry "O sweet creature!", then kiss me hard,

---

**411 supervisor** onlooker    **414 Damn them then** i.e., they would have to be really incorrigible
**415 bolster** go to bed together, share a bolster    **416 More** other    **own** own eyes    **419 prime**
lustful    **420 salt** wanton, sensual    **pride** heat    **422 imputation . . . circumstances** strong cir-
cumstantial evidence    **427 sith** since    **428 Pricked** spurred

As if he plucked up kisses by the roots
That grew upon my lips; then laid his leg
Over my thigh, and sighed, and kissed, and then          *440*
Cried, "Cursèd fate that gave thee to the Moor!"

**OTHELLO:** O monstrous! Monstrous!

**IAGO:**                       Nay, this was but his
dream.

**OTHELLO:** But this denoted a foregone conclusion.°
'Tis a shrewd doubt,° though it be but a dream.

**IAGO:** And this may help to thicken other proofs          *445*
That do demonstrate thinly.

**OTHELLO:**               I'll tear her all to pieces.

**IAGO:** Nay, but be wise. Yet we see nothing done;
She may be honest yet. Tell me but this:
Have you not sometimes seen a handkerchief
Spotted with strawberries° in your wife's hand?          *450*

**OTHELLO:** I gave her such a one. 'Twas my first gift.

Iago: I know not that; but such a handkerchief—
I am sure it was your wife's—did I today
See Cassio wipe his beard with.

**OTHELLO:**              If it be that—

**IAGO:** If it be that, or any that was hers,          *455*
It speaks against her with the other proofs.

**OTHELLO:** O, that the slave° had forty thousand lives!
One is too poor, too weak for my revenge.
Now do I see 'tis true. Look here, Iago,
All my fond° love thus do I blow to heaven.          *460*
'Tis gone.
Arise, black vengeance, from the hollow hell!
Yield up, O love, thy crown and hearted° throne
To tyrannous hate! Swell, bosom, with thy freight,°
For 'tis of aspics'° tongues!          *465*

**IAGO:** Yet be content.°

**OTHELLO:** O, blood, blood, blood!

---

**443 foregone conclusion** concluded experience or action    **444 shrewd doubt** suspicious circumstance    **450 Spotted with strawberries** embroidered with a strawberry pattern    **457 the slave** i.e., Cassio    **460 fond** foolish (but also suggesting "affectionate")    **463 hearted** fixed in the heart    **464 freight** burden    **465 aspics'** venomous serpents'    **466 content** calm

**IAGO:**   Patience, I say. Your mind perhaps may change.

**OTHELLO:**   Never, Iago. Like to the Pontic Sea,° 

Whose icy current and compulsive course          470

Ne'er feels retiring ebb, but keeps due on

To the Propontic° and the Hellespont,°

Even so my bloody thoughts with violent pace

Shall ne'er look back, ne'er ebb to humble love,

I that a capable° and wide revenge          475

Swallow them up. Now, by yond marble° heaven,

[*Kneeling*] In the due reverence of a sacred vow

I here engage my words.

**IAGO:**                              Do not rise yet.

[*He kneels.*]° Witness, you ever-burning lights above,

You elements that clip° us round about,          480

Witness that here Iago doth give up

The execution° of his wit,° hands, heart,

To wronged Othello's service. Let him command,

And to obey shall be in me remorse,°

What bloody business ever.° [*They rise.*]

**OTHELLO:**                              I greet thy love,          485

Not with vain thanks, but with acceptance bounteous,

And will upon the instant put thee to 't.°

Within these three days let me hear thee say

That Cassio's not alive.

**IAGO:**                              My friend is dead;

'Tis done at your request. But let her live.          490

**OTHELLO:**   Damn her, lewd minx!° O, damn her, damn her!

Come, go with me apart. I will withdraw

To furnish me with some swift means of death

For the fair devil. Now art thou my lieutenant.

**IAGO:**   I am your own forever.                    *Exeunt.*          495

---

**469 Pontic Sea** Black Sea    **472 Propontic** Sea of Marmara, between the Black Sea and the Aegean **Hellespont** Dardanelles, straits where the Sea of Marmara joins with the Aegean    **475 capable** ample, comprehensive    **476 marble** i.e., gleaming like marble and unrelenting    **479 [s.d.] He kneels** (In the Quarto text, Iago kneels here after Othello has knelt at line 477.)    **480 clip** encompass    **482 execution** exercise, action    **wit** mind    **484 remorse** pity (for Othello's wrongs) **485 ever** soever    **487 to 't** to the proof    **491 minx** wanton

## Scene IV [Before the Citadel.]

*Enter Desdemona, Emilia, and Clown.*

DESDEMONA:  Do you know, sirrah,° where Lieutenant Cassio
lies?°

CLOWN:  I dare not say he lies anywhere.

DESDEMONA:  Why, man?

CLOWN:  He's a soldier, and for me to say a soldier lies, 'tis
stabbing.

DESDEMONA:  Go to. Where lodges he?                                           5

CLOWN:  To tell you where he lodges is to tell you where I lie.

DESDEMONA:  Can anything be made of this?

CLOWN:  I know not where he lodges, and for me to devise a
lodging and say he lies here, or he lies there, were to lie in
mine own throat.°                                                             10

DESDEMONA:  Can you inquire him out, and be edified by report?

CLOWN:  I will catechize the world for him; that is, make questions, and by them answer.

DESDEMONA:  Seek him, bid him come hither. Tell him I have
moved° my lord on his behalf and hope all will be well.                       15

CLOWN:  To do this is within the compass of man's wit, and
therefore I will attempt the doing it.                    *Exit Clown.*

DESDEMONA:  Where should I lose that handkerchief, Emilia?

EMILIA:  I know not, madam.

DESDEMONA:  Believe me, I had rather have lost my purse           20
Full of crusadoes;° and but my noble Moor
Is true of mind and made of no such baseness
As jealous creatures are, it were enough
To put him to ill thinking.

EMILIA:                              Is he not jealous?

DESDEMONA:  Who, he? I think the sun where he was born           25
Drew all such humors° from him.

EMILIA:                              Look where he comes.

---

**1 sirrah** (A form of address to an inferior.)    **lies** lodges (But the Clown makes the obvious pun.)
**9–10 lie . . . throat** (1) lie egregiously and deliberately (2) use the windpipe to speak a lie
**15 moved** petitioned    **21 crusadoes** Portuguese gold coins    **26 humors** (Refers to the four bodily
fluids thought to determine temperament.)

*Enter Othello.*

**DESDEMONA:**  I will not leave him now till Cassio
Be called to him.—How is 't with you, my lord?
**OTHELLO:**  Well, my good lady. [*Aside.*] O, hardness to
dissemble!—
How do you, Desdemona?
**DESDEMONA:**                    Well, my good lord.                    30
**OTHELLO:**  Give me your hand. [*She gives her hand.*] This hand is
moist, my lady.
**DESDEMONA:**  It yet hath felt no age nor known no sorrow.
**OTHELLO:**  This argues° fruitfulness° and liberal° heart.
Hot, hot, and moist. This hand of yours requires                    35
A sequester° from liberty, fasting and prayer,
Much castigation,° exercise devout;°
For here's a young and sweating devil here
That commonly rebels. 'Tis a good hand,
A frank° one.
**DESDEMONA:**      You may indeed say so,                    40
For 'twas that hand that gave away my heart.
**OTHELLO:**  A liberal hand. The hearts of old gave hands,°
But our new heraldry is hands, not hearts.°
**DESDEMONA:**  I cannot speak of this. Come now, your
promise.
**OTHELLO:**  What promise, chuck?°                    45
**DESDEMONA:**  I have sent to bid Cassio come speak with you.
**OTHELLO:**  I have a salt and sorry rheum° offends me;
Lend me thy handkerchief.
**DESDEMONA:**  Here, my lord. [*She offers a handkerchief.*]
**OTHELLO:**  That which I gave you.
**DESDEMONA:**                    I have it not about me.                    50
**OTHELLO:**  Not?

---

**34 argues** gives evidence of   **fruitfulness** generosity, amorousness, and fecundity   **liberal** generous and sexually free   **36 sequester** separation, sequestration   **37 castigation** corrective discipline   **exercise devout** i.e., prayer, religious meditation, etc.   **40 frank** generous, open (with sexual
suggestion)   **42 The hearts . . . hands** i.e., in former times, people would give their hearts when
they gave their hands to something   **43 But . . . hearts** i.e., in our decadent times, the joining of
hands is no longer a badge to signify the giving of hearts   **45 chuck** (A term of endearment.)
**47 salt . . . rheum** distressful head cold or watering of the eyes

**DESDEMONA:** No, faith, my lord.

**OTHELLO:** That's a fault. That handkerchief
Did an Egyptian to my mother give.
She was a charmer,° and could almost read          *55*
The thoughts of people. She told her, while she kept it
'Twould make her amiable° and subdue my father
Entirely to her love, but if she lost it
Or made a gift of it, my father's eye
Should hold her loathèd and his spirits should hunt          *60*
After new fancies.° She, dying, gave it me,
And bid me, when my fate would have me wived,
To give it her.° I did so; and take heed on 't;
Make it a darling like your precious eye.
To lose 't or give 't away were such perdition°          *65*
As nothing else could match.

**DESDEMONA:**                    Is 't possible?

**OTHELLO:** 'Tis true. There's magic in the web° of it.
A sibyl, that had numbered in the world
The sun to course two hundred compasses,°
In her prophetic fury° sewed the work;°          *70*
The worms were hallowed that did breed the silk,
And it was dyed in mummy° which the skillful
Conserved of° maidens' hearts.

**DESDEMONA:**                    I' faith! Is 't true?

**OTHELLO:** Most veritable. Therefore look to 't well.

**DESDEMONA:** Then would to God that I had never seen 't!          *75*

**OTHELLO:** Ha? Wherefore?

**DESDEMONA:** Why do you speak so startingly and rash?°

**OTHELLO:** Is 't lost? Is 't gone? Speak, is 't out o' the way?°

**DESDEMONA:** Heaven bless us!

**OTHELLO:** Say you?          *80*

**DESDEMONA:** It is not lost; but what an if° it were?

**OTHELLO:** How

---

**55 charmer** sorceress    **57 amiable** desirable    **61 fancies** loves    **63 her** i.e., to my wife
**65 perdition** loss    **67 web** fabric, weaving    **69 compasses** annual circlings (The *sibyl*, or
prophetess, was two hundred years old.)    **70 prophetic fury** frenzy of prophetic inspiration.
**work** embroidered pattern    **72 mummy** medicinal or magical preparation drained from mummified
bodies    **73 Conserved of** prepared or preserved out of    **77 startingly and rash** disjointedly and
impetuously, excitedly    **78 out o' the way** lost, misplaced    **81 an if** if

**DESDEMONA:**   I say it is not lost.
**OTHELLO:**                    Fetch 't, let me see 't.
**DESDEMONA:**   Why, so I can, sir, but I will not now.
  This is a trick to put me from my suit.
  Pray you, let Cassio be received again.                    85
**OTHELLO:**   Fetch me the handkerchief! My mind misgives.
**DESDEMONA:**   Come, come,
  You'll never meet a more sufficient° man.
**OTHELLO:**   The handkerchief!
**DESDEMONA:**                    I pray, talk° me of Cassio.         90
**OTHELLO:**   The handkerchief!
**DESDEMONA:**                    A man that all his time°
  Hath founded his good fortunes on your love,
  Shared dangers with you—
**OTHELLO:**   The handkerchief!
**DESDEMONA:**   I' faith, you are to blame.                    95
**OTHELLO:**   Zounds!                    *Exit Othello.*
**EMILIA:**   Is not this man jealous?
**DESDEMONA:**   I ne'er saw this before.
  Sure, there's some wonder in this handkerchief.
  I am most unhappy in the loss of it.                    100
**EMILIA:**   'Tis not a year or two shows us a man.°
  They are all but stomachs, and we all but° food;
  They eat us hungerly,° and when they are full
  They belch us.

  *Enter Iago and Cassio.*

                    Look you, Cassio and my husband.
**IAGO** [*to Cassio*]:   There is no other way; 'tis she must do 't.         105
  And, lo, the happiness!° Go and importune her.
**DESDEMONA:**   How now, good Cassio? What's the news with
  you?
**CASSIO:**   Madam, my former suit. I do beseech you
  That by your virtuous° means I may again

---

**89 sufficient** able, complete   **90 talk** talk to   **91 all his time** throughout his career   **101 'Tis . . . man** i.e., you can't really know a man even in a year or two of experience (?), or, real men come along seldom (?)   **102 but** nothing but   **103 hungerly** hungrily   **106 the happiness** in happy time, fortunately met   **109 virtuous** efficacious

Exist and be a member of his love                                       110
Whom I, with all the office° of my heart,
Entirely honor. I would not be delayed.
If my offense be of such mortal° kind
That nor my service past, nor° present sorrows,
Nor purposed merit in futurity                                          115
Can ransom me into his love again,
But to know so must be my benefit;°
So shall I clothe me in a forced content,
And shut myself up in° some other course,
To fortune's alms.°
**DESDEMONA:**          Alas, thrice-gentle Cassio,                      120
My advocation° is not now in tune.
My lord is not my lord; nor should I know him,
Were he in favor° as in humor° altered.
So help me every spirit sanctified
As I have spoken for you all my best                                    125
And stood within the blank° of his displeasure
For my free speech! You must awhile be patient.
What I can do I will, and more I will
Than for myself I dare. Let that suffice you.
**IAGO:** Is my lord angry?
**EMILIA:**               He went hence but now,                         130
And certainly in strange unquietness.
**IAGO:** Can he be angry? I have seen the cannon
When it hath blown his ranks into the air,
And like the devil from his very arm
Puffed his own brother—and is he angry?                                 135
Something of moment° then. I will go meet him.
There's matter in 't indeed, if he be angry.
**DESDEMONA:** I prithee, do so.                 *Exit [Iago].*
                    Something, sure, of state,°

---

**111 office** loyal service    **113 mortal** fatal    **114 nor . . . nor** neither . . . nor    **117 But . . .**
**benefit** merely to know that my case is hopeless will have to content me (and will be better than
uncertainty)    **119 shut . . . in** confine myself to    **120 To fortune's alms** throwing myself on
the mercy of fortune    **121 advocation** advocacy    **123 favor** appearance.    **humor** mood
**126 within the blank** within point-blank range (The *blank* is the centre of the target.)
**136 of moment** of immediate importance, momentous    **138 of state** concerning state affairs

Either from Venice, or some unhatched practice°
Made demonstrable here in Cyprus to him,     *140*
Hath puddled° his clear spirit; and in such cases
Men's natures wrangle with inferior things,
Though great ones are their object. 'Tis even so;
For let our finger ache, and it indues°
Our other, healthful members even to a sense     *145*
Of pain. Nay, we must think men are not gods,
Nor of them look for such observancy°
As fits the bridal.° Beshrew me° much, Emilia,
I was, unhandsome° warrior as I am,
Arraigning his unkindness with° my soul;     *150*
But now I find I had suborned the witness,°
And he's indicted falsely.

**EMILIA:**                Pray heaven it be
State matters, as you think, and no conception
Nor no jealous toy° concerning you.

**DESDEMONA:** Alas the day! I never gave him cause.     *155*

**EMILIA:** But jealous souls will not be answered so;
They are not ever jealous for the cause,
But jealous for° they're jealous. It is a monster
Begot upon itself,° born on itself.

**DESDEMONA:** Heaven keep that monster from Othello's mind!     *160*

**EMILIA:** Lady, amen.

**DESDEMONA:** I will go seek him. Cassio, walk hereabout.
If I do find him fit, I'll move your suit
And seek to effect it to my uttermost.

**CASSIO:** I humbly thank your ladyship.     *165*

                        *Exit [Desdemona with Emilia].*

*Enter Bianca.*

**BIANCA:** Save° you, friend Cassio!

---

**139 unhatched practice** as yet unexecuted or undiscovered plot    **141 puddled** muddied
**144 indues** brings to the same condition    **147 observancy** attentiveness    **148 bridal** wedding
(when a bridegroom is newly attentive to his bride.)    **Beshrew me** (A mild oath.)    **149 unhand-**
**some** insufficient, unskillful    **150 with** before the bar of    **151 suborned the witness** induced the
witness to give false testimony    **154 toy** fancy    **158 for** because    **159 Begot upon itself** generated solely from itself    **166 Save** God save

**CASSIO:** What make° you from home?
How is 't with you, my most fair Bianca?
I' faith, sweet love, I was coming to your house.

**BIANCA:** And I was going to your lodging, Cassio.
What, keep a week away? Seven days and nights?          *170*
Eightscore-eight° hours? And lovers' absent hours
More tedious than the dial° eightscore times?
O weary reckoning!

**CASSIO:** Pardon me, Bianca.
I have this while with leaden thoughts been pressed;
But I shall, in a more continuate° time,          *175*
Strike off this score° of absence. Sweet Bianca,

[*giving her Desdemona's handkerchief*]

Take me this work out.°

**BIANCA:** O Cassio, whence came this?
This is some token from a newer friend.°
To the felt absence now I feel a cause.
Is 't come to this? Well, well.

**CASSIO:** Go to, woman!          *180*
Throw your vile guesses in the devil's teeth,
From whence you have them. You are jealous now
That this is from some mistress, some remembrance.
No, by my faith, Bianca.

**BIANCA:** Why, whose is it?

**CASSIO:** I know not, neither. I found it in my chamber.          *185*
I like the work well. Ere it be demanded°—
As like° enough it will—I would have it copied.
Take it and do 't, and leave me for this time.

**BIANCA:** Leave you? Wherefore?

**CASSIO:** I do attend here on the General,          *190*
And think it no addition,° nor my wish,
To have him see me womaned.

**BIANCA:** Why, I pray you?

166 **make** do    171 **Eightscore-eight** one hundred sixty-eight, the number of hours in a week
172 **the dial** a complete revolution of the clock    175 **continuate** uninterrupted    176 **Strike . . .**
**score** settle this account    177 **Take . . . out** copy this embroidery for me    178 **friend** mistress
186 **demanded** inquired for    187 **like** likely    191 **addition** i.e., addition to my reputation

**CASSIO:**  Not that I love you not.
**BIANCA:**  But that you do not love me.                                    *195*
  I pray you, bring° me on the way a little,
  And say if I shall see you soon at night.
**CASSIO:**  'Tis but a little way that I can bring you,
  For I attend here; but I'll see you soon.
**BIANCA:**  'Tis very good. I must be circumstanced.°                        *200*

*Exeunt omnes.*


# ACT IV

## Scene I [Before the Citadel.]

*Enter Othello and Iago.*

**IAGO:**  Will you think so?
**OTHELLO:**                 Think so, Iago?
**IAGO:**                                     What,
  To kiss in private?
**OTHELLO:**           An unauthorized kiss!
**IAGO:**  Or to be naked with her friend in bed
  An hour or more, not meaning any harm?
**OTHELLO:**  Naked in bed, Iago, and not mean harm?                         *5*
  It is hypocrisy against the devil.
  They that mean virtuously and yet do so,
  The devil their virtue tempts, and they tempt heaven.
**IAGO:**  If they do nothing, 'tis a venial° slip.
  But if I give my wife a handkerchief—                                      *10*
**OTHELLO:**  What then?
**IAGO:**  Why then, 'tis hers, my lord, and being hers,
  She may, I think, bestow 't on any man.
**OTHELLO:**  She is protectress of her honor too.
  May she give that?                                                         *15*
**IAGO:**  Her honor is an essence that's not seen;
  They have it° very oft that have it not.

---

**196 bring** accompany    **200 be circumstanced** be governed by circumstance, yield to your conditions
**9 venial** pardonable    **17 They have it** i.e., they enjoy a reputation for it

But, for the handkerchief—

**OTHELLO:**  By heaven, I would most gladly have forgot it.

Thou saidst—O, it comes o'er my memory                    20

As doth the raven o'er the infectious house,°

Boding to all—he had my handkerchief.

**IAGO:**  Ay, what of that?

**OTHELLO:**            That's not so good now.

**IAGO:**                        What

If I had said I had seen him do you wrong?

Or heard him say—as knaves be such abroad,°               25

Who having, by their own importunate suit,

Or voluntary dotage° of some mistress,

Convincèd or supplied° them, cannot choose

But they must blab—

**OTHELLO:**            Hath he said anything?

**IAGO:**  He hath, my lord; but, be you well assured,      30

No more than he'll unswear.

**OTHELLO:**            What hath he said?

**IAGO:**  Faith, that he did—I know not what he did.

**OTHELLO:**  What? What?

**IAGO:**  Lie—

**OTHELLO:**  With her?

**IAGO:**            With her, on her; what you will.

**OTHELLO:**  Lie with her? Lie on her? We say "lie on her" when    35
they belie° her. Lie with her? Zounds, that's fulsome.°—
Handkerchief—confessions—handkerchief!—To confess and
be hanged for his labor—first to be hanged and then to confess.°—I tremble at it. Nature would not invest herself in
such shadowing passion without some instruction.° It is not    40
words° that shakes me thus. Pish! Noses, ears, and lips.—Is
't possible?—Confess—handkerchief!—O devil!

---

**21 raven . . . house** (Allusion to the belief that the raven hovered over a house of sickness or infection, such as one visited by the plague.)    **25 abroad** around about    **27 voluntary dotage** willing
infatuation    **28 Convincèd or supplied** seduced or sexually gratified    **36 belie** slander    **fulsome**
foul    **38–39 first . . . to confess** (Othello reverses the proverbial *confess* and *be hanged*; Cassio is
to be given no time to confess before he dies.)    **39–40 Nature . . . instruction** i.e., without some
foundation in fact, nature would not have dressed herself in such an overwhelming passion that comes
over me now and fills my mind with images, or in such a lifelike fantasy as Cassio had in his dream of
lying with Desdemona    **41 words** mere words

*Falls in a trance.*

**IAGO:**   Work on,
My medicine, work! Thus credulous fools are caught,
And many worthy and chaste dames even thus,                          45
All guiltless, meet reproach.—What, ho! My lord!
My lord, I say! Othello!

*Enter Cassio.*

                                How now, Cassio?
**CASSIO:**   What's the matter?
**IAGO:**   My lord is fall'n into an epilepsy.
This is his second fit. He had one yesterday.                        50
**CASSIO:**   Rub him about the temples.
**IAGO:**                              No, forbear.
The lethargy° must have his° quiet course.
If not, he foams at mouth, and by and by
Breaks out to savage madness. Look, he stirs.
Do you withdraw yourself a little while.                             55
He will recover straight. When he is gone,
I would on great occasion° speak with you.

                                    [*Exit Cassio.*]

How is it, General? Have you not hurt your head?
**OTHELLO:**   Dost thou mock me?°
**IAGO:**                            I mock you not, by heaven.
Would you would bear your fortune like a man!                        60
**OTHELLO:**   A hornèd man's a monster and a beast.
**IAGO:**   There's many a beast then in a populous city,
And many a civil° monster.
**OTHELLO:**   Did he confess it?
**IAGO:**   Good sir, be a man.                                        65
Think every bearded fellow that's but yoked°
May draw with you.° There's millions now alive

---

**52 lethargy** coma   **his** its   **57 on great occasion** on a matter of great importance   **59 mock me** (Othello takes Iago's question about hurting his head to be a mocking reference to the cuckold's horns.)   **63 civil** i.e., dwelling in a city   **66 yoked** (1) married (2) put into the yoke of infamy and cuckoldry   **67 draw with you** pull as you do, like oxen who are yoked, i.e., share your fate as cuckold

That nightly lie in those unproper° beds
Which they dare swear peculiar.° Your case is better.°
O, 'tis the spite of hell, the fiend's arch-mock,                    70
To lip° a wanton in a secure° couch
And to suppose her chaste! No, let me know,
And knowing what I am,° I know what she shall be.°

**OTHELLO:**   O, thou art wise. 'Tis certain.

**IAGO:**   Stand you awhile apart;                                75
Confine yourself but in a patient list.°
Whilst you were here o'erwhelmèd with your grief—
A passion most unsuiting such a man—
Cassio came hither. I shifted him away,°
And laid good 'scuse upon your ecstasy,°                          80
Bade him anon return and here speak with me,
The which he promised. Do but encave° yourself
And mark the fleers,° the gibes, and notable° scorns
That dwell in every region of his face;
For I will make him tell the tale anew,                          85
Where, how, how oft, how long ago, and when
He hath and is again to cope° your wife.
I say, but mark his gesture. Marry, patience!
Or I shall say you're all-in-all in spleen,°
And nothing of a man.

**OTHELLO:**                         Dost thou hear, Iago?         90
I will be found most cunning in my patience;
But—dost thou hear?—most bloody.

**IAGO:**                                   That's not amiss;
But yet keep time° in all. Will you withdraw?

[*Othello stands apart.*]

Now will I question Cassio of Bianca,
A huswife° that by selling her desires                           95
Buys herself bread and clothes. It is a creature

---

**68 unproper** not exclusively their own   **69 peculiar** private, their own   **better** i.e., because you
know the truth   **71 lip** kiss   **secure** free from suspicion   **73 what I am** i.e., a cuckold   **she
shall be** will happen to her   **76 in . . . list** within the bounds of patience   **79 shifted him away**
used a dodge to get rid of him   **80 ecstasy** trance   **82 encave** conceal   **83 fleers** sneers
**notable** obvious   **87 cope** encounter with, have sex with   **89 all-in-all in spleen** utterly governed
by passionate impulses   **93 keep time** keep yourself steady (as in music)   **95 huswife** hussy

That dotes on Cassio—as 'tis the strumpet's plague
To beguile many and be beguiled by one.
He, when he hears of her, cannot restrain°
From the excess of laughter. Here he comes.                                    *100*

*Enter Cassio.*

As he shall smile, Othello shall go mad;
And his unbookish° jealousy must conster°
Poor Cassio's smiles, gestures, and light behaviors
Quite in the wrong.—How do you now, Lieutenant?

**CASSIO:**   The worser that you give me the addition°                        *105*
Whose want° even kills me.

**IAGO:**   Ply Desdemona well and you are sure on 't.
[*Speaking lower.*] Now, if this suit lay in Bianca's power,
How quickly should you speed!

**CASSIO** [*laughing*]:   Alas, poor caitiff!°                                 *110*

**OTHELLO** [*aside*]:   Look how he laughs already!

**IAGO:**   I never knew a woman love man so.

**CASSIO:**   Alas, poor rogue! I think, i' faith, she loves me.

**OTHELLO:**   Now he denies it faintly, and laughs it out.

**IAGO:**   Do you hear, Cassio?

**OTHELLO:**                          Now he importunes him                    *115*
To tell it o'er. Go to!° Well said,° well said.

**IAGO:**   She gives it out that you shall marry her.
Do you intend it?

**CASSIO:**   Ha, ha, ha!

**OTHELLO:**   Do you triumph, Roman?° Do you triumph?                          *120*

**CASSIO:**   I marry her? What? A customer?° Prithee, bear some
charity to my wit;° do not think it so unwholesome. Ha,
ha, ha!

**OTHELLO:**   So, so, so, so! They laugh that win.°

**IAGO:**   Faith, the cry° goes that you shall marry her.                      *125*

**CASSIO:**   Prithee, say true.

---

**99 restrain** refrain   **102 unbookish** uninstructed   **conster** construe   **105 addition** title
**106 Whose want** the lack of which   **110 caitiff** wretch   **116 Go to** (An expression of remonstrance.)   **Well said** well done   **120 Roman** (The Romans were noted for their *triumphs* or triumphal processions.)   **121 customer** i.e., prostitute   **121–122 bear . . . wit** be more charitable to my judgment   **124 They . . . win** i.e., they that laugh last laugh best   **125 cry** rumour

**IAGO:** I am a very villain else.°
**OTHELLO:** Have you scored me?° Well.
**CASSIO:** This is the monkey's own giving out. She is persuaded
    I will marry her out of her own love and flattery,° not out of     *130*
    my promise.
**OTHELLO:** Iago beckons me.° Now he begins the story.
**CASSIO:** She was here even now; she haunts me in every place.
    I was the other day talking on the seabank° with certain
    Venetians, and thither comes the bauble,° and, by this     *135*
    hand,° she falls me thus about my neck—

[*He embraces Iago.*]

**OTHELLO:** Crying, "O dear Cassio!" as it were; his gesture
    imports it.
**CASSIO:** So hangs and lolls and weep upon me, so shakes and
    pulls me. Ha, ha, ha!     *140*
**OTHELLO:** Now he tells how she plucked him to my chamber.
    O, I see that nose of yours, but not that dog I shall throw
    it to.°
**CASSIO:** Well, I must leave her company.
**IAGO:** Before me,° look where she comes.     *145*

*Enter Bianca* [*with Othello's handkerchief*].

**CASSIO:** 'Tis such another fitchew!° Marry, a perfumed one.—
    What do you mean by this haunting of me?
**BIANCA:** Let the devil and his dam° haunt you! What did you
    mean by that same handkerchief you gave me even now? I
    was a fine fool to take it. I must take out the work? A likely     *150*
    piece of work,° that you should find it in your chamber and
    know not who left it there! This is some minx's token, and I
    must take out the work? There; give it your hobbyhorse.°

---

**127 I . . . else** call me a complete rogue if I'm not telling the truth    **128 scored me** scored off me,
beaten me, made up my reckoning, branded me    **130 flattery** self-flattery, self-deception
**132 beckons** signals    **134 seabank** seashore    **135 bauble** plaything    **135–136 by this hand**
I make my vow    **142–143 not . . . to** (Othello imagines himself cutting off Cassio's nose and throwing it to a dog.)    **145 Before me** i.e., on my soul    **146 'Tis . . . fitchew** what a polecat she is! Just
like all the others (Polecats were often compared to prostitutes because of their rank smell and pre-
sumed lechery.)    **148 dam** mother    **151 A likely . . . work** a fine story    **153 hobbyhorse** harlot

[*She gives him the handkerchief.*] Wheresoever you had it, I'll take out no work on 't.                                          155

CASSIO:  How now, my sweet Bianca? How now? How now?

OTHELLO:  By heaven, that should be° my handkerchief!

BIANCA:  If you'll come to supper tonight, you may; if you will not, come when you are next prepared for.°

*Exit.*

IAGO:  After her, after her.                                      160

CASSIO:  Faith, I must. She'll rail in the streets else.

IAGO:  Will you sup there?

CASSIO:  Faith, I intend so.

IAGO:  Well, I may chance to see you, for I would very fain speak with you.                                                  165

CASSIO:  Prithee, come. Will you?

IAGO:  Go to.° Say no more.                    [*Exit Cassio.*]

OTHELLO [*advancing*]:  How shall I murder him, Iago?

IAGO:  Did you perceive how he laughed at his vice?

OTHELLO:  O, Iago!                                                170

IAGO:  And did you see the handkerchief?

OTHELLO:  Was that mine?

IAGO:  Yours, by this hand. And to see how he prizes the foolish woman your wife! She gave it him, and he hath given it his whore.                                                       175

OTHELLO:  I would have him nine years a-killing. A fine woman! A fair woman! A sweet woman!

IAGO:  Nay, you must forget that.

OTHELLO:  Ay, let her rot and perish, and be damned tonight, for she shall not live. No, my heart is turned to stone; I strike    180
it, and it hurts my hand. O, the world hath not a sweeter creature! She might lie by an emperor's side and command him tasks.

IAGO:  Nay, that's not your way.°

OTHELLO:  Hang her! I do but say what she is. So delicate with    185
her needle! An admirable musician! O, she will sing the sav-

---

**157 should be** must be    **159 when . . . for** when I'm ready for you (i.e., never)    **167 Go to**
(An expression of remonstrance.)    **184 your way** i.e., the way you should think of her

ageness out of a bear. Of so high and plenteous wit and invention!°

IAGO:   She's the worse for all this.

OTHELLO:   O, a thousand, a thousand times! And then, of so     190
gentle a condition!°

IAGO:   Ay, too gentle.°

OTHELLO:   Nay, that's certain. But yet the pity of it, Iago! O,
Iago, the pity of it, Iago!

IAGO:   If you are so fond° over her iniquity, give her patent° to     195
offend, for if it touch not you it comes near nobody.

OTHELLO:   I will chop her into messes.° Cuckold me?

IAGO:   O, 'tis foul in her.

OTHELLO:   With mine officer?

IAGO:   That's fouler.     200

OTHELLO:   Get me some poison, Iago, this night. I'll not ex-
postulate with her, lest her body and beauty unprovide° my
mind again. This night, Iago.

IAGO:   Do it not with poison. Strangle her in her bed, even the
bed she hath contaminated.     205

OTHELLO:   Good, good! The justice of it pleases. Very good.

IAGO:   And for Cassio, let me be his undertaker.° You shall hear
more by midnight.

OTHELLO:   Excellent good. [*A trumpet within.*] What trumpet
is that same?     210

IAGO:   I warrant, something from Venice.

*Enter Lodovico, Desdemona, and attendants.*

'Tis Lodovico. This comes from the Duke.
See, your wife's with him.

LODOVICO:   God save you, worthy General!

OTHELLO:                                                With all my heart,° sir.

LODOVICO [*giving him a letter*]:   The Duke and the senators of     215
Venice greet you.

OTHELLO:   I kiss the instrument of their pleasures.

---

**188 invention** imagination     **191 gentle a condition** well-born and well-bred     **192 gentle** generous, yielding (to other men)     **195 fond** foolish.     **patent** licence     **197 messes** portions of meat,
i.e., bits     **202 unprovide** weaken, render unfit     **207 be his undertaker** undertake to dispatch him
**214 With all my heart** i.e., I thank you most heartily

[*He opens the letter, and reads.*]

**DESDEMONA:**   And what's the news, good cousin Lodovico?
**IAGO:**   I am very glad to see you, signor.
    Welcome to Cyprus.                                                          220
**LODOVICO:**   I thank you. How does Lieutenant Cassio?
**IAGO:**   Lives, sir.
**DESDEMONA:**   Cousin, there's fall'n between him and my lord
    An unkind° breach; but you shall make all well.
**OTHELLO:**   Are you sure of that?                                            225
**DESDEMONA:**   My lord?
**OTHELLO** [*reads*]:   "This fail you not to do, as you will—"
**LODOVICO:**   He did not call; he's busy in the paper.
    Is there division twixt my lord and Cassio?
**DESDEMONA:**   A most unhappy one. I would do much                            230
    T' atone° them, for the love I bear to Cassio.
**OTHELLO:**   Fire and brimstone!
**DESDEMONA:**   My lord?
**OTHELLO:**   Are you wise?
**DESDEMONA:**   What, is he angry?
**LODOVICO:**                               Maybe the letter moved him;         235
    For, as I think, they do command him home,
    Deputing Cassio in his government.°
**DESDEMONA:**   By my troth, I am glad on 't.°
**OTHELLO:**   Indeed?
**DESDEMONA:**   My lord?                                                        240
**OTHELLO:**   I am glad to see you mad.°
**DESDEMONA:**   Why, sweet Othello—
**OTHELLO** [*striking her*]:   Devil!
**DESDEMONA:**   I have not deserved this.
**LODOVICO:**   My lord, this would not be believed in Venice,                  245
    Though I should swear I saw 't. 'Tis very much.°
    Make her amends; she weeps.
**OTHELLO:**                               O devil, devil!

---

**224 unkind** unnatural, contrary to their natures; hurtful   **231 atone** reconcile   **237 government**
office   **238 on 't** of it   **241 I am . . . mad** i.e., I am glad to see that you are insane enough to
rejoice in Cassio's promotion (? Othello bitterly plays on Desdemona's *I am glad.*)   **246 very much**
too much, outrageous

If that the earth could teem° with woman's tears,
Each drop she falls would prove a crocodile.°
Out of my sight!

**DESDEMONA:**       I will not stay to offend you. [*Going.*]        250

**LODOVICO:**   Truly, an obedient lady.
I do beseech your lordship, call her back.

**OTHELLO:**   Mistress!

**DESDEMONA** [*returning*]:   My lord?

**OTHELLO:**   What would you with her, sir?°        255

**LODOVICO:**   Who, I, my lord?

**OTHELLO:**   Ay, you did wish that I would make her turn.
Sir, she can turn, and turn, and yet go on
And turn again; and she can weep, sir, weep;
And she's obedient,° as you say, obedient,        260
Very obedient.—Proceed you in your tears.—
Concerning this, sir—O well-painted passion!°—
I am commanded home.—Get you away;
I'll send for you anon.—Sir, I obey the mandate
And will return to Venice.—Hence, avaunt!        265

[*Exit Desdemona.*]

Cassio shall have my place. And, sir, tonight
I do entreat that we may sup together.
You are welcome, sir, to Cyprus.—Goats and monkeys!° *Exit.*

**LODOVICO:**   Is this the noble Moor whom our full Senate
Call all in all sufficient? Is this the nature        270
Whom passion could not shake? Whose solid virtue
The shot of accident nor dart of chance
Could neither graze nor pierce?

**IAGO:**               He is much changed.

**LODOVICO:**   Are his wits safe? Is he not light of brain?

**IAGO:**   He's that he is. I may not breathe my censure      275
What he might be. If what he might he is not,

---

**248 teem** breed, be impregnated   **249 falls . . . crocodile** (Crocodiles were supposed to weep hypocritical tears for their victims.)   **255 What . . . sir** (Othello implies that Desdemona is pliant and will do a *turn*, lines 257–259, for any man.)   **260 obedient** (With much the same sexual connotation as *turn* in lines 257–259.)   **262 passion** i.e., grief   **268 Goats and monkeys** (See Act III, Scene iii, line 419.)

I would to heaven he were!°
**LODOVICO:**                          What, strike his wife?
**IAGO:** Faith, that was not so well; yet would I knew
That stroke would prove the worst!
**LODOVICO:**                          Is it his use?°          *280*
Or did the letters work upon his blood°
And new-create his fault?
**IAGO:**                          Alas, alas!
It is not honesty in me to speak
What I have seen and known. You shall observe him,
And his own courses will denote° him so
That I may save my speech. Do but go after,          *285*
And mark how he continues.
**LODOVICO:** I am sorry that I am deceived in him.          *Exeunt.*

## SCENE II [THE CITADEL.]

*Enter Othello and Emilia.*

**OTHELLO:** You have seen nothing then?
**EMILIA:** Nor ever heard, nor ever did suspect.
**OTHELLO:** Yes, you have seen Cassio and she together.
**EMILIA:** But then I saw no harm, and then I heard
Each syllable that breath made up between them.          *5*
**OTHELLO:** What, did they never whisper?
**EMILIA:** Never, my lord.
**OTHELLO:** Nor send you out o' the way?
**EMILIA:** Never.
**OTHELLO:** To fetch her fan, her gloves, her mask, nor nothing?          *10*
**EMILIA:** Never, my lord.
**OTHELLO:** That's strange.
**EMILIA:** I durst, my lord, to wager she is honest,
Lay down my soul at stake.° If you think other,
Remove your thought; it doth abuse your bosom.°          *15*

---

275–277 **I may . . . were** i.e., I dare not venture an opinion as to whether he's of unsound mind, as you suggest, but, if he isn't, then it might be better to wish he were in fact insane, since only that could excuse his wild behaviour          279 **use** custom          280 **blood** passions          284 **courses will denote** actions will reveal
14 **at stake** as the wager          15 **abuse your bosom** deceive you

If any wretch have put this in your head,
Let heaven requite it with the serpent's curse!°
For if she be not honest, chaste, and true,
There's no man happy; the purest of their wives
Is foul as slander.

OTHELLO:             Bid her come hither. Go.                                20

*Exit Emilia.*

She says enough; yet she's a simple bawd
That cannot say as much.° This° is a subtle whore,
A closet lock and key° of villainous secrets.
And yet she'll kneel and pray; I have seen her do 't.

*Enter Desdemona and Emilia.*

DESDEMONA:   My lord, what is your will?                                    25
OTHELLO:   Pray you, chuck, come hither.
DESDEMONA:   What is your pleasure?
OTHELLO:                       Let me see your eyes.
Look in my face.
DESDEMONA:           What horrible fancy's this?
OTHELLO [*to Emilia*]:   Some of your function,° mistress.
Leave procreants° alone and shut the door;                                  30
Cough or cry "hem" if anybody come.
Your mystery, your mystery!° Nay, dispatch.

*Exit Emilia.*

DESDEMONA [*kneeling*]:   Upon my knees, what doth your
speech import?
I understand a fury in your words,
But not the words.                                                          35
OTHELLO:   Why, what art thou?
DESDEMONA:                     Your wife, my lord, your true
And loyal wife.

---

**17 the serpent's curse** the curse pronounced by God on the serpent for deceiving Eve, just as some
man has done to Othello and Desdemona (See Genesis 3:14.)   **21–22 she's . . . much** i.e., any pro-
curess or go-between who couldn't make up as plausible a story as Emilia's would have to be pretty
stupid   **22 This** i.e., Desdemona   **23 closet lock and key** i.e., concealer   **29 Some . . . function**
i.e., practise your chosen profession, that of bawd (by guarding the door)   **30 procreants** mating
couples   **32 mystery** trade, occupation

**OTHELLO:**          Come, swear it, damn thyself,
Lest, being like one of heaven,° the devils themselves
Should fear to seize thee. Therefore be double damned:
Swear thou art honest.

**DESDEMONA:**                    Heaven doth truly know it.          *40*

**OTHELLO:**   Heaven truly knows that thou art false as hell.

**DESDEMONA:**   To whom, my lord? With whom? How am I false?

**OTHELLO** [*weeping*]:   Ah, Desdemon! Away, away, away!

**DESDEMONA:**   Alas the heavy day! Why do you weep?
Am I the motive° of these tears, my lord?          *45*
If haply you my father do suspect
An instrument of this your calling back,
Lay not your blame on me. If you have lost him,
I have lost him too.

**OTHELLO:**                    Had it pleased heaven
To try me with affliction, had they° rained          *50*
All kinds of sores and shames on my bare head,
Steeped me in poverty to the very lips,
Given to captivity me and my utmost hopes,
I should have found in some place of my soul
A drop of patience. But, alas, to make me          *55*
A fixèd figure for the time of scorn°
To point his° slow and moving finger° at!
Yet could I bear that too, well, very well.
But there where I have garnered° up my heart,
Where either I must live or bear no life,          *60*
The fountain° from the which my current runs
Or else dries up—to be discarded thence!
Or keep it as a cistern° for foul toads
To knot° and gender° in! Turn thy complexion there,°
Patience, thou young and rose-lipped cherubin—          *65*

---

**38 being . . . heaven** looking like an angel   **45 motive** cause   **50 they** i.e., heavenly powers
**56 time of scorn** i.e., scornful world   **57 his** its   **slow and moving finger** i.e., hour hand of the
clock, moving so slowly it seems hardly to move at all (Othello envisages himself as being eternally
pointed at by the scornful world as the numbers on a clock are pointed at by the hour hand.)
**59 garnered** stored   **61 fountain** spring   **63 cistern** cesspool   **64 knot** couple   **gender** engen-
der   **Turn . . . there** change your colour, grow pale, at such a sight

Ay, there look grim as hell!°
**DESDEMONA:**  I hope my noble lord esteems me honest.°
**OTHELLO:**  O, ay, as summer flies are in the shambles,°
  That quicken° even with blowing.° O thou weed,
  Who art so lovely fair and smell'st so sweet                                   70
  That the sense aches at thee, would thou hadst ne'er been
  born!
**DESDEMONA:**  Alas, what ignorant° sin have I committed?
**OTHELLO:**  Was this fair paper, this most goodly book,
  Made to write "whore" upon? What committed?
  Committed? O thou public commoner!°                                            75
  I should make very forges of my cheeks,
  That would to cinders burn up modesty,
  Did I but speak thy deeds. What committed?
  Heaven stops the nose at it and the moon winks;°
  The bawdy° wind, that kisses all it meets,                                     80
  Is hushed within the hollow mine° of earth
  And will not hear 't. What committed?
  Impudent strumpet!
**DESDEMONA:**                  By heaven, you do me wrong.
**OTHELLO:**  Are not you a strumpet?
**DESDEMONA:**  No, as I am a Christian.                                          85
  If to preserve this vessel° for my lord
  From any other foul unlawful touch
  Be not to be a strumpet, I am none.
**OTHELLO:**  What, not a whore?
**DESDEMONA:**  No, as I shall be saved.                                         90
**OTHELLO:**  Is 't possible?
**DESDEMONA:**  O, heaven forgive us!
**OTHELLO:**                  I cry you mercy,° then.
  I took you for that cunning whore of Venice
  That married with Othello. [*Calling out.*] You, mistress,
  That have the office opposite to Saint Peter                                   95

---

**65–66 Patience . . . hell** (Even Patience, that rose-lipped cherub, will look grim and pale at this spectacle.)  **67 honest** chaste  **68 shambles** slaughterhouse  **69 quicken** come to life  **with blowing** i.e., with the puffing up of something rotten in which maggots are breeding  **72 ignorant sin** sin in ignorance  **75 commoner** prostitute  **79 winks** closes her eyes (The moon symbolizes chastity.)  **80 bawdy** kissing one and all  **81 mine** cave (where the winds were thought to dwell)  **86 vessel** body  **92 cry you mercy** beg your pardon

And keep the gate of hell!

*Enter Emilia.*

You, you, ay, you!
We have done our course.° There's money for your
pains.[*He gives money.*]
I pray you, turn the key and keep our counsel.          *Exit.*

EMILIA:    Alas, what does this gentleman conceive?°
How do you, madam? How do you, my good lady?          100

DESDEMONA:    Faith, half asleep.°

EMILIA:    Good madam, what's the matter with my lord?

DESDEMONA:    With who?

EMILIA:    Why, with my lord, madam.

DESDEMONA:    Who is thy lord?

EMILIA:                         He that is yours, sweet lady.          105

DESDEMONA:    I have none. Do not talk to me, Emilia.
I cannot weep, nor answers have I none
But what should go by water.° Prithee, tonight
Lay on my bed my wedding sheets, remember;
And call thy husband hither.          110

EMILIA:    Here's a change indeed!          *Exit.*

DESDEMONA:    'Tis meet I should be used so, very meet.°
How have I been behaved, that he might stick°
The small'st opinion° on my least misuse?°

*Enter Iago and Emilia.*

IAGO:    What is your pleasure, madam? How is 't with you?          115

DESDEMONA:    I cannot tell. Those that do teach young babes
Do it with gentle means and easy tasks.
He might have chid me so, for, in good faith,
I am a child to chiding.

IAGO:    What is the matter, lady?          120

EMILIA:    Alas, Iago, my lord hath so bewhored her,
Thrown such despite and heavy terms upon her,
That true hearts cannot bear it.

---

97 **course** business (with an indecent suggestion of "trick," turn at sex)    99 **conceive** suppose, think    101 **half asleep** i.e., dazed    108 **go by water** be expressed by tears    112 **meet** fitting    113 **stick** attach    114 **opinion** censure.    **least misuse** slightest misconduct

**DESDEMONA:** Am I that name, Iago?

**IAGO:** What name, fair lady? 125

**DESDEMONA:** Such as she said my lord did say I was.

**EMILIA:** He called her whore. A beggar in his drink
Could not have laid such terms upon his callet.°

**IAGO:** Why did he so?

**DESDEMONA** [*weeping*]: I do not know. I am sure I am none
such. 130

**IAGO:** Do not weep, do not weep. Alas the day!

**EMILIA:** Hath she forsook so many noble matches,
Her father and her country and her friends,
To be called whore? Would it not make one weep?

**DESDEMONA:** It is my wretched fortune.

**IAGO:**                                         Beshrew° him for 't! 135
How comes this trick° upon him?

**DESDEMONA:**                               Nay, heaven doth know.

**EMILIA:** I will be hanged if some eternal° villain,
Some busy and insinuating° rogue,
Some cogging,° cozening° slave, to get some office,
Have not devised this slander. I will be hanged else. 140

**IAGO:** Fie, there is no such man. It is impossible.

**DESDEMONA:** If any such there be, heaven pardon him!

**EMILIA:** A halter° pardon him! And hell gnaw his bones!
Why should he call her whore? Who keeps her company?
What place? What time? What form?° What likelihood? 145
The Moor's abused by some most villainous knave,
Some base notorious knave, some scurvy fellow.
O heaven, that° such companions° thou'dst unfold,°
And put in every honest hand a whip
To lash the rascals naked through the world 150
Even from the east to th' west!

**IAGO:**                               Speak within door.°

**EMILIA:** O, fie upon them! Some such squire° he was

---

**128 callet** whore    **135 Beshrew** curse    **136 trick** strange behaviour, delusion    **137 eternal** inveterate    **138 insinuating** ingratiating, fawning, wheedling    **139 cogging** cheating    **cozening** defrauding    **143 halter** hangman's noose    **145 form** appearance, circumstance    **148 that** would that    **companions** fellows    **unfold** expose    **151 within door** i.e., not so loud    **152 squire** fellow

That turned your wit the seamy side without°
And made you to suspect me with the Moor.
**IAGO:**  You are a fool. Go to.°
**DESDEMONA:**                    Alas, Iago,                               155
What shall I do to win my lord again?
Good friend, go to him; for, by this light of heaven,
I know not how I lost him. Here I kneel. [*She kneels.*]
If e'er my will did trespass 'gainst his love,
Either in discourse° of thought or actual deed,                            160
Or that° mine eyes, mine ears, or any sense
Delighted them° in any other form;
Or that I do not yet,° and ever did,
And ever will—though he do shake me off
To beggarly divorcement—love him dearly,                                   165
Comfort forswear° me! Unkindness may do much,
And his unkindness may defeat° my life,
But never taint my love. I cannot say "whore."
It does abhor° me now I speak the word;
To do the act that might the addition° earn                                170
Not the world's mass of vanity° could make me.

[*She rises.*]

**IAGO:**  I pray you, be content. 'Tis but his humor.°
The business of the state does him offense,
And he does chide with you.
**DESDEMONA:**  If 'twere no other—                                        175
**IAGO:**  It is but so, I warrant. [*Trumpets within.*]
Hark, how these instruments summon you to supper!
The messengers of Venice stays the meat.°
Go in, and weep not. All things shall be well.

                    *Exeunt Desdemona and Emilia.*

*Enter Roderigo.*

---

153 **seamy side without** wrong side out    155 **Go to** i.e., that's enough    160 **discourse of thought**
process of thinking    161 **that** if (Also in line 163.)    162 **Delighted them** took delight    163 **yet**
still    166 **Comfort forswear** may heavenly comfort forsake    167 **defeat** destroy    169 **abhor** (1)
fill me with abhorrence (2) make me whorelike    170 **addition** title    171 **vanity** showy splendour
172 **humor** mood    178 **stays the meat** are waiting to dine

How now, Roderigo?                                          *180*

**RODERIGO:**  I do not find that thou deal'st justly with me.

**IAGO:**  What in the contrary?

**RODERIGO:**  Every day thou daff'st me° with some device,°
Iago, and rather, as it seems to me now, keep'st from me all
conveniency° than suppliest me with the least advantage° of      *185*
hope. I will indeed no longer endure it, nor am I yet persuaded to put up° in peace what already I have foolishly suffered.

**IAGO:**  Will you hear me, Roderigo?

**RODERIGO:**  Faith, I have heard too much, for your words and   *190*
performances are no kin together.

**IAGO:**  You charge me most unjustly.

**RODERIGO:**  With naught but truth. I have wasted myself out
of my means. The jewels you have had from me to deliver°
Desdemona would half have corrupted a votarist.° You have      *195*
told me she hath received them and returned me expectations and comforts of sudden respect° and acquaintance, but
I find none.

**IAGO:**  Well, go to, very well.

**RODERIGO:**  "Very well"! "Go to"! I cannot go to,° man, nor   *200*
'tis not very well. By this hand, I think it is scurvy, and begin
to find myself fopped° in it.

**IAGO:**  Very well.

**RODERIGO:**  I tell you 'tis not very well.° I will make myself
known to Desdemona. If she will return me my jewels, I will    *205*
give over my suit and repent my unlawful solicitation; if not,
assure yourself I will seek satisfaction° of you.

**IAGO:**  You have said now?°

**RODERIGO:**  Ay, and said nothing but what I protest
intendment° of doing.                                         *210*

---

**183 thou daff'st me** you put me off    **device** excuse, trick    **185 conveniency** advantage,
opportunity    **advantage** increase    **187 put up** submit to, tolerate    **194 deliver** deliver to
**195 votarist** nun    **197 sudden respect** immediate consideration    **200 I cannot go to** (Roderigo
changes Iago's go to, an expression urging patience, to *I cannot go to*, "I have no opportunity for success in wooing.")    **202 fopped** fooled, duped    **204 not very well** (Roderigo changes Iago's *very
well*, "all right, then," to *not very well*, "not at all good.")    **207 satisfaction** repayment (The term
normally means settling of accounts in a duel.)    **208 You . . . now** have you finished?
**210 intendment** intention

**IAGO:** Why, now I see there's mettle in thee, and even from this
instant do build on thee a better opinion than ever before.
Give me thy hand, Roderigo. Thou hast taken against me a
most just exception; but yet I protest I have dealt most
directly in thy affair.                                      *215*

**RODERIGO:** It hath not appeared.

**IAGO:** I grant indeed it hath not appeared, and your suspicion
is not without wit and judgment. But, Roderigo, if thou hast
that in thee indeed which I have greater reason to believe
now than ever—I mean purpose, courage, and valor—this      *220*
night show it. If thou the next night following enjoy not
Desdemona, take me from this world with treachery and
devise engines for° my life.

**RODERIGO:** Well, what is it? Is it within reason and compass?

**IAGO:** Sir, there is especial commission come from Venice to    *225*
depute Cassio in Othello's place.

**RODERIGO:** Is that true? Why, then Othello and Desdemona
return again to Venice.

**IAGO:** O, no; he goes into Mauritania and takes away with him
the fair Desdemona, unless his abode be lingered here by    *230*
some accident; wherein none can be so determinate° as the
removing of Cassio.

**RODERIGO:** How do you mean, removing of him?

**IAGO:** Why, by making him uncapable of Othello's place—
knocking out his brains.                                     *235*

**RODERIGO:** And that you would have me to do?

**IAGO:** Ay, if you dare do yourself a profit and a right. He sups
tonight with a harlotry,° and thither will I go to him. He
knows not yet of his honorable fortune. If you will watch his
going thence, which I will fashion to fall out° between twelve *240*
and one, you may take him at your pleasure. I will be near to
second your attempt, and he shall fall between us. Come,
stand not amazed at it, but go along with me. I will show
you such a necessity in his death that you shall think

---

**223 engines for** plots against    **231 determinate** conclusive    **238 harlotry** slut    **240 fall out**
occur

yourself bound to put it on him. It is now high° suppertime,     *245*
and the night grows to waste.° About it.

RODERIGO:   I will hear further reason for this.

IAGO:   And you shall be satisfied.                              *Exeunt.*


SCENE III [THE CITADEL.]

*Enter Othello, Lodovico, Desdemona, Emilia, and atten-*
*dants.*

LODOVICO:   I do beseech you, sir, trouble yourself no further.

OTHELLO:   O, pardon me; 'twill do me good to walk.

LODOVICO:   Madam, good night. I humbly thank your
ladyship.

DESDEMONA:   Your honor is most welcome.

OTHELLO:                                     Will you walk, sir?
O, Desdemona!                                                  *5*

DESDEMONA:   My lord?

OTHELLO:   Get you to bed on th' instant.
I will be returned forthwith. Dismiss your attendant there.
Look 't be done.

DESDEMONA:   I will, my lord.                                   *10*

*Exit [Othello, with Lodovico and attendants].*

EMILIA:   How goes it now? He looks gentler than he did.

DESDEMONA:   He says he will return incontinent,°
And hath commanded me to go to bed,
And bid me to dismiss you.

EMILIA:   Dismiss me?                                           *15*

DESDEMONA:   It was his bidding. Therefore, good Emilia,
Give me my nightly wearing, and adieu.
We must not now displease him.

EMILIA:   I would you had never seen him!

DESDEMONA:   So would not I. My love doth so approve him     *20*
That even his stubbornness,° his checks,° his frowns—
Prithee, unpin me—have grace and favor in them.

---

**245 high** fully    **246 grows to waste** wastes away
**12 incontinent** immediately    **21 stubbornness** roughness    **checks** rebukes

[*Emilia prepares Desdemona for bed.*]

**EMILIA:** I have laid those sheets you bade me on the bed.
**DESDEMONA:** All's one.° Good faith, how foolish are our
minds!
If I do die before thee, prithee shroud me                                   25
In one of these same sheets.
**EMILIA:**                                   Come, come, you talk.°
**DESDEMONA:** My mother had a maid called Barbary.
She was in love, and he she loved proved mad°
And did forsake her. She had a song of "Willow."
An old thing 'twas, but it expressed her fortune,                            30
And she died singing it. That song tonight
Will not go from my mind; I have much to do
But to go hang° my head all at one side
And sing it like poor Barbary. Prithee, dispatch.
**EMILIA:** Shall I go fetch your nightgown?°                                 35
**DESDEMONA:** No, unpin me here.
This Lodovico is a proper° man.
**EMILIA:** A very handsome man.
**DESDEMONA:** He speaks well.
**EMILIA:** I know a lady in Venice would have walked barefoot               40
to Palestine for a touch of his nether lip.
**DESDEMONA** [*singing*]:
    "The poor soul sat sighing by a sycamore tree,
    Sing all a green willow;°
    Her hand on her bosom, her head on her knee,
    Sing willow, willow, willow.                                             45
    The fresh streams ran by her and murmured her moans;
    Sing willow, willow, willow;
    Her salt tears fell from her, and softened the stones—"
    Lay by these.
        [*Singing.*] "Sing willow, willow, willow—"                         50
    Prithee, hie thee.° He'll come anon.°

---

**24 All's one** all right, it doesn't really matter    **26 talk** i.e., prattle    **28 mad** wild, i.e., faithless
**32–33 I . . . hang** I can scarcely keep myself from hanging    **35 nightgown** dressing gown
**37 proper** handsome    **43 willow** (A conventional emblem of disappointed love.)    **51 hie thee**
hurry    **anon** right away

[*Singing.*] "Sing all a green willow must be my
garland.
Let nobody blame him; his scorn I approve—"
Nay, that's not next.—Hark! Who is 't that knocks?
EMILIA:  It's the wind.                                                  55
DESDEMONA [*singing*]:
"I called my love false love; but what said he then?
Sing willow, willow, willow;
If I court more women, you'll couch with more men."
So, get thee gone. Good night. Mine eyes do itch;
Doth that bode weeping?
EMILIA:                          'Tis neither here nor there.              60
DESDEMONA:  I have heard it said so. O, these men, these
men!
Dost thou in conscience think—tell me, Emilia—
That there be women do abuse° their husbands
In such gross kind?
EMILIA:                There be some such, no question.
DESDEMONA:  Wouldst thou do such a deed for all the world?    65
EMILIA:  Why, would not you?
DESDEMONA:                     No, by this heavenly light!
EMILIA:  Nor I neither by this heavenly light;
I might do 't as well i' the dark.
DESDEMONA:  Wouldst thou do such a deed for all the world?
EMILIA:  The world's a huge thing. It is a great price          70
For a small vice.
DESDEMONA:  Good troth, I think thou wouldst not.
EMILIA:  By my troth, I think I should, and undo 't when I had
done. Marry, I would not do such a thing for a joint ring,°
nor for measures of lawn,° nor for gowns, petticoats, nor     75
caps, nor any petty exhibition.° But for all the whole world!
Uds° pity, who would not make her husband a cuckold to
make him a monarch? I should venture purgatory for 't.
DESDEMONA:  Beshrew me if I would do such a wrong
For the whole world.                                              80

63 **abuse** deceive  74 **joint ring** a ring made in separate halves  75 **lawn** fine linen  76 **exhibition** gift  77 **Uds** God's

**EMILIA:**  Why, the wrong is but a wrong i' the world, and having the world for your labor, 'tis a wrong in your own world,
and you might quickly make it right.

**DESDEMONA:**  I do not think there is any such woman.

**EMILIA:**  Yes, a dozen, and as many                                          85
To th' vantage° as would store° the world they played° for.
But I do think it is their husbands' faults
If wives do fall. Say that they slack their duties°
And pour our treasures into foreign laps,°
Or else break out in peevish jealousies,                                        90
Throwing restraint upon us? Or say they strike us,°
Or scant our former having in despite?°
Why, we have galls,° and though we have some grace,
Yet have we some revenge. Let husbands know
Their wives have sense° like them. They see, and smell,                         95
And have their palates both for sweet and sour,
As husbands have. What is it that they do
When they change us for others? Is it sport?°
I think it is. And doth affection° breed it?
I think it doth. Is 't frailty that thus errs?                                  100
It is so, too. And have not we affections,
Desires for sport, and frailty, as men have?
Then let them use us well; else let them know,
The ills we do, their ills instruct us so.

**DESDEMONA:** Good night, good night. God me such uses° send                    105
Not to pick bad from bad, but by bad mend!°

*Exeunt.*

---

86 **To th' vantage** in addition, to boot    **store** populate    **played** (1) gambled (2) sported sexually
88 **duties** marital duties    89 **pour . . . laps** i.e., are unfaithful, give what is rightfully ours (semen)
to other women    91 **Throwing . . . us** i.e., jealously restricting our freedom to see other men
92 **scant . . . despite** reduce our allowance to spite us    93 **have galls** i.e., are capable of resenting
injury and insult    95 **sense** physical sense    98 **sport** sexual pastime    99 **affection** passion
105 **uses** habit, practice    106 **Not . . . mend** i.e., not to learn bad conduct from others' badness (as
Emilia has suggested women learn from men), but to mend my ways by perceiving what badness is,
making spiritual benefit out of evil and adversity

# ACT V

## SCENE I [A STREET IN CYPRUS.]

*Enter Iago and Roderigo.*

**IAGO:** Here stand behind this bulk.° Straight will he come.
Wear thy good rapier bare,° and put it home.
Quick, quick! Fear nothing. I'll be at thy elbow.
It makes us or it mars us. Think on that,
And fix most firm thy resolution.                                                    5
**RODERIGO:** Be near at hand. I may miscarry in 't.
**IAGO:** Here, at thy hand. Be bold, and take thy stand.

[*Iago stands aside. Roderigo conceals himself.*]

**RODERIGO:** I have no great devotion to the deed;
And yet he hath given me satisfying reasons.
'Tis but a man gone. Forth, my sword! He dies.                                      10

[*He draws.*]

**IAGO:** I have rubbed this young quat° almost to the sense,°
And he grows angry. Now, whether he kill Cassio
Or Cassio him, or each do kill the other,
Every way makes my gain. Live Roderigo,°
He calls me to a restitution large                                                  15
Of gold and jewels that I bobbed° from him
As gifts to Desdemona.
It must not be. If Cassio do remain,
He hath a daily beauty in his life
That makes me ugly; and besides, the Moor                                          20
May unfold° me to him; there stand I in much peril.
No, he must die. Be 't so. I hear him coming.

*Enter Cassio.*

**RODERIGO** [*coming forth*]: I know his gait, 'tis he.—Villain,
thou diest!

---

**1 bulk** framework projecting from the front of a shop    **2 bare** unsheathed    **11 quat** pimple, pus-
tule    **to the sense** to the quick    **14 Live Roderigo** if Roderigo lives    **16 bobbed** swindled
**21 unfold** expose

[*He attacks Cassio.*]

**CASSIO:** That thrust had been mine enemy indeed,
But that my coat° is better than thou know'st.            25
I will make proof° of thine.

[*He draws, and wounds Roderigo.*]

**RODERIGO:**                    O, I am slain! [*He falls.*]

[*Iago, from behind, wounds Cassio in the leg, and exits.*]

**CASSIO:** I am maimed forever. Help, ho! Murder! Murder!

*Enter Othello.*

**OTHELLO:** The voice of Cassio! Iago keeps his word.
**RODERIGO:** O, villain that I am!
**OTHELLO:** It is even so.                                30
**CASSIO:** O, help, ho! Light! A surgeon!
**OTHELLO:** 'Tis he. O brave Iago, honest and just,
That hast such noble sense of thy friend's wrong!
Thou teachest me. Minion,° your dear lies dead,
And your unblest fate hies.° Strumpet, I come.            35
Forth of° my heart those charms, thine eyes, are blotted;
Thy bed, lust-stained, shall with lust's blood be spotted.

*Exit Othello.*

*Enter Lodovico and Gratiano.*

**CASSIO:** What ho! No watch? No passage?° Murder! Murder!
**GRATIANO:** 'Tis some mischance. The voice is very direful.
**CASSIO:** O, help!                                      40
**LODOVICO:** Hark!
**RODERIGO:** O wretched villain!
**LODOVICO:** Two or three groan. 'Tis heavy° night;
These may be counterfeits. Let's think 't unsafe
To come in to° the cry without more help.                45

---

**25 coat** (Possibly a garment of mail under the outer clothing, or simply a tougher coat than Roderigo expected.)  **26 proof** a test  **34 Minion** hussy (i.e., Desdemona)  **35 hies** hastens on  **36 Forth of** from out  **38 passage** people passing by  **43 heavy** thick, dark  **45 come in to** approach

[*They remain near the entrance.*]

**RODERIGO:**   Nobody come? Then shall I bleed to death.

*Enter Iago* [*in his shirtsleeves, with a light*].

**LODOVICO:**   Hark!

**GRATIANO:**   Here's one comes in his shirt, with light and
weapons.

**IAGO:**   Who's there? Whose noise is this that cries on° murder?

**LODOVICO:**   We do not know.

**IAGO:**                            Did not you hear a cry?                    50

**CASSIO:**   Here, here! For heaven's sake, help me!

**IAGO:**                                      What's the matter?

[*He moves toward Cassio.*]

**GRATIANO** [*to Lodovico*]:   This is Othello's ancient, as I take it.

**LODOVICO** [*to Gratiano*]:   The same indeed, a very valiant
fellow.

**IAGO** [*to Cassio*]:   What° are you here that cry so grievously?

**CASSIO:**   Iago? O, I am spoiled,° undone by villains!                    55
Give me some help.

**IAGO:**   O me, Lieutenant! What villains have done this?

**CASSIO:**   I think that one of them is hereabout,
And cannot make° away.

**IAGO:**                            O treacherous villains!

[*To Lodovico and Gratiano.*]

What are you there? Come in, and give some help. [*They
advance.*]                                                                              60

**RODERIGO:**   O, help me there!

**CASSIO:**   That's one of them.

**IAGO:**                            O murderous slave! O villain!

[*He stabs Roderigo.*]

**RODERIGO:**   O damned Iago! O inhuman dog!

---

**49 cries on** cries out    **54 What** who (also at lines 60 and 66)    **55 spoiled** ruined, done for
**59 make** get

**IAGO:** Kill men i' the dark?—Where be these bloody
thieves?—

How silent is this town!—Ho! Murder, murder!—    65

[*To Lodovico and Gratiano.*] What may you be? Are you of
good or evil?

**LODOVICO:** As you shall prove us, praise° us.

**IAGO:** Signor Lodovico?

**LODOVICO:** He, sir.

**IAGO:** I cry you mercy.° Here's Cassio hurt by villains.    70

**GRATIANO:** Cassio?

**IAGO:** How is 't, brother?

**CASSIO:** My leg is cut in two.

**IAGO:** Marry, heaven forbid!

Light, gentlemen! I'll bind it with my shirt.    75

[*He hands them the light, and tends to Cassio's wound.*]

*Enter Bianca.*

**BIANCA:** What is the matter, ho? Who is 't that cried?

**IAGO:** Who is 't that cried?

**BIANCA:**                O my dear Cassio!

My sweet Cassio! O Cassio, Cassio, Cassio!

**IAGO:** O notable strumpet! Cassio, may you suspect

Who they should be that have thus mangled you?    80

**CASSIO:** No.

**GRATIANO:** I am sorry to find you thus. I have been to seek
you.

**IAGO:** Lend me a garter. [*He applies a tourniquet.*] So.—O,
for a chair,°

To bear him easily hence!

**BIANCA:** Alas, he faints! O Cassio, Cassio, Cassio!    85

**IAGO:** Gentlemen all, I do suspect this trash

To be a party in this injury.—

Patience awhile, good Cassio.—Come, come;

Lend me a light. [*He shines the light on Roderigo.*] Know
we this face or no?

---

**67 praise** appraise    **70 I cry you mercy** I beg your pardon    **83 chair** litter

Alas, my friend and my dear countryman            90
Roderigo! No.—Yes, sure.—O heaven! Roderigo!

**GRATIANO:** What, of Venice?

**IAGO:** Even he, sir. Did you know him?

**GRATIANO:** Know him? Ay.

**IAGO:** Signor Gratiano? I cry your gentle° pardon.      95
These bloody accidents° must excuse my manners
That so neglected you.

**GRATIANO:**                 I am glad to see you.

**IAGO:** How do you, Cassio? O, a chair, a chair!

**GRATIANO:** Roderigo!

**IAGO:** He, he, 'tis he. [*A litter is brought in.*] O, that's well
said;° the chair.                                          100
Some good man bear him carefully from hence;
I'll fetch the General's surgeon. [*To Bianca.*] For you,
mistress,
Save you your labor.°—He that lies slain here, Cassio,
Was my dear friend. What malice° was between you?

**CASSIO:** None in the world, nor do I know the man.      105

**IAGO** [*to Bianca*]: What, look you pale?—O, bear him out o'
th' air.°

                    [*Cassio and Roderigo are borne off.*]

Stay you,° good gentlemen.—Look you pale, mistress?—
Do you perceive the gastness° of her eye?—
Nay, if you stare,° we shall hear more anon.—
Behold her well; I pray you, look upon her.            110
Do you see, gentlemen? Nay, guiltiness
Will speak, though tongues were out of use.

    [*Enter Emilia.*]

**EMILIA:** 'Las, what's the matter? What's the matter, husband?

**IAGO:** Cassio hath here been set on in the dark

---

**95 gentle** noble    **96 accidents** sudden events    **100 well said** well done    **103 Save . . . labor**
i.e., never you mind tending Cassio    **104 malice** enmity    **106 bear . . . air** (Fresh air was thought
to be dangerous for a wound.)    **107 Stay you** (Lodovico and Gratiano are evidently about to leave.)
**108 gastness** terror    **109 stare** (Iago pretends to interpret Bianca's wild looks as an involuntary
confession of guilt.)

By Roderigo and fellows that are scaped.                                    *115*
He's almost slain, and Roderigo dead.

**EMILIA:** Alas, good gentleman! Alas, good Cassio!

**IAGO:** This is the fruits of whoring. Prithee, Emilia,
Go know° of Cassio where he supped tonight.
[*To Bianca.*] What, do you shake at that?                                  *120*

**BIANCA:** He supped at my house, but I therefore shake not.

**IAGO:** O, did he so? I charge you go with me.

**EMILIA:** O, fie upon thee, strumpet!

**BIANCA:** I am no strumpet, but of life as honest°
As you that thus abuse me.                                                  *125*

**EMILIA:** As I? Faugh! Fie upon thee!

**IAGO:** Kind gentlemen, let's go see poor Cassio dressed.°—
Come, mistress, you must tell's another tale.
Emilia, run you to the citadel
And tell my lord and lady what hath happed.—                                *130*
Will you go on afore? [*Aside.*] This is the night
That either makes me or fordoes° me quite.              *Exeunt.*

## SCENE II [A BEDCHAMBER IN THE CITADEL.]

*Enter Othello [with a light], and Desdemona in her bed.°*

**OTHELLO:** It is the cause,° it is the cause, my soul.
Let me not name it to you, you chaste stars!
It is the cause. Yet I'll not shed her blood,
Nor scar that whiter skin of hers than snow,
And smooth as monumental° alabaster.                                        *5*
Yet she must die, else she'll betray more men.
Put out the light, and then put out the light.°
If I quench thee, thou flaming minister,°
I can again thy former light restore,
Should I repent me;° but once put out thy light,                            *10*
Thou cunning'st pattern° of excelling nature,

---

**119 know** learn     **124 honest** chaste     **127 Cassio dressed** Cassio's wounds dressed     **132 fordoes**
undoes, ruins
**[s.d.] in her bed** (Either the curtains are drawn back to reveal the bed in a recessed area backstage,
or the bed is "thrust out" onstage as the scene begins.)     **1 cause** i.e., cause of justice, the offence
itself, which Othello must correct as an agent of justice     **5 monumental** i.e., used in making tombs
and funeral monuments     **7 the light . . . light** the torch or lamp . . . Desdemona's life     **8 flaming
minister** torch or lamp that serves me     **10 repent me** change my mind     **11 Thou . . . pattern** you
skillfully wrought perfect example

I know not where is that Promethean heat°
That can thy light relume.° When I have plucked thy rose,
I cannot give it vital growth again;
It needs must wither. I'll smell thee on the tree.                    *15*

[*He kisses her.*]

O balmy breath, that dost almost persuade
Justice to break her sword! One more, one more.
Be thus when thou art dead, and I will kill thee,
And love thee after. One more, and that's the last.

[*He kisses her.*]

So sweet was ne'er so fatal. I must weep,                             *20*
But they are cruel° tears. This sorrow's heavenly;
It strikes where it doth love.° She wakes.
DESDEMONA:   Who's there? Othello?
OTHELLO:   Ay, Desdemona.
DESDEMONA:   Will you come to bed, my lord?                           *25*
OTHELLO:   Have you prayed tonight, Desdemon?
DESDEMONA:   Ay, my lord.
OTHELLO:   If you bethink yourself of any crime°
Unreconciled as yet to heaven and grace,
Solicit° for it straight.°                                            *30*
DESDEMONA:   Alack, my lord, what may you mean by that?
OTHELLO:   Well, do it, and be brief. I will walk by.
I would not kill thy unprepared spirit.
No, heaven forfend!° I would not kill thy soul.
DESDEMONA:   Talk you of killing?
OTHELLO:                                    Ay, I do.
DESDEMONA:                                    Then heaven              *35*
Have mercy on me!
OTHELLO:                   Amen, with all my heart!
DESDEMONA:   If you say so, I hope you will not kill me.
OTHELLO:   Humh!

---

**12 Promethean heat** divine fire (Alluding to the theft of fire from heaven by Prometheus.)
**13 relume** rekindle   **21 cruel** unrelenting   **22 It . . . love** (Compare Hebrews 12:6: "For whom
the Lord loveth he chasteneth.")   **28 crime** sin   **30 Solicit** petition, pray   **straight** immediately
**34 forfend** forbid

**DESDEMONA:** And yet I fear you; for you're fatal then
  When your eyes roll so. Why I should fear I know not, 40
  Since guiltiness I know not; but yet I feel I fear.

**OTHELLO:** Think on thy sins.

**DESDEMONA:**                    They are loves I bear to you.°

**OTHELLO:** Ay, and for that thou diest.

**DESDEMONA:** That death's unnatural that kills for loving.
  Alas, why gnaw you so your nether lip? 45
  Some bloody passion shakes your very frame.
  These are portents; but yet I hope, I hope,
  They do not point on° me.

**OTHELLO:** Peace, and be still!

**DESDEMONA:** I will so. What's the matter? 50

**OTHELLO:** That handkerchief which I so loved and gave thee
  Thou gav'st to Cassio.

**DESDEMONA:**                    No, by my life and soul!
  Send for the man and ask him.

**OTHELLO:** Sweet soul, take heed, take heed of perjury.
  Thou art on thy deathbed. 55

**DESDEMONA:** Ay, but not yet to die.

**OTHELLO:**                    Yes, presently.°
  Therefore confess thee freely of thy sin;
  For to deny each article with oath
  Cannot remove nor choke the strong conception°
  That I do groan withal.° Thou art to die. 60

**DESDEMONA:** Then Lord have mercy on me!

**OTHELLO:**                    I say, amen.

**DESDEMONA:** And have you mercy too! I never did
  Offend° you in my life; never loved Cassio
  But with such general warranty° of heaven
  As I might love. I never gave him token. 65

**OTHELLO:** By heaven, I saw my handkerchief in 's hand.
  O perjured woman! Thou dost stone° my heart,
  And makes me call what I intend to do

---

**42 They are . . . you** i.e., if I sinned, it was in loving you more than my father or more than God
**48 point on** point at, predict what is to happen to   **56 presently** immediately   **59 conception** (1)
belief in your guilt (2) plan in my mind   **60 groan withal** (1) groan at in sorrow (2) as in giving
birth   **63 Offend** wrong   **64 warranty** sanction   **67 stone** turn to stone, harden

A murder, which I thought a sacrifice.
I saw the handkerchief.

DESDEMONA:                    He found it, then.                    70
I never gave it him. Send for him hither;
Let him confess a truth.

OTHELLO:                    He hath confessed.

DESDEMONA:    What, my lord?

OTHELLO:    That he hath used thee.

DESDEMONA:                    How? Unlawfully?

OTHELLO:                                        Ay.

DESDEMONA:    He will not say so.

OTHELLO:                    No, his mouth is stopped;    75
Honest Iago hath ta'en order° for 't.

DESDEMONA:    O, my fear interprets. What, is he dead?

OTHELLO:    Had all his hairs been lives, my great revenge
Had stomach for them all.

DESDEMONA:    Alas, he is betrayed and I undone!  [*She weeps.*]    80

OTHELLO:    Out, strumpet! Weep'st thou for him to my face?

DESDEMONA:    O, banish me, my lord, but kill me not!

OTHELLO:    Down, strumpet!

DESDEMONA:    Kill me tomorrow; let me live tonight!

OTHELLO:    Nay, if you strive—                    85

DESDEMONA:    But half an hour!

OTHELLO:                    Being done,° there is no pause.

DESDEMONA:    But while I say one prayer!

OTHELLO:                    It is too late.

*Smothers her.*

EMILIA [*at the door*]:    My lord, my lord! What, ho! My lord,
my lord!

OTHELLO:    What noise is this? Not dead? Not yet quite dead?
I that am cruel am yet merciful;                    90
I would not have thee linger in thy pain.

[*He dispatches her.*]

---

**76 ta'en order** taken measures    **86 Being done** i.e., since justice has begun its relentless course

So, so.

**EMILIA** [*within*]:    What, ho! My lord, my lord!

**OTHELLO:**                                                    Who's there?

**EMILIA** [*within*]:    O, good my lord, I would speak a word with
you!

**OTHELLO:**    Yes, 'tis Emilia.—By and by.—She's dead.
'Tis like° she comes to speak of Cassio's death.—                    95
The noise was here.° Ha! No more moving?
Still as the grave. Shall she come in? Were 't good?—
I think she stirs again. No. What's best to do?
If she come in, she'll sure speak to my wife.
My wife! My wife! What wife? I have no wife.                         100
O, insupportable! O heavy hour!
Methinks it should be now a huge eclipse
Of sun and moon, and that th' affrighted globe
Should yawn° at alteration.°

**EMILIA** [*within*]:                       I do beseech you
That I may speak with you. O, good my lord!                          105

**OTHELLO:**    I had forgot thee. O, come in, Emilia.—
Soft,° by and by. Let me the curtains draw.—

[*He closes the bed-curtains and opens the door.*]

Where art thou?

*Enter Emilia.*

                          What's the matter with thee now?

**EMILIA:**    O, my good lord, yonder's foul murders done!

**OTHELLO:**    What, now?                                           110

**EMILIA:**    But now, my lord.

**OTHELLO:**    It is the very error° of the moon;
She comes more nearer earth than she was wont,
And makes men mad.

**EMILIA:**    Cassio, my lord, hath killed a young Venetian         115
Called Roderigo.

---

**95 like** likely that    **96 here** (The Folio's *high* is possible, suggesting that the commotion of the attack on Cassio was loud.)    **104 yawn** gape in amazement, i.e., move in an earthquake (According to Pliny, earthquakes often happen during eclipses.)    **at alteration** at these cataclysmic events in nature, well-suited to express the horror of Desdemona's death    **107 Soft** wait a minute    **112 error** aberration, irregularity

**OTHELLO:**                Roderigo killed?
And Cassio killed?

**EMILIA:**                No, Cassio is not killed.

**OTHELLO:**   Not Cassio killed? Then murder's out of tune,
And sweet revenge grows harsh.

**DESDEMONA:**   O, falsely, falsely murdered!                    120

**EMILIA:**   O Lord, what cry is that?

**OTHELLO:**   That? What?

**EMILIA:**   Out° and alas, that was my lady's voice.

[*She opens the bed-curtains.*]

Help, help, ho, help! O lady, speak again!
Sweet Desdemona! O sweet mistress, speak!                    125

**DESDEMONA:**   A guiltless death I die.

**EMILIA:**   O, who hath done this deed?

**DESDEMONA:**   Nobody; I myself. Farewell.
Commend me to my kind lord. O, farewell!          [*She dies.*]

**OTHELLO:**   Why, how should she be murdered?

**EMILIA:**                Alas, who knows?     130

**OTHELLO:**   You heard her say herself it was not I.

**EMILIA:**   She said so. I must needs report the truth.

**OTHELLO:**   She's like a liar gone to burning hell!
'Twas I that killed her.

**EMILIA:**                O, the more angel she,
And you the blacker devil!                    135

**OTHELLO:**   She turned to folly,° and she was a whore.

**EMILIA:**   Thou dost belie° her, and thou art a devil.

**OTHELLO:**   She was false as water.

**EMILIA:**   Thou art rash as fire to say
That she was false. O, she was heavenly true!                    140

**OTHELLO:**   Cassio did top her. Ask thy husband else.°
O, I were damned beneath all depth in hell
But that I did proceed upon just grounds
To this extremity. Thy husband knew it all.

---

**123 Out** (A cry of dismay, intensifying *alas.*)     **136 folly** i.e., wantonness, fleshly sin     **137 belie** slander     **141 else** i.e., if you don't believe me

**EMILIA:** My husband?                                                          *145*

**OTHELLO:** Thy husband.

**EMILIA:** That she was false to wedlock?

**OTHELLO:** Ay, with Cassio. Nay, had she been true,
    If heaven would make me such another world
    Of one entire and perfect chrysolite,°                                     *150*
    I'd not have sold her for it.

**EMILIA:** My husband?

**OTHELLO:** Ay, 'twas he that told me on her first.
    An honest man he is, and hates the slime
    That sticks on filthy deeds.                                             *155*

**EMILIA:** My husband?

**OTHELLO:** What needs this iterance,° woman? I say thy
    husband.

**EMILIA:** O mistress, villainy hath made mocks with° love!
    My husband say she was false?

**OTHELLO:**                                    He, woman;
    I say thy husband. Dost understand the word?                            *160*
    My friend, thy husband, honest, honest Iago.

**EMILIA:** If he say so, may his pernicious soul
    Rot half a grain a day! He lies to th' heart.
    She was too fond of her most filthy bargain.

**OTHELLO:** Ha?                                                  [*He draws.*]   *165*

**EMILIA:** Do thy worst!
    This deed of thine is no more worthy heaven
    Than thou wast worthy her.

**OTHELLO:**                                    Peace, you were best.°

**EMILIA:** Thou hast not half that power to do me harm
    As I have to be hurt.° O gull!° O dolt!                                  *170*
    As ignorant as dirt! Thou hast done a deed—
    I care not for thy sword; I'll make thee known,
    Though I lost twenty lives.—Help! Help, ho, help!
    The Moor hath killed my mistress! Murder, murder!

*Enter Montano, Gratiano, and Iago.*

---

**150 chrysolite** precious topaz   **157 iterance** iteration, repetition   **158 made mocks with** derided, made sport of   **168 you were best** it would be best for you   **170 to be hurt** i.e., to endure hurt **gull** dupe

**MONTANO:** What is the matter? How now, General?          *175*

**EMILIA:** O, are you come, Iago? You have done well,

That men must lay their murders on your neck.

**GRATIANO:** What is the matter?

**EMILIA** [*to Iago*]: Disprove this villain, if thou be'st a man.

He says thou toldst him that his wife was false.          *180*

I know thou didst not; thou'rt not such a villain.

Speak, for my heart is full.

**IAGO:** I told him what I thought, and told no more

Than what he found himself was apt° and true.

**EMILIA:** But did you ever tell him she was false?          *185*

**IAGO:** I did.

**EMILIA:** You told a lie, an odious, damnèd lie!

Upon my soul, a lie, a wicked lie.

She false with Cassio? Did you say with Cassio?

**IAGO:** With Cassio, mistress. Go to, charm° your tongue.          *190*

**EMILIA:** I will not charm my tongue; I am bound to speak.

My mistress here lies murdered in her bed—

**ALL:** O heavens forfend!

**EMILIA:** And your reports have set the murder on.

**OTHELLO:** Nay, stare not, masters. It is true indeed.          *195*

**GRATIANO:** 'Tis a strange truth.

**MONTANO:** O monstrous act!

**EMILIA:**                    Villainy, villainy, villainy!

I think upon 't—I think I smell 't! O villainy!

I thought so then°—I'll kill myself for grief—

O villainy, villainy!          *200*

**IAGO:** What, are you mad? I charge you, get you home.

**EMILIA:** Good gentlemen, let me have leave to speak.

'Tis proper I obey him, but not now.

Perchance, Iago, I will ne'er go home.

Othello: O! O! O!          [*Othello falls on the bed.*°]

**EMILIA:**                    Nay, lay thee down and roar,          *205*

For thou hast killed the sweetest innocent

---

**184 apt** plausible     **190 charm** keep silent (as though by a magic spell)     **199 then** (Perhaps at Act III, Scene iii, lines 331–332 and Act IV, Scene ii, lines 137–154.)     **205 [s.d.] Othello . . . bed** (This direction is from the Quarto, as also *He kisses her* at line 19 and *She dies* at line 129.)

That e'er did lift up eye.°
OTHELLO [*rising*]:                 O, she was foul!
    I scarce did know you, uncle. There lies your niece,
    Whose breath indeed these hands have newly stopped.
    I know this act shows° horrible and grim.          *210*
GRATIANO:   Poor Desdemon! I am glad thy father's dead.
    Thy match was mortal to him, and pure grief
    Shore his old thread° in twain. Did he live now,
    This sight would make him do a desperate turn,°
    Yea, curse his better angel from his side,          *215*
    And fall to reprobance.°
OTHELLO:   'Tis pitiful. But yet Iago knows
    That she with Cassio hath the act of shame
    A thousand times committed. Cassio confessed it;
    And she did gratify° his amorous works          *220*
    With that recognizance° and pledge of love
    Which I first gave her. I saw it in his hand;
    It was a handkerchief, an antique token
    My father gave my mother.
EMILIA:   O God! O heavenly God!          *225*
IAGO:   Zounds, hold your peace.
EMILIA:               'Twill out, 'twill out! I peace?
    No, I will speak as liberal as the north.°
    Let heaven and men and devils, let them all,
    All, all, cry shame against me, yet I'll speak.
IAGO:   Be wise, and get you home.
EMILIA:              I will not.

[*Iago threatens Emilia.*]

GRATIANO:                Fie!          *230*
    Your sword upon a woman?
EMILIA:   O thou dull Moor! That handkerchief thou speak'st of
    I found by fortune and did give my husband;
    For often, with a solemn earnestness,

---

207 **lift up eye** i.e., lift her eyes to heaven    210 **shows** looks    213 **Shore . . . thread** sheared the thread of his old age (as Atropos, one of the three Fates, was thought to do)    214 **turn** deed 216 **reprobance** damnation, i.e., suicide    220 **gratify** reward    221 **recognizance** token 227 **liberal as the north** freely as the north wind (blows)

More than indeed belonged° to such a trifle,                           235
He begged of me to steal 't.

IAGO:                          Villainous whore!

EMILIA:   She give it Cassio? No, alas! I found it,
And I did give 't my husband.

IAGO:                          Filth, thou liest!

EMILIA:   By heaven, I do not, I do not, gentlemen.
O murderous coxcomb!° What should such a fool             240
Do with so good a wife?

OTHELLO:   Are there no stones° in heaven
But what serves for the thunder?—Precious° villain!

*[He runs at Iago; Montano disarms Othello. Iago, from behind, stabs Emilia.°]*

GRATIANO:   The woman falls! Sure he hath killed his wife.

EMILIA:   Ay, ay. O, lay me by my mistress' side.                    245

*Exit [Iago.]*

GRATIANO:   He's gone, but his wife's killed.

MONTANO:   'Tis a notorious villain. Take you this weapon,
Which I have here recovered from the Moor.
Come, guard the door without. Let him not pass,
But kill him rather. I'll after that same villain,                    250
For 'tis a damnèd slave.

*Exit [with all but Othello and Emilia, who has been laid by Desdemona's side].*

OTHELLO:   I am not valiant neither,
But every puny whipster° gets my sword.
But why should honor° outlive honesty?°
Let it go all.

EMILIA:          What did thy song bode, lady?                       255
Hark, canst thou hear me? I will play the swan,

---

**235 belonged** was appropriate    **240 coxcomb** fool (Addressed to Othello.)    **242 stones** bolts, such as those used for thunderbolts    **243 Precious** i.e., arrant, utter    **[s.d.] He . . . Emilia** (The Quarto text reads, "The Moor runs at Iago. Iago kills his wife." The Quarto also specifies the exit of Iago at line 245 and the death of Emilia at line 260.)    **253 whipster** contemptible fellow (one who is always ready to whip out his sword)    **254 honor** i.e., the bravery for which one enjoys a soldier's reputation    **honesty** true integrity

And die in music. [*She sings.*] "Willow, willow, willow."
Moor, she was chaste. She loved thee, cruel Moor.
So come my soul to bliss as I speak true.
So speaking as I think, alas, I die.                    [*She dies.*]    260
OTHELLO:   I have another weapon in this chamber;
It was a sword of Spain, the ice-brook's temper°—
O, here it is. [*He finds a sword.*] Uncle, I must come forth.
GRATIANO [*within*]:   If thou attempt it, it will cost thee dear.
Thou hast no weapon, and perforce must suffer.                    265
OTHELLO:   Look in upon me then and speak with me,
Or, naked° as I am, I will assault thee.

[*Enter Gratiano.*]

GRATIANO:   What is the matter?
OTHELLO:                      Behold, I have a weapon;
A better never did itself sustain
Upon a soldier's thigh. I have seen the day                    270
That, with this little arm and this good sword,
I have made my way through more impediments
Than twenty times your stop.° But O, vain boast!
Who can control his fate? 'Tis not so now.
Be not afraid, though you do see me weaponed;                    275
Here is my journey's end, here is my butt°
And very seamark° of my utmost sail.

[*Gratiano steps back.*]

Do you go back dismayed? 'Tis a lost° fear;
Man but a rush° against Othello's breast
And he retires. Where should Othello go?                    280

[*He turns to Desdemona.*]

Now, how dost thou look now? O ill-starred wench!
Pale as thy smock! When we shall meet at compt,°
This look of thine will hurl my soul from heaven,

---

262 **the ice-brook's temper** tempered in ice-cold water    267 **naked** unarmed    273 **stop** power
(to stop)    276 **butt** goal, limit (An archery term.)    277 **seamark** beacon (marking his destination
or limit)    278 **lost** wasted, unneeded    279 **Man . . . rush** wield no more than a reed    282 **compt**
account, judgment day

And fiends will snatch at it. Cold, cold, my girl?
Even like thy chastity. O cursèd, cursèd slave!°                285
Whip me, ye devils,
From the possession of this heavenly sight!
Blow me about in winds! Roast me in sulfur!
Wash me in steep-down gulfs of liquid fire!
O Desdemon! Dead, Desdemon! Dead! O! O!                290

*Enter Lodovico, Cassio [carried in a litter°], Montano, and*
*Iago [prisoner], with officers.*

**LODOVICO:**   Where is this rash and most unfortunate man?
**OTHELLO:**   That's he that was Othello. Here I am.
**LODOVICO:**   Where is that viper? Bring the villain forth.

*[Iago is led forward.]*

**OTHELLO:**   I look down towards his feet;° but that's a fable.
If that thou be'st a devil, I cannot kill thee.                295

*[He wounds Iago.]*

**LODOVICO:**   Wrench his sword from him.

*[Othello is disarmed.]*

**IAGO:**                                    I bleed, sir, but not
killed.
**OTHELLO:**   I am not sorry neither. I'd have thee live,
For in my sense° 'tis happiness to die.
**LODOVICO:**   O thou Othello, that was once so good,
Fall'n in the practice° of a cursèd slave,°                300
What shall be said to thee?
**OTHELLO:**                          Why, anything.
An honorable murderer, if you will,
For naught I did in hate, but all in honor.
**LODOVICO:**   This wretch hath part confessed his villainy.
Did you and he consent° in Cassio's death?                305

---

**285 slave** i.e., Othello himself    **290 [s.d.] in a litter** (The Quarto specifies that Cassio is "in a chair.")    **294 towards his feet** i.e., to see if they are cloven, as the devil's are fabled to be    **298 in my sense** to one who feels as I do    **300 in the practice** through the plotting, into the snare    **slave** villain    **305 consent** agree

**OTHELLO:**   Ay.

**CASSIO:**   Dear General, I never gave you cause.

**OTHELLO:**   I do believe it, and I ask your pardon.
  Will you, I pray, demand that demi-devil
  Why he hath thus ensnared my soul and body?                   310

**IAGO:**   Demand me nothing. What you know, you know.
  From this time forth I never will speak word.

**LODOVICO:**   What, not to pray?

**GRATIANO:**   Torments° will ope your lips.

**OTHELLO:**   Well, thou dost best.                              315

**LODOVICO:**   Sir, you shall understand what hath befall'n,
  Which, as I think, you know not. Here is a letter
  Found in the pocket of the slain Roderigo;
  And here another. [*He produces letters.*] The one of them imports
  The death of Cassio, to be undertook                         320
  By Roderigo.

**OTHELLO:**   O villain!

**CASSIO:**                    Most heathenish and most gross!°

**LODOVICO** [*showing another paper*]:   Now here's another discontented° paper
  Found in his pocket too. And this, it seems,
  Roderigo meant t' have sent this damnèd villain;
  But that belike° Iago in the interim                          325
  Came in and satisfied him.°

**OTHELLO:**   O thou pernicious caitiff!—
  How came you, Cassio, by that handkerchief
  That was my wife's?

**CASSIO:**                    I found it in my chamber;
  And he himself confessed but even now                        330
  That there he dropped it for a special purpose
  Which wrought to his desire.°

**OTHELLO:**                    O fool, fool, fool!

**CASSIO:**   There is besides in Roderigo's letter

---

**314 Torments** torture   **322 gross** monstrous   **323 discontented** full of discontent   **325 belike** most likely   **326 Came . . . him** interposed and gave him satisfactory explanation   **332 wrought . . . desire** worked out as he wished, fitted in with his plan

How he upbraids Iago, that he made him
Brave° me upon the watch, whereon it came°                                 335
That I was cast;° and even but now he spake,
After long seeming dead, Iago hurt him,
Iago set him on.

LODOVICO [*to Othello*]:   You must forsake this room and go
with us.
Your power and your command is taken off,°                                 340
And Cassio rules in Cyprus. For this slave,
If there be any cunning cruelty
That can torment him much and hold him long,°
It shall be his. You shall close prisoner rest°
Till that the nature of your fault be known                                345
To the Venetian state.—Come, bring away.

OTHELLO:   Soft you;° a word or two before you go.
I have done the state some service, and they know 't.
No more of that. I pray you, in your letters,
When you shall these unlucky° deeds relate,                                350
Speak of me as I am; nothing extenuate,
Nor set down aught in malice. Then must you speak
Of one that loved not wisely but too well;
Of one not easily jealous but, being wrought,°
Perplexed° in the extreme; of one whose hand,                             355
Like the base Indian,° threw a pearl away
Richer than all his tribe; of one whose subdued° eyes,
Albeit unusèd to the melting mood,
Drops tears as fast as the Arabian trees
Their medicinable gum.° Set you down this;                                360
And say besides that in Aleppo once,
Where a malignant and a turbaned Turk
Beat a Venetian and traduced the state,
I took by th' throat the circumcisèd dog

---

**335 Brave** defy   **whereon it came** whereof it came about   **336 cast** dismissed   **340 taken off** taken away   **343 hold him long** keep him alive a long time (during his torture)   **344 rest** remain   **347 Soft you** one moment   **350 unlucky** unfortunate   **354 wrought** worked upon, worked into a frenzy   **355 Perplexed** distraught   **356 Indian** (This reading from the Quarto pictures an ignorant savage who cannot recognize the value of a precious jewel. The Folio reading, *Iudean* or *Judean*, i.e., infidel or disbeliever, may refer to Herod, who slew Miriamne in a fit of jealousy, or to Judas Iscariot, the betrayer of Christ.)   **357 subdued** i.e., overcome by grief   **360 gum** i.e., myrrh

And smote him, thus.                    [*He stabs himself.°*]    *365*
LODOVICO:   O bloody period!°
GRATIANO:   All that is spoke is marred.
OTHELLO:   I kissed thee ere I killed thee. No way but this,
    Killing myself, to die upon a kiss.

[*He kisses Desdemona and dies.*]

CASSIO:   This did I fear, but thought he had no weapon;    *370*
    For he was great of heart.
LODOVICO [*to Iago*]:          O Spartan dog,°
    More fell° than anguish, hunger, or the sea!
    Look on the tragic loading of this bed.
    This is thy work. The object poisons sight;
    Let it be hid.° Gratiano, keep° the house,    *375*

[*The bed curtains are drawn*]

    And seize upon° the fortunes of the Moor,
    For they succeed on° you. [*To Cassio.*] To you, Lord
    Governor,
    Remains the censure° of this hellish villain,
    The time, the place, the torture. O, enforce it!
    Myself will straight aboard, and to the state    *380*
    This heavy act with heavy heart relate.          *Exeunt.*

—*1604?*

---

365 [s.d.] **He stabs himself** (This direction is in the Quarto text.)    **366 period** termination, conclusion    **371 Spartan dog** (Spartan dogs were noted for their savagery and silence.)    **372 fell** cruel    **375 Let it be hid** i.e., draw the bed curtains (No stage direction specifies that the dead are to be carried offstage at the end of the play.)    **keep** remain in    **376 seize upon** take legal possession of    **377 succeed on** pass as though by inheritance to    **378 censure** sentencing

*Henrik Ibsen (1828–1906), universally acknowledged as the first of the great modern playwrights, was born in Skien, a small town in Norway, the son of a merchant who went bankrupt during Ibsen's childhood. Ibsen first trained for a medical career, but drifted into the theatre, gaining, like Shakespeare and Molière, important dramatic training through a decade's service as a stage manager and director. Ibsen was unsuccessful in establishing a theatre in Oslo, and he spent almost thirty years living and writing in Germany and Italy. The fame he won through early poetic dramas like* Peer Gynt *(1867), which is considered the supreme exploration of the Norwegian national character, was overshadowed by the realistic prose plays he began writing with* Pillars of Society *(1877).* A Doll's House *(1879) and* Ghosts *(1881), which deal, respectively, with a woman's struggle for independence and self-respect and with the taboo subject of venereal disease, made Ibsen an internationally famous, if controversial, figure. Although Ibsen's type of realism, displayed in "problem plays" such as these and later psychological dramas like* The Wild Duck *(1885) and* Hedda Gabler *(1890), has become so fully assimilated into our literary heritage that now it is difficult to think of him as an innovator, his marriage of the tightly constructed plots of the conventional "well-made play" to serious discussion of social issues was one of the most significant developments in the history of drama. Interestingly, the conclusion of* A Doll's House *proved so unsettling that Ibsen was forced to write an alternative ending, in which Nora states her case but does not slam the door on her marriage. His most influential advocate in English-speaking countries was George Bernard Shaw, whose* The Quintessence of Ibsenism *(1891) is one of the earliest and most influential studies of Ibsen's dramatic methods and ideas.*

# *Henrik Ibsen*
# A Doll's House

[*Et dukkehjem*]

## Play in Three Acts

## *Characters*

*Torvald Helmer,* a lawyer
*Nora,* his wife
*Dr. Rank*

Translated by James McFarlane

*Mrs. Kristine Linde*
*Nils Krogstad*
*Anne Marie*, the nursemaid
*Helene*, the maid
*The Helmers' three children*
*A porter*

*The action takes place in the Helmers' flat.*

## ACT ONE

*A pleasant room, tastefully but not expensively furnished. On the back wall, one door on the right leads to the entrance hall, a second door on the left leads to Helmer's study. Between these two doors, a piano. In the middle of the left wall, a door; and downstage from it, a window. Near the window a round table with armchairs and a small sofa. In the right wall, upstage, a door; and on the same wall downstage, a porcelain stove with a couple of armchairs and a rocking-chair. Between the stove and the door a small table. Etchings on the walls. A whatnot with china and other small objets d'art; a small bookcase with books in handsome bindings. Carpet on the floor; a fire burns in the stove. A winter's day.*

*The front door-bell rings in the hall; a moment later, there is the sound of the front door being opened. Nora comes into the room, happily humming to herself. She is dressed in her outdoor things, and is carrying lots of parcels which she then puts down on the table, right. She leaves the door into the hall standing open; a Porter can be seen outside holding a Christmas tree and a basket; he hands them to the Maid who has opened the door for them.*

**NORA:** Hide the Christmas tree away carefully, Helene. The children mustn't see it till this evening when it's decorated. [*To the Porter, taking out her purse.*] How much?
**PORTER:** Fifty öre.
**NORA:** There's a crown. Keep the change.

[*The Porter thanks her and goes. Nora shuts the door. She continues to laugh quietly and happily to herself as she takes off her things. She takes a bag of macaroons out of her pocket and eats one or two; then she walks stealthily across and listens at her husband's door.*]

NORA:   Yes, he's in.

[*She begins humming again as she walks over to the table, right.*]

HELMER [*in his study*]:   Is that my little sky-lark chirruping out there?

NORA [*busy opening some of the parcels*]:   Yes, it is.

HELMER:   Is that my little squirrel frisking about?

NORA:   Yes!

HELMER:   When did my little squirrel get home?

NORA:   Just this minute. [*She stuffs the bag of macaroons in her pocket and wipes her mouth.*] Come on out, Torvald, and see what I've bought.

HELMER:   I don't want to be disturbed! [*A moment later, he opens the door and looks out, his pen in his hand.*] 'Bought', did you say? All that? Has my little spendthrift been out squandering money again?

NORA:   But, Torvald, surely this year we can spread ourselves just a little. This is the first Christmas we haven't had to go carefully.

HELMER:   Ah, but that doesn't mean we can afford to be extravagant, you know.

NORA:   Oh yes, Torvald, surely we can afford to be just a little bit extravagant now, can't we? Just a teeny-weeny bit. You are getting quite a good salary now, and you are going to earn lots and lots of money.

HELMER:   Yes, after the New Year. But it's going to be three whole months before the first pay cheque comes in.

NORA:   Pooh! We can always borrow in the meantime.

HELMER:   Nora! [*Crosses to her and takes her playfully by the ear.*] Here we go again, you and your frivolous ideas! Suppose I went and borrowed a thousand crowns today, and you went and spent it all over Christmas, then on New Year's Eve a slate fell and hit me on the head and there I was. . . .

NORA [*putting her hand over his mouth*]:   Sh! Don't say such horrid things.

HELMER: Yes, but supposing something like that did happen . . . what then?

NORA: If anything as awful as that did happen, I wouldn't care if I owed anybody anything or not.

HELMER: Yes, but what about the people I'd borrowed from?

NORA: Them? Who cares about them! They are only strangers!

HELMER: Nora, Nora! Just like a woman! Seriously though, Nora, you know what I think about these things. No debts! Never borrow! There's always something inhibited, something unpleasant, about a home built on credit and borrowed money. We two have managed to stick it out so far, and that's the way we'll go on for the little time that remains.

NORA [*walks over to the stove*]: Very well, just as you say, Torvald.

HELMER [*following her*]: There, there! My little singing bird mustn't go drooping her wings, eh? Has it got the sulks, that little squirrel of mine? [*Takes out his wallet.*] Nora, what do you think I've got here?

NORA [*quickly turning round*]: Money!

HELMER: There! [*He hands her some notes.*] Good heavens, I know only too well how Christmas runs away with the housekeeping.

NORA [*counts*]: Ten, twenty, thirty, forty. Oh, thank you, thank you, Torvald! This will see me quite a long way.

HELMER: Yes, it'll have to.

NORA: Yes, yes, I'll see that it does. But come over here, I want to show you all the things I've bought. And so cheap! Look, some new clothes for Ivar . . . and a little sword. There's a horse and a trumpet for Bob. And a doll and a doll's cot for Emmy. They are not very grand but she'll have them all broken before long anyway. And I've got some dress material and some handkerchiefs for the maids. Though, really, dear old Anne Marie should have had something better.

HELMER: And what's in this parcel here?

NORA [*shrieking*]: No, Torvald! You mustn't see that till tonight!

HELMER: All right. But tell me now, what did my little spendthrift fancy for herself?

NORA: For me? Puh, I don't really want anything.

HELMER: Of course you do. Anything reasonable that you think you might like, just tell me.

**NORA:** Well, I don't really know. As a matter of fact, though, Torvald . . .

**HELMER:** Well?

**NORA** [*toying with his coat buttons, and without looking at him*]: If you did want to give me something, you could . . . you could always . . .

**HELMER:** Well, well, out with it!

**NORA** [*quickly*]: You could always give me money, Torvald. Only what you think you could spare. And then I could buy myself something with it later on.

**HELMER:** But Nora. . . .

**NORA:** Oh, please, Torvald dear! Please! I beg you. Then I'd wrap the money up in some pretty gilt paper and hang it on the Christmas tree. Wouldn't that be fun?

**HELMER:** What do we call my pretty little pet when it runs away with all the money?

**NORA:** I know, I know, we call it a spendthrift. But please let's do what I said, Torvald. Then I'll have a bit of time to think about what I need most. Isn't that awfully sensible, now, eh?

**HELMER** [*smiling*]: Yes, it is indeed—that is, if only you really could hold on to the money I gave you, and really did buy something for yourself with it. But it just gets mixed up with the housekeeping and frittered away on all sorts of useless things, and then I have to dig into my pocket all over again.

**NORA:** Oh but, Torvald. . . .

**HELMER:** You can't deny it, Nora dear. [*Puts his arm around her waist.*] My pretty little pet is very sweet, but it runs away with an awful lot of money. It's incredible how expensive it is for a man to keep such a pet.

**NORA:** For shame! How can you say such a thing? As a matter of fact I save everything I can.

**HELMER** [*laughs*]: Yes, you are right there. Everything you *can*. But you simply can't.

**NORA** [*hums and smiles quietly and happily*]: Ah, if you only knew how many expenses the likes of us sky-larks and squirrels have, Torvald!

**HELMER:** What a funny little one you are! Just like your father. Always on the look-out for money, wherever you can lay your hands on it; but as soon as you've got it, it just seems to slip through your fingers. You never seem to know what you've done with it. Well, one must accept you as you are. It's in the blood. Oh yes, it is, Nora. That sort of thing is hereditary.

NORA: Oh, I only wish I'd inherited a few more of Daddy's qualities.

HELMER: And I wouldn't want my pretty little song-bird to be the least bit different from what she is now. But come to think of it, you look rather . . . rather . . . how shall I put it? . . . rather guilty today. . . .

NORA: Do I?

HELMER: Yes, you do indeed. Look me straight in the eye.

NORA [*looks at him*]: Well?

HELMER [*wagging his finger at her*]: My little sweet-tooth surely didn't forget herself in town today?

NORA: No, whatever makes you think that?

HELMER: She didn't just pop into the confectioner's for a moment?

NORA: No, I assure you, Torvald. . . !

HELMER: Didn't try sampling the preserves?

NORA: No, really I didn't.

HELMER: Didn't go nibbling a macaroon or two?

NORA: No, Torvald, honestly, you must believe me. . . !

HELMER: All right then! It's really just my little joke. . . .

NORA [*crosses to the table*]: I would never dream of doing anything you didn't want me to.

HELMER: Of course not, I know that. And then you've given me your word. . . . [*Crosses to her.*] Well then, Nora dearest, you shall keep your little Christmas secrets. They'll all come out tonight, I dare say, when we light the tree.

NORA: Did you remember to invite Dr. Rank?

HELMER: No. But there's really no need. Of course he'll come and have dinner with us. Anyway, I can ask him when he looks in this morning. I've ordered some good wine. Nora, you can't imagine how I am looking forward to this evening.

NORA: So am I. And won't the children enjoy it, Torvald!

HELMER: Oh, what a glorious feeling it is, knowing you've got a nice, safe job, and a good fat income. Don't you agree? Isn't it wonderful, just thinking about it?

NORA: Oh, it's marvellous!

**HELMER:** Do you remember last Christmas? Three whole weeks beforehand you shut yourself up every evening till after midnight making flowers for the Christmas tree and all the other splendid things you wanted to surprise us with. Ugh, I never felt so bored in all my life.

**NORA:** I wasn't the least bit bored.

**HELMER** [*smiling*]: But it turned out a bit of an anticlimax, Nora.

**NORA:** Oh, you are not going to tease me about that again! How was I to know the cat would get in and pull everything to bits?

**HELMER:** No, of course you weren't. Poor little Nora! All you wanted was for us to have a nice time—and it's the thought behind it that counts, after all. All the same, it's a good thing we've seen the back of those lean times.

**NORA:** Yes, really it's marvellous.

**HELMER:** Now there's no need for me to sit here all on my own, bored to tears. And you don't have to strain your dear little eyes, and work those dainty little fingers to the bone. . . .

**NORA** [*clapping her hands*]: No, Torvald, I don't, do I? Not any more. Oh, how marvellous it is to hear that! [*Takes his arm.*] Now I want to tell you how I've been thinking we might arrange things, Torvald. As soon as Christmas is over. . . . [*The door-bell rings in the hall.*] Oh, there's the bell. [*Tidies one or two things in the room.*] It's probably a visitor. What a nuisance!

**HELMER:** Remember I'm not at home to callers.

**MAID** [*in the doorway*]: There's a lady to see you, ma'am.

**NORA:** Show her in, please.

**MAID** [*to Helmer*]: And the doctor's just arrived, too, sir.

**HELMER:** Did he go straight into my room?

**MAID:** Yes, he did, sir.

[*Helmer goes into his study. The Maid shows in Mrs. Linde, who is in travelling clothes, and closes the door after her.*]

**MRS. LINDE** [*subdued and rather hesitantly*]: How do you do, Nora?

**NORA** [*uncertainly*]: How do you do?

**MRS. LINDE:** I'm afraid you don't recognize me.

**NORA:** No, I don't think I . . . And yet I seem to. . . . [*Bursts out suddenly.*] Why! Kristine! Is it really you?

**MRS. LINDE:** Yes, it's me.

**NORA:** Kristine! Fancy not recognizing you again! But how was I to, when . . . [*Gently.*] How you've changed, Kristine!

**MRS. LINDE:** I dare say I have. In nine . . . ten years. . . .

**NORA:** Is it so long since we last saw each other? Yes, it must be. Oh, believe me these last eight years have been such a happy time. And now you've come up to town, too? All that long journey in wintertime. That took courage.

**MRS. LINDE:** I just arrived this morning on the steamer.

**NORA:** To enjoy yourself over Christmas, of course. How lovely! Oh, we'll have such fun, you'll see. Do take off your things. You are not cold, are you? [*Helps her.*] There now! Now let's sit down here in comfort beside the stove. No, here, you take the armchair, I'll sit here on the rocking-chair. [*Takes her hands.*] Ah, now you look a bit more like your old self again. It was just that when I first saw you. . . . But you are a little paler, Kristine . . . and perhaps even a bit thinner!

**MRS. LINDE:** And much, much older, Nora.

**NORA:** Yes, perhaps a little older . . . very, very little, not really very much. [*Stops suddenly and looks serious.*] Oh, what a thoughtless creature I am, sitting here chattering on like this! Dear, sweet Kristine, can you forgive me?

**MRS. LINDE:** What do you mean, Nora?

**NORA** [*gently*]: Poor Kristine, of course you're a widow now.

**MRS. LINDE:** Yes, my husband died three years ago.

**NORA:** Oh, I remember now. I read about it in the papers. Oh, Kristine, believe me I often thought at the time of writing to you. But I kept putting it off, something always seemed to crop up.

**MRS. LINDE:** My dear Nora, I understand so well.

**NORA:** No, it wasn't very nice of me, Kristine. Oh, you poor thing, what you must have gone through. And didn't he leave you anything?

**MRS. LINDE:** No.

**NORA:** And no children?

**MRS. LINDE:** No.

**NORA:** Absolutely nothing?

**MRS. LINDE:** Nothing at all . . . not even a broken heart to grieve over.

**NORA** [*looks at her incredulously*]: But, Kristine, is that possible?

**MRS. LINDE** [*smiles sadly and strokes Nora's hair*]:   Oh, it sometimes happens, Nora.

**NORA:**   So utterly alone. How terribly sad that must be for you. I have three lovely children. You can't see them for the moment, because they're out with their nanny. But now you must tell me all about yourself. . . .

**MRS. LINDE:**   No, no, I want to hear about you.

**NORA:**   No, you start. I won't be selfish today. I must think only about your affairs today. But there's just one thing I really must tell you. Have you heard about the great stroke of luck we've had in the last few days?

**MRS. LINDE:**   No. What is it?

**NORA:**   What do you think? My husband has just been made Bank Manager!

**MRS. LINDE:**   Your husband? How splendid!

**NORA:**   Isn't it tremendous! It's not a very steady way of making a living, you know, being a lawyer, especially if he refuses to take on anything that's the least bit shady—which of course is what Torvald does, and I think he's quite right. You can imagine how pleased we are! He starts at the Bank straight after New Year, and he's getting a big salary and lots of commission. From now on we'll be able to live quite differently . . . we'll do just what we want. Oh, Kristine, I'm so happy and relieved. I must say it's lovely to have plenty of money and not have to worry. Isn't it?

**MRS. LINDE:**   Yes. It must be nice to have enough, at any rate.

**NORA:**   No, not just enough, but pots and pots of money.

**MRS. LINDE** [*smiles*]:   Nora, Nora, haven't you learned any sense yet? At school you used to be an awful spendthrift.

**NORA:**   Yes, Torvald still says I am. [*Wags her finger.*] But little Nora isn't as stupid as everybody thinks. Oh, we haven't really been in a position where I could afford to spend a lot of money. We've both had to work.

**MRS. LINDE:**   You too?

**NORA:**   Yes, odd jobs—sewing, crochet-work, embroidery and things like that. [*Casually.*] And one or two other things, besides. I suppose you know that Torvald left the Ministry when we got married. There weren't any prospects of promotion in his department, and of course he needed to earn more money than he had before. But the first year he wore himself out completely. He had to take on all kinds of extra jobs, you know, and he found himself working all hours of the day and night. But he couldn't go on like that; and he became seriously ill. The doctors said it was essential for him to go South.

MRS. LINDE: Yes, I believe you spent a whole year in Italy, didn't you?

NORA: That's right. It wasn't easy to get away, I can tell you. It was just after I'd had Ivar. But of course we had to go. Oh, it was an absolutely marvellous trip. And it saved Torvald's life. But it cost an awful lot of money, Kristine.

MRS. LINDE: That I can well imagine.

NORA: Twelve hundred dollars. Four thousand eight hundred crowns. That's a lot of money, Kristine.

MRS. LINDE: Yes, but in such circumstances, one is very lucky if one has it.

NORA: Well, we got it from Daddy, you see.

MRS. LINDE: Ah, that was it. It was just about then your father died, I believe, wasn't it?

NORA: Yes, Kristine, just about then. And do you know, I couldn't even go and look after him. Here was I expecting Ivar any day. And I also had poor Torvald, gravely ill, on my hands. Dear, kind Daddy! I never saw him again, Kristine. Oh, that's the saddest thing that has happened to me in all my married life.

MRS. LINDE: I know you were very fond of him. But after that you left for Italy?

NORA: Yes, we had the money then, and the doctors said it was urgent. We left a month later.

MRS. LINDE: And your husband came back completely cured?

NORA: Fit as a fiddle!

MRS. LINDE: But . . . what about the doctor?

NORA: How do you mean?

MRS. LINDE: I thought the maid said something about the gentleman who came at the same time as me being a doctor.

NORA: Yes, that was Dr. Rank. But this isn't a professional visit. He's our best friend and he always looks in at least once a day. No, Torvald has never had a day's illness since. And the children are fit and healthy, and so am I. [*Jumps up and claps her hands.*] Oh God, oh God, isn't it marvellous to be alive, and to be happy, Kristine! . . . Oh, but I ought to be ashamed of myself. . . Here I go on talking about nothing but myself. [*She sits on a low stool near Mrs. Linde and lays her arms on her lap.*] Oh, please, you mustn't be angry with me! Tell me, is it really true that you didn't love your husband? What made you marry him, then?

MRS. LINDE: My mother was still alive; she was bedridden and help-less. And then I had my two young brothers to look after as well. I didn't think I would be justified in refusing him.

NORA: No, I dare say you are right. I suppose he was fairly wealthy then?

MRS. LINDE: He was quite well off, I believe. But the business was shaky. When he died, it went all to pieces, and there just wasn't anything left.

NORA: What then?

MRS. LINDE: Well, I had to fend for myself, opening a little shop, run-ning a little school, anything I could turn my hand to. These last three years have been one long relentless drudge. But now it's finished, Nora. My poor dear mother doesn't need me any more, she's passed away. Nor the boys either; they're at work now, they can look after themselves.

NORA: What a relief you must find it. . . .

MRS. LINDE: No, Nora! Just unutterably empty. Nobody to live for any more. [*Stands up restlessly.*] That's why I couldn't stand it any longer being cut off up there. Surely it must be a bit easier here to find something to occupy your mind. If only I could manage to find a steady job of some kind, in an office perhaps. . . .

NORA: But, Kristine, that's terribly exhausting; and you look so worn out even before you start. The best thing for you would be a little holiday at some quiet little resort.

MRS. LINDE [*crosses to the window*]: I haven't any father I can fall back on for the money, Nora.

NORA [*rises*]: Oh, please, you mustn't be angry with me!

MRS. LINDE [*goes to her*]: My dear Nora, you mustn't be angry with me either. That's the worst thing about people in my position, they become so bitter. One has nobody to work for, yet one has to be on the look-out all the time. Life has to go on, and one starts thinking only of oneself. Believe it or not, when you told me the good news about your step up, I was pleased not so much for your sake as for mine.

NORA: How do you mean? Ah, I see. You think Torvald might be able to do something for you.

MRS. LINDE: Yes, that's exactly what I thought.

NORA: And so he shall, Kristine. Just leave things to me. I'll bring it up so cleverly . . . I'll think up something to put him in a good mood. Oh, I do so much want to help you.

MRS. LINDE: It is awfully kind of you, Nora, offering to do all this for me, particularly in your case, where you haven't known much trouble or hardship in your own life.

NORA: When I . . . ? I haven't known much . . . ?

MRS. LINDE [*smiling*]: Well, good heavens, a little bit of sewing to do and a few things like that. What a child you are, Nora!

NORA [*tosses her head and walks across the room*]: I wouldn't be too sure of that, if I were you.

MRS. LINDE: Oh?

NORA: You're just like the rest of them. You all think I'm useless when it comes to anything really serious. . . .

MRS. LINDE: Come, come. . . .

NORA: You think I've never had anything much to contend with in this hard world.

MRS. LINDE: Nora dear, you've only just been telling me all the things you've had to put up with.

NORA: Pooh! They were just trivialities! [*Softly.*] I haven't told you about the really big thing.

MRS. LINDE: What big thing? What do you mean?

NORA: I know you rather tend to look down on me, Kristine. But you shouldn't, you know. You are proud of having worked so hard and so long for your mother.

MRS. LINDE: I'm sure I don't look down on anybody. But it's true what you say: I am both proud and happy when I think of how I was able to make Mother's life a little easier towards the end.

NORA: And you are proud when you think of what you have done for your brothers, too.

MRS. LINDE: I think I have every right to be.

NORA: I think so too. But now I'm going to tell you something, Kristine. I too have something to be proud and happy about.

**MRS. LINDE:** I don't doubt that. But what is it you mean?

**NORA:** Not so loud. Imagine if Torvald were to hear! He must never on any account . . . nobody must know about it, Kristine, nobody but you.

**MRS. LINDE:** But what is it?

**NORA:** Come over here. [*She pulls her down on the sofa beside her.*] Yes, Kristine, I too have something to be proud and happy about. I was the one who saved Torvald's life.

**MRS. LINDE:** Saved . . . ? How . . . ?

**NORA:** I told you about our trip to Italy. Torvald would never have recovered but for that. . . .

**MRS. LINDE:** Well? Your father gave you what money was necessary. . . .

**NORA** [*smiles*]: That's what Torvald thinks, and everybody else. But . . .

**MRS. LINDE:** But . . . ?

**NORA:** Daddy never gave us a penny. I was the one who raised the money.

**MRS. LINDE:** You? All that money?

**NORA:** Twelve hundred dollars. Four thousand eight hundred crowns. What do you say to that!

**MRS. LINDE:** But, Nora, how was it possible? Had you won a sweepstake or something?

**NORA** [*contemptuously*]: A sweepstake? Pooh! There would have been nothing to it then.

**MRS. LINDE:** Where did you get it from, then?

**NORA** [*hums and smiles secretively*]: H'm, tra-la-la!

**MRS. LINDE:** Because what you couldn't do was borrow it.

**NORA:** Oh? Why not?

**MRS. LINDE:** Well, a wife can't borrow without her husband's consent.

**NORA** [*tossing her head*]: Ah, but when it happens to be a wife with a bit of a sense for business . . . a wife who knows her way about things, then. . . .

**MRS. LINDE:** But, Nora, I just don't understand. . . .

**NORA:** You don't have to. I haven't said I did borrow the money. I might have got it some other way. [*Throws herself back on the sofa.*] I might even have got it from some admirer. Anyone as reasonably attractive as I am. . . .

**MRS. LINDE:** Don't be so silly!

**NORA:** Now you must be dying of curiosity, Kristine.

**MRS. LINDE:** Listen to me now, Nora dear—you haven't done anything rash, have you?

**NORA** [*sitting up again*]: Is it rash to save your husband's life?

**MRS. LINDE:** I think it was rash to do anything without telling him. . . .

**NORA:** But the whole point was that he mustn't know anything. Good heavens, can't you see! He wasn't even supposed to know how desperately ill he was. It was me the doctors came and told his life was in danger, that the only way to save him was to go South for a while. Do you think I didn't try talking him into it first? I began dropping hints about how nice it would be if I could be taken on a little trip abroad, like other young wives. I wept, I pleaded. I told him he ought to show some consideration for my condition, and let me have a bit of my own way. And then I suggested he might take out a loan. But at that he nearly lost his temper, Kristine. He said I was being frivolous, that it was his duty as a husband not to give in to all these whims and fancies of mine—as I do believe he called them. All right, I thought, somehow you've got to be saved. And it was then I found a way. . . .

**MRS. LINDE:** Did your husband never find out from your father that the money hadn't come from him?

**NORA:** No, never. It was just about the time Daddy died. I'd intended letting him into the secret and asking him not to give me away. But when he was so ill . . . I'm sorry to say it never became necessary.

**MRS. LINDE:** And you never confided in your husband?

**NORA:** Good heavens, how could you ever imagine such a thing! When he's so strict about such matters! Besides, Torvald is a man with a good deal of pride—it would be terribly embarrassing and humiliating for him if he thought he owed anything to me. It would spoil everything between us; this happy home of ours would never be the same again.

**MRS. LINDE:** Are you never going to tell him?

**NORA** [*reflectively, half-smiling*]: Oh yes, some day perhaps . . . in many years time, when I'm no longer as pretty as I am now. You mustn't laugh! What I mean of course is when Torvald isn't quite so much in love with me as he is now, when he's lost interest in watching me dance, or get dressed up, or recite. Then it might be a good thing to have something in reserve. . . . [*Breaks off.*] What nonsense! That day will never come. Well, what have you got to say to my big secret, Kristine? Still think I'm not much good for anything? One thing, though, it's meant a lot of worry for me, I can tell you. It hasn't always been easy to meet my obligations when the time came. You know in business there is something called quarterly interest, and other things called instalments, and these are always terribly difficult things to cope with. So what I've had to do is save a little here and there, you see, wherever I could. I couldn't really save anything out of the housekeeping, because Torvald has to live in decent style. I couldn't let the children go about badly dressed either—I felt any money I got for them had to go on them alone. Such sweet little things!

**MRS. LINDE:** Poor Nora! So it had to come out of your own allowance?

**NORA:** Of course. After all, I was the one it concerned most. Whenever Torvald gave me money for new clothes and such-like, I never spent more than half. And always I bought the simplest and cheapest things. It's a blessing most things look well on me, so Torvald never noticed anything. But sometimes I did feel it was a bit hard, Kristine, because it is nice to be well dressed, isn't it?

**MRS. LINDE:** Yes, I suppose it is.

**NORA:** I have had some other sources of income, of course. Last winter I was lucky enough to get quite a bit of copying to do. So I shut myself up every night and sat and wrote through to the small hours of the morning. Oh, sometimes I was so tired, so tired. But it was tremendous fun all the same, sitting there working and earning money like that. It was almost like being a man.

**MRS. LINDE:** And how much have you been able to pay off like this?

**NORA:** Well, I can't tell exactly. It's not easy to know where you are with transactions of this kind, you understand. All I know is I've paid off just as much as I could scrape together. Many's the time I was at my wit's end. [*Smiles.*] Then I used to sit here and pretend that some rich old gentleman had fallen in love with me. . . .

**MRS. LINDE:** What! What gentleman?

**NORA:** Oh, rubbish! . . . and that now he had died, and when they opened his will, there in big letters were the words: "My entire fortune is to be paid over, immediately and in cash, to charming Mrs. Nora Helmer."

**MRS. LINDE:** But my dear Nora—who is this man?

**NORA:** Good heavens, don't you understand? There never was any old gentleman; it was just something I used to sit here pretending, time and time again, when I didn't know where to turn next for money. But it doesn't make very much difference; as far as I'm concerned, the old boy can do what he likes, I'm tired of him; I can't be bothered any more with him or his will. Because now all my worries are over. [*Jumping up.*] Oh God, what a glorious thought, Kristine! No more worries! Just think of being without a care in the world . . . being able to romp with the children, and making the house nice and attractive, and having things just as Torvald likes to have them! And then spring will soon be here, and blue skies. And maybe we can go away somewhere. I might even see something of the sea again. Oh yes! When you're happy, life is a wonderful thing!

[*The door-bell is heard in the hall.*]

**MRS. LINDE** [*gets up*]: There's the bell. Perhaps I'd better go.
**NORA:** No, do stay, please. I don't suppose it's for me; it's probably somebody for Torvald. . . .
**MAID** [*in the doorway*]: Excuse me, ma'am, but there's a gentleman here wants to see Mr. Helmer, and I didn't quite know . . . because the Doctor is in there. . . .
**NORA:** Who is the gentleman?
**KROGSTAD** [*in the doorway*]: It's me, Mrs. Helmer.

[*Mrs. Linde starts, then turns away to the window.*]

**NORA** [*tense, takes a step towards him and speaks in a low voice*]: You? What is it? What do you want to talk to my husband about?
**KROGSTAD:** Bank matters . . . in a manner of speaking. I work at the bank, and I hear your husband is to be the new manager. . . .
**NORA:** So it's . . .
**KROGSTAD:** Just routine business matters, Mrs. Helmer. Absolutely nothing else.
**NORA:** Well then, please go into his study.

[*She nods impassively and shuts the hall door behind him; then she walks across and sees to the stove.*]

**MRS. LINDE:** Nora . . . who was that man?
**NORA:** His name is Krogstad.

**MRS. LINDE:** So it really was him.

**NORA:** Do you know the man?

**MRS. LINDE:** I used to know him . . . a good many years ago. He was a solicitor's clerk in our district for a while.

**NORA:** Yes, so he was.

**MRS. LINDE:** How he's changed!

**NORA:** His marriage wasn't a very happy one, I believe.

**MRS. LINDE:** He's a widower now, isn't he?

**NORA:** With a lot of children. There, it'll burn better now.

[*She closes the stove door and moves the rocking-chair a little to one side.*]

**MRS. LINDE:** He does a certain amount of business on the side, they say?

**NORA:** Oh? Yes, it's always possible. I just don't know. . . . But let's not think about business . . . it's all so dull.

[*Dr. Rank comes in from Helmer's study.*]

**RANK** [*still in the doorway*]: No, no, Torvald, I won't intrude. I'll just look in on your wife for a moment. [*Shuts the door and notices Mrs. Linde.*] Oh, I beg your pardon. I'm afraid I'm intruding here as well.

**NORA:** No, not at all! [*Introduces them.*] Dr. Rank . . . Mrs. Linde.

**RANK:** Ah! A name I've often heard mentioned in this house. I believe I came past you on the stairs as I came in.

**MRS. LINDE:** I have to take things slowly going upstairs. I find it rather a trial.

**RANK:** Ah, some little disability somewhere, eh?

**MRS. LINDE:** Just a bit run down, I think, actually.

**RANK:** Is that all? Then I suppose you've come to town for a good rest—doing the rounds of the parties?

**MRS. LINDE:** I have come to look for work.

**RANK:** Is that supposed to be some kind of sovereign remedy for being run down?

**MRS. LINDE:** One must live, Doctor.

**RANK:** Yes, it's generally thought to be necessary.

**NORA:** Come, come, Dr. Rank. You are quite as keen to live as anybody.

**RANK:** Quite keen, yes. Miserable as I am, I'm quite ready to let things drag on as long as possible. All my patients are the same. Even those with a moral affliction are no different. As a matter of fact, there's a bad case of that kind in talking with Helmer at this very moment. . . .

**MRS. LINDE** [*softly*]: Ah!

**NORA:** Whom do you mean?

**RANK:** A person called Krogstad—nobody you would know. He's rotten to the core. But even he began talking about having to *live*, as though it were something terribly important.

**NORA:** Oh? And what did he want to talk to Torvald about?

**RANK:** I honestly don't know. All I heard was something about the Bank.

**NORA:** I didn't know that Krog . . . that this Mr. Krogstad had anything to do with the Bank.

**RANK:** Oh yes, he's got some kind of job down there. [*To Mrs. Linde.*] I wonder if you've got people in your part of the country too who go rushing round sniffing out cases of moral corruption, and then installing the individuals concerned in nice, well-paid jobs where they can keep them under observation. Sound, decent people have to be content to stay out in the cold.

**MRS. LINDE:** Yet surely it's the sick who most need to be brought in.

**RANK** [*shrugs his shoulders*]: Well, there we have it. It's that attitude that's turning society into a clinic.

[*Nora, lost in her own thoughts, breaks into smothered laughter and claps her hands.*]

**RANK:** Why are you laughing at that? Do you know in fact what society is?

**NORA:** What do I care about your silly old society? I was laughing about something quite different . . . something frightfully funny. Tell me, Dr. Rank, are all the people who work at the Bank dependent on Torvald now?

**RANK:** Is *that* what you find so frightfully funny?

**NORA** [*smiles and hums*]: Never you mind! Never you mind! [*Walks about the room.*] Yes, it really is terribly amusing to think that we . . . that Torvald now has power over so many people. [*She takes the bag out of her pocket.*] Dr. Rank, what about a little macaroon?

**RANK:** Look at this, eh? Macaroons. I thought they were forbidden here.

**NORA:** Yes, but these are some Kristine gave me.

**MRS. LINDE:** What? I . . . ?

**NORA:** Now, now, you needn't be alarmed. You weren't to know that Torvald had forbidden them. He's worried in case they ruin my teeth, you know. Still . . . what's it matter once in a while! Don't you think so, Dr. Rank? Here! [*She pops a macaroon into his mouth.*] And you too, Kristine. And I shall have one as well; just a little one . . . or two at the most. [*She walks about the room again.*] Really I am so happy. There's just one little thing I'd love to do now.

**RANK:** What's that?

**NORA:** Something I'd love to say in front of Torvald.

**RANK:** Then why can't you?

**NORA:** No, I daren't. It's not very nice.

**MRS. LINDE:** Not very nice?

**RANK:** Well, in that case it might not be wise. But to us, I don't see why. . . . What is this you would love to say in front of Helmer?

**NORA:** I would simply love to say: 'Damn'.

**RANK:** Are you mad!

**MRS. LINDE:** Good gracious, Nora. . . !

**RANK:** Say it! Here he is!

**NORA** [*hiding the bag of macaroons*]: Sh! Sh!

[*Helmer comes out of his room, his overcoat over his arm and his hat in his hand.*]

**NORA** [*going over to him*]: Well, Torvald dear, did you get rid of him?

**HELMER:** Yes, he's just gone.

**NORA:** Let me introduce you. This is Kristine, who has just arrived in town. . . .

**HELMER:** Kristine. . . ? You must forgive me, but I don't think I know . . .

**NORA:** Mrs. Linde, Torvald dear. Kristine Linde.

**HELMER:** Ah, indeed. A school-friend of my wife's, presumably.

**MRS. LINDE:** Yes, we were girls together.

**NORA:** Fancy, Torvald, she's come all this long way just to have a word with you.

**HELMER:** How is that?

**MRS. LINDE:** Well, it wasn't really. . . .

**NORA:** The thing is, Kristine is terribly clever at office work, and she's frightfully keen on finding a job with some efficient man, so that she can learn even more. . . .

**HELMER:** Very sensible, Mrs. Linde.

**NORA:** And then when she heard you'd been made Bank Manager— there was a bit in the paper about it—she set off at once. Torvald please! You *will* try and do something for Kristine, won't you? For my sake?

**HELMER:** Well, that's not altogether impossible. You are a widow, I presume?

**MRS. LINDE:** Yes.

**HELMER:** And you've had some experience in business?

**MRS. LINDE:** A fair amount.

**HELMER:** Well, it's quite probable I can find you a job, I think. . . .

**NORA** [*clapping her hands*]: There, you see!

**HELMER:** You have come at a fortunate moment, Mrs. Linde. . . .

**MRS. LINDE:** Oh, how can I ever thank you. . . ?

**HELMER:** Not a bit. [*He puts on his overcoat.*] But for the present I must ask you to excuse me. . . .

**RANK:** Wait. I'm coming with you.

[*He fetches his fur coat from the hall and warms it at the stove.*]

**NORA:** Don't be long, Torvald dear.

**HELMER:** Not more than an hour, that's all.

**NORA:** Are you leaving too, Kristine?

**MRS. LINDE** [*putting on her things*]: Yes, I must go and see if I can't find myself a room.

**HELMER:** Perhaps we can all walk down the road together.

**NORA** [*helping her*]: What a nuisance we are so limited for space here. I'm afraid it just isn't possible. . . .

**MRS. LINDE:** Oh, you mustn't dream of it! Goodbye, Nora dear, and thanks for everything.

**NORA:** Goodbye for the present. But . . . you'll be coming back this evening, of course. And you too, Dr. Rank? What's that? If you are up to it? Of course you'll be up to it. Just wrap yourself up well.

[*They go out, talking, into the hall; children's voices can be heard on the stairs.*]

**NORA:** Here they are! Here they are! [*She runs to the front door and opens it. Anne Marie, the nursemaid, enters with the children.*] Come in! Come in! [*She bends down and kisses them.*] Ah! my sweet little darlings. . . . You see them, Kristine? Aren't they lovely!

**RANK:** Don't stand here chattering in this draught!

**HELMER:** Come along, Mrs. Linde. The place now becomes unbearable for anybody except mothers.

[*Dr. Rank, Helmer and Mrs. Linde go down the stairs: the Nursemaid comes into the room with the children, then Nora, shutting the door behind her.*]

**NORA:** How fresh and bright you look! My, what red cheeks you've got! Like apples and roses. [*During the following, the children keep chattering away to her.*] Have you had a nice time? That's splendid. And you gave Emmy and Bob a ride on your sledge? Did you now! Both together! Fancy that! There's a clever boy, Ivar. Oh, let me take her a little while, Anne Marie. There's my sweet little baby-doll! [*She takes the youngest of the children from the Nursemaid and dances with her.*] All right, Mummy will dance with Bobby too. What? You've been throwing snowballs? Oh, I wish I'd been there. No, don't bother, Anne Marie, I'll help them off with their things. No, please, let me—I like doing it. You go on in, you look frozen. You'll find some hot coffee on the stove. [*The Nursemaid goes into the room, left. Nora takes off the children's coats and hats and throws them down anywhere, while the children all talk at once.*] Really! A great big dog came running after you? But he didn't bite. No, the doggies wouldn't bite my pretty little dollies. You mustn't touch the parcels, Ivar! What are they? Wouldn't you like to know! No, no, that's nasty. Now? Shall we play something? What shall we play? Hide and seek? Yes, let's play hide and seek. Bob can hide first. Me first? All right, let me hide first.

[*She and the children play, laughing and shrieking, in this room and in the adjacent room on the right. Finally Nora hides under the table; the children come rushing in to look for her but cannot find her; they hear her stifled laughter, rush to the table, lift up the tablecloth and find her. Tremendous shouts of delight. She creeps out and pretends to frighten them. More shouts. Meanwhile there has been a knock at the front door, which nobody has heard. The door half opens, and Krogstad can be seen. He waits a little; the game continues.*]

KROGSTAD:  I beg your pardon, Mrs. Helmer. . . .

NORA [*turns with a stifled cry and half jumps up*]:  Ah! What do you want?

KROGSTAD:  Excuse me. The front door was standing open. Somebody must have forgotten to shut it. . . .

NORA [*standing up*]:  My husband isn't at home, Mr. Krogstad.

KROGSTAD:  I know.

NORA:  Well . . . what are you doing here?

KROGSTAD:  I want a word with you.

NORA:  With . . . ? [*Quietly, to the children.*] Go to Anne Marie. What? No, the strange man won't do anything to Mummy. When he's gone we'll have another game. [*She leads the children into the room, left, and shuts the door after them; tense and uneasy.*] You want to speak to me?

KROGSTAD:  Yes, I do.

NORA:  Today? But it isn't the first of the month yet. . . .

KROGSTAD:  No, it's Christmas Eve. It depends entirely on you what sort of Christmas you have.

NORA:  What do you want? Today I can't possibly . . .

KROGSTAD:  Let's not talk about that for the moment. It's something else. You've got a moment to spare?

NORA:  Yes, I suppose so, though . . .

KROGSTAD:  Good. I was sitting in Olsen's café, and I saw your husband go down the road . . .

NORA:  Did you?

KROGSTAD:  . . . with a lady.

NORA:  Well?

KROGSTAD:  May I be so bold as to ask whether that lady was a Mrs. Linde?

NORA:  Yes.

KROGSTAD:  Just arrived in town?

NORA:  Yes, today.

**KROGSTAD:** And she's a good friend of yours?

**NORA:** Yes, she is. But I can't see . . .

**KROGSTAD:** I also knew her once.

**NORA:** I know.

**KROGSTAD:** Oh? So you know all about it. I thought as much. Well, I want to ask you straight: is Mrs. Linde getting a job in the Bank?

**NORA:** How dare you cross-examine me like this, Mr. Krogstad? You, one of my husband's subordinates? But since you've asked me, I'll tell you. Yes, Mrs. Linde *has* got a job. And I'm the one who got it for her, Mr. Krogstad. Now you know.

**KROGSTAD:** So my guess was right.

**NORA** [*walking up and down*]: Oh, I think I can say that some of us have a little influence now and again. Just because one happens to be a woman, that doesn't mean. . . . People in subordinate positions, ought to take care they don't offend anybody . . . who . . hm . . .

**KROGSTAD:** . . . has influence?

**NORA:** Exactly.

**KROGSTAD** [*changing his tone*]: Mrs. Helmer, will you have the goodness to use your influence on my behalf?

**NORA:** What? What do you mean?

**KROGSTAD:** Will you be so good as to see that I keep my modest little job at the Bank?

**NORA:** What do you mean? Who wants to take it away from you?

**KROGSTAD:** Oh, you needn't try and pretend to me you don't know. I can quite see that this friend of yours isn't particularly anxious to bump up against me. And I can also see now whom I can thank for being given the sack.

**NORA:** But I assure you. . . .

**KROGSTAD:** All right, all right. But to come to the point: there's still time. And I advise you to use your influence to stop it.

**NORA:** But, Mr. Krogstad, I *have* no influence.

**KROGSTAD:** Haven't you? I thought just now you said yourself . . .

**NORA:** I didn't mean it that way, of course. Me? What makes you think I've got any influence of that kind over my husband?

**KROGSTAD:** I know your husband from our student days. I don't suppose he is any more steadfast than other married men.

**NORA:** You speak disrespectfully of my husband like that and I'll show you the door.

**KROGSTAD:**  So the lady's got courage.

**NORA:**  I'm not frightened of you any more. After New Year I'll soon be finished with the whole business.

**KROGSTAD** [*controlling himself*]:  Listen to me, Mrs. Helmer. If necessary I shall fight for my little job in the Bank as if I were fighting for my life.

**NORA:**  So it seems.

**KROGSTAD:**  It's not just for the money, that's the last thing I care about. There's something else . . . well, I might as well out with it. You see it's like this. You know as well as anybody that some years ago I got myself mixed up in a bit of trouble.

**NORA:**  I believe I've heard something of the sort.

**KROGSTAD:**  It never got as far as the courts; but immediately it was as if all paths were barred to me. So I started going in for the sort of business you know about. I had to do something, and I think I can say I haven't been one of the worst. But now I have to get out of it. My sons are growing up; for their sake I must try and win back what respectability I can. That job in the Bank was like the first step on the ladder for me. And now your husband wants to kick me off the ladder again, back into the mud.

**NORA:**  But in God's name, Mr. Krogstad, it's quite beyond my power to help you.

**KROGSTAD:**  That's because you haven't the will to help me. But I have ways of making you.

**NORA:**  You wouldn't go and tell my husband I owe you money?

**KROGSTAD:**  Suppose I did tell him?

**NORA:**  It would be a rotten shame. [*Half choking with tears.*] That secret is all my pride and joy—why should he have to hear about it in this nasty, horrid way . . . hear about it from *you*. You would make things horribly unpleasant for me. . . .

**KROGSTAD:**  Merely unpleasant?

**NORA** [*vehemently*]:  Go on, do it then! It'll be all the worse for you. Because then my husband will see for himself what a bad man you are, and then you certainly won't be able to keep your job.

**KROGSTAD:**  I asked whether it was only a bit of domestic unpleasantness you were afraid of?

**NORA:**  If my husband gets to know about it, he'll pay off what's owing at once. And then we'd have nothing more to do with you.

**KROGSTAD** [*taking a pace towards her*]: Listen, Mrs. Helmer, either you haven't a very good memory, or else you don't understand much about business. I'd better make the position a little bit clearer for you.

**NORA:** How do you mean?

**KROGSTAD:** When your husband was ill, you came to me for the loan of twelve hundred dollars.

**NORA:** I didn't know of anybody else.

**KROGSTAD:** I promised to find you the money. . . .

**NORA:** And you did find it.

**KROGSTAD:** I promised to find you the money on certain conditions. At the time you were so concerned about your husband's illness, and so anxious to get the money for going away with, that I don't think you paid very much attention to all the incidentals. So there is perhaps some point in reminding you of them. Well, I promised to find you the money against an IOU which I drew up for you.

**NORA:** Yes, and which I signed.

**KROGSTAD:** Very good. But below that I added a few lines, by which your father was to stand security. This your father was to sign.

**NORA:** Was to . . . ? He did sign it.

**KROGSTAD:** I had left the date blank. The idea was that your father was to add the date himself when he signed it. Remember?

**NORA:** Yes, I think. . . .

**KROGSTAD:** I then gave you the IOU to post to your father. Wasn't that so?

**NORA:** Yes.

**KROGSTAD:** Which of course you did at once. Because only about five or six days later you brought it back to me with your father's signature. I then paid out the money.

**NORA:** Well? Haven't I paid the instalments regularly?

**KROGSTAD:** Yes, fairly. But . . . coming back to what we were talking about . . . that was a pretty bad period you were going through then, Mrs. Helmer.

**NORA:** Yes, it was.

**KROGSTAD:** Your father was seriously ill, I believe.

**NORA:** He was very near the end.

**KROGSTAD:** And died shortly afterwards?

**NORA:** Yes.

**KROGSTAD:** Tell me, Mrs. Helmer, do you happen to remember which day your father died? The exact date, I mean.

**NORA:** Daddy died on 29 September.

**KROGSTAD:** Quite correct. I made some inquiries. Which brings up a rather curious point [*takes out a paper*] which I simply cannot explain.

**NORA:** Curious . . . ? I don't know . . .

**KROGSTAD:** The curious thing is, Mrs. Helmer, that your father signed this document three days after his death.

**NORA:** What? I don't understand. . . .

**KROGSTAD:** Your father died on 29 September. But look here. Your father has dated his signature 2 October. Isn't that rather curious, Mrs. Helmer? [*Nora remains silent.*] It's also remarkable that the words "2 October" and the year are not in your father's handwriting, but in a handwriting I rather think I recognize. Well, perhaps that could be explained. Your father might have forgotten to date his signature, and then somebody else might have made a guess at the date later, before the fact of your father's death was known. There is nothing wrong in that. What really matters is the signature. And *that* is of course genuine, Mrs. Helmer? It really was your father who wrote his name here?

**NORA** [*after a moment's silence, throws her head back and looks at him defiantly*]: No, it wasn't. It was me who signed father's name.

**KROGSTAD:** Listen to me. I suppose you realize that that is a very dangerous confession?

**NORA:** Why? You'll soon have all your money back.

**KROGSTAD:** Let me ask you a question: why didn't you send that document to your father?

**NORA:** It was impossible. Daddy was ill. If I'd asked him for his signature, I'd have had to tell him what the money was for. Don't you see, when he was as ill as that I couldn't go and tell him that my husband's life was in danger. It was simply impossible.

**KROGSTAD:** It would have been better for you if you had abandoned the whole trip.

**NORA:** No, that was impossible. This was the thing that was to save my husband's life. I couldn't give it up.

**KROGSTAD:** But did it never strike you that this was fraudulent . . . ?

**NORA:** That wouldn't have meant anything to me. Why should I worry about you? I couldn't stand you, not when you insisted on going through with all those cold-blooded formalities, knowing all the time what a critical state my husband was in.

**KROGSTAD:** Mrs. Helmer, it's quite clear you still haven't the faintest idea what it is you've committed. But let me tell you, my own offence was no more and no worse than that, and it ruined my entire reputation.

**NORA:** You? Are you trying to tell me that you once risked everything to save your wife's life?

**KROGSTAD:** The law takes no account of motives.

**NORA:** Then they must be very bad laws.

**KROGSTAD:** Bad or not, if I produce this document in court, you'll be condemned according to them.

**NORA:** I don't believe it. Isn't a daughter entitled to try and save her father from worry and anxiety on his deathbed? Isn't a wife entitled to save her husband's life? I might not know very much about the law, but I feel sure of one thing: it must say somewhere that things like this are allowed. You mean to say you don't know that—you, when it's your job? You must be a rotten lawyer, Mr. Krogstad.

**KROGSTAD:** That may be. But when it comes to business transactions—like the sort between us two—perhaps you'll admit I know something about *them?* Good. Now you must please yourself. But I tell you this: if I'm pitched out a second time, you are going to keep me company.

[*He bows and goes out through the hall.*]

**NORA** [*stands thoughtfully for a moment, then tosses her head*]: Rubbish! He's just trying to scare me. I'm not such a fool as all that. [*Begins gathering up the children's clothes; after a moment she stops.*] Yet . . . ? No, it's impossible! I did it for love, didn't I?

**THE CHILDREN** [*in the doorway, left*]: Mummy, the gentleman's just gone out of the gate.

**NORA:** Yes, I know. But you mustn't say anything to anybody about that gentleman. You hear? Not even to Daddy!

**THE CHILDREN:** All right, Mummy. Are you going to play again?

**NORA:** No, not just now.

**THE CHILDREN:** But Mummy, you promised!

**NORA:**  Yes, but I can't just now. Off you go now, I have a lot to do. Off you go, my darlings. [*She herds them carefully into the other room and shuts the door behind them. She sits down on the sofa, picks up her embroidery and works a few stitches, but soon stops.*] No! [*She flings her work down, stands up, goes to the hall door and calls out.*] Helene! Fetch the tree in for me, please. [*She walks across to the table, left, and opens the drawer; again pauses.*] No, really, it's quite impossible!

**MAID** [*with the Christmas tree*]:  Where shall I put it, ma'am?

**NORA:**  On the floor there, in the middle.

**MAID:**  Anything else you want me to bring?

**NORA:**  No, thank you. I've got what I want.

[*The Maid has put the tree down and goes out.*]

**NORA** [*busy decorating the tree*]:  Candles here . . . and flowers here.—Revolting man! It's all nonsense! There's nothing to worry about. We'll have a lovely Christmas tree. And I'll do anything you want me to, Torvald; I'll sing for you, dance for you. . . .

[*Helmer, with a bundle of documents under his arm, comes in by the hall door.*]

**NORA:**  Ah, back again already?

**HELMER:**  Yes. Anybody been?

**NORA:**  Here? No.

**HELMER:**  That's funny. I just saw Krogstad leave the house.

**NORA:**  Oh? O yes, that's right. Krogstad was here a minute.

**HELMER:**  Nora, I can tell by your face he's been asking you to put a good word in for him.

**NORA:**  Yes.

**HELMER:**  And you were to pretend it was your own idea? You were to keep quiet about his having been here. He asked you to do that as well, didn't he?

**NORA:**  Yes, Torvald. But . . .

**HELMER:**  Nora, Nora, what possessed you to do a thing like that? Talking to a person like him, making him promises? And then on top of everything, to tell me a lie!

**NORA:**  A lie . . . ?

HELMER: Didn't you say that nobody had been here? [*Wagging his finger at her.*] Never again must my little song-bird do a thing like that! Little song-birds must keep their pretty little beaks out of mischief; no chirruping out of tune! [*Puts his arm round her waist.*] Isn't that the way we want things to be? Yes, of course it is. [*Lets her go.*] So let's say no more about it. [*Sits down by the stove.*] Ah, nice and cosy here!

[*He glances through his papers.*]

NORA [*busy with the Christmas tree, after a short pause*]:  Torvald!

HELMER: Yes.

NORA:  I'm so looking forward to the fancy dress ball at the Stenborgs on Boxing Day.

HELMER:  And I'm terribly curious to see what sort of surprise you've got for me.

NORA:  Oh, it's too silly.

HELMER:  Oh?

NORA:  I just can't think of anything suitable. Everything seems so absurd, so pointless.

HELMER:  Has my little Nora come to *that* conclusion?

NORA [*behind his chair, her arms on the chairback*]:  Are you very busy, Torvald?

HELMER:  Oh. . . .

NORA:  What are all those papers?

HELMER:  Bank matters.

NORA:  Already?

HELMER:  I have persuaded the retiring manager to give me authority to make any changes in organization or personnel I think necessary. I have to work on it over the Christmas week. I want everything straight by the New Year.

NORA:  So that was why that poor Krogstad. . . .

HELMER:  Hm!

NORA [*still leaning against the back of the chair, running her fingers through his hair*]:  If you hadn't been so busy, Torvald, I'd have asked you to do me an awfully big favour.

HELMER:  Let me hear it. What's it to be?

NORA:  Nobody's got such good taste as you. And the thing is I do so want to look my best at the fancy dress ball. Torvald, couldn't you give me some advice and tell me what you think I ought to go as and how I should arrange my costume?

HELMER: Aha! So my impulsive little woman is asking for somebody to come to her rescue, eh?

NORA: Please, Torvald, I never get anywhere without your help.

HELMER: Very well, I'll think about it. We'll find something.

NORA: That's sweet of you. [*She goes across to the tree again; pauses.*] How pretty these red flowers look.—Tell me, was it really something terribly wrong this man Krogstad did?

HELMER: Forgery. Have you any idea what that means?

NORA: Perhaps circumstances left him no choice?

HELMER: Maybe. Or perhaps, like so many others, he just didn't think. I am not so heartless that I would necessarily want to condemn a man for a single mistake like that.

NORA: Oh no, Torvald, of course not!

HELMER: Many a man might be able to redeem himself, if he honestly confessed his guilt and took his punishment.

NORA: Punishment?

HELMER: But that wasn't the way Krogstad chose. He dodged what was due to him by a cunning trick. And that's what has been the cause of his corruption.

NORA: Do you think it would . . . ?

HELMER: Just think how a man with a thing like that on his conscience will always be having to lie and cheat and dissemble; he can never drop the mask, not even with his own wife and children. And the children—*that's* the most terrible part of it, Nora.

NORA: Why?

HELMER: A fog of lies like that in a household, and it spreads disease and infection to every part of it. Every breath the children take in that kind of house is reeking with evil germs.

NORA [*closer behind him*]: Are you sure of that?

HELMER: My dear Nora, as a lawyer I know what I'm talking about. Practically all juvenile delinquents come from homes where the mother is dishonest.

NORA: Why mothers particularly?

HELMER: It's generally traceable to the mothers, but of course fathers can have the same influence. Every lawyer knows that only too well. And yet there's Krogstad been poisoning his own children for years with lies and deceit. That's the reason I call him morally depraved. [*Holds out his hands to her.*] That's why my sweet little Nora must promise me not to try putting in any more good words for him. Shake hands on it. Well? What's this? Give me your hand. There now! That's settled. I assure you I would have found it impossible to work with him. I quite literally feel physically sick in the presence of such people.

NORA [*draws her hand away and walks over to the other side of the Christmas tree*]:   How hot it is in here! And I still have such a lot to do.

HELMER [*stands up and collects his papers together*]:   Yes, I'd better think of getting some of this read before dinner. I must also think about your costume. And I might even be able to lay my hands on something to wrap in gold paper and hang on the Christmas tree. [*He lays his hand on her head.*] My precious little singing bird.

[*He goes into his study and shuts the door behind him.*]

NORA [*quietly, after a pause*]:   Nonsense! It can't be. It's impossible. It *must* be impossible.

MAID [*in the doorway, left*]:   The children keep asking so nicely if they can come in and see Mummy.

NORA:   No, no, don't let them in! You stay with them, Anne Marie.

MAID:   Very well, ma'am.

[*She shuts the door.*]

NORA [*pale with terror*]:   Corrupt my children . . . ! Poison my home? [*Short pause; she throws back her head.*] It's not true! It could never, never be true!

## ACT TWO

*The same room. In the corner beside the piano stands the Christmas tree, stripped, bedraggled and with its candles burnt out. Nora's outdoor things lie on the sofa. Nora, alone there, walks about restlessly; at last she stops by the sofa and picks up her coat.*

NORA [*putting her coat down again*]:   Somebody's coming! [*Crosses to the door, listens.*] No, it's nobody. Nobody will come today, of course, Christmas Day—nor tomorrow, either. But perhaps. . . . [*She opens the door and looks out.*] No, nothing in the letter box; quite empty. [*Comes forward.*] Oh, nonsense! He didn't mean it seriously. Things like that *can't* happen. It's impossible. Why, I have three small children.

[*The Nursemaid comes from the room, left, carrying a big cardboard box.*]

NURSEMAID:  I finally found it, the box with the fancy dress costumes.

NORA:  Thank you. Put it on the table, please.

NURSEMAID [*does this*]:  But I'm afraid they are in an awful mess.

NORA:  Oh, if only I could rip them up into a thousand pieces!

NURSEMAID:  Good heavens, they can be mended all right, with a bit of patience.

NORA:  Yes, I'll go over and get Mrs. Linde to help me.

NURSEMAID:  Out again? In this terrible weather? You'll catch your death of cold, Ma'am.

NORA:  Oh, worse things might happen.—How are the children?

NURSEMAID:  Playing with their Christmas presents, poor little things, but . . .

NORA:  Do they keep asking for me?

NURSEMAID:  They are so used to being with their Mummy.

NORA:  Yes, Anne Marie, from now on I can't be with them as often as I was before.

NURSEMAID:  Ah well, children get used to anything in time.

NORA:  Do you think so? Do you think they would forget their Mummy if she went away for good?

NURSEMAID:  Good gracious—for good?

NORA:  Tell me, Anne Marie—I've often wondered—how on earth could you bear to hand your child over to strangers?

NURSEMAID:  Well, there was nothing else for it when I had to come and nurse my little Nora.

NORA:  Yes but . . . how could you *bring* yourself to do it?

NURSEMAID:  When I had the chance of such a good place? When a poor girl's been in trouble she must make the best of things. Because *he* didn't help, the rotter.

NORA:  But your daughter will have forgotten you.

**NURSEMAID:** Oh no, she hasn't. She wrote to me when she got confirmed, and again when she got married.

**NORA** [*putting her arms round her neck*]: Dear old Anne Marie, you
were a good mother to me when I was little.

**NURSEMAID:** My poor little Nora never had any other mother but me.

**NORA:** And if my little ones only had you, I know you would. . . . Oh,
what am I talking about! [*She opens the box.*] Go in to them.
I must . . . Tomorrow I'll let you see how pretty I am going to look.

**NURSEMAID:** Ah, there'll be nobody at the ball as pretty as my Nora.

[*She goes into the room, left.*]

**NORA** [*begins unpacking the box, but soon throws it down*]: Oh, if
only I dare go out. If only I could be sure nobody would come. And
that nothing would happen in the meantime here at home.
Rubbish—nobody's going to come. I mustn't think about it. Brush
this muff. Pretty gloves, pretty gloves! I'll put it right out of my
mind. One, two, three, four, five, six. . . . [*Screams.*] Ah, they are
coming. . . . [*She starts towards the door, but stops irresolute.
Mrs. Linde comes from the hall, where she has taken off her things.*]
Oh, it's you, Kristine. There's nobody else out there, is there? I'm so
glad you've come.

**MRS. LINDE:** I heard you'd been over looking for me.

**NORA:** Yes, I was just passing. There's something you must help me
with. Come and sit beside me on the sofa here. You see, the
Stenborgs are having a fancy dress party upstairs tomorrow
evening, and now Torvald wants me to go as a Neapolitan fisher lass
and dance the tarantella. I learned it in Capri, you know.

**MRS. LINDE:** Well, well! So you are going to do a party piece?

**NORA:** Torvald says I should. Look, here's the costume, Torvald had it
made for me down there. But it's got all torn and I simply don't
know. . . .

**MRS. LINDE:** We'll soon have that put right. It's only the trimming
come away here and there. Got a needle and thread? Ah, here's
what we are after.

**NORA:** It's awfully kind of you.

**MRS. LINDE:** So you are going to be all dressed up tomorrow, Nora?
Tell you what—I'll pop over for a minute to see you in all your

finery. But I'm quite forgetting to thank you for the pleasant time we had last night.

NORA [*gets up and walks across the room*]:  Somehow I didn't think yesterday was as nice as things generally are.—You should have come to town a little earlier, Kristine.—Yes, Torvald certainly knows how to make things pleasant about the place.

MRS. LINDE:  You too, I should say. You are not your father's daughter for nothing. But tell me, is Dr. Rank always as depressed as he was last night?

NORA:  No, last night it was rather obvious. He's got something seriously wrong with him, you know. Tuberculosis of the spine, poor fellow. His father was a horrible man, who used to have mistresses and things like that. That's why the son was always ailing, right from being a child.

MRS. LINDE [*lowering her sewing*]:  But my dear Nora, how do you come to know about things like that?

NORA [*walking about the room*]:  Huh! When you've got three children, you get these visits from . . . women who have had a certain amount of medical training. And you hear all sorts of things from them.

MRS. LINDE [*begins sewing again; short silence*]:  Does Dr. Rank call in every day?

NORA:  Every single day. He was Torvald's best friend as a boy, and he's a good friend of *mine*, too. Dr. Rank is almost like one of the family.

MRS. LINDE:  But tell me—is he really genuine? What I mean is: doesn't he sometimes rather turn on the charm?

NORA:  No, on the contrary. What makes you think that?

MRS. LINDE:  When you introduced me yesterday, he claimed he'd often heard my name in this house. But afterwards I noticed your husband hadn't the faintest idea who I was. Then how is it that Dr. Rank should. . . .

NORA:  Oh yes, it was quite right what he said, Kristine. You see Torvald is so terribly in love with me that he says he wants me all to himself. When we were first married, it even used to make him sort of jealous if I only as much as mentioned any of my old friends from back home. So of course I stopped doing it. But I often talk to Dr. Rank about such things. He likes hearing about them.

**MRS. LINDE:** Listen, Nora! In lots of ways you are still a child. Now, I'm a good deal older than you, and a bit more experienced. I'll tell you something: I think you ought to give up all this business with Dr. Rank.

**NORA:** Give up what business?

**MRS. LINDE:** The whole thing, I should say. Weren't you saying yesterday something about a rich admirer who was to provide you with money. . . .

**NORA:** One who's never existed, I regret to say. But what of it?

**MRS. LINDE:** Has Dr. Rank money?

**NORA:** Yes, he has.

**MRS. LINDE:** And no dependents?

**NORA:** No, nobody. But . . . ?

**MRS. LINDE:** And he comes to the house every day?

**NORA:** Yes, I told you.

**MRS. LINDE:** But how can a man of his position want to pester you like this?

**NORA:** I simply don't understand.

**MRS. LINDE:** Don't pretend, Nora. Do you think I don't see now who you borrowed the twelve hundred from?

**NORA:** Are you out of your mind? Do you really think that? A friend of ours who comes here every day? The whole situation would have been absolutely intolerable.

**MRS. LINDE:** It *really* isn't him?

**NORA:** No, I give you my word. It would never have occurred to me for one moment. . . . Anyway, he didn't have the money to lend then. He didn't inherit it till later.

**MRS. LINDE:** Just as well for you, I'd say, my dear Nora.

**NORA:** No, it would never have occurred to me to ask Dr. Rank. . . . All the same I'm pretty certain if I were to ask him . . .

**MRS. LINDE:** But of course you won't.

**NORA:** No, of course not. I can't ever imagine it being necessary. But I'm quite certain if ever I were to mention it to Dr. Rank. . . .

**MRS. LINDE:** Behind your husband's back?

**NORA:** I have to get myself out of that other business. That's also behind his back. I *must* get myself out of that.

**MRS. LINDE:** Yes, that's what I said yesterday. But . . .

**NORA** [*walking up and down*]:   A man's better at coping with these things than a woman. . . .

**MRS. LINDE:**   Your own husband, yes.

**NORA:**   Nonsense! [*Stops.*]   When you've paid everything you owe, you do get your IOU back again, don't you?

**MRS. LINDE:**   Of course.

**NORA:**   And you can tear it up into a thousand pieces and burn it—the nasty, filthy thing!

**MRS. LINDE** [*looking fixedly at her, puts down her sewing and slowly rises*]:   Nora, you are hiding something from me.

**NORA:**   Is it so obvious?

**MRS. LINDE:**   Something has happened to you since yesterday morning. Nora, what is it?

**NORA** [*going towards her*]:   Kristine! [*Listens.*] Hush! There's Torvald back. Look, you go and sit in there beside the children for the time being. Torvald can't stand the sight of mending lying about. Get Anne Marie to help you.

**MRS. LINDE** [*gathering a lot of the things together*]:   All right, but I'm not leaving until we have thrashed this thing out.

[*She goes into the room, left; at the same time Helmer comes in from the hall.*]

**NORA** [*goes to meet him*]:   I've been longing for you to be back, Torvald, dear.

**HELMER:**   Was that the dressmaker . . . ?

**NORA:**   No, it was Kristine; she's helping me with my costume. I think it's going to look very nice . . .

**HELMER:**   Wasn't that a good idea of mine, now?

**NORA:**   Wonderful! But wasn't it also nice of me to let you have your way?

**HELMER** [*taking her under the chin*]:   Nice of you—because you let your husband have his way? All right, you little rogue, I know you didn't mean it that way. But I don't want to disturb you. You'll be wanting to try the costume on, I suppose.

**NORA:**   And I dare say you've got work to do?

**HELMER:**   Yes. [*Shows her a bundle of papers.*] Look at this. I've been down at the Bank. . . .

[*He turns to go into his study.*]

**NORA:** Torvald!

**HELMER** [*stopping*]: Yes.

**NORA:** If a little squirrel were to ask ever so nicely . . . ?

**HELMER:** Well?

**NORA:** Would you do something for it?

**HELMER:** Naturally I would first have to know what it is.

**NORA:** Please, if only you would let it have its way, and do what it wants, it'd scamper about and do all sorts of marvellous tricks.

**HELMER:** What is it?

**NORA:** And the pretty little sky-lark would sing all day long. . . .

**HELMER:** Huh! It does that anyway.

**NORA:** I'd pretend I was an elfin child and dance a moonlight dance for you, Torvald.

**HELMER:** Nora—I hope it's not that business you started on this morning?

**NORA** [*coming closer*]: Yes, it is, Torvald. I implore you!

**HELMER:** You have the nerve to bring that up again?

**NORA:** Yes, yes, you *must* listen to me. You must let Krogstad keep his job at the Bank.

**HELMER:** My dear Nora, I'm giving his job to Mrs. Linde.

**NORA:** Yes, it's awfully sweet of you. But couldn't you get rid of somebody else in the office instead of Krogstad?

**HELMER:** This really is the most incredible obstinacy! Just because you go and make some thoughtless promise to put in a good word for him, you expect me . . .

**NORA:** It's not that, Torvald. It's for your own sake. That man writes in all the nastiest papers, you told me that yourself. He can do you no end of harm. He terrifies me to death. . . .

**HELMER:** Aha, now I see. It's your memories of what happened before that are frightening you.

**NORA:** What do you mean?

**HELMER:** It's your father you are thinking of.

**NORA:** Yes . . . yes, that's right. You remember all the nasty insinuations those wicked people put in the papers about Daddy? I honestly think they would have had him dismissed if the Ministry hadn't sent you down to investigate, and you hadn't been so kind and helpful.

HELMER: My dear little Nora, there is a considerable difference between your father and me. Your father's professional conduct was not entirely above suspicion. Mine is. And I hope it's going to stay that way as long as I hold this position.

NORA: But nobody knows what some of these evil people are capable of. Things could be so nice and pleasant for us here, in the peace and quiet of our home—you and me and the children, Torvald! That's why I implore you. . . .

HELMER: The more you plead for him, the more impossible you make it for me to keep him on. It's already known down at the Bank that I am going to give Krogstad his notice. If it ever got around that the new manager had been talked over by his wife. . . .

NORA: What of it?

HELMER: Oh, nothing! As long as the little woman gets her own stubborn way . . . ! Do you want me to make myself a laughing stock in the office? . . . Give people the idea that I am susceptible to any kind of outside pressure? You can imagine how soon I'd feel the consequences of that! Anyway, there's one other consideration that makes it impossible to have Krogstad in the Bank as long as I am manager.

NORA: What's that?

HELMER: At a pinch I might have overlooked his past lapses. . . .

NORA: Of course you could, Torvald!

HELMER: And I'm told he's not bad at his job, either. But we knew each other rather well when we were younger. It was one of those rather rash friendships that prove embarrassing in later life. There's no reason why you shouldn't know we were once on terms of some familiarity. And he, in his tactless way, makes no attempt to hide the fact, particularly when other people are present. On the contrary, he thinks he has every right to treat me as an equal, with his 'Torvald this' and 'Torvald that' every time he opens his mouth. I find it extremely irritating, I can tell you. He would make my position at the Bank absolutely intolerable.

NORA: Torvald, surely you aren't serious?

**HELMER:** Oh? Why not?

**NORA:** Well, it's all so petty.

**HELMER:** What's that you say? Petty? Do you think I'm petty?

**NORA:** No, not at all, Torvald dear! And that's why . . .

**HELMER:** Doesn't make any difference! . . . You call my motives petty; so I must be petty too. Petty! Indeed! Well, we'll put a stop to that, once and for all. [*He opens the hall door and calls.*] Helene!

**NORA:** What are you going to do?

**HELMER** [*searching among his papers*]: Settle things. [*The Maid comes in.*] See this letter? I want you to take it down at once. Get hold of a messenger and get him to deliver it. Quickly. The address is on the outside. There's the money.

**MAID:** Very good, sir.

[*She goes with the letter.*]

**HELMER** [*putting his papers together*]: There now, my stubborn little miss.

**NORA** [*breathless*]: Torvald . . . what was that letter?

**HELMER:** Krogstad's notice.

**NORA:** Get it back, Torvald! There's still time! Oh, Torvald, get it back! Please for my sake, for your sake, for the sake of the children! Listen, Torvald, please! You don't realize what it can do to us.

**HELMER:** Too late.

**NORA:** Yes, too late.

**HELMER:** My dear Nora, I forgive you this anxiety of yours, although it is actually a bit of an insult. Oh, but it is, I tell you! It's hardly flattering to suppose that anything this miserable pen-pusher wrote could frighten *me!* But I forgive you all the same, because it is rather a sweet way of showing how much you love me. [*He takes her in his arms.*] This is how things must be, my own darling Nora. When it comes to the point, I've enough strength and enough courage, believe me, for whatever happens. You'll find I'm man enough to take everything on myself.

**NORA** [*terrified*]: What do you mean?

**HELMER:** Everything, I said. . . .

**NORA** [*in command of herself*]: That is something you shall never, never do.

**HELMER:**  All right, then we'll share it, Nora—as man and wife. That's what we'll do. [*Caressing her.*] Does that make you happy now? There, there, don't look at me with those eyes, like a little frightened dove. The whole thing is sheer imagination.—Why don't you run through the tarantella and try out the tambourine? I'll go into my study and shut both the doors, then I won't hear anything. You can make all the noise you want. [*Turns in the doorway.*] And when Rank comes, tell him where he can find me.

[*He nods to her, goes with his papers into his room, and shuts the door behind him.*]

**NORA** [*wild-eyed with terror, stands as though transfixed*]:  He's quite capable of doing it! He would do it! No matter what, he'd do it.— No, never in this world! Anything but that! Help? Some way out . . . ? [*The door-bell rings in the hall.*] Dr. Rank. . . ! Anything but that, anything! [*She brushes her hands over her face, pulls herself together and opens the door into the hall. Dr. Rank is standing outside hanging up his fur coat. During what follows it begins to grow dark.*] Hello, Dr. Rank. I recognized your ring. Do you mind not going in to Torvald just yet, I think he's busy.

**RANK:**  And you?

[*Dr. Rank comes into the room and she closes the door behind him.*]

**NORA:**  Oh, you know very well I've always got time for you.

**RANK:**  Thank you. A privilege I shall take advantage of as long as I am able.

**NORA:**  What do you mean—as long as you are able?

**RANK:**  Does that frighten you?

**NORA:**  Well, it's just that it sounds so strange. Is anything likely to happen?

**RANK:**  Only what I have long expected. But I didn't think it would come quite so soon.

**NORA** [*catching at his arm*]:  What have you found out? Dr. Rank, you must tell me!

**RANK:**  I'm slowly sinking. There's nothing to be done about it.

**NORA** [*with a sigh of relief*]:  Oh, it's *you* you're . . . ?

**RANK:**  Who else? No point in deceiving oneself. I am the most wretched of all my patients, Mrs. Helmer. These last few days I've made a careful analysis of my internal economy. Bankrupt! Within a month I shall probably be lying rotting up there in the churchyard.

NORA:   Come now, what a ghastly thing to say!

RANK:   The whole damned thing is ghastly. But the worst thing is all the ghastliness that has to be gone through first. I only have one more test to make; and when that's done I'll know pretty well when the final disintegration will start. There's something I want to ask you. Helmer is a sensitive soul; he loathes anything that's ugly. I don't want him visiting me. . . .

NORA:   But Dr. Rank. . . .

RANK:   On no account must he. I won't have it. I'll lock the door on him.—As soon as I'm absolutely certain of the worst, I'll send you my visiting card with a black cross on it. You'll know then the final horrible disintegration has begun.

NORA:   Really, you are being quite absurd today. And here was I hoping you would be in a thoroughly good mood.

RANK:   With death staring me in the face? Why should I suffer for another man's sins? What justice is there in that? Somewhere, somehow, every single family must be suffering some such cruel retribution. . . .

NORA [*stopping up her ears*]:   Rubbish! Do cheer up!

RANK:   Yes, really the whole thing's nothing but a huge joke. My poor innocent spine must do penance for my father's gay subaltern life.

NORA [*by the table, left*]:   Wasn't he rather partial to asparagus and *pâté de foie gras?*

RANK:   Yes, he was. And truffles.

NORA:   Truffles, yes. And oysters, too, I believe?

RANK:   Yes, oysters, oysters, of course.

NORA:   And all the port and champagne that goes with them. It does seem a pity all these delicious things should attack the spine.

RANK:   Especially when they attack a poor spine that never had any fun out of them.

NORA:   Yes, that is an awful pity.

RANK [*looks at her sharply*]:   Hm. . . .

NORA [*after a pause*]:   Why did you smile?

RANK:   No, it was you who laughed.

NORA:   No, it was you who smiled, Dr. Rank!

RANK [*getting up*]:   You are a bigger rascal than I thought you were.

NORA:   I feel full of mischief today.

RANK:   So it seems.

NORA [*putting her hands on his shoulders*]:   Dear, dear Dr. Rank, you mustn't go and die on Torvald and me.

RANK:   You wouldn't miss me for long. When you are gone, you are soon forgotten.

NORA [*looking at him anxiously*]:   Do you think so?

RANK:   People make new contacts, then . . .

NORA:   Who make new contacts?

RANK:   Both you and Helmer will, when I'm gone. You yourself are already well on the way, it seems to me. What was this Mrs. Linde doing here last night?

NORA:   Surely you aren't jealous of poor Kristine?

RANK:   Yes, I am. She'll be my successor in this house. When I'm done for, I can see this woman. . . .

NORA:   Hush! Don't talk so loud, she's in there.

RANK:   Today as well? There you are, you see!

NORA:   Just to do some sewing on my dress. Good Lord, how absurd you are! [*She sits down on the sofa.*] Now Dr. Rank, cheer up. You'll see tomorrow how nicely I can dance. And you can pretend I'm doing it just for you—and for Torvald as well, of course. [*She takes various things out of the box.*] Come here, Dr. Rank. I want to show you something.

RANK [*sits*]:   What is it?

NORA:   Look!

RANK:   Silk stockings.

NORA:   Flesh-coloured! Aren't they lovely! Of course, it's dark here now, but tomorrow. . . . No, no, no, you can only look at the feet. Oh well, you might as well see a bit higher up, too.

RANK:   Hm. . . .

NORA:   Why are you looking so critical? Don't you think they'll fit?

RANK:   I couldn't possibly offer any informed opinion about that.

NORA [*looks at him for a moment*]:   Shame on you. [*Hits him lightly across the ear with the stockings.*] Take that! [*Folds them up again.*]

RANK:   And what other delights am I to be allowed to see?

NORA: Not another thing. You are too naughty. [*She hums a little and searches among her things.*]

RANK [*after a short pause*]: Sitting here so intimately like this with you, I can't imagine . . . I simply cannot conceive what would have become of me if I had never come to this house.

NORA [*smiles*]: Yes, I rather think you do enjoy coming here.

RANK [*in a low voice, looking fixedly ahead*]: And the thought of having to leave it all. . .

NORA: Nonsense. You aren't leaving.

RANK [*in the same tone*]: . . . without being able to leave behind even the slightest token of gratitude, hardly a fleeting regret even . . . nothing but an empty place to be filled by the first person that comes along.

NORA: Supposing I were to ask you to . . . ? No . . .

RANK: What?

NORA: . . . to show me the extent of your friendship . . .

RANK: Yes?

NORA: I mean . . . to do me a tremendous favour. . . .

RANK: Would you really, for once, give me that pleasure?

NORA: You have no idea what it is.

RANK: All right, tell me.

NORA: No, really I can't, Dr. Rank. It's altogether too much to ask . . . because I need your advice and help as well. . . .

RANK: The more the better. I cannot imagine what you have in mind. But tell me anyway. You do trust me, don't you?

NORA: Yes, I trust you more than anybody I know. You are my best and my most faithful friend. I know that. So I will tell you. Well then, Dr. Rank, there is something you must help me to prevent. You know how deeply, how passionately Torvald is in love with me. He would never hesitate for a moment to sacrifice his life for my sake.

RANK [*bending towards her*]: Nora . . . do you think he's the only one who . . . ?

NORA [*stiffening slightly*]: Who . . . ?

RANK: Who wouldn't gladly give his life for your sake.

NORA [*sadly*]: Oh!

RANK: I swore to myself you would know before I went. I'll never have a better opportunity. Well, Nora! Now you know. And now you know too that you can confide in me as in nobody else.

NORA [*rises and speaks evenly and calmly*]: Let me past.

RANK [*makes way for her, but remains seated*]: Nora. . . .

NORA [*in the hall doorway*]: Helene, bring the lamp in, please. [*Walks over to the stove.*] Oh, my dear Dr. Rank, that really was rather horrid of you.

RANK [*getting up*]: That I have loved you every bit as much as anybody? Is *that* horrid?

NORA: No, but that you had to go and tell me. When it was all so unnecessary. . . .

RANK: What do you mean? Did you know . . . ?

[*The Maid comes in with the lamp, puts it on the table, and goes out again.*]

RANK: Nora . . . Mrs. Helmer . . . I'm asking you if you knew?

NORA: How can I tell whether I did or didn't. I simply can't tell you. . . . Oh, how could you be so clumsy, Dr. Rank! When everything was so nice.

RANK: Anyway, you know now that I'm at your service, body and soul. So you can speak out.

NORA [*looking at him*]: After this?

RANK: I beg you to tell me what it is.

NORA: I can tell you nothing now.

RANK: You must. You can't torment me like this. Give me a chance— I'll do anything that's humanly possible.

NORA: You can do nothing for me now. Actually, I don't really need any help. It's all just my imagination, really it is. Of course! [*She sits down in the rocking-chair, looks at him and smiles.*] I must say, you are a nice one, Dr. Rank! Don't you feel ashamed of yourself, now the lamp's been brought in?

RANK: No, not exactly. But perhaps I ought to go—for good?

NORA: No, you mustn't do that. You must keep coming just as you've always done. You know very well Torvald would miss you terribly.

RANK: And *you*?

NORA: I always think it's tremendous fun having you.

RANK: That's exactly what gave me wrong ideas. I just can't puzzle you out. I often used to feel you'd just as soon be with me as with Helmer.

NORA: Well, you see, there are those people you love and those people you'd almost rather *be* with.

RANK: Yes, there's something in that.

NORA: When I was a girl at home, I loved Daddy best, of course. But I also thought it great fun if I could slip into the maids' room. For one thing they never preached at me. And they always talked about such exciting things.

RANK: Aha! So it's their role I've taken over!

NORA [*jumps up and crosses to him*]: Oh, my dear, kind Dr. Rank, I didn't mean that at all. But you can see how it's a bit with Torvald as it was with Daddy. . . .

[*The Maid comes in from the hall.*]

MAID: Please, ma'am. . . !

[*She whispers and hands her a card.*]

NORA [*glances at the card*]: Ah!

[*She puts it in her pocket.*]

RANK: Anything wrong?

NORA: No, no, not at all. It's just . . . it's my new costume. . . .

RANK: How is that? There's your costume in there.

NORA: That one, yes. But this is another one. I've ordered it. Torvald mustn't hear about it. . . .

RANK: Ah, so that's the big secret, is it!

NORA: Yes, that's right. Just go in and see him, will you? He's in the study. Keep him occupied for the time being. . . .

RANK: Don't worry. He shan't escape me.

[*He goes into Helmer's study.*]

NORA [*to the Maid*]: Is he waiting in the kitchen?

MAID: Yes, he came up the back stairs. . . .

NORA: But didn't you tell him somebody was here?

MAID: Yes, but it was no good.

NORA: Won't he go?

**MAID:** No, he won't till he's seen you.

**NORA:** Let him in, then. But quietly. Helene, you mustn't tell anybody about this. It's a surprise for my husband.

**MAID.** I understand, ma'am. . . .

[*She goes out.*]

**NORA:** Here it comes! What I've been dreading! No, no, it can't happen, it *can't* happen.

[*She walks over and bolts Helmer's door. The Maid opens the hall door for Krogstad and shuts it again behind him. He is wearing a fur coat, over-shoes, and a fur cap.*]

**NORA** [*goes towards him*]: Keep your voice down, my husband is at home.

**KROGSTAD:** What if he is?

**NORA:** What do you want with me?

**KROGSTAD:** To find out something.

**NORA:** Hurry, then. What is it?

**KROGSTAD:** You know I've been given notice.

**NORA:** I couldn't prevent it, Mr. Krogstad, I did my utmost for you, but it was no use.

**KROGSTAD:** Has your husband so little affection for you? He knows what I can do to you, yet he dares. . . .

**NORA:** You don't imagine he knows about it!

**KROGSTAD:** No, I didn't imagine he did. It didn't seem a bit like my good friend Torvald Helmer to show that much courage. . . .

**NORA:** Mr. Krogstad, I must ask you to show some respect for my husband.

**KROGSTAD:** Oh, sure! All due respect! But since you are so anxious to keep this business quiet, Mrs. Helmer, I take it you now have a rather clearer idea of just what it is you've done, than you had yesterday.

**NORA:** Clearer than *you* could ever have given me.

**KROGSTAD:** Yes, being as I am such a rotten lawyer. . . .

**NORA:** What do you want with me?

**KROGSTAD:** I just wanted to see how things stood, Mrs. Helmer. I've been thinking about you all day. Even a mere money-lender, a hack journalist, a—well, even somebody like me has a bit of what you might call feeling.

NORA: Show it then. Think of my little children.

KROGSTAD: Did you or your husband think of mine? But what does it matter now? There was just one thing I wanted to say: you needn't take this business too seriously. I shan't start any proceedings, for the present.

NORA: Ah, I knew you wouldn't.

KROGSTAD: The whole thing can be arranged quite amicably. Nobody need know. Just the three of us.

NORA: My husband must never know.

KROGSTAD: How can you prevent it? Can you pay off the balance?

NORA: No, not immediately.

KROGSTAD: Perhaps you've some way of getting hold of the money in the next few days.

NORA: None I want to make use of.

KROGSTAD: Well, it wouldn't have been very much help to you if you had. Even if you stood there with the cash in your hand and to spare, you still wouldn't get your IOU back from me now.

NORA: What are you going to do with it?

KROGSTAD: Just keep it—have it in my possession. Nobody who isn't implicated need know about it. So if you are thinking of trying any desperate remedies . . .

NORA: Which I am. . . .

KROGSTAD: . . . if you happen to be thinking of running away . . .

NORA: Which I am!

KROGSTAD: . . . or anything worse . . .

NORA: How did you know?

KROGSTAD: . . . forget it!

NORA: How did you know I was thinking of *that*?

KROGSTAD: Most of us think of *that*, to begin with. I did, too; but I didn't have the courage. . . .

NORA [*tonelessly*]: I haven't either.

KROGSTAD [*relieved*]: So you haven't the courage either, eh?

NORA: No, I haven't! I haven't!

KROGSTAD: It would also be very stupid. There'd only be the first domestic storm to get over. . . . I've got a letter to your husband in my pocket here. . . .

**NORA:** And it's all in there?

**KROGSTAD:** In as tactful a way as possible.

**NORA** [*quickly*]: He must never read that letter. Tear it up. I'll find the money somehow.

**KROGSTAD:** Excuse me, Mrs. Helmer, but I've just told you. . . .

**NORA:** I'm not talking about the money I owe you. I want to know how much you are demanding from my husband, and I'll get the money.

**KROGSTAD:** I want no money from your husband.

**NORA:** What do you want?

**KROGSTAD:** I'll tell you. I want to get on my feet again, Mrs. Helmer; I want to get to the top. And your husband is going to help me. For the last eighteen months I've gone straight; all that time it's been hard going; I was content to work my way up, step by step. Now I'm being kicked out, and I won't stand for being taken back again as an act of charity. I'm going to get to the top, I tell you. I'm going back into that Bank—with a better job. Your husband is going to create a new vacancy, just for me. . . .

**NORA:** He'll never do that!

**KROGSTAD:** He will do it. I know him. He'll do it without so much as a whimper. And once I'm in there with him, you'll see what's what. In less than a year I'll be his right-hand man. It'll be Nils Krogstad, not Torvald Helmer, who'll be running that Bank.

**NORA:** You'll never live to see that day!

**KROGSTAD:** You mean you . . . ?

**NORA:** Now I have the courage.

**KROGSTAD:** You can't frighten me! A precious pampered little thing like you. . . .

**NORA:** I'll show you! I'll show you!

**KROGSTAD:** Under the ice, maybe? Down in the cold, black water? Then being washed up in the spring, bloated, hairless, unrecognizable. . . .

**NORA:** You can't frighten me.

**KROGSTAD:** You can't frighten me, either. People don't do that sort of thing, Mrs. Helmer. There wouldn't be any point to it, anyway. I'd still have him right in my pocket.

**NORA:** Afterwards? When I'm no longer . . .

**KROGSTAD:** Aren't you forgetting that your reputation would then be entirely in my hands? [*Nora stands looking at him, speechless.*] Well, I've warned you. Don't do anything silly. When Helmer gets my letter, I expect to hear from him. And don't forget: it's him who is forcing me off the straight and narrow again, your own husband! That's something I'll never forgive him for. Goodbye, Mrs. Helmer.

[*He goes out through the hall. Nora crosses to the door, opens it slightly, and listens.*]

**NORA:** He's going. He hasn't left the letter. No, no, that would be impossible! [*Opens the door further and further.*] What's he doing? He's stopped outside. He's not going down the stairs. Has he changed his mind? Is he . . . ? [*A letter falls into the letter-box. Then Krogstad's footsteps are heard receding as he walks downstairs. Nora gives a stifled cry, runs across the room to the sofa table; pause.*] In the letter-box! [*She creeps stealthily across to the hall door.*] There it is! Torvald, Torvald! It's hopeless now!

**MRS. LINDE.** [*comes into the room, left, carrying the costume*]: There, I think that's everything. Shall we try it on?

**NORA** [*in a low, hoarse voice*]: Kristine, come here.

**MRS. LINDE** [*throws the dress down on the sofa*]: What's wrong with you? You look upset.

**NORA:** Come here. Do you see that letter? *There*, look! Through the glass in the letter-box.

**MRS. LINDE:** Yes, yes, I can see it.

**NORA:** It's a letter from Krogstad.

**MRS. LINDE:** Nora! It was Krogstad who lent you the money!

**NORA:** Yes. And now Torvald will get to know everything.

**MRS. LINDE:** Believe me, Nora, it's best for you both.

**NORA:** But there's more to it than that. I forged a signature. . . .

**MRS. LINDE:** Heavens above!

**NORA:** Listen, I want to tell you something, Kristine, so you can be my witness.

**MRS. LINDE:** What do you mean "witness"? What do you want me to . . . ?

**NORA:** If I should go mad . . . which might easily happen . . .

**MRS. LINDE:** Nora!

**NORA:** Or if anything happened to me . . . which meant I couldn't be here. . . .

**MRS. LINDE:** Nora, Nora! Are you out of your mind?

**NORA:** And if somebody else wanted to take it all upon himself, the whole blame, you understand. . . .

**MRS. LINDE:** Yes, yes. But what makes you think . . . ?

**NORA:** Then you must testify that it isn't true, Kristine. I'm not out of my mind; I'm quite sane now. And I tell you this: nobody else knew anything, I alone was responsible for the whole thing. Remember that!

**MRS. LINDE:** I will. But I don't understand a word of it.

**NORA:** Why should you? You see something miraculous is going to happen.

**MRS. LINDE:** Something miraculous?

**NORA:** Yes, a miracle. But something so terrible as well, Kristine—oh, it must *never* happen, not for anything.

**MRS. LINDE:** I'm going straight over to talk to Krogstad.

**NORA:** Don't go. He'll only do you harm.

**MRS. LINDE:** There was a time when he would have done anything for me.

**NORA:** Him!

**MRS. LINDE:** Where does he live?

**NORA:** How do I know . . . ? Wait a minute. [*She feels in her pocket.*] Here's his card. But the letter, the letter . . . !

**HELMER** [*from his study, knocking on the door*]: Nora!

**NORA** [*cries out in terror*]: What's that? What do you want?

**HELMER:** Don't be frightened. We're not coming in. You've locked the door. Are you trying on?

**NORA:** Yes, yes, I'm trying on. It looks so nice on me, Torvald.

**MRS. LINDE** [*who has read the card*]: He lives just round the corner.

**NORA:** It's no use. It's hopeless. The letter is there in the box.

**MRS. LINDE:** Your husband keeps the key?

**NORA:** Always.

**MRS. LINDE:** Krogstad must ask for his letter back unread, he must find some sort of excuse. . . .

**NORA:** But this is just the time that Torvald generally . . .

MRS. LINDE:   Put him off! Go in and keep him busy. I'll be back as soon as I can.

[*She goes out hastily by the hall door. Nora walks over to Helmer's door, opens it and peeps in.*]

NORA:   Torvald!

HELMER [*in the study*]:   Well, can a man get into his own living-room again now? Come along, Rank, now we'll see . . . [*In the doorway.*] But what's this?

NORA:   What, Torvald dear?

HELMER:   Rank led me to expect some kind of marvellous transformation.

RANK [*in the doorway*]:   That's what I thought too, but I must have been mistaken.

NORA:   I'm not showing myself off to anybody before tomorrow.

HELMER:   Nora dear, you look tired. You haven't been practising too hard?

NORA:   No, I haven't practised at all yet.

HELMER:   You'll have to, though.

NORA:   Yes, I certainly must, Torvald. But I just can't get anywhere without your help: I've completely forgotten it.

HELMER:   We'll soon polish it up.

NORA:   Yes, do help me, Torvald. Promise? I'm so nervous. All those people. . . . You must devote yourself exclusively to me this evening. Pens away! Forget all about the office! Promise me, Torvald dear!

HELMER:   I promise. This evening I am wholly and entirely at your service . . . helpless little thing that you are. Oh, but while I remember, I'll just look first . . .

[*He goes towards the hall door.*]

NORA:   What do you want out there?

HELMER:   Just want to see if there are any letters.

NORA:   No, don't, Torvald!

HELMER:   Why not?

NORA:   Torvald, *please!* There aren't any.

HELMER:   Just let me see.

[*He starts to go. Nora, at the piano, plays the opening bars of the tarantella.*]

HELMER [*at the door, stops*]: Aha!

NORA: I shan't be able to dance tomorrow if I don't rehearse it with you.

HELMER [*walks to her*]: Are you really so nervous, Nora dear?

NORA: Terribly nervous. Let me run through it now. There's still time before supper. Come and sit here and play for me, Torvald dear. Tell me what to do, keep me right—as you always do.

HELMER: Certainly, with pleasure, if that's what you want.

[*He sits at the piano. Nora snatches the tambourine out of the box, and also a long gaily-coloured shawl which she drapes round herself, then with a bound she leaps forward.*]

NORA [*shouts*]: Now play for me! Now I'll dance!

[*Helmer plays and Nora dances; Dr. Rank stands at the piano behind Helmer and looks on.*]

HELMER [*playing*]: Not so fast! Not so fast!

NORA: I can't help it.

HELMER: Not so wild, Nora!

NORA: This is how it has to be.

HELMER [*stops*]: No, no, that won't do at all.

NORA [*laughs and swings the tambourine*]: Didn't I tell you?

RANK: Let me play for her.

HELMER [*gets up*]: Yes, do. Then I'll be better able to tell her what to do.

[*Dr. Rank sits down at the piano and plays. Nora dances more and more wildly. Helmer stands by the stove giving her repeated directions as she dances; she does not seem to hear them. Her hair comes undone and falls about her shoulders; she pays no attention and goes on dancing. Mrs. Linde enters.*]

MRS. LINDE [*standing as though spellbound in the doorway*]: Ah . . . !

NORA [*dancing*]: See what fun we are having, Kristine.

HELMER: But my dear darling Nora, you are dancing as though your life depended on it.

NORA: It does.

HELMER:   Stop, Rank! This is sheer madness. Stop, I say.

[*Dr. Rank stops playing and Nora comes to a sudden halt.*]

HELMER [*crosses to her*]:   I would never have believed it. You have forgotten everything I ever taught you.

NORA [*throwing away the tambourine*]:   There you are, you see.

HELMER:   Well, some more instruction is certainly needed there.

NORA:   Yes, you see how necessary it is. You must go on coaching me right up to the last minute. Promise me, Torvald?

HELMER:   You can rely on me.

NORA:   You mustn't think about anything else but me until after tomorrow . . . mustn't open any letters . . . mustn't touch the letter-box.

HELMER:   Ah, you are still frightened of what that man might . . .

NORA:   Yes, yes, I am.

HELMER:   I can see from your face there's already a letter there from him.

NORA:   I don't know. I think so. But you mustn't read anything like that now. We don't want anything horrid coming between us until all this is over.

RANK [*softly to Helmer*]:   I shouldn't cross her.

HELMER [*puts his arm round her*]:   The child must have her way. But tomorrow night, when your dance is done. . . .

NORA:   Then you are free.

MAID [*in the doorway, right*]:   Dinner is served, madam.

NORA:   We'll have champagne, Helene.

MAID:   Very good, madam.

[*She goes.*]

HELMER:   Aha! It's to be quite a banquet, eh?

NORA:   With champagne flowing until dawn. [*Shouts.*] And some macaroons, Helene . . . lots of them, for once in a while.

HELMER [*seizing her hands*]:   Now, now, not so wild and excitable! Let me see you being my own little singing bird again.

NORA:   Oh yes, I will. And if you'll just go in . . . you, too, Dr. Rank. Kristine, you must help me to do my hair.

RANK [*Softly, as they leave*]:   There isn't anything . . . anything as it were, impending, is there?

HELMER: No, not at all, my dear fellow. It's nothing but these childish fears I was telling you about.

[*They go out to the right.*]

NORA: Well?

MRS. LINDE: He's left town.

NORA: I saw it in your face.

MRS. LINDE: He's coming back tomorrow evening. I left a note for him.

NORA: You shouldn't have done that. You must let things take their course. Because really it's a case for rejoicing, waiting like this for the miracle.

MRS. LINDE: What is it you are waiting for?

NORA: Oh, you wouldn't understand. Go and join the other two. I'll be there in a minute.

[*Mrs. Linde goes into the dining-room. Nora stands for a moment as though to collect herself, then looks at her watch.*]

NORA: Five. Seven hours to midnight. Then twenty-four hours till the next midnight. Then the tarantella will be over. Twenty-four and seven? Thirty-one hours to live.

HELMER [*in the doorway, right*]: What's happened to our little skylark?

NORA [*running towards him with open arms*]: Here she is!

## ACT THREE

*The same room. The round table has been moved to the centre of the room, and the chairs placed round it. A lamp is burning on the table. The door to the hall stands open. Dance music can be heard coming from the floor above. Mrs. Linde is sitting by the table, idly turning over the pages of a book; she tries to read, but does not seem able to concentrate. Once or twice she listens, tensely, for a sound at the front door.*

MRS. LINDE [*looking at her watch*]: Still not here. There isn't much time left. I only hope he hasn't . . . [*She listens again.*] Ah, there he is. [*She goes out into the hall, and cautiously opens the front door.*

*Soft footsteps can be heard on the stairs. She whispers.*] Come in.
There's nobody here.

KROGSTAD [*in the doorway*]:   I found a note from you at home. What
does it all mean?

MRS. LINDE:   I *had* to talk to you.

KROGSTAD:   Oh? And did it have to be here, in this house?

MRS. LINDE:   It wasn't possible over at my place, it hasn't a separate
entrance. Come in. We are quite alone. The maid's asleep and the
Helmers are at a party upstairs.

KROGSTAD [*comes into the room*]:   Well, well! So the Helmers are out
dancing tonight! Really?

MRS. LINDE:   Yes, why not?

KROGSTAD:   Why not indeed!

MRS. LINDE:   Well then, Nils. Let's talk.

KROGSTAD:   Have we two anything more to talk about?

MRS. LINDE:   We have a great deal to talk about.

KROGSTAD:   I shouldn't have thought so.

MRS. LINDE:   That's because you never really understood me.

KROGSTAD:   What else was there to understand, apart from the old,
old story? A heartless woman throws a man over the moment something more profitable offers itself.

MRS. LINDE:   Do you really think I'm so heartless? Do you think I
found it easy to break it off?

KROGSTAD:   Didn't you?

MRS. LINDE:   You didn't really believe that?

KROGSTAD:   If that wasn't the case, why did you write to me as you
did?

MRS. LINDE:   There was nothing else I could do. If I had to make the
break, I felt in duty bound to destroy any feeling that you had for
me.

KROGSTAD [*clenching his hands*]:   So that's how it was. And all
that . . . was for money!

MRS. LINDE:   You mustn't forget I had a helpless mother and two
young brothers. We couldn't wait for you, Nils. At that time you
hadn't much immediate prospect of anything.

KROGSTAD:   That may be. But you had no right to throw me over for
somebody else.

**MRS. LINDE:** Well, I don't know. Many's the time I've asked myself whether I was justified.

**KROGSTAD** [*more quietly*]: When I lost you, it was just as if the ground had slipped away from under my feet. Look at me now: a broken man clinging to the wreck of his life.

**MRS. LINDE:** Help might be near.

**KROGSTAD:** It was near. Then you came along and got in the way.

**MRS. LINDE:** Quite without knowing, Nils. I only heard today it's you I'm supposed to be replacing at the Bank.

**KROGSTAD:** If you say so, I believe you. But now you do know, aren't you going to withdraw?

**MRS. LINDE:** No, that wouldn't benefit you in the slightest.

**KROGSTAD:** Benefit, benefit. . . . ! I would do it just the same.

**MRS. LINDE:** I have learned to go carefully. Life and hard, bitter necessity have taught me that.

**KROGSTAD:** And life has taught me not to believe in pretty speeches.

**MRS. LINDE:** Then life has taught you a very sensible thing. But deeds are something you surely must believe in?

**KROGSTAD:** How do you mean?

**MRS. LINDE:** You said you were like a broken man clinging to the wreck of his life.

**KROGSTAD:** And I said it with good reason.

**MRS. LINDE:** And I am like a broken woman clinging to the wreck of her life. Nobody to care about, and nobody to care for.

**KROGSTAD:** It was your own choice.

**MRS. LINDE:** At the time there was no other choice.

**KROGSTAD:** Well, what of it?

**MRS. LINDE:** Nils, what about us two castaways joining forces?

**KROGSTAD:** What's that you say?

**MRS. LINDE:** Two of us on *one* wreck surely stand a better chance than each on his own.

**KROGSTAD:** Kristine!

**MRS. LINDE:** Why do you suppose I came to town?

**KROGSTAD:** You mean, you thought of me?

**MRS. LINDE:** Without work I couldn't live. All my life I have worked, for as long as I can remember; that has always been my one great joy. But now I'm completely alone in the world, and feeling horribly empty and forlorn. There's no pleasure in working only for yourself. Nils, give me somebody and something to work for.

KROGSTAD:   I don't believe all this. It's only a woman's hysteria, wanting to be all magnanimous and self-sacrificing.

MRS. LINDE:   Have you ever known me hysterical before?

KROGSTAD:   Would you really do this? Tell me—do you know all about my past?

MRS. LINDE:   Yes.

KROGSTAD:   And you know what people think about me?

MRS. LINDE:   Just now you hinted you thought you might have been a different person with me.

KROGSTAD:   I'm convinced I would.

MRS. LINDE:   Couldn't it still happen?

KROGSTAD:   Kristine! You know what you are saying, don't you? Yes, you do. I can see you do. Have you really the courage . . . ?

MRS. LINDE:   I need someone to mother, and your children need a mother. We two need each other. Nils, I have faith in what, deep down, you are. With you I can face anything.

KROGSTAD [*seizing her hands*]:   Thank you, thank you, Kristine. And I'll soon have everybody looking up to me, or I'll know the reason why. Ah, but I was forgetting. . . .

MRS. LINDE:   Hush! The tarantella! You must go!

KROGSTAD:   Why? What is it?

MRS. LINDE:   You hear that dance upstairs? When it's finished they'll be coming.

KROGSTAD:   Yes, I'll go. It's too late to do anything. Of course, you know nothing about what steps I've taken against the Helmers.

MRS. LINDE:   Yes, Nils, I do know.

KROGSTAD:   Yet you still want to go on. . . .

MRS. LINDE:   I know how far a man like you can be driven by despair.

KROGSTAD:   Oh, if only I could undo what I've done!

MRS. LINDE:   You still can. Your letter is still there in the box.

KROGSTAD:   Are you sure?

MRS. LINDE:   Quite sure. But . . .

KROGSTAD [*regards her searchingly*]:   Is that how things are? You want to save your friend at any price? Tell me straight. Is that it?

MRS. LINDE:   When you've sold yourself *once* for other people's sake, you don't do it again.

**KROGSTAD:** I shall demand my letter back.

**MRS. LINDE:** No, no.

**KROGSTAD:** Of course I will. I'll wait here till Helmer comes. I'll tell him he has to give me my letter back . . . that it's only about my notice . . . that he mustn't read it . . .

**MRS. LINDE:** No, Nils, don't ask for it back.

**KROGSTAD:** But wasn't that the very reason you got me here?

**MRS. LINDE:** Yes, that was my first terrified reaction. But that was yesterday, and it's quite incredible the things I've witnessed in this house in the last twenty-four hours. Helmer must know everything. This unhappy secret must come out. Those two must have the whole thing out between them. All this secrecy and deception, it just can't go on.

**KROGSTAD:** Well, if you want to risk it. . . . But one thing I can do, and I'll do it at once. . . .

**MRS. LINDE** [*listening*]: Hurry! Go, go! The dance has stopped. We aren't safe a moment longer.

**KROGSTAD:** I'll wait for you downstairs.

**MRS. LINDE:** Yes, do. You must see me home.

**KROGSTAD:** I've never been so incredibly happy before.

[*He goes out by the front door. The door out into the hall remains standing open.*]

**MRS. LINDE** [*tidies the room a little and gets her hat and coat ready*]: How things change! How things change! Somebody to work for . . . to live for. A home to bring happiness into. Just let me get down to it. . . . I wish they'd come. . . . [*Listens.*] Ah, there they are. . . . Get my things.

[*She takes her coat and hat. The voices of Helmer and Nora are heard outside. A key is turned and Helmer pushes Nora almost forcibly into the hall. She is dressed in the Italian costume, with a big black shawl over it. He is in evening dress, and over it a black cloak, open.*]

**NORA** [*still in the doorway, reluctantly*]: No, no, not in here! I want to go back up again. I don't want to leave so early.

**HELMER:** But my dearest Nora . . .

**NORA:** Oh, please, Torvald, I beg you. . . . *Please*, just for another hour.

**HELMER:** Not another minute, Nora my sweet. You remember what we agreed. There now, come along in. You'll catch cold standing there.

[*He leads her, in spite of her resistance, gently but firmly into the room.*]

**MRS. LINDE:** Good evening.

**NORA:** Kristine!

**HELMER:** Why, Mrs. Linde. You here so late?

**MRS. LINDE:** Yes. You must forgive me but I did so want to see Nora all dressed up.

**NORA:** Have you been sitting here waiting for me?

**MRS. LINDE:** Yes, I'm afraid I wasn't in time to catch you before you went upstairs. And I felt I couldn't leave again without seeing you.

**HELMER** [*removing Nora's shawl*]: Well take a good look at her. I think I can say she's worth looking at. Isn't she lovely, Mrs. Linde?

**MRS. LINDE:** Yes, I must say. . . .

**HELMER:** Isn't she quite extraordinarily lovely? That's what everybody at the party thought, too. But she's dreadfully stubborn . . . the sweet little thing! And what shall we do about that? Would you believe it, I nearly had to use force to get her away.

**NORA:** Oh Torvald, you'll be sorry you didn't let me stay, even for half an hour.

**HELMER:** You hear that, Mrs. Linde? She dances her tarantella, there's wild applause—which was well deserved, although the performance was perhaps rather realistic . . . I mean, rather more so than was strictly necessary from the artistic point of view. But anyway! The main thing is she was a success, a tremendous success. Was I supposed to let her stay after that? Spoil the effect? No thank you! I took my lovely little Capri girl—my capricious little Capri girl, I might say—by the arm, whisked her once round the room, a curtsey all round, and then—as they say in novels—the beautiful vision vanished. An exit should always be effective, Mrs. Linde. But I just can't get Nora to see that. Phew! It's warm in here. [*He throws his cloak over a chair and opens the door to his study.*] What? It's dark. Oh yes, of course. Excuse me. . . .

[*He goes in and lights a few candles.*]

**NORA** [*quickly, in a breathless whisper*]: Well?

**MRS. LINDE** [*Softly*]: I've spoken to him.

**NORA:** And . . . ?

**MRS. LINDE:** Nora . . . you must tell your husband everything.

**NORA** [*tonelessly*]: I knew it.

**MRS. LINDE:** You've got nothing to fear from Krogstad. But you must speak.

**NORA:** I won't.

**MRS. LINDE:** Then the letter will.

**NORA:** Thank you, Kristine. Now I know what's to be done. Hush . . . !

**HELMER** [*comes in again*]: Well, Mrs. Linde, have you finished admiring her?

**MRS. LINDE:** Yes. And now I must say good night.

**HELMER:** Oh, already? Is this yours, this knitting?

**MRS. LINDE** [*takes it*]: Yes, thank you. I nearly forgot it.

**HELMER:** So you knit, eh?

**MRS. LINDE:** Yes.

**HELMER:** You should embroider instead, you know.

**MRS. LINDE:** Oh? Why?

**HELMER:** So much prettier. Watch! You hold the embroidery like this in the left hand, and then you take the needle in the right hand, like this, and you describe a long, graceful curve. Isn't that right?

**MRS. LINDE:** Yes, I suppose so. . . .

**HELMER:** Whereas knitting on the other hand just can't help being ugly. Look! Arms pressed into the sides, the knitting needles going up and down—there's something Chinese about it. . . . Ah, that was marvellous champagne they served tonight.

**MRS. LINDE:** Well, good night, Nora! And stop being so stubborn.

**HELMER:** Well said, Mrs. Linde!

**MRS. LINDE:** Good night, Mr. Helmer.

**HELMER** [*accompanying her to the door*]: Good night, good night! You'll get home all right, I hope? I'd be only too pleased to . . . But you haven't far to walk. Good night, good night! [*She goes; he shuts the door behind her and comes in again.*] There we are, got rid of her at last. She's a frightful bore, that woman.

**NORA:** Aren't you very tired, Torvald?

**HELMER:** Not in the least.

**NORA:** Not sleepy?

**HELMER.** Not at all. On the contrary, I feel extremely lively. What about you? Yes, you look quite tired and sleepy.

**NORA:** Yes, I'm very tired. I just want to fall straight off to sleep.

**HELMER:** There you are, you see! Wasn't I right in thinking we shouldn't stay any longer?

**NORA:** Oh, everything you do is right.

**HELMER** [*kissing her forehead*]: There's my little sky-lark talking common sense. Did you notice how gay Rank was this evening?

**NORA:** Oh, was he? I didn't get a chance to talk to him.

**HELMER:** I hardly did either. But it's a long time since I saw him in such a good mood. [*Looks at Nora for a moment or two, then comes nearer her.*] Ah, it's wonderful to be back in our own home again, and quite alone with you. How irresistibly lovely you are, Nora!

**NORA:** Don't look at me like that, Torvald!

**HELMER:** Can't I look at my most treasured possession? At all this loveliness that's mine and mine alone, completely and utterly mine.

**NORA** [*walks round to the other side of the table*]: You mustn't talk to me like that tonight.

**HELMER** [*following her*]: You still have the tarantella in your blood, I see. And that makes you even more desirable. Listen! The guests are beginning to leave now. [*Softly:*] Nora . . . soon the whole house will be silent.

**NORA:** I should hope so.

**HELMER:** Of course you do, don't you, Nora my darling? You know, whenever I'm out at a party with you . . . do you know why I never talk to you very much, why I always stand away from you and only steal a quick glance at you now and then . . . do you know why I do that? It's because I'm pretending we are secretly in love, secretly engaged and nobody suspects there is anything between us.

**NORA:** Yes, yes. I know your thoughts are always with me, of course.

**HELMER:** And when it's time to go, and I lay your shawl round those shapely, young shoulders, round the exquisite curve of your neck . . . I pretend that you are my young bride, that we are just leaving our wedding, that I am taking you to our new home for the first time . . . to be alone with you for the first time . . . quite alone with your young and trembling loveliness! All evening I've been longing for you, and nothing else. And as I watched you darting and swaying in the tarantella, my blood was on fire . . . I couldn't bear it any longer . . . and that's why I brought you down here with me so early. . . .

NORA: Go away, Torvald! Please leave me alone. I won't have it.

HELMER: What's this? It's just your little game isn't it, my little Nora. Won't! Won't! Am I not your husband . . . ?

[*There is a knock on the front door.*]

NORA [*startled*]: Listen . . . !

HELMER [*going towards the hall*]: Who's there?

RANK [*outside*]: It's me. Can I come in for a minute?

HELMER [*in a low voice, annoyed*]: Oh, what does he want now? [*Aloud.*] Wait a moment. [*He walks across and opens the door.*] How nice of you to look in on your way out.

RANK: I fancied I heard your voice and I thought I would just look in. [*He takes a quick glance round.*] Ah yes, this dear, familiar old place! How cosy and comfortable you've got things here, you two.

HELMER: You seemed to be having a pretty good time upstairs yourself.

RANK: Capital! Why shouldn't I? Why not make the most of things in this world? At least as much as one can, and for as long as one can. The wine was excellent. . . .

HELMER: Especially the champagne.

RANK: You noticed that too, did you? It's incredible the amount I was able to put away.

NORA: Torvald also drank a lot of champagne this evening.

RANK: Oh?

NORA: Yes, and that always makes him quite merry.

RANK: Well, why shouldn't a man allow himself a jolly evening after a day well spent?

HELMER: Well spent? I'm afraid I can't exactly claim that.

RANK [*clapping him on the shoulder*]: But I can, you see!

NORA: Dr. Rank, am I right in thinking you carried out a certain laboratory test today?

RANK: Exactly.

HELMER: Look at our little Nora talking about laboratory tests!

**NORA:** And may I congratulate you on the result?

**RANK:** You may indeed.

**NORA:** So it was good?

**RANK:** The best possible, for both doctor and patient—certainty!

**NORA** [*quickly and searchingly*]: Certainty?

**RANK:** Absolute certainty. So why shouldn't I allow myself a jolly evening after that?

**NORA:** Quite right, Dr. Rank.

**HELMER:** I quite agree. As long as you don't suffer for it in the morning.

**RANK:** Well, you never get anything for nothing in this life.

**NORA:** Dr. Rank . . . you are very fond of masquerades, aren't you?

**RANK:** Yes, when there are plenty of amusing disguises. . . .

**NORA:** Tell me, what shall we two go as next time?

**HELMER:** There's frivolity, for you . . . thinking about the next time already!

**RANK:** We two? I'll tell you. You must go as Lady Luck. . . .

**HELMER:** Yes, but how do you find a costume to suggest *that?*

**RANK:** Your wife could simply go in her everyday clothes. . . .

**HELMER:** That was nicely said. But don't you know what you would be?

**RANK:** Yes, my dear friend, I know exactly what I shall be.

**HELMER:** Well?

**RANK:** At the next masquerade, I shall be invisible.

**HELMER:** That's a funny idea!

**RANK:** There's a big black cloak . . . haven't you heard of the cloak of invisibility? That comes right down over you, and then nobody can see you.

**HELMER** [*suppressing a smile*]: Of course, that's right.

**RANK:** But I'm clean forgetting what I came for. Helmer, give me a cigar, one of the dark Havanas.

**HELMER:** With the greatest of pleasure.

[*He offers his case.*]

**RANK** [*takes one and cuts the end off*]: Thanks.

**NORA** [*strikes a match*]: Let me give you a light.

**RANK:** Thank you. [*She holds out the match and he lights his cigar.*] And now, goodbye!

**HELMER:** Goodbye, goodbye, my dear fellow!

**NORA:** Sleep well, Dr. Rank.

**RANK:** Thank you for that wish.

**NORA:** Wish me the same.

**RANK:** You? All right, if you want me to. . . . Sleep well. And thanks for the light.

[*He nods to them both, and goes.*]

**HELMER** [*subdued*]: He's had a lot to drink.

**NORA** [*absently*]: Very likely.

[*Helmer takes a bunch of keys out of his pocket and goes out into the hall.*]

**NORA:** Torvald . . . what do you want there?

**HELMER:** I must empty the letter-box, it's quite full. There'll be no room for the papers in the morning. . . .

**NORA:** Are you going to work tonight?

**HELMER:** You know very well I'm not. Hello, what's this? Somebody's been at the lock.

**NORA:** At the lock?

**HELMER:** Yes, I'm sure of it. Why should that be? I'd hardly have thought the maids . . . ? Here's a broken hair-pin. Nora, it's one of yours. . . .

**NORA** [*quickly*]: It must have been the children. . . .

**HELMER:** Then you'd better tell them not to. Ah . . . there . . . I've managed to get it open. [*He takes the things out and shouts into the kitchen.*] Helene! . . . Helene, put the light out in the hall. [*He comes into the room again with the letters in his hand and shuts the hall door.*] Look how it all mounts up. [*Runs through them.*] What's this?

**NORA:** The letter! Oh no, Torvald, no!

**HELMER:** Two visiting cards . . . from Dr. Rank.

**NORA:** From Dr. Rank?

**HELMER** [*looking at them*]: Dr. Rank, Medical Practitioner. They were on top. He must have put them in as he left.

**NORA:** Is there anything on them?

**HELMER:** There's a black cross above his name. Look. What an uncanny idea. It's just as if he were announcing his own death.

**NORA:**  He is.

**HELMER:**  What? What do you know about it? Has he said anything to you?

**NORA:**  Yes. He said when these cards came, he would have taken his last leave of us. He was going to shut himself up and die.

**HELMER:**  Poor fellow! Of course I knew we couldn't keep him with us very long. But so soon. . . . And hiding himself away like a wounded animal.

**NORA:**  When it has to happen, it's best that it should happen without words. Don't you think so, Torvald?

**HELMER** [*walking up and down*]:  He had grown so close to us. I don't think I can imagine him gone. His suffering and his loneliness seemed almost to provide a background of dark cloud to the sunshine of our lives. Well, perhaps it's all for the best. For him at any rate. [*Pauses.*] And maybe for us as well, Nora. Now there's just the two of us. [*Puts his arms round her.*] Oh, my darling wife, I can't hold you close enough. You know, Nora . . . many's the time I wish you were threatened by some terrible danger so I could risk everything, body and soul, for your sake.

**NORA** [*tears herself free and says firmly and decisively*]:  Now you must read your letters, Torvald.

**HELMER:**  No, no, not tonight. I want to be with you, my darling wife.

**NORA:**  Knowing all the time your friend is dying . . . ?

**HELMER:**  You are right. It's been a shock to both of us. This ugly thing has come between us . . . thoughts of death and decay. We must try to free ourselves from it. Until then . . . we shall go our separate ways.

**NORA** [*her arms round his neck*]:  Torvald . . . good night! Good night!

**HELMER** [*kisses her forehead*]:  Goodnight, my little singing bird. Sleep well, Nora, I'll just read through my letters.

[*He takes the letters into his room and shuts the door behind him.*]

**NORA** [*gropes around her, wild-eyed, seizes Helmer's cloak, wraps it round herself, and whispers quickly, hoarsely, spasmodically*]:  Never see him again. Never, never, never. [*Throws her shawl over her head.*] And never see the children again either. Never, never. Oh, that black icy water. Oh, that bottomless . . . ! If only it were all over! He's got it now. Now he's reading it. Oh no, no! Not yet! Torvald, goodbye . . . and my children. . . .

[*She rushes out in the direction of the hall; at the same moment Helmer flings open his door and stands there with an open letter in his hand.*]

HELMER: Nora!

NORA [*shrieks*]: Ah!

HELMER: What is this? Do you know what is in this letter?

NORA: Yes, I know. Let me go! Let me out!

HELMER [*holds her back*]: Where are you going?

NORA [*trying to tear herself free*]: You mustn't try to save me, Torvald!

HELMER [*reels back*]: True! Is it true what he writes? How dreadful! No, no, it can't possibly be true.

NORA: It *is* true. I loved you more than anything else in the world.

HELMER: Don't come to me with a lot of paltry excuses!

NORA [*taking a step towards him*]: Torvald . . . !

HELMER: Miserable woman . . . what is this you have done?

NORA: Let me go. I won't have you taking the blame for me. You mustn't take it on yourself.

HELMER: Stop play-acting! [*Locks the front door.*] You are staying here to give an account of yourself. Do you understand what you have done? Answer me! Do you understand?

NORA [*looking fixedly at him, her face hardening*]: Yes, now I'm really beginning to understand.

HELMER [*walking up and down*]: Oh, what a terrible awakening this is. All these eight years . . . this woman who was my pride and joy . . . a hypocrite, a liar, worse than that, a criminal! Oh, how utterly squalid it all is! Ugh! Ugh! [*Nora remains silent and looks fixedly at him.*] I should have realized something like this would happen. I should have seen it coming. All your father's irresponsible ways. . . . Quiet! All your father's irresponsible ways are coming out in you. No religion, no morals, no sense of duty. . . . Oh, this is my punishment for turning a blind eye to him. It was for your sake I did it, and this is what I get for it.

NORA: Yes, this.

**HELMER:** Now you have ruined my entire happiness, jeopardized my whole future. It's terrible to think of. Here I am, at the mercy of a thoroughly unscrupulous person; he can do whatever he likes with me, demand anything he wants, order me about just as he chooses . . . and I daren't even whimper. I'm done for, a miserable failure, and it's all the fault of a feather-brained woman!

**NORA:** When I've left this world behind, you will be free.

**HELMER:** Oh, stop pretending! Your father was just the same, always ready with fine phrases. What good would it do me if you left this world behind, as you put it? Not the slightest bit of good. He can still let it all come out, if he likes; and if he does, people might even suspect me of being an accomplice in these criminal acts of yours. They might even think I was the one behind it all, that it was I who pushed you into it! And it's you I have to thank for this . . . and when I've taken such good care of you, all our married life. Now do you understand what you have done to me?

**NORA** [*coldly and calmly*]: Yes.

**HELMER:** I just can't understand it, it's so incredible. But we must see about putting things right. Take that shawl off. Take it off, I tell you! I must see if I can't find some way or other of appeasing him. The thing must be hushed up at all costs. And as far as you and I are concerned, things must appear to go on exactly as before. But only in the eyes of the world, of course. In other words you'll go on living here; that's understood. But you will not be allowed to bring up the children, I can't trust you with them. . . . Oh, that I should have to say this to the woman I loved so dearly, the woman I still. . . . Well, that must be all over and done with. From now on, there can be no question of happiness. All we can do is save the bits and pieces from the wreck, preserve appearances. . . . [*The front door-bell rings. Helmer gives a start.*] What's that? So late? How terrible, supposing. . . . If he should . . . ? Hide, Nora! Say you are not well.

[*Nora stands motionless. Helmer walks across and opens the door into the hall.*]

**MAID** [*half dressed, in the hall*]: It's a note for Mrs. Helmer.

**HELMER:** Give it to me. [*He snatches the note and shuts the door.*] Yes, it's from him. You can't have it. I want to read it myself.

**NORA:** You read it then.

**HELMER** [*by the lamp*]:   I hardly dare. Perhaps this is the end, for both of us. Well, I *must* know. [*He opens the note hurriedly, reads a few lines, looks at another enclosed sheet, and gives a cry of joy.*] Nora! [*Nora looks at him inquiringly.*] Nora! I must read it again. Yes, yes, it's true! I am saved! Nora, I am saved!

**NORA:**   And me?

**HELMER:**   You too, of course, we are both saved, you as well as me. Look, he's sent your IOU back. He sends his regrets and apologies for what he has done. . . . His luck has changed. . . . Oh, what does it matter what he says. We are saved, Nora! Nobody can do anything to you now. Oh, Nora, Nora . . . but let's get rid of this disgusting thing first. Let me see. . . . [*He glances at the IOU.*] No, I don't want to see it. I don't want it to be anything but a dream. [*He tears up the IOU and both letters, throws all the pieces into the stove and watches them burn.*] Well, that's the end of that. He said in his note you'd known since Christmas Eve. . . . You must have had three terrible days of it, Nora.

**NORA:**   These three days haven't been easy.

**HELMER:**   The agonies you must have gone through! When the only way out seemed to be. . . . No, let's forget the whole ghastly thing. We can rejoice and say: It's all over! It's all over! Listen to me, Nora! You don't seem to understand: it's all over! Why this grim look on your face? Oh, poor little Nora, of course I understand. You can't bring yourself to believe I've forgiven you. But I have, Nora, I swear it. I forgive you everything. I know you did what you did because you loved me.

**NORA:**   That's true.

**HELMER:**   You loved me as a wife should love her husband. It was simply that you didn't have the experience to judge what was the best way of going about things. But do you think I love you any the less for that; just because you don't know how to act on your own responsibility? No, no, you just lean on me, I shall give you all the advice and guidance you need. I wouldn't be a proper man if I didn't find a woman doubly attractive for being so obviously helpless. You mustn't dwell on the harsh things I said in that first moment of horror, when I thought everything was going to come crashing down about my ears. I have forgiven you, Nora, I swear it! I have forgiven you!

**NORA:** Thank you for your forgiveness.

[*She goes out through the door, right.*]

**HELMER:** No, don't go! [*He looks through the doorway.*] What are you doing in the spare room?

**NORA:** Taking off this fancy dress.

**HELMER** [*standing at the open door*]. Yes, do. You try and get some rest, and set your mind at peace again, my frightened little song-bird. Have a good long sleep; you know you are safe and sound under my wing. [*Walks up and down near the door.*] What a nice, cosy little home we have here, Nora! Here you can find refuge. Here I shall hold you like a hunted dove I have rescued unscathed from the cruel talons of the hawk, and calm your poor beating heart. And that will come, gradually, Nora, believe me. Tomorrow you'll see everything quite differently. Soon everything will be just as it was before. You won't need me to keep on telling you I've forgiven you; you'll feel convinced of it in your own heart. You don't really imagine me ever thinking of turning you out, or even of reproaching you? Oh, a real man isn't made that way, you know, Nora. For a man, there's something indescribably moving and very satisfying in knowing that he has forgiven his wife—forgiven her, completely and genuinely, from the depths of his heart. It's as though it made her his property in a double sense: he has, as it were, given her a new life, and she becomes in a way both his wife and at the same time his child. That is how you will seem to me after today, helpless, perplexed little thing that you are. Don't you worry your pretty little head about anything, Nora. Just you be frank with me, and I'll take all the decisions for you. . . . What's this? Not in bed? You've changed your things?

**NORA** [*in her everyday dress*]: Yes, Torvald, I've changed.

**HELMER:** What for? It's late.

**NORA:** I shan't sleep tonight.

**HELMER:** But my dear Nora. . . .

**NORA** [*looks at her watch*]: It's not so terribly late. Sit down, Torvald. We two have a lot to talk about.

[*She sits down at one side of the table.*]

**HELMER:** Nora, what is all this? Why so grim?

**NORA:**   Sit down. It'll take some time. I have a lot to say to you.

**HELMER** [*sits down at the table opposite her*]:   You frighten me, Nora. I don't understand you.

**NORA:**   Exactly. You don't understand me. And I have never understood you, either—until tonight. No, don't interrupt. I just want you to listen to what I have to say. We are going to have things out, Torvald.

**HELMER:**   What do you mean?

**NORA:**   Isn't there anything that strikes you about the way we two are sitting here?

**HELMER:**   What's that?

**NORA:**   We have now been married eight years. Hasn't it struck you this is the first time you and I, man and wife, have had a serious talk together?

**HELMER:**   Depends what you mean by "serious."

**NORA:**   Eight whole years—no, more, ever since we first knew each other—and never have we exchanged one serious word about serious things.

**HELMER:**   What did you want me to do? Get you involved in worries that you couldn't possibly help me to bear?

**NORA:**   I'm not talking about worries. I say we've never once sat down together and seriously tried to get to the bottom of anything.

**HELMER:**   But, my dear Nora, would that have been a thing for you?

**NORA:**   That's just it. You have never understood me . . . I've been greatly wronged, Torvald. First by my father, and then by you.

**HELMER:**   What! Us two! The two people who loved you more than anybody?

**NORA** [*shakes her head*]:   You two never loved me. You only thought how nice it was to be in love with me.

**HELMER:**   But, Nora, what's this you are saying?

**NORA:**   It's right, you know, Torvald. At home, Daddy used to tell me what he thought, then I thought the same. And if I thought differently, I kept quiet about it, because he wouldn't have liked it. He used to call me his baby doll, and he played with me as I used to play with my dolls. Then I came to live in your house. . . .

**HELMER:**   What way is that to talk about our marriage?

**NORA** [*imperturbably*]:   What I mean is: I passed out of Daddy's hands into yours. You arranged everything to your tastes, and I acquired the same tastes. Or I pretended to . . . I don't really know . . . I think it was a bit of both, sometimes one thing and sometimes the other. When I look back, it seems to me I have been living here like a beggar, from hand to mouth. I lived by doing tricks for you, Torvald. But that's the way you wanted it. You and Daddy did me a great wrong. It's your fault that I've never made anything of my life.

HELMER: Nora, how unreasonable . . . how ungrateful you are! Haven't you been happy here?

NORA: No, never. I thought I was, but I wasn't really.

HELMER: Not . . . not happy!

NORA: No, just gay. And you've always been so kind to me. But our house has never been anything but a play-room. I have been your doll wife, just as at home I was Daddy's doll child. And the children in turn have been my dolls. I thought it was fun when you came and played with me, just as they thought it was fun when I went and played with them. That's been our marriage, Torvald.

HELMER: There is some truth in what you say, exaggerated and hysterical though it is. But from now on it will be different. Play-time is over; now comes the time for lessons.

NORA: Whose lessons? Mine or the children's?

HELMER: Both yours and the children's, my dear Nora.

NORA: Ah, Torvald, you are not the man to teach me to be a good wife for you.

HELMER: How can you say that?

NORA: And what sort of qualifications have I to teach the children?

HELMER: Nora!

NORA: Didn't you say yourself, a minute or two ago, that you couldn't trust me with that job.

HELMER: In the heat of the moment! You shouldn't pay any attention to that.

NORA: On the contrary, you were quite right. I'm not up to it. There's another problem needs solving first. I must take steps to educate myself. You are not the man to help me there. That's something I must do on my own. That's why I'm leaving you.

HELMER [*jumps up*]: What did you say?

NORA: If I'm ever to reach any understanding of myself and the things around me, I must learn to stand alone. That's why I can't stay here with you any longer.

**HELMER:** Nora! Nora!

**NORA:** I'm leaving here at once. I dare say Kristine will put me up for tonight. . . .

**HELMER:** You are out of your mind! I won't let you! I forbid you!

**NORA:** It's no use forbidding me anything now. I'm taking with me my own personal belongings. I don't want anything of yours, either now or later.

**HELMER:** This is madness!

**NORA:** Tomorrow I'm going home—to what used to be my home, I mean. It will be easier for me to find something to do there.

**HELMER:** Oh, you blind, inexperienced . . .

**NORA:** I must set about *getting* experience, Torvald.

**HELMER:** And leave your home, your husband and your children? Don't you care what people will say?

**NORA:** That's no concern of mine. All I know is that this is necessary for *me*.

**HELMER:** This is outrageous! You are betraying your most sacred duty.

**NORA:** And what do you consider to be my most sacred duty?

**HELMER:** Does it take me to tell you that? Isn't it your duty to your husband and your children?

**NORA:** I have another duty equally sacred.

**HELMER:** You have not. What duty might *that* be?

**NORA:** My duty to myself.

**HELMER:** First and foremost, you are a wife and mother.

**NORA:** That I don't believe any more. I believe that first and foremost I am an individual, just as much as you are—or at least I'm going to try to be. I know most people agree with you, Torvald, and that's also what it says in books. But I'm not content any more with what most people say, or with what it says in books. I have to think things out for myself, and get things clear.

**HELMER:** Surely you are clear about your position in your own home? Haven't you an infallible guide in questions like these? Haven't you your religion?

**NORA:** Oh, Torvald, I don't really know what religion is.

**HELMER:** What do you say!

**NORA:** All I know is what Pastor Hansen said when I was confirmed. He said religion was this, that and the other. When I'm away from all this and on my own, I'll go into that, too. I want to find out whether what Pastor Hansen told me was right—or at least whether it's right for *me*.

HELMER:   This is incredible talk from a young woman! But if religion cannot keep you on the right path, let me at least stir your conscience. I suppose you do have some moral sense? Or tell me—perhaps you don't?

NORA:   Well, Torvald, that's not easy to say. I simply don't know. I'm really very confused about such things. All I know is my ideas about such things are very different from yours. I've also learnt that the law is different from what I thought; but I simply can't get it into my head that that particular law is right. Apparently a woman has no right to spare her old father on his death-bed, or to save her husband's life, even. I just don't believe it.

HELMER:   You are talking like a child. You understand nothing about the society you live in.

NORA:   No, I don't. But I shall go into that too. I must try to discover who is right, society or me.

HELMER:   You are ill, Nora. You are delirious. I'm half inclined to think you are out of your mind.

NORA:   Never have I felt so calm and collected as I do tonight.

HELMER:   Calm and collected enough to leave your husband and children?

NORA:   Yes.

HELMER:   Then only one explanation is possible.

NORA:   And that is?

HELMER:   You don't love me any more.

NORA:   Exactly.

HELMER:   Nora! Can you say that!

NORA:   I'm desperately sorry, Torvald. Because you have always been so kind to me. But I can't help it. I don't love you any more.

HELMER [*struggling to keep his composure*]:   Is that also a "calm and collected" decision you've made?

NORA:   Yes, absolutely calm and collected. That's why I don't want to stay here.

HELMER:   And can you also account for how I forfeited your love?

NORA:   Yes, very easily. It was tonight, when the miracle didn't happen. It was then I realized you weren't the man I thought you were.

**HELMER:** Explain yourself more clearly. I don't understand.

**NORA:** For eight years I have been patiently waiting. Because, heavens, I knew miracles didn't happen every day. Then this devastating business started, and I became absolutely convinced the miracle *would* happen. All the time Krogstad's letter lay there, it never so much as crossed my mind that you would ever submit to that man's conditions. I was absolutely convinced you would say to him: Tell the whole wide world if you like. And when that was done . . .

**HELMER:** Yes, then what? After I had exposed my own wife to dishonour and shame . . . !

**NORA:** When that was done, I was absolutely convinced you would come forward and take everything on yourself, and say: I am the guilty one.

**HELMER:** Nora!

**NORA:** You mean I'd never let you make such a sacrifice for my sake? Of course not. But what would my story have counted for against yours?—That was the miracle I went in hope and dread of. It was to prevent it that I was ready to end my life.

**HELMER:** I would gladly toil day and night for you, Nora, enduring all manner of sorrow and distress. But nobody sacrifices his *honour* for the one he loves.

**NORA:** Hundreds and thousands of women have.

**HELMER:** Oh, you think and talk like a stupid child.

**NORA:** All right. But you neither think nor talk like the man I would want to share my life with. When you had got over your fright—and you weren't concerned about me but only about what might happen to you—and when all danger was past, you acted as though nothing had happened. I was your little sky-lark again, your little doll, exactly as before; except you would have to protect it twice as carefully as before, now that it had shown itself to be so weak and fragile. [*Rises.*] Torvald, that was the moment I realised that for eight years I'd been living with a stranger, and had borne him three children. . . . Oh, I can't bear to think about it! I could tear myself to shreds.

**HELMER** [*sadly*]: I see. I see. There is a tremendous gulf dividing us. But, Nora, is there no way we might bridge it?

**NORA:** As I am now, I am no wife for you.

**HELMER:** I still have it in me to change.

NORA: Perhaps . . . if you have your doll taken away.

HELMER: And be separated from you! No, no, Nora, the very thought of it is inconceivable.

NORA [*goes into the room, right*]: All the more reason why it must be done.

[*She comes back with her outdoor things and a small travelling bag which she puts on the chair beside the table.*]

HELMER: Nora, Nora, not now! Wait till the morning.

NORA [*putting on her coat*]: I can't spend the night in a strange man's room.

HELMER: Couldn't we go on living here like brother and sister . . . ?

NORA [*tying on her hat*]: You know very well that wouldn't last. [*She draws the shawl round her.*] Goodbye, Torvald. I don't want to see the children. I know they are in better hands than mine. As I am now, I can never be anything to them.

HELMER: But some day, Nora, some day . . . ?

NORA: How should I know? I've no idea what I might turn out to be.

HELMER: But you are my wife, whatever you are.

NORA: Listen, Torvald, from what I've heard, when a wife leaves her husband's house as I am doing now, he is absolved by law of all responsibility for her. I can at any rate free you from all responsibility. You must not feel in any way bound, any more than I shall. There must be full freedom on both sides. Look, here's your ring back. Give me mine.

HELMER: That too?

NORA: That too.

HELMER: There it is.

NORA: Well, that's the end of that. I'll put the keys down here. The maids know where everything is in the house—better than I do, in fact. Kristine will come in the morning after I've left to pack up the few things I brought with me from home. I want them sent on.

HELMER: The end! Nora, will you never think of me?

NORA: I dare say I'll often think about you and the children and this house.

HELMER: May I write to you, Nora?

NORA: No, never. I won't let you.

HELMER: But surely I can send you . . .

NORA:   Nothing, nothing.

HELMER:   Can't I help you if ever you need it?

NORA:   I said "no." I don't accept things from strangers.

HELMER:   Nora, can I never be anything more to you than a stranger?

NORA [*takes her bag*]:   Ah, Torvald, only by a miracle of miracles. . . .

HELMER:   Name it, this miracle of miracles!

NORA:   Both you and I would have to change to the point where . . . Oh, Torvald, I don't believe in miracles any more.

HELMER:   But I *will* believe. Name it! Change to the point where . . . ?

NORA:   Where we could make a real marriage of our lives together. Goodbye!

[*She goes out through the hall door.*]

HELMER [*sinks down on a chair near the door, and covers his face with his hands*]:   Nora! Nora! [*He rises and looks round.*] Empty! She's gone! [*With sudden hope.*] The miracle of miracles . . . ?

[*The heavy sound of a door being slammed is heard from below.*]

—*1879*

**Gwen Pharis Ringwood (1910–1984)** *was born in Anatone in the state of Washington but moved at the age of three to a farm in southern Alberta. She studied at both the University of Montana and the University of Alberta, graduating with a B.A. in 1934. She worked for Elizabeth Sterling Haynes, co-founder of the Banff School of the Theatre, and it was there that her first stage play,* The Dragons of Kent, *was produced in 1935. A Rockefeller Fellowship took her to the University of North Carolina where a number of "folk" plays, including her famous one-act work,* Still Stands the House, *and* Pasque Flower *(developed into her first full-length play,* Dark Harvest*), were first produced by the Carolina Playmakers. In 1939, Pharis married Dr. J. B. Ringwood and moved to northern Saskatchewan, and in 1941 she received the Governor General's Award for her outstanding service to Canadian drama. She continued to write plays representing the life of the regions in which she lived, including* A Fine Coloured Easter Egg *(1948), a Native trilogy entitled* Drum Song, *a musical, and several plays for children. In 1968, she moved to Williams Lake, British Columbia, where she continued to write and teach, and where the Gwen Pharis Ringwood Civic Theatre was opened in her honour. In addition to the prize-winning* Still Stands the House, *which was widely performed and anthologized, she wrote more than sixty plays, including* A Remembrance of Miracles *(1976) and* The Garage Sale *(1981). Her* Collected Plays *were published in 1982, and she died of cancer in 1984.*

# *Gwen Pharis Ringwood*
# Still Stands the House

## CHARACTERS

Ruth Warren
Arthur Manning
Hester Warren
Bruce Warren

Scene: *A living room.*

*The icy wind of a northern blizzard sweeps across the prairie, lashes about the old Warren farmhouse, and howls insistently at the door and windows. But the Warren house was built to withstand the menace of the Canadian winter and scornfully suffers the storm to shriek about the chimney corner, to knock at the door and rattle the windows in a wild attempt to force an entrance.*

*The living-room of this house has about it a faded austerity, a decayed elegance that is as remote and cheerless as a hearth in which no fire is ever laid. The room has made a stern and solemn pact with the past. Once it held the warm surge of life: but as the years have gone by, it has settled in a rigid pattern of neat, uncompromising severity.*

*As if in defiance of the room, the frost has covered the window in the rear wall with a wild and exotic design. Beside the window is an imposing leather armchair, turned toward the handsome coal stove in the Right corner. A footstool is near the chair. A door at the Centre of the rear wall leads to the snow-sheeted world outside. Along the Left wall, between a closed door to a bedroom (now unused) and an open door to the kitchen, is a mahogany sideboard. Above it is a portrait of old Martin Warren, who built this house and lived in it until his death. The portrait is of a stern and handsome man in his early fifties, and in the expression of the eyes the artist has caught something of his unconquerable will.*

*An open staircase, winding to the bedrooms upstairs, extends into the room at Right. There is a rocking chair by the stove with a small stand-table beside it. A mahogany dining table and two matching chairs are placed at a convenient distance from the side-board and the kitchen door. The figured wall paper is cracked and faded. The dark rug, the heavy curtains, and the tablecloth show signs of much wear, but there is nothing of cheapness about them.*

*Two coal oil lanterns have been left beside the kitchen door. Blooming bravely on the table, in contrast to its surroundings, is a pot of lavender hyacinths.*

*(Ruth Warren is standing near the outside door, talking to Arthur Manning, who is about to leave. Ruth is small, fair-haired, and pretty, twenty-five or twenty-six years of age. There is more strength in her than her rather delicate appearance would indicate. She wears a soft blue house-dress, with a light wool cardigan over it. Manning is a middle-aged man of prosperous appearance. He wears a heavy overcoat over a dark business suit. His hat, gloves and scarf are on the armchair.)*

**RUTH:** Do you think you'd better try to go back tonight, Mr. Manning? The roads may be drifted.

**MANNING:** It's a bad blizzard, all right, but I don't think I'll have any trouble. There's a heater in the car, and I've just had the engine checked over.

**RUTH:** You'll be welcome if you care to spend the night.

**MANNING:** Thank you, but I'm afraid I've got to get back to town. I'd hate to try it in an old car, but this one of mine can pull through anything.

**RUTH:** I've never seen a storm come up so quickly.

**MANNING:** These prairie blizzards are no joke. One of my sheep-herders got lost in one last year, just half a mile from the house. He froze to death out there trying to find his way.

**RUTH:** How frightful!

**MANNING:** One of the ranch hands found him the next morning. Poor old fellow—he'd herded for me for twenty years. I never knew how he came to be out in a storm like that.

**RUTH:** They say when a person gets lost he begins to go round in a circle, although it seems straight ahead.

**MANNING:** Yes, I've always heard that. The winters are the one thing I've got against this country.

**RUTH** *(Wistfully)*: I used to like them in town. We went skating on the river and tobogganing. But out here it's different.

**MANNING:** If Bruce sells the farm and takes this irrigated place near town, you won't notice the winter so much, Mrs. Warren.

**RUTH:** No. I hope he does take your offer, Mr. Manning. I want him to.

**MANNING:** He'll never get a better. Five thousand dollars and an irrigated quarter is a good price for a dryland farm these days.

**RUTH:** If only we didn't have to decide so soon.

**MANNING:** I talked it all over with Bruce in town a couple of weeks ago, and I think he's pretty well made up his mind. All he needs to do is sign the papers.

**RUTH:** I thought he'd have until spring to decide.

**MANNING:** I've got orders to close the deal before I go South next week. You tell Bruce I'll come by tomorrow or the next day, and we can get it all settled.

**RUTH:** I'll tell him. I hope he does take it, Mr. Manning.

**MANNING:** I know you do and you're right. I think all he needs is a little persuading. He's had a hard time here these dry years.

**RUTH:** I don't know what Hester will say.

**MANNING:** I understand she's very much attached to the place. Is it
true that she never leaves the farm?

**RUTH:** Not often.

**MANNING:** She'd be better off where she could get out more.

**RUTH:** I don't know.

**MANNING:** I suppose all those years out here, keeping house for Bruce
and her father, were pretty hard on her.

**RUTH:** The house has come to mean so much to her. But maybe she
won't mind. *(Smiling hopefully.)* We'll see.

*The door to the bedroom, Left, is opened quietly, and Hester
Warren enters the room. She closes and locks the door behind her
and stands looking at the two in the room with cold surmise. Hester
is forty years old. She is tall, dark and unsmiling. The stern rigidity
of her body, the bitter austerity of her mouth, and the almost arrogant dignity of her carriage seem to make her a part of the room she
enters. There is bitter resentment in her dark eyes as she confronts
Ruth and Manning. She holds a leather-bound Bible close to her
breast.*

**RUTH** *(Startled)*: Why, Hester! I thought you never unlocked that
door.

**HESTER** *(Quietly)*: No. I keep Father's room as it was.

**RUTH:** Then why were you—

**HESTER:** I was reading in Father's room. I heard a stranger.

**RUTH:** You know Mr. Manning, Hester.

**MANNING** *(With forced friendliness)*: I don't suppose you remember
me, Miss Warren.

**HESTER** *(Without moving)*: How do you do?

**MANNING** *(Embarrassed at her coldness and anxious to get away)*:
Well, I'll be getting on home. I'll leave these papers for Bruce to
sign, Mrs. Warren. Tell him I'll come by tomorrow. He'll find it's all
there, just as we talked about it. *(He lays the document on the
table.)*

**RUTH:** Thank you, Mr. Manning.

**MANNING** *(Turning to go)*: Take care of yourselves. Good-night. *(To Hester.)* Good-night, Miss Warren.

*(Hester barely nods.)*

**RUTH:** You're sure you ought to try it in the storm?

**MANNING:** Sure. There's no danger if I go right away. *(He goes out.)*

**RUTH** *(Calling after him as she shuts the door)*: Good-night.

*(Hester watches Manning out and, as Ruth returns, she looks at her suspiciously. There is a silence which Hester finally breaks.)*

**HESTER:** What did he want here?

**RUTH** *(Uncomfortable under Hester's scrutiny)*: He just left some papers for Bruce to look over, Hester. He was in a hurry so he didn't wait to see Bruce.

**HESTER:** I see. What has Arthur Manning got to do with Bruce?

**RUTH:** It's something to do with the farm, Hester. I'll put these away. *(She starts to take up the document on the table, but Hester is before her.)*

**HESTER** *(After a long look at the document)*: A deed of sale. *(Turning angrily upon Ruth.)* So this is what you've been hiding from me.

**RUTH** *(Quickly)*: Oh, no! Nothing's settled, Hester. Mr. Manning made an offer, and Bruce wants to think it over. That's all.

**HESTER** *(Her eyes betraying her intense agitation)*: Bruce isn't going to sell this place!

**RUTH:** It's just an offer. Nothing has been decided.

**HESTER:** Your hand's in this! You've been after him to leave here.

**RUTH** *(Trying to conciliate her)*: Let's not quarrel. You can talk to Bruce about it, Hester.

**HESTER:** You hate this house, I know that.

**RUTH:** No. *(Facing Hester firmly.)* But I think Bruce ought to sell.

**HESTER:** You married him. You made your choice.

**RUTH** *(Quietly)*: I've not regretted that. It's just that we're so cut off and lonely here; and this is the best offer we could get. But let me put these away. *(Indicating the deed of sale.)* We'll talk about it later, the three of us.

**HESTER** *(Allowing Ruth to take the papers)*: You may as well burn them. He isn't going to sell.

**RUTH:** Please, Hester—we'll discuss it when Bruce comes. *(She places the document on the sideboard, then crosses to the stove.)* I'll build up the fire.

**HESTER** *(Takes the Bible to the sideboard and places it under her father's portrait. She stands looking up at the portrait)*: This house will not be sold. I won't allow it.

**RUTH** *(Puts some coal on the fire. Shivering)*: It's so cold it almost frightens me. The thermometer has dropped ten degrees within the hour.

**HESTER:** I hope Bruce knows enough to get the stock in. They'll freeze where they stand if they're left out tonight. *(She moves to the window and takes her knitting from the ledge.)*

**RUTH:** He'll have them in. *(Crossing to the table.)* Look, Hester, how the hyacinths have bloomed. I could smell them when I came in the room just now.

**HESTER:** Hyacinths always seem like death to me.

**RUTH** *(Her voice is young and vibrant)*: Oh, no. They're birth, they're spring! They say in Greece you find them growing wild in April. *(She takes an old Wedgwood bowl from the sideboard, preparing to set the pot of hyacinths in it.)*

**HESTER** *(In a dry, unfriendly tone)*: I've asked you not to use that Wedgwood bowl. It was my grandmother's. I don't want it broken.

**RUTH:** I'm sorry. *(Replacing the bowl, she gets a plain one from inside the sideboard.)* I thought the hyacinths would look so pretty in it, but I'll use the plain one.

**HESTER:** You've gone to as much trouble for that plant as if it were a child. *(Hester sits in the rocking chair by the stove.)*

**RUTH** *(Placing the hyacinths in the bowl)*: They're so sweet. I like to touch them.

**HESTER:** They'll freeze tonight, I'm thinking.

**RUTH:** Not in here. We'll have to keep the fire up anyway. *(Leaving the bowl of hyacinths on the table, Ruth returns to the sideboard, taking some bright chintz from the drawer. She holds it up for Hester to see.)* I've almost finished the curtains, Hester.

**HESTER** *(Tonelessly)*: You have?

**RUTH:** Don't you think they'll make this room more cheerful?

**HESTER:** The ones we have seem good enough to me.

**RUTH:** But they're so old.

**HESTER** *(Coldly)*:   Old things have beauty when you've eyes to see it. That velvet has a richness that you can't buy now.

**RUTH** *(Moving to the window)*:   I want to make the room gay and happy for the spring. You'll see how much difference these will make.

**HESTER:**   I've no doubt. *(Hester rises and goes to the table to avoid looking at the curtains.)*

**RUTH** *(Measuring the chintz with the curtains at the window)*:   I wonder if I have them wide enough.

*(The Wind rises.)*

*(As if the sound had quelled her pleasure in the bright curtains, Ruth turns slowly away from the window. A touch of hysteria creeps into her voice.)* The wind swirls and shrieks and raises such queer echoes in this old house! It seems to laugh at us in here, thinking we're safe, hugging the stove! As if it knew it could blow out the light and the fire and—*(Getting hold of herself.)* I've never seen a blizzard when it was as cold as this. Have you, Hester?

**HESTER** *(Knitting)*:   Bruce was born on a night like this.

*(Throughout this scene Hester seldom looks at Ruth but gives all her attention to her knitting. She seems reluctant to talk and yet impelled to do so.)*

**RUTH:**   I didn't know.

**HESTER:**   Father had to ride for the doctor while I stayed here with Mother.

**RUTH:**   Alone?

**HESTER:**   Yes. I was rubbing Father's hands with snow when we heard the baby crying. Then we helped the doctor bathe him.

**RUTH:**   You were such a little girl to do so much.

**HESTER:**   After Mother died I did it all.

**RUTH:**   I know, but it was too hard for a child. I don't see how you managed.

**HESTER:**   Father always helped me with the washing.

**RUTH:**   Not many men would stay in from the field to do that.

**HESTER:**   No. *(Her knitting drops to her lap, and for a moment she is lost in the past.)* "We'll have to lean on one another now,

Daughter."—Those were his words.—And that's the way it was. I was beside him until—I never left him.

RUTH *(At Hester's side)*: You've never talked of him like this before.

HESTER *(Unconscious of Ruth)*: He always liked the snow. *(Her eyes are on the portrait of her father.)* He called it a moving shroud, a winding-sheet that the wind lifts and raises and lets fall again.

RUTH: It is like that.

HESTER: He'd come in and say, "The snow lies deep on the summer fallow, Hester. That means a good crop next year."

RUTH: I know. It's glorious in the fall with the wheat like gold on the hills. No wonder he loved it.

HESTER *(Called out of her dream, she abruptly resumes her knitting)*: There hasn't been much wheat out there these last years.

RUTH: That isn't Bruce's fault, Hester.

HESTER: You have to love a place to make things grow. The land knows when you don't care about it, and Bruce doesn't care about it any more. Not like Father did.

RUTH *(Her hands raised to touch the portrait above the sideboard)*: I wish I'd known your father.

HESTER *(Rising and facing Ruth with a sudden and terrible anger)*: Don't touch that picture. It's mine.

RUTH *(Startled, she faces Hester)*: Why, Hester—

HESTER: Can't I have anything of my own? Must you put your fingers on everything I have?

RUTH *(Moving to Hester)*: Hester, you know I didn't mean—What is the matter with you?

HESTER: I won't have you touch it.

RUTH *(Gently)*: Do you hate my being here so much?

HESTER *(Turning away)*: You've more right here than I have now, I suppose.

RUTH *(Crossing over to the stove)*: You make me feel that I've no right at all.

HESTER *(A martyr now)*: I'm sorry if you don't approve my ways. I can go, if that's what you want.

RUTH *(Pleading)*: Please—I've never had a sister, and when Bruce told me he had one, I thought we'd be such friends—

HESTER *(Sitting in the chair by the stove)*: We're not a family to put words to everything we feel. *(She resumes her knitting.)*

RUTH *(Trying to bridge the gulf between them)*: I get too excited over things: I know it. Bruce tells me I sound affected when I say too much about the way I feel, the way I like people—or the sky in the evening. I—

HESTER *(Without looking up)*: Did you get the separator put up? Or shall I do it?

RUTH *(Discouraged, Ruth turns away, and going to the table, sits down with her sewing)*: It's ready for the milk when Bruce brings it. I put it together this morning.

HESTER: The lanterns are empty.

RUTH: I'll fill them in a minute.

HESTER: When I managed this house, I always filled the lanterns right after supper. Then they were ready.

RUTH *(Impatiently)*: I said I'd fill them, Hester, and I will. They're both there in the corner. *(She indicates the lanterns at the end of the sideboard.)*

HESTER: Bruce didn't take one, then?

RUTH: No.

HESTER: You'd better put a lamp in the window.

RUTH *(Lights a small lamp on the sideboard and takes it to the window)*: I wish he'd come. It's strange how women feel safer when their men are near, close enough to touch, isn't it? No matter how strong you think you are. *(As she speaks, Ruth drapes some of the chintz over the armchair.)*

HESTER: I can't say that I need my strength from Bruce, or could get it if I needed it.

RUTH: That's because he's still a little boy to you. *(A pause. Then Ruth speaks hesitantly.)* Hester—

HESTER: Yes?

RUTH: Will you mind the baby in the house?

HESTER *(After a silence, constrainedly)*: No, I won't mind. I'll keep out of the way.

RUTH *(Warmly, commanding a response)*: I don't want you to. You'll love him, Hester.

HESTER *(Harshly)*: I loved Bruce, but I got no thanks for it. He feels I stand in his way now.

RUTH *(Suddenly aware that Hester has needed and wanted love)*: You mustn't say that. It isn't true.

**HESTER:**   When he was little, after Mother died, he'd come tugging at my hand—He'd get hold of my little finger and say, "Come, Hettie—come and look." Everything was "Hettie" then.

**RUTH** *(Eagerly, moving to Hester)*:   It will be like that again. This baby will be almost like your own.

**HESTER** *(As if Ruth's words were an implied reproach)*:   I could have married, and married well if I'd had a mind to.

**RUTH:**   I know that. I've wondered why you didn't, Hester.

**HESTER:**   The young men used to ride over here on Sunday, but I stopped that. *(A pause.)* I never saw a man I'd let touch me. Maybe you don't mind that kind of thing. I do.

**RUTH** *(Involuntarily; it is a cry)*:   No! *(Attempting to put her arms around Hester.)* What hurt you?

**HESTER** *(Rising)*:   Don't try your soft ways on me. *(She moves behind the armchair, her hand falls caressingly on the back of the chair.)* I couldn't leave Bruce and Father here alone. My duty was here in this house. So I stayed. *(Hester notices the chintz material draped over the chair and, taking it up, turns to Ruth angrily.)* What do you intend to do with this?

**RUTH:**   I thought—there's enough left to make covers for the chair to match the curtains—

**HESTER** *(Throwing the chintz down)*:   This is Father's chair. I won't have it changed.

**RUTH:**   I'm sorry, Hester. *(With spirit.)* Must we keep everything the same forever?

**HESTER:**   There's nothing in this house that isn't good, that wasn't bought with care and pride by one of us who loved it. This stuff is cheap and gaudy.

**RUTH:**   It isn't dull and falling apart with age.

**HESTER:**   Before my father died, when he was ill, he sat here in this chair where he could see them threshing from the window. It was the first time since he came here that he'd not been in the fields at harvest. Now you come—you who never knew him, who never saw him—and you won't rest until—

**RUTH:**   Hester!

**HESTER:**   You've got no right to touch it! *(Her hands grip the back of the old chair as she stands rigid, her eyes blazing.)*

*(Bruce Warren enters from outside, carrying a pail of milk. He is tall and dark, about thirty years old, sensitive and bitter. His vain struggle to make the farm pay since his father's death has left him with an oppressive sense of failure. He is proud and quick to resent an imagined reproach. He has dark hair, his shoulders are a little stooped, and he moves restlessly and abruptly. Despite his moodiness, he is extremely likeable. He is dressed warmly in dark trousers, a sweater under his heavy leather coat; he wears gloves, cap and high boots. He brushes the snow from his coat as he enters.)*

BRUCE *(Carrying the milk into the kitchen)*: Is the separator up, Ruth?

RUTH: Yes, it's all ready, Bruce. Wait, I'll help you. *(She follows him into the kitchen.)*

*(Hester stands at the chair a moment after they have gone; her eyes fall on the plant on the table. Slowly she goes toward it, as if drawn by something she hated. She looks down at the lavender blooms for a moment. Then with a quick, angry gesture, she crushes one of the stalks. She turns away and is winding up her wool when Bruce and Ruth return.)*

You must be frozen.

BRUCE *(Taking off his coat and gloves)*: I'm cold, all right. God, it's a blizzard: thirty-eight below, and a high wind. *(He throws his coat over a chair at the table.)*

RUTH *(With pride)*: Did you see the hyacinths? They've bloomed since yesterday.

BRUCE *(Smiling)*: Yes, they're pretty. *(Touching them, he notices the broken stalk.)* Looks like one of them's broken.

RUTH: Where? *(She sees it.)* Oh, it is! And that one hadn't bloomed yet! I wonder—It wasn't broken when I— *(Ruth turns accusingly to Hester.)* Hester!

HESTER *(Returns look calmly. Coldly)*: Yes?

RUTH: Hester, did you—

BRUCE *(Going over to the fire)*: Oh, Ruth, don't make such a fuss about it. It can't be helped.

HESTER: I'll take care of the milk. *(She takes the small lamp from the window.)*

**RUTH:** I'll do it.

**HESTER** *(Moving toward the kitchen)*: You turn the separator so slow the cream's as thin as water.

**RUTH** *(Stung to reply)*: That's not true. You never give me a chance to—

**BRUCE** *(Irritably)*: For God's sake, don't quarrel about it. *(He sits in the chair by the stove.)*

**HESTER:** I don't intend to quarrel. *(She goes into the kitchen.)*

*(Ruth follows Hester to the door. The sound of the separator comes from the kitchen. Ruth turns wearily, takes up the pot of hyacinths, and places them on the stand near the stove. Then sits on the footstool.)*

**RUTH:** It's always that way.

**BRUCE** *(Gazing moodily at the stove)*: Why don't you two try to get along?

*(A silence.)*

**RUTH:** Did you put the stock in? *(The question is merely something to fill the empty space of silence between them.)*

**BRUCE:** Yes. That black mare may foal tonight. I'll have to look at her later on.

**RUTH:** It's bitter weather for a little colt to be born.

**BRUCE:** Yes.

*(Another silence. Finally Ruth, to throw off the tension between them, gets up and moves her footstool over to his chair.)*

**RUTH:** I'm glad you're here. I've been lonesome for you.

**BRUCE** *(Putting his hand on hers)*: I'm glad to be here.

**RUTH:** I thought of you out at the barn, trying to work in this cold.

**BRUCE:** I was all right. I'd hate to walk far tonight, though. You can't see your hand before your face.

**RUTH** *(After a look at the kitchen)*: Hester's been so strange again these last few days, Bruce.

**BRUCE:** I know it's hard, Ruth.

**RUTH:** It's like it was when I first came here. At everything I touch, she cries out like I'd hurt her somehow.

**BRUCE:** Hester has to do things her own way. She's always been like that.

**RUTH:** If only she could like me a little. I think she almost does sometimes, but then—

**BRUCE:** You think too much about her.

**RUTH:** Maybe it's because we've been shut in so close. I'm almost afraid of her lately.

**BRUCE:** She's not had an easy life, Ruth.

**RUTH:** I know that. She's talked about your father almost constantly today.

**BRUCE:** His death hit us both hard. Dad ran the farm, decided everything.

**RUTH:** It's been six years, Bruce.

**BRUCE:** There are things you don't count out by years.

**RUTH:** He wouldn't want you to go on remembering forever.

**BRUCE** *(Looking at the floor)*: No.

**RUTH:** You should get free of this house. It's not good for you to stay here. It's not good for Hester. *(Getting up, she crosses to the sideboard and returns with the deed of sale, which she hands to Bruce.)* Mr. Manning left this for you. He's coming back tomorrow for it, when you've signed it.

**BRUCE** *(Takes the papers. Annoyed by her assurance)*: He doesn't need to get so excited. I haven't decided to sign yet. He said he wouldn't need to know till spring. *(He goes over to the lamp at the table and studies the document.)*

**RUTH:** His company gave him orders to close the deal this week or let it go.

**BRUCE:** This week?

**RUTH:** That's what he said.

**BRUCE:** Well. I'll think about it.

**RUTH:** You'll have to decide tonight, Bruce. No one else will offer you as much. Five thousand dollars and an irrigated farm a mile from town seems a good price.

**BRUCE:** I'm not complaining about the deal. It's fair.

**RUTH** *(Urgently)*: You're going to take it, aren't you, Bruce?

**BRUCE:** I don't know. God, I don't know. *(He throws the document on the table.)* I don't want to sell, Ruth. I think I'll try it another year.

RUTH: Bruce, you've struggled here too long now. You haven't had a crop, a good crop, in five years.

BRUCE: I need to be told that!

RUTH: It's not your fault. But you've told me you ought to give it up, that it's too dry here.

BRUCE: We may get a crop this year. We're due for one.

RUTH: If you take this offer, we'll be nearer town. We'll have water on the place. We can have a garden, and trees growing.

BRUCE: That's about what those irrigated farms are—gardens.

RUTH: And, Bruce, it wouldn't be so lonely there, so cruelly lonely.

BRUCE: I told you how it was before you came.

RUTH *(Resenting his tone)*: You didn't tell me you worshipped a house. That you made a god of a house and a section of land. You didn't tell me that!

BRUCE *(Angrily)*: You didn't tell me that you'd moon at a window for your old friends, either. *(He stands up and throws the deed of sale on the table.)*

RUTH: How could I help it here?

BRUCE: And you didn't tell me you'd be afraid of having a child. What kind of a woman are you that you don't want your child?

RUTH: That's not true.

BRUCE: No? You cried when you knew, didn't you?

RUTH: Bruce!

BRUCE *(Going blindly on)*: What makes you feel the way you do, then? Other women have children without so much fuss. Other women are glad.

RUTH *(Intensely angry)*: Don't speak to me like that. Keep your land. Eat and sleep and dream land, I don't care!

BRUCE *(Turning to the portrait of his father)*: My father came out here and took a homestead. He broke the prairie with one plough and a team of horses. He built a house to live in out of the sod. You didn't know that, did you? He and Mother lived here in a sod shanty and struggled to make things grow. Then they built a one-roomed shack: and when the good years came, they built this house. The finest in the country! I thought my son would have it.

RUTH *(Moving to him)*: What is there left to give a son? A house that stirs with ghosts! A piece of worn-out land where the rain never comes.

**BRUCE:** That's not all. I don't suppose you can understand.

**RUTH** *(Turning away from him, deeply hurt)*: No. I don't suppose I can. You give me little chance to know how you feel about things.

**BRUCE** *(His anger gone)*: Ruth, I didn't mean that. But you've always lived in town. *(He goes to the window and stands looking out for a moment, then turns.)* Those rocks along the fence out there, I picked up every one of them with my own hands and carried them with my own hands across the field and piled them there. I've ploughed that southern slope along the coulee every year since I was twelve. *(His voice is torn with a kind of shame for his emotion.)* I feel about the land like Hester does about the house, I guess. I don't want to leave it. I don't want to give it up.

**RUTH** *(Gently)*: But it's poor land, Bruce.

*(Bruce sits down, gazing gloomily at the fire. Hester comes in from the kitchen with the small lamp and places it on the sideboard. Then she sits at the table, taking up her knitting. As Bruce speaks, she watches him intently.)*

**BRUCE:** Yes, it's strange that in a soil that won't grow trees a man can put roots down, but he can.

**RUTH** *(At his side)*: You'd feel the same about another place, after a little while.

**BRUCE:** I don't know. When I saw the wind last spring blowing the dirt away, the dirt I'd ploughed and harrowed and sowed to grain, I felt as though a part of myself was blowing away in the dust. Even now, with the land three feet under snow, I can look out and feel it waiting for the seed I've saved for it.

**RUTH:** But if we go, we'll be nearer other people, not cut off from everything that lives.

**BRUCE:** You need people, don't you?

**HESTER:** Yes. She needs them. I've seen her at the window looking toward the town. Day after day she stands there.

*(Bruce and Ruth, absorbed in the conflict between them, had forgotten Hester's presence. At Hester's words, Ruth turns on them both, flaming with anger.)*

**RUTH:** You two. You're so *perfect!*

**HESTER** *(Knitting)*:   We could always stand alone, the three of us. We didn't need to turn to every stranger who held his hand out.

**RUTH:**   No! You'd sit in this husk of a house, living like shadows, until these four walls closed in on you, buried you.

**HESTER:**   I never stood at a window, looking down the road that leads to town.

**RUTH** *(The pent-up hysteria of the day and the longing of months breaks through, tumbling out in her words)*:   It's not for myself I look down that road, Hester. It's for the child I'm going to have. You're right, Bruce. I am afraid. It's not what you think, though, not for myself. You two and your father lived so long in this dark house that you forgot there's a world beating outside, forgot that people laugh and play sometimes. And you've shut me out! *(There is a catch in her voice.)* I never would have trampled on your thoughts if you'd given them to me. But as it is, I might as well not be a person. You'd like a shadow better that wouldn't touch your house. A child would die here. A child can't live with shadows.

**BRUCE** *(Much disturbed, Bruce rises and goes to her)*:   Ruth! I didn't know you hated it so much.

**RUTH:**   I thought it would change. I thought I could change it. You know now.

**BRUCE** *(Quietly)*:   Yes.

**RUTH** *(Pleading)*:   If we go, I'll *want* this child, Bruce. Don't you see? But I'm not happy here. What kind of a life will our child have? He'll be old before he's out of school. *(She looks at the hyacinth on the stand.)* He'll be like this hyacinth that's broken before it bloomed.

**BRUCE** *(Goes to the table and stands looking down at the deed of sale. His voice is tired and flat, but resolved)*:   All right. I'll tell Manning I'll let him have the place.

**HESTER** *(Turning quickly to Bruce)*:   What do you mean?

**BRUCE:**   I'm going to sell the farm to Manning. He was here today.

**HESTER** *(Standing up, her eyes blazing)*:   You can't sell this house.

**BRUCE** *(Looking at the deed of sale)*:   Oh, Ruth's right. We can't make a living on the place. *(He sits down, leafing through the document.)* It's too dry. And too far from school.

**HESTER:**   It wasn't too far for you to go, or me.

**BRUCE** *(Irritably)*:   Do you think I want to sell?

**HESTER:** *She* does. But she can't do it. *(Her voice is low.)* This house belongs to me.

**BRUCE:** Hester, don't start that again! I wish to God the land had been divided differently, but it wasn't.

**HESTER:** Father meant for us to stay here and keep things as they were when he was with us.

**BRUCE:** The soil wasn't blowing away when he was farming it.

**HESTER:** He meant for me to have the house.

**RUTH:** You'll go with us where we go, Hester.

**HESTER** *(To Ruth)*: You came here. You plotted with him to take this house from me. But it's mine!

**BRUCE** *(His voice cracks through the room)*: Stop that, Hester! I love this place as much as you do, but I'm selling it. I'm selling it, I tell you. *(As he speaks, he gets up abruptly and, taking up his coat, puts it on.)*

*(Hester sinks slowly into the chair, staring. Ruth tries to put her hand on Bruce's arm.)*

**RUTH:** Bruce! Not that way! Not for me. If it's that way, I don't care enough.

**BRUCE** *(Shaking himself free)*: Oh, leave me alone!

**RUTH:** Bruce!

**BRUCE** *(Going to the door)*: I'll be glad when it's over, I suppose.

**RUTH:** Where are you going?

**BRUCE** *(Taking his cap and gloves)*: To look at that mare.

**RUTH:** Bruce!

*(But he has gone.)*

**HESTER** *(Getting up, she goes to her father's chair and stands behind it, facing Ruth; she moves and speaks as if she were in a dream)*: This is my house. I won't have strangers in it.

**RUTH** *(At the table, without looking at Hester)*: Oh, Hester! I didn't want it to be this way. I tried—

**HESTER** *(As if she were speaking to a stranger)*: Why did you come here?

**RUTH:** I've hurt you. But I'm right about this. I know I'm right.

**HESTER:** There isn't any room for you.

**RUTH:** Can't you see? It's for all of us.

*(Hester comes toward Ruth with a strange, blazing anger in her face.)*

**HESTER:** I know your kind. You tempted him with your bright hair.

**RUTH:** Hester!

**HESTER:** Your body anointed with jasmine for his pleasure.

**RUTH:** Hester, don't say such things!

**HESTER:** Oh, I know what you are! You and women like you. You put a dream around him with your arms, a sinful dream.

**RUTH** *(Drawing back)*: Hester!

**HESTER:** You lift your white face to every stranger like you offered him a cup to drink from. *(Turning from Ruth, as if she had forgotten her presence, Hester looks fondly at the room.)* I'll never leave this house.

**BRUCE** *(Opens the door and comes in quickly and stormily. He goes into the kitchen as he speaks)*: That mare's got out. She jumped the corral. I'll have to go after her.

**RUTH** *(Concerned)*: Bruce, where will she be?

**BRUCE** *(Returning with an old blanket)*: She'll be in the snowshed by the coulee. She always goes there when she's about to foal.

*(Hester sits in the chair by the stove, her knitting in her hand. She pays no attention to the Others.)*

**RUTH:** But you can't go after her in this storm.

**BRUCE:** I'll take this old blanket to cover the colt, if it's born yet. Where's the lantern? *(He sees the two lanterns by the kitchen door and, taking one of them to the table, lights it.)*

**RUTH:** It's three miles, Bruce. You mustn't go on foot. It's dangerous.

**BRUCE:** I'll have to. She'd never live through the night, or the colt either. *(He turns to go.)* You'd better go to bed. Good-night, Hester.

**RUTH:** Let me come with you.

**BRUCE:** No. *(Then, as he looks at her, all resentment leaves him. He puts down the lantern, goes to her, and takes her in his arms.)* Ruth, forget what I said. You know I didn't mean—

**RUTH** *(Softly)*: I said things I didn't mean, too—

**BRUCE:** I love you, Ruth. You know it, don't you?

**RUTH:** Bruce!

*(He kisses her, and for a moment their love is a flame in the room.)*

**BRUCE:**   Don't worry. I won't be long.

**RUTH:**   I'll wait.

*(Bruce goes out. Ruth follows him to the door, and, as it closes, she stands against it for a moment. There is a silence. Hester is slowly unravelling her knitting but is unaware of it. The black wool falls in spirals about her chair.)*

**HESTER** *(Suddenly)*:   It's an old house. I was born here. *(Then in a strange, calm voice that seems to come from a long distance.)* You shouldn't let Bruce be so much alone. You lose him that way. He comes back to *us* then. He'll see you don't belong here unless you keep your hand on him all the time.

*(Ruth looks curiously at Hester but does not give her all her attention.)*

*(Hester suddenly becomes harsh.)* This is my house. You can't change it.

*(Ruth starts to say something but remains silent.)*

Father gave it to me. There isn't any room for you. *(In a high, childlike tone, like the sound of a violin string breaking.)* No room. *(She shakes her head gravely.)*

**RUTH** *(Aware that something is wrong)*:   Hester—

**HESTER** *(As if she were telling an often-recited story to a stranger)*:   I stayed home when Mother died and kept house for my little brother and my father. *(Her voice grows stronger.)* I was very beautiful, they said. My hair fell to my knees, and it was black as a furrow turned in spring. *(Proudly.)* I can have a husband any time I want, but my duty is here with Father. You see how it is. I can't leave him.

**RUTH** *(Goes quickly to Hester. With anxiety and gentleness)*:   Hester, what are you talking about?

**HESTER:**   That's Father's chair, I'll put his Bible out. *(She starts from her chair.)*

**RUTH** *(Preventing her)*:   Hester, your father's not here—not for six years. You speak of him as if you thought—Hester—

**HESTER** *(Ignoring Ruth but remaining seated)*:   When I was a girl I always filled the lanterns after supper. Then I was ready for his coming.

**RUTH** *(In terror)*:   Hester, I didn't fill them! I didn't fill the lanterns!
*(She runs to the kitchen door and takes up the remaining lantern.)*

**HESTER** *(Calmly)*:   Father called me the wise virgin then.

**RUTH:**   Hester, Bruce took one! He thought I'd filled them. It will burn out and he'll be lost in the blizzard.

**HESTER:**   I always filled them.

**RUTH** *(Setting the lantern on the table)*:   I've got to go out after Bruce. If he gets down to the coulee and the lantern goes out, he'll never find the way back. I'll have to hurry! Where's the coal oil?

*(Ruth goes to the kitchen and returns with a can of coal oil and a pair of galoshes. Hester watches her closely. As Ruth comes in with the oil, Hester slowly rises and goes to her.)*

**HESTER:**   I'll fill the lantern for you, Ruth.

**RUTH** *(Trying to remove the top of the can)*:   I can't get the top off. My hands are shaking so.

**HESTER** *(Taking the oil can from Ruth)*:   I'll fill it for you.

**RUTH:**   Please, Hester. While I get my things on! *(Giving Hester the oil can, Ruth runs to the footstool and hurriedly puts on her galoshes.)* I'm afraid that lantern will last just long enough to get him out there. He'll be across the field before I even get outside. *(She runs up the stairs.)*

**HESTER** *(Standing motionless, the oil can in her hand)*:   You're going now. That's right. I told you you should go.

*(Ruth disappears up the stairs. Hester moves a step toward the lantern, taking off the top of the coal oil can. She hesitates and looks for a long moment after Ruth. With the strange lucidity of madness, slowly, deliberately, she places the top back again on the can and, moving behind the table, sets it on the floor without filling the lantern. Ruth hurries down the stairs excited and alarmed. She has on heavy clothes and is putting on her gloves.)*

**RUTH:**   Is it ready?

*(Hester nods.)*

Will you light it for me, Hester? Please.

*(Hester lights the lantern.)*

I'll put the light at the window. *(She crosses with the small lamp and places it at the window.)* Hurry, Hester! *(With a sob.)* Oh, if only I can find him!

*(Hester crosses to Ruth and gives her the lantern, Ruth takes the lantern and goes out. A gust of wind carries the snow into the room and blows shut the door after her. Hester goes to the window.)*

**HESTER** *(Her voice is like an echo):* The snow lies deep on the summer fallow—The snow is a moving shroud—a winding-sheet that the wind lifts and raises and lets fall again. *(Turning from the window.)* They've gone. They won't be back now. *(With an intense excitement, Hester blows out the lamp at the window and pulls down the shades. Her eyes fall on the bowl of hyacinths in the corner. Slowly she goes to it, takes it up and, holding it away from her, carries it to the door. Opening the door, she sets the flowers outside. She closes the door and locks it. Her eyes blazing with excitement, she stands with her arms across the door as if shutting the world out. Then softly she moves to the door of her father's bedroom, unlocks it, and goes in, returning at once with a pair of men's bedroom slippers. Leaving the bedroom door open, she crosses to the sideboard, takes up the Bible and, going to her father's chair, places the slippers beside it. She speaks very softly.)* I put your slippers out. *(She draws the footstool up to the chair.)* Everything will be the same now, Father. *(She opens the Bible.)* I'll read to you, Father. I'll read the one you like. *(She reads with quiet contentment.)* "And the winds blew, and beat upon the house; and it fell not: for it was founded upon a rock."

—*1939*

**Arthur Miller (1915–2005)** *gained a reputation as a major American dramatist with his second play, and continued to be productive in his mid-80s. Miller was born in Harlem, the son of prosperous Jewish immigrants who suffered badly during the Depression. He studied drama at the University of Michigan and was for a time employed by the Federal Theatre Project, a Roosevelt-era government program dedicated to bringing drama with social themes to audiences in areas outside New York. His first success was* All My Sons *(1947), an Ibsenesque problem play (Miller later adapted Ibsen's* An Enemy of the People *for the New York stage) about a manufacturer who profited during World War II by knowingly supplying defective parts that caused airplanes to crash.* All My Sons, *following closely on the heels of investigations of wartime profiteering, easily found appreciative audiences.* Death of a Salesman *(1949) won Miller a Pulitzer Prize. Originally a short story based to some degree on one of Miller's uncles,* Death of a Salesman *evolved into its final form over many years. When Miller finally sat down at the typewriter to write the play, he said, "All I had was the first two lines and a death." During the height of the play's success, Miller wrote a famous essay titled "Tragedy and the Common Man," in which he dismisses the ancient "rule" that true tragedy can concern only the lives and fates of the famous. "I believe," he said, "that the common man is as apt a subject for tragedy in its highest sense as kings were. . . . If the exaltation of tragic action were truly a property of the high-bred character alone, it is inconceivable that the mass of mankind should cherish tragedy above all other forms, let alone be capable of understanding it." Miller's fame was further increased by* The Crucible *(1953), a play about the Salem witch trials that had obvious contemporary political overtones, drawing on Miller's own McCarthy-era investigations by the House of Un-American Activities Committee into his past political affiliations. Miller risked a jail term for his refusal to cooperate with the committee. His marriage to Marilyn Monroe, which is in part the subject of* After the Fall *(1964), ended unhappily shortly after Miller completed work on the screenplay of* The Misfits, *which proved to be her final film. Other important plays include* A View from the Bridge *(1955), which has been revived several times on Broadway and also exists in an operatic version;* Incident at Vichy *(1964), a play about the Holocaust;* The Price *(1968);* Broken Glass, *another play about anti-Semitism; and* Ride Down Mount Morgan *(1998), which starred Patrick Stewart in its Broadway production. Miller's autobiography,* Timebends, *was published in 1987. In it he proudly recounts his experiences in 1983 directing a Chinese production of* Death of a Salesman *in Beijing, the first contemporary American play produced in China.*

# *Arthur Miller*
# Death of a Salesman

## *C*HARACTERS

Willy Loman
Linda
Biff
Happy
Bernard
The Woman
Charley
Uncle Ben
Howard Wagner
Jenny
Stanley
Miss Forsythe
Letta

Scene: *The action takes place in Willy Loman's house and yard and in various places he visits in the New York and Boston of today.*

## A*CT* 1

Scene: *A melody is heard, played upon a flute. It is small and fine, telling of grass and trees and the horizon. The curtain rises.*

*Before us is the Salesman's house. We are aware of towering, angular shapes behind it, surrounding it on all sides. Only the blue light of the sky falls upon the house and forestage; the surrounding area shows an angry glow of orange. As more light appears, we see a solid vault of apartment houses around the small, fragile-seeming home. An air of the dream clings to the place, a dream rising out of reality. The kitchen at center seems actual enough, for there is a kitchen table with three chairs, and a refrigerator. But no other fixtures are seen. At the back of the kitchen there is a draped entrance, which leads to the living room. To the right of the kitchen, on a level raised two feet, is a bedroom furnished only with a brass bedstead and a straight chair. On a shelf over the bed a silver athletic trophy stands. A window opens onto the apart-ment house at the side.*

*Behind the kitchen, on a level raised six and a half feet, is the boys' bedroom, at present barely visible. Two beds are dimly seen, and at the back of the room a dormer window. (This bedroom is above the unseen living room.) At the left a stairway curves up to it from the kitchen.*

*The entire setting is wholly or, in some places, partially transpar-ent. The roof-line of the house is one-dimensional; under and over it we see the apartment buildings. Before the house lies an apron, curving beyond the forestage into the orchestra. This forward area serves as the back yard as well as the locale of all Willy's imaginings and of his city scenes. Whenever the action is in the present the actors observe the imaginary wall-lines, entering the house only through its door at the left. But in the scenes of the past these boundaries are broken, and char-acters enter or leave a room by stepping "through" a wall onto the forestage.*

*From the right, Willy Loman, the Salesman, enters, carrying two large sample cases. The flute plays on. He hears but is not aware of it. He is past sixty years of age, dressed quietly. Even as he crosses the stage to the doorway of the house, his exhaustion is apparent. He unlocks the door, comes into the kitchen, and thankfully lets his burden down, feeling the soreness of his palms. A word-sigh escapes his lips—it might be "Oh, boy, oh, boy." He closes the door, then carries his cases out into the living room, through the draped kitchen doorway.*

*Linda, his wife, has stirred in her bed at the right. She gets out and puts on a robe, listening. Most often jovial, she has developed an iron repression of her exceptions to Willy's behavior—she more than loves him, she admires him, as though his mercurial nature, his temper, his massive dreams and little cruelties, served her only as sharp reminders of the turbulent longings within him, longings which she shares but lacks the temperament to utter and follow to their end.*

**LINDA** (*hearing Willy outside the bedroom, calls with some trepi-dation*):   Willy!

**WILLY:**   It's all right. I came back.

**LINDA:**   Why? What happened? (*Slight pause.*) Did something hap-pen, Willy?

**WILLY:** No, nothing happened.

**LINDA:** You didn't smash the car, did you?

**WILLY** (*with casual irritation*): I said nothing happened. Didn't you hear me?

**LINDA:** Don't you feel well?

**WILLY:** I'm tired to the death. (*The flute has faded away. He sits on the bed beside her, a little numb.*) I couldn't make it. I just couldn't make it, Linda.

**LINDA** (*very carefully, delicately*): Where were you all day? You look terrible.

**WILLY:** I got as far as a little above Yonkers. I stopped for a cup of coffee. Maybe it was the coffee.

**LINDA:** What?

**WILLY** (*after a pause*): I suddenly couldn't drive any more. The car kept going off onto the shoulder, y'know?

**LINDA** (*helpfully*): Oh. Maybe it was the steering again. I don't think Angelo knows the Studebaker.

**WILLY:** No, it's me, it's me. Suddenly I realize I'm goin' sixty miles an hour and I don't remember the last five minutes. I'm—I can't seem to—keep my mind to it.

**LINDA:** Maybe it's your glasses. You never went for your new glasses.

**WILLY:** No, I see everything. I came back ten miles an hour. It took me nearly four hours from Yonkers.

**LINDA** (*resigned*): Well, you'll just have to take a rest, Willy, you can't continue this way.

**WILLY:** I just got back from Florida.

**LINDA:** But you didn't rest your mind. Your mind is overactive, and the mind is what counts, dear.

**WILLY:** I'll start out in the morning. Maybe I'll feel better in the morning. (*She is taking off his shoes.*) These goddam arch supports are killing me.

**LINDA:** Take an aspirin. Should I get you an aspirin? It'll soothe you.

**WILLY** (*with wonder*): I was driving along, you understand? And I was fine. I was even observing the scenery. You can imagine, me looking at scenery, on the road every week of my life. But it's so beautiful up there, Linda, the trees are so thick, and the sun is warm. I opened the windshield and just let the warm air bathe over me. And then all of a sudden I'm goin' off the road! I'm tellin' ya,

I absolutely forgot I was driving. If I'd've gone the other way over the white line I might've killed somebody. So I went on again—and five minutes later I'm dreamin' again, and I nearly . . . (*He presses two fingers against his eyes.*) I have such thoughts, I have such strange thoughts.

LINDA: Willy, dear. Talk to them again. There's no reason why you can't work in New York.

WILLY: They don't need me in New York. I'm the New England man. I'm vital in New England.

LINDA: But you're sixty years old. They can't expect you to keep traveling every week.

WILLY: I'll have to send a wire to Portland. I'm supposed to see Brown and Morrison tomorrow morning at ten o'clock to show the line. Goddammit, I could sell them! (*He starts putting on his jacket.*)

LINDA (*taking the jacket from him*): Why don't you go down to the place tomorrow and tell Howard you've simply got to work in New York? You're too accommodating, dear.

WILLY: If old man Wagner was alive I'd a been in charge of New York now! That man was a prince, he was a masterful man. But that boy of his, that Howard, he don't appreciate. When I went north the first time, the Wagner Company didn't know where New England was!

LINDA: Why don't you tell those things to Howard, dear?

WILLY (*encouraged*): I will, I definitely will. Is there any cheese?

LINDA: I'll make you a sandwich.

WILLY: No, go to sleep. I'll take some milk. I'll be up right away. The boys in?

LINDA: They're sleeping. Happy took Biff on a date tonight.

WILLY (*interested*): That so?

LINDA: It was so nice to see them shaving together, one behind the other, in the bathroom. And going out together. You notice? The whole house smells of shaving lotion.

WILLY: Figure it out. Work a lifetime to pay off a house. You finally own it, and there's nobody to live in it.

LINDA: Well, dear, life is a casting off. It's always that way.

WILLY: No, no, some people—some people accomplish something. Did Biff say anything after I went this morning?

LINDA: You shouldn't have criticized him, Willy, especially after he just got off the train. You mustn't lose your temper with him.

**WILLY:** When the hell did I lose my temper? I simply asked him if he was making any money. Is that a criticism?

**LINDA:** But, dear, how could he make any money?

**WILLY** (*worried and angered*): There's such an undercurrent in him. He became a moody man. Did he apologize when I left this morning?

**LINDA:** He was crestfallen, Willy. You know how he admires you. I think if he finds himself, then you'll both be happier and not fight any more.

**WILLY:** How can he find himself on a farm? Is that a life? A farm hand? In the beginning, when he was young, I thought, well, a young man, it's good for him to tramp around, take a lot of different jobs. But it's more than ten years now and he has yet to make thirty-five dollars a week!

**LINDA:** He's finding himself, Willy.

**WILLY:** Not finding yourself at the age of thirty-four is a disgrace!

**LINDA:** Shh!

**WILLY:** The trouble is he's lazy, goddammit!

**LINDA:** Willy, please!

**WILLY:** Biff is a lazy bum!

**LINDA:** They're sleeping. Get something to eat. Go on down.

**WILLY:** Why did he come home? I would like to know what brought him home.

**LINDA:** I don't know. I think he's still lost, Willy. I think he's very lost.

**WILLY:** Biff Loman is lost. In the greatest country in the world a young man with such—personal attractiveness, gets lost. And such a hard worker. There's one thing about Biff—he's not lazy.

**LINDA:** Never.

**WILLY** (*with pity and resolve*): I'll see him in the morning; I'll have a nice talk with him. I'll get him a job selling. He could be big in no time. My God! Remember how they used to follow him around in high school? When he smiled at one of them their faces lit up. When he walked down the street . . . (*He loses himself in reminiscences.*)

**LINDA** (*trying to bring him out of it*): Willy, dear, I got a new kind of American-type cheese today. It's whipped.

**WILLY:** Why do you get American when I like Swiss?

**LINDA:** I just thought you'd like a change . . .

**WILLY:** I don't want a change! I want Swiss cheese. Why am I always being contradicted?

**LINDA** (*with a covering laugh*): I thought it would be a surprise.

**WILLY:** Why don't you open a window in here, for God's sake?

**LINDA** (*with infinite patience*): They're all open, dear.

**WILLY:** The way they boxed us in here. Bricks and windows, windows and bricks.

**LINDA:** We should've bought the land next door.

**WILLY:** The street is lined with cars. There's not a breath of fresh air in the neighborhood. The grass don't grow any more, you can't raise a carrot in the back yard. They should've had a law against apartment houses. Remember those two beautiful elm trees out there? When I and Biff hung the swing between them?

**LINDA:** Yeah, like being a million miles from the city.

**WILLY:** They should've arrested the builder for cutting those down. They massacred the neighborhood. (*Lost.*) More and more I think of those days, Linda. This time of year it was lilac and wisteria. And then the peonies would come out, and the daffodils. What fragrance in this room!

**LINDA:** Well, after all, people had to move somewhere.

**WILLY:** No, there's more people now.

**LINDA:** I don't think there's more people. I think . . .

**WILLY:** There's more people! That's what's ruining this country! Population is getting out of control. The competition is maddening! Smell the stink from that apartment house! And another one on the other side . . . How can they whip cheese?

*On Willy's last line, Biff and Happy raise themselves up in their beds, listening.*

**LINDA:** Go down, try it. And be quiet.

**WILLY** (*turning to Linda, guiltily*): You're not worried about me, are you, sweetheart?

**BIFF:** What's the matter?

**HAPPY:** Listen!

**LINDA:** You've got too much on the ball to worry about.

**WILLY:** You're my foundation and my support, Linda.

**LINDA:** Just try to relax, dear. You make mountains out of molehills.

**WILLY:** I won't fight with him any more. If he wants to go back to Texas, let him go.

**LINDA:** He'll find his way.

**WILLY:** Sure. Certain men just don't get started till later in life. Like Thomas Edison, I think. Or B. F. Goodrich. One of them was deaf. (*He starts for the bedroom doorway.*) I'll put my money on Biff.

**LINDA:** And Willy—if it's warm Sunday we'll drive in the country. And we'll open the windshield, and take lunch.

**WILLY:** No, the windshields don't open on the new cars.

**LINDA:** But you opened it today.

**WILLY:** Me? I didn't. (*He stops.*) Now isn't that peculiar! Isn't that a remarkable . . . (*He breaks off in amazement and fright as the flute is heard distantly.*)

**LINDA:** What, darling?

**WILLY:** That is the most remarkable thing.

**LINDA:** What, dear?

**WILLY:** I was thinking of the Chevvy. (*Slight pause.*) Nineteen twenty-eight . . . when I had that red Chevvy . . . (*Breaks off.*) That funny? I coulda sworn I was driving that Chevvy today.

**LINDA:** Well, that's nothing. Something must've reminded you.

**WILLY:** Remarkable. Ts. Remember those days? The way Biff used to simonize that car? The dealer refused to believe there was eighty thousand miles on it. (*He shakes his head.*) Heh! (*To Linda.*) Close your eyes, I'll be right up. (*He walks out of the bedroom.*)

**HAPPY** (*to Biff*): Jesus, maybe he smashed up the car again!

**LINDA** (*calling after Willy*): Be careful on the stairs, dear! The cheese is on the middle shelf. (*She turns, goes over to the bed, takes his jacket, and goes out of the bedroom.*)

*Light has risen on the boys' room. Unseen, Willy is heard talking to himself: "Eighty thousand miles," and a little laugh. Biff gets out of bed, comes downstage a bit, and stands attentively. Biff is two years older than his brother Happy, well built, but in these days bears a worn air and seems less self-assured. He has succeeded less, and his dreams are stronger and less acceptable than Happy's. Happy is tall, powerfully made. Sexuality is like a visible color on him, or a scent that many women have discovered. He, like his brother, is lost, but in a different way, for he has never allowed himself to turn his face toward defeat and is thus more confused and hard-skinned, although seemingly more content.*

**HAPPY** (*getting out of bed*):   He's going to get his license taken away if he keeps that up. I'm getting nervous about him, y'know, Biff?

**BIFF:**   His eyes are going.

**HAPPY:**   No, I've driven with him. He sees all right. He just doesn't keep his mind on it. I drove into the city with him last week. He stops at a green light and then it turns red and he goes. (*He laughs.*)

**BIFF:**   Maybe he's color-blind.

**HAPPY:**   Pop? Why he's got the finest eye for color in the business. You know that.

**BIFF** (*sitting down on his bed*):   I'm going to sleep.

**HAPPY:**   You're not still sour on Dad, are you, Biff?

**BIFF:**   He's all right, I guess.

**WILLY** (*underneath them, in the living room*):   Yes, sir, eighty thousand miles—eighty-two thousand!

**BIFF:**   You smoking?

**HAPPY** (*holding out a pack of cigarettes*):   Want one?

**BIFF** (*taking a cigarette*):   I can never sleep when I smell it.

**WILLY:**   What a simonizing job, heh!

**HAPPY** (*with deep sentiment*):   Funny, Biff, y'know? Us sleeping in here again? The old beds. (*He pats his bed affectionately.*) All the talk that went across those beds, huh? Our whole lives.

**BIFF:**   Yeah. Lotta dreams and plans.

**HAPPY** (*with a deep and masculine laugh*):   About five hundred women would like to know what was said in this room. (*They share a soft laugh.*)

**BIFF:**   Remember that big Betsy something—what the hell was her name—over on Bushwick Avenue?

**HAPPY** (*combing his hair*):   With the collie dog!

**BIFF:**   That's the one. I got you in there, remember?

**HAPPY:**   Yeah, that was my first time—I think. Boy, there was a pig. (*They laugh, almost crudely.*) You taught me everything I know about women. Don't forget that.

**BIFF:**   I bet you forgot how bashful you used to be. Especially with girls.

**HAPPY:**   Oh, I still am, Biff.

**BIFF:**   Oh, go on.

**HAPPY:**   I just control it, that's all. I think I got less bashful and you got more so. What happened, Biff? Where's the old humor, the old confidence? (*He shakes Biff's knee. Biff gets up and moves restlessly about the room.*) What's the matter?

**BIFF:** Why does Dad mock me all the time?

**HAPPY:** He's not mocking you, he . . .

**BIFF:** Everything I say there's a twist of mockery on his face. I can't get near him.

**HAPPY:** He just wants you to make good, that's all. I wanted to talk to you about Dad for a long time, Biff. Something's—happening to him. He—talks to himself.

**BIFF:** I noticed that this morning. But he always mumbled.

**HAPPY:** But not so noticeable. It got so embarrassing I sent him to Florida. And you know something? Most of the time he's talking to you.

**BIFF:** What's he say about me?

**HAPPY:** I can't make it out.

**BIFF:** What's he say about me?

**HAPPY:** I think the fact that you're not settled, that you're still kind of up in the air . . .

**BIFF:** There's one or two other things depressing him, Happy.

**HAPPY:** What do you mean?

**BIFF:** Never mind. Just don't lay it all to me.

**HAPPY:** But I think if you just got started—I mean—is there any future for you out there?

**BIFF:** I tell ya, Hap, I don't know what the future is. I don't know—what I'm supposed to want.

**HAPPY:** What do you mean?

**BIFF:** Well, I spent six or seven years after high school trying to work myself up. Shipping clerk, salesman, business of one kind or another. And it's a measly manner of existence. To get on that subway on the hot mornings in summer. To devote your whole life to keeping stock, or making phone calls, or selling or buying. To suffer fifty weeks of the year for the sake of a two-week vacation, when all you really desire is to be outdoors, with your shirt off. And always to have to get ahead of the next fella. And still—that's how you build a future.

**HAPPY:** Well, you really enjoy it on a farm? Are you content out there?

**BIFF** (*with rising agitation*): Hap, I've had twenty or thirty different kinds of jobs since I left home before the war, and it always turns out the same. I just realized it lately. In Nebraska when I herded cattle, and the Dakotas, and Arizona, and now in Texas. It's why I came home now, I guess, because I realized it. This farm I work on, it's spring there now, see? And they've got about fifteen new colts. There's nothing more inspiring or—beautiful than the sight of a mare and a new colt. And it's cool there now, see? Texas is cool now, and it's spring. And whenever spring comes to where I am, I suddenly get the feeling, my God, I'm not gettin' anywhere! What the hell am I doing, playing around with horses, twenty-eight dollars a week! I'm thirty-four years old, I oughta be makin' my future. That's when I come running home. And now, I get here, and I don't know what to do with myself. (*After a pause.*) I've always made a point of not wasting my life, and everytime I come back here I know that all I've done is to waste my life.

**HAPPY:** You're a poet, you know that, Biff? You're a—you're an idealist!

**BIFF:** No, I'm mixed up very bad. Maybe I oughta get married. Maybe I oughta get stuck into something. Maybe that's my trouble. I'm like a boy. I'm not married, I'm not in business, I just—I'm like a boy. Are you content, Hap? You're a success, aren't you? Are you content?

**HAPPY:** Hell, no!

**BIFF:** Why? You're making money, aren't you?

**HAPPY** (*moving about with energy, expressiveness*): All I can do now is wait for the merchandise manager to die. And suppose I get to be merchandise manager? He's a good friend of mine, and he just built a terrific estate on Long Island. And he lived there about two months and sold it, and now he's building another one. He can't enjoy it once it's finished. And I know that's just what I would do. I don't know what the hell I'm workin' for. Sometimes I sit in my apartment—all alone. And I think of the rent I'm paying. And it's crazy. But then, it's what I always wanted. My own apartment, a car, and plenty of women. And still, goddammit, I'm lonely.

**BIFF** (*with enthusiasm*): Listen, why don't you come out West with me?

**HAPPY:** You and I, heh?

**BIFF:** Sure, maybe we could buy a ranch. Raise cattle, use our muscles. Men built like we are should be working out in the open.

**HAPPY** (*avidly*): The Loman Brothers, heh?

**BIFF** (*with vast affection*): Sure, we'd be known all over the counties!

**HAPPY** (*enthralled*): That's what I dream about, Biff. Sometimes I want to just rip my clothes off in the middle of the store and outbox that goddam merchandise manager. I mean I can outbox, outrun, and outlift anybody in that store, and I have to take orders from those common, petty sons-of-bitches till I can't stand it any more.

**BIFF:** I'm tellin' you, kid, if you were with me I'd be happy out there.

**HAPPY** (*enthused*): See, Biff, everybody around me is so false that I'm constantly lowering my ideals . . .

**BIFF:** Baby, together we'd stand up for one another, we'd have someone to trust.

**HAPPY:** If I were around you . . .

**BIFF:** Hap, the trouble is we weren't brought up to grub for money. I don't know how to do it.

**HAPPY:** Neither can I!

**BIFF:** Then let's go!

**HAPPY:** The only thing is—what can you make out there?

**BIFF:** But look at your friend. Builds an estate and then hasn't the peace of mind to live in it.

**HAPPY:** Yeah, but when he walks into the store the waves part in front of him. That's fifty-two thousand dollars a year coming through the revolving door, and I got more in my pinky finger than he's got in his head.

**BIFF:** Yeah, but you just said . . .

**HAPPY:** I gotta show some of those pompous, self-important executives over there that Hap Loman can make the grade. I want to walk into the store the way he walks in. Then I'll go with you, Biff. We'll be together yet, I swear. But take those two we had tonight. Now weren't they gorgeous creatures?

**BIFF:** Yeah, yeah, most gorgeous I've had in years.

**HAPPY:** I get that any time I want, Biff. Whenever I feel disgusted. The only trouble is, it gets like bowling or something. I just keep knockin' them over and it doesn't mean anything. You still run around a lot?

**BIFF:** Naa. I'd like to find a girl—steady, somebody with substance.

**HAPPY:** That's what I long for.

**BIFF:** Go on! You'd never come home.

**HAPPY:** I would! Somebody with character, with resistance! Like Mom, y'know? You're gonna call me a bastard when I tell you this. That girl Charlotte I was with tonight is engaged to be married in five weeks. (*He tries on his new hat.*)

**BIFF:** No kiddin'!

**HAPPY:** Sure, the guy's in line for the vice-presidency of the store. I don't know what gets into me, maybe I just have an over-developed sense of competition or something, but I went and ruined her, and furthermore I can't get rid of her. And he's the third executive I've done that to. Isn't that a crummy characteristic? And to top it all, I go to their weddings! (*Indignantly, but laughing.*) Like I'm not supposed to take bribes. Manufacturers offer me a hundred-dollar bill now and then to throw an order their way. You know how honest I am, but it's like this girl, see. I hate myself for it. Because I don't want the girl, and, still, I take it and—I love it!

**BIFF:** Let's go to sleep.

**HAPPY:** I guess we didn't settle anything, heh?

**BIFF:** I just got one idea that I think I'm going to try.

**HAPPY:** What's that?

**BIFF:** Remember Bill Oliver?

**HAPPY:** Sure, Oliver is very big now. You want to work for him again?

**BIFF:** No, but when I quit he said something to me. He put his arm on my shoulder, and he said, "Biff, if you ever need anything, come to me."

**HAPPY:** I remember that. That sounds good.

**BIFF:** I think I'll go to see him. If I could get ten thousand or even seven or eight thousand dollars I could buy a beautiful ranch.

**HAPPY:** I bet he'd back you. 'Cause he thought highly of you, Biff. I mean, they all do. You're well liked, Biff. That's why I say to come back here, and we both have the apartment. And I'm tellin' you, Biff, any babe you want . . .

**BIFF:** No, with a ranch I could do the work I like and still be something. I just wonder though. I wonder if Oliver still thinks I stole that carton of basketballs.

**HAPPY:** Oh, he probably forgot that long ago. It's almost ten years. You're too sensitive. Anyway, he didn't really fire you.

**BIFF:** Well, I think he was going to. I think that's why I quit. I was never sure whether he knew or not. I know he thought the world of me, though. I was the only one he'd let lock up the place.

**WILLY** (*below*): You gonna wash the engine, Biff?

**HAPPY:** Shh!

*Biff looks at Happy, who is gazing down, listening. Willy is mumbling in the parlor.*

**HAPPY:** You hear that?

*They listen. Willy laughs warmly.*

**BIFF** (*growing angry*): Doesn't he know Mom can hear that?

**WILLY:** Don't get your sweater dirty, Biff!

*A look of pain crosses Biff's face.*

**HAPPY:** Isn't that terrible? Don't leave again, will you? You'll find a job here. You gotta stick around. I don't know what to do about him, it's getting embarrassing.

**WILLY:** What a simonizing job!

**BIFF:** Mom's hearing that!

**WILLY:** No kiddin', Biff, you got a date? Wonderful!

**HAPPY:** Go on to sleep. But talk to him in the morning, will you?

**BIFF** (*reluctantly getting into bed*): With her in the house. Brother!

**HAPPY** (*getting into bed*): I wish you'd have a good talk with him.

*The light on their room begins to fade.*

**BIFF** (*to himself in bed*): That selfish, stupid . . .

**HAPPY:** Sh . . . Sleep, Biff.

*Their light is out. Well before they have finished speaking, Willy's form is dimly seen below in the darkened kitchen. He opens the refrigerator, searches in there, and takes out a bottle of milk. The apartment houses are fading out, and the entire house and surroundings become covered with leaves. Music insinuates itself as the leaves appear.*

**WILLY:** Just wanna be careful with those girls, Biff, that's all. Don't make any promises. No promises of any kind. Because a girl, y'know, they always believe what you tell 'em, and you're very young, Biff, you're too young to be talking seriously to girls.

*Light rises on the kitchen. Willy, talking, shuts the refrigerator door and comes downstage to the kitchen table. He pours milk into a glass. He is totally immersed in himself, smiling faintly.*

**WILLY:**  Too young entirely, Biff. You want to watch your schooling first. Then when you're all set, there'll be plenty of girls for a boy like you. (*He smiles broadly at a kitchen chair.*) That so? The girls pay for you? (*He laughs.*) Boy, you must really be makin' a hit.

*Willy is gradually addressing—physically—a point offstage, speaking through the wall of the kitchen, and his voice has been rising in volume to that of a normal conversation.*

**WILLY:**  I been wondering why you polish the car so careful. Ha! Don't leave the hubcaps, boys. Get the chamois to the hubcaps. Happy, use newspaper on the windows, it's the easiest thing. Show him how to do it, Biff! You see, Happy? Pad it up, use it like a pad. That's it, that's it, good work. You're doin' all right, Hap. (*He pauses, then nods in approbation for a few seconds, then looks upward.*) Biff, first thing we gotta do when we get time is clip that big branch over the house. Afraid it's gonna fall in a storm and hit the roof. Tell you what. We get a rope and sling her around, and then we climb up there with a couple of saws and take her down. Soon as you finish the car, boys, I wanna see ya. I got a surprise for you, boys.

**BIFF** (*offstage*):  Whatta ya got, Dad?

**WILLY:**  No, you finish first. Never leave a job till you're finished— remember that. (*Looking toward the "big trees."*) Biff, up in Albany I saw a beautiful hammock. I think I'll buy it next trip, and we'll hang it right between those two elms. Wouldn't that be something? Just swingin' there under those branches. Boy, that would be . . .

*Young Biff and Young Happy appear from the direction Willy was addressing. Happy carries rags and a pail of water. Biff, wearing a sweater with a block "S," carries a football.*

**BIFF** (*pointing in the direction of the car offstage*):   How's that, Pop, professional?

**WILLY:**   Terrific. Terrific job, boys. Good work, Biff.

**HAPPY:**   Where's the surprise, Pop?

**WILLY:**   In the back seat of the car.

**HAPPY:**   Boy! (*He runs off.*)

**BIFF:**   What is it, Dad? Tell me, what'd you buy?

**WILLY** (*laughing, cuffs him*):   Never mind, something I want you to have.

**BIFF** (*turns and starts off*):   What is it, Hap?

**HAPPY** (*offstage*):   It's a punching bag!

**BIFF:**   Oh, Pop!

**WILLY:**   It's got Gene Tunney's signature on it!

*Happy runs onstage with a punching bag.*

**BIFF:**   Gee, how'd you know we wanted a punching bag?

**WILLY:**   Well, it's the finest thing for the timing.

**HAPPY** (*lies down on his back and pedals with his feet*):   I'm losing weight, you notice, Pop?

**WILLY** (*to Happy*):   Jumping rope is good too.

**BIFF:**   Did you see the new football I got?

**WILLY** (*examining the ball*):   Where'd you get a new ball?

**BIFF:**   The coach told me to practice my passing.

**WILLY:**   That so? And he gave you the ball, heh?

**BIFF:**   Well, I borrowed it from the locker room. (*He laughs confidentially.*)

**WILLY** (*laughing with him at the theft*):   I want you to return that.

**HAPPY:**   I told you he wouldn't like it!

**BIFF** (*angrily*):   Well, I'm bringing it back!

**WILLY** (*stopping the incipient argument, to Happy*):   Sure, he's gotta practice with a regulation ball, doesn't he? (*To Biff.*) Coach'll probably congratulate you on your initiative!

**BIFF:**   Oh, he keeps congratulating my initiative all the time, Pop.

**WILLY:**   That's because he likes you. If somebody else took that ball there'd be an uproar. So what's the report, boys, what's the report?

**BIFF:**   Where'd you go this time, Dad? Gee we were lonesome for you.

**WILLY** (*pleased, puts an arm around each boy and they come down to the apron*):   Lonesome, heh?

**BIFF:**   Missed you every minute.

**WILLY:**   Don't say? Tell you a secret, boys. Don't breathe it to a soul. Someday I'll have my own business, and I'll never have to leave home any more.

**HAPPY:**   Like Uncle Charley, heh?

**WILLY:**   Bigger than Uncle Charley! Because Charley is not—liked. He's liked, but he's not—well liked.

**BIFF:**   Where'd you go this time, Dad?

**WILLY:**   Well, I got on the road, and I went north to Providence. Met the Mayor.

**BIFF:**   The Mayor of Providence!

**WILLY:**   He was sitting in the hotel lobby.

**BIFF:**   What'd he say?

**WILLY:**   He said, "Morning!" And I said, "Morning!" And I said, "You got a fine city here, Mayor." And then he had coffee with me. And then I went to Waterbury. Waterbury is a fine city. Big clock city, the famous Waterbury clock. Sold a nice bill there. And then Boston— Boston is the cradle of the Revolution. A fine city. And a couple of other towns in Mass., and on to Portland and Bangor and straight home!

**BIFF:**   Gee, I'd love to go with you sometime, Dad.

**WILLY:**   Soon as summer comes.

**HAPPY:**   Promise?

**WILLY:**   You and Hap and I, and I'll show you all the towns. America is full of beautiful towns and fine, upstanding people. And they know me, boys, they know me up and down New England. The finest people. And when I bring you fellas up, there'll be open sesame for all of us, 'cause one thing, boys: I have friends. I can park my car in any street in New England, and the cops protect it like their own. This summer, heh?

**BIFF AND HAPPY** (*together*):   Yeah! You bet!

**WILLY:**   We'll take our bathing suits.

**HAPPY:**   We'll carry your bags, Pop!

**WILLY:**   Oh, won't that be something! Me comin' into the Boston stores with you boys carryin' my bags. What a sensation!

*Biff is prancing around, practicing passing the ball.*

**WILLY:**   You nervous, Biff, about the game?

**BIFF:** Not if you're gonna be there.

**WILLY:** What do they say about you in school, now that they made you captain?

**HAPPY:** There's a crowd of girls behind him everytime the classes change.

**BIFF** (*taking Willy's hand*): This Saturday, Pop, this Saturday—just for you, I'm going to break through for a touchdown.

**HAPPY:** You're supposed to pass.

**BIFF:** I'm takin' one play for Pop. You watch me, Pop, and when I take off my helmet, that means I'm breakin' out. Then you watch me crash through that line!

**WILLY** (*kisses Biff*): Oh, wait'll I tell this in Boston!

*Bernard enters in knickers. He is younger than Biff, earnest and loyal, a worried boy.*

**BERNARD:** Biff, where are you? You're supposed to study with me today.

**WILLY:** Hey, looka Bernard. What're you lookin' so anemic about, Bernard?

**BERNARD:** He's gotta study, Uncle Willy. He's got Regents next week.

**HAPPY** (*tauntingly, spinning Bernard around*): Let's box, Bernard!

**BERNARD:** Biff! (*He gets away from Happy.*) Listen, Biff, I heard Mr. Birnbaum say that if you don't start studyin' math he's gonna flunk you, and you won't graduate. I heard him!

**WILLY:** You better study with him, Biff. Go ahead now.

**BERNARD:** I heard him!

**BIFF:** Oh, Pop, you didn't see my sneakers! (*He holds up a foot for Willy to look at.*)

**WILLY:** Hey, that's a beautiful job of printing!

**BERNARD** (*wiping his glasses*): Just because he printed University of Virginia on his sneakers doesn't mean they've got to graduate him, Uncle Willy!

**WILLY** (*angrily*): What're you talking about? With scholarships to three universities they're gonna flunk him?

**BERNARD:** But I heard Mr. Birnbaum say . . .

**WILLY:** Don't be a pest, Bernard! (*To his boys.*) What an anemic!

**BERNARD:** Okay, I'm waiting for you in my house, Biff.

*Bernard goes off. The Lomans laugh.*

**WILLY:** Bernard is not well liked, is he?

**BIFF:** He's liked, but he's not well liked.

**HAPPY:** That's right, Pop.

**WILLY:** That's just what I mean. Bernard can get the best marks in school, y'understand, but when he gets out in the business world, y'understand, you are going to be five times ahead of him. That's why I thank Almighty God you're both built like Adonises. Because the man who makes an appearance in the business world, the man who creates personal interest, is the man who gets ahead. Be liked and you will never want. You take me, for instance. I never have to wait in line to see a buyer. "Willy Loman is here!" That's all they have to know, and I go right through.

**BIFF:** Did you knock them dead, Pop?

**WILLY:** Knocked 'em cold in Providence, slaughtered 'em in Boston.

**HAPPY** (*on his back, pedaling again*): I'm losing weight, you notice, Pop?

*Linda enters as of old, a ribbon in her hair, carrying a basket of washing.*

**LINDA** (*with youthful energy*): Hello, dear!

**WILLY:** Sweetheart!

**LINDA:** How'd the Chevvy run?

**WILLY:** Chevrolet, Linda, is the greatest car ever built. (*To the boys.*) Since when do you let your mother carry wash up the stairs?

**BIFF:** Grab hold there, boy!

**HAPPY:** Where to, Mom?

**LINDA:** Hang them up on the line. And you better go down to your friends, Biff. The cellar is full of boys. They don't know what to do with themselves.

**BIFF:** Ah, when Pop comes home they can wait!

**WILLY** (*laughs appreciatively*): You better go down and tell them what to do, Biff.

**BIFF:** I think I'll have them sweep out the furnace room.

**WILLY:** Good work, Biff.

**BIFF** (*goes through wall-line of kitchen to doorway at back and calls down*): Fellas! Everybody sweep out the furnace room! I'll be right down!

**VOICES:** All right! Okay, Biff.

**BIFF:** George and Sam and Frank, come out back! We're hangin' up the wash! Come on, Hap, on the double! (*He and Happy carry out the basket.*)

**LINDA:** The way they obey him!

**WILLY:** Well, that's training, the training. I'm tellin' you, I was sellin' thousands and thousands, but I had to come home.

**LINDA:** Oh, the whole block'll be at that game. Did you sell anything?

**WILLY:** I did five hundred gross in Providence and seven hundred gross in Boston.

**LINDA:** No! Wait a minute. I've got a pencil. (*She pulls pencil and paper out of her apron pocket.*) That makes your commission . . . Two hundred—my God! Two hundred and twelve dollars!

**WILLY:** Well, I didn't figure it yet, but . . .

**LINDA:** How much did you do?

**WILLY:** Well, I—I did—about a hundred and eighty gross in Providence. Well, no—it came to—roughly two hundred gross on the whole trip.

**LINDA** (*without hesitation*): Two hundred gross. That's . . . (*She figures.*)

**WILLY:** The trouble was that three of the stores were half-closed for inventory in Boston. Otherwise I woulda broke records.

**LINDA:** Well, it makes seventy dollars and some pennies. That's very good.

**WILLY:** What do we owe?

**LINDA:** Well, on the first there's sixteen dollars on the refrigerator . . .

**WILLY:** Why sixteen?

**LINDA:** Well, the fan belt broke, so it was a dollar eighty.

**WILLY:** But it's brand new.

**LINDA:** Well, the man said that's the way it is. Till they work themselves in, y'know.

*They move through the wall-line into the kitchen.*

**WILLY:** I hope we didn't get stuck on that machine.

**LINDA:** They got the biggest ads of any of them!

**WILLY:** I know, it's a fine machine. What else?

**LINDA:** Well, there's nine-sixty for the washing machine. And for the vacuum cleaner there's three and a half due on the fifteenth. Then the roof, you got twenty-one dollars remaining.

**WILLY:** It don't leak, does it?

**LINDA:** No, they did a wonderful job. Then you owe Frank for the carburetor.

**WILLY:** I'm not going to pay that man! That goddam Chevrolet, they ought to prohibit the manufacture of that car!

**LINDA:** Well, you owe him three and a half. And odds and ends, comes to around a hundred and twenty dollars by the fifteenth.

**WILLY:** A hundred and twenty dollars! My God, if business don't pick up I don't know what I'm gonna do!

**LINDA:** Well, next week you'll do better.

**WILLY:** Oh, I'll knock 'em dead next week. I'll go to Hartford. I'm very well liked in Hartford. You know, the trouble is, Linda, people don't seem to take to me.

*They move onto the forestage.*

**LINDA:** Oh, don't be foolish.

**WILLY:** I know it when I walk in. They seem to laugh at me.

**LINDA:** Why? Why would they laugh at you? Don't talk that way, Willy.

*Willy moves to the edge of the stage. Linda goes into the kitchen and starts to darn stockings.*

**WILLY:** I don't know the reason for it, but they just pass me by. I'm not noticed.

**LINDA:** But you're doing wonderful, dear. You're making seventy to a hundred dollars a week.

**WILLY:** But I gotta be at it ten, twelve hours a day. Other men—I don't know—they do it easier. I don't know why—I can't stop myself—I talk too much. A man oughta come in with a few words. One thing about Charley. He's a man of few words, and they respect him.

**LINDA:** You don't talk too much, you're just lively.

**WILLY** (*smiling*): Well, I figure, what the hell, life is short, a couple of jokes. (*To himself:*) I joke too much! (*The smile goes.*)

**LINDA:** Why? You're . . .

**WILLY:** I'm fat. I'm very—foolish to look at, Linda. I didn't tell you, but Christmas time I happened to be calling on F. H. Stewarts, and a salesman I know, as I was going in to see the buyer I heard him say something about—walrus. And I—I cracked him right across the face. I won't take that. I simply will not take that. But they do laugh at me. I know that.

**LINDA:** Darling . . .

**WILLY:** I gotta overcome it. I know I gotta overcome it. I'm not dressing to advantage, maybe.

**LINDA:** Willy, darling, you're the handsomest man in the world . . .

**WILLY:** Oh, no, Linda.

**LINDA:** To me you are. (*Slight pause.*) The handsomest.

*From the darkness is heard the laughter of a woman. Willy doesn't turn to it, but it continues through Linda's lines.*

**LINDA:** And the boys, Willy. Few men are idolized by their children the way you are.

*Music is heard as behind a scrim, to the left of the house; The Woman, dimly seen, is dressing.*

**WILLY** (*with great feeling*): You're the best there is. Linda, you're a pal, you know that? On the road—on the road I want to grab you sometimes and just kiss the life outa you.

*The laughter is loud now, and he moves into a brightening area at the left, where The Woman has come from behind the scrim and is standing, putting on her hat, looking into a "mirror" and laughing.*

**WILLY:** 'Cause I get so lonely—especially when business is bad and there's nobody to talk to. I get the feeling that I'll never sell anything again, that I won't make a living for you, or a business, a business for the boys. (*He talks through The Woman's subsiding laughter; The Woman primps at the "mirror."*) There's so much I want to make for . . .

**THE WOMAN:** Me? You didn't make me, Willy. I picked you.

**WILLY** (*pleased*): You picked me?

**THE WOMAN** (*who is quite proper-looking, Willy's age*): I did. I've been sitting at that desk watching all the salesmen go by, day in, day out. But you've got such a sense of humor, and we do have such a good time together, don't we?

**WILLY:** Sure, sure. (*He takes her in his arms.*) Why do you have to go now?

**THE WOMAN:** It's two o'clock . . .

**WILLY:** No, come on in! (*He pulls her.*)

**THE WOMAN:** . . . my sisters'll be scandalized. When'll you be back?

**WILLY:** Oh, two weeks about. Will you come up again?

**THE WOMAN:** Sure thing. You do make me laugh. It's good for me. (*She squeezes his arm, kisses him.*) And I think you're a wonderful man.

**WILLY:** You picked me, heh?

**THE WOMAN:** Sure. Because you're so sweet. And such a kidder.

**WILLY:** Well, I'll see you next time I'm in Boston.

**THE WOMAN:** I'll put you right through to the buyers.

**WILLY** (*slapping her bottom*): Right. Well, bottoms up!

**THE WOMAN** (*slaps him gently and laughs*): You just kill me, Willy. (*He suddenly grabs her and kisses her roughly.*) You kill me. And thanks for the stockings. I love a lot of stockings. Well, good night.

**WILLY:** Good night. And keep your pores open!

**THE WOMAN:** Oh, Willy!

*The Woman bursts out laughing, and Linda's laughter blends in. The Woman disappears into the dark. Now the area at the kitchen table brightens. Linda is sitting where she was at the kitchen table, but now is mending a pair of her silk stockings.*

**LINDA:** You are, Willy. The handsomest man. You've got no reason to feel that . . .

**WILLY** (*coming out of The Woman's dimming area and going over to Linda*): I'll make it all up to you, Linda, I'll . . .

**LINDA:** There's nothing to make up, dear. You're doing fine, better than . . .

**WILLY** (*noticing her mending*): What's that?

**LINDA:** Just mending my stockings. They're so expensive . . .

**WILLY** (*angrily, taking them from her*): I won't have you mending stockings in this house! Now throw them out!

*Linda puts the stockings in her pocket.*

**BERNARD** (*entering on the run*): Where is he? If he doesn't study!

**WILLY** (*moving to the forestage, with great agitation*): You'll give him the answers!

**BERNARD:** I do, but I can't on a Regents! That's a state exam! They're liable to arrest me!

**WILLY:** Where is he? I'll whip him, I'll whip him!

**LINDA:** And he'd better give back that football, Willy, it's not nice.

**WILLY:** Biff! Where is he? Why is he taking everything?

**LINDA:** He's too rough with the girls, Willy. All the mothers are afraid of him!

**WILLY:** I'll whip him!

**BERNARD:** He's driving the car without a license!

*The Woman's laugh is heard.*

**WILLY:** Shut up!

**LINDA:** All the mothers . . .

**WILLY:** Shut up!

**BERNARD** (*backing quietly away and out*): Mr. Birnbaum says he's stuck up.

**WILLY:** Get outa here!

**BERNARD:** If he doesn't buckle down he'll flunk math! (*He goes off.*)

**LINDA:** He's right, Willy, you've gotta . . .

**WILLY** (*exploding at her*): There's nothing the matter with him! You want him to be a worm like Bernard? He's got spirit, personality . . .

*As he speaks, Linda, almost in tears, exits into the living room. Willy is alone in the kitchen, wilting and staring. The leaves are gone. It is night again, and the apartment houses look down from behind.*

**WILLY:** Loaded with it. Loaded! What is he stealing? He's giving it back, isn't he? Why is he stealing? What did I tell him? I never in my life told him anything but decent things.

*Happy in pajamas has come down the stairs; Willy suddenly becomes aware of Happy's presence.*

**HAPPY:** Let's go now, come on.

**WILLY** (*sitting down at the kitchen table*): Huh! Why did she have to wax the floors herself? Everytime she waxes the floors she keels over. She knows that!

**HAPPY:** Shh! Take it easy. What brought you back tonight?

**WILLY:** I got an awful scare. Nearly hit a kid in Yonkers. God! Why didn't I go to Alaska with my brother Ben that time! Ben! That man was a genius, that man was success incarnate! What a mistake! He begged me to go.

**HAPPY:** Well, there's no use in . . .

**WILLY:** You guys! There was a man started with the clothes on his back and ended up with diamond mines! ·

**HAPPY:** Boy, someday I'd like to know how he did it.

**WILLY:** What's the mystery? The man knew what he wanted and went out and got it! Walked into a jungle, and comes out, the age of twenty-one, and he's rich! The world is an oyster, but you don't crack it open on a mattress!

**HAPPY:** Pop, I told you I'm gonna retire you for life.

**WILLY:** You'll retire me for life on seventy goddam dollars a week? And your women and your car and your apartment, and you'll retire me for life! Christ's sake, I couldn't get past Yonkers today! Where are you guys, where are you? The woods are burning! I can't drive a car!

*Charley has appeared in the doorway. He is a large man, slow of speech, laconic, immovable. In all he says, despite what he says, there is pity, and, now, trepidation. He has a robe over pajamas, slippers on his feet. He enters the kitchen.*

**CHARLEY:** Everything all right?

**HAPPY:** Yeah, Charley, everything's . . .

**WILLY:** What's the matter?

**CHARLEY:** I heard some noise. I thought something happened. Can't we do something about the walls? You sneeze in here, and in my house hats blow off.

**HAPPY:** Let's go to bed, Dad. Come on.

*Charley signals to Happy to go.*

**WILLY:** You go ahead, I'm not tired at the moment.

**HAPPY** (*to Willy*): Take it easy, huh? (*He exits.*)

**WILLY:** What're you doin' up?

**CHARLEY** (*sitting down at the kitchen table opposite Willy*): Couldn't sleep good. I had a heartburn.

**WILLY:** Well, you don't know how to eat.

**CHARLEY:** I eat with my mouth.

WILLY: No, you're ignorant. You gotta know about vitamins and things like that.

CHARLEY: Come on, let's shoot. Tire you out a little.

WILLY (*hesitantly*): All right. You got cards?

CHARLEY (*taking a deck from his pocket*): Yeah, I got them. Someplace. What is it with those vitamins?

WILLY (*dealing*): They build up your bones. Chemistry.

CHARLEY: Yeah, but there's no bones in a heartburn.

WILLY: What are you talkin' about? Do you know the first thing about it?

CHARLEY: Don't get insulted.

WILLY: Don't talk about something you don't know anything about.

*They are playing. Pause.*

CHARLEY: What're you doin' home?

WILLY: A little trouble with the car.

CHARLEY: Oh. (*Pause.*) I'd like to take a trip to California.

WILLY: Don't say.

CHARLEY: You want a job?

WILLY: I got a job, I told you that. (*After a slight pause.*) What the hell are you offering me a job for?

CHARLEY: Don't get insulted.

WILLY: Don't insult me.

CHARLEY: I don't see no sense in it. You don't have to go on this way.

WILLY: I got a good job. (*Slight pause.*) What do you keep comin' in here for?

CHARLEY: You want me to go?

WILLY (*after a pause, withering*): I can't understand it. He's going back to Texas again. What the hell is that?

CHARLEY: Let him go.

WILLY: I got nothin' to give him, Charley, I'm clean, I'm clean.

CHARLEY: He won't starve. None a them starve. Forget about him.

WILLY: Then what have I got to remember?

CHARLEY: You take it too hard. To hell with it. When a deposit bottle is broken you don't get your nickel back.

WILLY: That's easy enough for you to say.

CHARLEY: That ain't easy for me to say.

WILLY: Did you see the ceiling I put up in the living room?

982 • Arthur Miller

**CHARLEY:** Yeah, that's a piece of work. To put up a ceiling is a mystery to me. How do you do it?

**WILLY:** What's the difference?

**CHARLEY:** Well, talk about it.

**WILLY:** You gonna put up a ceiling?

**CHARLEY:** How could I put up a ceiling?

**WILLY:** Then what the hell are you bothering me for?

**CHARLEY:** You're insulted again.

**WILLY:** A man who can't handle tools is not a man. You're disgusting.

**CHARLEY:** Don't call me disgusting, Willy.

*Uncle Ben, carrying a valise and an umbrella, enters the forestage from around the right corner of the house. He is a stolid man, in his sixties, with a mustache and an authoritative air. He is utterly certain of his destiny, and there is an aura of far places about him. He enters exactly as Willy speaks.*

**WILLY:** I'm getting awfully tired, Ben.

*Ben's music is heard. Ben looks around at everything.*

**CHARLEY:** Good, keep playing; you'll sleep better. Did you call me Ben?

*Ben looks at his watch.*

**WILLY:** That's funny. For a second there you reminded me of my brother Ben.

**BEN:** I only have a few minutes. (*He strolls, inspecting the place. Willy and Charley continue playing.*)

**CHARLEY:** You never heard from him again, heh? Since that time?

**WILLY:** Didn't Linda tell you? Couple of weeks ago we got a letter from his wife in Africa. He died.

**CHARLEY:** That so.

**BEN** (*chuckling*): So this is Brooklyn, eh?

**CHARLEY:** Maybe you're in for some of his money.

**WILLY:** Naa, he had seven sons. There's just one opportunity I had with that man . . .

**BEN:** I must make a train, William. There are several properties I'm looking at in Alaska.

**WILLY:** Sure, sure! If I'd gone with him to Alaska that time, everything would've been totally different.

**CHARLEY:** Go on, you'd froze to death up there.

**WILLY:** What're you talking about?

**BEN:** Opportunity is tremendous in Alaska, William. Surprised you're not up there.

**WILLY:** Sure, tremendous.

**CHARLEY:** Heh?

**WILLY:** There was the only man I ever met who knew the answers.

**CHARLEY:** Who?

**BEN:** How are you all?

**WILLY** (*taking a pot, smiling*): Fine, fine.

**CHARLEY:** Pretty sharp tonight.

**BEN:** Is Mother living with you?

**WILLY:** No, she died a long time ago.

**CHARLEY:** Who?

**BEN:** That's too bad. Fine specimen of a lady, Mother.

**WILLY** (*to Charley*): Heh?

**BEN:** I'd hoped to see the old girl.

**CHARLEY:** Who died?

**BEN:** Heard anything from Father, have you?

**WILLY** (*unnerved*): What do you mean, who died?

**CHARLEY** (*taking a pot*): What're you talkin' about?

**BEN** (*looking at his watch*): William, it's half-past eight!

**WILLY** (*as though to dispel his confusion he angrily stops Charley's hand*): That's my build!

**CHARLEY:** I put the ace . . .

**WILLY:** If you don't know how to play the game I'm not gonna throw my money away on you!

**CHARLEY** (*rising*): It was my ace, for God's sake!

**WILLY:** I'm through, I'm through!

**BEN:** When did Mother die?

**WILLY:** Long ago. Since the beginning you never knew how to play cards.

**CHARLEY** (*picks up the cards and goes to the door*): All right! Next time I'll bring a deck with five aces.

**WILLY:** I don't play that kind of game!

**CHARLEY** (*turning to him*): You ought to be ashamed of yourself!

**WILLY:** Yeah?

**CHARLEY:** Yeah! (*He goes out.*)

**WILLY** (*slamming the door after him*): Ignoramus!

**BEN** (*as Willy comes toward him through the wall-line of the kitchen*): So you're William.

**WILLY** (*shaking Ben's hand*): Ben! I've been waiting for you so long! What's the answer? How did you do it?

**BEN:** Oh, there's a story in that.

*Linda enters the forestage, as of old, carrying the wash basket.*

**LINDA:** Is this Ben?

**BEN** (*gallantly*): How do you do, my dear.

**LINDA:** Where've you been all these years? Willy's always wondered why you . . .

**WILLY** (*pulling Ben away from her impatiently*): Where is Dad? Didn't you follow him? How did you get started?

**BEN:** Well, I don't know how much you remember.

**WILLY:** Well, I was just a baby, of course, only three or four years old . . .

**BEN:** Three years and eleven months.

**WILLY:** What a memory, Ben!

**BEN:** I have many enterprises, William, and I have never kept books.

**WILLY:** I remember I was sitting under the wagon in—was it Nebraska?

**BEN:** It was South Dakota, and I gave you a bunch of wild flowers.

**WILLY:** I remember you walking away down some open road.

**BEN** (*laughing*): I was going to find Father in Alaska.

**WILLY:** Where is he?

**BEN:** At that age I had a very faulty view of geography, William. I discovered after a few days that I was heading due south, so instead of Alaska, I ended up in Africa.

**LINDA:** Africa!

**WILLY:** The Gold Coast!

**BEN:** Principally diamond mines.

**LINDA:** Diamond mines!

**BEN:** Yes, my dear. But I've only a few minutes . . .

**WILLY:** No! Boys! Boys! (*Young Biff and Happy appear.*) Listen to this. This is your Uncle Ben, a great man! Tell my boys, Ben!

**BEN:** Why, boys, when I was seventeen I walked into the jungle, and when I was twenty-one I walked out. (*He laughs.*) And by God I was rich.

**WILLY** (*to the boys*): You see what I been talking about? The greatest things can happen!

**BEN** (*glancing at his watch*): I have an appointment in Ketchikan Tuesday week.

**WILLY:** No, Ben! Please tell about Dad. I want my boys to hear. I want them to know the kind of stock they spring from. All I remember is a man with a big beard, and I was in Mamma's lap, sitting around a fire, and some kind of high music.

**BEN:** His flute. He played the flute.

**WILLY:** Sure, the flute, that's right!

*New music is heard, a high, rollicking tune.*

**BEN:** Father was a very great and a very wild-hearted man. We would start in Boston, and he'd toss the whole family into the wagon, and then he'd drive the team right across the country; through Ohio, and Indiana, Michigan, Illinois, and all the Western states. And we'd stop in the towns and sell the flutes that he'd made on the way. Great inventor, Father. With one gadget he made more in a week than a man like you could make in a lifetime.

**WILLY:** That's just the way I'm bringing them up, Ben—rugged, well liked, all-around.

**BEN:** Yeah? (*To Biff.*) Hit that, boy—hard as you can. (*He pounds his stomach.*)

**BIFF:** Oh, no, sir!

**BEN** (*taking boxing stance*): Come on, get to me! (*He laughs.*)

**WILLY:** Go to it, Biff! Go ahead, show him!

**BIFF:** Okay! (*He cocks his fists and starts in.*)

**LINDA** (*to Willy*): Why must he fight, dear?

**BEN** (*sparring with Biff*): Good boy! Good boy!

**WILLY:** How's that, Ben, heh?

**HAPPY:** Give him the left, Biff!

**LINDA:** Why are you fighting?

**BEN:** Good boy! (*Suddenly comes in, trips Biff, and stands over him, the point of his umbrella poised over Biff's eye.*)

**LINDA:** Look out, Biff!

**BIFF:** Gee!

**BEN** (*patting Biff's knee*):  Never fight fair with a stranger, boy. You'll never get out of the jungle that way. (*Taking Linda's hand and bowing.*) It was an honor and a pleasure to meet you, Linda.

**LINDA** (*withdrawing her hand coldly, frightened*):  Have a nice—trip.

**BEN** (*to Willy*):  And good luck with your—what do you do?

**WILLY:**  Selling.

**BEN:**  Yes. Well . . . (*He raises his hand in farewell to all.*)

**WILLY:**  No, Ben, I don't want you to think . . . (*He takes Ben's arm to show him.*) It's Brooklyn, I know, but we hunt too.

**BEN:**  Really, now.

**WILLY:**  Oh, sure, there's snakes and rabbits and—that's why I moved out here. Why, Biff can fell any one of these trees in no time! Boys! Go right over to where they're building the apartment house and get some sand. We're gonna rebuild the entire front stoop right now! Watch this, Ben!

**BIFF:**  Yes, sir! On the double, Hap!

**HAPPY** (*as he and Biff run off*):  I lost weight, Pop, you notice?

*Charley enters in knickers, even before the boys are gone.*

**CHARLEY:**  Listen, if they steal any more from that building the watchman'll put the cops on them!

**LINDA** (*to Willy*):  Don't let Biff . . .

*Ben laughs lustily.*

**WILLY:**  You shoulda seen the lumber they brought home last week. At least a dozen six-by-tens worth all kinds a money.

**CHARLEY:**  Listen, if that watchman . . .

**WILLY:**  I gave them hell, understand. But I got a couple of fearless characters there.

**CHARLEY:**  Willy, the jails are full of fearless characters.

**BEN** (*clapping Willy on the back, with a laugh at Charley*):  And the stock exchange, friend!

**WILLY** (*joining in Ben's laughter*):  Where are the rest of your pants?

**CHARLEY:**  My wife bought them.

**WILLY:**  Now all you need is a golf club and you can go upstairs and go to sleep. (*To Ben.*) Great athlete! Between him and his son Bernard they can't hammer a nail!

**BERNARD** (*rushing in*): The watchman's chasing Biff!

**WILLY** (*angrily*): Shut up! He's not stealing anything!

**LINDA** (*alarmed, hurrying off left*): Where is he? Biff, dear! (*She exits.*)

**WILLY** (*moving toward the left, away from Ben*): There's nothing wrong. What's the matter with you?

**BEN:** Nervy boy. Good!

**WILLY** (*laughing*): Oh, nerves of iron, that Biff!

**CHARLEY:** Don't know what it is. My New England man comes back and he's bleedin', they murdered him up there.

**WILLY:** It's contacts, Charley, I got important contacts!

**CHARLEY** (*sarcastically*): Glad to hear it, Willy. Come in later, we'll shoot a little casino. I'll take some of your Portland money. (*He laughs at Willy and exits.*)

**WILLY** (*turning to Ben*): Business is bad, it's murderous. But not for me, of course.

**BEN:** I'll stop by on my way back to Africa.

**WILLY** (*longingly*): Can't you stay a few days? You're just what I need, Ben, because I—I have a fine position here, but I—well, Dad left when I was such a baby and I never had a chance to talk to him and I still feel—kind of temporary about myself.

**BEN:** I'll be late for my train.

*They are at opposite ends of the stage.*

**WILLY:** Ben, my boys—can't we talk? They'd go into the jaws of hell for me, see, but I . . .

**BEN:** William, you're being first-rate with your boys. Outstanding, manly chaps!

**WILLY** (*hanging on to his words*): Oh, Ben, that's good to hear! Because sometimes I'm afraid that I'm not teaching them the right kind of—Ben, how should I teach them?

**BEN** (*giving great weight to each word, and with a certain vicious audacity*): William, when I walked into the jungle, I was seventeen. When I walked out I was twenty-one. And, by God, I was rich! (*He goes off into darkness around the right corner of the house.*)

**WILLY:** . . . was rich! That's just the spirit I want to imbue them with! To walk into a jungle! I was right! I was right! I was right!

*Ben is gone, but Willy is still speaking to him as Linda, in night-gown and robe, enters the kitchen, glances around for Willy, then goes to the door of the house, looks out and sees him. Comes down to his left. He looks at her.*

LINDA:  Willy, dear? Willy?

WILLY:  I was right!

LINDA:  Did you have some cheese? (*He can't answer.*) It's very late, darling. Come to bed, heh?

WILLY (*looking straight up*):  Gotta break your neck to see a star in this yard.

LINDA:  You coming in?

WILLY:  Whatever happened to that diamond watch fob? Remember? When Ben came from Africa that time? Didn't he give me a watch fob with a diamond in it?

LINDA:  You pawned it, dear. Twelve, thirteen years ago. For Biff's radio correspondence course.

WILLY:  Gee, that was a beautiful thing. I'll take a walk.

LINDA:  But you're in your slippers.

WILLY (*starting to go around the house at the left*):  I was right! I was! (*Half to Linda, as he goes, shaking his head.*) What a man! There was a man worth talking to. I was right!

LINDA (*calling after Willy*):  But in your slippers, Willy!

*Willy is almost gone when Biff, in his pajamas, comes down the stairs and enters the kitchen.*

BIFF:  What is he doing out there?

LINDA:  Sh!

BIFF:  God Almighty, Mom, how long has he been doing this?

LINDA:  Don't, he'll hear you.

BIFF:  What the hell is the matter with him?

LINDA:  It'll pass by morning.

BIFF:  Shouldn't we do anything?

LINDA:  Oh, my dear, you should do a lot of things, but there's nothing to do, so go to sleep.

*Happy comes down the stair and sits on the steps.*

**HAPPY:** I never heard him so loud, Mom.

**LINDA:** Well, come around more often; you'll hear him. (*She sits down at the table and mends the lining of Willy's jacket.*)

**BIFF:** Why didn't you ever write me about this, Mom?

**LINDA:** How would I write to you? For over three months you had no address.

**BIFF:** I was on the move. But you know I thought of you all the time. You know that, don't you, pal?

**LINDA:** I know, dear, I know. But he likes to have a letter. Just to know that there's still a possibility for better things.

**BIFF:** He's not like this all the time, is he?

**LINDA:** It's when you come home he's always the worst.

**BIFF:** When I come home?

**LINDA:** When you write you're coming, he's all smiles, and talks about the future, and—he's just wonderful. And then the closer you seem to come, the more shaky he gets, and then, by the time you get here, he's arguing, and he seems angry at you. I think it's just that maybe he can't bring himself to—to open up to you. Why are you so hateful to each other? Why is that?

**BIFF** (*evasively*): I'm not hateful, Mom.

**LINDA:** But you no sooner come in the door than you're fighting!

**BIFF:** I don't know why. I mean to change. I'm tryin', Mom, you understand?

**LINDA:** Are you home to stay now?

**BIFF:** I don't know. I want to look around, see what's doin'.

**LINDA:** Biff, you can't look around all your life, can you?

**BIFF:** I just can't take hold, Mom. I can't take hold of some kind of a life.

**LINDA:** Biff, a man is not a bird, to come and go with the spring time.

**BIFF:** Your hair . . . (*He touches her hair.*) Your hair got so gray.

**LINDA:** Oh, it's been gray since you were in high school. I just stopped dyeing it, that's all.

**BIFF:** Dye it again, will ya? I don't want my pal looking old. (*He smiles.*)

**LINDA:** You're such a boy! You think you can go away for a year and . . . You've got to get it into your head now that one day you'll knock on this door and there'll be strange people here . . .

**BIFF:** What are you talking about? You're not even sixty, Mom.

**LINDA:** But what about your father?

**BIFF** (*lamely*): Well, I meant him too.

**HAPPY:** He admires Pop.

**LINDA:** Biff, dear, if you don't have any feeling for him, then you can't have any feeling for me.

**BIFF:** Sure I can, Mom.

**LINDA:** No. You can't just come to see me, because I love him. (*With a threat, but only a threat, of tears.*) He's the dearest man in the world to me, and I won't have anyone making him feel unwanted and low and blue. You've got to make up your mind now, darling, there's no leeway any more. Either he's your father and you pay him that respect, or else you're not to come here. I know he's not easy to get along with—nobody knows that better than me—but . . .

**WILLY** (*from the left, with a laugh*): Hey, hey, Biffo!

**BIFF** (*starting to go out after Willy*): What the hell is the matter with him? (*Happy stops him.*)

**LINDA:** Don't—don't go near him!

**BIFF:** Stop making excuses for him! He always, always wiped the floor with you. Never had an ounce of respect for you.

**HAPPY:** He's always had respect for . . .

**BIFF:** What the hell do you know about it?

**HAPPY** (*surlily*): Just don't call him crazy!

**BIFF:** He's got no character—Charley wouldn't do this. Not in his own house—spewing out that vomit from his mind.

**HAPPY:** Charley never had to cope with what he's got to.

**BIFF:** People are worse off than Willy Loman. Believe me, I've seen them!

**LINDA:** Then make Charley your father, Biff. You can't do that, can you? I don't say he's a great man. Willy Loman never made a lot of money. His name was never in the paper. He's not the finest character that ever lived. But he's a human being, and a terrible thing is happening to him. So attention must be paid. He's not to be allowed to fall into his grave like an old dog. Attention, attention must be finally paid to such a person. You called him crazy . . .

**BIFF:** I didn't mean . . .

**LINDA:** No, a lot of people think he's lost his—balance. But you don't have to be very smart to know what his trouble is. The man is exhausted.

**HAPPY:** Sure!

**LINDA:** A small man can be just as exhausted as a great man. He works for a company thirty-six years this March, opens up unheard-of territories to their trademark, and now in his old age they take his salary away.

**HAPPY** (*indignantly*): I didn't know that, Mom.

**LINDA:** You never asked, my dear! Now that you get your spending money someplace else you don't trouble your mind with him.

**HAPPY:** But I gave you money last . . .

**LINDA:** Christmas time, fifty dollars! To fix the hot water it cost ninety-seven fifty! For five weeks he's been on straight commission, like a beginner, an unknown!

**BIFF:** Those ungrateful bastards!

**LINDA:** Are they any worse than his sons? When he brought them business, when he was young, they were glad to see him. But now his old friends, the old buyers that loved him so and always found some order to hand him in a pinch—they're all dead, retired. He used to be able to make six, seven calls a day in Boston. Now he takes his valises out of the car and puts them back and takes them out again and he's exhausted. Instead of walking he talks now. He drives seven hundred miles, and when he gets there no one knows him any more, no one welcomes him. And what goes through a man's mind, driving seven hundred miles home without having earned a cent? Why shouldn't he talk to himself? Why? When he has to go to Charley and borrow fifty dollars a week and pretend to me that it's his pay? How long can that go on? How long? You see what I'm sitting here and waiting for? And you tell me he has no character? The man who never worked a day but for your benefit? When does he get the medal for that? Is this his reward—to turn around at the age of sixty-three and find his sons, who he loved better than his life, one a philandering bum . . .

**HAPPY:** Mom!

**LINDA:** That's all you are, my baby! (*To Biff.*) And you! What happened to the love you had for him? You were such pals! How you used to talk to him on the phone every night! How lonely he was till he could come home to you!

**BIFF:** All right, Mom. I'll live here in my room, and I'll get a job. I'll keep away from him, that's all.

**LINDA:** No, Biff. You can't stay here and fight all the time.

**BIFF:** He threw me out of this house, remember that.

**LINDA:** Why did he do that? I never knew why.

**BIFF:** Because I know he's a fake and he doesn't like anybody around who knows!

**LINDA:** Why a fake? In what way? What do you mean?

**BIFF:** Just don't lay it all at my feet. It's between me and him—that's all I have to say. I'll chip in from now on. He'll settle for half my paycheck. He'll be all right. I'm going to bed. (*He starts for the stairs.*)

**LINDA:** He won't be all right.

**BIFF** (*turning on the stairs, furiously*): I hate this city and I'll stay here. Now what do you want?

**LINDA:** He's dying, Biff.

*Happy turns quickly to her, shocked.*

**BIFF** (*after a pause*): Why is he dying?

**LINDA:** He's been trying to kill himself.

**BIFF** (*with great horror*): How?

**LINDA:** I live from day to day.

**BIFF:** What're you talking about?

**LINDA:** Remember I wrote you that he smashed up the car again? In February?

**BIFF:** Well?

**LINDA:** The insurance inspector came. He said that they have evidence. That all these accidents in the last year—weren't—weren't—accidents.

**HAPPY:** How can they tell that? That's a lie.

**LINDA:** It seems there's a woman . . . (*She takes a breath as:*)

**BIFF** (*sharply but contained*): What woman?

**LINDA** (*simultaneously*): . . . and this woman . . .

**LINDA:** What?

**BIFF:** Nothing. Go ahead.

**LINDA:** What did you say?

**BIFF:** Nothing. I just said what woman?

**HAPPY:** What about her?

**LINDA:** Well, it seems she was walking down the road and saw his car. She says that he wasn't driving fast at all, and that he didn't skid.

She says he came to that little bridge, and then deliberately
smashed into the railing, and it was only the shallowness of the
water that saved him.

**BIFF:** Oh, no, he probably just fell asleep again.

**LINDA:** I don't think he fell asleep.

**BIFF:** Why not?

**LINDA:** Last month . . . (*With great difficulty.*) Oh, boys, it's so hard
to say a thing like this! He's just a big stupid man to you, but I tell
you there's more good in him than in many other people. (*She
chokes, wipes her eyes.*) I was looking for a fuse. The lights blew
out, and I went down the cellar. And behind the fuse box—it happened to fall out—was a length of rubber pipe—just short.

**HAPPY:** No kidding!

**LINDA:** There's a little attachment on the end of it. I knew right away.
And sure enough, on the bottom of the water heater there's a new
little nipple on the gas pipe.

**HAPPY** (*angrily*): That—jerk.

**BIFF:** Did you have it taken off?

**LINDA:** I'm—I'm ashamed to. How can I mention it to him? Every
day I go down and take away that little rubber pipe. But, when he
comes home, I put it back where it was. How can I insult him that
way? I don't know what to do. I live from day to day, boys. I tell
you, I know every thought in his mind. It sounds so old-fashioned
and silly, but I tell you he put his whole life into you and you've
turned your backs on him. (*She is bent over in the chair, weeping,
her face in her hands.*) Biff, I swear to God! Biff, his life is in your
hands!

**HAPPY** (*to Biff*): How do you like that damned fool!

**BIFF** (*kissing her*): All right, pal, all right. It's all settled now. I've been
remiss. I know that, Mom. But now I'll stay, and I swear to you, I'll
apply myself. (*Kneeling in front of her, in a fever of self-reproach.*)
It's just—you see, Mom, I don't fit in business. Not that I won't try.
I'll try, and I'll make good.

**HAPPY:** Sure you will. The trouble with you in business was you never
tried to please people.

**BIFF:** I know, I . . .

**HAPPY:** Like when you worked for Harrison's. Bob Harrison said you were tops, and then you go and do some damn fool thing like whistling whole songs in the elevator like a comedian.

**BIFF** (*against Happy*): So what? I like to whistle sometimes.

**HAPPY:** You don't raise a guy to a responsible job who whistles in the elevator!

**LINDA:** Well, don't argue about it now.

**HAPPY:** Like when you'd go off and swim in the middle of the day instead of taking the line around.

**BIFF** (*his resentment rising*): Well, don't you run off? You take off sometimes, don't you? On a nice summer day?

**HAPPY:** Yeah, but I cover myself!

**LINDA:** Boys!

**HAPPY:** If I'm going to take a fade the boss can call any number where I'm supposed to be and they'll swear to him that I just left. I'll tell you something that I hate to say, Biff, but in the business world some of them think you're crazy.

**BIFF** (*angered*): Screw the business world!

**HAPPY:** All right, screw it! Great, but cover yourself!

**LINDA:** Hap, Hap!

**BIFF:** I don't care what they think! They've laughed at Dad for years, and you know why? Because we don't belong in this nuthouse of a city! We should be mixing cement on some open plain or—or carpenters. A carpenter is allowed to whistle!

*Willy walks in from the entrance of the house, at left.*

**WILLY:** Even your grandfather was better than a carpenter. (*Pause. They watch him.*) You never grew up. Bernard does not whistle in the elevator, I assure you.

**BIFF** (*as though to laugh Willy out of it*): Yeah, but you do, Pop.

**WILLY:** I never in my life whistled in an elevator! And who in the business world thinks I'm crazy?

**BIFF:** I didn't mean it like that, Pop. Now don't make a whole thing out of it, will ya?

**WILLY:** Go back to the West! Be a carpenter, a cowboy, enjoy yourself!

**LINDA:** Willy, he was just saying . . .

**WILLY:** I heard what he said!

**HAPPY** (*trying to quiet Willy*): Hey, Pop, come on now . . .

**WILLY** (*continuing over Happy's line*):   They laugh at me, heh? Go to Filene's, go to the Hub, go to Slattery's, Boston. Call out the name Willy Loman and see what happens! Big shot!

**BIFF:**   All right, Pop.

**WILLY:**   Big!

**BIFF:**   All right!

**WILLY:**   Why do you always insult me?

**BIFF:**   I didn't say a word. (*To Linda.*) Did I say a word?

**LINDA:**   He didn't say anything, Willy.

**WILLY** (*going to the doorway of the living room*):   All right, good night, good night.

**LINDA:**   Willy, dear, he just decided . . .

**WILLY** (*to Biff*):   If you get tired hanging around tomorrow, paint the ceiling I put up in the living room.

**BIFF:**   I'm leaving early tomorrow.

**HAPPY:**   He's going to see Bill Oliver, Pop.

**WILLY** (*interestedly*):   Oliver? For what?

**BIFF** (*with reserve, but trying; trying*):   He always said he'd stake me. I'd like to go into business, so maybe I can take him up on it.

**LINDA:**   Isn't that wonderful?

**WILLY:**   Don't interrupt. What's wonderful about it? There's fifty men in the City of New York who'd stake him. (*To Biff.*) Sporting goods?

**BIFF:**   I guess so. I know something about it and . . .

**WILLY:**   He knows something about it! You know sporting goods better than Spalding, for God's sake! How much is he giving you?

**BIFF:**   I don't know, I didn't even see him yet, but . . .

**WILLY:**   Then what're you talkin' about?

**BIFF** (*getting angry*):   Well, all I said was I'm gonna see him, that's all!

**WILLY** (*turning away*):   Ah, you're counting your chickens again.

**BIFF** (*starting left for the stairs*):   Oh, Jesus, I'm going to sleep!

**WILLY** (*calling after him*):   Don't curse in this house!

**BIFF** (*turning*):   Since when did you get so clean?

**HAPPY** (*trying to stop them*):   Wait a . . .

**WILLY:**   Don't use that language to me! I won't have it!

**HAPPY** (*grabbing Biff, shouts*):   Wait a minute! I got an idea. I got a feasible idea. Come here, Biff, let's talk this over now, let's talk some sense here. When I was down in Florida last time, I thought of a great idea to sell sporting goods. It just came back to me. You

and I, Biff—we have a line, the Loman Line. We train a couple of
weeks, and put on a couple of exhibitions, see?

WILLY: That's an idea!

HAPPY: Wait! We form two basketball teams, see? Two water-polo
teams. We play each other. It's a million dollars' worth of publicity.
Two brothers, see? The Loman Brothers. Displays in the Royal
Palms—all the hotels. And banners over the ring and the basketball
court: "Loman Brothers." Baby, we could sell sporting goods!

WILLY: That is a one-million-dollar idea!

LINDA: Marvelous!

BIFF: I'm in great shape as far as that's concerned.

HAPPY: And the beauty of it is, Biff, it wouldn't be like a business.
We'd be out playin' ball again.

BIFF (*enthused*): Yeah, that's . . .

WILLY: Million-dollar . . .

HAPPY: And you wouldn't get fed up with it, Biff. It'd be the family
again. There'd be the old honor, and comradeship, and if you
wanted to go off for a swim or somethin'—well, you'd do it!
Without some smart cooky gettin' up ahead of you!

WILLY: Lick the world! You guys together could absolutely lick the
civilized world.

BIFF: I'll see Oliver tomorrow. Hap, if we could work that out . . .

LINDA: Maybe things are beginning to . . .

WILLY (*wildly enthused, to Linda*): Stop interrupting! (*To Biff.*) But
don't wear sport jacket and slacks when you see Oliver.

BIFF: No, I'll . . .

WILLY: A business suit, and talk as little as possible, and don't crack
any jokes.

BIFF: He did like me. Always liked me.

LINDA: He loved you!

WILLY (*to Linda*): Will you stop! (*To Biff.*) Walk in very serious. You
are not applying for a boy's job. Money is to pass. Be quiet, fine, and
serious. Everybody likes a kidder, but nobody lends him money.

HAPPY: I'll try to get some myself, Biff. I'm sure I can.

WILLY: I see great things for you kids, I think your troubles are over.
But remember, start big and you'll end big. Ask for fifteen. How
much you gonna ask for?

BIFF: Gee, I don't know . . .

**WILLY:** And don't say "Gee." "Gee" is a boy's word. A man walking in for fifteen thousand dollars does not say "Gee!"

**BIFF:** Ten, I think, would be top though.

**WILLY:** Don't be so modest. You always started too low. Walk in with a big laugh. Don't look worried. Start off with a couple of your good stories to lighten things up. It's not what you say, it's how you say it—because personality always wins the day.

**LINDA:** Oliver always thought the highest of him . . .

**WILLY:** Will you let me talk?

**BIFF:** Don't yell at her, Pop, will ya?

**WILLY** (*angrily*): I was talking, wasn't I?

**BIFF:** I don't like you yelling at her all the time, and I'm tellin' you, that's all.

**WILLY:** What're you, takin' over this house?

**LINDA:** Willy . . .

**WILLY** (*turning to her*): Don't take his side all the time, goddammit!

**BIFF** (*furiously*): Stop yelling at her!

**WILLY** (*suddenly pulling on his cheek, beaten down, guilt ridden*): Give my best to Bill Oliver—he may remember me. (*He exits through the living room doorway.*)

**LINDA** (*her voice subdued*): What'd you have to start that for? (*Biff turns away.*) You see how sweet he was as soon as you talked hopefully? (*She goes over to Biff.*) Come up and say good night to him. Don't let him go to bed that way.

**HAPPY:** Come on, Biff, let's buck him up.

**LINDA:** Please, dear. Just say good night. It takes so little to make him happy. Come. (*She goes through the living room doorway, calling upstairs from within the living room.*) Your pajamas are hanging in the bathroom, Willy!

**HAPPY** (*looking toward where Linda went out*): What a woman! They broke the mold when they made her. You know that, Biff.

**BIFF:** He's off salary. My God, working on commission!

**HAPPY:** Well, let's face it: he's no hot-shot selling man. Except that sometimes, you have to admit, he's a sweet personality.

**BIFF** (*deciding*): Lend me ten bucks, will ya? I want to buy some new ties.

**HAPPY:** I'll take you to a place I know. Beautiful stuff. Wear one of my striped shirts tomorrow.

**BIFF:** She got gray. Mom got awful old. Gee, I'm gonna go in to Oliver tomorrow and knock him for a . . .

**HAPPY:** Come on up. Tell that to Dad. Let's give him a whirl. Come on.

**BIFF** (*steamed up*): You know, with ten thousand bucks, boy!

**HAPPY** (*as they go into the living room*): That's the talk, Biff, that's the first time I've heard the old confidence out of you! (*From within the living room, fading off*) You're gonna live with me, kid, and any babe you want just say the word . . . (*The last lines are hardly heard. They are mounting the stairs to their parents' bedroom.*)

**LINDA** (*entering her bedroom and addressing Willy, who is in the bathroom. She is straightening the bed for him*): Can you do anything about the shower? It drips.

**WILLY** (*from the bathroom*): All of a sudden everything falls to pieces. Goddam plumbing, oughta be sued, those people. I hardly finished putting it in and the thing . . . (*His words rumble off.*)

**LINDA:** I'm just wondering if Oliver will remember him. You think he might?

**WILLY** (*coming out of the bathroom in his pajamas*): Remember him? What's the matter with you, you crazy? If he'd've stayed with Oliver he'd be on top by now! Wait'll Oliver gets a look at him. You don't know the average caliber any more. The average young man today—(*he is getting into bed*)—is got a caliber of zero. Greatest thing in the world for him was to bum around.

*Biff and Happy enter the bedroom. Slight pause.*

**WILLY** (*stops short, looking at Biff*): Glad to hear it, boy.

**HAPPY:** He wanted to say good night to you, sport.

**WILLY** (*to Biff*): Yeah. Knock him dead, boy. What'd you want to tell me?

**BIFF:** Just take it easy, Pop. Good night. (*He turns to go.*)

**WILLY** (*unable to resist*): And if anything falls off the desk while you're talking to him—like a package or something—don't you pick it up. They have office boys for that.

**LINDA:** I'll make a big breakfast . . .

**WILLY:** Will you let me finish? (*To Biff.*) Tell him you were in the business in the West. Not farm work.

**BIFF:** All right, Dad.

**LINDA:** I think everything . . .

**WILLY** (*going right through her speech*): And don't undersell yourself. No less than fifteen thousand dollars.

**BIFF** (*unable to bear him*): Okay. Good night, Mom. (*He starts moving.*)

**WILLY:** Because you got a greatness in you, Biff, remember that. You got all kinds of greatness . . . (*He lies back, exhausted. Biff walks out.*)

**LINDA** (*calling after Biff*): Sleep well, darling!

**HAPPY:** I'm gonna get married, Mom. I wanted to tell you.

**LINDA:** Go to sleep, dear.

**HAPPY** (*going*): I just wanted to tell you.

**WILLY:** Keep up the good work. (*Happy exits.*) God . . . remember that Ebbets Field game? The championship of the city?

**LINDA:** Just rest. Should I sing to you?

**WILLY:** Yeah. Sing to me. (*Linda hums a soft lullaby.*) When that team came out—he was the tallest, remember?

**LINDA:** Oh, yes. And in gold.

*Biff enters the darkened kitchen, takes a cigarette, and leaves the house. He comes downstage into a golden pool of light. He smokes, staring at the night.*

**WILLY:** Like a young god. Hercules—something like that. And the sun, the sun all around him. Remember how he waved to me? Right up from the field, with the representatives of three colleges standing by? And the buyers I brought, and the cheers when he came out— Loman, Loman, Loman! God Almighty, he'll be great yet. A star like that, magnificent, can never really fade away!

*The light on Willy is fading. The gas heater begins to glow through the kitchen wall, near the stairs, a blue flame beneath red coils.*

**LINDA** (*timidly*): Willy dear, what has he got against you?

**WILLY:** I'm so tired. Don't talk any more.

*Biff slowly returns to the kitchen. He stops, stares toward the heater.*

**LINDA:** Will you ask Howard to let you work in New York?

**WILLY:** First thing in the morning. Everything'll be all right.

*Biff reaches behind the heater and draws out a length of rubber tubing. He is horrified and turns his head toward Willy's room, still dimly lit, from which the strains of Linda's desperate but monotonous humming rise.*

**WILLY** (*staring through the window into the moonlight*): Gee, look at the moon moving between the buildings! (*Biff wraps the tubing around his hand and quickly goes up the stairs.*)

## Act 2

*Scene: Music is heard, gay and bright. The curtain rises as the music fades away. Willy, in shirt sleeves, is sitting at the kitchen table, sipping coffee, his hat in his lap. Linda is filling his cup when she can.*

**WILLY:** Wonderful coffee. Meal in itself.

**LINDA:** Can I make you some eggs?

**WILLY:** No. Take a breath.

**LINDA:** You look so rested, dear.

**WILLY:** I slept like a dead one. First time in months. Imagine, sleeping till ten on a Tuesday morning. Boys left nice and early, heh?

**LINDA:** They were out of here by eight o'clock.

**WILLY:** Good work!

**LINDA:** It was so thrilling to see them leaving together. I can't get over the shaving lotion in this house!

**WILLY** (*smiling*): Mmm . . .

**LINDA:** Biff was very changed this morning. His whole attitude seemed to be hopeful. He couldn't wait to get downtown to see Oliver.

**WILLY:** He's heading for a change. There's no question, there simply are certain men that take longer to get—solidified. How did he dress?

**LINDA:** His blue suit. He's so handsome in that suit. He could be a—anything in that suit!

*Willy gets up from the table. Linda holds his jacket for him.*

**WILLY:** There's no question, no question at all. Gee, on the way home tonight I'd like to buy some seeds.

**LINDA** (*laughing*): That'd be wonderful. But not enough sun gets back there. Nothing'll grow any more.

**WILLY:** You wait, kid, before it's all over we're gonna get a little place out in the country, and I'll raise some vegetables, a couple of chickens . . .

**LINDA:** You'll do it yet, dear.

*Willy walks out of his jacket. Linda follows him.*

**WILLY:** And they'll get married, and come for a weekend. I'd build a little guest house. 'Cause I got so many fine tools, all I'd need would be a little lumber and some peace of mind.

**LINDA** (*joyfully*): I sewed the lining . . .

**WILLY:** I could build two guest houses, so they'd both come. Did he decide how much he's going to ask Oliver for?

**LINDA** (*getting him into the jacket*): He didn't mention it, but I imagine ten or fifteen thousand. You going to talk to Howard today?

**WILLY:** Yeah. I'll put it to him straight and simple. He'll just have to take me off the road.

**LINDA:** And Willy, don't forget to ask for a little advance, because we've got the insurance premium. It's the grace period now.

**WILLY:** That's a hundred . . . ?

**LINDA:** A hundred and eight, sixty-eight. Because we're a little short again.

**WILLY:** Why are we short?

**LINDA:** Well, you had the motor job on the car . . .

**WILLY:** That goddam Studebaker!

**LINDA:** And you got one more payment on the refrigerator . . .

**WILLY:** But it just broke again!

**LINDA:** Well, it's old, dear.

**WILLY:** I told you we should've bought a well-advertised machine. Charley bought a General Electric and it's twenty years old and it's still good, that son-of-a-bitch.

**LINDA:** But, Willy . . .

**WILLY:** Whoever heard of a Hastings refrigerator? Once in my life I would like to own something outright before it's broken! I'm always in a race with the junkyard! I just finished paying for the car and it's on its last legs. The refrigerator consumes belts like a goddam maniac. They time those things. They time them so when you finally paid for them, they're used up.

**LINDA** (*buttoning up his jacket as he unbuttons it*):   All told, about two hundred dollars would carry us, dear. But that includes the last payment on the mortgage. After this payment, Willy, the house belongs to us.

**WILLY:**  It's twenty-five years!

**LINDA:**  Biff was nine years old when we bought it.

**WILLY:**  Well, that's a great thing. To weather a twenty-five year mortgage is . . .

**LINDA:**  It's an accomplishment.

**WILLY:**  All the cement, the lumber, the reconstruction I put in this house! There ain't a crack to be found in it any more.

**LINDA:**  Well, it served its purpose.

**WILLY:**  What purpose? Some stranger'll come along, move in, and that's that. If only Biff would take this house, and raise a family . . . (*He starts to go.*) Good-by, I'm late.

**LINDA** (*suddenly remembering*):  Oh, I forgot! You're supposed to meet them for dinner.

**WILLY:**  Me?

**LINDA:**  At Frank's Chop House on Forty-eighth near Sixth Avenue.

**WILLY:**  Is that so! How about you?

**LINDA:**  No, just the three of you. They're gonna blow you to a big meal!

**WILLY:**  Don't say! Who thought of that?

**LINDA:**  Biff came to me this morning, Willy, and he said, "Tell Dad, we want to blow him to a big meal." Be there six o'clock. You and your two boys are going to have dinner.

**WILLY:**  Gee whiz! That's really somethin'. I'm gonna knock Howard for a loop, kid. I'll get an advance, and I'll come home with a New York job. Goddammit, now I'm gonna do it!

**LINDA:**  Oh, that's the spirit, Willy!

**WILLY:**  I will never get behind a wheel the rest of my life!

**LINDA:**  It's changing, Willy, I can feel it changing!

**WILLY:**  Beyond a question. G'by, I'm late. (*He starts to go again.*)

**LINDA** (*calling after him as she runs to the kitchen table for a handkerchief*):   You got your glasses?

**WILLY** (*feels for them, then comes back in*):  Yeah, yeah, got my glasses.

**LINDA** (*giving him the handkerchief*):   And a handkerchief.

**WILLY:**  Yeah, handkerchief.

LINDA: And your saccharine?

WILLY: Yeah, my saccharine.

LINDA: Be careful on the subway stairs.

*She kisses him, and a silk stocking is seen hanging from her hand. Willy notices it.*

WILLY: Will you stop mending stockings? At least while I'm in the house. It gets me nervous. I can't tell you. Please.

*Linda hides the stocking in her hand as she follows Willy across the forestage in front of the house.*

LINDA: Remember, Frank's Chop House.

WILLY (*passing the apron*): Maybe beets would grow out there.

LINDA (*laughing*): But you tried so many times.

WILLY: Yeah. Well, don't work hard today. (*He disappears around the right corner of the house.*)

LINDA: Be careful!

*As Willy vanishes, Linda waves to him. Suddenly the phone rings. She runs across the stage and into the kitchen and lifts it.*

LINDA: Hello? Oh, Biff! I'm so glad you called, I just . . . Yes, sure, I just told him. Yes, he'll be there for dinner at six o'clock, I didn't forget. Listen, I was just dying to tell you. You know that little rubber pipe I told you about? That he connected to the gas heater? I finally decided to go down the cellar this morning and take it away and destroy it. But it's gone! Imagine? He took it away himself, it isn't there! (*She listens.*) When? Oh, then you took it. Oh—nothing, it's just that I'd hoped he'd taken it away himself. Oh, I'm not worried, darling, because this morning he left in such high spirits, it was like the old days! I'm not afraid any more. Did Mr. Oliver see you? . . . Well, you wait there then. And make a nice impression on him, darling. Just don't perspire too much before you see him. And have a nice time with Dad. He may have big news too! . . . That's right, a New York job. And be sweet to him tonight, dear. Be loving to him. Because he's only a little boat looking for a harbor. (*She is trembling with sorrow and joy.*) Oh, that's wonderful, Biff, you'll save his life. Thanks, darling. Just put your arm around him when he comes into the restaurant. Give him a smile. That's the boy . . .

Good-by, dear. . . . You got your comb?. . . That's fine. Good-by, Biff dear.

*In the middle of her speech, Howard Wagner, thirty-six, wheels in a small typewriter table on which is a wire-recording machine and proceeds to plug it in. This is on the left forestage. Light slowly fades on Linda as it rises on Howard. Howard is intent on threading the machine and only glances over his shoulder as Willy appears.*

**WILLY:** Pst! Pst!

**HOWARD:** Hello, Willy, come in.

**WILLY:** Like to have a little talk with you, Howard.

**HOWARD:** Sorry to keep you waiting. I'll be with you in a minute.

**WILLY:** What's that, Howard?

**HOWARD:** Didn't you ever see one of these? Wire recorder.

**WILLY:** Oh. Can we talk a minute?

**HOWARD:** Records things. Just got delivery yesterday. Been driving me crazy, the most terrific machine I ever saw in my life. I was up all night with it.

**WILLY:** What do you do with it?

**HOWARD:** I bought it for dictation, but you can do anything with it. Listen to this. I had it home last night. Listen to what I picked up. The first one is my daughter. Get this. (*He flicks the switch and "Roll Out the Barrel" is heard being whistled.*) Listen to that kid whistle.

**WILLY:** That is lifelike, isn't it?

**HOWARD:** Seven years old. Get that tone.

**WILLY:** Ts, ts. Like to ask a little favor if you . . .

*The whistling breaks off, and the voice of Howard's daughter is heard.*

**HIS DAUGHTER:** "Now you, Daddy."

**HOWARD:** She's crazy for me! (*Again the same song is whistled.*) That's me! Ha! (*He winks.*)

**WILLY:** You're very good!

*The whistling breaks off again. The machine runs silent for a moment.*

HOWARD:   Sh! Get this now, this is my son.

HIS SON:   "The capital of Alabama is Montgomery; the capital of Arizona is Phoenix; the capital of Arkansas is Little Rock; the capital of California is Sacramento . . ." (*and on, and on.*)

HOWARD (*holding up five fingers*):   Five years old, Willy!

WILLY:   He'll make an announcer some day!

HIS SON (*continuing*):   "The capital . . ."

HOWARD:   Get that—alphabetical order! (*The machine breaks off suddenly.*) Wait a minute. The maid kicked the plug out.

WILLY:   It certainly is a . . .

HOWARD:   Sh, for God's sake!

HIS SON:   "It's nine o'clock, Bulova watch time. So I have to go to sleep."

WILLY:   That really is . . .

HOWARD:   Wait a minute! The next is my wife.

*They wait.*

HOWARD'S VOICE:   "Go on, say something." (*Pause.*) "Well, you gonna talk?"

HIS WIFE:   "I can't think of anything."

HOWARD'S VOICE:   "Well, talk—it's turning."

HIS WIFE (*shyly, beaten*):   "Hello." (*Silence.*) "Oh, Howard, I can't talk into this . . ."

HOWARD (*snapping the machine off*):   That was my wife.

WILLY:   That is a wonderful machine. Can we . . .

HOWARD:   I tell you, Willy, I'm gonna take my camera, and my band-saw, and all my hobbies, and out they go. This is the most fascinating relaxation I ever found.

WILLY:   I think I'll get one myself.

HOWARD:   Sure, they're only a hundred and a half. You can't do without it. Supposing you wanna hear Jack Benny, see? But you can't be at home at that hour. So you tell the maid to turn the radio on when Jack Benny comes on, and this automatically goes on with the radio . . .

WILLY:   And when you come home you . . .

HOWARD:   You can come home twelve o'clock, one o'clock, any time you like, and you get yourself a Coke and sit yourself down, throw the switch, and there's Jack Benny's program in the middle of the night!

**WILLY:** I'm definitely going to get one. Because lots of times I'm on the road, and I think to myself, what I must be missing on the radio!

**HOWARD:** Don't you have a radio in the car?

**WILLY:** Well, yeah, but who ever thinks of turning it on?

**HOWARD:** Say, aren't you supposed to be in Boston?

**WILLY:** That's what I want to talk to you about, Howard. You got a minute? (*He draws a chair in from the wing.*)

**HOWARD:** What happened? What're you doing here?

**WILLY:** Well . . .

**HOWARD:** You didn't crack up again, did you?

**WILLY:** Oh, no. No . . .

**HOWARD:** Geez, you had me worried there for a minute. What's the trouble?

**WILLY:** Well, tell you the truth, Howard. I've come to the decision that I'd rather not travel any more.

**HOWARD:** Not travel! Well, what'll you do?

**WILLY:** Remember, Christmas time, when you had the party here? You said you'd try to think of some spot for me here in town.

**HOWARD:** With us?

**WILLY:** Well, sure.

**HOWARD:** Oh, yeah, yeah. I remember. Well, I couldn't think of anything for you, Willy.

**WILLY:** I tell ya, Howard. The kids are all grown up, y'know. I don't need much any more. If I could take home—well, sixty-five dollars a week, I could swing it.

**HOWARD:** Yeah, but Willy, see I . . .

**WILLY:** I tell ya why, Howard. Speaking frankly and between the two of us, y'know—I'm just a little tired.

**HOWARD:** Oh, I could understand that, Willy. But you're a road man, Willy, and we do a road business. We've only got a half-dozen salesmen on the floor here.

**WILLY:** God knows, Howard. I never asked a favor of any man. But I was with the firm when your father used to carry you in here in his arms.

**HOWARD:** I know that, Willy, but . . .

**WILLY:** Your father came to me the day you were born and asked me what I thought of the name Howard, may he rest in peace.

HOWARD:   I appreciate that, Willy, but there just is no spot here for you. If I had a spot I'd slam you right in, but I just don't have a single solitary spot.

*He looks for his lighter. Willy has picked it up and gives it to him. Pause.*

WILLY (*with increasing anger*):   Howard, all I need to set my table is fifty dollars a week.

HOWARD:   But where am I going to put you, kid?

WILLY:   Look, it isn't a question of whether I can sell merchandise, is it?

HOWARD:   No, but it's business, kid, and everybody's gotta pull his own weight.

WILLY (*desperately*):   Just let me tell you a story, Howard . . .

HOWARD:   'Cause you gotta admit, business is business.

WILLY (*angrily*):   Business is definitely business, but just listen for a minute. You don't understand this. When I was a boy—eighteen, nineteen—I was already on the road. And there was a question in my mind as to whether selling had a future for me. Because in those days I had a yearning to go to Alaska. See, there were three gold strikes in one month in Alaska, and I felt like going out. Just for the ride, you might say.

HOWARD (*barely interested*):   Don't say.

WILLY:   Oh, yeah, my father lived many years in Alaska. He was an adventurous man. We've got quite a little streak of self-reliance in our family. I thought I'd go out with my older brother and try to locate him, and maybe settle in the North with the old man. And I was almost decided to go, when I met a salesman in the Parker House. His name was Dave Singleman. And he was eighty-four years old, and he'd drummed merchandise in thirty-one states. And old Dave, he'd go up to his room, y'understand, put on his green velvet slippers—I'll never forget—and pick up his phone and call the buyers, and without ever leaving his room, at the age of eighty-four, he made his living. And when I saw that, I realized that selling was the greatest career a man could want. 'Cause what could be more satisfying than to be able to go, at the age of eighty-four, into twenty or thirty different cities, and pick up a phone, and be remembered and loved and helped by so many different people? Do you know? when he died—and by the way he died the death of a salesman, in his green velvet slippers in the smoker of the New York, New Haven and Hartford, going into Boston—when he died, hundreds of salesmen and buyers were at his funeral. Things were sad on a lotta trains for months after that. (*He stands up, Howard has not looked at him.*) In those days there was personality in it, Howard. There was respect, and comradeship, and gratitude in it. Today, it's all cut and dried, and there's no chance for bringing friendship to bear—or personality. You see what I mean? They don't know me any more.

**HOWARD** (*moving away, to the right*):   That's just the thing, Willy.

**WILLY:**   If I had forty dollars a week—that's all I'd need. Forty dollars, Howard.

**HOWARD:**   Kid, I can't take blood from a stone, I . . .

**WILLY** (*desperation is on him now*):   Howard, the year Al Smith was nominated, your father came to me and . . .

**HOWARD** (*starting to go off*):   I've got to see some people, kid.

**WILLY** (*stopping him*):   I'm talking about your father! There were promises made across this desk! You mustn't tell me you've got people to see—I put thirty-four years into this firm, Howard, and now I can't pay my insurance! You can't eat the orange and throw the peel away—a man is not a piece of fruit! (*After a pause.*) Now pay attention. Your father—in 1928 I had a big year. I averaged a hundred and seventy dollars a week in commissions.

**HOWARD** (*impatiently*):   Now, Willy, you never averaged . . .

**WILLY** (*banging his hand on the desk*):   I averaged a hundred and seventy dollars a week in the year of 1928! And your father came to me—or rather, I was in the office here—it was right over this desk—and he put his hand on my shoulder . . .

**HOWARD** (*getting up*):   You'll have to excuse me, Willy, I gotta see some people. Pull yourself together. (*Going out.*) I'll be back in a little while.

*On Howard's exit, the light on his chair grows very bright and strange.*

**WILLY:**   Pull myself together! What the hell did I say to him? My God, I was yelling at him! How could I? (*Willy breaks off, staring at the light, which occupies the chair, animating it. He approaches this chair, standing across the desk from it.*) Frank, Frank, don't you remember what you told me that time? How you put your hand on my shoulder, and Frank . . . (*He leans on the desk and as he speaks the dead man's name he accidentally switches on the recorder, and instantly*)

HOWARD'S SON: ". . . of New York is Albany. The capital of Ohio is Cincinnati, the capital of Rhode Island is . . ." (*The recitation continues.*)

WILLY (*leaping away with fright, shouting*): Ha! Howard! Howard! Howard!

HOWARD (*rushing in*): What happened?

WILLY (*pointing at the machine, which continues nasally, childishly, with the capital cities*): Shut it off! Shut it off!

HOWARD (*pulling the plug out*): Look, Willy . . .

WILLY (*pressing his hands to his eyes*): I gotta get myself some coffee. I'll get some coffee . . .

*Willy starts to walk out. Howard stops him.*

HOWARD (*rolling up the cord*): Willy, look . . .

WILLY: I'll go to Boston.

HOWARD: Willy, you can't go to Boston for us.

WILLY: Why can't I go?

HOWARD: I don't want you to represent us. I've been meaning to tell you for a long time now.

WILLY: Howard, are you firing me?

HOWARD: I think you need a good long rest, Willy.

WILLY: Howard . . .

HOWARD: And when you feel better, come back, and we'll see if we can work something out.

WILLY: But I gotta earn money, Howard. I'm in no position to . . .

HOWARD: Where are your sons? Why don't your sons give you a hand?

WILLY: They're working on a very big deal.

HOWARD: This is no time for false pride, Willy. You go to your sons and you tell them that you're tired. You've got two great boys, haven't you?

WILLY: Oh, no question, no question, but in the meantime . . .

HOWARD: Then that's that, heh?

WILLY: All right, I'll go to Boston tomorrow.

**HOWARD:** No, no.

**WILLY:** I can't throw myself on my sons. I'm not a cripple!

**HOWARD:** Look, kid, I'm busy this morning.

**WILLY** (*grasping Howard's arm*): Howard, you've got to let me go to Boston!

**HOWARD** (*hard, keeping himself under control*): I've got a line of people to see this morning. Sit down, take five minutes, and pull yourself together, and then go home, will ya? I need the office, Willy. (*He starts to go, turns, remembering the recorder, starts to push off the table holding the recorder.*) Oh, yeah. Whenever you can this week, stop by and drop off the samples. You'll feel better, Willy, and then come back and we'll talk. Pull yourself together, kid, there's people outside.

*Howard exits, pushing the table off left. Willy stares into space, exhausted. Now the music is heard—Ben's music—first distantly, then closer, closer. As Willy speaks, Ben enters from the right. He carries a valise and umbrella.*

**WILLY:** Oh, Ben, how did you do it? What is the answer? Did you wind up the Alaska deal already?

**BEN:** Doesn't take much time if you know what you're doing. Just a short business trip. Boarding ship in an hour. Wanted to say good-by.

**WILLY:** Ben, I've got to talk to you.

**BEN** (*glancing at his watch*): Haven't the time, William.

**WILLY** (*crossing the apron to Ben*): Ben, nothing's working out. I don't know what to do.

**BEN:** Now, look here, William. I've bought timberland in Alaska and I need a man to look after things for me.

**WILLY:** God, timberland! Me and my boys in those grand outdoors!

**BEN:** You've a new continent at your doorstep, William. Get out of these cities, they're full of talk and time payments and courts of law. Screw on your fists and you can fight for a fortune up there.

**WILLY:** Yes, yes! Linda, Linda!

*Linda enters as of old, with the wash.*

**LINDA:** Oh, you're back?

**BEN:** I haven't much time.

**WILLY:** No, wait! Linda, he's got a proposition for me in Alaska.

**LINDA:** But you've got . . . (*To Ben.*) He's got a beautiful job here.

**WILLY:** But in Alaska, kid, I could . . .

**LINDA:** You're doing well enough, Willy!

**BEN** (*to Linda*): Enough for what, my dear?

**LINDA** (*frightened of Ben and angry at him*): Don't say those things to him! Enough to be happy right here, right now. (*To Willy, while Ben laughs.*) Why must everybody conquer the world? You're well liked, and the boys love you, and someday—(*To Ben*)—why, old man Wagner told him just the other day that if he keeps it up he'll be a member of the firm, didn't he, Willy?

**WILLY:** Sure, sure. I am building something with this firm, Ben, and if a man is building something he must be on the right track, mustn't he?

**BEN:** What are you building? Lay your hand on it. Where is it?

**WILLY** (*hesitantly*): That's true, Linda, there's nothing.

**LINDA:** Why? (*To Ben.*) There's a man eighty-four years old . . .

**WILLY:** That's right, Ben, that's right. When I look at that man I say, what is there to worry about?

**BEN:** Bah!

**WILLY:** It's true, Ben. All he has to do is go into any city, pick up the phone, and he's making his living and you know why?

**BEN** (*picking up his valise*): I've got to go.

**WILLY** (*holding Ben back*): Look at this boy!

*Biff, in his high school sweater, enters carrying a suitcase. Happy carries Biff's shoulder guards, gold helmet, and football pants.*

**WILLY:** Without a penny to his name, three great universities are begging for him, and from there the sky's the limit, because it's not what you do, Ben. It's who you know and the smile on your face! It's contacts, Ben, contacts! The whole wealth of Alaska passes over the lunch table at the Commodore Hotel, and that's the wonder, the wonder of this country, that a man can end with diamonds here on the basis of being liked! (*He turns to Biff.*) And that's why when you get out on that field today it's important. Because thousands of people will be rooting for you and loving you. (*To Ben, who has again begun to leave.*) And Ben! when he walks into a business office his name will sound out like a bell and all the doors will open to him! I've seen it, Ben, I've seen it a thousand times! You can't feel it with your hand like timber, but it's there!

**BEN:** Good-by, William.

**WILLY:** Ben, am I right? Don't you think I'm right? I value your advice.

**BEN:** There's a new continent at your doorstep, William. You could walk out rich. Rich! (*He is gone.*)

**WILLY:** We'll do it here, Ben! You hear me? We're gonna do it here!

*Young Bernard rushes in. The gay music of the Boys is heard.*

**BERNARD:** Oh, gee, I was afraid you left already!

**WILLY:** Why? What time is it?

**BERNARD:** It's half-past one!

**WILLY:** Well, come on, everybody! Ebbets Field next stop! Where's the pennants? (*He rushes through the wall-line of the kitchen and out into the living room.*)

**LINDA** (*to Biff*): Did you pack fresh underwear?

**BIFF** (*who has been limbering up*): I want to go!

**BERNARD:** Biff, I'm carrying your helmet, ain't I?

**HAPPY:** No, I'm carrying the helmet.

**BERNARD:** Oh, Biff, you promised me.

**HAPPY:** I'm carrying the helmet.

**BERNARD:** How am I going to get in the locker room?

**LINDA:** Let him carry the shoulder guards. (*She puts her coat and hat on in the kitchen.*)

**BERNARD:** Can I, Biff? 'Cause I told everybody I'm going to be in the locker room.

**HAPPY:** In Ebbets Field it's the clubhouse.

**BERNARD:** I meant the clubhouse. Biff!

**HAPPY:** Biff!

**BIFF** (*grandly, after a slight pause*): Let him carry the shoulder guards.

**HAPPY** (*as he gives Bernard the shoulder guards*): Stay close to us now.

*Willy rushes in with the pennants.*

**WILLY** (*handing them out*): Everybody wave when Biff comes out on the field. (*Happy and Bernard run off.*) You set now, boy?

*The music has died away.*

**BIFF:** Ready to go, Pop. Every muscle is ready.

**WILLY** (*at the edge of the apron*):   You realize what this means?

**BIFF:**   That's right, Pop.

**WILLY** (*feeling Biff's muscles*):   You're comin' home this afternoon captain of the All-Scholastic Championship Team of the City of New York.

**BIFF:**   I got it, Pop. And remember, pal, when I take off my helmet, that touchdown is for you.

**WILLY:**   Let's go! (*He is starting out, with his arm around Biff, when Charley enters, as of old, in knickers.*) I got no room for you, Charley.

**CHARLEY:**   Room? For what?

**WILLY:**   In the car.

**CHARLEY:**   You goin' for a ride? I wanted to shoot some casino.

**WILLY** (*furiously*):   Casino! (*Incredulously.*) Don't you realize what today is?

**LINDA:**   Oh, he knows, Willy. He's just kidding you.

**WILLY:**   That's nothing to kid about!

**CHARLEY:**   No, Linda, what's goin' on?

**LINDA:**   He's playing in Ebbets Field.

**CHARLEY:**   Baseball in this weather?

**WILLY:**   Don't talk to him. Come on, come on! (*He is pushing them out.*)

**CHARLEY:**   Wait a minute, didn't you hear the news?

**WILLY:**   What?

**CHARLEY:**   Don't you listen to the radio? Ebbets Field just blew up.

**WILLY:**   You go to hell! (*Charley laughs. Pushing them out.*) Come on, come on! We're late.

**CHARLEY** (*as they go*):   Knock a homer, Biff, knock a homer!

**WILLY** (*the last to leave, turning to Charley*):   I don't think that was funny, Charley. This is the greatest day of his life.

**CHARLEY:**   Willy, when are you going to grow up?

**WILLY:**   Yeah, heh? When this game is over, Charley, you'll be laughing out of the other side of your face. They'll be calling him another Red Grange. Twenty-five thousand a year.

**CHARLEY** (*kidding*):   Is that so?

**WILLY:**   Yeah, that's so.

**CHARLEY:**   Well, then, I'm sorry, Willy. But tell me something.

**WILLY:**   What?

**CHARLEY:** Who is Red Grange?

**WILLY:** Put up your hands. Goddam you, put up your hands!

*Charley, chuckling, shakes his head and walks away, around the left corner of the stage. Willy follows him. The music rises to a mocking frenzy.*

**WILLY:** Who the hell do you think you are, better than everybody else? You don't know everything, you big, ignorant, stupid . . . Put up your hands!

*Light rises, on the right side of the forestage, on a small table in the reception room of Charley's office. Traffic sounds are heard. Bernard, now mature, sits whistling to himself. A pair of tennis rackets and an old overnight bag are on the floor beside him.*

**WILLY** (*offstage*): What are you walking away for? Don't walk away! If you're going to say something say it to my face! I know you laugh at me behind my back. You'll laugh out of the other side of your goddam face after this game. Touchdown! Touchdown! Eighty thousand people! Touchdown! Right between the goal posts.

*Bernard is a quiet, earnest, but self-assured young man. Willy's voice is coming from right upstage now. Bernard lowers his feet off the table and listens. Jenny, his father's secretary, enters.*

**JENNY** (*distressed*): Say, Bernard, will you go out in the hall?

**BERNARD:** What is that noise? Who is it?

**JENNY:** Mr. Loman. He just got off the elevator.

**BERNARD** (*getting up*): Who's he arguing with?

**JENNY:** Nobody. There's nobody with him. I can't deal with him any more, and your father gets all upset every time he comes. I've got a lot of typing to do, and your father's waiting to sign it. Will you see him?

**WILLY** (*entering*): Touchdown! Touch—(*He sees Jenny.*) Jenny, Jenny, good to see you. How're ya? Workin'? Or still honest?

**JENNY:** Fine. How've you been feeling?

**WILLY:** Not much any more, Jenny. Ha, ha! (*He is surprised to see the rackets.*)

**BERNARD:** Hello, Uncle Willy.

**WILLY** (*almost shocked*): Bernard! Well, look who's here! (*He comes quickly, guiltily, to Bernard and warmly shakes his hand.*)

BERNARD:  How are you? Good to see you.

WILLY:  What are you doing here?

BERNARD:  Oh, just stopped by to see Pop. Get off my feet till my train leaves. I'm going to Washington in a few minutes.

WILLY:  Is he in?

BERNARD:  Yes, he's in his office with the accountant. Sit down.

WILLY (*sitting down*):  What're you going to do in Washington?

BERNARD:  Oh, just a case I've got there, Willy.

WILLY:  That so? (*Indicating the rackets.*) You going to play tennis there?

BERNARD:  I'm staying with a friend who's got a court.

WILLY:  Don't say. His own tennis court. Must be fine people, I bet.

BERNARD:  They are, very nice. Dad tells me Biff's in town.

WILLY (*with a big smile*):  Yeah, Biff's in. Working on a very big deal, Bernard.

BERNARD:  What's Biff doing?

WILLY:  Well, he's been doing very big things in the West. But he decided to establish himself here. Very big. We're having dinner. Did I hear your wife had a boy?

BERNARD:  That's right. Our second.

WILLY:  Two boys! What do you know!

BERNARD:  What kind of a deal has Biff got?

WILLY:  Well, Bill Oliver—very big sporting-goods man—he wants Biff very badly. Called him in from the West. Long distance, carte blanche, special deliveries. Your friends have their own private tennis court?

BERNARD:  You still with the old firm, Willy?

WILLY (*after a pause*):  I'm—I'm overjoyed to see how you made the grade, Bernard, overjoyed. It's an encouraging thing to see a young man really—really . . . Looks very good for Biff—very . . . (*He breaks off, then.*) Bernard . . . (*He is so full of emotion, he breaks off again.*)

BERNARD:  What is it, Willy?

WILLY (*small and alone*):  What—what's the secret?

BERNARD:  What secret?

WILLY:  How—how did you? Why didn't he ever catch on?

BERNARD:  I wouldn't know that, Willy.

**WILLY** (*confidentially; desperately*): You were his friend, his boyhood friend. There's something I don't understand about it. His life ended after that Ebbets Field game. From the age of seventeen nothing good ever happened to him.

**BERNARD:** He never trained himself for anything.

**WILLY:** But he did, he did. After high school he took so many correspondence courses. Radio mechanics; television; God knows what, and never made the slightest mark.

**BERNARD** (*taking off his glasses*): Willy, do you want to talk candidly?

**WILLY** (*rising, faces Bernard*): I regard you as a very brilliant man, Bernard. I value your advice.

**BERNARD:** Oh, the hell with the advice, Willy. I couldn't advise you. There's just one thing I've always wanted to ask you. When he was supposed to graduate, and the math teacher flunked him . . .

**WILLY:** Oh, that son-of-a-bitch ruined his life.

**BERNARD:** Yeah, but, Willy, all he had to do was go to summer school and make up that subject.

**WILLY:** That's right, that's right.

**BERNARD:** Did you tell him not to go to summer school?

**WILLY:** Me? I begged him to go. I ordered him to go!

**BERNARD:** Then why wouldn't he go?

**WILLY:** Why? Why! Bernard, that question has been trailing me like a ghost for the last fifteen years. He flunked the subject, and laid down and died like a hammer hit him!

**BERNARD:** Take it easy, kid.

**WILLY:** Let me talk to you—I got nobody to talk to. Bernard, Bernard, was it my fault? Y'see? It keeps going around in my mind, maybe I did something to him. I got nothing to give him.

**BERNARD:** Don't take it so hard.

**WILLY:** Why did he lay down? What is the story there? You were his friend!

**BERNARD:** Willy, I remember, it was June, and our grades came out. And he'd flunked math.

**WILLY:** That son-of-a-bitch!

**BERNARD:** No, it wasn't right then. Biff just got very angry, I remember, and he was ready to enroll in summer school.

**WILLY** (*surprised*): He was?

BERNARD: He wasn't beaten by it at all. But then, Willy, he disappeared from the block for almost a month. And I got the idea that he'd gone up to New England to see you. Did he have a talk with you then?

*Willy stares in silence.*

BERNARD: Willy?

WILLY (*with a strong edge of resentment in his voice*): Yeah, he came to Boston. What about it?

BERNARD: Well, just that when he came back—I'll never forget this, it always mystifies me. Because I'd thought so well of Biff, even though he'd always taken advantage of me. I loved him, Willy, y'know? And he came back after that month and took his sneakers—remember those sneakers with "University of Virginia" printed on them? He was so proud of those, wore them every day. And he took them down in the cellar, and burned them up in the furnace. We had a fist fight. It lasted at least half an hour. Just the two of us, punching each other down the cellar, and crying right through it. I've often thought of how strange it was that I knew he'd given up his life. What happened in Boston, Willy?

*Willy looks at him as at an intruder.*

BERNARD: I just bring it up because you asked me.

WILLY (*angrily*): Nothing. What do you mean, "What happened?" What's that got to do with anything?

BERNARD: Well, don't get sore.

WILLY: What are you trying to do, blame it on me? If a boy lays down is that my fault?

BERNARD: Now, Willy, don't get . . .

WILLY: Well, don't—don't talk to me that way! What does that mean, "What happened?"

*Charley enters. He is in his vest, and he carries a bottle of bourbon.*

CHARLEY: Hey, you're going to miss that train. (*He waves the bottle.*)

BERNARD: Yeah, I'm going. (*He takes the bottle.*) Thanks, Pop. (*He picks up his rackets and bag.*) Good-by, Willy, and don't worry about it. You know, "If at first you don't succeed . . ."

**WILLY:** Yes, I believe in that.

**BERNARD:** But sometimes, Willy, it's better for a man just to walk away.

**WILLY:** Walk away?

**BERNARD:** That's right.

**WILLY:** But if you can't walk away?

**BERNARD** (*after a slight pause*): I guess that's when it's tough. (*Extending his hand.*) Good-by, Willy.

**WILLY** (*shaking Bernard's hand*): Good-by, boy.

**CHARLEY** (*an arm on Bernard's shoulder*): How do you like this kid? Gonna argue a case in front of the Supreme Court.

**BERNARD** (*protesting*): Pop!

**WILLY** (*genuinely shocked, pained, and happy*): No! The Supreme Court!

**BERNARD:** I gotta run. 'By, Dad!

**CHARLEY:** Knock 'em dead, Bernard!

*Bernard goes off.*

**WILLY** (*as Charley takes out his wallet*): The Supreme Court! And he didn't even mention it!

**CHARLEY** (*counting out money on the desk*): He don't have to—he's gonna do it.

**WILLY:** And you never told him what to do, did you? You never took any interest in him.

**CHARLEY:** My salvation is that I never took any interest in anything. There's some money—fifty dollars. I got an accountant inside.

**WILLY:** Charley, look . . . (*with difficulty.*) I got my insurance to pay. If you can manage it—I need a hundred and ten dollars.

*Charley doesn't reply for a moment; merely stops moving.*

**WILLY:** I'd draw it from my bank but Linda would know, and I . . .

**CHARLEY:** Sit down, Willy.

**WILLY** (*moving toward the chair*): I'm keeping an account of everything, remember. I'll pay every penny back. (*He sits.*)

**CHARLEY:** Now listen to me, Willy.

**WILLY:** I want you to know I appreciate . . .

**CHARLEY** (*sitting down on the table*):   Willy, what're you doin'? What the hell is going on in your head?

**WILLY:**   Why? I'm simply . . .

**CHARLEY:**   I offered you a job. You make fifty dollars a week. And I won't send you on the road.

**WILLY:**   I've got a job.

**CHARLEY:**   Without pay? What kind of a job is a job without pay? (*He rises.*) Now, look, kid, enough is enough. I'm no genius but I know when I'm being insulted.

**WILLY:**   Insulted!

**CHARLEY:**   Why don't you want to work for me?

**WILLY:**   What's the matter with you? I've got a job.

**CHARLEY:**   Then what're you walkin' in here every week for?

**WILLY** (*getting up*):   Well, if you don't want me to walk in here . . .

**CHARLEY:**   I'm offering you a job.

**WILLY:**   I don't want your goddam job!

**CHARLEY:**   When the hell are you going to grow up?

**WILLY** (*furiously*):   You big ignoramus, if you say that to me again I'll rap you one! I don't care how big you are! (*He's ready to fight.*)

*Pause.*

**CHARLEY** (*kindly, going to him*):   How much do you need, Willy?

**WILLY:**   Charley, I'm strapped. I'm strapped. I don't know what to do. I was just fired.

**CHARLEY:**   Howard fired you?

**WILLY:**   That snotnose. Imagine that? I named him. I named him Howard.

**CHARLEY:**   Willy, when're you gonna realize that them things don't mean anything? You named him Howard, but you can't sell that. The only thing you got in this world is what you can sell. And the funny thing is that you're a salesman, and you don't know that.

**WILLY:**   I've always tried to think otherwise, I guess. I always felt that if a man was impressive, and well liked, that nothing . . .

**CHARLEY:**   Why must everybody like you? Who liked J. P. Morgan? Was he impressive? In a Turkish bath he'd look like a butcher. But with his pockets on he was very well liked. Now listen, Willy, I know you don't like me, and nobody can say I'm in love with you, but I'll give you a job because—just for the hell of it, put it that way. Now what do you say?

**WILLY:** I—I just can't work for you, Charley.

**CHARLEY:** What're you, jealous of me?

**WILLY:** I can't work for you, that's all, don't ask me why.

**CHARLEY** (*angered, takes out more bills*): You been jealous of me all your life, you damned fool! Here, pay your insurance. (*He puts the money in Willy's hand.*)

**WILLY:** I'm keeping strict accounts.

**CHARLEY:** I've got some work to do. Take care of yourself. And pay your insurance.

**WILLY** (*moving to the right*): Funny, y'know? After all the highways, and the trains, and the appointments, and the years, you end up worth more dead than alive.

**CHARLEY:** Willy, nobody's worth nothin' dead. (*After a slight pause.*) Did you hear what I said?

*Willy stands still, dreaming.*

**CHARLEY:** Willy!

**WILLY:** Apologize to Bernard for me when you see him. I didn't mean to argue with him. He's a fine boy. They're all fine boys, and they'll end up big—all of them. Someday they'll all play tennis together. Wish me luck, Charley. He saw Bill Oliver today.

**CHARLEY:** Good luck.

**WILLY** (*on the verge of tears*): Charley, you're the only friend I got. Isn't that a remarkable thing? (*He goes out.*)

**CHARLEY:** Jesus!

*Charley stares after him a moment and follows. All light blacks out. Suddenly raucous music is heard, and a red glow rises behind the screen at right. Stanley, a young waiter, appears, carrying a table, followed by Happy, who is carrying two chairs.*

**STANLEY** (*putting the table down*): That's all right, Mr. Loman, I can handle it myself. (*He turns and takes the chairs from Happy and places them at the table.*)

**HAPPY** (*glancing around*): Oh, this is better.

**STANLEY:** Sure, in the front there you're in the middle of all kinds of noise. Whenever you got a party, Mr. Loman, you just tell me and I'll put you back here. Y'know, there's a lotta people they don't like it private, because when they go out they like to see a lotta action around them because they're sick and tired to stay in the house by theirself. But I know you, you ain't from Hackensack. You know what I mean?

**HAPPY** (*sitting down*): So how's it coming, Stanley?

**STANLEY:** Ah, it's a dog life. I only wish during the war they'd a took me in the Army. I coulda been dead by now.

**HAPPY:** My brother's back, Stanley.

**STANLEY:** Oh, he come back, heh? From the Far West.

**HAPPY:** Yeah, big cattle man, my brother, so treat him right. And my father's coming too.

**STANLEY:** Oh, your father too!

**HAPPY:** You got a couple of nice lobsters?

**STANLEY:** Hundred per cent, big.

**HAPPY:** I want them with the claws.

**STANLEY:** Don't worry, I don't give you no mice. (*Happy laughs.*) How about some wine? It'll put a head on the meal.

**HAPPY:** No. You remember, Stanley, that recipe I brought you from overseas? With the champagne in it?

**STANLEY:** Oh, yeah, sure. I still got it tacked up yet in the kitchen. But that'll have to cost a buck apiece anyways.

**HAPPY:** That's all right.

**STANLEY:** What'd you, hit a number or somethin'?

**HAPPY:** No, it's a little celebration. My brother is—I think he pulled off a big deal today. I think we're going into business together.

**STANLEY:** Great! That's the best for you. Because a family business, you know what I mean?—that's the best.

**HAPPY:** That's what I think.

**STANLEY:** 'Cause what's the difference? Somebody steals? It's in the family. Know what I mean? (*Sotto voce.*) Like this bartender here. The boss is goin' crazy what kinda leak he's got in the cash register. You put it in but it don't come out.

**HAPPY** (*raising his head*): Sh!

**STANLEY:** What?

**HAPPY:** You notice I wasn't lookin' right or left, was I?

**STANLEY:** No.

**HAPPY:** And my eyes are closed.

**STANLEY:** So what's the . . . ?

**HAPPY:** Strudel's comin'.

**STANLEY** (*catching on, looks around*):  Ah, no, there's no . . .

*He breaks off as a furred, lavishly dressed Girl enters and sits at the next table. Both follow her with their eyes.*

**STANLEY:**  Geez, how'd ya know?

**HAPPY:**  I got radar or something. (*Staring directly at her profile.*) Oooooooo . . . Stanley.

**STANLEY:**  I think that's for you, Mr. Loman.

**HAPPY:**  Look at that mouth. Oh, God. And the binoculars.

**STANLEY:**  Geez, you got a life, Mr. Loman.

**HAPPY:**  Wait on her.

**STANLEY** (*going to the Girl's table*):  Would you like a menu, ma'am?

**GIRL:**  I'm expecting someone, but I'd like a . . .

**HAPPY:**  Why don't you bring her—excuse me, miss, do you mind? I sell champagne, and I'd like you to try my brand. Bring her a champagne, Stanley.

**GIRL:**  That's awfully nice of you.

**HAPPY:**  Don't mention it. It's all company money. (*He laughs.*)

**GIRL:**  That's a charming product to be selling, isn't it?

**HAPPY:**  Oh, gets to be like everything else. Selling is selling, y'know.

**GIRL:**  I suppose.

**HAPPY:**  You don't happen to sell, do you?

**GIRL:**  No, I don't sell.

**HAPPY:**  Would you object to a compliment from a stranger? You ought to be on a magazine cover.

**GIRL** (*looking at him a little archly*):  I have been.

*Stanley comes in with a glass of champagne.*

**HAPPY:**  What'd I say before, Stanley? You see? She's a cover girl.

**STANLEY:**  Oh, I could see, I could see.

**HAPPY** (*to the Girl*):  What magazine?

**GIRL:**  Oh, a lot of them. (*She takes the drink.*) Thank you.

**HAPPY:**  You know what they say in France, don't you? "Champagne is the drink of the complexion"—Hya, Biff!

*Biff has entered and sits with Happy.*

**BIFF:**  Hello, kid. Sorry I'm late.

**HAPPY:**  I just got here. Uh, Miss . . . ?

**GIRL:**   Forsythe.

**HAPPY:**   Miss Forsythe, this is my brother.

**BIFF:**   Is Dad here?

**HAPPY:**   His name is Biff. You might've heard of him. Great football player.

**GIRL:**   Really? What team?

**HAPPY:**   Are you familiar with football?

**GIRL:**   No, I'm afraid I'm not.

**HAPPY:**   Biff is quarterback with the New York Giants.

**GIRL:**   Well, that is nice, isn't it? (*She drinks.*)

**HAPPY:**   Good health.

**GIRL:**   I'm happy to meet you.

**HAPPY:**   That's my name. Hap. It's really Harold, but at West Point they called me Happy.

**GIRL** (*now really impressed*):   Oh, I see. How do you do? (*She turns her profile.*)

**BIFF:**   Isn't Dad coming?

**HAPPY:**   You want her?

**BIFF:**   Oh, I could never make that.

**HAPPY:**   I remember the time that idea would never come into your head. Where's the old confidence, Biff?

**BIFF:**   I just saw Oliver . . .

**HAPPY:**   Wait a minute. I've got to see that old confidence again. Do you want her? She's on call.

**BIFF:**   Oh, no. (*He turns to look at the Girl.*)

**HAPPY:**   I'm telling you. Watch this. (*Turning to the Girl.*) Honey? (*She turns to him.*) Are you busy?

**GIRL:**   Well, I am . . . but I could make a phone call.

**HAPPY:**   Do that, will you, honey? And see if you can get a friend. We'll be here for a while. Biff is one of the greatest football players in the country.

**GIRL** (*standing up*):   Well, I'm certainly happy to meet you.

**HAPPY:**   Come back soon.

**GIRL:**   I'll try.

**HAPPY:**   Don't try, honey, try hard.

*The Girl exits. Stanley follows, shaking his head in bewildered admiration.*

**HAPPY:** Isn't that a shame now? A beautiful girl like that? That's why I can't get married. There's not a good woman in a thousand. New York is loaded with them, kid!

**BIFF:** Hap, look . . .

**HAPPY:** I told you she was on call!

**BIFF** (*strangely unnerved*): Cut it out, will ya? I want to say something to you.

**HAPPY:** Did you see Oliver?

**BIFF:** I saw him all right. Now look, I want to tell Dad a couple of things and I want you to help me.

**HAPPY:** What? Is he going to back you?

**BIFF:** Are you crazy? You're out of your goddam head, you know that?

**HAPPY:** Why? What happened?

**BIFF** (*breathlessly*): I did a terrible thing today, Hap. It's been the strangest day I ever went through. I'm all numb, I swear.

**HAPPY:** You mean he wouldn't see you?

**BIFF:** Well, I waited six hours for him, see? All day. Kept sending my name in. Even tried to date his secretary so she'd get me to him, but no soap.

**HAPPY:** Because you're not showin' the old confidence, Biff. He remembered you, didn't he?

**BIFF** (*stopping Happy with a gesture*): Finally, about five o'clock, he comes out. Didn't remember who I was or anything. I felt like such an idiot, Hap.

**HAPPY:** Did you tell him my Florida idea?

**BIFF:** He walked away. I saw him for one minute. I got so mad I could've torn the walls down! How the hell did I ever get the idea I was a salesman there? I even believed myself that I'd been a salesman for him! And then he gave me one look and—I realized what a ridiculous lie my whole life has been! We've been talking in a dream for fifteen years. I was a shipping clerk.

**HAPPY:** What'd you do?

**BIFF** (*with great tension and wonder*): Well, he left, see. And the secretary went out. I was all alone in the waiting room. I don't know what came over me, Hap. The next thing I know I'm in his office—paneled walls, everything. I can't explain it. I—Hap. I took his fountain pen.

**HAPPY:** Geez, did he catch you?

**BIFF:** I ran out. I ran down all eleven flights. I ran and ran and ran.

**HAPPY:** That was an awful dumb—what'd you do that for?

**BIFF** (*agonized*): I don't know, I just—wanted to take something, I don't know. You gotta help me, Hap. I'm gonna tell Pop.

**HAPPY:** You crazy? What for?

**BIFF:** Hap, he's got to understand that I'm not the man somebody lends that kind of money to. He thinks I've been spiting him all these years and it's eating him up.

**HAPPY:** That's just it. You tell him something nice.

**BIFF:** I can't.

**HAPPY:** Say you got a lunch date with Oliver tomorrow.

**BIFF:** So what do I do tomorrow?

**HAPPY:** You leave the house tomorrow and come back at night and say Oliver is thinking it over. And he thinks it over for a couple of weeks, and gradually it fades away and nobody's the worse.

**BIFF:** But it'll go on forever!

**HAPPY:** Dad is never so happy as when he's looking forward to something!

*Willy enters.*

**HAPPY:** Hello, scout!

**WILLY:** Gee, I haven't been here in years!

*Stanley has followed Willy in and sets a chair for him. Stanley starts off but Happy stops him.*

**HAPPY:** Stanley!

*Stanley stands by, waiting for an order.*

**BIFF** (*going to Willy with guilt, as to an invalid*): Sit down, Pop. You want a drink?

**WILLY:** Sure, I don't mind.

**BIFF:** Let's get a load on.

**WILLY:** You look worried.

**BIFF:** N-no. (*To Stanley.*) Scotch all around. Make it doubles.

**STANLEY:** Doubles, right. (*He goes.*)

**WILLY:** You had a couple already, didn't you?

**BIFF:** Just a couple, yeah.

**WILLY:** Well, what happened, boy? (*Nodding affirmatively, with a smile.*) Everything go all right?

**BIFF** (*takes a breath, then reaches out and grasps Willy's hand*): Pal . . . (*He is smiling bravely, and Willy is smiling too.*) I had an experience today.

**HAPPY:** Terrific, Pop.

**WILLY:** That so? What happened?

**BIFF** (*high, slightly alcoholic, above the earth*): I'm going to tell you everything from first to last. It's been a strange day. (*Silence. He looks around, composes himself as best he can, but his breath keeps breaking the rhythm of his voice.*) I had to wait quite a while for him, and . . .

**WILLY:** Oliver?

**BIFF:** Yeah, Oliver. All day, as a matter of cold fact. And a lot of— instances—facts, Pop, facts about my life came back to me. Who was it, Pop? Who ever said I was a salesman with Oliver?

**WILLY:** Well, you were.

**BIFF:** No, Dad, I was a shipping clerk.

**WILLY:** But you were practically . . .

**BIFF** (*with determination*): Dad, I don't know who said it first, but I was never a salesman for Bill Oliver.

**WILLY:** What're you talking about?

**BIFF:** Let's hold on to the facts tonight, Pop. We're not going to get anywhere bullin' around. I was a shipping clerk.

**WILLY** (*angrily*): All right, now listen to me . . .

**BIFF:** Why don't you let me finish?

**WILLY:** I'm not interested in stories about the past or any crap of that kind because the woods are burning, boys, you understand? There's a big blaze going on all around. I was fired today.

**BIFF** (*shocked*): How could you be?

**WILLY:** I was fired, and I'm looking for a little good news to tell your mother, because the woman has waited and the woman has suffered. The gist of it is that I haven't got a story left in my head, Biff. So don't give me a lecture about facts and aspects. I am not interested. Now what've you got to say to me?

*Stanley enters with three drinks. They wait until he leaves.*

**WILLY:** Did you see Oliver?

**BIFF:** Jesus, Dad!

**WILLY:** You mean you didn't go up there?

**HAPPY:** Sure he went up there.

**BIFF:** I did. I—saw him. How could they fire you?

**WILLY** (*on the edge of his chair*): What kind of a welcome did he give you?

**BIFF:** He won't even let you work on commission?

**WILLY:** I'm out! (*Driving.*) So tell me, he gave you a warm welcome?

**HAPPY:** Sure, Pop, sure!

**BIFF** (*driven*): Well, it was kind of . . .

**WILLY:** I was wondering if he'd remember you. (*To Happy.*) Imagine, man doesn't see him for ten, twelve years and gives him that kind of a welcome!

**HAPPY:** Damn right!

**BIFF** (*trying to return to the offensive*): Pop, look . . .

**WILLY:** You know why he remembered you, don't you? Because you impressed him in those days.

**BIFF:** Let's talk quietly and get this down to the facts, huh?

**WILLY** (*as though Biff had been interrupting*): Well, what happened? It's great news, Biff. Did he take you into his office or'd you talk in the waiting room?

**BIFF:** Well, he came in, see, and . . .

**WILLY** (*with a big smile*): What'd he say? Betcha he threw his arm around you.

**BIFF:** Well, he kinda . . .

**WILLY:** He's a fine man. (*To Happy.*) Very hard man to see, y'know.

**HAPPY** (*agreeing*): Oh, I know.

**WILLY** (*to Biff*): Is that where you had the drinks?

**BIFF:** Yeah, he gave me a couple of—no, no!

**HAPPY** (*cutting in*): He told him my Florida idea.

**WILLY:** Don't interrupt. (*To Biff.*) How'd he react to the Florida idea?

**BIFF:** Dad, will you give me a minute to explain?

**WILLY:** I've been waiting for you to explain since I sat down here! What happened? He took you into his office and what?

**BIFF:** Well—I talked. And—and he listened, see.

**WILLY:** Famous for the way he listens, y'know. What was his answer?

**BIFF:** His answer was—(*He breaks off, suddenly angry.*) Dad, you're not letting me tell you what I want to tell you!

**WILLY** (*accusing, angered*):   You didn't see him, did you?

**BIFF:**   I did see him!

**WILLY:**   What'd you insult him or something? You insulted him, didn't you?

**BIFF:**   Listen, will you let me out of it, will you just let me out of it!

**HAPPY:**   What the hell!

**WILLY:**   Tell me what happened!

**BIFF** (*to Happy*):   I can't talk to him!

*A single trumpet note jars the ear. The light of green leaves stains the house, which holds the air of night and a dream. Young Bernard enters and knocks on the door of the house.*

**YOUNG BERNARD** (*frantically*):   Mrs. Loman, Mrs. Loman!

**HAPPY:**   Tell him what happened!

**BIFF** (*to Happy.*):   Shut up and leave me alone!

**WILLY:**   No, no! You had to go and flunk math!

**BIFF:**   What math? What're you talking about?

**YOUNG BERNARD:**   Mrs. Loman, Mrs. Loman!

*Linda appears in the house, as of old.*

**WILLY** (*wildly*):   Math, math, math!

**BIFF:**   Take it easy, Pop!

**YOUNG BERNARD:**   Mrs. Loman!

**WILLY** (*furiously*):   If you hadn't flunked you'd've been set by now!

**BIFF:**   Now, look, I'm gonna tell you what happened, and you're going to listen to me.

**YOUNG BERNARD:**   Mrs. Loman!

**BIFF:**   I waited six hours . . .

**HAPPY:**   What the hell are you saying?

**BIFF:**   I kept sending in my name but he wouldn't see me. So finally he . . . (*He continues unheard as light fades low on the restaurant.*)

**YOUNG BERNARD:**   Biff flunked math!

**LINDA:**   No!

**YOUNG BERNARD:**   Birnbaum flunked him! They won't graduate him!

**LINDA:**   But they have to. He's gotta go to the university. Where is he? Biff! Biff!

**YOUNG BERNARD:**   No, he left. He went to Grand Central.

**LINDA:**   Grand—You mean he went to Boston!

**YOUNG BERNARD:** Is Uncle Willy in Boston?

**LINDA:** Oh, maybe Willy can talk to the teacher. Oh, the poor, poor boy!

*Light on house area snaps out.*

**BIFF** (*at the table, now audible, holding up a gold fountain pen*): . . . so I'm washed up with Oliver, you understand? Are you listening to me?

**WILLY** (*at a loss*): Yeah, sure. If you hadn't flunked . . .

**BIFF:** Flunked what? What're you talking about?

**WILLY:** Don't blame everything on me! I didn't flunk math—you did! What pen?

**HAPPY:** That was awful dumb, Biff, a pen like that is worth—

**WILLY** (*seeing the pen for the first time*): You took Oliver's pen?

**BIFF** (*weakening*): Dad, I just explained it to you.

**WILLY:** You stole Bill Oliver's fountain pen!

**BIFF:** I didn't exactly steal it! That's just what I've been explaining to you!

**HAPPY:** He had it in his hand and just then Oliver walked in, so he got nervous and stuck it in his pocket!

**WILLY:** My God, Biff!

**BIFF:** I never intended to do it, Dad!

**OPERATOR'S VOICE:** Standish Arms, good evening!

**WILLY** (*shouting*): I'm not in my room!

**BIFF** (*frightened*): Dad, what's the matter? (*He and Happy stand up.*)

**OPERATOR:** Ringing Mr. Loman for you!

**WILLY:** I'm not there, stop it!

**BIFF** (*horrified, gets down on one knee before Willy*): Dad, I'll make good, I'll make good. (*Willy tries to get to his feet. Biff holds him down.*) Sit down now.

**WILLY:** No, you're no good, you're no good for anything.

**BIFF:** I am, Dad, I'll find something else, you understand? Now don't worry about anything. (*He holds up Willy's face.*) Talk to me, Dad.

**OPERATOR:** Mr. Loman does not answer. Shall I page him?

**WILLY** (*attempting to stand, as though to rush and silence the Operator*): No, no, no!

**HAPPY:** He'll strike something, Pop.

**WILLY:** No, no . . .

**BIFF** (*desperately, standing over Willy*):   Pop, listen! Listen to me! I'm telling you something good. Oliver talked to his partner about the Florida idea. You listening? He—he talked to his partner, and he came to me . . . I'm going to be all right, you hear? Dad, listen to me, he said it was just a question of the amount!

**WILLY:**   Then you . . . got it?

**HAPPY:**   He's gonna be terrific, Pop!

**WILLY** (*trying to stand*):   Then you got it, haven't you? You got it! You got it!

**BIFF** (*agonized, holds Willy down*):   No, no. Look, Pop. I'm supposed to have lunch with them tomorrow. I'm just telling you this so you'll know that I can still make an impression, Pop. And I'll make good somewhere, but I can't go tomorrow, see.

**WILLY:**   Why not? You simply . . .

**BIFF:**   But the pen, Pop!

**WILLY:**   You give it to him and tell him it was an oversight!

**HAPPY:**   Sure, have lunch tomorrow!

**BIFF:**   I can't say that . . .

**WILLY:**   You were doing a crossword puzzle and accidentally used his pen!

**BIFF:**   Listen, kid, I took those balls years ago, now I walk in with his fountain pen? That clinches it, don't you see? I can't face him like that! I'll try elsewhere.

**PAGE'S VOICE:**   Paging Mr. Loman!

**WILLY:**   Don't you want to be anything?

**BIFF:**   Pop, how can I go back?

**WILLY:**   You don't want to be anything, is that what's behind it?

**BIFF** (*now angry at Willy for not crediting his sympathy*):   Don't take it that way! You think it was easy walking into that office after what I'd done to him? A team of horses couldn't have dragged me back to Bill Oliver!

**WILLY:**   Then why'd you go?

**BIFF:**   Why did I go? Why did I go! Look at you! Look at what's become of you!

*Off left, The Woman laughs.*

**WILLY:**   Biff, you're going to go to that lunch tomorrow, or . . .

**BIFF:**   I can't go. I've got no appointment!

**HAPPY:** Biff, for . . . !

**WILLY:** Are you spiting me?

**BIFF:** Don't take it that way! Goddammit!

**WILLY** (*strikes Biff and falters away from the table*): You rotten little louse! Are you spiting me?

**THE WOMAN:** Someone's at the door, Willy!

**BIFF:** I'm no good, can't you see what I am?

**HAPPY** (*separating them*): Hey, you're in a restaurant! Now cut it out, both of you! (*The girls enter.*) Hello, girls, sit down.

*The Woman laughs, off left.*

**MISS FORSYTHE:** I guess we might as well. This is Letta.

**THE WOMAN:** Willy, are you going to wake up?

**BIFF** (*ignoring Willy*): How're ya, miss, sit down. What do you drink?

**MISS FORSYTHE:** Letta might not be able to stay long.

**LETTA:** I gotta get up very early tomorrow. I got jury duty. I'm so excited! Were you fellows ever on a jury?

**BIFF:** No, but I been in front of them! (*The girls laugh.*) This is my father.

**LETTA:** Isn't he cute? Sit down with us, Pop.

**HAPPY:** Sit him down, Biff!

**BIFF** (*going to him*): Come on, slugger, drink us under the table. To hell with it! Come on, sit down, pal.

*On Biff's last insistence, Willy is about to sit.*

**THE WOMAN** (*now urgently*): Willy, are you going to answer the door!

*The Woman's call pulls Willy back. He starts right, befuddled.*

**BIFF:** Hey, where are you going?

**WILLY:** Open the door.

**BIFF:** The door?

**WILLY:** The washroom . . . the door . . . where's the door?

**BIFF** (*leading Willy to the left*): Just go straight down.

*Willy moves left.*

**THE WOMAN:** Willy, Willy, are you going to get up, get up, get up, get up?

*Willy exits left.*

**LETTA:** I think it's sweet you bring your daddy along.

**MISS FORSYTHE:** Oh, he isn't really your father!

**BIFF** (*at left, turning to her resentfully*): Miss Forsythe, you've just seen a prince walk by. A fine, troubled prince. A hardworking, unappreciated prince. A pal, you understand? A good companion. Always for his boys.

**LETTA:** That's so sweet.

**HAPPY:** Well, girls, what's the program? We're wasting time. Come on, Biff. Gather round. Where would you like to go?

**BIFF:** Why don't you do something for him?

**HAPPY:** Me!

**BIFF:** Don't you give a damn for him, Hap?

**HAPPY:** What're you talking about? I'm the one who . . .

**BIFF:** I sense it, you don't give a good goddam about him. (*He takes the rolled-up hose from his pocket and puts it on the table in front of Happy.*) Look what I found in the cellar, for Christ's sake. How can you bear to let it go on?

**HAPPY:** Me? Who goes away? Who runs off and . . .

**BIFF:** Yeah, but he doesn't mean anything to you. You could help him—I can't! Don't you understand what I'm talking about? He's going to kill himself, don't you know that?

**HAPPY:** Don't know it! Me!

**BIFF:** Hap, help him! Jesus . . . help him . . . Help me, help me, I can't bear to look at his face! (*Ready to weep, he hurries out, up right.*)

**HAPPY** (*starting after him*): Where are you going?

**MISS FORSYTHE:** What's he so mad about?

**HAPPY:** Come on, girls, we'll catch up with him.

**MISS FORSYTHE** (*as Happy pushes her out*): Say, I don't like that temper of his!

**HAPPY:** He's just a little overstrung, he'll be all right!

**WILLY** (*off left, as The Woman laughs*): Don't answer! Don't answer!

**LETTA:** Don't you want to tell your father . . .

**HAPPY:** No, that's not my father. He's just a guy. Come on, we'll catch Biff, and, honey, we're going to paint this town! Stanley, where's the check! Hey, Stanley!

*They exit. Stanley looks toward left.*

**STANLEY** (*calling to Happy indignantly*): Mr. Loman! Mr. Loman!

*Stanley picks up a chair and follows them off. Knocking is heard off left. The Woman enters, laughing. Willy follows her. She is in a black slip; he is buttoning his shirt. Raw, sensuous music accompanies their speech:*

**WILLY:** Will you stop laughing? Will you stop?

**THE WOMAN:** Aren't you going to answer the door? He'll wake the whole hotel.

**WILLY:** I'm not expecting anybody.

**THE WOMAN:** Whyn't you have another drink, honey, and stop being so damn self-centered?

**WILLY:** I'm so lonely.

**THE WOMAN:** You know you ruined me, Willy? From now on, whenever you come to the office, I'll see that you go right through to the buyers. No waiting at my desk any more, Willy. You ruined me.

**WILLY:** That's nice of you to say that.

**THE WOMAN:** Gee, you are self-centered! Why so sad? You are the saddest, self-centeredest soul I ever did see-saw. (*She laughs. He kisses her.*) Come on inside, drummer boy. It's silly to be dressing in the middle of the night. (*As knocking is heard.*) Aren't you going to answer the door?

**WILLY:** They're knocking on the wrong door.

**THE WOMAN:** But I felt the knocking. And he heard us talking in here. Maybe the hotel's on fire!

**WILLY** (*his terror rising*): It's a mistake.

**THE WOMAN:** Then tell him to go away!

**WILLY:** There's nobody there.

**THE WOMAN:** It's getting on my nerves, Willy. There's somebody standing out there and it's getting on my nerves!

**WILLY** (*pushing her away from him*): All right, stay in the bathroom here, and don't come out. I think there's a law in Massachusetts about it, so don't come out. It may be that new room clerk. He looked very mean. So don't come out. It's a mistake, there's no fire.

*The knocking is heard again. He takes a few steps away from her, and she vanishes into the wing. The light follows him, and now he is facing Young Biff, who carries a suitcase. Biff steps toward him. The music is gone.*

**BIFF:** Why didn't you answer?

**WILLY:** Biff! What are you doing in Boston?

**BIFF:** Why didn't you answer? I've been knocking for five minutes, I called you on the phone . . .

**WILLY:** I just heard you. I was in the bathroom and had the door shut. Did anything happen home?

**BIFF:** Dad—I let you down.

**WILLY:** What do you mean?

**BIFF:** Dad . . .

**WILLY:** Biffo, what's this about? (*Putting his arm around Biff.*) Come on, let's go downstairs and get you a malted.

**BIFF:** Dad, I flunked math.

**WILLY:** Not for the term?

**BIFF:** The term. I haven't got enough credits to graduate.

**WILLY:** You mean to say Bernard wouldn't give you the answers?

**BIFF:** He did, he tried, but I only got a sixty-one.

**WILLY:** And they wouldn't give you four points?

**BIFF:** Birnbaum refused absolutely. I begged him, Pop, but he won't give me those points. You gotta talk to him before they close the school. Because if he saw the kind of man you are, and you just talked to him in your way, I'm sure he'd come through for me. The class came right before practice, see, and I didn't go enough. Would you talk to him? He'd like you, Pop. You know the way you could talk.

**WILLY:** You're on. We'll drive right back.

**BIFF:** Oh, Dad, good work! I'm sure he'll change it for you!

**WILLY:** Go downstairs and tell the clerk I'm checkin' out. Go right down.

**BIFF:** Yes, sir! See, the reason he hates me, Pop—one day he was late for class so I got up at the blackboard and imitated him. I crossed my eyes and talked with a lithp.

**WILLY** (*laughing*): You did? The kids like it?

**BIFF:** They nearly died laughing!

**WILLY:** Yeah? What'd you do?

**BIFF:** The thquare root of thixthy twee is . . . (*Willy bursts out laughing; Biff joins.*) And in the middle of it he walked in!

*Willy laughs and The Woman joins in offstage.*

**WILLY** (*without hesitation*): Hurry downstairs and . . .
**BIFF:** Somebody in there?
**WILLY:** No, that was next door.

*The Woman laughs offstage.*

**BIFF:** Somebody got in your bathroom!
**WILLY:** No, it's the next room, there's a party . . .
**THE WOMAN** (*enters, laughing; she lisps this*): Can I come in? There's something in the bathtub, Willy, and it's moving!

*Willy looks at Biff; who is staring open-mouthed and horrified at The Woman.*

**WILLY:** Ah—you better go back to your room. They must be finished painting by now. They're painting her room so I let her take a shower here. Go back, go back . . . (*He pushes her.*)
**THE WOMAN** (*resisting*): But I've got to get dressed, Willy, I can't . . .
**WILLY:** Get out of here! Go back, go back . . . (*Suddenly striving for the ordinary.*) This is Miss Francis, Biff, she's a buyer. They're painting her room. Go back, Miss Francis, go back . . .
**THE WOMAN:** But my clothes, I can't go out naked in the hall!
**WILLY** (*pushing her offstage*): Get outa here! Go back, go back!

*Biff slowly sits down on his suitcase as the argument continues offstage.*

**THE WOMAN:** Where's my stockings? You promised me stockings, Willy!
**WILLY:** I have no stockings here!
**THE WOMAN:** You had two boxes of size nine sheers for me, and I want them!
**WILLY:** Here, for God's sake, will you get outa here!
**THE WOMAN** (*enters holding a box of stockings*): I just hope there's nobody in the hall. That's all I hope. (*To Biff.*) Are you football or baseball?

**BIFF:** Football.

**THE WOMAN** (*angry, humiliated*): That's me too. G'night. (*She snatches her clothes from Willy, and walks out.*)

**WILLY** (*after a pause*): Well, better get going. I want to get to the school first thing in the morning. Get my suits out of the closet. I'll get my valise. (*Biff doesn't move.*) What's the matter! (*Biff remains motionless, tears falling.*) She's a buyer. Buys for J. H. Simmons. She lives down the hall—they're painting. You don't imagine—(*He breaks off. After a pause.*) Now listen, pal, she's just a buyer. She sells merchandise in her room and they have to keep it looking just so . . . (*Pause. Assuming command.*) All right, get my suits. (*Biff doesn't move.*) Now stop crying and do as I say. I gave you an order. Biff, I gave you an order! Is that what you do when I give you an order? How dare you cry! (*Putting his arm around Biff.*) Now look, Biff, when you grow up you'll understand about these things. You mustn't—you mustn't overemphasize a thing like this. I'll see Birnbaum first thing in the morning.

**BIFF:** Never mind.

**WILLY** (*getting down beside Biff*): Never mind! He's going to give you those points. I'll see to it.

**BIFF:** He wouldn't listen to you.

**WILLY:** He certainly will listen to me. You need those points for the U. of Virginia.

**BIFF:** I'm not going there.

**WILLY:** Heh? If I can't get him to change that mark you'll make it up in summer school. You've got all summer to . . .

**BIFF** (*his weeping breaking from him*): Dad . . .

**WILLY** (*infected by it*): Oh, my boy . . .

**BIFF:** Dad . . .

**WILLY:** She's nothing to me, Biff. I was lonely, I was terribly lonely.

**BIFF:** You—you gave her Mama's stockings! (*His tears break through and he rises to go.*)

**WILLY** (*grabbing for Biff*): I gave you an order!

**BIFF:** Don't touch me, you—liar!

**WILLY:** Apologize for that!

**BIFF:** You fake! You phony little fake! You fake! (*Overcome, he turns quickly and weeping fully goes out with his suitcase. Willy is left on the floor on his knees.*)

**WILLY:** I gave you an order! Biff, come back here or I'll beat you! Come back here! I'll whip you!

*Stanley comes quickly in from the right and stands in front of Willy.*

**WILLY** (*shouts at Stanley*): I gave you an order . . .

**STANLEY:** Hey, let's pick it up, pick it up, Mr. Loman. (*He helps Willy to his feet.*) Your boys left with the chippies. They said they'll see you home.

*A second waiter watches some distance away.*

**WILLY:** But we were supposed to have dinner together.

*Music is heard, Willy's theme.*

**STANLEY:** Can you make it?

**WILLY:** I'll—sure, I can make it. (*Suddenly concerned about his clothes.*) Do I—I look all right?

**STANLEY:** Sure, you look all right. (*He flicks a speck off Willy's lapel.*)

**WILLY:** Here—here's a dollar.

**STANLEY:** Oh, your son paid me. It's all right.

**WILLY** (*putting it in Stanley's hand*): No, take it. You're a good boy.

**STANLEY:** Oh, no, you don't have to . . .

**WILLY:** Here—here's some more, I don't need it any more. (*After a slight pause.*) Tell me—is there a seed store in the neighborhood?

**STANLEY:** Seeds? You mean like to plant?

*As Willy turns, Stanley slips the money back into his jacket pocket.*

**WILLY:** Yes. Carrots, peas . . .

**STANLEY:** Well, there's hardware stores on Sixth Avenue, but it may be too late now.

**WILLY** (*anxiously*): Oh, I'd better hurry. I've got to get some seeds. (*He starts off to the right.*) I've got to get some seeds, right away. Nothing's planted. I don't have a thing in the ground.

*Willy hurries out as the light goes down. Stanley moves over to the right after him, watches him off. The other waiter has been staring at Willy.*

**STANLEY** (*to the waiter*): Well, whatta you looking at?

*The waiter picks up the chairs and moves off right. Stanley takes the table and follows him. The light fades on this area. There is a long pause, the sound of the flute coming over. The light gradually rises on the kitchen, which is empty. Happy appears at the door of the house, followed by Biff. Happy is carrying a large bunch of long-stemmed roses. He enters the kitchen, looks around for Linda. Not seeing her, he turns to Biff, who is just outside the house door, and makes a gesture with his hands, indicating "Not here, I guess." He looks into the living room and freezes. Inside, Linda, unseen, is seated, Willy's coat on her lap. She rises ominously and quietly and moves toward Happy, who backs up into the kitchen, afraid.*

HAPPY: Hey, what're you doing up? (*Linda says nothing but moves toward him implacably.*) Where's Pop? (*He keeps backing to the right, and now Linda is in full view in the doorway to the living room.*) Is he sleeping?

LINDA: Where were you?

HAPPY (*trying to laugh it off*): We met two girls, Mom, very fine types. Here, we brought you some flowers. (*Offering them to her.*) Put them in your room, Ma.

*She knocks them to the floor at Biff's feet. He has now come inside and closed the door behind him. She stares at Biff, silent.*

HAPPY: Now what'd you do that for? Mom, I want you to have some flowers . . .

LINDA (*cutting Happy off, violently to Biff*): Don't you care whether he lives or dies?

HAPPY (*going to the stairs*): Come upstairs, Biff.

BIFF (*with a flare of disgust, to Happy*): Go away from me! (*To Linda.*) What do you mean, lives or dies? Nobody's dying around here, pal.

LINDA: Get out of my sight! Get out of here!

BIFF: I wanna see the boss.

LINDA: You're not going near him!

BIFF: Where is he? (*He moves into the living room and Linda follows.*)

LINDA (*shouting after Biff.*): You invite him for dinner. He looks forward to it all day—(*Biff appears in his parents' bedroom, looks around, and exits)*—and then you desert him there. There's no stranger you'd do that to!

HAPPY: Why? He had a swell time with us. Listen, when I—(*Linda comes back into the kitchen*)—desert him I hope I don't outlive the day!

LINDA: Get out of here!

HAPPY: Now look, Mom . . .

LINDA: Did you have to go to women tonight? You and your lousy rotten whores!

*Biff re-enters the kitchen.*

HAPPY: Mom, all we did was follow Biff around trying to cheer him up! (*To Biff.*) Boy, what a night you gave me!

LINDA: Get out of here, both of you, and don't come back! I don't want you tormenting him any more. Go on now, get your things together! (*To Biff.*) You can sleep in his apartment. (*She starts to pick up the flowers and stops herself.*) Pick up this stuff, I'm not your maid any more. Pick it up, you bum, you!

*Happy turns his back to her in refusal. Biff slowly moves over and gets down on his knees, picking up the flowers.*

LINDA: You're a pair of animals! Not one, not another living soul would have had the cruelty to walk out on that man in a restaurant!

BIFF (*not looking at her*): Is that what he said?

LINDA: He didn't have to say anything. He was so humiliated he nearly limped when he came in.

HAPPY: But, Mom, he had a great time with us . . .

BIFF (*cutting him off violently*): Shut up!

*Without another word, Happy goes upstairs.*

LINDA: You! You didn't even go in to see if he was all right!

BIFF (*still on the floor in front of Linda, the flowers in his hand; with self-loathing*): No. Didn't. Didn't do a damned thing. How do you like that, heh? Left him babbling in a toilet.

LINDA: You louse. You . . .

BIFF: Now you hit it on the nose! (*He gets up, throws the flowers in the wastebasket.*) The scum of the earth, and you're looking at him!

**LINDA:**   Get out of here!

**BIFF:**   I gotta talk to the boss, Mom. Where is he?

**LINDA:**   You're not going near him. Get out of this house!

**BIFF** (*with absolute assurance, determination*):   No. We're gonna have an abrupt conversation, him and me.

**LINDA:**   You're not talking to him.

*Hammering is heard from outside the house, off right. Biff turns toward the noise.*

**LINDA** (*suddenly pleading*):   Will you please leave him alone?

**BIFF:**   What's he doing out there?

**LINDA:**   He's planting the garden!

**BIFF** (*quietly*):   Now? Oh, my God!

*Biff moves outside, Linda following. The light dies down on them and comes up on the center of the apron as Willy walks into it. He is carrying a flashlight, a hoe, and a handful of seed packets. He raps the top of the hoe sharply to fix it firmly, and then moves to the left, measuring off the distance with his foot. He holds the flashlight to look at the seed packets, reading off the instructions. He is in the blue of night.*

**WILLY:**   Carrots . . . quarter-inch apart. Rows . . . one-foot rows. (*He measures it off.*) One foot. (*He puts down a package and measures off.*) Beets. (*He puts down another package and measures again.*) Lettuce. (*He reads the package, puts it down.*) One foot—(*He breaks off as Ben appears at the right and moves slowly down to him.*) What a proposition, ts, ts. Terrific, terrific. 'Cause she's suffered, Ben, the woman has suffered. You understand me? A man can't go out the way he came in, Ben, a man has got to add up to something. You can't, you can't—(*Ben moves toward him as though to interrupt.*) You gotta consider now. Don't answer so quick. Remember, it's a guaranteed twenty-thousand-dollar proposition. Now look, Ben, I want you to go through the ins and outs of this thing with me. I've got nobody to talk to, Ben, and the woman has suffered, you hear me?

**BEN** (*standing still, considering*):   What's the proposition?

**WILLY:** It's twenty thousand dollars on the barrelhead. Guaranteed, gilt-edged, you understand?

**BEN:** You don't want to make a fool of yourself. They might not honor the policy.

**WILLY:** How can they dare refuse? Didn't I work like a coolie to meet every premium on the nose? And now they don't pay off? Impossible!

**BEN:** It's called a cowardly thing, William.

**WILLY:** Why? Does it take more guts to stand here the rest of my life ringing up a zero?

**BEN** (*yielding*): That's a point, William. (*He moves, thinking, turns.*) And twenty thousand—that is something one can feel with the hand, it is there.

**WILLY** (*now assured, with rising power*): Oh, Ben, that's the whole beauty of it! I see it like a diamond, shining in the dark, hard and rough, that I can pick up and touch in my hand. Not like—like an appointment! This would not be another damned-fool appointment, Ben, and it changes all the aspects. Because he thinks I'm nothing, see, and so he spites me. But the funeral . . . (*Straightening up.*) Ben, that funeral will be massive! They'll come from Maine, Massachusetts, Vermont, New Hampshire! All the old-timers with the strange license plates—that boy will be thunderstruck, Ben, because he never realized—I am known! Rhode Island, New York, New Jersey—I am known, Ben, and he'll see it with his eyes once and for all. He'll see what I am, Ben! He's in for a shock, that boy!

**BEN** (*coming down to the edge of the garden*): He'll call you a coward.

**WILLY** (*suddenly fearful*): No, that would be terrible.

**BEN:** Yes. And a damned fool.

**WILLY:** No, no, he mustn't, I won't have that! (*He is broken and desperate.*)

**BEN:** He'll hate you, William.

*The gay music of the Boys is heard.*

**WILLY:** Oh, Ben, how do we get back to all the great times? Used to be so full of light, and comradeship, the sleigh-riding in winter, and the ruddiness on his cheeks. And always some kind of good news coming up, always something nice coming up ahead. And never

even let me carry the valises in the house, and simonizing, simonizing that little red car! Why, why can't I give him something and not
have him hate me?

**BEN:** Let me think about it. (*He glances at his watch.*) I still have a
little time. Remarkable proposition, but you've got to be sure you're
not making a fool of yourself.

*Ben drifts off upstage and goes out of sight. Biff comes down from
the left.*

**WILLY** (*suddenly conscious of Biff, turns and looks up at him, then
begins picking up the packages of seeds in confusion*): Where the
hell is that seed? (*Indignantly.*) You can't see nothing out here!
They boxed in the whole goddam neighborhood!

**BIFF:** There are people all around here. Don't you realize that?

**WILLY:** I'm busy. Don't bother me.

**BIFF** (*taking the hoe from Willy*): I'm saying good-by to you, Pop. (*Willy
looks at him, silent, unable to move.*) I'm not coming back any more.

**WILLY:** You're not going to see Oliver tomorrow?

**BIFF:** I've got no appointment, Dad.

**WILLY:** He put his arm around you, and you've got no appointment?

**BIFF:** Pop, get this now, will you? Everytime I've left it's been a—fight
that sent me out of here. Today I realized something about myself
and I tried to explain it to you and I—I think I'm just not smart
enough to make any sense out of it for you. To hell with whose fault it
is or anything like that. (*He takes Willy's arm.*) Let's just wrap it up,
heh? Come on in, we'll tell Mom. (*He gently tries to pull Willy to left.*)

**WILLY** (*frozen, immobile, with guilt in his voice*): No, I don't want to
see her.

**BIFF:** Come on! (*He pulls again, and Willy tries to pull away.*)

**WILLY** (*highly nervous*): No, no, I don't want to see her.

**BIFF** (*tries to look into Willy's face, as if to find the answer there*):
Why don't you want to see her?

**WILLY** (*more harshly now*): Don't bother me, will you?

**BIFF:** What do you mean, you don't want to see her? You don't want
them calling you yellow, do you? This isn't your fault; it's me, I'm a
bum. Now come inside! (*Willy strains to get away.*) Did you hear
what I said to you?

*Willy pulls away and quickly goes by himself into the house. Biff follows.*

**LINDA** (*to Willy*):   Did you plant, dear?

**BIFF** (*at the door, to Linda*):   All right, we had it out. I'm going and I'm not writing any more.

**LINDA** (*going to Willy in the kitchen*):   I think that's the best way, dear. 'Cause there's no use drawing it out, you'll just never get along.

*Willy doesn't respond.*

**BIFF:**   People ask where I am and what I'm doing, you don't know, and you don't care. That way it'll be off your mind and you can start brightening up again. All right? That clears it, doesn't it? (*Willy is silent, and Biff goes to him.*) You gonna wish me luck, scout? (*He extends his hand.*) What do you say?

**LINDA:**   Shake his hand, Willy.

**WILLY** (*turning to her, seething with hurt*):   There's no necessity—to mention the pen at all, y'know.

**BIFF** (*gently*):   I've got no appointment, Dad.

**WILLY** (*erupting fiercely*):   He put his arm around . . . ?

**BIFF:**   Dad, you're never going to see what I am, so what's the use of arguing? If I strike oil I'll send you a check. Meantime forget I'm alive.

**WILLY** (*to Linda*):   Spite, see?

**BIFF:**   Shake hands, Dad.

**WILLY:**   Not my hand.

**BIFF:**   I was hoping not to go this way.

**WILLY:**   Well, this is the way you're going. Good-by.

*Biff looks at him a moment, then turns sharply and goes to the stairs.*

**WILLY** (*stops him with*):   May you rot in hell if you leave this house!

**BIFF** (*turning*):   Exactly what is it that you want from me?

**WILLY:**   I want you to know, on the train, in the mountains, in the valleys, wherever you go, that you cut down your life for spite!

**BIFF:**   No, no.

**WILLY:**   Spite, spite, is the word of your undoing! And when you're down and out, remember what did it. When you're rotting somewhere beside the railroad tracks, remember, and don't you dare blame it on me!

**BIFF:** I'm not blaming it on you!

**WILLY:** I won't take the rap for this, you hear?

*Happy comes down the stairs and stands on the bottom step, watching.*

**BIFF:** That's just what I'm telling you!

**WILLY** (*sinking into a chair at a table, with full accusation*): You're trying to put a knife in me—don't think I don't know what you're doing!

**BIFF:** All right, phony! Then let's lay it on the line. (*He whips the rubber tube out of his pocket and puts it on the table.*)

**HAPPY:** You crazy . . .

**LINDA:** Biff! (*She moves to grab the hose, but Biff holds it down with his hand.*)

**BIFF:** Leave it there! Don't move it!

**WILLY** (*not looking at it*): What is that?

**BIFF:** You know goddam well what that is.

**WILLY** (*caged, wanting to escape*): I never saw that.

**BIFF:** You saw it. The mice didn't bring it into the cellar! What is this supposed to do, make a hero out of you? This supposed to make me sorry for you?

**WILLY:** Never heard of it.

**BIFF:** There'll be no pity for you, you hear it? No pity!

**WILLY** (*to Linda*): You hear the spite!

**BIFF:** No, you're going to hear the truth—what you are and what I am!

**LINDA:** Stop it!

**WILLY:** Spite!

**HAPPY** (*coming down toward Biff*): You cut it now!

**BIFF** (*to Happy*): The man don't know who we are! The man is gonna know! (*To Willy.*) We never told the truth for ten minutes in this house!

**HAPPY:** We always told the truth!

**BIFF** (*turning on him*): You big blow, are you the assistant buyer? You're one of the two assistants to the assistant, aren't you?

**HAPPY:** Well, I'm practically . . .

**BIFF:**  You're practically full of it! We all are! and I'm through with it. (*To Willy.*) Now hear this, Willy, this is me.

**WILLY:**  I know you!

**BIFF:**  You know why I had no address for three months? I stole a suit in Kansas City and I was in jail. (*To Linda, who is sobbing.*) Stop crying. I'm through with it.

*Linda turns away from them, her hands covering her face.*

**WILLY:**  I suppose that's my fault!

**BIFF:**  I stole myself out of every good job since high school!

**WILLY:**  And whose fault is that?

**BIFF:**  And I never got anywhere because you blew me so full of hot air I could never stand taking orders from anybody! That's whose fault it is!

**WILLY:**  I hear that!

**LINDA:**  Don't, Biff!

**BIFF:**  It's goddam time you heard that! I had to be boss big shot in two weeks, and I'm through with it!

**WILLY:**  Then hang yourself! For spite, hang yourself!

**BIFF:**  No! Nobody's hanging himself, Willy! I ran down eleven flights with a pen in my hand today. And suddenly I stopped, you hear me? And in the middle of that office building, do you hear this? I stopped in the middle of that building and I saw—the sky. I saw the things that I love in this world. The work and the food and time to sit and smoke. And I looked at the pen and said to myself, what the hell am I grabbing this for? Why am I trying to become what I don't want to be? What am I doing in an office, making a contemptuous, begging fool of myself, when all I want is out there, waiting for me the minute I say I know who I am! Why can't I say that, Willy? (*He tries to make Willy face him, but Willy pulls away and moves to the left.*)

**WILLY** (*with hatred, threateningly*):  The door of your life is wide open!

**BIFF:**  Pop! I'm a dime a dozen, and so are you!

**WILLY** (*turning on him now in an uncontrolled outburst*):  I am not a dime a dozen! I am Willy Loman, and you are Biff Loman!

*Biff starts for Willy, but is blocked by Happy. In his fury, Biff seems on the verge of attacking his father.*

**BIFF:** I am not a leader of men, Willy, and neither are you. You were never anything but a hard-working drummer who landed in the ash can like all the rest of them! I'm one dollar an hour, Willy! I tried seven states and couldn't raise it. A buck an hour! Do you gather my meaning? I'm not bringing home any prizes any more, and you're going to stop waiting for me to bring them home!

**WILLY** (*directly to Biff*): You vengeful, spiteful mutt!

*Biff breaks from Happy. Willy, in fright, starts up the stairs. Biff grabs him.*

**BIFF** (*at the peak of his fury*): Pop! I'm nothing! I'm nothing, Pop. Can't you understand that? There's no spite in it any more. I'm just what I am, that's all.

*Biff's fury has spent itself and he breaks down, sobbing, holding on to Willy, who dumbly fumbles for Biff's face.*

**WILLY** (*astonished*): What're you doing? What're you doing? (*To Linda.*) Why is he crying?

**BIFF** (*crying, broken*): Will you let me go, for Christ's sake? Will you take that phony dream and burn it before something happens? (*Struggling to contain himself, he pulls away and moves to the stairs.*) I'll go in the morning. Put him—put him to bed. (*Exhausted, Biff moves up the stairs to his room.*)

**WILLY** (*after a long pause, astonished, elevated*): Isn't that—isn't that remarkable? Biff—he likes me!

**LINDA:** He loves you, Willy!

**HAPPY** (*deeply moved*): Always did, Pop.

**WILLY:** Oh, Biff! (*Staring wildly.*) He cried! Cried to me. (*He is choking with his love, and now cries out his promise.*) That boy—that boy is going to be magnificent!

*Ben appears in the light just outside the kitchen.*

**BEN:** Yes, outstanding, with twenty thousand behind him.

**LINDA** (*sensing the racing of his mind, fearfully, carefully*): Now come to bed, Willy. It's all settled now.

**WILLY** (*finding it difficult not to rush out of the house*):   Yes, we'll sleep. Come on. Go to sleep, Hap.

**BEN:**   And it does take a great kind of a man to crack the jungle.

*In accents of dread, Ben's idyllic music starts up.*

**HAPPY** (*his arm around Linda*):   I'm getting married, Pop, don't forget it. I'm changing everything. I'm gonna run that department before the year is up. You'll see, Mom. (*He kisses her.*)

**BEN:**   The jungle is dark but full of diamonds, Willy.

*Willy turns, moves, listening to Ben.*

**LINDA:**   Be good. You're both good boys, just act that way, that's all.

**HAPPY:**   'Night, Pop. (*He goes upstairs.*)

**LINDA** (*to Willy*):   Come, dear.

**BEN** (*with greater force*):   One must go in to fetch a diamond out.

**WILLY** (*to Linda, as he moves slowly along the edge of the kitchen, toward the door*):   I just want to get settled down, Linda. Let me sit alone for a little.

**LINDA** (*almost uttering her fear*):   I want you upstairs.

**WILLY** (*taking her in his arms*):   In a few minutes, Linda. I couldn't sleep right now. Go on, you look awful tired. (*He kisses her.*)

**BEN:**   Not like an appointment at all. A diamond is rough and hard to the touch.

**WILLY:**   Go on now. I'll be right up.

**LINDA:**   I think this is the only way, Willy.

**WILLY:**   Sure, it's the best thing.

**BEN:**   Best thing!

**WILLY:**   The only way. Everything is gonna be—go on, kid, get to bed. You look so tired.

**LINDA:**   Come right up.

**WILLY:**   Two minutes.

*Linda goes into the living room, then reappears in her bedroom. Willy moves just outside the kitchen door.*

**WILLY:**   Loves me. (*Wonderingly.*) Always loved me. Isn't that a remarkable thing? Ben, he'll worship me for it!

**BEN** (*with promise*):   It's dark there, but full of diamonds.

**WILLY:**   Can you imagine that magnificence with twenty thousand dollars in his pocket?

**LINDA** (*calling from her room*):   Willy! Come up!

**WILLY** (*calling into the kitchen*):   Yes! Yes. Coming! It's very smart, you realize that, don't you, sweetheart? Even Ben sees it. I gotta go, baby. 'By! 'By! (*Going over to Ben, almost dancing.*) Imagine? When the mail comes he'll be ahead of Bernard again!

**BEN:**   A perfect proposition all around.

**WILLY:**   Did you see how he cried to me? Oh, if I could kiss him, Ben!

**BEN:**   Time, William, time!

**WILLY:**   Oh, Ben, I always knew one way or another we were gonna make it, Biff and I.

**BEN** (*looking at his watch*):   The boat. We'll be late. (*He moves slowly off into the darkness.*)

**WILLY** (*elegiacally, turning to the house*):   Now when you kick off, boy, I want a seventy-yard boot, and get right down the field under the ball, and when you hit, hit low and hit hard, because it's important, boy. (*He swings around and faces the audience.*) There's all kinds of important people in the stands, and the first thing you know . . . (*Suddenly realizing he is alone.*) Ben! Ben, where do I . . . ? (*He makes a sudden movement of search.*) Ben, how do I . . . ?

**LINDA** (*calling*):   Willy, you coming up?

**WILLY** (*uttering a gasp of fear, whirling about as if to quiet her*):   Sh! (*He turns around as if to find his way; sounds, faces, voices, seem to be swarming in upon him and he flicks at them, crying.*) Sh! Sh! (*Suddenly music, faint and high, stops him. It rises in intensity, almost to an unbearable scream. He goes up and down on his toes, and rushes off around the house.*) Shhh!

**LINDA:**   Willy?

*There is no answer. Linda waits. Biff gets up off his bed. He is still in his clothes. Happy sits up. Biff stands listening.*

**LINDA** (*with real fear*):   Willy, answer me! Willy!

*There is the sound of a car starting and moving away at full speed.*

**LINDA:**   No!

**BIFF** (*rushing down the stairs*):   Pop!

*As the car speeds off the music crashes down in a frenzy of sound, which becomes the soft pulsation of a single cello string. Biff slowly returns to his bedroom. He and Happy gravely don their jackets. Linda slowly walks out of her room. The music has developed into a dead march. The leaves of day are appearing over everything. Charley and Bernard, somberly dressed, appear and knock on the kitchen door. Biff and Happy slowly descend the stairs to the kitchen as Charley and Bernard enter. All stop a moment when Linda, in clothes of mourning, bearing a little bunch of roses, comes through the draped doorway into the kitchen. She goes to Charley and takes his arm. Now all move toward the audience, through the wall-line of the kitchen. At the limit of the apron, Linda lays down the flowers, kneels, and sits back on her heels. All stare down at the grave.*

## REQUIEM

**CHARLEY:**   It's getting dark, Linda.

*Linda doesn't react. She stares at the grave.*

**BIFF:**   How about it, Mom? Better get some rest, heh? They'll be closing the gate soon.

*Linda makes no move. Pause.*

**HAPPY** (*deeply angered*):   He had no right to do that. There was no necessity for it. We would've helped him.

**CHARLEY** (*grunting*):   Hmmm.

**BIFF:**   Come along, Mom.

**LINDA:**   Why didn't anybody come?

**CHARLEY:**   It was a very nice funeral.

**LINDA:**   But where are all the people he knew? Maybe they blame him.

**CHARLEY:**   Naa. It's a rough world, Linda. They wouldn't blame him.

**LINDA:**   I can't understand it. At this time especially. First time in thirty-five years we were just about free and clear. He only needed a little salary. He was even finished with the dentist.

**CHARLEY:**   No man only needs a little salary.

**LINDA:** I can't understand it.

**BIFF:** There were a lot of nice days. When he'd come home from a trip; or on Sundays, making the stoop; finishing the cellar; putting on the new porch; when he built the extra bathroom; and put up the garage. You know something, Charley, there's more of him in that front stoop than in all the sales he ever made.

**CHARLEY:** Yeah. He was a happy man with a batch of cement.

**LINDA:** He was so wonderful with his hands.

**BIFF:** He had the wrong dreams. All, all, wrong.

**HAPPY** (*almost ready to fight Biff*): Don't say that!

**BIFF:** He never knew who he was.

**CHARLEY** (*stopping Happy's movement and reply; to Biff*): Nobody dast blame this man. You don't understand: Willy was a salesman. And for a salesman, there is no rock bottom to the life. He don't put a bolt to a nut, he don't tell you the law or give you medicine. He's a man way out there in the blue, riding on a smile and a shoeshine. And when they start not smiling back—that's an earthquake. And then you get yourself a couple of spots on your hat, and you're finished. Nobody dast blame this man. A salesman is got to dream, boy. It comes with the territory.

**BIFF:** Charley, the man didn't know who he was.

**HAPPY** (*infuriated*): Don't say that!

**BIFF:** Why don't you come with me, Happy?

**HAPPY:** I'm not licked that easily. I'm staying right in this city, and I'm gonna beat this racket! (*He looks at Biff, his chin set.*) The Loman Brothers!

**BIFF:** I know who I am, kid.

**HAPPY:** All right, boy. I'm gonna show you and everybody else that Willy Loman did not die in vain. He had a good dream. It's the only dream you can have—to come out number-one man. He fought it out here, and this is where I'm gonna win it for him.

**BIFF** (*with a hopeless glance at Happy, bends toward his mother*): Let's go, Mom.

**LINDA:** I'll be with you in a minute. Go on, Charley. (*He hesitates.*) I want to, just for a minute. I never had a chance to say good-by.

*Charley moves away, followed by Happy. Biff remains a slight distance up and left of Linda. She sits there, summoning herself. The flute begins, not far away, playing behind her speech.*

**LINDA:** Forgive me, dear. I can't cry. I don't know what it is, but I can't cry. I don't understand it. Why did you ever do that? Help me, Willy, I can't cry. It seems to me that you're just on another trip. I keep expecting you. Willy, dear, I can't cry. Why did you do it? I search and search and I search, and I can't understand it, Willy. I made the last payment on the house today. Today, dear. And there'll be nobody home. (*A sob rises in her throat.*) We're free and clear. (*Sobbing mournfully, released.*) We're free. (*Biff comes slowly toward her.*) We're free . . . We're free . . .

*Biff lifts her to her feet and moves out up right with her in his arms. Linda sobs quietly. Bernard and Charley come together and follow them, followed by Happy. Only the music of the flute is left on the darkening stage as over the house the hard towers of the apartment buildings rise into sharp focus and the curtain falls.*

—*1949*

**Samuel Beckett (1906–1989)** *was born near Dublin, Ireland. As a young man he enjoyed sports, studied French and Italian, and discovered the silent films of Buster Keaton and Charlie Chaplin, whose influence can be seen in his work. Teaching English in Paris in the 1920s, he joined the circle of fellow Irish writer James Joyce. He began to write novels and travelled in Europe, finally settling in Paris in 1937, where he later worked for the French Resistance during World War II. Most of his plays and novels were originally written in French, including his most famous play,* Waiting for Godot *(1953), in which two lost characters endlessly wait, though they are not sure for what or whom. Other important plays include* Endgame *(1957) and* Happy Days *(1961). Beckett's attempt to portray the bare essentials of the human condition meant that his plays became increasingly spare.* Act Without Words I: A Mime for One Player, *as the title suggests, dispenses with language entirely and, like other examples of the "theatre of the absurd," conveys a sense of incoherence and improvisation that represents modern life. As the solitary and silent character reaches for various tools, these are withdrawn from him until he no longer reacts, a response that can be interpreted as despair or defiance. This "mime" was first produced in Paris in April 1957 as an afterpiece to* Endgame. *Beckett was awarded the Nobel Prize in 1969 and is considered one of the most original and influential writers of the twentieth century.*

# Samuel Beckett
# Act Without Words I

*A Mime for One Player*

Desert. Dazzling light.

The man is flung backwards on stage from right wing. He falls, gets up immediately, dusts himself, turns aside, reflects.

Whistle from right wing.

He reflects, goes out right.

Immediately flung back on stage he falls, gets up immediately, dusts himself, turns aside, reflects.

Whistle from left wing.

He reflects, goes out left.

Immediately flung back on stage he falls, gets up immediately, dusts himself, turns aside, reflects.

Whistle from left wing.

He reflects, goes towards left wing, hesitates, thinks better of it, halts, turns aside, reflects.

A little tree descends from flies, lands. It has a single bough some three yards from ground and at its summit a meager tuft of palms casting at its foot a circle of shadow.

He continues to reflect.

Whistle from above.

He turns, sees tree, reflects, goes to it, sits down in its shadow, looks at his hands.

A pair of tailor's scissors descends from flies, comes to rest before tree, a yard from ground.

He continues to look at his hands.

Whistle from above.

He looks up, sees scissors, takes them and starts to trim his nails.

The palms close like a parasol, the shadow disappears.

He drops scissors, reflects.

A tiny carafe, to which is attached a huge label inscribed WATER, descends from flies, comes to rest some three yards from ground.

He continues to reflect.

Whistle from above.

He looks up, sees carafe, reflects, gets up, goes and stands under it, tries in vain to reach it, renounces, turns aside, reflects.

A big cube descends from flies, lands.

He continues to reflect.

Whistle from above.

He turns, sees cube, looks at it, at carafe, reflects, goes to cube, takes it up, carries it over and sets it down under carafe, tests its stability, gets up on it, tries in vain to reach carafe, renounces, gets down, carries cube back to its place, turns aside, reflects.

A second smaller cube descends from flies, lands.

He continues to reflect.

Whistle from above.

He turns, sees second cube, looks at it, at carafe, goes to second cube, takes it up, carries it over and sets it down under carafe, tests its stability, gets up on it, tries in vain to reach carafe, renounces, gets down, takes up second cube to carry it back to its place, hesitates, thinks better of it, sets it down, goes to big cube, takes it up, carries it over and puts it on small one, tests their stability, gets up on them, the cubes collapse, he falls, gets up immediately, brushes himself, reflects.

He takes up small cube, puts it on big one, tests their stability, gets up on them and is about to reach carafe when it is pulled up a little way and comes to rest beyond his reach.

He gets down, reflects, carries cubes back to their place, one by one, turns aside, reflects.

A third still smaller cube descends from flies, lands.

He continues to reflect.

Whistle from above.

He turns, sees third cube, looks at it, reflects, turns aside, reflects.

The third cube is pulled up and disappears in flies.

Beside carafe a rope descends from flies, with knots to facilitate ascent.

He continues to reflect.

Whistle from above.

He turns, sees rope, reflects, goes to it, climbs up it and is about to reach carafe when rope is let out and deposits him back on ground.

He reflects, looks around for scissors, sees them, goes and picks them up, returns to rope and starts to cut it with scissors.

The rope is pulled up, lifts him off ground, he hangs on, succeeds in cutting rope, falls back on ground, drops scissors, falls, gets up again immediately, brushes himself, reflects.

The rope is pulled up quickly and disappears in flies.

With length of rope in his possession he makes a lasso with which he tries to lasso carafe.

The carafe is pulled up quickly and disappears in flies.

He turns aside, reflects.

He goes with lasso in his hand to tree, looks at bough, turns and looks at cubes, looks again at bough, drops lasso, goes to cubes, takes up small one, carries it over and sets it down under bough, goes back for big one, takes it up and carries it over under bough, makes to put it on small one, hesitates, thinks better of it, sets it down, takes up small one and puts it on big one, tests their stability, turns aside and stoops to pick up lasso.

The bough folds down against trunk.

He straightens up with lasso in his hand, turns and sees what has happened.

He drops lasso, turns aside, reflects.

He carries back cubes to their place, one by one, goes back for lasso, carries it over to cubes and lays it in a neat coil on small one.

He turns aside, reflects.

Whistle from right wing.

He reflects, goes out right.

Immediately flung back on stage he falls, gets up immediately, brushes himself, turns aside, reflects.

Whistle from left wing.

He does not move.

He looks at his hands, looks around for scissors, sees them, goes and picks them up, starts to trim his nails, stops, reflects, runs his finger along blade of scissors, goes and lays them on small cube, turns aside, opens his collar, frees his neck and fingers it.

The small cube is pulled up and disappears in flies, carrying away rope and scissors.

He turns to take scissors, sees what has happened.

He turns aside, reflects.

He goes and sits down on big cube.

The big cube is pulled from under him. He falls. The big cube is pulled up and disappears in flies.

He remains lying on his side, his face towards auditorium, staring before him.

The carafe descends from flies and comes to rest a few feet from his body.

He does not move.

Whistle from above.

He does not move.

The carafe descends further, dangles and plays about his face.

He does not move.

The carafe is pulled up and disappears in flies.

The bough returns to horizontal, the palms open, the shadow returns.

Whistle from above.

He does not move.

The tree is pulled up and disappears in flies.

He looks at his hands.

Curtain

*—1957*

*Sharon Pollock (b. 1936) is considered one of Canada's foremost playwrights. She was born Mary Sharon Chalmers in Fredericton, New Brunswick, the daughter of a doctor who appears as a character in her play* Doc *(1984). In 1966 she moved to Calgary, where her first play, written while she was pregnant with her sixth child, won the Alberta Playwriting Competition. Many of the plays that followed — including* Walsh *(1973),* Whiskey Six Cadenza *(1983),* Fair Liberty's Call *(1993),* End Dream *(2000), and* Kabloona Talk *(2006) — examine real incidents in Canadian history; they reveal that, as Pollock says in her introduction to* The Komagata Maru Incident *(1976), "much of our history has been misrepresented and even hidden from us. Until we recognize our past, we cannot change our future." Her most famous play, the Governor General's Award–winning* Blood Relations *(1980), examines Lizzie Borden's supposed murder of her parents in 1892, which is immortalized in the children's skipping rhyme that begins "Lizzie Borden took an axe. . . ." Of late, Pollock has created more female protagonists, including Zelda Fitzgerald in* Angel's Trumpet *(2001) and Nell Shipman in* Moving Pictures *(1999). The latter, a Canadian-born actor/filmmaker who worked in Edison's medium in the early decades of the twentieth century when filmmaking was shifting from "art to industry," faced many challenges. Appropriately, Pollock herself starred in a 2004 production of this play about "the artist's addiction to creation whatever the cost." In a lifetime of plays gathered in three volumes of* Collected Works, *Pollock challenges audiences to think about ideas, conflicts, and choices. She explores power politics and the process of inquiry through multiple perspectives resulting in complex characters but no easy answers.*

# *Sharon Pollock*
# Moving Pictures

## Playwright's Notes

Moving Pictures *is a theatrical tracing of the life of Nell Shipman, who as an actress sang, danced and hammed her way across North America in the early 1900s. In silent films she was a hit, known as the girl from God's Country from the title of her most successful film, "Back to God's Country." She established an independent production company and made movies in which strong women played principal roles, and a holistic view of the natural environment, the animal kingdom, and humankind prevailed. But as movie-making shifted from art to industry, the precepts that guided Nell to success became threats to her life as well as her career. Her last film script, written under a pseudonym, was produced in 1934. Her death in 1972 went unnoticed.*

Moving Pictures *explores the meaning of story-telling in our lives, and the artist's addiction to creation whatever the cost.*

## CHARACTERS

| | |
|---|---|
| *Helen* | Nell Shipman, an actress, early years. |
| *Nell* | Nell Shipman, director & producer, mid years. |
| *Shipman* | Nell Shipman, towards the end of her life. |
| *Man #1* | |
| Bert Van Tuyle | American born; independent movie director and producer; Nell's lover and creative partner. |
| Sam Goldwyn | Polish immigrant; founder of Goldwyn Pictures. |
| *Man #2* | |
| Carl Laemmle | German immigrant, founder of Universal Studios. |
| Ernie Shipman | Canadian immigrant; theatre and movie entrepreneur; Nell's first husband. |
| *Thomas Edison* | An old but still powerful man, inventor of the medium in which Nell Shipman creates, and a voice of authority. |
| *Barry* | The 8-year-old son of Nell and Ernie—never seen, all lines are voiceover. |

*MAN #1 and MAN #2, when not directly engaged in a scene with the women, are always present on stage and observing the action. While they may seem to play roles assigned by the women, real power is vested in them. They have an ultimate interest in maintaining that power, in blocking any challenge to it, and in preventing any loss of it. As the play progresses, their assuming of character becomes more overt. Wardrobe bits or hand props that identify them are merely suggestions and may be as a production concept dictates. It's important that such bits or props be minimal, easily integrated into the action, and not impede the flow of the play. The degree and specifics of interplay between MAN #1 and MAN #2 and/or between the women and EDISON is left to the discretion and imagination of the director and his/her creative team.*

*There are 3 Nell Shipmans in the Play: HELEN, the young vaudeville and stock actress; NELL, the successful film star, director, screenwriter and producer; and SHIPMAN, the elderly has-been. They confront each other in the reconstruction of a life dedicated to the creation of play on stage and on screen. In that play, and in the transforming of her life experience into fiction, the woman discovers meaning that the actual living of her life did not reveal to her.*

## Note on Punctuation

*In the script a dash followed by square-bracketed dialogue indicates an interruption of the line; within the square bracket are the words that complete the line were the character not interrupted.*

## MOVING PICTURES

*Black. A light picks out SHIPMAN sitting in a chair behind a desk. Less visible is NELL who stands behind SHIPMAN, and HELEN who is holding a script and standing behind NELL. A hand gun lies on the desk. MAN #1 and MAN #2 are on the periphery observing. EDISON is isolated from the others. SHIPMAN is reading a letter which she places on the desk. A moment of emptiness, the void. NELL leans forward and whispers in SHIPMAN's ear.*

**NELL:**  Play.

**SHIPMAN:**  Can't.

**NELL:**  Come on plaaay.

**SHIPMAN:**  Can't.

**NELL:**  Can so. *(snaps her fingers, then the sound of the rhythmic click of film running through a projector)* Play!

> *Black and white film plays on the set and the bodies of the characters, which provide the "screen." Elusive images flicker and flash, a strobe-like effect, illuminating SHIPMAN, NELL and HELEN. All are looking out as if watching a film they see playing on a distant screen, as the film plays on them.*

**EDISON:**  *(a victorious public statement describing his greatest achievement; savours the words as they grow in volume and power)* The . . . illusion . . . of . . . continuous . . . movement . . . through persistence . . . of vision the . . . illusion of continuous movement . . . through . . . persistence of vision The Illusion of Continuous Movement *(the film freezes)* through Persistence of Vision!

> *Twilight fills the space. The frozen film image bleeds out. Silence. A small moment frozen in time. The image of the "three in one"*

*breaks apart. HELEN in her Lady Teazle costume steps away a bit, looking down at a script and resumé in her hand. She's studying her lines. NELL continues to gaze out as if she were still seeing the film. Neither acknowledges SHIPMAN.*

**SHIPMAN:** *(considering the implications of the words as they apply to her—a personal intimate statement of her failure)* The illusion of continuous ... movement ... through persistence of vision The illusion of ... *(pause)* I ... have nothing to say ... I have nothing to—*(She looks at NELL and an irritation grows at NELL's focus on something that is not accessible to SHIPMAN.)* I said I have nothing to say! *(no reaction from NELL)* I'm talking to you!! *(no response)* Do you know what everyone hates? ... They hate it when you do that.... I said they hate it when you do that! Nell! ... Nell! ... I said everyone hates it! When your eyes glaze over. When they know you're not paying one bit of attention to anything they're saying. They could be telling you they're dropping dead in a month ... "I am dropping dead in a month!" ... They hate it! I hate it! And you've always done it! As long as I can remember! ... I said I'm dropping dead in a month!! *(NELL still deep in thought makes a small sound of assent or dissent; she's not listening.)* Would it make any difference if I were? *(pause)* What are you thinking? ... Are you thinking about dropping dead? No, not likely. You're writing, aren't you? Inside your head you're writing. After everything you are still writing! You're not listening! You're writing!

**NELL:** *(still absent)* No.

**SHIPMAN:** No what? No what!

**NELL:** *(less absent)* What?

**SHIPMAN:** Exactly.

**NELL:** What did you say?

**SHIPMAN:** I said no what!

**NELL:** And I said I don't know what you're talking about.

**SHIPMAN:** And I said "exactly." I said "you're not listening, you're writing!" And you said "no" and I said "no what!" I said "no what" meaning "go on" and you don't know what I'm talking about so you can't go on because you aren't listening and I said "Exactly!"

**NELL:** And I'm saying "What the hell are you talking about!"

**SHIPMAN:** Oh for Christ's sake. I just want to hear you say no I'm not writing. Inside my head I'm not writing!

**NELL:** Why would you want me to say that?

**SHIPMAN:** Because it would be such a bloody lie!

*HELEN looks up from her script to SHIPMAN, then, as the banter between the two other women seems to have ended she returns to studying her lines. NELL has returned to her inner contemplation. SHIPMAN studies NELL. After a moment she speaks. She's not letting go of the rant she's on. NELL is listening with only half an ear.*

**SHIPMAN:** So what're you doing now—considering sub-text?

**NELL:** I'm making something up.

**SHIPMAN:** You're a lousy mother, make something of that.

**NELL:** I could.

**SHIPMAN:** So you're writing. Alright. Here's something. Are you listening?

**NELL:** Ah-huh.

**SHIPMAN:** I'm telling you something.

**NELL:** Ah-huh.

*A pause. After a bit the silence penetrates NELL's consciousness. She looks at SHIPMAN. SHIPMAN says nothing.*

Well? . . . Have you told me yet?

**SHIPMAN:** You're not that old, you're not senile, have you been told something or not?

**NELL:** You told me *(She thinks for a moment.)* I'm a lousy mother. Was that it?

**SHIPMAN:** No that's not it! I said "telling" not "told." This is it. You— have an incurable disease. The tests have come back and the doctor said you wanted to know.

**NELL:** Is this how he said to tell me?

**SHIPMAN:** Let's say—he gave no specific directive. So. Make something of that.

**NELL:** Did he say how long?

**SHIPMAN:** No.

**NELL:** *(She prepares to write, gets out paper. Pauses and looks at SHIPMAN.)* Are you lying?

**SHIPMAN:** About the story line—or the time line?

**NELL:** Either.

**SHIPMAN:** Everything's fiction. Isn't that what you say? So. Do you think you could write a script about that?

**NELL:** About what?

**SHIPMAN:** About dying! Pay attention! Do you think you could write a script about dying!

**NELL:** If I've got the time. The question is—

**SHIPMAN:** Why bother.

**NELL:** That's not the question.

**SHIPMAN:** Who'd buy it, who would produce it?

**NELL:** I said that's not the question!

**SHIPMAN:** It would be for any rational person.

**NELL:** I don't think about that.

**SHIPMAN:** Liar. *(pause)* What were you thinking about before?

**NELL:** Before? The flickers. I was thinking about the flickers.

*HELEN looks up from the script; she loves the flickers, as early movies were called. She watches and listens to NELL and SHIPMAN.*

Standing at the back of the vaudeville house watching the flickers.

**SHIPMAN:** That was years ago. Past. Gone. Not important any more, no use.

**NELL:** Says who?

**SHIPMAN:** Says me. *(pause)* Now what're you thinking?

**NELL:** Now?

**SHIPMAN:** Yes now! After receiving the news.

**NELL:** What news?

**SHIPMAN:** The news, the news, we're back to that now! The doctor, the tests, the dying, the dead!

**NELL:** The fictional news?

**SHIPMAN:** You say the fictional news. I say Now, as I sit here, essentially destitute in my little rent-free cottage, courtesy of affluent old friends, Now as I digest the meat of the message, Now as The End looms up there on the screen—what can you make of it?

**NELL:** What can you make of it?

**SHIPMAN:** Nothing.

**NELL:** Make something.

**SHIPMAN:** Can't.

**NELL:** Can so.

**SHIPMAN:** Can't.

**NELL:**  You always could.

**SHIPMAN:**  Nothing to say.

**HELEN:**  So play.

**SHIPMAN:**  "The End." How's that?

**NELL:**  Noo. The beginning, the middle, the bits in between, then the end, make something of it! Go on!

**HELEN:**  Do it! *(She offers her script to SHIPMAN who refuses to take it.)*

**NELL:**  Oh for God's sake! Play!

> *NELL grabs a pair of glasses from the desk and shoves them on her face; snatches the script and resumé from HELEN'S hands, and plays, has fun with, sending up Mr. Gilmore, a Chicago producer of a third rate national stock touring company. He sounds like a Mafia wiseguy or Brando's Godfather.*

**NELL:**  *(as Mr. Gilmore)* Next!

**HELEN:**  Helen Barham, Mr. Gilmore, student at Frank Egan Drama School Seattle—Lady Teazle.

> *Wears a Lady Teazle costume made by her mother, not a bad seamstress. She never falters, and steps into the scene playing to an invisible Sir Peter. NELL as Mr. Gilmore feeds HELEN her cues. HELEN's performance is rather extravagant even for restoration comedy and done with a veddy English accent. It's not a bad performance from a 13-year-old, and reveals punk, nerve, talent and daring. If she doesn't get the part it's not because she didn't give it everything she's got.*

As you please, Sir Peter, you may bear it or not, but I ought to
have my own way in everything, and what's more I will too.

**NELL:**  *(as Mr. Gilmore)* So da husband has no aut'ority?

**HELEN:**  If you wanted authority over me you should have adopted me and not married me. I am sure you were old enough.

**NELL:**  *(as Mr. Gilmore)* T'ou my life may be made unhappy by your temper, I'll not be ruined by your extravagance.

**HELEN:**  Am I to blame because flowers are dear in cold weather? You should find fault with the climate and not with me. For my part I wish it were spring all the year round and that roses grew under one's feet!

**NELL:**  *(as Mr. Gilmore)* Yuh forget where yuh was when I married yuh.

**HELEN:**   Yes 'twas most disagreeable or I should never have married you.

**NELL:**   *(as Mr. Gilmore)* I have made yuh a woman of fashion, of fortune, of rank—in short I have made yuh my wife.

**HELEN:**   There is but one thing more you can make me to add to the obligation and that is—

**NELL:**   *(as Mr. Gilmore)* My widow I suppose?

**HELEN:**   Why do you make yourself so disagreeable to me and thwart me in every little elegant expense?

**NELL:**   *(as Mr. Gilmore)* Had yuh any of dose little "elegant expenses" when yuh married me?

**HELEN:**   I should think you would like your wife thought a woman of taste.

**NELL:**   *(as Mr. Gilmore)* Yuh had no taste when yuh married me.

**HELEN:**   And after having married you I shall never pretend to taste again! And now, Sir Peter *(with an elaborate curtsy, and a pretty exit out of the scene)* goodbye to you!

**NELL:**   *(as Mr. Gilmore)* Not bad.

**HELEN:**   *(the high of performance still sustains her)* Did you really think so, Mr. Gilmore? I did my best.

**NELL:**   *(as Mr. Gilmore)* Ah-huh

**HELEN:**   *(that high is fading)* Although one can always do better.

**NELL:**   *(as Mr. Gilmore, searching for the info on the resumé, trying to goad SHIPMAN into a response, into playing)* Address, ah-huh . . . Age Age . . . Age Age Age, Age Age Age Age—

**SHIPMAN:**   Thirteen!

**HELEN:**   But I'm tall for my age! And I've finished school. Seattle Grammar School, class of 1905, that was in the spring, and I am not interested in further education . . . *(faltering a bit with the strain of the "interview")* . . . except—as it—pertains . . . to the stage. I intend to be—an actress.

*NELL as Mr. Gilmore considers her in silence, sniffs, looks at the resumé and back at HELEN who speaks with greater strength and conviction, almost daring NELL or SHIPMAN to contradict her.*

I intend to be an actress!

**NELL:**   *(as Mr. Gilmore)* Dis your right age?

**SHIPMAN:**   I said thirteen.

**HELEN:**   Thirteen, Mr. Gilmore, I'm tall for my age.

**NELL:** *(as Mr. Gilmore)* I can see dat. What would da folks say?

**HELEN:** Weeelll—my Great Aunt Marion—she lives in Scotland—I'm not American you know, I hope that doesn't matter, it shouldn't matter, but I'm Canadian and my parents are British and my cousin you see, or maybe an aunt, I've never met her, married a D'Oyly Carte so my parents are used to that and my Great Aunt Marion, I mentioned her before, well she would send the money for my musical education in Leipzig she said "A proper goal" she called it so—so everyone is used to the idea because ever since the age of the, age of the—but I'm not interested in that I've—I've taken piano and dancing and singing of course and now I'm here at Mr. Egan's and . . . *(pause)* . . . I don't think my family would mind.

**NELL:** *(as Mr. Gilmore)* We'll ask. *(removing the glasses)*

**HELEN:** That means?

*A cue for SHIPMAN to contribute to the story, to join in the play.*

**NELL:** Come on Shipman, give a little.

*No response from Shipman.*

**HELEN:** I've got it! Isn't that right? I'm cast! I'm going on tour with Paul Gilmore's National Stock Company! Ta Dum!

**SHIPMAN:** *(attempting to puncture HELEN's balloon)* Third rate national stock.

**NELL:** *(helping HELEN out of her costume)* But you done good.

**HELEN:** I did, didn't I? I really did. I knew they'd never let me in to audition so I had to sneak in. *(to SHIPMAN)* Isn't that right? I just—snuck in! And now I'm playing the *ingenue* in Mr. Gilmore's production of—Ta dum!—*AT YALE*!

**SHIPMAN:** It was only a knock-off of the real hit.

**HELEN:** I know I know, but this is it, this is the beginning, why aren't you excited? It's alright to get excited you know, you miss a lot when you don't. Just say Hooray! real loud. Hooray!! Come on Nell, show her how. I think she's forgot.

**NELL:** *(going to a gramophone and cranking it)* She saves it for *chimeras*, none left for life.

**HELEN:** Come on Shipman, real loud, Hooray! *(HELEN who is now in her bloomers and chemise does a cartwheel)* You did it! Come on.

*The gramophone plays. HELEN sings and dances for SHIPMAN. HELEN is sending up an act from a children's singing & dancing troupe at the turn of the century: The Boston Lilliputians. She does so with much physical illustration and a silly child's voice, attempting to seduce SHIPMAN into playing.*

Please go 'way and let me sleep
Don't disturb my slumber deep
I would rather sleep than eat
For sleep to me is such a treat, treat, treat,
I never had a dream so nice
Thought I was in Paradise
Waking up makes me feel cheap
So please let me sleep!

You did it, Shipman, yes you did! Hooray! Come on, Nell, your cue! How about Universal Pictures and—Mr. Carl Laemmle! *(With a clap of her hands MAN #2 buttons up a double-breasted suit jacket and dons eyeglasses.)* Play!

**SHIPMAN:** You don't have to yell.

**NELL:** *(to SHIPMAN)* Well, this should interest you—it's all about Money!

**HELEN:** You're on Nell!

**SHIPMAN:** I said you don't have to yell!

**NELL:** I'm not!

**HELEN:** Cue!

**CARL:** Why does it seem like you are?

**NELL:** Because nothing makes me feel more like yelling than you telling me to stop yelling when I'm not yelling!

**CARL:** Maybe that's it.

**NELL:** I want my check, Carl. *(CARL makes a move.)* And don't even think about putting your hand on my ass.

**CARL:** It's a friendly gesture and it's a nice ass. If you were a man I'd offer a drink.

**NELL:** I could use a drink.

**CARL:** A little hand on ass—it's how business is done.

**NELL:** I said a drink would be nice.

**CARL:** No one else complains.

**NELL:** You put your hand on my ass, first I'm going to complain and second I'm going to shove—[this scenario]

**CARL:** Now I feel like you're yelling again.

**NELL:** Look Carl, my last picture made 300 per cent for investors, and no check for me yet, why is that? And now Bert's—[out raising money]

**CARL:** That would be Mr. Van Tuyle, Bert?

**HELEN:** *(a whisper to SHIPMAN)* I'd say so *(snaps her fingers, MAN #1 slips on an ascot)* wouldn't you?

**NELL:** Don't get cute.

**CARL:** Only asking—former company manager Bert?

**HELEN:** *(to SHIPMAN)* What would you say?

**SHIPMAN:** I'm not playing.

**CARL:** He says you walk on water.

**HELEN:** Tell her, Bert. *(She tosses a cane to BERT. He has no disability.)*

**BERT:** So I say where are you shooting this film? And Nell looks over at Ernie and she knocks back her drink, bangs the glass down on the table, and she says, she leans forward and says "God's Country Mr. Van Tuyle." I say ah-huh. She says "where elephants can walk on water, and so can I." I say ah-huh. Ernie says "cut the bullshit Nell! It's Lesser Slave Lake, middle of winter, so what do you say, Bert."

**NELL:** I said I want my money.

**CARL:** Be nice Nell.

**NELL:** I'm a hell of a lot nicer than you deserve and I'm asking what's going on?

**CARL:** So—as a friend, Nell—I tell you. *(He pours himself and NELL a drink.)* You did two stupid things.

**NELL:** Only two?

**CARL:** Please. Keep your mouth shut, drink your drink, and listen. Two, let's say three, things. Who the hell knows how many things. Right now we are talking three things. Number one stupid thing. Cost overruns. You get brilliant idea on set and you execute that idea. Schedule or no schedule, budget or no budget. Kern River shots, end of movie, fall into this category. Number two stupid thing. Original writer is one of your producing partners. So you adapt his dog story for film, you beef up the woman's role—your role—and the dog gets a walk-on.

**NELL:** Hardly.

**CARL:** An improvement, but you don't handle him well. You intimidate this writer who is also producer.

**NELL:** It's hard not to. The top of his head touches my chin.

**CARL:** Comic potential. Use it in something.

**NELL:** How about I walk on my knees?

**CARL:** Whatever.

**NELL:** Look, you know "Back To God's Country" was a technical and an artistic success. It was worth every penny. So to hell with your cost overruns! And I improved Curwood's story, you said so yourself. The dog did not get a walk-on. The dog was very important. I love that dog! So what if the writer's peeved and we went over budget. The movie made money and I want my take.

**CARL:** You will get it—when Ernie signs the check.

**NELL:** I need you to ask him.

**CARL:** Why don't you ask Ernie yourself?

**NELL:** Ernie.

**CARL:** Yes Ernie. You remember Ernie. Your other producing partner? The one raising the money? Disbursing the funds? Signing the checks? That producing partner. Ernie. Your husband, Ernie.

**NELL:** Ex-husband.

**CARL:** Soon to be ex-husband. Which brings us to stupid thing number three. Second producing partner happens to be your husband. It is not good idea Nell, technically or artistically, to sleep with company manager when producer signing the checks is husband. If you had thought about that, I am sure you could have figured it out.

**NELL:** I made "Back To God's Country" a hit. I got incredible footage out of those animals with care and honey sticks, no electric prods or trip wires! And believe me it was no picnic. You knew Ron Bryant? He died of pneumonia on location for Christ's sake! This ass you're so fond of? It damn near froze off, and poor Bert froze his foot off!

**CARL:** Totally off?

**NELL:** He froze his foot!

**CARL:** Fuck Bert.

**NELL:** I did.

**CARL:** I know. Don't fuck around, Nell. Write that on something. Refer to it often.

**NELL:** I wonder how often you've preached marital monogamy to Ernie Shipman, the great Canadian cocksman, over the years he and I have been married.

**CARL:** Ernie is a friend.

**NELL:** Does that mean you just stood in line for seconds?

**CARL:** You've a funny way of getting me on side.

**NELL:** I am owed money! You're the distributor and a friend and you can get it for me! I want it!

**CARL:** Ernie won't sign your check. End of discussion.

**NELL:** I! . . . he can't do that.

**CARL:** He can.

**NELL:** So he can. Alright. Yes. I accept that. I was stupid. You're right.

**CARL:** And now you do what with this Bert.

**NELL:** Make my next movie, that's what. A winner. Building on the success of the last one, the one I'm not getting paid for.

**CARL:** Neeell . . .

**NELL:** Everyone wants to see The Girl from God's Country. I am The Girl from God's Country! And this time I'm not tied to a writer whose nose hits my nipple, and I'm working with a man I respect who's not boffing everything in skirts—no offense to Ernie.

**CARL:** Ernie would not feel offended.

**NELL:** No he wouldn't.

**CARL:** I tell you Nell where it is you go wrong—it's the way you make movies, and the movies you make.

**NELL:** How can you say that?

**CARL:** The lips move, the words come out.

**NELL:** I make good movies. Successful movies. How many have I written to keep Ernie in poker games and tarts?

**SHIPMAN:** You married him.

**NELL:** I was eighteen he was thirty-five that's the story, and we're not talking Ernie, we're talking movies, my movies, how many have I written, directed and played in, you tell me, how many?

**CARL:** You're a good little actress, Nell.

**NELL:** A good little actress?

**CARL:** Sam Goldwyn offered you a Studio contract year or so ago, no?

**SHIPMAN:** That's right.

**CARL:** You should have taken it Nell. See your name up in lights.

**NELL:** My name is up in lights!

**CARL:** You could have been a Star. *(CARL will exit the scene, but not leave the stage.)*

**SHIPMAN:** Could have been a star?

**CARL:** None of this bullshit, Nell. You could've been a star!

**NELL:** *(yelling after him)* Can you see me in a slinky dress, blond curls, and cupid lips! Could have been a star?! *(to SHIPMAN)* I am a star!

**BERT:** She's got sparks coming out of her hair and ideas pouring out of her head, she's got an eye for film and story, and a kick-ass attitude and by God if you aren't willing and able to follow her out on the ice you better pack your bags and hightail it home. *(will exit the scene but not leave the stage)* She's a beautiful woman ... I can't walk on water but she—she sure as hell ... she sure as Hell ...

**HELEN:** *(yelling after him)* I sure as hell can!

**NELL:** *(as Mr. Gilmore, bellowing from the shadows)* Who told me yuh was an actress?

**HELEN:** *(shielding her eyes from the stage lights, looking into the balcony)* I did, Mr. Gilmore?

**NELL:** *(as Mr. Gilmore)* What's dat on your face?

**HELEN:** Make-up Mr. Gilmore?

**NELL:** *(as Mr. Gilmore)* Speak up! Can't hear yuh!

**HELEN:** Make-up Mr. Gilmore!

**NELL:** *(as Mr. Gilmore)* Never hear yuh past da sixth row! *(pause)* What! *(pause)* What! *(pause)* I said what!

**HELEN:** I've—forgotten the line, Mr. Gilmore.

**NELL:** *(as Mr. Gilmore)* What da hell are yuh wearin'?

**HELEN:** My costume?

**NELL:** *(as Mr. Gilmore)* No no no!

**HELEN:** My mother made it, Mr. Gilmore, she—[thought it was appropriate]

**NELL:** *(as Mr. Gilmore)* Find somet'ing else!

**SHIPMAN:** Give the kid a break!

*HELEN changes into her HELEN costume as SHIPMAN watches.*

**HELEN:** *(not complaining, it was a glorious time for her)* Provide my own wardrobe ... pay my own way. ... Cheapest hotels ... *(struggling with her costume change)* Can't do it. A hand please? (SHIPMAN, after a momentary hesitation, helps.)* Mattress this thin! *(half an inch between her fingers)* Remember? And the smell?

**SHIPMAN:** *(anything but a glorious memory)* Still prickles my nose.

**HELEN:** I never noticed after a while. The luxury of an upper berth! *(SHIPMAN is about to contradict her.)* I know! Most often the hardest seat in the day coach, but sometimes? Right?

*No response. The luxury of an upper berth was a rare event in SHIPMAN's opinion.*

Laundry—mine and what I wear in the show? I wash it—and me— in a small metal basin—and it's always at the end of the iciest hall why is that?!

*For HELEN even the eternal iciest was a magical occurrence.*

And I dream—do you know what I dreamt?

**SHIPMAN:** My name up in lights. *(A foolish dream in SHIPMAN's opinion.)*

**HELEN:** Wrong! Hot water and food! Got a good review by a name critic at the Hundred and Twenty-fifth St. Theatre!

**SHIPMAN:** Closest I ever got to Broadway.

**HELEN:** Wrote letters home and never told them a thing that was true! *(an exceptional and fantastic achievement)*

**NELL:** Missed them.

**SHIPMAN:** Not really.

**NELL:** Not true.

**SHIPMAN:** Play then. *(She'll force NELL to acknowledge true family history.)*

**NELL:** Mummy

**HELEN:** who could make something out of nothing, whether it was meals for a week out of just enough meat for Sunday

**NELL:** or a glorious dress for the dance recital and a sailor suit for my elocution bit

**HELEN:** both of them made from some lacy bits and a dress sent by an English cousin

**SHIPMAN:** along with the Remittance check for Daddy, Black Expatriate Sheep of the British tribe. Admit it.

**HELEN:** *(to NELL)* Don't listen to her! Mummy was "an English Lady."

**SHIPMAN:** A Tragedy if she forgot her gloves.

**HELEN:** *(horrified)* Oh I don't think she ever forgot her gloves, do you?

**NELL:** Never!

**SHIPMAN:** So how about when brother Maurice was at war and Daddy and the dogs—

**NELL:** Daddy's war effort! A plan to raise meat for the table!

**SHIPMAN:** You're avoiding.

**HELEN:** I was a *bona fide* movie star then, least I'm saying I was.

**SHIPMAN:** Admit it.

**NELL:** He bought two rabbits!

**HELEN:** and before we knew it

**NELL:** there were hundreds of rabbits out in the yard.

**HELEN:** He'd sit out there

**NELL:** by the rabbit hutch

**HELEN:** smoking, he'd smoke out there, what did he smoke?

**SHIPMAN:** Navy cut.

**HELEN:** Navy cut! That's what he smoked!

**NELL:** But finally

**HELEN:** finally he took

**NELL:** five rabbits down to the butcher, and Mummy served them up for dinner!

**HELEN:** But! A terrible hush fell over the table

**NELL:** Nobody spoke

**HELEN:** Nobody ate

**NELL:** And finally

**HELEN:** by some kind of uncommon unspoken consent

**NELL:** we all got up, carried the pot to the yard

**HELEN:** Daddy got out a shovel

**NELL:** And we gave them a proper burial!

**SHIPMAN:** The dogs, the three of them, Daddy and the dogs.

**HELEN:** Four of them counting Daddy.

**SHIPMAN:** Out for a walk and a sit on the bench and a good smoke of that Navy Cut. He was old then.

**NELL:** No.

**SHIPMAN:** No what? Go on?

**NELL:** No!

**HELEN:** So take it back! New Play. Play! He loved being silly and singing his songs what were the songs? Come on Nell!

**NELL:** Gilbert and Sullivan.

**SHIPMAN:** And?

**NELL:** And he'd sing and he'd whirl round!

**SHIPMAN:** Yes, in a dance with—what? Come on, alliteration, you love it, dance with—what, with Death?

**HELEN:** A nice story, come on!

**SHIPMAN:** A dance with what?

**HELEN:** A handkerchief on his head!

**NELL:** He never fit in so he left Somerset

**HELEN:** and the family pottery works

**SHIPMAN:** That's not the story I'm thinking of.

**NELL:** and settled for a remittance. Alright?!

**SHIPMAN:** The End?

**NELL:** Shut up.

**HELEN:** Music Nell. Music!

*HELEN begins to hum softly "Three Little Maids." NELL gestures and the gramophone plays. HELEN places a handkerchief on her head and sings, lowering her voice and dancing, an imitation of her father with his English accent, doing his silly bit singing and dancing.*

Three little maids from school are we
Pert as a schoolgirl well can be

*HELEN places a handkerchief on NELL's head and pulls NELL into her song and dance.*

**SHIPMAN:** Come on Nell, what's the story?

**HELEN & NELL:**
*(singing)* Filled to the brim with girlish glee
Three little maids from school!

**SHIPMAN:** Daddy out for a walk and

**NELL:** No.

**HELEN & NELL:**
Everything is a source of fun
Nobody's safe for we care for none

**SHIPMAN:** Finish the story.

**HELEN & NELL:**
Life is a joke that's just begun
Three little maids from school!

**SHIPMAN:** You afraid?

**NELL:** No!

**HELEN:** From three little maids take one away—

**SHIPMAN:** So finish the story!

**NELL:** My story!

**SHIPMAN:** The Daddy story?

**NELL:** My way!

**SHIPMAN:** I can hardly wait.

**HELEN:** So stop fighting and tell it!

**NELL:** *(as she helps MAN #2, formerly CARL, off with his jacket which he hooks casually over one shoulder)* It's "Back To God's Country," Lesser Slave Lake. Where's the hat, he's got to have the hat. *(HELEN throws a cocky red hat to NELL who passes it to MAN #2 who tilts it back on his head.)* There. Ernie Shipman!

**SHIPMAN:** He needs to speak to you alone, Nell.

**NELL:** *(to SHIPMAN)* So we're alone, and we're speaking, alright?

**HELEN:** How the hell do the

**ERNIE:** How the hell do the boys keep the cameras going?

**NELL:** I know. Ron's got a cold. It's all in his chest.

**ERNIE:** So I hear.

**NELL:** Can't afford a work stoppage.

**ERNIE:** That wouldn't be good.

**NELL:** I suppose Bert reports all of this so it's old news.

**ERNIE:** I get reports. From Bert. About Bert. I keep in touch.

**NELL:** He's good at his job.

**ERNIE:** Something like that. So I hear.

**NELL:** Ah-huh. Sooo. We're alone, Ernie. Why're you here? It's not Maurice is it? Nothing's happened to Maurice?

**SHIPMAN:** Avoiding.

**ERNIE:** He's fine.

**NELL:** Bloody war.

**SHIPMAN:** It's Daddy.

**NELL:** *(to SHIPMAN)* Daddy is fine! *(to ERNIE)* I know he's drinking a little too much but that's . . . that's because he's alone, with Mummy gone and, me here. He's fine. He looks after the dogs and the dogs look after him. . . . When I get home . . . not so busy, I'll see about . . . I'll see about someone to stay with him, or . . . or something like that. That's what I'll do when I'm back. He'll be fine, he's just

**ERNIE:** Stop talking Nell.

**NELL:** You know that's what I do when I'm nervous. Tell me I've nothing to be nervous about! Brother Maurice is fine, Daddy is fine so, get on with it, what's this about?

**ERNIE:** No, he's not fine. But we thought—I thought—it would be better to wait a bit. Not interfere too much with the picture. I knew you wouldn't want that.

**NELL:** No . . . . No . . . . Nothing, should interfere with the picture. Daddy. . . . That's good of you Ernie.

**SHIPMAN:** Nothing should interfere with the picture.

**NELL:** It's good work! And I'll. . . . After this one I'll definitely be The Girl from God's Country. You'll see.

**SHIPMAN:** And Daddy?

**ERNIE:** Had a stroke. They think it was a stroke. He was walking the dogs. Sat down for a smoke and, some passerby got him home. Not really much they could do. He was an old man, Nell.

**NELL:** He was an old man.

**ERNIE:** *(as he's leaving the scene)* And I thought it best if we just waited a bit till we told you. Get most of it in the can. I figured that would be what you'd want.

**NELL:** That's right . . . I wouldn't want—

**SHIPMAN:** He's right. It is what you want.

**ERNIE:** The Colvins looked after the funeral, Forest Lawn, by your mum, so it's all taken care of, don't worry. *(He doesn't leave the stage.)*

**SHIPMAN:** Worry? All that matters is the movie, isn't that right?

**NELL:** Other things matter.

**SHIPMAN:** Nothing matters, only the movie.

**NELL:** Daddy matters! And Ron, and Ernie he matters!

**SHIPMAN:** "The dogs will look after Daddy"—Was that supposed to be funny?

**NELL:** No not funny.

**SHIPMAN:** "When I'm not so busy I'll see about someone for Daddy"—when would that be? The not so busy part, when would that be in this story?

**NELL:** I don't know.

**SHIPMAN:** Sure you know, tell me when?

**NELL:** I don't know.

**SHIPMAN:** Never! That's when. Another movie. An opportunity not to be missed. This one will be different! I'm an actress! I'm a star! I'm The Girl from God's Country! Pick it up! Say something!

**NELL:** I loved Daddy!

**SHIPMAN:** You loved work more. I heard that was the story.

**NELL:** No.

**SHIPMAN:** And "Ernie he matters." Did you ever love Ernie?

**NELL:** Yes but—

**SHIPMAN:** You were an unemployed actress whose norm was third-rate national stock and Pantages vaudeville when you met Ernie Shipman! You fell in love with his blue eyes and blond curly hair, and the jokes he made, and the people he knew, and the deals he cut, and it didn't hurt that he ran a better Stock company than you'd ever played in before! With lots of leading roles for you! Isn't that how it went?

**NELL:** All wrong, that's not the way that it goes.

**SHIPMAN:** And Barry, what about Barry?

**NELL:** Barry?

**SHIPMAN:** Your son, Ernie's son, where've you parked him this time?

**NELL:** You can't remember.

*The shadow of a child begins to grow on the floor of the stage.*

**SHIPMAN:** Military academy isn't it? And how old would he be now? Let me see, seven I think, and how long has he been there? Since he was six, and he'll be there for a bit, on and off

**NELL:** Play something different!

**SHIPMAN:** tuition paid by those wonderful English relatives, the ones you make fun of, "that British tribe" whose nice little cheques saved your neck more than once.

**NELL:** I don't have to listen.

**BARRY:** *(voiceover)* I hate it when you do that! I said I hate it when you do that! I hate it! Mummy!

**SHIPMAN:** It's not Mummy, Barry, it's Nell. She says call her Nell.

**BARRY:** *(voiceover)* You're not paying one bit of attention to me. I could be telling you I'm dropping dead in a month. I'm dropping dead in a month Mummy! And you've always done it. As long as I can remember. Listen to me! Some things are important you know. What're you thinking? Are you thinking about me dropping dead?

No not likely. Are you writing? Yes you're writing aren't you. Inside
your head you're writing. You're not listening to me. You're writing.

**NELL:**   *(Her dialogue overlaps with BARRY'S voiceover.)* No

**BARRY:**   *(voiceover)* No what! . . . No what!

**NELL:**   What

**BARRY:**   *(voiceover)* Exactly!

**NELL:**   What did you say

**BARRY:**   *(voiceover)* I said no, what!

**NELL:**   I don't know what you're talking about

**BARRY:**   *(voiceover)* And I said exactly. You're not listening to me,
you're writing. You said no and I said no what. I said no what
meaning go on, and you don't know what I'm talking about so you
can't go on because you aren't listening and I said exactly!

**NELL:**   I said I don't know— [what you're talking about]

**BARRY:**   *(voiceover)* Pay attention to me! I just want to hear you say no
I'm not writing! Inside my head I am not writing! Say it!

**NELL:**   Why would I want to say that?

**BARRY:**   *(voiceover)* Because it would be a great big lie! *(pause)*

**SHIPMAN:**   True?

**NELL:**   Not like that, no, you're twisting the story.

*The shadow of the child starts to fade away.*

**BARRY:**   *(voiceover, distant)* Mummy! Mummy!

**SHIPMAN:**   Bert then. "Tell me, Miss Shipman, how is Mr. Van Tuyle?"
Or is that just the Daddy story inside out?

**NELL:**   I loved Daddy! If I'd known in time I'd have—

**SHIPMAN:**   What?

**NELL:**   I'd have gone to him yes I would!

**SHIPMAN:**   "She leaves the picture to go to her father."

**NELL:**   Maybe she would. I don't know if she would.

**SHIPMAN:**   I do.

**NELL:**   You're old. She never grows old.

**SHIPMAN:**   You will.

**NELL:**   She never grows old like you.

**SHIPMAN:**   You will.

**NELL:**   She never forgets the things that count.

**SHIPMAN:**   What things would they be? Lay them out! Let's see! A list
of her movies? The stories she's written? Is that what you mean?

**HELEN:** Stop!

**NELL:** I cried for Daddy. Not with Ernie. Not in front of the crew or the cast or the people milling around. I kept it inside. I said why wasn't I there, how could I leave him, what was I thinking. But—I thought I was doing something that mattered!

**SHIPMAN:** You thought recognition would come.

**NELL:** Now that you're old and no one remembers and you can't even remember you wonder if it was worth it! I know it was worth it!

**SHIPMAN:** Worth it. What is "it," what is it?

**HELEN:** Start over!

**SHIPMAN:** *(to HELEN)* What about Mummy? The real Mummy story? Title "How Mummy Died for Nell." Her movie, which one was it that time? You know she's spent her entire career peering through pine boughs, or swimming round waterfalls, or having a significant moment with a member of the animal kingdom. *(to NELL)* Don't you ever feel that?

**NELL:** You do. I don't.

**SHIPMAN:** *(to HELEN)* It was water that time. She was wet. Wet and cold. She'd been dunked more times than a doughnut and the take still wasn't right. She came down with the flu. *(to NELL)* When was it, 19 something or other? *(SHIPMAN knows the date.)*

**NELL:** You figure it out.

**SHIPMAN:** 1918. *(to HELEN)* Yes, a bad flu. And Mummy tended poor Nell. Washed the flushed face, wet the dry lips, hovered over her like an angel. Looked after Barry. And poor Nell fell into a sleep. Like the princess no one could waken? A terrible sleep. Then do you know what happened? Once Mummy had made a pact with God. And she'd almost forgotten. God hadn't forgotten. *(to NELL)* She'd made a pact with God when you were ten days old on the night the doctor said you were dead. That night, she ran to the hill overlooking the bay with you in her arms. She held you tight in her arms, you, a little blue baby. She made a pact. And a light breath of wind off the water, hardly a wind, an ever so slight movement of air rose up from the water below and spiralled around her. And the dead baby started to cry. The night of the flu and your terrible sleep, she sat by your bed. When there was nothing more to be done, could be done, would be done, except wait for the sleep to take its terrible toll, Mummy remembered. Mummy went up and lay on her bed. She had made a pact. And in the morning, you woke up. She didn't. *(silence)* Play. *(no response)* Somebody. *(no response)* Play.

**NELL:**  No.

**SHIPMAN:**  *(defeated)* I win. *(silence)*

**HELEN:**  *(a whispered valiant attempt to start a new story)* Daddy's voice was a tenor, and Mummy's, a very sweet alto . . . Nell? *(HELEN looks to NELL who doesn't respond.)*

**EDISON:**  pin-point photographic images, spun to the accompaniment of a phonograph playing the sound track, resulting in a harmonious relationship with the moving pictures

**HELEN:**  Play Nell.

**NELL:**  *(whispers)* Can't.

**SHIPMAN:**  Told you so.

**EDISON:**  the motion of the subjects is documented simultaneously by three cameras—the subjects' movement is captured in bright relief

**HELEN:**  *(to NELL)* Daddy lies on the sidewalk and Laddie stands over Daddy and won't let anyone near till they find someone who knows what to do. And the three dogs stay by his bed. Never leaving his bed. They look after him, Nell, like you said. Really, they do. That is the story.

**EDISON:**  with a transparent, translucent film fed through the camera producing pictures of subjects in motion over an extended period of time

**HELEN:**  *(to SHIPMAN)* This is the story! Ernie tells her and then she's alone. She goes to the place where they chain the dog from the movie. Two dogs really, Great Danes! Tresore for the vicious scenes because he is vicious and Rex for the gentle scenes because he is gentle, and the two of them looking like twins. She sits between them and she cries for Daddy. She cries, while Tresore and Rex each stretch to the end of their chains, put their heads in her lap and make small little comforting sounds. They love her.

**EDISON:**  Persistence of Vision is the Central Illusion: the idea that isolated, fixed, and single images can appear to flow together, when brought successively into view, and intermittently advanced

**HELEN:**  It's a love story, Shipman! Not old and not dying but living! National stock theatre on tour in Alaska? Exhilarating, Shipman! Going broke in Alaska? Stimulating, Shipman! Playing on pool tables shoved together for a stage? Galvanizing, Energizing—and bloody dangerous, Shipman! Why can't you remember?!

SHIPMAN: I remember.

HELEN: I know you remember. Boarding with an old lady and her forty canaries in Alaska? I never knew they shed feathers like snow in a blizzard. Educational Shipman, remember? Before movies and Ernie. Remember. That's when you fall in love. Really in love. In love for keeps. With the sky and the earth and the mountains.

SHIPMAN: I did do that . . . I did.

HELEN: You feel like a migrating bird flying home in Alaska.

SHIPMAN: Not there yet, but close, getting close.

HELEN: Charlie Taylor writes a play just for you, and what did he call it Nell? Nell?

SHIPMAN: "The Girl From Alaska?"

HELEN: Everyone thinks you're the girl from Somewhere Away. From Not Where You're At. Isn't that funny? What does it mean?

EDISON: There is a tendency to overheat if the picture passes too close to the light source.

HELEN: I know what it means! Our last night in Alaska, I go for a walk with a husky. A big black silver-tipped dog. The Northern Lights are out, and I run with the dog, my feet pounding the ground with great shafts of light overhead. I run and I run with the dog. *I'm turning the earth with my running under a kaleidoscope sky.* That's what it means. We can play that Nell. Because that's how it was, and that's how it is, and that's how it always will be!

SHIPMAN: Was it ever really like that?

EDISON: *(fading although still audible)* This defect is not a major problem so long as the moving picture stays within certain parameters and distance from the source.

NELL: Priest Lake?

HELEN: We aren't playing that story.

SHIPMAN: Not yet.

NELL: But soon.

HELEN: Don't think of it.

NELL: Bert and the gun—

HELEN: Not yet! Try summer on stage in New York . . . try the toney Wall St. Cousins! . . . Try their painful teas for the poor relation, me! . . . Try . . . try Fun out with the Boys in the Chorus!

**SHIPMAN:** Fun. Till the leading lady pulls you aside, sits you down, and tells you all about "whoopsies" "muffhounds" "queers" and "other unnatural acts."

**HELEN:** "Do you want to be thought one of "them?" she says. She says "You will if you hang about with "them!" She says "Everyone'll think you're one of "them"—so ignore "them" she says—let "them" hang about with "themselves"—and she says "you hang about with . . . "Yourself!"

**NELL:** So I did.

**HELEN:** You didn't.

**SHIPMAN:** Well the end's the same. Alone.

**HELEN:** Get over it.

**NELL:** Did I cry?

**HELEN:** Of course you cried.

**NELL:** "She cried because they'd been her friends." That's how the story goes.

**SHIPMAN:** Does it?

**HELEN:** *(to SHIPMAN)* Would I lie? *(to NELL)* And you laughed. It was funny and sad. And you told the whole chorus what she'd said about "whoopsies!" and "muffhounds" and you and the boys all laughed together and then you were sad and—Playing, keep playing!

**SHIPMAN:** Playing! For the Larger Lot in the Seats! For the Customers! For the Audience! For the Ones Paying the Shot!

**HELEN:** New York! *(does a little tap dance)* Got Fired! For? *(a "da da da da da dum!" hand off to NELL who doesn't pick up the cue; a second "da da da da da dum!" tap dance and hand off bit of business again)* For refusing to take a cut in pay when? Come on Nell—when?

**NELL:** *(with no great enthusiasm)* When audiences failed to appear.

**SHIPMAN:** So play for the Smaller Lot, for the Lot that you have to Pretend for, in order to Be In, in order to Get Out, in order to Learn, in order to Get Jobs, in order to Keep Jobs, in order to—

**HELEN:** Got a job with—come on Nell, with

**NELL:** With Jesse Lasky

**HELEN:** Jesse Lasky! Me playing the piano with five others on stage for—ta dum—*The Pianophiends! (as always, "performing" her story, and in the course of it managing to engage SHIPMAN and*

*NELL more fully)* My piano downstage right. I could not get the piece of music ending the first act into my head and I couldn't use sheet music so—I fake it! Who could tell? Six pianos playing on stage? No one can tell! My fingers fly over the keys! They don't once touch the keys! Till a brush-up rehearsal when, as we approach the end of the act, and at a sign from Jesse's congenitally suspicious sister Blanche, everyone stops playing. But me. Who continues a beautifully mimed performance of this particular bit. As silence fills the air I gradually . . . bring . . . it . . . to . . . a . . . close.

**NELL:** How did I ever get hired?

**HELEN:** You know how! You played a bit of piano for Miss Lasky at the audition, and then, for Jesse, performed a highly effective crotch-splitting high-kicking bump and grind rendition of Alexander's Ragtime Band! *(the audition that seduced Lasky into hiring her; she sings while performing her "highly effective crotch-splitting high-kicking bump and grind rendition" of the first verse)* And did a reprise for my audition for Ernie Shipman!

*Full orchestration comes in as HELEN continues her song and dance routine into the chorus of the song. ERNIE watches with a high degree of appreciation as she plays to him. He holds her resumé in his hand. The song and dance ends, and ERNIE redirects with difficulty his attention to reading the resumé.*

*During the following dialogue ERNIE studies HELEN'S resumé with a bit of eye play between them as he does so. They are the focus of SHIPMAN and NELL who approach the couple.*

**SHIPMAN:** In order to Find Love, in order to Keep Love, in order to

**NELL:** *(to SHIPMAN)* Alright. You were right. It was partly his hair. It was curly. He had blond curly hair. And he wore this funny little red hat that looked like a hunting cap and—didn't look like a hunting cap . . . I don't know what the hell it was, but on him it looked good. Made him look different. Not arty, or corporate or. . . . No bullshit. Ernie was not a bullshitter. Eyes . . . blue. A particular blue. Like a flower. Periwinkle blue. You don't see a blue like that very often. Little laugh lines. He was funny. It's hard to explain. He knew how to do things. How to get things done. He. . . . He just . . . I don't know, he just . . . I did love him. I did.

**SHIPMAN:**  He was an asshole.

**NELL:**  I don't know how I missed that.

**SHIPMAN:**  A bullshitter.

**NELL:**  I know. I know. . . . And he did get me jobs. . . . *(She is amused by, and kind of admires, ERNIE's blatant behaviour.)* Took all my money and spent it or lost it. Pregnant with Barry, I didn't have a thing for the baby. The morning after I delivered, the baby furniture and clothing and pram start arriving. All of this infant wear and apparel and. . . . He'd won it. While I gave birth, he played poker for all of these baby things. I don't know what we'd have done if he'd lost. I don't know what he'd put up for his ante. . . . Probably Barry! He would do that. He would bet the baby!

**SHIPMAN:**  And his hair?

**NELL:**  You know it wasn't that blond. A dirty blond. More of a sandy colour. Kind of dark. And he wasn't that tall, not really short . . . but

**SHIPMAN:**  I know what you mean.

**NELL:**  He was short. But I've got to stand by the eyes. They really were blue. This miraculous blue. . . . Sort of blue.

**SHIPMAN:**  Muddy blue?

**HELEN:**  *(as she eyes ERNIE)* Like a flower? Delphinium Blue?

**SHIPMAN:**  Prairie slough Blue?

**NELL:**  Leave me something. Come on.

**ERNIE:**  *(He's coming on to HELEN, she knows it and returns the ball, having fun.)* Call me Ernie. I like the piece. You do it well. What else have you done?

**HELEN:**  Two tours with national stock; *Pianophiends* with Mr. Lasky and his lovely sister Blanche.

**ERNIE:**  *(chuckles catching a subtle sub-text on "lovely sister")* Bet there's a story there.

**HELEN:**  You win.

**ERNIE:**  I do.

**HELEN:**  And a national and Alaska tour with Charlie Taylor; next with Sullivan and Considine in Seattle.

**ERNIE:**  Playing what?

**HELEN:**  Ingenues, Leading Ladies and Sads. It's on the resumé.

**ERNIE:**  I like your voice, to hear you talk, go on.

**HELEN:**  Aahh, vaudeville, Pantages, Cora Mullaley and I have *The Apple Sisters Act*, we do a kind of parody of

**ERNIE:**   Heard it's funny. Maybe a little too smart but funny. How old are you? Hate to ask a lady but you look

**HELEN:**   Eighteen?

**ERNIE:**   What's your name again?

**HELEN:**   Helen Barham.

**ERNIE:**   Helen Barham. Sounds very—English.

**HELEN:**   It is English. So's Ernie Shipman.

**ERNIE:**   It's American—North American. Helen Barham. Sounds kind of—stuffy. You don't look like a stuffy kind of girl. Are you?

**HELEN:**   Am I what?

**ERNIE:**   Stuffy.

**HELEN:**   It depends.

**ERNIE:**   On what?

**HELEN:**   On what the role calls for.

**ERNIE:**   *(laughs)* You've got style. I like that . . . I manage a lot of people. They get work. They call me 10% Ernie because when I get you work, 10% is mine. Would you mind turning around? *(She does so.)* Looks good. . . . You're tall.

**HELEN:**   I'm just right.

**ERNIE:**   I like tall women. You've got something. It's partly the face. Something else. I dunno. I may be falling in love.

**HELEN:**   I hear you do that on a fairly regular basis.

**ERNIE:**   *(laughs)* I like you. You got something. How'd you like to play the lead in . . . *The Barrier?*

**HELEN:**   Sounds good to me.

**ERNIE:**   How does dinner sound? You see the order of things is important. If I'd asked you for dinner first you might've gotten the wrong idea.

**HELEN:**   I still might.

**ERNIE:**   *(laughs)* I like you.

*During the following dialogue MAN #1 slips off his ascot, puts on a tie, clenches a dead cigar in his teeth and moves into the scene as SAM Goldwyn.*

**SAM:**   Sam Goldwyn.

**ERNIE:**   You're worth keeping an eye on.

*The SAM/NELL scene, as it begins, interfaces with the ERNIE/ HELEN scene as it ends.*

**SAM:** I been keepin' an eye on you. You done some good work for Vitagraph.

**ERNIE:** But we gotta do something about the name. How about Nell— Nell Wilson Nell Harris Nell Thompson Nell

**SAM:** Ernie had you churnin' out a lotta stuff for a lotta people

**ERNIE:** Shipman!

**SAM:** de Mille saw you on set at Vitagraph

**ERNIE:** It calls for discussion.

**SAM:** he mentioned your name

**ERNIE:** over dinner what do you say

**SAM:** Now you know we're contractin' some players and we're thinkin' of contractin' you.

**ERNIE:** Nell Shipman!

**SAM:** I got a contract right here. Seven years. Legal limit. You sign at the bottom.

**NELL:** Don't you think I should read it?

**SAM:** Never said don't read it. Always read the contract. Ernie teach you that?

**NELL:** It's a little something I discovered myself.

**SAM:** Smart girl. Don't let it get in the way of the camera.

**NELL:** I'm not smart enough to know what that means.

**SAM:** Movies're about one thing. *He wants it. Is he gonna get it?* Now go ahead and read, and sign there at the bottom. You know we're in the business of makin' money and one of the things that makes money is Stars, so in the business of makin' money, we make Stars. We can make you a Star. A commodity that sells the commodity we make.

**NELL:** I don't think of it that way.

**SAM:** Why should you? Nothin' to do with you. The deal is you're gonna make a lotta money, and we're gonna make a lotta money. Hell, when this business started nobody realized there was money to be made. But once we started throwin' movin' pictures up on that screen—'stead of some little kinescope parlour one machine one person—everything changed. Mass Audience! And when Carl Laemmle invested some money into makin' Florence Lawrence a Star and the box office took off, the industry realized hey, you make Stars you sell pictures! For a start you sell pictures. Then you sell what she wears. You sell what she drives. You sell how she looks. You sell how she lives, what she drinks, where she goes and you sell it on screen and off! You sell what she thinks! You sell what she stands for! You got yourself a vehicle to sell any goddamn material or immaterial thing you want! You can change the face and mind of America. *(pause)* You signed that yet?

NELL: I've read it.

SAM: For you we're gonna create a whole new look.

NELL: My name?

SAM: The name suits you, I like it. But the hair, the clothes, kinda roles you been playin'

NELL: And what kind is that?

SAM: and the stuff that you write, I've seen it on screen

NELL: What about it?

SAM: the female role, the kinda role you been playin'?—have you signed that yet?

NELL: The terms seem onerous.

SAM: Omerous!—omerous? What the hell does that mean?

NELL: Well, this says I work any hours you want, I play any roles you want, I make any movies you want. You can rent me out to any company you want for any reason you want. I'm to live where you want, go where you want, do what you want, and if I have a problem with any of this, I'm out at a moment's notice! That's what "onerous" means.

SAM: And you make a lotta money.

NELL: You make a lot of money. I don't. At least not in this contract.

SAM: I thought Ernie was smarter than this.

NELL: Say, if you see Ernie here you got a big problem.

SAM: I thought he had a thoroughbred, turns out you don't have the legs for it. Bit of mud on the track and you're runnin' last.

NELL: I'm finished at Vitagraph. I'm going into independent production. So—how about congratulations, Sam?

SAM: *(starting to leave)* All the world needs, another independent producer.

NELL: Hold it! Here's another hot flash! *(SAM slowly, leisurely, undoes and removes his tie and any other "Sam" bits as he listens to her.)* I'm writing the screenplay and I'm playing the role. Guess what? Female lead: strong woman. Male lead: sick husband. She beats arctic weather and villains. Saves husband and self with the aid of a great vicious hound everyone's afraid of but her. The villains all *want it*. But none of them *get it*.

Here's your contract. *(MAN #1, formerly SAM, smiles at her, ignores the contract and moves out of the scene but not off stage. NELL calls after him as he leaves.)* Why don't you try changing the name at the top and see if you can buy someone else? I'm not for sale!

SHIPMAN:   Bad tag line. It puts him off. *(takes the contract and looks at it)*

NELL:   He's an ass! I wasn't sure that he'd get it.

HELEN:   An important ass?

SHIPMAN:   In any version we care to create.

NELL:   *(grabbing the contract from SHIPMAN and tearing it up)* And stupid!

HELEN:   Well we can make him stupid—but was he?

NELL:   They're always the ones running things.

SHIPMAN:   Dangerous supposition, even in fiction.

NELL:   Alright!

SHIPMAN:   And you know another thing that you do?

NELL:   What is it now?

SHIPMAN:   You dick around with time, and with place—And with people! It complicates things.

NELL:   It clarifies things!

SHIPMAN:   How?

NELL:   Gets to the essence, you know, fresh insight when you rearrange life? when you

SHIPMAN:   Critics would differ.

NELL:   "Cri-tics would differ?"

HELEN:   It's alright to differ.

NELL:   *(to SHIPMAN)* First structure, then critics? What the hell has that got to do with the story? *(to HELEN)* Why am I even talking to her? *(to SHIPMAN)* Maybe the real problem's content eh? *(to HELEN)* I bet that it's content. She—does not know—her own life!

SHIPMAN:   Not the way that you tell it!

NELL:   Nor apparently the way that you lived it You gave me your so-called "fictional news" remember? The End looming up there on the screen and you said make something of that, and I'm trying!

**SHIPMAN:** Oh you're trying alright.

**HELEN:** She means she can see that you're trying.

**NELL:** So! We have toured with the Gilmores, we have married Ernie, we've made movies, we've had Barry, we have lost Mummy and Daddy, we are The Girl from God's Country, we have turned down Sam Goldwyn, we have produced with Ernie, we have been screwed by Universal and we have screwed Bert! Does any of this ring a bell?

**SHIPMAN:** I find it painful you know.

**NELL:** *(to HELEN)* She finds it painful—while I struggle on, trapped by the burden of bad teeth, failing eyesight, clogged arteries, stomach problems with spicy food and never remembering where I've left the keys, she finds it painful? Who is this old woman? I can't believe that it's me!

**SHIPMAN:** So where are we now?

**NELL:** *(to SHIPMAN)* With Bert! Dumped Ernie! With Bert!

**HELEN:** "The Nell Shipman Finance Company" remember?

**NELL:** She remembers alright! Producer, Star, Vice-president, me!

**SHIPMAN:** Oh yes—all the accoutrements, right?

**NELL:** That's right. A new car. Drove by the showroom, I saw it and bought it.

**SHIPMAN:** And a big house, right?

**NELL:** Are you suggesting that I was overly concerned with the acquisition of material goods? Is that what you're saying? Yes, I had a big house, a new car, motion picture company, hordes of animals, great clothes! I admit it! Do you feel better now? *(to HELEN)* She has a thing for material goods. I never had a thing for material goods. If I did, I'd remember.

**SHIPMAN:** How can I have a thing for material goods when at this stage of my life I have no material goods?! And you want to know why I have no material goods? Because you had a thing for material goods!

**NELL:** *(to SHIPMAN)* Well get this. Brownie the bear from "Back To God's Country?" I let her ride in the rumble seat of the car. I do. She has totally destroyed the rumble seat of the car. Does that sound like a thing for material goods?

**SHIPMAN:** It sounds like wanton destruction of material goods and irresponsible care of a bear.

**NELL:**   And I've got raccoons, chipmunks, a skunk and a squirrel, a desert rat called Ignatz, two wild cats, and Nikki a desert gray fox, Tex who's a malamute and Angelic Nikisia the panama deer!

**SHIPMAN:**   Don't forget Barry the boy.

**NELL:**   And never forget the housekeeper for Barry. Housekeeper for Barry! Give me a death sentence for that! And I've got a room, special room, my room, where I, I cut and I edit!

**SHIPMAN:**   And Bert?

**NELL:**   What about Bert?

**SHIPMAN:**   You tell me what about Bert.

**HELEN:**   How about something new?

**NELL:**   "Something New!" That's the title of a crazy marvellous picture! Him. And me. Bert. Nell. Driving a Maxwell through the Mojave! 120 degrees heat. Horses or mules can't even go where we went. And we film it all. Good Work and I'm not afraid to say that out loud. Good Work! Are you listening out there! Good Work! This is the beginning! Real beginning. I am going to make movies that'll make people laugh and cry, and think a little. What the hell is wrong with that story?

**SHIPMAN:**   Incomplete.

**NELL:**   What's complete?! You tell me, what's complete? Who wants complete? Do you want complete?! I have never wanted complete! And neither have you!

*MAN #1 has slipped on his ascot and picked up the cane to become BERT. He has a slight limp, the after-effects of the foot frozen during the filming of "Back To God's Country."*

**BERT:**   You lost it, Nell.

**NELL:**   I'm not cut out to stand up in front of a bunch of pigeons, and justify every penny spent.

**BERT:**   It's over budget.

**NELL:**   It's not over budget! It was under budgeted!

**BERT:**   You and I understand that. The investors don't. And you've got to explain it in a way they can understand and support.

**NELL:**   They're in too deep, they can't pull the plug now.

**BERT:**   They need reassurance and they need it from you.

**NELL:**   We've changed the title. It's "The Girl From God's Country," I like it.

**BERT:** It's not titles they're worried about!

**NELL:** Whose side are you on?

**BERT:** It's the overtime on the flight shots.

**NELL:** So we have miles of film. I'd love more miles. Up there in the blue, blue sky, and those World War One Jennies skipping across the clouds, and you've got it on film, Bert, it's all there. The planes, wing tip to wing tip. Joe standing up in his Jenny cranking the camera, and me standing up in my Jenny playing the heart out of Marion. You on the ground. No communication between us. Director. Cameraman. Actress. We're reading each other's minds. A tiny mistake from the pilots? End of movie. Real end of movie. We've got to be crazy but just look at the footage!

**BERT:** And it's the cost overruns on the Canyon sequence!

**NELL:** We're fighting weather and we've got to pack everything in!

**BERT:** The menagerie keeps growing!

**NELL:** The animals are an asset! And I resent having to defend them on financial grounds!

**BERT:** They're expensive, not only to buy, but to house, to feed, and to transport!

**NELL:** But you can't put a price tag on what they give back! It's special between me and them! No fear. No abuse to make them perform. It's pure and it's spiritual and it reads. It all comes out on the film! For God's sake you're the director, you've seen the rushes, you know that!

**BERT:** But we can't afford to piss off the Backers and you know that!

**NELL:** All right! *(pause)*

**BERT:** You can't walk out of Board meetings, luv.

**NELL:** I know.

**BERT:** Tonight was a do-zer.

**NELL:** I was tired! And talk, talk, talking doesn't put footage on film.

**BERT:** It's their game in the Board Room. You've got to play their game.

**NELL:** I'm an artist, not an accountant.

**BERT:** But if you can't make the movie—

**NELL:** But I do make movies, so do you!

**BERT:** If you can't make the movie—or nobody sees it! What are you then!?

**NELL:** What am I then? *(pause)* Well, Bert, I'm trying to think of an answer to that . . . Zero! Zilch! Blank Page in the Script! Do not waste my time asking questions that don't have an answer, Bert! Don't do that!

*Pause.*

**SHIPMAN:** If you can't make the movie. Or nobody sees it. What am I then?

**NELL:** *(speaking to BERT who is still and does not acknowledge her)* I tell him I love him. I tell him we will finish this movie. I tell him it will be a success. I tell him Believe.

**SHIPMAN:** He says he believes.

**NELL:** I believe. What's wrong with that?

**MAN #1:** *(as he removes ascot and jacket, rolls up his shirt sleeves, drops his cane and anything that identifies him as BERT or SAM)* Timing, Nell!

*Fading in on tape, the background noise of a small gathering of major players, a conspiracy, with glasses of good scotch in a smoke-filled room. The background noise plays under the following dialogue.*

**MAN #2:** *(similarly removing anything that identifies him as ERNIE or CARL)* Timing and Time and the Major Players!

**MAN #1:** We make product! And makin' product is gettin' very expensive. Movies are gettin' expensive.

**MAN #2:** Unregulated Competition!?

**MAN #1:** Financial risk.

**MAN #2:** Unacceptable!

**MAN #1:** Creation?

**MAN #2:** I say each of us produces only the kind of movie each of us produces best

**MAN #1:** given our stable of Stars and directors!

**MAN #2:** Standardization of Product—Makes sense for makin' cars, makes sense for us too.

**MAN #1:** Chryslers make Chryslers, Fords make Fords

**MAN #2:** So You—Westerns, you—Costume Dramas,—you—Musicals, and Comedies you!

**MAN #1:** Distribution?

**MAN #2:** We gotta control the means of distributin' product to the guys who exhibit.

**MAN #1:** Gotta control all distribution companies

**MAN #2:** Preference is own em!

**MAN #1:** Exhibition?

**MAN #2:** We gotta control the means of Showing our product

**MAN #1:** We're talkin' movie houses here.

**MAN #2:** Preference is own the theatres!

**MAN #1:** Or place em under contractual obligation to us.

**MAN #2:** Packagin' of Product?

**MAN #1:** Every movie we make won't be a hit.

**MAN #2:** Every movie we make won't have a Star.

**MAN #1:** Every movie we make with a Star won't be a hit

**MAN #2:** So we control

**MAN #1:** Control the mix of movies our theatres exhibit

**MAN #2:** Some good movies, some B movies, some bad movies—they want a Pickford or Chaplin

**MAN #1:** they gotta take a whole package which is gonna contain— let's face it—some dogs.

*MAN #1 begins donning those items which identify him as BERT; similarly MAN #2 is donning those items which identify him as CARL.*

**MAN #2:** No takin' one film.

**MAN #1:** It's a package of a number of films or nothin'

*MAN #1 and MAN #2 pause.*

**MAN #2:** Independent Producers?
*Pause.*

**MAN #1:** If . . .

**MAN #2:** . . . they make a movie we like

**MAN #1:** if . . . it fits in the package

**MAN #2:** if we can make a deal for distribution

**MAN #1:** and exhibition that works

*MAN #1 and MAN #2 resume "dressing."*

**MAN #2:** for us

**MAN #1:** we pick up the rights!

**MAN #2:** No problem with independent producers. *(He addresses NELL.)* It can't run nine reels. *(He puts on the glasses, he's CARL.)*

**NELL:** What do you mean, can't? It just did. The premiere was a roaring success.

CARL: Rented theatre, invited audience, roses for the Star, lots of friends.

NELL: Does that make it any less real? Everyone loved it!

CARL: It's too long for the market. If you want Universal to distribute, cut it.

NELL: I took a lot of care with the edit.

CARL: You took as long to edit as you took to shoot it. Right?

NELL: The length of the film is the length of the film.

CARL: And went 100% over budget.

NELL: Do you want to distribute this film or not?

CARL: Nine reels, no distribution.

NELL: Get that time thing out of your head!

CARL: Nine reels does not fit the program.

NELL: Do you like the movie?

CARL: You cut the film to market requirements or—

NELL: Or what?

CARL: Or your investors will take it, re-edit, and offer for distribution themselves.

NELL: This film is my film.

CARL: Not true.

NELL: I've got a contract! And clauses! One being no interference from them with the edit!

CARL: Contracts are made to be broken, what the hell do you think lawyers live on?

NELL: It's my film!

CARL: It's product! They invested in product! The length of your product takes it out of the market! Shorten the product then you got market! We're talking value of investment dollars and their right to pay-back against what? What are you putting against their dollars, Nell? What the hell is there goes up against dollars?

NELL: If they cut it they'll ruin it.

CARL: Believe me no one will notice.

NELL: I'll notice.

CARL: Who are you? People see what they get. They don't know the difference.

NELL: If I ever thought that, I'd quit!

CARL: So do yourself a favour. I got to go.

NELL: I'll sue.

**CARL:** The investors are shaking, the lawyers are laughing. *(starting to exit the scene)*

**NELL:** I'll write every exhibitor! I'll tell them the film's been butchered! Don't show it!

**CARL:** *(stops)* That would be stupid thing number—what, Nell. I'd think about it.

**NELL:** You bet I will! Take out a full-page ad! Tell everyone! I won't let them do it! It's not gonna happen, you'll see!

**HELEN:** I'll tell it! I want to go back and this time I'll tell it.

**SHIPMAN:** Do you think you can change it?

**NELL:** With a little song and dance maybe?

**HELEN:** "Carl Laemmle scene, Distribution of "The Girl From God's Country," an Independent Production"

**NELL:** I know, I know! How about he says "nine reels Nell? A little long maybe?" and she says "no problem, I'll cut it"!! . . .

Or it goes like this! Carl says "an epic film I am proud to distribute Nell" and she smiles modestly accepting the compliment!!! . . .

I know! She says "I'm so ashamed of the marvelous reception given the premiere of my film that I can not offer it for distribution unless it is cut! I insist that the film be cut!!!" *(a little tap dance to)* Da da da da dah! Is that it? Do you think you can tell it like that? Do you?!

**HELEN:** I know what they did. They killed "The Girl From God's Country."

**BERT:** *(to NELL)* They can't cut a third of a film and keep it coherent!

**HELEN:** *(to BERT who does not acknowledge HELEN; he's talking to NELL)* She knows what they did! *(to NELL)* Fresh start Nell. Fresh start.

**SHIPMAN:** No.

**BERT:** Do you think you were right about running that ad?

**HELEN:** *(to BERT)* We had to! *(to SHIPMAN)* And we have to. *(to NELL)* Go on, tell him. Priest Lake.

**BERT:** I don't regret your running the ad. Do you?

**HELEN:** Pine trees and mountains. Tell him. With the angle of sun and the light on the trees—the landscape, it changes.

**BERT:** It's going to cause trouble but—

**HELEN:** It changes in colour. It tells different stories different times of the day, different times of the year. See? Fiction. Even in nature.

**BERT:**   I don't regret it.

**HELEN:**   We have to, Nell.

**BERT:**   You know it could kill us.

**HELEN:**   Everything big. Nothing small, Nell. Puts things in perspective.

**SHIPMAN:**   Don't want to.

**HELEN:**   Have to!

**BERT:**   We're lucky we aren't blacklisted, that's—assuming we aren't.

**SHIPMAN:**   She's afraid.

**NELL:**   Not afraid.

**BERT:**   What?

**NELL:**   I said Coolin, a little place called Coolin. Go there by train, then by boat to the end of the Lake. Wilderness, nothing but wilderness.

**BERT:**   Why the hell would we want to go there?

**NELL:**   Sell everything, start over.

**BERT:**   I said why?

**NELL:**   Create a spiritual home for the kind of films we make! Not just for the next picture, but a long-term location! Have you read my scenario? Working title "The Grubstake"—

**BERT:**   But Studio work—

**NELL:**   In Spokane! Not LA. Keep the cost down. We'll move the animals, bears, wolves, wild cats, the whole lot of them. Transport em. Build a lodge on the water—Lionhead Lodge for Film Casts and Crew! A Home for the Animals! What do you think? *(BERT is rubbing his foot)* What's wrong?

**BERT:**   It's nothing. Sell everything, the house, the—?

**NELL:**   Move to Priest Lake! Shoot "Grubstake" in Idaho! What do you think?

**BERT:**   I dunno.

**NELL:**   Come on Bert. "Lionhead Lodge for Film Casts and Crew" a spiritual home for our films!

**BERT:**   Do you really think we could do it?

**NELL:**   Remember making "The Girl From God's Country?" When I nearly drowned twice? When the plane pitched and I almost fell out of the sky? The time my foot slipped and I almost fell off a mountain? When my dress caught and I could have burnt to death in the fire? I was never afraid. Not once. I knew we could do it. It just took another take. And it was a good movie, Bert. The investors cut it and killed it but even then—there're moments still in it, wonderful moments! I'm not afraid, and yes, of course we can do it!

**SHIPMAN:** When you say that—

**NELL:** Say what?

**SHIPMAN:** Say you're never afraid? When you think you can do anything? You are a danger. That's something I know.

**HELEN:** A danger to who?

**SHIPMAN:** To herself. And to others.

**HELEN:** Why's that?

**SHIPMAN:** She's either a fool or a liar.

**NELL:** So which am I? Tell me.

**SHIPMAN:** A . . . maker of fiction? A liar.

**HELEN:** And which one are you?

**SHIPMAN:** Me?

**HELEN:** Yes you. The Fool? Or The Liar?

**SHIPMAN:** Ah. . . . Which one am I.

**EDISON:** *(faintly)* the illusion of continuous movement with the appearance of truth is achieved through a persistence of vision in which the image dwells on the eye.

**NELL:** Never show fear. It grows and it spreads. Let them do what they want. Keep the film rolling. If Dumka the wolf wants to chew on my hair, don't move. Don't move. Pretend a slow soft awakening. Low baby babble of sound. Always that sound. Open eyes. Brown eye sees yellow. All caught by glass eye in black box. Lock brown eye with yellow. Film rolling. Keep rolling. If Brownie the bear hugs a little too tight, no fear. No fear. Glass eye, black box, babble words, almost words, always words, hear the words babble words always words you know me you trust me, trust me and know me and trust, the glass eye, the black box, the film, and the story.

**SHIPMAN:** Trust? . . . Trust you? . . . And the story. . . . Trust in the Story, and Telling the Story?

**BERT:** How'd it go?

**NELL:** A disaster.

**BERT:** How could it be a disaster?

**NELL:** I don't know! I've never done a trade show before. Room full of distributors backed by the majors and a couple of poor independents like me. It was supposed to be you! You're the one knows the distribution game, not me! And I'm the one's supposed to sell "Grubstake?"

**BERT:** So . . . how . . . did . . . it . . . go?

**NELL:** How's your flu or your foot and whatever it is that's kept you in bed?

**BERT:** I feel— [like hell]

**NELL:** Actually I don't care. At this moment I really don't care.

**BERT:** You can't keep it a secret. How did it go?

**NELL:** They hated it! They sat there like lumps, smoking cigars and belching. They got up and filed out at the end like the funeral service was over and if they got away quick, duty having been done, they could escape the graveside ritual. That would have been me. I was the graveside ritual!

**BERT:** Help me up.

**NELL:** I had to cut and edit this film at night sneaking up and down fire exits to avoid actors we owe money to! We've spent everything to make this movie and build Lionhead Lodge! We've hocked everything we own to get to this Trade Show! We're running out of money for feed and we need three thousand more for winter feed, and they hate the movie! Not a word to me, not a word!

**BERT:** Help me up.

**NELL:** I will not help you up! Who the hell's helping me up?

**BERT:** It's alright, Nell. It'll be okay.

**NELL:** Are you crazy? It is not alright or okay. It's a bloody disaster. And the worst thing is, the very worst is . . . I don't think the movie is bad! That's what's so terrifying! I don't think it's bad. I think "Grubstake" is good! Goddamn it, it is good! . . . But no sale. . . . So now what do we do?

*Sound of a phone ring.*

**SHIPMAN:** Fred Warren, independent distributor, makes a bid for "Grubstake"

**BERT:** Take it

**SHIPMAN:** Projected gross five hundred thousand, but a 75–25 split in His favour

**BERT:** Take it.

**SHIPMAN:** No money up front.

**BERT:** For God's sake, take it!

**NELL:** Not a good deal!

**BERT:** No other offers!

**NELL:** It's worth a lot more!

**SHIPMAN:** You'll take it.

**NELL:** I won't!

**SHIPMAN:** You'll take it.

**NELL:** I will not take it! I won't! I—! *(pause)* I . . . *(to SHIPMAN)* But I. . . . Have. . . . To . . . I have to. It's not a good deal but, I'll take it. . . . Maybe . . . I can raise some money on the strength of the deal maybe . . . work a deal, shoot some two reelers till the money comes in maybe sell . . . sell a coupla stories till, till . . . I can do it . . . I know I can do it. *(to BERT)* We can do it. We'll take it, and we can do it. But I—! . . . But I'm telling you Bert! I think "Grubstake" is good. I do! It's good. What do you think? *(pause)* What do you think? . . .

I said I think "Grubstake" is good! What Do You Think?! *(no response)* For God's sake, say something! Just say it! It was bad! It was good! It was—

*Sound of phone.*

**CARL:** *(moving into the scene, speaking directly to NELL)* I watched your film this morning, really enjoyed it.

**SHIPMAN:** Did you.

**CARL:** Beautiful scenery. Fantastic shots with the animals. Got excitement, got a neighbourly feel. Holiday fare. We like it.

**SHIPMAN:** Do you.

**CARL:** Universal thinks it will sell.

**SHIPMAN:** It'll sell.

**CARL:** Seventy-five thousand up front, 50–50 split, in your favour.

**SHIPMAN:** Can't do it.

**CARL:** It's a very good deal. *(pause)* So. We can talk more advance but the percentage offer—[is solid]

**SHIPMAN:** I've signed with Fred Warren

*Sound of phone ringing and continuing to ring.*

**NELL:** I thought nobody liked it. Nobody said that they liked it.

**CARL:** Nell, Nell, Nell, no one ever says anything at a trade show. *(sound of a second phone ringing.)* Warren eh? Not a major player. *(As he speaks he is removing any items of dress or hand props that identify him as CARL.)* You know the bankruptcy rate for fellows like him? *(sound of third phone ringing)* Too bad. A good little movie.

**SHIPMAN:** I've already signed.

*Sound of four phones ringing*

**CARL:** You should stick with the majors, Nell. *(He snaps his fingers and the ringing phones stop.)* Independent distribution will kill you. *(Silence. He moves to the periphery watching as MAN #2.)*

**HELEN:** Play.... It's alright. We can play! ... *(She laughs.)* Remember, remember that time driving into Seattle!? And seeing the billboard "Back To God's Country?" And your face? How big was your face?

**NELL:** *(It was a nightmarish enlargement, not a cheering thought.)* It was huge.

**SHIPMAN:** It was frightening.

**HELEN:** "See Nell Shipman in 'Back To God's Country'!" Ta dum! Not a paltry "with Nell Shipman" plus names in a cast list. No sir. It said "She's The Girl from God's Country!" And you were! The Girl From God's Country!

**SHIPMAN:** See Nell Shipman in!

**NELL:** Whatever.

**HELEN:** Remember those forty canaries in Alaska? The din and the feathers? It was funny. And seeing your name and the ad for the play on the floor of the birdcage? Finding that very same page and the ad and your face replacing the Sears Roebuck catalogue for use in the outhouse. You laughed.

**SHIPMAN:** It was funny. *(SHIPMAN and NELL can't resist smiling.)*

**HELEN:** And behind Pantages Vaudeville House in Spokane? Who was it put the apple on top of his head? Who gave you the gun? It was loaded. And you just took twelve big paces, you turned and you fired!

**NELL:** I did. I just did it! I fired!

*The three of them laugh.*

**SHIPMAN:** You did, you fired. Ka-pow!

**HELEN:** One lucky shot! No takers for seconds! Who was it you called the Top Top Banana?

*Pause as she realizes who that was, and what became of the top top banana; she has inadvertently brought up something that causes depression.*

**SHIPMAN:** That was Bert.

**NELL:** Trusting.

**SHIPMAN:** Too trusting.

**NELL:** Followed precisely the advice he got for his foot the first time he froze it.

**HELEN:** Prolonged immersion of said foot in kerosene in a washtub accompanied by the smoking of many cigarettes and the simultaneous imbibing of much hard liquor.

**NELL:** Bad advice.

**SHIPMAN:** And suffered the consequences everafter.

**HELEN:** Ending up with a permanent log. A log at the end of his leg. A dead piece of wood. At the end of his leg this—thing. It never really unfreezes he says. When it's cold, it hurts he says. When he walks, foot hits the ground, and it hurts.

**NELL:** Loved actors.

**SHIPMAN:** Loved me.

**NELL:** He believed.

**SHIPMAN:** After breakfast, up from the table, "Let's make motion pictures, Nell, let's go!"

**BERT:** What the hell has this place got that no other place has?

**NELL:** Charm! Simplicity! Reflects the purity, the spirituality of the Big Places! This Big Place! Priest Lake, Idaho! The mountains, the forest, the water, the scale of it all!

**BERT:** Oh yes, the natural setting we have in abundance!

**NELL:** It is not a compromise! It's the essence! We want that. If we weren't here we'd have to come here!

**BERT:** Not unless we were crazy. Well? Go on!

**NELL:** Movement and plot, plot based on small human incident in a natural setting.

**BERT:** And when they ask where's the cleavage?

**NELL:** You say "It's a reprieve from human villainy and sexual exploits." Do you think you could say that! Would it hurt you to say that!

**BERT:** Translation no sex and no villain.

**NELL:** How many times do I have to say it! The only villain is the tumultuous nature of the natural world! It works for our characters, and against them! We place our characters in that world as part of that world!

**BERT:** What characters?

**NELL:** The characters in the scenarios! Would you read the scenarios. Read them!

**BERT:** We've no actors! We've no money for actors!

**NELL:** We've got Barry for the kid's role, we've got me, I'm an actor, we've got Lloyd, I can get a guy from the lumber camp and Belle from the—

**BERT:** It's pathetic.

**NELL:** Listen! The animals. The animals play a big role.

**BERT:** Better be one helluva big role is all I can say.

**NELL:** Do you think I enjoy begging for film stock? Do you think I revel in pleading for a small cheque from the British Tribe while we wait for the money from "Grubstake?" Do you think I relish mixing flour, cornmeal, bran, rye, and lake water, arms in a trough up to my elbows, for feed? Do you think I savour poaching white-fish for dog food? Well let me tell you I don't! Let me tell you I would like it to be otherwise. But I make movies! This is what I have to do to make movies! To make my kind of movies! *(The shadow of the child is growing on the stage.)* They are set here because this is their setting! Animals work with us! Work for food and for housing and for care and affection because that is the world in which my movies live! And I work with people who give me the best they can give! I won't have you taking potshots—

**BARRY:** *(voiceover)* Mummy!

**NELL:** Call me Nell!

**BARRY:** *(voiceover)* Why can't I call you mummy?

**NELL:** I'm busy, Barry!

**BARRY:** *(voiceover)* Mummy?

**NELL:** *(a strong vicious attack springing from her impotence in other areas of her life)* You don't call Brownie bear do you! And you don't call Laddie dog, and you don't call Angelic Nikisia panama deer! You don't call King horse! and I don't want to be called mum or mummy or mother!

**BARRY:** *(voiceover)* Okay.

**NELL:** I'm!

**BARRY:** *(voiceover)* Okay.

**NELL:** I am your mother. That's What I am. But it's not Who I am. Call me Nell please call me Nell and I'll call you Barry, Okay?

**BARRY:** *(voiceover)* Let's run away Nell. Let's pack a lunch and go. Let's run away and find happiness over the hill. Do you think we could do that, Nell?

**SHIPMAN:** Pack a lunch and find happiness over the hill. . . . Do you think we could do that Nell?

*Silence. Although HELEN feels unable to "sing" or "perform" at this moment, she tries to provide some image of affection, love, happiness. The shadow of the child fades away during her speech.*

**HELEN:** Brownie the bear sings. She has five songs that she sings. The sweetest when Barry and you lie down on a bed of pine needles beside her; most blissful when she sucks her paw pads; the saddest when she sees you leave with the huskies. Brownie still sings. She still can sing.

*Pause. SHIPMAN picks up a yellow telegram, looks at it, holds it out. NELL takes it, opens it.*

**NELL:** Fred Warren's gone under. Bankrupt. "Grubstake" held as an asset by creditors. No money from "Grubstake."

**HELEN:** Winter Tales.

**NELL:** Not yet.

**SHIPMAN:** Stories of. Winter.

**NELL:** Soon winter soon. Not yet! . . . Five little dramas're finished. We're sure to get something for them. An advance. Some money. Some . . . some

**SHIPMAN:** Barry?

**NELL:** I'll send Barry to friends.

**SHIPMAN:** We'll need

**NELL:** Food. For Bert. The handyman Robson. And me. Winter kitchen supplies for us three. Then there's supplies for

**HELEN:** the animals. Brownie and the two other bears; Sweetie, the mule who's kept by the creek, the sled dogs, the great Danes and Laddie

**SHIPMAN:** the eagles, the coyotes, the wolves, the foxes, the deer and the elk

**HELEN:** the raccoon and skunk; Bobs and Babs the two wildcats, Coalie my mare and Bert's gelding King; there's Angelic Nikisia and—

**NELL:** Feed for the animals, three tons of carrots and apples, the hard biscuits I bake, we've still got some hay, there's the game Robson hunts if the snow isn't deep. Then there's. . . . There's . . .

**SHIPMAN:**  Not enough.

*Pause.*

**HELEN:**  Remember the flickers? Vaudeville and the flickers. I'd rush from back stage to stand in the house just to watch. Over and over. I'd stand there and watch. Eyes glued to the Flickers.

*Pause.*

**SHIPMAN:**  So ... we ... can. ... Play. ... Play for money. Charge money for tickets at Bonners Ferry and Sandpoint, they're big enough towns, you'd get a crowd. Show your copy of "Grubstake." Strut your stuff. You're a star.

**NELL:**  I'm a what?

**HELEN:**
(*sings*) Buffalo gal won't you come out tonight
Come out tonight come out tonight

*Lights dim. The three "perform" for the Bonners Ferry and Sandpoint audiences as black and white film is projected. The images can't be made out but shadow and light play across their faces, bodies and the stage. They'll perform as music plays. Reaction and the odd rude catcall from MAN #1 and MAN #2 at the audience. Although the three women are unified, working together, the strobe-like effect of the flickers fragments their unified actions.*

**HELEN, NELL & SHIPMAN:**
Buffalo gal won't you come out tonight
And dance by the light of the moon
Darktown strutters play this song
Play this song play this song—(*music stops*)

**NELL:**  A politician? Why that's an animal that can sit on the fence and keep both ears to the ground!

*Drum punctuation and the music plays.*

**HELEN, NELL & SHIPMAN:**
Come on along come on along
Let me take you by the hand
Up to the man up to the man
Who's the leader of the band

> And if you care to hear the Swanee River
> Played in ragtime—*(music stops)*

**SHIPMAN:** What's a critic? Why that's a legless man who teaches running.

*Drum punctuation and the music plays.*

**HELEN, NELL & SHIPMAN:**
> Come on and hear come on and hear
> Alexander's Ragtime band—*(music stops)*

**HELEN:** An associate producer? Well . . . that's the only person who'll associate with a producer.

*Drum punctuation and the music plays.*

**HELEN, NELL & SHIPMAN:**
> I never had a dream so nice
> Thought I was in paradise
> Waking up makes me feel cheap—*(music stops)*

*The three play this one moment from HELEN'S audition for Mr. Gilmore as one individual sharing the line, with simultaneous robotic duplication of movement.*

**HELEN:** Am I to blame be
**NELL:** cause flowers are dear
**SHIPMAN:** in cold weather
**NELL:** you should find
**HELEN:** fault with the cli
**SHIPMAN:** mate and not with
**NELL:** me for my part I
**SHIPMAN:** wish it was
**HELEN:** spring all year round and
**NELL:** that roses grew
**HELEN:** under one's feet!

*Sound effects for a pratfall, then music plays.*

**HELEN, NELL & SHIPMAN:**
> Everything is a source of fun
> Nobody's safe for we care for none
> Life is a joke that's just begun

*Flickering and music abruptly stop.*

**BERT:** Nell! Nell!! *(He staggers, walking with difficulty, wrapping a blanket round his shoulders. The three women observe his struggles.)* Where are you. *(silence)* Where are you? Where've you gone!? *(silence)* I'm talkin' to you! *(silence)* I'm talkin' to someone! Where are you, where—*(He falls down, and tries to get up unsuccessfully.)* Answer me! . . . Robson, Robson are you here, where are you? Where's Nell? *(silence)* Robson!. . . . Get up . . . come on get up . . . get the foot . . . under you . . . foot under. . . . You . . . get up—can't . . . get up . . . Robson! *(silence)* Help me! . . . Nell! . . . Nell! . . . I'm here, Nell! *(He starts to cry.)* Help me. I need help, Nell! . . . Get up. It's cold. Somebody help me! Somebody! Nell! Where are you, Nell! Nell. Help me Nell! Nell!!!

**NELL:** Where's Robson?

**BERT:** Robson? Where is he? I called, no one came.

**NELL:** Angelic Nikisia is dead.

**BERT:** A blizzard came in. Twenty below Robson said.

**NELL:** And Nikisia is dead! Was extra bedding put out?

**BERT:** I've been calling for you. Where were you?

**NELL:** Were they fed? Did anyone feed them? Or did you just sit here with the blanket around you and whine!?

**BERT:** I can't get up! My foot hurts and I can't get up! There's been a blizzard outside. Where were you when I called?

**NELL:** Think! At the Benefit at Bonnet's Ferry and Sandpoint!

**BERT:** That isn't true, that's a lie.

**NELL:** Don't start.

**BERT:** There's a blizzard so how did you get here?

**NELL:** I walked! And yes, there is a blizzard out there! I've hiked from Coolin to here, over the Lake where it's frozen and by beach where it's not. Forty miles. If I hadn't made Reader Creek last night I'd be dead. By rights I ought to be dead!

**BERT:** I know. I know where he is. He took the gun. He went hunting. The snow stopped and the wind died, and *(BERT struggles to get up.)* Robson said I'll see if I can get us some meat. That's where he is. He went hunting, Nell. That's where he is.

**NELL:** And Nikisia is dead of the cold. And the others—*(NELL leans down to help him.)* I asked you before! Were they fed? Did you feed them? Was extra bedding put out?

**BERT:** *(grabs her arm, a steel-like firm grip and quickly levers himself up)* You should be dead! Before you kill any more of us. You're killing us. Crazy ideas. You're crazy. Who said you were an actress? Who said it? I never said it! You couldn't direct. No. No, I could direct! You couldn't direct. I direct. What do you write? You write garbage and trash. You write little scenarios. Little—little notes. Little pieces of paper, not real writing. Little pieces of paper and I—I—I take them and I try—I try to make that garbage into story on film. Moving! Moving Pictures! Pictures! Pictorial! Action! That Moves! That's what I do. I do it! This place is killing me. You are killing me. You're killing me. I won't let you kill me. No, no I won't. That's what it is. Killing me, kill you. Kill you, I'll kill you!

*He shoves her away from him. Without touching her, a mimed realistic violent attack. He hits her in the stomach, backhands her across the face, grabs her round the throat, punches her in the face knocking her down. His frenzied attack is carried out in isolation from NELL although she reacts physically and audibly as if she were hit. She does not fall down. The sound of his laboured breathing and exertions and her audible reaction are enhanced subtly on tape. Physically exhausted, BERT stops. Inertia permeates the ambience of the space. Silence.*

**SHIPMAN:** He goes to the cookhouse. She walks down to the creek. She walks out on the ice. She walks close to where water streams into the lake, and she stands on the ice. A low sound, not a rumble. A clean sound, not a snap. She stands there. She waits. Laddie comes. Laddie sits on her feet.

*HELEN picks up the hand gun.*

**NELL:** I remember it's time.
**SHIPMAN:** Time.
**NELL:** Time to feed Brownie and the others. Extra bedding. I—Robson helps. No success with his hunt.
**HELEN:** I feed King the gelding the last of the hay. I tie my kerchief round his head and his eyes. I shoot him for meat for the huskies. I take Bert into Coolin by sled with the dogs.

*HELEN replaces the gun on the desk.*

**SHIPMAN:** He says it was the pain. It was because of the pain.

**NELL:** End result of the foot frozen how long ago? Now, blood poisoning, and threat of gangrene, and amputation of toes.

**SHIPMAN:** He'll be back when it's over.

**HELEN:** Why?

**SHIPMAN:** He Believes.

**NELL:** Do you believe that?

**SHIPMAN:** He . . . won't be away . . . long.

**HELEN:** Still winter still winter still winter still

**NELL:** Film. Keep shooting film!

**SHIPMAN:** I mire Coalie the mare on a trail. We shoot her at dawn. There's meat for the dogs.

**HELEN:** The two wildcats go mad, chew each other to death.

**SHIPMAN:** The eagle turns on its mate. Tresore the Great Dane is poisoned.

**HELEN:** Who poisoned the dog?

**NELL:** The mule packing cameras stops in her tracks. She sways as she stands there in the snow. Robson will build a fire under her belly. Even this will not move her. Sweetie refuses to move. When Venus appears in the sky, Robson will shoot her.

**HELEN:** Carry on. This is the story.

*HELEN goes to the phonograph and winds it as dialogue continues.*

**NELL:** I write. Little things.

**SHIPMAN:** He's better. Bert's better.

**NELL:** For *The Saturday Evening Post.*

**SHIPMAN:** Don't you think that he's better?

*NELL looks at SHIPMAN. The phonograph starts to play a dreamy piece of music. BERT watches the three women. He is very slowly, carefully, casually, stalking them. He sees the gun, casually picks it up, carries it in an absent-minded way. The women appear quiescent, almost languid, as they search an internal landscape for details of this story.*

**NELL:** *The Atlantic Monthly,* sell a series of pieces.

**HELEN:** Spring. Spring comes. Spring always comes.

**NELL:** Feed and care for the animals, Laddie always close on my heels.

**HELEN:** And spring always comes?

**NELL:** Wait for the mail. A shipment of film. A magazine cheque.

**SHIPMAN:** Some word of success?

**HELEN:** Plans. New story, tell a new story. *(She starts to sway to the music.)*

**NELL:** A feature. Working title "The Purple Trail." Scenario. A woman—*(She falters before continuing strongly.)* A Strong Woman.

**EDISON:** Take, for example, a song on a phonograph record. Cut away seventy-five per cent of the record, and what remains would, of course, give the tune, but would it produce the desired illusion of hearing the song?

*HELEN dances slowly. She's playing for herself. There is a false- ness, a sadness, in her attempt to recreate fun. BERT's focus will centre on her.*

**HELEN:** So the two of us are in a spotlight downstage and it's a long piece of dialogue in which he's telling me off. Now he's a very spitty actor, my poor face is getting drenched and this spitty spray can be seen by the house because of the light. So—I take out one of those miniature Japanese umbrellas and open it, holding it up in front of my face. The audience breaks up and Gilmore fines me ten bucks, 50% of my salary!

*She laughs, but it's forced and fades away. She continues dancing for several moments before attempting another story.*

By the end . . . by the end there's . . . there's six horses on stage along with six piles of you know what which I think they must have been saving all day for their moment on stage. So I get shot and I die. There I am, whirling round in my death throes, head tilted sideways like a bird, eyes squinty shut, trying to locate a spot where I can fall down and expire without landing in a pile of manure!

Many's the night I took a curtain call picking road apples out of my hair! *(The music quickens a bit, HELEN dances, and begins again.)* At the flickers, at the vaudeville house watching the flickers I'd stand—

*BERT grabs her, holding her tightly. He doesn't seem angry, very con- versational at first. HELEN doesn't struggle; his grip is painful. She stays very still, as do NELL and SHIPMAN the way one does with an animal that might attack if one makes the wrong move. Show no fear.*

**BERT:** *(to the audience)* Glamour. They all said she had glamour. *(He smiles, perhaps even a small chuckle.)* Not the usual kind. Not that kind. Special. Her own kind of glamour. Do you think she's glamorous? . . . Do you think she's lovely? . . . Do you think you could love her? . . . I love her. . . . Yes, I do. I love her. I. Love. Her. Do you think you could love her? . . . Look at her. Look really closely! Look close! *(He grabs HELEN's face, pushing her face forward so the audience can examine it.)* Look at her! . . . I said look! Can you see her? . . . I love her. . . . Glamorous. Glamorous screen star! Does that look glamorous to you? Does it? Destroys everything. Everything. Lose everything everything lost. Everything lost everything gone! *(He shoves, throws, her towards the audience.)* Take her! Go on take her! I don't want her, you take her! You take her!!

*He turns on NELL, who is isolated from SHIPMAN; he aims the gun at her.*

**EDISON:** Isolated snapshots selected from all three strips of film and reassembled afterwards achieve the most detailed representation.

**SHIPMAN:** The End.

**HELEN:** *(getting up)* Never Ends.

**SHIPMAN:** New story?

**BERT:** Don't leave me.

*Pause. NELL and BERT lock eyes as he continues to point the gun at her.*

**HELEN:** Play.

**BERT:** Please. . . . Nell!

*BERT puts the gun to his own head. NELL makes no move to stop him.*

**SHIPMAN:** In order to—

**NELL:** *(to BERT)* Go on!

*After a moment BERT lowers the gun, it hangs loosely from his hand. The sound and flare of flame as MAN #2 scratches a match, lights a cigar. MAN #1 drops the persona of BERT, turns and tosses the gun to MAN #2 who catches it, puts it in his pocket. There is an ambiance of threat or danger as the women watch MAN #1 as he joins MAN #2.*

*The two men are on the periphery in shadow. They remain, watching, barely silhouetted, as the cigar smoke drifts around them.*

**NELL:** *(to MAN #1 and MAN #2 in defiance)* Play! *(NELL turns her gaze from the men to HELEN and SHIPMAN.)* In order—to go on.

**SHIPMAN:** The animals will be lost.

**NELL:** To the San Diego zoo.

**HELEN:** Better than starving.

**NELL:** The lease on the land at Priest Lake

**SHIPMAN:** Will be lost.

**NELL:** I'll finish "The Purple Trail."

**HELEN:** Hokey title.

**SHIPMAN:** No one will back it.

**NELL:** Idea for a novel

**HELEN:** It'll be published

**NELL:** Magazine pieces and novels

**SHIPMAN:** Will anyone read them?

**NELL:** Movies.

**SHIPMAN:** Will anyone see them? *(pause)*

**NELL:** Never stop. Never stop, never.

*Light starts to change.*

**SHIPMAN:** Why not? . . . why not, Nell Shipman?

**HELEN:** Why not?

**NELL:** No choice!

**EDISON:** There is a tendency to overheat as the picture passes too close to the light source.

**SHIPMAN:** But we know the devil sits on the doorstep.

**HELEN:** Yes! But he'll never get in.

**SHIPMAN:** Why not?

**HELEN:** Because stories are barring the door! So—plaaaay. *(She picks up the script she was studying at the beginning.)*

**NELL:** *(smiles)* No choice.

**EDISON:** This defect is not a major problem so long as the moving picture stays within certain parameters and distance from the source.

**SHIPMAN:** *(looks at EDISON)* No choice!

*EDISON's light goes out. SHIPMAN picks up the letter she'd had in her hand at the beginning. She glances at it, passes it to NELL.*

**SHIPMAN:** The "fictional" news . . . *(She looks up at the lighting booth.)* Gooo—to Black. *(lights start to fade)*

**NELL:** *(to unseen techie in booth)* Never! *(lights bump back up)*

**SHIPMAN:** Would you give me one moment's peace? I'm an old woman you know. *You're* an old woman!

**NELL:** *We're* an old woman.

**HELEN:** Never!

**NELL:** Never?

*HELEN and NELL look to SHIPMAN.*

**SHIPMAN:** Alright. You've got me. Never! So—Play!

*A tinny music hall piano accompanies a silent black and white film as it plays on the set and the bodies of the characters, which provide the "screen." Elusive images flicker and flash illuminating SHIPMAN, NELL and HELEN looking out as if watching a film they see playing on a distant screen, as the film plays on them. The shadows/silhouettes of MAN #1 and MAN #2 remain. The sound and the flickering black and white film stop. Hot pools of light on the three women. A moment frozen in time. Blackout.*

*The end.*

—*1999*

*Tomson Highway (b. 1951) was born on a remote island in Maria Lake near the Brochet Reserve in northern Manitoba. His father was a trapper, fisherman, and champion dog-sled racer, and he spent his early life in a nomadic existence as the eleventh of twelve children. At age six, he was legally required to go to residential school in The Pas, which expanded his educational horizons, especially in the area of music, but separated him from his family and cultural roots and exposed him to traumatic abuse. He eventually went to England, where he studied to be a concert pianist, and later completed his Bachelor of Music at the University of Western Ontario. It was there that he met and studied with playwright James Reaney and was exposed to the work of Michel Tremblay, whose influence can be seen in Highway's plays. He then did social work in Native communities and became artistic director of an Aboriginal theatre company entitled Native Earth, which co-produced his first major play,* The Rez Sisters, *with Theatre Passe Muraille in 1986. This play won the Dora Mavor Moore Award for Best New Play, and was nominated for the Governor General's Award.* The Rez Sisters, *along with its sequel,* Dry Lips Oughta Move to Kapuskasing *(1989), brought Highway to national prominence. Tracing the efforts of seven remarkable women to win* The BIGGEST BINGO IN THE WORLD, *the text of* The Rez Sisters *is sprinkled with Cree and Ojibway and features the Trickster figure of Native mythology in the guise of Nanabush, who "straddles the consciousness of man and that of God, the Great Spirit." Highway has also written several other plays, including* Rose *(2000) and* Ernestine Shuswap Gets Her Trout *(2004); a novel,* Kiss of the Fur Queen *(1998); and books for children.*

# Tomson Highway
# The Rez Sisters

## A Note on Nanabush

*The dream world of North American Indian mythology is inhabited by the most fantastic creatures, beings, and events. Foremost among these beings is the "Trickster," as pivotal and important a figure in the Native world as Christ is in the realm of Christian mythology. "Weesageechak" in Cree, "Nanabush" in Ojibway, "Raven" in others, "Coyote" in still others, this Trickster goes by many names and many guises. In fact, he can assume any guise he chooses. Essentially a comic, clownish sort of character, he teaches us about the nature and the meaning of existence on the planet Earth; he straddles the consciousness of man and that of God, the Great Spirit.*

*Some say that "Nanabush" left this continent when the whiteman came. We believe he is still here among us—albeit a little the worse for wear and tear—having assumed other guises. Without him—and without the spiritual health of this figure—the core of Indian culture would be gone forever.*

## CHARACTERS

*Pelajia Patchnose*, 53
*Philomena Moosetail*, 49, sister of Pelajia
*Marie-Adele Starblanket*, 39, half-sister of Pelajia & Philomena
*Annie Cook*, 36, sister of Marie-Adele & half-sister of the other two
*Emily Dictionary*, 32, sister of Annie & ditto
*Veronique St. Pierre*, 45, sister-in-law of all the above
*Zhaboonigan Peterson*, 24, mentally disabled adopted daughter of
    Veronique
*Nanabush*—who plays the Seagull (the dancer in white feathers), the
    Nighthawk (the dancer in dark feathers), and the Bingo Master.

Time: *Late summer, 1986.*
Place: *The Wasaychigan Hill Indian Reserve, Manitoulin Island,
Ontario. (Note: "Wasaychigan" means "window" in Ojibway.)*

## ACT ONE

*It is mid-morning of a beautiful late August day on the Wasaychigan Hill Indian Reserve, Manitoulin Island, Ontario. Pelajia Patchnose is alone on the roof of her house, nailing shingles on. She wears faded blue denim men's cover-alls and a baseball cap to shade her eyes from the sun. A brightly-colored square cushion belonging to her sister, Philomena Moosetail, rests on the roof beside her. The ladder to the roof is offstage.*

**PELAJIA:**   Philomena. I wanna go to Toronto.
**PHILOMENA** (*From offstage*):   Oh, go on.
**PELAJIA:**   Sure as I'm sitting away up here on the roof of this old house. I
    kind of like it up here, though. From here, I can see half of Manitoulin
    Island on a clear day. I can see the chimneys, the tops of apple trees,

the garbage heap behind Big Joey's dumpy little house. I can see the seagulls circling over Marie-Adele Starblanket's white picket fence. Boats on the North Channel I wish I was on, sailing away somewhere. The mill at Espanola, a hundred miles away . . . and that's with just a bit of squinting. See? If I had binoculars, I could see the superstack in Sudbury. And if I were Superwoman, I could see the CN Tower in Toronto. Ah, but I'm just plain old Pelajia Rosella Patchnose and I'm here in plain, dusty, boring old Wasaychigan Hill . . . Wasy . . . waiting . . . waiting . . . nailing shining shingles with my trusty silver hammer on the roof of Pelajia Rosella Patchnose's little two-bedroom welfare house. Philomena. I wanna go to Toronto.

*Philomena Moosetail comes up the ladder to the roof with one shingle and obviously hating it. She is very well-dressed, with a skirt, nylons, even heels, completely impractical for the roof.*

PHILOMENA:   Oh, go on.

PELAJIA:   I'm tired, Philomena, tired of this place. There's days I wanna leave so bad.

PHILOMENA:   But you were born here. All your poop's on this reserve.

PELAJIA:   Oh, go on.

PHILOMENA:   You'll never leave.

PELAJIA:   Yes, I will. When I'm old.

PHILOMENA:   You're old right now.

PELAJIA:   I got a good 30 years to go . . .

PHILOMENA:   . . . and you're gonna live every one of them right here beside me . . .

PELAJIA:   . . . maybe 40 . . .

PHILOMENA:   . . . here in Wasy.

*Tickles Pelajia on the breasts.*

Chiga-chiga-chiga.

PELAJIA (*Yelps and slaps Philomena's hand away*):   Oh, go on. It's not like it used to be.

PHILOMENA:   Oh, go on. People change, places change, time changes things. You expect to be young and gorgeous forever?

PELAJIA:   See? I told you I'm not old.

PHILOMENA:   Oh, go on. You.

PELAJIA:   "Oh, go on. You." You bug me like hell when you say that.

**PHILOMENA:** You say it, too. And don't give me none of this "I don't like this place. I'm tired of it." This place is too much inside your blood. You can't get rid of it. And it can't get rid of you.

**PELAJIA:** Four thirty this morning, I was woken by . . .

**PHILOMENA:** Here we go again.

**PELAJIA:** . . . Andrew Starblanket and his brother, Matthew. Drunk. Again. Or sounded like . . .

**PHILOMENA:** Nothing better to do.

**PELAJIA:** . . . fighting over some girl. Heard what sounded like a base-ball bat landing on somebody's back. My lawn looks like the shits this morning.

**PHILOMENA:** Well, I like it here. Myself, I'm gonna go to every bingo and I'm gonna hit every jackpot between here and Espanola and I'm gonna buy me that toilet I'm dreaming about at night . . . big and wide and very white . . .

**PELAJIA:** Aw-ni-gi-naw-ee-dick.[1]

**PHILOMENA:** I'm good at bingo.

**PELAJIA:** So what! And the old stories, the old language. Almost all gone . . . was a time Nanabush and Windigo and everyone here could rattle away in Indian fast as Bingo Betty could lay her bingo chips down on a hot night.

**PHILOMENA:** Pelajia Rosella Patchnose. The sun's gonna drive you crazy.

*And she descends the ladder.*

**PELAJIA:** Everyone here's crazy. No jobs. Nothing to do but drink and screw each other's wives and husbands and forget about our Nanabush.

*From offstage Philomena screams. She fell down the ladder.*

Philomena!

*As she looks over the edge of the roof.*

What are you doing down there?

**PHILOMENA:** What do you think? I fell.

**PELAJIA:** Bring me some of them nails while you're down there.

[1]**Oh, go on**. (Ojibway)

**PHILOMENA** (*Whining and still from offstage, from behind the house*): You think I can race up and down this ladder? You think I got wings?

**PELAJIA:** You gotta wear pants when you're doing a man's job. See? You got your skirt ripped on a nail and now you can see your thighs. People gonna think you just came from Big Joey's house.

**PHILOMENA** (*She comes up the ladder in a state of disarray*): Let them think what they want. That old cow Gazelle Nataways . . . always acting like she thinks she's still a spring chicken. She's got them legs of hers wrapped around Big Joey day and night . . .

**PELAJIA:** Philomena. Park your tongue. My old man has to go the hundred miles to Espanola just to get a job. My boys. Gone to Toronto. Only place educated Indian boys can find decent jobs these days. And here I sit all broken-hearted.

**PHILOMENA:** Paid a dime and only farted.

**PELAJIA:** Look at you. You got dirt all over your backside.

*Turning her attention to the road in front of her house and standing up for the first and only time.*

And dirt roads! Years now that old chief's been making speeches about getting paved roads "for my people" and still we got dirt roads all over.

**PHILOMENA:** Oh, go on.

**PELAJIA:** When I win me that jackpot next time we play bingo in Espanola . . .

**PHILOMENA** (*Examining her torn skirt, her general state of disarray, and fretting over it*): Look at this! Will you look at this! Ohhh!

**PELAJIA:** . . . I'm gonna put that old chief to shame and build me a nice paved road right here in front of my house. Jet black. Shiny. Make my lawn look real nice.

**PHILOMENA:** My rib-cage!

**PELAJIA:** And if that old chief don't wanna make paved roads for all my sisters around here . . .

**PHILOMENA:** There's something rattling around inside me!

**PELAJIA:** . . . I'm packing my bags and moving to Toronto.

*Sits down again.*

**PHILOMENA:** Oh, go on.

*She spies Annie Cook's approach a distance up the hill.*

Why, I do believe that cloud of dust over there is Annie Cook racing down the hill, Pelajia.

**PELAJIA:** Philomena. I wanna go to Toronto.

**PHILOMENA:** She's walking mighty fast. Must be excited about something.

**PELAJIA:** Never seen Annie Cook walk slow since the day she finally lost Eugene to Marie-Adele at the church 19 years ago. And even then she was walking a little too fast for a girl who was supposed to be broken-heart . . . (*Stopping just in time and laughing*) . . . heartbroken.

*Annie Cook pops up the top of the ladder to the roof.*

**ANNIE** (*All cheery and fast and perky*): Halloooo! Whatchyou doing up here?

**PELAJIA:** There's room for only so much weight up here before we go crashing into my kitchen, so what do you want?

**ANNIE:** Just popped up to say hi.

**PELAJIA:** And see what we're doing?

**ANNIE:** Well . . .

**PELAJIA:** Couldn't you see what we're doing from up where you were?

**ANNIE** (*Confidentially, to Philomena*): Is it true Gazelle Nataways won the bingo last night?

**PHILOMENA:** Annie Cook, first you say you're gonna come with me and then you don't even bother showing up. If you were sitting beside me at that bingo table last night you would have seen Gazelle Nataways win that big pot again with your own two eyes.

**ANNIE:** Emily Dictionary and I went to Little Current to listen to Fritz the Katz.

**PELAJIA:** What in God's name kind of a band might that be?

**ANNIE:** Country rock. My favorite. Fritz the Katz is from Toronto.

**PELAJIA:** Fritzy . . . ritzy . . . Philomena! Say something.

**PHILOMENA:** My record player is in Espanola getting fixed.

**ANNIE:** That's nice.

**PHILOMENA:** Good.

**ANNIE:** Is it true Gazelle Nataways plans to spend her bingo money to go to Toronto with . . . with Big Joey?

**PHILOMENA:** Who wants to know? Emily Dictionary?

**ANNIE:** I guess so.

**PELAJIA:** That Gazelle Nataways gonna leave all her babies behind and let them starve to death?

**ANNIE:** I guess so. I don't know. I'm asking you.

**PELAJIA AND PHILOMENA:** We don't know.

**ANNIE:** I'm on my way to Marie-Adele's to pick her up.

**PELAJIA:** Why? Where you gonna put her down?

*Pelajia and Philomena laugh.*

**ANNIE:** I mean, we're going to the store together. To the post office. We're going to pick up a parcel. They say there's a parcel for me. They say it's shaped like a record. And they say it's from Sudbury. So it must be from my daughter, Ellen . . .

**PELAJIA AND PHILOMENA:** . . . "who lives with this white guy in Sudbury" . . .

**ANNIE:** How did you know?

**PHILOMENA:** Everybody knows.

**ANNIE:** His name is Ray*mond*. Not *Ray*mond, but Ray*mond*. Like in Bon Bon.

*Philomena tries out "bon bon" to herself.*

He's French.

**PELAJIA:** Oh?

**ANNIE:** Garage mechanic. He fixes cars. And you know, talking about Frenchmen, that old priest is holding another bingo next week and when I win . . . (*To Philomena.*) Are you going?

**PELAJIA:** Does a bear shit in the woods?

**ANNIE:** . . . when I win, I'm going to Espanola and play the bingo there. Emily Dictionary says that Fire Minklater can give us a ride in her new car. She got it through Ray*mond*'s garage. The bingo in Espanola is bigger. And it's better. And I'll win. And then I'll go to Sudbury, where the bingos are even bigger and better. And then I can visit my daughter, Ellen . . .

**PELAJIA:** . . . "who lives with this white guy in Sudbury" . . .

**ANNIE:** . . . and go shopping in the record stores and go to the hotel and drink beer quietly—not noisy and crazy like here—and listen to the live bands. It will be so much fun. I hope Emily Dictionary can come with me.

PHILOMENA: It's true. I've been thinking . . .

PELAJIA: You don't say.

PHILOMENA: It's true. The bingos here are getting kind of boring . . .

ANNIE: That old priest is too slow and sometimes he gets the numbers all mixed up and the pot's not big enough.

PHILOMENA: And I don't like the way he calls the numbers. (*Nasally.*) B 12, O 64.

ANNIE: When Little Girl Manitowabi won last month . . .

PHILOMENA: She won just enough to take a taxi back to Buzwah.

ANNIE: That's all.

*Both Annie and Philomena pause to give a quick sigh of yearning.*

PHILOMENA: Annie Cook, I want that big pot.

ANNIE: We all want big pots.

PELAJIA: Start a revolution!

PHILOMENA AND ANNIE: Yes!

ANNIE: All us Wasy women. We'll march up the hill, burn the church hall down, scare the priest to death, and then we'll march all the way to Espanola, where the bingos are bigger and better . . .

PHILOMENA: We'll hold big placards!

ANNIE: They'll say: "Wasy women want bigger bingos!"

PELAJIA: And one will say: "Annie Cook Wants Big Pot!"

PHILOMENA: . . . and the numbers at those bingos in Espanola go faster and the pots get bigger by the week. Oh, Pelajia Patchnose, I'm getting excited just thinking about it!

ANNIE: I'm going.

PELAJIA: You are, are you?

ANNIE: Yes. I'm going. I'm running out of time. I'm going to Marie-Adele's house and then we'll walk to the store together to pick up the parcel—I'm sure there'll be a letter in it, and Marie-Adele is expecting mail, too—and we'll see if Emily Dictionary is working today and we'll ask her if Fire Minklater has her new car yet so we can go to Espanola for that big pot.

*She begins to descend the ladder.*

**PELAJIA:** Well, you don't have much to do today, do you?
**ANNIE:** Well. Toodle-oo!

*And she pops down the ladder and is gone.*

**PELAJIA:** Not bad for someone who was in such a hurry to get her parcel. She talks faster than she walks.

*Noticing how dejected and abandoned Philomena looks, she holds up her hammer.*

Bingo money. Top quality. $24.95.

**PHILOMENA:** It's true. Bingos here in Wasy are getting smaller and smaller all the time. Especially now when the value of the dollar is getting lesser and lesser. In the old days, when Bingo Betty was still alive and walking these dirt roads, she'd come to every single bingo and she'd sit there like the Queen of Tonga, big and huge like a roast beef, smack-dab in the middle of the bingo hall. One night, I remember, she brought two young cousins from the city—two young women, dressed real fancy, like they were going to Sunday church—and Bingo Betty made them sit one on her left, with her three little bingo cards, and one on her right, with her three little ones. And Bingo Betty herself sat in the middle with 27 cards. Twenty seven cards! Amazing.

*Pelajia starts to descend the ladder, and Philomena, getting excited, steps closer and closer to the edge of the roof.*

And those were the days when they still used bingo chips, not these dabbers like nowadays, and everyone came with a little margarine container full of these bingo chips. When the game began and they started calling out the numbers, Bingo Betty was all set, like a horse at the race-track in Sudbury, you could practically see the foam sizzling and bubbling between her teeth. Bingo Betty! Bingo Betty with her beady little darting eyes, sharp as needles, and her roly-poly jiggledy-piggledy arms with their stubby little claws would go: chiga-chiga-chiga-chiga-chiga-chiga arms flying across the table smooth as angel's wings chiga-chiga-chiga-chiga-chiga-chiga-woosh! Cousin on the left chiga-chiga, cousin on the right chiga, chiga-eeee!

*She narrowly misses falling off the roof and cries out in terror.*

**PELAJIA:** Philomena!

PHILOMENA (*Scrambling on hands and knees to Pelajia, and coming to rest in this languorous pose, takes a moment to regain her composure and catch her breath*):   And you know, to this very day, they say that on certain nights at the bingo here in Wasy, they say you can see Bingo Betty's ghost, like a mist, hovering in the air above the bingo tables, playing bingo like it's never been played before. Or since.

PELAJIA:   Amazing! She should have gone to Toronto.

*Black-out.*

*The same day, same time, in Wasaychigan Hill. Marie-Adele Starblanket is standing alone outside her house, in her yard, by her 14-post white picket fence. Her house is down the hill from Pelajia Patchnose's, close to the lake. A seagull watches her from a distance away. He is the dancer in white feathers. Through this whole section, Nanabush (i.e., Nanabush in the guise of the seagull), Marie-Adele, and Zhaboonigan play "games" with each other. Only she and Zhaboonigan Peterson can see the spirit inside the bird and can sort of (though not quite) recognize him for who he is. A doll belonging to a little girl lies on the porch floor. Marie-Adele throws little stones at the seagull.*

MARIE-ADELE:   Awus! Wee-chee-gis. Ka-tha pu-g'wun-ta oo-ta pee-wee-sta-ta-gu-mik-si. Awus! Neee. U-wi-nuk oo-ma kee-tha ee-tee-thi-mi-soo-yin holy spirit chee? Awus! Hey, maw ma-a oop-mee tay-si-thow u-wu seagull bird. I goo-ta poo-goo ta-poo. Nu-gu-na-wa-pa-mik. Nu-gu-na-wa-pa-mik.

NANABUSH:   As-tum.

MARIE-ADELE:   Neee. Moo-tha ni-gus-kee-tan tu-pi-mi-tha-an. Moo-tha oo-ta-ta-gwu-na n'tay-yan. Chees-kwa. (*Pause.*) Ma-ti poo-ni-mee-see i-goo-ta wee-chi-gi-seagull bird come shit on my fence one more time and you and anybody else look like you cook like stew on my stove. Awus![2]

---

[2]**Marie-Adele:** Go away! You stinking thing. Don't coming messing around here for nothing. Go away! Neee. Who the hell do you think you are, the Holy Spirit? Go away! Hey, but he won't fly away, this seagull bird. He just sits there. And watches me. Watches me.
**Nanabush:** Come.
**Marie-Adele:** Neee. I can't fly away. I have no wings. Yet. (*Pause.*) Will you stop shitting all over the place you stinking seagull bird, etc. (Cree).
(Note: "Neee" is a very common Cree expression with the approximate meaning of "Oh you.")

*Veronique St. Pierre "passes by" with her adopted daughter Zhaboonigan Peterson.*

**VERONIQUE:** Talking to the birds again, Marie-Adele Starblanket?

**MARIE-ADELE:** Aha. Veronique St. Pierre. How are you today?

**VERONIQUE:** Black Lady Halked's sister-in-law Fire Minklater, Fire Minklater's husband, just bought Fire Minklater a car in Sudbury.

**MARIE-ADELE:** New?

**VERONIQUE:** Used. They say he bought it from some Frenchman, some garage. Cray-*on.*

**MARIE-ADELE:** Ray*mond.*

**VERONIQUE:** These Frenchmen are forever selling us their used cars. And I'm sure that's why Black Lady Halked has been baring those big yellow teeth of hers, smiling all over the reserve recently. She looks like a hound about to pounce on a mouse, she smiles so hard when she smiles. I'd like to see her smile after plastic surgery. Anyway. At the bingo last night she was hinting that it wouldn't be too long before she would be able to go to the bingo in Espanola more frequently. Unfortunately, a new game started and you know how Black Lady Halked has to concentrate when she plays bingo— her forehead looks like corduroy, she concentrates so hard—so I didn't get a chance to ask her what she meant. So. Fire Minklater has a used car. Imagine! Maybe I can make friends with her again. NO! I wouldn't be caught dead inside her car. Not even if she had a brand-new Cadillac. How are your children? All 14 of them.

**MARIE-ADELE:** Okay, I guess.

**VERONIQUE:** Imagine. And all from one father. Anyway. Who will take care of them after you . . . ahem . . . I mean . . . when you go to the hospital?

**MARIE-ADELE:** Eugene.

**ZHABOONIGAN:** Is he gentle?

**MARIE-ADELE:** Baby-cakes. How are you?

**ZHABOONIGAN:** Fine. (*Giggles.*)

**VERONIQUE:** She's fine. She went berry-picking yesterday with the children.

**ZHABOONIGAN:** Where's Nicky?

**MARIE-ADELE:** Nicky's down at the beach.

**ZHABOONIGAN:** Why?

| | |
|---|---|
| **MARIE-ADELE:** | Taking care of Rose-Marie. |
| **ZHABOONIGAN:** | Oh. |
| **MARIE-ADELE:** | Yup. |
| **ZHABOONIGAN:** | Me and Nicky, ever lots of blueberries! |
| **MARIE-ADELE:** | Me and Nicky picked lots of blueberries. |
| **ZHABOONIGAN:** | I didn't see you there. |
| **MARIE-ADELE:** | When? |
| **ZHABOONIGAN:** | Before today. |
| **MARIE-ADELE:** | How come Nicky didn't come home with any? |
| **ZHABOONIGAN:** | Why? |

*Marie-Adele shrugs. Zhaboonigan imitates this, and then pretends she is stuffing her mouth with berries.*

| | |
|---|---|
| **MARIE-ADELE:** | Aw, yous went and made pigs of yourselves. |
| **ZHABOONIGAN:** | Nicky's the pig. |
| **MARIE-ADELE:** | Neee. |
| **ZHABOONIGAN:** | Are you going away far? |
| **MARIE-ADELE:** | I'm not going far. |
| **ZHABOONIGAN:** | Oh. Are you pretty? |

*Marie-Adele, embarrassed for a moment, smiles and Zhaboonigan smiles, too.*

**MARIE-ADELE:**   You're pretty, too.

*Zhaboonigan tugs at Marie-Adele's shoelaces.*

Oh, Zhaboonigan. Now you have to tie it up. I can't bend too far cuz I get tired.

*Zhaboonigan tries to tie the shoelaces with great difficulty. When she finds she can't she throws her arms up and screams.*

**ZHABOONIGAN:**   Dirty trick! Dirty trick!

*She bites her hand and hurts herself.*

| | |
|---|---|
| **MARIE-ADELE:** | Now, don't get mad. |
| **VERONIQUE:** | Stop it. Stop it right now. |
| **ZHABOONIGAN:** | No! No! |
| **MARIE-ADELE:** | Zha. Zha. Listen. Listen. |
| **ZHABOONIGAN:** | Stop it! Stop it right now! |

**MARIE-ADELE:** Come on Zha. You and I can name the koo-koos-suk.[3] All 14 of them.

**ZHABOONIGAN:** Okay. Here we go.

*Marie-Adele leads Zhaboonigan over to the picket fence and Veronique follows them.*

**ZHABOONIGAN** (*To Veronique*): No.

*Veronique retreats, obviously hurt.*

**MARIE-ADELE** (*Taking Zhaboonigan's hand and counting on the 14 posts of her white picket fence*): Simon, Andrew, Matthew, Janie, Nicky, Ricky, Ben, Mark, Ron, Don, John, Tom, Pete, and Rose-Marie. There.

*Underneath Marie-Adele's voice, Zhaboonigan has been counting.*

**ZHABOONIGAN:** One, two, three, four, five, six, seven, eight, nine, ten, eleven, twelve, thirteen, fourteen. (*Giggles.*)

**MARIE-ADELE:** Ever good counter you, Zhaboonigan.

**ZHABOONIGAN:** Yup.

**VERONIQUE:** This reserve, sometimes I get so sick of it. They laugh at me behind my back, I just know it. They laugh at me and Pierre St. Pierre because we don't have any children of our own. "Imagine, they say, she's on her second husband already and she still can't have children!" They laugh at Zhaboonigan Peterson because she's crazy, that's what they call her. They can't even take care of their own people, they'd rather laugh at them. I'm the only person who would take Zhaboonigan after her parents died in that horrible car crash near Manitowaning on Saturday November 12 1964 may they rest in peace (*She makes a quick sign of the cross without skipping a beat.*) I'm the only one around here who is kind enough. And they laugh at me. Oh, I wish I had a new stove, Marie-Adele. My stove is so old and broken down, only two elements work anymore and my oven is starting to talk back at me.

**MARIE-ADELE:** Get it fixed.

**VERONIQUE:** You know that Pierre St. Pierre never has any money. He drinks it all up.

*She sighs longingly.*

[3]The little pigs. (Cree)

Some day! Anyway. Zhaboonigan here wanted to go for a swim so I thought I'd walk her down—drop by and see how you and the children are doing—it will do my weak heart good, I was saying to myself.

**MARIE-ADELE:** Awus!

*As she throws a pebble at the seagull on the stone, Veronique, for a second, thinks it's her Marie-Adele is shooing away. There is a brief silence broken after awhile by Zhaboonigan's little giggle.*

**VERONIQUE:** Anyway. I was walking down by that Big Joey's shameless little shack just this morning when guess who pokes her nose out the window but Gazelle Nataways—the nerve of that woman. I couldn't see inside but I'm sure she was only half-dressed, her hairdo was all mixed up and she said to me: "Did you know, Veronique St. Pierre, that Little Girl Manitowabi told me her daughter, June Bug McLeod, just got back from the hospital in Sudbury where she had her tubes tied and told her that THE BIGGEST BINGO IN THE WORLD is coming to Toronto?"

**MARIE-ADELE:** When?

**VERONIQUE:** I just about had a heart attack.

**MARIE-ADELE:** When?

**VERONIQUE:** But I said to Gazelle anyway: Is there such a thing as a BIGGEST BINGO IN THE WORLD? And she said: Yes. And she should know about these things because she spends all her waking and sleeping hours just banging about in bed with the biggest thing on Manitoulin Island, I almost said.

**MARIE-ADELE:** This bingo. When?

**VERONIQUE:** She didn't know. And now that I think of it, I don't know whether to believe her. After all, who should believe a woman who wrestles around with dirt like Big Joey all night long leaving her poor babies to starve to death in her empty kitchen? But if it's true, Marie-Adele, if it's true that THE BIGGEST BINGO IN THE WORLD is coming to Toronto, I'm going and I want you to come with me.

**MARIE-ADELE:** Well . . .

**VERONIQUE:** I want you to come shopping with me and help me choose my new stove after I win.

**MARIE-ADELE:** Hang on . . .

**VERONIQUE:** They have good stoves in Toronto.

**MARIE-ADELE:** Let's find out for sure. Then we start making plans.

**VERONIQUE:** Maybe we should go back and ask that Gazelle Nataways about this. If she's sure.

**MARIE-ADELE:** Maybe we should go and ask June Bug McLeod herself.

**VERONIQUE:** We can't walk to Buzwah and I'm too old to hitch-hike.

**MARIE-ADELE:** There's Eugene's van. He'll be home by six.

**VERONIQUE:** I want to find out NOW. But what if people see us standing at Big Joey's door?.

**MARIE-ADELE:** What do you mean? We just knock on the door, march right in, ask the bitch, and march right out again.

**VERONIQUE:** Zhaboonigan dear, wait for me over there.

*She waits until Zhaboonigan is safely out of earshot and then leans over to Marie-Adele in a conspiratorial whisper.*

Anyway. You must know, Marie-Adele, that there's all kinds of women who come streaming out of that house at all hours of the day and night. I might be considered one of them. You know your youngest sister, Emily Dictionary, was seen staggering out of that house in the dead of night two nights ago?

**MARIE-ADELE:** Veronique St. Pierre, what Emily Dictionary does is Emily's business.

*Annie Cook enters, walking fast, and comes to a screeching halt.*

**ANNIE:** Hallooooo! Whatchyou doin'?

**VERONIQUE** (*Giving Annie the baleful eye*): How are you?

**ANNIE:** High as a kite. Just kidding. Hi, Zha.

**ZHABOONIGAN:** Hi.

*Giggles. She runs toward Marie-Adele, bumping into Annie en route.*

**ANNIE:** Hey, Marie-Adele.

**ZHABOONIGAN:** Marie-Adele. How's your cancer?

*Giggles and scurries off laughing.*

**VERONIQUE:** Shkanah, Zhaboonigan, sna-ma-bah . . .[4]

---

[4]Shush, Zhaboonigan, don't say that. (Ojibway)

**MARIE-ADELE:** Come on, before the post office closes for lunch.

**VERONIQUE:** You didn't tell me you were going to the store.

**ANNIE:** Well, we are. (*To Marie-Adele.*) Hey, is Simon in? I'm sure he's got my Ricky Skaggs album. You know the one that goes (*Sings.*) "Honeee!"

*Calling into the house.*

Yoo-hoo, Simon!

**MARIE-ADELE:** He's in Espanola with Eugene.

**VERONIQUE:** Expecting mail, Annie Cook?

**ANNIE:** A parcel from my daughter, Ellen, who lives with this white guy in Sudbury . . .

**VERONIQUE:** So I've heard.

**ANNIE:** And my sister here is expecting a letter, too.

**VERONIQUE:** From whom?

**ANNIE:** From the doctor, about her next check-up.

**VERONIQUE:** When?

**MARIE-ADELE:** We don't know when. Or where. Annie, let's go.

**ANNIE:** They say it's shaped like a record.

**VERONIQUE:** Maybe there'll be news in that parcel about THE BIGGEST BINGO IN THE WORLD!

*Shouts toward the lake, in a state of great excitement.*

Zhaboonigan! Zhaboonigan! We're going to the store!

**ANNIE:** THE BIGGEST BINGO IN THE WORLD?

**VERONIQUE:** In Toronto. Soon. Imagine! Gazelle Nataways told me. She heard about it from Little Girl Manitowabi over in Buzwah who heard about it from her daughter June Bug McLeod who just got back from the hospital in Sudbury where she had her tubes tied I just about had a heart attack!

**ANNIE:** Toronto?

**MARIE-ADELE:** We gotta find out for sure.

**ANNIE:** Right.

**MARIE-ADELE:** We could go to Big Joey's and ask Gazelle Nataways except Veronique St. Pierre's too scared of Gazelle.

**VERONIQUE:** I am not.

**ANNIE:** You are too.

**MARIE-ADELE:** We could wait and borrow Eugene's van . . .

**VERONIQUE:** I am not.

**ANNIE:** . . . drive over to Buzwah . . .

**MARIE-ADELE:** . . . and ask June Bug McLeod . . .

**ANNIE:** . . . but wait a minute! . . .

**MARIE-ADELE AND ANNIE:** Maybe there IS news in that parcel about this BIGGEST BINGO IN THE WORLD!

**MARIE-ADELE:** Come on.

**VERONIQUE** (*Shouting toward the lake*): Zhaboonigan! Zhaboonigan!

**ANNIE:** And here I was so excited about the next little bingo that old priest is holding next week. Toronto! Oh, I hope it's true!

**VERONIQUE:** Zhaboonigan! Zhaboonigan! Zhaboonigan! Dammit! We're going to the store!

*And the "march" to the store begins, during which Nanabush, still in the guise of the seagull, follows them and continues to play tricks, mimicking their hand movements, the movement of their mouths, etc. The three women appear each in her own spot of light at widely divergent points on the stage area.*

**ANNIE:** When I go to THE BIGGEST BINGO IN THE WORLD, in Toronto, I will win. For sure, I will win. If they shout the B 14 at the end, for sure I will win. The B 14 is my lucky number after all. Then I will take all my money and I will go to every record store in Toronto. I will buy every single one of Patsy Cline's records, especially the one that goes (*Sings.*) "I go a-walking, after midnight," oh I go crazy every time I hear that one. Then I will buy a huge record player, the biggest one in the whole world. And then I will go to all the taverns and all the night clubs in Toronto and listen to the live bands while I drink beer quietly—not noisy and crazy like here—I will bring my daughter Ellen and her white guy from Sudbury and we will sit together. Maybe I will call Fritz the Katz and he will take me out. Maybe he will hire me as one of his singers and I can (*Sings.*) "Oooh," in the background while my feet go (*Shuffles her feet from side to side.*) while Fritz the Katz is singing and the lights are flashing and the people are drinking beer and smoking cigarettes and dancing. Ohhh, I could dance all night with that Fritz the Katz. When I win, when I win THE BIGGEST BINGO IN THE WORLD!

**MARIE-ADELE:** When I win THE BIGGEST BINGO IN THE WORLD, I'm gonna buy me an island. In the North Channel, right smack-dab in the middle—eem-shak min-stik[5]—the most beautiful island in the world. And my island will have lots of trees—great big bushy ones—and lots and lots and lots of sweetgrass. MMMMM! And there's gonna be pine trees and oak trees and maple trees and big stones and little stonelets—neee—and, oh yeah, this real neat picket fence, real high, long and very, very, very white. No bird shit. Eugene will live there and me and all my Starblanket kids. Yup, no more smelly, stinky old pulp and paper mill in Espanola for my Eugene—pooh!—my 12 Starblanket boys and my two Starblanket girls and me and my Eugene all living real nice and comfy right there on Starblanket Island, the most beautiful incredible goddamn island in the whole goddamn world. Eem-shak min-stik! When I win THE BIGGEST BINGO IN THE WORLD!

**VERONIQUE:** Well, when I win THE BIGGEST BINGO IN THE WORLD. No! After I win THE BIGGEST BINGO IN THE WORLD, I will go shopping for a brand-new stove. In Toronto. At the Eaton Centre. A great big stove. The kind Madame Benoit has. The kind that has the three different compartments in the oven alone. I'll have the biggest stove on the reserve. I'll cook for all the children on the reserve. I'll adopt all of Marie-Adele Starblanket's 14 children and I will cook for them. I'll even cook for Gazelle Nataways' poor starving babies while she's lolling around like a pig in Big Joey's smelly, sweaty bed. And Pierre St. Pierre can drink himself to death for all I care. Because I'll be the best cook on all of Manitoulin Island! I'll enter competitions. I'll go to Paris and meet what's-his-name Cordon Bleu! I'll write a cookbook called "The Joy of Veronique St. Pierre's Cooking" and it will sell in the millions! And I will become rich and famous! Zhaboonigan Peterson will wear a mink while she eats steak tartare-de-frou-frou! Madame Benoit will be so jealous she'll suicide herself. Oh, when I win THE BIGGEST BINGO IN THE WORLD!

*Zhaboonigan comes running in from swimming, "chasing" after the other three women, counting to herself and giggling.*

---

[5]A great big island. (Cree)

**ZHABOONIGAN:** One, two, three, four, five, six, seven, eight, nine, ten, eleven, twelve, thirteen, fourteen.

*At the store. Annie Cook, Marie-Adele Starblanket, Veronique St. Pierre, and Zhaboonigan Peterson have arrived. Emily Dictionary makes a sudden appearance, carrying a huge bag of flour on her shoulder. She is one tough lady, wearing cowboy boots, tight blue jeans, a black leather jacket—all three items worn to the seams— and she sports one black eye.*

**EMILY** (*In a loud, booming voice that paralyzes all movement in the room while she speaks*): Zhaboonigan Peterson! What in Red Lucifer's name ever possessed you to be hangin' out with a buncha' dizzy old dames like this?

*Bag of flour hits the floor with a "doof."*

**MARIE-ADELE:** Emily. Your eye.

**EMILY:** Oh, bit of a tussle.

**VERONIQUE:** With who?

**EMILY:** None of your goddamn business.

**MARIE-ADELE:** Emily, please.

**ANNIE** (*Following Emily about the store while Veronique tries, in vain, to hear what she can*): I wasn't able to find out from Pelajia Patchnose or Philomena Moosemeat if Gazelle Nataways is going to Toronto this weekend with . . . Big Joey . . . they didn't know . . . Gazelle did win the bingo last night though.

**EMILY:** Aw shit. Veronique St. Pierre, you old bag. Is it true Gazelle Nataways is takin' off for Toronto with that hunk Big Joey?

**VERONIQUE:** It WAS you coming out of that house two nights ago. I walked by as quickly as I could . . .

**EMILY:** . . . shoulda come out and nailed your big floppy ears to the door . . .

**VERONIQUE:** . . . and I would have called the police but I was too scared Big Joey might come after me and Zhaboonigan later . . .

**EMILY:** . . . yeah, right.

**ZHABOONIGAN:** Yeah, right.

**VERONIQUE:** . . . and I have a weak heart, you know? Who hit you? Big Joey? Or Gazelle Nataways?

**EMILY:** The nerve of this woman.

**VERONIQUE:** Well?

**EMILY** (*Calls Zhaboonigan, who is behind the counter, on the floor, playing with the merchandise*): Zhaboonigan Peterson! Where in Red Lucifer's name is that dozy pagan?

**VERONIQUE:** You keep hanging around that house and you're gonna end up in deep trouble. You don't know how wicked and vicious those Nataways women can get. They say there's witchcraft in their blood. And with manners like yours, Emily Dictionary, you'd deserve every hex you got.

**EMILY:** Do I know this woman? Do I know this woman?

**VERONIQUE** (*During this speech, Marie-Adele and Annie sing "Honeee" tauntingly*): I'm sorry I have to say this in front of everyone like this but this woman has just accused my daughter of being a pagan. I didn't call her Zhaboonigan. The people on this reserve, who have nothing better to do with their time than call each other names, they called her that. Her name is Marie-Adele. Marie-Adele Peterson. You should talk. I should ask you where in Red . . . Red . . . whatever, you got a circus of a name like Emily Dictionary.

*Emily grabs Veronique and throws her across the room. Veronique goes flying right into Pelajia, who has entered the store during the latter part of this speech.*

**PELAJIA:** Veronique St. Pierre! Control yourself or I'll hit you over the head with my hammer.

**VERONIQUE** (*Blows a "raspberry" in Pelajia's face*): Bleah!

**ANNIE:** No, Pelajia, no.

**EMILY:** Go ahead, Pelajia. Make my day.

**ANNIE:** Down, put it down.

**PHILOMENA** (*As she comes scurrying into the store.*): I have to use the toilet.

*Running to Emily.*

I have to use your toilet.

*And goes scurrying into the toilet.*

**ANNIE** (*To Pelajia*): Remember, that's Veronique St. Pierre and if you get on the wrong side of Veronique St. Pierre she's liable to spread rumors about you all over kingdom come and you'll lose every bit of respect you got on this reserve. Don't let those pants you're wearing go to your head.

**PELAJIA** (*Catching Annie by the arm as she tries to run away*): Annie Cook! You got a mouth on you like a helicopter.

**ANNIE:** Veronique's mad at you, Emily, because you won't tell her what happened the other night at Big Joey's house. And she's jealous of Gazelle Nataways because Gazelle won the bingo again last night and she hopes you're the one person on this reserve who has the guts to stand up to Gazelle.

**VERONIQUE** (*Making a lunge at Annie, who hides behind Emily*): What's that! What's that! Ohhh! Ohhh!

**ANNIE:** Leave me alone, you old snoop. All I wanna know is this big bingo really happening in Toronto.

**VERONIQUE:** Annie Cook. You are a little suck.

**EMILY** (*To Veronique*): Someday, someone oughta stick a great big piece of shit into that mouth of yours.

**PELAJIA** (*To Emily*): And someday, someone ought to wash yours out with soap.

**PHILOMENA** (*Throwing the toilet door open, she sits there in her glory, panties down to her ankles*): Emily Dictionary. You come back to the reserve after all these years and you strut around like you own the place. I know Veronique St. Pierre is a pain in the ass but I don't care. She's your elder and you respect her. Now shut up, all of you, and let me shit in peace.

*And slams the washroom door. Veronique, scandalized by this, haughtily walks through toward the door, bumping into Pelajia en route.*

**PELAJIA:** Philomena. Get your bum out here. Veronique St. Pierre is about to lose her life.

*She raises her hammer at Veronique.*

**VERONIQUE** (*To Pelajia*): Put that hammer away. And go put a skirt on, for heaven's sake, you look obscene in those tight pants.

**ANNIE:** Hit her. Go on. Hit the bitch. One good bang is all she needs.

**EMILY:** Yeah, right. A gang-bang is more like it.

*And a full-scale riot breaks out, during which the women throw every conceivable insult at each other. Emily throws open the toilet door and Philomena comes stomping out, pulling her panties on and joining the riot. All talk at the same time, quietly at first, but then getting louder and louder until they are all screaming.*

**PHILOMENA** (*To Annie*): What a slime. Make promises and then you go do something else. And I always have to smile at you. What a slime. (*To Emily.*) All that tough talk. I know what's behind it all. You'll never be big enough to push me around. (*To Marie-Adele.*) Fourteen kids! You look like a wrinkled old prune already. (*To Pelajia.*) At least I'm a woman. (*To Veronique.*) Have you any idea how, just how offensive, how obnoxious you are to people? And that halitosis. Pooh! You wouldn't have it if you didn't talk so much.

**EMILY** (*To Philomena*): So damned bossy and pushy and sucky. You make me sick. Always wanting your own way. (*To Veronique.*) Goddamned trouble-making old crow. (*To Pelajia.*) Fuckin' self-righteous old bitch. (*To Marie-Adele.*) Mental problems, that's what you got, princess. I ain't no baby. I'm the size of a fuckin' church. (*To Annie.*) You slippery little slut. Brain the size of a fuckin' pea. Fuck, man, take a Valium.

**VERONIQUE** (*To Emily*): You have no morals at all. You sick pervert. You should have stayed where you came from, where all the other perverts are. (*To Pelajia.*) Slow turtle. Talk big and move like Jell-o. (*To Annie.*) Cockroach! (*To Philomena.*) You big phony. Flush yourself down that damned toilet of yours and shut up. (*To Marie-Adele.*) Hasn't this slimy little reptile (*Referring to Annie.*) ever told you that sweet little Ellen of hers is really Eugene's daughter? Go talk to the birds in Sudbury and find out for yourself.

**PELAJIA** (*To Veronique*): This reserve would be a better place without you. I'm tired of dealing with people like you. Tired. (*To Marie-Adele.*) You can't act that way. This here's no time to be selfish. You spoiled brat. (*To Philomena.*) You old fool. I thought you were coming back to help me and here you are all trussed up like a Thanksgiving turkey, putting on these white lady airs. (*To Annie.*) Annie Cook. Move to Kapuskasing! (*To Emily.*) "Fuck, fuck, fuck!" Us Indian women got no business talking like that.

**MARIE-ADELE** (*To Pelajia*): You don't have all the answers. You can't fix everything. (*To Annie.*) White guys. Slow down a minute and see how stupid you look. (*To Emily.*) Voice like a fog-horn. You ram through everything like a truck. You look like a truck. (*To Veronique.*) Some kind of insect, sticking insect claws into everybody's business. (*To Philomena.*) Those clothes. You look like a giant Kewpie doll. You make me laugh.

ANNIE (*To Marie-Adele*): You always make me feel so . . . small . . . like a little pig or something. You're no better than me. (*To Philomena.*) Why can't you go to bingo by yourself, you big baby? At least I got staying power. Piss off. (*To Veronique.*) Sucking off everybody else's life like a leech because you got nothing of your own. Pathetic old coot. Just buzz off. (*To Emily.*) You call me names. I don't call you names. You think you're too smart. Shut up. (*To Pelajia.*) "Queen of the Indians," you think that's what you are. Well, that stupid hammer of yours doesn't scare me. Go away. Piss me off.

*Then Pelajia lifts her hammer with a big loud "Woah"! And they come to a sudden dead stop. Pause. Then one quick final volley, all at once, loudest of all.*

PHILOMENA (*To Annie*): You slimy buck-toothed drunken worm!
EMILY (*To Veronique*): Fuckin' instigator!
VERONIQUE (*To Marie-Adele*): Clutching, clinging vine!
PELAJIA (*To Veronique*): Evil no-good insect!
MARIE-ADELE (*To Veronique*): Maggot-mouthed vulture!
ANNIE (*To Philomena*): Fat-assed floozy, get off the pot!

*Marie-Adele, stung to the quick, makes a vicious grab for Veronique by the throat. In a split-second, all freeze. Lights out in store interior. Lights on on Zhaboonigan, who has run out in fright during the riot, outside the store. Nanabush, still in his guise as the seagull, makes a grab at Zhaboonigan. Zhaboonigan begins talking to the bird.*

ZHABOONIGAN: Are you gentle? I was not little. Maybe. Same size as now. Long ago it must be? You think I'm funny? Shhh. I know who you are. There, there. Boys. White boys. Two. Ever nice white wings, you. I was walking down the road to the store. They ask me if I want ride in car. Oh, I was happy I said, "Yup." Took me far away. Ever nice ride. Dizzy. They took all my clothes off me. Put something up inside me here. (*Pointing to her crotch, underneath her dress.*) Many, many times. Remember. Don't fly away. Don't go.

I saw you before. There, there. It was a. Screwdriver. They put the screwdriver inside me. Here. Remember. Ever lots of blood. The two white boys. Left me in the bush. Alone. It was cold. And then. Remember. Zhaboonigan. Everybody calls me Zhaboonigan. Why? It means needle. Zhaboonigan. Going-through-thing. Needle Peterson. Going-through-thing Peterson. That's me. It was the screwdriver. Nice. Nice. Nicky Ricky Ben Mark. (*As she counts, with each name, feathers on the bird's wing.*) Ever nice. Nice white birdie you.

*During this last speech, Nanabush goes through agonizing contortions. Then lights change instantly back to the interior of the store. The six women spring back into action. Philomena stomps back into the toilet.*

**MARIE-ADELE** (*To Veronique*):   Fine. And the whole reserve knows the only reason you ever adopted Zhaboonigan is for her disability cheque.

**ANNIE:**   You fake saint.

*Annie, Marie-Adele, and Emily start pushing Veronique, round-robin, between the three of them, laughing tauntingly until Veronique is almost reduced to tears.*

**VERONIQUE** (*Almost weeping*):   Bastards. The three of you.

*Marie-Adele grabs Veronique by the throat and lifts her fist to punch her in the face. But the exertion causes her body to weaken, almost to the point of collapse, from her illness. At this point, Philomena emerges from the toilet.*

**PHILOMENA** (*Crinkling her nose*):   Emily. Your toilet.

**WOMEN:**   Shhhh.

**MARIE-ADELE** (*Holding her waist, reeling, barely audible*):   Oh, shit.

**PHILOMENA:**   I can't get it to flush.

**WOMEN:**   Shhhh.

**PELAJIA** (*Rushing to Marie-Adele*):   Marie-Adele. You're not well.

**MARIE-ADELE** (*Screams*):   Don't touch me.

*Complete silence from all while Marie-Adele weaves and struggles to keep herself from collapsing. Annie scurries offstage, to the back part of the store, where the post office would be.*

**EMILY** (*To Veronique*):   You f'in' bitch!

**PHILOMENA:**   What did I just tell you? Who did that to your eye?

**VERONIQUE:**   Big Joey.

**EMILY** (*To Veronique*):   Look here, you old buzzard. I'll tell you a few things. You see this fist? You see these knuckles? You wanna know where they come from? Ten years. Every second night for 10 long ass-fuckin' years that goddamn Yellowknife asshole Henry Dadzinanare come home to me so drunk his eyes was spittin' blood like Red Lucifer himself and he'd beat me purple.

**VERONIQUE:**   I wish I'd been there to see it all.

**EMILY:**   Yeah, scumbag. I wish you'd been there to watch me learn to fight back like you've never seen a woman fight for her life before. Take a look at this eye. I earned it, Veronique St. Pierre, I earned it.

**PHILOMENA:**   Henry Dadzinanare, Big Joey. They're all the same. Emily, use your brains.

**EMILY:**   Use my brains. Yeah, right. I used them alright the night he came at me with an axe and just about sank it into my spine, I grabbed one bag, took one last look at the kids and walked out of his life forever.

**ANNIE** (*From offstage*):   And she took the bus to San Francisco.

**PHILOMENA:**   And gets herself mixed up with a motorcycle gang, for God's sake.

**EMILY** (*Now addressing all in the room*):   Rosabella Baez, Hortensia Colorado, Liz Jones, Pussy Commanda. And me. The best. "Rose and the Rez Sisters," that's us. And man, us sisters could weave knuckle magic.

**VERONIQUE:**   So why did you bother coming back?

**PHILOMENA:**   You stay out of this.

**EMILY:**   Come back to the Rez for a visit, get all wedged up with that hunk Big Joey one night . . . (*Grunts.*)

**PHILOMENA:**   I give up.

**EMILY:**   . . . and I was hooked. Couldn't leave. Settlin' back on a cou-pla beers with Big Joey the other night when Gazelle Nataways come sashayin' in like she's got half the Rez squished down the crack of her ass. She was high. I was high. Hell, we were all high. Get into a bit of a discussion, when she gets me miffed and I let fly, she let fly, Big Joey let fly, misses that nympho and lands me one in the eye instead.

**VERONIQUE:** So it was Big Joey.

**EMILY:** Damn right. And that's as close as he got cuz I put him out for the night right then and there. Just one of these. (*Brandishing her fist.*) One. That's all it took.

*Veronique runs off to look for Zhaboonigan.*

**ANNIE AND PHILOMENA:** Emily Dictionary.

*Philomena with exasperation, Annie with adulation, from offstage.*

**ANNIE:** You're amazing!

**EMILY:** Not Dictionary. Dadzinanare. Henry Dadzinanare. The man who made me learn to fight back. Never let a man raise one dick hair against me since.

**VERONIQUE** (*Calling out to Zhaboonigan*): Zhaboonigan. Don't you be talking to the birds like that again. You're crazy enough as it is.

**ANNIE** (*As she comes running back in from the post office with her parcel, already unwrapped, and two letters, one for herself, already unfolded, and one still in its envelope*): See? I told you. It's a record. Patsy Cline.

**PHILOMENA:** Never mind Patsy Cline.

**ANNIE** (*As she hands Marie-Adele the letter in the envelope*): Hey, Marie-Adele.

**EMILY:** Read your friggin' letter, Annie Cook.

**ANNIE:** Listen to this.

*Zhaboonigan walks back in as Annie reads her own letter very haltingly.*

Dear Mom: Here is the record you wanted. I thought you'd like the picture of Patsy Cline on the cover. (*Annie shows off her record.*) See? It's Patsy Cline. (*Returns to her letter.*) I also thought you might like to know that there is a bingo called THE BIGGEST BINGO IN THE WORLD. Can you fu . . . ture that?

**EMILY** (*Who has been looking over Annie's shoulder*): Feature. Feature.

**ANNIE:** Can you . . . feature . . . that? . . . that's coming to Toronto. The jackpot is $500,000. It's on Saturday, September 8. Ray*mond*'s

Mom was in Toronto. Aunt Philomena will hit the roof when she hears this. Much love, your daughter Ellen.

*Annie announces once more.*

*There is a brief electric silence followed by an equally electric scream from all the women. Even Zhaboonigan screams. Excitement takes over completely.*

VERONIQUE: So it's true! It's true!

PHILOMENA: The Espanola bingo. Piffle. Mere piffle.

VERONIQUE: My new stove!

PHILOMENA: My new toilet! White! Spirit white!

EMILY (*Grabbing Zhaboonigan and dancing around the room with her*): I'd take the money, come back to the Rez, beat the shit out of Gazelle Nataways and take you down to Frisco with me. Whaddaya think?

ZHABOONIGAN: Yup.

MARIE-ADELE (*In the background, where she has been reading her letter quietly to herself*): September 10.

ANNIE (*Taking the letter from Marie-Adele*): Look, Pelajia. Marie-Adele's tests are in Toronto just two days after THE BIGGEST.

*There is a brief embarrassed silence.*

MARIE-ADELE: Kill two birds with one stone.

*To Nanabush.*

I wanna go.

*To Pelajia and Philomena.*

I wanna go.

VERONIQUE: Goood!

EMILY (*Mimicking Veronique*): Goood! Now how the hell are you guys gonna get down to Toronto? You're all goddamn welfare cases.

ANNIE: Fire Minklater.

VERONIQUE: Mary, mother of Jesus! I refuse, I absolutely refuse to be seen anywhere near that sorceress! We'll chip in and rent a car.

EMILY: Zhaboonigan Peterson here gonna chauffeur you down?

ZHABOONIGAN: Yup.

VERONIQUE: Don't you make fun of my daughter.

**EMILY:** What kind of stove you gonna buy, Veronique St. Pierre? Westinghouse? Electrolux? Yamaha? Kawasaki?

**VERONIQUE:** Oh my god, Marie-Adele, I never thought about it. They will have so many stoves in Toronto, I'll get confused.

**ANNIE:** If you go to Toronto and leave Wasy for even one day, Emily, you'll lose Big Joey forever . . .

**VERONIQUE:** To that witch!

**ANNIE:** . . . and then whose thighs will you have to wrestle around with in the dead of night? You'll dry up, get all puckered up and pass into ancient history.

**EMILY:** Annie Cook. I don't know what the fuck you're yatterin' on about now but I'd like to hear you say two words of French to that white guy in Sudbury you're so damn proud of.

**ANNIE:** Oh my god, Marie-Adele, she's right. I won't know what to say to this Ray*mond*. I've never met him. I can't speak French. All I can say in French is Ray*mond* and Bon Bon and I don't even know what that means. I can't go and live with them, not even after I win THE BIGGEST BINGO IN THE WORLD. What am I gonna do?

*She collapses on the floor and rolls around for a bit.*

**EMILY:** And Philomena Moosemeat's so fulla shit she'd need five toilets to get it all out.

**PHILOMENA** (*Going at Emily.*): And just who do you think you're talking to, Miss Dictionary, just who the hell do you think you're talking to?

*With a resounding belly butt from Emily, they begin to wrestle.*

**PELAJIA** (*Banging her hammer on the counter*): Alright, alright. It's obvious we've got a problem here.

**EMILY** (*Throwing Philomena off to the side*): I'll say.

**MARIE-ADELE:** It's true. None of us has any money.

*But Veronique, standing behind Pelajia, winks at the others and makes a hand motion indicating that Pelajia, for one, does have money. All the other women slowly surround Pelajia. But Pelajia catches the drift and quickly collects herself to meet the onslaught. During Pelajia's speech, the women respond at periodic intervals with a "yoah" and "hmmm," etc., as when a chief speaks at a council meeting.*

**PELAJIA:** I say we all march down to the Band Office and ask the Band Council for a loan that will pay for the trip to this bingo. I know how to handle that tired old chief. He and I have been arguing about paved roads for years now. I'll tell him we'll build paved roads all over the reserve with our prize money. I'll tell him the people will stop drinking themselves to death because they'll have paved roads to walk on. I'll tell him there'll be more jobs because the people will have paved roads to drive to work on. I'll tell him the people will stop fighting and screwing around and Nanabush will come back to us because he'll have paved roads to dance on. There's enough money in there for everyone, I'll say. And if he doesn't lend us the money, I'll tell him I'm packing my bags and moving to Toronto tomorrow.

**EMILY:** That oughta twist his arm but good.

**PELAJIA:** And if he still says no, I'll bop him over the head with my hammer and we'll attack the accountant and take the money ourselves. Philomena, we're going to Toronto!

*The seven women have this grand and ridiculous march to the band office, around the set and all over the stage area, with Pelajia leading them forward heroically, her hammer just a-swinging in the air. Nanabush trails merrily along in the rear of the line. They reach the "band office"—standing in one straight line square in front of the audience. The "invisible" chief "speaks": cacophonous percussion for about seven beats, the women listening more and more incredulously. Finally, the percussion comes to a dead stop.*

**PELAJIA:** No?

*Pelajia raises her hammer to hit the "invisible" chief, Nanabush shrugs a "don't ask me, I don't know," Emily fingers a "fuck you, man." Blackout. End of Act One.*

## Act Two

*All seven women are holding a meeting in the basement of Pelajia Patchnose's house. This is a collection of chairs and stools off to the side of the stage area. The only light comes from an old, beat-up trilight pole lamp. Some have tea, Emily and Annie a beer.*

**VERONIQUE:** We should have met at the priest's house.

**PELAJIA:** No! We're gonna work this out on our own. Right here. Emily Dictionary, you chair.

*And she lends Emily her hammer.*

**VERONIQUE:** She's good at ordering people around.

**PHILOMENA:** Shut up.

**EMILY:** First. When are we leaving? (*She bangs the hammer regularly throughout the meeting.*)

**VERONIQUE:** How much is the trip going to cost?

**EMILY:** When are we leaving?

**PHILOMENA:** How long to Toronto?

**ANNIE:** Four hours.

**EMILY:** When are we leaving?

**PHILOMENA:** The only human being who can make it in four hours is Annie Cook.

**VERONIQUE:** I'm not dying on the highway.

**PHILOMENA:** Eight hours.

**PELAJIA:** No way we're gonna stop at every toilet on the highway.

**MARIE-ADELE:** Six hours. Eugene's driven there.

**VERONIQUE:** Maybe we can borrow his van.

**ANNIE:** Maybe we can borrow Big Joey's van.

*A quick little aside to Pelajia.*

Hey, can I have another beer?

**PELAJIA:** No.

**VERONIQUE:** What about Gazelle Nataways?

**EMILY:** We're gonna borrow his van, not his buns, for Chris'sakes.

**MARIE-ADELE:** The only thing we have to pay for is gas.

**ANNIE:** Philomena's got gas.

**EMILY:** Right! Six hours. Eugene's van.

**MARIE-ADELE:** We still don't know when we're leaving.

**PHILOMENA:** Bingo's on Saturday night.

**ANNIE:** Leave Saturday morning.

**VERONIQUE:** Oh! I'll be so tired for the bingo. I'll get confused. Wednesday. Rest on Thursday.

**ANNIE:** And rest again on Friday? Too much resting. I can't go for that.

**PELAJIA:**   And we can't afford such a long stay.

**PHILOMENA:**   Where are we gonna stay?

**EMILY:**   Whoa!

*Pause.*

**PELAJIA:**   Friday night.

**EMILY:**   Right. Leave Friday night. Next.

**PHILOMENA:**   Coming home right after the bingo.

**MARIE-ADELE:**   And leave me behind? Remember my tests Monday morning.

**EMILY:**   Right. Monday noon, we come back. Next.

**VERONIQUE:**   Don't go so fast. My mind is getting confused.

**EMILY:**   Goood! Next.

**MARIE-ADELE:**   Where are we gonna stay?

**ANNIE:**   The Silver Dollar!

**MARIE-ADELE:**   You can't stay there.

**ANNIE:**   There's rooms upstairs.

**PELAJIA:**   You wanna sleep in a whorehouse?

**VERONIQUE:**   Zhaboonigan! Don't listen to this part.

**PELAJIA:**   There's room at my son's.

**PHILOMENA:**   Two washrooms! He's got a wonderful education.

**EMILY:**   Next.

**VERONIQUE:**   Who's going to drive?

**ANNIE:**   Emily. She can drive anything.

**VERONIQUE:**   I believe it.

**ANNIE:**   But I can drive, too.

**VERONIQUE:**   Oh my god.

**ANNIE:**   Long as I don't have to drive in the city. You drive the city.

**VERONIQUE:**   Me?

**ANNIE AND MARIE-ADELE:**   No!

**PELAJIA:**   Long as you don't drive too fast, Annie Cook.

**PHILOMENA:**   And we'll pack a lunch for the trip and then eat in restaurants. Chinese.

**PELAJIA:**   Can't afford it. We chip in, buy groceries and cook at my son's.

**VERONIQUE:**   I'll give $10.

**EMILY:**   You old fossil. You want us to starve?

**PHILOMENA:**   $50 a day. Each.

**EMILY:** Philomena Moosemeat! That's $50 times seven people times four days. That's over $1,000 worth of groceries.

**VERONIQUE:** Imagine!

**MARIE-ADELE:** Okay. Veronique St. Pierre. You cook. $20 apiece. Right?

**EMILY:** Right. Next.

**PHILOMENA:** Anybody writing this down?

**ANNIE:** I'm gonna go to Sam the Recordman.

**MARIE-ADELE:** I'll make the grocery list.

**PELAJIA:** How much for gas?

**VERONIQUE** (*Still in dreamland over the groceries*): $1,000!

**PHILOMENA** (*Flabbergasted*): Nooo! You goose.

**ANNIE:** $40.

**EMILY:** $150. Period. Next.

**PELAJIA:** We got 10 days to find this money.

**MARIE-ADELE:** What's it cost to get into the bingo?

**VERONIQUE:** All the Indians in the world will be there!

**PHILOMENA:** $50.

**ANNIE:** And we're gonna be the only Indians there.

**PELAJIA:** Silence.

*There is a long, thoughtful silence, broken only after awhile by a scream from Zhaboonigan. Nanabush has knocked her off her stool. The women laugh.*

Can't think of anything else.

**PHILOMENA:** Add it up. (*She hands a pencil to Emily.*)

**EMILY** (*Calculates*): $1,400. You guys need $200 each.

**VERONIQUE:** Where am I going to get $400?

**EMILY:** Make it. End of meeting.

*And the women start their fundraising activities with a vengeance. The drive is underlined by a wild rhythmic beat from the musician, one that gets wilder and wilder with each successive beat, though always underpinned by this persistent, almost dance-like pulse. The movement of the women covers the entire stage area, and like the music, gets wilder and wilder, until by the end it is as if we are looking at an insane eight-ring circus, eight-ring because through all this, Nanabush, as the seagull, has a holiday, particularly with*

*Marie-Adele's lines of laundry, as Marie-Adele madly strings one line of laundry after another all over the set, from Pelajia's roof to Emily's store, etc. For the garage sale, Annie sells off Pelajia's lamp, chairs, etc., so that Pelajia's "basement" simply dissolves into the madness of the fundraising drive.*

*Beat one.*

*Pelajia is hammering on the roof.*
*Emily is at the store cash register and rings up each sale as Annie, Philomena, Marie-Adele, Zhaboonigan, and Veronique stand shoulder to shoulder and pass the following from one side of the stage to the other:*
*seven large sacks marked "FLOUR"*
*two giant tubs marked "LARD"*
*one bushel of apples*

*Beat two.*

*Zhaboonigan brings small table on and puts it stage left.*
*Annie brings table on and puts it stage right.*
*Philomena brings a basket full of beer bottles to centre and empties it. She has a baby attached to her.*
*Veronique comes on with cloth and Windex and starts "cleaning windows" rhythmically, listening to whatever gossip she can hear.*
*Marie-Adele strings two lines of clothing across the stage.*
*Pelajia hammers on her roof.*
*Emily brings on several empty beer cases and fills them with Philomena's bottles.*

*Beat three.*

*Zhaboonigan brings in six quarts of blueberries and then takes over window cleaning from Veronique.*
*Annie brings on basket of old clothes and a broken kitchen chair.*
*Philomena brings on another basket full of beer bottles, empties it. She now has two babies attached to her, like a fungus.*
*Emily fills beer cases rapidly, expertly.*

*Pelajia gets down off roof, hammering everything until she is on hands and knees, hammering the floor.*
*Marie-Adele strings third and fourth lines of laundry across the stage.*
*Veronique comes in burdened with seven apple pies and puts them on Annie's table.*

*Beat four.*

*Pelajia hammers as she crawls across the floor.*
*Zhaboonigan washes windows like a person possessed.*
*Emily runs and rings up a sale on the cash register and then brings on more empty beer cases and loads them up.*
*Philomena brings on a third load of bottles. Three babies are now attached to her.*
*Annie brings on an old trilight pole lamp and an old record player, which she opens and stacks alongside the rest of her stuff.*
*Annie and Emily sing a line of their song with very bad harmony.*
*Marie-Adele strings fifth and sixth lines of laundry across stage.*
*Veronique comes on with seven loaves of bread and puts them neatly by the pies.*

*Beat five.*

*Pelajia hammers as she crawls across the floor, hammering everything in sight. The women protect their poor feet.*
*Zhaboonigan washes windows even faster; she's starting to cry.*
*Emily and Philomena work together filling the empty beer cases as fast as they can. Emily runs to the register, rings in seven sales and sings a bit of song with Annie, better this time. Philomena now has four kids attached to her body.*
*Annie comes on with a small black and white TV with rabbit ears and an old toaster.*
*Veronique comes on with six dozen buns and dumps them out of their tins all over the table.*
*Pelajia hammers faster and faster.*
*Zhaboonigan is now working like a maniac and is sobbing.*
*Marie-Adele strings seventh and eighth lines of laundry across the stage.*

*Beat six.*

*Emily goes to cash register and tallies their earnings; she works the register with tremendous speed and efficiency all this beat.*
*Zhaboonigan continues washing windows.*
*Philomena sticks a sign in beer bottles: World's Biggest Bottle Drive. She now has five babies attached to her.*
*Veronique sticks a sign on her table: World's Biggest Bake Sale.*
*Annie sticks a sign up around her stuff: World's Biggest Garage Sale.*
*Marie-Adele sticks a sign up on Zha's table: Big Blueberries and Laundry While You Wait.*
*Pelajia begins hammering the air. She may have lost her marbles.*

*Beat Seven.*

**EMILY:** Whoa!

*The "music" comes to a sudden stop. The women all collapse. The women look at each other. They then quickly clear the stage of everything they've brought on as Pelajia speaks, consulting her list. By the end of Pelajia's speech, the stage area is clear once more, except for a microphone stand that one of the women has brought on as part of the "clean-up" activities.*

**PELAJIA:** Bottle drive. Ten cents a bottle, 24 bottles a case, equals two dollars and 40 cents. 777 bottles collected divided by 24 is 32 cases and nine singles that's 32 times $2.40 equals $77.70. Blueberries equals $90. Good pickin' Zha and the Starblanket kids. Washing windows at $5.00 a house times 18 houses. Five eights are 40, carry the four and add the five is 90 bucks less two on account of that cheap Gazelle Nataways only gave three dollars. That's $88. Household repairs is four roofs including the Chief's and one tiled floor is $225. Garage sale brung in $246.95, the bake sale equals $83 after expenses, we make 110 bucks on doing laundry, 65 bucks babysitting, 145 from Emily doing a double shift at the store and I have generously donated $103 from my savings. That brings us to a grand total of $1233.65. So!

*Emily and Annie move forward as the music starts up. They are lit only by tacky floor flood-lighting, and are, in effect, at the Anchor Inn, Little Current. Emily speaks into the microphone.*

**EMILY:**   Thank-you. Thank-you, ladies and gentlemen. I thank you very much. And now for the last song of the night, ladies and gents, before we hit the road. A song that's real special to me in my heart. A song I wrote in memory of one Rosabella Baez, a Rez Sister from way back. And Rose baby, if you're up there tonight, I hope you're listenin' in. Cuz it's called: "I'm Thinkin' of You." Here goes . . .

*Emily and Annie grab their microphones; Emily sings lead, Annie sings backup. And it's "country" to the hilt.*

I'm thinkin' of you every moment,
As though you were here by my side;
I'll always remember the good times,
So darlin' please come back to me.

I'm dreamin' of you every night,
That we were together again;
If time can heal up our partin'
Then love can remove all this pain.

*Instrumental—dance break*

If love is the secret of livin',
Then give me that love, shinin' light;
When you are again by my side,
Then livin' will once more be right.

*The audience claps. Emily says, "Thank-you." And then she and Annie join the other women, who have, during the song, loaded themselves, their suitcases, and their lunches into the "van." This van consists of three battered old van seats stuck to the walls of the theatre, on either side and up high. The back seat is on the "stage left" side of the theatre and the other two are on the other side, the middle seat of the van towards the back of the theatre, the front seat, complete with detachable steering wheel, just in front and "stage right" of the stage area. Each seat is lit by its own light.*

**EMILY:** How much did me and Annie take in singin' at the Anchor Inn?

**PELAJIA:** $330 at the door.

**MARIE-ADELE:** Solid packed house, eh? Shoulda charged more.

**ANNIE:** Fifty bucks for the oom-chi-cha machine. Twenty bucks for Ronnie's guitar. That's our only costs.

**EMILY:** Ha! We're laughin'.

*A cappella reprise of a verse of their song, which fades into highway sounds, and they drive, for a few moments, in silence.*

*In the van, driving down the highway to Toronto, at night. The women have intimate conversations, one on one, while the rest are asleep or seated at the other end of the van. Annie is driving. Emily sits beside her listening to her Walkman, while Marie-Adele is "leaning" over Annie's shoulder from her place in the middle seat. Veronique sits beside Marie-Adele, sleeping. Pelajia and Philomena are in the very back seat with Zhaboonigan between them.*

**MARIE-ADELE:** Nee, Annie, not so fast.

*Pause. Annie slows down.*

So. You couldn't get Ellen and *Ray*mond to come along? I'd like to meet this *Ray*mond someday.

**ANNIE** (*Angrily insisting on the correct pronunciation*): Raymónd! Ellen says he's got a whole library full of cassette tapes.

**MARIE-ADELE:** Annie. You ever think about getting married again?

**ANNIE:** Not really. I can hear the band at the Silver Dollar already.

**MARIE-ADELE:** Do you still think about . . . Eugene?

**ANNIE:** What're you talkin' about? Of course, I think about him, he's my brother-in-law, ain't he?

**MARIE-ADELE:** He made his choice.

**ANNIE:** Yeah. He picked you.

**MARIE-ADELE:** Annie. I never stole him off you.

**ANNIE:** Drop dead. Shit! I forgot to bring that blouse. I mean. In case I sing. Shit.

**MARIE-ADELE:** If I'm gone and Eugene if he starts drinkin' again. I see you going for him.

**ANNIE:** Why would I bother? I had my chance 20 years ago. Christ!

**MARIE-ADELE:** Twenty years ago, I was there.

**ANNIE:** Why would I want 14 kids for?

**MARIE-ADELE:** That's exactly what I'm scared of. I don't want them kids to be split up. You come near Eugene you start drinking messing things up me not here I come back and don't matter where you are . . .

**ANNIE:** I don't want him. I don't want him. I don't want him. I don't want him. I don't want him.

**EMILY:** Put us all in the fuckin' ditch!

**PELAJIA:** Hey, watch your language up there.

**ANNIE:** Shit! I don't care. There's nothing more to say about it. Why don't you take your pills and go to sleep.

*Pelajia and Philomena begin talking.*

**PHILOMENA:** September 8 again.

**PELAJIA:** Hmmm? What about September 8?

**PHILOMENA:** You don't remember?

**PELAJIA:** What?

**PHILOMENA:** How could you?

**PELAJIA:** Mama died?

**PHILOMENA:** No! Remember?

**PELAJIA:** I can't remember. Got so much on my mind. So many things to forget.

**ZHABOONIGAN** (*To Philomena*): You like me?

**PHILOMENA:** Yes, Zhaboonigan. I like you.

**ZHABOONIGAN:** I like the birdies.

**PHILOMENA:** You like talking to the birdies?

**ZHABOONIGAN:** Yup.

*She falls asleep.*

**PHILOMENA:** Zhaboonigan . . . sometimes I wonder . . .

**PELAJIA:** It's dark . . . warm . . . quiet . . .

**PHILOMENA:** Toronto. Had a good job in Toronto. Yeah. Had to give it all up. Yeah. Cuz mama got sick. Philomena Margaret Moosetail. Real live secretary in the garment district. He'd come in and see my boss. Nice man, I thought. That big, red, fish-tail Caddy. Down Queen Street. He liked me. Treated me like a queen. Loved me. Or I thought he did. I don't know. Got pregnant anyway. Blond, blue-eyed, six foot two. And the way he smelled. God! His wife walks in on us.

*Long silence.*

He left with her.

*Long silence.*

I don't even know to this day if it was a boy or a girl. I'm getting old. That child would be . . . 28 . . . 28 years old. September 8. You know what I'm gonna do with that money if I win? I'm gonna find a lawyer. Maybe I can find that child. Maybe I wouldn't even have to let him . . . her . . . know who I am. I just . . . want to see . . . who . . .

**PELAJIA:** I hope you win.

*Annie and Emily, at the front of the van with Annie driving, are laughing and singing, "I'm a little Indian who loves fry bread." From time to time, they sneak each other a sip of this little bottle of whiskey Annie has hidden away inside her purse.*

I'm a little Indian who loves fry bread,
Early in the morning and when I go to bed;
Some folks say I'm crazy in the head,
Cuz I'm a little Indian who loves fry bread.

Now, some folks say I've put on a pound or two,
My jeans don't fit the way they used to do;
But I don't care, let the people talk,
Cuz if I don't get my fry bread, you'll hear me squawk.

**ANNIE:** So tell me. What's it like to go to a big bar like . . . I mean like . . . the Silver Dollar.

**EMILY:** Lotta Nishnawbs.[6]

**ANNIE** (*Disappointed*): Yeah? Is the music good?

**EMILY:** Country rock.

**ANNIE** (*Screams gleefully*): Yee-haw! Maybe the band will ask me up to sing, eh? I'll sing something fast.

**EMILY:** You would, too.

**ANNIE** (*Sings real fast*): "Well, it's 40 below and I don't give a fuck, got a heater in my truck and I'm off to the rodeo. Woof!" Something like that.

**EMILY:** Yup. That's pretty fast.

[6]Indians. (Ojibway)

**ANNIE:** Hey. Maybe Fritz the Katz will be there. Never know. Might get laid, too, eh? Remember Room 20 at the Anchor Inn? Oh, that Fritz! Sure like singin' with him. Crazy about the way . . .

**EMILY** (*Starts singing Patsy Cline's famous "Crazy . . . crazy for feelin' so lonely . . ." all the way through Annie's next speech.*)

**ANNIE:** . . . he stands there with his guitar and his 10-gallon hat. Is that what you call them hats? You know the kind you wear kind of off to the side like this? That's what he does. And then he winks at me. (*Sings.*) "Crazy . . ." Oooh, I love, just love the way the lights go woosh woosh in your eyes and kinda' wash all over your body. Me standing there shuffling my feet side to side, dressed real nice and going (*Sings.*) "Oooh darlin' . . ." with my mike in my hand just so. Oh! And the sound of that band behind me. And Fritz. (*Sings.*) "Crazy, crazy for feelin' so lonely . . ."

**EMILY:** Yeah. You look good on stage.

**ANNIE:** Yeah?

**EMILY:** How come you're so keen on that guy anyway?

**ANNIE:** Sure Veronique St. Pierre isn't just pretending to be asleep back there?

*Emily and Marie-Adele check Veronique in the middle seat.*

**MARIE-ADELE:** Nah. Out like a lamp.

**EMILY:** Hey! We'll get her drunk at the Silver Dollar and leave her passed out under some table. Take two beers to do that.

**ANNIE:** Hey. Too bad Big Joey had to come back from Toronto before we got there, eh?

**EMILY:** Man! That dude's got buns on him like no other buns on the face of God's entire creation. Whooo! Not to mention a dick that's bigger than a goddamn breadbox.

*Annie screams gleefully.*

How about Fritz? What's his look like?

**ANNIE** (*After an awkward pause*): He's Jewish, you know.

**EMILY** (*Laughing raucously*): World's first Jewish country singer!

**ANNIE:** Don't laugh. Those Jews make a lot of money, you know.

**EMILY:** Not all of them.

**ANNIE:** Fritz buys me jeans and things. I'm gonna be one of them Jewish princesses.

**EMILY:**   What's wrong with being an Indian princess?

**ANNIE:**   Aw, these white guys. They're nicer to their women. Not like Indian guys. Screw you, drink all your money, and leave you flat on your ass.

**EMILY:**   Yeah, right. Apple Indian Annie. Red on the outside. White on the inside.

**ANNIE:**   Emily!

**EMILY:**   Keep your eye on the road.

**ANNIE:**   Good ol' highway 69.

**EMILY:**   Hey. Ever 69 with Fritz?

**MARIE-ADELE:**   Neee.

**ANNIE:**   White guys don't make you do things to them. You just lie there and they do it all for you. Ellen's real happy with her Ray*mond*. You can tell the way she sounds on the phone. Maybe someday I'll just take off with a guy like Fritz.

**EMILY:**   Then what? Never come back to the rez?

*Annie is cornered. Emily then slaps her playfully on the arm.*

Hey. Know what?

*Sings.*

When I die, I may not go to heaven,
I don't know if they let Indians in;
If they don't, just let me go to Wasy, lord,
Cuz Wasy is as close as I've been.

**ANNIE:**   Lots of white people at this Silver Dollar?

**EMILY:**   Sometimes. Depends.

**ANNIE:**   How much for beer there?

**EMILY:**   Same as up here. Nah! Don't need money, Annie Cook. You just gotta know how to handle men. Like me and the Rez Sisters down in Frisco.

**ANNIE:**   Yeah?

**EMILY:**   I'll take care of them.

**ANNIE:**   Maybe we can find a party, eh? Maybe with the band.

**EMILY:**   Whoa! Slow down, Annie Cook! Easy on the gas!

**MARIE-ADELE:**   Annie!

*Pow. Black-out. They have a flat tire.*

*The flat tire. Everything now happens in complete darkness.*

**VERONIQUE:**   Bingo!

**PHILOMENA:**   What was that? What happened?

**ANNIE:**   I don't know. Something just went "poof"!

**EMILY:**   Alright. Everybody out. We got a fuckin' flat.

*They all climb out of the van.*

**VERONIQUE:**   Oh my god! We'll never get to the bingo.

**ZHABOONIGAN:**   Pee pee.

**PELAJIA:**   I can't fix a flat tire.

**ANNIE:**   Emily can.

**PELAJIA:**   Get the jack. Spare tire.

**ANNIE:**   Philomena's wearing one.

**ZHABOONIGAN:**   Pee pee.

**PHILOMENA:**   This is all your fault, Annie Cook.

**MARIE-ADELE:**   It's in the back.

**ANNIE:**   So what do we do?

**PELAJIA:**   What's the matter with Zha?

**PHILOMENA:**   Gotta make pee pee.

**VERONIQUE:**   I knew there was something wrong with this van the moment I set eyes on it. I should have taken the bus.

**PHILOMENA:**   Oh shut up. Quack, quack, quack.

**ANNIE:**   Don't look at me. It's not my fault the tires are all bald.

**PHILOMENA:**   Nobody's blaming you.

**ANNIE:**   But you just did.

**PHILOMENA:**   Quack, quack, quack.

**VERONIQUE:**   Where are we?

**ANNIE:**   The Lost Channel. This is where you get off.

**VERONIQUE** (*Groans*):   Ohhh!

**EMILY:**   Yeah, right.

**PHILOMENA:**   Shhh!

**PELAJIA:**   Jack's not working too well.

**EMILY:**   Okay. Everybody. Positions.

**VERONIQUE:**   Not me. My heart will collapse.

**EMILY:**   You wanna play bingo?

**VERONIQUE** (*Groans.*):   Ohhhh!

**ANNIE:**   Hurry up! Hurry up!

**EMILY:** Okay. One, two, three lift.

*Everybody lifts and groans.*

**PELAJIA:** Put the jack in there.

*All lift, except Marie-Adele and Zha, who wander off into the moonlit darkness. Dim light on them.*

**ZHABOONIGAN:** Ever dark.
**MARIE-ADELE:** You'll be fine, Zhaboonigan.

*Suddenly, a nighthawk—Nanabush, now in dark feathers— appears, darting in the night.*

**ZHABOONIGAN:** The birdies!
**MARIE-ADELE:** Yes, a birdie.
**ZHABOONIGAN:** Black wings!

*Marie-Adele begins talking to the bird, almost as if she were talking to herself. Quietly, at first, but gradually—as the bird begins attacking her—growing more and more hysterical, until she is shrieking, flailing, and thrashing about insanely.*

**MARIE-ADELE:** Who are you? What do you want? My children? Eugene? No! Oh no! Me? Not yet. Not yet. Give me time. Please. Don't. Please don't. Awus! Get away from me. Eugene! Awus! You fucking bird! Awus! Awus! Awus! Awus! Awus!

*And she has a total hysterical breakdown.*

*Zhaboonigan, at first, attempts to scare the bird off by running and flailing her arms at it. Until the bird knocks her down and she lies there on the ground, watching in helpless astonishment and abject terror. Underneath Marie-Adele's screams, she mumbles to herself, sobbing.*

**ZHABOONIGAN:** One, two, three, four, five, six, seven . . . Nicky Ricky Ben Mark . . . eight, nine, ten, eleven, twelve . . .

*Until the other women come running. Total darkness again.*

**EMILY:** What the . . .
**ANNIE:** Marie-Adele!
**PELAJIA:** Stop her! Hold her!
**VERONIQUE:** What's happening?

**PHILOMENA:**  Marie Adele. Now, now . . . come . . . come . . .

**EMILY** (*In the background*):  Stop that fucking screaming will ya, Marie-Adele!

**PHILOMENA:**  Emily. There's no need to talk to her like that now.

**PELAJIA:**  Help us get her in the van.

**PHILOMENA:**  Come . . . come, Marie-Adele . . . everything's fine . . . you'll be fine . . . come . . . shhh . . . shhh . . .

*And they ease Marie-Adele back into the van. Once all is beginning to settle down again:*

**PELAJIA:**  Everything okay now?

**PHILOMENA:**  Yes. She's fine now.

**PELAJIA:**  Emily, take over.

**VERONIQUE:**  Yes. I don't trust that Annie Cook. Not for one minute.

**EMILY:**  All set?

**MARIE-ADELE:**  What time is it?

**PELAJIA:**  Twenty after four.

**ANNIE:**  Oh! We're over two hours behind schedule. Hurry up. Hurry up.

**VERONIQUE:**  I'll be exhausted for the bingo tomorrow night. Maybe I should just take 15 cards.

**EMILY:**  You can rest your heart. And your mouth. All day tomorrow. All set?

*And she starts up the van. The van lights come back on.*

*The dialogues resume. Marie-Adele now sits in the front with Emily, who is driving. Zhaboonigan sits between them. Pelajia and Philomena are now in the middle seat, Annie and Veronique in the back.*

**EMILY:**  You scared the shit out of me out there.

*Silence.*

Don't do that again.

*Silence.*

Feeling better now?

*Silence.*

**MARIE-ADELE:** I could be really mad, just raging mad just wanna tear his eyes out with my nails when he walks in the door and my whole body just goes "k-k-k-k". . . . He doesn't talk, when something goes wrong with him, he doesn't talk, shuts me out, just disappears. Last night he didn't come home. Again, it happened. I couldn't sleep. You feel so ugly. He walks in this morning. Wanted to be alone, he said. The curve of his back, his breath on my neck, "Adele, ki-sa-gee-ee-tin oo-ma,"[7] making love, always in Indian, only. When we still could. I can't even have him inside me anymore. It's still growing there. The cancer. Pelajia, een-pay-seek-see-yan.[8]

**PELAJIA:** You know one time, I knew this couple where one of them was dying and the other one was angry at her for dying. And she was mad because he was gonna be there when she wasn't and she had so much left to do. And she'd lie there in bed and tell him to do this and do that and he'd say "Okay, okay." And then he'd go into the kitchen and say to me, "She's so this and she's so that and she's so damned difficult." And I watched all this going on. That house didn't have room for two such angry people. But you know, I said to her, "You gotta have faith in him and you gotta have faith in life. He loves you very much but there's only so much he can do. He's only human." There's only so much Eugene can understand, Marie-Adele. He's only human.

**EMILY:** Fuckin' right. Me and the Rez Sisters, okay? Cruisin' down the coast highway one night. Hum of the engine between my thighs. Rose. That's Rosabella Baez, leader of the pack. We were real close, me and her. She was always thinkin' real deep. And talkin' about bein' a woman. An Indian woman. And suicide. And alcohol and despair and how fuckin' hard it is to be an Indian in this country. (*Marie-Adele shushes her gently.*) No goddamn future for them, she'd say. And why, why, why? Always carryin' on like that. Chris'sakes. She was pretty heavy into the drags. Guess we all were. We had a fight. Cruisin' down the coast highway that night. Rose in the middle. Me and Pussy Commanda off to the side. Big 18-wheeler come along real fast and me and Pussy Commanda get out of the way. But not Rose. She stayed in the middle. Went head-on

[7]Adele, I love you. (Cree)
[8]Pelajia, I'm scared to death. (Cree)

into that truck like a fly splat against a windshield. I swear to this day I can still feel the spray of her blood against my neck. I drove on. Straight into daylight. Never looked back. Had enough gas money on me to take me far as Salt Lake City. Pawned my bike off and bought me a bus ticket back to Wasy. When I got to Chicago, that's when I got up the nerve to wash my lover's dried blood from off my neck. I loved that woman, Marie-Adele, I loved her like no man's ever loved a woman. But she's gone. I never wanna go back to San Francisco. No way, man.

**MARIE-ADELE** (*Comforting the crying Emily*):   You should get some rest. Let Annie take over.

**EMILY:**   I'll be fine. You go to sleep. Wake you up when we get to Toronto.

*Emily puts her Walkman on and starts to sing along quietly to "Blue Kentucky Girl" by Emmylou Harris with its "I swear I love you . . ." while Marie-Adele leans her head against the "window" and falls asleep.*

*After a few moments, Zhaboonigan, who has been dozing off between Emily and Marie-Adele in the front seat, pokes her head up and starts to sing along off-key. Then she starts to play with Emily's hair.*

**EMILY** (*Shrugging Zhaboonigan's hand off*):   Don't bug me. My favorite part's comin' up.

*Initiated by Zhaboonigan, they start playing "slap." The game escalates to the point where Emily almost bangs Zhaboonigan over the head with her elbow.*

**EMILY:**   Yeah, right. You little retard.

*Mad at this, Zhaboonigan hits Emily in the stomach.*

Don't hit me there, you little . . . Hey, man, like ummm . . . I'm sorry, Zha.

**ZHABOONIGAN:**   Sorry.

**EMILY** (*Emily feels her belly thoughtfully. After a brief silence*):   You gonna have kids someday, Zha?

**ZHABOONIGAN:**   Ummm . . . buy one.

**EMILY:** Holy! Well, kids were alright. Aw geez, Zha, that man treated me real bad. Ever been tied to a bed post with your arms up like this? Whoa!

*Grabbing the steering wheel.*

Maybe you should drive.

**ZHABOONIGAN:** Scary.

**EMILY:** Aw, don't be scared. Fuck.

**ZHABOONIGAN:** Fuck.

**EMILY:** Zhaboonigan Peterson! Your ma'll give me a black eye.

*Zhaboonigan turns her head toward the back seat, where Veronique sits sleeping, and says one more time, really loud.*

**ZHABOONIGAN:** Fuck!

**EMILY:** Shhh! Look, Zha. You don't let any man bother you while we're down in T.O. You just stick close to me.

**ZHABOONIGAN:** Yup.

**EMILY:** We're sisters, right? Gimme five.

*They slap hands.*

Alright. Bingo!!!

*Instantly, the house lights come on full blast. The Bingo Master—the most beautiful man in the world—comes running up centre aisle, cordless mike in hand, dressed to kill: tails, rhinestones, and all. The entire theatre is now the bingo palace. We are in: Toronto!!!!*

**BINGO MASTER:** Welcome, ladies and gentlemen, to the biggest bingo the world has ever seen! Yes, ladies and gentlemen, tonight, we have a very, very special treat for you. Tonight, ladies and gentlemen, you will be witness to events of such gargantuan proportions, such cataclysmic ramifications, such masterly and magnificent manifestations that your minds will reel, your eyes will nictitate, and your hearts will palpitate erratically.

Because tonight, ladies and gentlemen, you will see the biggest, yes, ladies and gentlemen, the very biggest prizes ever known to man, woman, beast, or appliance. And the jackpot tonight? The jackpot, ladies and gentlemen, is surely the biggest, the largest, the hugest, and the most monstrous jackpot ever conceived of in the entire history of monstrous jackpots as we know them. $500,000!

Yes, ladies and gentlemen, $500,000 can be yours this very night! That's half a million—A HALF MILLION SMACKEROOS!!! IF you play the game right.

And all you have to do, ladies and gentlemen, is reach into your programs and extract the single bingo card placed therein. Yes, ladies and gentlemen, the single bingo card placed therein, which bingo card will entitle you to one chance at winning the warm-up game for a prize of $20. $20! And all you have to do is poke holes in that single bingo card. Yes, ladies and gentlemen, just poke holes in that single bingo card and bend the numbers backward as the numbers are called. And don't forget the free hole in the middle of the card. Twenty dollars, ladies and gentlemen, that's one line in any direction. That means, of course, ladies and gentlemen, that the first person to form one line, just one straight line in any direction on their card, will be the very lucky winner of the $20 prize. $20! Are you ready, ladies and gentlemen? Are you ready? Then let the game begin! Under the G 56. Etc. . . .

*The audience plays bingo, with the seven women, who have moved slowly into the audience during the Bingo Master's speech, playing along. Until somebody in the audience shouts, "Bingo!"*

**BINGO MASTER:** Hold your cards, ladies and gentlemen, bingo has been called.

*The Bingo Master and the assistant stage manager check the numbers and the prize money is paid out.*

**BINGO MASTER:** And now for the game you've all been waiting for, ladies and gentlemen. Now for the big game. Yes, ladies and gentlemen, get ready for THE BIGGEST BINGO IN THE WORLD! For the grand jackpot prize of $500,000! Full house, ladies and gentlemen, full house! Are you ready? Are you ready? Then let the game begin!

*The house lights go out. And the only lights now are on the bingo balls bouncing around in the bingo machine—an eerie, surreal sort of glow—and on the seven women who are now playing bingo with a vengeance on centrestage, behind the Bingo Master, where a long bingo table has magically appeared with Zhaboonigan at the table's centre banging a crucifix Veronique has brought along for good luck. The scene is lit so that it looks like "The Last Supper."*

*The women face the audience. The bingo table is covered with all the necessary accoutrements: bags of potato chips, cans of pop, ashtrays (some of the women are smoking), etc. The Bingo Master calls out number after number—but not the B 14—with the women improvising responses. These responses—Philomena has 27 cards!—grow more and more raucous:* "B 14? Annie Cook? One more number to go! The B 14! Where is that B 14?! Gimme that B 14! Where the fuck is that B 14?!!!" *etc. Until the women have all risen from the table and come running downstage, attacking the bingo machine and throwing the Bingo Master out of the way. The women grab the bingo machine with shouts of:* "Throw this fucking machine into the lake! It's no damn good!" *etc. And they go running down centre aisle with it and out of the theatre. Bingo cards are flying like confetti. Total madness and mayhem. The music is going crazy.*

*And out of this chaos emerges the calm, silent image of Marie-Adele waltzing romantically in the arms of the Bingo Master. The Bingo Master says "Bingo" into her ear. And the Bingo Master changes, with sudden bird-like movements, into the nighthawk, Nanabush in dark feathers. Marie-Adele meets Nanabush.*

*During this next speech, the other women, one by one, take their positions around Marie-Adele's porch, some kneeling, some standing. The stage area, by means of "lighting magic," slowly returns to its Wasaychigan Hill appearance.*

**MARIE-ADELE:** U-wi-nuk u-wa? U-wi-nuk u-wa? Eugene? Neee. U-wi-nuk ma-a oo-ma kee-tha? Ka. Kee-tha i-chi-goo-ma so that's who you are . . . at rest upon the rock . . . the master of the game . . . the game . . . it's me . . . nee-tha . . . come . . . come . . . don't be afraid . . . as-tum . . . come . . . to . . . me . . . ever soft wings . . . beautiful soft . . . soft . . . dark wings . . . here . . . take me . . . as-tum . . . as-tum . . . pee-na-sin . . . wings . . . here . . . take me . . . take . . . me . . . with . . . pee-na-sin . . .[9]

---

[9]Marie-Adele: Who are you? Who are you? Eugene? Nee. Then who are you really? Oh. It's you, so that's who you are . . . at rest upon the rock . . . the master of the game . . . the game . . . it's me . . . me . . . come . . . come . . . don't be afraid . . . come . . . come . . . to . . . me . . . ever soft wings . . . beautiful soft . . . soft . . . dark wings . . . here . . . take me . . . come . . . come . . . come and get me . . . wings here . . . take me . . . take . . . me . . . with . . . come and get me . . . (Cree)

*As Nanabush escorts Marie-Adele into the spirit world, Zhaboonigan, uttering a cry, makes a last desperate attempt to go with them. But Emily rushes after and catches her at the very last split second. And the six remaining women begin to sing the Ojibway funeral song. By the beginning of the funeral song, we are back at the Wasaychigan Hill Indian Reserve, at Marie-Adele's grave.*

**WOMEN:**
Wa-kwing, wa-kwing,
Wa-kwing nin wi-i-ja;
Wa-kwing, wa- kwing,
Wa-kwing nin wi-i-ja.[10]

*At Marie-Adele's grave. During Pelajia's speech, the other women continue humming the funeral song until they fade into silence. Pelajia drops a handful of earth on the grave.*

**PELAJIA:**  Well, sister, guess you finally hit the big jackpot. Best bingo game we've ever been to in our lives, huh? You know, life's like that, I figure. When all is said and done. Kinda' silly, innit, this business of living? But. What choice do we have? When some fool of a being goes and puts us Indians plunk down in the middle of this old earth, dishes out this lot we got right now. But. I figure we gotta make the most of it while we're here. You certainly did. And I sure as hell am giving it one good try. For you. For me. For all of us. Promise. Really. See you when that big bird finally comes for me.

*Whips out her hammer one more time, holds it up in the air and smiles.*

And my hammer.

*Back at the store in Wasaychigan Hill. Emily is tearing open a brand-new case of the small cans of Carnation milk, takes two cans out and goes up to Zhaboonigan with them.*

**EMILY:**  See, Zha? The red part up here and the white part down here and the pink flowers in the middle?

[10]Women: Heaven, heaven, heaven, I'm going there; Heaven, heaven, heaven, I'm going there. (Ojibway)

**ZHABOONIGAN:** Oh.

**EMILY:** Carnation milk.

**ZHABOONIGAN:** Carnation milk.

**EMILY:** And it goes over here where all the other red and white cans are, okay?

**ZHABOONIGAN:** Yup.

> *Zhaboonigan rushes to Emily and throws her arms around her affectionately. Emily is embarrassed and struggles to free herself. Just then, Annie enters. She's lost some of her speed and frenetic energy. There's obviously something wrong with her.*

**ANNIE:** Hallooo! Whatchyou doing.

**EMILY:** Red Lucifer's whiskers! It's Annie Cook.

**ANNIE:** Well, we seem to have survived the biggest bingo in the world, eh? Well . . . ummm . . . not all of us . . . not Marie-Adele . . . but she knew she was . . . but we're okay. (*Laughs.*) . . . us? . . .

**EMILY:** Annie Cook. Sometimes you can be so goddamn ignorant. (*Pause.*) Too bad none of us won, eh.

**ANNIE:** Philomena Moosemeat won $600. That's something.

**EMILY:** Yup. That's one helluva jazzy toilet she's got there, eh?

**ANNIE:** She's got eight-ply toilet paper. Dark green. Feels like you're wiping your ass with moss!

**EMILY:** Holy!

**ANNIE:** I'm singing back-up for Fritz weekends. 25 bucks a gig. That's something, eh?

**EMILY:** Katz's whore . . .

**ANNIE:** What?

**EMILY:** You heard me.

**ANNIE:** The Katz's what?

**EMILY:** Chris'sakes. Wake up.

**ANNIE:** I love him, Emily.

**EMILY:** You been drinkin'.

**ANNIE:** Please, come with me tonight.

**EMILY:** Have to wait for the old buzzard to come pick up this dozy daughter of hers and that's not 'til seven.

**ANNIE:** Okay?

**EMILY:** Alright. But we're comin' right back to the Rez soon as the gig's over. Hear?

**ANNIE:** Thanks. Any mail today?

**EMILY:** Sorry.

**ANNIE:** That's okay. See you at seven.

*And she exits.*

**ZHABOONIGAN:** Why . . . why . . . why do you call me that?

**EMILY:** Call you what?

**ZHABOONIGAN:** Dozy dotter.

*Awkward silence, broken after awhile by Zhaboonigan's little giggle.*

**EMILY:** Look, Zha. Share a little secret with you, okay?

**ZHABOONIGAN:** Yup.

**EMILY:** Just you and me, promise?

**ZHABOONIGAN:** Yup.

**EMILY:** Gazelle Nataways'll see fit to kill . . . but I'm gonna have a baby.

**ZHABOONIGAN** (*Drops the Carnation milk cans she's been holding all this time and gasps*): Ohhh! Big Joey!

**EMILY** (*In exasperation*): This business of having babies . . .

*And the last we see of them is Zhaboonigan playfully poking Emily in the belly and Emily slapping Zhaboonigan's hand away.*

*At Eugene Starblanket's house. Veronique St. Pierre is sitting on the steps, glowing with happiness, looking up at the sky as though looking for seagulls. She sees none so she picks up the doll that lies under her chair and cradles it on her lap as though it were a child. At this point, Annie Cook enters.*

**ANNIE:** Hallooo!

*Surprised to see Veronique sitting there.*

Veronique St. Pierre. What are you doing here?

**VERONIQUE:** Annie Cook. Haven't you heard I'm cooking for Eugene and the children these days? It's been four days since the funeral as you know may she rest in peace (*Makes a quick sign of the cross without missing a beat.*) but I was the only person on this reserve who was willing to help with these 14 little orphans.

**ANNIE:** That's nice. But I came to see if Simon Star . . .

**VERONIQUE:** The stove is so good. All four elements work and there is even a timer for the oven. As I was saying to Black Lady Halked at the bingo last night, "Now I don't have to worry about burning the fried potatoes or serving the roast beef half-raw."

**ANNIE:** Well, I was about to . . .

**VERONIQUE:** Yes, Annie Cook. I bought a roast beef just yesterday. A great big roast beef. Almost 16 pounds. It's probably the biggest roast beef that's been seen on this reserve in recent years. The meat was so heavy that Nicky, Ricky, Ben, and Mark had to take turns carrying it here for me. Oh, it was hard and slippery at first, but I finally managed to wrestle it into my oven. And it's sitting in there at this very moment just sizzling and bubbling with the most succulent and delicious juices. And speaking of succulent and delicious juices, did you come to call on Eugene? Well, Eugene's not home.

**ANNIE:** Yeah, right. I came to see if Simon had that new record.

**VERONIQUE:** Why?

**ANNIE:** I'm singing in Little Current tonight and I gotta practice this one song.

**VERONIQUE** (*Contemptuously*): That Ritzie Ditzie character.

**ANNIE:** It's Fritz the Katz, Veronique St. Pierre. FREDERICK STEPHEN KATZ. He's a very fine musician and a good teacher.

**VERONIQUE:** Teacher?! Of what?! As I was saying to Little Girl Manitowabi and her daughter June Bug McLeod at the bingo last night, "You never know about these non-Native bar-room types." I said to them, "We have enough trouble right here on this reserve without having our women come dragging these shady white characters into the picture." Before you know it, you will end up in deep trouble and bring shame and disrespect on the name of Pelajia Patchnose and all your sisters, myself included.

**ANNIE:** Myself included, my ass! Veronique St. Pierre. I wish you would shut that great big shitty mouth of yours at least once a year!

**VERONIQUE** (*Stunned into momentary silence. Then*): Simon Starblanket is not home.

*With this, she bangs the doll down viciously.*

**ANNIE:** Good day, Veronique St. Pierre.

*And exits.*

*Veronique, meanwhile, just sits there in her stunned state, mouth hanging open and looking after the departing Annie.*

*On Pelajia Patchnose's roof. As at the beginning of the play, Pelajia is alone, nailing shingles on. But no cushion this time.*

**PELAJIA:**  Philomena. Where are those shingles?

**PHILOMENA** (*From offstage*):  Oh, go on. I'll be up in just a minute.

**PELAJIA** (*Coughs*):  The dust today. It's these dirt roads. Dirt roads all over. Even the main street. If I were chief around here, that's the very first thing I would do is . . .

**PHILOMENA** (*Coming up the ladder with one shingle and the most beautiful pink, lace-embroidered, heart-shaped pillow you'll ever see*):  Oh, go on. You'll never be chief.

**PELAJIA:**  And why not?

**PHILOMENA:**  Because you're a woman.

**PELAJIA:**  Bullshit! If that useless old chief of ours was a woman, we'd see a few things get done around here. We'd see our women working, we'd see our men working, we'd see our young people sober on Saturday nights, and we'd see Nanabush dancing up and down the hill on shiny black paved roads.

*Annie Cook pops up at the top of the ladder.*

**ANNIE:**  Pelajia for chief! I'd vote for you.

**PHILOMENA:**  Why, Annie Cook. You just about scared me off the edge of this roof.

**PELAJIA:**  Someday, we'll have to find you a man who can slow you down. So what do you want this time, Annie Cook?

**ANNIE:**  Well, to tell you the truth, I came to borrow your record player, Philomena Moosemeat . . . I mean, Moosetail. I'm going to practice this one song for tonight. Emily Dictionary is coming to Little Current to watch me sing with the band.

**PELAJIA:**  It's back from Espanola.

**PHILOMENA** (*To Pelajia*):  Pelajia Rosella Patchnose!

*To Annie.*

It's still not working very well. There's a certain screeching, squawking noise that comes out of it every time you try to play it.

**PELAJIA:**  That's okay, Philomena. There's a certain screechy, squawky noise that comes out of Annie Cook every time she opens her mouth to sing anyway.

**PHILOMENA:**  Yes, Annie Cook. You can borrow it. But only for one night.

**ANNIE:**  Good. Hey, there's a bingo in Espanola next week and Fire Minklater is driving up in her new car. There might be room.

*To Philomena.*

Would you like to go?

**PELAJIA:**  Does a bear shit in the woods?

**PHILOMENA** (*Glares at Pelajia first*):  Yes.

*Then quickly to Annie.*

Make . . . make sure you don't leave me behind.

**ANNIE:**  I'll make sure. Well. Toodle-oo!

*And she pops down the ladder again, happy, now that she's finally got her record player.*

**PELAJIA:**  That Annie Cook. Records and bingo. Bingo and records.

**PHILOMENA:**  You know, Pelajia, I'd like to see just what this Fritz looks like. Maybe he IS the man who can slow her down, after all.

**PELAJIA:**  Foolishness! Annie Cook will be walking fast right up until the day she dies and gets buried beside the two of us in that little cemetery beside the church.

**PHILOMENA:**  Oh, go on.

*Pause. As Philomena sits down beside her sister, leaning with her elbow on her heart-shaped pillow.*

So, Pelajia Patchnose. Still thinking about packing your bags and shipping off to Toronto?

**PELAJIA:**  Well . . . oh . . . sometimes. I'm not so sure I would get along with him if I were to live down there. I mean my son Tom. He was telling me not to play so much bingo.

**PHILOMENA:**  His upstairs washroom. Mine looks just like it now.

**PELAJIA:**  Here we go again.

**PHILOMENA:**  Large shining porcelain tiles in hippity-hoppity squares of black and white . . . so clean you can see your own face, like in a mirror, when you lean over to look into them. It looks so nice. The shower curtains have a certain matching blackness and whiteness to them—they're made of a rich, thick plasticky sort of material—and they're see-through in parts. The bathtub is beautiful, too. But the best, the most wonderful, my absolute most favorite part is the toilet bowl itself. First of all, it's elevated, like on a sort of . . . pedestal, so that it makes you feel like . . . the Queen . . . sitting on her royal throne, ruling her Queendom with a firm yet gentle hand. And the bowl itself—white, spirit white—is of such a shape, such an exquisitely soft, perfect oval shape that it makes you want to cry. Oh!!! And it's so comfortable you could just sit on it right up until the day you die!

*After a long, languorous pause, Philomena snaps out of her reverie when she realizes that Pelajia, all this time, has been looking at her disbelievingly and then contemptuously. Pelajia cradles her hammer as though she'd like to bang Philomena's head with it. Philomena delicately starts to descend the ladder. The last we see of her is her Kewpie-doll face. And beside it, the heart-shaped pillow, disappearing like a setting sun behind the edge of the roof. Once she's good and gone, Pelajia dismisses her.*

PELAJIA:   Oh, go on!

*Then she pauses to look wistfully at the view for a moment.*

Not many seagulls flying over Eugene Starblanket's house today.

*And returns once more to her hammering on the roof as the lights fade into black-out. Split seconds before complete black-out, Nanabush, back once more in his guise as the seagull, "lands" on the roof behind the unaware and unseeing Pelajia Patchnose. He dances to the beat of the hammer, merrily and triumphantly.*

*—1986*

*Djanet Sears (b. 1959) was born Janet Sears in London, England, to parents of Caribbean heritage who moved to Canada in 1974, settling in Ontario. Sears added the "D" to her first name after discovering the West African oasis town of Djanet. Her plays include the semi-autobiographical quest play* Afrika Solo *(1990),* Harlem Duet *(1997), and* A Black Girl in Search of God *(2003), a play about an African-Canadian doctor in western Ontario, which takes its title from a George Bernard Shaw fable published in 1932.* Harlem Duet *(1997), which won the Chalmers Award, four Dora Mavor Moore Awards, and the Governor General's Award, is a prequel to Shakespeare's* Othello *(1603) set in Harlem at the corner of Martin Luther King and Malcolm X boulevards. This new look at Othello, the first African to appear in Western drama, and his first wife, Billie, is part exorcism and part exploration of "the effects of race and sex on the lives of people of African descent." Though the play is set in the United States, a Canadian presence is felt in the character of Canada, Billie's father, who, despite his flaws, remains a strong symbol of hope—just as Canada was for the slaves, and the playwright's adopted country is for her. In addition to writing plays, Sears has been active as a director, actor, and anthologist, as well as helping to establish Toronto's Obsidian Theatre and the AfriCanadian Playwrights Festival. In her work she continues to explore issues of gender, identity, and race through a variety of theatrical techniques, including the use of a chorus, musical instruments, audio clips, projected images, and a wealth of allusions to African and Western cultures and dramaturgy.*

# Djanet Sears
# Harlem Duet

## CHARACTERS

*Othello,* a man of 40, present day
*He,* Othello, 1928
*Him,* Othello, 1860

*Billie,* a woman of 37, present day
*She,* Billie, 1928
*Her,* Billie, 1860

*Canada,* Billie's father, 67
*Amah,* Billie's sister-in-law, 33
*Magi,* the landlady, 41

*Mona,* White, 30s (an off-stage voice)

# SETTING

Late summer.

Harlem: 1928, a tiny dressing room.

Harlem: the present, an apartment in a renovated brownstone, at the corner of Martin Luther King and Malcolm X boulevards (125th & Lennox)

Harlem: 1860, on the steps to a blacksmith's forge

Style note: Ellipsis marks vary; this is intentional.

> . . . That handkerchief
> Did an Egyptian to my mother give.
> She was a charmer . . .
> There's magic in the web of it.
> A sibyl . . . in her prophetic fury sewed the work.
>
> William Shakespeare, *Othello* (3.4.53–70)

# ACT I

## PROLOGUE

*(Harlem, 1928: late summer—night. As the lights fade to black, the cello and the bass call and respond to a heaving melancholic blues. Martin Luther King's voice accompanies them. He seems to sing his dream in a slow polyrhythmic improvisation, as he reaches the climax of that now famous speech given at the March on Washington. Lights up on a couple in a tiny dressing room. SHE is holding a large white silk handkerchief, spotted with ripe strawberries. She looks at HE as if searching for something. He has lathered his face and is slowly erasing the day's stubble with a straight razor. She looks down at the handkerchief.)*

**SHE:** We keep doing this don't we?

**HE:** I love you . . . But—

**SHE:** Remember . . . Remember when you gave this to me? Your mother's handkerchief. There's magic in the web of it. Little strawberries. It's so beautiful—delicate. You kissed my fingers . . . and with each kiss a new promise you made . . . swore yourself to me . . . for all eternity . . . remember?

**HE:**  Yes. Yes . . . I remember.

*(Pause.)*

**SHE:**  Harlem's the place to be now. Everyone who's anyone is coming here now. It's our time. In our place. It's what we've always dreamed of . . . isn't it?

**HE:**  Yes.

**SHE:**  You love her?

**HE:**  I . . . I wish—

**SHE:**  Have you sung to her at twilight?

**HE:**  Yes.

**SHE:**  Does your blood call out her name?

**HE:**  Yes.

**SHE:**  Do you finger feed her berries dipped in dark and luscious sweets?

**HE:**  Yes.

**SHE:**  Have you built her a crystal palace to refract her image like a thousand mirrors in your veins?

**HE:**  Yes.

**SHE:**  Do you let her sip nectar kisses from a cup of jade studded bronze from your immortal parts?

**HE:**  Yes.

**SHE:**  Does she make your thoughts and dreams and sighs, wishes and tears, ache sweet as you can bear?

**HE:**  Yes.

**SHE:**  Do you prepare her bed, deep in fragrant posies, rosemary, forget-me-nots and roses, anoint her feet with civet oil, lotus musk and perfumes, place them in gossamer slippers with coral clasps, amber beads and buckles of the purest gold, kiss her ankles and knees, caress her fragrant flower, gently unfolding each petal in search of the pearl in her velvet crown?

**HE:**  Yes.

**SHE:**  You love her.

**HE:**  Yes. Yes. Yes.

*(He wipes his face with a towel. She stares at the handkerchief laying in her bare hand.)*

**SHE:**  Is she White?

*(Silence)*

Othello?

*(Silence.)*

She's White.

*(Silence.)*

Othello . . .

*(She holds the handkerchief out to him. He does not take it. She lets it fall at his feet. After a few moments, he picks it up.)*

## SCENE 1

*(Harlem, present: late summer—morning. The strings thump out an urban melody blues/jazz riff, accompanied by the voice of Malcolm X, speaking about the nightmare of race in America and the need to build strong Black communities.*

*MAGI is on the fire escape, leaning on the railing, reading a magazine with a large picture of a blonde woman on the cover. As the sound fades, she closes the magazine, surveying the action on the street below.)*

**MAGI:** Sun up in Harlem. *(She spots the postman.)* Morning Mr. P.! Don't bring me no bill now—I warned ya before, I'm having a baby. Don't need to get myself all worked up, given my condition . . . I'm gonna have me a Virgo baby, makes me due 'bout this time next year . . . I can count. I just haven't chosen the actual father/husband candidate as yet. Gotta find me a man to play his part. I wanna conceive in the middle of December, so I've booked the Convent Avenue Baptist church for this Saturday. The wedding's at three. You sure look to be the marrying kind. What you up to this weekend, yourself sweetness? Oh well then, wish your wife well for me. Package from where? California? Oohh. Yeh, yeh, yeh. I'll be right— Hey, hey, Amah girl . . . Up here . . . Let yourself in . . . *(She throws a set of keys down to AMAH.)* Mr. P., give that young lady the package . . . Yeh, she'll bring it up for me. *(Beat.)* Thank you, sugar. *(Beat.)* You have yourself a nice day now. Alright, sweetness. Mmn, mmn, mmn!

*(AMAH unlocks the door, enters and makes her way to the fire escape.)*

**AMAH:** Magi, look at you, out on the terrace, watching the summer blossoms on the corner of Malcolm X and Martin Luther King Boulevards.

**MAGI:** Nothing but weeds growing in the Soweto of America, honey. *(Shouting out.)* Billie!

**AMAH:** Where is she?

**MAGI:** I didn't want to wake her up 'till you got here. She didn't get to sleep 'till early morning. I could hear her wailing all the way downstairs.

**AMAH:** I can see a week. A couple of weeks at the most. But what is this?

**MAGI:** Two months—it's not like she's certifiable though.

*(Shouting gently to BILLIE in the bedroom.)*

Billie! Billie, Amah's here!

**AMAH:** Well, least she sleeps now.

**MAGI:** She's stillness itself. Buried under that ocean of self help books, like it's a tomb. Like a pyramid over her. Over the bed. *(Calling out once more.)*

Billie!

*(BILLIE'S body moves slightly and an arm listlessly carves its way to the surface, shifting the tomb of books, several dropping to the floor.*

*MAGI and AMAH make their way inside. On a large table is a vase filled with blossoming cotton branches. There is also a myriad of bottles and bags, and a Soxhlet extraction apparatus: flask, extractor and thimble, condenser, siphoning hoses, all held up by two metal stands. A Bunsen burner is placed under the flask.)*

I'm just making her some coffee, can I get you a cup?

*(AMAH inspects the table and searches for a space to put the small package.)*

**AMAH:** Thanks Magi. Where d'you want this? It looks like a science lab in here.

**MAGI:** Some healing concoction I've been helping her make—but she's way ahead of me these days. She's got a real talent for herbs, you know. She's been sending away for ingredients—I can't even figure out what most of them are—put the package down anywhere.

**AMAH:** If I can find a space.

**MAGI:** Right there. On top of that alchemy book—right in the middle. Yeh. Thanks for doing this Amah. For coming. It'll make her feel like a million dollars again.

**AMAH:** Please. Billie and me go so far back, way before Andrew. Besides, sister-in-laws are family too, you know. Jenny's been simply begging to come and see her, you know, for their once a week thing. They eat sausages, mashed potatoes, and corn. Some Canadian delicacy I guess—

**MAGI:** Aren't you guys vegetarians?

**AMAH:** Vegan.

**MAGI:** Vegan?

**AMAH:** We don't eat anything that has eyes. The sausages are tofu. You know they eat exactly the same thing every time. I was glad for the break. I guess I was kinda . . . well . . . it bugged me. Jenny's always full of Auntie Billie this, Auntie Billie that. Now I miss our one night a week without her. I mean—our time alone. And I see how it's a kind of security for her.

**MAGI:** Security for who?

**AMAH:** Oh, I can't rent your ground floor. They won't give me any insurance 'cause I don't have a licence. And I can't get a licence until I get a cosmetician's certificate. And I can't get a cosmetician's certificate until I finish this two year course on how to do White people's hair and make-up. I told them ain't no White people in Harlem. I'd learn how to do work with chemical relaxers and Jheri curls. Now, I do dreadlocks. And do they teach that? Oh no. They're just cracking down on people who do hair in private homes—something about lost tax revenues. I don't know . . . I want my own salon so bad I can taste it. 'The Lock Smiths'.

**MAGI:** 'The Lock Smiths'.

**AMAH:** Billie's supposed to be helping me with the business plan. Besides we've started trying for kid number 2. I need the space.

**MAGI:** You're trying?

**AMAH:** I'm 10 days late.

**MAGI:** No!

**AMAH:** It's still early. Don't tell Billie . . . you know. I'll tell her.

**MAGI:** Good for you, girl! Did I tell you I was having a baby?

**AMAH:** Oh yeh. How was he, that new candidate you were telling me about . . . Warren, no Waldo—

**MAGI:** Wendel? Wedded Wendel as I've discovered.

**AMAH:** He didn't tell—

**MAGI:** Oh no. He believes that the nuclear family is the basis for a healthy society. That's why he's married. He keeps his own personal nuclear family at home in the event that he might someday want to spend time with it.

**AMAH:** Why'd you stop seeing George. I liked George.

**MAGI:** Well I liked him too.

**AMAH:** You two looked pretty serious there for a while.

**MAGI:** We'd been seeing each other the better part of . . . . . . what . . . two years. I'm just not getting any younger. I mean, I kept dropping hints I was ready for him to pop the question. Seems like he don't know what question I'm referring to. So I decided to give him some encouragement. See, I've been collecting things for my trousseau, and I have this negligée . . . all white, long, beautiful lacy thing. Looks like a see-through wedding gown. So, I'm out on my balcony—you know, 'cause it's too hot inside, and I still ain't got around to putting in air conditioning. Anyway, I see him coming up the street. So I rush in and put on the wedding dress negligée, thinking, he'll see me in it, all beautiful like—want to pop the question, you know. So I open the door, me in the negligee, and he . . . He stands there. Mouth wide open. And he says, he guess he should go get a bottle of wine, seeing how this was gonna be some kind of special occasion an' all. Now I don't know whether he got lost . . . or drunk . . . But I ain't seen or heard from him since.

**AMAH:** Aahh nooo.

**MAGI:** I should have margarined his butt when I had the chance.

**AMAH:** Margarined his backside?

**MAGI:** If you want to bind a man—

**AMAH:** You don't mean, what I think you mean?

**MAGI:** If you want to keep a man then, you rub his backside with margarine.

**AMAH:** And it works?

**MAGI:** I don't know. When I'd remember, I could never figure out how to get from the bed to the refrigerator.

**AMAH:** Margarine, huh?

**MAGI:** But you've got to be careful. He might be a fool. You don't want to be dragging no damn fool behind you the rest of your days.

**AMAH:** You're a regular charmer, girl.

**MAGI:** Don't get me wrong. I don't cut the heads off chickens, or anything now.

**AMAH:** You know, a Jamaican lady told me about one where you rinse your underwear and use the dirty water to cook the meal.

**MAGI:** Nooo! Really?

**AMAH:** Really.

**MAGI:** Ooh, I like that. Boil down some greens in panty stock. Hmm!

**AMAH:** Once I buried his socks under the blackberry bush by the front door. Sure enough, he always finds his way back home.

**MAGI:** How is True Drew?

**AMAH:** Oh, Andrew's real good. You know him. He was up here 'till late, night before last, even, playing broad shouldered brother.

**MAGI:** Yep, he's a good man. They're rare. And he went all the way down to D.C. for the Million Man March. Yeh, he's one in a million. If you ever think of trading him in . . .

**AMAH:** Don't even think about it!

**MAGI:** Can't blame a girl for trying. *(Calling out again.)* Billie! Billie you up yet?

*(MAGI gets no response. She goes into the bedroom.)*

Billie? Billie, sorry to wake you, but Amah's here. She waiting.

*(BILLIE emerges. We recognize her as the woman in the prologue. She slowly makes her way to the edge of the bed.)*

**BILLIE:** If I could only stop dreaming, I might be able to get some rest.

**MAGI:** You should jot them down. They're messages from other realms, you know.

**BILLIE:** Jenny's in a large white room—the walls start pressing in all around her . . .

**MAGI:** You OK?

**BILLIE:** Mm mm. Yeh. I'm fine. I'm good.

**MAGI:** *(Gently.)* Come on sweetheart, Amah's waiting.

**BILLIE:** Let me just wash my face, and my mouth.

*(MAGI leaves BILLIE to join AMAH, who is now on the fire escape.)*

**MAGI:** She's coming . . .

*(AMAH hands MAGI a cup of coffee.)*

Ooh . . . Thanks.

**AMAH:** How is she?

**MAGI:** Better. Dreaming hard, though. Like she's on some archeological dig of the unconscious mind.

**AMAH:** His words hit her hard, huh.

**MAGI:** Like a baseball bat hits a mango. Like he was trying for a home run or something. The bat breaks through the skin, smashing the amber flesh, propelling her core out of the park, into the clouds. And she lays there, floating.

**AMAH:** Feeling sorry for herself.

**MAGI:** A discarded fruit sitting in a dish, surrounded by its own ripening mould.

**AMAH:** She feels so much.

**MAGI:** Yeh. Each of her emotions sprout new roots, long, tangled things, intersecting each other like strangle weed.

**AMAH:** She should go out though, get some fresh air once in a while.

**MAGI:** She does. Her trips out into the real world are brief, though. The grocer's for tubs of things you add water to, she calls food; the pharmacy for the pills, and the bookstore. All her money goes up in smokes and writings that tell her she really ain't out of her mind. They'd make her feel better, more beautiful, more well, until she'd see some nice chocolate brown-skinned man, dangling his prize in front of her. 'Cause all the rot inside her would begin to boil, threaten to shoot out. So she comes home, takes some pills and sleeps again that fitful sleep 'till she wakes.

**AMAH:** So she knows?

**MAGI:** Ooh she knows. She knows she's still up there in the clouds.

**AMAH:** She never used to be like that, you know, about colour.

**MAGI:** Guess it ain't never been personal before.

**AMAH:** But it seems bigger than that . . .

**MAGI:** Girl, you've been married what . . . six years?

**AMAH:** Seven this February coming . . .

**MAGI:** How'd you feel if Drew just upped and left you?

**AMAH:** I can't even imagine . . .

**MAGI:** They've been together nine.

**AMAH:** She still moving?

**MAGI:** So she say . . . asked me to pick up some boxes.

**AMAH:** *(Quietly.)* Rumour has it he's getting married.

**MAGI:** So soon. He hasn't told her anything. He still hasn't even moved his stuff yet.

**AMAH:** And she sacrificed so much. Gave up her share of the trust from her mother's life insurance to send him through school.

**MAGI:** No!

**AMAH:** So when it's her turn to go . . . All those years.

**MAGI:** And those babies.

**AMAH:** Yeh, thank god they didn't have any babies.

**MAGI:** No, no . . . Twice . . .

**AMAH:** No!

**MAGI:** First time, he told her he believed in a woman's right to choose, but he didn't think that the relationship was ready for—

**AMAH:** We didn't—

**MAGI:** Nobody did. Second time she miscarried.

**AMAH:** When? I don't—

**MAGI:** 'Bout the same time he left—no, it was before that. She was by herself . . . Set down in a pool of blood. She put it in a ziplock bag . . . in the freezer . . . all purple and blue . . .

**AMAH:** Oohh God . . . No . . . Really?

**MAGI:** Yeh.

**AMAH:** Nooo . . . For real. I'm serious . . .

**MAGI:** Yeh!

**AMAH:** Show me.

*(MAGI turns toward the living area and heads for the kitchen; AMAH follows closely behind. They approach the fridge and MAGI is about to open the freezer door when BILLIE enters from the bedroom. AMAH and MAGI stop abruptly, as if caught in the act.)*

**AMAH:** Billie!

**MAGI:** *(Overlapping.)* Hey girl!

*(BILLIE waves to them as she exits into the bathroom. MAGI turns to AMAH.)*

Or maybe I lied. Gotcha!

**AMAH:** You . . . You . . . little heifer—*(MAGI laughs. AMAH gets infected and joins her.)*

## SCENE 2

*(Harlem, 1860: late summer—twilight. The instruments sing a blues from deep in the Mississippi delta, while a mature northern American voice reads from the Declaration of Independence. HIM steeps hot metal into cool water. He places the shackles on an anvil and hammers the metal into shape. HER is making repairs to a shawl with a needle.)*

**HER:** I pray Cleotis is in heaven.

**HIM:** Yeh . . . I . . . um . . . I . . .

**HER:** You think Cleotis went to heaven?

**HIM:** Well, I . . . I don't . . .

**HER:** You think he's in hell?

**HIM:** No. No.

**HER:** Probably somewhere in between, though. Not Hades. Not God's kingdom. He's probably right there in the hardware store. Probably right there watching every time that Mr. Howard proudly hoists the mason jar. Every time they pay their penny to see through the formaldehyde. Cleotis is probably right there watching them gawk at his shriveled, pickled penis . . . You seen it?

**HIM:** No.

**HER:** You know who did the cutting, though?

**HIM:** No . . . Oh no . . .

**HER:** In France they got the vagina of a sister entombed for scientific research.

**HIM:** No!

**HER:** Venus, the Hottentot Venus. I read it in one of Miss Dessy's books. Saartjie—that's her real name, Saartjie Baartman. When Saartjie was alive they paraded her naked on a pay per view basis. Her derrière was amply endowed. People paid to see how big her butt was, and when she died, how big her pussy was.

**HIM:** Wooo!

**HER:** Human beings went and oohed and ahhed and paid money to see an endowment the creator bestowed on all of us.

**HIM:** That's . . . that's . . . so . . . so . . .

**HER:** They probably go to a special place though—Cleotis and Venus, Emmett. Purgatory. Venus and Cleotis fall in love, marry, but have no tools to consummate it. Must be a lot of us there walking around in purgatory without genitals.

*(Beat.)*

**HIM:** I've been meaning to . . . I want . . . *(Laughing to himself)* I would like to . . .

**HER:** Yes . . . ?

**HIM:** Talk. We should talk.

**HER:** Talk-talk?

**HIM:** Talk-talk.

**HER:** About what . . . ? What's wrong?

**HIM:** Why must something be wrong—

**HER:** I . . . I just figured . . . figure . . .

*(HIM takes HER's hand and kisses it, then places a white handkerchief into her palm.)*

**HIM:** My heart . . .

*(HIM closes HER's fingers around the handkerchief. He kisses her fingers. Opening her hand, she examines the cloth.)*

**HER:** Little strawberries on a sheet of white. Berries in a field of snow . . . *(Sighing.)* Ah silk. It's beautiful.

**HIM:** It was my mother's. Given her by my father . . . from his mother before that. When she died she gave it me, insisting that when I found . . . chose . . . chose a wife . . . that I give it to her . . . to you heart.

**HER:** Oh . . . It is so beautiful.

**HIM:** There's magic in the web of it.

**HER:** So delicate . . . so old.

**HIM:** A token . . . an antique token of our ancient love.

**HER:** My ancient love . . .

**HIM:** My wife. My wife before I even met you. Let's do it. There's a war already brewing in the south. Canada freedom come.

**HER:** Yes?

**HIM:** Yes.

**HER:** We're really gonna go?

**HIM:** People will come to me and pay me for my work.

**HER:** Yes sir, Mr. Blacksmith, sir.

**HIM:** Can we have us a heap of children?

**HER:** Four boys and four girls.

**HIM:** And a big white house.

**HER:** A big house on an emerald hill.

**HIM:** Yeh . . . a white house, on an emerald hill, in Canada. *(Pause.)* I want to be with you 'till I'm too old to know. You know that.

**HER:** Even when my breasts fall to my toes?

**HIM:** I'll pick them up and carry them around for you.

**HER:** And when I can't remember my own name?

**HIM:** I'll call it out a thousand times a day.

**HER:** Then I'll think you're me.

**HIM:** I am you.

**HER:** And when I get old, and wrinkled, and enormously fat, you'll—

**HIM:** Fat? Naw. If you get fat, I'll have to leave your ass.

*(HIM kisses inside the crook of HER's arm.)*

**HER:** Oh-oh. You're prospecting again.

**HIM:** I'm exploring the heightening Alleghenies of Pennsylvania.

*(HIM kisses HER.)*

The curvaceous slopes of California.

*(HIM kisses HER.)*

The red hills of Georgia, the mighty mountains of New York.

*(HIM kisses HER again.)*

I'm staking my claim.

**HER:** I don't come cheap, you know.

**HIM:** I know . . . I'm offering more than money can buy.

**HER:** How much more?

**HIM:** This much.

*(HIM kisses HER.)*

**HER:** I could buy that.
**HIM:** Could you buy this?

*(HIM kisses HER deeply.)*

**HER:** Beloved . . .

*(HER kisses HIM.)*

SCENE 3

*(Harlem, the present: late summer—morning. Strains of a melodious urban blues jazz keeps time with an oral address by Marcus Garvey on the need for African Americans to return to Africa.)*

**MAGI:** No, I hate it.
**AMAH:** Come on. No one hates it.
**MAGI:** I do.
**AMAH:** Bah humbug?
**MAGI:** What?
**AMAH:** Scrooge?
**MAGI:** Oh no, no, no. You know what I hate about Christmas? Seven days to New Year's Eve. And I hate New Year's Eve. And you know what I really hate about New Year's Eve? It's not the being alone at midnight. It's not the being a wallflower at some bash, because you fired your escort, who asked for time and a half, after 10:00 p.m. It's not even because you babysat your friend's kids the previous two. I really hate New Year's Eve, because it's six weeks to Valentines Day. And what I really really hate about Valentines Day—well, maybe that's too strong. No. I really hate it. What I really hate about Valentines Day is . . . it's my birthday. Don't get me wrong, now. I'm glad I was born. But I look at my life—I'm more than halfway through it, and I wonder, what do I have to show for it? Anyway . . .
**AMAH:** Well you come and spend Kwanzaa with us this year.
**MAGI:** I don't know about the seven days, girl? Look, I gotta go. I'm seeing a certain minister about a certain wedding.
**AMAH:** Whose wedding?
**MAGI:** Mine. And don't say a thing—you know, about him getting married, or anything.

*(MAGI indicates the refrigerator.)*

**AMAH:** Sealed.

**MAGI:** I'll drop by later.

**AMAH:** Alright.

**MAGI:** *(Shouting.)* Billie? I'm gonna drop by later with some boxes, OK?

**BILLIE:** *(Offstage.)* Thanks, Magi.

*(MAGI exits. AMAH goes to the table and examines the small chemical factory.)*

**AMAH:** Saracen's Compound . . . Woad . . . Hart's tongue . . . Prunella vulgaris . . .

*(She picks up a book lying among the small packages and vials.)*
*Egyptian Alchemy: A Chemical Encyclopedia . . .*
*(She puts the book back in its place and picks up another vial.)*

Nux Vomica, warning: Extremely poisonous. Can be ingested on contact with skin . . .

*(AMAH quickly replaces the vial, wiping her hand on her clothes. She turns her attention to the kitchen. She cautiously approaches the refrigerator, and is about to open the freezer section when BILLIE comes out of the bathroom.)*

**BILLIE:** Hey Amah.

**AMAH:** Oh—hi girl, how you feeling?

**BILLIE:** Thanks for making the house call, Amah.

**AMAH:** Child, you look so thin.

**BILLIE:** Well, I'm trying to lose a little baby fat before I die.

**AMAH:** Coffee?

**BILLIE:** Oh . . . Thanks. *(Pours coffee.)* You didn't have to come. I'm fine you know.

**AMAH:** You're very welcome. Come sit down.

*(AMAH hands her the cup.)*

**BILLIE:** I didn't mean . . . Thank you.

**AMAH:** You washed your hair?

**BILLIE:** Yesterday.

**AMAH:** Good. A package came for you this morning.

**BILLIE:** Where?

**AMAH:** I put it beside the chemistry set. What is all that?

**BILLIE:** Don't touch anything!

AMAH:   Alright—alright. I—

BILLIE:   No. No. I—I mean, some of this stuff can be deadly unless mixed . . . or . . . or diluted. Some ancient Egyptian rejuvenation tonic. If it don't kill me, it'll make me brand new—or so it says. How's my baby?

AMAH:   Jenny's fine. Andrew's taking her to her first African dance class today. You should see her in the little leotard . . .

BILLIE:   I should be there.

AMAH:   She's dying to come over for sausages and mashed potatoes.

BILLIE:   Yeh, yes, soon. Real soon.

*(AMAH prepares to twist BILLIE'S hair. She opens a jar of hair oil and takes a generous portion of the oil, rubs it onto her hands and gently works it into BILLIE's hair.)*

AMAH:   She was so cute, today—you know what she did? She overheard me talking to Andrew about you, and I was saying I thought your breakdown was—

BILLIE:   You told her I had a nervous breakdown?

AMAH:   Oh—No. No. She overheard me—

BILLIE:   I am not having a nervous breakdown.

AMAH:   She didn't really understand. She thinks you've broken your legs and can't walk, you can't dance. She thinks you've broken your throat, and that's why she can't talk to you on the phone, that's why you don't sing to her on the phone anymore.

BILLIE:   Please don't tell her I'm crazy.

AMAH:   I never said you were crazy.

BILLIE:   I've just been . . . tired. Exhausted. I . . . I didn't want her to see this in me. She'd feel it in me. I never want her to feel this . . .

AMAH:   I know.

BILLIE:   But I'm fine now. Really, I'll be fine. I registered for school, I'm only taking one course this term, but that's cool. And first thing next week, I'm redoing the business plan for the salon.

AMAH:   You need to give me some of that tonic too, girl. That's the best kind of revenge, you know—living the good life.

BILLIE:   I thought I was living that life.

AMAH:   Maybe you were just dreaming.

*(AMAH takes a new lock of BILLIE's hair. Taking a large dab of oil, she applies it to the lock, rubbing the strand between her palms.)*

**BILLIE:** Remember when we moved in? The day Nelson and Winnie came to Harlem, remember? Winnie and Nelson—our welcoming committee. They'd blocked off the whole of 125th—it took us 45 minutes to convince the cops to let us through. And me and you and Othe and Drew went down to hear them speak. And Drew went off in search of some grits from a street vendor. And you asked me to hold baby Jenny while you went to the restroom, when this man came up to us and took our picture. Asked to take our picture. Jenny in my arms. Othello beside me. "The perfect Black family". That's what he called us. "The perfect Black family".

*(The phone rings.)*

**AMAH:** I'll get it.

**BILLIE:** No. Let it ring. I know who it is. I can still feel him—feel when he's thinking of me. We've spoken . . . Must be three times, in the last two months. Something about $500 on my portion of his American Express card, which they'd cancel if I didn't pay the bill. Seems I did me some consumer therapy. Last time he called—mad—to announce that the card had been cancelled by AMEX, and that he hoped that I was pleased.

*(Beat.)*

And I was. Is that crazy?

**AMAH:** Don't sound crazy. Hold the hair oil for me.

**BILLIE:** I used to pray that he was calling to say he's sorry. To say how he'd discovered a deep confusion in himself. But now . . .

*(The phone stops ringing.)*

I have nothing to say to him. What could I say? Othello, how is the fairer sexed one you love to dangle from your arm the one you love for herself and preferred to the deeper sexed one is she softer does she smell of tea roses and baby powder does she sweat white musk from between her toes do her thighs touch I am not curious just want to know do her breasts fill the cup of your hand the lips of your tongue not too dark you like a little milk with your nipple don't you no I'm not curious just want to know.

**AMAH:** You tell Jenny colour's only skin deep.

**BILLIE:** The skin holds everything in. It's the largest organ in the human body. Slash the skin by my belly and my intestines fall out.

**AMAH:** Hold the hair oil up.

*(AMAH takes a dab of oil from the jar.)*

**BILLIE:** I thought I saw them once, you know—on the subway. I had to renew my prescription. And I spot them—him and her. My chest is pounding. My legs can't move. From the back, I see the sharp barber's line, separating his tightly coiled hair from the nape of the skin at the back of his neck. His skin is soft there . . . and I have to kick away the memory nudging its way into my brain. My lips on his neck, gently . . . holding him . . . Here, before me—his woman—all blonde hair and blonde legs. Her weight against his chest. His arm around her shoulders, his thumb resting on the gold of her hair. He's proud. You can see he's proud. He isn't just any Negro. He's special. That's why she's with him. And she . . . she . . . she flaunts. Yes, she flaunts. They are before. I am behind, stuck there on the platform. My tongue is pushing hard against the roof of my mouth . . . trying to hold up my brain, or something. 'Cause my brain threatens to fall. Fall down through the roof of my mouth, and be swallowed up. Slowly, slowly, I press forward, toward them. I'm not aiming for them though. I'm aiming with them in mind. I'm aiming for beyond the yellow line, into the tracks. The tunnel all three of us will fall into can be no worse than the one I'm trapped in now. I walk—no, well hover really. I'm walking on air. I feel sure of myself for the first time in weeks. Only to be cut off by a tall grey man in a grey uniform, who isn't looking where he's going, or maybe I'm not—Maybe he knew my aim. He looks at me. I think he looks at me. He brushes past. Then a sound emanating from . . . from . . . from my uterus, slips out of my mouth, shatters the spell. They turn their heads—the couple. They see me. It isn't even him.

*(The phone rings again.)*

**AMAH:** It could be your father, you know. He's been trying to get in touch with you. Says he doesn't know if you're dead or alive. He was calling Drew even up to this morning.

**BILLIE:** My father . . . I wouldn't have anything to say. It's been so long. What would I say?

*(The phone stops ringing.)*

**AMAH:**  He's been in the hospital, you know. Something about his liver.

**BILLIE:**  He hauled us all the way back to Nova Scotia from the Bronx, to be near Granma, when Mama died.

**AMAH:**  I love that Nova Scotia was a haven for slaves way before the underground railroad. I love that . . .

**BILLIE:**  He's a sot. That's academia speak for alcoholic. My Dad, the drunk of Dartmouth.

**AMAH:**  You're still his children.

**BILLIE:**  A detail I'm glad he's recalled.

**AMAH:**  Better late than never.

**BILLIE:**  Too little, too late.

**AMAH:**  Forgiveness is a virtue.

**BILLIE:**  What?

**AMAH:**  Forgiveness is a virtue.

**BILLIE:**  Girl, patience is a virtue.

**AMAH:**  Well. . . . . .forgiveness is up there . . .

**BILLIE:**  Did Drew tell you about the time my father sang to me at my high school graduation dinner?

**AMAH:**  Nooo. That's lovely. My father never sang to me at my graduation.

**BILLIE:**  We were eating. He was standing on top of the banquet table.

**AMAH:**  Nooo!

**BILLIE:**  It's the truth!

*(Pause.)*

**AMAH:**  Can I get a glass of water?

**BILLIE:**  Yeh. Yeh, help yourself.

*(AMAH goes into the kitchen.)*

I've got O. J. in the fridge, if you want.

**AMAH:**  Water will do, thanks. Do you have any . . . ice in your freezer?

**BILLIE:**  I'll get it.

**AMAH:**  I can get it.

*(BILLIE gets up quickly, and heads toward the kitchen.)*

**BILLIE:**  It's OK. It's OK. I'll get it for you.

*(BILLIE opens the freezer and gets her the ice, closing the freezer door immediately behind her.)*

**AMAH:** Thanks. *(Beat.)* What's in there?

**BILLIE:** Frozen shit.

*(The phone begins to ring again. Both women look toward it.)*

## Scene 4

*(Same day: noontime. Accompanying the sound of rushing water and the polyrhythmic chorus of strings, Martin Luther King continues to assert his dream, its relationship to the American Constitution, and the Declaration of Independence.)*

**OTHELLO:** *(Offstage.)* Billie!

*(Silence. He knocks again.)*

Billie?! *(To MONA.)* I don't think she's there.

*(OTHELLO unlocks the door. He enters. We recognize him as the man in both 1860 and 1928.)*

Billie? Mona and I are here to pick up the rest of my things. Billie?

*(He hears the shower. He goes over to the bathroom door. He knocks.)*

Billie? . . .

*(BILLIE screams. We hear something crash.)*

It's just me . . . I tried to call. You should get that machine fixed.

**BILLIE:** *(Offstage.)* I'll be out in a minute

*(OTHELLO returns to MONA at the entrance. We see nothing of her but brief glimpses of a bare arm and a waft of light brown hair.)*

**OTHELLO:** It's OK Mona, she's in there. Why don't you wait in the car.

**MONA:** *(Offstage.)* She'll have to get used to me sometime.

**OTHELLO:** I'll be down in a flash. It won't take me that long. *(She doesn't answer.)*

Hey, hey, hey!

**MONA:** *(Offstage.)* Hey yourself. I do have other things to take care of, you know.

*(He kisses her.)*

OK . . . I still haven't found anything blue. I'll scour the stores.
I'll be back in a couple of hours.

**OTHELLO:** Alright.

**MONA:** *(Offstage.)* Alright.

*(He brings in several large empty boxes. He closes the door and looks
around. He sees a burning cigarette, picks it up, looks at it, then puts
it out. He takes off his jacket. Then he takes several albums from a
shelf and places them on the floor. He begins to form two piles. He
picks up one of the albums and begins to laugh. BILLIE enters
dressed in a robe.)*

**BILLIE:** What are you doing here?

**OTHELLO:** I came over to pack my things. The movers are coming in
the morning. I tried to call . . .

**BILLIE:** You took my pot.

**OTHELLO:** What . . .

**BILLIE:** My pot. The cast iron Dutch pot.

**OTHELLO:** Oh . . . Well, you never use it.

**BILLIE:** I want it back.

**OTHELLO:** You never use it.

**BILLIE:** The one with the yellow handle.

**OTHELLO:** We need it to make gumbo.

**BILLIE:** She uses it?

**OTHELLO:** I need it to make gumbo.

**BILLIE:** She needs my pot? The one with the carrying rings.

**OTHELLO:** It was a gift to both of us.

**BILLIE:** From my father.

**OTHELLO:** I'll bring it back tomorrow.

**BILLIE:** If you don't have it here for me inside of 30 minutes, I will
break every jazz recording on that shelf.

**OTHELLO:** You want me to go all the way back for something you
don't even use.

**BILLIE:** Let me see . . .

**OTHELLO:** You never used it.

**BILLIE:** Abbey Lincoln . . .

*(She takes the album from the table. Takes the record from the jacket
and breaks it in two. She reaches for another album. OTHELLO
picks up the broken record.)*

Aah. Max Roach.

*(She takes the cover off the Max Roach album.)*

**OTHELLO:**  The Abbey Lincoln was yours.

*(She breaks the Max Roach record too.)*

OK. OK, I'll go and get it.

*(He picks up his jacket and proceeds to the door.)*

**BILLIE:**  Fine. It's fine.
**OTHELLO:**  Excuse me?
**BILLIE:**  It's fine. Tomorrow's fine.

*(Pause. He turns toward her.)*

**OTHELLO:**  OK.

*(Pause. He puts his jacket down again. Pause.)*

How are you? You look well.
**BILLIE:**  I'm fine. And you?
**OTHELLO:**  Great . . . Good.

*(Pause.)*

**BILLIE:**  Well you know where your stuff is.
**OTHELLO:**  Yep . . . Yes.

*(Pause.)*

**BILLIE:**  Drink?
**OTHELLO:**  What?
**BILLIE:**  Would you like something to drink?
**OTHELLO:**  Sure . . . Yes . . . What do you—
**BILLIE:**  Peppermint, fennel, chamomile . . . No . . . Just peppermint
and fennel. Coffee, wine, cognac, water.
**OTHELLO:**  What are you having?
**BILLIE:**  Cognac.
**OTHELLO:**  Oh. Well . . . That'll do.

*(BILLIE goes to the kitchen.)*

Where's my suitcase?

**BILLIE:**   Where you left it.

   *(Pause.)*

**OTHELLO:**   So you're staying on then?

**BILLIE:**   No.

**OTHELLO:**   Where are you . . . You know . . . I mean, things are tight, money-wise, but I'll still put money in your account . . . When I can . . . I mean, I hope we can keep in touch.

   *(She hands him a glass of cognac.)*

   Thank you.

**BILLIE:**   You're welcome.

   *(Pause.)*

**OTHELLO:**   You've lost weight. You look great. *(He takes a large gulp.)* Aaahh! Yes!

   *(OTHELLO looks at BILLIE for a moment. He then takes one of the boxes and places it at his feet. He approaches the bookshelf. He takes down a large book.)*

   *African Mythology* . . . Is this mine or yours?

**BILLIE:**   Mine . . . I think . . . I don't know.

**OTHELLO:**   This is going to be interesting.

**BILLIE:**   Take what you like. I don't care.

   *(OTHELLO takes another book.)*

**OTHELLO:**   *The Great Chain of Being?*

**BILLIE:**   From man to mollusk. The scientific foundation for why we're not human. An African can't really be a woman, you know. My department agreed to let me take only one course this year—I'm taking a reading course.

**OTHELLO:**   Yours . . . Yours . . . Mine . . . *Black Psychology;* you keeping this?

**BILLIE:**   Yeh. *(She takes the books from him.)* You'd think there was more information on Black people and mental health. You know . . . Christ, we've been here, what, 400 years. No money in it I guess . . .

**OTHELLO:**   What's money got to do with it?

**BILLIE:**   You know, grants . . . Scholarships . . .

**OTHELLO:**   Race is not an obscure idea.

*(He places several books into a box.)*

**BILLIE:**   In genetics, or the study of what's wrong with people of African descent—The Heritage Foundation will give you tons of dough to prove the innate inferiority of . . . The Shakespeare's mine, but you can have it.

**OTHELLO:**   Sure, if you don't—

**BILLIE:**   No. The Heritage Foundation—that's where that guy Murray, et al, got most of their money for Bell Curve—I think . . . There's just no-one out there willing to give you a scholarship to prove that we're all mad.

**OTHELLO:**   We're all mad. This is the founding principle of your thesis?

**BILLIE:**   Well, not mad . . . I mean . . . Well . . . Psychologically dysfunctional, then. All cultural groups are to some degree ethnocentric: We—they. But not all intercultural relations are of an inferior/superior type.

**OTHELLO:**   Thus we're not all mad.

*(He returns to the bookshelf.)*

**BILLIE:**   No, no. In America, this race shit is classic behavioural disorder. Obsessions. Phobias. Delusions. Notions of persecution. Delusions of grandeur. Any one or combination of these can produce behaviours which categorize oneself as superior and another as inferior. You see, this kind of dysfunction is systemically supported by the larger society. Psychology only sees clients who can no longer function in society. We're all mad. We just appear to be functional.

**OTHELLO:**   And your solution?

**BILLIE:**   You'll have to buy my book.

*(Pause. They continue packing.)*

How's the teaching?

**OTHELLO:**   Fine . . . Great . . .

**BILLIE:**   Good.

*(Pause.)*

**OTHELLO:** I'll be heading the department's courses in Cyprus next summer.

**BILLIE:** I thought you told me Christopher . . . What's his name?

**OTHELLO:** Chris Yago?

**BILLIE:** Yeh, Yago.

**OTHELLO:** Well everyone thought he would get it. I thought he'd get it. So a whole bunch of them are challenging affirmative action.

**BILLIE:** Rednecks in academia.

**OTHELLO:** No, no . . . Well. . . . .I think it's a good thing.

**BILLIE:** Pul-eese.

**OTHELLO:** Using discrimination to cure discrimination is not—

**BILLIE:** We're talking put asides of 5%. 5% of everything available to Whites. They've still got 95.

**OTHELLO:** Billie . . . Injustice against Blacks can't be cured by injustice against Whites . . . you know that.

**BILLIE:** And younger people won't have the same opportunities you had.

**OTHELLO:** Now look who's sounding White.

**BILLIE:** Who said you sounded White?

**OTHELLO:** It's implied . . . No-one at school tells me I don't know how to do my job . . . it's implied. I'll be at a faculty meeting, I'll make a suggestion and it'll be ignored. Not five minutes later, someone else will make the exact same suggestion and everyone will agree to it. Mona noticed it too. They think I'm only there because I'm Black. I've tested it.

**BILLIE:** So let me get this straight, you're against affirmative action in order for White people to respect you.

*(Pause.)*

**OTHELLO:** For my peers. . . . . .my peers to respect me. You know what it's like. Every day I have to prove to them that I can do my job. I feel that any error I make only goes to prove them right.

**BILLIE:** Well you must be perfect. Mona respects you.

**OTHELLO:** Well, she really sees me. She was the only other faculty to support me on the MLK Day assembly. When we played the video—

**BILLIE:** The 'I have a dream' speech?

**OTHELLO:** They understood. For a moment I got them to understand.

*(He picks up several books and places them in a box.)*

**BILLIE:** "America has defaulted on this promissory note insofar as her . . .

**OTHELLO & BILLIE:** . . . citizens of colour are concerned.

**OTHELLO:** Instead of honouring this sacred obligation, America has given its coloured people a . . .

**OTHELLO & BILLIE:** bad cheque . . .

**BILLIE:** . . . a cheque that has come back marked . . .

**OTHELLO & BILLIE:** . . . 'insufficient funds'."

**BILLIE:** The man was a . . . a . . .

**OTHELLO:** Poet . . . Visionary.

**BILLIE:** A prophet.

**OTHELLO:** After all he'd been through in his life, he could still see that at a deeper level we're all the same.

*(Pause.)*

**BILLIE:** I'm not the same.

**OTHELLO:** In the eyes of God, Billie, we're all the same.

**BILLIE:** One day little Black boys and little White girls—

**OTHELLO:** You're delusional.

**BILLIE:** You're the one looking for White respect.

**OTHELLO:** Wrong again! White respect, Black respect, it's all the same to me.

**BILLIE:** Right on brother man!

**OTHELLO:** When I was growing up. . . . .in a time of Black pride—it was something to say you were Black. Before that, I'd say . . . My family would say we're Cuban . . . It takes a long time to work through some of those things. I am a member of the human race.

**BILLIE:** Oh, that's a switch. What happened to all that J. A. Rogers stuff you were pushing. Blacks created the world, Blacks are the progenitors of European civilization, gloriana . . . Constantly trying to prove you're as good, no, better than White people. White people are always the line for you, aren't they? The rule . . . the margin . . . the variable of control. We are Black. Whatever we do is Black.

**OTHELLO:** I'm so tired of this race shit, Billie. There are alternatives—

**BILLIE:** Like what? Oh yes, White.

**OTHELLO:** Oh, don't be so—

**BILLIE:** Isn't that really what not acting Black, or feeling Black means.

**OTHELLO:** Liberation has no colour.

**BILLIE:** But progress is going to White schools . . . proving we're as good as Whites . . . like some holy grail . . . all that we're taught in those White schools. All that is in us. Our success is Whiteness. We religiously seek to have what they have. Access to the White man's world. The White man's job.

**OTHELLO:** That's economics.

**BILLIE:** White economics.

**OTHELLO:** God! Black women always—

**BILLIE:** No. Don't even go there . . .

**OTHELLO:** I . . . You . . . Forget it!

**BILLIE:** *(Quietly at first.)* Yes, you can forget it, can't you. I don't have that . . . that luxury. When I go into a store, I always know when I'm being watched. I can feel it. They want to see if I'm gonna slip some of their stuff into my pockets. When someone doesn't serve me, I think it's because I'm Black. When a clerk won't put the change into my held-out hand, I think it's because I'm Black. When I hear about a crime, any crime, I pray to God the person who they think did it isn't Black. I'm even suspicious of the word Black. Who called us Black anyway? It's not a country, it's not a racial category, it's not even the colour of my skin. And don't give me this content of one's character B.S. I'm sorry . . . I am sorry . . . I had a dream. A dream that one day a Black man and a Black woman might find . . . Where jumping a broom was a solemn eternal vow that . . . I . . . Let's . . . Can we just get this over with?

*(She goes to the window.*
*Silence.*
*He moves toward her.)*

**OTHELLO:** I know . . . I know. I'm sorry . . .

**BILLIE:** Yeh . . .

**OTHELLO:** I care . . . you know that.

**BILLIE:** I know.

*(Silence.)*

**OTHELLO:** I never thought I'd miss Harlem.

*(Pause.)*

**BILLIE:** You still think it's a reservation?

**OTHELLO:** Homeland/reservation.

**BILLIE:** A sea of Black faces.

**OTHELLO:** Africatown, USA.

*(Pause.)*

**BILLIE:** When we lived in the Village, sometimes, I'd be on the subway and I'd miss my stop. And I'd just sit there, past midtown, past the upper west side, and somehow I'd end up here. And I'd just walk. I love seeing all these brown faces.

**OTHELLO:** Yeh . . .

**BILLIE:** Since they knocked down the old projects, I can see the Schomberg Museum from here. You still can't make out Harlem Hospital. I love that I can see the Apollo from our—from my balcony.

**OTHELLO:** Fire escape.

**BILLIE:** Patio.

**OTHELLO:** You never did find a pair of lawn chairs, and a table to fit in that space.

**BILLIE:** Terrace.

**OTHELLO:** I never saw the beauty in it.

**BILLIE:** Deck. My deck.

**OTHELLO:** I wish . . .

*(He looks at her.)*

**BILLIE:** That old building across the street? I didn't know this, but that used to be the Hotel Theresa. That's where Castro stayed when he came to New York . . . Must have been the fifties. Ron Brown's father used to run that hotel.

**OTHELLO:** I. . . . . .I. . . . . .I miss you so much sometimes. Nine years . . . it's a long time.

**BILLIE:** I know.

**OTHELLO:** I'm really not trying to hurt you, Billie.

**BILLIE:** I know.

**OTHELLO:** I never meant to hurt you.

*(He strokes her face.)*

**BILLIE:** I know.

**OTHELLO:** God you're so beautiful.

*(He kisses her. She does not resist.)*

**BILLIE:** I. . . . don't. . . . I feel . . .

*(He kisses her again.)*

**BILLIE:** What are you doing?

**OTHELLO:** I . . . I'm . . . I'm exploring the heightening Alleghenies of Pennsylvania.

*(He kisses her again.)*

The curvaceous slopes of California.

*(He kisses her again.)*

The red hills of Georgia, the mighty mountains of New York. Such sad eyes.

*(He kisses her again.)*

I'm an equal opportunity employer.

*(Pause.)*

I am an equal opportunity employer.

*(Pause.)*

I say, I'm an equal opportunity employer, then you say, I don't come . . .

**BILLIE:** I don't come cheap, you know.

**OTHELLO:** I'm offering more than money can buy.

**BILLIE:** How much more?

**OTHELLO:** This much.

*(He kisses her.)*

**BILLIE:** I could buy that.

**OTHELLO:** Could you buy this?

*(He kisses her deeply.)*

**BILLIE:** Be . . . Be . . . Beloved.

*(She kisses him.)*

## Scene 5

*(Same day: early afternoon. The stringed duet croons gently as Malcolm X speaks about the need for Blacks to turn their*

*gaze away from Whiteness so that they can see each other with new eyes. OTHELLO is lying in the bed. BILLIE is in the living room, smoking a cigarette.)*

**OTHELLO:** I've missed you.

**BILLIE:** That's nice.

**OTHELLO:** By the looks of things, I miss you even now.

**BILLIE:** I'm coming.

**OTHELLO:** I noticed.

**BILLIE:** Sometimes . . . Sometimes when we make love. Sometimes every moment lines up into one moment. And I'm holding you. And I can't tell where I end, or you begin. I see everything. All my ancestors lined up below me. . . . . .like a Makonde statue, or something. It's like . . . I know. I know I'm supposed to be here. Everything is here.

**OTHELLO:** Sounds crowded to me.

**BILLIE:** It's actually quite empty.

**OTHELLO:** Not as empty as this bed is feeling right about now.

**BILLIE:** I'm coming. I'm coming.

*(She hurriedly stubs the cigarette out, and heads toward the bedroom. The apartment buzzer rings. BILLIE goes to the intercom.)*

**BILLIE:** Hi Magi. I . . . er . . . I'm kinda busy right now.

**MONA:** *(Through intercom.)* It's Mona. Could I have a word with Othello.

**OTHELLO:** *(Overlapping)* Shit!

**BILLIE:** One second please.

*(He rushes to the intercom, while attempting to put his clothes back on. BILLIE tries to hold back her laughter. Her laughter begins to infect OTHELLO. He puts a finger over his mouth indicating to BILLIE to be quiet.)*

**OTHELLO:** Hey Mone . . . Mone, I'm not done yet. There's more here than I imagined. Why don't I call you when I'm done.

*(MONA does not respond. OTHELLO's demeanour changes.)*

Mone? Mona? I'm coming, OK? I'll be right . . . Just wait there one second, OK? OK?

*(BILLIE is unable to hide her astonishment.)*

**MONA:** *(Through intercom.)* OK.
**OTHELLO:** OK.

*(He steps away from the intercom to finish putting on his clothes. BILLIE stares at him.)*

I'll be back in . . . Uh . . . I just have to go straighten . . . Uh . . . She wants to help . . . help pack. You'll have to get used to her sometime. I mean . . . I . . .

*(BILLIE continues to stare steadily at OTHELLO as he struggles with the buttons on his shirt.)*

I'm sorry . . . Well I'll be right . . . I'll be back.

*(He exits. BILLIE does not move.)*

SCENE 6

*(Harlem, 1860: late summer—night. A whining delta blues slides and blurs while the deeply resonant voice of Paul Robeson talks of his forbears, whose blood is in the American soil. HIM is hammering a newly-forged horseshoe, HER rushes in holding a large carrying bag.)*

**HER:** Oh . . . let me catch—catch my breath . . . I thought I was seen . . . Oh my . . . I . . . I've packed a change of clothes for both of us, some loaves . . . I liberated the leftover bacon from yesterday's meal, from out the pantry, seeing how it was staring me right in the face when I was cleaning. It won't be missed. I wish I could pack old Betsy in my bag. She'd be sure an' give us some good fresh milk each mornin'. Oh—and I packed a fleece blanket. I hear the nights get good and cold further north you go. And . . . did I forget . . . no . . . Nothing forgotten. Oh yes, I borrowed the big carving knife—for the bacon, a' course. You still working on those shoes for Miss Dessy's stallion . . . Let her send it to town, or get some other slave to do that . . . She's going to be mad as hell you took off in any event . . . May as well not finish the shoes, it won't placate her none . . .

*(HIM picks up the horseshoe with a pair of tongs. HIM inspects it carefully. HIM puts the shoe to one side and retrieves the shackles. HIM takes a chamois and begins to polish the metal.)*

*(Pause.)* O? O? Othello? The moon'll be rising. We've got to make any headway under cover of dark . . . Othello, why you trying to please her. I'm so tired of pleasing her. I'm so tired of pleasing White folks. Up in Canada, we won't have to please no White folks no how. I hear they got sailing ships leaving for Africa every day. Canada freedom come . . . O? Othello? Are you coming?

**HIM:** I can't.

**HER:** If we make it to the border there's people there'll help us wade that water—help us cross over.

**HIM:** I'm not going.

**HER:** A big white house on an emerald hill . . .

**HIM:** I know.

**HER:** You need more time, O? I can wait for you. Finish her shoes, I'll . . . I can wait—

**HIM:** No. No.

*(Pause.)*

**HER:** You love her.

**HIM:** Her father going to war.

**HER:** You love her?

**HIM:** I love you. It's just . . . She needs me. She respects me. Looks up to me, even. I love you. It's just . . . When I'm with her I feel like . . . a man. I want . . . I need to do for her . . .

**HER:** Do you love her?

**HIM:** Yes.

**HER:** Fight with me. . . . . .I would fight with you. Suffer with me, O . . . I would suffer with you . . .

*(Silence.)*

## SCENE 7

*(Harlem, present: late summer—late afternoon. Dulcet blue tones barely swing as Louis Farrakhan waxes eloquent on African Americans being caught in the gravity of American society.)*

**MAGI:** And you know what he says, after turning on the baseball game, in the middle of my romantic dinner? Eyes glued to the screen, he says, I bet you've never made love to a man with 26-inch biceps!

**BILLIE:**  *(Smiles.)* Oh . . . no . . .

**MAGI:**  I'm telling you, girl. Macho Mack, spot him at any locale selling six-packs. Easily recognizable, everything about him is permanently flexed. His favourite pastime? Weekend NFL football, Monday night football, USFL football—even Canadian foot . . . You look like you're feeling better. Amah did a great job with your hair.

**BILLIE:**  What's her motto? We lock heads and minds.

**MAGI:**  Hey, can I borrow that beautiful African boubou—I got me a date with an African prince. The brother has it going on! Oh . . . you already have boxes.

*(BILLIE begins placing some of the wrapped objects into a box.)*

**BILLIE:**  They're his box—

**MAGI:**  When . . . He came over?

**BILLIE:**  I even spoke to her.

**MAGI:**  You saw her?

**BILLIE:**  No. Want this mask?

**MAGI:**  You met her?

**BILLIE:**  No. Want this mask?

**MAGI:**  I'll keep it for you—

**BILLIE:**  I . . . er. . . . . .I don't know how long these things will have to stay in storage.

**MAGI:**  You don't have to move, you know. It's not rented yet. I mean, I can always lower the—

**BILLIE:**  No, no . . . I'm moving on.

**MAGI:**  Good. Good. To where? Where are you going? You haven't given me a date or anything. I've got bills to pay too, you know. When d'you plan to leave? Where are you going?

**BILLIE:**  I might go. . . . . .stay with Jenny. I could go home.

**MAGI:**  I'll keep it for you—

**BILLIE:**  I don't want anything that's—that was ours. If you don't want it, that's OK, I'll just trash it.

*(BILLIE throws the mask onto the floor. It breaks into several pieces.)*

**MAGI:**  Something happened. What happened?

**BILLIE:**  Nothing.

**MAGI:**  Did he tell you about . . . What did he say to you?

**BILLIE:** I'm just tired. Tired of sleeping. Tired of night. It lays over me like a ton of white feathers. Swallows me up. The movers are coming in the morning to pick up his things. It's OK. I'm fine. You know . . . I've lived all my life believing in lies.

**MAGI:** Well, getting your Masters isn't a lie.

**BILLIE:** It's about proving, isn't it? Proving I'm as good as . . . I'm as intelligent as . . .

**MAGI:** Nothing wrong with that.

**BILLIE:** I don't want anything . . . Believe in anything. Really. I've gotta get out of here. I don't even believe in Harlem anymore.

**MAGI:** Come on . . .

**BILLIE:** It's all an illusion. All some imagined idealistic . . . I dunno.

**MAGI:** When I go out my door, I see all the beauty of my Blackness reflected in the world around me.

**BILLIE:** Yeh, and all my wretchedness by the time I get to the end of the block.

**MAGI:** Billie, he's the one who wants to White wash his life.

**BILLIE:** Corporeal malediction.

**MAGI:** Corp-o-re-all mal-e . . . Oooh that's good.

**BILLIE:** A Black man afflicted with Negrophobia.

**MAGI:** Girl, you on a roll now!

**BILLIE:** No, no. A crumbled racial epidermal schema . . .

**MAGI:** Who said school ain't doing you no good.

**BILLIE:** . . . causing predilections to coitus denegrification.

**MAGI:** Booker T. Uppermiddleclass III. He can be found in predominantly White neighbourhoods. He refers to other Blacks as "them". His greatest accomplishment was being invited to the White House by George Bush to discuss the "Negro problem."

**BILLIE:** Now, that is frightening.

**MAGI:** No, what's frightening is the fact that I dated him.

**BILLIE:** What does it say . . . about us?

**MAGI:** Who?

**BILLIE:** You and me.

**MAGI:** Girl, I don't know. I can't even want to go there.

**BILLIE:** Ohh . . . Oh well . . . Least he's happy though. What does he say? Now he won't have to worry that a White woman will emotionally mistake him for the father that abandoned her.

**MAGI:** Isn't he worried the White woman might mistake him for the butler?

**BILLIE:** He'd be oh so happy to oblige.

**MAGI:** I see them do things for White women they wouldn't dream of doing for me.

**BILLIE:** It is a disease. We get infected as children, and . . . and the bacteria . . . the virus slowly spreads, disabling the entire system.

**MAGI:** Are we infected too?

*(There is knocking at the apartment door.)*

Speaking of White minds parading around inside of Black bodies—you want me to stay?

**BILLIE:** Don't you have a date?

**MAGI:** Hakim. But I can cancel . . .

*(There is knocking at the door again.)*

**BILLIE:** I'm OK. I'm OK. I'm fine . . . Truly.

*(BILLIE opens the door. OTHELLO enters.)*

**OTHELLO:** The pot!

*(He hands the pot to BILLIE.)*

Magi!

**MAGI:** How's Harlumbia?

**OTHELLO:** Columbia?

**MAGI:** Harlumbia—those 10 square blocks of Whitedom, owned by Columbia University, set smack dab in the middle of Harlem.

**OTHELLO:** Harlumbia, as you call it, is dull without you.

**MAGI:** You could steal honey from a bee, couldn't you. Better watch you don't get stung. Well, I'm off to doll myself up. Billie . . .

**BILLIE:** Yeh, I'll get that boubou . . .

*(BILLIE goes into the bedroom. After a few moments of silence.)*

**MAGI:** Why haven't you told her yet?

**OTHELLO:** About?—Oh yes . . . Yeh . . . I wanted to . . .

*(BILLIE returns with a beautiful multicoloured boubou.)*

**BILLIE:** He won't be able to resist you . . .

**MAGI:** Thank you, thank you. Later you two.

**OTHELLO:** I'll be in touch . . .

**BILLIE:** I'm keeping my fingers crossed for you.

**MAGI:** Good, I'm running out of time.

*(MAGI exits. OTHELLO enters. BILLIE closes the door. There is a long awkward silence. BILLIE continues placing wrapped objects into her boxes. OTHELLO steps on a piece of the broken mask. He picks it up, looks at it, then places it on the mantel. He goes over to the bookshelf and begins to pack more of his possessions into his boxes.)*

**OTHELLO:** They're coming at nine.

**BILLIE:** Oh . . . Er . . . I'll be out of your way.

**OTHELLO:** You can be here . . .

**BILLIE:** No. No. No. I have an appointment. . . . . .an early appointment.

**OTHELLO:** Either way . . .

*(They continue packing.)*

Ah . . . I've been meaning to tell you. . . . .things are real. . . . . money's real tight right now, what with buying the apartment, and moving and everything . . . I won't be able to cover your tuition this semester. I'll try and put money in your account when I can. Maybe—

**BILLIE:** I told you, I'm only taking one course. If you cover that, I won't be taking a full load 'till next—

**OTHELLO:** I know, that's what I'm saying. . . . I can't . . . I just can't do it right now.

**BILLIE:** It's one course . . .

**OTHELLO:** It's $5000.

**BILLIE:** You promised . . .

**OTHELLO:** I'm mortgaged up the wazoo. I don't have it. I just don't have $5000, right now.

**BILLIE:** Ooh. . . . . .okay.

**OTHELLO:** I would if I could, you know that.

*(He continues to pack.)*

I think I brought the bookshelf with me when we first—

**BILLIE:** Take it all.

**OTHELLO:**  I don't want all of it.

**BILLIE:**  I'm keeping the bed.

**OTHELLO:**  What about the rest . . .

**BILLIE:**  If you don't want it . . . I'm giving it away . . .

**OTHELLO:**  OK, if you're throwing it out . . .

**BILLIE:**  I'm keeping the bed.

*(They continue packing in silence.)*

**OTHELLO:**  We're getting married.

*(Pause.)*

Me and Mona. We're engaged . . . Officially.

*(Very long pause.)*

**BILLIE:**  Congratulations.

**OTHELLO:**  I wanted to tell you . . . Hear it from the horse's mouth . . . Hear it from me first. You know . . .

*(Pause.)*

**BILLIE:**  Yeh . . . Yes. Yes. Congratulations.

**OTHELLO:**  Mona wanted me to tell you.

**BILLIE:**  Yes. Yes. Being a feminist and everything—A woman's right to know—since we're all in the struggle. . . . I thought you hated feminists.

**OTHELLO:**  Well . . . I didn't mean that. I mean . . . the White women's movement is different.

**BILLIE:**  Just Black feminists.

**OTHELLO:**  No, no . . . White men have maintained a firm grasp of the pants. I mean, White men have economic and political pants that White women have been demanding to share.

**BILLIE:**  White wisdom from the mouth of the mythical Negro.

**OTHELLO:**  Don't you see! That's exactly my point! You . . . The Black feminist position as I experience it in this relationship, leaves me feeling unrecognized as a man. The message is, Black men are poor fathers, poor partners, or both. Black women wear the pants that Black men were prevented from wearing . . . I believe in tradition. You don't support me. Black women are more concerned with their careers than their husbands. There was a time when women felt satisfied, no, honoured being a balance to their spouse, at home, supporting the family, playing her role—

BILLIE: Which women? I mean, which women are you referring to? Your mother worked all her life. My mother worked, her mother worked . . . Most Black women have been working like mules since we arrived on this continent. Like mules. When White women were burning their bras, we were hired to hold their tits up. We looked after their homes, their children . . . I don't support you? My mother's death paid your tuition, not mine . . .

OTHELLO: Can't we even pretend to be civil? Can't we? I know this isn't easy. It's not easy for me either. Do you ever consider that?

BILLIE: You like it easy, don't you.

OTHELLO: The truth is, this is too fucking difficult.

BILLIE: You wouldn't know the truth if it stood up and knocked you sideways.

OTHELLO: You don't want the truth. You want me to tell you what you want to hear. No, no, you want to know the truth? I'll tell you the truth. Yes, I prefer White women. They are easier— before and after sex. They wanted me and I wanted them. They weren't filled with hostility about the unequal treatment they were getting at their jobs. We'd make love and I'd fall asleep not having to beware being mistaken for someone's inattentive father. I'd explain that I wasn't interested in a committed relationship right now, and not be confused with every lousy lover, or husband that had ever left them lying in a gutter of unresolved emotions. It's the truth. To a Black woman, I represent every Black man she has ever been with and with whom there was still so much to work out. The White women I loved saw me—could see me. Look, I'm not a junkie. I don't need more than one lover to prove my manhood. I have no children. I did not leave you, your mother, or your aunt, with six babies and a whole lotta love. I am a very single, very intelligent, very employed Black man. And with White women it's good. It's nice. Anyhow, we're all equal in the eyes of God, aren't we? Aren't we?

*(BILLIE stares at OTHELLO. He continues to pack.)*

## Scene 8

*(Harlem, 1928: late summer—night. The cello and bass moan, almost dirge-like, in harmonic tension to the sound of Jesse Jackson's oratory. SHE holds a straight-edged razor in her bloodied palms. HE lies on the floor in front of her, motionless, the handkerchief in his hand.)*

**SHE:**  Deadly deadly straw little strawberries it's so beautiful you kissed my fingers you pressed this cloth into my palm buried it there an antique token our ancient all these tiny red dots on a sheet of white my fingernails are white three hairs on my head are white the whites of my eyes are white too the palms of my hands and my feet are white you're all I'd ever and you my my I hate Sssshh. Shhhhh OK. OK. OK. I'm OK alright don't don't don't don't my eyes on the shadow sparrow my sense in my feet my hands my head shine the light there please scream no sing sing *(SHE tries to sing.)* and if I get a notion to jump into the ocean, ain't nobody's business if I do do do do If I go to church on Sunday then shimmy down on Monday t'ain't nobody's business if I . . .

## Scene 9

*(Harlem, present: late summer—early evening. The instruments sound out a deep cerulean blues, while Malcolm X almost scats the question, "What difference does colour make?" OTHELLO continues to pack. BILLIE sits on the floor by the bed watching him from the bedroom.)*

**OTHELLO:**  I didn't mean—what I said. You know that. I just . . . Sometimes you make me so mad I . . . People change, Billie. That's just human nature. Our experiences, our knowledge transforms us. That's why education is so powerful, so erotic. The transmission of words from mouth to ear. Her mouth to my ear. Knowledge. A desire for that distant thing I know nothing of, but yearn to hold for my very own. My Mama used to say, you have to be three times as good as a White child to get by, to do well. A piece of that pie is mine. I don't want to change the recipe. I am not minor. I am not a minority. I used to be a minority when I was a kid. I mean my culture is not my mother's culture—the culture of my ancestors.

My culture is Wordsworth, Shaw, *Leave it to Beaver, Dirty Harry.*
I drink the same water, read the same books. You're the problem if
you don't see beyond my skin. If you don't hear my educated
English, if you don't understand that I am a middle class educated
man. I mean, what does Africa have to do with me. We struttin'
around professing some imaginary connection for a land we don't
know. Never seen. Never gonna see. We lie to ourselves saying,
ah yeh, mother Africa, middle passage, suffering, the Whites did it
to me, it's the White's fault. Strut around in African cloth pretending we human now. We human now. Some of us are beyond that
now. Spiritually beyond this race shit bullshit now. I am an
American. The slaves were freed over 130 years ago. In 1967 it was
illegal for a Black to marry a White in sixteen states. That was less
than thirty years ago . . . in my lifetime. Things change, Billie. I am
not my skin. My skin is not me.

## SCENE 10

*(Harlem, same day: night. A rhapsody of sound keeps time with
Christopher Darden as he asks O. J. Simpson to approach the jury
and try on the bloody glove. The apartment is virtually full of
boxes. BILLIE is by the chemical factory at the table. The book of
Egyptian Alchemy sits open upon it. Something is boiling in the
flask and steam is coming out of the condenser. With rubber gloved
hands she adds several drops of a violet liquid into the flask. She
picks up a large white handkerchief with pretty red strawberries
embroidered on it.)*

**BILLIE:**    I have a plan, my love. My mate. . . . throughout eternity. Feel
what I feel. Break like I break. No more—no less. You'll judge me
harsher. I know. While Susan Smith . . . She blamed some imaginary Black man for the murder of her two boys and that's why
authorities didn't suspect her for nearly two weeks. Stopping every
Black man with a burgundy sedan from Union, South Carolina, to
the Oranges of New Jersey. And you're still wondering what made
her do it. What was she going through to make her feel that this
was her only way out. Yet I'll be discarded as some kind of uncon-
scionable bitter shadow, or something. Ain't I a woman? This is my
face you take for night—the biggest shadow in the world. I . . .

I have nothing more to lose. Nothing. Othello? I am preparing something special for you . . . Othe . . . Othello. A gift for you, and your new bride. Once you gave me a handkerchief. An heirloom. This handkerchief, your mother's. . . . .given by your father. From his mother before that. So far back . . . And now . . . then . . . to me. It is fixed in the emotions of all your ancestors. The one who laid the foundation for the road in Herndon, Virginia, and was lashed for laziness as he stopped to wipe the sweat from his brow with this kerchief. Or, your great great grandmother, who covered her face with it, and then covered it with her hands as she rocked and silently wailed, when told that her girl child, barely thirteen, would be sent 'cross the state for breeding purposes. Or the one who leapt for joy on hearing of the Emancipation Proclamation, fifteen years late mind you, only to watch it fall in slow motion from his hand and onto the ground when told that the only job he could now get, was the same one he'd done for free all those years, and now he's forced to take it, for not enough money to buy the food to fill even one man's belly. And more . . . so much more. What I add to this already fully endowed cloth, will cause you such. . . . . .such . . . Wretchedness. Othe . . . Othello.

*(The contents of the flask have been transformed from violet to clear. BILLIE places the handkerchief onto a large tray. Then with tongs, she takes the hot flask and pours the contents over the handkerchief. She retrieves a vial from the table, opens it.)*

My sable warrior . . . Fight with me. I would fight with you . . . Suffer with me . . . I would suffer—

*(She starts to pour, but the vial is empty. The buzzer rings. BILLIE is surprised. The buzzer rings again. BILLIE turns off the Bunsen burner. She takes the flask into the kitchen and pours it into the sink. The buzzer rings once more. Going back to the table, she carefully takes the tray and heads toward the bathroom. There is a knock at her door.)*

**BILLIE:**  *(From the bathroom.)* You have a key, let yourself in . . . Make yourself right at home, why don't you—

**MAGI:**  *(Offstage.)* Billie? Billie, it's me. Magi.

**BILLIE:**  Magi?

**MAGI:** *(Offstage.)* Are you OK?

**BILLIE:** Yes. Yes. I'm fine. Let me call you later, OK Magi?

*(We hear the sound of liquid being poured. The toilet flushes.)*
*(MAGI offstage mumbles something about BILLIE having a visitor.)*

**BILLIE:** What?

**MAGI:** *(MAGI mumbles something about a visitor again.)*

**BILLIE:** What? Door's open!

*(MAGI enters and stands in the doorway. She is speaking quietly, as if not wanting someone to hear.)*

**MAGI:** Sweetie, you have a visitor. Shall I—

**BILLIE:** *(Entering the living area.)* Look I'm tired. He's been here practically all day already—

**MAGI:** No, no, no. He said his name is Canada. *(BILLIE turns to MAGI.)* He says he's your father. That's what he said. He said he was your father.

*(A man in his late sixties, brushes past MAGI. He wears a hat, and has a small suitcase in his hand.)*

**CANADA:** Sybil? Sybil! There's my girl. Come and give your Daddy a big hug.

*(End of ACT I.)*

## ACT II

### Scene 1

*(Harlem, present: late summer—night. The cello and bass pluck and bow a funky rendition of Aretha Franklin's "Spanish Harlem" against the audio sound of Michael Jackson and Lisa Marie Presley's interview on ABC's "Dateline". CANADA is sitting on one of the chairs, amidst stacks of boxes.)*

**CANADA:** The first time I came to Harlem, I was scared. Must have been '68 or '69. Yeh . . . We were living in the Bronx, and your mother was still alive. Everything I'd ever learned told me that I wasn't safe in this part of town. The newspapers. Television. My friends. My own family. But I'm curious, see. I says, Canada you can't be in New York City and not see Harlem. So I make my way to 125th. "A" train. I'm gonna walk past the Apollo, I'm gonna see this place. I'm gonna walk the ten city blocks to Lexington and catch the "6" train back, if it's the last thing I do. So out of the subway, I put on my 'baddest mother in the city' glare. I walk—head straight. All the time trying to make my stride say, "I'm mean . . . I'm mean. Killed somebody mean." So I'm doing this for 'bout five, ten minutes, taking short furtive glances at this place I really want to see, when I begin to realize . . . No-one is taking any notice of me . . . Not a soul. Then it dawns on me: I'm the same as them. I look just like them. I look like I live in Harlem. Sounds silly now. But I just had to catch myself and laugh out loud. Canada, where did you get these ideas about Harlem from?

*(The kettle whistles.)*

**BILLIE:**   How do you like it?

*(BILLIE heads to the kitchen to make tea.)*

**CANADA:**   Brown sugar. No milk.

**BILLIE:**   I don't even know why I asked, I don't have any milk anyway.

**CANADA:**   You can't take milk. Never could. When your mother stopped feeding you from her milk, that cow's milk just gave you colic. And those diapers . . . Now that's an image I'll never forget.

**BILLIE:**   So what brings you to these parts?

**CANADA:**   Just passing through. Since I was in the neighbourhood, thought I'd stop on in.

**BILLIE:**   Nova Scotia's nearly a thousand miles away.

**CANADA:**   Well, I thought I should see my grandchild. Jenny's almost six and I've only talked to her on the phone. And Andrew and his wife, and you. Nothing wrong with seeing family is there?

**BILLIE:**   Strong or weak?

**CANADA:**   Like a bear's bottom.

**BILLIE:**   Polar or Grizzly?

**CANADA:**   Grizzly.

*(BILLIE returns with a tray.)*

Andrew told me what happened.

**BILLIE:**   He did, did he?

**CANADA:** Said you were taking it kinda hard.

**BILLIE:** Oh, I'll be fine. I'm a survivor. But then again, you already know that.

**CANADA:** Tea should be ready. Shall I be mother?

**BILLIE:** Go ahead.

*(CANADA pours the tea.)*

**BILLIE:** I hear you were in the hospital.

**CANADA:** My liver ain't too good. Gave out on me. I guess you reap what you sow.

**BILLIE:** Still drinking?

**CANADA:** Been sober going on five years now.

**BILLIE:** Good. Good for you.

**CANADA:** Don't mean I don't feel like it sometimes though . . .

**BILLIE:** Well . . . How long do you plan to be in town?

**CANADA:** Just a few days. See Andrew and his family. See the sights. I'm staying there—at Andrew's. Went by there earlier . . . No one home. Must have given them the wrong time. Left a note though. Told them to find me at Sybil's.

**BILLIE:** Billie. I've always despised that name. Sybil.

**CANADA:** I gave you that name. It's a good name. It was your Grandmother's name. It means prophetess. Sorceress. Seer of the future. I like it. I don't see anything wrong with that name.

**BILLIE:** Sounds like some old woman living in a cave.

*(CANADA reaches for his suitcase.)*

**CANADA:** I brought something for you.

*(He takes out a small red box.)*

Go on . . . Open it. The box is a bit too big, but . . .

*(BILLIE opens the box.)*

It's your mother's ring. I figured she'd want you to have it.

**BILLIE:** I hardly remember her anymore. I get glimpses of this ghostly figure creeping in and out of my dreams.

**CANADA:** When Beryl first passed on, I couldn't get her off my mind, like she'd gone and left us somehow. Left me . . . With two kids, one a young girl ripening to sprout into womanhood. I was sad, but I was good and mad too. One minute I'd be trying to etch her face

into my mind, cause I didn't want to forget. Next thing, I'd be
downing another shot of rye . . . I couldn't carry the weight. I just
couldn't do it by myself. That's when we moved to Dartmouth.
What's that them old slaves used to say? "I can't take it no more, I
moving to Nova Scotia."

**BILLIE:** I'm thinking of heading back there myself . . .

*(Pause.)*

**CANADA:** 'Cause he left you, or 'cause she's White?

*(Pause.)*

**BILLIE:** I remember that White woman . . . That hairdresser you used
to go with . . . The one with the mini skirts . . . What was her name?

**CANADA:** That's going way back . . . You remember her?

**BILLIE:** She was boasting about knowing how to do our kind of hair.
And she took that hot comb to my head . . . Sounded like she was
frying chicken . . . Burnt my ears and half the hair on my head. I
hated her stubby little beige legs and those false eyelashes. She
taught me how to put on false eyelashes.

**CANADA:** Deborah.

**BILLIE:** Debbie . . . Yes . . . Debbie.

*(Pause.)*

**CANADA:** I wish . . . I wish things between . . .

*(The buzzer rings.)*

**BILLIE:** That must be Drew.

*(BILLIE goes to the console by the door.)*

Drew?

**AMAH:** *(Through intercom.)* It's me. Amah. Is your—

**BILLIE:** He's here. Come on up.

**CANADA:** You know, an old African once told me the story of a man
who was struck by an arrow. His attacker was unknown. Instead
of tending to his wound, he refused to remove the arrow until the
archer was found and punished. In the meantime, the wound
festered, until finally the poison infected his entire body, eventually killing him . . . Now, who is responsible for this man's

death, the archer for letting go the arrow, or the man for his foolish holding on?

*(There is a knock at the door. BILLIE gets up and heads toward it.)*

**BILLIE:** The drunk?

**CANADA:** A drunken man can get sober but a damn fool can't ever get wise.

*(BILLIE opens the door. AMAH enters with some rolls of paper in her arms.)*

**AMAH:** *(Kissing BILLIE's cheek.)* Hi sweetie. And you must be Canada.

**CANADA:** Drew's wife . . .

**AMAH:** So very pleased to meet you at last.

**CANADA:** Delighted . . .

**AMAH:** We weren't expecting you until tomorrow. We ate out tonight. We would have come pick you up. Jenny's so excited.

**CANADA:** No, no . . . No need to fuss. I arrived safe and sound. And Sybil—Billie's been taking good care of me.

**AMAH:** Drew would have come himself. Jenny insisted he give her a bath tonight. You know, it's a father–daughter thing.

*(Silence.)*

Anyway, we should get going. *(To CANADA)* You're probably starving. I can rustle something up for you in no time.

*(CANADA reaches for his coat.)*

*(To BILLIE.)* Look, I'm gonna have to bring that child of mine over here. She's driving me crazy asking for you—

**BILLIE:** No. No. . . . not yet.

**AMAH:** Well, if I go mad, you and Drew will have to take care of her. I want you to know that. Oh, Jenny asked me to give these to you. She made them specially for you. She wanted to give you some inspiration. You might not be able to tell, but one's of her dancing, and the other's of her singing.

**BILLIE:** Tell I miss her.

**AMAH:** I will.

**BILLIE:** Tell her I'll see her real soon.

**AMAH:** I will.

**BILLIE:**   *(To AMAH.)* I still have a bone to pick with you, though.

(*Indicating CANADA.*)

**AMAH:**   No, no. You have a bone to pick with Drew.

**CANADA:**   I'll drop in again tomorrow, if that's OK with you.

**BILLIE:**   Tomorrow might not be so good. He's moving his stuff in the morning. We'd probably be in the way. I won't even be here until sometime in the afternoon.

**CANADA:**   Well then . . . We'll see how things go. *(He kisses BILLIE on the forehead.)*

**AMAH:**   Come join us over something to eat—

**BILLIE:**   No. Thanks. I'm fine.

**CANADA:**   Good to see you, Sybil—Billie.

**BILLIE:**   Well it certainly was a surprise. Bye y'all.

*(AMAH and CANADA exit. BILLIE closes the door, then leans against it as she studies the pictures Jenny drew.)*

## SCENE 2

*(Harlem, the present: the next day—late morning. Lyrical strains give way to an undulating rhythm while Malcolm X recounts the tale of how George Washington sold a slave for a gallon of molasses. The apartment looks empty of furniture, save for the bed, several piles of books, and boxes strewn around the living area. OTHELLO walks into the bedroom with a large green garbage bag. After a few moments, the door is unlocked and BILLIE peers through the doorway. She hears someone in the bedroom. She quietly closes the door behind her and places a small brown paper bag in her pocket. She makes her way into the kitchen area. She waits. OTHELLO exits the bedroom, green garbage bag in tow. He walks to the centre of the living room where he stands for a few moments taking it all in.)*

**BILLIE:**   Got everything?

**OTHELLO:**   *(Startled.)* Ahh! *(Dropping the garbage bag, he turns around.)* Christ . . .

**BILLIE:**   Got everything?

**OTHELLO:**   God, I didn't hear you come in.

**BILLIE:**   My meeting ended earlier than I expected. I was able to get what I needed . . . I didn't see a van. I figured you'd be done by now.

**OTHELLO:** They just left. I was doing a final check. See if I'd forgotten anything.

**BILLIE:** So the move went well.

**OTHELLO:** Yes . . . yeh. It's amazing how much stuff there is.

**BILLIE:** Yeh. It's hard to throw things away.

**OTHELLO:** I know what you mean. We've got a huge place though.

**BILLIE:** Good. Good for you.

*(Pause.)*

**OTHELLO:** This place looks pretty huge right now, though. Remember when we first came to look at this place?

**BILLIE:** Yes.

*(Pause.)*

**OTHELLO:** Well . . . I guess that's it.

**BILLIE:** I guess . . .

*(Pause.)*

**OTHELLO:** Anyway . . . So when do you plan on leaving?

**BILLIE:** Oh, I don't . . . I don't know.

**OTHELLO:** Ah.

**BILLIE:** I haven't decided.

**OTHELLO:** I see . . . Well . . .

**BILLIE:** So when's the big day?

**OTHELLO:** Oh well. . . . .Er . . . Three weeks.

**BILLIE:** So soon?

**OTHELLO:** Just a small affair.

**BILLIE:** Good. Good for you. Good for you both.

**OTHELLO:** Yeh . . .

**BILLIE:** I . . . I've been meaning . . . Well . . . I've been thinking.

**OTHELLO:** Hmn Hmn . . .

**BILLIE:** I . . . er . . . I . . . um . . . I want to return something you gave me . . . centuries ago.

**OTHELLO:** Oh?

**BILLIE:** The handkerchief?

**OTHELLO:** Oh! Really? Wow . . . No. No. It's not necessary. Really—

**BILLIE:** No, no, let me finish. I've been. . . . . . .foolish. I understand that now. You can understand why. And . . . . . . I'm sorry. That's

what I wanted to tell you. And the handkerchief . . . it's yours. Held
by me for safekeeping really. To be passed on to our children—if
we had any. Since we don't, it should be returned to you, to your
line . . .

**OTHELLO:** Why are you doing this?

**BILLIE:** I just thought you might . . . I thought you would . . . After
all . . . it's the only thing your mother left you . . .

**OTHELLO:** I don't know what to say.

**BILLIE:** I thought you'd be glad.

**OTHELLO:** Oh, I'm more than glad.

**BILLIE:** But I have to find it first.

**OTHELLO:** Are you sure about—

**BILLIE:** I'm sure. Give me a couple of days, to find it. . . . . .clean it up
a bit.

**OTHELLO:** I could come by.

**BILLIE:** Yes. You should have it before . . . You know . . . before
your . . . big day.

**OTHELLO:** Thank you.

**BILLIE:** Just trying to play my part well.

**OTHELLO:** Thanks.

**BILLIE:** Forgive me . . .

**OTHELLO:** I know it's been hard.

**BILLIE:** Yeh.

**OTHELLO:** OK. Well . . .

*(He reaches to touch her face. She retreats.)*

**BILLIE:** I'll see you in a couple of days then.

**OTHELLO:** Alright.

**BILLIE:** Alright.

**OTHELLO:** Alright. And say Hello to Jenny for me. *(Silence.)* Alright.

*(OTHELLO exits. BILLIE takes the small package out of her
pocket. She unwraps it, revealing a small vial of fluid. She goes into
the kitchen, vial in hand, turns toward the fridge, opens the freezer
door and stares into it.)*

**BILLIE:** Look this way and see . . . your death . . . Othe . . . Othe . . .

*(She places the vial into the freezer.)*

## Scene 3

*(Harlem, 1862: late summer—night. Indigo blues groan as if through a delta, while echoes of a presidential voice reads from the Emancipation Proclamation. The sound fades. HER holds HIM in her arms like Mary holds Jesus in Michelangelo's 'The Pieta'. There is a rope around his neck. He does not move.)*

**HER:** *(Caressing him.)* Once upon a time, there was a man who wanted to find a magic spell in order to become White. After much research and investigation, he came across an ancient ritual from the caverns of knowledge of a psychic. "The only way to become White," the psychic said, "was to enter the Whiteness." And when he found his ice queen, his alabaster goddess, he fucked her. Her on his dick. He one with her, for a single shivering moment became . . . her. Her and her Whiteness.

## Scene 4

*(Harlem, present: late summer—night. A cacophony of strings grooves and collides as sound bites from the Anita Hill and Clarence Thomas hearings, the L.A. riots, the O. J. Simpson trial, Malcolm X, and Martin Luther King, loop and repeat the same distorted bits of sound over and over again. BILLIE is alone in the apartment. She goes into the freezer and removes the vial. Wearing rubber gloves, she places several drops of a liquid substance onto the handkerchief. She replaces the cap of the vial. BILLIE carefully folds the handkerchief, hesitates for a moment, looks around and spots the red box on the mantel. She puts the handkerchief back down on the tray and, with her hands in the air, like a surgeon scrubbing for surgery, she gets up and goes to the red box. With one hand she takes off one of the gloves. With the ungloved hand, she opens the red box and slips her mother's ring on her finger. She then takes the red box with her to the table. She very carefully replaces the one glove, picks up the handkerchief, and neatly places it in the small red box. She works slowly, and is mindful not to touch the sides of the box with the handkerchief itself.*

*She removes a single rubber glove once more, picks up the cover to the box, and places it on top of the other half. She is still for a few moments, staring at the box.*

*BILLIE gets up and crosses the room, as if looking for something, only to stop in her tracks and return to the box. She paces. Her pacing appears more methodical than hysterical. Suddenly she stops. She turns to look at the small red box.*

*She shakes her head and takes a seat on a large, full, cardboard box at her feet. Her breathing becomes more apparent as she begins to rock, almost imperceptibly at first. Finally she places her head in her hands.*

*After several moments, BILLIE's face slowly emerges from her hands.*

*She glares at the gloved hand incredulously, as she realizes that she has inadvertently transferred some of the potion onto her own skin. She quickly removes the second glove, and proceeds to wipe her face with her own clothes.)*

**BILLIE:** *(To herself.)* Oh god! Oh my god! Shit! Shit! Shit! Shit!

*(BILLIE gets up and rushes to the kitchen sink, turns on the tap and frantically washes her hands and face in the water.)*

## SCENE 5

*(The following day: early evening. In counterpoint to the cello and bass, the distorted sound loop becomes a grating repetition. MAGI and CANADA are on either side of a large box, sitting on two smaller ones. The larger box is covered by a scarf to resemble a table cloth, on top of which is a small feast. They are eating. MAGI gets up and goes to the door of the bedroom. She peeks in. After a few moments she closes the door and returns to her seat.)*

**MAGI:** She's in distant realms. I checked in on her when I got back from church. I thought she was speaking in tongues. I couldn't understand a thing she was saying. I don't think she slept a wink all night. Those pills work like a charm, though. *(Beat.)* How is it?

**CANADA:** Mmn! Those greens . . . She looks like an angel and cooks like one too.

**MAGI:** Can I get you some more?

**CANADA:** No, no, I don't want to appear too greedy now.

**MAGI:** Here . . . *(Serving him another helping.)* There you go. And I won't tell a soul. Promise.

**CANADA:** I haven't tasted cooking like this in a long time.

**MAGI:**   My Mama would say, some food is good for the mind, some is good for the body, and some food is good for the soul.

**CANADA:**   Your Mama taught you how to cook like this?

**MAGI:**   Once she even taught me how to cook a soufflé. She used to have a restaurant downstairs from as far back as I can recall. And I guess the boys returning home from the war in Europe kept asking for the Parisian food, and it ended up on her menu. She'd say, now this Parisian food ain't good for nothing. Soufflé ain't nothing more than baked eggs. And eggs is for breakfast. Eggs don't do no one no good past noon.

**CANADA:**   So you've lived here all your life?

**MAGI:**   And my mother before me, and her mother before her. My great grandmother, worked for the family that lived here, most of her life. She never married, but she had two children by the man she worked for—seems his wife never knew they were his. One brown baby looks just like another to most White folks. And when the wife died, my great grandmother just stayed on. Everybody thinking she's just the maid, but she was living like the queen of the manor— him being her babies' father and everything. And his other children were all grown by then. So when he died, he left everything to his White children, 'cept this house. He left it in my great grand- mother's name, and it's been in my family ever since.

**CANADA:**   So the White man's children ever find out? About their brown skinned relatives.

**MAGI:**   I don't know. The Van Dykes—they were Dutch. We used to watch the Dick Van Dyke show, and my Grandmother used to always say, "That there's your relative!" But we didn't pay her too much mind. More greens?

**CANADA:**   If I eat another thing, I will truly burst. This was wonderful. Thank you. Thank you very much.

**MAGI:**   You're more than welcome.

**CANADA:**   When I was a boy, I used to love to sop the pot liquor.

**MAGI:**   It's nearly the best part.

**CANADA:**   You sure know the way to a man's heart.

**MAGI:**   Haven't had any luck so far.

**CANADA:**   Yet.

*(There is an awkward silence between them, after which they both start speaking at once.)*

**MAGI:** *(Overlapping.)* Well I better get started with these dishes . . .

**CANADA:** *(Overlapping.)* I should go in and check on Sybil . . . Let me give you a hand.

**MAGI:** No, no, it's quite alright. I can handle this.

*(BILLIE enters.)*

**CANADA:** Billie! Marjorie was kind enough to share her dinner with me.

**MAGI:** Billie, come and have something to eat.

**BILLIE:** I'm not hungry. I heard voices. I need to go back and lay down . . . get some reading done.

**MAGI:** You can't have eaten anything for the day, girl.

**BILLIE:** I'm fine.

**CANADA:** What you need is a good meal inside you.

**BILLIE:** I said I was fine.

**MAGI:** I'll just take these things downstairs. *(MAGI exits.)*

**CANADA:** I'll make you some tea, OK.

**BILLIE:** I don't—don't need any tea. I don't want anything to eat. I'm fine. I'm sorry. I don't—don't—don't mean . . . to be like this . . . But I haven't seen you in God knows how long . . . And you just show up, and expect things to be all hunky dory.

*(Pause.)*

**CANADA:** Well, I'll be off then.

*(He goes for his coat.)*

**BILLIE:** I'm sorry.

**CANADA:** Me too.

*(He heads for the door.)*

**BILLIE:** And I am glad you came . . . Maybe this can be . . . You know. . . . like a beginning of something . . . I don't know.

**CANADA:** I nearly came before . . . Two or three times . . . You know, when I heard. I wished your mother was here. I really wished for her . . . Her wisdom. I mean Beryl would know what to do. A girl needs her mother. And I know you didn't have her all those times . . . I mean, I couldn't tell you. What could I tell you? I kept seeing your face. It's your mother's face. You've got my nose. My mouth. But those eyes . . . The shape of your face . . . The way your head tilts to one side when you're thinking, or just listening. It's all her.

You've got her moods. I used to call them her moods. Once 'bout every three months, on a Friday, when she'd have the weekend off, she'd come home from that hospital, take off her clothes and lay down in her bed and stay there 'till Sunday afternoon. She'd say she'd done turned the other cheek so many times in the past little while, she didn't have no more smiles for anybody. She'd say, better she just face God and the pillow than shower me and the children with the evil she had bottled up inside her. See, if you spend too much time among White people, you start believing what they think of you. So I'd take you and Drew and we'd go visiting. We'd take the whole weekend and visit all the folks we knew, in a fifteen mile radius . . . When we'd get home, she'd have cleaned the house, washed the clothes and even made a Sunday dinner. And after I'd pluck the guitar . . . And she'd start to sing . . . And you'd dance . . . You remember? You'd dance. You'd stomp on that floor like you were beating out some secret code to God or something . . . I know you—we don't see eye to eye. I know you haven't wanted to see very much anything of me lately. But I've known you all your life. I carried you in my arms and on my back, kissed and spanked you when you needed, and I watched you start to talk, and learn to walk, and read and I just wanted to come . . . I just wanted to come. And I know I can't make everything alright. I know. But I was there when you arrived in this world. And I didn't think there was space for a child, I loved your mother so much. But there you were and I wondered where you'd been all my life, like something I'd been missing and didn't know I'd been missing. And I don't know if you've loved anybody that long. But behind your mother's face you're wearing, I still see the girl who shrieked with laughter, and danced to the heavens sometimes . . .

*(CANADA slowly approaches BILLIE. She does not move. He takes her in his arms. He holds her in his arms for a long time.)*

## Scene 6

*(Harlem, 1928: late summer—night. The strident movement of the strings is joined by the rising tempo of the distorted sound loop. HE and SHE are both in a tiny dressing room, as in the prologue. On a counter is a shaving brush, a straight-edged razor, greasepaint and*

*a top hat. HE wipes his face with a towel. SHE holds the handkerchief out to him. He does not take it. She lets it fall at his feet. After a few moments, he picks it up.)*

HE: *(Referring to the handkerchief at first.)* White, red, black, green, indigo . . . What difference does it make? That makes no sense . . . makes no difference. "If virtue no delighted beauty lack, Your son-in-law is far more fair than black." Far more fair than black. I want . . . I need to do this . . . For my soul. I am an actor. I—

SHE: *(Kindly.)* A minstrel. A Black minstrel . . .

*(He places the towel on the counter beside the toiletries.)*

HE: It's paid my way.

*(She caresses the towel.)*

SHE: Stay, my sable warrior . . .

*(Her hand stumbles upon the razor.)*

HE: I'll not die in black-face to pay the rent. I am of Ira Aldrigde stock. I am a classical man. I long to play the Scottish king. The prince of Denmark. "The slings and arrows of outrageous . . ." Or . . . Or . . . "There's a divinity that shapes our ends, Rough-hew them how we will" . . . Those words . . . I love those words. They give me life. Mona sees my gift. She's cast me as the prince of Tyre. She's breathed new life into a barren dream. She . . . She . . . She has a serene calmness about her. That smile . . . I bet they named her Mona because even at birth, she had that constant half smile, like the Mona Lisa. Skin as smooth as monumental alabaster . . . As warm as snow velvet.

*(She exposes the blade.)*

SHE: My onyx prince . . .
HE: Ooohh . . .

*(She approaches him from behind.)*

SHE: My tourmaline king . . .

*(She leans her head on his back.)*

HE: S'alright . . .

**SHE:**  My raven knight . . .

*(She wraps her arms around him. He turns his head toward her.)*

**HE:**  Oh sweet . . .

**SHE:**  My umber squire . . .

**HE:**  I wish . . . I wish—

*(Her hand rises, the razor is poised, nearly touching the skin of his neck, just below his ear, within his peripheral vision.)*

**SHE:**  My Cimmerian lord . . .

*(He turns around, as if to see what she's holding, and in that turn, his neck appears to devour the blade. The razor's shaft at once hidden by his flesh, swiftly withdraws, leaving a rushing river of red like a scarf billowing around his neck and her hands. He yields to gravity.)*

SCENE 7

*(Harlem, the present: late summer night. The plucked strings and the distorted audio loop have become even more dissonant. BILLIE is clutching the small red box.)*

**MAGI:**  . . . You know, Hakim has seven children, and he's never been married. Brother Hakim. Spot him at any street rally where the subject is prefaced by the words "Third World". He's the one with the "Lumumba Lives" button prominently displayed on his authentic kente cloth dashi—Billie? Billie, what's up? You don't look so good.

*(Pause.)*

Billie?

**BILLIE:**  Sybil. I'm Sybil.

**MAGI:**  That's what your Daddy calls you.

**BILLIE:**  Yes.

**MAGI:**  Your Daddy sure is one good-looking gentleman.

**BILLIE:**  Trapped in history. A history trapped in me.

**MAGI:**  I'm serious. I mean . . . I wanna know if you mind? Really. You were still a little girl when your mama died.

**BILLIE:**  I don't remember Beryl's funeral. I see my father dressed in black, sewing a white button, on to his white shirt, with an enormous needle. He attaches the button and knots the thread so many times it's like he's trying to hold onto more than just the button. Like he can't bear for anything else in his life to leave him.

**MAGI:** He's a nice man. Would you mind?

**BILLIE:** Am I nice?

**MAGI:** Billie, I bet you haven't eaten today.

**BILLIE:** Can you keep a secret?

**MAGI:** No, but that's never stopped you before.

**BILLIE:** Then sorry . . .

**MAGI:** OK, OK. I promise.

**BILLIE:** I am about to plunge into very dangerous waters. Give me your word.

**MAGI:** You're not going to do something stupid, now.

**BILLIE:** Your word?

**MAGI:** Yeh, OK.

**BILLIE:** I've drawn a line.

**MAGI:** A line? A line about what?

**BILLIE:** I'm returning the handkerchief—the one his mother give him. The one he gave to me when we first agreed to be together . . .

**MAGI:** I don't understand.

**BILLIE:** I've concocted something . . . A potion . . . A plague of sorts . . . I've soaked the handkerchief . . . Soaked it in certain tinctures . . . Anyone who touches it—the handkerchief, will come to harm.

**MAGI:** Now that is not a line, Billie, that is a trench!

**BILLIE:** I'm supposed to . . .

**MAGI:** Billie, if this kind of stuff truly worked, Africans wouldn't be in the situation we're in now. Imagine all them slaves working magic on their masters—didn't make no difference. If it truly worked, I'd be married to a nice man, with three little ones by now. But if it makes you feel better—

**BILLIE:** He's going to marry her . . . Officially . . .

**MAGI:** I know . . . I know. Remember, what goes around comes around. Karma is a strong and unforgiving force.

**BILLIE:** I haven't seen it affect White people too much.

**MAGI:** Is everything about White people with you? Is every living moment of your life eaten up with thinking about them? Do you know where you are? Do you know who you are anymore? What about right and wrong? Racism is a disease my friend, and your test just came back positive. You're so busy reacting, you don't even know yourself.

**BILLIE:** No, no, no . . . It's about Black. I love Black. I really do. And it's revolutionary . . . Black is beautiful . . . So beautiful. This Harlem sanctuary. . . . . .here. This respite . . . Like an ocean in the middle of a desert. And in my mirror, my womb, he has a fast growing infestation of roaches. White roaches.

**MAGI:** Billie?

**BILLIE:** Did you ever consider what hundreds of years of slavery did to the African American psyche?

**MAGI:** What? What are you . . . ?

**BILLIE:** Every time someone mentions traditional values or the good old days—who exactly were those days good for?

*(The phone rings. BILLIE goes over it. She sits on the bare floor but does not answer.)*

Jenny . . . Is that you Jenny. My beauty. My little girl. It's Sybil . . . Auntie Sybil . . . The woman who lives in the cave.

*(BILLIE laughs.)*

**MAGI:** I'll get it for you.

*(BILLIE picks up the receiver.)*

**BILLIE:** Yes, yes, I'm here. Oh, Othe . . . Othello. I didn't recognize your voice. You sound. . . . . .different. No. No, no, you can't pick it up. I mean—I've got it, yes. It's right here. No. No, I won't be in . . . No, no. I haven't changed my mind. But—I mean . . . I have to go . . . Roaches. Yeh, blue roaches. Green roaches. So I have to go now. I—I just have to go.

*(BILLIE replaces the receiver.)*

**MAGI:** He's coming over?

**BILLIE:** I don't want a Mona Lisa smile . . .

**MAGI:** Oh Billie . . . Billie, you're all in bits and pieces.

**BILLIE:** I know. I know. A tumour. Suddenly apparent, but it's been there, tiny, growing slowly for a long time. What kind of therapy to take? Chop it out? Radiate it? Let it eat me alive? I see roaches all around me. In me. Blue roaches. Green roaches. Aah! Get off! Get it off. I eat roaches. I pee roaches. Help! I'm losing . . . I don't don't . . . I'm falling . . .

**MAGI:** Billie? Billie?

**BILLIE:** I have a dream today.

**MAGI:** You had a dream?

**BILLIE:** I have a dream that one day every valley shall be engulfed, every hill shall be exalted and every mountain shall be made low . . . oh . . . oh . . . the rough places will be made plains and the crooked places will be made . . .

**MAGI:** *(Overlapping.)* It's gonna be alright, Billie.

*(MAGI goes to the phone and dials.)*

**BILLIE:** *(Overlapping.)* . . . straight and the glory of the Lord shall be revealed and all flesh shall see it together.

**MAGI:** *(Overlapping.)* It's Magi. You all better get over here, now. No, no, no. NOW. Alright. Alright.

*(MAGI puts down the receiver and returns to BILLIE. She gently takes the red box from out of BILLIE's hands, and places it on the mantel.)*

**BILLIE:** *(Overlapping.)* . . . This is our hope . . .

**MAGI:** *(Overlapping.)* It's gonna be alright. I know . . . I know . . .

**BILLIE:** *(Overlapping.)* . . . With this faith we will be able to hew out of the mountain of despair a stone of hope . . .

**MAGI:** *(Overlapping.)* It's OK. It's OK. Let's start with a little step. Come on. Come with me. *(MAGI helps BILLIE up.)* Come on . . . Good. Let's get some soup into you. Warm up that frozen blood of yours. *(MAGI leads her to the door.)* Warm up your insides. Come . . . Come on . . . Chase all the roaches out . . .

*(BILLIE breaks loose of MAGI and rushes to the window.*

*MAGI is no longer in the room. OTHELLO appears wearing a brightly coloured dashiki. He is inspecting a broom, laying against the fridge. It is now Fall, seven years earlier. Save for the broom, and the fridge, the apartment is empty.)*

**BILLIE:** Look . . . Come, look . . . You can see the Apollo from the window. I love it.

**OTHELLO:** Where?

**BILLIE:** Over there. See.

**OTHELLO:** Oh yeh—If I crane my neck.

**BILLIE:** I could find some lawn chairs and table and we'd have a city terrace.

**OTHELLO:** On the fire escape?

**BILLIE:** We'd have our own little balcony.

**OTHELLO:** Patio.

**BILLIE:** Terrace . . .

**OTHELLO:** We could buy a house up here.

**BILLIE:** We can't afford to buy a house until I finish school. If I'm going to go to school full-time, this fall, like we agreed—you'd go to school, then I'd go to school—how can we afford a down payment on a house?

**OTHELLO:** I know. I know.

*(Pause.)*

**BILLIE:** I love it. Don't you love it?

**OTHELLO:** I love you.

**BILLIE:** I love you and I love it.

**OTHELLO:** Think Chris Yago and Mona and the other faculty will feel uncomfortable coming up here . . . for meetings and the like . . .

**BILLIE:** It's on the subway line.

**OTHELLO:** And boy do they need to take the journey. I'll take them on a cultural field trip—blow their minds.

**BILLIE:** I've longed for this sanctuary.

**OTHELLO:** I know what you mean.

**BILLIE:** Black boutiques.

**OTHELLO:** Black bookstores.

**BILLIE:** Black groceries.

**OTHELLO:** Filled with Black doctors and dentists. Black banks.

**BILLIE:** Black streets teeming with loud Black people listening to loud Jazz and reggae and Aretha . . . *(Singing.)* "There is a rose in Spanish Harlem. *(He joins her.)* A rose in Black and Spanish Harlem. Da da da, da da da . . . " Maybe later we could buy a place on 'strivers row', that's where all the rich Black folks live.

**OTHELLO:** Strivers row.

**BILLIE:** Owned by Blacks hued from the faintest gold to the bluest bronze. That's my dream.

**OTHELLO:** By then you'd have your Ph.D.

**BILLIE:** And a small lecturer's position at a prestigious Manhattan university. We might even have enough money to get a small house in the country too.

**OTHELLO:** A big house in the country too?

**BILLIE:** A big house with a white picket fence.

**OTHELLO:** On a rolling emerald hill.

**BILLIE:** I want 2.5 kids.

*(He kisses her lightly.)*

**OTHELLO:** You're mad, you know that.

**BILLIE:** That makes you some kinda fool for loving me, baby.

**OTHELLO:** Let's do it. There's an old broom right over there. Wanna jump it with me?

*(OTHELLO retrieves the broom.)*

**BILLIE:** Are you asking me to m—

**OTHELLO:** Yes . . . Yes, I am asking.

**BILLIE:** Yes . . . *(Silence.)* Then yes.

*(OTHELLO kisses her. He places the broom in the middle of the floor. He takes BILLIE's hand. They stand in front of it.)*

What will we use for rings?

**OTHELLO:** Think them old slaves had rings? Slave marriages were illegal, remember. This broom is more than rings. More than any gold. *(He whispers.)* My ancient love.

**BILLIE:** *(She whispers.)* My soul.

*(OTHELLO kisses her hand. The couple gaze at each other, preparing to jump over the broom. They jump. They hold each other. The landlady enters.)*

**MAGI:** Oh—I'm sorry.

**BILLIE:** No, no. We were just . . . just—

*(OTHELLO picks up the broom and places it to one side.)*

**OTHELLO:** I think we'll take it.

**MAGI:** I didn't mean to rush you. I can give you another few minutes if you need to make good and sure?

**BILLIE:** I think we're sure. *(To OTHELLO.)* You sure? *(To MAGI.)* We're sure.

*(MAGI looks gravely at BILLIE. They are the only ones in the room. We are back in the present. MAGI carefully approaches BILLIE. BILLIE stares at where OTHELLO stood, only moments ago.)*

**MAGI:** Come on. Come with me. Come on . . . Good. Let's get some soup into you. Warm up that frozen blood of yours. *(MAGI leads her to the door.)* Warm up your insides. Come . . . come on . . . Chase all the roaches out . . . One by one . . . One by one . . .

*(They exit.)*

## SCENE 8

*(Harlem, present: late summer, afternoon. A lyrical rhapsody swings to the sound of a commentator describing the scene at the Million Man March. The apartment is virtually empty. CANADA is cleaning the kitchen, taking tubs and bags from out of the freezer. He gives them a brief once-over and then throws them into the trash. OTHELLO enters.)*

**OTHELLO:** Billie? Billie?

**CANADA:** Othello! Othello, good to see you son.

*(They shake hands.)*

Good to see you.

**OTHELLO:** I didn't know . . . When did you get here?

**CANADA:** A few days.

**OTHELLO:** Billie didn't say a word.

**CANADA:** Well, Billie's in . . . she's . . . Billie's not here right now.

**OTHELLO:** *(Scanning the apartment.)* Did she leave anything for me. An envelope . . . A package—

*(He sees the red box on the mantel.)*

Oh. Maybe . . .

*(He goes over to it.)*

CANADA:  Oh, she said no one was to touch that . . . I'm supposed to throw it out.

OTHELLO:  Great! *(He opens the red box and takes out the handker-chief.)* It's OK, this is it. It's mine. This is what I was looking for.

CANADA:  I was just about to throw it in with the trash from the fridge.

OTHELLO:  Just in time, huh?

CANADA:  Yeh, some of this stuff's about ready to crawl out by itself.

OTHELLO:  I can imagine.

CANADA:  I swear, one thing had actually grown little feet.

OTHELLO:  Well, Billie wasn't one for cleaning . . . I guess neither of us was.

*(There is an awkward silence between them.)*

Well . . . I should be off.

*(He takes some keys from out of his pocket and places them where the red box was laying.)*

CANADA:  She tells me you're getting married.

OTHELLO:  I do confess the vices of my blood.

CANADA:  I'm real sorry it didn't work out . . . Between you and Billie . . . I mean . . . I was hoping . . .

OTHELLO:  Yes. I know.

CANADA:  She's my child, so—

OTHELLO:  I know, I know.

CANADA:  You young'uns don't know the sweetness of molasses . . . Rather have granulated sugar, 'stead of a deep clover honey, or cane sugar juice from way into the Demerara. Better watch out for that refined shit. It'll kill ya. A slow kinda killin'. 'Cause it kills your mind first. So you think you living the life, when you been dead a long time.

*(Silence.)*

OTHELLO:  Well sir . . . I should be somewhere.

CANADA:  *(Nodding.)* Well, I hope we can catch up sometime . . .

*(OTHELLO goes to the door.)*

OTHELLO:  That would be great. Tell Billie I came by.

CANADA:  I'll tell her that. She'll be glad to know.

OTHELLO:  Good seeing you.

**CANADA:** You too . . . son . . . You too.

*(OTHELLO takes one last look at the apartment, takes out a tiny cellular phone, and exits. CANADA is still for a few moments. From the hallway we hear OTHELLO.)*

**OTHELLO:** *(Offstage.)* Chris Yago, please.

*(CANADA returns to the fridge, and continues to clean.)*

SCENE 9

*(Harlem, 1928: late summer—night. The music softly underscores the voice of Paul Robeson speaking about not being able to get decent acting roles in the U.S., and how fortunate he feels to be offered a contract to play OTHELLO in England. HE is alone. He proceeds to cover his face in black grease paint. He begins to speak, as if rehearsing, at first.)*

**HE:** It is most true; true, I have married her.
It is most . . .
It is most true; true, I have married her.
For know, but that I love the gentle Desdemona,
(She) questioned me the story of my life
From year to year—the battles, sieges, fortunes,
That I have passed. These things to hear
Would Desdemona seriously incline;
But still the house affairs would draw her thence,
Which ever as she could with haste dispatch
she'd come again, and with a greedy ear
Devour up my discourse. Which I, observing,
Took once a pliant hour . . .
And often did beguile her of her tears,
When I did speak of some distressful stroke
That my youth suffered . . .

*(In the background we can hear a children's song. HE begins to add a white greasepaint to his lips, completing the mask of the minstrel.)*

. . . My story being done,
She gave me for my pains a world of sighs.
She wished she had not heard it, yet she wished

That heaven had made her such a man. She thanked me,
She thanked me . . .
She thanked me . . .
She thanked me . . .

## SCENE 10

*(Harlem, the present: late summer—night. A beryline blues impro-
visation of "Mama's Little Baby" cascades alongside a reading of
the Langston Hughes poem "Harlem". AMAH sits beside BILLIE in
the visitors lounge of the psychiatric ward. AMAH is clearly saddened by BILLIE's state.)*

**BILLIE:** *(Singing.)* . . . Step back Sal-ly, all night long.
Strut-in' down the al-ley, al-ley, al-ley,
Strut-in' down the al-ley, all night long.
**AMAH & BILLIE:** I looked over there, and what did I see?
A big fat lady from Ten-nes-see.

*(BILLIE gets up and begins to dance.)*

I bet you five dollars I can beat that man,
To the front, to the back, to the side, side, side.
To the front, to the back, to the side, side, side.

*(The two women laugh.)*

**BILLIE:** I haven't done that in . . . in years.
**AMAH:** I never knew that one—I just saw Jenny do it the other day.
**BILLIE:** I even remember the dance. *(Singing under her breath.)* . . .
Bet you five dollars I can beat that man . . .
**AMAH:** It's not so bad here.
**BILLIE:** You'd think the doctors at Harlem hospital would be Black.
Especially in psychiatrics. Most of the nurses are Black.
**AMAH:** But they're nice to you—the doctors?
**BILLIE:** They help. I don't—don't want anymore pills. And that's OK.
They don't really understand, though. I had this dream. Lucinda—
she's my main doctor. Lucinda was sitting at the edge of a couch
and I asked her a question. But she couldn't answer because her
eyes kept flashing. Like neon lights. Flash, flash, flash. That was it.
That was the dream. I knew it was important, but I didn't get it.

And I told her. And she didn't get it either. But it gnawed away at me . . . For days . . . The flashing eyes. And that was it! The eyes were flashing blue. Her eyes were flashing blue. She could only see my questions through her blue eyes.

**AMAH:** Something in you really wants to heal.

**BILLIE:** Exorcism.

**AMAH:** Pardon?

**BILLIE:** Repossess.

**AMAH:** Self-possession?

**BILLIE:** I hate. I know I hate. And he loves. How he loves.

**AMAH:** Billie?

**BILLIE:** Why is that, you think?

**AMAH:** Some of us spend our entire lives making our own shackles.

**BILLIE:** Canada freedom come.

**AMAH:** And the experienced shackle-wearer knows the best polish for the gilt.

**BILLIE:** I wanna be free.

**AMAH:** It must be hard, though. I feel for him.

**BILLIE:** I'm not that evolved.

**AMAH:** Forgiveness.

**BILLIE:** Forgiveness . . .

**AMAH:** If I don't forgive my enemy, if I don't forgive him, he might just set up house, inside me.

**BILLIE:** I just . . . I—I despise—I know . . . I know . . . Moment by moment. I forgive him now. I hate—I love him so—I forgive him now. And now.

*(She moves as if to speak, but stops herself.)*

And I forgive him now.

**AMAH:** My time's up, sweetie.

**BILLIE:** I have a dream . . .

**AMAH:** Sorry?

**BILLIE:** I had a dream . . .

**AMAH:** Yes . . . I know.

**BILLIE:** Tell Jenny . . . Tell her for me . . . Tell her that you saw me dancing.

**AMAH:** I will tell her.

**BILLIE:** And tell her . . . Tell her that you heard me singing.

**AMAH:** I will.

**BILLIE:** And tell her . . . I'll see her real soon.

**AMAH:** I will tell her, Billie. I will tell her.

*(AMAH kisses BILLIE on the cheek and begins to exit. CANADA enters.)*

**BILLIE:** *(In the background softly.)*
Betcha five dollars I can beat that man.
To the front, to the back, to the side, side, side.
To the front, to the back, to the side, side, side.

**CANADA:** How's she doing?

**AMAH:** Mmm, so-so.

**CANADA:** Okay. Thanks.

**AMAH:** We'll really miss you when you go—back to Nova Scotia.

**CANADA:** Oh, I don't think I'm going anywhere just yet—least if I can help it. Way too much leaving gone on for more than one lifetime already.

*(BILLIE stops singing for a moment, then segues into a version of Aretha Franklin's "Spanish Harlem", more hummed than sung.*

*CANADA pats AMAH on the back. AMAH turns and exits. CANADA approaches BILLIE and sits down beside her.*

*Shortly, he joins her in the song. He rests his hand on hers.*

*After several moments: The lights fade to black.)*

*The End*

—*1997*

*Djanet Sears*

# nOTES oF a cOLOURED gIRL 32 sHORT rEASONS wHY i wRITE fOR tHE tHEATRE

1  Carved from that same tree
in another age
counsel/warriors who
in the mother tongue
made drums talk
now in another tongue
make words to walk in rhythm
'cross the printed page
carved from that same tree
in another age
      Khephra
      Talking Drums #1 <sup>(Khephra 125)</sup>

2 Two years ago I found myself speaking with esteemed writer and Nobel laureate, Derek Walcott, about an upcoming staged reading I was directing of his play, *A Branch of the Blue Nile*. Toward the end of our conversation I politely requested an opportunity to ask him, what I termed, a stupid question. His eyebrows seemed to crawl up to his hairline, but he didn't say no. Not that I gave him a chance. Swiftly managing to kick all second thoughts out of my mind, I boldly asked him to tell me why he wrote. He retreated to the back of his seat, and after several long moments of pondering, he replied, "I don't know." He said that writing really wasn't a choice for him. From as far back as he could recall, he had written. He described it as a type of organic urge. He didn't know why he wrote, but when he experienced this urge, he felt compelled to act on it. Be it on a plane, first thing in the morning, or last thing at night.

**3** From as far back as I can recall, I never believed in miracles. My life had taught me not to. Then I witnessed the birth of my sister's daughter. I'd seen birth films. I'd even studied human reproduction at the undergraduate level. But this child came out of my sister—already alive. I mean, not yet fully born, her head alone protruding from between her mother's legs, she wailed. Full of voice, she slipped out of the velvety darkness that was her mother's womb, into the light. I was overcome. I watched as this tiny, golden-umber coloured soul, caught by an opaque rubber gloved doctor, in a white coat, was separated from the placenta and bundled into blanched cloth. I stood there for a moment and wondered how she would come to know of herself, blinded by the glare of snow? What would this fair world tell her? I experienced such a sadness for her—or maybe it was for myself. I wanted something different for her.

**4** I wanted there to be no question of her right to take up space on this planet.

**5** I was already eighteen when I saw Ntozake Shange's *For Coloured Girls Who Have Considered Suicide When The Rainbow Is Enuf* in New York City. This was the first live stage production by a writer of African descent I had ever seen. **6** This will not be Qwyn's fate. **7** She must have access to a choir of African voices, chanting a multiplicity of African experiences. One voice does not a chorus make. And I will not wait. **8** I harbour deep within me tales that I've never seen told. **9** I too must become an organ and add my perspective, my lens, my stories, to the ever growing body of work by and about people of African descent.

**10** Thirty-seven years ago, and nine months before I was born, in a country over three thousand miles away, Lorraine Hansberry began rehearsals for her first play. In the season of my birth, *Raisin in the Sun* opened to extraordinary critical and popular acclaim.

**11** ... *Raisin in the Sun* marked a turning point, for until this time no black writer, black actor, black director, or technician had benefited financially from any of the plays about black people that had been presented (in the commercial theatre). [King vii]

**12** An old West African proverb states that, as a people, we stand on the shoulders of our ancestors. **13** Lorraine Hansberry is my mother—in the theatre—and she accompanies me wherever I go. **14** I have been known to drop her a few lines, now and then. **15** Yes, she responds. **16** As a woman of African descent, and a writer for the stage, I stand on her shoulders. They are a firm and formidable foundation on which to rest my large and awkward feet.

**17** Acting is a craft that I have been called to by my nature. Writing is a craft that I have chosen to nurture. **18** As a young actor, I soon realized that a majority of the roles that I would be offered did not portray me in the way I saw myself, my family, or my friends, in life. I became consumed by my own complaining. **19** Complaining, imploring, and protesting only served to disperse my energy.

**20** Protest takes an enormous toll. We can and should make noise; however, in most cases our screams fall upon deaf ears.

**21** Don't get me wrong here, without protest we'd never have had the likes of Martin, Malcolm, or Angela. Activism is a craft in and of itself. My skills are as a theatre practitioner, and this is the medium I must use.

That's why I am so impressed by artists like Baraka, Sanchez, Bullins, Caldwell, Hansberry, Baldwin, Giovanni, Milner, and Ahmad, many of whom were involved in the Black Arts Movement of the 1960's. The fact is they used their work as a vehicle with which to express personal and political passions.

**22** In early 1993, Christine Moynihan approached me, on behalf of the Toronto Theatre Alliance and Equity Showcase Productions, about coordinating the spring 'Loon Cafe' (a one-off evening of presentations involving a host of performers, directors, writers, production workers, designers and supporters). I agreed, on the condition that I could do anything. In the ensuing weeks I developed the blueprint for the evening which I titled: *Negrophilia: An African American Retrospective: 1959–1971.* The three studio spaces of Equity Showcase were renamed Obsidian, Onyx and Jet. And the events taking place, three in each room over the course of the evening, involved readings, performances and discussions around Black theatre in America. There were plays that I had loved and had only read. One new piece, *Jimmy and Lolo,* was a collaboration, based on an idea that had been brewing inside of me for ages. Performed on the rooftop of an adjacent building, the play tells the story of the relationship between James Baldwin and Lorraine Hansberry.

The entire event was inspirational; a rousing celebration of Blackness.

**23** I have a dream. A dream that one day in the city where I live, at any given time of the year, I will be able to find at least one play that is filled with people who look like me, telling stories about me, my family, my friends, my community. For most people of European descent, this is a privilege they take for granted.

**24** Like Derek Walcott, I too have no choice. I must write my own work for the theatre. I must produce my own work, and the work of other writers of African descent. Then my nieces' experience of this world will almost certainly be different from my own. **25** But where do I start? How do I find the words?

**26** My good friend Clarissa Chandler, a business consultant, educator, and motivational speaker, shared with me a process for using my nagging mind and raging heart, as a way to get back in touch with my innermost knowing and creative desires. She identified three steps of transformation that I could use like footprints leading me back home.

**27** First: identify the place of complaint. (This can sometimes be evident in the complaining we do in hiding, in conversation with friends, and/or in the privacy of our own minds.) Second: Say it out loud. Create a mantra out of it. (Give it room in the world). Third: locate a creative point of expression for this mantra. **28** Paint it, dance it, sculpt it, or write about it. Why limit yourself?

**29** As a veteran theatre practitioner of African Descent, Shakespeare's *Othello* had haunted me since I first was introduced to him. Sir Laurence Olivier in black-face. Othello is the first African portrayed in the annals of western dramatic literature. In an effort to exorcise this ghost, I have written *Harlem Duet*. *Harlem Duet*, a rhapsodic blues tragedy, explores the effects of race and sex on the lives of people of African descent. It is a tale of love. A tale of Othello and his first wife, Billie. Set in 1860, 1928 and contemporary Harlem at the corner of Malcolm X and Martin Luther King Boulevards, this is Billie's story. The exorcism begins.

**30** For the many like me, black and female, it is imperative that our writing begin to recreate our histories and our myths, as well as integrate the most painful of experiences . . . (Philip 25) Writing for me is a labour of love, probably not unlike the experience of giving birth. In a very deep way, I feel that I am in the process of giving birth to myself. Writing for the stage allows me a process to dream myself into existence.

**31** In a recent clinical study at Duke University researchers found that racist comments can not only lead directly to an overworked heart, but the internal stress caused by racism was found to tear the lining of blood vessels. I must write to save my own life.

**32** There are a great many times when I forget. I forget why I'm doing this. Days when the blues move from a deep cerulean to icy cold pale. So I have the following words by Langston Hughes from "Note on Commercial Theatre", on my wall, just above my desk, for those times when I most need reminding.

SOMEDAY SOMEBODY'LL
STAND UP AND TALK ABOUT ME,
AND WRITE ABOUT ME—
BLACK AND BEAUTIFUL
AND SING ABOUT ME,
AND PUT ON PLAYS ABOUT ME!
I RECKON IT'LL BE
ME MYSELF!

YES, IT'LL BE ME.

## Works Cited

Franklin, Deborah, Lehrman, Sally & Mason, Michael. "Vital Signs: Racism Hurts the Heart Twice." *Health*. Vol. 10, No. 4. (October, 1996)

Hughes, Langston. Excerpt from "Note on Commercial Theatre." *Selected Poems Langston Hughes*. (New York: Random House, Inc., 1974), p. 190

Khephra. "Talking Drums #1." *Essence Magazine*. Vol. 20, No. 11. (March 1990)

King, Woodie & Ron Milner. "Evolution of a People's Theatre." *Black Drama Anthology*. (New York: Signet, 1971)

Philip, Marlene. *She Tries Her Tongue*. (Charlottetown: Ragweed Press, 1989)

*—1997*

# *Appendix*

## Literature: Thematic and Critical Approaches

Because it is possible to classify the stories, poems, and plays in the anthology in many different ways, the following appendix is not exhaustive. It should, however, provide suggestions for reading and writing about works from the same genre or works from different genres that share thematic similarities. Following the thematic listing is a brief discussion of several key critical approaches and their applications to the thematic groups.

Works are listed by genre, and works in each genre are listed in chronological order. Consult the *Index of Authors, Titles, and First Lines* for their page numbers in the text.

## Thematic Approaches

### Aging (See also Carpe Diem)

#### Stories

Mansfield, "Miss Brill"
García Márquez, "A Very Old Man with Enormous Wings"
Carrier, "Perhaps the Trees Do Travel"
Vanderhaeghe, "The Home Place"

#### Poems

Queen Elizabeth I, "When I Was Fair and Young"
Shakespeare, "Sonnet 73"
Scott (D. C.), "The Forsaken"
Williams, "To a Poor Old Woman"

Eliot, "The Love Song of J. Alfred Prufrock"
Thomas, "Do Not Go Gentle into That Good Night"
Pastan, "Ethics"
Phillips, "Compartments"

#### Plays

Miller, *Death of a Salesman*
Pollock, *Moving Pictures*

### Allegorical and Symbolic Works

#### Stories

Hawthorne, "The Birthmark"
Borges, "The Book of Sand"

García Márquez, "A Very Old Man
with Enormous Wings"
Barthelme, "The Glass Mountain"
Schoemperlen, "Forms of Devotion"

### Poems

Blake, "The Sick Rose"
Dickinson, "I Died for Beauty—But
Was Scarce"
Dickinson "I had Been Hungry All
the Years"
Rossetti, "Goblin Market"
Lampman, "The City of the End
of Things"
Yeats, "The Second Coming"
Frost, "Neither out Far nor in Deep"
Stevens, "Thirteen Ways of Looking
at a Blackbird"
Eliot, "Journey of the Magi"
Plath, "Metaphors"

### Plays

Miller, *Death of a Salesman*
Beckett, *Act Without Words I*
Highway, *The Rez Sisters*

## Animals

### Stories

Munro, "Boys and Girls"

### Poems

Smart, *from* "Jubilate Agno"
Blake, "The Tyger"
Stevens, "Thirteen Ways of Looking
at a Blackbird"
Moore, "The Fish"
Zukofsky, "Mantis"
Stafford, "Traveling Through the
Dark"
Hughes, "The Thought-Fox"

Plath, "Black Rook in Rainy
Weather"
Nowlan, "The Bull Moose"
Lowther, "Octopus"

## Art

### Stories

Carr, "Kitwancool"

### Poems

Spenser, "Amoretti: Sonnet 75"
Shakespeare, "Sonnet 18"
Shelley, "Ozymandias"
Keats, "Ode on a Grecian Urn"
Browning (Robert), "My Last
Duchess"
Yeats, "Sailing to Byzantium"
Birney, "El Greco: *Espolio*"
Auden, "Musée des Beaux Arts"
Livesay, "The Three Emilys"
Olson, "The Ring Of"
Ferlinghetti, "In Goya's greatest
scenes"
Sexton, "The Starry Night"
Pastan, "Ethics"
Bolster, "*Le Far-West* (1955)"

## Ballads and Narrative Poetry

Anonymous, "Sir Patrick Spens"
Keats, "La Belle Dame sans
Merci"
Tennyson, "The Lady of Shalott"
Randall, "Ballad of Birmingham"
Rogers, "The Mary Ellen Carter"

## Carpe Diem Poetry

Queen Elizabeth I, "When I Was
Fair and Young"
Marvell, "To His Coy Mistress"

# Childhood and Adolescence (Initiation)

## Stories

Joyce, "Araby"
Cheever, "Reunion"
Angelou, *from* "I Know Why the Caged Bird Sings"
Munro, "Boys and Girls"
MacLeod, "The Boat"
Walker, "The Flowers"
Kincaid, "Girl"
Winter, "Archibald the Arctic"
Thien, "Simple Recipes"

## Poems

Kogawa, "When I Was a Little Girl"
Lane, "Because I Never Learned"
Dove, "Persephone, Falling"
Robinson (Matt), "when skates break"

## Plays

Miller, *Death of a Salesman*

# Conceit and Extended Metaphor (Poetry)

Donne, "Holy Sonnet 14"
Herbert, "Easter Wings"
Bradstreet, "The Author to Her Book"
Cavendish, "Nature's Cook"
Crawford, "The Dark Stag"
Plath, "Metaphors"
Chappell, "Narcissus and Echo"

# Conceit: Petrarchan (Poetry)

Shakespeare, "Sonnet 130"

# Death

## Stories

Poe, "The Cask of Amontillado"
Chopin, "The Story of an Hour"
Woolf, "A Haunted House"
Achebe, "Dead Men's Path"
MacLeod, "The Boat"
Walker, "The Flowers"

## Poems

Cavendish, "Nature's Cook"
Browning (Robert), "My Last Duchess"
Dickinson, "I Died for Beauty—But Was Scarce"
Scott (D. C.), "The Forsaken"
Thomas, "Do Not Go Gentle into That Good Night"
Jarrell, "The Death of the Ball Turret Gunner"
Cohen, "The Future"
Atwood, "Death of a Young Son by Drowning"

## Plays

Shakespeare, *The Tragedy of Othello, the Moor of Venice*
Miller, *Death of a Salesman*

# Dramatic Dialogues (Poetry)

Randall, "Ballad of Birmingham"
Chappell, "Narcissus and Echo"

# Dramatic Monologues and Related Poetry

Browning (Robert), "My Last Duchess"

Pound, "The River-Merchant's Wife:
   A Letter"
Eliot, "Journey of the Magi"
Eliot, "The Love Song of J. Alfred
   Prufrock"
Jarrell, "The Death of the Ball Turret
   Gunner"
Wayman, "Did I Miss Anything?"
Muldoon, "Anseo"

## Duty

### Stories

MacLeod, "The Boat"

### Poems

Anonymous, "Sir Patrick
   Spens"
Lovelace, "To Lucasta, Going to
   the Wars"

### Plays

Shakespeare, *The Tragedy of
   Othello, the Moor of Venice*

## Fate

### Stories

Russ, "Mr. Wilde's Second
   Chance"

### Poems

Hardy, "The Convergence of the
   Twain"
Randall, "Ballad of Birmingham"

### Plays

Shakespeare, *The Tragedy of
   Othello, the Moor of Venice*
Miller, *Death of a Salesman*

## Future

### Poems

Lampman, "The City of the End of
   Things"
Yeats, "The Second Coming"
Cohen, "The Future"
Crozier, "Packing for the Future:
   Instructions"

## History

### Stories

Achebe, "Dead Men's Path"
King, "A Coyote Columbus Story"

### Poems

Hayman, *from Quodlibets*, "The
   Four Elements in
   Newfoundland"
Kelsey, "Now Reader Read"
Shelley, "Ozymandias"
Hardy, "The Convergence of the
   Twain"
Yeats, "The Second Coming"
Pratt, "From Stone to Steel"
Scott (F. R.), "Laurentian Shield"
Curnow, "Landfall in Unknown
   Seas"
Kroetsch, "Stone Hammer
   Poem"
Webb, "Leaning"
Brathwaite, "Colombe"
Walcott, "Central America"
Williams, "The Book"
Atwood, "Notes Towards a Poem
   That Can Never Be Written"
Shomer, "Women Bathing at
   Bergen-Belsen"
Armstrong, "History Lesson"
Forché, "The Colonel"
Simpson, "The Body Tattoo of World
   History"

## Plays

Shakespeare, *The Tragedy of Othello, the Moor of Venice*
Pollock, *Moving Pictures*

## Humanity

### Stories

Hawthorne, "The Birthmark"
Maupassant, "The Piece of String"

### Poems

Milton, *from* "Paradise Lost"
Pope, *from* "An Essay on Man"
Arnold, "Dover Beach"
Pratt, "From Stone to Steel"
cummings, "pity this busy monster,manunkind"
Stafford, "Traveling Through the Dark"
Ginsberg, "A Supermarket in California"
Phillips, "Compartments"
Mayers, "All-American Sestina"
Bringhurst, "Essay on Adam"
Steele, "Sapphics Against Anger"
Carson, "God's List of Liquids"

## Language

### Stories

Shields, "Words"
Atwood, "Happy Endings"

### Poems

Hass, "Picking Blackberries with a Friend Who Has Been Reading Jacques Lacan"
Raine, "A Martian Sends a Postcard Home"

NourbeSe Philip, "Discourse on the Logic of Language"
Clarke, "Casualties"
Bök, "Vowels"

### Plays

Highway, *The Rez Sisters*

## Love

### Stories

Wilde, "The Sphinx Without a Secret"
Montgomery, "How Betty Sherman Won a Husband"
Lawrence, "The Horse Dealer's Daughter"
Hemingway, "Hills like White Elephants"
Atwood, "Happy Endings"
Bissonnette, "Dresses"

### Poems

Shakespeare, "Sonnet 30"
Wroth, "In This Strange Labyrinth How Shall I Turn"
Behn, "Love Armed"
Burns, "A Red, Red Rose"
Browning (E.B.), "Sonnets from the Portuguese 1 & 43"
Johnson, "The Idlers"
Hale, "This Oblivion"
Eliot, "The Love Song of J. Alfred Prufrock"
Jones (D. G.), "Kate, These Flowers . . ."
Marlatt, "(is love enough?)"
Nichol, "blues"
Wallace, "Common Magic"
Addonizio, "First Poem for You"
Langlais, "Elle récite cent fois . . ."

### *Plays*

Shakespeare, *The Tragedy of Othello, the Moor of Venice*

## *Love, Loss of*

### *Poems*

Anonymous, "Western Wind"
Wyatt, "They Flee from Me"
Shelley, "When the Lamp Is Shattered"
Keats, "La Belle Dame sans Merci"
Poe, "The Raven"
Millay, "What Lips My Lips Have Kissed"
Bishop, "One Art"
Atwood, "you fit into me"

## *Love: Marital Relationships*

### *Stories*

Hawthorne, "The Birthmark"
Chopin, "The Story of an Hour"
MacLeod, "The Boat"
Carver, "Cathedral"
Atwood, "Happy Endings"
Lahiri, "Interpreter of Maladies"

### *Poems*

Browning (Robert), "My Last Duchess"
Arnold, "Dover Beach"
Pound, "The River-Merchant's Wife: A Letter"

### *Plays*

Shakespeare, *The Tragedy of Othello, the Moor of Venice*
Ibsen, *A Doll's House*
Ringwood, *Still Stands the House*
Miller, *Death of a Salesman*
Sears, *Harlem Duet*

## *Myth and Fairy Tale*

### *Stories*

Wilde, "The Sphinx Without a Secret"
Borges, "The Book of Sand"
García Márquez, "A Very Old Man with Enormous Wings"
Barthelme, "The Glass Mountain"
King, "A Coyote Columbus Story"

### *Poems*

Inuit Traditional Song, "Magic Words/Aua"
Southern First Nations Traditional Orature, "Fragment of a Song"
Wordsworth, "The World Is Too Much with Us"
Poe, "To Helen"
H. D., "Helen"
Eliot, "The Love Song of J. Alfred Prufrock"
Auden, "Musée des Beaux Arts"
Olson, "The Ring Of"
Rukeyser, "Myth"
Sexton, "Cinderella"
Chappell, "Narcissus and Echo"
MacEwan, "Poem Improvised Around a First Line"
McKay, "Icarus"
Keeshig-Tobias, "How to Catch a White Man (Oops) I Mean Trickster"
Moses, "Inukshuk"
Dove, "Persephone, Falling"

### *Plays*

Highway, *The Rez Sisters*

## *Nature and God*

### *Poems*

Hopkins, "God's Grandeur"
Nelligan, "Evening Bells"

Plath, "Black Rook in Rainy
    Weather"
Duffy, "Prayer"

### Nature: Descriptive Poetry

Swift, "Description of a City
    Shower"
Wordsworth, "I Wandered Lonely as
    a Cloud"
Brontë, "[Ah! why, because the
    dazzling sun . . .]"
Hopkins, "Pied Beauty"
Crawford, "The Dark Stag"
Roberts, "Tantramar Revisited"
Frost, "Stopping by Woods on a
    Snowy Evening"
Smith, "The Lonely Land"
Roethke, "Root Cellar"
Thomas, "Fern Hill"
Lowell, "Water"
Larkin, "Water"
MacEwan, "Water"
Nichol, "landscape: I"
Thurston, "Miracle"

### Nature: The Environment

#### Stories

Le Guin, "Sur"
Van Camp, "the uranium leaking
    from port radium and rayrock
    mines is killing us"

#### Poems

Hopkins, "God's Grandeur"
cummings, "pity this busy
    monster,manunkind"
Stafford, "Traveling Through the
    Dark"
Page, "Planet Earth"
Oodgeroo, "We Are Going"
Kumin, "Noted in the *New York Times*"
Godbout, "Trees"
Marlatt, "(is love enough?)"

Keeshig-Tobias, "How to Catch a
    White Man (Oops) I Mean
    Trickster"

### Nature: Seasons of the Year

#### Poems

Hébert, "Snow"
Avison, "Snow"

#### Plays

Ringwood, *Still Stands the House*

### Parents and Children

#### Stories

Hemingway, "Hills like White
    Elephants"
Cheever, "Reunion"
Findley, "Stones"
Munro, "Boys and Girls"
MacLeod, "The Boat"
Aidoo, "The Message"
Winter, "Archibald the Arctic"
Thien, "Simple Recipes"

#### Poems

Hensley, "Courage"
Livesay, "The Three Emilys"
Thomas, "Do Not Go Gentle into
    That Good Night"
Wilbur, "The Writer"
Atwood, "Death of a Young Son
    by Drowning"
Heaney, "Digging"
Olds, "I Go Back to May 1937"
Keefer, "My Mother, a Closet Full
    of Dresses"

#### Plays

Shakespeare, *The Tragedy
    of Othello, the Moor of Venice*
Ibsen, *A Doll's House*

Miller, *Death of a Salesman*
Pollock, *Moving Pictures*

## Physical Handicaps

### Stories

Carver, "Cathedral"

### Poems

Owen, "Disabled"
Knighton, "Braille"

### Plays

Shakespeare, *Tragedy of Othello, the Moor of Venice*

## Poetry: Inspiration

Bradstreet, "The Author to Her Book"
Coleridge, "Kubla Khan"
Brontë, "[Ah! why, because the dazzling sun . . .]"
Whitman, "Song of Myself"
Stevens, "The Motive for Metaphor"
Ezra Pound, "In a Station of the Metro"
Neruda, "In Praise of Ironing"
Klein, "Portrait of the Poet as Landscape"
Layton, "The Fertile Muck"
Wilbur, "The Writer"
Kroetsch, "Stone Hammer Poem"
Ashbery, "Paradoxes and Oxymorons"
Ramanujan, "A River"
Hughes, "The Thought-Fox"
Plath, "Black Rook in Rainy Weather"
Nowlan, "The Broadcaster's Poem"
Bowering, "Play & Work & Art"
Heaney, "Digging"
Gwynn, "Approaching a Significant Birthday . . ."

## Political and Social Themes

### Stories

Chekhov, "An Upheaval"
Hemingway, "Hills like White Elephants"
Achebe, "Dead Men's Path"

### Poems

McLachlan, "We Live in a Rickety House"
Purdy, "A Handful of Earth"
Carter, "University of Hunger"
Walcott, "Central America"
Cohen, "The Future"
Atwood, "Notes Towards a Poem That Can Never Be Written"
Chiasson, "Red"
Forché, "The Colonel"

### Plays

Shakespeare, *The Tragedy of Othello, the Moor of Venice*
Ibsen, *A Doll's House*
Highway, *The Rez Sisters*

## Race and Ethnicity

### Stories

Carr, "Kitwancool"
Angelou, *from* "I Know Why the Caged Bird Sings"
Aidoo, "The Message"
King, "A Coyote Columbus Story"
Walker, "The Flowers"
Lahiri, "Interpreter of Maladies"
Thien, "Simple Recipes"

### Poems

Wheatley, "On Being Brought from Africa to America"
Scott (D. C.), "The Forsaken"
Dunbar, "Sympathy"

### Plays

Miller, *Death of a Salesman*

## Suicide

### Stories

Lawrence, "The Horse Dealer's
Daughter"

### Poems

Robinson (E.A.), "Richard Cory"
Sexton, "The Starry Night"
Dewdney, "Ten Typically Geological
Suicides"

### Plays

Othello, *The Tragedy of Othello,
the Moor of Venice*
Miller, *Death of a Salesman*

## War

### Stories

Findley, "Stones"

### Poems

Lovelace, "To Lucasta, Going
to the Wars"
Byron, "Stanzas: When a Man Hath
No Freedom to Fight for at Home"
Hensley, "Courage"
Owen, "Dulce et Decorum Est"
Owen, "Disabled"
Brecht, "The God of War"
Jarrell, "Death of the Ball Turret
Gunner"
Ciardi, "To Lucasta, About That War"

Kogawa, "When I Was a Little Girl"
Forché, "The Colonel"
Muldoon, "Anseo"
Clarke, "Casualties"

### Plays

Shakespeare, *The Tragedy of
Othello, the Moor of Venice*

## Women's Issues

### Stories

Chopin, "The Story of an Hour"
Hemingway, "Hills like White
Elephants"
Le Guin, "Sur"
Munro, "Boys and Girls"
Atwood, "Happy Endings"
Kincaid, "Girl"

### Poems

Finch, "Adam Posed"
Leapor, "An Essay on Women"
Rossetti, "Goblin Market"
Parker, "One Perfect Rose"
Rukeyser, "Myth"
Levertov, "In Mind"
Sexton, "Cinderella"
Rich, "Power"
Plath, "Metaphors"
Piercy, "Barbie Doll"
Cope, "Rondeau Redoublé"
Campbell, "Woolf"

### Plays

Ibsen, *A Doll's House*
Pollock, *Moving Pictures*

# Critical Approaches to Literature

An extensive overview of strategies for reading and analyzing fiction, poetry, and drama lies outside the scope of this book, but it may safely be said that each era in the history of literature has given rise to critics and theorists who redefine the very nature of what literature is. Neoclassical critics of the eighteenth century, with their insistence on balance, reason, and order, yielded in the next century to their romantic successors, who stressed qualities that were diametrically opposed. The so-called New Critics of the mid-twentieth century focused on literary works as autonomous verbal texts that should be read with little or no reference to the writers' biographies or to the social conditions under which they lived. More recent theories of poetic interpretation focus precisely on those things the New Critics avoided, stressing matters of race, class, and gender as essential to understanding texts. Now that we have entered a new century, new strategies for reading and understanding literature will doubtless emerge to challenge the preconceptions of the past and offer readers further ways to "make it new."

You may be asked to analyze works from two or three genres at once; the themes that one encounters in short stories will also be found in poems and plays. Similarly, a single critical approach—deconstruction, feminist criticism, new historicist techniques—may be employed to look at literary works by employing a specific methodology. For example, suppose you are asked to explore a general topic like "Parent/Child Relations." You might pick Thien's "Simple Recipes," MacLeod's "The Boat," and Munro's "Boys and Girls" as three examples. A thematic approach to such a topic might find some common thread that links the three. A feminist approach might examine the role of gender in each story, whereas a psychological approach might explore the backgrounds and experiences of the central characters to explain the choices they make. The possibilities are numerous, and these groupings of stories, poems, and plays that would lend themselves to shared thematic or critical approaches are offered as suggestions. The brief discussion of several leading theoretical strategies that follows will further assist you in using the thematic index.

## Formalism

### Formalist Criticism

Formalism, in its American incarnation as the New Criticism, devoted much of its early attention to the works of metaphysical poets like Donne, Marvell, and Herbert. In the hands of such New Critics as Cleanth Brooks, William K. Wimsatt, Jr., and Monroe Beardsley, the formalist approach stressed the internal qualities of literary works by close reading and explication, attempting to demonstrate unity of form and content in successful poems. Such matters as authors' biographies, historical situations, or intentions, and the effect that works produced on readers were considered less important than analysis that would demonstrate and justify the "tensions" in a given work as contributing to a unified whole. In essence, the New Criticism stressed that in literature the whole is always more than the sum of the individual parts. Formalist approaches may be used to examine any kind of literary work, but they are perhaps most useful in explications of short poems (especially those, like sonnets, that have a clear formal structure), or in explications of selected passages from stories and plays. Because this book contains a number of contemporary poems written in traditional forms, a formalist approach to them might focus on the relationship of poetic form to content and use of language. As far as short stories and plays are concerned, works translated from other languages would not be good candidates for explication because many of the nuances of the original language may have been lost in translation.

## Biographical Criticism

Writers whose life stories continue to intrigue us are always likely choices for biographical criticism, which tries to locate literary works and their genesis within the known facts about the lives and working habits of authors. Although you should be wary of making connections between life and art that are too direct, biographical criticism can be useful in examining the sources of stories, poems, and plays and, in the case where an author's preliminary drafts have been preserved, in articulating the process of literary creation. Among fiction writers, Poe, Chopin, Hemingway, Walker, and Munro, to mention only a few, have undergone quite a bit of scrutiny by biographers and memoirists. In poetry, one obvious source of much biographical speculation has been Shakespeare's sonnets, which have been read, in the absence of any substantial biographical information about Shakespeare, as revelatory of the poet's friendships, sexual preferences, and jealousies. It is only with the rise of romanticism that the poet becomes the true subject of the poem, and it is easy to see why Wordsworth made such an impact on literary history and, in his long autobiographical poem, *The Prelude*, made his own life his primary subject. In this respect, Wordsworth parallels Coleridge; indeed, John Livingston Lowes's *The Road to Xanadu* remains a classic critical biography that traces the sources of Coleridge's "Kubla Khan" through rigorous examination of the poet's education and reading. In more recent times, the confessional poetry of the 1960s, as practised by Plath and Sexton, still attracts interest, especially because multiple biographies and memoirs of these writers are now available. In drama, none of the plays can be considered autobiographical, though *The Rez Sisters* builds upon Highway's knowledge of life on the reserve, and Arthur Miller's own autobiography, *Timebends*, gives quite a bit of information about how *Death of a Salesman* grew into its present form over a number of years.

## Historical and Sociological Criticism

Old-style historical and sociological criticism focused on the contexts of the authors' historical eras, demonstrating how events and cultural forces influenced their works. With the rise of naturalism in the late nineteenth century, critics began to apply the theories and practices of "social Darwinism" to literary works, often finding that the emphasis on heredity and environment in them was directly influenced by many of the new ideas of what we now term the social sciences. In recent times, the new historicism, which reevaluates such matters as race, class, and gender as essential forces shaping literary creation, and various types of Marxist criticism (we note especially critics Fredric Jameson and Terry Eagleton in this regard) have been prominent. Works that deal with such likely topics for historical and sociological analysis as war and political ideology are listed above thematically and would lend themselves to historical/sociological approaches. The use of historical and sociological contexts to analyze fiction requires an understanding of the culture out of which the story arose, so you may need to investigate this background possibly as part of a research assignment. An obvious choice among short stories would be Findley's "Stones," which reveals the long reach of war across oceans and time. Virtually all of the selections listed thematically under *Race and Ethnicity* would be good choices for sociological/historical analysis. An investigation of the policies of segregation in the American South and the cross-currents of the African-American struggle for liberation would enhance an understanding of Maya Angelou's *I Know Why the Caged Bird Sings* or Djanet Sears's *Harlem Duet*. "Mr. Wilde's Second Chance" is best read with some understanding of attitudes toward homosexuality during the lifetime of Oscar Wilde. Highway's play *The Rez Sisters*, along with a number of poems and stories, speaks to the Aboriginal experience, and those stories and poems that directly deal with such historical topics as war are good subjects for historical analysis.

## Feminist and Gender Criticism

Feminist critical approaches focus on both the woman as reader of (male) literature and the woman-as-writer. To look at the latter first, the thematic listing under *Women's Issues* or under *Love: Marital Relationships* would be a starting point for feminist analysis of how women writers have viewed these subjects. The recent rediscovery of writers like Chopin has been a chief concern of feminist criticism, and there are many writers here who are outspoken feminists and critics as well (Atwood and Rich are the two most prominent). As far as the perspective of woman-as-reader is concerned, one potentially useful topic for analysis from the feminist perspective would be to examine the role of the silent auditors in such classic love poems as "To His Coy Mistress" and "Dover Beach." Students might be asked to examine the stereotypes of female behaviour that male authors perpetuate in these works. Some women fiction writers, interestingly, have not yet attracted a great deal of response from feminist critics. Among poets, Dickinson has perhaps been the subject of the most feminist scrutiny, with Plath a close second; some others have not received much attention at all. The relatively late but prominent arrival of women playwrights as a major force in drama can only be hinted at with the limited selection of plays this book contains, but Pollock clearly uses feminist themes in her work. Obviously, many of the stories, poems, and plays listed under *Sexual Themes* would also benefit from feminist or other types of gender-based analysis, such as gay studies (also known as queer theory), the study of how a writer's sexual orientation shapes his or her work. Shakespeare's sonnets have long provided fuel for this kind of speculation, as have Whitman's and Dickinson's poems in recent years. Obvious subjects are writers who were either openly gay or whose sexual orientation has been the subject of study: Wilde, Bishop, Walker, Rich, Findley, Highway, and Brand are a few who are commonly mentioned in this regard.

## Structuralism: Mythological and Psychological Approaches

Under the structuralist banner are included mythological (archetypal or Jungian) and Freudian approaches, as well as a number of other structuralist methods of critical analysis that began to appear in the 1970s in the works of Roland Barthes, Tzvetan Todorov, Jacques Lacan, and others. The thematic category of *Myth and Fairy Tale* lists works that draw heavily on traditional mythology and folklore and would be ideal for Jungian analysis; you may find the Bill Moyers/Joseph Campbell video series *The Power of Myth* helpful in recognizing some of these archetypes. Some of the choices from earlier eras of works that derive from myth are obvious here (Poe and H. D.'s poems on Helen of Troy), but more intriguing might be contemporary works by such writers as King that adapt ancient myths to new cultural settings. King's story "A Coyote Columbus Story" reveals his debt to the rich tradition of Native trickster tales. One area of fiction that has been deeply concerned with mythic subtexts has been magic realism, as practised by García Márquez. Freudian psychological approaches can be used on virtually any selection from the fiction section of the anthology, although the obvious choices are those that present characters like Poe's, Maupassant's, or Findley's, who are in extreme situations. Poets who are of interest for their psychological histories—Blake, Lowell, Sexton—will readily lend themselves to psychological approaches. *Death of a Salesman* deals directly with mental illness, and violent behaviour is explored in several plays. Purely structuralist approaches such as those employed by Todorov in *The Fantastic* might be employed to distinguish between the different uses of fantastic material in such fiction writers as Hawthorne, Poe, and Barthelme.

## Post-Structuralism: Reader-Response Theory and Deconstruction

These more recent critical methods, both of which attempt to demonstrate that language itself cannot impose a definite meaning upon a reader's interpretation of a given work, involve in-depth study, and the critical theories of Stanley Fish, Jacques Derrida, and Paul de Man may be too abstruse for serious application in lower-division courses. Still, in theory (so to speak), reader-response criticism and deconstruction can be applied to any literary text, and a brief demonstration of their main points might lead to some lively classroom discussion about how language and meaning operate. A demonstration of how reader-response theory proceeds might be performed by having you, without any prior preparation, write about such a short, cryptic modernist poem as Williams's "The Red Wheelbarrow." Because it stresses the indeterminacy of language itself, deconstruction seems a likely choice for works that clearly use experimental techniques; Ashbery's or NourbeSe Philip's poems might provide good examples for post-structuralist analysis, as would stories that employ unconventional techniques, such as Barthelme's "The Glass Mountain" or Atwood's "Happy Endings."

## *Post-Colonial Theory*

Like other contemporary theoretical approaches, post-colonial theory is complex and difficult to define, but it concerns a shift in the way previously and currently colonized people and places are viewed. Though the literatures of former colonies like Canada, Australia, and New Zealand are considered post-colonial, much of the focus is on nations of the developing world that have gained political independence and are now seeking ways to talk back to the empires that once imposed their rule. Post-colonial theory challenges the disparity between the Western (Europe and North America) and the non-Western continents (Africa, Asia, Latin America) by giving prominence to the literature, culture, and politics of the latter. In his seminal text *Orientalism* (1978), Edward Said argued that the Orient (the East) was an idea of "otherness" invented for the purposes of domination. Those once considered subordinate or subaltern now seek to resist such domination through a variety of cultural and political strategies that have become the subject of study for post-colonial scholars. Though globalization has increasingly broken down trade and other barriers, this has not meant the end of economic disparity or exploitation. Post-colonialism is about challenging our understanding of margin and centre, and attempting to transform our world into a place where fairness is sought and difference is respected. Among the texts that might be fruitfully explored from a post-colonial perspective are Shakespeare's *Othello*, Aidoo's "The Message," and Carter's "University of Hunger."

# *Credits*

## Fiction

# Poetry

# Drama

# Index of
# Critical Terms

# Index of Authors, Titles, and First Lines